"Sets the bar impossibly high for anyone else wanting to contribute to the field. Remember the thrill that came from your first horror movie book, when everything was new and magical? I felt that excitement again as I began paging through Nightmare USA."
- David Annandale, Brain Blasters -

"When it comes to exploitation films, Stephen Thrower has shot it, smoked it, snorted it and perhaps even inserted it rectally. The definitive book on the subject. Stunning."
- Jimmy McDonough, author of 'The Ghastly One: The Sex Gore Netherworld of Andy Milligan' -

"Thrower's personal insight and enthusiasm make Nightmare USA a consistent pleasure to read. Too much writing on the darker corners of cinema is just functional, but his prose throbs with twisted love. This is a truly important film book, in itself as a piece of writing but also as a direction to areas of film history that remain to be explored."
- Kim Newman, Video Watchdog -

"The best book ever written about the golden era of American independent horror cinema… an encyclopedic tome of arcane cinematic lore and knowledge."
- Matthew Dean Hill, Atrocities Cinema -

"Thrower's tome deserves a spot next to Carlos Clarens's 'An Illustrated History of the Horror Film,' Carol Clover's 'Men, Women, and Chainsaws,' Michael Weldon's 'The Psychotronic Encyclopedia of Film,' and Bill and Michelle Landis's 'Sleazoid Express' on a healthily horrific bookshelf."
Johnny Ray Huston, San Francisco Bay Guardian

"Thrower brings a finely-honed analytical eye to the material, but his writing is never dry. It's all sizzle and all steak!"
- Mark Pilkington, Fortean Times -

"Nightmare USA prises up the star-stamped paving slabs of American cinema and reveals the strange and sometimes strangely beautiful bugs glistening beneath. A must-have roadmap for those either innocent or insane enough to want to explore the byroads and backwaters of low-budget horror."
- Alec Worley, Dredd Zine -

"Digs right down into the fetid underbelly of the filmmaking scene. Perhaps the finest book ever produced on the subject of American exploitation cinema - skilfully and informatively written and packed throughout with some of the rarest and most beautifully garish imagery ever to see print. Book of the year? No doubt."
- Alan Simpson, SexGoreMutants -

"As Madonna is inducted into the Rock'n'Roll hall of fame and the world flushes itself further down a spiraling vortex of meaningless brown bile, along comes this great book. Understand this…YOU will buy this book NOW or I will rip out your fat-headed intestines from your gutless bodypit and hang them over the telephone wires like tennis shoes!"
- Lux Interior, The Cramps -

NIGHTMARE USA
THE UNTOLD STORY OF THE EXPLOITATION INDEPENDENTS

This second edition published by FAB Press Ltd, July 2008
(The first edition was published by FAB Press, May 2007)

FAB Press Ltd.
2 Farleigh
Ramsden Road
Godalming
Surrey
GU7 1QE
England, UK

www.fabpress.com

Edited and designed by Harvey Fenton, with thanks to Francis Brewster for production assistance.

A CIP catalogue record for this book is available from the British Library.
hardback:
ISBN 978-1-903254-46-2
paperback:
ISBN 978-1-903254-52-3

Nightmare USA
The Untold Story of the Exploitation Independents

Stephen Thrower

ACKNOWLEDGEMENTS I
TEXT

For their time and patience in granting interviews conducted over several months, the author wishes to extend his deepest gratitude and thanks to the following people:

John Ballard, George Barry, Wayne Bell, Charles Bernstein, Wayne Berwick, James Bryan, Robert Dadashian, Walter Dallenbach, Tom Dalton, Daniel DiSomma, David Durston, Garth Eliassen, Joseph Ellison, Robert Endelson, Morgan Fisher, Frederick Friedel, Michael Gornick, Renee Harmon, Ellen Hayes, William Heick, Fredric Hobbs, Jeremy Hoenack, Chris Huntley, Willard Huyck, Don Jones, Kalassu, Gloria Katz, Gary Kent, Don Leifert, Sidney Ann Mackenzie, Douglas McKeown, Rue McClanahan, Tony Malanowski, Matthew Mallinson, Joseph Masefield, Ron Medico, Joan Mocine, Ted Newsom, Art Piatt, Marc B. Ray, Steve Sandkuhler, Mark Sawicki, Robert Allen Schnitzer, Christopher Speeth, Annie Sprinkle, John Stoglin, Stephen Traxler, Norman Thaddeus Vane, Robert Voskanian, Richard Wadsack, Roger Watkins, Straw Weisman, James Wilson, John Wintergate, Oliver Wood.

For their assistance in setting up interviews, passing on helpful leads, sourcing rare films, and co-ordinating contacts with the filmmakers, much gratitude is due to: Daniel Craddock, Tom Fitzgerald, Cheryl Harmon, Worth Keeter, Arthur Marks, Ron Medico, Marc Morris, Pete Tombs.

For letting me paraphrase his online comments about drive-in cinemas, thanks to Robert Monell.

For sterling work on 'post-production' thanks to Harvey Fenton and Francis Brewster.

For the most invaluable help in all areas, and for his constant inspiration and support, sincerest gratitude goes to my good friend Julian Grainger..

Thanks to Abigail King for help with transcription; to Thighpaulsandra for hospitality and peaceful working atmosphere at his farmhouse in South Wales; and to David Michael Tibet, Andrea Degens and their four legged family, for letting me stay at their beautiful home in Hastings.

Cover design by James Mannox, with Stephen Thrower and Harvey Fenton.

ACKNOWLEDGEMENTS II
VISUALS

This book would have been a great deal less fun to read without the generosity of those who responded to my request at www.fabpress.com by offering stills, pressbooks, advertising materials, video covers and posters.
The author wishes to thank everyone who replied:

in particular the following:
Matt Blankner, Suzanne Donahue, Michael Gingold, Michael Greenwood, Eric Jenkins, Armin Junge, Wes Vance

also many thanks to:
Francis Brewster, Julian Grainger, David Gregory, Alan Jones, Marc Morris (The Mondo Erotico Archive) and Harvey Fenton (The FAB Press Archive)

and for their generous loan of personal materials:
George Barry, James Bryan, David Durston, Joseph Ellison, Robert Endelson, Frederick Friedel, Fredric Hobbs, Chris Huntley, Don Jones, Gary Kent, Douglas McKeown, Tony Malanowski, Mark Sawicki, Robert Allen Schnitzer, Richard Stange, Norman Thaddeus Vane, Richard Wadsack, James Wilson

All other images are from the author's collection.

THIS BOOK IS DEDICATED TO OSSIAN BROWN

IN MEMORY OF
Tomi Barrett
Bhaskar
Robert Burns
Don Dohler
Renee Harmon
John Peyser
Roger Watkins

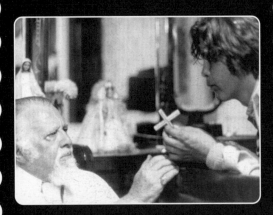

Section III:
Reviews

Section IV:
Appendices and Index

| KEEPS YOU INFORMED | # THE CITY NEWS | EXTRA |

Vol. 1 No. 1

Los Angeles, California

PYSCHOPATHIC KILLER ON THE LOOSE!

Have You Seen This Man?

ALBERT ROBERTSON, 21-year-old scion of prominent local family, today slashed the throat of an attendant and fled from private mental institution. With a psychopathic hatred of all women, he has been adjudged criminally insane and any knowledge of his whereabouts should be reported to police immediately.

BULLETIN

Albert Robertson, 21-year-old killer who escaped from a local mental hospital, eluded police and entered his mother's home in the Hollywood Hills here earlier today.

Two officers reported seeing a red sports car with a man and young girl pass them on the road minutes before they arrived to throw a protective cordon around the Robertson hillside mansion and grounds. It is now supposed that the psycopath entered a short time before, murdered the housekeeper before her young daughter returned from school, and then when the unsuspecting child arrived invited her to go for a ride, perhaps for an ice cream soda, for which she is known to have a fondness.

All servants had been ordered removed from the house when the manhunt began but it was later learned that the housekeeper had been on an errand and no one thought of the little girl at school.

Little Annie's mother was found dead in her bedroom, brutally slashed and nude. Coroner's report indicated she had not been raped. Fear for the child's life mounts and an all-out search is on for the pair.

Murdered Victim

A 43 year old attendant at a local mental hospital today was viciously slashed to death by Albert Robertson, an inmate who stole his car keys and fled.

It is reported that the victim showed sadistic tendencies and frequently teased

ATTENDANT

the inmates which is given as one reason for his slaying.

Reconstruction of the tragedy indicates that he was lured to his death on the pretext of seeing smuggled stag films in the room of the criminally insane Robertson. The attendant was found seated in front of a small portable motion picture screen, slumped over dead while the film continued to unreel.

ESCAPES MENTAL HOSPITAL WOMEN IN AREA WARNED

LOS ANGELES, CA. — Southland women today were warned by police authorities to stay indoors at night, bolt all doors and windows, and report any suspicious strangers at once.

Albert Robertson, age 21, scion of the socially prominent Robertson family here, and heir to millions, today brutally murdered a male attendant at a local mental hospital where he has been a patient, stole the murdered man's car keys, and made good his escape. Earlier he was thwarted in an attempt to murder a nurse who had reprimanded him for an infringement of hospital regulations.

According to Dr. J. W. Burton, the psychiatrist in charge, the institution is more a rest home than an asylum and he had repeatedly warned the youth's mother that her son needed stronger security, and more stringent treatment than his hospital was prepared to offer. Refusing to accept that the young man is insane, the wealthy matron insisted, "Poor Albert is only a little disturbed."

The escaped psychopath is reported as youthful, handsome, with affable personality and disarming manner and might easily pass for any normal, cultured young man. He is reported as having a deep hatred of women—particularly his mother—and refers to them as evil, degraded, not fit to live.

It is the belief of both the psychiatrist and the detective assigned to the case that Albert will try to seek out his mother at the palatial Hollywood Hills home in which he grew up and which she now occupies with a staff of servants. A special police cordon has been thrown around the house and grounds. Heavy security, of a type undisclosed to newsmen, is being given the killer's mother.

He has no hatred of men and murdered the attendant only to get his keys in the opinion of the police detective. The law enforcement officer warned TV and radio audiences and newspaper readers that they must take absolutely no chances. "The man," he says, "is criminally insane and will stop at nothing."

NEXT ON MADMAN'S LIST?

This sweet-faced, blue-eyed blonde child is 12 years of age, and in the company of psychopathic killer Albert Robertson, son of Mrs. Albert Robertson, prominent Southland socialite. The little girl is unaware that her companion has already murdered two people, one of them her own mother, who was the housekeeper in the beautiful Hollywood Hills home of Albert's mother.

In school when her mother was slain, the child must have arrived at the house minutes later and was unaware of the

ANNIE

tragedy. Said to be a good child who never disobeys, it is supposed that Annie must have been told that her mother had given permission for her to go for a ride with Albert.

It was later learned that large sum of money is missing from a safe in his mother's bedroom where Mrs. Robertson was known to keep it for possible emergencies. It is therefore believed that the killer has enough money to take the child and go far away should his disturbed mind think along those lines.

But what concerns police and others even more is that some little trifle may tip the killer's mind in another direction and little Annie will become his next victim. It is hoped that his hatred of women does not include what he regards as "the innocent young" and that the child's life will be spared.

Anyone seeing the pair is urgently requested to contact the police with details.

Author's Preface

*N*ightmare USA has changed shape many times since I began writing it, in 2001. I first intended, naively as it turned out, to compile a comprehensive guide to every non-studio horror film made in America between 1970 and 1985, complete with supporting interview material. I made lists, I placed asterisks next to favourites, I planned an A-Z. I imagined the ultimate encyclopaedia: the freakiest decade of the freakiest genre, an American Film Necronomicon…

Of course, the list grew longer. And longer. It was easy to dismiss the studio pictures and the foreign co-productions – I even set a rule against the classics. After all, was there really anything else to say about *The Texas Chain Saw Massacre*? Could the embers of Romero spit a few more sparks? Did *The Evil Dead* require a cheerleader? David Szulkin's book 'Wes Craven's Last House on the Left: The Making of a Cult Classic' left successive commentators with about as much hope as a victim of Weasel Padowski. So where to go for that sense of discovery?

I began by making telephone calls, writing letters and e-mails, note-taking, research, immersion in the minutiae, scouring through thirty years of documentation. I wanted a big, immersive project, and by God I'd found one. It had a beckoning, alluring quality, the promise of untrodden snow, unsullied greenery, the swamps and the deserts of horror, the nameless gas stations and wrong turnings and ghost towns.

What really took me by surprise, however, was the warmth and friendliness of the people with whom I made contact, and their willingness to discuss their work. Everyone I've spoken to has been tirelessly patient, tolerating a veritable locust-storm of questions spread over four or five years. Even those with whom I've enjoyed just a fleeting exchange of e-mails gave me frankness, thoughtfulness and wit.

Nightmare USA would have been so much easier to complete if my initial pessimism had been borne out: I naively imagined I would reach maybe four out of ten of my targets. Instead, the strike rate was closer to 90%. My list of 250 films, to be covered in equal depth, was merely mad ambition. I felt like the Borges character who tried to map reality at a ratio of 1:1. I had to concede defeat. A 'map' like *Nightmare USA* cannot *be* the territory.

For instance: *Don't Go in the Woods* was one of my 'must-cover' horror favourites. Director James Bryan was known almost solely for a critically reviled rural slasher film which I happened to love. Perfect! The chance to rally to a cause, to hold forth at length about why everyone else was wrong… who could resist? I knew nothing about Bryan except that he'd made an obscure vigilante movie a couple of years later. However, after interviewing Jim, and seeing his earlier films (so obscure that back then they didn't even turn up on the Internet Movie Database), the idea that I might cover his career in 5,000 words was simply absurd. Frankly, one could write a book – a pertinent and detailed and far-reaching book – about this one director. The chapter that follows on James Bryan is twenty thousand words long, and I'm pretty sure you'll agree it's all meat and no fat. If one previously reviled video nasty could be the springboard for so much material, how the hell could I ever finish this book?

In the name of sanity and for the sake of your back muscles, dear reader, I've divided *Nightmare USA* into two halves (see the last page for details of Volume 2), and still it's just about half of what could be done. If the book you're now holding is less comprehensive than I set out to write, it's also more detailed, wider-ranging (and better, I think): even if it does trail a few loose threads. *Nightmare USA*, for all its size, is a beginning, not an end.

We'll be examining an era in which anything was possible, when the horror genre became unshackled by convention. The anticipation of success, though devoutly to be wished, was not a tourniquet to invention. Through a combination of eccentricity, amateur inspiration and wild guesswork, these films, by filmmakers I call 'the Exploitation Independents', achieve a strangeness and variety and imaginativeness to which Hollywood horror films rarely aspire. In the museum of film history, the Exploitation Independents are shades and hants and interlopers, tripping alarms and disappearing, too free to be boxed and evaluated by the mainstream of film criticism.

Why 1970-1985? Well even I'm not crazy enough to attempt 1930-2006 - although a bit of me feels guilty for not doing so. Essentially, the period I've chosen tallies with a trend in the movies I love, towards greater visceral extremes and a greater flexibility of form. Before 1970 there were only a few films that would match the extremes of the 1970s. And after 1985, the genre diminished and receded, renouncing its confrontational power under pressure from the majors and the MPAA. If there's a book to be written about indie horror after 1985, I look forward to reading it, not writing it.

Stephen Thrower

The Exploitation Independents

The 1970s were fertile years for American cinema. Directors like Bob Rafelson, Brian De Palma, Robert Altman, Francis Ford Coppola, Martin Scorsese and Woody Allen were at the height of their powers, with movies such as *Five Easy Pieces* (1970), *Sisters* (1973), *Nashville* (1975), *The Conversation* (1974), *Taxi Driver* (1976), and *Annie Hall* (1977) redefining American cinema. Low-budget horror films too were developing in a vivid parallel world: Wes Craven's *The Last House on the Left* (1972), Tobe Hooper's *The Texas Chain Saw Massacre* (1974) and George Romero's *Martin* (1976) were bold, idiosyncratic works by hugely talented directors, with energy, imagination, and a confrontational approach to their subject matter; while John Carpenter's *Halloween* (1978) and Romero's *Dawn of the Dead* (1978) were as polished, dynamic and technically innovative as anything the majors could offer.

And then there was the subterranean film industry, the exploitation arena, where some of the wildest and most shocking films imaginable proliferated, unchecked by censorship or the dictates of 'good taste'. Horror, an evergreen exploitation genre, enjoyed a surge in production, and as distributors strove to maintain their business edge against television and the major studios, the race was on to be more extreme, more shocking, more bizarre. Advances were also being made in film style: some of the strangest midnight blooms of the horror genre emerged from the 1970s, and the equally fertile soil of the early 1980s. A multitude of creative individuals took the opportunity offered by independent producers to explore their own obsessions, advance their personal vision, and make money. As long as the films were startling enough to support an exploitation hard sell, the filmmaker could expect the sort of writing, casting and directing freedom many a Hollywood director would sell his own grandmother to possess.

Before we get carried away, it is of course worth admitting that the exploitation industry of the 1970s also gave us some of the slowest, silliest, most hopelessly inept celluloid swarf ever to run through a projector. Some examples are hilarious, others are just dull beyond belief: what matters is that *taken together*, both good and bad constitute an alternative, parallel cinema, where big money or the lack of it was no obstacle. Just as a sumptuous, expensive film made by a talented director can sometimes tank ignominiously, so too a cheap, threadbare movie made by an amateur can transcend its limitations, touching some part of us beyond the reach of the merely proficient. There are exploitation films of real class, and others of awesome ineptitude: nevertheless, even the latter can *sometimes* achieve a kind of insane apotheosis. Searching through the thousands of low-budget exploitation pictures made since the 1930s is compulsive for this very reason. Years after one has seen the major contenders, the *Texas Chain Saw Massacre*s and *Halloween*s, one can still discover unexpected marvels: maybe whole films, like *Victims* (Daniel DiSomma, 1977) or *Death Bed* (George Barry, 1977); or maybe just amazing scenes or images, in movies largely unremarked-upon before. In the attics and cellars of American cinema, under its floorboards, behind the weighty furniture and between the layers of linoleum, strange cine-life forms still lurk, and if sometimes your passion for the obscure gives you the mien of a deranged entomologist, holding aloft a weird insect and trying to convince others of its beauty while they wrinkle their noses in distaste, well, that's obsession: it's not for everybody…

opposite:
Shooting **Don't Go in the Woods**, a quintessential rural slasher film, in the Rocky Mountains, summer 1980.
left to right:
Hank Zinman (director of photography); Eric Jenkins (camera assistant); James Bryan (director).

below:
A chilling and beautifully crafted scene from George Romero's masterpiece of low-budget American horror, **Martin** (1976).

So, what exactly are exploitation films? Put simply, they are independently made non-studio films produced either: a) to exploit the financial possibilities of a popular genre; b) to respond quickly to current interest in a contemporary topic; or c) to milk an existing market success. The term 'exploitation' thus refers primarily to the intention to 'exploit' audience interest in a topic (or, in mainstream terms, 'to meet demand'). In essence there is little difference here between the business practices of the exploitation film industry and the majors. The studios may have indulged the occasional star director with an offbeat personal project (Paramount allowing Hitchcock to make *Vertigo* in 1958), or polished their artistic credibility by bankrolling a project by a visiting European art-house *maestro* (Antonioni, courted by MGM to make *Zabriskie Point* in 1970), but they generally wanted a ready audience for their output. Where exploitation filmmakers, producers and distributors differed was in their willingness to strip away all but the most essential elements from a package, hyping the selling points with shameless hyperbole, and then produce as many variants as possible, quickly and cheaply, to maximise financial reward while audience demand was still fresh. Unlike Hollywood films, with their large crews, astronomical star wages, and temperamental directors, an exploitation film could be hurried from script to screen in just three or four months, with another on the

way soon after. The results might lack the airs and graces of a *High Society* (MGM, 1956) or a *Breakfast at Tiffany's* (Paramount, 1961) but at their best they possessed a rude energy and vitality capable of upstaging major product. The word 'exploitation' is therefore merely a synonym for 'giving the people what they want'; a time-honoured credo for business big and small.

To some, the word 'exploitation' carries negative connotations, especially in the wake of feminism and its influence on film criticism. An 'exploitation film' can sound somehow sinister, as if the cast and crew are being exploited by immoral working practises, or worse… Given the exploitation industry's love of nudity and sexual extremes, the word inevitably echoes with concerns about the exploitation of women. This however is an ancillary connotation, and not part of the term's original meaning. Besides, women were at least as likely to experience exploitation on a Hollywood casting couch as in the smoky backroom of an independent film hustler. It's tempting to seek a different label, and exploitation's small business roots and *ad-hoc* distribution arrangements have often suggested the term 'Independent' as an alternative. However, the word 'Independent', or 'Indie' has come to mean something quite different in the last fifteen years, referring instead to the work of mainstream auteurs like Steven Soderbergh and The Coen Brothers, so instead I will use the expanded term 'Exploitation Independents' to represent the filmmakers, producers and distributors covered here.

The 1970s saw a period of intense development in the ambition and extremity of the exploitation film. Censorship was relaxed and the gate to excess thrown wide open. Massively popular in drive-ins and urban hardtops, exploitation movies – in particular the exploitation genre *par excellence*, horror – offered a vibrant and varied alternative to the mainstream of American cinema. Luridly-titled wonders like *The Headless Eyes* (Kent Bateman, 1971), *I Drink Your Blood* (David Durston, 1971), *Scream Bloody Murder* (Marc B. Ray, 1972) and *Hitch Hike To Hell* (Irv Berwick, 1977) were everywhere, a cross-country phenomenon, from Texas and Illinois to the grindhouses of New York and Los Angeles. Frequently offered to audiences in double or even triple bills, low-budget horror was at last in step with the hyperbole of the poster-writers; for decades, horror film ads had been promising '*An Unbelievable Orgy of Terror!*' – and for decades audiences had been trooping off home after seeing the movie, passably entertained but somewhat unfulfilled. As exploitation entrepreneur David Friedman once put it, the early exploitation market offered viewers "the sizzle without the steak". The person being exploited was the 'mark', the gullible audience member sucked in by 'Coming Attractions' hinting at depravity '*too shocking to be described in this trailer!*' It was only really in the 1960s and 1970s that exploitation films stopped teasing and delivered on those dangled promises. The technical aspects could be crude, to say the least, but when it came to the meat of the matter, you frequently got it all – the sizzle *and* the steak.

Coming at the horror genre from a different angle were movies that bred horror with something not unlike the stranger reaches of European art cinema. In this realm we encounter poetic chillers like *Let's Scare Jessica To Death* (John Hancock, 1971); *Lemora: A Child's Tale of the Supernatural* (Richard Blackburn, 1973); *Messiah of Evil*

(Willard Huyck and Gloria Katz, 1973); *The Premonition* (Robert Allen Schnitzer, 1975); *The Witch Who Came from the Sea* (Matt Cimber, 1976); and *Friday the 13th: The Orphan* (John Ballard, 1977) – films that take a dreamy, impressionistic approach to the genre. Implicit in horror is the erosion of boundaries, be they physical, psychological or metaphysical, and this allows filmmakers a license, unique in commercial genre cinema, to employ stylistic effects that would normally reside in *avant-garde* or 'art cinema' settings. In some cases, such as the extraordinary *Alabama's Ghost* (Fredric Hobbs, 1973), these ellipses and stylistic flourishes were employed deliberately; in others they resulted from lack of money, lack of conventional skill, or sheer mutant waywardness. Sometimes, as in beautiful, haunting movies like *Axe* (Frederick Friedel, 1974) or delirious nightmares like the under-rated *Death Trap* (Tobe Hooper, 1976), a combination of accident *and* artistic ambition played a part. To the startled viewer, though, it scarcely matters: the effect is frequently the same whether intentional or not. One can feel a powerful sense of alienation and disorientation oozing from the frankly insane *Frozen Scream* (Frank Roach and Renee Harmon, 1981) that rivals anything achieved by more self-conscious means. As the search for shocks morphs into weirdness as an end in itself, horror takes on a hallucinatory quality that leaves the viewer agape: *Malatesta's Carnival of Blood* (Christopher Speeth, 1973) and *BoardingHouse* (John Wintergate, 1982) are among the most extraordinary examples, while *The Last House on Dead End Street* (Roger Watkins, 1977) goes furthest of all, combining mind-bruising violence, drug-soaked delirium, and – to cap it all – genuine artistic self-awareness.

The USA boasts an incredible wealth of geographical and cultural variety – from the baking-hot alien landscapes of Death Valley to the sweltering marshlands of Louisiana, from the synthetic overload of Las Vegas to the old world elegance of New Orleans – and low-budget film productions sprang up in all manner of such unlikely locations, giving us glimpses into small towns and rural corners generally ignored by the majors. The impetus for these regional productions varied: they could be the result of a local entrepreneur venturing to fulfil a life-long dream of movie-making, or they could spring from thriving mini-studios dedicated to local production. The hot-spots for low-budget exploitation in the seventies and early eighties were still chiefly New York and Los Angeles, but significant movie-makers emerged from Miami, Florida (Harry Kerwin, William Grefé); Pittsburgh, Pennsylvania (George Romero, Christopher Speeth); Dallas, Texas (S.F. Brownrigg, Larry Buchanan); Texarkana, Texas (Charles B. Pierce); Shreveport, Louisiana (Joy Houck Jr., James Wilson); New Orleans, Louisiana (Jack Weis); Louisville, Kentucky (William Girdler); Gleason, Wisconsin (Bill Rebane); Baltimore, Maryland (Don Dohler, Tony Malanowski); and the North Carolina towns of Shelby (Earl Owensby, Worth Keeter) and Charlotte (Pat Patterson, Frederick Friedel). As time went by, some of these filmmakers headed off for California or New York to pursue their goals in the industry; others took one spin of the roulette wheel before retiring, fingers burned after being defrauded by distributors, or simply losing their shirt on a film that failed to appeal to an audience.

Such small film production was scattered wide across the United States, adding immensely to the richness of the exploitation field. In Hollywood, film is planned, shaped,

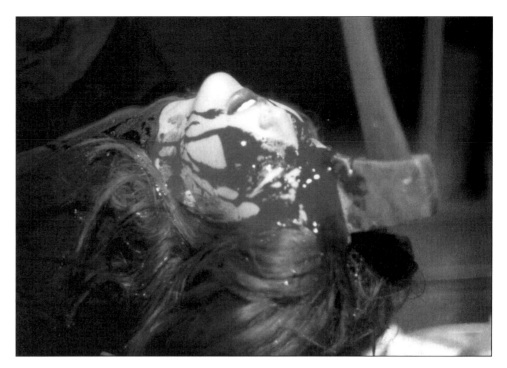

cultivated, harvested: it's a garden for the medium, with all of the strict control that implies. Exploitation films are more like the uncultivated countryside of the American film landscape, where weeds and wild flowers alike grow more freely. The Exploitation Independents contributed something of real value to American cinema: choice, variety, 'cultural plurality' if you will. From the 1930s to the mid-1980s, low-budget exploitation pictures provided a vital alternative to the prestige productions of the majors. They made good money for cinema owners and drive-in chains, thrived in urban and rural locations alike, and responded rapidly to current youth trends and issues. Unlike the majors, who were always looking over their shoulders at the gossip mags or mainstream press, or worrying about the absurd demands of the Hays Code, exploitation moviemakers could badger away at the limits of what was legally allowed onscreen; and since most mainstream movie critics disdained to review them, much of what went on in the wilder world of exploitation films passed by without nationwide howls of outrage (of the sort that eventually put paid to the horror genre's development in the early 1980s when the majors began taking an interest in the 'slasher film' subgenre). An alternative history of American cinema can be mapped through a study of these ephemeral products, and as the modern American film industry regresses to the monolithic form of its early days, it's a breath of fresh air to experience the products of a freer, less mediated film environment. Although the claims to be made for individual exploitation pictures must not be overstated, their great value was in decentring the film industry, providing variance, aesthetic and topical; offering pleasures above and beyond the more conservative major products; and even suggesting to the viewer that their home towns, their friends and acquaintances, could partake in the dream-structure of America. They provided balance against the feeling that cultural power in cinema was located entirely in Hollywood, and encouraged optimism and engagement in the medium at a local level. For these reasons – as well as for the sheer pleasure of the films themselves – the Exploitation Independents are worthy of detailed examination.

above:
There's certainly *something* oozing from this victim in **Frozen Scream**... Directors Frank Roach and Renee Harmon, proving that axe murders and alienation are far from mutually exclusive...

opposite bottom left:
Italian poster for **I Drink Your Blood**.

below:
Crude but amusing promo artwork for Tobe Hooper's **Death Trap**, his wonderfully weird follow-up to **The Texas Chain Saw Massacre**.

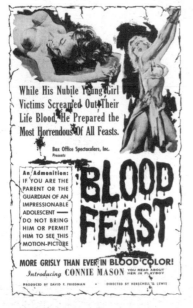

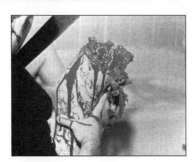

The Roots of Exploitation, and The Godfather of Gore

The traditions of carnival or 'carny' trading were a key factor in the development of exploitation cinema. Influential producer-director David Friedman, for instance, was a huckster who brought to the movie business all the skills he'd learned in the roadshow trade. Of course, carnivals often promised you marvels, only to leave you with a deflated beachball, food poisoning, and a dead goldfish in a bag of tap-water. It's no surprise that horror films should have been one of the favourite products of the exploitation entrepreneurs: persuading an audience to queue up for the '*shriekingest ghastliest thrill of your life!*' before offloading a duff Larry Buchanan film was not unlike shoving you into a tawdry tunnel of fake bats and cardboard witches masquerading as a ghost train ride.

But, even in the early days, exploitation films *occasionally* delivered, just as the sideshows occasionally featured a real two-headed calf, or a genuine human oddity strange enough to send you home unsettled and subdued. In the 1940s it was the unscrupulous producer/distributor Kroger Babb who, with director William Beaudine, first delivered a movie that really did startle the audience. The otherwise inane educational film *Mom and Dad* (1945) featured footage shot at a real human birth, triggering stunned reactions all the more powerful for having been preceded by the expectation of erotica. The film was marketed to suggest that here was the chance to see a woman expose herself to scrutiny of the most intimate kind – only to deliver the distended vaginal contortions, rupturing membranes and escaping fluids of the birth process.

Babb was a major influence on the wily Friedman, who worked with him for a while and realised that it was possible to make a profit by showing just a little of what people wanted. As he said, "The whole secret to exploitation and our successful little racket was the carnival tease: Boy, we didn't see it this week, but next week they're really going to show it to us."[1] But it was when a man called Herschell Gordon Lewis entered the picture that Friedman's place in exploitation film legend was assured…

Lewis first came to Friedman's attention in 1960 when he marched into the Chicago office of Modern Film Distributors, Friedman's company, and said he needed money to make his first feature. Friedman and Lewis got to talking and discovered they were very much of a mind about the industry. Their first collaboration was as producers of *The Prime Time* (1960), a mildly titillating romp directed by Gordon Weisenborn, which offered fleeting glimpses of female flesh to ape the 'nudie-cutie' style of Russ Meyer's *The Immoral Mr. Teas* (1959). The nudie cuties were tame fare, offering mere tinges of toplessness and glimpses of quivering bottoms, padded out with light unsophisticated comedy. Lewis immediately upped the stakes by directing *Living Venus* (1961), a slightly more risqué nudie-cutie than Weisenborn's film, following it with a sex comedy, *The Adventures of Lucky Pierre* (1961), and a string of nudist films, including *Daughter of the Sun* (1962), *Nature's Playmates* (1962) and a parody of the nudie industry called *Boin-n-g* (1963).

With qualifications for teaching High School English, Lewis was a smart, ambitious guy; smart enough to know that if he was going to advance beyond the limits of the nudies he had to do something that would stop the audience in their tracks. In an increasingly crowded market he needed something new to set his work apart from both major studios and other exploitation purveyors. Despite moderate financial success peddling smut, Lewis was growing restless with the rather dull material and looking for alternatives. Fully explicit sex was still a no-no, so it had to be something else…

That 'something' was gore. It occurred to Lewis and Friedman that although violence and death were staples of the cinema, no one ever showed the grisly details – instead the camera always flinched, the picture always faded to black. There was a taboo against showing the torn, mangled and twisted flesh of bleeding screaming victims. As soon as this taboo was remarked upon, the two men set about violating it.

Lewis directed his first gore film, *Blood Feast*, in 1963, and from the very start he knew he was onto a winner: "We opened the film at a drive-in in Peoria, feeling that if we dropped dead in Peoria no one would know. The film opened on a Friday. Saturday we couldn't stand it any longer, and we drove down to Peoria. Even though there was a major fair in town, theater traffic was backed up so far the State Police were directing it. We were still about a quarter mile from the theater when I turned to Dave, held out my hand, and said, 'I guess we've started something.'"[2]

If there's a fertilizing moment in the Cinema of Bad Taste, it's *Blood Feast*. Made for $24,000, it transcended its niche to become a runaway drive-in hit of the early sixties. Its importance to the horror genre in particular cannot be over-estimated. *Blood Feast* was the first horror film not only to shock its viewers, but also to wilfully *revolt* them. When it comes to Bad Taste, H.G. Lewis is the Daddy, to whom even John Waters genuflects. Not all of the films covered here in *Nightmare USA* embrace Lewis's liberating vulgarity, but there's no doubt that the modern horror film owes a chromosome to this man, one that can be seen today in the bloodline of everything from *Friday the 13th* (1980) to *Hostel* (2006).

Blood Feast is so crude and simplistic that it can seem positively *avant-garde* today, with its wonky music and bold primary colour backgrounds lit so flatly you'd think a comic-strip page was pressing itself on the lens. Blocky,

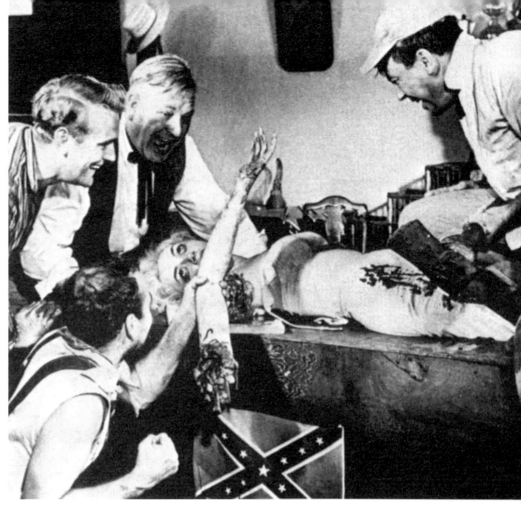

stilted editing patterns thwart the usual flow of visual information, and close-ups are so startlingly graceless it's worth coining a new technical term to prevent Gloria Swanson spinning in her grave. Gruesome murders are presented with blunt defiance, or the obstreperous relish of a child showing a mouthful of chewed-up food. This is where the film really lives, and it's the feeling of gleeful pathological childishness that amuses or offends, as much as the gore itself. Lewis treated audiences to the sight of a woman's tongue (a foot-long mass of cranberry coloured excreta) being ripped from her mouth, while another victim has her leg cut off at the knee. The *pièce de résistance*, a tabletop evisceration, achieves a *Grand Guignol* tableau that's simultaneously repulsive and astounding. Certainly, audiences in 1963 had seen nothing remotely like it before.

Disgusting? Of course. Misogynous? Debatable. There's hilarity in all this butcher shop mayhem, and to be outraged is to play straight man to Lewis's wind-up. *Blood Feast*'s exuberant eruptions of gore are as funny as they are revolting, like something from a cheap-and-nasty carnival act, and the film's villain, 'caterer' Fuad Ramses, is as bizarrely emphatic as a circus clown. Let go of the need to disapprove, and the score for horn and kettledrums alone is so leadenly foreboding it can only raise a smile.

Despite all these things, *Blood Feast* is more than just a cluster of 'bad film' signifiers. It has power because of, not despite, its amateur elements. There's no need to coddle Lewis, as some movie buffs do Edward D. Wood – *Blood Feast* does not cry out for the pity of an indulgent audience. Lewis will never need some future Tim Burton to cheerlead his *oeuvre*. Implicit in *Blood Feast*, and explicit in Lewis's later films, is a feeling that we're being played, like fish by an angler; that the filmmaker is having a laugh at the expense of anyone unprepared for his butcher-shop hi-jinx.

Lewis followed *Blood Feast* with another violent saga, *Two Thousand Maniacs!* (1964). From its hyperbolic title onwards we're tipped off to the presence of a showman. *Two Thousand Maniacs!* was one of Lewis's most plausible films, with fair acting and a story of some originality (the musical *Brigadoon* excepted) to bolster the bouts of violence. The gore wasn't *quite* as disgusting as that of *Blood Feast*, but still it must have sent many a wobbly-kneed drive-in patron out of his car to 'call Ralph'. Take the film's first eruption of mayhem: during a countryside tryst, a grinning hick suddenly severs a city girl's thumb before dragging her screaming back into town for dismemberment by a gloating cadre of good ole boys. The scene has impact, not only for what you see (the thumb slicing, and a girl's limbs hacked off by an axe) but because of the sheer onscreen duration – the horror is drawn out, with the victim transferred from one location to another for further abuse. Amid the carnage, the gleeful performances of the killers add a tinge of aggressive absurdity. Audiences accustomed to short bursts of implied violence were having their faces rubbed in something quite different...

The energy diminished somewhat for the third in Lewis's 'Gore Trilogy', *Color Me Blood Red* (1965), a film that shows the beginnings of artistic self-consciousness in its depiction of a painter who discovers that the perfect shade of red needed for his work is human blood. But after splitting from producer David Friedman and directing a few non-horror items, Lewis bounced back with even grislier films: chiefly *The Gruesome Twosome* (1967), *The Wizard of Gore* (1970) and *The Gore Gore Girls* (1972). As

the titles suggest, they bring a rough, satirical humour to the table, along with even more of the red stuff. *The Gruesome Twosome* sees the start of Lewis's decadent period – don't laugh! – as the set-up is relentlessly satirized and no one behind or in front of the camera takes the horror seriously. That said, the visceral shocks are as potent as ever. Quite what an unsuspecting 1960s audience made of these simultaneously gross and unconvincing scalp-slitting charades is anyone's guess. The killer is a poorly acted retard cooed over by his equally deranged mother, and the threadbare plotting is sarcastically endowed with several minutes of blatant padding, as in the opening scene (added to bring the running time up to spec') in which two Styrofoam heads swap small-talk in the window of a downtown wig shop.

The Wizard of Gore is simultaneously the strangest and the slowest of Lewis's movies: jaw-droppingly ghastly, bizarrely inventive, but infuriatingly repetitive. Telling the

above:
A visiting Yankee (Shelby Livingston) finds that being 'guest of honour' in a Confederate centenary celebration isn't all it's cracked up to be in **Two Thousand Maniacs!**, H.G. Lewis's rip-roarin' follow-up to **Blood Feast**.

bottom left:
Promotional art for
Two Thousand Maniacs!

opposite:
The movie that started it all: **Blood Feast**...
from top:
Original US poster art;
Fuad Ramses (Mal Arnold) whips a young woman before adding her to his 'Egyptian feast';
More ingredients, as Fuad prepares a dish fit for a *Playboy* centerfold (well, wooden heroine Connie Mason, anyway...) using pieces of Sandra Sinclair.

above and right:
For the third entry in his 'gore trilogy', **Color Me Blood Red**, Lewis toned down the violence somewhat, although the rest of his hallmarks – terrible acting, leaden pacing and static framing – continued as normal.

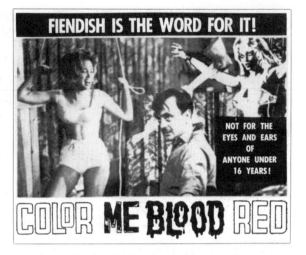

below:
Night of the Living Dead – original UK quad poster. Note the breathless lack of punctuation in the ad-line!

story of a deranged stage magician whose grisly illusions turn to reality after the show is over, it establishes a high watermark for exploitation weirdness that would not be challenged until Doris Wishman birthed *A Night To Dismember* in 1983. Lewis constructs an ambitious tale of Illusion versus Reality; the ideas are audacious, although his narrative skills are, if anything, more regressive and painfully amateur than ever. Nevertheless, since the film depicts reality as contradictory and mutational, and since the principle of cause-and-effect is deliberately and flagrantly violated, author and Lewis expert Daniel Krogh was right to suggest, however facetiously, a kinship between *Wizard* and the work of Sicilian novelist and dramatist Luigi Pirandello! Finally, *The Gore Gore Girls* (see review section) plays like a macabre comedy, with Lewis slapping on perhaps the most extreme, extraordinary violence of his career. Indeed, the man himself felt that he'd done as much as he could with *The Gore Gore Girls*, which gained an 'X' certificate in March 1972; a rare distinction at the time for a non-porno movie. He would not return to directing until tempted by cash to make the ill-advised *Blood Feast 2* in 2002.

Romero, and the Modern Horror Pantheon

As time goes by and film history settles into a mould set by theoreticians and film journalists, it has become a staple observation that the golden age of American horror cinema began in 1968 with George Romero's *Night of the Living Dead*. In truth, Herschell Gordon Lewis was the progenitor of graphic American horror, but what Romero added was exceptional filmmaking skill – something Lewis could never claim – and genuine *on-screen* intelligence (Lewis, as interviews have shown, is a very smart guy, but his films are not the best vehicles to prove it). Romero's astonishing debut has been analysed, rejected, celebrated, berated, discovered, rediscovered, colorized, extended, remade and re-released until it's almost impossible to regain a sense of what really changed when audiences were initially exposed to it. What is worth saying once again is that Romero brought a new urgency to the genre. Something changed when his zombies began their march into film history, something that left even the jocular sadism of H.G. Lewis behind.

Night of the Living Dead is without doubt a turning point, a class act emerging from what initially looked like just a simple Pennsylvania business enterprise. Although it was initially condemned, mocked, sneered at and blamed for all manner of negative effects on its poor audience, its now well-established position of respect can be even more obscuring than the fury of those early attacks. One of the first things you have to do is to stop thinking of it as perfect. It has a significant degree of stylization, despite its reputation as the film that brought *verité* ambience to the horror genre. It's almost as talky as that other great black and white monster movie, *Fiend Without a Face*: but where *Fiend* only springs to life for its hokey but exciting climax, *Night of the Living Dead* kicks off as a true nightmare, falls back into dialogue-heavy stodge in the middle, then lunges for the audience's throats again in the final reel.

Romero's debut brought a chilling seediness to the genre, a shabbiness of cast and *mise-en-scène*. As for the monsters: here was a grubby blue-collar apocalypse made from life's rejects, the flotsam and jetsam of the grave. In the movement of the undead there was a lack of dignity, a terribly plausible gaucheness. The zombies weren't just horrible because they wanted to eat you – it was the way they embodied an irredeemable abjection as they did so. These pathetic, mangled figures weren't the snarling beasts of folklore, werewolves or vampires, red in tooth and claw, with the gleam of a savage vitality in their eye. Fighting over scraps of human flesh, they possessed none of the sovereignty or glamour of the wild. You find yourself feeling somehow embarrassed for them, these ghouls half-dressed in the tatters of their baggy underclothes, stumbling around on a chilly November night, pasty and plump and bedraggled. Their actions are not the expression of some revolutionary aggression – just a sad, listless compulsion. The performers, non-actors conscripted from the local community – shopkeepers, businessmen, housewives – are like the unchosen hordes who fail auditions for talent shows, trailing around in their 'model's own' costumes. Romero gave us an invasion of the quotidian: *we* were the ghouls, you and I, our families, our neighbours. A terrible intimacy changes the way we see the monsters in this film: take the old woman plucking a large bug from a tree trunk and eating it, caught indulging some mindless joyless compulsion, as if we'd turned on the hallway light and seen a favourite but now senile Aunt on the kitchen floor in her nightie, eating cat food, eyes glazed and confused. Horror was mixed with a confusing pathos.

Then there was Barbara, whose failure to adjust to the film's nightmarish reality marked a defining shift from the sophisticated heroines and spirited screamers of Lewton and Hammer. The dismaying honesty of her characterisation said, 'Who are you kidding? What makes you think you'd cope with this level of horror?' The screams and swoons of Universal or Hammer heroines were more sexual in nature, the closest men got to hearing the female orgasm onscreen before the days of sexual liberation. Barbara isn't part of that game, her trauma isn't titillating; it's scary and all-too believable. As survivor of the first zombie attack, she becomes audience surrogate for the first reel, pulling us deeper into the story as she runs across open countryside and attempts to fetch help at a decrepit old farmhouse. This surrogacy is then challenged by her collapse into disconnection. Some viewers can't take the turn of events: 'Pull yourself together you stupid bitch!' is not an unusual audience catcall. Romero shows how we hate to believe that events might be 'too much' for us. Barbara's collapse into near-catatonia, her pathetic clinging to the fringes of normality (fiddling with a piece of fabric etc.), even her belated effort to rejoin the group by ineptly barricading the door, all offend the audience's wish to experience a sense of control. For me, the ironic finale in which Barbara falls into the hands of her undead brother just as she's begun to fight back gives the film one of its most authentic notes of horror.

Night of the Living Dead said that things were *not* going to turn out alright. The hero was not in control of events, good people did not have a right to live, love didn't conquer all, the family was not a sanctuary. Even the monsters weren't 'evil', so there was no consoling moral dimension. The threat wasn't Communism or Fascism. It was too close to be defined as an 'other' of some sort. Instead of an enemy in the clear and righteous sense, a depersonalized slurry of humanity roamed the Earth in a sort of reproachful mortification. As such, the film presents an irresistible symbolic enticement for critics and theorists. American social upheavals of the sixties, such as the Kent State anti-war demonstrations, the Kennedy assassination and the Civil Rights movement, have all been cited as catalysts for Romero's film. Fruitful connections can indeed be made, but beware – in our desire to make grand narratives of history and culture, we can often accept high-minded theorizing as gospel. Romero himself has been cautious on the subject: "I was sort of conscious of the iconoclastic aspect of it. We were doing a film that was shattering a lot of conventions, and we weren't adverse [sic] to shattering those conventions because we wanted to give our film every chance we could to attract attention." Beyond cinematic conventions and the etiquette of screen horror, though, Romero is more guarded: "It was 1968, man. *Everybody* had a 'message'. Maybe it crept in. I was just making a horror film, and I think the anger and the attitude and all that's there is just there because it was 1968 […] I think that if you make something that seems real and true to people, it then becomes possible for them to have the little kinds of insights and feelings and rationales that they call 'hidden meanings' and 'statements' and whatever."[3]

Americans *d'un certain age* may share a social background that dovetails with theories seeing modern horror as borne of the political upheavals of the 1960s. But these films have made sense to viewers all over the world,

regardless of social context, which would suggest that something broader and deeper is at play. The social-response thesis (as expanded upon in 2000 by Adam Simon's documentary *The American Nightmare*) smacks of a middle-aged grasp for respectability by those uncomfortable with the atavistic, sadistic, masochistic and sensationalist qualities of the genre. British audiences didn't respond to *Night of the Living Dead* because their sons were coming home from a war in body bags. Nor did they feel stirred by *The Texas Chain Saw Massacre* in the mid-seventies because of sympathetic twinges of anxiety about the US fuel crisis, or the mechanisation of agriculture. Audiences worldwide react to the syntax and rhythm of these movies, their kinetic and auditory power, their grasp of nightmare logic and the embodiment of primal fears about bad places and bad people. You no more need political and social context to 'read' them than a lover of Grimm's fairytales needs to bone up on 19th Century German forestry practices.

above:
The Texas Chain Saw Massacre, or to the Spanish, **La matanza de Texas** – an authentic movie nightmare in any language or social context...

Critical Responses to Exploitation Cinema

Prevailing critical opinion in the 1970s would have insisted that horror films, 'mere exploitation', were certainly *not* to be ranked alongside the mavericks and masters of the New Hollywood. Even a powerful, thoughtful work like *Dawn of the Dead* (which, unlike *Night of the Living Dead*, has a conscious, deliberate and deeply pessimistic political dimension) was just as likely to be dismissed as revolting garbage as it was to be admired for its bleak social satire and self-consciously cartoonish spectacle. However, time has changed the way in which critics see these films. As a result of two factors – changing social views on screen violence, and (perhaps more tellingly) the subsequent mainstream careers of the filmmakers concerned – many of the most high profile Exploitation Independents are now safely ensconced in a critical film discourse that recognises the value of their work as 'texts'.

It's uncontroversial to suggest that styles and tastes change over time; the horror genre, alongside comedy, has long been a good barometer for mapping the way in which social taboos and boundaries shift, dissolve and reform. But what does it mean to suggest that the subsequent career of a filmmaker plays a part in redefining attitudes to their earlier output? The answer lies in the auteur theory, a commonly adopted theoretical viewpoint in which privilege is given to the perceived author of a work; usually the director.

There is much to be said for the auteur approach. Prominent voices in the horror genre such as George Romero or David Cronenberg are writer-directors, justly celebrated for their authorial signature, their 'auteur consistency'. But there's a drawback: before such value judgements can be made, the auteur theory requires multiple films by the same director – preferably more than two – as a sanction for serious consideration, and a safeguard against the ultimate critical crime: *reading too much* into a single film. The auteurist approach, with its concern for *sustained* artistic signatures, has obvious deficiencies when assessing 'one-off' films made by

'unknown' directors. Few theorists, even now, would admit individual exploitation films into serious consideration *without* the imprimatur of previous critical recognition. Such films have generally been disregarded in overviews of American cinema because they make risky subjects for learned theses. If lightning can be shown to have struck twice, theorists feel they can safely start looking for the 'hand of God' – i.e. the auteur.

Specialist or fan publications have more diligently scrutinised the exploitation arena, and admittedly, in the last five or six years, an increasing number of academic writers address it too, but to illustrate the blind-spot in wider film discourse it's worth looking briefly at two books which act as bridging points for film students entering academic study: *The Cinema Book*, by Pam Cook and Mieke Bernink; and *Film Art*, by David Bordwell and Kristin Thompson. Although admirably wide-ranging in almost every other respect, neither volume grants exploitation due credit as a distinct cinematic force: indeed, the category is barely acknowledged. In *The Cinema Book*, a chapter called 'Alternatives to Classic Hollywood' lists the following: 'Early Cinema after Brighton'; 'New Hollywood'; 'Art Cinema'; 'East Asian Cinema'; 'Avant-Garde and Counter-Cinema'; 'Third World and Postcolonial Cinema'; and 'Hindi Cinema'. In *Film Art*, exploitation movies are referred to in just three paragraphs (in a book of over five hundred pages): by comparison, Experimental Film (another form in which individual effort is spread widely over the whole USA) receives scrutiny over seventeen pages. Considering cultural reach alone, the imbalance is regrettable.

The oversight is almost certainly due to a combination of factors: the perceived lowbrow nature of exploitation, its ephemeral, decentralized nature (lots of one-off films, with many different writers and directors), and its reliance on genre. When general film reference works dip into exploitation cinema it's nearly always to mention Sam Arkoff's American International Pictures (AIP) or Roger Corman Productions: two solid mini-major set-ups whose exploitation movies account for just a fraction of those produced. Corman and AIP have also been reasonably well documented because several alumni of the two (such as Coppola and Scorsese) went on to mainstream careers, thus drawing attention to the 'seed-bed' from which they grew. (Corman's own career as director of such classic films as *The Masque of the Red Death* and *The Tomb of Ligeia* no doubt helped as well.) Sometimes an iconic figure from the margins of exploitation, a David Cronenberg or a Wes Craven, is raised on the shoulders of critical recognition, especially if their work fits neatly with the discursive trends of the day. Suddenly the director metamorphoses from exploitation pariah to maverick hero: which is fine, except that their films are then admitted to a 'charmed circle' of critical celebration at the expense of legions of others ignored at the periphery. It's not the purpose of this book to dismiss the value of established auteurs: I just believe that critics should extend to interesting strangers the same courtesy they offer familiar faces. And besides, the 'charmed circle' of critical acceptance is itself a problem: it can become a petrified forest in which vital talents are frozen mid-step. Such is the fate of the Italian director Dario Argento, a true maverick of the horror genre whose work became mired in sterile self-consciousness some time in the early 1990s; suspiciously enough, *after* he became the subject of serious study.

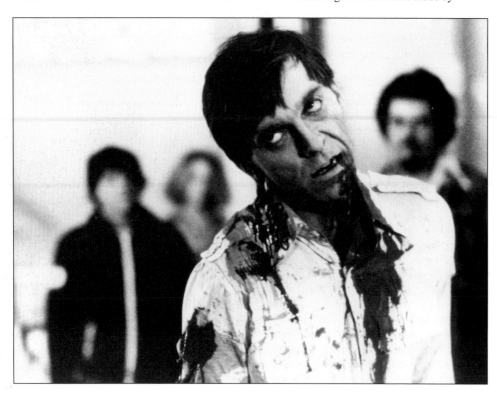

Drive-In Massacres
with thanks to Robert Monell

From the thirties to the eighties, a parallel network of film production and exhibition flourished in the USA. Thousands of low-budget genre movies were made, and central to their success was a uniquely American phenomenon: the drive-in movie theatre.

A 'drive-in' is basically an open-air cinema, comprising: a large white surface upon which a movie can be projected (anything from a whitewashed wall to a specially constructed high-tension canvas); a projection booth; a large car-parking area; and (last but not least) a concession stand for the sale of snacks. The first drive-in was patented in 1933 by Richard M. Hollingshead Jr., the son of a chemical company magnate. Feeling unchallenged by his post in the family business, Hollingshead came up with the idea after noting two problems with existing cinemas: if parents with young children wanted to go to a movie, they had to find a babysitter in the evenings, and since most theatres of the day were on main streets without parking lots, finding a parking space was a major headache. Hitting on the idea of outdoor screenings to be viewed from the family car, he set up a prototype on his own land, using a screen nailed to trees in his garden, and cars arranged in the driveway. After experimenting with different options to achieve optimum audio and visual range, Hollingshead obtained a patent and set up the world's first drive-in theatre in Camden, New Jersey, opening on 6 June, 1933. The idea was a big success, and soon others were springing up elsewhere.

The early drive-ins relied on a single audio source, usually a three-way speaker mounted near the screen. But there were two drawbacks to this approach: firstly, since sound travels more slowly than light, the cars furthest away from the screen would hear the sound lag behind the image; and secondly, although drive-in sites were often out of town, the speakers would broadcast the movie across fields to adjacent properties, making them unpopular with local residents. The problem was solved when in-car speaker systems were introduced: patrons were offered portable speakers attached to posts beside each parking space, to be inserted through the side window and propped on the dashboard. (Later technological advances led to the sound being transmitted to the car radio at low-radius output on the AM or FM band, enabling stereo in place of the classic 'tinny' monaural speaker system.)

By 1948 there were over 800 drive-ins dotted around America, rising to over 4,000 by 1958. Numbers remained between 3,300 and 3,500 for the next fifteen years. This decreased a little, to around 2,800 by 1977, and 2,200 by the early 1980s. However by the end of the eighties – the home video decade – the numbers slid to below 1,000; by which time the major studios had bought up the chains and insisted the screens be used to promote the same first run product that dominated hardtop cinemas elsewhere.[4]

America's love affair with the motorcar is well known, and has always been adoringly fostered by the cinema. The image of a young white male driving an open-topped car down the streets of his home town, whistling at girls and pulling over at a diner to hang out with buddies, is as pervasive a slice of American iconography as one can find. From the youth-oriented films of the 1950s like *Rebel Without a Cause* (1955), to the purposeful mythologizing of *American Graffiti* (1973) – not to mention ambivalent exploitation films like *Death Race 2000* (1975) and videogames like *Carmageddon* – the car is clearly the central icon of American success. Drive-ins brought the automobile and the silver screen together, then added yet another potent energy to the mix: teenage sex.

While the inventor of the drive-in may have been thinking of hard-worked parents struggling to find babysitters and parking spaces, it wasn't long before teenagers discovered another advantage to his brainchild. Drive-ins – of course – made perfect venues for dating. By necessity, they operated after twilight, and the mixture of semi-privacy and safety they offered horny teenage lovers led to disapproving press articles damning drive-ins as 'passion-pits'. Adding to the appeal of 'sitting in the backseat at the movies' by cocooning young couples in their automobiles, the drive-in gave baby-boomers the ideal location for intimacy. What moralizers failed to see was that for girls it was probably better to make out in a car surrounded by lots of other cars, all perhaps similarly occupied, and bathed in the intermittent flare of the movie screen, rather than acceding to a drive down some lonely 'Lover's Lane'.

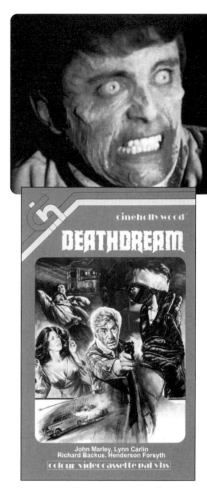

Meanwhile, horror offered reliable frights, driving couples together in a ritual of shock-embrace-and-fondle that has long been self-consciously recorded by the genre itself. Seventies horrors that feature key scenes at the drive-in include *Deathdream* (Bob Clark, 1972); *Kiss of the Tarantula* (Chris Munger, 1975); and, you guessed it, *Drive-In Massacre* (Stu Segall, 1976). In each case, the films spring horrific backseat surprises – a zombie; killer spiders; a psycho-killer – on the requisite necking couples. Perhaps the most potent use of the drive-in as an icon in its own right came in *Targets* (Peter Bogdanovich, 1968), in which a teenage sniper takes pot-shots at drive-in patrons, during a screening in honour of a soon-to-retire horror icon (Boris Karloff). The film suggested that the old Gothic horror films of the 1930s and '40s (and the Corman Gothics of the early 1960s) had been rendered obsolete by the horror of real-life random violence (the film was inspired by the Charles Whitman 'Texas Tower Sniper' killings of 1966). This slightly smug formulation was itself rendered obsolete when the horror genre took up the challenge of addressing real-world horror, in such uncompromising films as *The Last House on the Left* (1972), *The Texas Chain Saw Massacre* (1974), *I Spit on Your Grave* (Meir Zarchi, 1978) and *Maniac* (1980) – movies Bogdanovich is unlikely to admire…

You never knew quite what to expect at the drive-in. For sure, the posters and admats designed by the distributors declared that you were in for the shock of your life, but all sorts of other forces were at work too, and they differed from territory to territory, chain to chain. Drive-in owners wilfully changed the titles of the films they were showing, crudely inserting new title cards, drawn with magic marker if necessary. A manager might order the projectionist to edit a film, particularly if the screen faced a street where people pulled onto the Interstate. After all, a grisly shocker like *I Drink Your Blood* could cause accidents if some hapless traveller caught a glimpse of, say, a deranged hippy chick touting a severed limb! Films were also butchered as successive managers and projectionists snipped out favourite violent or sexy moments for their own collections. And while the producers and distributors edited different versions for different regional drive-ins (a film that played well in the

above: A horror classic set in the streets around Times Square – **Basket Case** (1981). *below:* If any country rivals America for that no-holds-barred exploitation sizzle it's Japan, as we can see from this fantastic poster for **The Texas Chain Saw Massacre** (1974).

Deep South, for instance, might need some coaxing in Upstate New York), they weren't the only ones playing the game: the term 'Franchise Print' was coined in the industry to describe a version cut together not by the producer or distributor but by the owner of the drive-in circuit. As fans began to compare notes, certain titles gained mythic reputations, and thus repeat business whenever they turned up again. Wildly different degrees of extremity were discovered in prints strewn nationwide, so committed fans would drive hundreds of miles to see a film in a neighbouring state, hoping to catch it uncut. And if the drive-ins were letting you down, you could always make the ultimate exploitation pilgrimage and trek to New York, where, running West to East across Manhattan Island, the Satanic El Dorado of exploitation awaited you…

42nd Street Monsters

For Exploitation fans born too late to go there, the image of New York's 42nd Street as a Dantean circle-and-stalls of hell is incredibly seductive. Other cities could boast their share of sleazy cinemas,[5] but as a nerve centre of illicit stimulation this dense cluster of movie theatres and porno houses possessed a diabolical glamour, something that still excites the imagination today. Bill Landis, writer of *Sleazoid Express*, the essential chronicle of the New York grindhouse scene, describes the area: "Times Square was America's most notorious red-light district, located within the esteemed Broadway theater hub. From the early 1960s its main artery was known as the Deuce, a tiny strip of grimy neon and concrete that coldly fleshed out 42nd Street between 7th and 8th Avenues. The street was wall-to-wall grindhouses, down-at-the-heels creations left over from the Minsky's Burlesque days, old theaters that retained a stained, velour elegance and an imposing physicality, with large auditoriums, balconies, big screens, velvet curtains, and long-ago closed off opera seats."[6]

To brave a screening of *Torture Dungeon* (Andy Milligan, 1970), *Ilsa, She Wolf of the SS* (Don Edmonds, 1975) or *Fight for Your Life* (Robert Endelson, 1977) in one of these notorious venues you needed either nerves of steel, blissful ignorance, or a bit of the psycho in your own mental baggage. Ushers admitted anyone with a ticket, and once in the theatre an assortment of winos, weirdos and jerkoffs could settle in for the day, uninterrupted. Drugs were scored and consumed, sex sought and obtained in the toilets or tenebrous balcony seats, and arguments you wouldn't want to get involved with played out in row after sticky-floored row of crud-flecked seating.

Hunkering down amid this Boschean circus were a few, just a few, who had come specifically for the movie. Film fans like John Waters, up from Baltimore to soak up as much trash cinema as possible. Landis, of course. Others such as Rick Sullivan, editor of the *Sleazoid*-influenced *Gore Gazette*, and Bob Martin, editor of the more mainstream *Fangoria*, were among the writers eager to venture into these environs in search of trash epiphanies; or failing that just a handful of memorable moments in the parade of horror/action/sexploitation dross. Landis in particular was at home there. A fervent drug-user and hard-nosed cynic, he documented the cinema ambience as much as the movies: later editions of *Sleazoid Express* are notable more as gonzo reports from the brink of amphetamine psychosis than as film journalism *per se*. Landis seemed to take Nietzsche's aphorism about the abyss looking into you more as a challenge than a warning…

Others who frequented the 42nd Street grindhouses included filmmakers who were themselves soon to contribute to the excesses served up there. William Lustig, who made his directing debut in 1977 at the age of 22 with a porno flick called *The Violation of Claudia* (directed under the pseudonym Billy Bagg) was already a regular 42nd Street patron, soaking up a constant diet of sex, horror and imported Italian action flicks. He told Eric Caidin and John McCarty: "I was addicted to movies! I used to cut school and go to 42nd Street and that area to see movie after movie. I fell in love with everything I saw, from the art pictures to the Harry Novak type of sexploitation pictures I used to sneak into."[7] Lustig especially loved horror movies, and so struck a deal with executive producer Judd Hamilton and actor Joe Spinell to make their own. The result was *Maniac* (1980), a legendarily grim exercise in violence and sleaze that divided horror fans at the time. These days the film has been partially reclaimed by the fans but in the early 1980s it was treated as symbolic of all that was 'sick' and 'irresponsible' about the modern horror genre. For those of us who have always loved this nasty tale (see my comments in the review section), such arguments were just a side-salad to the meat of Lustig's film. Here was a director who had obviously studied hard at the 42nd Street lecture halls of sleaze!

Another self-taught aficionado of horror to be found haunting the sleaziest screens of the area was Frank Henenlotter, soon to be the celebrated director of *Basket Case* (1981). Henenlotter began by making Super-8mm shorts, with titles like *Slash of the Knife* and *The Shameful Women*, homemade horrors that mimicked the bad taste of his favourite trash films. Moving on to the glories of 16mm, Henenlotter made *Basket Case*, one of the few films to act both as a *bona fide* 42nd Street movie and a self-conscious homage to its predecessors. It's interesting to note that both Lustig and Henenlotter eventually withdrew from filmmaking to pursue their love of grindhouse films by releasing them on DVD – Henenlotter through an association with Something Weird, and Lustig with Anchor Bay and his own company, Blue Underground.

Not everyone felt the ambivalent affection-repulsion for the region expressed by writers like Bill Landis. For critics and moralists, 42nd Street came to epitomise a brand of cynical, amoral cinema, and if an upright filmmaking citizen wanted to suggest that screen horror and real life horror were causally interlinked, he could always film a murderous character strolling down the very streets where such joys as *The Bloodthirsty Butchers* (Andy Milligan, 1970) or *Shriek of the Mutilated*

(Michael Findlay, 1974) were playing. In a region where drugs and prostitution were at epidemic levels, and which was effectively decimated by crack during the mid-eighties, one might counter that social policies on these issues, and not sleazy movies, were the real reason that the streets seemed to crawl with the viciousness seen on the screens of the Deuce. But it nevertheless became typical for a screen killer to be shown prowling the 42nd Street drag, as if there was some inexorable link between the screaming billboards and the actions of the patrons. 42nd Street became synonymous with sickness, and, by implication, the habits of an American icon at least as influential as those smooth fifties boys in their Chevy convertibles we talked about earlier: I'm referring to the serial killer, the sex sadist, the psychopath…

Serial Killers

Serial killing impacted heavily on America's collective psyche in the sixties and seventies, when Charles Manson, David Berkowitz, Dean Corll, John Wayne Gacy, Edmund Kemper, Ted Bundy, Henry Lee Lucas and a blizzard of others slammed the concept into mass consciousness. It's hardly surprising that cinema should react to this by offering audiences a staged glimpse of the horrors so darkly hinted at in TV and newspaper coverage. Crimes such as Ted Bundy's savage assault on a Florida co-ed dorm in the January of 1978, killing two girls and severely bludgeoning two others, sent ripples of terror across America, and it wasn't long before the genre responded by inviting filmgoers to confront their worst imaginings of such crimes onscreen.

A serial killer is defined as someone who commits at least three murders, separated in time, with a 'cooling off' period in between, during which time they will seem perfectly normal, holding down a regular job or even (like Bundy) maintaining a marriage in which the partner is

all illustrations this page:
Shriek of the Mutilated was produced by Ed Adlum (the man responsible for **Invasion of the Blood Farmers**) and directed by New York exploitation pioneer Michael Findlay. Although the brilliantly excessive title far outstrips the contents, it's still a cheesy low-rent treat – in fact it's positively adorable next to Findlay's most notorious New York cine-crime, **Snuff**…

unaware of their spouse's criminal activity. Crucially, it's this 'cooling-off period' that makes the serial killer such an enticing villain for the horror genre. Maniacs who can't hide their madness tend to foreshorten narrative; so it's better to feature a killer who keeps the audience guessing, hidden behind an ordinary-Joe persona. In the 1970s, the horror genre began to take the real-world nightmare of serial slaying as source material, and as the crimes of sadistic killers were reported with increasing prurience in the news, the genre's response, further fostered by the relaxation of censorship, grew more explicit and uncompromising.

While some will find the notion of a film producer taking inspiration from such crimes despicable, it's worth considering the way in which horror films help us to deal with our fears. A fear left unscrutinised festers and grows, but a fear confronted is at least containable. No power in America could stem the tide of mass slayings; therefore young people, for whom horror films are so attractive, and who comprise the most likely target for killers, need some way of visualising and thus dealing with the threat. Violent horror films offered a way of doing so, as well as feeding the morbid fascination that real life brutality inspires. The slasher movies and sorority house horrors of the late 1970s and 1980s may have been mounted primarily for money's sake, but they appealed to a huge 16-25 audience, perhaps because of the way they deprive frightening, often salacious news reports of their exclusivity, drawing 'beyond-the-pale' imagery into the

fantasy arena where it can be subject to the process of imagination. Looked at in this way, it seems only right that the perpetrators of atrocity should be denied the last word – to allow such crimes to be *literally* unspeakable, and thus to be honoured by taboo, is to confer a spurious authority upon the criminal.

For those concerned with the issue of bad taste in exploitation's response to reality, it's worth pointing out that Alfred Hitchcock was there very early with *Psycho* (1960), based on the crimes of Wisconsin necrophile and murderer Ed Gein. From a 21st Century standpoint, it's remarkable that *Psycho*, a studio picture by one of the industry's most respected directors, was released only *three years* after Gein was apprehended, in November 1957, making it something of an 'exploitation' film in its own right. Hitchcock, a frequent visitor to the horror genre in his film and TV work, was an artist of rampaging morbidity, but even he found it necessary to draw a veil over some of the more revolting details of the Gein case (however, as David Cronenberg has suggested, this probably had more to do with the restrictions of the time than with any innate reserve on Hitchcock's part).[8] Gein's crimes, which went on to inspire radically visceral treatments like *The Texas Chain Saw Massacre* (1974) and *Deranged* (Jeff Gillen, 1974), were *so* macabre, and the imagery associated with them in the public imagination so bizarre, that in many ways they joined the Jack the Ripper killings in that odd moral purgatory where salaciousness and sadism meet myth and fantasy.

However, this 'comfort zone' of the macabre, in which dastardly Victorian slashers and folksy grave-robbers are allowed to cavort, was unable to contain all the horrors unleashed in the news stories of the 1970s. Horror films responded by adopting a grimmer, darker tone: the genre was no longer guaranteed to be spooky escapist fun. The Exploitation Independents took notice of the headlines and media scare stories and began crafting films with a downbeat, upsetting vibe. Among the films that address the subject of serial murder are: *Abducted* (Don Jones, 1973); *Victims* (1977); *Hitch Hike to Hell* (1977); *The Toolbox Murders* (Dennis Donnelly, 1977); *Sketches of a Strangler* (Paul Leder, 1978); *Bloodrage* (Joseph Zito, 1979); *Don't Answer the Phone!* (Robert Hammer, 1979); *Don't Go in the House* (Joseph Ellison, 1979); and *Maniac* (1980).

If there's one thing such films agree upon, it's that hitchhiking is a shortcut to death. In the early 1970s increasing numbers of disaffected youths, influenced by the promise of social and sexual liberation, were eagerly relocating to the big cities looking for fun and freedom, but in order to 'live the dream' they had to cross the wide-open spaces of America, hitchhiking through county after county, state after state. A boy or girl could get lost on such a journey, and there were predators on the highways worse than any wolf or bear. Considering the alarming number of serial killers operating in California during the 1970s, it seemed as if these human monsters were picking up the very scent of the country's youth, hunting them down as they flocked to free-thinking San Francisco and Los Angeles. Perhaps it's a testament to the groundbreaking changes of the hippy era that a new strain of evil emerged in the seventies to provide the shadow to sexual and social liberation.

Meanwhile, the counterculture produced its own iconic monster in the form of Charles Manson, whose role as murder-guru to acid-guzzling dropouts like Charles 'Tex' Watson, Patricia Krenwinkel, Susan Atkins and Leslie Van Houten sent shockwaves through bourgeois America. Hot on the heels of the Manson Family's capture, *Janie* (Jack Bravman, 1970) depicted a young female killer whose blithe psychopathy echoes that of the Manson girls; *Sweet Savior* (Bob Roberts, 1972) had ex teen heart-throb Troy Donahue in long hair as a Manson figure exhorting the kids to murder; the disturbing docudrama *The Other Side of Madness* (Frank Howard, 1970) and the inaccurate and unconvincing *The Manson Massacre* (Kentucky Jones, 1972) went so far as to depict the case directly; and *The Centerfold Girls* (John Peyser, 1974) had it both ways, with a nerdy serial killer whose first victim falls into his hands having already suffered a night of rape and humiliation at the hands of a Mansonesque hippy gang. *Snuff* (1976), originally shot in 1971 as *Slaughter* by Michael and Roberta Findlay, features a Mansonesque cult, but the film was unreleased at the time and only came to notoriety when Allan Shackleton and Simon Nuchtern added a fake snuff sequence to the ending, thus tapping into rumours of the Manson family's own supposed 8mm snuff atrocities (none of which have ever been found). On a related note, there's a counterculture vibe to the killer artist in that extraordinary grindhouse classic *The Headless Eyes* (1971); *Trip with the Teacher* (Earl Barton, 1975) resurrects another counterculture bad-guy, the psychotic biker; and the two female psychos in the

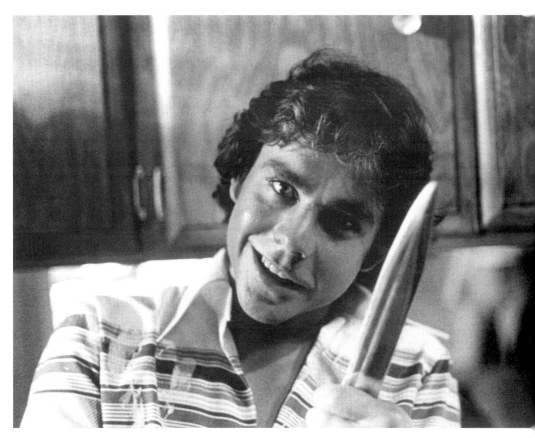

lurid *Death Game* (Peter Traynor, 1976) share the anti-bourgeois attitudes and grinning, unsympathetic sadism of the Family girls.

Coming at murder from quite a different angle to Manson and his gang of sociopaths, the psycho Vietnam veteran brought it all back home for American filmgoers in equally disturbing fashion. The ultra-obscure *The Ravager* (Charles Nizet, 1970), about a Vietnam vet with an explosives fetish, may have been the first to make it to the screen; *My Friends Need Killing* (Paul Leder, 1976) takes a thoughtful, downbeat spin on the subject; but the most shocking treatment of the topic has to be the horror-porn nightmare *Forced Entry* (Shaun Costello, 1972), a virtually indefensible piece of nastiness that nevertheless authentically summons the rage and bitterness felt by devalued soldiers who found themselves back in menial jobs after participating in the most terrible State-sanctioned atrocities. Oddly though, the most persuasive and intelligent horror-film treatment of the returning Vietnam veteran came in a fantasy context, *Deathdream* (1972), in which a young man called Andy returns home from the war, apparently to resume his small-town family life. What his family and friends don't realise is that Andy is really dead – killed in action during the prologue. Brought back to life by the feverish prayers of his mother (in a steal from the classic ghost story *The Monkey's Paw* by W.W. Jacobs), he has returned without conscience, without warmth, without humanity. In order to stay mobile, he needs blood, and he wastes no time in obtaining it. *Deathdream* is full of bitter ironies about the mental state of soldiers returning to 'normal' life – no one can quite believe that Andy is capable of strangling a pet dog that annoys him, and when police quiz locals about a mysterious soldier seen hitching a ride on the night a lorry-driver was horribly killed, one woman says, "I can't believe a soldier would *do* a thing like that!"

above:
Wesley Eure as Kent, the deceptively wholesome killer in double-trouble murder tale **The Toolbox Murders**, a film which takes its inspiration from cases such as real life killer Ted Bundy, who enacted the multiple slaying of nurses in a single apartment block.

below:
Promo art for Michael Findlay's infamous **Snuff**, the film that, more than any other, exploited the audience's fearful curiosity regarding real life murder and mutilation: a curiosity that must frequently have been extinguished by the sixty minutes of boredom preceding the film's faux-snuff climax…

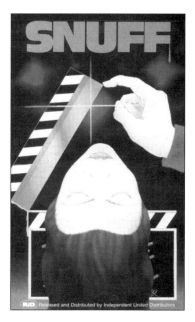

In the serial-killing seventies, death lurked on every street corner: John Carpenter's stylish and intelligent slasher film, **Halloween** (*above*) made the most of its widescreen photography to scare audiences, with danger leaping out from the periphery of the frame. Earlier films like Paul Leder's **Poor Albert & Little Annie** (*right*) relied more on tried and tested ballyhoo techniques, such as retitling the movie **I Dismember Mama**…
below:
A rather jaunty jack o'lantern advertises **Halloween** in this amusing German poster.

But while hippies and soldiers alike were now potentially threatening figures, it was far from plain sailing at points in between – frankly, you'd be hard pressed to rule out *anyone*. If there's one message American horror films of the 1970s have for their audiences, it's 'Trust no one!' The killer is a skinny momma's boy in *Scream Bloody Murder* (1972); a soft-spoken hunk in *Abducted* (1973); a pretty teenage girl in *Kiss of the Tarantula* (1975); a bible-thumpin' broad in *Evil Come Evil Go* (Walt Davis, 1972); a massively overweight middle-aged woman in *"Criminally Insane"* (Nick Philips, 1975); a middle-aged lawyer in *Swingers Massacre* (Ron Garcia, 1973); a good-looking well-spoken rich kid in *I Dismember Mama* (Paul Leder, 1972), and William Shatner in flares in *Impulse* (William Grefé, 1974) – if *Captain Kirk* couldn't be trusted, America was *really* in trouble…

Perhaps, the despairing viewer may have mused, only our children offer respite from the threat of random violence? The movies were having none of it… *The Exorcist* (William Friedkin, 1973) is perhaps the most celebrated mainstream horror film of the 1970s, and it brashly declared, perfectly in synch with the fallout from Manson, that youth was revolting; puking on priests, swearing at parents, indulging in grossly inappropriate sexual activity, and essentially crushing the nuts and mocking the values of anyone who got in its way. The fact that the specific youngster in question was a girl entering puberty (the true demon of Catholicism being female desire) raised the spectre of childhood itself as a locus of evil. Picking up on this, and taking cues from earlier models like *The Bad Seed* (1956) and *Village of the Damned* (1960), the seventies introduced killer kids as a viable horror subgenre. *Devil Times Five* (Sean MacGregor, 1973), *The Child* (Robert Voskanian, 1976), *Bloody Birthday* (Ed Hunt, 1980), *The Children* (Max Kalmanowicz, 1980), and *Friday the 13th: The Orphan* (1977), all featured kids with a grudge, gleefully determined to turn the tables on their elders and upset natural law. The *reductio ad absurdum* can be found in Larry Cohen's twin titles for Warner Brothers, *It's Alive* (1974) and *It Lives Again* (1978), about marauding killer babies. Both films have interesting concepts floundering in a stodgy, uninvolving directorial style, and are totally eclipsed by the Canadian David Cronenberg's far more compelling meditation on family dysfunction, *The Brood* (1979).

Among the most interesting films about multiple murder are those that try in some way to understand or explore the humanity of their sick protagonists. Homicidal madness is depicted within a broadly sympathetic framework in films like *Dream No Evil* (John Hayes, 1972), *Psychopath* (Larry Brown, 1972), *Pigs* (Marc Lawrence, 1972), *Homebodies* (Larry Yust, 1973), *Abducted* (1973), *Axe* (Frederick Friedel, 1974), *The Premonition* (1975), and *The Mafu Cage* (Karen Arthur, 1977). Even the much maligned *Don't Go in the House* (1979) and *Maniac* (1980) take time out from the violence to show us their killers' weakness and pain. The challenge for the filmmaker is to find an actor capable of withstanding the necessary scrutiny (a challenge most of the above rise to admirably), but perhaps the real reason such treatments are rare in the horror genre is that they tend to alleviate suspense, thus removing from the director's arsenal one of the major sources of dramatic energy. We tend to view killers we've come to know less with fear than despair; and despair is an emotion that's rather less commercially persuasive.

Not all of the films covered in this book take the darkest of routes through their subject matter, but there was in the 1970s a general turning away from frivolity in the genre and a greater will to face the truly horrific. It may seem perverse to those who regard movies like *Maniac* as the scummiest the genre has to offer, but I would argue that the darker, more grisly or downbeat horror films of the era are morally justified, thanks to their determination to send you home feeling stunned and/or nauseated. Bearing in mind the real-life inspirations for such filmic excesses, it seems only right that we should take a 'reality-check' here and there. The horror genre is a place where fantasies and morbid wish-fulfilment can cavort unshackled, but as we vicariously dance around in the moonlight with our imaginary victim's face and tits strapped to ours, it's perhaps worth glancing over at the real world, in which most of us conspicuously fail to 'get a kick' from torture and murder. Fantasy violence is a rush, there's no doubt about it, but it's a game, a charade, a luxurious indulgence; and when the game's over, you have to admit it's a far cry from reality. For all the thrill of a truly nasty horror film, how many of us *really* want murder and mutilation to play a part in our lives? Films that acknowledge this, even as they push the boundaries of what can be shown, demonstrate a realism that balances the more superficial thrills of horror's *bona fide* big hitter circa 1979-85: the slasher genre.

Psycho-Killer, Qu'est-ce que c'est?

Long before John Carpenter's stylish *Halloween* (1978) received the cineastes' seal of approval for knife-wielding maniacs, there were already quite a few slashers stalking the darkened corridors of the silver screen. *Halloween* is a great film that survives multiple viewings, because it establishes the ideal way of presenting its hackneyed material, but let no one be deceived that it arrived out of a clear blue sky. Effective it may have been, innovative it was not. The slasher genre had been around for quite some time and there were already some formidable contenders.

Putting aside the Italian *giallo* genre (a major influence on slasher cinema), one of the most accomplished North American precursors was *Black Christmas* (1974), a Canadian production directed by American citizen Bob Clark, who eventually became renowned for the 'tits-and-zits' teen comedy *Porky's* (1982). *Black Christmas* substantially pre-empts both the plotting and stylistic strategies of *Halloween*, and takes place around a major public holiday, while possessing a chilly approach to characterisation that matches the iciness of its winter *mise-en-scène*. In comparison, *Halloween* is an experience as warmly creepy as the orange glow of a jack-o'-lantern. *Black Christmas* can give even post-*Scream* viewers a serious case of the shudders, as it employs techniques more typical of the Hollywood Movie Brats to unsettle our sense of moral and emotional security. Characters initially designated as decent people are given spiky and foul-mouthed qualities (especially Margot Kidder, who if we're to believe Peter Biskind's account of her in *Easy Riders, Raging Bulls* probably ad-libbed her own profanity). The film has that 'trust no one' aura redolent both of early seventies paranoia (Coppola, Watergate etc.) and the aforementioned *giallo* genre. An artistic, 'sensitive' character is prone to bouts of petty destructiveness, adults are given tics that blur the line of generational responsibility (the sorority's 'den mother' is a well-meaning but inept alcoholic) and the overall threat emerges from what was to become one of the most shop-worn of sources, the menacing telephone caller (see Mario Bava's 1963 classic, *Black Sabbath*). The film begins with a party atmosphere (modishly conveyed with overlapping dialogue) which is then twisted by the sheer savagery of the 'phone pervert'. So much hinges on him that the voice artist deserved higher pay than the onscreen actors. It's a screeching, painful, nails-down-a-blackboard performance, wandering into the absurd here and there, but with a control that conveys utter malice rather than whimsical scariness. By the time the film delivers its big twist – a fresh one at the time – the combination of chilly winter setting, skilled acting and prowling camerawork is likely to have thoroughly unnerved its audience.

Communion (Alfred Sole, 1976) also deserves a mention for its tricky plotting, strong performances and shocking eruptions of violence. There's a knife attack here that rivals anything the genre has to offer; not in terms of its graphic special effects (although they're very good), but in the timing, editing, staging, acting and overall conception. *Communion*, concerning murders that may or may not be committed by a disturbed teenage girl, is such a strong, intelligent film that in many ways one would have placed money on Sole as a future big wheel rather than John Carpenter. It's really a shame this never came to pass.

With *Black Christmas* already out there, it wasn't long before film producers realised there was something

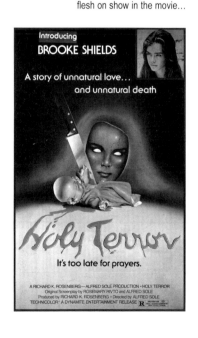

above: A classic 'Special Occasion Slasher', and the King of the Killer-Santa films! **Silent Night, Deadly Night** (1984) beats the almost equally wonderful **Christmas Evil** (1980) by a reindeer's neck thanks to its inspired promotional ballyhoo. The original poster art depicted Santa climbing down a chimney on Christmas Eve, toting a bloody axe in place of the customary presents. The film was immediately attacked by Christian and Family groups in America: as Adam Rockoff has reported, demonstrators gave horror fans a Yuletide belly-laugh by toting placards which read, "Deck the Halls with Holly, Not Blood" and "Santa Does Not Slay"! Although these protests killed the film theatrically when the startled distributor got cold feet, **Silent Night, Deadly Night** sold like hot mince pies on home video. (Note how the video art above effaces all evidence of Christmas, Santa or the trappings of the Season...)

opposite: Hal Borske in grisly scenes from **The Ghastly Ones** (1968), Andy Milligan's tale of bloody murder, kinky sex, family intrigue and mental retardation that's either stupendous or stupefying, depending on your trash-horror mileage...

below: **X-Ray** (1982) is a slasher film at the cheesier end of the subgenre, directed by **Lemon Popsicle** creator Boaz Davidson, and starring Barbi Benton, one-time girlfriend of *Playboy* boss Hugh Hefner.

compelling (and inherently marketable) about horror films set during a specific time of year. Firstly of course, the promotional advantage of a ready-made red-letter launch day is immense. Then there's the way in which teen audiences experience seasonal intervals: as each yearly celebration goes by, even the most carefree of fifteen-year-olds grows aware of the passage of time. When you're a teenager, to be a year older than another is to occupy an entirely different social milieu. Teenagers thus have a very different temporal awareness. Three years is a long time: five years is tantamount to a generation gap. In general it's only with yearly holidays and special dates that younger people are reminded of the passage of time, and thus perhaps their own mortality. Yearly rituals let the future as well as the past leak through: once again, like last year, you're trick-or-treating; once again, like last year, it's Christmas; once again, like last year, it's Valentine's Day; but how many more will you see? Many successful slasher flicks take a 'significant annual event' as their cue for violence and death, and in so doing touch a raw nerve for a teenage target audience otherwise shored up with a sense of their own invulnerability.

There are subdivisions in slasherdom, as elsewhere in the horror genre. Besides the 'Special Occasion Slashers' (*Bloody Birthday, Happy Birthday to Me, My Bloody Valentine, April Fool's Day, Halloween, Silent Night, Deadly Night, Christmas Evil, New Year's Evil*) there were the 'Summer Camp Slaughterthons' (*Friday the 13th, The Burning, Madman, Sleepaway Camp*); the 'Sorority Abattoirs' (*The House on Sorority Row, Sorority House Massacre, To All a Goodnight*); the 'Hiker-Hackers' (*Don't Go in the Woods, The Forest, The Prey*); the 'Stalk-and-Slash Colleges' (*Final Exam, Graduation Day, The Killing Touch, Pranks, The Scaremaker, Prom Night, Night School*); and the 'Horror Hospitals' (*X-Ray, Visiting Hours*).

What's notable is how many slashers were bankrolled by major studios: after picking up the first as an independent, Paramount handled the *Friday the 13th* series, as well as *Night School, April Fool's Day* and the Canadian *My Bloody Valentine*; Columbia stumped up for *When a Stranger Calls* and the Canadian *Happy Birthday to Me*; and MGM produced *He Knows You're Alone*. The list grows longer when you include independently produced films that nonetheless received nationwide distribution from the majors. In the course of this book, however, we'll be looking at some of the less frequently celebrated examples of the format, made and distributed solely by the Exploitation Independents.

Slashers – J'adore!

There's something wonderfully satisfying about the slasher film. Yes, it's unsophisticated. No, there's not much of a case for it as 'a valuable contribution to cinema'. It exists by and large to do what its detractors claim it does. It's cheap and nasty. It trades in the devaluation of the individual. The craft of the actor is neglected. Audiences are offered the most primitive of stimuli: death, mutilation, skinny-dipping teens. This is all true. It sounds awful; and yet, for me, these films are some of the most thrilling and enjoyable slices of genre hokum you can find. I adored these films, whether overstuffed (*Happy Birthday to Me*) or undernourished (*Pranks*, Stephen Carpenter & Jeff Obrow, 1982), when they first came out, and I still love seeing

them today. Just as fans of other eras found that their taste for schlock endowed Rondo Hatton or Monogram B-movies with a certain retro charm, so too the slashers, once admittedly overshadowed by the artistic wonders of Dario Argento, David Cronenberg and George Romero, look distinctly more fun today.

It isn't just a matter of gore, arterial sprays, close-ups of wounds (although such considerations are of course right up there). What really propels these movies is the satisfying chase-and-kill formula, leading inexorably to a shameless enjoyment of the moment of death: *gruesome* death, given maximum impact by taut editing, voyeuristic camera angles and nerve-scraping music. The murder scene in a good slasher film is a production number, with screams and blood instead of song and dance. Creativity, such as it is, can be found in the choreography between the essentials. Scary music leads the apprehensive viewer to a swiftly edited, percussively orchestrated frenzy of now-you-see-it now-you-don't delirium, as the slash of the editor's razor spins you into ecstatic appreciation of another minor character's demise. The formula is perfect. Set up a crowd of inane teens and let them feel the joy of the audience's surrogate blade for ninety minutes. Bliss.

In fact it's often *so* blissful that I find myself liking these doomed High School klutzes as soon as they begin touting their dumb-ass trademarks. What a paradox! Precisely *because* they are so inane and clichéd, I know these hormonal jocks and dope-smoking cheerleaders will soon give me immense pleasure by meeting hideous, violent death. As I anticipate it, I find myself looking benevolently on the sort of characters I might otherwise have despised. I *love* the dumb teens of these films, I feel a warm glow as they act out their silly practical jokes, their breast-fondling liaisons, and their flimsily anti-authoritarian acts. As they fulfil in that wonderfully bovine way the requirements of the slasher movie victim, traits that could have been contemptible become cute and loveable. Watching the materialistic beach-babes and sexist volleyball hunks of *Slumber Party Massacre 3* (Sally Mattison, 1990) driving down a coastal road in an open-topped car, listening to awful AM pop-rock, I hug myself with excitement, treasuring my affection for these bubble-heads and jackasses. They are my friends and I can't wait to see them die. I feel the thrill of betrayal as I gleefully anticipate the deaths they are yet to suffer. Re-watching these films seems to make them not less but *more* fun. I confess that I sometimes watch only the first half of the movies, when the characters are yet to die, because the dimwit poignancy of their empty lives is even more satisfying to observe than their death throes...[9]

There are some truly riveting examples of the format and there are a few that try even my patience – and I consider myself an easy convert to any passing slasher with half a will to offend. *Be* formulaic! *Be* obvious! By God, rip off *Friday the 13th* as much as you like! Just be sure to chase people, maim them and kill them, and follow any displays of 'zany college humour', 'dope-smoking' or 'teenage sex' with the intrusion of a serrated metallic tool. I'm an easily pleased consumer of this 'degraded' form of cinema, so go for it. Just kill them all – is it asking too much? I *want* the mindless repetition; it's one of the few effluents of the mechanised era that I find entirely pleasurable. I would watch a ten-hour slasher film. I'd watch a *twenty-four*-hour slasher film. As long as the victims were increased in proportion to the running time,

I would be there, best seat in the house, with matchsticks propping my eyelids, eager to see it all, including the beach-ball games and skinny-dipping, the fake tarot readings and campsite canoodling.

Okay, after I've waxed lyrical on the morality of depressing horror films, this eulogy to superficial schlock may seem a trifle callous, but in essence I try to keep both responses in mind when I discuss the genre. Personally I don't think horror fans have a leg to stand on if they try to reject the more tasteless elements. Stephen King, who wrote entertainingly about all kinds of horror films in his excellent non-fiction book *Danse Macabre* (1980), made an uncharacteristically puritanical judgement when he tried to drive a wedge between classy, even 'arty' horrors like *Dawn of the Dead*, and what I presume was a dim recollection of an Andy Milligan double bill (King attacked a non-existent movie called 'The Bloody Mutilators' for an alleged buzz-saw killing, which sounds like he's merging the title of *The Bloodthirsty Butchers* with the mayhem of *The Ghastly Ones*). Milligan's deeper idiosyncrasies aside for the moment, it seems to me that if you want to raise a flag for the modern horror film there's no point getting prissy about screen violence. When King himself writes short stories built entirely around a single gross idea, it seems pretty rich to criticise the cinema equivalent. Granted, his craftsmanship leaves Milligan standing; but judging by his affection for hopelessly bad movies elsewhere in his book, I don't think that's why King refers to grindhouse filmmakers as "morons with cameras". Somehow, the grubby likes of *The Ghastly Ones* or *The Last House on the Left* offend not only because they show grisly violence, but also because in their grainy, low-lighting shaky-cam amateurism they transgress notions of filmic decorum as they do so.

Although my expression of enthusiasm for the slasher format has so far emphasised just the sadistic component of my responses, my guess is that the audience's enjoyment runs the gamut across a spectrum that also includes the masochistic desire to be shocked and in some way vicariously assaulted. It certainly works that way with me. In films such as the slashers, where an atavistic narrative devoid of plausible three-dimensional characterisation effectively shuts off the possibility of engagement with real people in the wider world, and instead draws its energy from varying parts of the viewer's own psyche, the thrill one feels is a closed loop incorporating the actions of aggressor and victim. A good slasher movie withholds the murders with mounting suspense, tantalising but also tormenting the viewer, then paying off with a jolting, shocking attack. It's quite obvious that all this tease-and-slap, tension-and-release stuff is engaging the viewer's underlying libidinal desires, whether conscious or unconscious. And if that sounds dangerous, it's worth pedantically emphasising that, like the sexual practice of sadomasochism, it all takes place within a consensual environment. The audience buy their tickets for a slasher horror film, revelling in the adrenaline rush of aggression and the concomitant flinch of fear. No one really gets hurt, and if the film has some skill the audience leaves the theatre on a high. As for what happens later, in the street or the home, I have *never* subscribed to the theory that violence in films begets violence in real life: they are two utterly distinct regions of reality, and to treat them as causally linked is to offer a blank cheque to moral cowards. No film can take responsibility for our actions in the real world; to

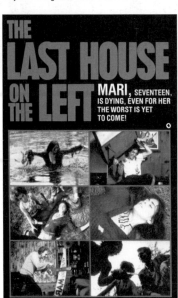

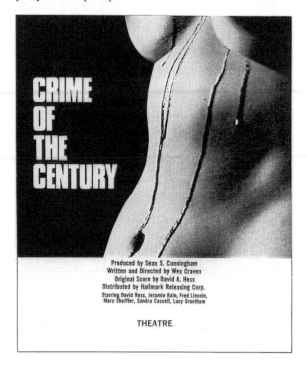

say so is to dismiss choice and abnegate responsibility. No one (except the hopelessly insane, perhaps, for whom even *Shrek* could be the trigger for psychosis) ever got so deeply involved in a film that they sat in their seat waiting for a jump-cut rather than their legs to take them home. Nothing you see on the movie screen can be blamed for your actions in the real world: to say so is either legal chicanery, moral dishonesty (Sartre's 'bad faith'), or stupidity.

Many of the lesser criticisms levelled at slasher movies are built on false premises. For instance, it's now common-place for audiences to scoff at the irrational, terrorized actions of slasher film heroines, always opening the wrong door at the worst possible time, always straying into darkened rooms without turning on the light, always splitting up from their friends when it's 'obvious' they're about to get it. Obvious to *us*, that is. These protests about unlikeliness show our fears in high relief: we hate it when characters make dangerous mistakes, because they're acting just like us. It's not as if there's *really* any reason why victim number two should hesitate to wander off, just because victim number one hasn't returned from the summer-camp showers. We walk into darkened rooms all the time in our daily lives; even when briefly we think there's something 'funny' going on, we hardly ever believe that we're *really* going to die – more likely we'll dismiss the misgiving as caused by too many horror films!

No, a slasher film may be dumb, but despite its flagrantly mechanical technique it has the power to frustrate the audience's sense of control, and that creates anxiety – pleasurable to some, upsetting to others. Sure, we know there's a maniac at large somewhere, we can read the signs, we're aware of the genre conventions – but the moment, the exact form, the intensity and duration of the attack, are things that we can't entirely predict. Hence, pleasure.

Scream (Wes Craven, 1996) was hailed as the moment that post-modern reflexivity entered the horror genre. In fact it merely crashed an ongoing party. An exposé and satire of genre? Audiences were already well aware of the 'codes' and 'strategies' of the slasher film back in the early 1980s. The post-modern horror film merely tries to feed you your own perceptiveness. For *Scream*'s director Wes

Craven, the film offered a 'fixed fight', in which he gaudily pulled rank on a genre to which he clearly feels superior. Much as I dislike *Scream* and its satellites, I have to admit that Craven does have one reason to feel superior, although it has nothing to do with the trendy pop-cynicism of his recent work: his best movie, and his first, *The Last House on the Left* (1972), far outdoes the slashers in brutality and sexual violence – and it's to this particular combination that we now turn…

When Blood Is Not Enough

"I wonder what the meanest, foulest, rottenest, woodsiest sex crime ever was? Hey Sadie, what do you think the sex crime of the century was?"
– 'Weasel' Padowski in *The Last House on the Left*

Sex and violence are the Alpha and Omega of exploitation, and filmmakers in the seventies found ever more bizarre and startling ways to ricochet between them. Horror films got sexier and sleazier, and sex films got bloodier and nastier. Although the really extreme material remained obscure, located far from the attentions of mainstream American film critics like Pauline Kael and Vincent Canby, enough of it reached an audience to create a demand for more.

Censorship restrictions were gradually relaxed during the late sixties and early seventies, and as a result sex films rose to another level. The Grove Press-distributed *I Am Curious Yellow* (1967) was the twelfth highest grossing picture in 1969 ($6,600,000 that year), just behind the zeitgeist-defining youth hit *Easy Rider* (1969). Softcore turned to hardcore, kinkiness went ballistic, eccentricity and bizarre fantasy edged their way into the fray: the levee was breaking and all manner of exotic flora and fauna were being carried down the Deuce on the currents of exploitation. As the decade turned, Times Square became home to the furthest reaches of hardcore sex and horror. Looking back at the early 1970s, it's hard to believe just how sudden the transition was. Jack Gennaro's 1971 sleaze-pic *D.O.G.* (*Deviations On Gratifications*) – distributed by Sherpix, who handled Jim Bidgood's amazing art-house epic *Pink Narcissus* – includes a scene (mentioned casually by *Variety*, no less) in which, "A gay youth unsuccessfully attempts to arouse a German Shepherd." This casual reference to queer bestiality in the leading trade paper of the American film industry gives you some idea of the unimagined excesses towards which cinema was leaping as the 1970s dawned.

Foremost among those pushing the envelope of what could or could not be shown were Sean Cunningham and Wes Craven. In 1972 they declared open season on taste and restraint with a mind-blowing horror film called *The Last House on the Left*, written and directed by Craven and produced by Cunningham. Telling the story of two teenage girls who fall into the hands of a gang of sadists while scoring dope before a rock concert, it featured tough, realistic performances (alongside some frankly awful ones, truth be told), and an unblinking depiction of sexual humiliation and violence. The vision of pitilessness summoned in the first half is so powerful that it can't even be erased by a contrived revenge twist in the second, in which Craven's script attempts to retrieve the situation for moral purposes. For many years, *The Last House on the Left*, if referred to at all, was used by critics as evidence of the utmost depravity to which the horror genre could sink.

Its current rehabilitation – released on DVD by MGM no less, with prestige extras and much celebration of its pivotal genre status – is truly remarkable. The recuperative process was triggered in the late 1970s by the critic Robin Wood, who identified in the film political themes he considered 'progressive'. Later, Craven mentioned the Vietnam War a lot in interviews, and cheerfully admitted stealing a key plot twist from an Ingmar Bergman picture, thus assuring himself of future artistic redemption. It could so easily have been different: Craven's script had initially featured even more gross and humiliating brutality, much of which was sexual in nature. Ultimately, in a decision he must cherish to this day, Craven decided that the explicit sex-torture material would have to be cut back for practical reasons. As David Szulkin reports in his definitive book *Wes Craven's Last House on the Left: The Making of a Cult Classic*: "One scene featured Krug and Weasel engaging in necrophilia with Phyllis's mutilated corpse; the sequence of Mari's rape and defilement was also rougher and more prolonged. Other incidental sex scenes included Mari masturbating in the shower at the opening of the film and fantasy sequences of Mari and Phyllis getting it on with the rock group Bloodlust." Fred Lincoln, a porno actor who was among the first to be cast in the film, told Szulkin, "I read the script, and it was absolutely the most disgusting thing I'd ever seen… I mean, it was *really* hideous."

Even as it is, the film has a rawness that feels poised to take that extra step into pornography – it's not hard to imagine hardcore close-ups of Mari and Phyllis's enforced lesbianism, Mari's rape by Krug, and of course Mrs. Collingwood's terminal fellatio scene with Weasel. It's perhaps just as well that it didn't go the whole nine yards, though, and not just because Craven and Cunningham would never have crossed over into mainstream cinema: with hardcore porno scenes the film would have sunk to an even lower rung of the exploitation ladder, and would rarely have been seen today. After all, how big is the cult for Michael Hugo (*Hardgore*) or Zebedy Colt (*Unwilling Lovers*)? Certainly we could kiss goodbye to that prestigious DVD release!

There's another reason why we should be glad Craven held back from pornoland. Combining pornography and horror can seem like the ultimate exploitation dream, but in practice the blend rarely works. There's something stubbornly anti-cinematic about hardcore sex. It refuses to yield itself to genre. When someone tries to force the issue, the resulting mutant is a static, uncomfortable beast. With porno, the viewer needs about thirty seconds to decide if they find the participants attractive. If the answer is no, that means it's *very* unlikely the film will hold their attention. Seeing two *un*attractive people having sex in graphic detail is an experience few of us would list in our dreams for a new form of cinema. On the other hand, if the couple are attractive, or the sex is so powerful and compelling that you make allowances for the odd hunchback or stretch mark, a different problem occurs. You cease to be *interested* in the aesthetic realm and lose all concern with the plot, even resenting the reintroduction of these factors when the sex scene is over (assuming you haven't already 'upped' and left the theatre). Essentially, pornography causes the mind to be seduced, chemically changed; the viewer's focus narrows to take in only salient details, which are then scrutinised to an intense degree. Variables are reduced to a minimum; context, background and framing are considered only inasmuch as they foster sexual enjoyment.

above:
Going beyond the limits. **Hardgore** (1974), which is also known as **Horror Whore** (*left*) and **Sadoasylum**, takes the horror genre and pornography and fuses them in a barrage of sparks, screams and spunk.

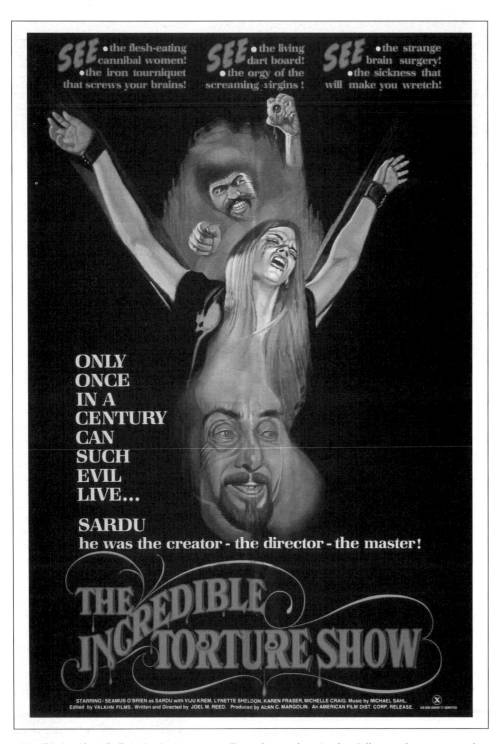

SEE ● the flesh-eating cannibal women! ● the iron tourniquet that screws your brains!

SEE ● the living dart board! ● the orgy of the screaming virgins!

SEE ● the strange brain surgery! ● the sickness that will make you wretch!

ONLY ONCE IN A CENTURY CAN SUCH EVIL LIVE...

SARDU he was the creator - the director - the master!

THE INCREDIBLE INCREDIBLE TORTURE SHOW

STARRING: SEAMUS O'BRIEN as SARDU with VIJU KREM, LYNETTE SHELDON, KAREN FRASER, MICHELLE CRAIG. Music by MICHAEL SAHL. Edited by VALKHN FILMS. Written and Directed by JOEL M. REED. Produced by ALAN C. MARGOLIN. An AMERICAN FILM DIST. CORP. RELEASE.

above: Frivolous 'Carry-On Torture' or the heir to the crown of Herschell Gordon Lewis? It's all a matter of taste... One-sheet for Joel M. Reed's New York-lensed atrocity exhibition **The Incredible Torture Show** (1976), better known as **Bloodsucking Freaks**.

below: Small press ad for **Sex Wish** (1976), from the King of 'knives-out maliciousness', Zebedy Colt...

TAURUS PRODUCTIONS PRESENTS — SEAVUE II — Rated XXX
Sex Wish
YOU'VE NEVER SEEN ANYTHING LIKE IT!
Starring THE WORLD FAMOUS HARRY REEMS
C.J. Lang - Zebedy Colt Terry Hall & Candy Love with a line up like that how can you miss.
In Color XXX

From time to time, 'serious' directors have expressed a wish to make porno that engages the broader complexities of cinema – in the late sixties Stanley Kubrick and Terry Southern discussed working together on a film treatment of Southern's book *Blue Movie*, the impetus being Kubrick's fascination with the challenge of making the first porno that might also be considered a work of art. The film was never made, but perhaps we saw just a little of 'what might have been' in the film that Alex is shown in *A Clockwork Orange* (1971), during his brainwashing against violence? Given the darkness expressed elsewhere in his work, it's not hard to imagine that a Kubrick porno film – as opposed to his 'erotic' film *Eyes Wide Shut* (1999) – would be one in which violence was an essential component.

Still, a handful of filmmakers have given the porno-horror film a shot, and scored a few successes. In Europe,

Joe D'Amato and Jess Franco ventured repeatedly into the terrain between genre narrative and hardcore non-narrative. In America, Armand Weston, who began as a porno director before crossing over to horror to make the effective haunted whorehouse tale, *The Nesting* (1980), demonstrated his aptitude with *The Defiance of Good* (1974), a sex-horror hybrid based around themes of mind-control, abduction and rape. Massively indebted to the Marquis de Sade (in particular his books *Justine ou les malheurs de la vertu* and *L'histoire de Juliette*), *Defiance* tells the story of Cathy Taylor (Jean Jennings), a teenage girl committed to a mental institute by her puritanical parents because she's had sex with a boy against their wishes. In the asylum she causes more trouble, and so is placed in the care of Dr. Gabriel, a sinister fellow with some radical therapeutic ideas. Carting her off to his private sanatorium, Dr. Gabriel reprograms Cathy as a masochistic slave who will forever crave sexual violence… This is a dark and twisted work, revelling in torment, and (just to make things nastier) it stars Fred Lincoln, sex-killer 'Weasel' from *The Last House on the Left*, as the sadistic doctor.

Michael Hugo is a mystery figure often said to have directed the mind-boggling sex-horror opus *Hardgore* (1974), although his name does not appear on the print. *Hardgore* is another sexy-asylum picture, although the tone of the film is more absurd, featuring such once-in-a-lifetime images as flying severed penises spitting sparks (an image that perhaps shows an awareness of Kenneth Anger's 1947 debut, *Fireworks*). Amid the intimate vaginal examinations and group sex scenes, *Hardgore* casually inserts horrific imagery, not least a dauntingly matter-of-fact penis amputation sure to have sent a few unsuspecting theatre patrons fleeing in dismay. Worldly viewers today will know how the trick was done, but in a theatre in 1974, it must have packed quite a wallop…

Also in a medical sex-horror vein, though more silly than sleazy, is *The Sex Machine* (1971) by Eric Jeffrey Haims (director of the awful but entertaining cheapie *The Jekyll and Hyde Portfolio*). In another isolated medical institute, yet more sexual experiments are being conducted on female subjects (or "surrogates"), supposedly to help with "libidinal problems". The 'Sex Machine' itself is a Rube Goldberg contraption able to "photograph the interior of the vagina" and "heal frigidity". Surprisingly, despite these complex medical aims, most of its functional application stems from a protruding, rapidly spinning dildo. All is well until the arrival of Jessica (Debra Christian), an aggressive SM dyke known as 'Big Daddy', who throws the hitherto hetero institute into erotic confusion. In a development that could – and probably should – result in Haims being beaten up by enraged lesbian activists, Jessica becomes addicted to the phallic Sex Machine and has to be barred from the Institute. After taking out her frustration on one of the female staff with the help of a whip and a gang of obliging bikers, 'Big Daddy' torches the lab before strapping herself into The Sex Machine for one last ride. "If I can't have it, nobody will!" she cries, before the machine electrocutes her in a shower of sparks…

The pinnacle of the horror-porn genre is *Sex Wish* (1976), variously credited to Tim McCoy, Victor Milk, and Zebedy Colt (see review section). Colt's other films often include scenes of brutality and sexual violence that double-book them as both horror and porn. As we'll see, they point through other doorways in the horror genre, leading to two of the most offensive cinematic indulgences of all…

Torture

Before Herschell Gordon Lewis, death in the movies was a swift, clean and painless affair. But while Lewis dragged out the demise of victims with a host of simultaneously grotesque and unconvincing special effects, the result was to push screen suffering into the realms of black comedy. Wes Craven's *The Last House on the Left* was a very different experience, taking the fun and hi-jinx out of the recipe, and inaugurating real horror. The key difference was that although Lewis depicted graphic mutilation, his actors and actresses were utterly inept at showing emotion, and so there was never any sense of real suffering. *Last House* on the other hand was (mostly) well acted and directed, and thus showed suffering in a stark and plausible form. Craven and Cunningham can probably claim the credit for bringing realistic torture and rape into the genre...

Torture-killings inflict upon an individual the antithesis of the 'good death'. For the perpetrator it's pure hedonistic obscenity, a feasting upon another's pain, a total immersion in the sadistic drive. Torture is also heavily in cahoots with the voyeuristic urge. The sadist wants to *see* how much it hurts. Cinema is therefore the torture medium *par excellence*. Whatever happens we have to *see*, and to see it for longer and longer (which is why Michael Haneke's *Funny Games* is so powerful: although it shows hardly any physical violence, the fact that it lingers for such a long time on the agony, fear and anguish of the victims is more than enough to compensate; this is Haneke's personal contribution to the cinema of sadism).

Torture is about achieving a hyper-redundancy of suffering. It violates the idea of limits, of what's necessary, of how much is too much. This is where we leave the realm of simple aggression and jump up a register. It's all about duration – the nastiest torture scenes are those that open onto vistas unimpeded by the genre's conventional narrative clock. Roger Watkins's *The Last House on Dead End Street* (1977) is a perfect example: constraints like plot, narrative and characterisation are gradually pushed out of the frame, and we have no idea how long the victims' pain, torture and humiliation will last.

However, even in the Exploitation Independent arena, drawn-out depictions of *physical* torture are quite rare. Humiliation, degradation, incarceration, and psychological torture are all more common. Among the Exploitation Independent films to depict sustained cruelty in some form are *Pets* (Raphael Nussbaum, 1972), featuring humiliation and confinement, both male and female; *Abducted* (1973), with its incarceration and forced medical 'games'; *I Drink Your Blood* (1971), which features a ritualised torture scene; *The Witch Who Came from the Sea* (1976), which features a woman's double castration of two bound men but fades on the screams of the first; *Bloodsucking Freaks* (Joel M. Reed, 1976), of which more in a moment; *Death Game* (1976), with more humiliation and confinement of a male victim; *Fight for Your Life* (1977), with verbal humiliation and confinement; *Don't Answer the Phone!* (1979), with its psychological torture prior to murder; *Don't Go in the House* (1979), with drawn-out preparations for murder as a naked woman is slowly dowsed in petrol; *Human Experiments* (Gregory Goodell, 1979), concentrating on psychological torture and the fear of creepy-crawlies; *Mother's Day* (Charles Kaufman, 1980) – rape and confinement; and of course *The Texas Chain Saw Massacre* (1974), featuring intermittent physical and sustained

left and above:
Robert Hammer's **Don't Answer the Phone!** (1979) features a nasty bout of psychological torture as the killer mockingly uses his grasp of a victim's childhood trauma to pose as her abusive 'daddy' in a vicious role-play scenario.

psychological torment. Of these, the only one to dwell on physical brutality for its own sake is *Bloodsucking Freaks*. So what does it offer the jaded horror film consumer?

Torture as Titillation! Blood as Belly Laugh! Pain as Panto! You gotta love it! And may anyone who disagrees with me roll down the hillside in my eight-inch-spiked barrel of laughs! Well, that's the pitch anyway... By tipping off the audience that this is just a big grisly joke, however, *Bloodsucking Freaks* – originally released as *The Incredible Torture Show* – ends up relegating itself to the suburbs of sleaze. Jolly japes and knowing winks in a torture film are as welcome as a slug in a salad: and *Bloodsucking Freaks* not only winks, it also digs you in the ribs and gets on your nerves like *Monty Python*'s Mr. Say-No-More. It's a very early example of a trend that would spiral out of control in the 1980s: the 'shocking' film that laughs at its own jokes, or feigns to puke at its own gross-outs (see Troma Films). As a result, despite its misogyny, sadism, etc. etc., it's oddly inoffensive. It so desperately wants to be the high watermark of bad taste that it loses out by fathoms. There's something smug and silly about the sadism on offer: the sexual brutality is so safely corralled by tongue-in-cheek humour that you long for the knives-out maliciousness of Zebedy Colt or Walt Davis. Whereas *Sex Wish* or *Sex Psycho* are both blackly hilarious and truly disturbing, *Bloodsucking Freaks* is 'Carry-On Torture', a comedy sketch dragged out over eighty minutes. The lead actor provides the only fun: Seamus O'Brien as Sardu is wonderfully arch, delivering his lines with the epicurean relish of a depraved Kenneth Williams.[10]

No, from the standpoint of the 1970s, depictions of sustained physical torture are surprisingly rare. They would only flourish into full flower in the 1980s and 1990s, when the Japanese took control of the concept with the shot-on-video *Za Ginipiggu: Akuma No Jikken* aka *Guinea Pig: Devil's Experiment* (1985) by Hideshi Hino; the similarly monomaniacal *Akai Misshitsu (Heya): Kindan No Ôsama Geemu* aka *Red Room* (1999) by Daisuke Yamanouchi; and the extraordinary cyberpunk horror film *Rubber's Lover* (1996) by Shozin Fukui. But if the American Exploitation Independents were reluctant to get into torture, when it came to another brand of atrocity they were *way* ahead...

below:
Pets (1972) was Raphael Nussbaum's sleazy adaptation of three one-act plays written by Richard Reich, which were first performed onstage in Greenwich Village during May 1969. The stories were: 'Baby with a Knife', about a lesbian painter trying to discourage her sexy young girlfriend from lusting after men; 'The Silver-Grey Toy Poodle', in which two pretty hitch hikers abduct, humiliate and rob a middle aged man; and 'Pets', in which a liberated young woman goes home with an insane chauvinist who delights in showing off his collection of caged animals, including a runaway girl. The film's poster art, however (as seen on this rare Intervision video) chose to emphasise only the latter scenario...

Rape

If one word sets the pulse of the exploitation addict racing it's rape. Gore is exciting, glimpses of erections and vulvas are fine for lightweights and newcomers, but rape is the swooningly delicious truffle hidden in the loam of exploitation cinema. Like the centipede's "black meat" in William Burroughs's *Naked Lunch*, it's both sickening and compulsively more-ish, carrying a charge of vicarious fantasy excitement and the powerful aura of badness. If you want to explore the heart of darkness in seventies exploitation, you have to come to terms with the entertainment value of rape.

Mere murders are ten a penny in the movies, so mundane and overexposed that it's excruciatingly difficult to come up with a new and vital depiction. To kill, to extinguish a person's being, to take someone unwillingly to the very brink of life, and then to push them into oblivion… It sounds terrible, but think again: it's the meat and two veg' of television, the burger and fries of cinema, the cheap plonk of literature. No one raises an eyebrow – murder is okay. Rape on the other hand is still swathed in taboo. Grisly screen slaughter can be repeated *ad nauseam*, but add one graphic rape and you have a test case for audience morality. And as long as rape is considered to be a fate *worse* than death, this moral incongruity will remain unchallenged.

Rape is the unwanted, frequently violent, intrusion of one person into another. I would argue that this means the rape film belongs, if not entirely within the Body-Horror genre, then at least conjoined to it. The horror of rape is twofold: it's about the disgust factor of unwanted intimacy; and it's about loss of control, the subversion of the victim's autonomy, and the terror that goes with it. Normally, cognitive and sexual modes have to be re-set by arousal before we're willing to come into close contact with each other's fluids and organs: if a stranger in a café drools saliva on a slice of bread and then offers us a bite, most of us would find the idea of eating it repugnant. Real life rape is similarly characterized by disgust at the invasion of tactile boundaries. The second, psychological dimension is often worse after the fact, with victims feeling guilty for having 'participated' in sexual behaviour abhorrent to them. Social responses to victims then compound the problem, as the words 'soiled', 'ruined' and 'scarred for life' unhelpfully surround discourses on rape and its aftermath.

But what makes rape so distressing is also what makes it so fascinating. It's the same with everything we reject. It's one of life's callous ironies that there's a lure tucked away in that which we wish to avoid. It's an irony we're frequently indisposed to recognise; hence, Freud would say, neurosis.

You may be wondering what all this has to do with rape in the movies. After all, when we talk about *Friday the 13th* we don't feel obliged to debate the rights and wrongs of murder. The reason is that rape has been enshrined, fenced off, so that it becomes necessary to brandish a moral border-pass of real-world awareness, papers all in order, before we can discuss the subject in its spectacular form as cinema.

In terms of shock value and wilful offensiveness, there can be no denying the magnetism of a really explicit rape scene – not at this level of the industry. Sex and violence, as David Cronenberg provocatively put it in an interview in Cannes to promote his film *A History of Violence*, go together "like bacon and eggs."[11] Rape *fantasies* bear witness to this, and to the way in which our sexual tastes

are defined in the teeth of negative forces – bad parenting, social hypocrisies – which seek to constrict, divert or deny sexual pleasure. Although you would never guess from the protestations of moral guardians, rape fantasies occur in both males and females, and they are common in a wide range of advanced cultures. Michael J. Bader's *Arousal: The Secret Logic of Sexual Fantasies*, which discusses sex fantasy as a psychological antidote to unconscious dangers, estimates that 24% of men and 36% of women have had a rape fantasy, adding that 10% of women report them as their favourite type. The cinema has always responded to the fantasy lives of its audience and, as the walls of taboo came tumbling down in the 1970s, the exploitation film industry was there to fulfil its part of the bargain. Rape fantasy was liberated from the allusion-heavy realm of literature, with its 'ravishment' and 'bodice-ripping', and allowed to appear in all its savagery onscreen.

A prominent title in any discussion of screen rape is *I Spit on Your Grave* (1978), although it actually belongs in its own sub-category, being both extremely brutal and disturbing, and highly moral in its construction. The most raw and 'irredeemable' depictions of rape in film are the shorts or 'loops' released to porno theatres during the 1970s, lasting ten to fifteen minutes maximum, and offering hardcore simulated sex attacks in isolation, with no narrative save the most basic of set-ups. These often-untitled films are rape-horror's Degree Zero, and they're about as far from cinematic and moral decency as it's possible to get. A step up the ladder from these grimy experiences are the rape-themed hardcore feature films. Those that push the boundaries of bad taste include the forced-incest shocker *Wet Wilderness* (Lee Cooper, 1975); the race-war rape tale *Hot Summer in the City* (Gail Palmer, 1976), which would have benefited from more street-life and less hanging out in a dismal shack; Shaun Costello's aforementioned *Forced Entry* (1972) and his mind-boggling *Waterpower* (1977); and Zebedy Colt's horror-porn sleaze quartet, *The Farmer's Daughter* (1973), *Terri's Revenge* (1976), *Sex Wish* (1976) and *Unwilling Lovers* (1977); some of the most diabolically honest products of American erotic cinema.

Borderline soft-'X' features like Jack Gennaro's gory *San Francisco Ball* (1971), about three thugs who kidnap a girl as a hostage, but then rape, slice and bludgeon her to death before they can collect, take the rape-murder format into overdrive, with a balls-to-the-wall ferocity that Ray Williams, director of the simultaneously sleazy and unconvincing softcore rape flick *Wrong Way* (1971) could only dream about (Williams proves, if nothing else, that having a non-penetrative gang rape scene go on for twenty minutes does nothing to increase its intensity). And rape would crop up for a scene or two in any number of downbeat hardcore features, such as the blistering *Baby Rosemary* ('Harold Perkins', 1976), the existentially gloomy *I Love You I Love You Not* (James Bryan, 1973) and countless others.

Rape involving male victims is unsurprisingly rare, even in exploitation. Zebedy Colt's films frequently steer into bisexual terrain (as well as other, even more specialized, fantasy arenas such as incest and necrophilia), and his rape classic *Terri's Revenge*, about women hunting down rapists and turning the tables, is as nasty and assaultive as you'd imagine from the man who made *Sex Wish*, but Colt's work is about as far out on a limb as anyone ever went in American sex-horror production, and he remains a benchmark for shot-on-film porno nastiness. Certainly Colt

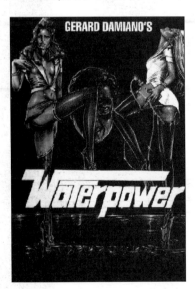

"ORIENTAL, CAUCASIAN, BLACK...BLONDES, BRUNETTES, REDHEADS... THE MOST EXCITING FOXY LADIES AND THE MOST BIZARRE PORNO ACTION EVER FANTASIED!" - (M. Williams)

"If you think you've seen all there is to see, then you must see deRenzy's 'Femmes deSade'. There's a whole lot more going on than you think!" - (Jeff Gates)

Alex deRenzy's
femmes deSade

Love is a hurting thing.

IN COLOR

ADULTS ONLY

completely eclipses AIP's idiotic *Rape Squad* (Bob Kelljan,
1974), another film about women's revenge for sexual
assault that's so badly made you end up disliking the victims.

That's not the case with the electrifyingly nasty *Femmes
de Sade* (dir: Alex De Renzy, 1976), in which one of the
meanest, freakiest sex-maniacs in porno history (Ken Turner)
rapes and bullies his way across San Francisco. We see him
brutally raping his prison buddy's girl, after which he takes
off to the red light district, cajoling prostitutes into vicious,
abusive sex. He looks pretty old – check out those pale fifty-
something dugs – but he's supple with it, even demonstrating
blowjob technique to a trembling hooker by sucking his own
wang. However, it's a game of two halves, and Turner ends
up trussed like a chicken at an S&M orgy he thought was
just a joke – which it is, but the joke's on him. A gang of
working girls, pissed off at his incessant attacks, subject him
to anal rape, an unsolicited golden shower, and the deposit of
a chocolate treat that, let's just say, must have slipped from
the dinner-table in Pasolini's *Salò*...

However, the doorway to excess through which De
Renzy, Colt and others like them gambolled in the
seventies was soon closed again in the eighties. The rape
scene as spectacle of cruelty in American exploitation
cinema bit the dust with porn's migration from cinema to
videotape. The MPAA's stranglehold on film production in
the early 1980s, the major studios' increasing dominance,
and the clean-up campaign inflicted upon sleazy oases like
42nd Street, meant that story-driven genre pictures were
largely forced to abandon such extremes. Rape fantasies
still turned up as grist to the porno-video mill in the ever
more provocative 'gonzo porn' videos of Ron Black, Max
Hardcore and others, but the atavistic intensity and gritty
storytelling of the seventies theatrical releases were lost.
Instead, rape joined cancer, paedophilia and drug-addiction
as an 'issue-of-the-month' to be explored in lachrymose TV
movies for the titillation of bored housewives.

right:
Hot Summer in the City (1976), directed by
one of hardcore's female directors, Gail
Palmer, deals with the abduction and gang
rape of a white woman by a gang of would-be
black revolutionaries. While nasty enough
when it wants to be, the film lacks the
explosive political thrust it seems to have
been aiming for.

It Came from the Stars/Swamp/Bushes/Caves (delete as appropriate)

Having travelled to the heart of darkness, exploitation-style,
we can now emerge refreshed to look at the more 'user-
friendly' areas of the horror genre. The seventies and
eighties were not *all* about extremes; horror continued to
offer what we might loosely call 'traditional' scares, and the
Exploitation Independents were as willing to do so as the
majors, albeit on a fraction of the budget. As ever, the
mainstream success of this or that idea would suggest all
number of variants; for every *Alien* and *Exorcist* there were
scores of low-budget alternatives. Ghost stories, occult tales
and assorted supernatural manifestations account for much
of what we're about to examine – but shambling to the front
of the queue, leaving muddy footprints in the vestibule and
chewing next door's dog, is the Monster Movie...

Monsters of the hairy, scaly or bug-eyed variety have
always appealed to cinemagoers, and the seventies saw
many a hulking leviathan stagger across the screens of
America's drive-ins and hardtops. Now, cheaply made
monster *movies* can be a painful affair, but personally I have
a lot of time for cheaply made *monsters*. They're a visible
triumph of optimism over plausibility, and they're often
extremely charismatic, possessing an intriguing wrongness
that their expensive cousins lack. The only thing that
hampers such a monster is the shyness of its creator, who
often flinches from showing us what he's come up with. It's
a shame, because a low-budget horror flick with a jaw-
droppingly strange or unlikely monster has a charm that can
imprint itself on your memory for decades. The unforgettable apeman-with-space-helmet in *Robot Monster* (Phil
Tucker, 1953) for instance, keeps you glued to the screen
despite being possibly the least plausible alien menace ever
created. Thank goodness Tucker had the courage of his
convictions and gave us shot after shot of 'Ro-Man'
ambling implacably back and forth, tuning his 'bubble-
machine' and carrying young ladies over hill and rise. The
thing is, if you *hide* your raggedy-ass monster, and drag
everything else out to compensate for the lack of it, then
what could have been prime B-movie fun sinks like a
plesiosaur's turd to the bottom of the Black Lagoon. Many
of the inexpensive monster flicks covered in the review
section of this book induce a see-sawing ambivalence in the
viewer, as over-scripted tedium alternates with glimpses of a
weird prosthetic wonder.

The monster movie was pretty much born in the fifties
(I'm excluding here such megastars as Frankenstein,
Dracula and the Wolf Man), and many of the seventies
variants carried on where classics like *The Thing from
Another World* (1951) and *Creature from the Black Lagoon*
(1954) left off. The template was set early on: earnest
lawmen, straight-arrow doctors and dedicated scientists
battle space monsters on the rampage; journalists and local
teenagers try to get to the truth; girls find themselves
menaced just as they're about to go swimming.
Affectionate revivals of the fifties approach, with some
added gore to liven things up, became common in low-
budget horror. Two Greydon Clark movies, *Without
Warning* (1980) and *The Return* (1980), and two Don
Dohler movies, *The Alien Factor* (1977) and *NightBeast*
(1982), deserve special mention – Clark's for their
exemplary B-movie energy and well-placed character
actors like Martin Landau, Jack Palance and Neville Brand;
and Dohler's for their down-home settings and mind-

boggling monster designs. But the crown for this subgenre goes to a New Jersey-lensed wonder, *The Deadly Spawn* (Doug McKeown, 1982), an exuberant, intelligent riff on fifties alien invasion movies that delivers the ultimate in low-budget mayhem – likeable characters, gripping action, and monsters by the vanload! If only the same could be said for bigger-budgeted snoozers like *The Dark* (John 'Bud' Cardos, 1978), which suffers from the curse of seventies horror – a workaday TV-movie feel.

Taking cues from the Black Lagoon's most famous resident are those movies depicting something nasty in the local creek, stirred into action either by falling meteors, like *The Crater Lake Monster* (William R. Stromberg, 1977), or more pointedly, human interference in the environment. Pollution from a lakeside cement factory rouses the eponymous *Monstroid* (Kenneth Hartford & Herbert R. Strock, 1979); fishing with dynamite pisses off the swamp-dwelling rubber-fetishist in *Bog* (Don Keeslar, 1978); and *Spawn of the Slithis* (Stephen Traxler, 1977), the most evolved of these movies, has a monster emerging from irradiated sea-slime, revisiting nuclear worries in a prescient way (the Three Mile Island accident was just a year away).

As with all genres, subgenres and sub-subgenres, there are exceptions, misfits and God-Knows-Whats. A half-man half-turkey runs amok in *Blood Freak* (Brad F. Grinter, 1972) – for which drugs are to blame – and a half-man half-octopus romps around in (you guessed it) *Octaman* (Harry Essex, 1971) – for which atomic radiation takes the rap. *Track of the Moonbeast* (Richard Ashe, 1976) has some schmuck turned into a monster by exposure to what can hardly have been the most threatening substance known to seventies man, a lump of moonrock; and *Rana: The Legend of Shadow Lake* (Bill Rebane, 1981) can't decide whether the monster is an Indian demon or a hominid mutant. Charmingly demonstrating a sort of 'and now, local news!' spin on the monster movie, a badly-tended municipal rubbish tip gestates *The Milpitas Monster* (Robert L. Burrill, 1975), a film made entirely by High School students and local community volunteers in the town of Milpitas, near San Francisco, CA. Also hailing from the San Francisco region, but operating on a far more complex level, is *Godmonster of Indian Flats* (Fredric Hobbs, 1973). This is a movie that owes as much to the idiosyncrasies of its uncate-gorisable director as it does to the horror genre, blending political allegory with California history, and topping it all off with a magnificently stubborn belief in its outrageously weird monster. New York's finest hour monster-wise came with *Basket Case* (1981), which asks what *is* a monster, and via a passing nod to *Freaks* (Tod Browning, 1932) suggests that there but for the grace of genes go you and I. Perhaps the most inexplicable monsters in low-budget horror are those stalking a handful of shipwrecked toffs in *Attack of the Beast Creatures* (Michael Stanley, 1983); since they resemble nothing more than tiny hand-puppets with stuck-on razor teeth it's hard to say whether they should be considered either as monsters or supernaturally animated manikins – certainly the filmmaker isn't letting on, and the cast struggle gamely through the horror without a word about the nature of their attackers.

If you discount oceans, lakes and waterways as hiding places for your monster, then surely the next best location is a cave or abandoned mine. Caves have undergone a horror renaissance recently, with the highly successful British film *The Descent* (Neil Marshall, 2005) wowing audiences on both sides of the Atlantic. Britain seems to do this sort of

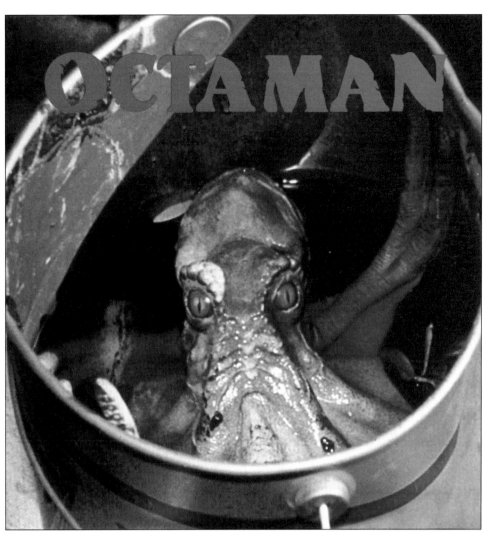

thing very well: the long-running BBC TV series *Doctor Who* has made capital from caves and mines many times, with horrors such as a race of cave-dwelling reptile men in *The Silurians* (1970), giant maggots emerging from abandoned mineworks in *The Green Death* (1973), and the alien cavern domain of the Devil himself (possibly) in *The Satan Pit* (2006). There's something almost too perfect about a cave or mine setting: it's likely to stir up claustro-phobia; it offers an environment with no reassuring physical markers; and for the Kristevans among us it resonates with deep unconscious connections to the pre-natal state. No wonder one of the best stalk-and-slash films to follow in the footsteps of *Friday the 13th* was the Canadian *My Bloody Valentine* (George Mihalka, 1981), set in a mining town where the killer's activities eventually lure the requisite teen cast underground. Chief among the low-budget cave-monster stories are *The Strangeness* (David Michael Hillman, 1980), which summons a believable cave complex in a garage-built set before revealing one of the best Lovecraftian monsters this side of *The Deadly Spawn*, and *The Boogens* (James L. Conway, 1982), a gripping little B-movie that hides genuine scares behind a title that unfortu-nately sounds like a failed joke.

Of course there's no doubt that the home-grown, All-American star of the Monster Show is Bigfoot, the as-yet mythical hominid whose possible existence still excites imaginations across the United States. It's just a shame that this creature has so often failed to set the screen alight. *The Legend of Boggy Creek* (Charles B. Pierce, 1972), a Bigfoot

above:
The irresistible **Octaman** (1971), courtesy of filmmaker Harry Essex and future Oscar-winning effects maestro Rick Baker.

below:
One of two pre-cert UK video covers for enjoyable monster-in-the-caves story, **The Strangeness** (1980).

America has a long-standing tradition of welcoming immigrant communities from the 'old world' and so it's not surprising that a few hardy, pioneering Transylvanians should have established themselves there over the years. As wrought by Bela Lugosi, Count Dracula enjoyed a balmy period at the top of the monster hierarchy with *Dracula* (1931), but his star soon diminished in American cinema, until reduced to playing fourth fiddle (unbilled, yet) in *Abbott and Costello Meet Frankenstein* (1948). For a few years, perhaps from shame, the Count slipped from view in American movies (finding salve for his wounds in the loving attentions of the British Hammer studio). Meanwhile, the family moniker was dragged through the dirt in TV comedy sketches, cereal commercials and kids' cartoons. A change of name, and a few hints that that's *all* it was, eventually saw a kind of renaissance when the American actor Robert Quarry – as *Count Yorga, Vampire* (Bob Kelljan, 1970) – stepped up to the plate. Here was Dracula updated for the me-generation, far from the Carpathian mountains or the drawing rooms of Hammer, willing to 'mix it up' with the ego-swingers and party-pussycats of modern California. A sequel followed (*The Return of Count Yorga*, Bob Kelljan, 1971), but probably the most high-profile new arrival from the old country appeared in *The Night Stalker* (1972), a gripping, influential and widely seen TV movie that had Chandleresque reporter Carl Kolchak (Darren McGavin) hunting down a (surprisingly nasty) vampire in modern-day Las Vegas. It too was successful enough to inspire a sequel (*The Night Strangler*, 1973, in which the threat is a murderous immortal alchemist), and even extended to a short but fondly remembered TV series, *Kolchak: The Night Stalker*, running from 1974-75.

Eight episodes of *Kolchak: The Night Stalker* were penned by a talented young writer called David Chase, future creator of TV mega-hit *The Sopranos* (1999-2007). Chase already had form when it came to the undead: he had written an unusual Exploitation Independent movie called *Grave of the Vampire* (John Hayes, 1972), in which a vampire rapes a young woman who, nine months later, gives birth to his bloodsucking baby. *Grave of the Vampire* is a truly odd film, a downbeat one-off that morphs into an explicitly Oedipal battle between vampire father and his abandoned son. In the hands of John Hayes, an unsung talent of the Exploitation Independents (see *Chapter 12*), it perhaps lacks some of the cultish brio of the more expensive (AIP-distributed) films like *Yorga*, but it forgoes their borderline campiness too, and prefers to play the game straight-faced, leading to scenes that can give unsuspecting viewers quite a chill.

Lemora: A Child's Tale of the Supernatural (Richard Blackburn, 1973) also rings a number of highly individual changes on by then rather trite vampire lore. Blackburn, a genuine artistic talent largely unheeded at the time, embraces the lesbian vampire theme so beloved of Hammer, but spins from it a bewitching fable (a young girl fleeing religious orthodoxy who meets a seductive vampiress) that's more fairytale than sex fantasy. Fortunately, a recent DVD release by Synapse restoring the film to its original lustrous hues has ensured that Blackburn's sole directorial outing joins Herk Harvey's *Carnival of Souls* (1962) as proof that it's always worth checking out the 'one-offs' of the genre.

above:
Evocative artwork for Charles B. Pierce's influential monster movie **The Legend of Boggy Creek** (1972).

below:
The ad-line on this poster for AIP's **Count Yorga, Vampire** (1970) would seem to have inspired the titling of their subsequent vampire tale **The Deathmaster** (1972), which also stars Robert Quarry...

pseudo-docudrama, is the leader of the pack by a country mile. This widely distributed exploitation hit actually marshals some honest scares, first through its moody photography, and then by its use of (fake) footage purporting to be the eye-witness testimony of real people. Twenty-five years later, *The Blair Witch Project* (1999) would hit the big time by revisiting the stylistic innovations of Pierce's film and bolting them to Ruggero Deodato's 'lost film crew' idea from *Cannibal Holocaust* (1980). *Boggy Creek* itself was followed by a dreadful sequel in 1977 by Tom (*Mark of the Witch*) Moore, and a third film, blandly directed by Pierce in '85, that completely ignores the second. The original is the only one to see: it's a great piece of Southern exploitation ballyhoo that reportedly scared the *bejeezus* out of children when it was unaccountably released to cinemas with a 'G' rating in the seventies! Of the others, *Creature from Black Lake* (Joy N. Houck Jr., 1976) can hold its shaggy head up high as an actual kids' movie variant; *Shriek of the Mutilated* (1974) lacks the guts to live up to its magnificent title, but its cornball set-up and spectacularly awful Bigfoot creature will have you giggling after a few beers; and no whistle-stop tour of the subgenre can possibly ignore the astounding *Night of the Demon* (James Wasson, 1980), in which Bigfoot leaps aboard the explicit horror bandwagon with a penis-ripping vengeance. But as for the blurry footprints left by such tedious tramplers as *The Beauties and the Beast* (Ray Nadeau, 1973), *Revenge of Bigfoot* (Harry Thomason, 1979), and *The Capture of Bigfoot* (Bill Rebane, 1979), well, let's just say they're less likely to lead to cult re-evaluation.

Sadly, successful innovation was *not* the main feature of vampire cinema in the 1970s: Dracula himself changes his name to Count Adrian, adopts a camp persona (obviously intended as a fitting disguise in California) and fiddles around with Voodoo in *Guess What Happened to Count Dracula?* (Laurence Merrick, 1970); Dracula's gay sons have hissy fits in the ultra-obscure *Dragula* (Jim Moss & Andy Milligan, 1971); a cursed bloodline creates vampires in the incoherent Florida Gothic *The Brides Wore Blood* (Robert R. Favorite, 1972); Dracula's daughter marries the son of the Wolf Man and moves to Staten Island, where the unhappy couple raise man-eating plants in the frankly demented *Blood* (Andy Milligan, 1974); a Satanic priest drags a brother and sister into incest and vampirism in the loopy *Satan's Black Wedding* (Philip Miller [Nick Millard], 1975); vampires hit the disco in *Nocturna* (Harry Hurwitz, (1979), starring John Carradine as Dracula (maybe) and narcissistic actress Nai Bonet in the title role; and the dignitaries of a small town have a neat line in sucking the blood of road accident victims in *Last Rites* (Domonic Paris, 1979). While there's fun to be had with a few of these films (especially Milligan's *Blood*, which is a riot), they can hardly be said to preserve the dignity of the vampire mythos, and instead it fell to George Romero to deliver the *coup de grâce* by demystifying the vampire completely in his superlative *Martin* (1976).

Of course, nothing can keep a good fiend down, and the vampire eventually resumed a place at the top of the monsters' table. A well-made Exploitation Independent

movie, *The Black Room* (Norman Thaddeus Vane & Elly Kenner, 1981) got the ball rolling again with the introduction of a soon to be popular notion, the vampire as stylish swinger, but it took the (unaccountable) cult success of the fangs, fetish and furnishings item *The Hunger* (Tony Scott, 1983) to relaunch the monster's mainstream career, followed by the re-imagining of vampires in three popular hits: the horror comedy *Fright Night* (Tom Holland, 1985), the gritty, 'alternative' culture inflected *Near Dark* (Kathryn Bigelow, 1987), and the glossy teen flick *The Lost Boys* (Joel Schumacher, 1987). Eventually, Dracula was fit enough for reinterpretation by one of Hollywood's big hitters, Francis Ford Coppola, who essayed the visually amazing though completely unscary

above:
Vampires? C'est chic!
Nocturna (1979) hits the dancefloor.

left:
A member of **Count Yorga**'s harem.

THE OUTING

...no one ever returns from this phantom town of TERROR!

above:
UK video art for Byron Quisenberry's
The Outing (1981).
and right:
The cast's befuddled expressions say it all...

Bram Stoker's Dracula (1992). More influential by far was Neil Jordan's screen adaptation of the bestselling Anne Rice novel *Interview with the Vampire* (1994), which dispensed with elegant old fiends like Christopher Lee and resold the mythos as a sensual pact between sexy young men (well, Brad Pitt and Tom Cruise).

Vampires, for all their 'beyond-the-grave' stylings, retain drives, needs, obsessions, compulsions that they themselves *understand*, and that link them not only to our dreams but also to our bodies. Ghosts, on the other hand, lack this corporeal connection, and thus present difficulties for screen representation. A real ghost caught on film today would have a hard time not to look like a Photoshop joke, or a pastiche of the cruder images of a bygone age in which fake mediums and spirit witnesses attempted to convince us of an other-world's existence, using crude superimpositions and optical trickery. The photographic image of a ghost can never be believed (which is why *The Blair Witch Project* succeeds, by refusing to show the ghost at the end). Ghosts have a hard time these days: when even the photographic image of cold reality is in doubt, spirits have it tough getting the good press. If we can doubt the veracity of a video clip showing a man being beheaded by terrorists, what chance has a phantom? None – not without a good publicist, anyway. Your haunting profile can be raised, your 'unearthly wail' heard loud and clear; just don't expect to be treated as real. Even the living can't be sure of *that* endorsement any more...

Ghostly visitations have been a mainstay of horror since their first literary stirrings in the medieval Gothic novel, and despite the seventies' onslaught of tales about murder and sadism, their unearthly cinematic offspring continued to pop up throughout the decade. However, the ghost story needs, if not 'class', then a certain elegance, something that often eludes low-budget films. Perhaps because hauntings in the cinema depend a great deal on the credible reactions of actors, horror filmmakers found that they couldn't get away with just a few flapping doors and a cheap optical overlay. Often, what liberates low-budget films from the demands of mainstream moviemaking is that they can dispense with quality acting (which is generally expensive) and instead prioritize sensationalism, outré style, and sheer directorial fancy. That's not to say good acting doesn't help, or that it never surfaces, but if you're making a slasher film or a bizarro horror you can go a long way without it. The ghost tale however rarely lends itself to 'cheap-and-cheerful'. Hauntings, with all their concomitant auras of doubt and uncertainty, are so much less visually sensational than murder, rape and mutilation; they require finesse, both in the acting and in the way the subtle gradations of fear are deployed. Or else, they require sly deliberation and co ordination. To give the viewer that shiver of the uncanny, you must trick your way to their nerve-endings by subtlety and misdirection, or take a psychological approach that sees the uncanny as a mental process. In both cases a considerable degree of caution, measurement, and insight are required.

Much as I admire the tenacity of Wisconsin's low-budget *maestro* Bill Rebane, his spook-story *The Demons of Ludlow* (1983) takes an intriguingly off-kilter idea – a haunted piano given as a centennial gift to an isolated rural community – and fumbles it in a murky, plodding fashion that robs the story of impact. I would happily nominate *The Hearse* (George Bowers, 1980) – a well-mounted ghost story rarely defended by critics – as a better film, despite

the fact that it's fairly predictable. Lead actress Trish Van Devere plays the role of lonely middle-aged newcomer to a small rural town so well that you feel for her even as the director serves up plot developments as if from a checklist of haunted-house paraphernalia. *The Demons of Ludlow* is interesting only as a plucky low-budget endeavour; *The Hearse*, for all its limitations, works as a ghost story. And while I extend my great admiration to those who try and fail to evoke the supernatural on a shoestring, this is one subgenre of horror that is probably best served by money.

Among the also-rans on the scary house market are *The House of Seven Corpses* (Paul Harrison, 1973) and *The Evil* (Gus Trikonis, 1978). Both films squander potentially intriguing ideas: in the first, a film crew shooting a horror movie in a genuinely haunted house are picked off by an evil force (an idea partially revisited in Norman J. Warren's 1978 Brit-horror classic, *Terror*); and in the second, an inner-city drug rehabilitation project relocates to a big house in the sticks, and exposes the druggies to demonic forces lurking within. Someone could still make a marvellous film from these simple set-ups, but there's a crippling lack of meta-drama in Harrison's film, and a lack of social edge to the Trikonis effort.

Another great premise – a haunted cinema – is screwed up royally in *Movie House Massacre* (Alice Raley [Rick Sloane], 1984), in which the 'camp' card is played by a director who lacks the deftness of touch needed to bring it off. *Natas: The Reflection* (Jack Dunlap, 1983) surrounds its best ideas (a haunted desert town full of zombies, a mountain-demon) with so much stodge and silt that you have to be a genre completist (or film reviewer) to discover them; *Till Death* (Walter Stocker, 1974) ought to be, but isn't, a necrophiliac poem, about a man visited by the ghost of his dead wife when he's accidentally locked in her tomb; and *The Outing* (Byron Quisenberry, 1981), a painfully slow and inscrutable film set in an abandoned Wild West village, is so guarded about what's actually going on that I

don't know whether to dismiss it as the worst spook story ever told or to seek out an audience with its mysterioso director. *Dark Eyes* (James Polakof, 1980) proves that 'class' is in the eye of the beholder with a ghost story (admittedly enjoyable on a camp level) that's heavy on chiffon negligees and billowing curtains yet low on incident or atmosphere. But the best ghost tales in low-budget horror are those that innovate sideways into other regions. *The Forest* (Don Jones, 1981) takes what initially feels like a rural slasher and gradually imports ghosts both benevolent and vengeful; *Haunted* (Michael De Gaetano, 1976) floats more ideas than it knows what to do with but at least keeps viewers on their toes, with non-sequitur visuals, a reincarnated American-Indian princess, and some curious post-Hollywood melodrama *á là* Curtis Harrington. Without a doubt the most stylish and affecting of all ghost stories in this field is *Let's Scare Jessica To Death* (John Hancock, 1971), in which the heroine, recovering from a breakdown, encounters horrors at first indistinguishable from her own mental distortions. Hancock's finely acted, beautifully shot and genuinely uncanny film stands as the best supernatural tale to be produced by the Exploitation Independents during the 1970s.

Swelling the ranks of the supernatural horror film, at least numerically, are those concerned with the occult. After the smash success of *Rosemary's Baby* (Roman Polanski, 1968) and the even greater commercial and cultural impact of *The Exorcist* (William Friedkin, 1973), tales of sorcery and Satanism were, if you will, legion. Witches of a not especially threatening variety pop up in *Mark of the Witch* (Tom Moore, 1972), *Blood Orgy of the She Devils* (Ted V. Mikels, 1972), and the rather more likeable *Madame Zenobia* (Eduardo Cemano, 1973) and *Blood Sabbath* (Brianne Murphy, 1972).

More complex and intelligent are *Simon, King of the Witches* (Bruce Kessler, 1971), *Season of the Witch* (George Romero, 1972), *Dark August* (Martin Goldman,

above:
Unusual compositions abound in Romero's
Season of the Witch, although it has to be
said that this one looks almost like a parody
of the tricksy framing associated with
'art' cinema!

right:
J.G. 'Pat' Patterson's incredibly tacky and
inept first film **The Body Shop** (1972) – now
better known on DVD under its early eighties
video retitling, **Doctor Gore** – so horrified his
friend, the young director of **Axe**, Frederick
Friedel, that the latter swore never to take
Patterson's advice when it came to
filmmaking!

1975), and *The Devonsville Terror* (Ulli Lommel, 1983),
films that actually engage with the phenomenon of
witchcraft, either as a belief-system or a cultural
phenomenon. *Simon…* is examined in detail in the review
section; suffice to say here that it's an uncommonly even-
handed engagement with occult ideology. *Season of the
Witch* is from Romero's oft-derided 'slump' period, post-
Night of the Living Dead and pre-*Martin*. It does have
some near-crippling problems, not least a far too leisurely
pace, and passages where forced scripting can have you
grinding your knuckles against your teeth. The lead
character, an unhappily-married suburban housewife, is so
emotionally reserved that many tend to dismiss the film
for lacking a compelling lead presence. Personally I like
it, but it's a close call. I suspect Romero, with his lead
actress Jan White, was striving for a Bergmanesque
portrait of emotional withdrawal comparable to Liv
Ullmann in *Persona* (1966) or Harriet Andersson in
Through a Glass Darkly (1961) – a not-unlikely notion
considering that in the early 1970s Bergman's films still
commanded popular attention in the USA. However, what
really makes *Season of the Witch* special is its
commitment to the imagery of Joan's dreams as an index
of her social and sexual anxieties, and its placing of
occult beliefs within a larger framework that addresses
female marginalisation in the patriarchal culture of the
early seventies. *Dark August*, a lesser-known work that
deserves to be seen more widely, is a serious-minded tale
addressing the occult's appeal to the vengeful, and is
covered in more detail in the review section. *The
Devonsville Terror* is likewise a thoughtful attempt to
inject some sociological context into the 'scary witch'
archetype, insisting, in a slightly mangled but sincere
way, that witchcraft is a fair response by women to the
injustices of patriarchy.

Elsewhere in horror, the occult was mostly a modish
excuse to get group sex up on the screen. Judging from
both cinema and the porn mags of the 1970s, the idea of
'gang-bangs' both gripped and appalled the collective
imagination of 'squares', leading to all sorts of

unconvincing screen depictions. Quite why group sex is
so fascinating depends on how you view Protestant,
Catholic and Jewish notions of shame. To a Protestant,
group sex is a sin because it's profligate, excessive,
grandiose, and of course Pagan. To Catholics, it's not only
Pagan, it's also dirty, and if sex is dirty what could be
dirtier than doing it in full view of others? Judaism has
explicit laws against such behaviour, and besides, you
might see a neighbour in a compromising position and
then how are you going to face them over dinner next
week? Ninety percent of what passes for Satanism and
occultism in the horror genre is simply square society's
attempt to visualize what it is they suspect 'sinners' are
getting up to after lights-out, and by and large it's as
unconvincing as their attempts to visualize heaven. Given
that 'Satanists' are just Christians in drag, their rituals are
about as erotic as Sunday Service. Sacrificial victims in
occult-horror cinema, for instance, are traditionally
hypnotized or drugged, so we get none of the fervid
struggling that enlivens the pitch for unbelievers. Satanic
ritual cuts eroticism off at the knees, as everyone
maintains a staunchly serious air that would scarcely
shame a Cardinal working his way through a Catechism.

Pornographers, naturally keen to exploit the
audience's wish to witness 'sin' at work, frequently went
for the occult group-sex trip, but never with much
success. Perhaps a few lapsed Catholics were excited by
the tired juxtaposition of quasi-religious hokum and bared
breasts, but the Devil of desire rarely got a look-in: lust,
and true animal enjoyment, were forever over the horizon.
(Frankly, group sex in such settings is a bore; a bunch of
ostentatiously undressed squares cavorting in a poor
imitation of abandon while some twit with a piccolo plays
nursery rhymes backwards.)

With the notable exception of David Cronenberg, sci-
fi horror also accounts for little of worth in the
Exploitation Independent field. Silly mad scientist motifs
are garnished with mouldy horror in *Flesh Feast* (Brad F.
Grinter, 1970), *The Possessed!* (Charles Nizet, 1974), and
Doctor Gore (J.G. 'Pat' Patterson, 1972). *Mansion of the
Doomed* (Michael Pataki, 1976), a mad doctor film, has
some schlocky energy, but can't leap high enough to
escape the gravitational pull of *Les yeux sans visage*
(1959), the masterpiece from which it borrows its big
idea. An odour of Dr. Moreau and sundry other thirties
offcuts lingers in the air like old cookery on *Frankenstein
Island* (Jerry Warren, 1981). And speaking of cooking
smells, given the current debates about GM foods, E-
additives and nutritional standards, I suppose *The Corpse
Grinders* (Ted V. Mikels, 1971) takes on science-fiction

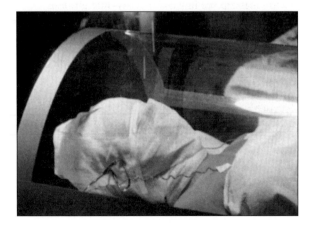

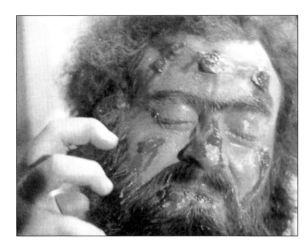

overtones in its exposé of a company using human flesh in cat food manufacture… but I'm joking of course; it's a weirdo horror film really. Chief among the true sci-fi horrors is *The Crazies* (George Romero, 1973), of which more in the review section. *Stigma* (David Durston, 1972) is more science-fact than science-fiction but employs a vibe redolent of the old sci-fi horrors of the fifties to get a less-than-cosy health warning across; and *Blue Sunshine* (Jeff Lieberman, 1977) enters Philip K. Dick terrain with a marvellously unsettling study of what happens to a bunch of one-time druggies, now firmly ensconced in normal life, who start losing their minds because of bad acid they all took back in the sixties. A vogue for psi-fi horror swept through the genre in the aftermath of *Carrie* (1976): interestingly, a few smaller films got there first. *Psychic Killer* (Ray Danton, 1975) is a tolerably entertaining example, although the more intriguing and complex *The Premonition* (1975), which also predates the De Palma film, has the edge.

Rounding off this tour of monsterdom is the Zombie. *Night of the Living Dead* was followed by such diverse American oddities as: *Messiah of Evil* (1973) – a fantastically strange and imaginative film touting a 'hippy-dream gone sour' meets 'consumer-society gone crazy' theme well before Romero's *Dawn*; the aforementioned *Deathdream* (Bob Clark, 1972) – a *Monkey's Paw* variant in which a Vietnam soldier dies in combat, then returns home to resume his old life; *Children Shouldn't Play with Dead Things* (Alan Ormsby, 1972) – a tale about grave-robbing that starts out like a student film lark but turns surprisingly creepy; the awful but endearing *Garden of the Dead* (John Hayes, 1972) – with its talking, formaldehyde-addicted chain-gang zombies; and *The Child* (Robert Voskanian, 1976) – a delirious bizarro masterpiece in which a nasty little girl uses psychic powers to terrorize her family and tutor, before introducing them to her 'friends' from the graveyard. A second wave came after Romero rekindled the zombie's box-office draw with *Dawn of the Dead*, as backyards across America provided locations for a variety of ultra-low-budget spin-offs. Tony Malanowski's mind-bogglingly minimalist *Night of Horror* (1981) and its energetic pulp-horror update *The Curse of the Screaming Dead* (1982) are explored in detail elsewhere in this book; *The Day It Came to Earth* (Harry Thomason, 1979), features a Mafia boss revived from the dead by a falling meteor; Fred Olen Ray's inept but amusing *The Alien Dead* (1980) is worth a look for its Florida swamp-zombies; *Fiend* (Don Dohler, 1980) is a rare example of

a post-*Dawn* zombie film that owes nothing to Romero, with a reanimated cadaver, possessed by a demon, giving violin tutorials in deepest Baltimore; *Night of the Zombies* (Joel M. Reed, 1981) meanders in a truly dismal way through a plot involving the CIA, Nazi zombies and a heroic commitment to nothingness; *The Dark Power* (Phil Smoot, 1985) unleashes zombie Toltec Indians and then shoehorns them into a Sorority slasher film; *Forest of Fear* (Chuck McCrann, 1979) shows that living in Pittsburgh is no guarantee you can direct zombie flicks; the epically deranged *Frozen Scream* (Frank Roach & Renee Harmon, 1981) has dead people stored in cryogenic suspension ordered to kill by radio control; and the action-schlock smorgasbord *Raw Force* (Edward D. Murphy, 1982) features cannibalistic monks who raise the dead.

above:
Romero's **The Crazies** (1973) carries a political punch that makes it a dry run for the world-wide apocalypse depicted in **Dawn of the Dead** (1978).

top left:
More shabby mayhem from **Doctor Gore**.

A crypt is a place where the dead
are laid to rest...or are they?

One Dark Night

Julie MEG TILLY   Steve DAVID MASON DANIELS

above:
UK video art for **One Dark Night**
(1983), a spirited ghost story that
takes hackneyed sorority dare
material and weaves an enjoyably
pulp-inflected B-movie out of it.

right:
A supernatural manifestation in
One Dark Night.

Two post-*Dawn* films to achieve something striking and nuanced are *Sole Survivor* (Thom Eberhardt, 1982) and *One Dark Night* (Tom McLoughlin, 1983). The wonderfully creepy *Sole Survivor* has a great twist: the Undead don't attack indiscriminately but instead focus on just one unfortunate individual, the 'sole survivor' of a plane crash. *One Dark Night* plays the hackneyed 'sorority dare' scenario, and then enlivens it with heavily stylized effects and a kineticism that occasionally recalls Sam Raimi. No one is going to have their life changed by *One Dark Night*, but it's visually inventive and McLoughlin knows how to make the 'walking down a dark corridor' scenes feel fresh. When the undead appear, their fantastical appearances anticipate the ghost-zombie visions of Steven Spielberg (*Raiders of the Lost Ark*; *Poltergeist*) and Peter Jackson (*The Frighteners*) – all on a fraction of the budget.

Art of Perversity – Horror and Incoherence

Some films are genuinely hard to classify. Take *Phantasm* (Don Coscarelli, 1978) – a rubber-reality teen adventure sci-fi horror film (eat your heart out *Donnie Darko*); and *The Bogey Man* – a slasher film that thinks it's a supernatural possession story, or vice-versa. Then there's *Double Jeopardy* (Ulli Lommel, 1983) – on the surface a sort of female serial killer story, although London Bridge's relocation to the Arizona desert acts as a decentring motif and the whole thing comes on like Krzysztof Kieslowski remaking *Ms.45* based on a mumbled conversation with a heavily sedated Abel Ferrara.

Those are perhaps 'arty' examples, or at least self-consciously crafted ones. But what are we to make of *Soul Vengeance* (Jamaa Fanaka, 1975), a film that takes the persistent cultural image of the black man as sexually super-endowed, and has its put-upon black hero actually *murder* people with his enormous snake-like schlong? How about *Ghosts That Still Walk* (James T. Flocker, 1977) – a psi-horror film about Indian artefacts, a possessed boy, and giant rolling rocks that appear from nowhere? Or *A Scream in the Streets* (directed by Carl Monson and three other idiots in 1972), which spends forever mooching around after a couple of nasty cops like a snivelling police informant, only giving the audience a break by depicting a roughie-style beating at a massage parlour and several cameos from a day in the life of a serial killing female impersonator? Keeping the flame alive for bizarro horror into the eighties, *The Jar* (Bruce Toscano, 1985) tells of a man malevolently driven to the brink of madness by a bottled homunculus left behind by a hit-and-run victim. Why he doesn't show it to anyone, or smash it, or put it in the cooker, we never learn...

Even these films are partially comprehensible (I'm being mean about *The Jar*; I suspect it actually works as an allegory of sexual identity). Perhaps I'm shilly-shallying, dragging my heels as I approach both the critic's nemesis and, paradoxically, one of my favourite wastes of time; a region of American horror that defies criticism and freaks your credulity while feeding your jaded palate the most exquisite cinematic truffles...

Sometimes, films just elude you. For all your experience and would-be sophistication, for all your critical dexterity, they escape your terms of reference, like neutrinos blithely passing through all that is solid and orderly. They aren't *trying* to do it; but they do. These are films so *damaged*, so wonky and graceless and brilliant, that you feel a need for an anti-semiosis, where movies gain points for being *beyond* bad, for being truly incoherent. These are the films that fall between the cracks: too skewed and dishevelled to be hailed as art, too mind-bendingly weird to be patronised as kitsch. They hatch in the interstices between 'bad' and 'unique' – bearing in mind that the only *truly* bad film is a boring one, and 'unique' can just mean 'no one else would want to do this'. The terrain is one of dazed ambivalence, the appropriate attitude for the viewer stunned helplessness.

Here are preposterous stories told stonily, blankly, by terrified or medicated actors, though it's all disconcertingly real; here are plain-Jane heroines mumbling incomprehensible lines foiled by *ad hoc* editors cursed with a thought-disease unknown to man, following scripts written by blithe surfers of the senses, adrift on their own untranscribable dreams, wrecked on the shores of bloody-minded persistence; encouraged by camera-toting dope-hound mediums whose ectoplasmic smoke-dreams fail to show up on celluloid, despite achingly beautiful long shots invaded by human wrecking balls swinging lazily and destructively in the foreground; here are sensitive self-taught actors giving it their utmost, pressed into service as straight men at the mercy of blood-clottingly comical music, their spastic emotion-ellipses grazed upon by directorial idiot-savants grasping the profound by accident and squashing it into a messy insect pulp, exciting verbose collectors of ingrown arcana…

It has often been said that 'bad' films overlap the surreal, although those who make this claim tend to refer back mainly to the black-and-white era. Few critics have insisted that the cinema of the 1970s and 1980s can contribute; I hope we can agree that a few astounding candidates are dotted throughout this book… Such filmmakers may stumble upon techniques normally associated with the *avant-garde*, while remaining stubbornly – or helplessly – cut off from the safe haven of art theory. A clever idea can be mired in mundane expression, and a senseless film can sometimes capture in fleeting form a penetrating truth. Buñuel is an example of a director who was unafraid of the most ludicrous notions because he intuited that in art deemed low and idiotic there were jewels of insight. There's nothing to stop the characters in *The Exterminating Angel* (1962) from leaving their dinner party – and yet they stay, befuddled by their relentless 'sophistication'. Similarly ludicrous notions crop up all the time in 'bad' movies, and it's as intriguing to encounter Doris Wishman in this mode as it is to confront the giants of surrealism: the only difference is self-consciousness, and since the surrealists were desperately seeking to evade rational thought, we can hardly be blamed for assessing those incapable of it just as favourably.

Rather than sneering at the perceived shortcomings of a low-budget film like, say, Wishman's *A Night To Dismember* (1983) or John Wintergate's *BoardingHouse* (1982), perhaps a more illuminating, reasonable and enjoyable method of viewing is to imagine one is 'through the looking glass' into a world where films are *meant* to look this way, where all the 'shortfalls' of technique are actually artistic achievements. Instead of being condescending to 'bad movies', why not treat the 'errors' and 'shortcomings' as a sort of art-in-negative, where divergences from the norm, whether accidental or not, make up a parallel film universe? A place where tracking

above:
Angus gives good 'Scrimm' as The Tall Man in Don Coscarelli's indie horror classic, **Phantasm** (1978).

left:
The man with the murdering penis – Marlo Monte in the unforgettable **Soul Vengeance** (1975).

shots are *supposed* to stumble, editing *always* obscures, and actors characteristically *refuse* to give even the basics of a plausible performance. It's by taking this trip to another world that we can really start to enjoy 'bad' films, and also to discover their aesthetics. We need an imaginary film grammar to account for movies in which a high concentration of ostensible failure – technical, logical, discursive – transcends mere kitsch.

The horror genre, it seems, has a special dispensation; it can get away with disorientation and incoherence under cover of the genre's habitual erosion of safe boundaries. The critic Verina Glaessner once reviewed a Jess Franco film in the U.K.'s film journal *Monthly Film Bulletin*, saying that it featured, "Chilly, robot-like actresses at an obvious loss". Such powerful words… 'Chilly, robot-like actresses' – who could resist such an image? Chilly, as in cold and forbidding. Robot-like, as in human but not human. 'At an obvious loss' meaning that these disturbing half-humans were somehow malfunctioning in a sort of automaton's graveyard. Marry such compelling creatures to a lack of dramatic focus that makes even a relatively simple plot hard to follow, and erratic editing that intervenes aggressively between the viewer and the action, and you have me in the palm of your hand. You are, in fact, Renee Harmon. Harmon's *Frozen Scream* is everything you could hope for from the words of Ms. Glaessner, and more: why, the chilliness is underlined by a plot that not only has actresses playing cold, manipulative, or distant characters,

below:
Suzanna Love as the troubled Olivia, in Ulli Lommel's fractured horror thriller **Double Jeopardy** (1983).

but also features cryogenic suspension. Ms. Harmon remains an inscrutable though gracious character (see interview), while co-director Frank Roach has disappeared, despite my best efforts; but I implore you to watch *Frozen Scream* again, and apply the 'looking glass' perception…

Obviously, low-budget films made by ambitious friends in California suburbs or Alabama back-yards can hardly aspire to a perfect match of theme and imagery: set dressing and art design go to the wall when you can barely afford film stock. In Italy, where sleazy subject matter is supported by establishment money, design is something even the cheaper flicks consider. Take a look at Joe D'Amato's brutal, often repellant 1979 horror film *Beyond the Darkness*: the interiors are beautiful, the locations well chosen, camerawork surprising and creative. Examples from the USA such as *Lemora, Messiah of Evil* and *Martin* boast creative art direction without going to Cinecittà levels of indulgence: but more often than not American horror films are design-free zones, their principal visual charm arising from good locations. An American director like Frederick Friedel made his stylish and distinctive movies in a production context where tuition came in the form of a chat with the director of *Doctor Gore*, and where six months contact with the industry was considered sufficient to equip you with the skills to helm a feature. That this unschooled, unmoderated environment can produce truly extraordinary films like Friedel's *Lisa, Lisa* (*Axe*) or *The Kidnap Lover* (*Kidnapped Coed*) is a testament to the Exploitation Independent way of doing things…

Sadly, the innocence, naiveté, freedom, self-obsession, blissful ignorance, call it what you will, of the Exploitation Independents was eroded and dissipated in the mid-1980s. By the nineties, it was gone. Standardization, organisation, de-clawing; such was the effect that the majors exerted on the Exploitation Independents; first through their take-over at the business level, and then via the corruption of the B-movie style by aggressive irradiations of cash.

Decline – Carpenter, Hooper, Romero, Craven

In the 1980s, as the Exploitation Independents were locked out of theatres by block-bookings of mainstream movies, the writing was on the wall. Investors drifted away as the majors tied up the money-bags and closed the loopholes. Since then, of the leading players in the seventies' horror boom, only David Cronenberg has consistently parlayed his abilities into projects that reach the multiplexes (*The Fly, Dead Ringers, A History of Violence, Eastern Promises*) or the headlines (*Naked Lunch, Crash*). Others have not been so adaptable.

John Carpenter, who after the commercial success of *Halloween* soon crossed over to studio pictures, is still a frequent visitor to the horror genre. His wonderful spook story *The Fog* (1980) has enjoyed a well-deserved reappraisal in recent years (while suffering desecration-by-remake), but his best work remains *The Thing* (1982); a sci-fi horror, made at Universal, that may be the most morbid film ever produced by a major studio. Carpenter's later efforts to return to the smaller, more intimate scale of his early work, such as *Prince of Darkness* (1987) and *In the Mouth of Madness* (1995) have their charms, but they struggle to simulate, and thus miss by miles, the effortless confidence of his early work.

The strangest and most prolonged decline befell Tobe Hooper, director of *The Texas Chain Saw Massacre*.

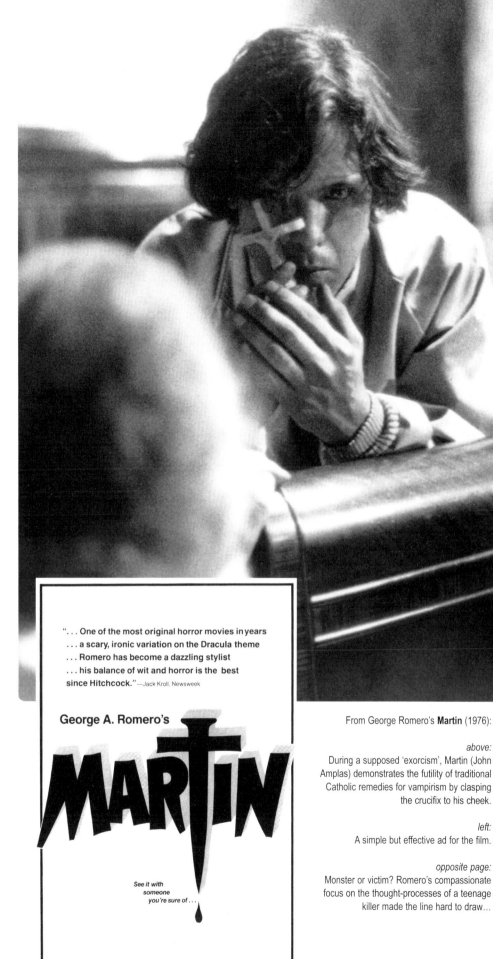

"…One of the most original horror movies in years …a scary, ironic variation on the Dracula theme …Romero has become a dazzling stylist …his balance of wit and horror is the best since Hitchcock." —Jack Kroll, Newsweek

George A. Romero's

MARTIN

See it with someone you're sure of …

Introducing JOHN AMPLAS as "MARTIN" featuring LINCOLN MAAZEL · CHRISTINE FORREST · ELYANE NADEAU
… SARAH VENABLE · TOM SAVINI · FRAN MIDDLETON · AL LEVITSKY · Produced by RICHARD RUBINSTEIN · Original Score: DONALD RUBINSTEIN · Photography by: MICHAEL GORNICK
A Laurel Film · IN COLOR
A Libra Films Release

From George Romero's **Martin** (1976):

above:
During a supposed 'exorcism', Martin (John Amplas) demonstrates the futility of traditional Catholic remedies for vampirism by clasping the crucifix to his cheek.

left:
A simple but effective ad for the film.

opposite page:
Monster or victim? Romero's compassionate focus on the thought-processes of a teenage killer made the line hard to draw…

Like Orson Welles, Hooper made his one perfect film first (well, strictly second, after a rarely screened 1969 item called *Eggshells*) and was then seemingly ever after prone to production interference, acrimonious behind-the-scenes disagreements and questionable career choices. He suffered setbacks to the distribution arrangements of *The Texas Chain Saw Massacre*, signing the rights over to the Mafia-run Bryanston Distributing, resulting in massive defrauding of the ticket receipts for that wildly successful movie. *Death Trap* (1976) suffered at the hands of producer Mardi Rustam, whose attitude to his *wunderkind* director was less than cordial. He was thrown off the productions of *The Dark* (1978) and *Venom* (1981) after just a few days shooting. Production difficulties allegedly beset the making of *The Funhouse* in 1979. Fortunately, Hooper's television debut, the mini-series *Salem's Lot* (1979), was a popular success, and played a big part in netting his most prestigious mainstream assignment, MGM's supernatural roller coaster, *Poltergeist* (1982). It looked as if Hooper was about to make the most effective margins-to-mainstream transition of all. However, during the shooting of *Poltergeist*, Hooper experienced difficulties with producer Steven Spielberg and the rumour mill went into overdrive, claiming that Spielberg was taking the reins away from an out-of-his-depth Hooper and directing the movie himself. Spielberg took out a full page ad in the trade paper *Variety*, stating that he had every confidence in his director, but while this may partially have saved Hooper's reputation it

did not entirely quell the stories, especially when the film as released looked and sounded far more like the work of Spielberg than Hooper. After this unpleasant experience Hooper went on to strike a three-picture deal with Menahem Golan and Yoram Globus, Israeli producers who had clawed their way to the top of the industry heap in the early 1980s. In many ways it was the high watermark of his career as a bankable director, with two medium-budget sci-fi action films, *Lifeforce* (1985) and *Invaders from Mars* (1986), commissioned, along with *The Texas Chainsaw Massacre 2* (1986). Unfortunately, the results were a mixed bag: *Lifeforce* is a riot, but suffers from unintentional laughs and an uncertain tone; *Invaders* was just appalling; and while *Chainsaw 2* was a qualified success, in my opinion, it failed to win over enough fans. For Hooper, the story thereafter was one of compromise, interference, and loss of focus, leading him to the direct-to-DVD dungeon where recent efforts like *The Mangler* (1995) and *Crocodile* (2000) reside. Some have hailed his 'remake' of *[The] Toolbox Murders* (2004) as a return to form: I honestly wish I could agree.

George Romero's decline is more insidious. The Pittsburgh-based director seems to have found it increasingly difficult to get projects bankrolled and, when he has, there have usually been gremlins in the works to prevent the films reaching an audience. Add this to a case of interesting concepts sunk by pedestrian direction, and you have another unhappy autumn for a once excellent director.

The rot began with the cheap and cheerful horror-whimsy of *Creepshow* (1982), a collaboration with Stephen King, which failed to live up to the duo's breathless *Fangoria* promises of "the scariest film ever – you'll literally have to crawl out of the cinema!" King may have ruled the paperback racks, but he was less reliable as a screenwriter, giving Romero a clutch of flimsy, lightweight tales to play with. Despite having fun with the coloured gels and comic-strip backdrops, Romero ended up with little more than a cute diversion. After *Day of the Dead* (1985), a grim masterpiece that nevertheless suffered significant pre-production hassles, Romero made *Monkey Shines* (1988), an unusual tale with strong performances and some impressive suspense sequences. Unfortunately it also suffers from a persistent 'afternoon TV' vibe, thanks to a sedate shooting style and a bland, sensible score that sounds pilfered from an episode of *Quincy*. The same problem beset a return engagement with Italian titan Dario Argento. Having enjoyed cordial relations during the making of *Dawn of the Dead*, and substantial box-office too, the pair were keen to make lightning strike twice. The result was the diptych *Two Evil Eyes* (1990). Argento scored a qualified success with his half of the deal, merging several Poe stories into a curate's omelette that at least has a feel for the grotesque. Romero opted for *The Facts in the Case of M. Valdemar*, but allowed a 'made-for-TV' aura to creep in again. Devoid of menace or atmosphere, Romero's part of the bargain displayed all the morbid psychological shading of *The Rockford Files… The Dark Half* (1993), another Stephen King adaptation, had its moments, but it was starting to look as if Romero was relying on the King brand name. *Bruiser* (2000) at least marked Romero's return to self-written work, but it took a crackpot notion, embedded it in a mundane *mise-en-scène*, attached it to a tired revenge plot, and then threw in a few wild jabs of surreal allegory that failed to reach a target. It may well be the most frustrating and annoying film the director has ever made. More recently, *Land of the Dead* (2005) saw Romero back in the mainstream with a fair but hardly epic new entry in his zombie mythos. As a director whose skill with character was always his best suit, he disappoints here with a corny super-villain and bland hero. By suggesting that the zombies are now the real locus of sympathy, yet neglecting to explore them in detail, he leaves us with a sketch of a movie, a hollow theoretical abstraction. It must have looked good on paper but it fails to ignite onscreen. To make matters worse, recent interviews have shown a man uneasy with the excesses of his earlier work and retreating into a 'what about the children' position that can only embarrass his admirers.

Wes Craven, on the other hand, has enjoyed perhaps the most unexpected career trajectory of all. If anyone leaving a screening of *The Last House on the Left* back in 1972 (or, for that matter, catching it on video in 1982) had been accosted by a visitor from the future telling them that the the director would be a big wheel in 21st Century Hollywood, they'd have concluded that time travel rots the brain. Yet thirty-six years later, in March 2008, *Last House* was granted a certificate for uncut DVD release in, of all places, the *United Kingdom*. The impossible has been achieved: Craven's rehabilitation is complete.

But if *Last House on the Left* wasn't enough of a bad-taste barricade between Craven and the Hollywood Hills, a string of failed efforts afterwards should have kept him off Mulholland for good.

Crocks like *Deadly Blessing* (1981), *Swamp Thing* (1982), *The Hills Have Eyes 2* (1985), *Deadly Friend* (1986), and *Shocker* (1989) ought to have ensured that his Country Club card was forever marked 'visitor' not 'resident'. However, Craven was to demonstrate an amazing knack for pulling the occasional ace from the pack. *The Hills Have Eyes* (1977) was a solid, effectively scary exploitation flick that toned down the excesses of *Last House* without castrating it, but the franchise-floating, culture-defining *A Nightmare On Elm Street* (1984) and the po-mo snarkfest *Scream* (1996) clinched his reputation, with both fans and studio heads. To give the world Freddy Krueger and then to do the same zeit-heist again with *Scream*, another multi-sequel hit, is evidence of Craven's rare talent to read and even anticipate the mood and desires of the mass teen market.

Hollywood Trash

"An exploitation film is a motion picture in which the elements of plot and acting become subordinate to elements that can be promoted. In that respect, I would regard Jurassic Park *as the ultimate exploitation film. If you look at* Jurassic Park *with a cold-blooded eye, the acting level is junior high school. People read their lines as though they're seeing them on a TelePrompTer for the first time."* – Herschell Gordon Lewis, to John McCarty, in *The Sleaze Merchants.*

The relationship between the majors and the Independents changed forever with the advent of Steven Spielberg's *Jaws* (1975) and the runaway success of George Lucas's *Star Wars* (1977). Grisly shocks and fairground thrills were no longer the sole province of the Exploitation Independents. Twenty years after Herschell Gordon Lewis assaulted the audience with the image of a woman's tongue yanked out of her gullet, Steven Spielberg's *Indiana Jones and the Temple of Doom* (1984) featured a scene in which a villain pulls a steaming human heart from a victim's chest (in a 'PG' certificated film, no less). From the kinetic grisliness of *Jurassic Park* (1993) to the portentously 'sober' treatment of graphic violence in *Saving Private Ryan* (1998) and the barnstorming terror of *War of the Worlds* (2005), Hollywood's golden boy has consistently used his position at the top of the tree to indulge his childhood love of B-movie shocks.

Brian De Palma has wrought a series of films that play as stylish variations on B-movie formats, decked out with copious film allusions (most notoriously to Hitchcock) and Byzantine explorations of the voyeuristic urge. When De Palma tips a bucket of pig's blood over the radiant Carrie White, queen of the prom for a few brief seconds, it's fair to say that the director of *Blood Feast* has been trumped. Films like *Friday the 13th*, initially an independent production but swiftly bought up for distribution by Paramount, added the requisite flesh wounds and one-on-one carnage, and the majors were at last playing the game as bloodthirstily as the independents. And so came the backlash. By taking this overt slashing and maiming into the wider arena of mainstream cinema, with its TV and newspaper advertising and hardtop blanket releases, the producers courted an emasculation of the rude energy they were exploiting. The fate of *Friday the 13th Part 2* is a case in point. It was another enjoyable romp through the woods, with plenty of tension and a few startling moments of

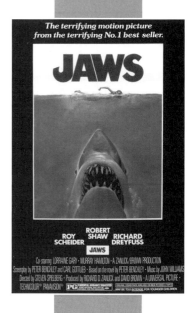

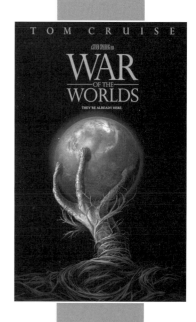

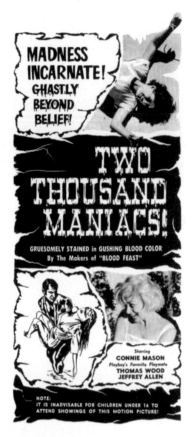

above and below:
In the 21st Century, the rough-and-ready exuberance and sublime bad taste exhibited by Herschell Gordon Lewis feels a lifetime away. The makers of recent US horror films like **Hostel** (2006) or **The Devil's Rejects** (2005) have gorged themselves on the excesses of the Exploitation Independents, and who can blame them? That's what we are here to do too! And yet a self-consciousness intrudes in these new movies, reminding us that all is now reference and quotation, homage and pastiche. That's just the way it is in this postmodern world, no way out. But at least we can still enjoy films like **Two Thousand Maniacs!** or **The Gruesome Twosome** – Lewis was vaulting into self-parody before anyone else had even topped his straight-faced approach to butchery!

violence, but the film had to be severely watered-down before release – grisly killings shown via production stills in America's gore-film bible *Fangoria* were never to emerge intact in the cinema, and even today the missing scenes have not been reinstated on DVD. Dedicated *Fangoria* readers in the early eighties grew ever more wearily disappointed, as optimistic on-set reports promising grisly special prosthetic effects were contradicted, when mutt after neutered mutt hit the cinemas. Between *Fango* picture-spreads and the actual release, the MPAA insisted that oodles of nastiness be removed to secure an 'R' rating. This, not to put too fine a point on it, is how cheese-wire was looped around the nuts of the genre. The majors were willing to get their hands just a *little* dirty with the disreputable, lucrative slashers, but they absolutely insisted on an 'R' rating, without which their advertising would be shorn of its traditional avenues. Newspapers mostly refused to run ads for an unrated film, and major TV stations would refuse a trailer. Although it was technically possible to release a film without the MPAA-approved 'R', restricted advertising was a real drawback. Sadly, most people mistook unrated films for 'X' films; in other words, pornography. The stigma was enough to scare off newspaper ad departments, offend those with a will to be offended, and petrify studio bosses. In marketing terms, the freedom to go unrated was the freedom to go fuck yourself.

The *Friday the 13th* series, probably the lynch-pin deal between mainstream cinema and the Exploitation Independents, turned out to be a genuine cash cow for Paramount – but in getting their corporate fingerprints all over the sequels they managed to erase the contours that made the series distinctive in the first place. Each successive *F13* was less violent, less gory, and less satisfying, until watching the latest effort was like visiting an old friend who used to be a live wire but who lately spends his days doped up on Prozac. There's a genuinely poignant moment in *Jason X* (2001), one of New Line's additions to the franchise, when Jason – now an immortal monster attacking teens in outer space – wanders onto a 'holodeck' programmed to simulate his earliest killing grounds. The scene plays wittily, even affectionately, with the early format, but of course the holographic image is part of the intended victims' self-defence, the emphasis having long ago shifted to survival and resistance – cosy reassurances that 'we' can cope. Horror becomes an exercise in problem solving, a 'can-do' lecture in which those who die are tainted as 'losers' and the survivors are those who 'deserve' to live. Such was the gift the 1980s gave to horror… But *Jason X is* very funny – it's a world away from the Exploitation Independent roots of the series but it keeps the faith in a handful of nasty scenes; and for a while you visit, as if in a dream, the grisly days of yore, when studio squeamishness and misguided sexual politics did not demand that the killer be a joke, or a schmuck, defeated *a priori*. When the only survivor was there to keep the sequel open, not to 'empower' the viewer…

Genres wax and wane, and in this respect the horror genre is like any other. The phenomenal explosion of activity in the 1970s was bound to end sooner or later. It's just a shame that the industry has been restructured so profoundly that a cheap, gritty, artfully odd or endearingly off-beam horror film stands little chance of reaching movie screens. There are occasional exceptions, but they basically prove the rule. The Exploitation Independents are a historical category now, and it's hard to see how a similar blend of market conditions and creative forces could ever be repeated. It's only through video, DVD, and the tireless obsession of fans that these movies survive today. And, like FM radio, where the same 'golden oldies' are peddled from a play-list that ignores 95% of the past, it's easy to let the modern entertainment machine push these all-too human oddities, these rough gems of the awkward squad, out of the picture. It's called airbrushing: and it's a mild but insidious form of fascism. *Nightmare USA*, with its cavalcade of perversions and idiosyncrasies, is my beacon for those films and filmmakers either avoided, disrespected, forgotten or ignored by all but the most dedicated fan discourse. Not in the name of art, not to ennoble a new list of greats, but for variance, diversity, strangeness – and all the pleasures they can bring.

Footnotes

[1] From John McCarty's *The Sleaze Merchants*, p.69.

[2] *The Sleaze Merchants*, p.41.

[3] All Romero quotes are from *The Zombies That Ate Pittsburgh*; Paul R. Gagne, pub: Dodd, Meade and Co, 1987.

[4] Figures courtesy of www.driveintheater.com

[5] Los Angeles was the West Coast Mecca for sleaze movie fans; less iconic than New York's Deuce but still a major source of exhibition revenue for the Exploitation Independents. James Bryan, L.A.-based director of *Don't Go in the Woods* (1980), describes the city's exhibition circuit: "The L.A. movie theater scene in the early seventies pre-mall Cineplex era centred on Hollywood Blvd. and Sunset Blvd. in Hollywood, and to some extent Westwood Village (UCLA) and Beverly Hills along Wilshire Blvd. That's where the big films had their opening engagements. Downtown L.A. was home to the Grindhouses that were once the Movie Palaces of the thirties (Million Dollar and Mayan and others). The east end of Hollywood saw the invasion of the grindhouse policy, as the Mall Cineplexes began developing around outlying L.A. The original major revival house was the Cinema on Western at Santa Monica Blvd. While numerous other revival houses soon sprang up in the early seventies the beginning of the VHS revolution closed most of them down just as quickly. There are a few struggling on today but the last one still going strong is the New Beverly on Beverly Blvd. at La Brea. The most likely reason for this long healthy run is the wildly successful Grindhouse Film Festival presented by Eric Caidin and Brian Quinn once a month at the grand old New Beverly."

[6] Sleazoid Express, Bill Landis and Michelle Clifford, Fireside/Simon & Schuster, 2002.

[7] *The Sleaze Merchants*, p.133.

[8] *Cronenberg on Cronenberg*, Chris Rodley, Faber & Faber, 1992.

[9] Perhaps I'm getting a little peculiar in my old age.

[10] Sad to say, O'Brien was stabbed to death soon after making this movie, killed in his home on 14 May, 1977 while trying to fend off a burglar.

[11] See the British DVD extras.

You may only dare to see it once but once will be enough . . .

FRIDAY THE 13TH

It may not have been the first slasher film, but **Friday the 13th** (1980), director Sean Cunningham's thrilling invitation to slaughter, simplified the format and added extra gore – a decision enthusiastically embraced by the Exploitation Independents.

DON'T GO IN THE WOODS

Don't Go in the Woods (1980), James Bryan's rural slasherfest, took the **Friday the 13th** style and added a wonderfully ramshackle weirdness.

opposite page, clockwise from top left:

A victim has an arm lopped off after witnessing the maniac in action.

Joanne, strung up from a tree in her sleeping bag, struggles to free herself as the Mountain Man (Tom Drury) approaches.

l to r: Ingrid (Mary Gail Artz), Peter (Jack McLelland), Craig (James Hayden) and Joanne trek on through the woods.

The Mountain Man in his woodland abode.

this page:

top: The killer takes a hit.

right: The brilliantly lurid US one-sheet for **Don't Go in the Woods**.

below: Dick (Frank Millen) loses face while camping with his wife.

Everyone has nightmares about the ugliest way to die.

DON'T GO IN THE WOODS ...alone!

WARNING: This motion picture depicts scenes of graphic violence!

Starring NICK McCLELLAND • JAMES P. HAYDEN • MARY GAIL ARTZ & TOM DRURY as "The Monster

ANGIE BROWN Director of Photography HENRY ZINMAN Music By H. KINGSLEY THURBER Original Story & Screenplay By GARTH ELIASSE

Produced & Directed By JAMES BRYAN Distributed By SEYMOUR BORDE & ASSOCIATE

R RESTRICTED UNDER 17 REQUIRES ACCOMPANYING PARENT OR ADULT GUARDIAN

HARRY NOVAK Presents
KIDNAPPED COED
He only wanted the ransom— until he saw HER!
Starring JACK CANON · LESLIE ANN RIVERS
GLADYS LAVITAN · LARRY LAMBETH · JIM BLANKINSHIP · Written, Produced and
Directed by FREDERICK R. FRIEDEL · Executive Producer IRWIN FRIEDLANDER
IN COLOR · A BOXOFFICE INTERNATIONAL PICTURES Release
R RESTRICTED
Under 17 requires accompanying Parent or Adult Guardian

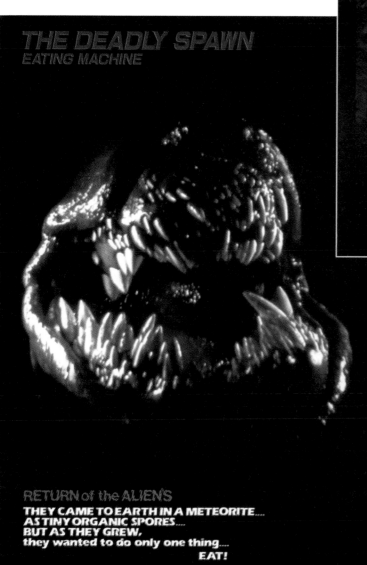

THE DEADLY SPAWN
EATING MACHINE

RETURN of the ALIENS

**THEY CAME TO EARTH IN A METEORITE....
AS TINY ORGANIC SPORES....
BUT AS THEY GREW,
they wanted to do only one thing....
EAT!**

opposite:
Distributor Harry Novak took Frederick Friedel's **The Kidnap Lover** (1975), retitled it as **Kidnapped Coed**, and graced it with this quintessential exploitation artwork.

this page from top left:
The Deadly Spawn (1982):

Director Douglas McKeown tends to the creature between takes.

Japanese pressbook for the film.

Barbara (Elissa Neil) suffers a fatal encounter in the basement.

More fantastic pressbook art.

The Deadly Spawn

this page clockwise from top:

David Durston demonstrating his strict directorial style on **I Drink Your Blood**!

A flyer for one of Bhaskar's dance spectaculars.

Bhaskar as Horace Bones, with friend.

this page, clockwise from bottom left: **I Drink Your Blood** (1971): An infected construction worker brandishes the severed head of nice-guy Satanist Andy (Tyde Kierney), while the crazed Rollo (George Patterson, *right*) looks on gleefully; Japanese press-sheet for the film, featuring Lynn Lowry; Sylvia (Iris Brooks), the rabid nympho of a construction-worker's nightmares.

above: James Wilson's low-budget portmanteau horror **Screams of a Winter Night** (1979) became **Howlings of a Winter's Night** for this Australian video release.

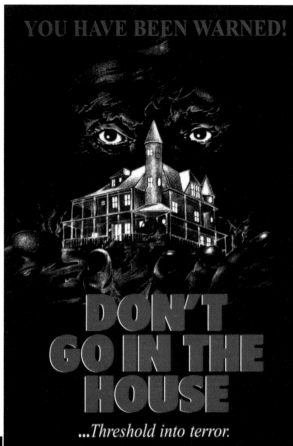

this page: **Don't Go in the House** (1979) was initially marketed under the title **The Burning**:
left: American budget DVD artwork.
above: The fiery climax as Donny (Dan Grimaldi) is set upon by vengeful cadavers.
below: Disco inferno… the appropriately coiffured Farrah (Nikki Collins) goes up in flames during a night out with Donny.

THE BURNING

atlas
international

this page: **Don't Go in the House**.
The burning: Kathy Jordan (Johanna Brushay [Debra Richmond]) is doused in petrol *(top right)*, and burned to death *(bottom left)*, after which her charred carcass is propped in an armchair with Donny's other victims *(bottom right)*.

opposite page: Great promotional artwork for David Michael Hillman's spirited monster romp **The Strangeness** (1980).

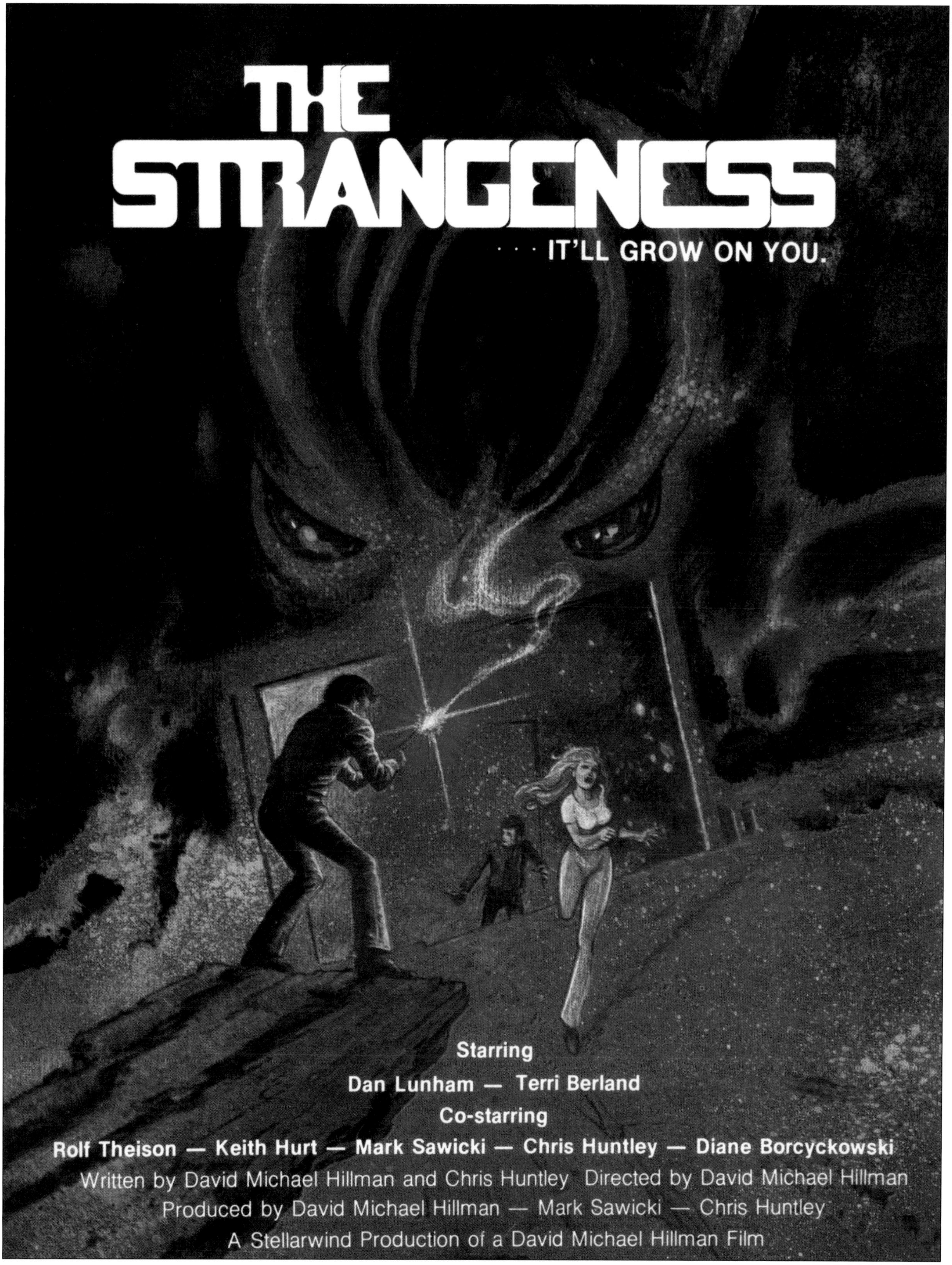

THE STRANGENESS

···IT'LL GROW ON YOU.

Starring

Dan Lunham — Terri Berland

Co-starring

Rolf Theison — Keith Hurt — Mark Sawicki — Chris Huntley — Diane Borcyckowski

Written by David Michael Hillman and Chris Huntley   Directed by David Michael Hillman

Produced by David Michael Hillman — Mark Sawicki — Chris Huntley

A Stellarwind Production of a David Michael Hillman Film

this page:
Images from **The Strangeness**:
right: Cindy Flanders (Terri Berland) gets a look at the monster.
far right: Designer Chris Huntley's creature in all its glory.
below: Ruggles (Chris Huntley) is slimed to death.

opposite page:
top left: The American one-sheet for **Fight for Your Life** (1977) depicting Kane (William Sanderson) and Pastor Turner (Robert Judd) locked in combat.
top right: Rare promotional sheet for **Victims**, Daniel DiSomma's fantastically bleak psycho-thriller, made in 1977 but not released until 1982.
bottom: more race-war mayhem in **Stigma** (1972).

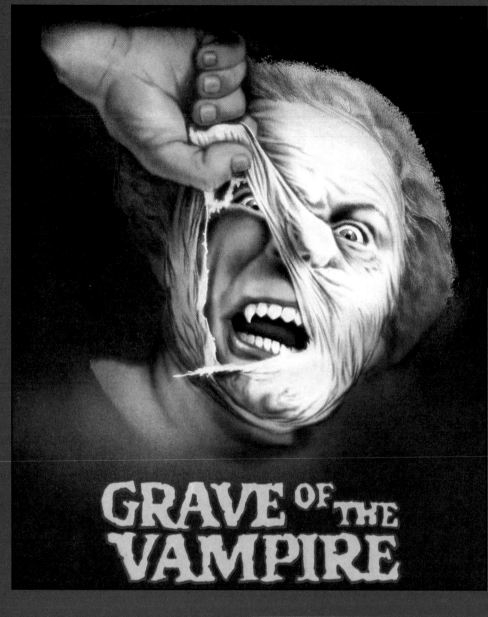

GRAVE OF THE VAMPIRE

this page:
above: US promo sheet for John Hayes's
Grave of the Vampire (1972).
right top: The vampire strikes…
above bottom right: Caleb Croft (Michael Pataki) reveals his fangs.
right, top row:
Grace (Vicki Shreck),
the disturbed heroine of Hayes's
Dream No Evil (1971);
Grace's father (Edmond O'Brien).
right, bottom row: Gangster movie veteran Marc Lawrence plays the sinister undertaker-cum-brothelkeeper in
Dream No Evil;
Grace sinks further into her madness in
Dream No Evil.

opposite:
main picture: Video artwork for John Hayes's melancholy psycho-killer tale, **Dream No Evil**.
others, from top:
Hot Lunch (1978) was a late outing from Hayes's porno alter-ego 'Harold Perkins';
Artwork for Hayes's sexploitation nudie
Fandango (1969);
Original US one-sheet for the extremely rare Hayes film **The Farmer's Other Daughter** (1965).

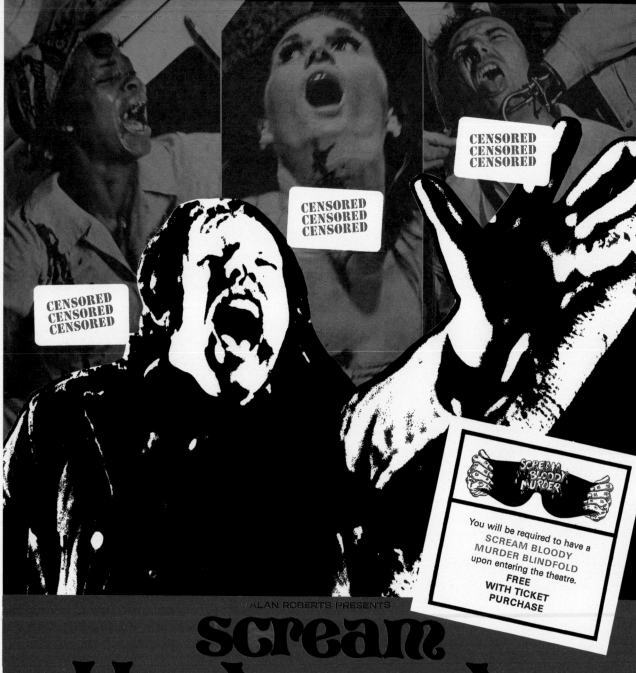

The First Motion Picture to be Called
GORE-NOGRAPHY!!!

CENSORED CENSORED CENSORED

CENSORED CENSORED CENSORED

CENSORED CENSORED CENSORED

You will be required to have a SCREAM BLOODY MURDER BLINDFOLD upon entering the theatre.
FREE WITH TICKET PURCHASE

ALAN ROBERTS PRESENTS

scream bloody murder

STARRING

FRED HOLBERT • LEIGH MITCHELL • ROBERT KNOX • A MAANA TANELAH • RON BASTONE • SUZETTE HAMILTON

SCREENPLAY by **LARRY ALEXANDER** and **MARC B. RAY** EXECUTIVE PRODUCER **ALAN ROBERTS** PRODUCED and DIRECTED by **MARC B. RAY** An INDEPIX Release

FILMED IN VIOLENT VISION and GORY COLOR

WARNING!!!
Because of the explicit violence depicted in the film, theatre-goers must have a sound mind and strong stomach.

COLOR by CREST

R **RESTRICTED**
Under 17 requires accompanying Parent or Adult Guardian

—COLBY POSTER PRINTING CO. 1322 W. 12th Pl. L.A. 90015

right:
Daniel DiSomma's debut, **Come One Come All** (1970) spoofed the sexploitation industry.

far right:
Irv Berwick's **Hitch Hike to Hell** (1977), another exploitation picture to benefit from a classic poster design, courtesy of Harry Novak's Box Office International.

below:
Scenes from Wayne Berwick's horror-comedy **Microwave Massacre** (1978).

opposite page:
John Ballard's only feature film began life as a script called 'Killers of the Dream.' Shot mostly in 1968, it finally reached the screen in 1978 as **Friday the 13th: The Orphan**.

You have a date... with death!

GILMAN-WESTERGAARD ENTERPRISES and **CINEMA INVESTMENTS COMPANY**
in association with **TRIMEDIA SOUTHWEST ASSOCIATES II** presents
"THE ORPHAN" Written and Directed by **JOHN BALLARD**

Starring PEGGY FEURY, JOANNA MILES, DONN WHYTE, and introducing MARK OWENS as David / with STANLEY CHURCH, ELEANOR STEWART, AFOLABI AJAYI,
JANE HOUSE, ED FOREMAN, JIM BRODER / Art Director, Production Supervisor SIDNEY ANN MACKENZIE / Production Supervisor PETER MULLER
Theme song by JANIS iAN / Read the JOVE NOVEL

R RESTRICTED
UNDER 17 REQUIRES ACCOMPANYING
PARENT OR ADULT GUARDIAN

Distributed by WORLD NORTHAL CORPORATION

A
masterpiece
of terror and
suspense.

The
PREMONITION

"THE PREMONITION" starring SHARON FARRELL
RICHARD LYNCH • JEFF COREY
Executive Producer M. WAYNE FULLER
Produced and directed by ROBERT ALLEN SCHNITZER
Screenplay by ANTHONY MAHON and
ROBERT ALLEN SCHNITZER • PANAVISION®
Music by HENRY MOLLICONE
In Color • A ROBERT ALLEN SCHNITZER FILM
A [CREATIVE FORCE] / GALAXY FILMS PRODUCTION
 AVCO EMBASSY PICTURES RELEASE

PG PARENTAL GUIDANCE SUGGESTED

R790058

"THE PREMONITION"

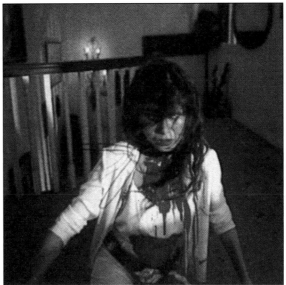

opposite:
Moody US one-sheet for Robert Allen
Schnitzer's stylish paranormal horror tale,
The Premonition (1975).

this page, left:
Slasher gore enlivens Norman Thaddeus
Vane's **The Black Room** (1981).

main picture below:
From **The Premonition** - Andrea (Ellen
Barber) appears in a dream, or is it a vision?

THE HORROR ST★R

starring FERDINAND MAYNE as "THE HORROR STAR"
JENNIFER STARRET, NITA TALBOT with special appearance by LEON ASKIN
and introducing "The Horror Film Society"

this page: Coffin montage, from Norman Thaddeus Vane's **Midnight** (1988): Mr. B. (Tony Curtis) discusses his schemes with an associate; Midnight (Lynne Redgrave) entertains; Mr. B. and Mickey Modine (Steve Parrish); Midnight in her happy place.
above: Poster art depicting Ferdinand Mayne as Conrad Ragzoff in Norman Thaddeus Vane's **The Horror Star** (1981).
left: Three years before shooting to horror stardom in Stuart Gordon's **Re-Animator**, Jeffrey Combs played an obnoxious film fan who gets his just desserts for tampering with Ragzoff's coffin.
below: Eve (Carlene Olson) on her way to a date with doom in **The Horror Star**.
opposite page: Amusingly cheesy artwork for **The Horror Star**'s initial U.S. release.

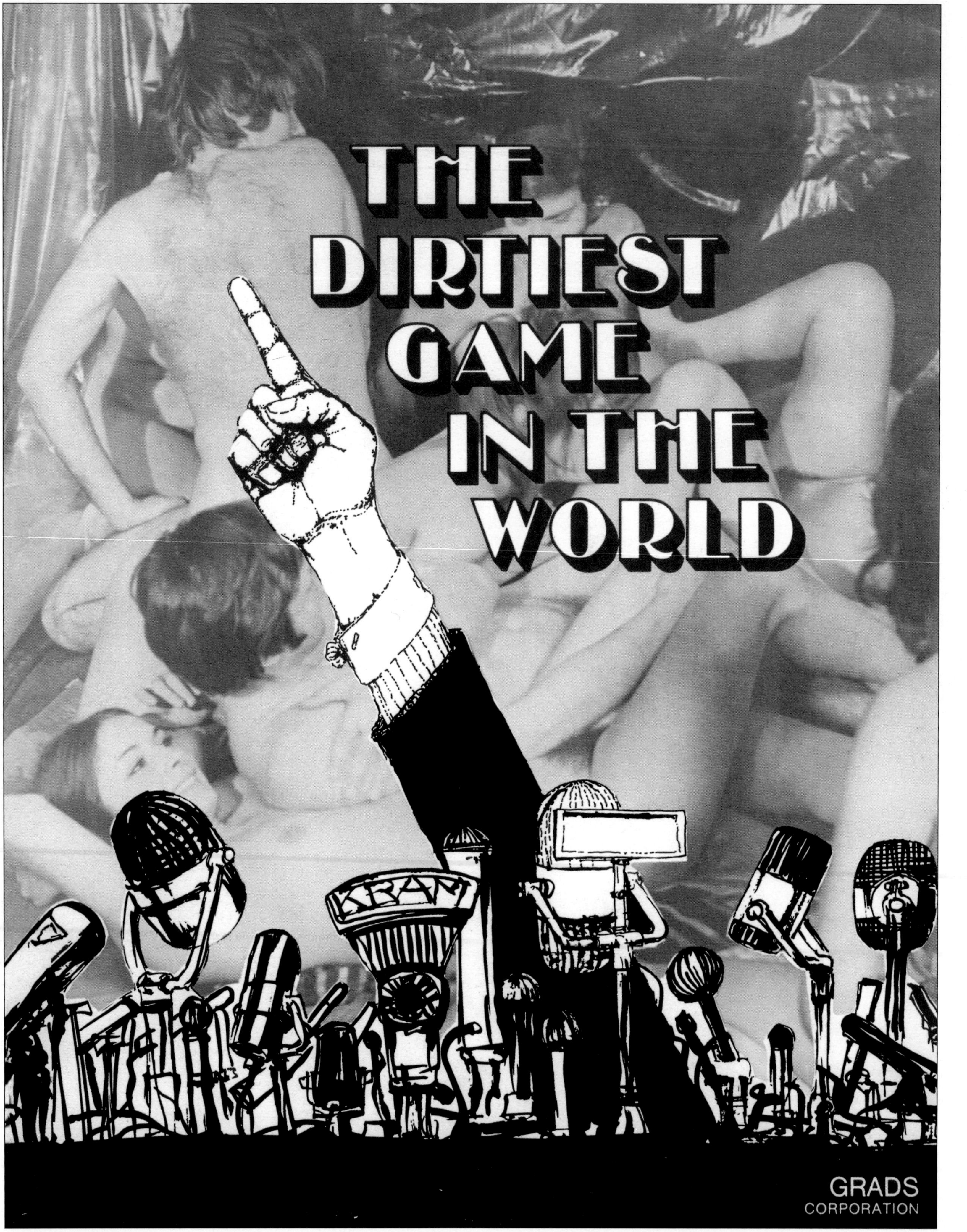
THE DIRTIEST GAME IN THE WORLD
GRADS
CORPORATION

Dirty Games in Hollywood

The Career of James Bryan

Don't Go in the Woods (1981)

When James Bryan embarked on this low-budget horror flick, shot in Utah in the summer of 1980, he had no way of knowing that two or three years later, in Great Britain, it would become so controversial. *Don't Go in the Woods* was classified by the British Director of Public Prosecutions as a 'video nasty' – a threat to common decency, childhood innocence, family values, and the sanity of the great unwashed. First came the hostile police raids and newspaper headlines. Then, as if indignity enough had not been heaped on his modest production, came brickbats from a few genre critics, eager to justify their viewing habits to the conservative thought police. Some 'video nasties' were redeemable, even artistic, Your Honour. Others were 'just trash', not worth the effort.

I arrived late at the scene of the crime, but I soon smelled a rat. If you're asking me what's wrong with the film, well, go figure. For the record, I enjoyed the hell out of it, one of the last of the 'nasties' I saw. Nostalgia for the good old days was *not* a factor – Bryan's movie needed no misty recollections of tabloid controversy to hit all of my trash-horror buttons. Let's not mince words: it's senseless; it's gratuitously violent; it has *very* shaky tech credits; I forgot who was who and yet I watched it avidly from start to finish. The crude but oddly realistic violence had me squirming with delight, as foursquare conventions of 'proper' film-making were trampled, quite figuratively, into the mountain mud. On the day I saw it I was ill and feeling down: by the time it was over I felt much, much better. I ask for little more from my 'nasties': a pox on those who can't share!

A film about being lost in the woods, *Don't Go in the Woods* underlines the idea by wandering from its core characters here there and everywhere, bringing the slash of the killer's blade to as many incidental victims as possible. If that leaves the storyline incoherent, so what? Let's make that incoherence a badge of honour. It amazes me that I have to say it, but: this is a *very gory film with lots of violence and murder*. Bryan is giving us precisely what we deserve and desire from a film called *Don't Go in the Woods*! Would Godard use that nomenclature? Peter Greenaway? *Don't Go in the Woods* (and yes, the grammatically inelegant title does seem to forbid *al fresco* urination) offers all that you could reasonably expect from a low-budget horror flick about murder in the country: indeed, it goes further and tosses in psychotronic dementia and bizarre electronic music too. Anyone who ever paid a penny for this experience has only himself to blame if it fails to deliver the existential insight, metaphysical scope or action-adventure thrills they were seeking. In many ways this is the *quintessential* video nasty. Arty aberrations like Abel Ferrara's *The Driller Killer* are hardly the point; *Don't Go in the Woods* is cheap, gruesome, and yet operating on some sublime atavistic pleasure-frequency. The many savage killings are like truffles hidden in the dirt of the film's *mise-en-scène* (or maybe that's just the transfer), and they keep on coming, leaving no time for distracting subplots or time-wasting nods to the mainstream. The story has a gadfly irritability; no sooner despatching one luckless camper than moving on to the next. It's the logic of commercial horror filmmaking taken to the extreme. I just wish it had been a hit: can you imagine Part II?

The term 'video nasty' is now an absurdity, invented by the press years ago and pounced upon by the likes of British media campaigner Mary Whitehouse (deceased); it means nothing today, when all of the films once banned are easily available on eBay. I'm using it here as a historical marker, but even ignoring the glamour of illegality, I would always have felt attracted to this quasi-art-brut horror flick. It may be fetishistic (or worse still nostalgic) to carry a torch for the nasties, but let's not forget: many of the films on the banned list were there simply because they were cheap, lacking in the niceties of studio production, and lacking moreover the industry muscle to defend themselves. That confluence of cash-based aesthetics and business manipulation lives on today. It's actually a sign of something special that this reviled little movie should have alarmed lawmakers and moralists, when some big-budget lump like *The Omen* failed to provoke a single governmental goosebump. Yet, of all cases for reappraisal, *Don't Go in the Woods* has the lowest profile. Personally, I would screen it at my own fantasy cinematheque in a second; and here's why…

opposite:
What's **The Dirtiest Game in the World**? It's James Bryan's first feature film, made in 1970 – a political sex satire and a neglected low-budget gem…

below:
Grisly mayhem as another luckless camper bites the mud, in Bryan's 'go-hiking-and-die' classic, **Don't Go in the Woods** (1981).

Don't Go in the Woods
aka **Don't Go in the Woods... Alone!** (poster title)
aka **Sierra** (script title)
© none [1981]
JBF presents.
director: James Bryan. producer: Roberto Gomez and Suzette Gomez. associate producer: William Stockdale. original story and screenplay: Garth Eliassen. director of photography: Hank Zinman. music: H. Kingsley Thurber. title song written and sung by H. Kingsley Thurber. editor [uncredited]: James Bryan. production design: S.K. James [Sally Kathleen Bryan]. costumes: Suzette Bryan-Gomez. assistant to the producer: Matthew Muller. production manager: Jonathan Bliss. camera assistant: Eric Jenkins. location sound: Gerry Klein. post production sound: Sound Cinema Services. casting: McCarty Agency, Inc. additional casting: Richard Olivier. production assistants: Leon Brown, Jr., Phoebe Montague. den mother: Linda Martell. wrangler: Tom Ruff. dialogue editors: Willie Allen, Van Christensen. effects editors: Kate Clark, Leon Brown. negative cutter: B.F. Matt Muller. make up: Nim Telson [sic]. special thanks to: Dean R. Bullock (Emblem Tape & Label Co.); Don Lindsey (Hafer's Inc.); Don Despain (Brighton Village Store); Capt. Webb (Webb Security); John Earle (Utah Film Commission); Stockdales.
Cast: Jack McClelland (Peter). Mary Gail Artz. (Ingrid) James P. Hayden (Craig). Angie Brown (Joanne). Ken Carter (sheriff). David Barth (Deputy Benson). Larry Roupe (store owner). Amy Martell (artist's child). Tom Drury (maniac). Laura Trefts (Dr. Maggie). Victims Alma Ramos (running girl). Carolyn Braza (Cherry). Frank Clitus Muller [Frank Millen] (Dick). Mc Cormick Dalten (bird watch). Cecelia Fannon (lady artist). Dale Angell (tourist at falls). Ruth Grose (tourist's mother). Hank Zinman (fisherman). Leon Brown, Jr. (camper in sleeping bag). Linda Brown (camper in sleeping bag). Gerry Klein (man in wheelchair). Tom Ruff (man in tree). Police Department Valetta Saunders (dispatcher). John Williams (cop #1). Jeff Wood (cop #2). Randy Kleffer (cop #3). Jarne Harbrecht (detective). Ann St. Michael (jail trustee). On The Trail Bonnie Harris (skater). Matt Noone (man on trail). Matt Muller (pilot). Garth Eliassen (cop at the lake). Susan Farris (cop at the falls). T. Ruff (boy at the falls). Bill Stockdale (photographer). Ebin Whiting (angry posse member). Brad Carter (tired posse member). Posse Members Jeffery Wood. Randy Kleffer. Mark Prager. Eben Whitney. Randy Prager. David Wiggins. Randy Iverson. John Warren. Michael Smith. Paul Thorpe. Hospital Joan Forester (hospital receptionist). Pam Srubaugh-Littig (head nurse). Tawnya Crespin (girl in wheelchair). Pat J. Winn (intern). Franky Crespin (nurse). Amy Oliphant (candy striper). Patrick Satterthwaithe (doctor). Anne Marie Nagenga (personnel). Suzy Folsom (receptionist). uncredited: Eric Jenkins (victim poked with spear). James Bryan (dubbed voice of Dick).

The four main characters, Peter (Jack McClelland), Craig (James Hayden), Joanne (Angie Brown) and Ingrid (Mary Gail Artz) bicker, pull pranks and fall out with each other in time-honoured slasher film fashion, and they are joined in this supposedly remote and unspoiled mountain region by so many other hikers that it feels like rush-hour on an ant-hill. A painter and her baby daughter, *two* pairs of newly-weds, a fisherman, a chick on roller-skates, an elderly couple, and even some guy in a wheelchair: all seem drawn to the same patch of mountain, only to fall foul of the best psychotic mountain dweller since the cannibal family in *The Hills Have Eyes* (Tom Drury, wonderfully gross and threatening in the killer's role).

The fragmented, episodic feel is amplified by composer Kingsley Thurber, and by Bryan's hectic sound editing. The score is much given to sudden spurts of electronic weirdness, brief snatches of country guitar, and – my favourite – the maddening "steel puke" effect that Bryan explains in the following interview. All of Thurber's music cues are short, and Bryan peppers them liberally throughout. Their brevity and variability add a jagged, hiccupping madness to the movie. However, two music cues are employed frequently enough to be called themes. One is a moody synthesizer tune (not unlike the main theme from Ulli Lommel's *The Bogey Man*) which plays over later scenes, adding a sombre hue that sits well with the dusk-lit locations. The other is a rhythmic piece for synthesizer, so caveman-crude it could have been played by the murderous mountain-man himself (and sounding for all the world like early DAF or Throbbing Gristle).

The music cues confuse the film's time-frame. We're used to horror films beginning with a shock-cum-tease, then progressing in a lighter vein, before darkening in mood as the nightmare encroaches. Bryan, however, uses comedy music over two or three scenes at the beginning of the film, then returns to it again well past the half-way stage, by which point the lead characters have suffered casualties and the aforementioned sombre cue has already begun to work its magic. This has the effect of looping the viewer's emotional orientation: it's as if we're back near the beginning of the movie, as lost in time as the characters are lost in the woods. Bryan hastens through transitions from sunlight to darkness in a way that shuffles evening and morning, and the resulting time confusion is exacerbated by the often shaky day-for-night scenes. For sure, much of this is accidental, but I tend to just go with the flow, allowing the mistakes to determine my feelings in tandem with the more intentional elements. The result is a film whose errors and technical failings actually improve rather than impede the overall experience.

Unlike a more run-of-the-mill slasher film, there's a distinct tinge of humour to some of the action, which while not exactly sophisticated (the wheelchair-bound 'hiker' for example), does mean that we're a long way from bores like Edwin Brown's *The Prey* (1984) or bland efforts like Andrew Davis's *The Final Terror* (1983). The script has its share of amusing lines: when Craig recommends looking out for rabid animals *"acting contrary to nature,"* Peter replies, *"You mean there are little furry perverts running around out here?";* and I love the anguished cry of *"I'm sorry!"* from Peter when he accidentally stabs a passer-by he's mistaken for the killer. Meanwhile, the acting of the newly-wed couple in the camper-van scene is so oddball you wonder if Curt *Thundercrack!* McDowell directed it.

Bryan's violence, while lacking the graphic (read: expensive) detail of a Tom Savini assignment, is spirited, impressive, and *very* frequent. It's a wonder the killer can fit everyone into his schedule, as he works flat out, murdering an unlikely array of secondary characters and ensuring the movie never gets bogged down in unnecessary deviations from slaughter. We're treated to a limb-severing in the first five minutes, there's a wonderfully gory stabbing through a painter's canvas, and a scene where a young couple are tied up in their sleeping bags and then stuck with knives, which is as good as anything in *Friday the 13th*. The awful fate of Joanne is another grisly highlight, with the editing and set design making her demise, hacked to death in a rickety closet garlanded with rotting fabric, quite horribly memorable. (It reminded me of the gruesome first murder in *Theatre of Blood*: Michael Hordern butchered by tramps amid sheets of polythene). Speaking of the shack scenes, the Mountain Man's home is startlingly similar to that of Jason

Nightmare USA

James Bryan Interviewed

Voorhees in *Friday the 13th Part 2*, which was shot the following year, and it wouldn't be the first time the famous horror franchise had 'borrowed' ideas from less well-known films, now would it?

There are lots of details to enjoy, but it's the overall feel of the movie that works for me. There's something intensely satisfying about the film's minimalism, its simple but fragmented structure, and its streamlined visual palette. It is free of the prosaic grounding in sensible filmmaking reality that weighs down many other slasher tales. You could call it an impressionist slasher film, with the hard detail of (plot)line removed and the contents left to swill around in a defocused drift of greenery and gore. It feels like a borderless amalgam of several different slasher horror tales, taking the raw essence and discarding the mundanities of each. The scenes where Pete is first rescued and hospitalised, then absconds to return to the woods and avenge Joanne – probably the closest thing to a plot development in the movie – are over so quickly you could easily forget them. Your mind wanders, and somehow Pete is back in the woods: you have a vague feeling he's been away, as if a fugue had lifted momentarily. To me, *Don't Go in the Woods* is psychedelic: not in a clichéd sense, with swirling colours and fish-eye lenses, but in its wrenching contrast between the simplest of horror tales and its fractured, lurchingly off-kilter realisation. When occasionally the acting veers from serviceable to lousy (as in a terribly dubbed campfire scene where the actors seem to be vying with each other to deliver the worst line readings), you get the conventional pleasure associated with 'bad' movies; but Bryan has brought something unschooled, unsophisticated and truly idiosyncratic to the table: it's not just a case of the desire to make 'normal' films being thwarted by lack of skill. I love *Friday the 13th* and I don't want to run it down, but *Don't Go in the Woods* feels to me like a *Friday the 13th* left out in the rain, with its colours smeared and its characters washed into their backgrounds – and that's an entirely more exciting prospect for an incorrigible aesthete like myself…

British horror fans know James Bryan as the director of the banned 'video-nasty' *Don't Go in the Woods*, a wonderful low-budget slice of rural mayhem classified as obscene in a series of British legal trials, and banned under the terms of the 1984 Video Recordings Act. The rest of Bryan's filmography has, until now, remained largely obscure, which is a shame, since his early films deserve much wider exposure. His debut, *The Dirtiest Game in the World*, offers scenes more shocking than anything in his notorious gore classic, and even today it would likely never receive an uncut release in this country. Bryan's movie career began in the late 1960s and his early work, though primitive in many respects, is influenced by the hippie era's dream of artistic subversion through sexual frankness and the confrontation of taboos.

Not all of Bryan's films repay the closest scrutiny: in the 1980s his ongoing friendship with idiosyncratic actress and producer Renee Harmon led to a couple of hastily-shot action movies lacking in focus and thrills (not to mention money), although they still have points of interest for fans willing to put aside their many flaws. With an ethos that demanded he should keep working come what may, it's not surprising that the quality of his workmanship varies, but Bryan nevertheless exemplifies a classic American tenacity. Although his intentions were frequently thwarted or diverted, he never gave up on a project, sometimes struggling for several years to get a film onto the screen. From the shocking extremes of *The Dirtiest Game in the World* to the melancholy pessimism of *I Love You I Love You Not*, and from the makeshift action of *The Executioner Part II* to the hangdog capers of *Escape to Passion*, Bryan demonstrates a true passion for filmmaking; *Don't Go in the Woods* is really just the tip of the iceberg…

*All images from **Don't Go in the Woods**.*

opposite page bottom left, group of four, clockwise from top left:
A woman (Cecelia Fannon) painting a landscape achieves a merger of artist and artwork far beyond her usual capacities; Peter (Jack McClelland) and Ingrid (Mary Gail Artz) find the mountain-dwelling savage that dwells within their selves, as they confront the maniac in a fight to the death; The nervous Dick (Frank Millen, a Bryan regular) plays the fearless protector less than convincingly; Joanne (Angie Brown) cowers in the undergrowth as the Mountain Man approaches.

opposite page top right:
James Bryan at the Arriflex, with Hank Zinman, DP.

this page top left:
The Mountain Man (Tom Drury) takes time out from his primitive ways to appreciate the practical benefits of a quick beer…

above:
Bryan sets up a shot with DP Hank [Henry] Zinman

left:
James Bryan publicity photo, taken for Cannes 1997.

Early Days

James Bryan was born in Houston, Texas on the 15 May, 1943 (he's the same age as fellow Texan Tobe Hooper). He grew up in East Texas where, as he explains, "the Spanish crypto-Jewish side of my family settled in 1720 and the Irish-Welsh-French Protestant side settled in 1854." His father and mother came from sharecropper farming backgrounds: "The relatives on both sides all had that Dorothea Lange Depression look about them, refugees from a very poor rural South. I spent a lot of time at the movies – my parents, who were products of the Great Depression, were big movie fans as well."

Young James was soon drawn to an active engagement with film: "It was standard 8mm that I first encountered. I used pliers to splice the film, which crimped it, creating an odd optical effect at a cut," he recalls. This wouldn't be the last time that technical restrictions would leave their mark on his work: fortunately, splicing tape was soon available. "I shot lots of 8mm, enjoyed seeing lots of films and afterwards spent hours trying to break down the way special effects were achieved. I read everything and anything available about filmmaking. Old back issues of *Life* magazine at the library and the motion picture chapter of our *Compton's Encyclopedia* along with TV documentaries like the Wolper series.[1] After reading reviews in *Time* I would drive a hundred miles to see a new release that wouldn't play locally for months."

For Bryan, nurturing a teenage obsession with the movies, cinema was more than just a distraction: life was film. In the days before home video, to actually own a copy of something seen on the silver screen was the stuff of dreams, and celluloid itself possessed talismanic significance. Bryan rummaged through bins behind old movie theatres, collecting discarded film rolls, trailers, and damaged offcuts from release prints. His quest was to see how the magic worked, to absorb the lessons and learn how to make it all happen. When AIP released their first low-budget drive-in movies, he was thrilled not only by the stories, but also by the accessibility suggested by their lack of polish (just as

subsequent generations would find the technical primitivism of punk rock inspiring). "I thought hey, I can do this!" he recalls. "I really enjoyed AIP films, pre-Corman, that was an awakening for me. I liked the beach party films too. I liked the Poe films later, but it was the drive-in pictures I loved, *The Killer Shrews* or *The Giant Claw*, all that nonsense! They were liberating because there was nothing like them. It didn't matter how bad it was, they finished the film and got it on the screen. They were so bad they were great."

From Laboratory to Film School

In 1963 Bryan graduated from the Stephen F. Austin University in Nacogdoches, Texas, with a Bachelor of Science degree in Biology. He worked the summer at a cancer hospital in Houston, prepping and observing dogs that were the subjects of experimental organ transplant surgery. November of '63 saw him interviewed for a job at the Medical School at Parkland Hospital in Dallas, on the day after J.F. Kennedy was shot. Conspiracy theorists may want to add Bryan's recollection to their data: "Our guide through ER was a resident who was present at the JFK ER scene. In 1981, his TV demonstration of JFK's wound differed from his 1963 version to us Med School applicants, in that he moved his hand from the front side of the face to the rear side of the head."

The following year, Bryan took a scholarship funded by a US Army grant, for Graduate Studies at the Vanderbilt University Medical School in Nashville. There he indulged in the traditional college excesses of sex, drugs, rock'n'roll, and vivisection: "I fell in with the wannabe music crowd, went out a few times with the young Tammy Faye (yet to be Bakker) and spent a year removing fat pads from the gonads of euthanized lab rats," he deadpans. By 1965, Bryan had seen enough of animal innards (for a while at least) and opted for a career change; he applied for a place at film school with The University of California, Los Angeles (UCLA), beginning his studies in September of 1965.

Bryan's first real job in the movie industry came in '66, as cameraman for a documentary called *Operation Bootstrap*, funded by the Rand Corporation (a non-profit organisation set up after World War Two, "*To further and promote scientific, educational, and charitable purposes, all for the public welfare and security of the United States of America,*" as their mission statement put it). The subject was a community computer-training program set up in the Watts neighbourhood of Los Angeles after the 1965 Watts riots. Bryan also worked as an usher at the Beverly Theatre in nearby Beverly Hills for a short time and followed that with a stint as a UCLA film class projectionist. Around this time, he decided to move from his campus residence at Westwood and head for Venice Beach, drawn there by what he saw as its "enticing New Bohemian reputation."

In 1967, after a job as gaffer-cum-grip on a documentary about the death penalty called *Religion in Jail*, made by Michael Parks for The American Civil Liberties Union, Bryan directed his first film, an animated short called *Inner Limits*. Bryan describes it as a sci-fi concept, "in the *Outer Limits* vein, a visual pun on the unified field theory using a series of dissolves and pull backs starting from a close-up on one of many busy pens making notes in a lecture hall and quickly moving back to global, planetary, galactic and ultimately universal views. The universe is revealed to be a small glowing mass in a particle generator, and the voice-over physics lecture is cut short when the glowing mass/universe is bombarded with accelerated particles by a pair of ambitious researchers in search of new grant funding." With gratifying speed, *Inner Limits* received immediate television exposure as part of a CBS Special called *The New Communicators*, overseen by Lee Mendelson, the producer of the *Charlie Brown* cartoons. With this cosmic comedy under his belt, Bryan took an interest in darker ideas: they were to cause him serious psychological complications…

California in the late 1960s was a socio-cultural hotspot, a lodestone of 20th Century Western culture. Bryan was embroiled in the fantasies and dreams of the day, and UCLA was an electric environment, if you were so attuned. Studying there, says Bryan, "was empowering in a social artistic sense. Given the 'Dawning of the Age of Aquarius' and the experimenting with drugs and sex, any level of film production was a chance to create a Happening-like state. We all walked the walk and talked the talk and wore the Hippie uniform and had the long hair and practiced creative nonconformity and believed our joy would go on forever. Civil disobedience and police riots put a different spin on it. So while we all giggled finding Francis Ford Coppola's 'Nudie' outtakes in the editing room and gossiped about the last year's film students who centred their rock band around an electric organ and opened at the Whisky-a-Go-Go and became The Doors, another of our merry pals indulged inclinations toward sexual mutilation and murder while partaking of LSD. A couple more exercised their rights to perform as police agents at local and federal levels, compiling personal data and attempting to encourage illegal political gestures as a means of protecting the greater good."

Aware of the huge cultural changes going on around him, Bryan sought to develop his aesthetic awareness, and was not satisfied with a merely passive relationship to Art. In particular, he felt drawn to the category of aesthetics referred to as 'the Grotesque': "It was during this period that I stumbled onto the primitive power of the aversion reflex," he recalls. "When purposely embracing those things that normally seem horrifying or repulsive, my aversion sense mechanism shifted, refocusing onto new associations; in my case, natural textures. I spent a terrifying few months having exaggerated, even psychotic, reactions to usually neutral things like the texture of bark on trees. After a gradual and fitful recovery, I treated aversion with a great deal of respect. I believe my texture-directed aversion was the result of trying to embrace the common things of aversion by a deliberate force of will. It seemed to me that aversion was a primal reflex, a raw non-rational mechanism that, by it's gross negative reaction, creates an opposite: that which we see rationally as attractive, desirable beauty."[2]

The displaced aversion that Bryan refers to has similarities to the synaesthetic experience accessible through LSD: I asked Bryan if he thinks the drug could have played a part in his alarming reaction: "The LSD experience was in the air at that time," he admits, "and was a huge influence on me and all my fellow students who lusted after the artistic liberation of an altered consciousness. R.D. Laing had just published ideas on mental problems as positive creative artistic influences, so it seemed the drugs your brain made were just as good as the drugs recommended by radical Harvard professors.[3] My aversion interest was part of my particular personal psychology. My interests moved me to attempt to formalize in some small way an aesthetic for the grotesque, at least in terms of images. I was leaning toward ideas of deformity as biological violence. Images of rot and decay fascinated me, but I was too socially well-behaved to go so directly to the boundaries of accepted or conditioned taste. I was excited by the notion of causing my audience discomfort on an artistic level but not to the degree of damage of a psychic sort. Not 'full on' torture, maybe only a tease at torture. *And yes, it was all humorous to me!* – up until the aversion demon turned on me."

Bryan would eventually incorporate his love of decay imagery in *Don't Go in the Woods*, with its filthy mountain man living in a rotten, tumbledown shack, but before that he attempted to explore his fascination with 'biological violence' in his second film: "I did a student project involving a female character who was an amputee, and approached a coed who had lost a leg as the result of an out-of-control Frat Party colliding with an out-of-control police officer, who fired into the crowd. She explained to me that her friends thought it a great idea but her parents worried that I was disturbed and might be planning a nude scene for sick reasons of my own. We talked about it for a while and agreed it was not a situation that could please everyone, so I went to the blonde actress who sings with Mike Hall in *Escape to Passion*, and she wore a special device that worked just fine from one angle."

Bryan was essentially looking for ways to represent a dissident attitude, and playing with ideas in a sufficiently intense way to cause himself some psychological problems (the sort which, when added to vast amounts of LSD, would result in a significant number of so-called 'acid-casualties' lost in their own private hells in the fallout of the hippie era). Although Bryan's use of LSD was not quite so extreme, he didn't emerge entirely unscathed from this period of his life: "My pseudo-deformity ultimately was made manifest when a life time of trauma-induced selective blackouts finally erased enough brain cells to leave a big empty space at the centre of my brain. The doctors who gave me the MRI results asked if I had been a prisoner of war or suffered some extreme chemical exposure. A certain kind of anxiety would cause people, events or situations to disappear. At one point I began to be aware of them as they happened, people as black outlines that I didn't recognize and objects that I couldn't see or find until after the anxiety was no longer attached to the object. At odd times the erased situations reappear as half-real recollections, like scenes from a script I might have written; I'm never sure if they are real. These things are relatively mundane and don't seem to be antisocial or horrifying. The effects are just a little disturbing, in that recall is a bitch. I remember a name I should know, or the spelling of a word, or even a specific word sometimes hours after I reached for it. Word recognition is sometimes interrupted in the midst of conversation. I do find this situation humorous and have worked out a few ways to kick-start my brain when it stalls. It seems the brain keeps duplicate files in odd places and most cells are interchangeable, so that any synapse will keep the wheels turning over as impulses search for alternative connections until a circuit is complete. I just have to keep a steady supply of stimulations coming and the grey matter snaps into place."

While these experiences relate mainly to Bryan's personal life, he did follow through when it came to pushing the boundaries of what could be shown onscreen. The violent imagery of his first feature film is more sexual than textural, but it nonetheless acts as a gross confrontation with taboo, and must have created its own aversion responses in unsuspecting audiences who wandered in to early screenings of *The Dirtiest Game in the World*…

above:
Shooting **The Dirtiest Game in the World**, originally known as **Blood, Flesh and Tears**, in Venice Beach, 1970:
left to right (ignoring the children):
James Bryan (holding script); DP Chris Munger (seated); assistant cameraman Howard Lester (standing); grip Richard Bohn (holding reflectors); script girl Andrea Fishel (wearing poncho); actor Bruce Beard; sound assistant Earl Sampson (kneeling, with boom); and actresses Jean Stone and Sheryl Powell (in the car).

below:
Felicia (Sheryl Powell) takes self-destruction to orgiastic extremes in **The Dirtiest Game in the World**.

Dirty Games in Pornoland

Like many a film graduate in the late sixties, Bryan found the swiftly tumescing adult movie scene a valuable resource when it came to hands-on filmmaking experience. One of his fellow students at UCLA was director, producer and soon-to-be one-man porn empire Bob Chinn: "Bob and I were there at the same time and worked on class projects together," Bryan remembers, "the camera course, for example, which involved being put in small groups to shoot a selected type of scene, silent, with each person doing camera in turn with a hundred feet of 16mm black and white film, while the others acted as crew and talent. I didn't know that he'd gone major into pornography. We used to make jokes but no one was very serious about it. Bob Chinn is a really nice guy; he's easy to talk to. He's not insane like some people are in that world. We both did 'nudie' and hardcore films independently with the same producer, Dick Aldrich, in the early seventies. That was the last time I had contact with him."

In sympathy with the tenor of the times, Bryan saw sex films as subversive: "Everybody was in a race to be more sexual than the next person," he remembers, "that was the attitude of the day. I made some low-budget nudie features after getting out of UCLA Film School during the hippie epoch, in an effort to thumb my nose at society and convention and the Studio system." These features – *The Dirtiest Game in the World* (1970), *Escape to Passion* (1970) and *I Love You I Love You Not* (1973) – were cheaply made, shot largely hand-held on 16mm, but each of them is an effective, dramatic feature with a smattering of mostly plot-driven sex scenes,

unlike the wave of true hardcore that would eventually predominate, in which narrative was so rudimentary and disposable that it frequently disappeared altogether.

Bryan made his feature debut in 1970 with *The Dirtiest Game in the World*, and it's undoubtedly his most shocking film. Titus Moody plays Titus Moore, a struggling politician unhappily married to Felicia (Sheryl Powell), an alcoholic with whom he refuses to have sex. In order to gain the youth vote and win a forthcoming election, he is advised by corpulent party bigwig R.J. (Coleman Francis, the director of *The Beast of Yucca Flats*) to involve himself with the campaign to legalise marijuana: *"I want you to infiltrate these pot users and LSD smokers and suck 'em over on our side,"* he's told. Titus, accompanied by his nerdy sidekick Frank (Frank Millen), makes contact with hippie campaigner Bruce (Bruce Beard), who introduces them to his housemate Jean (Jean Stone). She offers the two politicians a joint. Frank runs away in horror, but Titus 'turns on' and inhales. Soon he's being initiated into the hippie lifestyle by Jean, who invites him to eat raspberry jam from her snatch, and then turns him on to something else he's never tried before – namely a strap-on dildo up the *derrière*. Titus initially seems to embrace the lifestyle and values of his new friends: he tells R.J., *"These people are more enlightened than we thought. Their style of living is unique and natural. They respond to a universal cosmic energy source."* *"Horseshit,"* snaps R.J. *"What I want to know is how many votes can we squeeze out of 'em?"* Back at home, lonely frustrated Felicia falls into bed with Titus's buddy Frank, who reveals that he's in love with her. Titus returns and sees them *in flagrante* but steals off again, unperturbed. Felicia gets wind of her hubby's new life in Bohemian La-La land and sets out to confront Jean, who promptly seduces her too, drawing her into a roadside lesbian clinch by the oil pumps at the edge of town. ("My inspiration was The Beatles' *Why Don't We Do It in the Road?*," Bryan says.) However, Jean abruptly rejects her afterwards, and after spurning the genuine if goofy affections of Frank, Felicia starts to crack. She arranges an orgy: the guests include Titus, Jean and Bruce. Once the party is swinging, Felicia dresses in SM garb and stalks the room, whip in hand. Flying into a rage, she whips Jean and gashes Bruce with a knife. Jean retaliates by raping Felicia with a strap-on dildo, while Bruce, Titus and the other guests hold her down. Humiliated and out of her mind, she staggers to Frank's apartment and lets herself in. Finding he's not at home, she goes crazy and slashes her legs, her vagina and her nipples with a razorblade, smearing herself head to foot in blood before committing suicide by firing a gun up her snatch. Frank finds her blood-caked corpse and goes on the rampage, gate-crashing the orgy and shooting both Bruce and Titus, who dies complaining that his career is ruined.

Jean survives the bloodbath and, after hearing Titus's dying words about his political ambitions, takes his place, turning up as the new candidate at R.J.'s Party fundraiser.

The Dirtiest Game in the World is a political satire, a snapshot of the sexual revolution and its discontents, and an act of cinematic provocation that climaxes with a truly alarming burst of violence. In terms of sexual explicitness, it's at the leading edge of what was permissible at the time. There's full-frontal female – and occasionally male – nudity, but no erections, no penetration, and no split-beaver shots (i.e. no manual spreading of the labia, although some does occur due to actresses' postures).[4] Bryan himself calls it, "A three day wonder born out of this crazed era, inspired by *Un chien andalou*. My goal was to have audiences either go directly into orgy mode in the theater or crawl out to the street and throw up in the gutter. A good many of the audience did head for the exits but no one ever asked for their money back. At least one patron in Montana threw up before he made it to the exit. The picture had a political theme and was so popular in Washington, DC that

a bar hangout for government workers purchased a 16mm print and screened it every night for a year."

Just as in Europe, where directors like José Bénazéraf were dabbling with porno as artistic rebellion, so too West Coast youngbloods were excited by the implications of porn as a sort of cinematic civil disobedience, and it wasn't hard to attract the requisite misfits and malcontents. Although the film at first seems based around Titus Moody's character, it's not long before the women run away with the acting honours, dominating proceedings to such a degree that when Titus is killed at the end, it fails to register as a dramatic climax – he has in truth been deposed from the starring role for quite a while. Sheryl Powell and Jean Stone, on the other hand, both give strong, forthright performances. Stone, as the cynical hippie who seduces first Titus then Felicia, is pivotal to the story. Bryan recalls of his star: "Jean Stone, an Australian girl, had a political background. She was one of a family of Australian Communists who went to Russia in the 1950s, so her idea of politics and sex was really different! I ran into her when

The Dirtiest Game in the World
aka **Blood, Flesh and Tears** (shooting title)
© none [1970]
director: James Bryan. assistant director: Frank Millen. camera: Chris Munger. music: Country Al Ross. assistant [camera]: Howard Lester. sound: Mike Hall. assistant [sound]: Earl Sampson. script girl: Andrea Fischel. make-up: Signe Marlene. food service: Sally O'Connor. grips: Fred Lorenzen, Richard Bohn. assistant editors: Frank Millen, John Gough. titles: Villagran. filmed on location in Venice Beach (California, USA).
Cast: *Jean Stone (Jean Stone). Sheryl Powell (Felicia). Titus Moody [Moede] (Titus Moore, the candidate). Frank Millen (Frank, the intell-ectual). Coleman Francis (R.J.). Bruce Beard (Bruce Beard).*

below:
Party-time... prepping the S&M scene.
Seated at rear: Jean Stone and Titus Moody.
Standing: Bruce Beard and Sheryl Powell.
Holding slate: Frank Millen.

she was working in a bar where they were supposed to have nude dancers but she would get nude and then give health lectures, sexual health lectures, to the guys! So it was different. Somebody said 'You should get her.' There was a political theme to the picture, and because the film was weird and strange and the whole approach was different, I said okay."

Stone makes her entrance doing an energetic reverse striptease in her sunny apartment (actually James Bryan's Venice Beach house at the time – it later featured in Vernon Zimmerman's *Fade to Black*), starting off nude and then getting dressed while dancing to one of the rollicking Country Al Ross songs dotted throughout the film. The next time we see her she's turning Titus on to grass, before engaging him in a polymorphous sexual tryst that must have had a few unsuspecting punters spluttering into their raincoats (if you get my drift). The strap-on scene is a real brown-eye-opener, but it's played as part of a montage, including shots where Titus fucks Jean too: in effect, Bryan declines to exploit the shock value of male penetration and substitutes a playfulness and sense of erotic exploration. Stone, who resembles a young Patty D'Arbanville, also shines during dialogue scenes, coming across as a natural screen performer whose casual line readings are all the more impressive next to the palpably awkward Moody.

The Dirtiest Game in the World is a compelling debut that holds your attention throughout its (admittedly brief) running time: at just over an hour it seems the ideal length for a sex drama of this kind. But it's a cold film and not for everyone, filled as it is with mean, loveless, cynical and unsympathetic characters. Titus is needlessly cruel and callous to his wife (*"The only reason I'm here is that a senator needs a wife to get votes. After the election we're through."*), the initially likeable Jean turns nasty after seducing Felicia (*"Ha! Are you kidding? You didn't think that was for real, did you?"*), while minor character Frank, although honestly devoted to Felicia, is two-faced with Titus – willing to screw his buddy's wife behind his back while trying to stoke up trouble with R.J. 'No-one can be trusted' seems to be the (rather paranoid) theme.

As for poor Felicia… She's an alcoholic, she can't arouse her husband, her lesbian lover dumps her after one munch, and her desperate attempt to 'swing' her way back into hubby's heart leads to rape and humiliation. She's doomed because she can't let go of her bourgeois values: instead she's consumed by fantasies of vengeance against the woman who's 'stolen' her husband. Her attempt to take control as an S&M Goddess (*"Tonight what I say is law. Understand?"*) ends in mockery and degradation as she gets raped by her love-rival (*"Right, this is it you neurotic cunt."*). Sheryl Powell's sexually frustrated Felicia would have fitted neatly into John Waters's *Desperate Living*, thanks to a performance that is at times melodramatic to the point of camp. She's always impressive though, and makes a credible, tormented focus of attention as the film gathers pace for its gruesome, upsetting *pièce de résistance*. Her decline into madness may be a little overdone, but by the time we see her gouging a razorblade into her pussy-lips only a few diehards will be laughing.

Certainly, the film was a shock to the system for those who saw it first, as Bryan recalls: "I showed the film to a lot of people, it was a few months ahead of its time and no-one knew what to do with it. They felt it was way over the top. Some distributors got really upset as to why I would make such a film. I was mixing sex, an exploitation

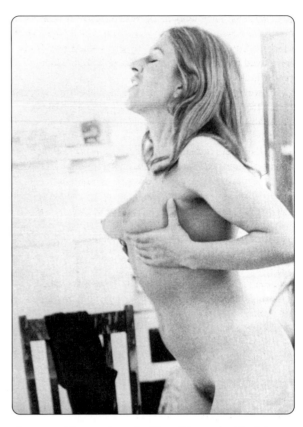

element, with comedy and with politics and with violence. And you didn't do that! David Friedman was one of the first people I brought it to, and he said, 'Well, I'll make you this deal' – but I didn't trust him. He owns carnivals, and I'm gonna trust him? I don't know, maybe I should have! So I said, 'I'm sorry'. Everybody was in one little compound on Cordova Street. Seymour Borde, who distributed *Don't Go in the Woods* a few years later, rented a space from Friedman – I showed it to Seymour in 1970, right after him. I'm sure Friedman said go next door and show it to Seymour. But it was too much for him. Seymour wasn't the one who had the strongest reaction though, that was Hal Herzon[5] – he was *very* upset. 'How could you do this? What do you think you're trying to do?!' I was pushing too many buttons with that movie. I'd thought, they're coming to see a sex film, they're open for anything!"

The Dirtiest Game in the World hasn't received much attention recently from fans of 'X' entertainment, although it has an edge that prefigures the porno films of Walt Davis, Zebedy Colt and Jess Franco. Shot in March of 1970, its theatrical release was delayed until 1972, when *Deep Throat* cleared the way for further extremes. It missed the boat on video too: by the time it emerged as one of 'Titus Moody's Cult Classics' in the early 1990s, the mould had been set and Bryan's contribution to savage cinema was, by and large, excluded from the history books. Bryan is always going to be best-known for his enjoyable slasher romp *Don't Go in the Woods*, but I recommend you seek out *Dirtiest Game*: you can be sure that it too would have fallen foul of the Video Recordings Act if anyone had dared to release it in the UK!

Dirtiest Game's star Titus Moody, best known to trash-movie fans as 'Boo Boo' from Ray Dennis Steckler's immortal if unwatchable *Rat Pfink a Boo Boo* (1966) was one of Bryan's closest friends in the industry. "The only character I remember fondly from that period – what a guy," he says. They worked together on *Dirtiest Game* and *Escape to Passion*, set up the short-lived video label 'Titus Moody's Cult Classics' in 1991 to release their own films, and stayed friends right up until Moody's death from cancer in 2001.

However, I don't think I'm being too harsh if I say that Titus Moody is, on the face of it, one of the least likely candidates for a career in porno. Not that good looks and a fine physique were a requirement in heterosexual porn, where hunks are rare and troglodytes far more common – it's his milquetoast manner that seems to militate against his chosen profession, as much as his lank hair and bank-teller looks. Moody always looks nervous, he stumbles and hesitates on his lines, and during *The Dirtiest Game*'s orgy scenes he's the only guy who insists on wearing his boxer shorts. At times he cuts loose a bit to show he can perform more credibly – ironically, it's during a rape scene that this essentially gentle man seems to get the bit between his teeth, snarling at Sheryl Powell and half-throttling her with a leather belt. Perhaps he was afraid of his own propensity for anger? Whatever, it's hard to hold these shortcomings against him – he's an eccentrically likeable fellow who was obviously popular in the industry. Bryan recalls: "When I did *Dirtiest Game* I went to Titus to find a cast since he did stills for everybody and knew all the actors and actresses in the adult film biz. At our first meeting Coleman Francis was staying at Titus's apartment, so I cast him in the film."[6]

Escape to Passion and *I Love You I Love You Not*

Bryan's next film, *Escape to Passion*, began shooting in the Autumn of 1970, just a few months after *Dirtiest Game*. As if chastened by the extreme response to his debut, Bryan, assisted by co-writer Warren Wintergreen (aka Joseph Adamson), concocted a lighter tale: it's an out-and-out comedy for much of the time, albeit one with the essence of dead-end Loserville oozing from every pore. "*Escape* was, by the distributor's request, not so explicit as *Dirtiest Game*," Bryan explains. "The difference between 'X' and soft 'X' was more important in terms of what theatre a film could be played in, rather than the community standards that determine what might be illegal. The distributors owned the Pussycat Theater chain, which maintained a legal truce with all the local police authorities."

Leo (Leonard Schumaker aka Leo Lyons, a friend from Bryan's days at the Beverly Hills Theater) is a nice but weak-willed and chronically unambitious guy, working in a dead-end packing job, who is drawn to the lowest level of petty crime: pilfering handbags from parked cars. His apartment is decked out with giant pictures of his idols, Edward G. Robinson and James Cagney, but for Leo, life ain't like it is in the movies. His shrewish 'moll' Judy is unimpressed with the 'loot' he brings home, and constantly berates him for being a loser. His only solace is in bragging about his criminal activities to Neds (Frank Millen), a simpleton who drinks with Leo at his favourite downtown bar. When his mean-spirited boss (Coleman Francis) refuses his request for a raise, and his girlfriend's moaning gets too much, Leo arranges a more ambitious robbery, involving Neds and budding porn entrepreneur Jason, another bar patron; but despite assaulting a night watchman ("*You criminals… you just got no respect for the law, have you!*") he emerges with a measly fifteen bucks. This is the last straw for his girl: "*You're not a man, you're a wimp, a ball-less wimp! You never were a man. I laugh every time I think of you trying to get on top of me!*" she screams. Leo throws her out and shacks up instead with bubble-headed Cherry (Kathie Hilton), whose willingness to *help* Leo, rather than scorn him, more than makes up for her ditziness. Frank decides to go for broke, now or never: a bank job. Jason opts out and Cherry opts in, so with simpleton Neds and space-cadet Cherry as his 'gang', Leo stages a heist. Needless to say, things do not go according to plan…

Escape to Passion begins with a well-edited sequence of the 'hero' breaking into parked cars. Giving up empty-handed, he walks disconsolately down an L.A. back alley, where he sees a busty blonde strutting her stuff in an upstairs window. He appears to break in, brandishing a gun, and we think for a second that he's dangerous, until the girl responds with weary familiarity and chastises him for his immature behaviour. So begins the catalogue of petty humiliations that propels Leo into action. The sexploitation angle is limited to full-frontal nudity, but takes a turn for the grotesque (that word again) when Bryan films a prolonged scene involving the hugely obese Coleman Francis and two pretty girls getting it on in a 'Crisco orgy' organised by Jason and his wife Marlene. For the uninitiated, this involves being smeared all over in gloopy handfuls of white animal fat, used as a cheap lubricant in the days before KY gel. Quite how the room must have smelled as this muck basted the actors under the klieg lamps is probably best unimagined! Things take an even weirder turn as Neds, Cherry and the injured Leo

above: The pressbook for Bryan's comedy-action-melodrama **Escape to Passion** (1970) features Leo Lyons and Kathie Hilton as woefully unskilled criminals, out of their depth after robbing a bank.

left: Sheryl Powell goes into self-mutilation overdrive in **The Dirtiest Game in the World**, attacking her own sex with a viciousness only Hisayasu Sato's **Naked Blood** (1995) and Michael Haneke's **The Piano Teacher** (2001) have since revisited.

opposite page, photostrip: Behind the scenes on **The Dirtiest Game in the World**.

opposite page top right: Jean Stone strips for Titus Moody, before turning him on to weed and buggering him with a strap-on. These liberated girls…

below: You want collectible? 'The Titus Moody Collection' is your poison! We're talking rare video catnip, film fanatics: don't walk, don't run, but *sprint like a gazelle* to obtain this cassette, and others in the range including Bryan's **Escape to Passion** and **I Love You I Love You Not**, and Moody's **Outlaw Motorcycles** (1966) and **The Last American Hobo** (1967).

Escape to Passion
aka **Hard Orgy** (US theatrical reissue title)
aka **A Good Orgy Is Hard to Find**
(shooting title)
© none [1970]
director: James Bryan. screenplay: Warren
Wintergreen [Joseph Adamson] and James
Bryan. associate producers: P. McGurk, F.
[Fred] Lorenzen, C.E. [Chris] Munger. director
of photography: Bob Eberlien. camera: Chris
Munger. [camera] assistants: Fred Lorenzen,
Rupert Macnee. sound: Mike Hall. music: Al
Ross, Mike Hall, Roy Lopez, Richard Bohn.
titles: [Nancy] Villagran. asst. director: Frank
Millen. asst. editor: Melody Brennen. script girl:
Andrea Fischel. make-up: Signe Marlene
[Marlene Selsman]. food service: Nancy
Villagran, Frances Bohn, Walt Brando, Paul
Overby, Bennette Rottman.
Cast: Leonard Schumaker [Leonard
Shoemaker, aka Leo Lyons] (Leo). Frank
Millen (Neds). Kathie Hilton (Cherry). Barbara
Caron [Barbara Mills] (Audrey). Sebastian Figg
(Jason). Marvin Vanderventer (J.J. Billingsley).
Fred Spruel (gangsta wannabe). Linda Levin
(Marlene). Holly Woodstar (Judy). Bruce Beard
(loud-mouthed drunk). Titus Moody [Moede]
(bank guard). Jack Duga (porno actor). Jean
Stone (porno actress). Signe Marlene
[Marlene Selsman] (bar singer). Hal John
Norman (security guard). Doug Kirby (hardhat
in bar). uncredited: Coleman Francis (the
boss). Gene Sturman (motorcyclist). Mike Hall
(bar singer). Joseph Adamson (customer in
restaurant, hippie).

top:
You wanna know what happens at a Crisco
orgy? **Escape to Passion** shows it all, in
skin-blemishing detail...

above:
Frank Millen, Kathie Hilton and Leo Lyons
pose for the camera in an **Escape to
Passion** promo shot that irresistibly reminds
one of Mario Bava's **Danger: Diabolik!**

right:
Frank Millen gets distracted from his
desperado act...

gatecrash the scene after their bungled bank-robbery, and
hide out from the police. The party atmosphere staggers on,
like a shabby *dolce vita* for the gutterporn underworld,
until the police add blood and bullets to the festivities.
Escape to Passion lacks the grimy intensity of *Dirtiest
Game* but it's still worth seeking out. With its shaky
gangsterism and weird sex, it's like a soft-porn variant of
an early Woody Allen film, with the element of genre
parody lending a sardonic edge to the clichés.

During post-production on *The Dirtiest Game in the
World* and *Escape to Passion*, Bryan occupied an office-
cum-editing room on Market Street near Venice Beach,
shared with Chris Munger, his cameraman and associate
producer on *Escape to Passion* (Munger would go on to
direct the enjoyably hokey *Kiss of the Tarantula* in 1975).
It was a prime location with hip credentials: local legend
held that Jim Morrison had stayed at the address early in
his career, and Orson Welles had used Market Street
locations for his masterly *Touch of Evil*. In early 1971, with
Escape to Passion completed, Bryan moved downstairs in
the same building, adapted an unused studio space
belonging to L.A. sculptor Larry Bell, and set up the
Market Street Studio, shared communally with several
local artists and filmmakers.

It was here that he began work on a satire of the sex
industry called *The Young Moviemakers* (aka *Girlie*), which
eventually emerged, six years later, as *Boogie Vision*.
Bryan pulled the cast together at Market Street to
improvise scenes, which he then wrote up into script form.
Meanwhile a sound stage was created, and sets built. *The
Young Moviemakers* was shot during 1971, and post-
production began in '72: however, the project fizzled and
stalled several times due to lack of money and energy.

In the meantime, Bryan worked as sound effects editor
on Larry G. Brown's incredible horror opus *An Eye for an
Eye*, better known on video as *Psychopath*: "*Psychopath*
was basically a soundstage picture," he says, "it was a
drama, an actor's piece. It was okay but very strange. The
'Mr. Rabbey' guy, Tom Basham, was a very strange
character. When I first saw Pee-wee Herman I wondered if
it was him or an interpretation of him. I was involved with
the music, with Al Ross. I remember those sessions well:
Al Ross was a devotee of alcohol... The path of least
resistance for me was editing, because like with Larry's
film, he just needed someone to get it done, he didn't see it
so much in post-production, that was beyond his
involvement in a way. And so I felt I should get it done as
cheaply as possible and just cover the bases."

With *The Young Moviemakers* dragging on, Bryan put
it aside to direct another three adult-themed movies. The
first of these, *I Love You I Love You Not* (the onscreen title
omits punctuation), was written and directed in 1973, and
released in 1974. The impetus came from a job that he
snagged as cameraman on an educational short,
Introduction to Numbers, for Encyclopaedia Britannica
Films. Bryan used the camera he was issued with to shoot
his own movie. *I Love You I Love You Not*, "a more
realistic psychological portrait, one woman's life in sex," as
Bryan puts it, gathers towards another impressively
downbeat finale, but there are signs this time of directorial
fatigue. The sex scenes, though still not hardcore, are
longer and more numerous, and they sometimes lack the
plotting dynamics that gave them purpose in *Dirtiest
Game*. The sound edit gives the impression of being
completed in a hurry, with occasional blank patches lacking

I Love You I Love You Not
© none [1973]
director: James Bryan. producer: Gerry Klein. director of photography [uncredited]: James Bryan. editor: Bill Haugse. sound: Mike Hall, Leslie Schatz. [production] assts: Jacquie Sturman [Jacqueline Cambas], David Whitten, Frances Bohn. songs "Put Your Trust in Me", "Carry Me Back" written and performed by Keypashine [Kay Pashine].
Cast: Lynn Harris (Lynn). Leo Lyons [Leonard Shoemaker] (Leo). Frances Fey (Frances). Frank Michaels [Frank Millen] (Frank). Marsha Jordan. Fred Lorenzen. Richard Salem. Gilles Ducharme. uncredited: Gene Sturman (a rapist).

left:
Frank Millen and Kathie Hilton freak out during the chaotic shoot-out that climaxes **Escape to Passion**.

below:
The trio of would-be criminals head for the hills after the heist goes horribly wrong.

both music and dialogue (a problem that would recur in *The Executioner Part II*, another rush-job). That said, the film is a slow burner that transcends its limitations: despite my initial reservations it stuck in my mind for days afterwards…

The story follows the fortunes of Lynn (Lynn Harris) who, although she's married to Vietnam veteran Frank (Frank Millen, here billed as 'Frank Michaels'), likes to sleep around with other men. Her friend Frances (Frances Fey) warns her that she's losing control of her life, but Lynn won't listen, and battens onto married man Leo (Leo Lyons aka Leonard Shoemaker), who treats her gently in bed but remains reluctant to leave his nagging wife Marjorie. Frank tolerates Lynn's infidelity, but leaves in disgust when Frances reveals that Lynn has told her of his bedroom 'shortcomings'. With Frank out of the way, Frances attempts a lesbian seduction. Lynn rejects it, so Frances turns against her – and jumps into bed with Frank. Leo too rejects Lynn, when she commits the cardinal adulterer's sin of telephoning his family home. Gradually, all of those closest to Lynn peel away, leaving her to sink into alcoholic loneliness and depression. Walking home one day, friendless and desperate, she's raped by a gang of three men, who abandon her in the midst of a muddy and deserted urban development. Life seems to have reached rock bottom. Is there time to turn things around, or is Lynn's tragic fate sealed?

This is a film probably best approached only after you first acclimatize to the rites and rhythms of seventies porn. An unsympathetic viewer, looking at it cold, would likely give up after twenty minutes, associating the frequent sex scenes with a lack of artistic imagination. And fair enough – but if you mentally sideline the 'sexy stuff', there *is* a directorial identity to be found. Besides all the screwing, the actors give serious, understated performances: and slowly, a perspective emerges on sexual alienation and the dangers of deferring emotional commitment. The opening

Directed and Produced
by JAMES BRYAN

ESCAPE TO PASSION©

STARRING
Leonard Schumaker | Sebastian Figg
Kathie Hilton | Marvin Vanderverter
Barbara Caron | Frank Millen

scene, where Lynn cavorts with a casual partner who keeps up a stream of jokes and quips, gets the sex off to an amusing start, but the man, though clever and funny, is clearly using wit and intellect to keep emotions at bay. This is not a distinction you would expect from a mindless fuckfest, nor is it arty pretension: it's a classic case of a director exploring psychological reality within the flawed framework of sexploitation.

If there's a drawback to this movie, it's more structural than sexual: the story of Lynn, her failed ambitions and her indecision regarding the men in her life, lacks focus and meanders. You could argue that the film and the leading lady suffer the same malaise. While some of this may well have been deliberate, it's always going to be a challenge to reflect a character like Lynn without weakening your narrative, and Bryan slips into disarray here and there: he initially withholds information about the characters, leaving us to piece together not only the status of the men with whom Lynn shares her bed but also the chronology of their relations. He's not exactly alone in this: it's a classic 1970s maverick strategy, redolent of such obliquely 'difficult' directors as Henry Jaglom and Robert Altman. I wouldn't stress the similarities too much but there's no doubt in my mind that there was 'something in the air' at the time; the film's looseness is partially a function of the seventies maverick sensibility and not merely laziness.

If you think this all sounds too bleak and serious, there's always Bryan regular Frank Millen, who brings his comedic skills to a scene where he riffs, Scorsese-style, on the revelation that love-rival Leo has only one testicle; and he later shines during a scene in which Lynn's boozy mother seduces him (it's a classic of drunken embarrassment: he tells her he has a small dick; she pipes up with a rendition of 'I'm a Little Teapot').

I Love You I Love You Not is a curio, a post-hippie comedown caught on film. 'Free love' has become more of an unsatisfactory habit for Lynn than a source of lasting joy or liberation. While the sex is at first presented as pleasurable, there's a gradually more enervated vibe to the story that makes Lynn's vacillating emotional life the real focus of concern. Nice guy Leo seems to want nothing more than a bit on the side, but when Lynn starts to cling, threatening his marriage, Mr. Nice Guy turns into a hot-tempered loudmouth. Girlfriend Frances tries to talk Lynn out of sleeping around, but her motivation proves to be selfish – her objection to Lynn's promiscuity is merely a prelude to a lesbian advance. When this fails she selfishly spoils an attempted truce between Lynn and Frank by betraying a confidence about Frank's small penis. Humiliated, Frank leaves his wife for good. Even Lynn's sluttish mother turns her back. To cap it all, once Lynn has retreated into depression, Frances and Frank get it together, refusing to answer the phone when Lynn calls for help.

All of this makes for a rather downbeat view of the free-love ideal. As often in seventies porno, the spectacle of orgies and multiple couplings is served up to audiences who are then told how ruinous these things are in real life. It's a combination of prurience and moralising that permeates many an American sex film of the era. While I would applaud the film for its commitment to slowly draining the light from its narrative, it's a pity that Bryan offers no alternative/positive spin on sexual hedonism. It seems the choice is between unhappy, unsatisfying marriage, or loneliness and exploitation in a string of hollow sexual encounters. Like Felicia in *The Dirtiest Game in the World*,

Lynn tries to achieve happiness through sex but ends up finding only bitterness and misery. In *Dirtiest Game*, Felicia's problems are caused by her inability to see beyond bourgeois notions of fidelity. *I Love You I Love You Not* seems to explore the reverse angle – what happens in open relationships? – only to conclude that they lead to the same depression, alcoholism and tragedy as before. Perhaps the sex film industry is inclined to spread this message because it leaves only porno itself as an option – 'virtual' infidelity without the dangers of sexual freedom or the stifling dictates of monogamy! I wouldn't make so cynical a case here – if James Bryan wants to tell sad tales of unhappy souls failing to find solace in sex, I can 'dig' that. I just feel that this film would have been enriched by a parallel story exploring a less catastrophic interpretation of sexual freedom. Perhaps the overall bleakness of the movie inspired what followed, as Bryan turned to greater explicitness within a more light-hearted context…

Enter Morris Deal…

In 1974, having paused at the brink of hardcore with *I Love You I Love You Not*, Bryan decided to follow the example of others in the field, and make true hardcore films under a pseudonym, thus leaving his real name free of potentially damaging associations: and so 'Morris Deal' was born. The first film to appear from this alter ego was *High School Fantasies*, which Bryan wrote and directed in February 1974 for producer Dick Aldrich (aka Damon Christian). It starred Larry Barnhouse, alongside adult-movie regulars Rene Bond and her husband/frequent co-star Ric Lutze, Nicole Riddell (who appeared in *Ilsa, She Wolf of the SS* the following year), and Leo Lyons (aka Leonard Shoemaker) (from *Escape to Passion* and *I Love You I Love You Not*).

Freddy (Larry Barnhouse) is a teenage nerd suffering the time-honoured difficulty of bedding girls, in particular his dream-date Mary (Rene Bond). His friends, Buddy (Ric Lutze) and Moose (Tony Mazziotti), have no such problems and try all sorts of ideas to help him, but all they seem to do is cost Freddy a lot of dough. One day they convince him to try a dose of Spanish Fly (which in truth they have made up themselves in their basement.) Somehow, their homemade brew actually works – when girls taste a soda spiked with the concoction they go crazy with lust. But the proud inventors discover they are unable to repeat their recipe...

Unusually for a porno film, an original soundtrack album was released[7]: the film's rock'n'roll revival score, according to those who've seen the film, is one of its most persuasive features. Gene Sturman, an artist-sculptor Bryan met whist working as production assistant on Terry Sanders's Academy Award-nominated documentary *Four Stones for Kanemitsu*, did the music along with his buddy Bill Spater. "Gene Sturman had a band back in New York in the late fifties, early sixties," Bryan remembers. "He cut a single and was picked up by Paul Revere and the Raiders for an East Coast tour. He really enjoyed doing the *High School Fantasies* music." Sturman and his wife Jacqueline Cambas first met Bryan when they moved to a rented studio in Venice where Bryan was shooting the climactic orgy shoot-out from *Escape to Passion*.[8] Sturman appeared as a motorcyclist who's shot down in that film, and played one of the rapists in *I Love You I Love You Not*. Jacqueline Cambas worked for a while on the stop-start project *The Young Moviemakers*: an ex-UCLA student, she

above:
Bryan's alter-ego Morris Deal enters the seventies porno fray with **High School Fantasies** (1974).

opposite page:
More cavorting and confusion in **Escape to Passion**.

Lady Street Fighter
© none [1978]
director: James Bryan [uncredited onscreen]. producer: Renate [Renee] Harmon. camera: Max Reid. assistants: Woody Hamilton, David Jones, Eric Jenkins. key grip: Jeff Slike. sound: Gerry Klien. make-up: Sue Cabral. production assistant: Susan Bryan. assistant director: G'Abrielle Topping. aerial sequence: Ricky Cardoni. assistant to the producer: F.L. Millen. *Cast:* Joel D. McCrea, Jr. (Pollitt). Renee Harmon (Linda Allen). Trace Carradine. Liz Renay (burlesque dancer). Tony Romano. Bob Morris. Steve Sexton. Elisa M. Kipp. Mio Shy Astarr. Tom Eiesly. Stephen Machey. Gil Grace. Lalania Castinni. Frank Millen. Robin Hood. Mark Glover. Scott Barrington. Bob Barnes.
Re-versioned, with added footage as:
Revenge of Lady Street Fighter
© 1991. James Bryan Films.
James Bryan Films. Bravo - Kilo presents a Kenna Productions film.
aerial sequence: Ricky Cardoni. assistant to the producer: F.L. [Frank] Millen.
Cast: Ruth Peebles. Rene Harmon. Sandford Hampton. Nick Random. Doug Hart. Frank Neuhaus. Byron Clark. Louis B. Perez. Timothy de Haas. Jay Wright.

began as editor for Tom Laughlin, and moved on to a successful editing career working on Paul Schrader's *Hardcore* and *Cat People*, and mainstream fare like the Al Pacino vehicle *Frankie and Johnny*.

'Morris Deal' followed *High School Fantasies* with the appealingly titled *Beach Blanket Bango*, shot in September 1974. It again starred horny couple Rene Bond and Ric Lutze, as well as several other cast members from *High School Fantasies*, joined this time by Bryan's buddies Frank Millen (as Frank Michaels) and Titus Moody. A spoof on the sixties AIP beach movies, it works in references to LSD, a haunted house piss-take, and the obligatory surfing footage. Perhaps still carrying a torch for the provocations of his first movie, in the midst of this frivolity Bryan has some of the characters sent to Vietnam, cutting through the

SHE MAKES THE GOOD GUYS HAPPY . . .
SHE MAKES THE BAD GUYS BLEED ! ! !

SHE GIVES
GOOD KUNG FU!

Lady Street Fighter

STARRING MARITAL ARTS QUEEN
RENEE HARMON • JOEL D. McCREA, Jr.
TRACE CARRADINE and LIZ RENAY

good-time ambience with actual war footage. For the period soundtrack, Dick Aldrich clinched a deal with a Hollywood music entrepreneur who owned a huge library of old demos by 'sound-alike' bands of the sixties.

Given that the sex industry was plumbing dark waters at the time, with the grimy violence of Zebedy Colt, Alex De Renzy, Shaun Costello and Armand Weston going further than even *The Dirtiest Game in the World* had dared, it's interesting that Bryan's first two hardcore films are such frothy, light-hearted confections, based around nostalgia and pastiche. Having directed the downbeat, pessimistic *I Love You I Love You Not*, one could hardly call Bryan a brazen hedonist, and *Dirtiest Game*'s denouement is still shocking today; but in both cases the acts onscreen were simulated. When it came to making fuck films with no-one faking it, Bryan essentially had no thirst to explore the more violent possibilities. His view of the industry was coloured by wariness about the psychological fallout, as he explains: "The sex film biz is a universe of its own, bizarre and dark, hidden from the light, growing like a mushroom prospering in the collected dung. It was a weird journey filled with excessive people. I'm glad to be past that chapter. The porno industry will tend to make you neurotic. I think, after having worked with some people who really churn it out, and have very specific rules, like a factory, it's just the constant exposure that does it. You're getting the stimulation, things happen to you psychologically and physiologically, and, you know, there's no completion, no recognition of that reality, so it's creating a certain level of frustration, like a short circuit. Looking at the images and all the stimulation you'd have, you're genetically disposed to react but you're not reacting. You're not supposed to be involved in it, you're supposed to be working! If somebody is involved in it they're usually not working for very long! The consumer can exist in a sexual universe but the producer cannot. It's the factory situation, I realised that it was too much. I started noticing people I had worked with a long time, and I thought, well… everyone is a little bit crazy here, and I think I know the reason why! I did *High School Fantasies*, *Beach Blanket Bango* and some videos under the name of Morris Deal. But after doing two or three, the third time it's like 'Oh no, this is pornography, this is not what I wanted to do, where's the joy in this?' I was thinking in terms of art with *Dirtiest Game*, although I consider myself more like pulp fiction, in terms of effect. The first two hardcore films I made were like a fascinating journey into a strange land and reinforced that rebel/black sheep thing. By the third one the fun had worn thin, and a not-so-good feeling of being just an everyday garden-variety pornographer began to colour the experience. Then AIDS put it all in the bad place as far as I was concerned. So I left."

Other things colluded to make working in the porn industry stressful, such as the constant difficulty getting paid, as Bryan explains: "That was everybody's big concern, all the time, so what I wanted was paying up front or a guaranteed amount paid in a certain schedule." Porn's connection to organised crime and the Mafia has been well documented, but Bryan had little direct connection: "I was aware of the mob influence to some degree but it was all very quiet and distant, something to do with the other guy in someplace faraway. I wasn't a threat to any grand empires. But the 'Godfather' craze created a nasty change when wannabe producers with a few bucks started carrying guns and acting tough. That was annoying."

Stalled and Mothballed:
Boogie Vision and *Lady Street Fighter*

The Market Street Studio set-up dissolved in 1974, and Bryan moved to Silverlake on the Eastside of L.A. In 1975, keen to build a new working environment, he set up Bungalow A, an editing facility at Scott Sound in Hollywood ("a place where really bad movies went to die," he jokes). Bryan himself was in-house sound effects editor on a variety of projects that came through Bungalow A between '75 and '77, including: Bill Rebane's *The Giant Spider Invasion*; Robert Voskanian's *The Child*; Larry Buchanan's *Goodbye Norma Jean*; Frank Packard's *Abar, the First Black Superman*; Don Hulette's *Breaker! Breaker!*; one of the many recuts of *Wolfen* (a film that didn't make it into cinemas for another four years); and a Polish import called *The Two Who Stole the Moon*. He also made himself available as second unit production manager on Gene Corman's *Vigilante Force*: "Peter Jamison, who had been the production designer on *High School Fantasies* and *Beach Blanket Bango*, was now picking up jobs from Julie, Roger and Gene Corman and rented space for props and costumes at Bungalow A," Bryan explains. "Peter had talked Gene into letting him direct the second unit for *Vigilante Force* and came to me to be unit production manager. I also did some camera work – sunsets, special effects explosions and the like."

With *The Young Moviemakers* still limping onwards, Bryan started *Lady Street Fighter*, an action film with a martial arts slant, starring German-born actress turned writer/producer Renee Harmon. Bryan explains, "For reasons of economy we shot *Lady Street Fighter* with my recently acquired variable speed unblimped 35mm Arriflex, recording a 'scratch' soundtrack that could be replaced with a matched clean re-recorded dialogue track, since Renee had a flat deal with Scott Sound which included dialogue replacement; and so we stayed on budget. While filming, a camera assistant manually adjusted the speed control to keep the camera as close to constant sound speed as possible. Director Bill Rebane had finished *The Giant Spider Invasion* and was redoing an earlier UFO production[9] and prepping a picture that required some rock and roll music. We met in the Scott Sound transfer room and traded scores, *High School Fantasies* for the UFO score, which was used on *Lady Street Fighter*."

With a version of *Lady Street Fighter* completed in '76, Bryan screened the cut to distributor Harry Novak, whose pickup *The Child* (see feature elsewhere in this book) was at that time in post-production at Bungalow A. Novak showed interest but then stalled for a year, before finally declining the film in '77. During this time, Bryan was not only working at Bungalow A but also working for Brandon Chase at Group I, re-editing Italian theatrical imports for US domestic release and assembling their theatrical trailers.[10] Bryan had many discussions with the veteran distributor and huckster, and he recalls Chase explaining that the commercial winds were changing: "He told me all the leading independent distributors were notified in an informal way, by the major studios, that the majors would be taking over the independents' share of the production and distribution business: essentially putting them *out* of business by producing the kind of exploitation films that previously had been low-budget summer drive-in movies, with studio name casts and studio budgets. Also every theatre and drive-in would thereafter be considered 'first

run' or dedicated to major studio product, thus eliminating all the screens that had been available for 'Indy' product. The studios' Indy squeeze would be interrupted in a few years by the home video revolution, which effectively derailed their plans of total domination, but only for a decade or so. Their dream of ultimate control was soon back on track – until the present-day film business became truly international and the rules changed yet again."

Bryan's headaches were just beginning with *Lady Street Fighter*, but in 1977 he did at last manage to heave his pet project *The Young Moviemakers* over the finishing line. Six years on from its inception, however, times had really changed, and Bryan's adult-movie comedy satire was out of date. After showing the fine cut to just about every distributor or studio in Hollywood, and finding no interest, he recut, reshot and retitled it, as *Boogie Vision*.

above:
Boogie Vision was Bryan's ambitious attempt to satirise modern media, the hippie milieu, and the porno scene. Can a movie featuring a film-within-a-film called 'The Lizardwoman from Outer Space Meets the Radical Feminoids' be anything other than marvellous? Certainly the Robert Crumb influenced poster art suggests we're missing something. Sadly, **Boogie Vision** remains extremely difficult to see.

Boogie Vision
aka **The Young Moviemakers** (shooting title)
aka **Girlie**
1977
director / writer / editor: James Bryan.
producers: S.K. Bryan, James Bryan.
executive producers: Leonard Shoemaker,
Gloria Shoemaker, Susan Kathleen Bryan.
associate producers: Tom Powell, Frances
Bohn. director of photography: Frank Mills.
music: Gene Sturman, Bill Spater. production
design: Dale Oderman. costumes: Belladonna
Ace [Rosanna Norton]. props: Dale Oderman.
balloon sculpture: Nancy Villagran. animation:
Top Peg of Santa Barbara. animated title
sequence: John Haugse. production
assistants: Rodger Bowers, John Gough,
Rodger Denmar, Eric Jenkins. assistant
editor: Eric Jenkins. sound: Gerry Radger,
Mike Hall, Leslie Schatz.
Cast: Michael Laibson. Marlene Selsman
(Marlene). Bert Belant (Bert). Frank Millen
(Frank). Leo Lyons [Leonard Shoemaker].
Victoria Miller (Mouse). Robin Hood. Steve
Gillman. Tom Malinchak. Mary Montray (nudie
actress). Steve White (Roberto). Burt
Littlebeau (info-mercial spokesman). Peter
Turner (TV reporter). Michael Laibson (Mick).
Leonard Shoemaker (nudie actor). uncredited:
Jacqueline Cambas (feminist car pooler).
Michael Ahnemann (hippie with six shooter).
Barbara Mills (feminist protester). Calista
Carradine.

The templates for this new version were *The Groove Tube* (1974), at the time a ground-breaking spoof on TV, directed by Ken Shapiro; and *Tunnelvision* (1976), its immediate successor/rip-off: "The first company I signed with was Crest, from L.A.," he explains. "They did a few dates, started building it up. Then Universal, who had picked up *The Kentucky Fried Movie* (1977) and discovered they didn't know how to release this offbeat satire, approached Jerry Persell at Crest with a sweet business deal he couldn't refuse. The unfortunate part for me, and *Boogie Vision*, was that Jerry had to be exclusive to *The Kentucky Fried Movie* and he regretfully told me, in the nicest of terms, I was being dropped. So I decided to try releasing *Boogie Vision* myself, using the education I had received from working at Group I, having listened closely in those long conversations with Brandon Chase."

Bryan sighs: "I released it through my own company, but it didn't appear in the right publications to be noticed. Releasing it solo destroyed my bank balance to such a degree that when Peter Turner offered me an option on the *Alien* script for $100 I had to pass and gave him the number of the guy who was putting together *The First Nudie Musical*!"

Peter Turner was an up-and-coming writers' agent newly arrived from Chicago, and he brought with him a school chum called Garth Eliassen. Turner talked himself onto the crew and provided talent, including Eliassen, to handle pick-up shots for the restructured *Boogie Vision*. It was this association that brought Bryan and Eliassen together, and the two of them would shortly go on to create *Don't Go in the Woods* in the State of Utah, home of the friendly and inviting Mormon Church…

Life Among the 'Destroying Angels'….

Working around Bungalow A in 1977 was Craig Hill, an employee of Sunshine Releasing, a company that immediately felt the effects of the 'Indy Squeeze' Brandon Chase had described. Says Bryan, "Hill saw his job disappearing and explained to me there was still business here and there, and if he could pick up some reasonable product there was yet a little money to be made. I went to Charles Ver Halen, a producer and lab owner who would sometimes bankroll films, and explained our plan. He agreed to give us several of his not-so-recent films that had been sitting on the shelf for a while. The titles included Curtis Harrington's *The Killing Kind*, and *Messiah of Evil* by Gloria Katz and Willard Huyck. New advertising was printed, the dates set, the prints shipped, but difficulties with collections soon had Craig back in Houston surviving as an accountant. I'm sure Mr. Ver Halen saw some money but I never did, and Craig wouldn't discuss it. After getting play dates around the country, and knowing collections would be a long wait, I jumped at the chance to take a sound effects job at Schick-Sunn Classics in Salt Lake City, on the *Grizzly Adams* TV series."

Bryan worked on the Utah-based TV production *Grizzly Adams* for three seasons. At that time, Schick-Sunn Classics (often referred to as Sunn Classics) were thriving, producing 'NBC Movies of the Week' and TV pilots like *The Deerslayer*, *Earthbound*, *Nancy Drew* and *The Adventures of Tom Sawyer*. Bryan was involved with both their broadcast and theatrical output, editing sound effects on docu-features like *Beyond Death's Door*, *Encounter with Disaster*, *The Lincoln Conspiracy* and *The Bermuda Triangle*. He explains the set-up: "Sunn Classics released high concept Nature, Bible and UFO theatrical documentaries or docu-dramas, using a 'four-wall' deal with theatres, essentially renting the auditorium at a flat rate and covering all other expenses, spending large sums on advertising, heavy on TV spots, to get a huge viewer turn out, then keeping all the ticket sales. It was a very successful strategy for a few years. Entrepreneur Patrick Frawley got into the 'four wall' game with a nature show starring Dan Haggerty about Siberian tigers, and after making a generous investment in a small Utah production company, Sun Pictures, he subsequently took control, renamed it Schick-Sunn Classics and set out to produce a theatrical docu-drama, *The Life and Times of Grizzly Adams*, starring animal-handler/actor/producer Dick Robinson. In the course of shooting, Dick Robinson was badly injured by a bear. Charles Sellier, who began making airline safety films in Denver before producing nature shows for Sunn, stepped in as Frawley's agent, recast the film with Dan Haggerty and had it completely reshot. Sellier's successful formula got the attention of Fred Silverman at NBC and so the *Grizzly Adams* series was born. Frawley believed Dick Robinson broke his contract and advised him to sue if he thought he had any money coming out of the deal.[11] That's when I showed up in that second team of sound effects editors. My boss left Salt Lake, and the series, at the end of that season, and I stepped into the supervisor spot with instructions to use local editors. NBC was throwing one contract after another at Sunn Classics for TV specials, mini-series and 'Movies of the Week'. Since the only qualified local editors were already on staff, I picked from the untrained and had to train them very quickly. The first lesson was that the film used to space out or fill between sound effects had two different sides, a clean or cell side and a coated or emulsion side. The second lesson was how to splice two ends of this film with tape while matching the two sides. Next the film was wound onto thousand-foot reels, with the cell or clear side up or exposed on the roll of film. And so simple step by simple step the training progressed. Developing the physical skills with various pieces of equipment was a matter of basic repetition and each trainee was instructed to notify me when they were ready to progress to the next level. Our little sound editors' handbook that I put together to keep each sound editor's work consistent within the department was passed on to the Sound Department at Paramount to train their new people."

Bryan spent four years working for Sellier at Schick-Sunn Classics. His recollections of the unusual pressures working there offer a glimpse into a world within a world within a world: the Mormon American Film Industry: "In Salt Lake City, at the time I arrived to work for Sunn Classics, the Mormon Church was changing to accommodate a faction of its young membership who were not fitting into the standard image of the young Mormon. Following up on the popularity of Donny and Marie Osmond, the approved Farrah Fawcett hairdo could be replaced by the short and perky Marie Osmond cut. The Donny style in men's fashion, seen in *American Gigolo*, was accepted as well. The Church had a boy's and girl's youth auxiliary where teenagers were taught proper grooming, which turned out to be a bit of a joke outside Utah since it was stuck in the Brady Bunch mould. Also, this conformity marginalized the growing geek or nonconforming academic types, so the Church started a separate

opposite:
In the woods with Bryan and Co. Snapshots taken during the making of **Don't Go in the Woods,** from the director's collection.

program for its young exceptional weirdos and updated the standard training for socialization, since the old-school approach was driving kids away from the Church."

You might think that if you suggested a film about the Mormon Church and its revered founders, you would ingratiate yourself with the establishment: "Many Mormon film people have proposed projects about the very popular figure Porter Rockwell, but all have been persuaded not to follow up. I found that even the most intellectual and opened-minded of Mormons really resented outsiders like myself who commented on 'the culture.' I heard, 'When outsiders talk about 'the culture' I say if you don't like it here, just leave' enough times to get the idea and shut up about my observations. While I was working at Sunn Classics, Charles Sellier converted to the Church, as many who have successful businesses there find it wise to do."

Bryan persisted in trying to link the film industry in Utah to the broader cinema establishment. "In 1981 I was a founding member of the Utah Association of Motion Picture and Television Artists (UAMPTA) and was a member of the Magazine Committee. I didn't realize at the time, contrary to the bylaws, the true purpose of the organization was to control and limit production in Utah, making sure the 'right' people kept a tight grasp on the film and video business. Since I got lots of people to pay dues and join up I felt we should deliver the Association's magazine to prove we were serious about promoting the film business in Utah. When it came time for the magazine to start publication the rest of the committee was too busy, so I just did it all myself, thinking that once it was going other members could take over – since I really didn't want to do it anyway. I sold all the ads, got the printer, got the articles promoting film in Utah, got photos together and pasted it up camera-ready. I mailed copies out to the union production managers in L.A. and dumped copies at labs and suppliers there too. The effort to pass out free issues at the US Film Festival (which evolved into the Sundance Festival) was quickly ruled to be too much trouble, and so they were left at the door in their cartons. When the Church sent in for a subscription after I had set up other members to take over the second issue, the officers got nervous and finally became involved. The third issue was scaled down to a four-page news letter, and it was allowed to die after the fourth issue. In response I organized Salt Lake City's first Midnight Movie Series with titles like *F for Fake*, *Sword of Vengeance*, *Rock 'n' Roll High School* and Mae West's last film *Sextette*, to raise money for UAMPTA. Each program had a specially honoured short film by a local filmmaker. I shot a trailer promoting the series and it was a big success, but there was fallout. All the Salt Lake City movie chains responded by having their own midnight shows. The management of the building got heat because our champagne receptions for the local filmmakers would hurt the bar downstairs. Finally, UAMPTA rescinded any support or involvement and demanded that their name be removed from all ads and posters. When I was too much trouble for Sunn Classics it was time for me to go. I hired their first and last African-American employee, an editor. When I joined the Elks Club across the street from the editing rooms, so I could have a Department lunch at the end of the *Grizzly Adams* season, it caused a tremor, since we brought that black editor. The local Elks Order had to have a special regional meeting to get organization approval for racial integration of their restaurant-bar. Sellier and pals were making lots of movies over-budget, since the

company was put up for sale at its earnings peak and certain people were creating production problems to throw money at. As post-production supervisor I was being hit by these unending major roadblocks. When I finally tumbled to the runaround scheme and spoke to one of the players, they moved me out of the stooge's spot and soon eased me out altogether. I blew no whistles nor threatened the established order of the day. Just took my paycheck and said my thanks. The film business is the film business."

Into the Woods...

Shot in the summer of 1980, during Bryan's seven-year sojourn in Utah, *Don't Go in the Woods* is a lively, ramshackle horror picture with a devil-may-care approach to story construction, and lots of gory deaths. The story, concerning two couples on a camping holiday who run into a maniacal 'mountain man' while trekking through the Rockies, may lack originality, but it plays the slasher horror game to the hilt and proved to be Bryan's most visible and commercially successful picture.

Bryan was thirsty for a successful theatrical release: *Boogie Vision* had foundered and his career had gravitated towards more and more work on other people's movies, so an 'overcome all odds' approach was essential. "I really wanted to make a general release theatrical picture that would play nationally through a regular distributor," he says. There was just one extra proviso: "It had to be done with no money! Or at least with the money I had. I bought out-of-date raw stock that was slated to be sold for the reclaimable silver in the emulsion. The cost was under $500 with shipping. A major coup. The lab really had to strive to get acceptable colour but they made it work. It was very cheap. And it tickled me to finish it that way."

Initially, it was the existence of a new cut of *Lady Street Fighter* that made *Don't Go in the Woods* possible. Bryan explains: "In order to collect from sub-distributors you needed the next picture to be ready to go into release before the subs would let go of your money, sort of the reverse of a ransom. They had to have product to survive, so naturally any money they let go of, by the Law of the Indy Jungle, had to be going to a source of new pictures. Working in Utah I was able to recut *Lady Street Fighter* and make a trailer that would ensure a release on the kung fu circuit, and then found a place for it in an oversubscribed tax shelter package. So Renee Harmon and I sold out and split the cash. A few subs, seeing I was still producing product, let go of some more cash. Renee and I both started separate productions, since she was in L.A. and I was in Salt Lake City."[12]

Bryan decided upon a horror film set in the Rocky Mountains, with the scenery providing production value. Shooting on outdoor locations would save money on lighting, so he opted for a story based on local rumours about a number of hikers who were said to have fallen victim to a suspected serial killer. Peter Turner heard the word back in L.A.: "He had Garth send me an outdoor script about hikers in danger and also recommended talent who would travel to Salt Lake on their own dime," Bryan recalls, adding dryly: "So Garth became a victim twice, once on screen and simultaneously behind the scenes as I rewrote his script with a vicious disregard for his artistic intentions!"

The shooting schedule was arranged to make careful use of resources, and with a storyline based around four campers as leads, and a succession of unrelated secondary victims, it made sense to begin shooting each individual

victim scene one at a time, saving the assembled cast shots for last. "All-told we shot for a couple of months, mostly weekends, using local actors," says Bryan. "The store owner in the scene with the sheriff was the head of a local casting company. Finally we got the main cast assembled and shot the rest in under two weeks, with a couple of down days to recover our breath and prepare for the finish. The locations were spread around a bit but we always made it back to Salt Lake for the evenings. It was a struggle in the mountains because of the altitude; we were always out of breath. Coming back down to Salt Lake really left everybody fatigued. We worked above the snake line in the mountains so we didn't worry about the rattlesnakes, which meant the mice were a plague as far as catering was concerned. We were usually on our way home when the porcupines came out, and after dark we could hear some larger furry friends; but we never met them face to face!"

Don't Go in the Woods has a gloriously high body-count, and the murders are frequently as grisly as one could wish for in such a low-budget production. "I really enjoyed the bloody violence," says Bryan, "believing it stayed safely in a fun or comic zone. Only one scene, once it was edited, crossed the line for me and created a very disturbing reaction, like the scene of a bloody accident or a factual medical record of a crime. That was the killing of Joanne. I recut it and brought down the level of horror to something that would be seen as entertainment, not some bit of police evidence material. The special effects were really simple and really cheap, but for whatever reason that killing was like *Mark of the Devil*, you know, too far." Later, back in the cutting room, Bryan also realised he had inadvertently shot an homage to Orson Welles in the Joanne-slashing sequence – "It was only later, once I had cut it and saw the way I shot it, that I realised I was replicating, unintentionally, Akim Tamiroff's death in *Touch of Evil*, you know, trying to get up through the window. When I saw it later I thought, 'Oh no, what have I done!'"

When shooting wrapped, there were problems getting post-production money together, at which point Bryan's sister Suzette, and her husband Roberto Gomez, entered the picture as producers: "We got the film in the can and had no budget left for the lab costs. Suzette, who hustled up costumes (helping my artist wife who sculpted the blood and body parts and special effect devices), was married to a forest ranger from Honduras, Roberto Gomez. At this moment Roberto was hired by a major corporation in Texas. They bought a house, sold their trailer and decided to invest the new cash in *Don't Go in the Woods*."

For the score, Bryan turned to H. Kingsley Thurber, and his primitive but distinctive contributions really help to sell the film. "When I started out with H. Kingsley Thurber he was in this groove of writing music for industrial films," recalls Bryan, "sort of cheerful and bland. He started writing cues and I said, 'This isn't going to work, we can maybe use it on a few hiking scenes but mostly I think we should go to John Carpenter's notebook and replicate his cues' – obviously in the way Thurber would do it, but that was the approach. He really had a good time doing it; it was like a release for him because he could do anything he wanted to. He gave me cues for different scenes and I used them or moved them around, doubled them up… Looking at the film, I thought okay, it's gotta have a lot of music! I tried to use music everywhere, looking back at it maybe I went too far, but at the time I thought, I'll just keep going, do it scene by scene and not

worry about progression so much. After *Woods* I recommended Kingsley to Renee for *Frozen Scream*."

Frozen Scream and *Don't Go in the Woods* share several cues, including one very distinctive sound like a deranged bedspring. Bryan knows it well: "Thurber was a quiet-spoken fellow with a dry sense of humour – he referred to the cue you liked as 'Steel Puke', in that it was made with a steel guitar distortion. I wasn't around for the recording so I don't know how he made it do what it did."

Post-production was fine, but Bryan found the actual shoot less enjoyable than it had been on his previous movies, as he explains: "*Don't Go in the Woods* was the most difficult film that I had made. It just happens that each film has a character to it; problems happen in a certain vein, everything follows a certain line. That film was almost impossible to make, with all kinds of resistance. I did have some problems with actors. The psychology of the acting population had changed. The reason I was making films was no longer possible, and I was approaching things in an antique way. I thought everyone should enjoy making movies: that you couldn't help but enjoy making a film. People wanted something different out of it. Garth was very upset because I chose to put in some scenes that he would never put in. I was interested in certain things, so I wrote a scene so that characters could deal with them. At the time and place we were shooting there was an acknowledgement of urban myths. I included an urban myth in the campfire story, which nobody – the cast, and Garth who was in the crew – wanted to do. Garth was upset and perturbed, and lobbied with the cast not to do it."

The scene Bryan is referring to – in which the lead quartet play at scare stories round the campfire – is atrociously acted; the reason becomes clearer as Bryan reveals they were essentially sulking at its inclusion and trying to mess it up! However, their strategy backfired; they had not reckoned with Bryan's temperament. "It's like when actors want a close-up to be used," he explains, "they'll give a bad performance in the three shot!" This spoiler technique, used so blatantly by the leading players, cut no ice with Bryan: "They didn't see it as drama, or whatever. I think they were hoping I wouldn't use the scene. They were dealing with the wrong person! My attitude – and I get in trouble telling actors this – is, 'It's your face that's going to be up there on the screen, so if you want to give a bad performance, and do it wrong, be my guest! They're not gonna be thinking *I'm* lousy as a director, they're going to be thinking *you're* lousy!' And some people *really* don't appreciate that!"

The key to the cast's ill grace, according to Bryan, was that they arrived with unrealistic expectations, especially about the financial status of the production: "I did a lot of things, getting away with stuff on the budget. They didn't like the Arriflex. It made their experience of filming 'less than Hollywood'. I was recording a scratch track, and that was also something they were not familiar with. It wasn't a Nagra, it was a little Sony, stereo, with one track recording the synch pulse off the camera; but it worked. All I know is you spend as little money as you can and you move as fast as you can – but they didn't get it. All the cast dubbed themselves, except one of the victims. I had to dub Frank Millen, who played Dick, the guy with the van, myself. I've known him all of my life and he's been in nearly all of my films. I thought I could do it, but it went way beyond what he does. He has a real comic delivery, but I think I maybe went too far!"

With so many practical and monetary pressures squeezing down on the production, there was no way Bryan was going to let a handful of pernickety actors destabilize him: "My attitude is to finish. The harder they pushed the harder *I* pushed, and ultimately it was okay. It was only like seven days total for the four of them, but for the last few days everybody accepted it. I think they were just glad it was over!"

Garth Eliassen on *Don't Go in the Woods*

I contacted Garth Eliassen, the writer of *Don't Go in the Woods*, in 2003. No longer active in the industry, he is an amiable man with a great deal of warmth towards his progeny. He knows that his script could well have been the one to reach genre heaven: after all, it preceded *Friday the 13th* and anticipates its setting. Slasher stories set in the woods milled around in the late 1970s like spermatozoa vying to fertilize the commercial egg. Sean Cunningham was the lucky donor, but he made it to the finish line by the mere swish of a protozoic tail, metaphorically speaking.

Eliassen describes the genesis of *Don't Go in the Woods*, called *Sierra* at its script stage: "It was originally a brutal survival film taking place in the Sierra when some backpackers become lost. I remember as a child, going camping and snuggling in our sleeping bags around the fire late into the night, telling ghost stories and scaring each other; the shadows and darkness in the trees beyond the flickering firelight… We knew that animals were watching but we couldn't see them. Your imagination would run wild with gruesome thoughts, but the morning always came and the fears of the previous night disappeared. *Sierra* told the story of what would happen if those worst fears suddenly

above:
Woodland qualms and desiduous dilemmas…

right, clockwise from top left:
Angie Brown gives it her all, as Joanne dies;
Tom Drury, looking positively heroic;
Peter and Ingrid on their way to a rendezvous with a monster;
The sheriff (Ken Carter) explores the killer's lair, and wishes he hadn't…

opposite:
Trapper Jim!

below:
A film crew shooting a horror movie in the mountains mysteriously disappeared, leaving only a slate, a script, and a case full of film. And if you believe that you'll love **The Blair Witch Project**…

became a reality. (*Jaws* did the same thing with the ocean). It was a good script, and the first of its kind. *Friday the 13th* and all the others would come later."

Eliassen appears in the film as a cop, although he is modest about his acting: "I'm available as a sleeping extra (my specialty) in any motion picture! I first met Jim Bryan when he was making *Boogie Vision* and my wife and I had a scene emerging from a car and looking at a piece of property – but that was pretty complicated. During the filming of *Woods* he coerced me into playing a sheriff's deputy in the background. That was complicated, too. He first wanted me to be a victim, but I refused because I didn't want to get killed in my own movie. A friend of ours, Eric Jenkins, who helped the production by repacking the film canisters (a busy job because we were shooting with shot tail ends), got poked by the spear instead. The Jim Bryan roles are the most active I've ever had. Now I refuse to play difficult parts, and will certainly never speak in a movie. I work cheap – SAG minimums – in my sleeping roles." he laughs: "I'm usually paid in cash."

Eliassen remembers his first meeting with Bryan: "Jim read *Sierra* and decided to buy it. Lenore and I drove to Salt Lake City to meet the Bryans and get more information. I wanted to make any rewrites or changes to the script that Jim wanted. The main thing he wanted was more murders. I need to have things spelled out, so I wanted to know how many. Bryan was reluctant to commit to an exact number. I kept pressing. Finally, out of frustration I guess, he said something like 'Fourteen!' So I went back to Sonoma and added a bunch of murders. I don't think I added as many as he wanted. I was also under the impression that he had a fairly high budget, so I wrote more description than I would have if I'd known it was going to be done with hardly any money (Bryan had a backer pull out at the last minute). At any rate, I did two rewrites. My script was about 110 pages.

When we showed up for filming Jim gave out handwritten scripts, about thirty or forty pages long. Everything was trimmed. It was quite a surprise, but what did I know?"

Eliassen feels that, despite their differences of opinion, Bryan deserves credit for the work he put in: "Jim and Kathie Bryan worked the hardest, probably averaging a couple of hours sleep per night. The rest of us had it pretty easy. Jim and Kathie offered us their house to stay in, but that would have been too crowded for me. I moved into a local motel and most of the out-of-town cast and crew followed. I had to have some quiet time every day. Jim Bryan is a grand master of the low-budget film. He is a bit compulsive, I think, and possibly the process itself is to him more important than the quality of the finished product. But he is a genius, and anyone with $50,000 who wants to make a movie can get it done. He deserves to get the funding and a good script to direct a real film, and I hope he gets it some day. The problem with shooting with tail ends is that you only have a few takes, if that, for each scene, few chances to get it right. So usually it's not right. Also, in a low-budget movie the film and processing is the largest cost, and actors are usually paid very little or not at all. With a real budget, that reverses and the amount of film is not a consideration so the number of takes increase and the quality rises. He did the best he could with the pittance of a budget he had to do it with."

He adds: "We first saw *Don't Go in the Woods* at some strange screening room in a dive in downtown L.A. During the filming I'd had a fight with one of the actors, who had just graduated from some damned method acting school and was way overplaying his lines. I tried to tell him he didn't have to emote so much because the effect of the camera was to bring him in closer than stage acting. I tried to tone down his performance. He thought I didn't know what I was talking about. In the first ten minutes of the screening he leaned over to me and said, 'I'm sorry. You were right.'"

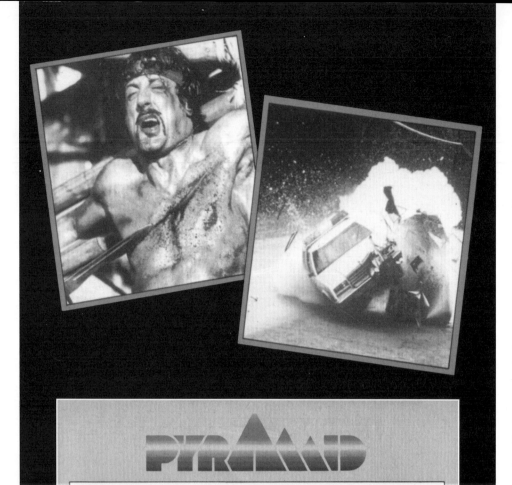

PYRAMID

Be thankful its not
you he's after

THE
EXECUTIONER

By the time *Don't Go in the Woods* wrapped, Renee
Harmon and Frank Roach's L.A. production *Frozen
Scream* was also in the can. Bryan arranged for *Frozen
Scream*'s post-production to take place in Salt Lake City
early in 1981, shooting pickups and cutaways as needed.

Bryan's creative relationship with Renee Harmon, who
passed away in 2006, was one of the most important of his
life. Even today, several failed or underfunded projects
down the line, he remains full of admiration: "Renee was
120% determination. As a producer, she was unstoppable.
As an actress she was above all a trouper and knew no fear.
When Renee came looking for a deal for post-sound for her
$20,000 script, Bruce Scott sent her over to me in
Bungalow A. Renee had persuaded her acting students to
invest their first acting jobs in a production she would star
in as well as produce; then they could all have a film of
themselves. Asked if I believed it was do-able, I said yes,
up to a point, and showed her how to go through shooting
and editing to the first fine cut, ready for viewing by a
distributor. Renee absorbed it all and came out of her first
film hungry for more. She grew with each production and
ultimately published a number of how-to books on
producing your own low-budget movie."[13]

The marketing of *Frozen Scream* led Renee Harmon
to a company called TransWorld (soon to be absorbed by
21st Century Cinema Corp). In 1983 they agreed to fund
two more pictures, the first of these being *The
Executioner Part II* (1983), an unofficial riff on *The
Exterminator* (1980), James Glickenhaus's efficient B-pic
about a vigilante taking on rapists and mafia scumbags in
New York. Harmon called Bryan back to direct it, but *The
Executioner Part II* proved to be a hasty affair, made
under difficult financial conditions, with an inexperienced
crew and a constantly changing script. The resulting mess,
though enjoyable, is probably the closest thing to a *bona
fide* 'bad movie' Bryan has made.

A vigilante known as 'The Executioner' is on the
loose in L.A. His targets? The lowlife rapists and
scumbags of the city. His slogan? *"All the Way!"* This
puts him at odds with both the police and the Syndicate.
News reporter Celia Amherst (Renee Harmon) is investigating the case, as is Detective Roger O'Malley (Chris
Mitchum), who comes to suspect his ex-Vietnam buddy
Mike (Antoine John Mottet). Unbeknownst to O'Malley,
his daughter Laura has a drug habit, which brings her into
contact with Antonio Casales, a gangland boss and sexual
sadist known to the city's hookers as 'The Tattoo Man'.
Casales sends one of his goons to kill Mike, but Mike
overpowers him and forces him to reveal who he's
working for. Casales has Laura abducted for one of his
sex-and-torture sessions, but her friend Kitty witnesses
Laura being bundled into a car by one of Casales's pimps
and passes on the information to Celia. Casales then has
Celia abducted too: who will come to the rescue – Cop or
Executioner?

Amid the rubble of this impoverished production,
there are still a few scenes that stand out. I treasure the
moment when Renee Harmon stabs one on Casales's
henchmen with a samurai sword, pinning him to a couch:
seconds later Mike bursts in, and the victim tries to grab
them with the settee still pinned to his back, looking like
an upholstered snail. The minimalist synth and drums

theme at the climax is a killer, like early Human League meets Dave Brubeck. And there is one scene that enters the pantheon of Top 100 strangest cinema moments, as Laura and her college girlfriend Kitty get stoned on grass and giggle through a swathe of poorly dubbed dialogue (*"I wish this was coke; oh, heavenly coke!"*). Kitty's bizarre, insistent laugh, a bovine hurh-hurh-hurh!!!, is worth the video rental fee all by itself, and for a short while you feel as stoned as the characters.

The Executioner Part II is the most primitive and threadbare of all Bryan's 'real' films: its technical flaws and lack of polish are impossible to ignore. The sound editing is the worst offender; it's obvious that Bryan, a skilled sound-editor himself, had no time to begin a decent assembly: the audio is riddled with frequent bald patches where basic foley and ambient tracks are missing, leaving the dubbed dialogue hovering against the audio equivalent of a blank canvas. It has to be said that Bryan's first three films are probably cheaper on a dollar-for-dollar basis, but they're conceived as dramas, not action-adventure. What sinks *Executioner* is that its reach so badly exceeds its grasp. To aim for spectacle on a budget this low, with Vietnam battle scenes similar to those in any number of Italian war knockoffs, was brave, but doomed to failure. I don't think I'm being mean if I say that the Vietnam scenes lack a certain verisimilitude: the one helicopter on show is a sleek black number that was probably more in demand for ferrying L.A. celebrities to swanky parties than shipping troops into a war zone! What really damages the film, though, more than any deficiencies in budget, is the acting: why is it that low-budget flicks in the 1980s always seem to feature woefully unconvincing street gangs? And why do the guys' supposedly street-hardened girlfriends always look like Cyndi Lauper, or The Bangles? Bryan is lumbered here with a posse of L.A. queens wearing leather jackets rolled up at the sleeves. Danger is not really part of their vibe – they brandish a flick-knife with all the enthusiasm of a gay man helping a woman insert a tampon. Actually, I liked the scene in a convenience store where these naff hoodlums smear the middle-aged proprietors with food before beating them up: everyone is so careful not to smash anything and bankrupt the production that they hardly dare move, their 'violent' gestures as prim and inhibited as a nervous ballet class. The actor playing Casales is fairly menacing, and you can believe he's a danger to women, but the film founders on the rocks of Antoine John Mottet's performance as Mike; his wild grimacing and *Planet of the Apes*-style bodily contortions show, I guess, an admirable commitment to physical acting, but... well, let's just say he could have done with a bit more rehearsal.

Bryan is frank about what went wrong with the production: "*Executioner II* was difficult. That was a situation where Renee got the money, she put the crew together, and then I showed up. Most of the cast and crew were willing, but they had never been involved in theatrical production. The cameraman was a studio cameraman for a TV station; he'd done some work but not much. He could operate the camera but he didn't know about the aspect ratio, or taking a light reading, as he was used to a studio environment where everything was set. So we just started and I said, 'Okay, here's what we're going to do...' So I started taking the equipment out of the trunk and setting it up, saying this is how you

do it, this is how you load the film, this is how you set up the camera, this is how you set up the lights; and they sort of picked it up."

As if nursemaiding a crew of novices wasn't enough, Bryan had to contend with executive producers who wanted their product the day before: "The time ran out. We had to deliver, we couldn't wait. We were handing it over a reel at a time. The people who put up the money, Art Schweitzer and friend, operated a company out of New York called Cinevest, who distributed such items as Brett Piper's *Mutant War*."[14]

Harmon's script was originally called *Crime Fighter*, until Schweitzer's company demanded a change, to tie the film in with *The Exterminator*. "That was a picture that could get booked," Bryan explains, "it was playing in Europe. We had European money and the European distributors wanted certain elements. They'd say, 'You've got to have this, we need more helicopters,' so we would go and shoot more of what they wanted. They would tell Renee, and Renee would tell me. The problem for me with Renee's script was we had no budget, and so I had to work out how to get *anything* on the screen! It was not easy! We needed explosions, and so a tin that once held olive oil was opened top and bottom, coated on the inside with rubber cement, mounted in front of the camera lens, set alight and hair spray was shot into the flames to create a miniature foreground explosion for combat scenes. I was reacting to the experience; I was not 'in charge' in any way. I did what I could – it was like reflex filmmaking. It was written way beyond what we could do. The shoot was two weeks, post-production another two weeks." Bryan drafted some friends from Salt Lake City to work on the movie: "I said, 'We don't have any money, but if you want to start a job in L.A. thinking that you'll get other jobs, this is the one to do, I'll hire you, we'll just bang it out,' and they did. Chris Mitchum really made it work. He was there, he showed up, and I thought, oh great, this is what happens when someone actually knows what they're doing! I didn't expect that, but I was glad to be surprised. I was surprised that it worked at all or that anybody accepted it."

The Executioner Part II
(US theatrical & UK video title)
aka **The Executioner** (UK video title)
aka **Crime Fighter** (original title)
aka **Vengeance Is Mine** (shooting title)
© 1983. [no company] / ©1984. 21st Century Distribution Corporation
director: James Bryan. producer: Renee Harmon. writer: Renee Harmon. cinematographer: James Bryan. filmed in 1981 on location in Hollywood (Los Angeles) by [uncredited] Renee Harmon Productions.
Cast: Chris Mitchum (Lt. Roger O'Malley). Aldo Ray (Police Commissioner Fred Hubnell). Antione [Antoine] John Mottet (Mike). Renee Harmon (Celia Amhurst). Dan Bradley (Big Dan). Frank Albert (Pete Vance). Bianca Phillipi (Laura). Frisco Estes (Antonio Casallas). Ricco Mancini (Danny). Marisi Courtwright (Kitty). Bruce Barrington (Mr. Eastbrook). Debra Martell (Libby). Karen Luce (Diana). Cheryl Harmon (student). Arline Specht (baglady). Dennis Mancini (Miller). Carla Barbour (girl 1). Tania Kim (girl 2). June Mellon (landlady). Al Doro (landlord). Jerry Rattay (storeowner). Donna Esser (his wife). Belle (dancer). Shawn Klugman, Larry Soffer, Andre France, Carl Solomon, Marc Villa, Lynn Wiedemaier, Christine Haramis, Rochelle Kanter (the hoods).
Note: Different versions of the this film are available, one that bears both a 1983 and a 1984 copyright has Bryan's name misspelled as 'Bryant'.

opposite page:
After ten years making horror films, downbeat sex films and far-out satires, Bryan returned to the action template of **Lady Street Fighter** with **The Executioner Part II** (1983), once again starring the incomparable Renee Harmon. The film was released on video in the UK by Pyramid, who were incidentally also responsible for putting out Don Jones's **The Forest** (see page 151).

left:
So pretty, so innocent, so demure... who would suspect that Laura (Bianca Phillipi) craves hard drugs even as she honks away on a joint?

top, back row:
The Hell Riders.
top, front row:
Dianne Miller, James Bryan, Renee Harmon.

above:
Bryan on-set of **Hellriders** (1984).

below:
Bryan and Titus Moody convince a temperamental Chi-Chi (Moody's chihuahua) to go for another take...

The second Renee Harmon project Bryan directed in 1984 was *Hellriders*. This tale of marauding bikers making life miserable for the townsfolk of a dusty desert town is my least favourite of Bryan's films. It's not as technically dishevelled as *Executioner Part II*, but it's nowhere near as much fun either: the story, involving 'Batman' Adam West and one-time *Gilligan's Island* star Tina Louise, is simply tedious, and the relatively minor role for Renee Harmon deprives fans of her unique screen presence. The film has the feel of a Ted V. Mikels production, lacking the extremes of Bryan's best work and conveying nothing but an aimless wandering through uninteresting locations. The 'Hell Riders' themselves lack menace, and besides, the biker movie cycle was already long played out, having overstretched its palette in the late sixties and early seventies.

Desperate to keep the momentum going, Bryan returned to his earlier film with Renee Harmon, *Lady Street Fighter*: "Originally I was supposed to get the film in the can, do a cut so that we could show it to the distributors, and the idea was that the distributor would finish it. But after the years went by and it wasn't going anywhere, I said okay, let's finish it. I spent my money; I tried not to spend any! I had some stock left over from other things. I invented an extra Carradine brother – Trace Carradine – on *Lady Street Fighter*, because sub-distributors didn't want to give bookings without a name and any Carradine brother was a name that would sell tickets. By the way, David Carradine's daughter Calista has an uncredited minor part in *Boogie Vision*."

With 'legitimate' productions drying up, Bryan decided it was time for 'Morris Deal' to put food on the table again: so *Bizarre Encounters* (1986) and *Sex Aliens* (1987) marked an eighties bloom for the director of *High School Fantasies* and *Beach Blanket Bango*. "*Bizarre Encounters* was a video effort to make S&M seem fun," Bryan explains, "The stars, Nick Random and Tantala, wanted

everybody to enjoy something they found very comfortable and natural. No, really, that's what they told me. I took a whack at it." Well, indeed. Fun certainly seems to have been the watchword: having seen a few screen grabs from this production, I was startled to recognize none other than Miss Piggy, lover of Kermit and formidable dominatrix in her own right, embroiled in the action. What madness was this? Bryan explains how he came to work with perhaps the biggest star of his career: "It was shot at an S&M club in Hollywood and the Miss Piggy mask was part of the club's fantasy outfits, most likely because the club's initial location was a rental property picked up by one of Jim Henson's investment companies. When Henson's people found out, they discreetly arranged for the club to move to a new non-Muppet location."

Bryan made two Morris Deal videos for porno kingpins Caballero Home Video: *Swedish Erotica 73* (1986) and *Sex Aliens* (1987). Both were co-directed with Ted Gorley aka Illo Appleby. About his co-director, Bryan notes, "Illo had worked with Ed Wood. I suggested an idea for a musical, 'The Ed Wood Story', with production numbers transforming his low-budget scenes into dream visions of MGM-level quality; but it hit Illo the wrong way. Illo said Ed Wood was a great director and had taught him all he knew about filmmaking." Bryan has little more to add about this shady figure: "I think he's shy of any attention either legal or overly non-legal," he laughs. "The Justice Department once characterized him as 'a general in the army of pornography.'" Bryan/Deal also added to his straight-to-video filmography with *Phone Sex Girls* (1987) – shot and then edited together with another director's work, and given a wraparound by porno specialist John T. Bone, whose name is the only one to turn up on the credits – and *Two on the Rack* (1990), possibly his most difficult to trace porno movie, being another vehicle for SM maestros Nick Random and Mistress Tantala.

The same year saw yet another attempt to make some money from the now elderly *Lady Street Fighter* concept. *Revenge of Lady Street Fighter* (1990), Bryan admits, was, "A rehash of *Lady Street Fighter* with twenty minutes of new scenes bringing in the character of Renee's niece in trouble, so Renee retells the original story. It was a video release and rights were sold to Korea, but the US video company went bankrupt before a cassette was shipped." *Lady Street Fighter*'s long and chequered journey from its inception in 1976 to this final manifestation in 1990 makes it Bryan's most nagging and troublesome production. Many would simply have put it aside and forgotten about it, but as Bryan explains, "Because of my personality I have a need to finish, I haven't always finished every film, but that's the strongest part. I have to finish. Many times, the experience has led me to another point of view, or something else is more important, then I really have to force myself to finish it, because the film is not the same as I originally intended."

Jim Bryan Today

In the nineties, directing work finally dried up. Bryan concentrated on post-production jobs, and touted a number of old film acquisitions (including Peter Semelka's teenage-crewed seventies sci-fi *The Varrow Mission*, and an ultra-obscure slasher – try finding a reference to it anywhere else! – called *Weekend of Terror* by Bobby Davis) at the international film markets. In 1994 he set out to release some of his early work on video. With his old friend Titus Moody, Bryan developed *Titus Moody's Cult Classics*, featuring Titus himself (and Chi-Chi, his pet Chihuahua) introducing films like *The Dirtiest Game in the World*, *Escape to Passion*, and *I Love You I Love You Not*; plus Moody's own debut as director, *Outlaw Motorcycles* (1966), and his follow-up *The Last American Hobo* (1967). "We even talked about doing a Part 2 of *Rat Pfink a Boo Boo*," muses Bryan, "but we didn't get very far along." Moody died of cancer in 2001, and soon after Bryan decided he'd had enough of the film industry: "I followed the dwindling market of low-budget films through video and porno to its bitter conclusion," he says. "I rode that failing horse until it dropped dead, then I dragged it a little further still until the rotting corpse pulled apart in the road!"

Nowadays, Bryan lives in the hills outside L.A., having spent several years building his own house and studio there. He's dubbed it 'Rozannadoo' after his wife Rosanna; with a humorous nod to Charles Foster Kane. Says Bryan, "It's a steel kit designed by computer in 10 ft. increments and delivered in numbered pieces that require no welding, only the correct placement of self tapping screws and a variety of nuts and bolts. We built on property that is directly north of the centre of downtown L.A. and at the boundary of the City limits and the Angeles National Forest. The street level is 2,100 ft. above the beach at Venice and about twenty miles away from our old place at the shore."

For me, this has been a fascinating journey. *Don't Go in the Woods* was once just a name on the list of banned video nasties, and James Bryan an unknown. I now find that I could double the length of this already substantial chapter with ease. Bryan has journeyed through the subterranea of American filmmaking and provided a wonderfully vivid and detailed account of his experiences along the way. Of course, every low-budget director has a story to tell, but few have been so entwined with the industry, and few have such good recall! Life hasn't exactly been easy for Bryan, but he's a man with guts and drive, and an eccentric intelligence that generates the blend of counter-culture and commerce running through his filmography. He has steeped himself in movie-making for nearly forty years, and seen drastic changes sweep through the industry. For him, the immersion is what it's all about, an immersion that brings the director's emotional life into step with a fantasy world.

His films are not high art, and no one, not him, nor me or anyone else, would say they were. For Bryan, that's not the point anyway; to be making a film is the key, to have that magical synchronisation between real life sweat and endeavour, and a dream-world made tangible: "The thing that appealed to me personally," he explains, "without me actually realising it, is emotion. It's a way of dealing with emotions. So making the film or seeing the film, I can be in that emotional world. The strongest element for me is actual production. I go into a state of grace where I know no fear, I have no doubts, and I believe everything is possible. It's that simple. And it doesn't matter what the movie is. I enjoyed turning down those odd offers from Hollywood. I felt free, on top of the world. I didn't need Hollywood. This was before I had even heard of 'burnout'. I don't actually remember when those offers stopped coming, but they're truly a thing of the past. And 'burnout' – what a concept! What a goal! It was all a terrific joke!"

Footnotes

[1] David Wolper, whose company, Wolper Productions, produced many well-known and widely syndicated TV documentaries included the series' *Biography*, *The National Geographic Society Special*, *The Undersea World of Jacques Cousteau*, and *David C. Wolper Presents: Legendary Creatures*, which also enjoyed a successful cinema run in the early '70s. The TV version was known as *Monsters: Myth Or Mystery?* – made for the prestigious 'Smithsonian Series'. One of those interviewed in Wolper's documentary was Bigfoot researcher, and director of the horror film *Blood Stalkers*, Robert W. Morgan, whose obsession with Bigfoot resulted in him directing his own documentary, *In Search of Bigfoot*, (aka *Bigfoot: Man Or Beast?*) in 1976.

[2] Bryan believes that his experience has at least one corollary in the cinema: "I saw *Eraserhead* as a new frontier. I recall dream images from the Jung book *Man and His Symbols* that related to Lynch's own images. Which would prove?... Maybe Lynch is part of the Family of Man; or that aversion was and is an indirect focus of his art."

[3] Bryan is referring here of course to Dr. Timothy Leary.

[4] If this litany seems rather clinical, it's exactly the sort of precision that filmmakers of the time had to exercise to avoid prosecution.

[5] A Hollywood talent agent and ex-big band musician.

[6] Moody once claimed co-directorship of *Dirtiest Game* – Bryan laughs and says, "No, but - he's welcome, if he wants to say that."

[7] on Ducee Coupe Records.

[8] About the same time that Larry Hagman was shooting *Beware! The Blob* there too.

[9] Probably *Invasion from Inner Earth*, 1974.

[10] Examples include *Mussolini: ultimo atto* by Carlo Lizzani, with Rod Steiger and Franco Nero; and *Doppio delitto* by Steno, with Marcello Mastroianni and Ursula Andress.

[11] Dick Robinson won his lawsuit against Sunn Classic in 1982, and started a new production company under the name Ranger Rob.

[12] The L.A. production was Frank Roach and Renne Harmon's *Frozen Scream*, about which more in the section on Renee Harmon.

[13] Renee Harmon's filmmaking books are: *The Actor's Survival Guide for Today's Film Industry* (1984); *The Complete Book of Success: Your Guide to Becoming a Winner* (1984); *Complete Guide to Low-Budget Film Production* (1984); *How to Audition for Movies and TV* (1992); *The Beginning Filmmaker's Guide to Directing* (1992); *The Beginning Filmmaker's Business Guide: Financial, Legal, Marketing, and Distribution Basics of Making Movies* (1994); *Teaching a Young Actor: How to Train Children of All Ages for Success in Movies, TV, and Commercials* (1994); *The Beginning Filmmaker's Guide to a Successful First Film* (1997 - co-written with Jim Lawrence).

[14] Schweitzer is now Vice President of Castle Hill Productions, who handle upmarket titles like the Liv Ullmann-directed Swedish movie *Private Confessions*, written by Ingmar Bergman.

above:
Jim Bryan today.

below:
Bryan at Ranger Rob's editing room, Salt Lake City, Utah, circa 1982, while working for Schick-Sunn Classics.

JAMES BRYAN: FILMOGRAPHY AS DIRECTOR

1967	*Inner Limits* (animated short)
1968	*Camden, Texas* (documentary short)
1969	*Give 'em What They Want* (documentary feature) (also cameraman/editor)
1970	*The Dirtiest Game in the World* aka *Blood, Flesh and Tears* (released 1972)
1970	*Escape to Passion* aka *Hard Orgy*
1973	*I Love You I Love You Not* (released 1974)
1974	*High School Fantasies* aka *The Martians* (as 'Morris Deal' - hardcore)
1974	*Beach Blanket Bango* aka *Beach Party Bango* aka *Teenage Throat* (as 'Morris Deal' - hardcore)
1977	*Boogie Vision* aka *The Young Moviemakers* aka *Girlie* (begun in 1971)
1978	*Lady Street Fighter* (released 1980)
1981	*Don't Go in the Woods*
1983	*The Executioner Part II* aka *Crime Fighter*
1984	*Hellriders* aka *Hell Riders*
1985	*Run, Coyote, Run* (re-edit of *Lady Street Fighter*)
1986	*Jungle Trap* (unreleased)
1986	*Bizarre Encounters* (as 'Morris Deal' - hardcore)
1986	*Swedish Erotica 73* (as 'Morris Deal' – co-dir: Ted Gorley [Illo Appleby]) (two segments - hardcore)
1987	*Sex Aliens* (as 'Morris Deal' – co-dir Ted Gorley [Illo Appleby] - hardcore)
1987	*Thanks for the Mammaries* (sic) (as 'M. Deal' – co-dir Ted Gorley [Illo Appleby] - hardcore)
1988	*Phone Sex Girls* (as 'Morris Deal' – hardcore) (teamed with other material, wraparound dir: John T. Bone. 'Morris Deal' uncredited)
1990	*Two on the Rack* (as 'Morris Deal' – hardcore)
1990	*Revenge of Lady Street Fighter*
1994	*The Working Artist* (TV pilot)

OTHER CREDITS

The following list is drawn from James Bryan's own records and features production dates sometimes slightly different to those recorded by other sources. In the case of the Schick-Sunn Classics titles, this is due to the fact that the company shot many projects within a short period, subsequently releasing them more slowly. On occasion Bryan also re-edited films for US re-release – these have been noted where appropriate.

1966	*Operation Bootstrap* (documentary) – dir: unknown (cameraman)
1967	*Religion in Jail* (documentary) – dir: Michael Parks (gaffer / grip)
1968	*National Geographic Special: Reptiles and Amphibians* – dir: Walon Green (special effects cameraman)
1969	*California – The Year of the Commune* aka *The Good Life* – dir: Chris Munger (cameraman)
1969	*Charlie Chanstein Meets the Wild Bunch: Bob and Carol and Ted and Alice* [short] – dir: John Baron (cameraman)
1972	*Psychopath* aka *An Eye for an Eye* – dir: Larry G. Brown (sound editor)
1973	*Four Stones for Kanemitsu* (short) – dir: Terry Sanders (production assistant)
1973	*Lemora: A Child's Tale of the Supernatural* – dir: Richard Blackburn (cameraman for pickup shots)
1975	*The Giant Spider Invasion* – dir: Bill Rebane (sound effects editor)
1975	*Vigilante Force* – dir: Gene Corman (2nd unit production manager / cameraman for pickups)
1975	*Black Lolita* – dir: Stephen Gibson (sound effects editor)
1975	*Surfer Girls* – dir: Boots McCoy (supervising sund editor)
1975	*Goodbye Norma Jean* – dir: Larry Buchanan (sound effects editor)
1975	*Two Boys Who Stole the Moon* – dir: Jan Batory (recut sound on international version of *O Dwóch Takich, Co Ukradli Ksiezyc*)
1975	*Meatcleaver Massacre: Demon of Death* aka *Hollywood Meat Cleaver Massacre* aka *Evil Force* – dir: Evan Lee (re-edit, adding Christopher Lee)
1976	*The Child* – dir: Robert Voskanian (sound effects)
1977-8	*Double Murder* – dir: Steno (editor) (re-edited international release of *Doppio delitto*)
1977-8	*The Treasure of Jamaica Reef* – dir: Virginia Stone (editor) (re-edited version of the 1976 film *Evil in the Deep*)
1977-8	*The Last Four Days* – dir: Carlo Lizzani (editor) (re-edited version of the 1974 film *Mussolini: ultimo atto*)

1977-8	*Muddy Mama* – dir: Bob Favorite (editor) (re-edited version of the 1969 film *Riverboat Mama*)
1977-8	*Abar, the First Black Superman* – dir: Frank Packard (re-editing and sound effects)
1978	*The Life and Times of Grizzly Adams* (TV series) – dir: various (sound effects)
1978	*The Lincoln Conspiracy* – dir: James L. Conway (sound effects)
1978	*Last of the Mohicans* (TV) – dir: James L. Conway (sound effects)
1978	*Beyond Death's Door* – dir: Henning Schellerup (supervising sound editor)
1978	*The Deerslayer* (TV) – dir: Richard Friedenberg (sound effects/post-production supervisor [uncredited])
1978	*The Bermuda Triangle* – dir: Richard Friedenberg (sound effects)
1978	*The Adventures of Nellie Bly* (TV) – dir: Henning Schellerup (sound effects)
1979	*Encounter with Disaster* – dir: Charles E. Sellier Jr. (post-production supervisor)
1979	*Gulliver's Travels* (TV) – dir: Peter R. Hunt (post-production supervisor)
1979	*Fall of the House of Usher* (TV) – dir: James L. Conway (post-production supervisor)
1979	*Hangar 18* – dir: James L. Conway (post-production supervisor)
1979	*Donner Pass: The Road to Survival* – dir: James L. Conway (TV) (post-production supervisor)
1979	*In Search of Historic Jesus* – dir: Henning Schellerup (post-production supervisor)
1979	*The Time Machine* (TV) – dir: Henning Schellerup (post-production supervisor)
1979	*Greatest Heroes of the Bible* (TV) – dir: James L. Conway (post-production supervisor)
1979	*Adventures of Huckleberry Finn* (TV) – dir: Jack B. Hively (post-production supervisor)
1979	*Legend of Sleepy Hollow* (TV) – dir: Henning Schellerup (post-production supervisor)
1979	*She Came to the Valley* – dir: Albert Band (sound effects)
1979	*The Varrow Mission* – dir: Peter Semelka (sound effects advisor)
1981	*Frozen Scream* – dir: Frank Roach & [uncredited] Renee Harmon (second unit photography, post-production assistance)
1981	*Earthbound* (TV) – dir: James L. Conway (sound effects supervisor)
1981	*Wolfen* – dir: Michael Wadleigh (sound editor)
1982	*The Rogue and the Grizzly* – dir: unknown (post-production supervisor)
1982	*Grizzly Mountain* – dir: Richard Robinson (screenwriter/post-prod supervisor/editor/2nd Unit Cameraman on re-edited version of)
1982	*There'll Never Be a Reason* – dir: unknown (screenwriter/post-production supervisor/editor/2nd Unit Cameraman)
1985	*Swedish Erotica 69* – dir: unknown (sound editor)
1985	*Erotic Zones Vol.1* – dir: Paul Vatelli (sound editor)
1987	*Tennessee Stallion* – dir: Don Hulette (editor on re-cut of 1982 film, pickup cameraman)
1987	*Blood Vows: The Story of a Mafia Wife* – dir: Paul Wendkos (sound effects editor)
1987	*Police Academy 4: Citizens On Patrol* – dir: Jim Drake (sound effects editor)
1987	Six Pilots and Movies of the Week (including *Thirtysomething*) (sound effects editor)
1987	*Saigon (Off Limits)* – dir: Christopher Crowe (sound effects editor)
1988	*Salsa* – dir: Boaz Davidson (sound effects editor)
1988	*Hanna's War* – dir: Menahem Golan (sound effects editor)
1988	*Street Justice* – dir: Richard C. Sarafian (dialogue editor)
1988	*Haunted Summer* – dir: Ivan Passer (sound effects editor)
1988	*Mortuary Academy* – dir: Michael Schroeder (dialogue editor)
1988	*Braddock: Missing In Action III* – dir: Aaron Norris (sound effects editor)
1988	*Nightmare on Elm Street 4: The Dream Master* – dir: Renny Harlin (sound effects editor)
1989	*Return of Swamp Thing* – dir: Jim Wynorski (sound effects editor)
1989	*The Absent Minded Professor* (TV) – dir: Robert Scheerer (sound effects editor)
1989	*Underworld* – dir: unknown (sound effects editor)
1989	*Chopper Chicks in Zombietown* – dir: Dan Hoskins (sound re-recording mixer)
1990	*Caged in Paradiso* – dir: Mike Snyder (foley walker)
1990	*Julia Has Two Lovers* – dir: Bashar Shbib (post-production supervisor)
1991	*Weekend of Terror* – dir: unknown (post-production supervisor/writer of additional material/pickup cameraman)
1992	*Lakota Moon* (TV) – dir: Christopher Cain (sound effects editor)
1992	*My Cousin Vinny* – dir: Jonathan Lynn (sound effects editor)
1993	*The Dark Half* – dir: George Romero (sound effects editor)
1994	*A Worn Path* (educational short) – dir: Bruce Schwartz (sound designer)

The Frozen Scream Is a Clean Machine

An Interview with Renee Harmon

with thanks to Cheryl Harmon, and contributions from James Bryan & Art Piatt

Frozen Scream (1981)

"The lower temperature is the key: the chill factor."

Dr. Tom Girard (Wolf Muser) is working late at his surgery when a mysterious telephone caller warns him to expect a visit from 'the angels'. When he answers a knock at the door, two cowled figures overpower him and inject him with something nasty. His wife Ann (Lynne Kocol) sees the escaping figures and passes out… Ann regains consciousness in hospital to find sinister Doctor Lil Stanhope (Renee Harmon) informing her that Tom died of a heart-attack: she must have hallucinated the attackers. Ann protests, but allows herself to be overruled. *Dream sequence:* Ann sees Tom turn into a skeleton cowled in black. *Flashback:* The beach, on Halloween night. Doctors and students are gathered around a bonfire. Tom is deep in conversation with Doctor Johnson (Lee James) and a priest, Father O'Brian (Wayne Liebman). Doctor Johnson is impatient with Tom's existential angst: *"Listen Tom - I'm not going to let your little guilt trip spoil this project." "I'm not going to guilt. I'm going to hell!"* Tom replies. *Cutaway within the flashback:* A cowled figure smashes an axe into a young woman's face. *Return to flashback:* Father O'Brian tells the students that All Saints Eve was once a ceremony of resurrection, and the circle of fire they've built represents the sun. *"Love and Immortality,"* chant the students, linking hands around the fire. *"Call out now beyond the moon,"* Dr. Johnson implores. *"It's all a bit pagan, isn't it?"* Tom says to Father O'Brian. Cathrin (Sunny Bartholomew) advances towards Ann in slow motion. *Flashback ends.* Back at her house, Ann hallucinates Cathrin – or is it Tom? Speaking to Doctor Johnson at his laboratory, Doctor Stanhope says that their research is against nature. *A vision or remembered dream:* We're somewhere inside Doctor Stanhope's mind – she is lit against total darkness, a candle by her side. *"Immortality."* She cuts her wrists, blood flows, and she gnaws at the wound, smearing her face with it. *"Immortality."* Doctor Johnson assures her they are close to achieving their goal.

Vision/dream memory ends. *"Ann, I'm home; help me I'm so cold,"* Tom says, making a phone call from beyond the grave – or the refrigerator. A cowled figure attacks Ann and tells her to keep her suspicions to herself or else she'll have to join Tom in his hell, which is *"very cold"*. Ann finds three nude figures, including Tom, standing motionless in her walk-in fridge. Tom wakes up and grabs her. Ann screams and runs away. The frozen humanoids give chase. Private detective Kevin McGuire (Thomas Gowen) – don't ask – overpowers one of them by gouging its eyes until blood squirts from its neck. Ann hides in a white building (the hospital?) pursued by Kirk. The nightwatchman finds her, but he's killed by a shard of glass to the eye. Dr. Stanhope rescues Ann, and tells her, *"Immortals live in the cool of the clouds. But you are burning"*…

below:
Ann (Lynne Kocol) finds her supposedly dead husband stored in a walk-in refrigerator, in **Frozen Scream**.

Frozen Scream
© none [1981]
A Clara production.

director: Frank Roach. producer [and
uncredited co-director]: Renee Harmon.
screenplay: Doug Ferrin, Michael Soney &
Celeste Hammond. story: Renee Harmon &
Doug Ferrin. director of photography: Roberto
Quazada. music: H. Kingsley Thurber III.
editor: Matthew Muller. second unit camera:
Mark Israel. 1st assistant cameraman: Linda
C. Farmdale. gaffer: Lawrence L. Simeone.
electrician: Joseph Gluzinski. best boy:
Michael Zancanella. grips: Tom Witt, Tony
Silver, Gary Ries, Dale Almond. soundman:
Selwyn R. Sirot. post production supervisor:
Matthew Muller. sound effect editor: Dale
Angell. re-recording mixer: Tom Ruff. negative
cutter: Tom Ruff. stunt coordinator: Ben Perry.
choreographer: Chris Hammond. script
supervisor: Sue Hawes. key make-up artist:
Karen Calvert Luce. special effects make-up:
William A. Luce. art directors: Don Rohrbacher,
Bill Luce, Art Piatt. still photography: Art Piatt.
casting & assistant to the producer: Terri
Argula. production interns: Michael Tolin,
Heather E. Paul, William Reid Goodman.
colour by Pacific Film Lab, Inc. sound by
Sound Cinema Services. 2nd unit photography
& post-production assistance [uncredited]:
James Bryan.
Cast: Renee Harmon (Dr. Lil B. Stanhope).
Lynne Kocol (Ann Girard). Wolf Muser (Tom
Girard). Thomas Gowen (Kevin McGuire).
Wayne Liebman (Father O'Brian). Lee James
(Sven Johnson). Sunny Bartholomew (Cathrin).
Bill Oliver (Bob Russel). Bob Rochelle (Kirk
Richard). Terri Argula (nurse). Art Platt
(nightwatchman). Cheryl Harmon, Julie Ann
Meisels, Jennifer Flamen (trick o'treat children).
Chris Hammond, Sandie Gelbard (principal
dancers). Bill Luce (man in car). Cheryl Crandal
(girl in pool). Chris Russell (girl in house). Paul
Yamanian (killer). Ben Moase, Andy Nachtigall,
Stephan Fusci (men at party). Gary Pearl
(young man in pool). uncredited: Frank Roach
(drunk in alleyway).

below:
Dr. Lil Stanhope (Renee Harmon) explains
all to the captured Ann. Well, when I say
explain...

There's something deeply off-beam about *Frozen Scream*. It has a lurching, spasmodic quality, an arrhythmia induced by the bizarre music and the crashingly intrusive editing. An electric piano, the sort you might use to perform *Send in the Clowns* at a seaside nightspot, adds a queasy amateur feeling; crude tape loops and electronic whirring underscore conversations, along with the occasional dash of slasher-movie synth. (See James Bryan and *Don't Go in the Woods*.) Somehow though, it works. Dull normality never stands a chance; the mood sways unsteadily between occult cliché, sci-fi weirdness and juddering dislocation, with frequent cutaways to dreams or past events constantly fragmenting the action. When people talk about films being indigestible it's rarely as appropriate as here – the mind feels like it's trying to swallow something that it can't get down (believe me, mixed metaphors are wholly appropriate). The prologue appears to have been designed purely to get the film off to a violent start, and involves a couple swimming in a private pool who barely have time to clock in as 'lovers' before they're murdered. Two black-cloaked killers grimace comically as they strangle and slice their victims: is the film going to be a cheesy send-up?

No, not a send-up; nothing so easily definable. Full of stylistic flourishes that place it somewhere beyond the films of Doris Wishman, *Frozen Scream* achieves a rather deranged quality. I wish there were three more just like it from the same director; I'd happily watch them all. Tonight.

Given that the theme of the film is the freezing of humans to achieve – you got it – immortality, at the price of a certain human energy or soul, it's ironic that the acting of even the non-immortals is rife with flat enunciation, 'elsewhere' mannerisms and awkward acting tics. Their jarring performances make even the most mundane exchanges feel drugged, dislodged from reality. In a story full of zombified robotic people, Sunny Bartholomew as 'Cathrin' is perhaps the most memorable. She projects something quite convincingly alienated. *"Have you ever noticed how cold Cathrin is? She's like walking ice!"* someone says. I love her; she resembles a small-town beauty queen with a Quaalude problem, a chilly, factory-damaged glamour-puss obsessed with her own haughtiness.

Cathrin collapses during a rock'n'roll dance, after trying to strangle her partner. *"Bring some ice"*, says Doc Stanhope. The late Renee Harmon, who plays Stanhope, would be perfectly at home in Andy Warhol's *Flesh for Frankenstein*, and deserves her own cult following: with her every utterance she embodies the ineffable strangeness of the film. Much of what is extraordinary about *Frozen Scream* emanates from Ms. Harmon, whose uniqueness and mystery resist analysis. She was an actress-producer (a rare enough thing), and according to her she was the true director of this film. I'm not sure what to make of that claim, having failed to trace the credited director Frank Roach, but one thing's for certain: she must have been a formidable ally. If I owned Grauman's Chinese Theater, her handprints would be right there: between Bette Davis and Darth Vader.

In keeping with the frozen-fingered artiness of the film, the dialogue fumbles for significance: *"Your dreams are full of mental symbols,"* Dr. Stanhope informs Ann. *"I don't want to talk about the mysteries of the mind,"* she retorts. Elsewhere, Stanhope helpfully draws her own character profile when she observes to Dr. Johnson: *"Sometimes I really don't know what I see in you, Sven. Maybe you appeal to some sense of danger and adventure in me."* As for Johnson, I'm still not entirely sure what his process really does. It involves drugs, but there's also a technological angle: the homicidal immortals bear metallic devices in their necks, so there must be radio mind-control going on. Dr. Stanhope suggests that the immortals are murdering people because Johnson has broken down their taboos by force, so no wonder they now kill independently. To make matters even harder to fathom, Ann really does seem to be hallucinating, even though we know Dr. Stanhope was lying when she made her diagnosis. This, added to the intermittent dream imagery, makes the film's perceptual centre difficult to ascertain. While none of the mind-control, chemical, cryogenic, or techno elements really come together into a coherent whole, the proliferation of these sci-fi-horror cyphers gives the film a gleefully garbled quality which aids its passage from the mundane to the insane. (It's like Ted V. Mikels's *The Astro-Zombies* made by a true creative lunatic.) The film also feels cut loose in time: the sci-fi trappings are imported from the fifties and sixties, but the slasher murder elements and stylistic distortions are defiantly seventies.

The dialogue is as haphazardly post-synced as any Italian gorefest, so if you care too much for realism you'll never be able to enjoy it. However, bad dubbing ceases to be a problem if you just give up and go with it. Try looking at people's eyes instead of their lips. Once you've adjusted you may even find that dubbing *adds* something to the experience. And at least everyone is speaking English onscreen. Heavily accented English, but English all the same...

Frozen Scream is so violently disorganised that the actual screen violence is secondary. Mind you, if that sounds like baloney to you, rest assured there's still enough bloodshed to soothe a gore-junkie's fevered brow. For reasons that remain narratively and symbolically obscure, Dr. Stanhope chooses to inject the interfering detective McGuire in the eyeball at the end of the film, but while it seems a little unnecessary, if the aim is to turn him into an immortal ice zombie, it does at least mean that the film

above and left:
Frozen Scream's axe-attack scene was constructed by special effects designer William Luce. Art Piatt, the film's art designer with Luce, provided these pictures showing the effect *in situ*, and how it was done.

below:
The shadowy figure of **Frozen Scream**'s credited director Frank Roach, as seen here in a production photograph taken on location for **Nomad Riders**, his only other known film. (It was made without the involvement of Renee Harmon in 1981, the same year as **Frozen Scream**). Inset is the US video release of **Nomad Riders**, from Vestron.

adds ocular trauma to its list of achievements. Gore, however, is not where the action is; if you measure this film by the usual standards, it won't give up its pleasures. Mere 'competence' makes for such boring films – and *Frozen Scream* is never ever boring. This fascinating piece of celluloid madness will have historians of future civilisations totally flummoxed as they try to understand the culture that made it. The line between haste and style has been blurred, leading to a general disconnectedness. There *are* some well-conceived moments, in which the director has clearly thought about how to make a scene unsettling, but they tend to be swallowed up by the inadvertent weirdness surrounding them. What finally emerges is a film of insane ambition mixed with technical primitivism: it exists in a ravine between intention and accident, with enough creepy synchronicity between theme and realisation to make you wonder whether Frank Roach and Renee Harmon knew exactly what they were doing all along. Chilling!

Establishing the provenance of this extraordinary piece of celluloid has proven a fraught endeavour. Art Piatt, the film's art designer, says it was shot on 16mm in no more than twenty-eight days for approximately $35,000. According to Piatt, Frank Roach was actually co-director: he directed on the set, but Renee Harmon edited and thus finished the film. Roach was apparently not consulted during the editing, leading to a fall-out between the two. Piatt recalls, "*Frozen Scream* was made for the European market, around 1980 or '81, I think. *Frozen Scream* and *Nomad Riders* [Roach's only other film, made without Harmon] were made pretty close together. Frank Roach was a little disturbed not to be there when they were editing the film. Renee didn't want to spend a lot of money because she didn't *have* a lot of money, so she had it edited out of town somewhere, and I think she paid about $700." Piatt met Harmon through one of her college classes: "Renee was teaching a course on how to get into television commercials, and that's where she found me, and the people she put into the movie. Sunny Bartholomew I think paid to get into the movie, to get a credit. Renee was a pretty shrewd businessperson! I was making $25 a day as

art director. Sometimes we would just go to sleep on the set and in the morning if you had a job to do they would wake you up and you'd do it. It was fun, and exciting and tiring. You wore a lot of hats, because it was non-union." His memories of Roach are few, but he does recall that he was a fairly 'hands-off' director: "The guy who played the detective was complaining to me that Frank wasn't giving him any direction, and I said, 'Well, how lucky you are! You can do anything you want!'"

Regretfully, I have been unable to trace Frank Roach – and boy have I tried. But at least now, thanks to Art Piatt who supplied the information, we know what he looks like: he plays the drunk seen in an alleyway, and is pictured in the photograph below. Maybe one day he'll emerge for a DVD commentary, but until then, here's Renee …

The Incomparable Renee Harmon

Author's Note: I was deeply saddened when James Bryan contacted me, early in 2007, to say that Renee Harmon had died of heart failure at her home in Visalia, California on 26 November, 2006. I've decided not to change the tense of the following material – Renee never really received her due, so I prefer to present this, her first published interview, as it was originally written....

Renee Harmon is unique. You can tell this from *Frozen Scream* and *Lady Street Fighter*, and her extraordinary production *The Executioner Part II*. In a light-hearted mood you might call her 'a character', but you really wouldn't want to patronise her: even when she smiles or laughs in her movies, she can flash a look that would peel a rattlesnake. Her German accent is another testament to her strength; she's lived in California since the late sixties, but when I spoke to her on the telephone recently, I heard not a single concession to L.A. cadences. Her English is fine, but there's no transatlantic twang, and definitely no valley-speak!

Harmon is not widely celebrated, in fact many who know about her cinema regard it as cheap and shoddy. They see the obvious limitations but miss the real pleasures. Those with a squeamish dislike for rough edges will never appreciate the strange energy and determination of her filmmaking. Harmon has worked on numerous projects with James Bryan, another filmmaker hardly over-blessed with funding. What united them in the seventies and eighties was their resolve: in the teeth of possible failure, in the absence of money or critical

top right:
A snapshot of Renee taken by Jim Bryan in the 1970s, possibly around the time of **Lady Street Fighter**.

below:
Radio-controlled zombie technology in **Frozen Scream**.

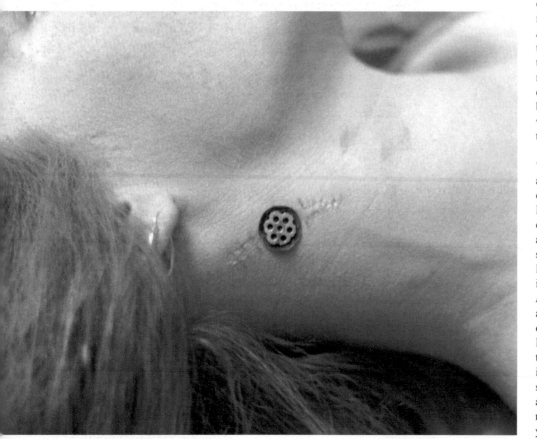

admiration, they strove long and hard to keep on working. If you banish the received wisdom of how films should look and sound, both Bryan and Harmon offer aesthetic sensations outside of the familiar; and in a climate where culture is currently being rendered into a glue of retroactive consensus, we really ought to cherish those who cannot be so easily absorbed.

It's always rather gruesome when critics try to force art motivations onto exploitation films, but there's an interesting overlap between the practises of low-budget commercial cinema and the avant-garde. One of the reasons that films like *Lady Street Fighter* or *Frozen Scream* feel so alien and unique is the haste with which they're shot: with an attitude that says, 'Who cares if the take was fluffed, if there's no more cash it goes in the movie!' The limitation becomes a distinction when you change the artistic context; hasty decision-making becomes spontaneity (a venerable aesthetic ideal) and what seems slapdash equates to bloody-mindedness (a trait we love in our 'crazy' artists).

Speaking as someone who's watched a lot of allegedly 'bad' movies, I know what matters to me: I want to enter another world, to visit somewhere new, and I don't really care how 'intentional' or 'involuntary' it is. Bryan and Harmon produce real surprises, leaving you incredulous, out of step with reality. The rulebook has been flung out, and it matters not to me if this was part of a creative strategy or a last-minute dash to get the scene in the can. I adore the attitude that says a film *must* be made, whether it transgresses normal standards of quality or not. (*The Executioner Part II* is especially far out in this respect, and Harmon, though onscreen too infrequently in my opinion, was a major contributor both onscreen and off.) It's probably only by ignoring the possibility of failure that Renee Harmon was able to complete her projects, so it's not surprising that she has little time for criticism or suggestions of variable quality. Enquiries along such lines are curtly shot down. She's an unswerving individual with no taste for compromise and if you don't like her work you know what you can do!

A Chat with Renee Harmon

Renee Harmon was born in Mannheim, Germany, in 1927. Her first ambition and creative passion was to dance. As a child, she was a fan of Shirley Temple, but nothing she saw in the movies, as a child at least, made her dream of the film industry. I asked her if she felt that she had stumbled into film by accident:

"Well, in a way, I did. I was a dancer with the Mannheim Ballet, I was in dancing classes since I was four years old, and then when I came to the US I danced for colleges and universities – mostly religious universities, because my outfits were very clean, and my dancing was very clean. What I don't like in dancing right now is that, to me, it is kind of dirty."

Ms. Harmon has an air of authority which stems from her family background: "My father was in the army. And the Army was a wonderful place to live. My father hated Hitler, so he was killed at the end of the War by one of his officers. Because he said, 'Well well well! We got rid of Hitler! Let's put up the white flags!' He was shot in the head. An American General helped my mother, and he came to the funeral. My grandmother was Jewish. My parents ran a store, which was completely destroyed during the War. My mother survived and came with us to America."

Harmon married an American serviceman in Germany on 13 August, 1955, and moved to the USA in 1957. (Their first child, a boy, was born on 17 July, 1957 in Augusta Georgia. Renee's daughter and companion Cheryl was born some time later, on 19 July, 1968, on an American Army base in Wiesbaden Germany.) "We arrived in New York and from there we went to Minnesota. My husband was in the army and he was transferred every so often, and we went all over the United States. I liked the army officers' wives, and I had a good time with them. We ended up in Woodland Hills Los Angeles in 1969, a very nice suburb, nice people. I was accepted into the Country Club. It was a nice place." As for California 1969, with all its changing morality: "There were no hippies in the suburbs. The hippies were downtown but we never went downtown."

In the mid-seventies, having settled in California, Harmon took a post at Moorpark College, Los Angeles, as an acting teacher. There she met James Bryan, who was teaching camera skills. During 1976, the two worked together on a project called *Lady Street Fighter*, which was eventually released in 1978 (see previous chapter on James Bryan). In 1980, Renee launched production of *Frozen Scream*, employing her Moorpark College students: "*Frozen Scream* was made in a haunted house. We didn't know it was a haunted house, we were told it was later. The lights would go off and on, and my people were shouting, 'Come on ghosts, let's get the lights back on!' It went all over the United States; not big theatres, small theatres. It was very clean; all my movies are clean."

Harmon's memory is a little vague; she doesn't remember Doug Ferrin or Celeste Hammond, who receive onscreen credit for writing the film, but she's sure they had no hand in the script: "I thought if I wrote and directed and produced and starred, it would be too much, so I gave the credits away. Frank Roach was a cameraman but I decided it would be better to have another director on the film. I didn't want to be credited as director, for business reasons. I directed the film."

Having failed to track down Frank Roach for his comments, it's hard for me to know how to respond to this assertion, although it is worth bearing in mind that Renee Harmon is not in the best of health. She is far clearer when quizzed about her own directorial style: "I find it easy to direct others. Because when I look at people I sit in the background and write things down, and then my director talks to them. I am not a very nice person when I am filming, okay? Very mean, yes? And demanding." Bearing in mind James Bryan's account of the making of *The Executioner Part II*, which she starred in and produced (see chapter on Bryan), I asked Ms. Harmon if she ever had to compromise when making her films on such very low budgets: "No, no, no. No one could interfere with me. The script was filmed as I wrote it. I had no interference." She is also very adamant that I stress one vitally important thing about her work: "All my films are clean. I don't have anything dirty in my films."

Ms. Harmon exited the film industry in the mid-eighties and took up writing: so was the industry changing? "Yes. It was not as clean as I wished it to be." Since then she has published a book of mystery stories called *The Three Red Satchels* some time around the late 1980s. A book adaptation of *Frozen Scream* exists, penned by Ms. Harmon herself, called *Evil Covenant* (a must for any fan of the film, if you can find it), and she has also written a book called *Hollywood Mysteries: The Hunting Party / Let the Dice Roll* (published 2000), about a female detective. Although she is incapacitated somewhat these days, she is animated and emphatic in conversation, she

below:
Renee Harmon at the height of her glamour in the early 1970s.

above:
Art Piatt, the art designer on **Frozen Scream** and **Nomad Riders**.

right:
Piatt made this giant sculpture for Tim Burton's **Batman Returns** (1992) – for a sense of the scale, Piatt can be seen at the base, in the white T-shirt.

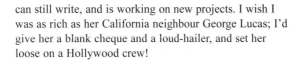

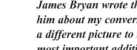

below:
You want obscure? How about this photograph of Renee Harmon and Bill Whittmeyer, taken from Bryan's video copy of **Run, Coyote, Run**; the unreleased 1985 re-edit of **Lady Street Fighter**!

can still write, and is working on new projects. I wish I was as rich as her California neighbour George Lucas; I'd give her a blank cheque and a loud-hailer, and set her loose on a Hollywood crew!

James Bryan wrote the following passage after I spoke to him about my conversation with Renee Harmon. He paints a different picture to the one that emerges above. This is a most important additional commentary. Ms. Harmon was in no way feeble when we spoke, and she directed our conversation adamantly, but she was quite ill, and obviously confused at times, especially when it came to names, dates, and the professional status of her one-time collaborators in film. Jim's recollections are of Renee in her prime, and provide an essential balance for our perception of her character.

"As producer, Renee kept a very effective tight control over her productions, planning and arranging for locations and cast. During actual production she was fully involved with her part as actress and with other cast members, who were usually her students. Renee spent a lot of time working with the cast, going over and over their performances in the days prior to actual production, so in that sense she was directing, and had shaped the actors and their work down to the smallest degree. When we were in production and on the set Renee never stopped as producer and worked behind the scenes to keep things on track, yet she didn't have much to say about the director's job other than to support his authority and to demand the same support from everyone else. When others came to her with questions outside the work done previously in her directing sessions, she would direct these people to consult with the director for the answers to their questions. Renee never was one to usurp the director's authority and never allowed anyone on the set to do it either. She was always working to support me and I worked to support her. I believe Renee would have worked the same way with any of her directors. She expected

everybody to do their job and she backed everyone on the production wholeheartedly. Renee used a lot of first-time people so there were always unprofessional types who had to learn the ropes, and they might start out finding fault with me or Renee; ultimately, due to Renee's ironclad demeanour on the set, those who began with ridicule would develop a respect and genuine affection for her. Perhaps now, with Renee in a weakened physical state, those old comments that used to bounce off a very tough hide have started to sting, or maybe the way the world sees our old efforts now seem less than kind to her. If Renee feels the need to reconsider the credits on her body of work then I'll go along with whatever she sees as correct in the light of a career to be proud of. The Renee I've known over the years gave everyone their credit and was generous in her praise. In my hearing she never once detracted from any of her directors' contributions, nor brought their credits into question."

RENEE HARMON:
FILMOGRAPHY AS PRODUCER AND ACTRESS

1978	*Lady Street Fighter* (released 1980) (dir: James Bryan)
1981	*Frozen Scream* (also co-director, with Frank Roach)
1984	*The Executioner Part II* (dir: James Bryan)
1984	*Hellriders* aka *Hell Riders* (dir: James Bryan)
1985	*Run, Coyote, Run* (re-edit of *Lady Street Fighter*) (dir: James Bryan)
1986	*Jungle Trap* (unreleased) (dir: James Bryan)
1990	*Revenge of Lady Street Fighter* (dir: James Bryan)

AS ACTRESS ONLY

1977	*Cinderella 2000* (dir: Al Adamson)
1979	*Van Nuys Blvd.* (dir: William Sachs)
1986	*Night of Terror* aka *Escape from the Insane Asylum* (dir: Felix Girard)

chapter 2

The Fiend from Prime-Time

John Peyser on The Centerfold Girls

The Centerfold Girls (1974)

Perhaps the strangest of the seventies proto-slasher films, *The Centerfold Girls* – in which pretty girls who pose for the same softcore calendar are stalked and killed by a puritanical misogynist – certainly rings some changes on the old three-act structure. It's divided into sections, as distinct from each other as the pages of a calendar. Nothing links the three settings except the maniac, who turns up like a bad penny to eradicate the objects of his desire. It's this mechanical, eerily callous structure that distinguishes the film, as it mirrors both the subject of the film (the commercial objectification of women) and the attitude of the killer. The effect is almost to mimic the portmanteau or anthology film, popular at the time thanks to the British company Amicus.

The credits rise over the killer (Andrew Prine) on a moonlit beach, burying a female corpse in a sandy grave. The only sound is the indifferent roar of the waves. Lacking any context or explanation, this opening gambit immediately unnerves us with its lack of emotion. There's no mystery, no suspense, just the flat, unadorned concealment of a corpse to 'get things rolling'. This objectified, affectless vibe recurs throughout and gives the film a special kick that makes it feel like a precursor of William Lustig's *Maniac*. And like *Maniac*, *The Centerfold Girls* rests firmly on a terrific performance by its star. Andrew Prine is creepy and convincing in this, the second of his lunatic roles that year, after *The Barn of the Naked Dead* (see review section). It's a part that was probably less than substantial on the page, but Prine just picks it up and runs with it – he's one of best low-budget stars of the era. I was reminded a little of Anthony Perkins's insane priest in Ken Russell's *Crimes of Passion*, though for my money Prine is scarier. He addresses his victims with a barely suppressed sneer, a superior air of disgust borne of a bitter Puritanism. Prine ought to be a genre celebrity along the same lines as Perkins, or Donald Pleasence: like the former, he has a gaunt, sardonic intensity, and like the latter, he can turn schlock into gold. With decent material like *The Centerfold Girls*, he's unstoppable. Peyser directs with hallucinatory camera angles to amplify the killer's actions, emphasising

his dangerous sense of omnipotence. Utterly convinced of his capabilities, he exudes a cold, shark-eyed simulation of post-sixties freedom: both comical and carnivorous. We see him stepping from a car in his too-short trousers and out-of-date spats, the camera's floor-level wide-angle lens conferring a sort of geekish anti-glamour. He's an unhip psycho in the 'permissive age', out of date but able to pass himself off as just another garish Me-Generation freak. (Bill Landis makes the following sharp observation in his book *Sleazoid Express*: "Andrew Prine plays a psychopath who stalks the monthly pinups that appear in a third-string men's stroke magazine. Curiously, Prine himself was a man of the month in *Viva* magazine at the time, so he brings an extra dimension of reality, zest, and understanding to the role.")

Unusually for a low-budget movie of this (supposedly debased) sort, art design decisions have clearly been made, with the killer's apartment decked out entirely in white: white bed, white wardrobe, white walls, various white accessories, and even a white record deck on which the killer plays an album. (If only it were white vinyl!) In contrast, the black, misogynous fantasies of the killer are immediately apparent: we see him slicing up a girlie calendar, enacting hypocritical violence on the primary symbolic currency allowed to women in patriarchal culture: the photographic image of beauty.

A groovy sixties horn arrangement introduces Jackie Carol (Jaime Lyn Bauer). The music, and Jackie's casual nudity, suggest the counterculture, until we see her arrive at her place of work – a hospital. In nurse's uniform, she immediately embodies a social role that has no truck with 'dropping out'. Kind-hearted Jackie then buys herself a night in hell by taking pity on a hippyish hitch hiker called Linda (Janet Wood), who's apparently been abandoned by her friends. Jackie invites her to spend the night. Only when the girl's friends (Dennis Olivieri, Teda Bracci and Talie Cochrane) invade the house does she realise she's dealing with a spiteful little psycho who'd have been more at home at the Spahn Ranch. (The name 'Linda' was perhaps intended by screenplay writers Arthur Marks and Robert Peete to echo Linda Kasabian, the Manson girl who turned State snitch.) Certainly, these aggressive, home-invading hippies seem freshly plucked from the post-Cielo Drive American psyche.

below:
Jaime Lyn Bauer as Carol, the unfortunate nurse and part-time model who encounters the killer in **The Centerfold Girls**.

Sharon Tate and her friends were arbitrarily killed by such people, even though they weren't the originally intended target: the Manson Family struck with an indiscriminate resentment, something that gave the killings their special horror. Likewise, the first part of *The Centerfold Girls* deals with the fear of being exploited, robbed, bullied and terrorized, just because you happen to fit an arbitrary mug-shot of the *bourgeoisie* carried around in a sociopath's head.

After a night of humiliation, Jackie escapes to a nearby residence, only to fall foul of Ed Walker (Aldo Ray), the frustrated husband of a shrewish wife (Paula Shaw). Instead of trying to help, he treats the distraught woman's partial nudity as an invitation to party. So much has gone wrong for this suffering heroine (the plot's quite Sadean in its mercilessness) that we can only wince when she escapes this new indignity and then wanders into the arms of the killer...

'Page Two' sets off in a much lighter vein. Three pretty centrefold models, Sandi (Kitty Carl), Glori (Ruthy Ross) and Charly (Jennifer Ashley), a young male actor, Sam (John Denos), an ageing modelling agent, Melissa (Francine York), and her photographer husband Perry (Ray Danton) – the latter pair enmeshed in a sort of Albee-lite relationship – head off for a photoshoot at a chic bachelor pad on an attractive but deserted island. From the trendy guitar music and shadowy colour-tinged lighting to the *Ten Little Indians* vibe and the black-clad killer wielding an open razor, this middle segment plays for all the world like a Continental *giallo* of the sort Sergio Martino or Silvio Amadio might have directed. If the sound recording had been blatantly post-synched, the illusion would be complete. And Peyser's taste for swift, artistically imaginative shots of blood splashing from victims' throats (across a plate glass window; into a deep-blue outdoor pool) is worthy of Dario Argento circa 1971. Perhaps because of the stylisation, the mood is much lighter: the body-count is cheerfully high and the whole island escapade is almost a holiday from the grimness that surrounds it.

The third part involves Vera (Tiffany Bolling), a pretty airline hostess, and her friend Patsy (Connie Strickland). Patsy hosts a fabulous shindig that's shot hand-held through a wide-angle lens (like all the best parties). Her friend however takes a raincheck, wondering about the creep who mailed her yellow roses and then followed them up with a phone call saying, *"Beautiful, aren't they. I hope they bury you in yellow."* It's the high-life, alright, but there's a shadow at the feast. Occasional glimpses of the roiling ocean cue a dark foreboding, borne in by the roaring waves. By now we've come to recognise the killer's soundtrack theme – a haunting, slightly precious mock-harpsichord tune: it's like something The Doors might have recorded around the time of *Strange Days*. In fact, as Prine murders Patsy (mistaking her for Vera) he looks uncannily like Ray Manzarek (crossed perhaps with Tom Verlaine). Alerted to the fact that there's a killer working his way through the calendar, Vera ducks out of town, but stupidly leaves her forwarding address with an equally careless friend...

Then we're back on the bad-luck trail, as Vera's car suffers a flat. The sailors (Scott Edmund Lane and Richard Mansfield) who pick her up slip a roofie into her beer, and by nightfall poor Vera is flyin' high. The boys pull in at a motel for a night of drugged debauchery – a scene that recalls Welles's *Touch of Evil*. When Vera emerges from her night of ravishment, Prine is there to greet her – posing as a concerned square called 'Clement Dunne' who thought he heard a commotion from the room next door. When he offers the shell-shocked girl a lift back to town, she's so disorientated by her experience that she mistakes this horn-rimmed Humphrey for a saviour. That is, until she finds a copy of her magazine centrefold on the back seat, with creepy graffiti scrawled over it...

This time, though, the relationship between killer and victim is different: Vera fights back and challenges the killer verbally: *"There are lots of pretty girls in the world you know, you can't kill the whole world!"* Again, Peyser displays an aesthete's eye as Vera makes a run for it through a fire-scorched forest, with trees reduced to brittle stumps and the ground thick with ash. And, in a scene that plays like a prototype of the 'Final Girl' scenes so beloved of critics, Vera makes a stand against her tormentor...

Like many of the best American horrors of the 1970s, *The Centerfold Girls* is a triumph of atmosphere over story. The choice of locations, the sparing sound design and the subtle rootlessness of the narrative unpick the viewer's genre moorings, leaving the overall sensation weirdly loose and defocused. For all the second section's frivolity, the film has little warmth – one feels that arbitrary narrative decisions are being made to steer the courses of characters towards disaster: a chilling analogue to the empty impulsiveness of serial murder. Several bleak and impressive scenes occur at coastal locations, adding to the morbid, end-of-the-line feel. It's not a complete downer – but it would be, were it not for Prine's compelling performance. Besides, 'down' is good as far as I'm concerned; a far grislier movie like *Bloodsucking Freaks* piles on the atrocity while attending to our prurience with all the smarm of a posh waiter. I prefer movies that bite rather than lick the horror-fan's hand, and I want my serial killer films to convey the sickness of the killer. *The Centerfold Girls* was directed by a television specialist known mainly for mainstream drama entertainment, yet he turns in this chilling piece of work that proves you don't have to love the genre to make a great horror film. I wish that Peyser had returned to horror more frequently, because *The Centerfold Girls* is a genuinely creepy and engaging drive-in classic which deserves much greater eminence in fan circles.

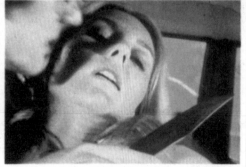

John Peyser Interviewed

Note: John Peyser died on 16 August, 2002 but I was fortunate enough to reach him for a brief interview. The quotes are from e-mails he sent me in June and July 2001.

John Peyser was born at 86th Street and Broadway in New York City, 10 August 1916, and raised in Woodmere, Long Island. "My father was an insurance man but also a frustrated Broadway producer," he recalls. "He produced two plays on Broadway, neither great successes, but our house was always filled with actors, actresses, writers, directors and assorted theatre people. From the time I was in high school I knew that I would be in 'The Business'. I started in radio and then on to television and into the cinema and back to television and then back to cinema etc. After high school I attended Colgate University for four years. While I was there I worked in a small radio station in Utica, New York, as assistant program manager. My first job after school was directing fifteen-minute and thirty-minute open-end dramatic shows to be sold to small radio stations. After I had made a hundred of them I went on the road to sell them to stations all over the New England States. Then I got the opportunity to become a page at NBC. After I had been there six months, besides paging and taking guided tours of the studios and acting as fill-in director on soap operas, I was afforded the chance to join the new television department. I was transferred to the RCA Exhibit at the 1939-40 World Fair in New York and put on live shows for the exhibit for two years. I continued to work for NBC until the war came and I went overseas to North Africa, Sicily, Italy, France, and Luxembourg to try to grab radio stations before the Germans blew them up, get them back on the air until another team relieved me, and I would move on to the next job."

After the War, Peyser came back to New York and worked as a director for CBS, under his former commanding officer and founder of CBS, William Paley, making "hundreds of live shows, including *Suspense*, *Prudential Theater*, *Studio One* and so many I can't remember." The early 1950s are frequently referred to as the Golden Age of American television, and Peyser was in the thick of it, directing live for *The Frank Sinatra Show*, *Starlight Theater*, *Kraft Television Theatre* and *Armstrong Circle Theater*. In 1953, Peyser directed the legendary James Dean in 'Death Is My Neighbor', an episode of the drama series *Danger*. Also appearing were Betsy Palmer (*Friday the 13th*'s Mrs. Voorhees) and Walter Hampden, a highly respected stage actor. Journalist Ronald Martinetti, who interviewed John Peyser in 1975, related a story that Peyser told him about working with Dean: "After the cast had gone over the script, [Peyser] called Dean and Hampden together to block the first scene. It was a highly dramatic one in which Jimmy told the old man of his misdeeds, and the old man felt pity. Peyser recalled that as Hampden began speaking his lines, tears welled up in the old man's eyes. His voice sounded choked and everyone appeared deeply moved. Then, abruptly, Hampden stopped and turned to the director. In a clear voice, he asked, 'Is that what you want, Mr. Peyser?' Peyser replied, 'Yes, thank you, Mr. Hampden.' Dean seemed stunned by the old actor's technique; his jaw dropped and he gazed at Hampden in

The Centerfold Girls
aka **Girl Hunter**
© 1974. Centerfold Ltd. Productions. General Film Corporation presents. director: John Peyser. screenplay: Robert Peete. story: Arthur Marks. producer: Charles Stroud. executive producer: William Silberkleit. executive in charge of production: Arthur Marks. music composed and conducted by Mark Wolin, performed by Wheeze. film editor: Richard Greer, A.C.E. director of photography: Robert Maxwell. sound mixer: John R. Peyser. casting: Geno Havens. stills by Beau Marks. makeup: Chuck House. key grip: Vossa Leach. property master: Chuck Stroud, Jr. boom man: Don Coufal. 2nd unit cameraman: John Simpson. sound effects editing: Conway Recorders. sound: Glen Glenn Sound. titles, opticals, processing: Consolidated Film Industries. assistant to the producer: Cary Glieberman. production manager: Robert Doudell. 2nd assistant director: William Sheehan. script supervisor: Patty Townsend. production assistants: Gary Shermaine, Glenn Iliff, Richard Mansfield, Rocky Quatrocky. production equipment by Production Systems, Inc.
Cast: Andrew Prine (Clement Dunne). The First Story: Jaime Lyn Bauer (Jackie). Aldo Ray (Ed Walker). Dennis Olivieri (Tim). Janet Wood (Linda). Teda Bracci (Rita). Talie Cochrane (Donna). Paula Shaw (Mrs. Walker). John Hart (sheriff). Jaki Dunn (nurse). Charlie (Miss January). The Second Story: Ray Danton (Perry). Francine York (Melissa). Jeremy Slate (the detective). Mike Mazurki (the caretaker). Jennifer Ashley (Charly). Kitty Carl (Sandi). Ruthy Ross (Glory). John Denos (Sam). Janis Lynn (roommate). The Third Story: Tiffany Bolling (Vera). Connie Strickland (Patsy). Anneka De Lorenzo (Pam). Scott Edmund Lane (sailor #1). Richard Mansfield (sailor #2). Dan Seymour (proprietor). Walden (himself).

amazement. Peyser recalled afterward that 'from then on, during rehearsals, Mr. Hampden could not start to sit down unless Jimmy was there placing a chair for him.'"[1]

In 1955, Peyser moved to California, maintaining an astonishing work-rate as a contract director for Warner and Universal: "I directed over a thousand filmed TV shows including *The Untouchables*, *Combat!*, *Caine's Hundred*, *Switch*, *Charlie's Angels* and on and on," he said. Peyser left the United States in 1966 and headed for Spain, directing the war series *The Rat Patrol*, which used Spanish locations for depictions of desert warfare. "Then I stayed on and did a bunch of pictures, including: *Honeymoon with a Stranger* with Janet Leigh; *Four Rode Out* with Sue Lyon, Leslie Nielsen and Pernell Roberts; and *Kashmiri Run* with Pernell Roberts, Julian Mateos and Alexandra Bastedo."[2]

Returning to the USA in 1973, Peyser ran into an old pal, film producer Arthur Marks. *The Centerfold Girls* was the result. As Peyser recalls, "I had just returned from eight years in Spain and had gone broke due to Nixon's devaluation of the dollar. My son and I had shipped our two Rovers to New York and had just driven them across the country to Woodland Hills, California. In the parking lot of a shopping centre not far from our house, my son decided he needed a McDonald's hamburger. As we parked our cars we ran into Art Marks: 'Hey John, am I glad to see you. I got a picture for you. It starts prep next week. Are you free?' That was my intro into the picture. Art and I were old friends. When I came out from New York, with a CBS series *The Man Behind the Badge*, Art was assigned to me as my First Assistant Director. It was his first shoot as a 1st AD. We stayed together for the whole series then moved on to Warner Brothers for a couple of years. We then went our separate ways. Art rose in the ranks and became producer of *Perry Mason*, where I directed for him."

above:
Prime US exploitation poster art for
The Centerfold Girls.

opposite page, strip of images from top:
Victim No.1 we never even meet;
Jackie Carol's night of horror;
This is one killer who can't be trusted with the scissors;
Lurking;
Prine in wide-angle giving the film the benefit of his creepiness.

opposite page, group of four images, clockwise from top left:
Jaime Lyn Bauer is humiliated;
Prine as 'Clement Dunne';
Vera (Tiffany Bolling) attacked after her rape by two sailors;
Bolling and Prine in the film's last segment.

above:
"The Most Beautiful Girls in the World. Some are for LOVING. Some are for KILLING." Yeah, but which ones are going to cook and clean?

The Centerfold Girls was a production of General Film Corp., a company owned and run by Marks. Peyser explained, "The money was put up by a small group of private investors who had been into three films prior to *The Centerfold Girls*. The film cost $181,000 complete, and was shot in twenty-one days on 16mm stock. It returned its money to the investors with a small profit." As part of the pre-shoot research for the project, questionnaires were sent out to exhibitors on the East Coast, mostly drive-in operators, along with a synopsis of the story. According to Marks, the questionnaires asked theatre owners how interested they were in booking stories featuring horror and nudity. "They responded enthusiastically," Peyser added, "so we made the picture."

The film was shot in December 1973 in Los Angeles, with the numerous shore scenes filmed in Paradise Cove, about twenty five miles north of the city. Peyser had nothing but praise for his star, Andrew Prine: "Andy was a doll to work with. We had done TV shows before so we were not strangers going into this film. His input was very important. As we had a very tight shooting schedule, we worked out his character, his dress and even the idea of his all-white living quarters before we started to shoot." Of the rest of the cast he recalled: "The actresses were hungry thespians. They understood the nudity problems and by the end of the first day of each segment lack of clothing was another costume. I worked with each girl every morning during make up. Some had a lot of working experience but most were tyros. I did the best with what I had in the time available. One thing I would have changed was to play down the hippies. I think I let them get out of hand. Unfortunately there was hardly time for 'take two'. We were doing about forty to fifty set-ups a day. I rehearsed with the actors during lighting. I worked with the people whenever I had a chance before shooting began."

I asked Peyser for his recollections about other key members of the production: "Mark Wolin, who did the soundtrack, had access to an extensive music library. Most all the music was 'library', already recorded. We selected the cues and themes from that library. Wolin did record some cues. Wheeze was a musical group we hired to record cues we could not find in the library. Charles Stroud, the producer, had been a child actor. He later became a production manager and worked in many films. He was promoted to producer by Art Marks. He did the film *Togetherness* [dir: Arthur Marks, 1970], filmed in Greece. He later produced a number of films for General Films and Arthur Productions. Robert Maxwell was a well-known independent director of photography. He was suggested to us by Roger Corman. His knowledge of low-key lighting and mood atmosphere was a must for the look of this film. Robert Peete, an Afro-American writer, collaborated with Art Marks after Marks had written the story. Peete wrote the screenplay and then he and Marks polished it."

When I asked Peyser if contemporary factors like the Manson case had played a part in the darkness of the story, he was adamant that such connections were superfluous: "Not the Manson case. Just the temper of the times. I think it was an era of how much we could get away with. We had been censored by television and the Hayes office for so long that the new freedom was a great relief, but still we were held within bounds by an innate sense of good taste and built in self-censorship. For instance, I think movie fucking is a bore." He was equally dismissive about possible influences from recent American shockers like *The Last*

House on the Left: "I was not aware of any other films in this genre. I had been away in Spain for eight years and nothing of that kind ever was shown in the time of Franco. What you saw was what I wanted you to see. I must say it was all mine!"

The Centerfold Girls was released in the late Spring of '74 when the drive-ins re-opened after the winter snow. It opened in six Eastern states: Massachusetts, Rhode Island, Connecticut, New York, New Jersey and Pennsylvania. Peyser recalled that, "The reviews and press were always favourable and enthusiastic. The picture was financially successful and went on to play drive-ins all over the USA."

After *Centerfold Girls*, Peyser went back to television, always his greatest pleasure. He contributed episodes to *Hawaii Five-O*, *Tales of the Unexpected*, *Quincy*, *CHiPs*, and *Charlie's Angels*, among many others. However, sources often give the wrong impression when it comes to credits on long-running television shows, frequently implying a director has worked throughout a series, when in fact he may only have directed a single episode; such is the case with Peyser's contribution to *Charlie's Angels*, for which he directed "Taxi Angels" in 1981. To call him 'best-known' for his work on the series, as some obituaries did, is somewhat misleading. (Other directors were far more intimately involved with the *Charlie's Angels* series: Dennis Donnelly, who made *The Toolbox Murders*; Bob Kelljan, director of *Rape Squad* for AIP; and George McCowan, director of the wonderful *Frogs*, all made numerous episodes each.) Putting aside the live dramas of the forties and fifties, for which complete credits are unavailable, Peyser's most sustained involvement appears to have been on shows like *Behind Closed Doors* (a late-fifties spy series for which he made sixteen episodes), *The Untouchables* (the classic crime series for which he made nine episodes), *Combat!* (a WWII war drama series of the sixties, for which he made twenty-seven episodes), and the series which he himself created for television, *The Rat Patrol* (a drama series set in WWII for which he shot ten episodes, three of which were edited together to make the TV movie *The Last Harbor Raid*).

With a career so deeply embedded in the heyday of American television, and a list of directing credits still to be definitively compiled, which Peyser himself claimed would reach over a thousand, it's perhaps a little strange that this essay – to my knowledge the most detailed ever written about him – should focus mainly on *The Centerfold Girls*, a film so untypical of his work; his 'black sheep', even. I found him courteous on the subject, but disinclined to discuss the film in detail. I suppose it's understandable: in a career that saw him directing the greats of the Hollywood screen, rubbing shoulders with Sinatra and Dean, and then ploughing though a phenomenal run of hit television shows, it's little wonder that for him, *The Centerfold Girls* was of minor interest. For the rest of us, who love and admire the film, it's amazing to think of a life so packed with achievement that this movie barely mattered to its maker! Rest in peace, John Peyser: if ever a man deserved a lie-down, it's you!

below:
Clement is all Dunne...

Footnotes

[1]   http://www.bigmagic.com/pages/blackj/column69i.html

[2]   Despite several erroneous credits elsewhere, John Peyser had nothing to do with the 1969 film *Anatomy of a Crime*.

JOHN PEYSER:
FILMOGRAPHY AS DIRECTOR

1957   *Undersea Girl* aka *Aqua Dive Girl* aka *Crime Beneath the Sea*
1961   *The Murder Men*
1967   *The Young Warriors* aka *Eagle Warriors*
1970   *Tibetana* aka *Kashmiri Run*
1971   *Four Rode Out* aka *Cuatro cabalgaron*
1974   *The Centerfold Girls* aka *Girl Hunter*

DIRECTED FOR RADIO:

1940-62 *Suspense* (live drama: precise credits unknown)

DIRECTED FOR TELEVISION:

1947-58 *Kraft Television Theatre* (live drama: precise credits unknown)
1949-54 *Suspense* (live drama: precise credits unknown. Note: this is a different credit to the radio series listed above)
1950   *The Prudential Family Playhouse* (live drama: precise credits unknown)
1950-51 *Studio One* (TV Anthology Series) episodes: "Mist with the Tamara Geba" (11-9-50); "Away from It All" (25-9-50); "The Spectre of Alexander Wolff" (9-10-50); "Lonely Boy" (25-6-51); "Nightfall" (9-7-51); "Tremolo" (23-7-51); "The Rabbit" (13-8-51); "Summer Had Better Be Good" (27-8-51)
        Starlight Theatre (TV Series)
        The Frank Sinatra Show (music show: precise credits unknown)
        The Armstrong Circle Theatre (live drama: precise credits unknown)
1951-53 *Crime Syndicate* (TV Series)
1953   *Danger* (TV Series) episode: "Death Is My Neighbor" (25-8-53: some sources claim 06-10-53) (starring James Dean)
1953-55 The Man Behind the Badge (Dramatizations of actual cases about real law enforcement personnel: precise credits unknown)
1957-58 *The Millionaire* aka *If You Had a Million* (TV Series) episodes: "The Millionaire: Ruth Ferris" (30-10-57); "The Millionaire: Michael Holm" (5-2-58); "The Millionaire: John Richards" (26-2-58); "The Millionaire: The Thorne Sisters" (16-4-58); "The Millionaire: Jack Garrison" (14-5-58); "The Millionaire: Betty Hawley" (3-9-58); "The Millionaire: Ralph the Cat" aka "Ralph" (29-10-58)
1958   *Naked City* (TV Series)
1958-59 *Behind Closed Doors* (TV Series) episodes: "The Alkaloid Angle" (22-1-59); "The Antidote" (2-4-59); "Assignment Prague" (9-4-59); "Double Agent" (26-3-59); "The Enemy on the Flank" (4-12-58); "The Gamble" (19-3-59); "The Geneva Story" (26-2-59); "It Was Learned on Good Authority" (27-11-58); "Man in the Moon" (6-11-58); "The Meeting" (5-3-59); "Message from Mardenburg" (8-1-59); "The Middle East Story" (18-12-58); "Mightier Than the Sword" (12-3-59); "The Nike Story" (13-11-58); "The Quemoy Story" (12-2-59); "Troubles in Test Cell #19" (30-10-58)
1959-60 *The Untouchables* (TV Series) episodes: "The Empty Chair" (10/15(?)-10-59); "Little Egypt" (11-2-60 – dir: unverified); "Kiss of Death Girl" (8-12-60); "The Big Train" (Eps 1 & 2: 5/12-1-61) "The Jamaica Ginger Story" (2-2-61); "The Otto Frick Story" (22-12-60); "The Waxey Gordon Story" (10-11-60); "Three Thousand Suspects" (24-3-60 – dir: unverified); "The Jack "Legs" Diamond Story" (20-10-60 – dir: unverified)
1959-60 *Law of the Plainsman* aka *The Westerners* (TV Series): episodes "Appointment in Santa Fe" (19-11-59); "Clear Title" (17-12-59); "The Comet" (21-1-60); "Common Ground" (11-2-60)
1960   *The Rifleman* (TV Series) episode: "A Case of Identity" (19-1-60)
1960   *Hong Kong* (TV Series) episode: "To Catch a Star" (30-11-60)
1961   *Adventures in Paradise* (TV Series) episode: "The Good Killing" (30-1-61)
1961-62 *Cain's Hundred* (TV Series) episodes: "Blues for a Junkman" (20-2-62); "In The Balance: Phillip Hallson" (28-11-61); "Blue Water, White Beach – Edward Hoagley (3-10-61)"
1961   *Perry Mason* (TV Series) episodes: "The Case of the Misguided Missile" (6-5-61); "The Case of the Difficult Detour" (25-3-61)
1962   *The Dick Powell Show* (TV Series) episode: "The Sea Witch" (23-10-62)
1962   *Alcatraz Express* aka *The Big Train* (TV Movie: amalgamation of 'The Untouchables Eps: "The Big Train" 1 & 2)
1962   *Bonanza* (TV Series) episode: "The Lady from Baltimore" (14-1-62)
1962   *G.E. True* (TV Series) episode(s) unknown
1962   *The Nurses* aka *The Doctors and the Nurses* (TV Series) episode: "The Perfect Nurse" (28-2-63)

1963   *The Virginian* (TV Series) episode: "Ride A Dark Trail" (18-9-63)
1963   *The Wide Country* episode: "The Girl from Nob Hill" (28-3-63)
1963   *The Eleventh Hour* episode: "A Medicine Man in This Day and Age?" (1-5-63)
1963-66 *Combat!* (TV Series) episodes: "Masquerade" (1-10-63); "The Little Jewel" (12-11-63); "A Distant Drum" (19-11-63); "Thunder from the Hill" (17-12-63); "The Party" (24-12-63); "Gideon's Army" (31-12-63); "Counter-Punch" (11-2-64); "What Are the Bugles Blowin' For" Part One & Two (3/10-3-64); "Infant of Prague" (14-4-64); "Vendetta" (22-9-64); "The Duel" (6-10-64); "Operation Fly Trap" (27-10-64); "Birthday Cake" (29-12-64); "The Enemy" (5-1-65); "The Steeple" (9-2-65); "A Walk with an Eagle" (2-3-65); "The Long Wait" (9-3-65); "The Hell Machine" (30-3-65); "Heritage" (13-4-65); "Beneath the Ashes" (27-4-65); "S.I.W." (28-9-65); "The Farmer" (12-10-65); "Evasion" (19-10-65); "Breakout" (14-12-65); "The Raider" (28-12-65); "The Mockingbird" (4-1-66)
1964   *Route 66* (TV Series) episode: "Is It True There Are Posies at the Bottom of Landfair Lake?" (10-1-64)
1964   *The Man from U.N.C.L.E.* (TV Series) episodes: "The Green Opal Affair" (27-10-64); "The Dove Affair" (15-12-64)
1965   *Burke's Law* aka *Amos Burke, Secret Agent* (TV Series) episodes: "The Prisoners of Mr. Sin" (27-10-65); "Deadlier Than the Male" (17-11-65)
1965   *Honey West* (TV Series) episode: "Whatever Lola Wants" (22-10-65); "A Stitch in Crime" (26-11-65)
1966   *The Legend of Jesse James* (TV Series) episode: "The Hunted and the Hunters" (11-4-66)
1966-67 *The Rat Patrol* (TV Series) episodes: "The Wildest Raid of All" (26-9-66); "The Chain of Death Raid" (19-10-66); "The Do Or Die Raid" (17-10-66); "The Fatal Chase Raid" (31-10-66); "The Moment of Truce Raid" (14-11-66); "The Lighthouse Raid" (5-12-66); "The Daredevil Rescue Raid" (12-12-66); "The Last Harbour Raid Eps 1,2,3 (19/26-12-66/2-1-67 - also writer)
        NB: This series created by John Peyser, with Tom Gries.
1967-68 *Garrison's Gorillas* (TV Series) episodes: "Thieves Holiday (7-11-67)***; "The Death Sentence" (16-1-68); "The Frame-Up" (27-2-68)
1968-75 *Hawaii Five-O* (TV Series) episodes: "And They Painted Daisies on His Coffin" (7-11-68); "Steal Now–Pay Later"; (1-10-74) "Ring of Life" (4-2-75); "Hit Gun for Sale" (25-2-75); "6,000 Deadly Tickets" (25-3-75)
1969   *Honeymoon with a Stranger* (TV Movie)
1969   *Massacre Harbour* aka *The Last Harbor Raid* (TV Movie)
1971   *Monty Nash* (TV Series) episodes: "The Death Squad" (1-10-71); "The Man in the Embassy" (8-10-71); "Tension in a Troubled Town" (15-10-71); "A Friendly Town in the South" aka "The Friendliest Town in the South" (5-11-71)
1974   *Shazam!* (TV Series) episode title(s) unknown
1975   *Bronk* (TV Series) episode title(s) unknown
1975   *Kate McShane* (TV Series) episode: "Conspiracy of Silence" (29-10-75)
1975   *Switch* (TV Series) episodes: "The Argonaut Special" (12-10-76); "Portraits of Death" (14-1-77); "Heritage of Death (3-4-77); "Legend of the Macunas" (21-10-77); "Siege at Bouzouki Bar" – writer only (9-7-78)
        this series co-produced by John Peyser.
1975   *Khan!* (TV Series) episode title(s) unknown
1976   *Baa Baa Black Sheep* aka *Black Sheep Squadron* (TV Series) episodes: "High Jinx" (5-10-76); "The Meatball Circus" (9-11-76)
1978   *The American Girls* aka *Have Girls Will Travel* (TV Series) episode: "A Crash Course in Survival" (21-10-78)
1979   *The Fantastic Seven* aka *Steel Glory* aka *Stunt Seven* (TV Movie)
1980   *Quincy* (TV Series) episode: "New Blood" (28-2-80)
1980-85 *Tales of the Unexpected* (TV Series) episodes: "A Glowing Future" (18-10-80); "Light Fingers" (4-7-82); "I Like It Here in Wilmington" (8-11-84); "In the Cards" (14-7-85); "Nothin' Short of Highway Robbery" (21-7-85)
1981   *Charlie's Angels* (TV Series): episode "Taxi Angels" (7-2-81)
1981   *240-Robert* (TV Series) episode: "First Loss" (14-3-81)
1981   *CHiPs* (TV Series) episode: "Finders Keepers" (29-11-81)
1981-86 *Ripley's Believe It Or Not* (many episodes: precise details unknown)

*** Has been credited to 'James Peyser' who apparently never directed anything else and doesn't show elsewhere: it's likely that this episode has been miscredited and was actually directed by John Peyser.

PRODUCED FOR TELEVISION:

1978   *B.J. and the Bear* (also 2nd unit director) TV Series

chapter 3

Carolina on My Mind

The Films of Frederick Friedel

Axe (1974)

Although genre movies from the Southern states are often perceived as simple fare, aimed at those for whom 'Art' is simply the name of the guy who runs the drugstore, there are a significant few whose work makes the clichés inoperable – Lone Star horror specialist S.F. Brownrigg is one of the foremost examples, and another is Frederick Friedel. Although Friedel – a Brooklynite who moved to Charlotte, North Carolina seeking film work – directed only two horror films in the 1970s, they are head and shoulders above the pack.

Best-known around the world as *Axe*, Friedel's debut initially sounds unlikely to inspire adjectives such as subtle, experimental or thoughtful: so, to set off on the right foot, let's begin by remembering that the director's original title for the film was *Lisa, Lisa*. The repetition of this gentle, childlike name sets the scene in quite a different way. It has a romantic and poetic cadence, placing a (doubled/split) female identity centre stage, and suggests yearning, sadness or regret (feelings often expressed through the repetition of a name). When we eventually meet Lisa we begin to appreciate both the tenderness of the original title and the irony; once we've seen her in action, the echoing title is like a futile cry reaching for a lost soul. It's also a reiteration of a first name without a surname – and unanswered questions about the role of a patriarchal character become increasingly significant as the film progresses.

The credits appear over a beautifully photographed view of a farmhouse at dusk (or dawn), with a tree beside it silhouetted against the sky, branches and twigs reaching out like delicate nerve fibres... Friedel holds the shot for a long time (due, in fact, to problems making the film run to feature length), but like most of the film's slower passages it dovetails beautifully with the emotional bias of the story. Austin McKinney, Friedel's invaluable director of photography, achieves many striking images throughout the film, but this painterly opening shot is especially fine, and feels more like something from Terrence Malick's *Badlands* (1973) than neighbouring fare like *Doctor Gore* (directed the same year by *Lisa*'s

producer J.G. Patterson). Although the early scenes veer away for a while, the mood of this first image, redolent of childhood and memory and the vulnerability of the mind, ultimately prevails...

Post-credits, it's a very masculine world in which we find ourselves, as we join three men breaking into a hotel room. This dysfunctional trio – Steele (Jack Canon), a temperamental, sardonic hood with a down-at-heel aura, Lomax (Ray Green), a bullish heavy, and Billy (Frederick Friedel himself), a nervous, lanky youngster – provide the first axis of the film. We stay with them as they settle down to wait for their prey, a man called Aubrey (Frank Jones). But what could have been ellipsed into a brief expository scene becomes a weirdly attenuated cinematic set-piece in its own right, running approximately four-and-a-half minutes. Nervous glances to the light under the hotel room door; fragments of detail as the three attempt to keep their cool; hallucinatory suspensions of time in the editing – all turn an otherwise 'dead air' scene into a sequence that cues the film's overall mood. By the time the unfortunate Aubrey arrives, our sense of time has changed, sucking us into the drama on Friedel's terms. And it's no caprice – what may seem merely perverse to begin with is a tip-off to the real metabolism of the movie.

The confrontation with Aubrey ends in his violent death. The gang of three go on the run, squabbling among themselves and revealing the dynamic of their group. The 'strongest' character is also the most compromised. Steele's role as leader is undercut by his bitterness and fake machismo; beneath the posturing we sense a man perpetually disappointed in himself. For all his bravado he's barely suited to guiding his own destiny, never mind that of his partners. Steele attempts to assert his leadership during a bullying interlude at a convenience store. Showing off to the brutish Lomax, he subjects a lone female shop assistant (Carol Miller) to a barrage of humiliation. The scene is disturbingly well-acted – Miller admirably conveys suppressed terror, making the degradation of this character (which in graphic terms amounts to little more than the removal of her blouse) acutely uncomfortable. The impact is conveyed through

opposite page, clockwise from top left:
A montage of scenes from **Axe**, featuring: Lomax (Ray Green) top left; Aubrey (Frank Jones) second and third top; Terrified storekeeper (Carol Miller) second row left and right; Lisa (Leslie Lee) third row left and right; ...and director Frederick Friedel, bottom row right.

below:
Austin McKinney's photography gives **Axe** a pictorial elegance quite at odds with the expectation conjured by the title.

Axe (US theatrical re-release title)
aka **Lisa, Lisa** (original theatrical title)
aka **California Axe Massacre**
(UK theatrical title, US/UK video title)
aka **The Virgin Slaughter**
aka **The Axe Murders**
© none [1974]
Frederick Productions presents.
writer/director: Frederick R. Friedel. executive
producer: Irwin Friedlander. produced by J.G.
Patterson, Jr. production company: Frederick
Productions. director of photography: Austin
McKinney. production manager: Philip Smoot.
soundman: George Newman Shaw. assistant
soundman: Carl Fuerstman. script girl:
Jaqueline Pyle. technical assistants: Scott
Smith, Richard W. Helms, Charles Rickard,
Harry H. Waters, Lenore Fuerstman. makeup:
Worth Keeter. editors: Frederick R. Friedel,
J.G. Patterson, Jr. script consultant: Alan J.
Pesin. assistant to the producer: Nita S.
Patterson. recording studio engineer: Hank
Poole, Jr. filmed in cooperation with Empire
Studios (Charlotte, N.C.). original score by
George Newman Shaw, John Willhelm. special
acknowledgement and appreciation: Mrs.
Clara Hood (Matthews, N.C.); Mr. & Mrs.
Richard Wolfe (Fort Mill, S.C.); Queens
College (Charlotte, N.C.); Dr. Mollie Abernathy
(Charlotte, N.C.); S & H Motors, Inc.
(Charlotte, N.C.); Munford Majik Mart
(Charlotte, N.C.); The WHite Horse Inn
(Charlotte, N.C.); Radio Shack #2304
(Charlotte, N.C.). Box Office International, Inc.
A Harry Novak presentation. filmed in
Charlotte, North Carolina.
Cast: Leslie Lee [Leslie Lee Moore] (Lisa).
Jack Canon (Steele). Ray Green (Lomax).
Frederick R. Friedel (Billy). Douglas Powers
(grandfather). Frank Jones (Aubrey). Carol
Miller (storewoman). George J. Monaghan
(Harold). Hart Smith (detective). Scott Smith
(policeman). Jeff MacKay, David Hayman,
Don Cummins, Jaqueline Pyle, Lynne
Bradley, Richie Smith (radio and television
shows). George Newman Shaw. Ronald
Watterson. Beverly Watterson. Graddie Lane.
Suzy Bertoni.

below:
Steele, as played by Jack Canon, the
compelling North Carolina actor whose skills
helped bring Friedel's best-known films to life.

the acting and direction, both of which refuse to deliver an illicit 'exploitation' thrill that isn't also balanced by a counter-weight of horror. Significantly, Billy, played by the director, remains in the car during the assault, and he refuses the bag of peanuts Steele offers him when he and Lomax return. In a perhaps slightly disingenuous fashion, Friedel thus establishes his detached relationship to the violence depicted.

After this gruelling episode, we encounter the second axis of the film: the relationship between strange, distant young Lisa (Leslie Lee) and her paralysed, mute, but perpetually aware grandfather (Douglas Powers). The two of them occupy an isolated farmhouse, standing in its own grounds like a pariah, off the road and away. It's the house seen in the credits sequence. Fraught with an air of anxiety, the building itself seems to vibrate with impending trauma.

Lisa calls the man for whom she cares 'grandfather' but he's not very old, in his fifties maybe, and our doubt about the truth of their relationship is stimulated by suggestive editing. It's difficult to be sure quite what feeling is trapped behind the staring eyes of this man as he witnesses the encroachment of Steele's gang into the house, and later, Lisa's bloody retaliation. No easy emotional cues are given. He cannot show love or hate, anger or fear. Somehow, though, it seems likely he's seen Lisa's darker side before. Douglas Powers, who has the unenviable task of conveying emotion without moving his face, is marvellous at achieving what's needed. His haunted eyes carry numerous scenes in which the camera homes in on his features. With so much mystery, so little explanation, the audience must scour his slightest change of expression for clues as to what has happened before. Through the editing, Friedel suggests all manner of possible explanations, none of them pleasant. When Lisa steps out into the back yard to kill a chicken, an edit takes us from a shot of her chopping the bird's head off to a close-up of her grandfather's intensely staring eyes. It's not a reaction shot – he's indoors and can't see her – but the editing links the two and carries intimations of castration, further elaborated when Lisa returns and feeds the old man raw eggs from a bowl. Perhaps grandfather was once a source of unwanted intimacy? After the house is invaded by the gang, a distressed Lisa shuts herself in the bathroom and sees a large worm in the bathtub plughole. Following on from the 'violation' of her house by male intruders, Lisa's hallucination has inevitable symbolic weight.

While it's perfectly normal for a country girl to kill a chicken for dinner, Lisa's demeanour as she's doing it is unsettlingly detached, and the scene where she lingers over a smashed egg when returning from the henhouse – a brief touch, but genuinely haunting – raises all sorts of questions: not least the whereabouts of her mother. It's also a clear nod to Roman Polanski's *Repulsion* – remember Catherine Deneuve's dreamy, disconnected Carole, gazing at a crack in the pavement? *Repulsion* also comes to mind during Lomax's attempted rape of Lisa, which Friedel stages in tight close-ups with a stifling quietness from the actors. And finally, the stubborn lack of dialogue explaining the past is as pervasive a directorial choice here as Polanski's refusal to spell out the source of Carole's childhood trauma.

Whatever our suspicions, they remain unanswered and we have to move on. The old man's immobility means that, disturbed or not, Lisa must act alone against the invaders. And act she certainly does. When Lomax tries to rape her, she slices him across the back of his neck (presumably opening arteries too, although we don't see it) using a cut-throat razor she was playing with earlier. Dragging Lomax's body into the bathroom, she dumps it in the tub and hacks it to bits with the axe she'd used earlier on the chicken. All the key props in the film have a follow-up scene (eggs, chicken, soup, axe, razor) – there's even an echo of the earlier worm hallucination, as we see the rapist's tie, soaked in blood, curled in the bathtub with one end in the plughole; further support for the notion that Lisa's original trauma is sexual in origin.

Billy's role in the film is to extend the director's sympathy to Lisa. He interrupts her when she's contemplating taking her own life, he (unwittingly) helps her to drag the trunk containing Lomax's corpse up into the attic; then, when he looks inside the trunk and sees Lomax's limbless corpse (a sight we don't share, dismemberment fans), he immediately asks Lisa who did it, displaying naïve trust in her innocence (or is it just an inability to believe that a sweet young girl could murder a big lummox like Lomax?). But whatever the rescue fantasy Billy has for Lisa, he's barking up the wrong tree. He only narrowly (and again inadvertently) diverts Lisa's plan to murder him too; and at the climax, after Lisa has murdered Steele, he finds Steele's ring in the suspiciously blood-hued soup Lisa serves him. The ring is her reproach for Billy's complicity with Steele and Lomax. It would seem that forgiveness is not part of Lisa's character!

Lisa's killing of Steele is compelling, but as a climax it's slightly undercooked. Lomax has already attempted rape, and died for it, so when Steele does the same it brings a feeling of depletion to the narrative. His decision to molest Lisa in front of her grandfather adds an extra frisson of sadism, but the duplication of a sexual attack, in a film as economical and minimalist as this, is a slight mis-step. The molestation, however, is conveyed with a return to the edgy, frantic editing of the opening hotel-room scenes, and there's no doubt that Lisa's axing of Steele is a welcome dramatic outcome: it's just that by having Lisa kill both Lomax and Steele for attempted rape, the film, which runs barely sixty-eight minutes, stands on its own toes somewhat. If Steele had turned his sadistic (rather than sexual) impulses on the paralysed grandfather, it might have been preferable in dramatic terms.

When Steele's ring turns up in the soup that Lisa serves to Billy, it changes the way we view Lisa. We've seen so little evidence of subterfuge in her that at first viewing I thought the twist was corny and senseless, a cheap jolt. When you consider, though, that Lisa must have placed the ring there deliberately, we must evaluate her anew as a judge of Billy's actions: not just a victim seeking to protect herself, and clearly not as disconnected from reality as we thought. If she's capable of passing judgement, her earlier actions take on a different hue. If Lisa can place the ring in the soup to remind Billy of his complicity, then perhaps feeding her grandfather raw eggs is not a sign of dissociation but a deliberate symbolic reproach. Then there's the soup itself: the climax is edited to imply that the bright red broth Lisa serves is mixed with Steele's blood. I say 'imply' because even at this late stage, Friedel declines to make things obvious. Billy drinks the soup, and hesitates; sips; hesitates; pulls a face; and continues sipping. To an almost infuriating degree, Friedel holds us on the brink of an answer that he then declines to give. Of all the scenes in the movie, this is the most acute example of his *modus operandi*. Friedel defers information, sets up questions and ambiguities, and leads us to make assumptions that he then refuses to endorse or refute. This has nothing to do with lack of money or lack of time; it's characteristic, personal. It would cost nothing to explain, it would take almost no time at all. Friedel's open-ended, tantalising storytelling is a mark of artistry and an imprimatur for audience interpretation. *Axe* is a small film, modest even, but it's beautiful, bordering on poetic, and it invites you to play an active part in making sense of what you're seeing.

It seems appropriate to discuss the music here, finally, as we get a long, uninterrupted draught of it over the end credits. Friedel stretched the credits out to four-and-a-half minutes, as the movie was too short and needed a cost-conscious boost to reach the bare minimum feature length. His thrift is our gain: composers George Newman Shaw and John Willhelm pick up on the undertow of

regret and tenderness in the film and, in a semi-improvised mode that complements the film beautifully, score to the heart of the movie and not the horror. Based around a simple but haunting synthesizer melody and gorgeous piano embellishments, with some equally lovely vibraphone and soprano saxophone on the run-out track, it reminds me of possibly my favourite film score of all time, Donald Rubinstein's breathtaking music for *Martin* by George Romero. It has that same eerie but sorrowful quality, like something heard emanating from a late night jazz radio station falling into sync' with an alcohol reverie. The same theme plays over the opening credits, a two-and-a-half minute version which concentrates on the electric keyboard, a keening high register sound possibly generated by a MiniMoog: both recordings are so perfectly in tune with the mood of the drama that it's impossible to imagine them separated. Frederick Friedel, with cinematographer Austin McKinney, and composers George Newman Shaw and John Willhelm, fashioned a film way outside the box for low-budget horror; and as if to prove it was no fluke, they did so again, immediately afterwards, with *Kidnapped Coed*…

above:
Leslie Lee played Lisa, the beautiful but chronically dislocated star of **Axe**.

below:
UK quad for **Axe**'s cinema release, with a title amplified for maximum horror shock value.

Kidnapped Coed (US theatrical re-release title) aka The Kidnap Lover (original theatrical title) aka Date with a Kidnapper (UK video title)
aka House of Terror (US video title)
aka Night of Mourning (early working title)
© none [1975]
Box Office International Pictures, Inc. - a Harry Novak presentation. Frederick Productions presents.
writer/producer/director: Frederick R. Friedel. executive producer: Irwin Friedlander. director of cinematography: Austin McKinney (colour by Movielab). soundman: Don Jones. soundman: Lloyd L. De France. assistant soundman: Douglas L. Deal. 2nd unit cameraman: Chris Allen. assistant cameraman: Phillip Smoot. makeup - special effects: Worth Keeter. scriptgirl: Caroline Batson. assistant to the producer: Nancy Durham. script consultant: Alan J. Pesin. editor: Avrum M. Fine. original score by George Newman Shaw and John Willhelm. Special acknowledgements and appreciation for their cooperation: The Hotel Concord (Concord, North Carolina); Monroe Room and Apts (Monroe, North Carolina); The Barn (Rock Hill, South Carolina); The Cavalier Hotel (Charlotte, North Carolina); Arnold Palmer Cadillac (Charlotte, North Carolina); The Fort Mill Police Dept. (Fort Mill, South Carolina); The Durham Farm (Chester, South Carolina); The Blakeney Farm (Charlotte, North Carolina); The Strawn Farm (Marshville, North Carolina). For Adolph.
Cast: Jack Canon (Eddie Mattlock). Leslie Ann Rivers (Sandra Morely). Gladys Lavitan (Mrs. Mattlock). Larry Lambeth (hotel clerk). Jim Blankinship (bellhop). Charles Elledge (old farmer). Susan McRae (daughter). Bob Martin (man with shotgun). Clonnie Baxter Strawn (old man in chair). Skip Lundby (blindman). Elizabeth Allan Burger (birdwatcher - Lady Lush). Nancy Pselos (blonde barfly). Rusty Smith (redheaded barfly). Buck Kraft Sr. (bartender). Mrs. Buck Kraft Sr. (old barfly). Larry Drake (age home attendant). Pinckney Greene (roadhouse gangleader). Junious L. Leak (gangmember). Marvin G. Crosland (lookout). Jack Murray (man at bar). Carole [Carol] Miller (birdwatcher). Mary Hartford (birdwatcher). Ron Campbell (beggar). John Gibson (barber). Shela May (angry mother). Kendall D. May (son). Ronald Duvall Davis (boy on street). Helen Kaye (Mrs. Morley). Frederick R. Friedel (voice of Mr. Morley).

Kidnapped Coed (1975)

"It started with Patti – where will it end?"
– original trailer, *The Kidnap Lover*

Teenager Sandra Morely (Leslie Rivers), daughter of a wealthy businessman, is abducted by kidnapper Eddie Mattlock (Jack Canon). Eddie makes a ransom demand to Sandra's father, then checks in at a rundown hotel with his terrified captive in tow. Room service arrives, but the two men at the door are toting guns, not towels. Sandra thinks she's being rescued by the cops, but instead the men beat up Eddie, tie her to the bed and rape her. Eddie, who's horrified to see Sandra molested, escapes from his bonds and shoots the two men, taking his captive back on the road. While waiting for the money to be dropped at the appointed spot, Eddie keeps on the move, from a disused barn in a remote beauty spot to a beach and a succession of farms. As hostage and kidnapper get acquainted, Sandra begins to find Eddie both funny and attractive. After an encounter with some hostile rednecks, the couple eventually pull in at a farmhouse and ask to stay the night. The farmer who greets them agrees to their request, and over dinner reveals that he used to be the local sheriff. Observing the tension between the visitors, and their beat-up appearance, the old man's suspicions are raised, but he's thrown off the scent when he sees evidence of the growing bond of intimacy that has developed between his two guests. Next morning, inexplicably, he flips and attacks them with a pitchfork; Eddie panics and shoots the old man, and Sandra runs away in horror. However, the two lovers eventually make up and decide to stay together, fleecing Sandra's father of the ransom and going on the run…

Friedel's companion piece to his wonderful *Axe* takes us on another engagingly downbeat journey through a melancholic rural America. Best known today as *Kidnapped Coed* (the Harry Novak retitling under which it has been released on DVD), the storyline of what started out as *The Kidnap Lover* is built up from a slow accumulation of fragments, cameos of rural and small-town decay, and apparent narrative discords. While the tension is sometimes diluted by slow pacing, *Kidnapped Coed* is riveting in its photographic beauty and its depiction of two increasingly warm and sympathetic lead characters. It has the structural looseness of certain 'artier' directors, and although the storyline is thin, the approach to the telling is creative and highly distinctive. It's really a tragedy that Friedel was not showered with plaudits and offers of further directing gigs after this, as I'd love to have seen what he could have achieved two or three years later.

Actress Leslie Rivers is strikingly subtle and convincing as Sandra Morely, the victim who grows to love her kidnapper, while Jack Canon is again an actor with the potential for greatness, playing Eddie Mattlock as a morally ambivalent character struggling against his finer feelings; a wannabe villain who's bitten off more than he can chew. Their relationship is developed in a spare and unshowy way that never misses a beat, thanks to the rapport between the actors, and to Friedel's gentle, considerate direction. Eddie is drawn with real delicacy: for instance, the first time we glimpse the character's vanity and insecurity is when he drives through a small town (Fort Mill, South Carolina, just a few miles over the border from Charlotte) and passes a young boy sat on the kerb who flips him the bird. *"Little bastard,"* Eddie mutters. We immediately understand that his ego is so fragile, even a five-year-old glimpsed on the roadside can get his goat. Canon breathes real life into the role: when Eddie wakes up after a night asleep in the car, he yawns and you see him wince and cuss under his breath – the yawn having hurt thanks to a kick in the face he received the day before, during the hotel room attack. This, in medium-to-long shot, is barely observed by the camera and so quietly added by the actor it's possible even Friedel was unaware he was planning it. Cinematographer Austin McKinney is on the ball too: a partially collapsed barn set in misty morning fields gives him another chance to show off his photographic skill, and Friedel the chance to set up some artful compositions, framing the landscape through broken wood and abandoned farm machinery.

You can imagine this movie played higher up the Hollywood scale: with a young Jack Nicholson as Eddie, and Sissy Spacek in the role of Sandra. You'd take the anti-authoritarian streak in Eddie and play it up to heroic heights, give Sandra's lack of concern for her family a sociological spin, and bingo: *Five Easy Pieces* meets *Badlands*. A director like Bob Rafelson might have milked the scenario for greater social comment, but Friedel's pacing, his eye for composition, and the careful, emotionally honest performances make such parlour-game recasting redundant. *Kidnapped Coed* is great the way it is, and there's enough here to suggest that Friedel could have scored a hit with the wider film-going public if he'd been supported at the right point in his career.

As you watch *Kidnapped Coed*, you feel doors open on all sides, permitting a glimpse into other stories, other narrative directions, shown for a second then swiftly left behind. The first of these occurs when Eddie takes his captive to a rundown hotel for the night, only to stumble into a crime scene without realising it. Two hoods have murdered the *maître d'* (presumably just minutes before) – but weirdly, instead of taking off they hang around, assuming the role of hotel staff and checking the 'couple'

in. We are given no more information about their criminal escapade; we don't know who they are, or why they're doing what they're doing. Their intrusion into the story of Eddie and Sandra has an existential quality. They are simply there, and it's random bad luck that brings them all into contact (as much for the two hoods, who end up dead, as for poor Sandra, whom they rape).

Loneliness, isolation, cries that go unheard, help that doesn't come – these are the motifs of the film, explored through sometimes wrenching, sometimes amusing vignettes. Sandra tries to write a plea for help on a toilet roll, chucking it out the hotel window ten storeys up: but when it lands in the gutter on the street below, two kids come along and kick it, leaving just a trail of soggy paper that no-one is going to read. When Eddie shoots the rapist and Sandra gets drenched in blood, her shriek echoes around the backyard of the hotel tenement block, but the only person we see is an old man sat impassively in a rocking chair, either too deaf or too senile to react. Later on, the quiet scenes at the barn are interrupted by noises Eddie thinks could be the police approaching. Instead it's a group of middle-aged women, birdwatchers, eyes glued to binoculars which they point resolutely upwards at the treetops, oblivious to Sandra's plight.

It may seem perverse to praise an exploitation flick for its gentleness, but it's as important to Friedel's films as exuberance was to David Durston's *I Drink Your Blood* (1971) or sadism to Wes Craven's *The Last House on the Left* (1972). Panic not, horror fans, there's still rape, bullets up the ass, and death by scythe to prevent the film becoming too laid-back, but the gentleness is something that extends beyond Sandra and Eddie's characterisations and into the overall climate of the film. In a review in the magazine *Shock Xpress* in 1989, writer David Kerekes described the film as "peaceful", and although it's a very oblique description, I think I know what he means. There's none of the rough handling that usually passes for narrative construction, no sense of the writer's ego yanking the viewer's chain, leading us from set-up to conflict to resolution. Actions are so embedded in the environment that we're often beguiled simply by where we are. More so here than in *Axe*, Friedel's style tends away from the main thread of the story, relaxing to take in snapshots and vivid tableaux of rural life, some of which have barely a tangential relationship to the plot. This digressive, non-linear approach brings three-dimensional life to the story, without insisting that the incidental details be sewn into a pattern pre-determined by the central relationship. The two leads are constantly being thrown off-course or thwarted by unexpected occurrences from the periphery. When Eddie's car breaks down and he walks to a nearby farm to ask for water, the almost psychopathic hostility of the farmers is shocking; not so much for what they say as for the rude and arbitrary way their stony-faced hatred cuts across the story arc. The pacing grants this *non sequitur* equal prominence with other more directly motivated scenes, and yet Eddie has to retreat, without water or assistance, in a scene that both humiliates and further humanises him. We are given no explanation for the farmers' hostility – better still, we sense that Eddie's arrival has occurred at some mysterious moment of crisis. He's an ace away from being shot for trespassing, and the fury that greets him suggests a whole subplot to which we're deliberately denied access. Canon plays the scene for awkward comedy, wringing maximum discomfort from the clash between his flimsy hard-man

ONCE YOU ENTER YOU MAY NEVER LEAVE!

HOUSE OF TERROR

persona and the mad-dog-on-a-frayed-leash fury of the old farmer. His actor's instinct to make the most of this scene gives Friedel's perverse narrative digression an emotional alibi. It all feels as if we're just a field away from the events of *The Texas Chain Saw Massacre*: in the bushes near the farm we see numerous clapped out cars, and in the driveway a filthy, battered old bus. What these derelict vehicles are doing there we never find out, but you feel the same ominous buzz that Hooper's film conjured so well.

Other incidental details accumulate, as Friedel makes choices that foreground incident over structure. (Compare his approach with Robert Endelson's stripped-to-the-bone functionalism in the excellent but diametrically opposed *Fight for Your Life*.) Perhaps the strangest and most opaque *non sequitur* in the film occurs when the fleeing couple, now aware of each other's growing affections, ask for

shelter at another isolated farm, owned by a taciturn old man and his silent daughter (shades of *Axe*). The farmer, a retired sheriff who invites the fugitives to eat at his table but suspects something isn't kosher, is a beat behind the truth, confused by the fact that the victim has fallen for her captor. So far so suspenseful. Next morning, though, all hell breaks loose: the old man attacks the couple in a fury, chasing Eddie with a scythe, and raving like a man possessed. There is simply no explanation for his rage: we have to fill in imaginary brushstrokes ourselves. It's as if the world itself is trying to reject the Kidnap Lovers; everyone with whom they come into contact poses an unpredictable threat. The attack precipitates a reckless act of self-defence from Eddie, who shoots the old man, causing him to fall on his scythe. Despite the evident provocation, Sandra is horrified to see Eddie kill and reverts to her spoilt rich-girl morality, running away into the open countryside, screaming *"Murderer!"* Eddie, himself appalled by the killing, runs after Sandra pleading for forgiveness.

One of the strangest, most oblique scenes in Friedel's work then occurs when Sandra, having run into the middle of nowhere, spots a man walking along a mud path nearby. She goes to him for help but is greeted with an anguished response: *"I'm blind, lady, can't you see that? I'm blind!"* We are in the middle of the countryside, with no buildings or signs of life around. The appearance of this strange, helpless man adds an absurdist dimension to a film that has already flirted with the arbitrary and random. He's like a character from Beckett, limping by on his lonely tangent. This is truly a universe where nothing can be trusted, and help is never at hand!

Where low-budget horror films are concerned, poor writing or post-production tampering often account for lapses of coherence, but when the lapses assume their own patterns we have to sit up and take notice. Accidents and commercial pressures acknowledged, these movies are cut from a different cloth to the straightforward likes of *The Toolbox Murders* or *Don't Answer the Phone!* If you insist on a utilitarian approach to Friedel's work, you could, I suppose, argue that lack of funds accounts for some of his idiosyncrasies. On the other hand, I would say that an artist's character is revealed by his choices under pressure; and Friedel's artistic choices are consistent enough to be considered the mark of a stylist. He himself says that he made *Kidnapped Coed* too soon after *Axe*: that he didn't have time to sit back and consider the mistakes he'd made in the first film and so made them again in the second. Perhaps over the years since he made these movies, he has had *too much* time to rue the impulsive, intuitive choices that set his work aside from the commercial mainstream. Personally, I feel that if Friedel had received sympathetic reviews and some fair recompense from distribution, he might have gone on to essay the style of these two films into something even better. From the vantage point of the 21st Century, they do indeed feel slow in comparison to the norm for horror and exploitation. But there's more to life than speed: the sympathy that Friedel extends to his characters, the loose, digressional narratives, and the focus on outsiders, be they criminals, the mentally ill or simply the lonely, as well as his beautiful and eerie portraits of rural Southern settings, all ensure that Frederick Friedel stands out from the crowd. Given the chance to make films for the drive-in circuit, he took the bare minimum of exploitation material and bought himself the license to direct unconventional movies that hover between genre and something closer to 'art' cinema.

Frederick Friedel Interviewed

Frederick Friedel's *Axe* and *Kidnapped Coed* are two of my favourite films in this book. Although their exploitational retitlings and lurid poster artwork suggest the more brutal end of the horror spectrum, they have a curious quality that beckons beyond the usual plot mechanics. Don't get me wrong; both films do indeed subject the audience to disturbing eruptions of violence: the horror hard-sell launched by distributor Harry Novak, who picked up these two independent regional productions in 1977, is based on actual content. It's just that there's something else going on; Friedel has real compassion for his characters, not a common attribute in the exploitation arena, and the unsettling quality of his work springs as much from his ability to evoke alienation and loneliness as from his visceral horror scenes. He was a young man when he made these movies, and he basically taught himself the job as he went along, bringing spontaneity to his work, an openness to his surroundings and circumstances. As well as being great exploitation films, *Axe* and *Kidnapped Coed* are lucid and evocative portraits of the places they were made. Because the stories are told so loosely, we have the chance to feel the surroundings through the images, in a way that would be ignored if the narrative were busier and more conventional. Some might find the films undisciplined, and if you're looking for stories that snap together with a satisfying 'click' at the end, you may feel unrewarded. Likewise, there's not a trace of the corkscrew in Friedel's plotting: instead of drawing clear lines and vortices to demarcate the story, his approach is to let things take form according to impulse. With the exception of the characters played by Jack Canon – his leading man in both films – and Leslie Rivers, the female lead in *Kidnapped Coed* (both of whom give detailed and credible performances), he favours enigma over psychology, and declines to divulge background information about the characters. The supporting cast are encountered like strangers, whose motivations are largely opaque. Friedel's training as a photographer may have informed this preference for enigma, as his characters appear in the frame with only their carefully chosen faces to suggest their character background. But more of this later…

Moving to Florida, a Dangerous Flirtation with Golf, and the Early Short Films

Frederick Friedel was born in Brooklyn, New York in 1948, and raised in Malverne, a small town on Long Island. His father was a prodigy who skipped five grades in school and graduated in Law before he was twenty one. Friedel Snr.'s cousin was also a prodigy, a doctor by the same age, and this high-flying family background was to prove both a spur to action and a burden of guilt for Friedel Jr. His mother provided the artistic side of the family equation: she was a professional dancer who headlined on Broadway when she was just fifteen – another family prodigy. "Walter Winchell, one of the most famous newspaper columnists, wrote that she was the most beautiful woman on Broadway," Friedel recalls. "She looked a bit like Vivien Leigh. Errol Flynn asked her out, but she was so young she was being chaperoned by my very religious grandmother to and from the theatre. She was asked to come to Hollywood for a screen test but she decided to marry my father instead." Friedel sees his mother's journey, from promising *ingénue* to wife of a successful lawyer, as a formative influence on his own ambitions: "Jung said that nothing affects a child more than the unlived dreams of their parents, and I'm sure my love of movies and my burning desire to make them came from her thwarted dreams. She was a tremendous combination of beauty and an incredible sense of humour. I believe had she pursued it she might have been another Carole Lombard or Lucille Ball."

With a host of early achievers in the family, it's no wonder that the cinema's foremost prodigy, Orson Welles, should have provided the inspiration for Friedel's film career: "My first memory of the cinema may have been seeing *Citizen Kane* on TV as a little child. My parents also took me to Radio City Music Hall in Manhattan for my birthdays to see movies like *The Ten Commandments*, *The Spirit of St. Louis* and *The Greatest Show on Earth*. The fabulous Rockettes, the long line of dancers, performed a stage show before the movies came on. I also remember them taking me to see *Psycho* and *An Affair to Remember*. We had a foreign movie theatre in Malverne and my mother took me as a little boy to see Brigitte Bardot in *And God Created Woman*. To this day I adore Brigitte Bardot. You never forget your first love, especially when you're three years old! I have the giant French poster of *Le mépris* hanging on my wall."

In the early sixties Friedel's father moved the family to Florida, having bought a motel and hotel on Miami Beach. After attending high school in Miami, Friedel – who at the time harboured fantasies of becoming a professional golfer – enrolled at The University of Florida, which had one of the country's best golf teams. However, he soon realised he was outclassed in the golfing arena and, thank goodness, looked for another outlet for his energies.

The University had no real film course but it did have an excellent photography department. Friedel was instantly drawn to movie-making: "In the one course available I did a short 16mm film starring my journalism teacher, Dwight Godwin,[1] and another student dressed up as a clown. Dwight is standing on a hillside, long grey hair, distinguished looking, with the clown sitting to his left. Two solitary figures in the landscape, against a grey sky. Between them, suspended from a long rope, dangles a knife. (I hadn't even thought about this for years, but, alas, it's slowly coming back...) The film opens in black with a cue card (influenced by my philosophy/theatre studies, no doubt) that reads: *It has been over a hundred years since God bowed out and left man in center stage. I do hope the audience is kind.* (Me, pretentious? Nah...) Anyhow Dwight begins to insult the little clown with a series of scathing remarks, like calling him a syphilitic tumour on the backside of an ape, until the clown rises and takes the knife and stabs Dwight repeatedly in the back with all the attendant agony and screams. It was pretty effective, if a bit depressing. Upon reflection I realise I was unconsciously dramatising, rather nakedly, my own relationship with my father, who could be verbally caustic and leave one feeling like a clown. I remember screening it later at MIT in class, and one of the students from Harvard came up to me and said he felt sorry for me. I didn't understand what he meant until now. I must have been pretty unhappy..."

above:
Frederick Friedel (centre), seen here directing his black comedy **My Next Funeral**.

Friedel showed the film to John Terry, a professor at the Massachusetts Institute of Technology (MIT), who offered to let him study there for a year. "I thought it would be a good way to get my hands on a camera and some film," Friedel says, "so I took him up on it, even though MIT really specialized in documentaries. They had Ricky Leacock there of Leacock-Pennebaker fame,[2] and another professor who wrote one of the textbook bibles of the day. I remember asking him a dumb question like, 'Which is better, a tracking shot or zoom?' and he replied, 'What's better, a kick in the arm or a kick in the leg?' Ah, once again that familiar clown-like feeling..."

Once installed at MIT, Friedel began work on an ambitious short film, using Walden Pond (the famous beauty spot near Concord Massachusetts immortalized by the American essayist Henry David Thoreau) as a location. As Friedel recalls, "I believe one of the key images dealt with actors emerging from the water in the foggy mist-filled dawn, their bodies whited from the waist up. I believe the lead was a Thoreau-like figure walking with a cane in silhouette against numerous sunrises/sunsets. And somehow it ended up with a man (my roommate David) reaching into the water and pulling out a mirror image of himself. All very symbolic in a very un-thought-out way. Anyway, armed with this dazzling concept I interviewed actors at Boston University's famous drama department. I even went to Emerson, another big theatre school in Boston, to look for actors. What chutzpah! I'm sure on some level I must have been trying to meet girls (I was pretty shy). So the moment arrives, it's winter and cold as hell, and my dutiful actors shed some of their clothes and don white makeup and wade into the classic American landmark, Walden Pond. We start filming and police cars come screaming up and 'Frederick Von Stroheim' yells out, 'Keep filming till they arrest us!' It all seemed so very important back then – I wish I could figure out what it all meant. A few years later when I was in New York casting *Kidnapped Coed*, an actor included a note with his 8 x10, saying, 'Does this sound familiar? It's six a.m. and I'm half-naked standing in Walden Pond, and the police pull up...'"

opposite page, strip of images, from top:
Eddie (Jack Canon) overpowers Sandra in **Kidnapped Coed**;
Two hoods (Larry Lambeth and Jim Blankinship) burst in to Eddie's hotel room;
...tie up Eddie;
...and rape Sandra;
Eddie and Sandra fall for each other;
The couple spend the night at a farm belonging to a grizzled ex-sheriff (Charles Elledge);
...who the following day attacks Eddie with a pitchfork.

above:
A childhood chopping chickens leaves Lisa adjusted to slaughter...

opposite page:
This admat hails from the early 1980s, when **Axe** was once again doing the rounds, this time in the wake of the post **Friday the 13th** psycho-slasher craze.

opposite page, strip of images:
More scenes from **Axe**, depicting the murder of Aubrey, the assault on the shopkeeper, Lisa at home, Lomax's assault, Lisa's retribution, and her despatching of Steele.

below:
Grandfather (Douglas Powers), locked immobile in his own hell, observes helplessly...

Miami – Los Angeles – New York – Columbus – Charlotte – *Lisa, Lisa*

After abandoning a further short film ("Christ walking on water only to divide his own image with a buzz saw... a very modern carpenter"), Friedel left college: "The first thing I did when I left was to play Macduff in a production of *Macbeth*; the second was to make *Axe*," he laughs. Things didn't move *quite* that swiftly, but Friedel, a young man in his early twenties, was certainly not wasting any time. "I moved to Los Angeles right after getting out of college," he recalls. "At the time my heroes were Woody Allen and Orson Welles. I was always inspired by the fact that Orson Welles had made *Citizen Kane* at twenty five. Not drawing any parallels between his unique genius and my abilities, but I was determined to make my first feature by that age. And the clock was ticking. I wrote a screwball comic western (before *Blazing Saddles* came out) that had the distinction of making Walter Shenson, the producer of the early Beatles comedies, call me and tell me he laughed so hard he fell off the toilet. (Apparently that's where he did his reading...) The script was outrageously funny but very raw and hardly a movie. It did convince my girlfriend Judy I had talent, and when I told her I was going to New York to see if I could raise money from my relatives to do a low-budget feature, she arranged for me to meet her businessman father from Georgia, who would be in New York at that time. I remember taking my last few dollars and travelling to New York, with the mindset that I would either get a movie made or 'die trying'. Really, very much that sort of fatalistic/romantic mission. I went to a number of my rich relatives to find investors. One gave me a five-dollar cab fare to get me home. The other said if I came up with other investors, he would invest $2,500. That's when I met Irwin Friedlander, Judy's father, in a hotel in Manhattan. We hit it off immediately, and he said if I met him in Columbus, Georgia, in a couple of days when he went back, he'd see if his friends were interested. I was out of money, so I went to a company that needs drivers to drive people's cars to other cities. I got a car and drove twenty four hours straight to Georgia and was waiting on Irwin's doorstep when he got home. Irwin owned a chain of clothing stores so he gave me some new clothes and got a group of his friends together (he became the executive producer) and that's how I raised the $25,000 to make the movie. He was a real angel who became like a second father to me."

Friedel originally intended to shoot his feature debut in Atlanta, but changed the location to Charlotte in North Carolina on the suggestion of Edward Montoro, a film distributor with whose company, Film Ventures International, Irwin Friedlander had investments. Charlotte, a thriving business centre built on the first verified gold mines to have been discovered in the USA, was already the home base for several low-budget productions in the early seventies: down the road was the small town of Shelby, where actor/producer/director Earl Owensby built his own studio facility. Montoro suggested that Friedel and Friedlander should approach North Carolina producer/director Pat Patterson. "Ed told us they were making low-budget movies in Charlotte, NC and gave me Pat's number," says Friedel. "Pat was a very interesting fellow. He was an ex-magician (his wife Nita was part of his magic act) who made low-budget horror movies. He had a giant warehouse in the middle of a field that he called Empire Studios because in his words, he was 'building an empire.' It was a tribute to my naiveté that I didn't smile at this remark. He was short, slightly built and a bit odd looking, but he said he knew how to make movies on a budget and I knew nothing, so I hired him to help me produce. He spoke with a Southern accent and had an imperious authoritative tone that convinced you he knew what he was doing." Friedel pauses: "So when I saw a few minutes of his movie *The Body Shop* [aka *Doctor Gore*], I was so shocked by its amateurishness that I made an immediate decision never to listen to any possible 'creative suggestions' he might ever have! I knew in that area, even though I had never done a movie, I would have to be on my own. I believe that resolve fuelled my decision to frame every shot myself and have total control of the film, for fear of being negatively influenced."

As anyone who has sat through *Doctor Gore* will agree, aesthetic judgement was indeed the least of Patterson's assets, but Friedel is quick to stress that he appreciated the support, and liked the man himself: "One time when we were in Empire Studios he screamed and showed me his bleeding finger. It turned out to be some sort of magic trick. Ironically a little time later he did slice his finger and was bleeding badly and I thought it was another trick! He went to a doctor and used self-hypnosis to avoid anaesthesia for the stitching. He claimed he could hypnotize anyone, including himself. I found out later from Jack Canon that Pat was actually suffering with the first stages of cancer during the filming of *Axe*. He would sometimes lie down to rest, but he never let on that he was ill. He died not very long after that. I felt terrible when I found out. I had decided that I'd learned enough to produce the second movie without him. And I know he was hurt by that. I remember him saying that *Axe* was the first real script he had ever had, and he kept saying I was a real pro, even though it was my first movie. Had I known how sick he was I would have used him for the second movie. He came to a screening of it and complimented me on it, saying he was proud of how much I had learned. He was a very sweet man."

Friedel's make-up artist on both films was Worth Keeter, who went on to work first as a low-budget director on movies for the Earl Owensby studio, such as *Wolfman* and *Rottweiler*, and then as a director on the hugely popular *Mighty Morphin' Power Rangers* TV series. "Pat introduced me to Worth, who made a valuable contribution to both films," says Friedel. "He was still in high school but he definitely had a way with blood!" Keeter was a native of the area and he knew the various movers and shakers in the local film scene. It was a far cry from the Los Angeles industry, as Keeter explains: "The early North Carolina film business had no reason to exist other than a bunch of us wanted to make movies. Most of us had no formal training, so we made it up as we went along. One producer, Henry Smith, had lost an arm and leg to a lightning strike while working for a power company. He used his financial settlement to become a film producer and was involved in an early drive-in hit, *Preacherman* [Albert T. Viola, 1971]. Pat Patterson was a carny and a magician. Earl Owensby was a tool salesman. Prior to the home-grown film industry there were mainly three reasons to shoot in North Carolina. There was the fabulous Biltmore Estate in Asheville, where Peter

Sellers's *Being There* was shot, and the Charlotte Motor Speedway. Other than that, there were the mountains made famous in Robert Mitchum's *Thunder Road*. The home-grown feature films and the commercials industry trained technicians, which later became a major draw for those producing films at a lower cost. The North Carolina Film Commission was originally an under-funded offshoot of the tourism office. In my opinion, it rode in on the coattails of Earl Owensby and local pioneers."

With a budget drawn up, and technical support from Patterson in the wings, Friedel was at action stations, his movie-making dream now within his grasp. He had written the script for *Axe* whilst raising the money, working quickly and bearing in mind a few words of wisdom from the King of the Indies, Roger Corman: "Corman said you could make *Doctor Zhivago* for $50,000 but it wouldn't be *Doctor Zhivago*. The trick was to make a low-budget movie that was really conceived as a low-budget movie. Ergo, a house in the country, few characters, few locations, etc. And since this was a drive-in movie there had to be horror, suspense, and people doing bad things to other people."

As it turned out, this pragmatic template was to lead to one of the moodiest, most haunting drive-in movies of the seventies…

Honing the Axe

"*Axe* possesses a sophisticated and unique cinematic syntax. […] A hallucinatory film, inducing a claustrophobic, intense feeling of being trapped with the characters." – *Bill Landis, Sleazoid Express (book)*.

Axe – under its original title *Lisa, Lisa* – was shot in a mere eight-and-a-half days, in the middle of February 1974. The cinematographer was Austin McKinney, a skilful but underused cameraman who, for his sins, had assisted Jack Hill on three Boris Karloff vehicles made at the end of the illustrious actor's career: *Isle of the Snake People*, *The Sinister Invasion* and *House of Evil*. As luck would have it, McKinney had just finished working on a Charlotte-based film, *Hot Summer in Barefoot County* (1974), directed by Will Zens,[5] and he remained in the region long enough to shoot both of Friedel's films: "Austin was recommended to me by Pat Patterson," says Friedel. "He was our big gun at $100 a day, and we'd refer to him as our 'Hollywood DP', trying to confer an air of legitimacy to our teeny-weeny production in the sticks. I really believe he was responsible for a lot of the look of the film. His lighting gave the film a style that made it look a lot better than its budget. He claims that I'm responsible for giving him interesting things to shoot. But I don't think I knew enough to visualize the lighting that we would end up with. It seems I'm always giving Austin the credit and he's always handing it right back to me!"

Bearing in mind Corman's dictum, Friedel had scouted for a single strong location that could act as the focus of the drama. As it turned out, two were needed to make the perfect screen composite: one providing the exterior and another the interior. "I went around and found that incredible old house and paid the people twenty five dollars to use it," he recalls. "The interior was actually a beautiful Gothic residence in Charlotte. That the two fit together as one place is part of the charm and magic of moviemaking."

With McKinney's lighting skills and Friedel's eye for the framing of a shot, honed during his days as a still photographer, *Axe* took shape with more style than one might expect for a low-budget horror flick. Notwithstanding the tiny budget, Friedel drew his imaginative palette from the greats. "Visually I was in the thrall of *Citizen Kane*," Friedel says, "so any time I could use low angles, deep focus, mood lighting, I was eager to do so. The first shot was the three hoods coming out of the elevator. I loved tracking shots, but had no tracks, so I stuck Austin in a grocery cart and someone pushed him down the hall. We had so little money and equipment. Austin joked that I was trying to kill him with all the low angles etc, but later said that my demanding this caused him to show just how good he really was. He never got asked to try for much on his other films."

One of Friedel's personal judgements was to limit the graphic depiction of gore and mutilation. Whilst the film has its share of horrific moments, the emphasis is on mood and suggestiveness. "Visually I agreed with Hitchcock, that playing horror off-camera was more disturbing because the audience fills in their own 'worst nightmare' – I also thought that it was a little cheap to be too graphic, and it just wasn't me," he admits. "I'm not a fan of horror movies and didn't go to them or study them. And that probably was one of the failings of the movie. On the other hand it brought an un-horror-like sensibility to the material. But I was a fan of the movie *Repulsion* by Polanski, and have always felt great sympathy for the mentally ill."

Working without scrutiny or prior training, Friedel was essentially taking a crash course in filmmaking whilst shooting a feature. It's this combination of naiveté, ambition and creativity that accounts for the personal feel of his work. "The first day of shooting was the first time I was ever on a movie set," he laughs. "Even the grips had more experience than me. My best friend was a teaching assistant for the critic Manny Farber, so I asked him to make a few suggestions. But it was pretty much pure instinct, and not much thought. I let it fly." Working with trained actors was also new to Friedel (his college films were cast from the faculty), but he soon rose to the challenge. "I felt the one thing I could count on was that I could tell when someone was being phoney or unreal. I had been a still photographer so I was aware of what faces can communicate, so it became a balancing act between those two instincts. Given the demands of such a short shooting schedule, I felt if they were just acceptable, i.e. didn't stink, we would be okay."

The script called for a young woman to play the withdrawn, emotionally disturbed Lisa. Enter Leslie Lee, who gives an unsettling performance. "Leslie had done a little modelling. She was the daughter of the State Senator from North Carolina and was actually quite down to earth despite her privileged upbringing. The key in casting is finding people that have those qualities the characters have, without them having to act. Leslie had a certain quiet angst in her at that time that I felt would be believable as Lisa. Since Leslie was not very comfortable with dialogue I kept hers to a minimum and let her face do her communicating."

Acting alongside Leslie as her mute, paralysed grandfather was Douglas Powers: "Douglas had so much humanity," says Friedel, "he was a child psychiatrist in real life. And those luminous eyes – I felt his face could convey the horror he would have to witness."

The third key role brought Friedel into contact with an actor whose screen presence would lift both of his Carolina-shot films. Hitchcock had Cary Grant, Scorsese had Robert De Niro, Orson Welles had, well, Orson Welles. Frederick Friedel, with one eye on the greats and the other on his minuscule budget, knew that he needed a compelling male lead to play the criminal gang leader Steele. An open casting was called in Charlotte, and Friedel waited to see who would turn up, knowing he might well have to take whoever walked through the door. Fortunately, fate was smiling. Jack Canon became Friedel's leading man in *Axe* and *Kidnapped Coed*. A talented actor adept at playing seedy but compelling characters with a sardonic edge, he was a godsend to both productions. "Jack was a director in dinner theatre in Charlotte at the time. So it was great luck to be able to find him, because I only cast locally. I felt he had real charisma and talent – sort of our low-budget 'Bogey'. Jack was so good that it was really just a matter of putting the camera in the right position to capture him. I believe he had previous film and television experience but I can't be sure. I remember him once saying, after I complimented his performance as special, that he was merely dipping into his old bag of tricks. He may have said that partly to underline my own inexperience. I do remember him almost grudgingly saying that while he could direct me under the table in theatre – in other words he knew a ton more than me – I certainly seemed to know more about directing movies. It was sort of a backhanded compliment, but such was my admiration for him I gladly took it anyway!"

Of the other leading cast-members, Friedel says: "Ray Green really looked like the character I wanted and that was more important than any ups and downs in his delivery. I don't remember much about him. I was lucky he came to the auditions too because he was quite a fit for the role. I remember not being that happy with him when he was delivering lines, but he embodied so much of Lomax by just walking into the room (or by being dragged down the hall...) that he was very effective. The one performance that really crossed the line in my view and is glaringly unreal is Aubrey (Frank Jones) when he is in the hotel before he's killed. But that was one of the first scenes we shot, and I totally missed it. I believe the director who said there are no bad actors, just bad directors, so the buck stops here on that one. If I had caught it, I could have given him better direction."

Rounding out the cast was Friedel himself as Billy, the younger member of Steele's gang. On the subject of his own acting, Friedel says: "I wasn't in too much of the film so I didn't find being an actor as well as director too difficult. Given the 'range' of my performance you can see why! I always harboured the belief – based on what, I'm not sure, probably ignorance – that acting was easy. As you can tell by the way I shot myself – straight down on my head so I resembled a 'bush man' – I gave a lot less thought to presenting myself than I gave to the other actors. In my recent movie, *My Next Funeral*, I was in every scene, so it was a bit more challenging."

The last scene to be shot was the one in which Steele and his gang hold up a convenience store and terrorize its lone female assistant, played by Carol Miller. "That sequence is very hard to watch now," shudders Friedel. "I chose Carol because of her innate shyness and dignity, not for any prurient value. As such you are seeing a real person's feelings and essence being violated and so it is very painful to watch, much more so than if the person is more an exhibitionist. Her suffering moved me to tears then, and it does now, because it was real. With any experience I would not have chosen a person for whom doing the role would cause so much pain. She was so shy we had to clear the set. I used Carol as one of the birdwatchers in *Kidnapped Coed* because of what I put her through on *Axe*. It was a role better suited to her temperament."

For Friedel, the shoot was a genuine seat-of-the-pants experience, requiring much improvisation. "We would all go to the location and I would sort of make it up on the spot," he says. "I'm embarrassed to admit that. I remember being so tired and feeling that I almost didn't have a minute to get there early and plan. On the last night, when we shot the convenience store mayhem, I remember getting there a half hour early and sitting down with a pad and paper and actually planning out the shots and shooting sequence. That was the only time I did. It went so smoothly that I made a mental note to do that in the future. Since this was my first movie and I didn't know how to make one and I had never seen one made, I didn't know people planned their shots until I tried it. Talk about the innocence of youth!"

One of *Axe*'s curious distinguishing features is its lack of back-story. Just how did Lisa and her disabled grandfather come to be living together? Where are Lisa's parents? The simplicity and the pared down dialogue lend the film a suitably isolated ambience but we're left with many unanswered questions at the end. Asked whether the actors did any theorizing about the history of their characters, Friedel says: "I don't know. Actually I didn't even know that was part of the actor's or writer's process at the time, such was my inexperience. I made the grandfather paralyzed simply to increase the jeopardy Lisa would be in and to have her character be someone who is both caring and trapped (and hopefully sympathetic) at the same time."

Another feature of the movie is its extremely short running time; it clocks in at a lean sixty eight minutes. Friedel explains how this came about: "I have never made a movie that was the proper running time. There is a maxim: one page of script to one minute of running time. It has never worked out that way for me. My last movie *My Next Funeral* had a ninety-three-page script and ended up seventy seven minutes. I believe *Axe*'s script was shortish to begin with. Those protracted opening and closing credits to lengthen it are embarrassing to me now.

An ill-conceived attempt to add screen time by essentially boring the audience to death. My solution to short running time has been, instead of writing longer scripts, to compound the problem by playing scenes longer than they should be. In other words playing scenes interminably to gain time and thereby slowing the whole movie down. Pretty clever, huh? It's sort of like the man who took longer strides to save his ten-dollar shoes and ripped his twenty-dollar pants. In *Lisa* we used almost everything we shot. We had to. I did cut out about five minutes of Lisa taking care of her grandfather – washing, shaving, etc. – because it was just excruciatingly slow. I actually snipped it from the final print with scissors when I came to my senses. The final shooting ratio was 1.8 to 1. Probably unheard of! We ended up using out-takes, bits of film right after the slates, the same shots over. I didn't know any better."

Post-production began immediately after the eight-day shoot, and lasted until the summer of '74. Friedel feels that the mood of the film emerged in the editing: "I don't think that it was really carefully thought out or planned out. I did think that there would be some innate suspense built in by setting in motion the collision of sadistic, capriciously violent thugs and an emotionally unbalanced farm girl with the capacity to kill. I started cutting the film on a Moviola in my living room in Charlotte. I remember cutting the killing scene in the hotel room first. I kept cutting it shorter and shorter because the more familiar I became with it, the more boring it became. Until I screened it for someone and it went by so fast they asked, 'What was that?' It was then I realized I was so close to the material that I needed a second opinion to keep me from going off the deep end. That's when someone recommended Avrum Fine, an editor in Atlanta, Georgia. So I moved to Atlanta for a couple of months while we finished the editing. We flew to Cleveland to get the music and sound mixed in a couple of days. I had an answer print made by Movielab in New York, and ten more prints struck."

Friedel's memories of making *Axe* are coloured by events in his personal life at the time. "I fell in love with Leslie shortly after I cast her. Apparently she had fallen first and would hang around me patiently until I woke up and realised we were in love. I remember the terrible discomfort of having to watch the two rape scenes with her as the target. It's one thing writing them, but quite another having the woman you love play them. (It certainly didn't help my affection for Ray Green as Lomax.) We went together for a while. She was separated from her husband at the time and she eventually went back to him. Our parting was very amiable and sweet. So in addition to the insecurities of directing my first movie there were the insecurities of young love. I think the movie sort of endowed me with the 'cool young director' aura. Worth Keeter once said he felt like Elvis when he started directing. Well I probably felt like a very, very minor rock star. But before the editing finally took off with Avrum I remember feeling pretty hopeless, like it wasn't going to turn out at all. And I had fantasies of just going off someplace to lead a 'quiet anonymous life'."

Once Avrum Fine became involved in the editing process, however, Friedel's spirits lifted, even more so when the marvellous, eerie score by George Newman Shaw and John Willhelm was added. Says Friedel: "George was a blue eyed angel with long blonde hair – think a Southern, more innocent Roger Daltrey. I thought

about casting him as Billy for a while. His mother was a famous American painter named Mary Todd Shaw. And John was a sweet, shy brown haired version. Both were smart, funny, and gifted musicians. They were like brothers and creative soul mates. George was also a soundman on the movie. We went to a studio in Charleston, South Carolina and did the music in one all-night session. Very spontaneous, watch the movie and let it fly. They also helped with the sound effects. I think we did the sound of the axe 'reconfiguring' Lomax by hitting

KIDNAPPED COED

a London broil with a spoon and snapping a piece of celery immediately afterward!"

Friedel's relief that his first feature film had been completed was matched by his enthusiasm for the results. "When *Axe* was completed I was happy with it. I felt it was as good as I could have done under the circumstances. And I sort of got swept up in everybody's positive reaction to it. What I wasn't prepared for was how horrifying and stomach-turning some people found it. The dichotomy between the exciting and playful experience of using 'red' in these scenes (food colour and corn syrup...) and how truly horrifying it becomes to an audience when music, effects, and editing are added, is truly head-spinning. It seems my just-out-of-college fun and games really bothered some people, my highbrow friends and relatives included. Some of them asked me how I could make such a horrifying movie, and do such terrible things to these people? Didn't they know it was just a movie? They believed it was evidence of something dark lurking beneath the surface! *The Los Angeles Times* reviewed it – imagine, the *L.A. Times* reviewing a $25,000 movie! – and attacked me for doing terrible things to an underage girl (Leslie was twenty-two...) Had I been less mortified I could have taken that review and parlayed it into a three-picture horror deal, but I really didn't want to do horror movies. I was already working on an adaptation of *Lady Chatterley's Lover*! I only screened *Lisa* once myself, at Movielab in New York, watching for colour correction with the executive for Movielab, and a college friend – they said they were impressed. The 'premiere' was in a drive-in, in Charlotte, North Carolina! There we all were, sitting in the front seats of our respective cars, listening to our opus on the tinny little sound boxes hanging inside our windows. When it was over we got out and went to the concession stand in back to see what reaction people had to the movie, looking for any excuse to 'exult over our triumph'. Actually I think I was too nervous to 'exult'..."

The positive reaction to the movie gave Friedel the confidence to roll the dice again: "People kept saying they thought it was the best thing to come out of this area – so I talked Irwin into immediately doing another so we'd have two 'successful' movies out there. I had read that the best time to get your second movie going is when your first is about to come out, before you know whether it's a hit or not. So when the first screening went well, I called Friedy (as my partner Irwin was known) and in my excitement somehow convinced him that having two successful movies was better than one. In other words let's just keep cranking them out. I was so enthralled with the experience of making them I couldn't bear the thought of stopping. This decision in a sense took my eye off the business end of selling *Axe*, which came back to haunt us, and I wasn't fully digesting the filmmaking lessons the first one could teach: so the second movie suffered from the same storytelling problems as the first..."

Kidnapped Coed

It was around this time that Friedel met another of the local players: studio boss, actor, director and one-man exploitation industry Earl Owensby. "I only met Earl at a screening of his movie *Challenge* (1974)," Friedel recalls. "I'm not sure I even was formally introduced. Worth Keeter said he asked me what I thought of it afterward and I said I thought the Pantera[4] was the best thing in it. I don't remember saying that, but the arrogance it conveys has a familiar ring to it. I probably was jealous about all the money he could spend on his movies. I think *Challenge* cost $250,000, ten times what I had for *Axe*. I guess I felt Earl was using his money to make himself a movie star, something that would never have happened any other way. I never saw any of his other movies or the ones that Worth made for him."

With *Axe* playing at the local drive-ins, work quickly began on the second of Friedel's North Carolina films. Known to British pre-cert video collectors as *Date with a Kidnapper* and to drive-in audiences in America as *Kidnapped Coed* (under which title it has surfaced on DVD), it started life as a rough outline called *Night of Mourning* and eventually made its screen debut as *The Kidnap Lover*. "It's odd seeing all the titles that have been hung on my movies by distributors in hopes of enticing an audience," Friedel says. "My first movie I called *Lisa, Lisa*, using the title to cue the protagonist in a rather innocent way in order to set up the irony of her turning into The Terminator. Calling it *Axe* (which distributor Harry Novak did in a second) was a way of announcing the impending bloodbaths in advance to lure horror fans to the film, which I felt totally undercut the element of surprise and irony." It was also Novak's decision to retitle *The Kidnap Lover* as the far more salacious *Kidnapped Coed* (no doubt trading on contemporary headlines about the so-called 'Coed Killer' Edmund Kemper, whose brutal serial murders terrorized the Santa Cruz area of California during 1973). Friedel shrugs: "I guess that's why they call them 'exploitation movies'!"

Buoyed by the experience of working with Jack Canon on *Axe*, Friedel cast the actor again in the central role of the kidnapper who falls in love with his captive. "I figured if a little bit of Jack was good, then a lot of him was great. I knew he was a terrific actor who could be menacing, touching, funny, intelligent, and so I simply

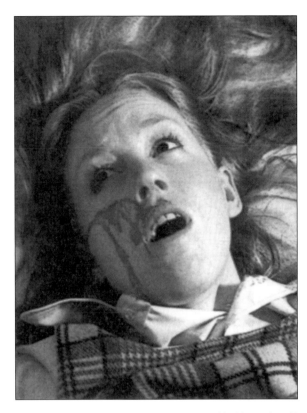

wrote a movie around him that would enable him to be all of that. I thought his scene with Leslie in the kitchen was the best thing in the first movie and I wanted more of that. I was very much under the spell of Bernardo Bertolucci's work at the time, especially *Last Tango in Paris*, so I sort of made Jack my version of Marlon Brando and wrote lots of scenes with him mining his past; you know, 'Last Tango in Charlotte'…" Referring to the slow, episodic plotting of *Kidnapped Coed*, Friedel wryly admits, "*Last Tango* was an unfortunate model to choose for an action movie, but such was its spell over me that I was blithely undeterred. I never studied the 'appropriate' movies! I was happy that Jack was able to get some work from his participation in my films, but I always felt with his talent and charisma he should have received more acclaim."

Also back on board was cinematographer Austin McKinney. "I figured with Jack in front of the camera and Austin behind it, I'd be in good shape," says Friedel. "I knew that Austin would bring a beautiful look to the second feature." With Canon as one of only two central characters, and a minimal supporting cast, Friedel was hoping to keep the budget right down: "But I was completely forgetting my weakness for beautiful images, which had us driving all over the North and South Carolina countryside, even hundreds of miles to the beach for one scene. A less sensible low-budget idea never existed! I don't know how I budgeted it because the shooting schedule was three times longer than *Axe* – twenty one or twenty three days instead of eight-and-a-half. Anyway, I came up with a budget of $49,000: that may have included getting an answer print from the lab."

Shooting started in the autumn of 1974, with a loose, still-unfinished script, lacking in structure but high on oblique incident. Friedel would endow the finished film with a unique episodic dreaminess, although he admits he was flying blind in terms of narrative style. "I actually didn't know what a story arc or a third act was, back

then," he laughs. "A lot of the choices of who and what the leads met up with came out of simple ideas – 'Wouldn't it be funny if this tough-as-nails character ran into some bird watchers? Or an old man who simply spits on him?' – people that would by their nature neutralise his first violent impulses, thwarting his ice-cold persona so he became more human and Sandra would have someone to fall in love with. Jack, in addition to playing hard-as-nails, could be so funny. That's why I let that scene with the old farmer play on and on. I just loved Jack when he mugged for the camera. The farmer with the shotgun never was really going to shoot him, just scare him off. I loved putting him in these ridiculous situations and just turning him loose: not the best strategy for making a tense kidnapping movie, but analysing and thinking things through was not something I indulged in much at that time. In fact, even though the scene is ostensibly about Jack getting water for an overheated car, I never really cared about that, and at a screening for distributors, one of them, Steve Kaplan, yelled out to me when the scene was over and we see Jack drive to the next farmhouse, 'Hey, where did he get the water?' I was pretty embarrassed! With Leslie I just thought, wouldn't it be interesting if the one time she decided to run away and get help the person she ran to turned out to be blind?" He pauses, and then with characteristic self-deprecation adds, "Pretty deep thinking, huh?"

Certain scenes, such as the one where the fleeing lovers meet a crazy old farmer and his catatonic daughter, seem to mirror the scenario of *Axe*, although Friedel stresses it's unintentional: "There was really no conscious connection between the farmer in *Kidnapped Coed* and the grandfather in *Axe*. A lot of the time when I was writing I would meet someone who evoked something for me and I would then write a scene for him or her. The actor who played the farmer looked like Santa Claus, and played him a lot around Christmas time. So I thought, wouldn't it be interesting if 'Santa Claus' turned out to be crazy – again, pretty deep thinking!"

"Back then if I had an idea or impulse I pretty much went with it."

It's worth pausing here to reflect on the (lack of) technique Friedel is describing. He consistently refers to his directing process with a disarming air of apology, self-deprecation. He clearly wishes to present his inexperience honestly, without artistic posturing, and this is entirely admirable: it would have been easy for him to make pretentious claims of an overarching directorial master plan, given the clear stylistic similarities between the two films. I think it would be a shame, though, if Friedel's modesty was allowed to overshadow his achievements. In the course of researching this book I've seen a great many films by inexperienced first-time directors, and they certainly don't all feel like *Axe* or *Kidnapped Coed*. Short schedules, tiny budgets, no exposure to the deathless wisdom of screenwriting guru Robert McKee: these are part and parcel of the low-budget horror film milieu; and yet there's a watermark of intelligence and creativity to Friedel's work that lifts it well above the average for movies made under such conditions.

In some cases, instead of predetermining character by writing a script and then looking for suitable actors, Friedel chose to build a story around people he wanted to film.

This allowed the real world to guide the structure of the story, through stray observations and chance meetings, rather than using actors as laboratory rats to run around a pre-determined storytelling maze. While this approach was clearly the result of inexperience, it's hardly controversial to point out that an untutored eye can sometimes see possibilities that the rigorously trained cannot. The very qualities that Friedel cites as failings – lack of preparation, impulsiveness, the influence of 'unsuitable' filmic models like *Last Tango in Paris* and *Citizen Kane* – contribute enormously to the idiosyncrasy of his work.

Friedel's habitual modesty is charming, but it shouldn't discourage viewers from regarding his work as creative and experimental in the true sense. Untutored, unpretentious, and bolstered only by his prior experience as a still photographer, Friedel possessed a natural inclination to look for personally satisfying solutions to the puzzles of filming, rather than responding to his inexperience by copying the conventions of less ambitious moviemakers. His photographic experience may explain why he chose to create characters on the basis of unusual-looking actors; still photography is not a narrative art, and sure enough both of Friedel's horror films are peppered with fleeting characters who appear in the movies like cameos or snapshots, and who then disappear never to return. They're like figures in the background of a photograph, captured in a split second in an instant of 'composition', their inclusion enigmatic and possibly accidental, leaving us to fantasize their possible relations.

Friedel's other great strength is to *trust* his impulses: as he says, "If I had an idea or impulse I pretty much went with it." This leads to a sequence of narrative events that can seem incredibly arbitrary: but it feels genuine and plausible too. I believe Friedel's spontaneity, and the courage to let it rule the storytelling, explain why his work is so much more interesting than, say, the contemporary efforts of his neighbour, Earl Owensby, whose business acumen is admirable but whose films lack intuitiveness and trail doggedly after the structural norms of mainstream cinema. By not trimming out his impulses, by allowing strange *non sequiturs*, Friedel created something unique. This also, I believe, accounts for the dream-like quality of the two films, their lucid sense of place soaked with an immanent malevolence. Friedel's impulses do not necessarily link up to make an entire subconscious structure that can be explored, like some sunken ship, by viewers snorkelling beneath the surface; but as in David Lynch's work they allow a sensation of 'floating' between narrative codes and storytelling currents, deferring closure in a highly individual and pleasurable way.

Friedel is candid about the way material circumstances dictated some aspects of his movies, aspects that a critic might have read as 'directorial intention'. *Axe* and *Kidnapped Coed* are still guided by intentional creative choices, however impulsive, but what's striking is how even the accidents Friedel describes – for instance when the shortfall in running time necessitated the use of longer takes in the editing – seem to fulfil some secret blueprint of the movie: things go right whilst seeming to go wrong. The elongated credits for *Axe* allow composers Shaw and Willhelm to shine, as their title theme plays out in its entirety, its mood perfectly matching the feeling of suspended time sustained by the lingering final shot. It

goes to show that creativity can be as much a case of circumstance drawing with your hand, as it is with conscious artistic choices. With solitary writing or music there's a greater degree of control over external factors, but cinema is a great fusion of media (writing, photography, music, art design etc.), and fused in there too we get the subtle DNA of real life, in the form of accidents, worldly pressures, all the organisational headaches and slip-ups that can occur on such a complex undertaking. Maybe that's why cinema, especially low-budget cinema, can feel more real than written storytelling. No one doubts that the extraordinary circumstances on the set of Francis Ford Coppola's *Apocalypse Now* fed into the onscreen story and lifted it to a higher state, but it's worth pointing out that even a 'bad' film can exude a casual verisimilitude, for which a novelist could sweat and labour gruellingly without success! Having said that, it's the temperament of the artist that determines whether an unintended intrusion should be incorporated or fought against. When Herschell Gordon Lewis saw that his 1967 film *The Gruesome Twosome* was running under feature length, his solution was to film a cheap five-minute prologue of two polystyrene heads in a wig-shop window, 'talking' to each other (via primitive animation) about the story to come. The same problem as Friedel had with *Axe* gave rise to two very different and idiosyncratic responses: Lewis's bizarro solution tells you a lot about his jocular attitude to his work; and Friedel's slowing down of the tempo is perfectly in keeping with the overall mood of his movie. Such 'accidents' of circumstance can reveal instead of obscure the character of the filmmaker.

Kidnap Completion

The film comes to life through its images. Friedel was highly attuned to the possibilities of the region's visual attractions and what *Kidnapped Coed* may lack in formal storytelling terms it more than makes up for in pictorial beauty and its ability to evoke a sense of place. "Part of the fun was just roaming around and letting my eye respond to the North Carolina countryside," he recalls. "It was like having the whole State for a movie set. The place where Eddie holed up with Sandra was actually two locations – they entered the lobby of a hotel in Concord, North Carolina and went upstairs, to a room in Monroe, North Carolina. In Charlotte, we were at most a few hours drive from everywhere: the small towns, the farms, etc. The only scene that required many hours driving and therefore staying overnight on location was the beach scene in South Carolina. We made that trek because I wanted to have Jack praying at sunrise by the water. We had only a few minutes of 'magic light' at sunset to shoot the exterior of the car on the beach. And it got stuck in the sand. So we had to quickly call a tow truck. Which also got stuck in the sand. So we had to call another tow truck to come and tow the first tow truck out... before it could get to our car. All of this was happening just outside of the frame while we were shooting! We had to keep shooting because the sun was going down. The next morning we shot the scene, which was quite beautiful."

He continues, "I had been a still photographer so I was always in love with beautiful images and that love pretty much drove the movie. I went overboard in shooting anything that my eye responded to. Even Austin chided me about it. Someone once said that when a director becomes old, he becomes a photographer – in other words he loses his discrimination between the essential and the pictorial. I was so young I had no discrimination at all, just a real love of shooting things. The one thing I didn't realise was how great Austin's lighting was until the dailies came back. I don't know that I even knew enough to ask for it back then, other than to say the mood I wanted."

Whilst the film is certainly one of the more oblique titles to have played American drive-ins, there is one scene at least that connects with the exploitable subject matter of its likely co-billers: a brutal rape scene in which Sandra is beaten and molested by two people she at first believes have come to rescue her from her captor. Although we see nothing remotely pornographic (not even Rivers's breasts), the tumultuously edited violence – a gun muzzle violently jammed into Sandra's crotch, just out of frame; the assailants shot dead with a bullet to the crotch and the rectum – when allied to four very convincing performances, turns this into probably the nastiest scene Friedel has ever shot. He describes his approach: "I felt about the rape scene as I did about the brutal killings, that I never wanted to show anything explicitly, but through suggestion. I felt that showing things explicitly was too easy (and wasn't in my nature) and required very little cinematic imagination. I followed Hitchcock's dictum of cinema being a series of pieces of film that add up to something greater in the viewer's imagination, which is one of the reasons the brutal scenes in both movies never felt brutal to shoot; because it was more like putting together the pieces of a puzzle. Leslie's emotions were real but all we shot were separate discon-nected images, like an arm tied here, a leg pulled there etc. Hitchcock said that in the *Psycho* shower scene you never actually see a knife touch the body but you are sure you've witnessed an incredibly brutal murder. In *Axe*, the axe never touches Steele, but you feel he's been brutally axe-murdered, you never see an axe strike the body of Lomax but you feel he's been dismembered. I only showed the razor on Lomax's neck really to show Lisa's pain and insanity; it's the only explicit image in either movie. In *Kidnapped Coed*, the combination of the images and Leslie Rivers's real emotion was designed to capture the essence of a brutal rape. In *Axe*'s rape scene, Leslie Lee, who was not an actress, never went to the emotional place that Leslie Rivers did, so it was not an emotionally compelling scene – it felt more abstract and disconnected, befitting her emotional state."

Leslie Rivers brings rich girl Sandra Morely to life in a subtle, economical performance. With her freckled face and long blonde hair, she's uncannily similar to Sissy Spacek, and her nervous fragility and occasional bursts of rage suggest she too would have made an excellent Carrie White! It's a shame that her movie career dried up: her committed performance for Friedel shows a talent that could have propelled her into the mainstream.

Amongst a supporting cast comprising mostly cameos, Friedel himself turns up again, but this time only on the soundtrack: "I decided to play Mr. Morely off-screen because I thought it was unnecessary to make a character of him in the movie. We know what a father's anguish would be in this situation without seeing him. Therefore I thought it wasn't necessary to involve more characters (and actors, another low-budget solution) into our mini-budgeted opus. Also, since I was playing Sandra's father

and I was the same age as Leslie Rivers who played Sandra, showing me wouldn't really have worked. I knew if I played him off camera I could gruff up my voice and sound a bit older."

With such a loose script, it was always going to be hard finding a satisfying ending. Friedel explains, "The original ending had Leslie being shot to death by the hoodlums. I shot it slow motion with Jack screaming and going to pieces. But it was such a downer that it didn't fit with the tone of the rest of the movie, so I had to rethink it. Since I had the footage of hoods pointing a gun at them and the long shot of them driving off into the sunset, the cheapest thing to do was have a voice-over line recorded – 'Alright, who's driving the Caddy... Hand over the keys!' and 'Do you believe what's in this suitcase!' – all designed to play over the footage we had. We couldn't afford to shoot anymore. It was a no-budget solution but the only one I could come up with that somehow gave it an ending consistent with the feel of the rest of the movie."

Kidnapped Coed was made in the midst of painful circumstances, as Friedel's father suffered a serious worsening of his health due to cancer. Friedel's mood was then further darkened by another tragedy that struck at the same time. He explains: "The incident involved Leslie Lee (her full name was Leslie Lee Moore). She and I were still close during the making of *Kidnapped Coed*. The long track down the hallway of the Morley residence was shot in her family's home. Leslie's mother, Beth Moore, was Carolina royalty, her husband was State Senator, and she was everything you would expect of the wife of Southern gentry. She was beautiful, vivacious, intelligent, witty – totally captivating. I adored her. She was also very, very unhappy, and I think quite lonely. During the period we were filming she would extend invitations to me to come and visit. We always had a great rapport and I think she just needed someone to talk to. With the filming and my father's progressively terminal illness I was a bit overwhelmed and was never able to take time to see her. I always regretted it." He pauses: "In short, Beth took her life in the most dramatic and horrible fashion. She set herself on fire. It was totally shocking. It became a national story."

As with *Axe*, when it was time to cut *Kidnapped Coed* together, it proved almost too short for an acceptable feature. Friedel had to use nearly all the exposed footage. Still, one scene in particular took padding a little too far: "I yanked about five minutes from the scene where Jack is pacing in the barn, after someone at the premiere said the scene was Andy Warholesque," he laughs.

For the music, Friedel once again called on the talents of musicians George Newman Shaw and John Willhelm. "We'd make up song lyrics on the spot and they'd create these wacky country songs for the soundtrack – *'You're my little baked potato, but you're alright with me. You don't put on airs like no Frenchy fry...'*" However, the mention of George and John saddens Friedel, as he explains: "George always idolised George Gershwin and had huge musical ambitions to match his talent. Very much relating to George's ambition, and wanting to help further it, when I got to New York with my movies I got a big agent and was discussing a film idea with a Vice President of Columbia Records, who I knew I could get to listen to their music. So George and John went back to that South Carolina studio to record some original

above:
Kidnapped Coed first played in North and South Carolina in 1975 as **The Kidnap Lover**.

opposite page, strip of images, from top:
Eddie approaches a taciturn old man to ask for gas;
...but the response is one of psychopathic hostility;
Eddie and Sandra meet a young girl playing in the dirt outside a farmhouse;
"I'm blind, lady! Can't you see that?";
The blind man ignores Sandra's desperate plea for help;
The money;
The celebration dance;
The twist ending.

doesn't the Symbionese Liberation Army want this story told?' It made us laugh, so I thought why not put it on the one-sheet, in typical misleading Hollywood fashion, not realizing in my youthful enthusiasm how offensive it might be! We only used that poster for the premiere."

The premiere of what was then still called *The Kidnap Lover* took place on 15 February, 1975, at The Great Western Music Hall theatre in Gainesville, Florida, Friedel's hometown. "I remember I ran into Lindsay Anderson, the great British director of *If...* and *O Lucky Man!*, who was lecturing at the school. They had me talking to the classes before my movie opened there, making a big deal of it, like 'local boy makes good', and I told him rather matter-of-factly that I had made two films in a year. He used to take many years between his films. I'm not drawing any comparison, his films are truly remarkable, and he looked at me, almost tired thinking about making two in one year and said, 'You must have a lot of pep!'

Friedel remembers the premiere screening well: "The actors flew in, klieg lights out front... they tried to make it as big a deal as possible. The print arrived by plane just hours before the opening. There was a reporter for the college newspaper there who was making himself a bit of a pest, pompous air and all, and I was less than gracious with him. He then wrote a scathing review in the college newspaper personally attacking me. Anyway I drove home three hundred miles south to Miami the next day to be with my very sick father, who was dying of cancer. When I came back a few days later and drove by the theatre I was shocked to see that the movie was no longer playing there. Apparently it had died at the box office amidst all the hoopla. It was quite humiliating. What made it even worse was that making the film kept me away from my father during the last few months of his life and I had dedicated it to him, so I felt doubly bad. I found out that he had cancer just when we were about to start shooting and he insisted I stay and finish the movie. I remember one week we didn't have the money and I called my father, and he sent me a check for $5,000 to keep it going. He was a very special man." Friedel's father died two months after the film opened. "Before he died I lied and told him the movie was a hit," Friedel says. "I didn't have the heart to tell him the truth."

The Charming Mr. Novak

At first, Friedel and Irwin Friedlander distributed the two films themselves, under their original titles *Lisa, Lisa* and *The Kidnap Lover*, scoring play dates in North and South Carolina. Two years later, hoping for wider distribution, they struck a deal with exploitation distributor Harry Novak and his company Box Office International. Dazzled by Novak's personal charm, they accepted his offer, a decision Friedel rues to this day...

"When Harry Novak took the films to distribute he paid $5,000 up front, then struck many prints and started playing them all over the country. Whenever he showed me a box office statement, it appeared that the more he played the movies and the more money he made, the more money he claimed I owed him. I was just out of college and was totally unaware of the duplicitous practice of many distributors. Two sets of books – pretty common, especially on the low end of the scale like Harry. When I hired a lawyer to go after him, he declared bankruptcy,

material. On their way home late one night a truck crossed into their lane and struck them head on, killing them instantly. They were just in their early twenties. To this day I find the grief of this loss is overwhelming."

As Friedel and Avrum Fine worked on the editing, they realised there was a similarity between the *Kidnap Lover* story and one of the biggest news events of the year: Patty Hearst's journey from spoiled little rich girl to revolutionary freedom fighter, which had begun in February 1974 with her abduction, and went stratospheric with her appearance as a gun-toting member of the SLA during a bank-robbery in April that year. "I only thought of the Patty Hearst connection after we had finished editing," Friedel says. "It was late and Avrum and I started joking about ways of seeking to tie it in to that event, which was all over the papers. 'What famous heiress doesn't want this story to come out?!' 'Why

and transferred the films into another company and took the negative from the lab and hid it. I was told by my lawyer that ever getting a penny from such a practiced con man would be nearly impossible, and would be financially prohibitive. He would just hide in the court system (and the sewers) for years... He's been sued many times before. I was advised to just get on with life and forget it. My partner Irwin who put up most of the money bore the brunt of the financial loss. His fortunes turned at this time and he was forced to move out of his large, luxurious home into a smaller, more modest one. The move was very hard on his beautiful wife Peggy, a vivacious Southern belle in the Scarlett O'Hara tradition. She became very depressed and eventually shot and killed herself. I have often thought that the money from the films if returned honestly would have kept them in their nicer home, and possibly this tragedy might have been averted. I'll never know. But it didn't stop there. Irwin's beautiful young daughter Jill was so distraught over Peggy's death that she attempted to take her own life. She shot herself in the throat, severing her spine, and remained paralyzed in a wheelchair. It was totally devastating. There were times I was so filled with rage I wanted to kill Novak."

The Later Films

The death of Friedel's father after *Kidnapped Coed* was completed meant he was obliged to take time away from the industry for a while to look after his mother and run the family business in Florida. "While I was there I wrote a script called *Dead Run* about two world-class serial killers and used it (and my two movies) to get a 'big time' agent in New York," he recounts. "I decided to shoot for the moon. My agent wrote a letter to the head of Universal Studios accompanying my script for *Dead Run* saying she thought I could be the next Steven Spielberg – pretty heady stuff for a young director. *Dead Run* never got made and I spent a few years trying to raise money to direct some even more ambitious projects. For my adaptation of *Lady Chatterley's Lover*, I actually had location scouts working in England when the financing fell through. I also spent some time writing and trying to raise money for *The Deed*, a movie about two young Israeli freedom fighters who helped create the state of Israel. It's based on a book by Gerold Frank, the man who wrote *The Boston Strangler*. In the eighties I got interested in making smaller, more personal movies, which I hoped to fund by writing and producing movie trailers for the studios. I probably worked on over a hundred movie campaigns: *Pretty Woman*, *War of the Roses*, *Rain Man*, *Die Harder*, etc. I also worked on TV spots for some popular American TV shows: *The X Files*, *Cops*, *America's Most Wanted*, *Beverly Hills 90210*, *Melrose Place*, etc. It was a bit schizophrenic, sort of like living in 'the belly of the beast'. Writing personal, un-Hollywood-like movie scripts while earning a living promoting big-budget fare, and television, which I never even watched. Along the way I wrote and starred in a play in Hollywood, called *Lost in the Movies*, about a mental patient who can only talk in movie dialogue. (I'll be doing that as a film in the next few years.) I collaborated with some other writers on material that was never produced: a studio picture called *Mama's Boys*, about two brothers who discover their father has a secret life as a successful criminal, and *Plots*, a murder

mystery set in the world of funeral homes. I also wrote a book called *The Complete Book of Hugs* (comic/romantic fare inspired by my beautiful wife Jill, an actress/singer who has performed with Frank Sinatra, Tony Bennett, Bob Hope, Tina Turner, and appeared on TV's *Happy Days*.) It has been published in ten countries including Great Britain. I spent some time doing stand-up comedy. More pertinently, I wrote a number of personal scripts dealing with subjects such as my father's death, and my mother's mental illness, that it appears I'll finally get to make due to the inexpensiveness of digital video."

In 1999, Friedel was brooding over the fate of his first two movies when he decided to act on an idea that had first struck him back in 1980: "I came up with an idea to create an original movie by combining the two – *Axe* and *Kidnapped Coed* – into one. Because Jack was the lead in both, I came up with a story about two identical twins who were separated at birth and never meet. But thirty five years later almost to the day, they both go on violent killing sprees within a few miles of each other. I called it *Bloody Brothers*. I did a rough cut in about a day and thinking it was probably a crazy idea – and that I'd actually get sued for releasing my own movies – I pretty much set it aside and forgot about it. Well a number of years later my best friend is teaching a college film course and for a lark shows the class the rough cut of *Bloody Brothers*... And they loved it. I finished re-cutting it and – I know this sounds crazy – it's actually a better movie than either of the other two, which were very slow and drawn out because I had to use every foot of film I shot. To make matters worse in the debacle with Novak, I failed to copyright my own films (remember, I was a small-town boy just out of college who didn't know nothin') so they have been copyrighted by a number of people who have been selling them all over the world without paying me a penny. So now I will finally own a bigger and better version of my own movies and at long last, God willing, get paid for it. The new movie actually looks like a period piece that could have been shot today. It will be interesting to see what happens. A lot of distributors want to see it. And I'd like to sell it to TV and video in Europe. All the money I make will go into my next movie. I'm intrigued as to how the story of a filmmaker who has his movies stolen but reinvents them to finally get the last laugh on a crooked distributor will play. So much of *Axe* and *Kidnapped Coed* was driven by not having enough footage to make a full length feature film, thereby using every bit of film but the slates and playing every scene on and on *ad nauseam*, that they are now almost impossible for me to watch without pain (or pain killers...) So when the opportunity came along to finally cut out some of the stuff that I find unwatchable, as well as to correct a long standing injustice, it was impossible to resist."

The scene originally cut by Novak where Leslie wakes to see Jack on the beach praying at sunrise has been reinstated in the cut of *Bloody Brothers*. Friedel always missed it, saying, "I felt it was important, to explain her change of heart towards him, but Novak cut it out without my knowing. Unfortunately the only source for this scene was an old 3/4 inch tape, so the poor quality of it you'll see in *Bloody Brothers* captures only a fraction of the visual beauty of the original."

Having made a cut of *Bloody Brothers*, Friedel turned his attention to a new project. In 2001, whilst working as

Bloody Brothers
© 2003 [no company].
writer/director: Frederick Friedel. director of cinematography: Austin McKinney. editor: Avrum M. Fine. original score and songs: George Newman Shaw and John Willhelm. soundmen: Don Jones, Lloyd L. DeFrance, George Newman Shaw. assistant soundmen: Carl Fuerstman, Douglas L. Deal. 2nd unit cameraman: Chris Allen. production manager / assistant cameraman: Phillip Smoot. special effects: Worth Keeter. editorial consultant: Perry Scofield. recording studio engineer: Hank Poole Jr. assistant to the producer: Nancy Durham. script girl: Jaqueline Plye [Jacqueline Pyle]. production assistance: Richard W. Helms, Charles Rickard, Harry H. Waters, Lenore Fuerstman. script consultant: Alan J. Pesin. executive producer: Irwin Friedlander. producer: Frederick Friedel and J.G. Patterson, Jr. colour by Movielab. This film is dedicated to the memory of George Newman Shaw and John Willhelm.
Cast: Jack Canon (Frank/Eddie). Leslie Ann Rivers (Sandra Morely). Leslie Lee [Leslie Lee Moore] (Lisa). Ray Green (Lomax). Frederick Friedel (Billy). Douglas Powers (grandfather). Larry Lambeth (hotel clerk). Carol Miller (store clerk/birdwatcher). Frank Jones (Aubrey). Jim Blankinship (bellhop). Charles Elledge (old farmer). Skip Lundby (blindman). George J. Monaghan (Harold). Susan McRae (daughter). Elizabeth Allan Burger (birdwatcher). Hart Smith, Scott Smith (policemen). Mary Hartford (birdwatcher). Ron Campbell (blind man on street). John Gibson (barber). Shela May (angry mother). Kendall D. May (son). Ronald Duvall Davis (boy on street). Helen Kaye (Mrs. Morley). Jeff MacKay, David Hayman, Don Cummins, Jacqueline Pyle, Lynne Bradley, Richie Smith, George Newman Shaw, Ronald Watterson, Beverly Watterson, Graddie Lane, Suzy Bertoni (radio and television show players).

below:
The face of a maniac? Patrick David Bradley in Friedel's latest movie, **Squish** (2007).

"suicide," Friedel says, "and a cousin of mine who killed herself. A beautiful twenty-three-year-old named Linda, who was actually a twin. I was always haunted by the idea that if someone somehow had just managed to get through to them before they did it, they might actually have decided to live. Like the Voltaire quote which I use in the movie, 'A man who kills himself today, would have wanted to live, if he had only waited a week.' A serious subject that I thought could be best approached comedically. Because I hadn't made a movie in a long time, I was eager to try anything and everything. I wrote the script while working at Fox Television, producing spots for *America's Most Wanted*, and I thought I'd lighten the load by writing as many jokes as I could think of. It turned out to be one of the most logistically complicated low-budget movies ever. Truly head spinning. Over a hundred and fifty actors, fifty locations, music numbers, and the shooting was completed for $25,000. (When finished it came to three times that, all out of my own pocket and on credit cards.) It took me a while to find a production manager who even wanted to work on it, because they all thought it was impossible to make for the money I had. I play the lead and I'm in every scene so the directing was interesting! I'm presently looking for a distributor for it."

Friedel continues to work on new stories, turning these days to the increasingly sophisticated possibilities of video technology. A script called *A Dog's Life* is one possible future project: "At this point it's a bit up in the air. I haven't found a way to approach the subject that's not hopelessly grim and off putting... It's a drama about the relationship between a homeless deaf mute and a dog he finds on the streets. The drama unfolds when the dog is put into a city pound where he'll be put down, and the city refuses to give the dog back to him because he's homeless. It's a powerful story that I hope brings some attention to the rather bleak treatment given to both homeless people and animals in this country."

Friedel is still only in his fifties, so it's more than likely he will direct another production some time soon. The structure of the film industry may have changed so that films like *Axe* no longer get made, but Friedel is clearly not a quitter. I look forward to seeing his next film, whatever the medium. Meanwhile, we have *Axe* and *Kidnapped Coed* to remind us just how fertile the American independent cinema could be, back in the days when the 'exploitation' film industry ran it's own merry way, separate and sovereign, generating its own pantheon of greats: a pantheon to which Friedel most definitely belongs.

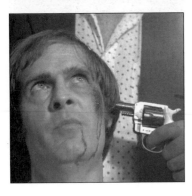

an acting teacher at the Angels Gate Cultural Center in San Pedro, California, Friedel saw an opportunity to launch his third feature film. The Angels Gate facility is an artists' enclave at a converted military base, and due to its practice of holding rents down low, it has become a haven for painters, sculptors, photographers and filmmakers. Friedel used the facility as a base for a 16mm feature film called *My Next Funeral*, a black comedy about a destitute, depressive comedian (played by Friedel himself) who decides to take his own life. However, oblivion proves just as elusive as stardom. "The story was probably inspired by Beth Moore's

Wet Off the Press…

As *Nightmare USA* was nearing completion, Frederick Friedel sent me a rough cut of his latest film, a thirty-five-minute 'short' marking his long-delayed return to the horror genre. So what would it be – another of his digressive journeys into melancholia? A downbeat character study? Not quite… The film in question is *Squish*, the moving tale of an escaped mental patient who hides out in a factory full of huge industrial presses!

We shouldn't be so surprised that Friedel has turned to black comedy this time. After the Woody Allen-ish gallows humour of *My Next Funeral*, and the problems of getting *A Dog's Life* into shape ("I haven't found a way to approach the subject that's not hopelessly grim and off putting" he says), Friedel clearly has a need to find an 'up' to counter his downbeat proclivities. And once you adjust to the idea of a film perhaps more in the mould of Frank Henenlotter or Stuart Gordon, Friedel's habitual tendency to root for the underdog is readily apparent.

The following synopsis is kindly provided by the director: *"A deranged mental patient escapes from the hospital after brutally murdering a security guard. He takes refuge in a deserted factory with heavy industrial presses, and soon becomes obsessed with a beautiful young girl. When Beauty rejects the Beast, he embarks on a gruesome killing spree. He turns the factory into a modern chamber of horrors, where death is accompanied by blood curdling screams, and punctuated by the sound of …squish. The manhunt begins. Can he be stopped before the river of blood becomes a tidal wave?"*

Although the demeanor of 'the patient' (Patrick David Bradley) suggests the forlorn undercurrents in which the director's previous characters so often swam, *Squish* is first and foremost a comedy horror film. Friedel derives deadpan humour from the means by which the tall, sallow-faced mental patient makes his escape. When a drunken male security guard comes to his cell to taunt him, dressed in a long blonde wig and women's clothing – *"D'you think this dress makes me look a little heavy?"* – the patient murders his tormentor and adopts the female garments as a disguise. Later, while tottering past a factory in red dress, blonde wig and high heels, he's bizarrely offered a job (*"Have you ever thought of a career in industry?"*) by a boss determined to win a wager with a lazy employee (the latter played by Friedel himself). And when the madman takes to a backstreet red light area looking for the john who molested his dream-girl (a fourteen-year-old innocent forced into prostitution by her

debt-ridden boyfriend) he again finds the dress, wig and heels invaluable. Meanwhile, in a broader comedy vein, the murdered guard's twin brother, a cop, suffers the jibes of colleagues who find it hilarious that the dead man was found wearing split-crotch pink knickers, fish-net stockings and a wonder-girdle. *"The nerve of that fuckin' Tony – drawing a bra and panties on the chalk outline of my brother's body,"* he exclaims.

On the downside, *Squish* suffers from a couple of shaky zooms and some even shakier performances, in particular the psychiatrist (Otto Brezina) whose line readings inexorably recall Bela Lugosi in *Glen Or Glenda* (1953). Brianna Walker also struggles to make much of innocent under-age Anna (and while beautiful she looks closer to nineteen than fourteen). Fortunately the cops (Joe Bonny and Bob Lucchesi) and Anna's selfish boyfriend T.J. (handsome up-an-coming horror star Jared Cohn, a protegé of prolific genre studio The Asylum) take up the slack, giving performances that would work just fine in a more expensive exploitation movie.

"*Squish* is an experiment to shoot a movie on Mini DV for under $5,000," Friedel explains. "It was shot mostly on weekends with mainly non-actors and almost no crew. Pretty much a mike and a camera. Its origin? A friend has a shop with heavy industrial presses. Another has a face like 'death'. I thought if I put the two together it might be a movie. I wrote the script in about the time it takes to cook a roast!"

Once again, Friedel is building his work from locations and faces rather than storytelling notions, a method that recalls his Carolina movies. One major difference this time is gore; or at least it will be, once the film is completed. The version I've seen is extremely bloody but lacking in grisly aftermath shots. Friedel explains: "It's still being edited. There are black holes, shots missing. Most of the killing, terror, and gore scenes are only 25% filled in. The sound hasn't been fixed and is unbelievably bad. There is no music, and sound effects yet, no colour correction, no titles/credits, and the last scene, which twists the story in a different direction, is missing." Asked about the film's modest running time, Friedel says, "It just played better shorter. And with some of the non-actor performances, less was definitely more…"

Made for $5,000 it may be, but *Squish* is a short with commercial DVD potential, so let's hope we see a finished version. Perhaps, with a second and third film to go with it, this could even be the birth of Friedel's first portmanteau horror movie?

Squish
© none [2007]
writer/producer/ director: Frederick Friedel.
camera: James Jay Sheldon. sound: Gordon
Michael, Wolf Bradley. lighting: Austin
McKinney. editor: Karl Jacobsen. special
effects: Greg McDougal. makeup: Jill Jaxx.
production assistant: Jonathan Stehney.
Cast: Patrick David Bradley (The Patient). Otto
Brezina (Dr. Wilhelm). Joe Bonny (Joe
Murphy). Joe Bonny (Lt. Frank Murphy). Bob
Lucchesi (Lt. Mike Barbera). Brianna Walker
(Anna). Jared Cohn (TJ). Paul Kuljis (Nick). Jill
Jaxx (Victoria). Jill Jaxx (Nurse). Jonathan
Cameron (JB). Frederick Friedel (Tony). Roger
Roman (Edward). Juan Jose Wing III (Juan).
Andrew Macatrao (Jaime).

opposite page, top:
Incarcerated, but why? 'The Patient' in
Squish.

opposite page, bottom:
Jack Canon's likeable Eddie from **Kidnapped Coed** (pictured) and his sadistic Steele from **Axe** share the screen in **Bloody Brothers** (2003).

this page, top left:
In a movie called **Squish**, set in a factory with huge industrial presses, it's inevitable that somebody's going to lose a few appendages…

above:
Will true love go **Squish**?

left:
Patrick David Bradley – mad, bad or sad?
Why not all three?

above:
More gruesome fun from **Squish**.

right:
Friedel directs **My Next Funeral**.

opposite page:
A gallery of images from **Kidnapped Coed**, starring Jack Canon and Leslie Rivers.

Postscript

It's not often that a film critic gets the chance to add a line to one of his favourite movies, especially when it's over thirty years old. The opportunity arose for me, however, whilst researching this chapter. During our correspondence, Frederick kindly sent me a cut of *Bloody Brothers*, asking for my opinion. I watched it with my friend Julian Grainger, who'd seen neither of the two films from which it was derived. Knowing that *Bloody Brothers* would need to work as a stand-alone movie, I figured a combination of my perspective and Julian's would be useful feedback. As it turned out, we both enjoyed the film. However, we agreed that the ending was a problem: because it was technically impossible for the two Jack Canons to meet, the film lacked a final payoff, although it was something the intercutting seemed to promise; events appeared to be heading for convergence as the film progressed, with captions revealing that the two brothers were getting closer and closer geographically. The original cut ended with Eddie and Sandra, from *Kidnapped Coed*, driving off together, and Steele, from *Axe*, dead in the farmhouse…

I suggested that one way to make the storylines cross would be to add a radio news bulletin over the final shot of Eddie and Sandra driving away, to the effect that Steele's body has been found at the farmhouse, and eye-witness reports have also identified him as the person responsible for the kidnapping of Sandra Morely, with Sandra declared missing presumed dead. Thus, the murderous Steele is blamed for Eddie's crime, and Sandra and Eddie can head off together with the ransom money, safe in the knowledge that the police have attributed Eddie's crime to his evil twin.

Friedel approved of the idea, saying: "It would cost nothing to do and is truly in the spirit of low-budget filmmaking." The final cut of *Bloody Brothers* now has the extra line dubbed over the requisite shot.

Footnotes

1 Godwin directed a documentary about the University of Florida called *The Magic Tower* (1966).

2 Leacock was a cinematographer and partner in the Leacock-Pennebaker company who made *Don't Look Back* (1967) and *Monterey Pop* (1968).

3 Distributed by Variety Film Inc., the company who handled Patterson's *The Body Shop* and the aforementioned Southern drive-in hit *Preacherman*; Variety also handled such explosive sex-horror hybrids as Shaun Costello's *Forced Entry* (1972) and Alex De Renzy's *Femmes de Sade* (1976), and circulated Doris Wishman's extraordinary sex-change saga *Let Me Die a Woman* (1978).

4 A brand of car.

FREDERICK FRIEDEL: FILMOGRAPHY AS DIRECTOR

1970	*Untitled Short*
1971	*Untitled Short*
1972	*Unfinished Short*
1974	*Axe* aka *Lisa, Lisa* aka *California Axe Massacre* aka *The Virgin Slaughter* aka *The Axe Murders* (also writer)
1975	*Kidnapped Coed* aka *The Kidnap Lover* aka *Date with a Kidnapper* aka *House of Terror* aka *Night of Mourning* (script title only) (also writer / producer)
2001	*My Next Funeral* (also writer / producer)
2003	*Bloody Brothers* (also writer / producer)
2007	*Squish* (short)

THE DEADLY SPAWN
EATING MACHINE

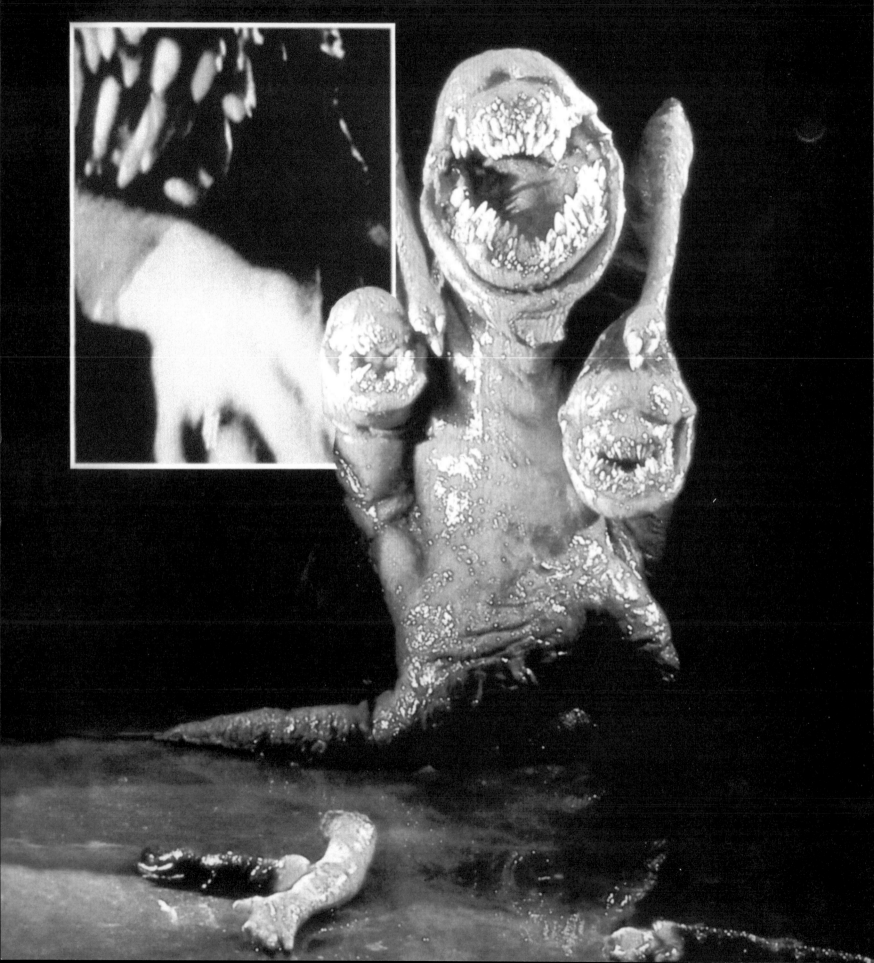

chapter 4

It Came from New Jersey!

Douglas McKeown on The Deadly Spawn

The Deadly Spawn (1982)

When a meteorite lands near a sleepy New Jersey village, tiny slithering creatures with fearsome teeth emerge and infest the locality. Next morning, thirteen-year-old Charles (Charles Hildebrandt) wanders down to the cellar of his family's hillside home and discovers gruesome evidence that his parents have been eaten by the Spawn, which now swarm the waterlogged basement. Charles must devise a way to destroy the creatures, which are growing at frightening speed, if he's to save his older brother Pete (Tom De Franco), and Pete's friends Frankie (Richard Lee Porter), Ellen (Jean Tafler) and Kathy (Karen Tighe), from a similarly grisly fate. A tall order for a thirteen-year-old, but perhaps an encyclopaedic knowledge of monster movies will prove useful…?

If a cynic were to give a 'high-concept' summary of *The Deadly Spawn*, it would sound like any one of a multitude of gory horrors – monsters, alien invasion, eyes eaten, girlfriends chased, etc., etc. But it's actually one of the most enjoyable and exciting low-budget horror films of its day. Let's be clear about one thing: the worst a horror movie can be is dull. *The Deadly Spawn* may be cheaply made and essentially frivolous but it has a brisk pace, grue and gristle galore, and lots of pleasing incidental detail along the way. It's a funny, gripping and atmospheric piece of work that puts many a monster flick of big studio pedigree in the shade.

A brief prologue showing the deaths of a couple of unwary campers is simply workmanlike, but the next few scenes draw us compellingly under the film's spell. Director Douglas McKeown takes time to introduce an entire household whose fate will be the focus of the story. These early scenes are so evocative and plausible you find, to your surprise, that you're not merely waiting for the Spawn to attack – with most low-budget monster mashes, all you really want to see is teeth and flesh-wounds, everything else is an irritant. Not so here – without over-doing it or being pointlessly arty, McKeown captures the gentle, sleepy domesticity of a Sunday morning, as everyone just eases their way into the day. The wonderful music has a dreamy calm-before-the-storm

feel, the acting is realistically low key, rain beats down on the windows: you would almost forgive the characters if they opted to deny us the usual screaming and bleeding and instead hopped back into bed like real people, for another forty winks…

But this is a horror film, and such idyllic laziness is not an option. Bloodthirsty sceptics can rest assured that the laid-back parents soon lose their happy thoughts after a trip to the cellar, and the mayhem proliferates (in step with good characterisation) from thereon.

The Deadly Spawn reminds me of another great American horror movie, Don Coscarelli's *Phantasm*: both films focus on believable, non-chippy teenage protagonists forced to deal with an attack on their families, presented within a fantastical framework. *The Deadly Spawn*, like *Phantasm*, is liberally packed with highly inventive special effects. And both are mood-pieces; the prevailing emotional ambience being a blend of humour, horror and melancholy.

opposite page:
The Spawn Queen in all her glory.

below:
McKeown applies some additional make-up to cast member Richard Lee Porter. In the centre background are Rita Hildebrandt (*left*) and Ted Bohus (*right*).

The Deadly Spawn
(US/UK theatrical & US/UK video title)
aka **Return of the Aliens: The Deadly Spawn**
(US theatrical re-release & video title)
aka **Return of the Alien's Deadly Spawn**
(US video cover title)
aka **The Deadly Spawn: Eating Machine**
(Japanese theatrical & video title)
© 1982. Filmline Communications
Filmline Communications presents.
director: Douglas McKeown. producer: Ted A.
Bohus. executive producers: Ron Giannotto,
Tim & Rita Hildebrandt, Jeff Kimelman,
Jonathan and Susan Harris. screenplay:
Douglas McKeown; story: Ted A. Bohus, John
Dods and Douglas McKeown. director of
special effects: John Dods. director of photog-
raphy: Harvey Birnbaum. editor: Marc Harwood.
additional music: Ken Walker & Paul Cornell.
music composed, arranged and produced by
Michael Perilstein. lighting director: Frank
Balsamo. special makeup: Arnold Gargiulo.
associate producer: John Dods. first assistant
cameraman and additional photography: Carl
Santoro. special effects unit director: John Dods.
chief technician: Greg Ramoundos. cinematog-
rapher: Frank Balsamo. makeup: Arnold
Gargiulo. effects technicians: Jack Piccuro,
Glenn Takakjian, Robert Bohus, John
Matthews, Kevin Shinnick, John Payne.
miniature & additional effects created by Tim
Hildebrandt, Glenn Takakjian. negative cutter:
Noelle Penraat. assistant to producer: Sue
Oster. production co-ordinator: Kathi Vent.
music editor: Ken Walker. continuity & stills:
Robert Bohus. unit manager: Mik Cribben.
sound editors: Tom Davis, David Szani, Glenn
Takakjian. additional dialogue: Tim Sullivan.
sound recordist: Frank Balsamo. camera
operators: Bernie Noble, Robbie Anderson,
Boris Zimilewski, Greg Ramoundos. sound
effects: Paul Cornell. production assistants:
Greg Ramoundos, Jack Piccuro, Glenn
Takakjian, Abigail Wieland, Robert Bohus, Ken
Brilliant. Special thanks to Filmcore: Gary
Knudsen; Charlie Chubak; John Rizzo; Ted and
Diane Bohus; Don Bohus; Donna Olive; John
Dods Sr.; June Dods; Norma Vent; Jim Palmer;
Bill and Linda Williams; Ron & Jo Vent; Joe
Tranz; World Cinnevision; Andrew Freiberg;
Sharon Weinstein; William Lynches; Neil
Pappalardo; Susan Dods; Helga Grev; Mary
Payne; Ken Freile; John Chatzky; John
Romberg; Jerry Shettig; Forry J. Ackerman;
Dave Hutchinson; Laura; Derek thorne; Tom
Roberts; Jill Stoudt; Kelly Dodds; Joe Russo;
Walter Brenen; Don Harvath; The Gladstone-
Peapack Fire and Ambulance Corps. colour by
Technicolor. processing by Studio 16. titles by
Movie Magic. music recorded at Veritable
Studio (Ardmore, PA). engineered by Joe
McSorley. music score copyright 1982 by
Michael Perilstein. Endnote: "Don't Try It, Gary"
Cast: Charles George Hildebrandt (Charles).
Tom De Franco (Pete). Richard Lee Porter
(Frankie). Jean Tafler (Ellen). Karen Tighe
(Kathy). James Brewster (Sam). Elissa Neil
(Barb). Ethel Michelson (Aunt Millie). John
Schmerling (Uncle Herb). Judith Mayes
(Bunny). Andrew Michaels (camper #1). John
Arndt (camper #2). Diane Stevens (Nibbs).
Darlene Kenley (Hilde). Madeline Charanis (Ju
Ju). Jack Piccuro (electrician). Ied A. Bohus
(medic). Robert Bohus (medic). William Sorgi
(policeman #1). Michael Mastrobaltista
(policeman #2). Michael Robert Coleman
(policeman #3). Tim Hildebrandt (doctor). Rita
Hildebrandt (nurse #1). Diane Bohus (nurse
#2). Ted Bohus Sr. (mayor). Joe Kanarek, Gabe
Bartalos, Cliff Rubin, Jonathan Neil Harris,
Susan Harris, Margaret Truit, Jon Cavaluzzo,
John Riley, Lucile Riley, James E. McPherson,
John Tiger, Eric C. Hammarstrom, Joseph
Haggerty, Skip Williamson, Gary De Franco,
Ken Burge, David Steck (extras).

above:
Japanese video cover.

But enough of the film's subtleties... What about the monsters? Well, they're *fantastic*, a triumph of low-budget dedication and design. The Spawn-on-human attacks are just priceless, and even the less successful prosthetics make up for in chutzpah what they lack in technical polish. Of all the effects in the movie, I'm always most startled by the ultra-realistic early stages of the Spawn, skittering around like mutated mudskippers in the flooded cellar. The more advanced Spawn inspire a mixture of repulsion and hilarity: they even have a bizarre sort of cuteness, their cartoonish facial expressions exuding a Tex Avery pleasure in going about their gory business. By the time these critters have grown into man-eating multi-headed giants the size of cattle they're riotously impressive, sure to stir the hearts of even the most jaded fans. John Dods, who designed these magnificently angry crimson creatures, their gaping mouths packed with teeth sprouting from swollen gums and dripping with alien mucous, gives us one of the most memorable screen nasties ever. I've applauded the film's other qualities but let's not mince words – this is one hell of a payday for monster fans. In many ways *The Deadly Spawn* is the apotheosis of the low-budget monster flick – instead of a cute but obvious man-in-a-suit (*Spawn of the Slithis*, *The Milpitas Monster*, *Bog*), here we have a rude, aggressive, dementedly phallic/grungily vaginal creation, proliferating through several differently designed and realised stages – all of them dangerous – executed with balls-to-the-wall dedication by John Dods and given the utmost impact by McKeown. It's obvious that the

inspiration came from Ridley Scott and H.R. Giger's *Alien*: but where Scott and Giger had vast resources, McKeown and Dods carved their niche in horror heaven with a thousandth of the budget. If you have any love for the craft of monster-making, you can't fail to be dazzled.

But then, everything works well here. The young cast hold the story together admirably: there's nothing phoney about their performances, even when they have to react *in extremis*. They may have been 'new to the screen' but they never feel clumsy or corny. The scene where Peter (Tom De Franco) refuses to accept that his cherished world of science and logic has been breached by an *"impossible"* invader is well acted and completely plausible within the generic context of the film. Thirteen-year-old Charles Hildebrandt, in the pivotal role of a clued-in horror fan, never hits a false note, and – a genuine rarity with child stars – never has you rooting for his death. The script foregrounds his interest in horror films, and in a clever, cannily written exchange, McKeown has him answering questions from a psychiatrist-uncle about the effect of scary movies, thus shooting down the criticisms parents often raise when they choose to stop their children reading horror comics, or watching horror films on TV. It's all done without ostentation, revealing the child's no-nonsense distinction between fantasy and reality, and then bolstering this by showing that he's actually more resourceful thanks to his passion for horror. Talk about understanding your audience: by cocking a snook at oppressive, pleasure-denying parents, McKeown's script is guaranteed to strike a ready spark with viewers! This genre-referential approach proved quite prescient, too: the self-aware use of movie lore was still infrequent in horror films of the time. McKeown's 'postmodern' appeal to fan sensibilities easily pre-dates the 'horror-irony' bandwagon of the 1990s and has the added virtue of offering a casual, playful setting for such ideas.

All horror films need their set pieces, and McKeown delivers in spades with a priceless scene in which the Spawn chow down on the guests at a housewives' vegetarian lunch. What gives it that extra bite (if you'll forgive me) is that we're not really used to seeing middle-aged women prey to gory monster attacks. There's something both funny and disturbing about it. I was reminded of David Cronenberg's *Shivers*: repellent slug-like monsters attacking the elderly in scenes that vibrate with both horror and hilarity. If all the movie had to offer was this one scene it would still be worth your money.

There are problems, of course: Charles Hildebrandt does his best to sell the scenes in the cellar, but they're dragged out far too long, seeming to strand the boy in a temporal limbo and interfering with the time-scale of the story. He's still down there after the mayhem at the vegetarian luncheon, which jars, because in screen terms we've been occupied for quite a long time with it, not to mention the plight of Pete and his friends. On the plus side though, these extended scenes (explained in the interview with Doug McKeown) do give us lots of lingering shots of the various Spawn: one caught in a mousetrap, another nibbling at a severed head, etc. Quibbles aside, the film's overwhelming drive and energy push the narrative beyond the nitpicker's tweezers. If you're a parent who hasn't forgotten the thrill of being a childhood horror fan, how about leaving a DVD of this movie lying around for your children to find? I bet even the seen-it-all 'kids of today' would get a kick from this spirited genre treasure.

Douglas McKeown was born in New York City on 14 January, 1947, and raised in Metuchen, New Jersey. He graduated with Honors from Emerson College in Boston and began teaching high school English courses (Shakespeare, World Literature and the Art of Film) in 1970, leaving after six years to work in the theatre. Among the film students he taught in the early seventies were: Richard Wenk, who went on to become writer-director of *Vamp* and *Just the Ticket*; Tom Ruegger, producer-writer of the TV shows *Tiny Toon Adventures* and *Animaniacs*; and David Copperfield, *née* Kotkin, the stage and TV magician. From 1976 to the present, McKeown has been an actor, stage director, stage and screen writer, stage designer and video maker, and, of course, has enthralled horror fans with his only theatrical feature *The Deadly Spawn*, released in 1983 and still wowing audiences on DVD today. McKeown is currently living in New York, writing and performing autobiographical material as a member of the storytelling group Queer Stories.

The Monster of Metuchen

"My earliest memories of movies are from Saturday matinees at the Forum Theatre in Metuchen," he recalls. "They used to run 'old' movies for kids. I remember the Weissmuller 'Tarzan' pictures and a host of sci-fi and horror, such as *Forbidden Planet*, *Tarantula*, *Them!*, *The Mole People*, *It Came from Outer Space*, *It! The Terror from Beyond Space*, *It Conquered the World*, and so forth. All the *It*s! I was completely in love with early Harryhausen, like *The Beast from 20,000 Fathoms* and *20 Million Miles to Earth*. I didn't care much for colour films, which I felt were garish and more suitable for children's musicals than terrifying monsters. Besides, the movies I liked were mostly bloodless and not gory, until Hammer films arrived and everything changed. I remember the first run of *The Curse of Frankenstein*, which my mother eagerly took me to, talking all the while about what a scary monster Frankenstein was, and how her high school class had met Boris Karloff backstage at *Arsenic and Old Lace* on Broadway. Then, with the opening credits of the Hammer film, I heard her whisper, 'I don't remember this being in colour...' Of course, I knew she was disappointed as it dawned on her it was a new film, but I was terribly excited. Christopher Lee's make-up I remember well, and the horrible pain of being pieced together without anaesthesia. I went home and copied the make-up as I remembered it. Later, I would copy pictures from the magazine *Famous Monsters of Filmland*, my bible. And then I began a little career of making-up as all the monsters, every one! But it is very important to note that my most vivid memories came not from the movie theatres but from television. In the mid-fifties, ABC and local stations realized they had cheap programming in some of the studios, old movie prints, which they could rent for a song. So it was *King Kong* on the *Million Dollar Movie* on Channel 11 and the Universal horrors of the early thirties and the forties screened on *The Night Show* and later on *Chiller Theatre*, that really influenced me."

For the young Douglas, it seemed natural to want to learn how the images onscreen were created, but his interest did not meet with parental encouragement. "I always wanted to make movies, from the first time I saw one, I believe. And I was an enormously exuberant and talented child. But I was discouraged in such dreams by my father and to a lesser extent by my mother. In a thousand ways they utterly convinced me that it was not possible for me to consider working in motion pictures, because it was not a real career you could go to school for and make money at, or because it cost too much, or because I had no 'connections,' without which nobody got anywhere. What did I think I was, after all, talented? Discouragement, irrationally based, as discouragement always is, was practically a way of life with my father."

Nevertheless, by the time he was sixteen, a teenage McKeown had made quite a name for himself in the locality: "I'd spent seven or eight years creating realistic monster make-ups, putting on shows, painting huge frightening murals in downtown store fronts for Halloween, etc. I was pretty damned inventive. I read in *Famous Monsters*, for example, that Lon Chaney, Sr. had employed mortician's wax for both Quasimodo and Erik, the Phantom, so I got on a bus to New Brunswick and found the stuff in an old theatrical shop, and melted it down with modern nose putty to arrive at the perfect blend, more malleable than the putty alone, but not as impossibly sticky. From age nine, I was sneaking out at night in my various guises and by twelve I had already terrorized the children in whole neighbourhoods who did not know my real identity. These 'appearances' got quite elaborate!"[1]

above:
McKeown receives his first film camera, a Bolex Standard-8.

below:
McKeown, with chatty guest star.

above:
McKeown in the 1970s.

through an improved jungle, intercut with live-action footage of my youngest brother trying to escape. In the final frames he runs into a clearing, where the dinosaur overtakes and wolfs him down."

This obsession with horror continued into college: "I shot two short 16mm films at Emerson College, one, called *The Dinosaur* (1966), that I am still happy with, small and simple though it is; the other a lugubrious story of madness and incest called *Dear Penny* (1968). I also shot filmed sequences for a play production about the Donner party (you know, the stranded pioneers who fell into cannibalism) that our college took to the Yale University drama festival in 1967. The play starred Henry Winkler, and I guess some of the sequences with him represent his film debut. They were well done, though I was certainly no technician."

After graduating from college, McKeown suffered a disappointment when his application to study film at the prestigious UCLA Graduate School was turned down. Instead, he took a job as an editorial coordinator for ABC-TV in New York. The job included putting the commercials into episodes of *The Avengers* and *Casper the Friendly Ghost*. It was less than exciting work: "I was frustrated and bored. I quit and went back to my family's home in New Jersey to re-group. I had no money and big student loans to pay off. I needed a job, but I didn't seem to be properly trained for anything except possibly teaching, so I started as a substitute at the high school I had attended only a few years before. I embarked on a teaching 'career' because I needed a job. In half a year, I was on the faculty. I spent summers putting on musicals at a children's camp, where I created a theatre arts program."

Living in New Jersey provided little in the way of film industry opportunities but, determined not to be thrown off the scent, McKeown set up a film society at the school where he was teaching, and with the students raised enough money to make a documentary. They won first prize in a New Jersey competition and the film was screened on public TV. "I should add that my inspiration to teach film came through a correspondence I was having with Lillian Gish," McKeown explains, "and I'm sure I was among the enthusiastic young film students in the sixties who gave her the idea to start touring with a show about her early filmmaking experiences. I believe it was those lectures that led to her book, *The Movies, Mr. Griffith and Me*."

Enter John Dods and Ted Bohus

In 1976 McKeown left teaching and moved back to New York. It was a period of poverty and struggle for him, working as an actor, scenic designer and theatre director. But it was through his persistence working in the theatre that one day, in 1980, the opportunity to make a feature film came knocking. "I got a call from John Dods.[3] He had worked for me on a couple of projects, notably Shakespeare's *The Winter's Tale*, a spectacular production I mounted in 1973. John created special visual effects for the play. He also did animation for a 'House of the Living Dead' attraction I designed at an amusement park in 1977. I'd known him since he was in junior high school; he made effects in his family's basement on Rector Street in Metuchen. I knew his older sister from school, and she brought me over to see his set-up: model animation on a

This early interest in film received its first practical boost when a photographer uncle persuaded McKeown's parents to go halves with him on buying the boy a Bolex 8mm camera for Christmas. "Ah, Uncle Tom," McKeown smiles, "only a photographer would know that the Bolex was equipped with the single-frame exposure capacity. Just what I needed to shoot a dinosaur movie!" At last the teenager's obsession with horror and sci-fi could make the transition from theatrical scares to moving images. The theme of his first film experiment, shot in Standard-8 in 1964, followed in the footsteps of the Father of the *cine-fantastique*, Georges Méliès: a rocket trip to the surface of the moon, recreated in McKeown's basement. "My second film was of a Tyrannosaurus rex crashing through a forest," he continues, "the prehistoric tree was a frozen broccoli stalk that gradually melted under the lights and looked like a time-lapse decay from *The Time Machine* when projected. I remember laboriously moving the wire-and-latex dinosaur model I had made through the miniature set, while my mother, sitting there peeling potatoes in a bowl in her lap, clicked the shutter after every incremental move. My second dinosaur film was with the same model, but moving more sophisticated scale than I had ever come up with in *my* basement, let me tell you! Anyway, he said he had met another horror film buff at a convention, named Ted Bohus, and they were interested in having me join them to make a low-budget film! Simple as that. They were both New Jersey residents and I was now a *bona fide* starving New York theatre type."

McKeown immediately set about writing scenes for the film. "I wrote the first scene in time for the auditions, which we did on videotape, and a couple of dummy scenes of dialogue to express projected characters. A lot of that ended up in the 'final script'." He pauses: "Final, hah! There *never was* a final script, as it turned out!"

The onscreen story credit goes to Bohus, Dods and McKeown, in that order, with McKeown credited as sole author of the screenplay. When I ask about the co-writing credit for story, McKeown laughs: "Now it gets funny. I'm chuckling at the term 'co-writers'. At our first meeting I realized neither one of them had given much thought to a script. None in fact! Well, they weren't writers, you see. It was to be a low-budget sci-fi horror film like the ones we had loved in the fifties, about a monster from space that eats people. Ted said they would like me to come on board to 'direct the actors,' since they didn't know about acting, but they would direct the film! I was momentarily taken aback, but I said there was no

such thing, as far as I knew, in the history of motion pictures, at least after 1916 or so! (Well, maybe briefly in the earlier sound period, with a position called 'dialogue director', I grant you.) I would only direct the movie, the whole movie, and I was afraid that would have to be final. They reluctantly agreed (as I remember it) and I asked to see a script or a treatment. Ted said, 'Oh, we were going to make the words up as we went along.' I thought, *what have I gotten into?* But I really, really wanted to make a film, so I said I would direct only if I could also write the script. I figured that way I could develop a theme or two and maybe make the characters more than just functionaries to the special effects. I certainly had years of experience writing dialogue for various stage projects, and of course had studied writing in college. However, I never considered the amount of work I was setting myself up for. Okay, they said, but they would have to be equal partners as far as the story was concerned. Agreed, absolutely! It was their film! And that was the way it stayed even to the final credits. At least so far as the writing was concerned. I wrote every word of the dialogue in the principal photography. The words added by other people to the film were added much later (including some boring mumbo-jumbo spoken into a walkie-talkie at the end), probably as much as a year after I had left the project, as I understand it."

above:
McKeown on the set of **The Deadly Spawn**.

below:
McKeown in 2005 [photo: Joe Henson].

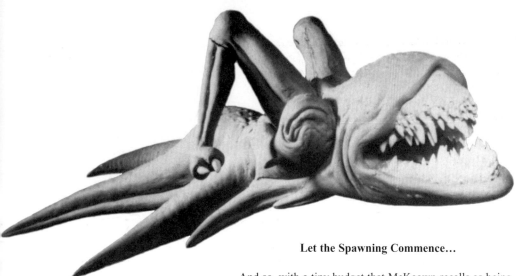

Let the Spawning Commence…

And so, with a tiny budget that McKeown recalls as being between $25,000 and $28,000, the production was underway. Shooting started in the autumn of 1980 ("late October or November") and continued throughout the winter and up to early summer of 1981. "We shot basically in sequence," McKeown explains, "Without knowing how the film was going to end! And on weekends only, since almost everyone had weekday jobs. Except me. I borrowed thousands of dollars from a friend to be free from a job to write the scenes as we shot, to have the scenes ready for the actors as early in the week before we shot as possible. Sometimes they only got hand-written speeches on the Saturday morning of the shoot, driving out to New Jersey in Kathy's car – she was Ted's girlfriend at the time, and she worked very hard as a general dogsbody."

McKeown set about writing a story that would be practical on the limited budget: "I suggested that we tell the story of a single family to keep it simple and cheap, that we don't try to bring in the larger world of, you know, military, government, officialdom of any kind – it couldn't be remotely convincing on our budget. Besides, I didn't know about those things personally; I only knew what I had seen in the movies (Hitchcock once said he could never make a western, for example, since he would not have known the price of a loaf of bread). However, I *did* know about a middle-class New Jersey family. I also said the whole thing should take place in one twenty-four-hour period. One setting, one main action, one day. I didn't tell the other guys, but I thought Aristotle and his dramatic unities were just made for a low budget! I also decided that an easy way to tie everything together without too much effort, and since we didn't have a single person charged with production design, and also since we had a monster called a Spawn that flourished in water, would be that it should rain for the entire twenty four hours. I envisioned the sky clearing only at the end. This would also provide general atmosphere, since the surroundings were *not* going to be a haunted castle, or anything remotely exotic."

With a setting and time-frame now chosen, McKeown turned to the characters, drawing on his own experiences as a movie-addicted youngster. "I went to work on the conflict between the two boys, as a set-up for the younger kid – a stand-in for me and my childhood, if you haven't already guessed as much – to be the hero later, with his love of monster movies and flexible imagination, while Pete would be helplessly in denial (probably another fragment of me in that trait, as well). I always assumed the kid would somehow find a way to kill the thing, probably by 'frying it' with electricity or something. Incidentally,

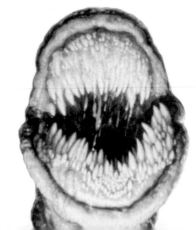

that's why I had him ask in the breakfast scene, 'Hey Pete, how did *The Thing from Another World* get killed?' A savvy audience would know it was 'cooked' like a big carrot! I followed convention by having two sets of 'lovers,' but neither would be lovers in terms of sexual content. I didn't want any sexual content. Ted said from the start that we had to get an 'R' rating to put his company on the map, and he said he wanted to see 'tits'. I thought that would be gratuitous, not to mention embarrassing, out in New Jersey with semi-pros and amateurs and their families around – besides, the teens I had in mind were relatively innocent. Ted did force the issue and made the poor actress who played the mother wear a see-through nightie. However, I said I thought violence – which could also earn an 'R' – would be quite natural, given the nature of the big Spawn, which we had all agreed should be a fierce, unstoppable eating machine. (I know we were thinking of recent films like *Alien* and *Jaws*). So I said, we will make it violent, *grossly* violent: we'll rip the mother's face off! It's ironic that I even thought this, since I had believed from childhood that such gore was revolting and not 'art'. I always preferred the subtler terrors to stomach-churning horror. While I was proposing these things in the weeks before shooting started, John was having me out to his New Brunswick apartment building to behold the armature of the Mother Spawn he was creating. I was dazzled by his precise work, but a little alarmed at his 'identification' with the creature... There was a moment when I happened to be nearby as Dods was crouching next to his mother spawn, making some adjustment or other. I believe he was unaware he was being overheard. He murmured to it, with a certain focus and intensity, and in a slow drawl, 'What kind of a creature are you?' I tip-toed away!"

The Bernardsville house where much of the action unfolds belonged to Tim and Rita Hildebrandt, parents of the film's young star Charles Hildebrandt. McKeown explains, "Ted had hooked up with Tim at one of those sci-fi movie conventions, and Tim had, I think, agreed to help produce the film at that time. He offered his house for the main location, as well as his considerable artistic talent and skills, and when I came up with the characters of the kid and the family, his son Charles joined the cast. They had no basement, however. The door in their kitchen opened on a stairwell of maybe five steps down to a crawl space. A tiny root cellar. So we shot up from that to the silhouette of Barb calling 'Sam, Sam?' but the reverse angle and all the basement footage itself was shot at John Dods's apartment building down in New Brunswick. He leased it as his workshop and studio, so it would now double as our movie family's *huge* basement. Pete's bedroom interior was in another house entirely: it was John Dods's actual childhood bedroom on Rector Street in Metuchen. The vegetarian luncheon interior was the house Ted Bohus shared with his parents in, I think, Hoboken, New Jersey."

The first scene to go before the camera was the prologue, in which two doomed campers meet the Spawn (off-camera). "I think it was Dods who later re-shot most of this and made it rather flat and trite, I'm afraid," McKeown asserts. "Today, I think he might half agree with me. In the original as I shot it, the guy attacked in the tent doesn't just do a bloody hand-grasping thing, as the camera tracks in to the shaking tent; instead, he suddenly gets flung out head-first all shredded and bloody and then wrenched back inside at high speed to be consumed with great violence. I thought the rushes looked great, leaving what the thing looked like to the imagination, yet shaking the tent so unnaturally and all, but Dods later re-shot the scene. I don't know why – maybe he just wanted to be a director. But the unintentional jump cut, the silly bloody hand reaching out, these I would never have done. Two shots of mine that remain show the campers actually coming upon the burning ground surrounding the meteorite. They are too dimly lighted, but I still like the energy and excitement in them."

I tell McKeown that I particularly admire the early stages of the film for their domestic sleepiness and pleasurable melancholy. "Thanks, I agree! And I was conscious at the time of trying to get almost exactly what you describe. It's very pleasing to know you felt that! I wanted to pull the spectators in to the ordinariness of life. I thought if I could convince them of that, the 'impossible' would become believable."

The rain outside during these scenes plays a big part in establishing mood, although it was by no means easy to make it work: "The rain was a big headache, though I think it was a good idea to have it. Not only did we always have to spare a crew member to stand out of camera range with a garden hose, and we had precious few crew members to spare – they were basically three or four college students and one or two local teenaged interns – but we shot the entire movie over the course of that year during the longest drought in the state's history to that point! Believe it or not, it never rained, but *never*. There was an emergency town ordinance against using garden

hoses! So we had to be very careful to watch out for the police on top of everything else. I also had to instruct the crew member each time in the correct angles of rainfall and so forth. What we really needed was a rain-wrangler! In the shot out the kitchen window at the end of the breakfast scene, the little tree outside is being shaken so violently it looks like a hurricane. But I couldn't pay attention to that since I had to operate the camera for that shot! The cinematographer of the day (our credited DP didn't always show up) said it was an impossible shot to get – he said he would have to scrunch up under a cabinet on the counter, and he couldn't do it. So, it fell to me, and I hand-held it. At the end of the film there is a high-angle panning shot when Millie runs into the yard to find Charles in shock with a medic (played by Tim, his father), and the DP of the day would not go on the roof of the garage to shoot it, so I did that shot too, as well as a high angle from a van in the front yard in that sequence – amazing how many people are afraid of heights, isn't it? When I wanted a shot, I wanted a shot. I kept saying that it couldn't be shot any *other* way, and that was the truth once I had envisioned it a certain way."

McKeown was full of admiration for the work at which John Dods excelled, namely creature design and special effects: "The monsters were marvellous. I was terribly excited when Dods and Bohus agreed with me initially that we should try to do as much effects work in the frame with the actors as possible, since this challenge was rarely if ever taken up by Hollywood. I had in mind the nearly impossible-to-achieve shot in *Jaws* when Roy

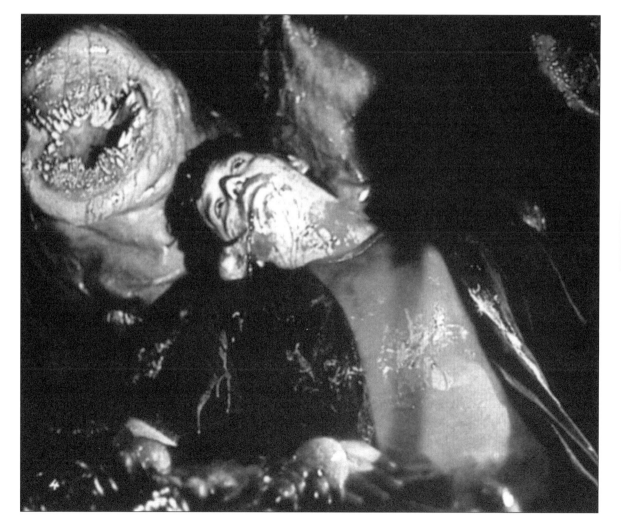

above:
Mom (Elissa Neil) regrets going down to the basement...

left:
A passing electrician (Jack Piccuro) provides a tasty treat.

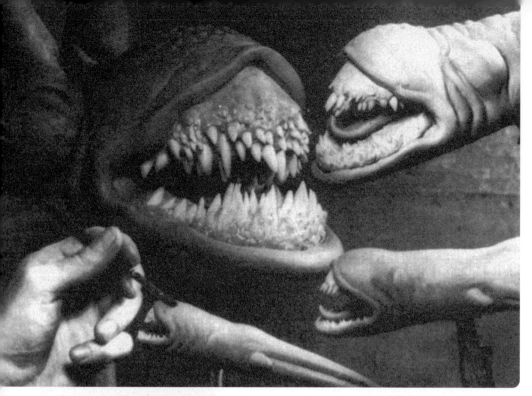

Scheider is throwing out chum and the shark surfaces behind him. I mean, can you imagine how hard it was to frame that so tightly, while moving in a fast boat, and have it work? I admire that so much. And I'm not even a Spielberg fan. A lazy cut-in, or 'fixing it in post', are Hollywood methods. I believe audiences know when they see a cut-in that whatever they are seeing isn't really happening, so the energy just drains out of so many scenes in other movies."

One of Dods's most imaginative and innovative ideas involved the early, 'mudskipper' manifestations of the Spawn, seen swimming around in the waterlogged cellar. "This was John Dods at his most brilliant," agrees McKeown. "I came in one morning and he had invented this effect almost literally overnight. Like all genius ideas, it was incredibly simple. Like, 'why didn't I think of that?' simple. Maybe he stole it from someplace, but I think he just invented it. He had a shallow box made, about eight feet by four feet and filled it with no more than a few inches of water. In this he inserted a plywood sheet in which narrow squiggling pathways had been cut out with a jigsaw. This panel lay flat just below the surface of the shallow pool. Little spawn, made of flexible foam latex over metal armatures, were attached by a tiny stud through to the underside of the plywood in each of the pathways. It was as if each had a cufflink on its ventral side. The camera framed out the sides of the big shallow box, as well as the crew members who stood at one end and pulled a fishline attached to the front of each spawn. The little flexible bodies, submerged exactly halfway into the shallow water, merely traced the course pre-cut in the plywood, as they were pulled from one end of the box to the other. Voila! They appeared to be swimming."

The film benefits not only from Dods's dedication to his creatures but also from the focus the mainly young cast bring to their roles. Had they been wooden or exaggerated, or drama-school precocious, it would have been the kiss of death: instead they help to assert the film's careful plausibility, despite a most implausible threat. McKeown agrees: "I liked that cast of actors very much and had great respect for them, working tirelessly and not complaining, and for no money! Your praise for them makes me feel justified in my contribution, in the high energy I brought to the set – energy and seriousness that were not always welcomed by the producer, I have to say, nor very often by the effects director. Only the actors seemed to appreciate these things. Ted and John often mistook seriousness of purpose for bad vibes, I think. They didn't thrive on tension, so they tried to undercut it with joking and distracting silliness. Once, I actually snapped at Dods and the crew when when one of the actresses was about to scream her head off for a POV through the monster's teeth, and they were making jokes and not realizing how hard it was for her to concentrate. I think I said something like, 'She's the one being seen up there on the screen, so shut up!' If I didn't say it, I said something *like* it, and I know she was grateful. The actor who played Pete was Tom De Franco, and I thought he was very, very good. He worked seriously and hard, and never complained. Except once, when I stupidly filled in for a missing actor in his close-up and we kept having to do re-takes. Finally he said, 'Doug, how would you feel having to play the scene with your director?' I was instantly humbled and apologetic. I had been the cause of his discomfort, though totally unwittingly. I really like the way he did the physical stunts himself, and Tom made some nearly unspeakable lines of dialogue trip off the tongue. I honestly don't know what he later did, though I believe he continued acting."[2]

One decision that could have backfired horribly was to make an untrained youngster, Charles Hildebrandt, the primary human focus of the narrative. McKeown says, "He took direction very well, like Tom, because he took the film seriously and trusted me. I gave him lines to memorise, and I also provided him with subtextual thinking, filling in beats that a professional actor would ordinarily do himself, and Charles grasped the whole deal effortlessly. I especially like him at the breakfast table with its carefully rehearsed overlapped dialogue, and in the 'psychoanalysis' scene. He was just thirteen I think, maybe younger, when we shot the film. But Dods later added a great deal of footage with Charles in the basement with the Mother Spawn, after he had begun to shoot inserts, etc., up to a year or two later. I don't think that material works as well, frankly. Though Charles certainly performs bravely under the circumstances – Charles told me Dods would yell at him directions like, 'Look more scared! You don't look scared enough!' I saw Charles in February of 2004 when we got together to record an audio commentary track for the DVD. This was a coup for Don May,[4] I am told, because apparently, with the lower budget features, the principal artists generally all end up never speaking to each other again! Charles never was interested in acting, and is now a successful entertainment lawyer living in Washington, DC."

In scenes that pre-date similar discussions in movies like Wes Craven's *Scream*, McKeown decided to include a number of exchanges, between Charles and the others, about monster movies and their effects on those who watch them: this was, as McKeown says, "to saturate the non-monster scenes with interest: irony, visuals, clues. It was also to pay off later when the boy's fantasy-world obsession leads to the shrewd deployment of a WSD – a Weapon of Spawn Destruction! He knows monsters, so he's ready. Pete doesn't believe in monsters, so he's not. He won't even be able to save his girlfriend. And it's not that Pete isn't strong, brave and true; he's just paralyzed by a rigid paradigm that Charles does not hold."

Among the adult cast, John Schmerling played the mildly patronizing psychoanalyst uncle (says McKeown: "He was an actor from the Jean Cocteau Repertory Company I was associated with in New York – he later sang and played a villain in my stage musical version of *The Count of Monte Cristo*, which I directed and designed"), and Ethel Michelson played the sweetly eccentric Aunt Millie ("She simply came to us in an audition when another actress, a comedienne I had wanted, turned down the part. I found her to be quirky, and New Jersey-like, and I wanted Millie to be funny. She was a nice lady, and I seem to recall, she was coming back to acting from a hiatus of some kind."). James Brewster, who played the father, was actually around the same age as his 'son' Tom De Franco: "I tried to make him up to look older," laughs McKeown, "but I think I only made him look hung over!"

Ratatouille!

In a film with so many wonderful scenes, it is still, when all's said and done, quite easy to choose the best. The ladies' vegetarian luncheon that goes horribly wrong must be one of the funniest scenes in a horror picture. I asked McKeown what he remembered about shooting this classic moment in monster movie history…

"I remember all of it! My favourite sequence in the film. Dods and I were in complete agreement about the tone of the sequence (it is really two scenes, the preparations with Millie and Bunny, and the actual luncheon). He was rather more prepared with effects for the two shooting sessions (on two successive Saturdays as I recall) than at some other times. Plus, I got enough concessions on shooting effects in shot with the actors that I accepted his insistence that he be allowed to do a lot later as inserts. This included the food processor gag, which I remember as my idea originally. I wish I had been called in for those close-ups. Especially the suspenseful one: I would have made Dods move that baby spawn faster, or in the final edit have cut the shot's duration in half, maybe more, and I would have made them put more slime on the spawn!! But it is a crowd-pleaser, and I am told it was stolen later for a film called *Gremlins*, though I never saw that. I especially enjoyed the cast of the luncheon scene, since three of the ladies were personal friends. 'Hilde and 'Nibbs' were Darlene Kenley and Diane Stevens, a comedy team I wrote for and directed at the time – they played nightclubs in New York – and 'Ju-Ju' was Dr. Madeline Charanis, who had been my French teacher in high school and later my colleague. She was the wife of a distinguished Byzantine scholar from Rutgers University in New Brunswick. We all had a great deal of fun! 'Bunnie' was Judith Mayes, a funny actress who had played the maid in an Off-Off Broadway production of Molière's *School for Wives* in which I had played Arnolphe, some years before. Her personal style was that of a ready-made 'character', something I thought would help put over the speech about peace-loving gorillas. She was quite game and without vanity, as the finished film I think shows. My favourite bit may be Madeline hammering at spawns with her shoe as the ladies all flee the house, a crew member standing outside spraying them all with a garden hose. The 'funny' (disgusting) food bit was really just a Hitchcockian touch: he was fond of food gags, like the supper scene in *Frenzy*, or Jessie Royce Landis putting out her cigarette in an egg

yolk in *To Catch a Thief*. I also loved when Millie screamed and tossed the baby spawn and Dods later inserted the picture frame exposing the spawns on the wall behind it, like cockroaches. All of this was planned and storyboarded in advance, of course, as was all of the principal photography, else we could never have shot such tight sequences on no budget. The DP was rarely happy that I had pre-planned so carefully the angles and movements – it left him little to do but light and shoot. And he knew almost nothing about lighting! He was probably hired because he owned the camera and the lights. I also remember Kathy having to come up with green sauce and brown rice for the scene, and Madeline herself making the centrepiece, using an aubergine (except she gave it whiskers, so it looks like a baby seal!) And Darlene (Hilde, spelt Hildey in the film) came up with a nice line after the one I had written: 'They're Swedish soy balls,' to which she added, 'You can freeze them, you know.' I remember we had to take care not to stain Ted's parents' furniture with the fake blood, so on the couch in one shot the pool of blood is a piece of red latex!"

Post-Production and Fall-Out…

Throughout principal photography, tensions had been mounting between McKeown and John Dods, and when it came time to physically integrate the monsters into dramatic context, with the actors present and the clock ticking, sparks began to fly: "I shot quickly," McKeown explains, "and I expected that the effects planned in advance would be up and ready on time, always allowing, of course, for the inevitable unplanned problems. I work fast in action sequences to keep the actors and crew 'up', to match energy. This is critical when scenes are shot in pieces; they don't mesh together well later if the energies don't match. And I always knew how they were to be edited; that's why I shot so little coverage. But Dods always wanted to take it slow whenever his monsters were in the shot. He usually said at the last minute that he needed more time, and when I refused to postpone, because the actors were on call, Ted would have to step in and insist that we improvise and proceed. I know this really upset Dods, but what was I to do? I had the cast for only a short time, and I knew the opportunity to work with them (for free) was not going to last. Dods seemed to have no grasp of any of this – which would have been fine, by which I mean he was focused on effects. But he had grander ideas, I think. He saw this as an effects film, a Dods film, the way *Jason and the Argonauts* is a Harryhausen film. My calling out directions to move the monster faster or more aggressively, or in some fashion he had not anticipated, right there on the set in front of everyone, really began to irk him, and he bridled more than once. I remember he absolutely refused to bring the thing upstairs behind Kathy to tear her blouse, said it wouldn't look right, what I was asking was not possible, he'd do it later as an insert, etc. But I remember really putting my foot down on that one and insisting. Luckily Ted persuaded him, saying it was only one shot, he'd help move it himself, not to worry. But I think the real problem was basically that Dods thought of the Mother Spawn as the protagonist – she was the star, the opera diva, to him. Plus, it was him, in a way. He was 'playing' the monster, and I don't think he could appreciate the emphasis I was placing on the human characters."

above:
Dutch video cover.

shared it with anyone, it was with Dods. I slaved over it as if I owned it, but I didn't. Contracts really didn't mean a lot. I signed one, but Ted never signed a copy of it. I had had my lawyer look it over and he had suggested some clarifying language, no substantive changes at all. Well, Ted said he would have to take those changes under consideration. Every time I asked about it, he put me off, and in the meantime, I was working day and night on the film, and had no energy left over for politics or negotiations. Seems naïve now, but I wanted badly to work, and didn't want to jeopardise that. Then, after Dods got itchy to direct, he told Ted he might consider leaving the film before it was finished, complained about my directing and delivered a 'him-or-me' ultimatum – Ted must have decided to cut me out, or at least downsize my participation. (Twenty three years on, Dods sent me a copy of the ultimatum letter he had sent Ted in 1981, and expressed his regret for having written it.) I remember in one frosty phone call, Ted suggested I would not be turned away if I wished to continue to come out to watch them film the effects and even look on as they began the editing process in New Brunswick, but I would certainly have to pay for my own transportation, etc. At that point, I was pretty demoralised. Besides, I owed a lot of money, and I was without a job. Couldn't have afforded to pay for daily transportation even if I hadn't minded being unwelcome on the film that I had just written and directed! Major bummer, as you can imagine. There was another factor, one that I now think was blown out of proportion by Bohus to help him justify ending my participation. There had been a stranger on the set during one of the all-night attic filming sessions. An older lady photographer from a local Jersey paper. I was never introduced to her, but I saw her taking pictures and was mildly irritated, since it was a little disruptive. We had way too much to get done that night and everyone was already tired and cranky. I was trying to move things along. Suddenly Ted announced we would 'break' and he would take everyone out for pizza or something. I was speechless. I hadn't slept in a couple of nights, but I was so ready to work, and I felt we could get it all done if we pushed. Now, everything sagged and dropped, and I was very discouraged and angry. They all took off. I sat outside on the porch smoking a cigarette and had a casual conversation with the lady photographer. I don't remember our conversation, but she seemed like a nice lady. Well, I'm sure you are ahead of me! Seems there was consequently a piece in that local paper about a 'feud' on the set between producer and director. Quoting me. The 'photographer' was a reporter! I never saw the article, but Ted accused me of trying to undermine his film. I was flabbergasted and protested that it was my film too and why would I undermine it? I guessed he must have just assumed that's the way everyone behaves – cutting off their noses to spite their own faces." McKeown pauses, adding ruefully, "The phone calls I got from these two guys were too much. I had this crazy idea they should be grateful for my contributions..."

Whatever the ultimatum Dods threw at the producer, this complete breakdown of working relations appears to have been handled poorly by Bohus, who allowed Dods to dictate an ungrateful and bitterly unfair treatment of the director. Absorbed in the nitty-gritty of the production, director and designer failed to take time out for reasoned communication, but such considerations could and should

Science-fiction film
Bestelnummer 459

Towards the end of shooting, the storm finally broke. "Very late in principal photography, virtually at the end, in fact (I think we were up to the attic sequence), he called me at home late at night, and in a low, affectless voice, said he wanted 'to direct the film'. I was speechless. Come again? I had just directed it. What did he mean? He merely repeated that he wanted to direct it. It was a weird call. I now realise it must have been a very difficult call for him to make."

Ted Bohus had so far been acting as mediator between the two men, but at this point he chose to side with Dods, and McKeown was removed from the picture: "In Ted's mind, I think, *The Deadly Spawn* was his film, and if he have been taken on board by the producer. McKeown's 'shoot it fast and gimme the monsters!' style may have chafed the pride and obsessiveness of the Spawn's creator, but it's unusual for a producer to side with someone intent on gobbling up financial resources against the one man who's trying to keep the budget on track. If, as it proved, there was more money available for effects reshoots and inserts, there's no reason why McKeown couldn't have been made aware of this and kept in the loop. To fire a director on the eve of completion, when he's fought to bring your movie in within the budget and on time, then neglect to inform him of the film's eventual release, is shabby treatment indeed. "I was no longer communicated with after the early summer of 1981," McKeown sighs, "and only learned of the finished film's release in April of 1983, when I saw the advert in the *New York Times*! I know John Dods took months after we finished what I would call 'principal photography' to plan and set up some of the most beautifully photographed shots in the film. Almost the entire Charles-meets-Mother-Spawn basement sequence was Dods's work, for example, and to my eye, Charles looks to be at least a year older. I ended up owing a lot of money. I tried to get a free poster after the picture opened – had to fight for it at some shabby office in mid-town. Kept saying indignantly to a snooty lady, 'But I directed it!' I finally got one. I only saw the completed film at its opening night. I almost missed the evening entirely because I had to work late at a restaurant! I arrived with four or five friends for moral support. I was anxious: remember, I had thought this movie would never be completed because no one had contacted me in almost two years! So I assumed that if there ever was a finished product, it would be messy and confused at best, incoherent at worst. While it was never exactly the latter, it often was the former. I had a brief reunion with Tim Hildebrandt and kind of waved at Ted Bohus and John Dods, but had no real conversation with anyone, except the editor, whom I had never met before. I remember he was amazed to learn I possessed the actual shooting script. 'There was a shooting script? Nobody told me that!' Said he wished he had known. He was full of compliments about the ease with which the pieces had fit together, but annoyed as hell there was so little coverage – he said I barely left room at the tail of a scene for it to finish before yelling 'cut'. Well, he was right to be annoyed, but I hadn't wanted anyone messing with the timing, you see. So I called 'cut' pretty much where it would splice together later. The only scene I got to edit myself was an early one: the mother going down to the basement looking for Sam and getting attacked. We took that sequence to a sci-fi convention shortly after I assembled it, to drum up publicity, and it remained in the finished film just as I cut it (with of course many trite additional shots of blood spattering and too much swinging light bulb, tacked on later by others. Beautifully lit, of course, since Dods had had all the time in the world without actors around). Up until the moment Ted effectively took the film away from me, he had planned to rent a Steenbeck editing table and put it in my apartment so I could assemble all the footage shot up to that point, with slugs where the cut-in effects would go. I was the only one holding the complete shooting script, which I had written week by week with the editing in mind, so it made sense. But no one even asked for it later on. No wonder I always assumed the picture would never come out!"

The Unseen *Deadly Spawn*: Douglas McKeown's cut

After McKeown was elbowed out, John Dods and Ted Bohus took creative decisions that flew in the face of McKeown's prior intentions. I asked him to explain where he thinks key mistakes were made once the movie was taken away from him: the following comments help us to visualise McKeown's intended cut.

Opening scenes: "The effects shot of the meteor shooting down appears to happen in daylight (and it is followed immediately by the campers hearing the crash in the dead of night). It looks like, at best, day-for-night, and why shoot a studio model in day-for-night!? And then the establishing shot of the house – at dawn during a rainstorm!!!! – shows a starry sky with crickets chirping and a dog barking! So ridiculous. (Though I adore the model work, technically)."

First basement scene: "Here was the Mother Spawn in the basement as I cut it, but there are wrong inserts suddenly; the cut-ins of the drain that both the father and mother see are stupid and confusing, blood when there shouldn't be blood, no blood when there should be; then the shots following that face-ripping shot we so carefully created include these overlong clichés of flailing hands and swinging light bulb and blood spattering on walls (and one red-filtered close-up of 'Barb' screaming that should not be there). Actions missing. There is no shot of the spawn actually biting off the ringed finger, for example! The finger is suddenly just there on the floor (in a beautifully, lovingly photographed close-up). Simply for continuity, we needed a shot, one quick horrific shot inserted of the spawn rearing its head back like a croc and gulping the forearm, snapping down, and perhaps another quick one of the finger flying, but instead – nothing! And suddenly the open mouth is empty and coming after Barb."

Missing characterisation: "The first 'love' scene between Pete and Ellen is also gone (their best-acted scene!), rendering some of their subsequent dialogue confusing. Dods told me when I saw him in 2004 that they deliberately trashed the scene because 'the movie would have been too long.' I did not reply that among sequences he *added* I could easily have trimmed about five minutes! I'm thinking in particular about the extended Charles-in-basement sequence."

Missing plot: "A whole bit that Dods and I had talked about at some length, showing that the spawns regenerate in an 'impossible' way, a kind of 'biological fallacy,' devouring portions of their own corpuses, was simply dropped, no effects created to show this as we had discussed: but a slow track into the kitchen sink, where we were actually to see this process (later causing the kids to rush excitedly downstairs to show Uncle Herb), among other elements created with this in mind, remained as shot. It puzzled the audience, I think, or at least the people I was with."

The vegetarian luncheon scene: "Dods added shots of spawn chewing on vegetable matter. He apparently thought this amusing, but it's wrong. The spawns like water and flesh... period. Having them chewing celery or parsley undercuts the irony of the vegetarian luncheon scene. There are so many examples of things like that that made me wince at the opening night on Broadway in 1983. However, there were also additions that delighted and surprised me. For example, someone wrote a clarifying voice-over to a shot of the luncheon, "I've added something *new* this time." Also, back in the kitchen breakfast scene, the radio weather reporter ends with, "It's going to be a really *bad* day." I did not write those lines, but I wish I had!

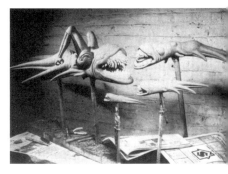

above:
Behind the scenes, some off-duty Spawn scan the morning papers…

below:
Alien teeth and pretty girls: what could go wrong?

above:
John Dods with the Super-Spawn seen in the film's spectacular coda.

below:
US poster artwork designed by Tim Hildebrandt, executive producer and father of young star Charles Hildebrandt.

footage of the crew packing up, and now it was in the film! I guess the editor used every extra bit he could lay his hands on. The very last shot they came up with surprised me. Not entirely unpleasantly, although it was a bit of a cartoon. Well, the movie can't be taken too seriously, I suppose, and the final shot *is* a pay off, in a way..."

McKeown finally breaks off and laughs: "Am I whining? Maybe I was just too darn fastidious, but it's attention to details like these that engages me as a filmmaker, even as a spectator of other people's films." Putting aside his grievances, though, McKeown admits, "There were lines of dialogue, added by others, that really help the film, and careful photography by Dods – again, technically excellent – that I simply couldn't get during the months I shot live action with other DPs. These things were a pleasure to see on the big screen, even if the dramatic content dismayed me. In general, the editor did a noble job of making sense of the jigsaw puzzle, but many pieces are placed nowhere near where I foresaw them in my editing plan, so I was bothered almost every other shot; it was hard to enjoy the film story unfolding with these constant jolts. I was pleasantly surprised at how well some of the scenes/shots worked, but I cringed, actually slumped down in my seat during others. The worst part was knowing that there was this bad stuff I didn't do. No, even worse perhaps, was knowing that some of the bad stuff I *did* do. But no: maybe even worse than *that*, some of the really *good* stuff I *didn't* do!"

Looking Back

Although McKeown's experiences at the time left him bruised, angry and disappointed, he has always remained willing to acknowledge the work of his colleagues. "I certainly don't mean to suggest that the other two guys weren't absolutely committed to the film," he stresses, "John Dods came up with some amazing effects on practically no budget at all, and Ted held the whole thing together and dealt with logistics that would be daunting for anyone. When it all worked out, it was more fun than I can say! I always loved work more than anything: eating or sleeping or even sex! – well, to be frank, maybe just as much as – and when it paid off, as for example in the vegetarian luncheon scene, I felt even at the time that we were making something quite special, something original. I suppose it should be clear by now that I love movie-making and would do nothing else if I could. I had the same intense passion when I shot my first 8mm footage in the early sixties as I had the last time I worked in video, and every time in between. *The Deadly Spawn*, with all its attendant craziness and obstacles, rancours and discouragements, was no different. Not only could I not wait to get to work every morning, I barely wanted to go to sleep the night before. (Still writing and sketching!) I suppose the most rewarding part was watching the dailies and seeing what I wanted to get, or maybe something better than I expected, suddenly on the screen. My intrepid actors were amazing, considering the conditions under which they laboured. I can very easily wax nostalgic for those early Saturday morning meetings with sleepy-eyed actors at the Camelot Coffee Shop on the corner of 8th Avenue and 45th Street, where we had coffee and breakfast and went over lines before the car picked us up and drove us to New Jersey. Of course the rehearsal process on any project is terribly exciting, always. But I was directing my own script from ideas hammered out maybe only days or

The discovery of the spawn-riddled corpse of Uncle Herb: "Those reverse angle effects shots of Uncle Herb being eaten up last too long (they were created after I left). Compare the duration with the shots leading up to and away from it, the action shots I did shoot, with the kids rushing in, spawns threatening at the edges of the frame, and the close-up of them kicking back spawns in trying to close the sliding door, just before Mother Spawn makes her appearance in the kitchen. Startling and over-the-top as the Uncle Herb effects are, the duration should have been much less, maybe half the time. We see too much, enough for the scariness to seep out, in my estimation."

Ellen's demise: "I really could go on and on. Don't even get me *started* on the sequence of 'effects' shots Dods did to cover Ellen's demise! The actress actually looks resentful instead of terrified in the very bad POV shot of her suddenly just sitting on the floor waiting to get her head bitten off!"

The ending: "This had me feeling most ambivalent. The idea I'd had for it was unsatisfactory, but I thought we would know how to make it work when the time came. Anyway, I now think the idea I had was 'soft' and slightly dull. You may remember Charles is assisted into the patrol car at the end of the final sequence and sits stupefied in the back seat. This whole shot was in the initial screening. From that point, I had proposed: Camera tracks in to the open cruiser window. Charles, now left alone in the back seat, blinks and jerks his head, as if jolted out of shock for a moment, and then anxiously leans his head out the window and looks up searchingly. The camera *cranes* slowly up, and then up and up, past the extras zapping spawns and the police and flashing lights, and up all the way to the edge of the Earth's atmosphere, where the blue gradually becomes black and star-studded. Zip! Zip! Zing! Suddenly these meteors scream past the lens, first a few and then a gazillion in a fiery shower... The End. Well, that 'ending' thrilled no one, rightly so, never got filmed of course, and instead there is a piece of film I immediately recognised as the camera rolling after 'cut': a long shot from the same angle as before, the one wherein Pete was being led tail-away to an ambulance (this reverse angle was shot far away from the actual house, near some development) – but there are no actors in the shot, only crew! Apparently, the DP, unbeknownst to me, had shot hours before! I remember doing script breakdowns here in my Times Square apartment late at night, sketching my storyboards, preparing for whatever sequence was coming up on the weekend. I remember getting to the Bernardsville set and running around removing all the tchotchkes and gewgaws with which Rita Hildebrandt decorated her home, thinking, as I pulled things off shelves and walls, 'I'll never remember where everything goes to put them back, and Rita will kill me.' I remember I did try to put some little bits of fish-like sculptures around in some framings just to keep shots from being empty, but they really don't read in the final film – principal photography was fairly murky. Also, I remember the fabulous feeling, early on in the production, of working well with Dods to integrate his home-made effects into our home-made drama. I always had enormous respect for his skill, and I've tried not to dwell since on the differences that made us part later on. I had one ambition only and always: to put on a good show. I really wasn't interested in anything else."

Life After *Spawn*

When the shenanigans over completion of *The Deadly Spawn* left its director personally out of pocket, he returned to the theatre for some much needed paying work: "After *Spawn* I designed a set for *An Evening with W.S. Gilbert* at the Cherry Lane Theatre (adapted from his actual study at Grimsdyke), and I directed *The Witch of Edmonton*, *The Oresteia*, and *Cymbeline*. I did a bit more acting (I had been doing occasional parts on soap operas). Then I went on a sort of hiatus from theatre. Around this time, I wrote several juvenile novels – ghost-wrote them for a former student. The student got the credit, but at least I got paid. Shortly after that I lost my parents to cancer (in their fifties), and my life took a different course: I began to look into the dynamics of the addictive family system and the resulting trauma to children. Specifically, alcoholism. I spent many years healing childhood wounds, and learning about this fascinating topic along the way, all during a period in the late eighties when the whole country, it seems, was caught up in the so-called 'self-help' movement. From the many wonderful groups of people I met who wanted to get on with their lives and rid themselves of demons that had either held them back or made monsters out of them (real monsters), I heard a great many amazing true stories. Fiction could not compete. I even came to think that an unconscious element of my story for *Deadly Spawn* was the insidious disease of alcoholism, represented by a voracious alien creature, setting about to destroy a family, beginning with the parents. Even prophetic: my father saw *The Deadly Spawn* in a New Jersey theatre only about two months before he died. My mother died eighteen months later. These little insights took me into an understanding of my own remarkable survival instincts as a child, acting out the horrors that remained hidden from the view of family and community. I was a child who did not exactly repress his feelings the way so many people do, but acted them out, theatrically. I think this may have saved me from alcohol or drug addiction myself. I played at addiction, acted it out, transforming myself into Mr. Hyde (the Stevenson novel reads like the story of a dope fiend), or the Wolfman (Larry Talbot always cries, 'I can't help myself!' and wants to die), and that relieved something in me, freed me just enough to not 'shut down' as others do in such families, or to 'act out' for real, and end up on skid row – or death row."

For McKeown, though, a temptation to return to the visual image came in the form of improved video technology: "When I began to get creative again, I bought a video camera and made home movies or short documentaries of artists, and so forth. I didn't attempt to contact anybody in the film business, I didn't really know anyone anyway, and the subjects I was interested in would not do as films. No, I spent years living my life, doing a little teaching, tutoring immigrants in Los Angeles county, California – some wonderful souls and memories – a lot of small art projects. I lived my life! I did contribute scenes to a film in 1996. I loved the idea of the script. It was called *The Watermelon Woman* [dir: Cheryl Dunye], and it was about a young woman who works in a video store, sees some (faux) old movies of the thirties and forties and falls in love with, becomes obsessed by, an old-time movie actress, a black woman who never even got billing in the credits at all or was simply referred to as 'The Watermelon Woman'. The film was being written and directed by a very charming and sexy young lesbian who was a first-time filmmaker, and had managed to get a grant from the National Endowment for the Arts.[5] Her lover, a teacher of media at a local college, was producing, and I called her up and said they needed me to film the fake thirties film scenes the character watches. I had a hard time convincing her. I shot a test in black and white video, finding the location myself, and putting a friend in costume. When I screened it for the filmmakers, they thought it was research, that it was an actual old film! So I ended up being asked to co-write and direct the two scenes. One of the scenes came off okay, in spite of the short shrift I got technically. It was a 'plantation' scene, and I am proud of some of that. But I received no credit on the final film (like the Watermelon Woman herself). It wasn't very well done otherwise, I'm afraid, but I still think it was a great idea."

These days Doug McKeown runs a storytelling workshop, Queer Stories, based at New York's Gay & Lesbian Center in Greenwich Village: "Most of the participants consider themselves writers of some sort or other, but only a few of them have theatrical experience (outside of the public performances they give with us). 'Queer' actually refers to both senses of the word, the stories are told from the point of view of the gay sensibility, however one wants to define that. I have run the workshop for about eight years now." He has edited a book of stories, called *Queer Stories for Boys*, drawn from the talent encouraged by his workshop. "My own stories are queer, but more in the old sense of the word," he says, "but all of the stories are true, with the elements of both surprise and inevitability that true stories convey. We don't do fiction. I'm pursuing the idea of expanding our public performance style into something a tad more theatrical, without losing the spontaneity. (My own stories are almost all about being a monster in New Jersey from the age of nine to the age of about fifteen.) I'm still reluctant to involve myself in what most people think of as theatre, fictional drama or –

heaven help me – musicals again. I'm fairly content on this side of the footlights. But if somebody asked me, well... that might be a different matter!"

McKeown's career has taken so varied a route over the years that we can no longer think of him primarily as a filmmaker. And yet *The Deadly Spawn* continues to guarantee him the admiration of horror fans the world over. It's a shame that his experiences making the movie were ultimately so distressing, but at least now we can understand what happened and attribute credit where credit is most certainly due. McKeown is listed as director on the print; and yet, at times, others involved with the production have given a different impression. As recently as 2004, I offered a piece on Doug McKeown and *The Deadly Spawn* to a respected horror film magazine, to be met with a puzzled, 'But that's directed by Ted Bohus!' John Dods's monsters are truly amazing, but let no-one be under any illusions: films don't direct themselves, and there are plenty of great monsters languishing in lousy films. Of course John Dods's creations are a knockout, but *The Deadly Spawn* is an exciting, compelling fiction, not just an effects movie, and that's thanks to Douglas McKeown.

below:
A difficult shoot – McKeown in 1980, looking tense behind the scenes of the movie. "I think I was trying to look fierce like a monster – or maybe Fritz Lang!" jokes McKeown.

Footnotes

1   They also form the basis for a series of stories McKeown has written for public performances with the Queer Stories group. A trilogy of these was published in *Queer Stories for Boys* (Thunder's Mouth Press, 2004).

2   Tom De Franco went on to appear in Joseph Ellison's coming-of-age drama *Joey*, the sci-fi actioner *Alien Nation*, and David DeCoteau's *Dr. Alien*.

3   Called Bruce Dods at the time.

4   President of Synapse Films.

5   Dunye directed six short films before *The Watermelon Woman*.

DOUGLAS MCKEOWN: FILMOGRAPHY AS DIRECTOR

1964	*Untitled* (8mm short: a trip to the moon)
1965	*Untitled* (8mm short: dinosaur film)
1966	*The Dinosaur* (16mm short)
1968	*Dear Penny* (16mm short)
1982	*The Deadly Spawn* aka *Return of the Aliens: The Deadly Spawn* aka *Return of the Alien's Deadly Spawn* aka *The Deadly Spawn: Eating Machine*

OTHER CREDITS:

1967	*Donner* (stage play with filmed sequences: director/cinematographer)
1975	*By Cycle* (documentary; advisor/co-writer/director, with students)
1996	*The Watermelon Woman* – dir: Cheryl Dunye (director of film inserts)

chapter 5

Let's Play Nasty

The Films of Don Jones

Abducted (1973)

Sue (Lynn Ross), a pretty young redhead, is stranded on the freeway after her car breaks down. A good-looking, soft-spoken man called Frank Barrows (Gary Kent) pulls over and offers to drive her to the nearest garage. Once on the road, friendly Frank becomes taciturn, and worse still his retarded brother John (John Stoglin) pops up from the back seat. Sue leaps from the car as it waits at a railway crossing, but the train blocks her escape and she's bundled back in. Once at the brothers' isolated house, she's thrown into the cellar, where she finds two more girls, Ginger (Suzanne Lund) and Stevie (T.R. Blackburn), already imprisoned. Stevie is delirious with pneumonia, but warns the new arrival, *"Wait 'til you meet Momma, then you'll be sorry you came here."* Sue wastes no time and bravely makes a run for it, but she's shot down by Frank before she can reach the highway.

John comes down to the cellar and insists on playing a game of doctors and nurses. He assaults Ginger with a hypodermic needle: she tries to sweet-talk Frank into letting her go, but instead he rapes her. Afterwards, in flashback, we learn that Frank was sexually abused by his mother (Greta Gaylord). John begs Momma to allow him a new playmate, and chooses Bonnie (Leah Tate aka Cheryl Waters), an attractive blonde he's spied upon while hanging around the local college campus. Momma gives her assent and Bonnie is brought to the rat-infested cellar. Can she escape where the others have failed?

Of all the exploitation films that trailed in the wake of Hitchcock's *Psycho*, Don Jones's *Abducted* stands out for its sleazy atmosphere and strong performances. Jones went on to make three more genre pieces, including the excellent terror-in-the-woods tale *The Forest*, but *Abducted* is his best: a classic rural horror tale with those uniquely dirty 1970s fingerprints all over it. In America the film is better known as *Schoolgirls in Chains*, a title bestowed on it by its second distributor in place of Jones's original choice, *Playdead*. There are, in truth, no school-girls caught up in the plot, but that's not to say the film isn't shocking at times: it's a classic of early seventies horror cinema, with all the lascivious dwelling upon women-in-peril you'd expect.

Jones and cinematographer Ron Garcia make good use of the attractive orange-grove locations and beautifully decorated farmhouse interiors, contrasting them to great effect with the dingy, rat-infested cellar where the victims are imprisoned. Good mileage too is gained from that trusty stand-by of the horror genre, the extreme wide-angle lens: used to rack up tension at the start of the film, with the bulbous grille of Frank's car looming menacingly into frame; and then later, in the cellar, after Ginger is poked and pierced with a syringe. Garcia's queasy wide-angle shots of John examining the girl's breasts, with a coat-hanger as a stethoscope, suggest either that a mind-bending drug has been administered or, more likely, that the director malevolently wishes to induce fainting in those who find injection scenes distressing…

Unlike most low-budget horrors, *Abducted* gains real leverage from its actors, which is a blessing because the film relies heavily on Gary Kent and John Stoglin to make things work. Corny psychos can be fun, in a campy way, but they're not going to elicit sympathy; and sympathy, for both victims and killers, is the surprise suit of this film. John Stoglin as 'John' is outstanding, given that the character could easily have veered into hamminess. An accomplished dancer and theatre actor, Stoglin gives a lot more than the script probably asked for, in a performance that tempts ridicule but quells it through sheer nerve; the unsettling mixture of pathos and menace he creates is the hallmark of a skilled and thoughtful individual. What's also interesting is the way the characterisation plays with the audience. 'John' not only torments young women, he also taunts the viewer, goading both our nervous discomfort and sleazy complicity. Stoglin plays John as a retarded child locked into an endless loop of excitement, rage and frustration. A lesser actor would simply have allowed the viewer to feel illicitly turned on watching the girls' violation and humiliation – instead Stoglin's performance makes us squirm, as we see male rape fantasies played out in a creepy, childish way.

Gary Kent has the quieter role, but he's perfect as the strong, soft-spoken Frank. Seemingly the more 'normal' brother, his damage is more subtle: his identity short-circuited by a mother who demanded her son be the 'man of the house' far too literally. Kent is a big, handsome fellow whose weathered masculinity would have won him roles in the classic Westerns twenty years previously, but he's skilful at subverting the machismo of this six-foot barn-door of a rapist: as with John, there's a child in Frank, and Kent makes sure we can see the character's trauma in his features, without sliding into bathos or exaggeration. We pity Frank, even after he's raped poor Ginger (of which more later). The flashback to his abuse at the hands of his

below:
Incredibly rare UK video cover for **Abducted** under its most notorious retitling, **Schoolgirls in Chains**; from Portland Films, who also released the bootlegged **Death Bed**.

Abducted (UK video title)
aka **Playdead** (US theatrical title)
aka **Let's Play Dead** (US theatrical title)
aka **Schoolgirls in Chains**
(US theatrical re-release title)
aka **The Black Widow** (shooting title)
© none [1973]
Mirror Releasing.
producer/director: Don Jones. executive
producer: Dave Arthur. screenplay: Don Jones.
director of photography: Ron Garcia (colour by
Pacific Film Industries). music and vocals by
Josef Powell. editor: Maria Lease. production
manager: Gary Kent. sound: Audio Services.
opticals: Van Der Veer. assistant director: Jon
Klotz. production sound: Mike Hall. gaffer: Ron
Batsdorf. assistant camera: Tom Kantrud. script
supervisor: Maria Lease. key grip: Steve Moon.
makeup: Ron Foreman. boom man: J.L. Clark.
Cast: Gary Kent (Frank). John Stoglin (John).
Robert Mathews (Bob). Suzanne Lund
(Ginger). Leah Tate [Cheryl Waters] (Bonnie).
Lynn Ross (Sue). T.R. Blackburn (Stevie).
Greta Gaylord (mother). Russell Lane. Ervin
Sanders. Herb Goldstein (local).

Don Jones's **Abducted**…

right:
Cover art for the UK video release from
Astra.

opposite page, strip of images, from top:
John (John Stoglin) threatens Sue (Lynn
Ross) in the first abduction scene;
On a leash;
Sue meets Frank (Gary Kent);
Frank talks to Momma;
Ginger (Suzanne Lund) plays along with
John's sick games;
John gets nasty;
Ginger is taken into the house;
…and tries to use her feminine wiles to
escape.

below:
Video art for the American video release of
The Love Butcher (from Monterey Home
Video).

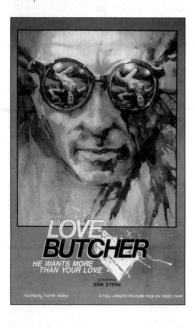

incestuously domineering mother could easily have been
played for sick laughter, thanks to Greta Gaylord's
marvellously over-ripe performance as the mother. Kent,
however, makes Frank believable (despite being decked out
in white clothes so luminous they're virtually radioactive);
his zoned-out demeanour as he obligingly 'massages'
Momma's breasts suggests the way that his mind has been
shut down by her dominance. And by the time we realise
Frank is actually *dressing* as Momma to keep her alive, for
John as well as for himself, we're saddened not amused; a
testament to Kent's composure in the role.

It's not just a case of 'pity the killer' though: Jones's
taut direction ensures we very much fear for the victims
who meet these all-too-human monsters. Two of the girls
are strong, rebellious characters who refuse to accept their
imprisonment and immediately try to escape. This of
course helps to propel the narrative, but it's also worth
noting, in a film often decried for misogyny, that
Abducted does at least portray *resistance* to captivity –
unlike, say, Alan Rudolph's *The Barn of the Naked Dead*.

Not that resistance pays off, exactly. Sue, a fiery
character who when thrown into the cellar with the others
immediately starts plotting for freedom, is a case in point.
We expect her to be the ringleader, goading the others to
rebellion against their captors. Wrong – Jones shocks the
audience by scratching her off the scorecard early, after a
tense and well-crafted chase. Shades of Janet Leigh, of
course, but the *Psycho* resonances are well absorbed into
the story, which never feels like a retread.

Psychology in *Abducted* hinges on the notion of
aggressive, clinging motherhood; the brothers' insanity is
born of a domineering matriarch whose hatred of men has
created monsters. (She's said to have murdered her husband
too, although nothing was proven.) Ungallant though this

may seem to viewers raised on feminism, a look at the
backgrounds of many serial killers (Ed Gein, Edmund
Kemper, Henry Lee Lucas, for example) bears out the
approach. As I've mentioned, though, it's possible to be
amused as well as shocked by this maternal monster. The
scene in which she reveals her incestuous relationship, to
Frank's superficially 'modern' yet rather prim girlfriend
Jane (Russell Lane), is a classic piece of American Gothic
melodrama, as she boastfully announces: *"We make love.
We make love like two lovers. We have since he was fifteen
[…] Come back any time… we'll let you watch!"* (Eagle-
eyed viewers with a sick sense of irony may notice that
behind Frank, as he starts to tell Ginger that his mother
abused him, there's a sheet-music score bearing the words
'Teaching Little Fingers How to Play'!)

Not all of the film's ploys are successful. Jones cheats
the audience to make us believe in Momma, showing us a
figure cowled in a shawl, sat in semi-profile and moving
slightly, lips just visible as she speaks to Frank. This
continues (*"Ah, it's good to have two fine boys"*) even after
Frank has left the room, making it hard to explain the scene
as simply a visualisation of his madness. Worse still, the
fine line between sleazy subject matter and sleazy direction
swings into view when Frank rapes Ginger, to the
accompaniment of a skirling saxophone, cheesily denoting
sensuality on the soundtrack. Given that Frank is impotent
with girls other than Momma, it's possible to argue that the
music mocks the affliction of the rapist, but it can just as
easily seem to suggest that rape victims secretly 'love it'.
There's also a grim irony here, because Ginger initially
tries to use her feminine charms to get Frank to release her.
When he turns nasty, it's almost as if she's brought the rape
upon herself, which gives the 'sexy' soundtrack an
unwelcome dose of sarcasm.

However, this is the only mis-step by Josef Powell,
who turns in an oddball but memorable score, playing
away from the obvious horror tropes by unsettling rather
than terrorizing the listener. (Incidentally, *Abducted* must
be the only grindhouse/drive-in movie to have made use
of Debussy's sublime *Prélude à l'après-midi d'un faune*!)
Powell's arrangements are creative and offbeat, based
around piano and electric piano, with ensemble work for
brass and woodwind. The inclusion of a minor-key flute
motif gives the film a tinge of the S.F. Brownriggs, while
the trumpets, trombones and weird ensemble vocals add
an unpredictable hint of derangement. The story's
'arrested childhood' theme is picked up by eerie arrangements of *Twinkle Twinkle Little Star* and *Three Blind Mice*
and, strangest of all, by a playground Greek Chorus of
shrieking voices yelling *"Run!! Run!!"* over Sue's fatal
sprint for freedom. Perhaps the title song, *Triangles,
Circles and Squares*, is a touch too mannered, its melody
rather archly delaying resolution via a dissonant semi-
tone, but for the final scene Powell comes up with a
successful variant, supporting Stoglin's emotional fade-
out with a sorrowful cello.

Storywise, *Abducted* falters slightly in the last reel by
introducing Bonnie, a young female student, and Bob
(Robert Mathews), her psychology professor/lover, a
couple whose intervention is meant to bring things to a
climax. Trouble is, we've spent too long watching events
at the farmhouse to engage with their anaemic love affair;
Waters is okay once she's endangered, but Mathews is
just a regulation cut-out hero, thudding to the rescue. It's
a shame the script didn't elaborate some of its fainter

148

implications about him: in a film about a mother who abuses her authority, it's interesting that Bob is abusing his authority too, by seducing a student and paying her off with good grades. He's nowhere near as bad, of course, but his lack of professional scruples makes the point that sexual exploitation is not the sole preserve of the mad. This is particularly acute given that Bob is a psychology professor – and not a very self-aware one either. After all, he drives a red Porsche – surely a bit of a *mea culpa* for a psych' professor with an overactive libido?

As the film reaches its climax there are a few striking similarities to *The Texas Chain Saw Massacre*, made a year later: Bonnie runs upstairs in the white-painted farmhouse and tries to take refuge in a bedroom, only to discover a corpse on the bed, withered to the point of mummification. Of course *Psycho* is the true source of this image, but the fact that the corpse is discovered on the first floor, by a young woman who runs screaming downstairs and out through a gauze screen-door, makes it feel like a dry run for Hooper's film. You can imagine Hooper at the drive-in, watching *Abducted* and thinking, 'Good idea!' *Abducted* can't compete with *The Texas Chain Saw Massacre* for sheer mind-bruising horror, but Jones pulls off a devastating finale of his own, ensuring that our last impressions are not sexual or visceral, but emotional. If there is perhaps just a smidgeon too much 'Pity the killers' here for some tastes, Jones does at least leave us glad that both their cruelty *and* their suffering is over.

The Love Butcher (1975)

The Love Butcher is something of a curate's egg, with its sleazy murder theme pulling against a broadly satirical depiction of the killer as super-nerd turned super-stud. It's also weirdly enjoyable, once you've resigned yourself to a bumpy ride. When I first saw this, back in the early 1980s, I was disappointed, essentially because it failed to live *down* to the savagery I'd imagined from the title. This was, after all, the era when films like *The Driller Killer* and *SS Experiment Camp* leered out at you from high street video shelves. *The Love Butcher* is the sort of title that promises all of the most reprehensible elements of sleaze cinema – graphic horror and cruel, nasty sex. When the film turns out instead to have humour and lots of dialogue, and a conspicuous absence of sadistic gynaecological butchery, you tend to feel let down, in that classic 'sizzle without the steak' exploitation way. Given that the film was originally called *The Gardener*, a title that errs too far in the opposite direction, it's little wonder that the producers chose to retitle the film so luridly! However, given a chance on its own terms, *The Love Butcher* deserves attention as a well-acted trip into horrific black-comedy.

Playing the schizophrenic Caleb/Lester, Erik Stern (from John Hayes's *The Hang-Up* and *Tomb of the Undead*) drives the film and makes an entertaining meal of both parts, his 'weirdo gimp' mannerisms contrasting wonderfully with his swanky Lothario. He essentially gives two star turns, and the movie would be a non-starter without him. Of course, it's amazing what a bald wig and a pair of jam-jar glasses can do, but there's more to his servile, diffident Caleb than comedy props. As for his egocentric misogynist Lester – with a script that feeds him some utterly absurd dialogue, the actor still manages to make the character frightening, even though we laugh at his deranged verbosity. Stern delivers the schizoid goods

without faltering, striking just the right tone and sailing blithely along despite the hiccupping plot construction. Jeremiah Beecher as the ostensible hero, Russell, is another matter. He's deeply unconvincing, turning in a performance that might have made the grade for Ted Mikels or Ray Dennis Steckler but lets the side down here. The female cast are without exception much better: Eve Mac in particular makes her Texan hussy come vividly to life in the brief time she has onscreen.

Lester's egomania takes the form of some eminently quotable rants about womankind (see below). His diatribes bring to mind General Jack D. Ripper in *Dr. Strangelove*, whose concern for the way women 'steal a man's essence' may have provided the script with a few hints about characterisation. The reversal of expectations in the final act, regarding the true relationship between Lester and Caleb, came from Don Jones, and it neatly ties the film into his own concerns, with callous words from a mother sowing the seeds of future mental illness in her son.

The credited director, Mikel Angel, was born of Greek parentage in Washington, D.C. in 1951, as Joseph Theakos. *The Love Butcher* was his only feature-directing credit. Angel acted in two Matt Cimber films, *The Black 6* and *The Candy Tangerine Man*, as well as Gary Graver's *Evil Spirits* and Joe Tornatore's *Grotesque* (the latter of which he also wrote). Two further writing credits, for Tornatore's *Demon Keeper*, and *Psychic Killer* in collaboration with actor/director Ray Danton and Greydon Clark, round out his brief filmography. (A 'Mike Angel' receives story and screenplay co-writing credit for *Rio Lambada* aka *Escape from Rio* (1990).)

Angel was a theatre director turned movie-maker, and you can see the fruits of his theatre training in the quality of the scenes where Caleb or Lester converse with their prospective victims. However, *The Love Butcher* suffered a rather stormy journey to the screen when Angel pulled out after principal shooting was completed. Don Jones, the film's cinematographer, was asked to step in and shoot new scenes, in order to shape the film into something releasable. The following synopsis is therefore accompanied by a 'co-director's commentary', kindly supplied by Don Jones. Don's comments precede the appropriate paragraphs.

"Hello, I'm Don Jones. I'll do my best – however until today I haven't seen this epic in thirty years. I suppose you know that it was shot in Techniscope. It's a two frame pull down patented by Technicolor. In essence 2:35 to 1. Most of the following scenes are Mike's, but since I also shot it I get confused as to which scenes were directed by me, and which scenes were directed by Mike (age you know)."

The camera tracks past a toy train and a flower bush to reveal a dead woman, with a garden fork shoved through her stomach. An unseen figure clips off a yellow rose and tosses it onto the corpse. The title *The Love Butcher* is superimposed over a close-up shot of a red rose. (This title card was added later, to replace the original title *The Gardener*). More flowers bloom beneath the rest of the credits.

At the crime scene, Russell Wilson (Jeremiah Beecher), an aggressive journalist, has a stand-up row with Captain Stark (Edward Roehm aka Wolfgang Roehm [Richard Kennedy]), who objects to Russell's photographer buddy taking pictures of the woman's corpse. In retaliation, Russell attacks the cops for their failure to catch the killer, whose murder tally now stands at six. Cut to another

below:
The Love Butcher's pre-credits sequence
gets things off to a good start, with some
always-welcome garden tool mayhem...

garden: Caleb (Erik Stern), a gardener-for-hire who gives the impression of mental retardation, offers a rose to Flo (Kay Neer), the lady of the house, before driving off to his next job. Once there, he asks Carla, a wealthy, irritable customer, for a glass of water. She asks him if he can recommend someone to fit air conditioning. He suggests a man called 'Les'.

Cut to Caleb's home. Caleb talks to 'Lester', who sits in an armchair. He mocks and disparages Caleb. *"You're a mental and physical cripple. And no-one loves a cripple."* The camera pans round to reveal that 'Lester' (*"I am Love. Total Love."*) is a black foam mannequin with a wig perched on top. Caleb grabs the wig and, removing his thick glasses, assumes the role of Lester, an arrogant lady's man, while looking at himself in the mirror. 'Lester' now visits Carla, the irritable lady, carrying a large knife. The film fades out before he kills her... Russell faces off with Captain Stark again at Carla's house.

This next could be mine, at least part of it, but I'm not sure.

Russell's lover Flo (Kay Neer) provokes a row by arguing that Russell spends too much time at work. They calm down and make love, but the next day the argument starts up again. Outside, Caleb is tending the couple's garden...

Anything with Pat I directed.

Cut to another garden, another customer. Pat (Eve Mac), a young woman with a Texan accent, complains to Caleb about the mess his sprinkler is causing. She mutters: *"Cripples. This fucking place is full of them. Doubt if there's a man in this state!"* Caleb overhears, and mutters, *"I know a good man, yes ma'am."* Later that day, 'Lester' knocks at Pat's door wearing a cowboy hat, posing as a Texan motorist in trouble, and asks to use the phone. Pat offers him a drink. Cut to the two of them in bed, post-coitus. Lester is about to stab Pat when a religious caller interrupts. She gets rid of the caller and Lester attacks her, chasing her into the kitchen. *"Your feminine pulchritude is detestable,"* he declares, before stabbing her to death.

Until further notice all is Mike's...

Carl (Louis Ojena), a bullying husband, and his wife Sheila (Robin Sherwood) get up for work. He complains about her taste in music, and she about their infrequent love-making. Later that day, after Carl has left for work, Caleb arrives. Sheila tells him not to come back for the rest of the month as her husband is away and she doesn't want any strange men around. When Caleb gets agitated she freaks out and dismisses him. Back at home, Lester, dressed in Spanish gigolo style, taunts Caleb (represented by his overalls on a coat-stand), before leaving to visit Sheila. He arrives at her door posing as a hip Latino record salesman. He puts the make on her but she turns him down. Back at home, Caleb goads 'Lester' about his failure to score. At the police station, Russell confronts Captain Stark with his (incorrect) theories about the killer's identity. Meanwhile, trying again with Sheila, Lester poses as a plumber, but Sheila recognises him from the night before. As Sheila swims in her private pool, Lester dives in (losing his wig in the process) and forces a hosepipe down her throat, drowning her. He puts the corpse in the bath to make it look like suicide. Back indoors, Caleb tells Lester the violence has to stop. Lester tells Caleb that their mother was a whore: 'Lester' is legitimate, 'Caleb' was born of his mother's affair with another man...

The next scene is probably mine...

Stark and Russell meet again, at the scene of the latest killing. Stark declares, *"There's one thing I do know for sure: whoever did this is weird. Not just sick, but a real weirdo!"*

This is Mike's:

Flo praises Caleb's work in the garden and invites Caleb in for a bite to eat.

Mine:

Cops at the police station examine various murder weapons. Consulting a map, they realise that the victims were all killed in the same neighbourhood.

Mike's:

Caleb talks to Flo, telling her that women have never been attracted to him: *"I'm a gimp, ma'am"* – he demonstrates by showing her his 'dead' hand – *"People don't take too well to cripples."* Flo goes to work and Russell tries to speak to her. She ignores him. When he persists, she says she's had lunch with Caleb – *"a gentleman […] He's okay, kind of a nice weirdo."* The word 'weirdo' rings a bell in Russell's mind. They wrangle for a while until Russell grabs her and kisses her, finally proposing marriage (if the kitsch version of Mendelssohn's *Wedding March* on the soundtrack is any indication). That night both Lester and Russell head for Flo's house. Russell stops at a phone and tries to call Captain Stark about his suspicions. Lester catches up with Russell on Flo's doorstep – *"Hey, Lover-Boy! Wait up!"* – and stabs him to death with the garden shears, before gaining entrance by posing as Caleb's doctor. Lester tells Flo his opinion of women: *"You emasculate a man with your bottomless body-pits. You leave him empty and unfulfilled. You drain him like a sewer into a cesspool. I am the Great Male Adonis of the Universe. I am Love."* Flo runs and locks herself in the kitchen. Seeing Russell outside, she opens the kitchen door, only for his corpse to tumble in. Lester stalks Flo around the house, rips off her clothes (*"You will leave this world as you entered it!"*), and when she begs for death rather than torture he smiles, *"But of course,"* before hacking her to death with a serrated hoe.

Police see Lester acting strangely as he walks back home, but his smooth performance under questioning throws them off the scent. Back at home, Caleb taunts Lester: Flo didn't find him attractive, she was more concerned for Caleb. The power relationship between the two personalities shifts in Caleb's favour. *"You're dead. You're nothin' […] You don't exist any more. You're a crawlin' slimy nothin'. You're a bad memory of somethin' that never was, and never shall be again."* Caleb attacks the mannequin with Lester's wig on it and tears it to pieces in a psychotic rage.

The rest is mine until the end. Little Lester's name is Marcus Flower son of Buck Flower.

Outside Flo's house, a tearful neighbour talks to Captain Stark about Flo and Caleb. Next morning, Caleb walks out into his own garden, celebrating his freedom from Lester. The sound of a car's screeching tyres triggers a flashback to a funeral. Little Lester (Marcus Flower) and his mother (Joan Vigman) are at Caleb's grave. Little crippled Caleb died in a car accident. Lester felt responsible for not saving his brother. *"I'll be good momma, just like Caleb, honest,"* he vows. *"You could never be like Caleb, never, never!"* his mother cries, *"It should have been you. Not him!"* Cut back to present day and: Captain Stark confronts Caleb. Caleb claims that his brother Lester was responsible for all the killings, but that he has put a stop to them by 'executing' him...

THE FOREST

You go down to the woods today — you might never get out alive!

The Forest (1981)

Murder in the woods, anyone? What do you mean you've heard enough already? If you don't relish yet another countryside slasher tale there may be little I can say to convince you, but it would be a shame to let jadedness get in the way of what is actually a very enjoyable excursion. Don Jones, already a director of talent after his psycho-killer flick *Abducted*, here fashions a good, solid riff on the old killer-in-the-woods formula, then leavens it with a left-field supernatural twist and some superior camerawork and photography. Location-wise too, the film is ahead of the game: instead of the rent-a-glade likes of *Forest of Fear*, *The Forest* is shot in the magnificent

Sequoia National Park, a natural resource of great beauty, with towering trees, plunging rapids and a giant's playground of rocks and boulders.

Two married couples – Steve (Dean Russell) and Sharon ('Elaine Warner' aka Tomi Barrett), and Charlie (John Batis) and Teddi (Ann Wilkinson) – embark on a camping trip in an attempt to revitalize their marriages. The women arrive first, defying their chauvinist husbands and striking out on their own to an arranged rendezvous point. After several hours hiking, they set up camp in a rocky glade by a river. Meanwhile, Steve and Charlie are seriously delayed by car trouble, arriving at the forest late afternoon. As night falls, Sharon and Teddi are visited by two strange, ghostly children (Corky Pigeon and Becki Burke) who warn them to beware of their daddy, before

above and left: Cover art and stills from the UK video of **The Forest**, one of two versions put out by Pyramid.

below: **The Forest**'s spooky children.

The Forest
aka Terror in the Forest
© 1981. Commedia Pictures, Inc.
producer/director: Don Jones. executive
producer: Frank Evans. associate producer:
Erv Sanders. writer: Evan Jones [Don Jones].
director of photography: Stuart Asbjornsen.
music: Richard Hieronymus and Alan Oldfield.
asst. camera: Tom Kantrud. key grip: Jack
Cochran. production sound: J.L. Clark. boom
person: Mary Jo Devenny. art director: Sandra
Sanders. script supervisor: Kathy Zatarga.
make up: Dana Wolski. editors: Robert Berk,
Nod Senoj [Don Jones]. additional photog-
raphy: Ken Barrows. associate producer:
Charles Aubuchon. negative cutter: Robert
Freeman. opticals: Alberto Soria. "I'm Comin'
On Strong" lyric by Nancy Hayden, music by
Richard Hieronymus, performed by Tami
Stevens; "The Dark Side of the Forest" lyric by
Stan Fidel, music by Richard Hieronymus,
performed by David Somerville; "You're My
Special Kind of Love" lyric by Tupper Turner,
music by Richard Hieronymus, performed by
Michelle Hart; "The Edge of Forever" lyric by
Stan Fidel, music by Richard Hieronymus,
performed by Carol Browning. steadicam
operator [uncredited]: Don Jones.
Cast: Dean Russell (Steve). Michael Brody
[Gary Kent] (John). Elaine Warner [Tomi
Barrett, aka Tomi Kent] (Sharon). John Batis
(Charlie). Ann Wilkinson (Teddi). Jeannette
[sic] Kelly (mother). Corky Pigeon (John Jr.,
boy). Becky Burke [sic] (Jennifer, girl). Tony
Gee (plumber). Stafford Morgan (man [male
hiker]). Marilyn Anderson (woman [female
hiker]). J.L. Clark (mechanic). Don Jones
(forest ranger).

opposite page, main picture:
Don Jones today.

opposite page, bottom right:
Jones's cameo appearance in **The Forest**.

below:
Marilyn Anderson as a hiker in **The Forest**'s
pre-credits sequence, who finds her holiday
sliding into slasher-horror territory...

disappearing into the darkness. Their equally ghostly mother (Jeanette Kelly) also pops up, but her concerns are less philanthropic: she's seeking her children in order to punish them. Frightened by these apparitions, Sharon runs away and hides. Teddi stays, refusing to believe the children's warning, only to be attacked by John ('Michael Brody' aka Gary Kent), a bearded man in a baseball cap who says he intends to eat her (*"I don't want to hurt you... but I'm starving."*). He kills Teddi and takes her body back to his lair. Arriving in the vicinity, Steve and Charlie enter a hillside cave decorated with candlesticks and cane furniture, where they meet John. He invites them to dinner and tells them he came to live in the hills after catching his wife in bed with another man. However, he declines to tell them the whole truth; that he murdered his wife and her lover and absconded into the hills with his two children, John Jr. and Jennifer. He also neglects to mention that he's murdered Teddi. Steve declines John's offer of meat from the roast he's tending on a spit, but Charlie gratefully accepts, only to shudder after a mouthful as some nameless apprehension hits him. Next morning, Steve and Charlie resume the search for their wives; more blood will be spilled before the day is through...

The Forest is a curious affair, a combination of flavours almost unique in the horror genre, as far as I can tell. (Lucio Fulci's *The House by the Cemetery* comes close: a ghostly child, slasher killings, and a ghoulish father. With Fulci as fellow traveller, Jones is in excellent company!) The woodland prologue sets up a straightforward stalk-and-slash tale, akin to *Don't Go in the Woods* or *Just Before Dawn*. The staging is efficient, the photography clean and attractive, and the first gouts of blood are gratifyingly realistic. If this was the extent of the film's ambitions you would basically be looking at a well-made *Friday the 13th* variant, nothing more, nothing less. With the introduction of the ghostly children, though, the film takes on another dimension. They bring a sweetness and sadness to the story, as if vacationing from a spooky TV drama for kids. We learn that they committed suicide when their life in the caves became intolerable, something they admit to with a blithe cheerfulness that makes the ghostly realm somehow more believable (*"It's okay. It's better than being alive. Being alive was so sad."*). Just as you think you've got a grip on the format, the children's father is revealed as a cannibal, and although we never *see* Gary Kent chewing on arms and legs or wolfing down a raw liver (I thought screen cannibals were obliged to do that by law?), we do get plenty of loaded close-ups of Kent chewing pieces of the roasted flesh he's cooking on a spit; presumably a tasty chunk of Teddi.

An underlying theme of matrimonial discord provides welcome real-world ballast for the story, although the treatment of female characters is occasionally patronising. Sharon and Teddi's decision to go off camping alone initially seems like a justifiable response to their husbands' chauvinistic sneering (*"We'd invite you along, but we kinda doubt you could take it,"* smirks Charlie, *"The first coyote howling would send you running for home."*). However, on the road the 'girls' are less sure of themselves (*"Why didn't we wait for them?"*) and once they're in the scary old forest, it's not long before they're struggling with tent pegs and pining for the menfolk to make them feel safe again (*"I wish the men were here." "Yeah – I hate to admit it, but me too."*). It's a shame that Jones wasn't able to make better use of the women's strengths, although he does

incapacitate Steve (with an impressively shuddersome greenstick fracture), leaving him reliant on Sharon. On the auteurist front, *The Forest* is the third Don Jones horror film to feature a nasty mother: in *Abducted* Momma was an incestuous dragon; in *The Love Butcher* she guilt-trips one son for surviving an accident that killed the other; while here she's a two-timing bitch who locks her kids in the bedroom closet while she screws the local repairman, then taunts her husband, *"Well, what do you expect me to do? You're practically impotent!"*

A couple of cheesy rock songs pop up here and there: the first is a feminist rock anthem called *Comin' On Strong*, complete with corny lyrics; followed later by a song that sounds like Echo and the Bunnymen fronted by Tony Bennett. Richard Hieronymus's score is functional, and at times evokes just the right combination of sweetness and menace, although his insistence on chasing a simple refrain up and down the keyboard gets annoying after a while. Perhaps my judgement is unreliable though, as I must admit the closing song *The Edge of Forever* has a certain camp appeal, of a sort that would be picked up and amplified in Jones's later *Molly and the Ghost*.

More frustrating than damaging are the plot's unexploited possibilities. We never learn why John resorted to cannibalism in a region teeming with wildlife. And I'm surely not alone in wishing that a few more peripheral characters had been slaughtered, to keep the film's slasher membership paid up in full. (I really am incorrigible when it comes to body counts!) The father's revenge on his wife and her lover – presented in a curious double flashback, only half of which represents information passed on to Steve and Charlie – has a dreamlike quality in which John veers from impotence to omnipotence. The cuckold's reprisal has the bizarrely emphatic feel of a child's revenge fantasy. He strangles his wife and then stalks her lover through the garden, toting various unlikely implements – a giant saw blade, a haybaler's fork – before goring the man to death on the rusty teeth of a mouldering circular saw.

The cast are all perfectly believable in their roles, but the honours must go to Kent, who makes the cannibal father strangely sympathetic. Instead of swivelling his eyes and drooling, he makes him gentle and hospitable, his madness restrained to a slight detachment. The scene where he offers Charlie a bite of his dead wife, Teddi, is one of the creepiest in the film, and it asks a question I don't recall being posed in the movies before: if you ate a piece of your lover, could you tell it was them from the taste? It's a pity that Kent only gets to act directly alongside his own wife Tomi at the end of the film, as she's another strong and credible presence. Which brings me to the head-scratching climax of the movie: John moves in for the kill as Steve lies injured, so Sharon attacks John with a knife, rapidly intercut with John's ghostly wife attacking him too. Quite what this is meant to convey I don't know; it surely can't be equating the two women, one of whom is a total harridan and the other a plucky heroine. Perhaps the ghost is using Sharon's actions as a chance to take vengeance for her own death, but if so, since she has been shown so unsympathetically throughout, we're not really rooting for her.

The Forest is a lighter film than Jones's classic *Abducted*, but there's still a lot to enjoy, and it leaves you with a curiously elusive emotional current afterwards. Made in 1981, it feels like a last gasp of seventies-style horror, and is more than enough to cement Jones's reputation as one of the best Exploitation Independents of the day.

Don Jones Interviewed

Although Don Jones is best known to fans of horror and exploitation cinema as director of the notorious *Schoolgirls in Chains*, the man himself is gentle in conversation; relaxed and pleasant, with a dry slant to his character. He's modest and down-to-earth in discussion of his work, he's at pains to stress that his nudies did not 'plumb the depths' of porno-excess, and he's clearly even a little sentimental, as a look at his less frequently celebrated horror film *The Forest* will reveal. I'm a big fan of *The Forest*, and I would recommend it to anyone who enjoys their ghost stories with a dash of the red stuff: even the later *Molly and the Ghost* is fun, although you may need a nodding acquaintance with camp to get the most out of that one. What emerges from Jones's story is a man who worked long and hard throughout the sixties and seventies, struggling to make ends meet in a variety of ways, and every few years gathering himself for another 'stab' at directing. Fortunately for us, Jones hit the target nearly every time – his ventures into the horror genre still have the power to startle and disturb viewers today.

Early Days

Donald E. Jones was born in Philadelphia, Pennsylvania in 1938 and enjoyed a happy childhood raised on a small farm about forty miles north of the city. His parents were both born in the United States: "My father was of Welsh descent, and my mother was a typical Anglo-Saxon - Scottish, Irish, English, and German," he says. "My older brother was a hellraiser – a professional boxer and race-car driver at the same time - but one great guy." Unlike the so-called movie brats, he saw few films as he was growing up, and the man who would come to be known for the classic exploitation shocker *Abducted* tended to milder fare at first. "The closest theatre was ten miles away and I went there very seldom, but I suppose that comedies were what I enjoyed the most. I had no interest in show business, and if I did I wouldn't have had the slightest idea of how to get into it."

In his teens, inspired by his brother's example, Jones embarked on a professional boxing career, but it was cut short by a period in the Army Signal Corps: "The desire that I had to fight before I went in the service had almost disappeared by the time I got out," he explains, "the fire had been banked." In 1958 his parents moved to Florida but Jones opted instead for Los Angeles. "Two things enticed me into the film business; one, my unemployment insurance ran out and I had to get a job. Fortunately a friend of mine offered me one in the major studios. I actually worked on *My Fair Lady* (1964) as a juicer (chief electrician). But that only lasted until something called the 'minority program' came in; and two, Gary Kent, whom I met when we were both parking cars, was probably most responsible for getting me into the low-budget film business. When one of us would find out about a job, we would tell the other and the majority of the time we would both work; but it was always hand-to-mouth."

Gary Kent (see sidebar for more on Kent's film career) takes up the story: "Don and I met at a restaurant called The Fog Cutter. I was the doorman, and he was a

car-parker. In L.A., many of the folks wanting into the business supported themselves working for the restaurants and bars at night, as it left the days open for interviews and film work. Jones was an aspiring boxer at the time, a middle-weight, fighting under the name of Irish Frankie Conway. He had done fairly well in the ring, but around us guys in film, he soon crossed over, and became another wannabe, like the rest of us. He came to L.A. for the opportunities as a boxer, and just got caught up in the whole film world and loved it. He was fairly handy, and I hired him on my stunt and effects jobs frequently. If you needed him to crash a car or fall a horse, he could do it. He was great to work with. He taught himself camera and

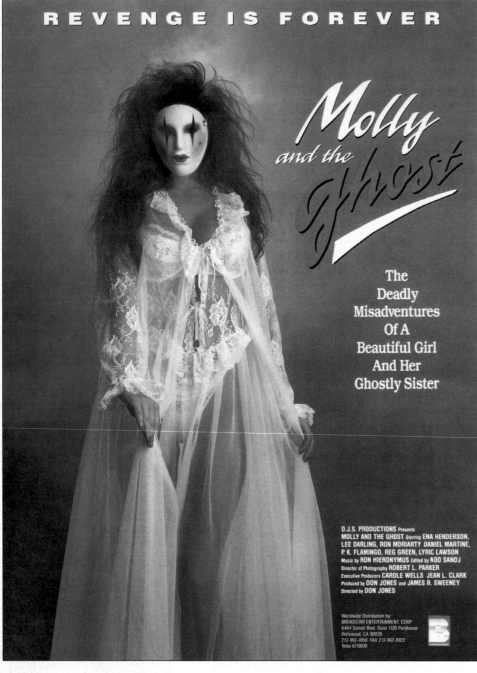

REVENGE IS FOREVER

Molly and the Ghost

The
Deadly
Misadventures
Of A
Beautiful Girl
And Her
Ghostly Sister

D.J.S. PRODUCTIONS Presents
MOLLY AND THE GHOST Starring ENA HENDERSON,
LEE DARLING, RON MORIARTY DANIEL MARTINE,
P. K. FLAMINGO, REG GREEN, LYRIC LAWSON
Music by RON HIERONYMUS Edited by NOO SANOJ
Director of Photography ROBERT L. PARKER
Executive Producers CAROLE WELLS JEAN L. CLARK
Produced by DON JONES and JAMES R. SWEENEY
Directed by DON JONES

Worldwide Distribution by
BROADSTAR ENTERTAINMENT, CORP
6464 Sunset Blvd. Suite 1130 Penthouse
Hollywood, CA 90028
213-962-4950 FAX 213-962-8922
Telex 6719038

above:
The promo sheet for Jones's most recent
horror film, **Molly and the Ghost** (1991).

opposite page, from top:
The first three images show Ginger trying to
placate Frank with sex;
Frank massages his mother (Greta Gaylord)'s
chest;
Shades of **Psycho**;
John forces Bonnie (Leah Tate aka Cheryl
Waters) to join in his games;
The horror in Momma's bedroom;
Tragedy or comeuppance?

Like many of the directors covered in this book, Don Jones found that the evolving adult film world of the late sixties and early seventies provided a few valuable extra paydays. Rapidly changing and expanding as successive legal developments pushed back the barriers of what was permissible, pornographic movies sprang from the much less explicit 'nudies' and their darker dramatic offspring the 'roughies'. The nudies were essentially frivolous films exemplified by the debut Russ Meyer film *The Immoral Mr. Teas* (1959), with glimpses of 'T&A' and scenarios based round nudist camps, holiday settings or strip-joints. The 'roughie' template was set by David Friedman's *The Defilers* (1965) – though it was barely more explicit in terms of the body areas visible, *The Defilers* added a cynical, aggressive strain of sadism and violence. As the law slowly relaxed, a pattern emerged: one especially bold new film would be made, then, if no prosecutions followed, a flurry of titles in a similar vein would rush to satisfy the punters' new demands, until eventually hardcore was established, and the 'nudies' and 'roughies', with their coyness and suggestiveness, died out.

For a young man eager to run film through a camera, this frenzy of activity in the erotic film arena was an ideal means of learning about the nuts and bolts of moviemaking. "I made a couple of black and white films – silly shows to be sure – where I did everything," Jones says. "It's the best way to learn." The first was *Excited* (1968), which Jones co-directed with the late Gary Graver, who was cameraman on the film and soon became an exploitation stalwart in his own right. Emerging from Ed De Priest's stable, and handled by Canyon Distribution, *Excited* has sadly proven to be an elusive debut: "I doubt if it's around any more," Jones says, "I haven't seen it in over thirty years."

He followed it swiftly with the darker, sleazier *Kiss-Off* (1968), also for Ed De Priest and Canyon Distribution. The story revolves around John, a pervert who makes obscene phone calls. Not satisfied with this pastime, he's also a rapist and murderer with a taste for slicing up hookers. Meanwhile, a private detective, whose girlfriend Terry works as a go-go dancer, is paid by an irate husband to locate his wife Mickey, who's left him for more exciting bisexual pastures. Mickey has embraced the dark side and is now a committed debauchee. She's also a friend of the killer's. The two of them form a Sadean partnership, and go out looking for kicks. One night they catch Terry's dance routine, and decide to follow her home for a rape and torture session…

Jones's next as director was *Who Did Cock Robin?* (1970), a detective melodrama about two brothers. It was his first film to be shot in colour. Easily confused with another 1970 nudie called *Who Killed Cock Robin?* (released by a company called Fleetan Films whose entire output seems to have been made anonymously), Jones's film opens with one man killing another and then throwing him into the ocean off Malibu pier. Jones explains, "This is the death of 'Cock Robin', the bad brother. The rest of the film concerns the good brother trying to find out who killed him. It's told in flashbacks, as he slowly finds out that his kid brother was a nasty piece of work. Then, when his girlfriend tells him that she was raped by him, he goes under Sodium Pentothal (suggested by the two detectives who are working on the case) and finds out that he was in fact the killer. His psyche had repressed the horrendous nature of his 'Cain and Abel' crime. It's a little more involved, but I think that's the gist of it. That one was

lighting. Knew very little about acting, so he hired the best he could get, and sort of left the performing up to them. He has that great Welsh sense of irony... it shows in his dialogue. He was a delight to work for, everyone wanted to do a good job for him, whether they understood the script or not, and his work has that improvised look and feel, but creatively so."

Jones's earliest experiences in the industry include work as a gaffer during the late sixties and early seventies, on TV spectaculars like *The Ann-Margret Show* and *Raquel*, along with classroom 'educationals' and industrial films. "Lighting and camera for some reason came to me pretty easy," says Jones. "The only mentor I had was an old German cameraman who I did a lot of classroom films with; he shot them and I lit them under his direction." Supplementing these paydays, Jones took on stunt work, mainly via Gary Kent, including motorcycle work on *2000 Years Later*, a 1969 film by Bert Tenzer for Warner Bros, and effects and stunts on *A Man Called Dagger* (Richard Rush, 1967).

written, produced, directed, edited and shot by me in 35mm colour. Final cost was pretty high, around $21,500."

Who Did Cock Robin? was made for distribution by Republic Amusements Corp., an outfit run by sexploitation king Bob Cresse. Republic Amusements picked up where Cresse's previous company Olympic International left off; their slate included *The Harem Bunch* (1968, directed by Cresse with Paul Hunt); *The Hot Spur* (1968, directed by Lee Frost, written and produced by Cresse);[1] and *The Scavengers* (1969, directed by Lee Frost, produced and written by Cresse). Cresse and Frost are perhaps most notorious for the sex-and-violence classic *Love Camp 7* (1968) which Cresse wrote, produced and starred in, playing a Nazi Kommandant. Jones's friend Ron Garcia had already co-directed a film handled by Republic Amusements called *The Pleasure Machines* (1967), and it was through Garcia that he came into contact with Cresse, although it was a brief association: "I made some money on *Cock Robin* but the distributor, Bob Cresse, stuck it to me. I'd left Ed De Priest and changed distributors because he was getting heavily into drugs and the money he owed me from *Kiss-Off* suddenly stopped coming."

There was more adult-movie work for Jones during the period, in his capacity as director of photography, although the details are vague: "As far as nudies go, I know I did a western (*Six Women* – dir: Mike Bennett, 1971) and a few others; the silliest one was named *One Million AC-DC* (dir: Ed De Priest, 1969, from a script by Edward D. Wood). *Who Did Cock Robin?* was one of the better ones. I probably only did a half-dozen or so. Porn came in soon after and I bailed."

Abducted!

Instead of wading into the hardcore porno scene, Jones set about making a name for himself on the horror film circuit, succeeding admirably with his best known film, *Abducted* (1973) – although you would never have guessed that smut was off the menu from its most notorious release title: "*Schoolgirls in Chains* was not the original title," laughs Jones, "it was simply called *Playdead*. It was changed to *Schoolgirls in Chains* when it was purchased by Mirror Releasing, because they wanted a more exploitative title. Mirror Releasing was formed by a friend of mine called Gary Gibbs. The shooting title however was *The Black Widow*, but the executive producer Dave Arthur thought that it would be misconstrued as a black picture so he came up with *Playdead*. I wrote it because I couldn't find a script that I liked and one that could be done for the money available. This was an unusual situation; I actually had the job before I had the script. Ron García found somebody who wanted to make a couple of low-budget features. One he would direct and I would shoot [*Swingers Massacre* aka *Inside Amy*], and the other he would shoot and I would direct. They were shot within a couple of months of each other. His was written by Dave Arthur's wife."

Ron García is a respected film and television cinematographer, nominated twice for Emmy awards (for the miniseries' *Murder in the Heartland* in 1993 and *The Day Lincoln Was Shot* in 1998) and four times by The American Society of Cinematographers, including a nomination in 1990 for his work on David Lynch's phenomenally successful TV series *Twin Peaks*. (García also shot the theatrical prequel *Twin Peaks: Fire Walk with Me*; one of the most stunning American films of the past twenty years.) He got his start in the industry directing adult films, ranging from *A Sweet Sickness* (1968, co-directed with Jon Martin)

and *The Pleasure Machines* (1967, co-directed with Paul Hunt) to the extravagantly bizarre sci-fi horror porno *The Toy Box* (1971). "I'm not exactly sure where I met García," says Jones, "but we were pretty good friends both on and off the set – until a girl came along. But that's another story!"

Abducted's star, Gary Kent, remembers García as "a friend of Don's. We'd all worked together on various projects. I hired Don as the cinematographer on [Paul Harrison's] *House of Seven Corpses*, and Ron García as art director. I also used Ron as DP on my film *Rainy Day Friends*. I remember a night on *Seven Corpses* when we all smoked a little too much ganja, drank a little too much Scotch, and ended up stealing a freight train and driving it through downtown Salt Lake City at midnight, blowing the whistle and singing bawdy songs. Hey, you have to let off pressure somehow!"

Abducted was financed entirely by executive producer Dave Arthur, and was budgeted at around $42,000. Jones received $5,000 for writing and directing. He came up with the idea quickly: "After reading about a young girl who disappeared from a freeway when her car broke down, I decided to begin with that premise. What happened to her? The original script took forty eight hours to write over three days, I believe. Dave Arthur liked it and after taking a couple of more days to rewrite, we shot it."

Regarding the genesis of the story, Kent says: "Don Jones swears he had no inspiration for the film other than his own warped sense of story telling. John Parker [Stoglin] and I were heavily influenced by the whole Ed Gein affair, and tried to incorporate this into our performances." "The only film that I can think of that might have influenced me was *Psycho*," concedes Jones.

Gary Kent remembers "*Abducted* was filmed in thirteen days, mainly on an orange farm just outside of Riverside, California, seventy miles east of L.A. The house we rented belonged to a wonderful old widow named Mrs. Barrons. Her husband had passed on and her children had all left the nest. She lived in that wonderful old house all alone, and was glad to have the company. Here we were, shooting this really bizarre horror film, and she treated us like we were her favourite children. She even cooked dinner for us several times.[2] Of course, for most of the shoot, we had her staying at a nice hotel in town, so she wouldn't panic at the destruction that always takes place around a film location. We also shot at Malibu beach, on the exact location they shot the Statue of Liberty scene for the original *Planet of the Apes*."

Recalling the shoot, Jones says, "The film was hard work. The crew was small, a gaffer, a grip, sound, props, make-up, boom, AD, asst. camera, and Ron Garcia the DP. The cast was composed of mostly small-theatre actors, especially the girls. The three leads were friends of mine, all good actors, so with the exception of the lead girl Cheryl Waters, whose boyfriend was on the set, we had a good time. Never let a boyfriend or girlfriend on the set! I tried to keep him away, or keep him occupied, but nothing really worked. Cheryl, whom I knew from before the film, had just done a lead in a film that was received pretty well. Anyway she and in particular her boyfriend thought she was on her way, so getting the nudity out of her as promised was difficult. He didn't like the way her breasts looked as she was crawling on her hands and knees. Suddenly they both smelled the roses and didn't want anything in her past to screw it up. She used a phoney name and threatened to sue if I used her real name. Sad to say neither her marriage nor her career went anywhere. Haven't seen her since.[3] The lead, her boyfriend

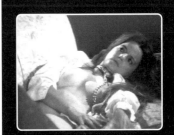

above:
College girl in chains in **Abducted**...

opposite page, from top:
The Love Butcher's pre-credits victim is
forked;
Lester (Erik Stern) in full flow;
Pat (Eve Mac) tries to fend off Lester;
...to no avail;
Sheila (Robin Sherwood) is murdered and
placed in the bathtub;
Flo (Kay Neer) is killed after begging for
death;
The picture pinned to the mannequin that
'Caleb' destroys;
Caleb or Lester?

below:
US one-sheet poster for Jones's **Who Did
Cock Robin?** (1970) – note the misspelling
of Freud on two separate occasions! Perhaps
it was after seeing this poster that Wes
Craven wrote Sadie's lines about "Sigmund
Frood" in **The Last House on the Left**?

in the movie, disliked Cheryl intensely. But the show had to
be shot so we put up with what we had to. The rest of the
cast was wonderful, cooperative, friendly, and fun. They
worked hard. In those days sex was probably looked at a
little differently than it is now, and nudity and the strange
aspects of the story didn't bother anyone."

Few of the cast can be traced today, as Jones explains:
"This was a non-union film, therefore the actors would not
use their real names. Gary and John were the exceptions;
they didn't seem to care. I think the mother used the name of
Greta Gaylord. If the SAG [Screen Actors Guild] caught
them they would fine the performer, and then after a few
times they could black-list them. Consequently any actor
who worked on a non-SAG show would use a different
name. Also as a rule, non-SAG films paid less money. The
agents usually didn't care as long as they got their 10%."

When it came to the casting of the two brothers, Jones
already knew where to turn: "I'd worked with Gary before,
both in stage and movies, and even though the part of Frank
was written specifically for somebody else, when Gary
showed interest the part was his. He comes off on camera as
very strong. John Stoglin was also a friend of both Gary's
and mine, and the part was written for him. He and Gary,
when they read the first draft, really liked it. When John was
crying at the end, when he found his 'mother' hung, boy you
should have seen that scene when he did it, everybody in the
room was crying. I shot it without sound, which was a stupid
thing to do, because he did such a good job."

Kent describes Stoglin as, "A talented actor I met at
group, from Clearwater, Florida. He'd been a professional
dancer, came to Hollywood to be the next James Dean. He
did a lot of theatre work in town, including directing for the
Glendale Center Theater, where he won several awards. I've
always respected John's unique talent, and I've cast him in
several of my films. He's always done a wonderful job, and
made his characters totally believable. We talked Don into
casting the rest of the show primarily from one of L.A.'s best
theatre groups, The Company Theater, so you had these
classically trained actors playing very bizarre parts usually
played by up and coming 'starlets'. We all worked really
well together. The usual, some love affairs going on, some
smoking of pot, lots of angst and a very serious attitude
toward Don's flick. John and I tried not to get too friendly
with the others, as we wanted to remain an enigma to them. I
don't know if it showed in the work or not..."

Stoglin himself confirms this was the approach: "I liked
to stay in character as much as I could, and so I stayed away
from the rest of the cast. This was something I developed on
my own, as opposed to some actors who like to be very
much the personality on-set, talking with the crew and being
Mr. Charming and Mr. Wonderful, or whatever. I just
preferred being somewhere away and it didn't matter where,
just being by myself."

While not pornographic, the film's content is still pretty
strong, as far as violent and abusive sexual situations are
concerned. "Dave Arthur wanted more, and it was a constant
battle," Jones admits. "Afterwards, to get the 'R' rating, the
MPAA made us shorten one of the scenes. I believe it was
the rape scene with Gary – it was really strong."

Thinking back to the shock tactics of early seventies
horror, Gary Kent recalls: "Most independents and
exploitation films were pushing the envelope a little. After
all, in the Big Apple they were showing all of the *Mondo
Cane* stuff... so we were actually a little tame in comparison.
Nevertheless, walls were coming down, and it was a great

time for breaking the rules! *Playdead* opened at a theatre in
San Diego, where it became a favourite midnight movie for
the US Marines on duty there. I understand that they still
play it now and then, just for old times sake, and the Marines
still go and hoot and holler and cheer for the bad guys!"

Jones continues: "I don't know where *Playdead* opened
and I didn't attend any screenings. It was not financially
successful as far as I know. When Dave Arthur tried to
release it, he found that he was in over his head. Distribution
is a dog-eat-dog business, and he was not prepared for it.
After some trial runs he pulled it, and it was bought – at a
profit – by Mirror Releasing. Right after, I shot Ron García's
film *Swingers Massacre*, and then *The House of Seven
Corpses* in Salt Lake City. As far as I know, the director Paul
Harrison came from TV, *The Untouchables* - and I don't
believe he did much after *House*. He died not too many
years after making the movie; cancer I believe. A nice guy."[4]

The Love Butcher and *Sweater Girls*

"*The Love Butcher* is interesting in that whilst its production
pre-dates the stalk-'n'-slash craze, its ironic tongue-in-cheek
script actually highlights and parodies the gross misogyny of
the subgenre." – *The Aurum Film Encyclopedia: Horror*.

In 1975, Jones accepted a job on a classic sleazy seventies
opus, *The Love Butcher*. To begin with, Mikel Angel was the
writer and director, with Jones hired as DP. "It was originally
called *The Gardener*," Jones recalls. "Unfortunately, after
viewing the rough cut we all knew that the film was
unreleasable. All except Mike, that is. He said, 'Well that's
the film' and walked out of the screening room, leaving the
producers in a quandary. So they hired me to try and fix it
and make it releasable. We hired another cameraman (*Axe*'s
Austin McKinney), did a little more casting and that's about
it. About half the film is Mike's and half is mine. I'd have to
see it again to remember which scenes I added (see review).
I'm sure close to half of the film was changed. The humour
was added. The film as originally cut just did not make any
sense, and what I remember most was the absolute silence
that followed the screening of the rough-cut. To make
matters worse, the editor as he was cutting it had been raving
about the film. This was of course before anybody saw it. He
also was very disappointed."

With four-and-a-half features under his belt but without a
conspicuous hit, Jones found that he still needed to keep
working in just about any capacity: "I had to make a living –
wives kids, etc. – and I would take anything to make a buck,
and that includes sound, lighting, gripping, editing, basically
anything. By then I was doing very little stunt work; mostly
I was working crew, camera, gaffing, etc. Except for
shooting another feature called *My Boys Are Good Boys*
(Bethel Buckalew, 1978) and some second unit shooting for
Roger Corman, I was mainly crew. By the last few years of
the seventies however, I was shooting a German TV show,
when they came to the States, called *The VIP Show*. Not
unlike *20/20* or perhaps *60 Minutes*, but interested more in
celebrities. I also shot a fun show travelling through the
Greek islands on a forty-metre schooner for German TV."

One of Jones's lighter screen offerings is the period
comedy *Sweater Girls*, which he directed in 1977. Written
with Neva Friedenn, who would shortly find work on *The
Toolbox Murders*, and giving seventeen-year-old Charlene
Tilton her last role before she went stellar as Lucy in the
smash TV soap *Dallas*, it's the tale of a group of girls in the

156

1950s who swear an oath that they'll save themselves for marriage, while the local juvenile delinquents try to persuade them otherwise. Jones recalls: "*Sweater Girls* was produced by Gary Gibbs, and I co-wrote and directed it. It suffers from a lack of money. The story's lame, but the actors are likeable and quite good. Gibbs expected great things from it, and although it didn't do as much as he would have liked, it did make a very nice profit."

The Forest

In 1981, Jones returned to the horror genre with *The Forest*, an under-rated slasher tale that's enlivened by a sudden leap into the supernatural: just the ticket for fans who think they've seen all the 'slice-and-dice' format has to offer. As Jones puts it, "There don't seem to be a lot of stories about ghost children and cannibalism!" Sadly, *The Forest* was a far from happy experience for its maker: "A shaft job of monumental proportions," to be precise…

Starting from the idea of ghost children ("Ghosts are always fun to use, they can do many things, and I like to write stories that are off the beaten trail," he says), Jones wrote the script in about thirty days. The movie was then shot over twelve days, in October of 1980, mostly in Sequoia National Park. "It was a pretty dry season up there, but they let us film," Jones remarks. "I put a $5,000 bond up – it's pretty cheap to burn down a national park you know! We had the park to ourselves, we did a lot of night shooting, and they left us alone." Jones not only wrote, directed and edited the film himself, he also shot the Steadicam material in the prologue. The majority of the film was lensed by DP Stuart Asbjornsen, and his photography of this prime American beauty-spot is lucid and attractive throughout.

Jones used pseudonyms for writing and editing *The Forest*, feeling that his name was already prominent enough in the credits. Gary Kent was back on board, this time using the name Michael Brody because of trouble with the SAG. He stars as the cannibal father living in a cave in the Sequoias (although the actual caves used are the famous Bronson Caves outside Los Angeles, well-known for their appearance in countless movies and TV shows, from *Robot Monster* to the sixties TV series *Batman*. "We had great accommodations at a little motel, the Blue Bird, inside the park," Kent remembers. "The people that owned it had just started business, and were eager to please. We had gourmet dinners every night. Shooting was a blast in all of that beautiful wilderness." Kent also handled the fights: "Yes, I staged them. Since Don had hocked his house to make the film, we had little money for other stuntmen, or fight props. I had to make do with whatever we found along the way. I thought the comic bit with the wife's lover was a chance to change the usual fisticuffs of that kind of confrontation, and threaten him with everyday farm objects: pitchfork, saw, etc."

The cast also includes Gary Kent's wife Tomi, using the name Elaine Warner, John Batis, Dean Russell, Ann Wilkinson, Jeanette Kelly, Stafford Morgan and Marilyn Anderson all used their real names, and came to an open casting. 'Tony Gee' is the only other pseudonym. Corky Pigeon and Becki Burke came from a children's agency. "He was eight, she was fifteen if you can believe it," Jones marvels. Along with his other credits on *The Forest*, Jones also appears in the movie, playing the forest ranger – however, there was no Hitchcockian reason for this: "I wrote the part for the production manager, but because of SAG he refused to do it. I didn't know until we got to the location."

Jones had plans for more scenic shooting around the waterfalls and giant Sequoia trees, but lack of time and money meant they were curtailed. However, when he made a rough cut of the film, he realised it was too short: "What I did was to add a prologue. The beginning, before we meet the protagonists, I shot in Frazier Park about fifty miles north of L.A. The chase scenes I shot with a Steadicam, and not too well I may add. If I had it to do over again I would not use the Steadicam. The only camera we had was a 35 BL, too heavy to do much hand-holding."

Once the necessary scenes had been captured at Sequoia, further shots were picked up elsewhere. Those at Steve and Sharon's house were shot at the home of Jones's friend Stafford Morgan, who played the hiker killed in the prologue, and the house in Gary Kent's cuckold flashback was located in Acton, fifty miles North East of Los Angeles. All told, the shooting budget was $42,000 into the can: "Not including around $30,000 deferred, which I paid by the way," Jones stresses: " I'm proud of that. Lost the house but I paid the deferrals."

Jones's unhappy memories of the film are rooted here. "Yeah, that film cost me my house, as I put it up for financing. Since I only had enough money to shoot it and not to finish it, I immediately took a job for Corman and gave the editing to somebody else who said that he would cut it on spec' and who was recommended to me by the composer. While I was working he got busy and gave it to Robert Berk to cut. This clown thought the film was terrible and in his wisdom decided that he would save it. Therefore he chose to tell the story in flashback. I didn't see it until I screened it for Caruth Byrd, one of the richest men in Texas, in an attempt to find finishing money. At the time I had every reason to believe that he would give me ten or fifteen thousand to finish it. After seeing it though he didn't, and I don't blame him. It was horrible, the screening was over and everybody's sitting there, not a word spoken. Just a heavy, heavy silence. I took the film back, put it back together the way it came from the lab, which was an absolute pain-in-the-ass, and started to re-cut it from scratch. What a mess. I want to kill the egoistic son-of-a-bitch."

From there, the problems snowballed. "I had trouble raising finishing money. I sold the film to Commedia for $200,000, which would have been a pretty nice profit for me, well over double my money, but they only paid about $75,000 of the $200,000, with which I paid off my deferrals, but I didn't pay my house off. I finished it with their money, they released it, (they made seventy or eighty prints but it pretty much failed in the theatres, as far as I know) and then they gave it to a guy named Jon Edwards to sell to video. Prism picked it up and made quite a bit of money with it, none of which, as far as I know, either Frank Evans (Commedia), nor I ever saw. Jon must have kept all the money. The profit was supposed to go back to Commedia but I don't think it did, I think it stayed with Edwards. So I'm one step removed from it, I'm not sure I have any legal recourse. The irony of the whole project is that it was originally shot to go straight to video. Frank however thought it could play big screen, hence the prints. Commedia was a penny stock company out of Utah. In reality what Frank wanted to do was drive up the price of the stock and then sell his shares. In later years he went to prison, not for that but something similar. Some kind of stock manipulation. Distributors think that they put it out there and any money it makes should be theirs. I've been through this with every movie I've ever made."

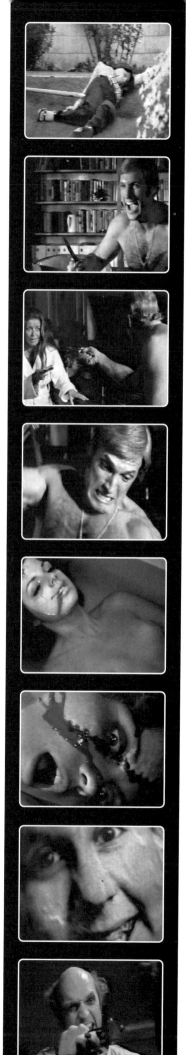

Lethal Pursuit
aka **Enraged**
© 1988. Shapiro Glickenhaus Entertainment
Corporation
Shapiro Glickenhaus Entertainment presents a
Gary Gibbs production.
director: Don Jones. producer: Gary Gibbs.
written by Roger Stone. executive producer: Alan
M. Solomon. director of photography: Stuart
Asbjornson. editor: Peter Schink. supervising
editor: Doug Jackson. music: Richard
Hieronymus. production designer: Yoram
Barazilai [Barzilai]. associate producer: Jerry
Landesman. casting by Joyce Maio and Louis
Goldman. costume designer: Karen Patch.
executive in charge of production: Frank Isaac.
co-associate producer: Mitzi Kapture. production
manager: Karen King. assistant director: Dutch
Haaland. location manager: Jim Sweeney. 1st
assistant cameraman: Tom Kantrud. 2nd
assistant cameraman: Johanna Derblowsky.
gaffer: Tom Evans. best boy: Randy Billian.
electrician: K.C. Pierson. key grip: Tiff Cooney.
dolly grip: Rod Farley. grip/driver: Antonio Onate.
set decorator: Stacy Doran. set dressers:
Richard Halke, Hernan Camacho, Anthony
Stabley. prop master: David Valdez. scenic
artists: Kelly Deco, David Clark. construction
coordinator: Chris Speer. carpenters: Ronald
Freeto, Cory Dawley, Tom Peachee, John
Langhammer, Richard Douglan, Steve Panetta.
wardrobe assistant: Kim Carleton. make-up and
hair: Angela Levin. assistant hair stylist: Haim
Adut. script supervisor: Marcy Pringle Price.
sound mixer: Mike Hall. boom man: Gilbert
Salas. 2nd unit sound mixer: Jeff Callaway. 2nd
unit boom man: Gary Schlintz. stunt coordinator:
Bob Ivy. vehicle preparation: Bill Jenkins.
production co-ordinator: Marla Fields. production
assistants: Paul Stone, John Aliano, Rick
Bronson, Julie Bryant, David Weeks, Jason
Gibbs. still photographer: Abe Perlstein. choreog-
raphy: Wenndy Leigh MacKenzie. special
effects: Players Special Effects. post production
supervisor: Adam Chuck. production accountant:
Elizabeth Soto. post production by Omni Post,
Inc. assistant editors: Ron Bingham, Joseph E.
Boren. associate editor: Thure Gustafson. sound
design by Omni Sound, Inc. sound editors:
Constance A. Kazmer, David Kulczycki, Kerry
Williams, Jeff Okun, Doug Jackson. electronic
sound effects: Mark Governor. re-recorded at
Cinesound Co., Inc. re-recording mixers: Hiroaki
'Zom' Yamamoto, Mark Rozett. opticals:
Hollywood Optical Systems, Inc. title design by
Jeff Okun. [songs] "I'm a Victim" performed by
Bebe Cross, words & music by Duane Sciacqua
& Richard Hieronymus, arranged by Duane
Sciacqua; "Still a lot of Country in This Girl"
performed by Bebe Cross, words & music by
Richard Hieronymus, arranged by Richard
Hieronymus; "Way to Love" performed by Bebe
Cross, words & music by Duane Sciacqua &
Richard Hieronymus, arranged by Duane
Sciacqua; "You Got the Last Laugh" performed
by Will Jones, words & music by Richard
Hieronymus; "Recuerdos" (Memories) performed
by Bebe Cross, words by Bebe Cross, composed
& arranged by Richard Hieronymus; "Rock-N-
Roll Rules" performed by Sandy Hollister, words
& music by Barry Schleifer, Sandra Salcone &
Richard Hieronymus. filmed in September 1987
in California (USA).
Cast: Mitzi Kapture (Debra J.). Blake Bahner
(Warren). John Stuart Wildman (Andy).
Stephanie Johnson. Blake Gibbons (Craig).
William Kerr (Philo). Mike Brody [Gary Kent]
(Bud). Alan Ross (Floyd). Fernando Gramaldo
(Armando). Linda Cox. Thom Adcox (Mike).
Dave Trice (Arnie). Ken Abraham. Jeff Culver.
Jean Don Brown (Lee). George Strine (cop #1).
Gregory Mortimer (cop #2). Erica Rodgers
(nurse). Willy Rosenblatt (liquor store clerk).
Deana Wells (girl in diner). country western
musicians Harry Orlove (lead guitar). Jay Dee
Maness (slide guitar). John Stuart Wildman
(rhythm guitar). Paul Marshall (bass guitar).
Steve Duncan (drums). Doug Atwell (fiddle
player). rock & roll musicians Mike Sherwood
(keyboards). Duane Sciacqua (lead guitar).
Steve Crane (bass guitar). Doug Madick
(drums). Ray Shaffer, Bill Jenkins (stunts).

LETHAL
PURSUIT

SOME LIVE
FOR THE HUNT.
OTHERS...

FOR THE KILL.

SHAPIRO GLICKENHAUS ENTERTAINMENT PRESENTS · GARY GIBBS PRODUCTION "LETHAL PURSUIT"
MITZI KAPTURE BLAKE BAHNER AND JOHN STUART WILDMAN CO-STARRING BLAKE GIBBONS WILLIAM KERR
AND THOM ADCOX FRANK ISAAC JERRY LANDESMAN KAREN PATCH
YORAM BARAZILAI RICHARD HIERONYMUS DOUG JACKSON STUART ASBJORNSON
ALAN M. SOLOMON ROGER STONE GARY GIBBS DON JONES

Lethal Pursuit and Molly and the Ghost

It would be seven years before Jones directed again. *Lethal Pursuit* (1988), a low-budget action movie, has a couple of nice stunts, and it's fun to see Gary Kent again, albeit in a minor role, but it's essentially the sort of late night cable TV filler that passes your eyes without your brain ever rising to the bait. The machismo is of that peculiarly eighties sort that has men with bad hair and trashy leather jackets throwing shapes at each other, while chicks with slightly bigger hair prove their worth in a man's world by wearing distressed jeans. *Lethal Pursuit* is the only Don Jones film I felt indifferent to as it played. The element of surprise, of the

perverse, seemed lost in an eighties mulch. Part of the problem is an extended prologue that takes place at night, amongst characters of interchangeable unpleasantness. The film gets cheesier, and thus slightly more fun, as it progresses, thanks to an ill-starred romance between good girl rock-chick Debra (Mitzi Kapture) and psycho-hunk Warren (Blake Bahner), to the dismay of nice-but-dull Andy (John Stuart Wildman). It's the sort of film where people say things like *"Warren's crazy but the dude ain't stupid, man"* in earnest tones that suggest half-time interviews in TV wrestling have taken the place of acting classes.

Fortunately, *Lethal Pursuit* was a short-lived dip in Jones's filmography. He himself dryly remarks that *Molly and the Ghost* (1991) is "not the best thing I ever did," but having tracked down a copy, I have to say I rather enjoyed it. Shot brightly and efficiently on 16mm, it tells the story of lascivious teenage tramp Susan (Ena Henderson, in a memorably tarty performance) a 'bad seed' who arrives penniless at the posh pad of her sister Molly (Lee Darling). Although welcomed into the house, within minutes she's stealing, prying and setting out to seduce Molly's buff husband Jeff (Ron Moriarty). Despite Susan's best efforts to implicate Jeff in an adulterous bedroom clinch, Molly remains unconvinced and the couple close ranks against the little minx. Pretending to withdraw, Susan instead psychotically ups the ante by paying a hired assassin (Daniel Martine) to murder the stubbornly happy Molly. All does not go according to plan. Due to unforeseen (and rather contrived) circumstances, Susan is murdered instead of her sister: but in a twist with faint echoes of Mario Bava's *Hatchet for the Honeymoon*, her hatred for Molly extends beyond the grave. Susan begins haunting the couple, appearing in bedroom mirrors during their lovemaking and generally spoiling the marital ambience. You want more? How about astral possession, professional ghost-debunkers, and spirit guides? *Molly and the Ghost* is way better than I expected; it's like an afternoon TV movie with a supernatural side-order and extra cheese. It has a flagrant, almost Italian tackiness that I found irresistible. It's easy to imagine the film made in the early 1970s, with Edwige Fenech as Molly and Erika Blanc as Susan, and some Euro-hunk like Howard Ross or George Hilton as the husband. Susan is such a spiteful little bitch that even death and the advice of a motherly spirit guide fail to quell her sexually frustrated stroppiness. It's not perfect by a long shot – the title music is so cable-TV soap you almost give up on the movie before it's begun – but a week later I found I was dying to watch it again.

Jones has mostly retired from the film industry today, and spends his time working on novels, such as his Southern-set ghost story, *Alma and the Poltergeist*. His memory is a little vague regarding the early days of his career, and he's unperturbed by the obscurity of his first three films; since he never did return to the adult cinema, we can assume that his interest in these pictures ended as soon as the last metre of film passed through the shutter. However, he's pleased to know that *Abducted* has been cherished and admired, and glad also that *The Forest* has picked up fans on video after its misfortune in theatrical distribution. The exploitation cinema scene that nurtured his best work may have disappeared, but Jones's films will continue to entertain as they find their way onto DVD. And as long as there are people out there who see that alternative title and think, 'Oh my God, they *can't* call a film *Schoolgirls in Chains*!!', his name will always be guaranteed some controversy!

Footnotes

1 This film is also frequently credited to Olympic International.

2 "The dolls in the credits scene belonged to the woman whose house it's all shot in," adds Jones.

3 Waters appeared in Max Baer Jr.'s *Macon County Line* (1974) in which she played one of the four leads, a hitch hiker. She followed *Abducted* with *Rape Squad*, a feminist vigilante film from AIP which is so poorly conceived and executed it actually makes the rape-killer look like less of a dope than the victims, and *Escape from Cellblock 3*, by Kent Osborne. If these choices represent the actress's rejection of sleaze, she was badly advised!

4 The IMDB confuses Harrison with his British namesake, a TV director of such fare as *Wycliffe* and *Ballykissangel*.

Molly and the Ghost
© 1991. D.J.S. Productions
D.J.S. Productions presents.
director: Don Jones. produced by Don Jones, James R. Sweeney. executive producers: Carole Wells, Jean L. Clark. director of photography: Robert L. Parker. music: Richard Hieronymus. editor: Nod Senoj [Don Jones]. casting: Judy Belshe. gaffer: Eric Lopez. camera op./asst.: Buzzi Burwell. location sound: Austin McKinney. boom man: Britton Jackson. make-up: Robin Slater. key grip: Jack Britton. camera package: Golden Eagle Prods. sound package: Lee Motion Pictures; Sound Recording Services. lighting: Cine-Video. film: Kodak. hi speed photography: Photosonics. ballistics expert: Erv Sanders. assistant to the producer: Judy Belshe. neg. processing: Foto-kem. paint box: Mike Bauer - C.C.I. telecine: R.G.B. Opticals. on-line: Mitch Fehr - C.C.I. titles: Bill Portune. neg. cutter: Robert Freeman. sound mix: Thomas Chan, Wally Burr Recording. insurance: Dewitt - Stern. catering: Colleen Stewart. "Flying Free" music by Tom Doenges, lyrics by Richard Hieronymus, performed by Tom Doenges; "On Love's Ride" music by Tom Doenges, Debra Gottesman, lyrics by Richard Hieronymus, performed by Debra Gottesman; "Walkin' Away from Love" music by Barry Schleifer, lyrics by Richard Hieronymus, performed by Lyn Chasteen; "Bang Bang" music by Tom Doenges, lyrics by Richard Hieronymus, performed by Tom Doenges.
Cast: Ena Henderson (Susan). Lee Darling (Molly). Ron Moriarty (Jeff). Daniel Martine (John). P.K. Flamingo (Vietnam vet.). Reg Green (professor). Lyric Lawson (spirit). Cliff Marlowe (David). Stephanie Johnson (Sammi). Kat Brown (Linda). Ian Warwick (Richard). Gene Collins (cab driver). Marty Boss (cafe waitress). B.C. Ousley (bar waitress). Lisa Dorshcé (Hywd. hooker). Ralph Pitt, Brian Brazil (boulevardiers). Rick Ward (cab driver).

opposite: Press-sheet for Jones's action film, **Lethal Pursuit** (1988).

DON JONES: FILMOGRAPHY AS DIRECTOR

1968	*Excited* (co-dir with Gary Graver)
1968	*Kiss-Off* aka *The Kiss Off* (also dp, directed as D.E. Jono)
1970	*Who Did Cock Robin?* (also writer/producer/editor/dp)
1973	*Abducted* aka *Playdead* aka *Schoolgirls in Chains* aka *Let's Play Dead* aka *The Black Widow* (also writer/producer)
1975	*The Love Butcher* aka *The Gardener* (co-director: also writer)
1977	*Sweater Girls* aka *The American Girls* (also writer)
1981	*The Forest* aka *Terror in the Forest* (also producer/actor/editor) (released 1983)
1988	*Lethal Pursuit* aka *Enraged*
1991	*Molly and the Ghost*

OTHER CREDITS:

1964	*My Fair Lady* – dir: George Cukor (electrician)
1965	*Ride in the Whirlwind* dir: Monte Hellman (stunts and grip)
1966	*The Wild Angels* – dir: Roger Corman (lighting)
1966	*Suburbia Confidential* – dir: Stephen C. Apostolof (actor)
1967	*A Man Called Dagger* – dir: Richard Rush (stunts)
1968	*Psych-Out* – dir: Richard Rush (stunts)
1968	*Targets* – dir: Peter Bogdanovich (stunts)
1968	*Nymphs Anonymous* – dir: Manuel Conde (actor)
1968	*Help Wanted Female* – dir: Harold Perkins [John Hayes] (actor)
1969	*2000 Years Later* – dir: Bert Trenzer (stunts)
1969	*One Million AC-DC* – dir: Ed De Priest (role uncertain)
1969	*Secret Sex Lives of Romeo and Juliet* – dir: Peter Perry (actor)
1969	*The Psycho Lover* – dir: Robert Vincent O'Neill (sound recordist)
1970	*The Hard Road* – dir: Greg Corarito & Gary Graver (role uncertain)
1970	*Fusion* – dir: Paul Hunt (sound)

1970	*The Postgraduate* – dir: unknown (actor)
1970	*Is This Trip Really Necessary?* – dir: Ben Benoit (sound)
1971	*Six Women* – dir: Mike Bennett (sound)
1973	*Swingers Massacre* aka *Inside Amy* – dir: Ron Garcia (dp)
1973	*The House of Seven Corpses* aka *Seven Times Dead* – dir: Paul Harrison (dp)
1976	*Woman in the Rain* – dir: Paul Hunt (co-dp with Gary Graver, also actor)
1978	*My Boys Are Good Boys* – dir: Peter Perry (dp)
1980	*Follow That Car* – dir: Daniel Haller (TV movie) (2nd unit dp)
1980	*Nur der Name bleibt... Henry Miller - Erkenntnisse und Bekenntnisse* – dir: Margret Dünser (TV movie) (dp)
1981	*Smokey Bites the Dust* – dir: Charles B. Griffith (2nd unit dp)
1985	*Rainy Day Friends* aka *L.A. Bad* – dir: Gary Kent (camera operator/2nd unit dp)

MADE FOR TELEVISION:

1968	*The Ann-Margret Show*
1970	*Raquel*
1976-80	*V.I.P.-Schaukel* aka *The VIP Show* (German/Austrian TV series. Jones was dp on episodes filmed in the USA.)

BOOKS:
Alma and the Poltergeist

ERRATA:
Many sources confuse Don Jones with Donald W. Jones, director of *Project Nightmare*, *Murderlust*, and others. Jones has never worked under this name, nor has he ever been credited as Donald M. Jones, another frequent misnomer.
Jones had nothing to do with the British film *The Firechasers* by Sidney Hayers.
Ken Barrows, cited as an uncredited 2nd unit director of *The Forest* on IMDB, was not involved in the production - "There was no second unit," says Jones

A Visit from Gary Kent

*G*ary Kent – actor, director, writer and stuntman – is one of Don Jones's closest friends and allies in the film industry. He's also a true gentleman and has been a constant source of friendly encouragement during the writing of this book. While his films as director fall outside the horror genre, his fascinating, genre-busting The Pyramid (1975) is a spiritual enlightenment odyssey that speaks the language of the sixties counterculture and deserves greater recognition. In the following pages, Gary describes his journey through the movie-making landscape of the sixties and seventies.

I was born and raised on a ranch, in Walla Walla, Washington. For me, getting to town once a month and seeing a movie was like a trip to a foreign country. Dad (Art) was a rancher and sheriff, macho to the bone. Mom (Viola) was a homemaker and a writer, a good poet, she was published in several Northwest papers. Four sisters, no brothers. I had my own horses all the way from grade school to high school, rode in some little punkin' roller rodeos, got some applause, thought I was Gary Cooper and Burt Lancaster, couldn't wait to get out in the big world and find out for sure; so second year of college, I joined the Naval Air Corps. In school, I had my nose broken playing football, so I turned out for the school play, fell in love with Drama and the stage. Hooked!

After discharge from service where I spent two years writing for the Blue Angels Flying Team, I did radio and theatre in Texas, where I had been stationed with Headquarters Flight Unit. I tried out for the Playhouse Theater in Houston, and was signed on as the juvenile lead for a season. I did a number of plays, including Shakespeare, and even directed a couple. The ingénue lead was Katherine Helmond. When the Playhouse ended the season, I grabbed a Greyhound bus for Los Angeles to see what movies were all about. Worked several jobs: private detective, bouncer, parking cars, etc. Finally wangled my way into a job in the mail room at Allied Artists Studios, and bugged everybody till I got a job doing some rough riding on a George Montgomery western, *King of the Wild Stallions* (1959). They gave me one line to say, and that got me in the union. I was off and running. Did three more flicks at Allied before we parted ways. At night, I belonged to several acting groups. The town was full of young, antsy and artsy actors from all over the spectrum, and much of the good work was being done at night, in the little theatres and acting groups. The studios were still pretty much of a 'Star Search' kind of operation, and, frankly, behind the times creatively. The groups had Jack Nicholson, Harry

Dean Stanton, Bruce Dern, Monte Hellman, etc. We were all young and too naïve to take no for an answer. A great, vital time to be young and in Hollywood. We just made up our own rules.

Devil Wolf of Shadow Mountain (1963)

I made friends with a stuntman actor named Bud Cardos. He had this script, *Devil Wolf of Shadow Mountain*. Bud had always wanted to play The Wolfman, and this story was about a young rancher who is bitten and infected by a devil wolf. It was somehow decided that I would direct it, having had the most film experience. (After all, I had worked in a mail room!) We shot quite a few scenes. Bud was great in the part. However, about halfway through, the producer, a horseman named Johnny Carpenter, ran out of money. We shelved the project. That was it, until years later I heard that Carpenter had gotten completion money, so he shot some pick-ups and released it. I have never seen the completed work, but I sure fell in love with film work getting it started. Bud Cardos has no knowledge of a completed film, either. Johnny Carpenter was known for working with disabled and blind children, for which he was much admired. Film-wise, he was a bit of a rounder, a scammer and schemer... but likable... a jolly fellow who felt that he and John Wayne were the only early cowboys who looked tall in the saddle. Johnny Carpenter was about five foot five. The photographer was Lewis Guinn, sound recorder was Bob Dietz, and as well as I can remember, a fellow named Beau Wilson did Bud's makeup. Beau was related to the famous Westmore make-up dynasty. John (Bud) Cardos is a good friend, although we see each other much too seldom. Like all of us old stunt guys, he has a few aches and pains but is otherwise hale and hearty. He lives in the San Fernando Valley, and keeps some horses and mules on property out in the mission hills. He still owns the rights to *Devil Wolf of Shadow Mountain* and has talked about re-doing it some day.

opposite page:
Lock up your daughters! Gary Kent in his J.D. phase, circa 1960.

below:
As the grizzled family-man turned cannibal, in **The Forest** (1981).

Scenes from **The Forest**:

above:
Kent menaces his love rival with a variety of unusual implements; here, a hay-baler's fork...

right:
Kent in the cave layer of his cannibal character.

below:
Holding court to his potential future meals...

Monte Hellman's *Ride in the Whirlwind* (1965), and *The Shooting* (1967)
Richard Rush's *Hells Angels on Wheels* (1967), and *Psych-Out* (1968)

I heard there were a couple of westerns going to Utah, and that they were looking for a stuntman. I went on the interview, told them I was a stuntman, and I got the job. Jack Nicholson and Monte Hellman had put the deal together with Roger Corman. Paul Lewis was the production manager. We became good friends, and that was the start of my work for AIP, as Jack and Paul were AIP regulars. The pictures we shot in Utah, *Ride in the Whirlwind* and *The Shooting*, have become more or less classics. Besides Jack, they had Warren Oates, Millie Perkins and Cameron Mitchell. The assistant cameraman, Gary Kurtz, later became a producer for George Lucas. It was Jack who hired me as stuntman on *The Shooting* and *Ride in the Whirlwind*, so I have known him for some time. He is a fairly handy guy, and easy to stage action with.

Dick Rush would always let his stunt coordinator decide where and when, regarding fights. This allowed me to be constantly creative. In *Hells Angels on Wheels*, I followed a theme in each fight: a 'Pier 6 donnybrook' in the bar; Roman Coliseum in the swimming pool (Christians and lions, bikers and rednecks); running the gauntlet when the sailors came off the merry-go-round. So, on *Psych-Out*, I just asked Dick, since we're gonna be in the junkyard anyway, I've always wanted to stage something there; all that metal and rot, I guess. Dick said yes, and I just took my guys there, stacked some cars, and a few props, etc. The stunt guys ran it on the master-shot, then Jack and Adam [Roarke] did the close-ups. Jack was always a dream guy to double, as he would watch the fights and repeat even the body language. He always approached his work very seriously, partied little except with his current love, alone somewhere. After the day's shoot, you wouldn't see

him until morn. Didn't drink, and back then he didn't smoke, except for pot. Loyal to his friends, loved his work.

There were, for me, certain directors who always raised the bar a little, both in treatment of their cast and crew, and overall artistic content of their films. Richard Rush was, for me, the top of that list. Frequently, when you don't have the time or money, then real creativity and inventiveness is called upon. I can recall the joy of being the 'special effects' man on *Psych-Out*, where I was asked to design a bad trip on acid (the fire sequence) and have a little girl vomit up "black ooze". I finally hit upon the combination of well chewed liquorice, backed up by a side shot of Shell thirty eight, squirted from a grease gun at just the right angle. The combination of the two was amazing, and served the purpose perfectly. Ah, the magic of it all!

Targets (1968)

I belonged to this acting group, and Peter [Bogdanovich] showed up as a possible director for one of our projects. He lived in a little house out in the San Fernando Valley with his wife at the time, Polly Platt. (an enormous talent in her own right). Peter had done some editing for Corman, and got the financing for this little film he and Polly had written based on the Texas Tower shootings. Polly had been in Texas when a fellow named Charles Whitman climbed to the top of the school tower and began shooting people. He killed sixteen before the police killed him. So, Polly and Pete wrote *Targets*, loosely based on that incident, and also, making a statement against guns. Peter remembered me from the group and called me in. Paul Lewis was his production manager. They hired me to play the oil field worker and do all of the special effects. I did all of the shooting in the film, including the big shootout in the drive-in at the end. The film was a good project, with many who went on to bigger things in the industry. (Lazlo Kovacs, Paul Lewis, Frank Marshall, Mike Farrell).

Swingers Massacre (1973)

I came on the picture late. I was in Seattle, staying with relatives, and recovering from a love affair gone south by nursing a large bottle of excellent Scotch, when I got a frantic call from Ron Garcia. An actor had to drop from his film, and Jonesy had suggested me as a replacement. Could I come back to L.A. right away?

I am not a fan of Ron Garcia as a film maker. I respect and rather fancy him as a cinematographer, but filmmaker? No... What sold me on the film was the idea that I would get to do a lingering death scene inside an automobile with the camera pretty much on me. Now, what actor doesn't want to do a lingering death scene? Its part of our hopes and dreams list. I remember this strange little fellow, Dave Arthur, who was the producer, and his wife, the writer, who hovered around the set, convinced that this would be a "winner". Mr. Arthur had made some sort of deal with Ron and Don (two pictures for the price of one, I imagine). I did not know the rest of the cast. The only exciting and creative thing that occured was when one of the actresses blew her fuse at her co-star, insisting that he had acted like a slob, and in doing so, had ruined a perfectly good love scene... Those fireworks I remember, and also that it took Ron Garcia forever to get a day's filming done. I was supposed to work two days, then return to Seattle and that bottle of Scotch. Well, Ron's days were longer and more tedious than his ultimate product. Two days streched into four 22-hour days, cast and crew reduced to going through motions. No wonder the film is a bore. Wish I had more to offer about the whole thing, but I was just in and out, so to speak, and have never really seen the entire film. How was the car scene? Bloody awful, I'll bet.

The House of Seven Corpses (1973)

Again, Paul Lewis, who was now working mainly as a producer, began to recommend me for Production Management jobs. This was one. We took the cast and crew to Salt Lake City, Utah, where we had talked the Mormon Church into letting us shoot in their Historical Society. Everyone in Salt Lake treated us great. The film was directed by Paul Harrison, (writer of *H.R. Pufnstuf*), and had those great old stalwarts, John Ireland and John Carradine. Ireland was into 'smoke', and rolled those funny maryjane cigarettes and passed them around. Carradine was strictly a drinker. Every night, after shooting, he would shower and dress for the evening, (suit and tie) and adjourn to the bar, where he would drink for hours and tell these incredibly funny stories about his years in show business. He was a crowd pleaser, that's for sure. Paul pretty much let me run the show, and I actually brought the picture in under budget! A first!

Phantom of the Paradise (1974)

I had just finished working stunts on *Freebie and the Bean* in San Francisco, for Richard Rush. I was anxious to direct. I got a call from an acquaintance in Dallas, Texas, asking me to come down and direct a movie for him. I got there and found he did not have the money. I took an apartment in town, as my love relationship had just gone sour back in L.A. and I decided to stay in Dallas and get a movie going (*The Pyramid*). While working on the script,

I got a call from Paul Lewis. He was bringing Brian De Palma to town for *Phantom of the Paradise*, and wanted me to help him on production. Brian hired me, Paul got in an argument with the producer, Ed Pressman, and quit. I inherited the production end of the film. The picture was in absolute chaos when it arrived in Dallas, no one speaking to anyone, no pre-production done, no sets, props or locations. Anyway, I put together a group of Dallasites who jumped in and helped me get it done. We had a ball trying to make Dallas look like New York.

A New York and L.A. crew, stuck in Dallas over the Xmas holidays... whew! Everyone was into a strange and personal scene, being away from home on the holidays, stuck in this redneck southern town. We partied hearty trying to keep spirits up. Everyone bonded at the Christmas banquet, which Paul Williams, the lead, had catered. A veritable feast – duck, ham, turkey, yams, grapes, the best wine and champagne – he was a class act, and put on a class dinner. After that evening, everyone got along pretty well, although we all caught the flu, and passed it around like popcorn. It seemed there was a doctor constantly on the set, giving everyone vitamin-B shots and Vicodin. Brian De Palma was a perfectionist who kept to himself and communicated with only a few members of his crew. We had trouble getting information from him regarding the schedule. A quiet, intense man, who believed in Ouija boards and the like. Did not have much of a sense of humour, but knew his camera angles. A good filmmaker, but I don't think a crew-person would feel comfortable having a laugh with him...

The Pyramid (1975)

At dinner one night back in San Francisco, one of the stuntmen on *Freebie and the Bean*, Al Wyatt, told us he had just returned from Egypt, visiting the pyramids. The dinner turned into a delightful discussion of all things mystical. The conversation and excellent Merlot lingered

above:
The cast and crew of **Phantom of the Paradise** partied hard during the winter lay-off...

below:
The undead vote five out of ten for **The House of Seven Corpses**...

BIJOUFLIX RELEASING
PRESENTS

PYRAMID

Meet Chris.
T.V. 'Journalist.'

"Movies like this always seem to have a lingering effect on me."
Don Safran, Dallas Morning News

"Recalls Haskell Wexler's ground-breaking film MEDIUM COOL."
L.A. Times

"Has caused strong reactions... exposes the real problems."
Parent's Magazine

"A brooding interface of looming malevolence."
Dallas Times Herald

Once, He Believed.
The Medium was the Message.
Now the Messenger Must Fight the Medium.

STARRING
C.W. BROWN   IRA HAWKINS   TOMI BARRETT
EDGAR MITCHELL   MYSTIC KOMAR   PSYCHIC JACK GRAY

BIJOUFLIX
Made in USA

CULT. FULL FRAME.
COLOR. STEREO. 92 MINS.

above:
After nearly thirty years in obscurity, Kent's experimental and philosophical film **The Pyramid** was re-released, via internet sales, by BijouFlix.

long after the evening ended. Remembering this, I sent a friend of mine some money – Tom Kelly, who had written *The House of Seven Corpses* – and asked him to write me a low-budget script. "What about?" says Tom. "Oh, I don't know, how about something about pyramids, and mysticism?" Well, Tom took the money and smoked a lot of very nice ganja, but never wrote a lick. The *Phantom of the Paradise* group returned to Hollywood, but I stayed in Dallas, convinced that, with the group of kids I had put together, I could make my own movie if I just had a script. Since Tom didn't get it done, I decided to write it myself.

Now, being an actor in Hollywood who also does stunts, you are usually the bad guy. You know, 'Thug #1' or 'Thug #2', and the films you work on are usually violent. I decided that, as a filmmaker, I wanted to try something different, something nobody else would even attempt. I wanted to do a very personal film. I sat in my little Dallas cubby-hole apartment and started writing. I soon found I had no real interest in the 'Pyramid Power' fad – I am neither a scientist nor mystic – but I was very open to positive forces, and needed to do some examination of my own inner consciousness at the time. I was on my own quest, so to speak, and decided to see if maybe I could encapsulate a fictional story into the process, and come up with a new and unusual film. This energy drew to me a variety of real mystics, scientists, spiritual gurus and nuts of all varieties and persuasions; I was introduced to astronauts, neuro-psychologists, people that talked to plants, etc. I cast some of these real people to interact with the imaginary characters. Ed

Mitchell, sixth man to walk on the moon, plays himself at the observatory. This was more or less a first. I talked them all into being in the film, threw them into the pot along with some music and stunts (I couldn't resist).

Then Gregory Peck's son committed suicide in a Santa Barbara TV studio. And a woman news announcer in Florida had actually done herself in on camera. Since I had at one time been a young news reporter, I knew some of the pressure there was to dwell on the sensationally sordid, or the sensationally insignificant. I looked up the word 'pyramid', found it translated as 'fire in the middle', and decided, well then, there's my story: a reporter who has grown tired of the usual crap, and takes his personal quest and nose for news into the forests of consciousness, whatever that turned out to mean. Sort of a 'Siddhartha of an American Newsman'.

When I started looking for money, wham, out of nowhere, the phone rings. An old friend from Sacramento, Mike McFarland. He had some money, and wanted to make a film. Would I be interested? Now, what are the chances of that happening other than 'in the movies'? It was not much money, I had to shoot the film on a nickel and a dime and a lot of favours. But the film got made, and along the way an incredible amount of unusual and mystical happenings occurred. Not just to me, but to the cast and crew. Some had their lives changed positively, and many developed a deeper awareness of this interconnected universe.

The male lead in the film, Charlie Brown, was shot and killed in a liquor store robbery before the film was out of the editing room. Charlie had just dropped in to run the cash register for a friend, who wanted to go see his girl. Two unknown assailants robbed the store, and needlessly shot Charlie in the back of the head. The female lead, Tomi Barrett, became my wife.

The Pyramid was a late entry at the Cannes Festival in 1975, but still got rave reviews and made several sales. When I told the suits this film was about consciousness they said, 'Huh?' But I can guarantee you that in Houston, in 1975, for thirteen weeks, *Pyramid* was the hot ticket for new-agers, stoners, bikers, intellectuals, film folk, etc. That alone made it worth the effort. At the USA Film Festival, in Park City, Utah, (now Sundance), *Pyramid* won best of category, Docu-Drama. We signed a deal with a distributor, and the film opened in Dallas, San Antonio, Houston, etc. It got rave reviews. Ed Mitchell was flown in and given the keys to the city of San Antonio – then I caught the distributor cheating with the numbers. I sued him to get the film back. The case went to trial, took a year. I won, but by then I was broke and on to other things. *Pyramid* sat in my garage for twenty some years, until a film writer for the *Austin Statesman* happened to see it sitting there and asked to see it. I set up a screening, cringing because the film was so long in the tooth. Well, he loved it. It became the opening film for an Austin Film Festival fund raiser, and sold out the house. Then BijouFlix made an offer to put it out over the internet, and at last, it's getting an audience.

Gary Kent is currently working on his autobiography, *Shadows and Light, Journeys with Outlaws in Revolutionary Hollywood*, a volume that should be on every self-respecting film fan's must-have list...

chapter 6

Louisiana Screamin'

James L. Wilson & Richard Wadsack on Screams of a Winter Night

Screams of a Winter Night (1979)

Released in 1979 and distributed by Dimension Pictures, the enticingly named *Screams of a Winter Night* was made in Natchitoches, Louisiana, far from the traditional film centres of Los Angeles and New York. Seen today, in a film market where sensation and excess rule the roost, it blows in like a sepulchral draft from a different age, when a horror story could safely take its time building its scares. It has its flaws, as with any low-budget film, but they're offset by a gradually thickening atmosphere of supernatural menace. The film was aimed at the early teens, so goriness and overt violence are not part of the package – however, as a scary campfire compendium for younger viewers, made before teenagers were familiar with such well-oiled death machines as *Alien* and *A Nightmare on Elm Street*, it has charm to go with the chills. It's also perhaps the only compendium horror film in which the wraparound tale is the best part of the show, building up into a genuinely unnerving climax that must have sent its young audience home with their nerves thrumming like phone wires in a high wind...

A group of ten friends take a weekend vacation in a remote lodge near Coyote Lake, so-called by the Indians because of the strange, howling winds that scour the region. As night falls, John (Matt Borel), a horror fan and practical joker determined to exploit the creepiness of the locale, tells the group a story about 'The Moss Point Man' – a monstrous wood-dweller whom a local girl and her boyfriend were reputed to have encountered when their car broke down in the woods. John's friend Steve (Gil Glasgow) joins in, with the tale of a hellish fraternity initiation in a nearby haunted house. Distracted by the ghost stories, no-one notices that the wind has begun to rise. Elaine (Mary Agen Cox), unimpressed by the spooky tales so far, recounts the story of a psychotic 'girl next-door' who embarked on a killing spree after a sexual assault tipped her over the edge. This unnerves the already jittery group, who by now can no longer ignore the howling wind outside. The intensity of the last tale spills over into the room. As the party descend into hysteria, violent forces tear at the lodge, eclipsing the scare-stories with a terrifying reality...

Screams of a Winter Night starts out as a fairly routine genre excursion but builds up in its second half into a

In the shadow of evil, in the echo of sins.
In the icy stare of moonlight, our ghostly tale begins...

It was a dark and stormy night when the kids arrived at the lake.

SCREAMS OF A WINTER NIGHT

How do you think those stories get started?

© 1979 DIMENSION PICTURES INC.

PG PARENTAL GUIDANCE SUGGESTED
SOME MATERIAL MAY NOT BE SUITABLE FOR CHILDREN

Dimension Pictures presents A Full Moon Pictures Production
"SCREAMS OF A WINTER NIGHT"
Starring **Matt Borel** • **Gil Glascow** • **Mary Agen Cox** • **Patrick Byers** • **Robin Bradley**
Ray Gaspard • **Beverly Allen** • **Brandy Barrett** • **Jan Norton** • **Charles Rucker**
Produced by **Richard H. Wadsack** & **James L. Wilson** • Directed by **James L. Wilson** • Screenplay by **Richard H. Wadsack**
Special Effects **William T. Cherry, III** • Original Score by **Don Zimmers** • Executive Producer **S. Mark Lovell**
DPi A DIMENSION PICTURES RELEASE

Screams of a Winter Night
aka **Howlings of a Winter's Night**
(Australian video title)
© none [1979]
Quinn-L Corporation & Rinconada, Inc. presents a Rinconada, Inc. film.
director: James L. Wilson. producers: Richard H. Wadsack & James L. Wilson. executive producer: S. Mark Lovell. special effects: William T. Cherry, III. film editors: Gary Ganote & Craig Mayes. original score: Don Zimmers. director of photography: Robert E. Rogers. original screenplay: Richard H. Wadsack. sound recording: Ron Judkins. set and wardrobe design: Mar'Sue Wilson. script supervisor: Deborah G. Wadsack. camera operator: Mark Beasley. gaffer: Keith Cunningham. key grip: Mike Charbonnet. assistant cameraman: Arthur Krausse. boom operator: Gary Potts. grip: Wes Harris, Jr. stillman/2nd unit camera: Raymond Groetsch. conformer: Mary Ganote. production manager: Cliff Blackburn. post-production manager: James L. Wilson. secretary to the producers: Betty Shettlesworth. production accountant: H. Wayne Wilson. special effects assistant: Sam Phillips. production aides: Joey Shettlesworth, Jeanmarie Sylvester. sound by Ryder Sound Services, Inc. colour by PSI Film Laboratories. Special assistance from: Charlie Whitaker; Norton Aviation; Pat Jaskula; G.W. Conlay; Nicole Brown; Chandler's Camp; Robert and Mary Smothers; Doyle Maynard; Sherman Cobb; Billy Kees; Lester Kees; Henry Cook Taylor; Becky Boswell; Kisatchee National Forest; Sadie Scott; The American Cemetery Ass'n., Inc.; Mary Townsend; Northwestern State University of La.; Cammie Deblieux; Mike and Charlotte Young; Roger LeBrescu; Peter and Conna Cloutier; John Mayfield; Edwin Dunahoe; Bill Jones; Minnie Ann Bamberg; Charles and Susan Norman; Hickory Village Sporting Goods; Don Sepulvado; Blackburn Productions; The Breezesle Family; Valley Farmers Co-op; Jan L. Wilson; The Crawford Young Estate; Lisa Bartmess; Cotton's Taxidermy; Ronald Dobson; Clemons Mathews; Syble Womack; Gargoyle's Antiques; Mrs. Leary Taylor; Harry Creighton. Special thanks to: Mr. and Mrs. James Lasyone; George Celles; Robert W. Ragsdale; Casper L. Smith; David S. Alphin; Glen Baker. filmed entirely on location in Natchitoches Parish (Louisana, USA).
Cast: Matt Borel (John). Gil Glasgow (Steve). Patrick Byers (Cal). Mary Agen Cox (Elaine). Robin Bradley (Sally). Ray Gaspard (Harper). Beverly Allen (Jookie). Brandy Barrett (Liz). Charles Rucker (Alan). Jan Norton (Lauri). Malcolm Edmonds. Nicole Salley. William Goodman. Jean Sweeney. Bill [William] Ragsdale (the kid).

bottom right:
Madness beckons in the second segment of
Screams of a Winter Night.

opposite page, strip of images, from top:
Beverly Allen plays a nice quiet girl who's pushed too far;
Fleeing through the woods;
Arriving at the lodge;
A feeling of foreboding at the threshold;
Terror in the night in the first fireside tale;
In the third tale, a girl's encounter with a brutish 'lover' triggers psychosis;
A room-mate suffers the murderess's rage...

tense supernatural suspenser. The onset of conviction arrives a tad too late to completely salvage the film's reputation, but it's nevertheless strong enough to pluck it from the mire. Originality isn't of the essence here: from the get-go, this unleashes a classic scenario that's part *Scooby-Doo*, part *Weird Tales*. The collection of rural grotesques who gather round the van when our gang of happy campers stop for gas are straight out of *Deliverance* (except for cute William Ragsdale, who eventually became a star in *Fright Night* six years later), and the hints of an Indian curse on the woods ensure the tale resides squarely in the comfort zone of seventies horror: and let's not get too snobby about comfort zones, after all they're frequently visited by royalty – Stephen King would be lost without them. Clearly we're not going to face anything *too* challenging or disturbing here, but you can't watch *The Last House on Dead End Street* every night, can you? The fact is, this is simple fare, bouncing merrily up and down the scale between hackneyed and thrilling – if the sight of a camper van driving through sinister woodland to a remote derelict cottage in the woods gives you a pleasurable frisson of expectation, you'll find there's some good creepy fun to be had.

The problem for a modern audience is that you have to be patient to get to the good stuff. The structure of the film is potentially ideal for an incremental series of scares, escalating from schlocky fright-stories to out-and-out supernatural terror. But after an innovative and genuinely unnerving opening (we hear the previous occupants of the lodge die in terror on the soundtrack, played against a black screen), and the arrival scenes mentioned above, the first story-within-the-story pays off so minimally it's a drag on the rest. There's an obvious commitment to the art of suggestion (gore is entirely absent) but such a vow of chastity requires a great deal of imaginative investment: fear and madness are fine spectres to call to the table, but they need a little more energy than *Screams of a Winter Night* initially possesses. Too much time is wasted on creeping around in the dark.

However, as the football pundits say, this is a game of two halves. (Actually, three halves with a wraparound, but that doesn't sound quite right…) Once the tide turns and the film begins to cook, it all gets distinctly alarming, and the actors do their utmost to crank up the tension. Granted, the girls are the main focus of terror: in fact female hysteria is so intense towards the end that you'd be well advised to turn down the treble on your TV set. But sexism be damned, not all women can be ass-kicking Amazons. In fact the shocks are so well marshalled in the final scenes that afterwards you come away with a vastly improved impression of the picture than you would have admitted earlier on. (I wish George Romero had seen this, because if ever a 'portmanteau' horror film needed a better wraparound, it's *Creepshow*.)

One of the film's best ideas is to have the actors in the wraparound story play the characters in the other stories. As well as making good use of the available cast, giving each actor a second bite of the cherry, it makes sense in a diegetic sense too: those listening would quite likely visualise the tales using their friends' faces to fill out the sketchy stories. You can imagine this technique paying off beautifully in a Fassbinder tale of warring couples regaling each other with mean vignettes at a party; and it's worth squirreling away for future reference if you're thinking of writing a low-budget script…

Story One, 'The Moss Point Man', is about as basic as a horror story can get, featuring some kind of Bigfoot in the night – the very dark picture on video does the episode no favours at all. Story Two, although hackneyed as hell, works itself up to a sucker-punch creep-out finale that brings to mind the end of *The Blair Witch Project*, with its reliance on a big build-up to a shuddery last image. A fraternity initiation dare to sleep overnight in a haunted house is accepted by three friends. After two have gone missing while exploring the upper reaches of the building, the third sets off to see what's become of them, and after much tenseness and shadowy apprehension, he opens a door to find… well, something haunting and subtle and likely to scare you if you're a twelve-year-old with an overactive imagination. There's still just enough of a thrill to please me now, so I'm sure that if I'd seen it when I was young it would have left me afraid to close my eyes at bedtime – in its horrid implication it feels like a moment from a Robert Aickman story, in which the horror is so understated you can almost, but not quite, miss it.

Mary Agen Cox is excellent as 'Elaine', the cynical odd-one-out, who mocks the ghost tales her friends have been telling, and offers in their place Story Three: about a sexually repressed girl turning psycho after an attempted rape. Beverly Allen acts out the role most convincingly, with shattered innocence turning to puritan bitterness, and it's also a relief to see what Wilson can do with scenes shot in daylight! Her performance segues into the wraparound story, where Matt Borel's 'John' is still giving us the classic nerdy horror-freak, always going too far with his practical jokes. For a fan of the slasher subgenre, 'John' is an old friend, and it's easy to imagine Borel turning up in much the same role in *Madman*, *The Burning*, *My Bloody Valentine* or *Final Exam*. He's distracting and enjoyable enough to act as a sleight of hand manoeuvre when the scares begin to ratchet up in the final scenes. The wind rises, whips up the hysteria, and you may find yourself wondering quite when the film got so scary – a neat piece of narrative construction. As for the destructive finale itself, the cast really go for it with some impressive shrieking and panicking, and rather surprisingly the whole thing works just fine *without* a giant optically-composited thingamajig putting in an appearance…

There's enough going right in *Screams of a Winter Night* to make you curious about what Wilson and Wadsack could have delivered next. Sure it's a bit shaky on its feet at times, but it's a fine calling card to the industry. It's really too bad the industry never got the message…

James Wilson & Richard Wadsack Interviewed

Natchitoches (pronounced Nack-a-tish, from an Indian word meaning Place of the Paw-Paw) is the oldest permanent settlement in Louisiana. A small but historic town, it was founded in 1714 by French colonists to promote trade with the local Indians and the Spanish in Mexico. Thanks to its status as an early river port, it played a key role in the commercial development of both Texas and Louisiana: goods, including livestock, deer hides, salt and tobacco were shipped by river from Natchitoches to New Orleans. Expansion occurred after 1803, when the Louisiana Purchase, often referred to as 'the greatest real estate deal in history', almost doubled the size of the United States. 828,000 square miles of what was then called The Louisiana Territory were bought "for a song"[1] from the French for $15 million: thirteen new states were carved from land stretching East-to-West, from the Mississippi River to the Rocky Mountains, and South-to-North from the Gulf of Mexico to the Canadian border. Natchitoches grew rapidly as Americans rushed into the area, introducing cotton plantations along the Cane River. However, in the 1830s, the river shifted its course about five miles east of town, leaving Natchitoches without a direct outlet to the sea except at high water. What remains today is the Cane River Lake, a beautiful, meandering body of water about thirty-two miles in length, flowing through downtown Natchitoches and on to the Plantation Country. The original inhabitants of the region, the Choctaw Indians, spread across Louisiana throughout the late 18th and throughout the 19th Century, sometimes displacing other smaller tribes, and refusing to be swept away by various Treaties designed to shuttle them off to the Oklahoma settlements.[2] Their influence can be felt in *Screams of a Winter Night*, with its wraparound tale, drawn from Indian legend, of a powerful wind that springs from nowhere.

The Louisiana Cavaliers

The writer of *Screams of a Winter Night*, Richard Wadsack, was born in San Antonio, Texas in 1946, but brought up in Shreveport, Louisiana, where his father, a noncommissioned officer in the US Air Force, was based. It's a town he still lives in today. "Neither of my parents graduated high school, but my father was one of the most intelligent people I've ever known and my mother strongly encouraged me to take interest in all kinds of music and the other arts," he recalls. "One of my earliest memories is of our outings to the 'Louisiana Hayride', staged at the Municipal Auditorium here in Shreveport. Slim Whitman lived about four blocks from our house in the early 1950s, and I have a photo of myself backstage at the 'Hayride', with Red Sovine." Wadsack's father, not your average officer type, enjoyed a brief stint in showbusiness: "He left his family's Kansas farm in the 1930s, looking for adventure, and joined the Floto-Tom Mix Circus, as groom to Mix's 'wonder horse', Tony. When the season ended, he joined the Army."

Wadsack's earliest movie memories are, "a jumble of scenes from cowboy pictures and scary jungle films in which the natives were generally something well beyond merely 'restless', and gorillas, lions, quicksand and a host of other dangers loomed large. My earliest intact memories are of *Invasion of the Body Snatchers*, *The Thing*, and *Invaders from Mars*. Most of what was on movie screens of my youth was little more than distraction, but those pictures compelled my attention, and they stuck."

After graduating high school Wadsack went on the road for a while, playing trumpet with a travelling lounge band before deciding to give college a try. Six-and-a-half years later, he'd earned a BA in History, and the question of what to do next arose once again: "I had no idea. I thought advertising might be an all-right job, if you had to have one, and I eventually landed a position with a small, backwater ad agency. Then, a fellow I had met in college became lead executive for an outdoor historical drama that was starting up in Natchitoches, and I conned him into hiring me as its public relations director. I also persuaded Jim Wilson to come to work for the theatre. I'd met him my freshman year at school and we had become friends. He wasn't having much fun where he was at the time, and agreed to design the stage for the theatre." The play, *Louisiana Cavalier*, was written by Paul Green (1894-1981), a North Carolina born playwright who had won the Pulitzer Prize in 1927 for his play, *In Abraham's Bosom*. Green, whose plays frequently spoke out against racial prejudice, lynchings and the brutal chain-gangs of the Deep South, wrote *Louisiana Cavalier* in 1976, and it received its Natchitoches outdoor premiere in 1977, but by then, Wadsack feels, his glory days were behind him: "*Cavalier* was just awful, so far as Jim and I were concerned, and we began working out what we thought would be great improvements, and conspiring together on how to get them introduced. A crazy notion, of course, and our schemes went nowhere. For reasons not limited to the script, the play's first season was a disaster."

James Wilson, the director and co-producer of *Screams of a Winter Night*, was born in 1947 in Shreveport, Louisiana to a middle class family background. "Our family's creative interests tended toward music," he recalls. "Two sisters and I sang in trio, did family events, church functions, etc. from time to time." Wilson began to take a serious interest in movies while at college: "I came of age in the late sixties/early seventies, a remarkable time for cinema. Films like *Midnight Cowboy*, *Five Easy Pieces*, *McCabe and Mrs Miller*, *M*A*S*H*, *A Clockwork Orange*, moved away from mere entertainment and suggested unlimited possibilities and a whole new way of looking at movies. After a couple of years of false starts in college, I discovered the theatre department and the performing arts. I moved quickly into directing, and in the last couple of years directed a half-dozen plays and several film shorts; Super-8 silent things, cops and robbers, car chases. After school, my first job was as director of an Arts Centre in Arkansas. The centre housed four arts organisations: a community theatre, symphony orchestra, ballet company and art league. The major part of my job was to direct five theatre productions a year. As a stage director, I took a serious interest in stage design and lighting."

With their joint experience in theatre production, Wilson and Wadsack were keen to apply their learning to something more permanent. Wadsack recalls, "One night my wife and I were visiting Jim and his wife at their home, all of us drinking wine and talking about our circumstances and the absence of future prospects. At some point, I

SCREAMS OF A WINTER NIGHT

1979 DIMENSION PICTURES INC.
A DIMENSION PICTURES RELEASE

PG PARENTAL GUIDANCE SUGGESTED
SOME MATERIAL MAY NOT BE SUITABLE FOR CHILDREN

above:
John (Matt Borel) spins a tale of rampaging monsters in the woods – and then *who* should pop up?

announced that I was either moving to Mexico, or making a movie. Everyone though it was a joke, but I wasn't joking. I didn't know squat about making movies, or the movie business, but I thought I understood about dramatic structure and considered I had a talent for marketing. Jim had directed several plays in college and at a small community theatre, both our wives and many friends had either majored or dabbled in theatre in school. I had never written a script of any kind, but from what I knew that was no impediment to success. And we had zero prospects in any other direction. So we agreed to try it for a year and see what developed, and our wives – incredibly, it seems now – did not discourage us."[3]

Research and Development

Prior to forming their own production company, Rincorda Inc., in late 1976, neither Wilson nor Wadsack had any experience directing features: *Screams of a Winter Night* was to be a combination of creative adventure, business course and film school. Wilson had directed numerous TV

spots and industrials, but nothing of a similar complexity to *Screams*. "We eked out a living doing advertising work and making a documentary about the plantation homes in the Natchitoches vicinity," Wadsack explains, "which also gave us a bit of experience putting together a 'Movie' - going through the process on at least a rudimentary level. We soon learned about a tax loophole that greatly benefited fundraising for film production in the 1970s here in the States."

Wilson picks up the story: "Everyone was producing these films via a unique financial strategy that you could use at the time. Limited partnerships allowed you to put investors together and guaranteed they wouldn't lose any money. When we first tiptoed into it, we were under the impression it was going to be easy because of these limited partnerships, but by the time we'd got our feet on the ground in 1977, the law had changed so you could no longer raise money that way."

Looking further into the possibility of local production, the duo realised that several filmmakers in the area had completed and sold their own movies, including:

Charles B. Pierce (Texarkana director of *The Legend of Boggy Creek* and *The Town That Dreaded Sundown*); Joy Houck and Jim McCullough (respectively the Louisiana-based director and producer of *Creature from Black Lake*); Harry Thomason (Arkansas-based director of *Encounter with the Unknown* and *The Day It Came to Earth*); and Bill Blackburn (the producer of *The Day It Came to Earth*). "I knew there was a good bit of independent production going on in our little region of Louisiana, Arkansas and Texas," Wadsack says.[4] "Charles Pierce was an advertising executive who had scored big with *The Legend of Boggy Creek* and gone on to semi-respectability with *The Town That Dreaded Sundown*; the McCulloughs here in Shreveport were grinding out a series of family-oriented features; and the lovable dog vehicle, *Benji*, had made a bundle for Joe Camp in Dallas. There were at least two other operations in Arkansas. Why not us?" Wilson concurs: "We decided if they could do it, so could we. We started an advertising agency to support us while we figured out how to finance and make a movie."

The most helpful local advice, according to Wadsack, came from Bill and Cliff Blackburn, two brothers from Arkansas. "We learned a whole lot about the details and many pitfalls of theatrical production. They had hit every rock in the road, and were generous in sharing their experience and know-how with us. We learned that many more movies were started than were finished, and that failing to complete and failing to find distribution were the greatest risks facing investors." Wilson, though also appreciative, found some of the Blackburns' wisdom questionable: "Bill and Cliff Blackburn advised us: 'Shoot on 16mm and blow up to 35mm so you can shoot lots of film.' Terrible advice, for a number of reasons, the main one being you spend a lot of time shooting stuff you don't need. At the time, the industry average was a 10:1 shooting ratio, and we were probably pushing a 30:1 ratio. Instead of a set-up taking a couple of hours you might spend four or five, and then when you get into the editing, you've got thirty takes, and at the level we were working the difference between them was, frankly, negligible." Wilson did, however, find some of their other words of warning valuable: " 'Hire an experienced production manager and start him well in advance of shooting.' Excellent advice. In fact we took on Cliff Blackburn for the post! And: 'If you had any idea how hard this was going to be, you wouldn't do it' – we figured that was true, but we did it anyway!"

Bill Blackburn introduced Wilson and Wadsack to his colleague Harry Thomason, who invited them to observe the filming of a monster movie he was making in Little Rock, Arkansas, called *The Day It Fell to Earth*. They stuck around for a few days but left feeling they'd seen enough. (See the review of Thomason's *Encounter with the Unknown*.) Wadsack also met up with Joy Houck Sr., who owned several theatres in Shreveport and New Orleans: "I didn't know until I met Joy Houck, Sr., that the names of a downtown theatre and a drive-in here in Shreveport derived from anyone's name. I spent some time in both of those theatres and always assumed that the Joy Theatre and the Joy Drive-In were named in the spirit of what their owners hoped for their audiences. Definitely a better choice than Rex, Venus, Saenger, Strand, Don, Capri, etc., the names of other local theatres: although I'd have appreciated *them* more had I known future movie palaces here would be called Tinseltown, Eastgate

Multiplex, Bossier Cineplex 9, etc.! When I visited the old man at his offices in a seedy stretch of Airline Highway in New Orleans, he showed me lobby cards of pictures he had produced in the 1950s. *Poor White Trash* is the only title I can recall, but they were all of the sexploitation variety. It took balls to produce something called *Poor White Trash*, I can tell you, certainly in the South in those days."

After brief meetings with Houck's son, Joy Houck Jr., director of *Creature from Black Lake*, and local-boy-made-good Charles Pierce, whose hit *The Town That Dreaded Sundown* had been picked up for nationwide distribution by AIP, the duo felt they were clued up enough to begin seeking finance for their own stab at the big time. Wadsack had already written the finished script early on to secure funding. Now it was time to go looking for the money. He describes the process: "From the start our business plan included completion insurance and funding for a test market. I reasoned that if we could show prospective distributors real-life box office receipts, we would eliminate some subjectivity and greatly enhance our chances – and our position from which to negotiate. I also figured that if we could succeed in reaching distribution with our first picture, we would position ourselves to move on, and learn how to make better movies as we went along. And our research revealed that, without question, the genre in which fledgling, low-budget filmmakers were most likely to be successful was 'horror'. So that was the kind of movie we needed to make. This businesslike approach seemed most likely to appeal to investors, too, and after many dead ends and missteps, we found S. Mark Lovell, a wealthy real estate developer with sophisticated tax savvy and the cash flow to fund the entire cost on his own. The sex appeal of backing a movie, and the potential for huge profits, certainly appealed to Mark, and once we had convinced him that we had our act together, and had eliminated every possible cause for failure – after many meetings and his own research – he said 'yes'. That was a pretty damn happy day!"

"We were introduced to Mark Lovell through a family member of mine," Wilson explains. "We pitched the movie to him and after several months of consideration he agreed to finance the entire project. As best we can figure, Mark saw it as a trial project, which, if successful, he could resell to his investor pool. But that's speculation; there's really no sound explanation. How a couple of kids from Louisiana who had never made a movie in their life were able to talk grown men into giving them several hundred thousand dollars to make one remains a mystery!"

So, with Lovell's financial assistance in the bag in 1977 or very early 1978, a total budget of around $300,000 was nailed down; pretty respectable for a small regional feature. Wilson recalls: "We had about $250,000 for production and another $50,000 for test marketing. That budget allowed us to do some things that we really thought were important. One was to have an original score recorded for the film. That cost six or eight grand. We knew there were a lot of sound effects, so we spent a lot of money there, and we went to Ryder Sound Services in L.A. to do the mix. We paid everybody, on time, we didn't ask for any deferment, and we paid ourselves: not a lot, but we paid ourselves a salary. I've seen productions round about here in Shreveport, and they ask everyone to do it for free, and they get a buddy to do the audio, and they've got sixty thousand dollars, to pay for the film in the camera."

above:
Terror grips the holidaymakers as the wind begins to rise... and rise...

below:
This beautifully crafted Gothic image greets one of the gang as they explore the dusty old lodge.

"The title was *Screams of a Winter Night* from the get-go," says Wadsack. "Like the story, it was marketing-driven. We started with the 'legends' and then sorted out the wraparound storyline within which to create a unified, rather than anthological piece. Two of the 'legends' existed in oral tradition and were widely known in this region of the US, and the activity – young couples getting together to frighten and titillate each other with tales of teenage terror – was very popular. Our original tagline, *'How do you think those stories get started?'*, played that up, and promised to legitimize it."

"We had a specific market in mind – one that research said did a lot of movie-going," Wilson explains. "We knew we needed a 'PG' rating to have access to that market, and at the time the rating system was still very conservative. So we were deliberate in avoiding graphic violence, drugs, and sex."

'How do you think those stories get started?' – shooting *Screams of a Winter Night*

Shooting took place during the summer of 1978, as Wadsack recalls: "It took over a year to reach funding, and about fifteen months from then until we broke the test market release. The principal filming spanned five or six weeks, I believe. Three weeks, then a break of a week or so, and then a final week's shooting." Wilson remembers a slightly longer schedule: "We shot a total of nine weeks, shooting seven straight weeks, then breaking for a couple of weeks, coming back for all the MOS shooting, pickups, etc."

"Everything was shot on location in Natchitoches Parish," adds Wadsack. "Having gone to college there and lived there, scouting and securing locations was one of the easiest aspects of the whole show for us. Most of the script was written with specific locations in mind. Grand Ecore Bluffs, where the crazy girl murders her overly-ardent date, has been a favourite make-out spot in the area for decades. The old hotel was a long-abandoned hotel in downtown Natchitoches. The dormitory was a dormitory on the local college campus. The cabin and much of the rural scenery was located around nearby Black Lake."

For a low-budget horror tale like this, the performances Wilson obtained from his cast are mostly above average. He shot the cabin scenes first, filming the cutaway stories afterwards, so for the most part all ten of the main cast were on the set together, which helped to develop an ensemble feeling. Wadsack recalls, "I wrote John and Cal, the characters portrayed by Matt Borel and Gil Glasgow, with them in mind. They and Ray Gaspard ['Harper'] were cast members for *Louisiana Cavalier*'s premiere season. Jim knew Beverly Allen ['Jookie'] from his stint at a community theatre in Arkansas and we cast the rest of the main players from Dallas and Houston."

Borel, in an interview with local paper *The Times Picayune* in 1979, explained: "Jim Wilson and Richard Wadsack asked members of *Louisiana Cavalier* to send résumés for a film they were putting together. What they had been doing was quietly watching us. They wrote the characters for us, so there were lines that sounded like things we would say. It worked out well." Of his employers, he said: "They're total collaborators, total partners, to such an extent that it makes some people uncomfortable."

The decision to use the same actors in multiple roles, Wadsack explains, "was probably motivated more out of practicality than sprung from inspiration. We had quite a few actors to contend with as it was, and none of them objected to the screen time. There was some concern about possible confusion, but the device made dramatic sense to me – that, in hearing the stories, listeners would tend to relate personalities in the stories to similar ones they knew, or who were telling the tales."

Two alumni of *Screams of a Winter Night* went on to mainstream success. Handsome young William Ragsdale, who plays a country-cuzzin garage attendant at the start of the film, found fame in *Fright Night* (1985), the hit vampire horror-comedy, and its sequel. "I had been working as director of an arts centre in El Dorado, Arkansas," Wilson remembers, "and Bill was in my children's group up there for about three years, I think he was about fifteen. He just loved acting so much that we created a part for him." On the crew side, sound mixer Ron Judkins has climbed to the top of his profession, in Hollywood terms, as sound mixer (recording the production sound on-set) for Steven Spielberg, having worked with him on *Minority Report*, *Catch Me If You Can*, *The Terminal* and *War of the Worlds*.

With production in full swing, Wadsack and Wilson experienced the thrills, the pressures and the horrors of a low-budget film shoot: "There was a night shoot for which the dailies came back so underdeveloped they appeared not to have been processed at all," shudders Wadsack. "Then there was a crew revolt - a stoppage over the slender variety of fruit juices and drinks served during breaks. One night not long after we had secured the financial backing, the old downtown building in Natchitoches in which we officed burned to the ground. We lost props and wardrobe, the production board, scripts, records, files, new furniture, many precious personal items. All gone. Jim and I both lived within walking distance of the office and generally left everything there. I happened to have taken a script home that night, or there would have been nothing left at all. On another occasion, law enforcement swarmed a remote location where we were filming the scene in which the boy is hung up over the car, with his terrified date inside. Some local happened to catch a glimpse and assumed the worst was going on… There were near fistfights between gaffers and sound folk in their age-old battle for supremacy. Arguments and insults. Accusations and recriminations. Stress breakdowns and anxiety attacks. The usual stuff. The helicopter pilot we hired for aerials, and to make our wind, announcing to assembled cast and crew that should they hear the helicopter engine stop, they should seek shelter immediately. Add to that the brutally long days and the awful heat and humidity – summers in Louisiana are not kind or gentle. On the other hand, many very happy moments when scenes were completed successfully – and the very strange feeling when filming was finished, and cast and crew departed."

On set, tension began to develop between Wilson and his director of photography, Robert E. Rogers. "Bob Rogers was experienced, but not at shooting movies. There's an enormous difference between shooting industrials and features. He knew the technical end, but the technical is not necessarily as important as the dynamics and the dramatics, or at least that's the conclusion we came to. I felt conflicted. I didn't have any experience, but I felt a shot needed to be done this way, or that way. I was just going on youth and instinct, but he was saying no, no, it needed to be done another way. At the same time I had my producer 'head' on and, you know, cinematographers are notorious for wanting to spend days lighting a shot. Fortunately, I connected with Mark Beasley, the camera operator, and by the end he and I were more or less running things, and Bob was overseeing to be sure we didn't get into serious trouble. Mark had a great eye, and a good sense of movement and composition, and he was shooting it anyway, while Bob was the director of cinematography and lighting. In Bob's defence, we didn't have the time to give him the script and let him go over it. He showed up, and two days later we started shooting. He didn't have the context."

Wilson's over-riding memory of the production period is the strain of knowing that so much money was riding on his efforts: "Virtually every aspect was a serious challenge because neither Wadsack nor I had any experience whatsoever with a project like this. Add to that the pressure of spending several hundred thousand dollars of someone else's money – a man who was fully expecting to get it all back and more – and we slept very little during the year. We were confident throughout that *Screams*, conceptually, would work, and that it was an okay, marketable scary movie. We were less sure how to get the concept on film and then make it all fit together more or less coherently. Having directed almost fifty plays by this time, I was fairly confident working with actors. Beyond that, the organisation, the scheduling, planning the setups, lighting, sound, continuity – all the technical and administrative demands – were almost overwhelming at times."

Post-Production and Test-Marketing

Post-production went on for a further six months, with the editing taking three-and-a-half to four: "I'd describe the editing process as miserable," says Wilson. "I had a three-year-old son, and we were living in Natchitoches and editing in Dallas, so I was away from home for almost four months. Secondly, we had an editor, Gary Ganote, who was experienced in industrials and commercials but did not have the experience editing a full length dramatic film. This was flatbed editing, you had to paste every cut; we were in this darkened room for fourteen to sixteen hours a day. We began by giving Gary an editor's cut, but the first sequence he cut together was not at all what we were thinking of. I felt I had to step in and take over the direction of the editing, relegating him to a functionary, and that's never pleasant. I understand his point of view: here's this kid that's never made a movie before telling him to do this and that and this and that. The second editor credited, Craig Mayes, he was a young man who came in about two weeks before we finished it and did a polish job, and he really did some things that made it nice." Wilson pauses, then laughs: "Looking back, Gary was probably cutting it right! I was stuck in that thing of 'character is important', so we would let scenes play out as written, whereas he wanted to get in and get out of it and move on to the next thing. On the rare occasion I look at it now, I think, 'Boy this thing drags!' At the time, I thought it was maybe a little too fast!"

Wadsack hated the editing too: "I stayed away, mostly. I worked with Don Zimmers on the music, and I did enjoy that. There wasn't much work to it, for me. Don had done well for years as a composer-arranger of music for commercials and an occasional pop or country recording session. He was truly excited about scoring a movie and got quite a lot out of a relatively-slim budget. We did the final sound mix and effects at Ryder Sound in Hollywood, and that was very enjoyable."

Originally there were four 'legends' in the test-market edit of the movie, the fourth being a cemetery scenario involving a malevolent witch-spirit. Wilson explains: "The distributor, Dimension Pictures, told us that our two-hour film had to be cut to about an hour and forty minutes. They said that movie houses needed to run features every two hours in order to get maximum showings per day, and they needed a twenty-minute break between showings to clear the theatre, to get the next group in. They cut an entire story – a twenty-minute story that took place in a cemetery. It was shot day-for-night for budgetary reasons. The result was fairly low contrast footage, and our distributor said that since this movie would be playing a lot of drive-ins, the ambient light at drive-ins would make this footage hard to see anyway. Plus, it was the corniest of the four stories, though no one said that outright." (Although this section was cut for the Dimension-distributed version, and for its various video releases, it still exists in the original 35mm print owned by Wilson.)

Wadsack recalls that, "*Screams* pretty much took over my entire existence for about three years. I haven't watched it in at least twenty. I don't need to. I remember it pretty well. My favourite moment in the process was the movie's opening in Shreveport - one of our test cities. We had no idea what to expect. Would anybody show up? What would be the reaction of whatever audience appeared? Nothing to go on but hopes and fears. I was a nervous wreck and Jim decided to opt out. Deborah and I took my parents, who were eager to see the picture and wanting to be supportive. I was shocked at the line in front of the theatre. We had to queue up for nearly twenty minutes to get inside, and the 400-plus seat theatre was jammed to capacity. It was thrilling, sitting there in the dark, that audience packed around us, all jolting in their seats, squealing, laughing in the appropriate places. And then smiling, talking animatedly among themselves, as they filed out, about a scene or a character they liked. The faces of the next crowd, waiting for the next showing, anxiously watching the demeanour of the departing groups and growing eager to go in. At the car, my Dad told me: 'If nothing else good ever happens to you for the rest of your life, you got no complaint coming.' He was dead right. I did the James Dean thing from *Giant* for about a week: 'I'm a rich boy. I'm a rich one!' Hopping around and giggling to myself. When the reports came in on the first week's box-office, I danced some more. It was held over on every screen and played for six weeks in three of the towns. The theatre owners were delighted, too. Life was sweet."

above:
An admat that renders any caption redundant.

opposite page, strip of images, from top:
Images from the climax of the film, as the wicked wind instils fear and madness in the occupants of the lodge:
Elaine (Mary Agen Cox) makes a run for it;
The window explodes inwards;
Elaine gets a faceful of glass, Argento-style;
Steve (Gil Glasgow) finally freaks out;
Sally (Robin Bradley) joins him;
Chaos reigns;
Liz (Brandy Barrett) is impaled on a falling light fitting;
...and after scaring the group with his ghost tales, John (Matt Borel) can't cope when it happens for real...

above:
The cast and crew pose for a production photograph. Director James Wilson can be seen front row, second from right. Wilson's wife Mar' Sue is to his left. Writer Richard Wadsack is behind him, immediately to the left. Wadsack's wife Deborah is to Wilson's right. Cliff Blackburn, advisor to the production, sits front row far left. Sound mixer Ron Judkins is to Wadsack's left (bearded) and special effects designer Bill Cherry can be seen third row, second left. Lead actor Matt Borel is second row, third from left.

below:
Sorority initiations can really screw you up...

Wilson concurs: "To a youthful audience, twelve to fifteen, at that time, in a darkened cinema, the film actually was suspenseful: it seemed to work well with that audience. We were told by our distributor that we should have shot additional graphic footage for the foreign markets, but by then, of course, it was too late."

"Are you sure you want to hear about distribution?" – Richard Wadsack

And so, after the thrills, comes the all-too-familiar tale of hopes ground into the dust. "We headed to L.A. with a print, our pocketful of box-office reports, and high expectations," says Wadsack. "We had enough money to hire the top Rodeo Drive entertainment law firm – Mark Lovell had insisted on that. By coincidence, our test market had coincided with the full initial release of the original *Halloween*. Our numbers compared very favourably. Gee, I was sure I was gonna be rich. After a week or so, we had only gotten a serious bite from one mid-level distributor, Dimension Pictures (not the same company as today's Dimension Pictures), and we eventually came to terms with them.[5] I wasn't completely happy, but they guaranteed at least two hundred prints and $150,000 in initial promotion – and there was no question they had the connections to place the picture. Especially if it performed well, as was expected. And they had the rights-sales contacts, too. Mark was satisfied. *Screams* hit No. 25 on Variety's '50 Top Grossers' chart the first week out of the box. It stayed on the chart for a while, too, and had over four hundred prints working at one point. Chicago, Philadelphia, Houston, Los Angeles, Portland, Miami, Long Island, Albuquerque, Indianapolis, Cleveland, St. Louis. The numbers were good."

He pauses: "They screwed us, of course. Ironclad hotshot contract or no. The movie grossed at least $8 million domestically and sold – cash deals in those days – to over a dozen primo overseas markets and to the just-starting-up Showtime Movie Channel. We collected a total of a little over $12,000. I actually threw a chair across their offices on a visit to the coast, when it became obvious they had put it to us. I was able to sort out what they'd done with a good bit of the money - used it to roll out four other pictures, all of which flopped heavily. Trying to break upwards in one big leap, and tumbled. But they could not have been as calm about events if they hadn't stashed a bunch away before they declared bankruptcy. It was good that I did not own a gun. Mark Lovell finally won the domestic rights back in court, but we knew that meant nada. It popped up in strange packaging in video stores for years and I'd hear from someone now and then that they'd seen it advertised as part of a drive-in bill or in some small town with a still-independent hardtop. While the picture hung on the charts, we could get in to see almost anybody in Hollywood, and we saw several. But we didn't get any offers or opportunities to make movies. We got offers to line-produce small-budget pictures. Which was something, and we knew that, but I didn't want to do that. It wasn't just 'breaking in to the biz' I was interested in. I didn't particularly *like* the business! I went a little depressive for six months or so, and then we moved back to Shreveport. I was a census taker for the 1980 US Census, and then I got on with a small but very professional ad agency. I've been doing advertising and marketing consultation work ever since. And the education I received from my experience with *Screams* – creatively, people-wise and business-wise – has been of no small value."

James Wilson and Richard Wadsack worked together for a few years after their movie-making ambitions were so unfairly curtailed, and they still see each other once in awhile. "We were going to do two more low-budget films," says Wilson. "You need leverage, and one way you can get leverage is by having some product flow. We understood that, but we were still dependent on Mark's money, and I think he decided these were not the waters he wanted to be swimming in, so he did not fund a second project. If we had gotten a bite on one of those other projects we would have continued, but it got to the point where I had to make a living, I had a wife and child, I didn't want to go to California. I had writerly ambitions so I went into the newspaper business for about seven years. I stayed in Natchitoches and became editor of the local newspaper. Now Wadsack and I each have our own small ad agency."

Richard Wadsack still has fond memories of his brief spell in the movie industry, and takes a philosophical attitude to the corruption he encountered: "You know, I learned that in the distribution business, 'theft' begins at the ticket window and continues right on up the line. It was as rough-and-tumble a racket as production, and equally risky, or pretty close to it. Indie theatre ownership was no piece of cake. When I drove town-to-town, selling our picture to theatres for the test market, I realised those guys loved the movies. I don't think any of them got rich. And I didn't even have a print of our movie yet – just the scenario, our promotional material, our planned media schedules and our promise to deliver a print and do the advertising. They risked a *week* in which they might not have had, essentially, 'product on their shelves' – or they could have suffered a dramatic decline in popcorn sales if nobody showed up wanting to see the movie. We offered a pretty good deal – we did all the promotion and they didn't have to pay a penny in rent up-front for the print – but the romance had to be a big part of why they bought into the thing. That, and there not being so much other product coming down the pike in January, when traditionally it's quiet distribution-wise. Indie distributors and, most importantly, independent theatres and small chains, had as much to do with the vitality and eccentricity of those times, as filmmakers. All the folk I met who were doing what we were doing had in common an obsessive drive and a hyper sense of responsibility in terms of getting their picture made, mixed with the soul of a pirate. Most were poor as church mice, like we were, and I never met a single 'rich kid' playing around in the movie game. There must have been some, but I only saw then sprinkled in with cast or crew types."

Despite the hardships and disappointments, Wilson still has fond memories of the filmmaking experience itself: "I was doing at the time exactly what I'd imagined I was supposed to be doing, although I'd not imagined it would be so damn hard. Still, it was about as much fun as one human should be allowed. I have no regrets at all about it – indeed, my kids think I'm cool because I once made a movie. So it seems it was all worth it!"

Footnotes

1 *"Let the Land rejoice, for you have bought Louisiana for a Song."* Gen. Horatio Gates to President Thomas Jefferson, on the signing of the Louisiana Purchase Treaty, July 18, 1803.

2 Source: *The Historic Indian Tribes of Louisiana from 1542 to the Present.* By Fred B. Kniffen, Hiram F. Gregory, George A. Stokes.

3 Both men are still married to the same women: Deborah Wadsack was script supervisor on the movie, and Mar Sue Wilson did the set and wardrobe design.

4 Shreveport is close to the border with Texas and Arkansas: approximately seventy miles from Texarkana, and two hundred miles from Dallas.

5 Dimension distributed quite a few low-budget horrors, including: S.F. Brownrigg's *Scum of the Earth*; Ferd and Beverly Sebastian's *Gator Bait*; Constantine Gochis's *The Redeemer: Son of Satan*; John 'Bud' Cardos's *Kingdom of the Spiders*; Curtis Harrington's *Ruby*; Tom Moore's *Return to Boggy Creek*; and Harry Kerwin's *Getting Even*.

below:
Alan (Charles Rucker), Sally (Robin Bradley), Jookie (Beverly Allen), Harper (Ray Gaspard) and Liz (Brandy Barrett) cower in terror as the wind tears down the lodge...

chapter 7

Satan Was an Acid Head!

The Career of David Durston

I Drink Your Blood (1971)

"Let it be known, sons and daughters, that Satan was an acid-head. Drink from his cup! Pledge yourselves! And together we'll all freak out!" – Horace Bones.

With these words, the late great Bhaskar cues the wild and wonderful *I Drink Your Blood*, an iconic seventies horror flick that lives right up to its reputation and delivers scares, gross-out images and (frequently intentional) laughs from beginning to end. It might seem strange to call such a bloodthirsty experience a good-time film, but there's an infectious wild humour to this tale of drug-addled hydrophobic Satanists, making it – in my opinion – the perfect mood-enhancer if you're inviting some friends over, or better still, planning a far-out acid party of your own…

The charismatic and dangerous Horace Bones (Bhaskar) and his travelling retinue 'The Sons and Daughters of Sados' – Rollo Yates (George Patterson), Sue-Lin (Jadine Wong), Sylvia (Iris Brooks), Molly (Ronda Fultz), Shelley (Alex Mann), Carrie (Lynn Lowry) and Andy (Tyde Kierney) – have been camping out on the edge of a small town. During the night, Horace conducts a black magic ceremony in which the group strip nude and take LSD, but the ritual is interrupted when Horace sees a local girl (Arlene Farber) spying on the group from the trees. Andy, one of the less committed of the group, explains that he's been taking time out from hellraising to pursue a romance with her. Horace sets his minions on the girl – she returns home, beaten and traumatized. The following day the group arrive in town. It's almost deserted: most of the population have been moved out to make way for a forthcoming dam project. Among the few remaining residents are the girl's veterinarian grandfather Doc Banner (Richard Bowler), and Pete (Riley Mills), her twelve-year-old brother. The gang occupy an abandoned, tumbledown hotel, and go looking for something to eat. The only place in town that's still open is a small bakery run by Mildred Nash (Elizabeth Marner-Brooks), who caters to the construction trade. Horace and his pregnant partner Molly buy meat pies and return to their new lair. That night,

Horace turns over control of the group to Rollo, who stipulates that Shelley be tortured for his lack of commitment. Shelley faints after Sue-Lin slices the soles of his bound feet with a knife. Doc Banner learns who is responsible for assaulting his granddaughter, and arrives to confront the gang in their hide-out. However, he's old and easily overpowered. Sylvia dopes him with LSD. Pete helps his grandfather home, and when he sees him in the throes of a bad trip, decides to avenge him. Having recently spied a rabid dog loose in the woods, he tracks it down, shoots it, and – using a syringe borrowed from Doc Banner's bag – collects some infected blood. The next morning he injects the blood into the pies at Mildred's shop, and sells them to the gang. With the exception of Andy and Shelley, the gang eat the pies; and by late afternoon they're nauseous and foaming at the mouth. Rollo is the first to go crazy, stabbing Shelley to death. Soon the others are running amok, and the situation escalates further after nightfall, when Sylvia picks up a truck-full of construction workers and beds the lot, passing the infection to them too. Thanks to Pete, the surrounding countryside is now crawling with crazed rabies victims, hell-bent on murder and mayhem!

Durston gets things off to a great start, with Bhaskar (pronounced Bash-kar) delivering Satanic mumbo-jumbo in front of a roaring campfire. The title music sets the mood perfectly, helping to define the film's cocktail-shaker blend of horror and sly send-up. As the story gets under way, the tone veers wildly between shuddery scare tactics and comic touches – for instance, as the local girl makes her escape through the woods, Clay Pitts's score has more in common with Nelson Riddle's music for the sixties *Batman* movie than the customary horror themes of the day. As Doc Banner and Mildred discuss what's happened to the poor girl, Durston – on the surface at least – plays the plight of these 'normal folk' sympathetically. And yet the acting (especially by Elizabeth Marner-Brooks as Mildred and Jack Damon as Roger, her super-square lover) has an earnest, melodramatic, daytime-TV quality, so although there's clearly *some* investment in these people and their plight, it's as if the sardonic attitude of the Satanists is beginning to seep through. No one labels the squares as

I Drink Your Blood
aka Phobia (original title)
© 1971. Cinemation Industries, Inc.
A Jerry Gross presentation. A Cinemation Industries release.
writer / director: David Durston. producer: Jerry Gross. director of photography: Jacques Demarecaux (colour by DeLuxe). music composed, conducted and directed by: Clay Pitts. editor: Lyman Hallowell. associate producer: Henry Kaplan. production manager: Loren Frank. assistant director: Peter Cox. lighting: Bob Vee. art director: Charles Baxter. sound: Stan Goldstein. boom man: Scott Warren. make up created by Irvin Carlton. uncredited: initial director of photography: Joseph Mangine.
Cast: Bhaskar (Horace Bones). Jadine Wong (Sue-Lin). Ronda Fultz (Molly). George Patterson (Rollo). Tyde Kierney (Andy). Riley Mills (Pete). Iris Brooks (Sylvia). John [Jack] Damon (Roger Davis). Alex Mann (Shelley). Elizabeth Marner-Brooks (Mildred Nash). Bruno Damon. Richard Bowler (Doc Banner). Mike Gentry. uncredited: Lynn Lowry (Carrie, mute hippie girl). David Durston (doctor). Mark La Roche (Ed). (construction worker). Arlene Farber (Sylvia Banner).

below:
Tyde Kierney's Andy is decapitated in the gory climax of **I Drink Your Blood**.

'piggies' (instead, one of the group daubs the word on Shelley), but you can't help feeling detached from the squeaky-clean life the 'normals' represent.

So the maniacs are far more interesting and compelling than the regular folk? I know, hold the front page… It wouldn't be the first time in the horror genre. Yet, when Bhaskar and his trailer-trash girlfriend Molly go to the pie shop, sarcastically adopting a polite bourgeois manner, Mildred swallows their ironic performance without a glimmer of suspicion, and responds with country generosity; not only selling the pies but also smiling, *"I threw in a few cakes, on the house."* *"The lord will bless you lady, the lord will bless you,"* mocks Bhaskar in pseudo-courtly manner. Now you find yourself irritated with the arrogance of the Satanists. So what's it to be: wild side or mild side? I'll spare you the rest of this battle between my inner Satanist and my inner Ned Flanders, although it's worth mentioning that this seesawing of sympathy is part of the way the film is written. It tosses you back and forth between the two sides, giving what could have been a simple horror tale an amusing sort of giddiness. The wildly varying tone of the film means we're always catching our step. Remember though that despite the blood and gore and dismemberment, all of this is achieved within an essentially light-hearted framework. As Bhaskar says to Doc Banner when the old man sees the unconscious, blood-dripping Shelley strung up from the rafters: *"I'm surprised you're taken in by all this. You see, we are a theatrical group, and we were rehearsing a horror scene that we perform in the theatre!"*

Nothing better conveys the arrogance and sublimated aggression of supposedly 'peace-loving' hippies than the practise of spiking 'straights' with LSD. (God, I sound so *square…*) *"You're pretty yummy for a dirty old man! Have a breath freshener, handsome!"* says nympho hippy-chick Sylvia, as she doses Doc Banner. It's perhaps a shame that Durston opts not to show the old man's hallucinations, but actor Richard Bowler makes his bad-trip scene work anyway, as we see him sobbing at the kitchen table, holding the salt and pepper shakers to his head like horns. Heavy trip, dad!

In a script full of great ideas, Durston's stroke of genius is to have young Pete inject meat pies with rabid dog's blood: a wonderful, malevolent notion so typical of a child's thought processes (children are The Devil's best disciples, after all). Unfortunately, young Riley Mills is the weakest link in the movie. There's something smug and porcine about him, which is a shame because I'm generally all in favour of children taking vengeance on adults (see *Devil Times Five*, or *Bloody Birthday*). Instead, Mills has the slappability of a *Waltons* character, a sort of truculent self-righteousness that had me hoping instead that Horace Bones would sacrifice him in the name of Sados…

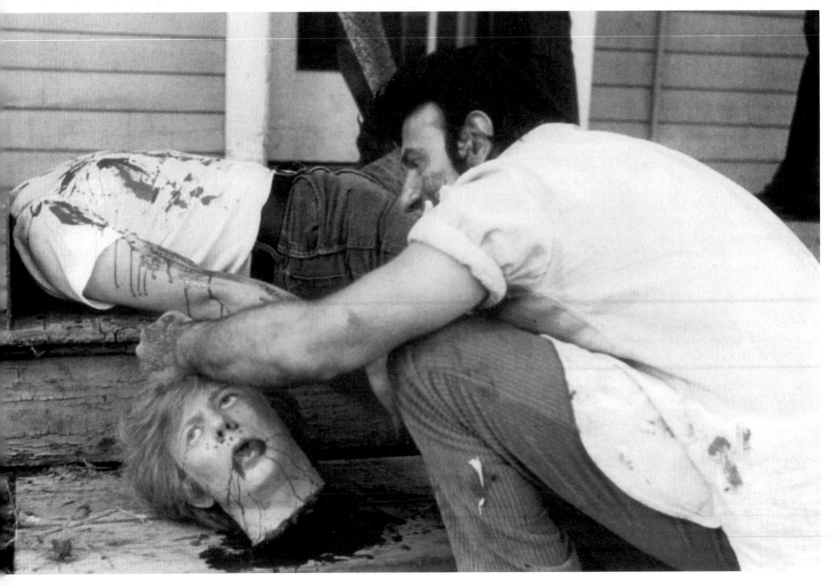

Of course, with a charismatic performer like Bhaskar in the lead role, it's no wonder we like the villain. The actor charges his performance with so much *joie de vivre* that Durston could have attached wires and run the klieg lights off him. He's impossible to dislike, and the laughter we can see in his eyes is the best advert for Lucifer the Light God that Anton LaVey could wish for! Horace's lieutenant has energy to burn too: George Patterson as Rollo Yates (*"Guess who's coming to din-dins!"* he smirks, referencing Stanley Kramer's 1967 race relations drama) is a strong contender for leading man status himself, and his scenes with Bhaskar (*"Satan was a Black Man!"*) highlight the advantages of casting two strong actors in the group. Patterson really goes for it, relishing his rabid scenes and creating one of the film's many iconic images: a handsome, wild-eyed black man foaming at the mouth and toting an axe! (Guess who's coming to din-dins indeed!) With blaxploitation riding high at the time, America's urban hardtops were ideally cued up for this, and the racial mix of the Satanist group – headed by an Indian man, a black man and an Oriental woman – must surely have struck a chord. (A double-bill of this and *Fight for Your Life* would be a hot ticket). Jadine Wong's character Sue-Lin may be drawn from a comic-strip vision of the inscrutable Oriental, but she's still a great presence. Her role as provocateur is especially sinister when she wordlessly directs Rollo to stab the unconscious Shelley by placing a Tarot Death card on him, and it's particularly cool that she's the only one of the infected able to suppress any glimmer of pain or anguish. Later, when she chooses self-immolation rather than allowing the crazed Horace Bones to kill her, Durston is clearly drawing on the infamous action of Quang Duc, a Buddhist monk who burned himself in Saigon in 1963 in protest at the Vietnamese government's suppression of Buddhism (A *New York Times* reporter who witnessed the event, wrote afterwards, "As he burned he never moved a muscle, never uttered a sound, his outward composure in sharp contrast to the wailing people around him.") Last but not least, the stunningly beautiful Lynn Lowry turns a silent role into one of the most memorable of the film, bringing her inimitable spaced-out demeanour to a standout scene where she attacks a woman with an electric carving knife and then wanders off, absent-mindedly carrying the woman's severed hand. Her appearance here for Durston, along with her knockout performances in David Cronenberg's *Shivers* and George Romero's *The Crazies*, ensure her position as one of the iconic faces of the genre.

Technically, *I Drink Your Blood* is well constructed and diligently shot, with vividly photographed night scenes (usually a weak-spot in low-budget horror) and only the odd boom-mike shadow in the brighter interiors to give away the haste of the shooting schedule. Durston's experience on fast-track TV productions must have helped a great deal, and his ability to fuse solid film craftsmanship with an understanding of how to milk the horror format pays dividends throughout. *I Drink Your Blood* arrived hot on the heels of the media frenzy surrounding the recently apprehended Manson cult (who were reputed to have practised black magic); so as well as being bold in visceral terms, it's one hell of a ballsy stab at topicality. Manson, arrested in October 1969 and charged with the Tate-LaBianca murders on 9 December '69, was finally found guilty in January 1971; *I Drink Your Blood* hit theatres just a month later. Although the passage of time means we can now view the film as fun entertainment, on its release the

Durston on Jadine Wong, who played **I Drink Your Blood**'s 'cool as a psychotic cucumber' Satanist Sue-Lin *(above)*: "She's still alive, working as an agent in NYC. Jadine was a good sport and a trouper. She never complained. She is the niece of the famous film star Anna May Wong, of silents and talkies."

Manson resonances and unusually extreme graphic violence must have sent quite a shudder through unsuspecting audiences. For the rest of us jaded gorehounds, many years later, *I Drink Your Blood* is marbled with black humour in a way that forestalls criticism. While the violent excess that made the film so shocking in 1971 has been overtaken today by the gore and gristle in mainstream movies, Durston's wit and the charm of the cast protect the film from the ravages of time. Today's young audiences, on the lookout for stereotypes and kitsch naiveté, may find, perhaps to their surprise, that *I Drink Your Blood*'s sly humour impedes the sort of retroactive viewer superiority encouraged by postmodern horror films. With the exception of some exchanges between the less interesting (i.e. 'good') characters, the dialogue and performances forge a sneaky, complicit relationship with the viewer, teasing and amusing us without stepping out of context. Energetic, infused with the liberating vitality of the truly tasteless, yet driven by real intelligence and wit, *I Drink Your Blood* is David Durston's blood-drenched gift to horror fans: I really can't think of a better way to get a Halloween party started.

Stigma

© 1972. The Stigma Company
writer/director: David E. Durston. producer: Charles B. Moss, Jr. director of photography: Robert M. Baldwin. film editor: Murray Solomon. in charge of production: Ronald Sullivan. music composed and conducted by Jacques Urbant. sound editors: George Craig, Joe Masefield. continuity: Claire Bradley. production co-ordinator: J. Boyce Harmon, Jr. gaffer: Bob Vee. best boy: F. Rickert Raphael. assistant cameraman: David M. Boehm. 2nd assistant cameraman: Bernard Breitbart. key grip: Chick Haynes. sound: Fred Kamiel. boom operator: Dierk Piffko. makeup: Irvin Carlton. production assistants: Robert Dozor, Elizabeth Hollister, Virginia A. Moss. assistant editor: Nancy Katz. The Producer wishes to thank Mr. Frank Santora, Chief, Venereal Disease Information & Education Unit, New York City Public Health Service, for his full cooperation. Cast: Philip M. Thomas (Dr. Calvin Crosse). Harlan Poe (Bill Waco). Peter H. Clune (Sheriff Whitehead). Josie Johnson (D.D. Whitehead). William Magerman (Jeremy). Connie Van Ess (Tassie). "Cousin" Bruce Morrow (himself). Richard Geisman (Joe). Kathy Joyce (Kathleen). Raina Barrett ("B" girl). Jean Parker (Jeanie). Carter Courtney (homosexual). Edwin Mills (choir leader). Rhonda Fuller [Fultz] (Rhoda). Jim Grace (Ed).

Stigma (1972)

"Put[s] a cast-iron boot on Hollywood's traditional pussyfoot around the subject of venereal disease." – *Variety*

"Will wonders never cease? *Stigma*, a screen warning about venereal disease, turns out to be not a luridly flapping sermon but a cracking good suspense melodrama. [It] is not a pretty picture. But it packs a vivid, crunching wallop that may do good where it should."
– *Howard Thompson, The New York Times.*

Doctor Calvin Crosse (Philip Michael Thomas) is released from jail after serving time for performing an illegal abortion. He heads for Stillford Island on the invitation of his former teacher Doctor Thor. On the way, he befriends Bill Waco (Harlan Cary Poe), a soldier returning home from Vietnam. However, when the two arrive on Stillford the locals are hostile to Calvin, who is black. At Doctor Thor's house, he discovers the old man dead in an upstairs bedroom. Sheriff Whitehead (Peter Clune), a racist cop who comes to investigate, makes it clear that Calvin is unwelcome on the island. Calvin finds a tape-recorded message from Doctor Thor warning of an epidemic sweeping Stillford, but the tape runs out before the nature of the problem is specified. Calvin goes to visit Bill and his girlfriend Dee-Dee Whitehead (Josie Johnson), the sheriff's daughter. Bill tells Calvin he needs to do something to 'win over' the town. The following day, Bill calls Calvin to the jetty saying that his younger brother has been pulled unconscious from the water. When Calvin arrives and administers the kiss of life, he realises that the boy is alive and well: the set-up is a fake designed by Bill to impress the townspeople. Calvin is furious but masks his feelings,

realising that the strategy has worked. That night, a weird old man, lighthouse-keeper Jeremy Burke (William Magerman), comes to the house seeking help for a mysterious affliction, which proves to be syphilis. Under pressure from Calvin, Jeremy claims to have had sex with someone called Tassie (Connie Van Ess), who runs a country brothel just out of town. Cal and Bill drive out to meet Tassie, and her girls: Kathleen (Kathleen Joyce), Jeanie (Jean Parker), and the educationally subnormal Rhoda (Rhonda Fuller aka Ronda Fultz). But when Calvin at last persuades them to undergo a health test, he finds nothing amiss. So who is passing the disease around town?

When you hear that the director of *I Drink Your Blood* followed up his 1971 gore classic with a film about VD, your stomach tends to quail at the prospect. Those of a squeamish disposition will survive the experience however, as long as they go to the john about a third of the way in, just in time to miss some gross-out scenes from a mondo-clappo educational short about syphilis. If you're made of sterner stuff, of course, you'll just hunker down in your seat, thank Eros for antibiotics, and admire the director's willingness to momentarily drain the fun from his movie in the name of public health. But apart from this brief medical shock-reel, and a close-up of a spinal injection, the rest of *Stigma* is less of a visceral assault than its predecessor. It's actually a well-written mystery-thriller that's as much about bigotry as venereal disease, and Durston works a neat angle by combining the two themes, associating the festering moral squalor of small-town racism with dishonesty, disgust and infection.

Durston's script makes telling points about racial prejudice without leaning from the pulpit, for instance by showing the difficulty Cal has hitching a ride compared to Bill, his white buddy. In fact the only way Cal can get a lift

above:
Dr. Calvin Crosse dispenses kill-or-cure justice to the abhorrent Sheriff Whitehead (Peter H. Clune).

right:
The sheriff and his corrupted daughter D.D. Whitehead (Josie Johnson) unite against Dr. Crosse.

is by borrowing Bill's spare army uniform, suggesting that racists have no time for black people unless they've accepted their lot as wartime cannon-fodder (it's a point Michael Moore was still having to make thirty years later, in *Fahrenheit 9/11*). Thankfully, Durston is careful not to make Cal some sort of saint who suffers insults without retaliation. His barbed tongue (*"It's enough to make a black boy lose his faith in Jeeezus!"*) ensures the character doesn't sink into the passivity that passed for dignity in earlier race dramas: Cal's confrontation with a slow-witted shopkeeper and his verbal trouncing of the repellent sheriff are sure to have all but the most pathological white-supremacists siding with the hero.

There's something almost Sirkian about the film's broad-brush moral set-up, although Durston has problems with the staging and handling of extras that would not have occurred in a studio picture. For instance, a few more takes would have improved the scene in which Bill fakes the drowning of his kid brother so that Cal can 'resuscitate' him. The way the scene's shot, it's difficult to believe that the illusion would work, given that onlookers and relatives are gathered so closely around. Likewise, Cal's anger at the subterfuge is too visible, endangering the illusion. Sirk embedded his potentially incendiary comments about American life in blatant melodrama, and thanks to the studio system he had the full arsenal of top-flight designers, as well as the darlings of the star system, to fluff the feathers of his hawk-like moral dissections. Durston has to make do with fair acting and good scripting, with *mise en scène* relegated to wishful thinking, but there's a definite link in Durston's films between genre games and a more active moral disposition. It makes you wonder just what he could have achieved as a filmmaker within the studio system.

If the design/*mise en scène* is lacking, the actors do their utmost to keep our attention on the foreground. Philip Michael Thomas has star quality written all over him, while Harlan Cary Poe, Josie Johnson and Peter Clune (reunited from Durston's *Blue Sextet*) strike a decent balance between cliché and passion. Look out too for Ronda Fultz, who follows her pregnant Satanist in *I Drink Your Blood* with a sad/hilarious turn as a whorehouse child-woman, whose response to Calvin's health inspection is to yell, *"I don't want to be venereal!"*

In one of the film's earliest scenes we encounter a city prostitute whose 'bad attitude' is crudely and obviously signalled. But while we might expect the rest of the film to follow suit, Durston pointedly declines to blame prostitutes for the epidemic on Stillford Island. This in itself is radical enough, but when eventually we learn who *is* responsible, the film's moral centre of gravity shifts definitively against the *status quo*. For sure, the film's critique of careless promiscuity is out of step with the free love rhythm of the day. But Durston fingers the collar of authority rather than make the all-too-easy link between disease and liberal tolerance. In *Stigma*, it's the uptight moral guardians, those who cannot face the truth and allow disease to fester untreated, who cause the plague: the youngsters merely suffer its effects. Perhaps the film's silliest scene is the one where Calvin interrupts a sand-dune orgy to deliver an STD lecture, and receives respectful attention instead of being told to butt out. But if nothing else it conveys Durston's sincere wish to offer good advice to his audience, risking his 'cred' by lecturing, and then regaining it by pointing the finger squarely at the older generation for their ignorance and denial.

David Durston Interviewed

The first thing you notice in conversation with David Durston is his wicked good humour. Ask him where he was born and you're quite likely to be told, "In a trunk at the Princess Theater!" before the man takes pity and admits, "No, that's Garland's story! Excuse me!" The next thing you detect is a generosity of spirit, laced with an occasional bluntness, suggesting both the will and the warmth of a man whose career in film and television has spanned some sixty years. Add to this the skill of a born raconteur and it's obvious this chapter could easily have been twice the length. So without further ado, let's start at the beginning, with Mr. Durston as our guide…

below:
David Durston comments: "My nephew Jack Damon, who is now a producer, and a officer in my company, the Seven Summits Group. That's me standing behind him, with mustache and glasses… just before that famous line: "My God, I've got to call the Red Cross." The kids today howl!"

Terrorized by Mary Pickford...

"Okay, for real - I was born on 10 September, 1921 in New Castle, Pennsylvania. Now you know how old that makes me - the same day, same year as Mickey Rooney, and I only stayed there for about a month before the police ran me out of town. Well, it might have been my father William E. Duersten, who was always leaving town. He was German. An engineer, a very good one, but he had style and a great appreciation of the arts, many pals and gals in show business. Bela Lugosi was a good friend of his when Bela was a matinee idol in the theatre in Budapest and Berlin, the early years before Bela came to New York and Hollywood. My father was very handsome and my mother Dea was very beautiful. She was a small town girl from Macon, Missouri, who became a concert pianist for a short period; until she had children and then she was the greatest, most supportive Mom anybody could hope for. She was a direct descendent of Pres. Andrew Jackson and Daniel Boone (Grandma was Molly Jackson, who married Finis Boone). As a child, I was in love with both my mother and father. How's that for a dark troubled beginning? I was a kid whose first ten years were during the Roaring Twenties. I could sing all the razzmatazz songs. My father 'Daddy Bill' was so liberal back in those days, (he was born in Berlin), but my Godfather was Jewish, Dad's very good friend Sigmund Romberg, the famous composer. I called him 'Rommy'. After that I was raised in Los Angeles; Chicago; Macon, Missouri; New Jersey; Milwaukee; and Ft. Lauderdale, Florida - with a few trips to New York."

below:
David Durston comments:
"I guess this was the peak of my career. Associate Producer of **Your Hit Parade**, living at the Sutton House, married to a New Orleans debutante. A happy period professionally; an unhappy time personally."

Durston's father took him to the big Broadway shows. Through his father's showbiz friends, he met many famous people, some of whom – Bela Lugosi, Ethel Waters, Patsy Ruth Miller, 'Rommy' Romberg – remained friends long afterwards. "I can't remember a time in my early years when I didn't want to be in show business," he says. "I didn't know what I wanted to do, I just knew I wanted to be a part of it."

Durston Senior also introduced his son to the cinema: it was to be an unexpectedly traumatic experience... "When I was five, I was taken to see my first movie – a Mary Pickford film my folks thought was safe enough in those days before the Hayes censorship and talkies. It was *Sparrows*, which turned out to be Pickford's only horror film. She takes ten orphans (the Sparrows) through swamp and quicksand, alligators snapping at their butts as they try to cross a stream via an overhanging branch from a tree that was ready to snap off. That's what sent this tot over the edge! They carried me out of the theatre screaming and crying. I was so impressionable, I wasn't allowed to see another movie for several years. When I was eight, I was allowed to see a stage production of *Dracula*, which was touring, and afterwards Dad took me backstage to meet Bela Lugosi. I was very impressed. I thought Bela was charming, aristocratic, gentle, a very dapper man, kind of like my father. They spoke several languages, were sharp dressers, and were connoisseurs of imported wines and beautiful women. Bela always mentioned that we had one thing in common. He came to America in 1921, the year I was born. At thirteen, I was already into Ernest Hemingway and Tiffany Thayer, so my folks figured seeing *Frankenstein* wasn't going to flip me emotionally. But it did! More so than when I saw the film *Dracula* a year earlier. I had already seen Dracula on stage, met Bela, and even been invited to his house. So I looked upon Bela as an actor, someone I had met personally, who was playing a part. But *Frankenstein* was such a departure: very sacrilegious at the time. As a result of seeing *Frankenstein*, I accidentally set fire to our house on Christmas Eve, and almost burned it down! I wrote to Boris Karloff about this, and he was very kind and considerate to answer my letter and give me some good advice about what is make-believe and what isn't. In later years I got to meet Boris, even wrote a script for him."

Durston's first participation in show business came with an acting role in high school. The play was called *The Valiant*: "Wow! I thought that was pretty heavy stuff. I played a convicted murderer on the eve he was to be executed and I had such lines as, 'Cowards die many times before their death; the valiant never taste of death but once.' I also did a production of *It's a Wise Child* [Laurence E. Johnson, 1929] when I was at Missouri University, majoring in journalism. By now I really wanted to be the next Ernest Hemingway, but I didn't mind having fun acting in one of the University drama club productions. I was a nice looking kid when I was eighteen to twenty. In those days they had talent scouts out there touring the country for Hollywood talent. I didn't have a lead role. I played a spoiled rich kid - and believe it or not, with all the good talent in that production praying to be discovered as actors, I was offered a trip to Hollywood (nothing special because I had lived out there) but also a screen test at 20th Century Fox: If I did well, I would be offered a stock contract at a hundred dollars a week. To a kid in college that was a lot of money in those days. I took it and never graduated from college. I didn't get a contract at the studio, but I was back there a few years later doing a film directed by George Cukor. I did meet some movie stars, directors and writers, and fell in love with the art of film production, and all the freedom you didn't have in the theatre."

Roles in plays such as *Night Must Fall*, *Young Man's Fancy* and *You Can't Take It With You* followed, but there was to be an inevitable diversion from his chosen path, when Durston was assigned to the 31st Army Air Force Unit out of Washington for much of World War Two. After the War, he began working in show business again, this time in the new arena of nationwide television. Commercial TV broadcasts in America had begun in 1941, but it was only after the war ended that production was stepped up. Durston went to live and work in Chicago to be near his mother, who was sick, and whilst there notched up credits writing for shows like *Foxhead 400* and *Top of the Weather*, as well as devising a successful music variety programme called *A Hit Is Made*. He also created and produced *The Woolworth Hour* on CBS Radio, which ran for two years from 1954-55. It was a musical program, with four big guest stars on each week, including talents such as Bob Hope, Rosemary Clooney and Duke Ellington. His success with ABC and CBS did not go unnoticed; when Durston returned to New York after the death of his mother in 1950, he was picked up by New York's NBC for their own hit music show: "I was the Associate Producer of *Your Hit Parade*. It walked off with seven Emmy Awards over eight years on TV. Every musical program on TV imitated it. It was produced live on NBC and was always sponsored by the American Tobacco Company, who owned the show. I created all the ideas used on the show and then, sort of as a line producer, I would follow through during the week, co-ordinating those ideas with the dancers, singers, stars, camera department, set designer, costumers, choreographer, prop men. We staged nine production numbers for each show and were on prime time Saturdays every week. I made good money!"

Intent on pursuing his passion for writing, Durston contributed scripts to some of the flagship TV drama shows of the era, including *Kraft Television Theatre* (one of the first popular drama series, launched by NBC in 1947). It was in the 1950s, as he enjoyed a sustained period of success in what is frequently referred to as American TV's 'Golden Age', that Durston had his first brush with the horror/sci-fi genre, writing for the hugely popular ABC series *Tales of Tomorrow*. One of the first sci-fi drama series to air in America, it was produced by Mort Abrahams, who went on to handle *The Man from U.N.C.L.E.*. Durston recalls, "I did things like *The Glacier Giant*, about the Abominable Snowman, and *Mr. Fish*, which was re-titled *The Discovered Heart*, but was a forerunner of the *Creature from the Black Lagoon*. A lot of plot ideas I stole from the newspapers, magazines and novels, but they were cleverly camouflaged, if I do say so myself."

When *Your Hit Parade* went off the air in 1959, The American Tobacco Company and the State Department sent Durston on a goodwill world tour with a two-hour stage production of the show. "There were 386 costumes, ten changes of scenery, a seven-piece orchestra, and two Army escort planes," he explains. ""I directed and produced it. We had some hair-raising experiences, there were some nightmares and one death…"

Felicia and *The Love Statue*

Before moving on to Durston's feature directing career, it's worth clearing up a misunderstanding regarding his alleged first film: some sources credit Durston as co-director on the Turkish film *Susuz Yaz* (1964) with Metin Erksan. So is this a true credit? "No! But I think I know how there might be a mix-up. I worked on a movie made in Turkey called *Dry Summer*. It starred and was produced by Ulvi Dogan, won the Golden Bear Award, 1st Prize at the Berlin Film Festival; the Golden Azteca, 1st prize at Acapulco; and the Cartagena, the Jury Prize at Colombia. *Dry Summer* wasn't a terrible movie. It was nicely made and acted, but it could not get released in the US. It was too bland for American audiences. Ulvi approached me about doing the translation and sub-titles. I had some ideas about making the film more commercial – some sequences where Ulvi suffers the horrors of a Turkish prison, some nude scenes in the shower, a sodomising scene and another short sequence when he gets out of prison and returns to his true love who has been suffering the cruelty of her old father or her landlord – I forget – and they manage to find time alone and make love. The nude and sex scenes were provocative, but not pornographic. Ulvi loved it and he put up the money to shoot those scenes in the States, circa 1971 – he couldn't get away with it in Turkey – and I edited them into the film. It made the film longer and gave it some texture. We changed the title to *Reflections* but it still didn't go any place. I didn't want any credit, but Ulvi insisted and I got a co-director, co-editor credit for the English translation and additional footage in the US version. End of story. I don't even have a video or film print of it."

In 1964, Durston made his true directorial feature debut, with *Felicia*, a big-budget romantic mystery about a woman under suspicion of murdering her wealthy and important husband. The film was shot over fourteen weeks in Puerto Rico with DP Saul Midwall (a distinguished camera operator whose estimable Hollywood credits include Sidney Lumet's *12 Angry Men*, Elia Kazan's *A Face in the Crowd*, Robert Rossen's *The Hustler*, and Otto Preminger's *The Cardinal*). The soundtrack featured music by Nat 'King' Cole, and Durston managed to coax forties beauty Louise Allbritton (memorable as the willing bride of Lon Chaney Jr.'s vampire in Robert Siodmak's *Son of Dracula*) out of retirement for the role. *Felicia* was a hit in Spanish-speaking countries, but is fiendishly hard to find today: chiefly because any further exhibition was thwarted when the backer withdrew the film thanks to complications in his divorce proceedings.

Durston followed *Felicia* with *The Love Statue* (1966), another movie that's extremely difficult to see, though Durston has access to a film print and is considering releasing it. Made for a little under $300,000, at a time when many young people were beginning to experiment with drugs and a freer sexual life, the film addressed the emerging counter-cultural agenda, telling the story of a group of Greenwich Village denizens and their experiences with LSD…

Tyler (Peter Ratray), a young Greenwich village artist, is having sexual and relationship problems with Lisa (Ondine Lise), his strong-willed, dominating girlfriend. Finally sick of her criticisms and mind-games, he throws her out of his apartment. Later, at a nightclub, a beautiful Japanese girl called Mashiko (Hisako Tsukuba) offers him LSD – Tyler accepts and spends his first acid trip at a debauched, uninhibited party where lesbianism and

The Love Statue
aka **The Love Drug** (original title)
aka **The Statue**
Robert A. Poore
© none [1966]
Vansan Productions. V & N Associates.
director: David Durston. executive producers: Evander Schley, Sandy Barnett. screenplay: Richard Kent. story: Robert A. Poore. cinematographer: Amin Chaudhri. camera: Hiroshi Kaku. Lighting: Ogden Lowell. special photography: Jurgen. editors: David Durston, Richard Kent. music composer & arrangers: Dottie Stallworth, Sandy Barnett. sound music editors & sound supervisors: Rudy Traylor; Robert Van Dyke. sound mix: Bill Stoddard. sound effects: Barney Beck. grateful acknowledgment is made by the producers to Aldo's of Bleeker Street and to The Bitter End Club. Stills: Martin Andrews. Paintings created by Maria Sobossek. Certain sequences were filmed at the Bitter End Club and Aldo's of Bleeker Street in New York City.
Cast: Peter Ratray (Tyler). Ondine Lise (Lisa). Harvey Goldenberg (Stan). Nancy Norman (the model). Hisako "Choko" Tsukuba (Mashiko). Coleman Younger. Cory Stevens. Liz Otto. Mario DeRosa. Lenore Rhein. Morgan Wilson. Maria Sobossek. David Roya.

below:
Durston's erotic fantasy drama **The Love Statue** (1966) caught the mid-sixties mood of sexual and chemical experimentation…

THE LOVE STATUE

"…a bizarre love affair between a sculptor and his sculpture"
— SIR MAGAZINE

"The most unusual 80 minutes ever filmed" —VARIETY

voyeurism are openly indulged. Still under the effects of the drug he returns to his apartment, where his sculptor friend Stan (Harvey J. Goldenberg) is also now staying. Tripping like crazy, Tyler becomes erotically fixated on a nude female sculpture Stan has been working on, and hallucinates a wild sex encounter with the statue coming to life. A few days later, Lisa returns and when Stan refuses to help her find Tyler she smashes the statue. Stan, driven to maniacal violence by her actions, murders her. Tyler comes home to find the corpse of his ex-girlfriend, and runs away from the horrible sight. Then, while roaming the streets, he encounters the woman who modelled for Stan's sculpture. The two of them strike up a relationship and go looking for Stan, who has gone completely off the deep end …

Commendably, Durston felt obliged to gain personal experience before the shoot began: "As long as I was writing about LSD and directing a film about it, I had to experience it, which I did under a doctor's supervision," he reveals. "I found out I was not suicidal or homicidal, but I did have two personalities – a conservative side and an extrovert side – which would be my mother and my father, and is why I sometimes sympathise with my antagonists. I know I didn't sleep for two days; my mind was clicking so fast. And I couldn't type fast enough to put down all my thoughts. I wondered about being a gum machine in the subway, but nobody would buy my peppermint, only my tutti-frutti. What really impressed me about the drug, dangerous as it can be for troubled people, is that, unlike alcohol, if you drink too much, you sometimes can't remember anything: after you come out of LSD, you remember most everything. Amazing, even the crazy things. Once the doctor was convinced I wasn't a person who would hurt myself or anybody else, he released me to go home."

Whilst filming *The Love Statue* (The original title, *The Love Drug*, was changed because it couldn't be used in advertising), Durston met Jerry Gross, a director/producer turned distributor who was to have a major impact on his future career. "This was before he formed Cinemation Industries and started producing some of his own movies," Durston explains. "He had a partner then and they dabbled in picking up foreign films that were sitting on the shelf. They would fix 'em up a bit and get distribution. Their big talent was in producing the trailers. They were good at that. Jerry had given the boys who produced *The Love Statue* a small investment in the film. These young guys, Harvard grads, had the story idea for the film. They paid me to write the script based on their idea and to direct the film. One day, during shooting in New York's Village and Little Italy (one of our locations was the now world famous club The Bitter End, which was just becoming popular in the Village), Jerry dropped in to check on his investment, and see how things were going. That's how I first met Jerry Gross. He had great energy and enthusiasm: a born hustler, and I liked that, because I wasn't. My downfall has always been that I have never been able to hustle. And that's not because I was lazy – I just couldn't pitch myself or my talent or manuscripts. Jerry and I got along well on that first meeting and it was the start of several years' association. Jerry had an eye for Betty Shea, and it upset her and made her angry that he kept staring at her. That was Jerry! The film opened at the World Playhouse, just off Broadway, a movie house that showed mostly foreign films, and for two or three days it did absolutely no business. It died and the exhibitor of the house was ready to pull it – but then, just in time, *Life* magazine broke the explosive Harvard Drug Scandal.[1] *The Love Statue* started doing great business, briefly, and tripled its investment in New York alone. Everybody wanted to know more about LSD. But it was a shabby film."

Durston did not enjoy a rapport with Sandy Barnett, the producer of *The Love Statue* ("Sandy and I didn't like each other. He was a society playboy who was heir to a chocolate candy fortune, a dilettante asshole who looked in the mirror and wondered what the other seven wonders of the world were doing.") but he speaks fondly of one particular cast member, with whom he enjoyed a warm relationship beyond the film: "Coleman Younger, III, the great grandson of the original American outlaw, played a small part in *The Love Statue*. He was a good-looking kid who looked a lot like James Dean, but I used him because he was good on a motorcycle. He got in a fight with another actor in the film who was bugging him, and a day or two later this guy tried to kill Coleman, and was arrested. Can't remember his name. He didn't even have a credit in the film. Coleman was a rebel, like his great grandfather, only he rode a motorcycle instead of a horse. We liked each other immediately, had the same sense of humour. He used to take me for some wild spins on his motorcycle, and Coleman was the first one to introduce me to pot. Wow! It was an experience the first few times, but I realized I could float just as well on dry martinis, and not cough as much."

Being a filmmaker in the 1960s, and acquainted socially with the younger generation as well as his own, Durston saw for himself the beginnings of the new cultural odyssey upon which American youth was embarked. However, by the time *The Love Statue* was enjoying its brief burst of box-office success, he was already in his mid-forties. I asked him what he'd thought of the counter-culture as it emerged: "Well, it was there. I didn't approve or disapprove of it. You must consider that I was a very liberal person. I had many black friends and gay friends. I could never stand to see any other human being intimidated or abused. I still can't. Of course I'm sure I inherited this trait from my father. But whenever I was in a situation where I thought I had the upper hand, I would defend these people. And the hippies, the flower-power groups, they were drawn to me like I was a magnet. I liked them and I helped them if I could. Mind you I didn't dress like the hippies, nor did I ride a motorcycle. I felt sorry for the hippies who were hooked on drugs, and tried to help, but there was so little real help I could offer – but I did go to many of their parties and activities. I of course loved *Easy Rider* – the freedom of its context and production. I knew that there was going to be an important place for independent films in the future. They didn't always have to be Hollywood studio controlled. My wife, Joan – a gal from New Orleans who was a socialite – hated it! We lived at the Sutton House on the East River, New York, and I was doing very well in TV then. But there's your difference. Socially prominent people and hippies did not approve of each other. I probably would have been a good hippie, but my life took a different turn. I didn't go to the big Woodstock event in New Jersey. Coleman invited me to go, and I would have, but Joan and I were in a crisis with our marriage, and her folks came up to New York to try to straighten us out that weekend. See what I mean? I may have had an easier, maybe more productive life, but I don't have the freedom of the hippies. I was married and I had a TV contract I had to live up to."

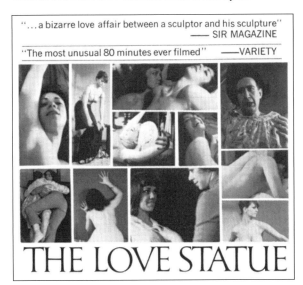

"...a bizarre love affair between a sculptor and his sculpture" —— SIR MAGAZINE

"The most unusual 80 minutes ever filmed" ——VARIETY

THE LOVE STATUE

WHAT BEGINS AS A SEARCH FOR TRUTH BECOMES AN EXPOSE OF A CHARMING HEEL WHO PLAYED WITH PEOPLES LIVES!

ALLEN BAZZINI and LLOYD MERTZ Present

BLUE SEXTET

...THEY PLAYED FOR KEEPS!

Starring JOHN DAMON · COCO SUMAKI · in COLOR

Written and Directed by DAVID DURSTON
Executive Producer JOHN DAMON

Released by UNISPHERE RELEASING CORPORATION

ONE SHEET

Giallo á là Durston: *Blue Sextet*

Four years passed before Durston was able to mount another production, the erotic thriller *Blue Sextet* (1970). It tells the story of a group of six people whose memories of a recently deceased friend are explored in extended flashbacks. The director is not keen to recommend it today: "It has some moments, but not very many. What I am proud of is that at the time I was the only one who would dare to write or direct a film that had two alternate endings – what could have happened and what did happen. J.B. Priestley was the only other writer who dared use two endings, in his play *Dangerous Corner*. They made a movie of the play (which he didn't adapt for the screen) and the asshole studio that produced it [RKO in 1934] only used the happy ending - the cowards! *Blue Sextet* was not a hit. I had trouble with that movie. They ran out of money, but I worked two weeks without pay just to finish what I started. And the French actress Adrienne Jalbert was a temperamental bitch. It just didn't have the team-work."

Sometimes, a filmmaker's unhappy experiences while making a picture can blind him to its charms. Durston eventually let me see a tape of *Blue Sextet*, and, despite his misgivings, I found it to be a wonderfully sly and perverse thriller, very much in the Italian mode of films like *The Sweet Body of Deborah*, or more accurately, Mario Bava's *Four Times That Night*. The plot revolves around the recently deceased Jeff Ambler (John Damon): friend, lover, businessman, art gallery owner, pornographic filmmaker, drug-dealer, ravisher and all-round amoral psychopath. His mysterious death at the start of the film triggers a cat's cradle of seamy revelations, as his friends congregate after

Blue Sextet
© none [1970].
writer/director: David E. Durston. producer: Pat Power. cinematography: Joseph Mangine (colour by Movielab, Inc.). musical director: Clif Edwards Bass. score: Ulpio Manucci and Guy Gilbert. camera: Richard Gray. lights: Robert Linda. production manager: Donald Hunt. sound: David Anderson. set decor: Shelly Guber. Technicolor supervisor: Charles Carmello. continuity: Marjorie Power. editor: David E. Durston. sound & editing facilities: Sound One. titles: Albert Paganelli. fashion consultant: Magda Bierman. gowns created by Kay Selig. furs by Rita Selig. costumes by Neil Cooper. jewelry created by Kramer Jewelry Creations. Mr. Damon's wardrobe by Chief Apparel. sculpture by Cepelia Corporation. fabrics created by Design Research, Inc. Jeff's portrait by CAM. songs "Blue Sextet", "Heh Go Now" music by Sylvester Bradford, lyrics by Stan Curtis, recorded by United Souls, at the piano: Henry Krieger.
Cast: John [Jack] Damon (Jeff Ambler). Harlan Cary Poe (Bud). Margaret Cathell (Liz Horner). Coco Sumaki (Tish). Mark La Roche (Ed Sinclair). Adrianne Jalbert (Felicia). Peter Clune (George). Dorian Wayne. Jacqueline Welter. Harry Skleros. Paul Chin and The Dynasty. Bhaskar (East Indian dance sequence). Tony Rivers (Grand Guignol sequence).

left:
The figures in this one-sheet for **Blue Sextet** (Durston's most decadent film) seem to echo the style of European comic-strip art, such as Guido Crepax's **Valentina** – although it has to be said the typography lacks a little *je ne sais quoi...*

bottom left:
Promotional art for **The Love Statue**.

opposite page, top left:
Poster art for **The Love Statue**.

opposite page, bottom left:
Durston's close friend Coleman Younger, in this publicity shot from **The Love Statue**. Durston says:
"This is my friend Coleman who worked in **The Love Statue** - with a scar from the cut on his lip. He loved doing the movie - he said "How often do I get the chance of having somebody try to kill me with a knife." But acting wasn't for him. He was the great grandson of the famed American outlaw, Coleman Younger, but he rode a Harley instead of a horse. He started a delivery service in Manhattan. I got him some good accounts like Movielab & Deluxe Labs, who had daily deliveries. Soon he had seven Harleys, and six guys working for him. He was doing great with 'Fleet Messengers', which is still delivering today. Then one day Coleman said he was in trouble. He showed me something like 120 parking citations he had never bothered to pay. They were confiscating his bikes, and he had to sell out fast before they slammed him in jail. Coleman left town on his Harley the next day, and I have never heard from him since. He was quite a guy! I wonder what has happened to him. If he's still alive or dead. We had some good times together. Just don't know."

the inquest for a long night of drinking and soul-baring: by morning they have at last understood the truth behind his apparent suicide, and the extent to which Jeff screwed, exploited and bamboozled them all. *Blue Sextet* only lets us glimpse Jeff through the perceptions of his friends, but apart from that he's like Patricia Highsmith's 'Talented Mr. Ripley'; an urbane seducer luring others to their doom without scarcely a care in the world (gazing idly into a mirror, he ponders, *"I never know whether it's me I'm looking at, or someone who looks like me. I'm always waiting to be introduced."*).

The fun comes from seeing how each of the six were, in one way or another, shafted by this callous Lothario (giving them all, in true *giallo* fashion, a motive for murder). George (Peter Clune), Jeff's business partner, learns that Jeff is actually the father of his child; Ed Sinclair (Mark La Roche) reveals that Jeff tricked him into sex with a wealthy transvestite (who proclaimed *"I adore the darkness!"* before switching off the lights and fellating him); Felicia (Adrienne Jalbert) claims that Jeff drugged her and then let strangers ravish her as punishment for rebuffing his sexual advances; and Tish (Coco Sumaki) explains how Jeff beat her during sex and then, when she left him, seduced her new boyfriend Bud (Harlan Cary Poe) into joining him in bisexual orgies. Bud appears to be the only one who still loves Jeff, but eventually even he can take no more…

The plot is a convoluted affair that requires close attention, but fans of the madly complicated Italian *giallo* will recognise this movie as a Stateside cousin. Durston plays his hand beautifully with plenty of twists and surprises, and just like the European thrillers mentioned, even the art design gets a look-in: for instance, on the walls of Jeff's apartment, a painting of a priapically horned demon sardonically counters another prominently

above, and right:
These stills from **Blue Sextet** show scenes from one of Jeff's parties, with something to please *all* tastes…

BLUE SEXTET   Released by UNISPHERE RELEASING CORPORATION

right:
Bud (Harlan Cary Poe) finds the party not entirely to his taste as he looks for Jeff…

below:
Another poster for the film, this time with a pithier adline…

Morals are for people who want to go to heaven… meet a group with other plans!

BLUE SEXTET

displayed portrait, portraying Jeff in the tasteful style of blue-period Picasso. (Considering the film's modernist, multi-faceted characterisation of Jeff, perhaps a cubist portrait would have been an overstatement?) The film explores the amorality of its central character, but it also skewers the machinations and hypocrisies of the 'Blue Sextet' themselves. Tish for instance is revealed as an unscrupulous manipulator who feigned suicide to wriggle her way into a rich man's affections. However, she gets more than she bargained for when it turns out that her target has a taste for rough sex: she can't cope with this and feels degraded, even having the nerve to complain that Jeff doesn't respect her as a person. As was perhaps inevitable given the time the film was made, Bud's desire for Jeff is slightly displaced, with his bemused attendance at an orgiastic gay party standing in for the love affair we suspect has taken place. The film is far from coy, though, about Bud's forlorn obsession: he forms a masochistic attachment to Jeff that can't even be dislodged by the others' revelations. *"I had happier times with him, even when he was laughing at me, than I had with anyone else,"* he sobs. Such tormented plaints may belong to the era that gave us such 'weep if you're sad to be gay' productions as *The Boys in the Band*, but Harlan Cary Poe is a likeable performer (as also seen in *Stigma*) and Durston gives Bud one of the least common attributes in the film: loyalty. It may be misplaced, but among the back-biting and double-crossing of the Blue Sextet, it's a veritable glimpse of saintliness.

Plotting aside, there are numerous lurid treats along the way. The aforementioned bisexual party is pretty daring for 1970, with semi-nude men kissing and fondling each other, and a floor show with two butch numbers wrestling. A *Grand Guignol* torture dungeon sequence (one of Jeff's porno reels) looks like out-takes from the fabulous Mickey Hargitay vehicle *Bloody Pit of Horror*, climaxing in a spot of grungy organ-ripping that brought back fond memories of René Cardona's *Night of the Bloody Apes*. And Jeff's drug-fuelled rape-ravishment of Felicia comes on like The Exploding Plastic Inevitable meets Roger Corman (*"It was a nightmare, I felt like I was drowning in a whirlpool of colour and freak images,"* Felicia recalls). But my favourite insight into Jeff's depraved world comes with a glimpse of his topless sculpting class (*"A kind of emotional striptease, in which the artistic endeavour does not flow until the soul lies free and naked,"* he declares, tongue firmly in cheek), in which it's the students not the models who sit around stripped to their undies.

For all the fun and frolics of *Blue Sextet*, Durston approaches the ending in a minor key, pastiching *Who's Afraid of Virginia Woolf?* as the confessions and revelations of the night leave everyone emotionally exhausted. *"If anybody says things'll look better in the morning, I'll scream,"* says Liz. Then, as if sending up the fears of those who'd rather die than watch a film with a downbeat ending, Durston skips back in time to the early stages of the movie, in which the six friends debated whether or not to let sleeping dogs stay in their closets. This time round, they agree to leave Jeff's secrets alone, and the film ends on the jolly banter of the no-longer-blue sextet, until the theme tune swoops over them with its Greek chorus lyric (*"Have you heard the story of the Blue Sextet?/They reached for the truth, and they found regret."*).[2]

Blue Sextet is a confection, an entertainment, but in its frivolity there's a great deal of style. Interleaved with the

cheerful sleaze and barbed wit, there's a chillier train of thought to do with loneliness and the mysteries of identity. The idea that no one ever really knows anyone else is taken a step further by the suggestion (now *de rigueur* in post-modernist discourse) that perhaps we're no more than the sum total of the impressions we make on others. After all, we can be totally re-defined by a single perception, as those accused of rape, for instance, know very well. Jeff is the hollow centre of the film, dead and gone, defined only by the memories and self-justifications of others, but Durston gives him one last laugh in the form of a shot from one of his dire little nudie reels, in which for a second he looks at the camera and winks. In that jolly, rogue-ish look, there's nothing of the maniacal egotist and psychopath we've just seen, the film once again stressing the impossibility of ever really knowing someone. It's this impossibility that propels the 'Blue Sextet' back into the past. Ignorance is bliss? Maybe not – the film expends far too much energy revealing the sordid truth for that to be Durston's conviction – but knowledge is certainly no guarantee of happiness.

above, clockwise from top left:
A montage of scenes from **Blue Sextet**:
Liz (Margaret Cathell) feels ambivalent about the amorous Jeff (Jack Damon);
Jeff the centre of attention as he would like to be remembered, in one of his home-made porno reels;
Tish (Coco Sumaki) comforts the sexually confused Bud;
Jeff on his way to the roof, and his date with destiny.

above:
Sylvia (Iris Brooks) – nymphomania and hydrophobia, a hellish combination in **I Drink Your Blood**.

below:
Sue-Lin self-immolates as Horace Bones looks on in **I Drink Your Blood**.

"Satan was an acid-head!"

"*I Drink Your Blood* is the pinnacle of the blood horror movie. It's fast, unrelentingly violent, and sexually explicit, dishing out a new shock every few minutes."
– *Bill Landis, Sleazoid Express (book).*

Hot on the heels of *Blue Sextet* came *I Drink Your Blood*, and now Durston was firing on all cylinders. As brash and energetic as a vintage Alice Cooper record, and easily as ghoulish, it ensured once and for all that horror fans would revere his name. Shot in 1970 and first released under its more notorious title in February 1971, *I Drink Your Blood* went before the cameras as *State Farm*, a fake title Durston used to protect his intended release title of *Phobia*, which he feared might be ripped off before he could finish the movie.[3]

By 1970, Durston was no longer under contract to a TV company, and his marriage to Joan was over. It was time for a change: "I moved out of Sutton House, from the East side to the West side, a bit of a social drop, but still very nice; on Central Park West, right off the park. Jerry called, said he admired my work, and invited me to his spacious production office for a chat. He was now CEO of Cinemation Industries, and was making a name for himself and his company. He asked me if I had seen *Night of the Living Dead*, and if I had, what did I think of it and did I think I could top it for graphic horror and original plotting? Jerry never minced words. What he had to say he came right out with. He said he wanted to make the most graphic horror film ever produced, but he didn't want any vampires, man-made monsters, werewolves, mad doctors or little people from outer space. I remember those words so clearly, which is why I blew my top when he changed the title to *I Drink Your Blood*! If I came up with a good idea, he would not give me a percentage of the picture, but he would double what my last writing and directing contract was with the Guilds. It was a challenge, but I said I would like to try."

Gross had seen Durston's work on ABC's *Tales of Tomorrow*: "Jerry said what he liked about it was that no matter how outlandish the story, it had roots in probability, everyday situations – which is what Mort Abrahams always demanded in the *Tales* scripts and what made it such a TV hit. For three weeks I wrestled with ideas – nothing unusual popped into my head. Then I saw this small piece in the newspaper about a mountain village in Iran (population eighty) – a pack of rabid wolves attacked the local schoolhouse, occupied by two school teachers and eighteen or nineteen children. One only has to read up on rabies and hydrophobia to know that it is highly contagious and attacks the central nervous system, driving victims mad and homicidal. I called a doctor, an authority on rabies, who had been flown over there to save the lives of as many as he could. He was from Nova Scotia, but he was in New York at the time and we got together. He showed me some 8mm film he took of little children locked in cages like animals and frothing at the mouth, gripping the bars of the cage like raving maniacs. It made the hair on the back of my head elevate. I had never seen anything so horrible, yet so real, in my life. This, I said, would be my story for Jerry, and I would take a page from Hitchcock and call it *Phobia* - like his *Psycho*! I started the story outline almost immediately without telling Jerry anything about the idea. The idea I

had was for a small town to come down with an epidemic of rabies. It hadn't been done. I knew Jerry would buy it. And, of course, he did. I think he said, 'Oh, shit! That's it. Go home. Go to work. You're on salary as of now!' And I did. During the time I was writing the script (It took about eight weeks, then I went back for revisions and adding stuff, another five weeks) there was so much newspaper and TV coverage on the capture and conviction of Charles Manson, his mean face on the cover of *Time* and *Life*. One couldn't avoid him, and as horrible as it was, everybody was fascinated or obsessed with him. Suddenly I thought, what greater horror than the invasion of a Satan-worshipping group along with the rabies epidemic? And it all tied together so easily. I rewrote, creating the character Horace Bones, inspired by Manson. It didn't change the mood of the story, it added to it. I changed very little. But he fit. It wasn't as if the Manson idea had just been stuck in there for more horror – Horace Bones created a real threat to the town and added some scenes that actually shocked the audience."

When Durston gave Jerry Gross his script, the veteran exploitation producer was over the moon. "Jerry flipped," he recalls. With Gross's enthusiasm ringing in his ears, Durston began work on pre-production. Firstly he hired a location finder, who earned his crust and then some by discovering a derelict berg called Sharon Springs in Upper State New York, near the Canadian border. It was perfect, giving the production a distinctive and memorable setting. It had once been a popular spa with warm mineral springs, but when the springs dried up the town did too. "It was a strange, lonely place," recalls Durston, "only about a hundred population hanging on, if you included the surrounding farms, but there was a sheriff and deputy – no restaurant, no movie theatre, but a general store. You had to drive twenty five miles to reach civilization as we New Yorkers knew it. We kind of had the pick of the town locations, including an old hotel, The Roosevelt that was going to be torn down within two months. We gave the town $300 and practically tore the hotel apart ourselves. And although we were very lucky, thinking we would be saving a lot of money, we were actually very foolish – or I was. All those glass windows we broke or smashed were not faked, but real glass. Some of the actors could have gotten seriously cut up. I think about that a lot and realize I must have been blessed, but nuts."

Gross proved to be a supportive, even indulgent producer: "There was no problem with getting paid, or the bills being paid, or getting what I needed," Durston recalls. "It was Jerry's company money and I had nothing to do with the financing except to make up a tentative budget, and submit it - and Jerry approved it. He gave me total control over casting, hoping I wouldn't mind a few suggestions. And I must say he left me completely alone when I was directing the film. He came to the location only once. He saw the dailies each day in New York, called me and said, 'It's looking better and better – better than anybody on the board expected it to be.' I think we only went over about $100,000. Jerry never complained. He knew he had something."

The film was shot entirely on location, in just eight weeks. "I spoke to God, and we had no weather problems," Durston jokes. "The locals were fascinated. A Hollywood film company coming to their sleepy little community to make a film – we didn't tell them it was a horror film. But they didn't know how to take us, especially the crew. Now the crew was a hundred percent professional – these were guys who knew what to do and how to do it quickly. If I asked for something on the spur of the moment, like 'source of light', or something tricky like that, they were right there with it. They were tough and worked hard, but they were also wild – some on drugs. I didn't know about that at the time. Stupid me! I got very friendly with the sheriff, as I knew we were going to need some help. He wasn't a redneck, but a very nice guy with a sense of humour. He was also quite moral-minded. He appears in the movie as the sheriff who comes in with his men in the shoot-out climax. He would show up sometimes, unexpectedly, which made some of the guys nervous about their sniffing and smoking!"

"One night the sheriff asked me if some of the locals could come out and watch us shooting. He said he would see that they didn't get in the way. They came out; the sheriff had bleacher seats for them, across the street from the Roosevelt Hotel. We were going to shoot a scene favouring Iris Brooks, playing the role of the promis-cuous girl, Frieda, who eventually infects the construction workers. That evening Iris was to run out of the hotel screaming and crying, a reaction to seeing Rollo chop off Shelley's leg. Now Iris was a good actress, but she always had to be motivated. She told me before we started shooting the scene that it was very difficult for her to cry on cue. What she suggested was that just before we started rolling the camera I talk very rough to her, call her some bad names, and smack her across the face so it hurt, and that would induce her to cry. Well this wasn't my method of getting somebody to cry (I liked to talk them into it), but I thought, anything to get the shot. At that point I hadn't counted on an audience. We were pretty keyed up that night. I yelled 'Stand by,' Iris ran out of the hotel, down to the camera position. I spoke very mean to her and smacked her across the face. Iris ran back into the hotel, I called for the camera to roll and Iris came out screaming and crying. It worked – for Iris and for the scene. We did four takes on that scene, and each time it got better – but the audience of locals were horrified. They told the sheriff that I was unbearably cruel to the actors – they thought I was a sadist and should be arrested or replaced by another director. They were really incensed!"

As various novel situations were played out before the camera, the locals started to fret over just what sort of movie they were allowing to be made in their town: "Rumour got around that we were a bunch of degenerates playing with rats," Durston laughs. "Those rats came from New York, I'll have you know! They had been raised in captivity, were very well trained, and were expensive by the day, with two handlers. We ordered twenty five, and didn't even have to fence them off for a scene. They could be turned loose and would all come back when the handler blew a high pitch whistle. Another funny story about the rats concerns the dead ones we had to buy from a medical centre forty miles away from our location. The trained rats were not to be harmed or abused in any way, so the prop man had to buy a box of dead white lab rats and spray-paint them the night before the shoot, to match the trained rats. They had to be kept on ice overnight in a cool place. The cottage I occupied had a refrigerator, so I suggested to the prop man that the rats be kept there. Well, I had a few cast members over for drinks that evening, including the sheriff. I forgot about the dead rats

in the bottom of the fridge, and while I was busy talking to the sheriff, I told a couple of actors to help themselves to drinks, and there were ice cubes in the fridge. When they opened the fridge and saw all those dead rats packed on ice, there was naturally an explosion of yelling, screaming and laughing over the discovery. What the sheriff thought I don't recall, or don't want to. I'm sure he thought we were insane. The townsfolk certainly did."

Durston has fond memories of working with his cast, many of whom he still knows today. "A lot of the actors in the movie went on to bigger and better films, like Arlene Farber, who played the only femme lead in *The French Connection*. And I want you to know that two of our rats went on to playing the title roles in two hit horror movies, *Willard* and *Ben* - and they were the leads! Talk about being a star-maker!"

above:
Horace Bones hangs an interfering construction worker (Mark La Roche) in **I Drink Your Blood**.

above:
George Patterson (Rollo) and Jadine Wong
(Sue-Lin) in **I Drink Your Blood**.

The Crazies) and Cronenberg (who put her in his 1975 feature debut, *Shivers* – of which, more later).

I Drink Your Blood is notable for many things, not least its casually multi-ethnic cast. The Satanic gang are made up of Black, White, Chinese and Indian members, with no explanation deemed necessary, which perhaps recalls Romero's *Night of the Living Dead* but is more likely just a function of Durston's gregarious liberal sensibility: "Another wonderful guy was George Patterson, who was a ballet dancer with the New York City Ballet Company. He played the part of Rollo, the black dude, who goes on the rampage. Everybody loved George. He had a wonderful sense of humour, a magnificent and graceful body, with a dick the size of a coke bottle. When we did the nude scene, I ordered everybody who was not involved in the scene off the set - only me, the cameraman, soundman, and one lighting technician, which made it more comfortable for those who did have to disrobe. But the gals in the company found a barn that overlooked the location, and they all sneaked up there quietly to get a look at George in the buff - with four pairs of binoculars!"

Of course, the most memorable character of all is cult-leader Horace Bones, played by Bhaskar (full name Bhaskar Roy Chowdhury), a strikingly handsome actor of Indian origin. "His father was a famous sculptor whose works became national treasures in India," Durston recalls. "Bhaskar became the world's foremost interpreter of East Indian dancing, which is quite an art of rhythm and muscular control. He had made a few films in India; he was even a singing Tarzan in one movie. He made a guest appearance playing himself in *Blue Sextet*, doing his famous Fire Dance. And then came *I Drink Your Blood*. Bhaskar wanted to act and was excited about playing the part of Horace Bones."

Bhaskar is a marvellously vital and daemonic presence in *I Drink Your Blood*, bringing to an essentially evil character a distinctly charming streak, which perhaps reflects his cultural background, where moral concepts are less absolute and Manichean. There's no doubt that Horace Bones is a monster, but the wicked sparkle in Bhaskar's eye goes a long way to explaining why we feel tempted, as viewers, to sympathise with the villains rather than the put-upon locals.

It's probably that same spark, visible in his onscreen persona, which gave him the strength to overcome a calamity that was soon to follow in real life… Not long after the film wrapped, Bhaskar's life took a painfully tragic turn, as Durston explains: "After he finished filming, he was scheduled on a nationwide concert tour. At one engagement in the Mid-West he was rehearsing on stage, making a series of pivots and leaps, when the stagehand at the light board backstage accidentally pulled the wrong switch and threw the stage and auditorium into darkness. Bhaskar pivoted off the stage into the orchestra pit. He has been paralyzed from the hips down ever since, cut short at the peak of his career." (For the full story, see the detailed interview with Bhaskar elsewhere in this chapter.)

Durston has nothing but praise too for his right-hand man on the shoot, DP Jacques Demarecaux: "Jacques was a rugged Frenchman with the heart of a poet. The first day we began working together, we instantly liked each other. He was an excellent cameraman and director of photography, and I immediately fell in love with his work.

One of the film's most iconic and extraordinary performers almost missed out on her role: "One morning, after the film was completely cast, a young lady walked into my office. There were no parts open for her to read, but she was so beautiful I just had to have her in the film. It was her first film – so you might say I discovered her. I wrote in the role of the mute girl, and gave her one big scene. Her name was Lynn Lowry and she went on to do films for some of our great horror film directors like George Romero and David Cronenberg. Lynn lives here in L.A. She's a helluva good actress, and today appears in the theatre, and even performs in nightclubs as a singer." Durston's instincts were impeccable: Lynn Lowry is a stunning presence. She has a pagan, elfin appearance that makes Cate Blanchett's 'Galadriel' in *The Lord of the Rings* look like a Russian shot-putter. Lowry draws the attention in a scene even when she's utterly silent, and has a knack for conveying a strange inner dissociation that must surely have gained her the attention of the aforementioned Romero (who cast her in his 1973 film

He gave me exactly what I wanted. He didn't come onto the film until we were one-third into production. Joe Mangine[4] began shooting the film with me, and the third week he left me, because somebody else made him an offer he couldn't refuse. Mangine and I had been together on *Blue Sextet* and one TV program that was part of the *Navy Log* series. We had been close, had the same ideas, and loved Hitchcock's theories about filmmaking, including 'the source of light' for atmosphere. We started lighting that way on *I Drink Your Blood*, and Jacques came right in and picked it up, so the film had the same look throughout. Mangine and Jacques were both good DPs. So I was lucky. Mangine did not get credit for his work on *I Drink Your Blood*. However, years later we did get together again for an elaborate forty-five-minute industrial film I wrote and directed for an art gallery, about the way art and paintings are promoted and sold."

I Drink Your Blood is distinguished by an all-time classic exploitation movie score, which positively encourages a humorous, even campy evaluation of the film. Durston recalls, "Clay Pitts did the score after I finished with the film and editing. I returned to L.A. so I wasn't around for the scoring, but I approved of what he did. In fact I liked it a lot. He gave the music a tongue-in-cheek kind of treatment, in some parts like an old-fashioned melodrama, which was the humour the film needed, after Cinemation re-edited my film to remove some of the humour. This was before the MPAA rating was delivered. Later, I wanted Clay Pitts to score something else I was doing, but I couldn't locate him, even through the musicians' union, and I heard that he had another name, and a successful reputation, which would explain why he didn't want his name on a film titled *I Drink Your Blood*!"

The film has many great qualities, but of course the violence, so extreme for the time it was made, is what really grabbed the audience by the balls back in 1971, and it still startles viewers today. Back then, *I Drink Your Blood* was one of very few films to reach Herschell

Gordon Lewis's level of grisliness. When I say this, Durston is thrilled: "Oh, wow! I'm compared to the Wizard of Blood!" Happy though he is to be appreciated in such a way, he then rightly makes a few distinctions: "Although *I Drink Your Blood* has become a cult classic, you must consider I was not a writer/director who specialised in horror at the time. Herschell Gordon Lewis was, and there are a few others who are very good at it. The in-your-face violence was not something I just threw into the picture. I was told to come up with a story that would out-do all other horror films. The violence was well thought out in advance, and I think it was well motivated, which would exonerate it from being an in-your-face horror picture. The fact that *I Drink Your Blood* is a landmark film – the first ever to be rated 'X' based on violence alone – indicates that I succeeded in giving Gross and the public what they wanted. I do not, however, think that *I Drink Your Blood* deserved the honour of the first 'X', making it the most gruesome horror film ever made at that time. I think the reason audiences reacted to it so dramatically was because it was a violent story that could probably have happened. The violence was not far-fetched or unmotivated. Hydrophobia is a reality. Manson is and was a reality. The point I'm making is that the more audiences can identify with a situation that might happen to them or could happen to them, the bigger the scare. Yes, when *I Drink Your Blood* first opened, the audience did scream and yell and talk to the actors on the screen – 'You're gonna get it!' – that sort of comment. One theatre tried to sue Cinemation Industries because, at a Saturday midnight showing, some of the audience tore up the seats. This may not have happened. It may have been a Jerry Gross press plug. Today, however, the young audiences who have rediscovered this film and brought it back to become a cult classic, find more 'camp' elements in it. They still scream and yell, but they also laugh a lot too. And my gore can't begin to match the special digital effects gore in today's films."

above, clockwise from top left:
Sue Lin and Horace Bones gaze in horror at the rabid Rollo;
A tasty moment;
Chaos in the wake of the rabies attackers;
Molly protects herself from her former cohorts.

left:
Jacques Demarecaux, the DP who replaced Joseph Mangine on **I Drink Your Blood**.
Durston recalls:
"What a fine man and DP. He was not well, but never said a word. I said to him one day "How ya doing?" and he answered "Just great! Working with you guys, I finally feel like I belong here." That was while we were doing **I Drink Your Blood**."

'I Ruin Your Title!' and 'I Eat Your Profits!'

Durston may have enjoyed the fun and frenzy of making the film, but what followed nearly soured the experience. The first unpleasant surprise was a change of title, from Durston's preferred *Phobia* to Gross's choice, *I Drink Your Blood*. Durston is scathing about the replacement title: "Ridiculous – there are no vampires in the film, not even a Bloody Mary! They might as well have called it 'I Shit in Your Saddlebag'!" He's right, of course, the title bears no real connection to what happens onscreen; but as Wes Craven was to discover the following year with his ultra-violent debut *The Last House on the Left*, a title can mysteriously transform the fortunes of a film, even if it has nothing at all to do with the movie. *Last House* initially played as *Krug and Company*, and briefly as *Sex Crime of the Century*, but it stiffed under these more apposite titles. Both Lee Lewis of Hallmark Releasing, who came up with the *Last House* title, and Barney Cohen, the Cinemation ad-man who invented the *I Drink Your Blood* moniker, applied a weird brand of business voodoo, concocting titles that seemed to leap off the marquees directly into the imaginations of cinemagoers. And speaking of voodoo…

The second surprise was that Gross had paired *I Drink Your Blood* on a double-bill with Del Tenney's black-and-white 1964 stiff *Voodoo Bloodbath*, now renamed *I Eat Your Skin* to match the new title of Durston's film. Although this double-bill and the attendant promotional campaign have gone down in exploitation history as one of the great horror hard-sells, Durston was understandably unimpressed: "I was never consulted. When I found out about the change of title and the plan to put it out on a double-bill, it was ready for release. I saw one of the ads they used but it was really too late to do anything about it. Quite obviously Cinemation Industries did not like losing money, even when they made a mistake. They had bought a dog of a film they could not sell or give away. *Phobia* was better than anybody expected, which is why it didn't have a drive-in opening. I try not to badmouth other filmmakers' work, but *I Eat Your Skin* was really amateurish, so shamefully badly acted, badly directed, badly written, and all the critics seemed to agree. It was a Cinemation Industry mistake buying it, and my film had to suffer so that *I Eat Your Skin* wasn't a loss for the damn stockholders."

He continues, "*Phobia* was supposed to play drive-ins - and I thought it was probably a drive-in movie, especially after they changed the title. But the surprise was that it opened at the first class Warner's Theater on Broadway – and there was already a line when the box office opened the first day. The film made money, even after the MPAA's rating meant the film had to be cut-cut-cut to get an 'R' rating. But what the MPAA did, bless their dear little two-faced hearts, without realizing it, was to make *I Drink Your Blood* a landmark film, a big controversy. So naturally everybody wanted to see it and decide for themselves if it deserved an 'X' rating, based solely on violence."

Happily, the scenes that were cut by Cinemation before the MPAA made their contribution have been reinstated in the DVD release. One unnerving sequence involving Doc Banner (Richard Bowler), in which the unsuspecting old man is dosed with LSD, was cut short for all prior versions, as Durston explains: "Richard Bowler, who is gone now I'm sorry to say, had appeared in a TV play I wrote, and I directed him in two summer stock productions (I worked for a while as a director at the Fairhaven Summer Theater in

Massachusetts). The scene was brutally cut short, and for the DVD it has been restored in full: under the influence of LSD he hallucinates that his grandchildren's parents have returned from the grave, accusing him of not bringing the kids up right, of not being a good parent, and he throws the ghosts out of the house. It's all back in, I'm happy to say, including the new ending taken from the outtakes where Pete, the boy, gives himself up to the sheriff, but they can't find a pair of handcuffs that don't slide off. They don't take his confession that he committed a horrible crime seriously. 'What did you do, kid? Break a window?' And also another never-before-seen sequence where my nephew Jack, who plays Roger, the engineer, gets his head blown off by his girlfriend, the bakery queen."

Durston's deal with Gross (no percentage of profits but double his established directing salary), though Spartan, was at least honoured in full: "I didn't have any problems with Jerry Gross and the original theatrical distribution. I didn't have anything to do with it. Cinemation Industries put up the money to make the film and they also had a major distribution arm in the US as well as the foreign market. I was paid off for the theatrical rights (video had not come in yet)." Born in New York City in 1940, Jerry Gross was an exploitation director (*Girl on a Chain Gang*, *Teenage Mother*, *Female Animal*) who put down the camera to concentrate on the business end of filmmaking. A man of varied interests, he was the only person willing to take a risk on *Sweet Sweetback's Baadasssss Song* in 1971, stepping up as producer when African-American movies were still considered unprofitable by the majors. He distributed art-house fare like *Juliet of the Spirits* and counter-culture efforts like *Fritz the Cat*, before starting his own company, The Jerry Gross Organisation, in the late seventies, and devoting his energies to marketing extreme horror films such as *I Spit on Your Grave* (1978) and *The Bogey Man* (1980).

Recalling the contradictions of the man, Durston muses: "Gross could be gross, but there was a fine line. He also appreciated arty films, and took chances nobody else would, such as *Johnny Got His Gun*, Dalton Trumbo's masterful but oh-so-depressing piece. Jerry did have an intellectual side. Years later, after he lost Cinemation Industries (it went bankrupt), he moved to L.A., met a wonderful woman called Marion whom he married and they formed another company with a big office in Century City. Marion was very smart and shrewd, and Jerry adored her. She was just what he needed to get going again. And they did, and were successful for a short period of time. I think if Jerry had known this woman when he had Cinemation Industries, it

never would have gone bankrupt. She really knew how to organise a company. I liked her, and she said she liked me the best of all Jerry's former associates. Jerry called me in and we forgot our differences on *I Drink Your Blood*. He wanted another horror story from me that his new company would produce. So he gave me some development money, and I went to work for him again. What I came up with this time was a classic type horror film, not all blood and guts. It was called *The Well of Darkness*. Jerry was sold on it, because Marion was sold on it. But here we go again. Before he got it produced, Marion died. Jerry just went to pieces. He was so in love with this woman and he never recovered from the loss of his first and only true love. I think Jerry was an original. He was a modern day P.T. Barnum. Most of his competitors, even if they didn't like him, at least respected his dauntlessness."

Sadly, Jerry Gross dropped out of the industry during the eighties, demoralised by his personal loss and by the squeeze tactics of the jealous major studios, who were crowding in on the independents. When he was found dead in Los Angeles, California, on 20 November, 2002, at the age of sixty two, he was without family and friends; except for Arlene Farber (Sylvia in *I Drink Your Blood*) who starred in *Teenage Mother*, and finally ensured that Gross received a proper funeral.

"I don't want to be venereal!"

Durston followed *I Drink Your Blood* with *Stigma* (1972), a 'catchy' title for a film about the horrors of venereal disease (imagine how Jerry Gross might have retitled *this* one…). In the event, Charles B. Moss Jr., the son of theatre-chain president Charles B. Moss Sr., put up the money and handled distribution. The film got quite a few rave notices, but failed to really pull them in at the box office. It received a minor video release but has never caught on as much as its predecessor.

"I think even Charles got a bad distribution deal, and his father owned a string of theatres on the East coast!" says Durston. "So, being exhibitors, they just pulled the film, as long as they weren't going to get a fair share of the profits from the distributor. I don't know this to be a fact, I only suspect this was the case. It never was a box office winner. Charles Moss was too smart to let anybody clean up on his picture, and he lost money. So he pulled it. My theory!"

Stigma is a strong story, well acted, but rather out-of-step given the 'free love' vibes of the time. So what convinced Durston to tackle such a potential audience turn-off? "I would never have tackled it on my own volition, but I needed a job - another picture. I'd been sitting on my ass for six months, managing the Ziegfeld Theater. TV and the advertising agencies had turned their backs on me, because I've always been an out-spoken loudmouth. I was interviewed by *Variety*, and complained about the sponsors producing the shows, who didn't know the first thing about professional showmanship. I said they should stick to selling their products, and allow the networks to produce the shows. So I wasn't very popular or in demand at that time. Charles Moss came along with this idea, something really grim and old hat: V.D.! And he paid me to come up with a story. V.D. was hot stuff back in the thirties: *Damaged Goods*, *The Road to Ruin*; but now it was corny, passé and no longer a threat with the discovery of penicillin. What could I do with this? Where was the twist? So I went to the health authorities. A young doctor working for the

Medical Examiner gave me the clue. I asked him what was the biggest threat to getting syphilis: without hesitation he said 'the attitudes of people' – the stigma on the character of anybody who got it. Like anybody with a prison record, or an illegitimate child, and trying to keep it quiet. That was it – I was off and running with a story. As I started developing the idea of people who were stigmatised – like blacks, prostitutes, gays – I started taking interest in what I was doing. I saw it as a mystery, and then once the mystery was revealed, it would explode into drama – it almost became melodrama, but I think the country whorehouse, painted 'titty pink', softened it a bit. I was determined it wasn't going to be a *Damaged Goods*, about teens having sex, or a soft porno. I think that's what Charlie was looking for. When I handed him a finished script, he didn't like it at all. And he said it wasn't what he wanted. But his father and mother read the script, didn't expect to like it because of the subject matter, and loved it. They thought it was intelligent and deftly handled for the times. I think they convinced Charles to go with it."

Durston believes that Moss Senior's intervention caused some friction: "I liked both the parents, and I think they liked me. He sat through *I Drink Your Blood*, screened at the Criterion on Broadway, one of his own theatres, and said it was well made. In other words, before Charlie got the money to make the movie, Mr. Moss had to approve of me and my work. Okay, fine – he approved. But I think if I had been Charles's father, I would not have read the script of *Stigma*, or told Charles to go with it. I would have let Charles make that decision for himself, and if he made a mistake it was Charles Jr.'s mistake. Charles had a lot to deal with to prove himself and be his own person."

Durston pauses, before explaining the course of his sometimes stormy relationship with Moss. "I grew to like Charles. But he was complex, and didn't make it easy getting to know him. He had a very successful father, who was a charmer and well liked by everybody. So it was something he had to live up to, to be as successful as his father. In the beginning Charles and I did not like each other, for whatever reasons. I could cite one case that was my fault; but let me say this first. After Charles and I started working together, and he was on the set every day throughout the shoot, we began to appreciate each other more. At least I began to appreciate Charles, and I think he did me, too. After the film was over and ready for release, he did a few things that made me feel like he approved of me. He invited me to attend a private screening of *Cabaret* with he and his young wife. I was wild about *Cabaret*; Charles was not. And when the *New York Times* review of *Stigma* came out (a rave from Howard Thompson), Charles had a blow-up of it made, autographed and framed and presented to me: it was inscribed, 'To David, Hope this is the start of many films together – Charles.' I still have it hanging over the bar. Well, we didn't make any more films together – I don't believe Charles produced any more films. I think he was disillusioned by the film business. But when he was interviewed by a major New York magazine, he was quoted as saying the best director he worked with was me."

"Now this is what I did that might have soured Charles against me in the beginning. I've never told this story, because it would have hurt somebody who was still alive, somebody I liked very much. He's dead now, and I can speak up. The part of the redneck sheriff in *Stigma* was a great part, with a dramatic death scene, the works – a juicy antagonist role. My very good friend Lawrence Tierney was

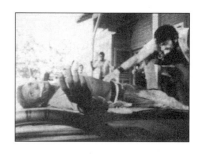

above:
Doctor Thor, Calvin's mentor, is found dead at his home in **Stigma**.

opposite page, main image:
US video cover for **Stigma**.

opposite page, bottom right:
Dr. Crosse with the resentful D.D. Whitehead, daughter of the sheriff in **Stigma**.

below:
Dr. Crosse confronts the bigoted Sheriff Whitehead.

perfect for the role. As Larry got older and outgrew all those gangster roles he became a great actor, I mean a natural. He was perfect for the role of the bigoted sheriff. I recommended him to Charles, and because Larry was still a recognised film star, Charles agreed to see him. When I told Larry, he was really excited, because he had already read the script. However, Larry had a drinking problem, so I begged him to stay overnight with me. I had an extra room he used many times. Larry thought it was a good idea. He was nervous about meeting Charles the next morning, and during the night Larry got up and left the house without me knowing it. I called Charles and said Larry had to cancel the appointment for another time. But Larry showed up for the appointment, and he was really drunk. He not only insulted Charles as the producer, but he threatened him. It was really disgraceful, and I literally had to pull Larry out of the office. I apologised to Charles, but Charles only wanted to know if I had known Larry was a serious alcoholic. I had to admit that I had, but he was a friend and I wanted to get him back on his feet. I think this is why Charles and I got off on the wrong foot. I think I would have felt the same way. I must add, however, that Larry did join Alcoholics Anonymous, and stopped drinking. He went on to do some memorable work in such films as *Tough Guys Don't Dance* and *Reservoir Dogs* – and some sober and brilliant work as a guest star on two major TV shows. I'm looking up at Larry's picture on the wall – and he seems to be saying 'It's okay to tell it as it was'. Anyway, Peter Clune took over the role and did a great job with it, probably the best performance of his career."

Fortunately for Durston, the casting of his leading man was not so fraught with difficulties. A young black actor called Philip Michael Thomas, now of course known principally as Tubbs in the hit eighties TV show *Miami Vice*, caught the director's eye and delivered a credible, likeably earnest performance. *Stigma* was his earliest screen role, as Durston recalls, "Yeah, Phil was one of a kind. I caught him in an Off-Broadway show that was so good it

went to Broadway. This was Phil's first movie. I saw him in the play and went backstage to introduce myself. He was just what I was looking for. Good looking, strong voice, a positive person. I remember he was so excited about the possibility of appearing in a movie, until he found out he wasn't going to be making a million dollars. He would be getting a few hundred above SAG scale. But he did the movie, never complained, was always on the set on time and knew his lines. The fact that he was the lead took some of the edge off not earning a million dollars. He was happily married at the time and had a beautiful little girl. I allowed him to bring his family to the location. Phil and I still stay in touch. When he became a big hit in *Miami Vice* and the girls were all over him, he was asked in a magazine interview, 'What was the happiest time of your life?' Phil replied, 'When I was making *Stigma* with Dave Durston.'"

With the script in place, shooting began in late September 1972, lasting eight weeks. The fictional Stillford Island was shot in the picturesque fishing village of Rockport near Gloucester in Massachusetts. In order to avoid offending the locals, the script claimed that the action was taking place not in mainland Rockport itself but an abandoned island off the mainland. Durston's cinematographer this time was Robert Baldwin, who shot John Hancock's chiller *Let's Scare Jessica To Death* (which *Stigma*'s producer Charles Moss also produced). "Bob Baldwin was another lucky break for me," Durston enthuses. "A great person and a good DP. I wasn't on speaking terms with Joe Mangine then, so Charles Moss recommended Baldwin, who had done *Jessica*. To show you how fine a person Baldwin was, one afternoon I wanted to shoot a couple of extra hours to get a beautiful sunset. Charles Moss was on the set every day, and said no. It was an added expense that wasn't necessary. So Baldwin went out on his own one evening, missed his dinner, and filmed me a beautiful sunset."

Like *I Drink Your Blood*, *Stigma* can be said to show a downside to the counter-culture. Where *I Drink Your Blood*, if viewed somewhat humourlessly, can be construed as a scare picture about out-of-control hippies, *Stigma* throws a bucket of cold water over the cherished hippie dream of free love and orgiastic revelry. Durston however rejects such interpretations, saying, "I've always been liberal – not too political, however, until recently with the Bush Administration." It's certainly the case that both films share an enlightened approach to issues of race and gender, and a freewheeling approach to sexuality. "I had and still have a lot of gay friends. They are a joy to be around. They're witty, have combustible senses of humour, are creative and talented, and also liberal. In my early days we weren't as open about our sexual preferences. It was understood, suggested or suspected, but never discussed openly. Not until the sixties did people start opening up about their sexual orientation. I've never said anything about it, but I'm not ashamed to admit I was bisexual. I really had the best of both sexual drives. Very few one-night stands, and only a handful of meaningful affairs, but with some of the most beautiful people in the world. I never went to bed with anybody that I didn't think I would be going to bed with again. I had to love that person as a person, male or female, not as a sex object, and if they felt the same way, the sex was always great. I had to enjoy being with that person, to admire him or her, to have sex. Free love I'm for. Group sex I'm not. And not that I don't know what I'm talking about. When I was younger, I was a clean-cut, nice looking kid. I had an athlete's body, and a fairly sizeable dick, and I knew how to use it. I was lured into one or two of these group sex situations (this was during the war) but the idea of having sex with somebody I had just met, didn't really know, or like, left me cold... man or woman, no matter how beautiful or sexually aggressive they were. Men have loved men and women have loved women for thousands of years - it just hasn't been very open, but it is and has been a part of life... and will be forever more, so why shouldn't I imply it in a script, if it fits the character or situation? Sex in films is like violence. It should always be motivated, never just there for shock value. Audiences do not feel or identify with anything that is presented like a pie in the face."

One aspect that does come out of *Stigma* like a slap in the face, though, is the grisly educational film about advanced syphilis that pops up around the half-way mark. I asked Durston whether the aim was to shock in a didactic sense: "Did you think it was a slap in the face? Not that I didn't worry about it doing just that. But the *New York Times* said the story was sturdy enough to sustain the graphic lecture. The film came from the Medical Examiner's office, a 16mm educational film. They had been so helpful, and asked if I could insert it in the script – it might do some good! Mind you, up to this point even I wasn't taking V.D. very seriously. The Medical Examiner said that was the major problem with teenagers. They weren't taking the infection seriously. They were laughing at it. They convinced me it would give weight to the subject matter of the film. I didn't, however, use their narration, I wrote my own. But from the beginning this was my worry; that audiences were not going to take V.D. seriously. Thankfully, the news and media were playing up a new European strain of V.D., using the old scare tactics. So why shouldn't I? If I do say so myself, I think my idea of getting Cousin Brucie, as the presenter delivering the lecture, was brilliant. At that time, he had the ear of every teenager in the country. The rating on his daily program was very high, and rock records became hits if Brucie played them on his show and recommended them. Unfortunately the MPAA stepped in and gave the film an 'R' rating, preventing teenagers from seeing it, but many sneaked past the ticket taker on the door. One critic said, 'Despite the 'R' rating, *Stigma* is a film that should be seen by teenagers' – and another suggested it should be shown in classrooms. Nobody, not me, not Charles, expected the rave reviews the film got. We were in shock. We had been afraid that my reputation from *I Drink Your Blood* was going to backfire on this film, but it didn't."

The plot strand involving a country cat-house whose whores turn out to have a clean bill of health, against the grain of our expectations, is certainly far more liberal than one might expect from the frequently reactionary exploitation movie scene – although Durston makes a distinction between urban and country prostitutes that shows he's no Almodóvar on the subject: "What I was going after was that the whore in the urban bar was a bitch, a mind destroyed by the hatred, the greed, the desperation of trying to survive in the city. I wanted to show the difference between the hardness of city prostitutes, as opposed to the domesticated, normal function of sex in country prostitutes. In urban life a mind can become warped. In suburban life the mind remains on normal healthy functions of the human body and mind. That's what those scenes were trying to say."

One curious feature of Durston's career is that both *I Drink Your Blood* and *Stigma* propose themes that the better-known Canadian director David Cronenberg explored soon after in his 'venereal horror' film *Shivers* (1975), and its follow-up *Rabid* (1976). Durston says, "I have never met David Cronenberg, but I have admired some of his work. I don't know if it is true or not, but I read that he admits to seeing *I Drink Your Blood* five times."[5] *Stigma*, which was

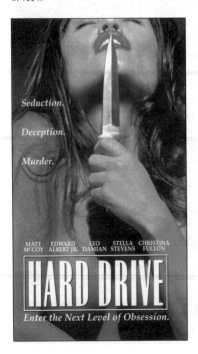

released to cinemas in August 1973, beat *Shivers* to the screen by two years, although Cronenberg has said that his script for *Shivers* was written two years before it finally went into production, making it contemporaneous with *Stigma*. He also says that whilst on a trip to California he met with Corman protégé Jonathan Demme, who revealed that Canadian producers Cinepix, for whom Cronenberg had written *Shivers*, had been touting his script around Hollywood, looking for a director other than the commercially untested Cronenberg himself.

Now, it's hardly necessary to suspect either David Cronenberg or David Durston of 'borrowing' from the other's work: even if the sudden appearance of two horror films about the spread of venereal disease written in the same year is quite a coincidence, given the *outré* nature of the subject. What is striking, however, is that the topic of Cronenberg's follow-up to *Shivers*, the excellent horror-thriller *Rabid*, is *also* anticipated by Durston's movie. Not only do both *Rabid* and *I Drink Your Blood* feature rabies-infected people attacking 'straight' society, but they also feature key scenes of a woman infecting men with rabies through sexual (or in the case of *Rabid*, quasi-sexual) contact. What's more, both films feature the beautiful waiflike actress Lynn Lowry! This time there's no question which story was written first: Durston's script predates *Rabid* by several years and Cronenberg has never suggested that *Rabid* was written before *Shivers*. It does seem plausible that Cronenberg, who has always denied cinematic inspirations for his movies, preferring to cite literary figures like William Burroughs and Vladimir Nabokov, should have seen *I Drink Your Blood* sometime in the early seventies, and then either forgotten it or decided to take the central premise (along with Lynn Lowry), and develop his own (it must be said, very individual) slant on the subject.

Phantom Projects

With *Stigma* performing modestly at the box office, Durston turned briefly to the adult film world with *Boynapped* (1975). However, the project proved to be more trouble than it was worth: "We were filming a fire escape scene on a Saturday, featuring a man with a gun, but the prop man had failed to get to the office where filmmakers can rent weapons and get a license to use them with blanks, before they closed on Friday evening. So he brought me a water pistol from Woolworths. It was as phoney as a three dollar bill. I refused to use it. I wanted the scene authentic, low-budget film be damned! I went to a friend of mine who had dealings with the Mafia. He loaned me an unlicensed gun. He warned me, however, to never admit where I got the gun, if I should get caught with it on me. God, what a chance I was taking. What if the gun was used to kill somebody? But I didn't think of that. The scene had to be authentic looking. The Saturday we shot the scene, I gave the gun to the actor a minute before the scene was shot, outside the tenement building we were using. The actor was to chase someone up a fire escape to the roof with a gun in his hand. That was it. And it was shot in one take. But a senile old woman saw the action from her kitchen window and called the police. Ten minutes after the scene was in the can and we returned inside, the tenement was surrounded by three patrol cars and we were invaded. The NYPD had enough sense to realize we were shooting a movie – they saw the camera equipment and the crew, recognized the men as actors in make-up. The first thing they said was

'Who's in charge?' I knew I was in trouble. I introduced myself, started to explain we were just shooting a movie outside. They didn't want to hear that. They were way ahead of me. 'Where's the gun you were using?' The actor had given it back to me as soon as the scene wrapped. I had to give it to them. They wanted to know if it was my gun, and did I have a license to carry it? I admitted the gun was not licensed to me, and I didn't have a license. That's a felony! I was handcuffed and taken to the station house, photographed and fingerprinted, and locked in a cell at the infamous Tombs Prison to await a trial hearing. In the cell with me was a Hispanic, who had been in a knife fight. His nose was cut, and it was bleeding as he tried to hold a small piece of flesh onto the nose until he could get medical attention. The Tombs was overcrowded, as it always was. The stench was terrible. My attorney got me into Night Court that evening. The Judge knew of me from some of the TV shows I did, that he and his wife watched. He reduced the felony charge to a misdemeanour. I was only using the gun as a prop – and an investigation proved they were not looking for that gun in any murder case. I was off the hook and allowed to have my mug-shots removed from their files, so I had no record. I was fined fifty bucks and released. But God what an experience..."

Keen to put this encounter with the authorities behind him, Durston began making plans in the Autumn of 1975 for a new feature film, based on a script he'd written called *Lord of the Dead*. The story tells of a revolution that occurs on a small island, and the incoming revolutionaries' attempts to track down and kill rebel opposition forces by using a traditional cult among the islanders. Durston explains why this project never made it to the screen: "My nephew, John 'Jack' Damon formed a company and partnership to do *Lord of the Dead*, to be filmed in Trinidad. Jack Damon was producing, I wrote the screenplay and was directing, and I called in Jacques Demarecaux as DP. Elke Sommer and John Forsythe were to be in it. Jacques accompanied Jack and me to Trinidad to select locations. Jack rented a small plane for us to survey the island – the forest and mountains, of which there were many. It was a wild bumpy flight and in that small plane, it could have been risky. However we landed safely, and Jacques went right back to his hotel room and went to bed. He had not told us he had a heart condition. To him it was as if he would be letting us down. The hotel doctor suggested we get him back to New York a.s.a.p. We left that night. Two weeks later Jacques was dead. *Lord of the Dead* was never produced, although there is some confusion as somebody else took the title."

Although Durston's filmography ends in the mid-seventies, he battled on through the following two decades, trying to mount an ambitious slate of projects that, had they reached fruition, would have shown him in a much broader light. In 1978 he signed a deal with Pathe Pictures International in New York to adapt Ernle Bradford's massive historic journal *The Great Siege: Malta 1565*. As he recalls, it was a highly prestigious project: "I was flown to Malta, where I was put up in a suite at a luxurious hotel, and lived like a King for two months researching the history of the great siege, which entailed a small unit of the Knights of Malta, say ninety or a hundred, who with the aid of a handful of Maltese natives, including some women, fought off two hundred thousand Turks. Kenneth Rooney, who was connected with Pathe Pictures, was also a member of the Knights of Malta. I was invited to the President's Palace and spent an evening with the President, who was a great guy

The Devil Is a Dancer – A Tribute to Bhaskar

"Bhaskar …is an extraordinary performer. His work seems above all dedicated to glorifying the vast possibilities involving the stretch, tension, and release of human muscle.
This is basically the underlying purpose of all dancing, when you come right down to it, however powerful the expressive goal of a particular dance may be.
It's just that Bhaskar's dances seem to be mainly about the power, grace, and the kinetic wit of the dancer himself." – *Leighton Kerner, The Village Voice*

Bhaskar, who played Horace Bones, the malevolent but charismatic cult-leader in *I Drink Your Blood*, never expected to become a horror icon. The character is based partly on Charles Manson, and yet his appeal is untainted by the sick horror of the Manson case. How can this be? Without a doubt, it's the wit and vitality of Bhaskar himself that we respond to: rather like Dyanne Thorne, the actress who created the fearsome but wonderful Ilsa in *Ilsa, She Wolf of the SS* and its sequels, Bhaskar takes a wicked character and persuades us to bestow a sneaking admiration.

He was born Bhaskar Roy Chowdhury on 11 February, 1930 in Madras (now Chennai), on the South-East coast of India. An only child of very wealthy parents, he enjoyed a happy childhood free from privation. "I had everything I wanted," he says. He was athletic, and excelled at running (particularly the hundred yard dash and the relay) and soon took up boxing, becoming a professional welterweight while still at school. His career in film started in 1949, although at first it was of little importance to him: "Showbusiness never even entered my mind. It was offered to me on a silver platter, and I said sure, but I didn't know anything about acting in movies. Those films, God knows what happened to them. I was nineteen, and from then on I did my films and dancing. In one I play a snake god, and in another, *Succubi*, I played Krishna. I was about twenty two, a ripe old age for Krishna!"

At the age of twenty five, Bhaskar was spotted by a visiting American, the heavyweight variety producer and director Max Liebman, whose *Max Liebman Spectaculars* were a keystone of NBC's evening schedules during the 1950s. Liebman had Bhaskar in mind for a forthcoming episode of his TV series *Max Liebman Presents* – the story, *The Adventures of Marco Polo*, starring Alfred Drake and Doretta Moreau, was first transmitted on 14 April, 1956. This quickly led to further TV assignments, including an episode of *Producers' Showcase* called *The Letter*, with Michael Rennie (transmitted on 15 October, 1956); and an episode of *The Alcoa Hour* called *The Protégé* starring Ed Wynn (transmitted 19 May, 1957).

When Bhaskar first arrived in New York in 1955 he was immediately taken on by a theatrical agent: "I was going to call myself just 'Roy Choudhury', but he said it sounded too Mid-Western, he couldn't sell Indian dancing with that name! He said, go home and find a name like Yma Sumac or something.[6] So I came back the next day and said, hey, how would 'Bhaskar' do? He didn't know that was my name!" Setting up his own dance company, 'Bhaskar Dances of India', he was soon in demand for stage musicals and movies. As work came in, Bhaskar moved from Forest Hill to the West Side, before landing a plum role in the 1960 Broadway show *Christine* with Maureen O'Hara. Based on the book *My Indian Family*, by Hilda Wernher, and written for the

with a wild sense of humor. After my research was complete and a treatment compiled, almost scene for scene, I was presented with a gold-plated Knight of Malta cross and chain, and I went back to New York to start on the script. Rooney said 'You're working for Pathe Pictures from here on. We complete this one, and go on to the next one.' Nothing was low-budget with Kenneth Rooney. He was tall, handsome, and built like a football player. He was born in Brooklyn, but dealing with the international set he had great manners, and was very diplomatic and poised. The production budget was somewhere in the neighborhood of $150 million, with a cast of twelve international stars. Jack Cardiff was to be our director of photography. It took me almost nine months to complete the script, which came to 189 pages. But there was great trouble trying to get it off the ground. Trouble with so many stars not being available at the same time, and for so many weeks. Then the Knights of Malta Committee would not allow one of the Knights in the script to bed a native girl who gets pregnant and commits suicide. Well, that had to go – no fucking and no suicides in our Society. They could kill but they couldn't fuck. Kenneth Rooney, though, had a mind of his own. He thought the Knights should be shown the way they really

lived in those days. There was a clash of minds and temperaments. I took the first draft of the script to Charlton Heston, who was considered for one of the starring parts, and instead of being honored he was insulted that I would present him with a 189-page script. I said it was a first draft and that the first draft of *Gone with the Wind* was over 200 pages! Anyway it ended on a bad note. After over a year, it was decided the picture was too big and expensive to produce. I stayed in touch with Kenneth Rooney for a few years more, tried to get him interested in doing a low-budget horror, or a thriller. But it didn't fire him up."

In the early 1980s Durston became interested in the Fox Sisters, two uneducated farm girls from Rochester, New York State who became world famous in the mid-19th Century as mediums, and around whom the founders of Spiritualism gathered. The sisters appeared before Kings, Queens and Presidents, before sinking into a later life marred by alcoholism, discord and penury. Durston recalls, "Somebody gave me a copy of a book about them, and I was fascinated. What an incredible life they had, much of it scary – some of it blows your mind. I started writing a script, 'The Walls Are Listening'. About 1983 I started getting involved in mounting this as a 3-part TV mini-series, with a cast of many stars. I had plenty of money, so I started a corporation, The Seven Summits Group. My nephew Jack Damon helped me, and became a partner. We got the networks interested, but eventually they all shied away from it as too big, with locations in New England, New York, London, Paris, Cuba, and a battle sequence during the Civil War."

After this potentially fascinating project fell through, Durston hovered on the verge of *Cannibal Holocaust* territory with another intriguing story idea: "My friend John Peverall became interested in a script called 'Souls and Savages' that I wrote for John Huston and producer Henry Blanke (*The Maltese Falcon*, *The Treasure of Sierra Madre*). It was put on the shelf after Mr. Blanke died in 1981, but then restored with a new title, 'Savage's Apprentice'. Peverall had an investor and we went off to Belem, Brazil, up the wild Amazon (before it was destroyed) to spot locations and make friends with a friendly tribe. This was in August 1986. We were there four weeks before pre-production came to a halt over creative differences. The script had a great deal of horror and violence between the savages and 'civilized' folk, though if I may say so it was a strong, valid drama, based on fact. But I think the backers were just looking for tits and ass amongst the natives…"

In 1992, Paragon Arts International contracted John Peverall as producer and Durston as writer to adapt for the screen the life of Belgian ecclesiastical hero Father Damien, the so-called 'Leper Priest': it was, as Durston recalls, "another big story – I got paid to write, but I didn't have control over the production. The script went from Paragon Arts to Tristar to Warners. Robin Williams was even approached, and agreed to play Father Damien – but again nothing came of it." (A film was eventually made on the subject in 1999: *Molokai: The Story of Father Damien*, directed by Paul Cox and written by *Cry Freedom* screen-writer John Briley.)

It's funny to think that in a parallel world David Durston's reputation expanded to include major historical dramas, anthropogical action adventures and religious biopics. He must have seen these phantom productions in his mind's eye many times – we can only regret that we can't see them too. What still remains, though, is Durston's

musical stage by Nobel Prize winner Pearl S. Buck, the production was a notorious flop, but it enabled him to move into the Columbus Avenue apartment where he would live for the rest of his life. The same year, he also appeared in a short musical film called *The Creation of Woman* (1960), which marked the start of producer Ismail Merchant's long career in the movies. This dance-and-music allegory of the origins of life helped to raise Bhaskar's profile in the USA: "It won a Cannes Film Festival award and was nominated for an Academy Award in America, in 1961. God creates Man and Woman, and he has a tie with them both, then he notices that they are always fighting and so he cuts the ties and says, 'Okay, go on and kill yourselves!' It was a cute little movie."[7]

After travelling to England a few times for several dance concerts at The Lambeth Theatre in 1963-64, he appeared in a British production of the play *The Kindly Monkeys* (1965), alongside Indian dance legend, Surya Kumari. Numerous foreign trips followed, including shows in Australia and South Africa. With his profile as a dancer and choreographer already assured, his next career move was, to say the least, surprising: a role in *I Drink Your Blood*. "I was sitting on the stoop, twiddling my thumbs, when one of my friends said, oh you must meet David Durston. David said, 'I'm making a movie based on Charles Manson, would you be interested in being in it?' and I said, 'Give me the script,' and I read it and said, 'Sure, why not.' Working with David was a great pleasure." Bhaskar was always alert to the film's double-edged appeal as both hardcore horror and black humour: "Sure, it was meant to be a tongue-in-cheek thing, but it became serious at times. With all that blood it was a serious movie, but when people come running down the hill with shaving cream around their mouths, if people don't laugh at that I don't know what they *can* laugh at. We in the cast got on very well, but the crew, that was a different matter. They were 'flying high' as the saying goes."

While shooting *I Drink Your Blood*, the cast found themselves as ostracised as their characters, thanks to some unexpected antagonism with the locals: "The cast got on well, but we were isolated because the townsfolk wouldn't let us come down into the town! They thought we were all crazy people who would go down there and corrupt them! We were not allowed in. No bar would open for us, so we had to have our own liquor sent in." Although the attitude of the locals could have felt intimidating to some, Bhaskar himself cut an imposing figure and would have been a formidable opponent in a fight: "I was, Stephen, let me tell you, I was! Both in New York and in India, if somebody said anything bad to me I attacked first and took the consequences later. If you're a dancer you're immediately categorized, you know, you can imagine, but I was always, 'Alright, let's step outside, we'll work this out…' I was a good boxer, and I studied a little bit of kung-fu and karate, so I could take care of myself."

Bhaskar was a great cook on top of his other talents. While digressing to talk about the importance of presentation in cookery, he commented on where he feels *I Drink Your Blood* fell down: "The publicity was so poorly done. You looked at the poster and thought, 'Oh my God, this is one of those 42nd street movies,' but *I Drink Your Blood* was not one of those movies. It's a couple of notches above that. It opened on Broadway; but the publicity was badly done. I was available but they didn't use me. I was being interviewed for my concerts, for everything else except the movie." He was also, like Durston, less than thrilled by producer Jerry Gross's decision to pair the film up on a double bill with *I Eat Your Skin*: "I met Jerry Gross, who billed those two together, and I said to him, 'What is this, a religious film you're selling? I drink your *blood* and I eat your *skin*? What are we talking about, a Catholic Mass?'"

Some of his snootier theatre colleagues raised an eyebrow at Bhaskar's latest cinematic adventure: "People in the dance world rang me and said, 'What are you *doing* Bhaskar?' And I said, 'I'm making a movie, what do you want from me? Dance concerts don't make enough, and I've got to make a living.'" He also received some bizarre calls from people who'd seen the film and taken against Horace Bones, like soap-fans writing to berate characters for their adulteries and misdemeanours: "I got so many bad phone calls because of *I Drink Your Blood*, I can't even tell you. A lot of people took it seriously and they think I am this person. Unfortunately, I was listed in the phonebook and all these Christians would call me and say, 'You'll go to hell, you're going to die!' I said, "Lady, it's a movie, I'm not that kind of a person! I'm all sugar and spice my dear, come and take a look at me!'" He laughed at the memory, adding, "There are some weird people in this world!"

After his brush with screen infamy, Bhaskar continued to dance for the theatre. In 1977 he signed up for a movie to be made in India, with Rex Harrison, Sylvia Miles and John Saxon, called *Shalimar*. While the film was in pre-production, Bhaskar was rehearsing a new dance spectacle for the theatre. Disaster struck: he fell from the stage during a difficult manoeuvre, and broke his spine. He was to spend the rest of his life

in a wheelchair: "It was traumatic. You feel anger first at the stupidity, then you feel sorry for yourself, and eventually you accept it and say hey, this is what's dealt to you, deal with it as best you can." With phenomenal strength of character, Bhaskar did just that, and moved on: "I started painting, I had an exhibition in New York, and I sold about forty paintings. I also started writing. I'm writing my autobiography, although I'm afraid it's probably too raunchy for publication!"

Bhaskar died in hospital on 4 August, 2003. I spoke to him on the phone just a few weeks before his death, and he was thrilled that *I Drink Your Blood* was being reissued on DVD, and very happy to hear how popular he had become among horror aficionados. The film may only have been a short vacation from his dance-oriented work in theatre and cinema, but he was immensely gratified that it was so well loved, and particularly glad to know that the humour as well as the horror were appreciated in his performance. I'd been informed prior to calling him that he was unlikely to leave hospital again, but to talk to him and to hear the energy that crackled in his voice was to indulge, just for a moment, the idea that he was unstoppable. One thing's for sure; as long as there are horror movie fans in the world, at least one facet of Bhaskar really is unstoppable. Horace Bones lives on, and on the screen we can see the fire and wit of his creator, laughing out at us again and again.

David Durston adds:

"Bhaskar passed away Sunday night. He was still in the hospital. They could not contain a bed-sore the size of a baseball on his hip. Two nights before, a close friend and associate, Tony Franco, arranged for him to see the DVD of *I Drink Your Blood* at the hospital. Bhaskar loved it and laughed a lot at the features on the menu, the interviews and stuff. He also read all the reviews and the good things they said about him. He was moved to tears. He also blasted me a few nights before on the phone when I was reading some clips from those reviews. He said, 'Get off your fucking ass and write another script with a big part for me in it - in a wheelchair, of course. Just think of all the great wheelchair parts there have been in movies - and we'll top them.' Those of us who were really close to Bhaskar are deeply broken up by his death. He was one of a kind. In the face of his misfortune, his spirit and zest for life was an inspiration to all of us."

animal or human, who is unconscious, drunk, drugged or in a deep sleep, these suckers can drain every ounce of blood out of your body within five hours and that victim never knows it. He's dead. Okay it's outlandish, but it's good for a scare and the Haemadipsa is a reality."

Whilst it would be a pleasure to see a Durston film on the big screen again, especially one as potentially gruesome and thrilling as *Leech*, the director has already made an indelible mark on the flesh of the horror genre: so here's a Bloody Mary to a consummate showbiz professional, and the man who gave us *I Drink Your Blood*, a seminal and unforgettable exploitation classic. Cheers, David!

Footnotes

1 Dr. Timothy Leary's escalating series of open-house drug experiments at Harvard are fascinatingly described in Jay Stevens's book *Storming Heaven.*

2 The title song has a mellow swing to it that resembles The Platters, and it's one of the film's foremost charms. It was written by r'n'b legend Sylvester Bradford, who with Al Lewis wrote the Fats Domino classic *Blueberry Hill* and Gene Vincent's *Right Now*, and whose song *Tears on My Pillow* appears on the soundtrack to *Grease.*

3 Ten years later, the producers of the ailing John Huston's snoreathon *Phobia* threatened legal action against sado-porn maestro Armand Weston, who tried to release a horror film of the same name the following year: Weston's *Phobia* became *The Nesting* – see review section.

4 Mangine's horror credits include *Squirm, Alligator, Alone in the Dark*, and *Mother's Day.*

5 I've been unable to trace this statement.

6 Yma Sumac is a Peruvian singer whose real name was changed by Capitol Records to make it sound more exotic.

7 *The Creation of Woman* is available as an extra on the DVD release of *The Householder* (1963), Ismail Merchant's first film with director James Ivory.

above:
Durston and friends at a recent revival screening of **I Drink Your Blood**. (*left to right:* Lynn Lowry, David Durston, Arlene Farber, Tyde Kierney.)

below, left to right:
Joe Mangine, Durston, and Grindhouse Releasing's Bob Murawski.

astonishing energy and spirit. In 2003, when *I Drink Your Blood* received its first DVD release, Durston happily took centre stage, and his charismatic contribution to the extras package made the disc a must-have for fans. Later that year, when Grindhouse Entertainment arranged a theatrical screening of the film in L.A., Durston was there in person to meet an adoring audience. Currently in his eighties, he is unfailingly gracious to his fans and exudes a degree of vim and vigour that suggests a man very happy with his life. If he suffers aches and pains you would never know it, as he's far more likely to fret over others than himself. Among several scripts he's written recently, a horror tale called *Leech* sounds the most likely to carry on the gory trade of the early seventies work: "It deals with a horde of vampire leeches that invade in the thousands during the mating season," explains Durston. "The vampire leech is a reality. It's technical term is the Haemadipsa, the most feared of blood-sucking leeches, because if it attaches itself to an

---

DAVID DURSTON: FILMOGRAPHY AS DIRECTOR

1964	*Felicia* (also writer)
1966	*The Love Statue* aka *The Love Drug* (also writer)
1970	*Blue Sextet* aka *Leap Into Hell* (also writer)
1971	*I Drink Your Blood* aka *Phobia* (also writer)
1972	*Stigma* (also writer)
1975	*Boynapped*

TV PROJECTS (some dates are approximate):

1947/8	*Foxhead 400 Houseparty* (live magazine show made for ABC, Chicago)
1947/8	*Top of the Weather* (made for ABC, Chicago)
1947/8	*Chicago Splash Party* (made for ABC, Chicago)
1948/9	*A Hit Is Made* (music show made for ABC, Chicago)
1948/9	*Street Singer* (music show made for ABC, Chicago)
1952-55	*Kraft Television Theatre* (writer) (made in New York City – episode title unknown)
1952-55	*Studio One* (writer) (made in New York City – episode title unknown)
1952-55	*Rheingold Playhouse* (writer) (made in New York City – episode title unknown)
1952-55	*Danger* (writer) (made in New York City – episode title unknown)
1952-55	*Playhouse 90* (writer) (made in New York City – episode title unknown)
1952-55	*Tales of Tomorrow* (writer) Episodes: "The Glacier Giant" (5 December 1952): "Mr. Fish" aka "The Discovered Heart": (16 January 1953): "Two Faced" (30 January 1953): "The Evil Within" (1 May 1953 - brief appearance by James Dean)
1953/4/5	*The Tournament of Roses Parade* (line producer for live broadcast of three successive New Year's Day Parades in Pasadena.)
1953/4/5	*Your Hit Parade* (associate producer)
1958	*Navy Log* (writer) Episode: "The Big White Albatross" (26 December 1958). Two more scripts: titles unknown.

OTHER CREDITS:

1971	*Dry Summer* aka *Susuz Yaz* aka *I Had My Brother's Wife* aka *Reflections* (dir: Metin Erksan) (directed inserts in US version retitled *Reflections*)
1971	*The Seduction of Inga* (dir: Joe Sarno) (re-edited and dubbed US version)
1994	*Hard Drive* (editorial supervisor)

RADIO:

1952-54	*Mr. Jolly's Hotel for Pets* aka *Hotel for Pets* (writer of NBC children's radio show starring Frank McHugh)
1954-55	*The Woolworth Hour* (music show: creator and producer)

chapter 8

Don't Make Me Do Anything Bad, Mother...

Joseph Ellison on Don't Go in the House

Don't Go in the House (1979)

Along with William Lustig's *Maniac* this is my favourite stalk-and-slash film, or perhaps I should say 'torch-and-stash' in this case? Ellison's grim tale of a lunatic kidnapping women in order to burn them with a flame-thrower in a purpose-built steel room is seemingly disinterested in turning its nastiness into *Halloween*-ish fun: and I'm sorry, but I like that in a movie. It's a film I've watched so often the neighbours are nervous, but what can I say – every time I see it, I'm struck by its powerful combination of violence, humour and genuine creepiness.

Ellison treads a knife-edge with the depiction of Donny Kohler (Dan Grimaldi), who is such a pathetic creature even *Maniac*'s Joe Spinell might have asked for re-writes. The victim of a cruel mother (Ruth Dardick) who punished him by holding his arms over the flames of a gas cooker, Donny can't so much as glance at a box of matches without suffering flashbacks to the abuse. Returning from work one day after witnessing an accident in which a fellow worker suffered severe burns, he discovers his mother has finally croaked. Free at last, he runs gleefully round the house, playing loud music and jumping up and down on soft furnishings like a naughty child left alone for the weekend. Relief turns to terror though, when he hears Mother's hated voice calling his name. She's still dead; but Donny has a few problems 'upstairs', in the form of whispering voices hissing murderous suggestions in his head. With pain, punishment and fire well-and-truly branded into his mind, he sets out to enact a few variations on the theme himself, turning an upstairs room of Mother's rambling old house into a steel-walled flameproof prison…

The film lurches from the macabre to the sadistic when Donny tricks a young woman called Kathy Jordan (Johanna Brushay aka Debra Richmond) back to his house, and bashes her round the head with a fire iron. She comes to in the steel-lined room, naked, and dangling by her wrists from the ceiling. In a protracted sequence that draws out the preparations to a shuddersome degree, Donny – wearing a heavy asbestos suit that obscures his features – douses his shrieking victim with petrol. As the music cranks the tension to the extreme, he pauses – then blasts her naked body with a flamethrower. She dies screaming and writhing in flames. It's one of the most outrageous scenes ever to feature in a horror film. Appallingly convincing, it takes the viewer through shock into a kind of stunned admiration.

For a while it seems Ellison may have shot his bolt with this excessive sequence, but while he doesn't show us anything quite so shocking again, other qualities hold our attention. Donny carries on killing, collecting the charred corpses of his female victims and dressing them up in his mother's old frocks, sitting them together in armchairs like attendees of some post-apocalyptic Tupperware party. The voices in his head identify themselves with the burnt remains, and Donny has conversations with them as if they

below:
The Kohler house, in Atlantic Highlands, New Jersey.

DON'T GO IN THE HOUSE Certificate: 'X'

Don't Go in the House
aka **The Burning** (shooting title)
© 1979. Turbine Films, Inc.
FVI - Film Ventures International/Turbine Films
presents.
director: Joseph Ellison. producer: Ellen
Hammill. story: Joseph R. Masefield.
screenplay: Joseph Ellison, Ellen Hammill,
Joseph R. Masefield. director of photography:
Oliver Wood. editor: Jane Kurson. music score:
Richard Einhorn. associate producers: Matthew
Mallinson, Dennis Stephenson. production
manager: Diane Sancetta. assistant director:
Monica Lange. art direction: Sarah Wood.
costumes: Sharon Lynch. assistant costumes:
Marlene Edlestein. sound mixer: Jimmy Kwei.
gaffer: George Giangrande. best boy: Richard
Mauro. 1st electrics: Ken Kelsch. 2nd electrics:
Jeff Etcher. 3rd electrics: Bob Zimmerman. key
grip: Jeff Sudzin. assistant camera: Arthur
Gardner. 2nd assistant camera: Steve Brecker.
script supervisor: Hallie Aaron. set design:
Peter Zsiba. set construction: Richard
DeStefano, Bob Wiederhorn, Uzi Parnes. hair
and make-up: Maryann Guar. assistant hair and
make-up: Tamara Hirschel. special effects co-
ordinator: Peter Kunz. special effects: Matt
Vogel. special effects make-up: Tom
Brumberger. catering: Tony Tucci, Angela Tucci,
Ginny Branca. post production consultant: Stan
Warnow. 1st assistant editor: Jimmy Kwei.
sound editor: John Lievsay. 2nd sound editor:
Lou Kleinman. editing room assistants: Lazley
Topping, Suzanna Pillsbury, Sanford Gendler,
Frances Politeo, Wendy Lydell, Frank Farrell,
Jeffrey Nevis, Jim Fitzgerald. re-recording mix:
Emil Neroda, The Sound Shop. post production
sound: Magno Sound. production assistants:
Darryl E. Holmes, Barry Shapiro, Vincent
Giordano, Harry Savides, Kim Martin, Jonathan
Alexander, Jan Carter, Isabella Verdini, Michael
Bates, Randi Melman, Tony Barone, Matthew
Polensky, Vilma Straino. "Dancin' Close to You"
and "Straight Ahead" produced by Murri Barber,
composed by Ted Daryll, performed by The
Daryll/Barber Band; "Late Night Surrender" and
"Boogie Lightning" composed by Bill Heller,
available on Reflection Records & Tapes,
recorded at Minot Sound (White Plains, NY).
negative matching: Match/Cut. opticals:
Optimum Effects. sound transfers: Accurate
Film Labs. titles: David L. Hoffman. Special
thanks: National Park Service; New Jersey Film
Commission; Jersey City Mayor's Office;
General Camera; Dick Dillons; August Films;
Simon Nuchtern; Royal Court Repertory;
Phyllis Craig; Lou Salvatore; Palace Disco
(New Rochelle, NY); Nap Holmes;
Phantasmagoria Prods. Inc.; Keith Robinson;
Mannerly Shop (New Rochelle, NY); William
Seef; Mark Goldberg; Shore Florist (Atlantic
Highlands, N.J.); Mary Ann Chin; Nancy Fraioli;
Jim Glass; Len Grainer; Scott Hello; Penny
Kunz; Larry Neroda; Beriau Picard; John Grey;
Y.C. Kwei. Lenses by Panavision. colour by
DeLuxe. filmed on location in New Rochelle
(New Jersey), USA.
Cast: Dan Grimaldi (Donny Kohler). Charlie
Bonet (Ben). Bill Ricci (Vito). Robert Osth
(Bobby Tuttle). Dennis M. Hunter, John
Hedberg (workers). Ruth Dardick (Mrs. Kohler).
Johanna Brushay [Debra Richmond] (Kathy
Jordan). Darcy Sheen (girl in car). Mary Ann
Chin (woman in street). Lois Verkruepse
(woman with kids). Susan Smith (girl in market).
Jim Donnegan (clerk). Claudia Folts (body #1).
Denise Woods (body #2). Pat Williams (body
#3). Colin McInnes (little Donny). Ralph D.
Bowman (Father Gerritty). Joey Peschi
(Bobby's son). Connie Oaks (Bobby's
daughter). David McComb (salesman). Jean
Manning (girl in store). Ken Kelsch (man in
store). Tom Brumberger (Alfred). Nikki Kollins
(Farrah). Kim Roberts (Karen). Louise Grimaldi
(Barbara). Commander Johnny G (himself).
Gloria Szymkovicz (Sylvia). David Brody (Tony).
O'Mara Leary (Suzanna). Gail Turner (Patty).
Christian Isidore (Michael). Eileen Dunn
(Michael's mother). Charlie Bonet (stunts).

were his guests. Is it just paranoia, or are they sniggering at him when his back's turned? Soon Donny's pyromaniac wet dreams turn to nightmares about being dragged down into the earth by his frazzled victims. He starts to get seriously freaked out by his own House of Horrors (one wonders if killers like Ed Gein, Jeffrey Dahmer or Robert Berdella had the same trouble), and – forced by panic into attempting a social life – he accepts the friendly overtures of a workmate, Bobby (Robert Osth), who invites him on a disco double date with two girls.

In case you were wondering what's so funny about all this, the following sequence delivers a welcome pinch of camp humour. Dreading his forthcoming disco-date but eager to get out of the house, Donny wanders into town. After catching a glimpse of himself in a shop window, clad in the same dreary windcheater and jeans he's been wearing throughout the film, he wanders nervously into a gentlemen's tailors to buy something more suited to the dance floor. He's swiftly pounced upon by the *so-o* offhand sales assistant (David McComb), who purrs, *"Why don't you let me set you up with an entire ensemble?"* Donny asks about a garish red shirt he'd seen a woman examining, pretending to recognise its brand name ('The Matador') when the assistant uses it. *"To tell you the truth, she thought it was tacky,"* snaps the salesman. Recognising a Grade-A sucker, he soon has Donny bamboozled with his expensive recommendations: *"Ahem... especially made for dancing. Elastic thread in the seams."*

Lovers of seventies disco-tack will cherish the gauche psycho's subsequent night out. Struggling within the restraints of a low budget, Ellison points his camera doggedly up from floor level to conceal how few extras there are. Donny tries to fit in with the dating game, socialising for the first time in his life and even trading lame puns with Bobby and the two girls he's brought with him. However, when his date tries to lure him onto the dance floor, she makes the mistake of pulling at his strobe-lit arms, stirring up memories of Donny's childhood punishments. He freaks (and I don't mean *"C'est chic"*), hurling a table candle at his unsuspecting date. As a frenzied disco song belts out on the soundtrack she staggers round the dance floor screaming, with her lavish hairdo in flames. It's a scene both horrible and hilarious, giving new meaning to the phrase 'bad hair day' and providing the film's second best set-piece. (What a pity they couldn't have stumped up for *Disco Inferno* on the soundtrack!)

Donny 'hot-foots' it out of the club pursued by the girl's enraged brother, but even after taking a beating he stubbornly persists in picking up two drunken girls and inviting them back to his house for a 'party'. Squeamish viewers will be fearing the worst, but as the story draws to a climax Ellison fights shy of further sadism, instead returning to the macabre tableau of burnt bodies for his finale ...

Don't Go in the House is an accomplished, atmospheric horror story that sustains a genuine mood of unease. It has one unforgettable explosion of violence which pulls the viewer up short in astonishment, but for me the film really does work as a whole. There's a unity of mood and purpose that speaks of a director firmly in control of his material. The movie was lensed in winter, and benefits from a canny contrast between frosty location work (a scene outside the incinerator plant where Donny

works is particularly effective), and the awful fiery fate of the victims. The photography adds to the chill, with many scenes shot in varying degrees of blue, culminating in Donny's deep-blue-tinted nightmares. Juxtaposing cold and fire throughout, Oliver Wood's deep-freeze photography provides a visual analogue for the story's extremes. If you compare the film with a superficially similar shocker of the period, like *The Toolbox Murders*, you'll see that even though both films feature extreme violence in urban locations, Ellison's direction and the simple but effective 'fire and iciness' of the cinematography pull theme and treatment together, whereas *Toolbox* lacks an aesthetic dimension and, apart from its brutal slayings, looks pretty run-of-the-mill.

There's something so compellingly despondent about much of the story, and Grimaldi's 'loser' performance has real emotional integrity. Alan Jones rightly described Grimaldi as "a low-rent Dustin Hoffman" when he reviewed the film for *Starburst* back in 1981. But while Jones saw nothing else to recommend, I have to disagree; simple and derivative though the plot may be, this alarming film-*flambé* has an undertow completely absent from the more mechanical slasher flicks of the period (Tony Maylam's *The Burning* for instance, a film that pipped Ellison's at the post for the *reductio ad toastem* title but which fizzles out of your memory with only a handful of severed fingers to show it was ever there). Joining the superior ranks of horror tales like Abel Ferrara's *The Driller Killer*, Meir Zarchi's *I Spit on Your Grave* and the aforementioned *Maniac*, Ellison serves us a story that's both sadistic and sombre – one of my favourite combinations. It seems to me that stories revolving around extreme cruelty ought to weight their prurience with some measure of bleakness. The failing of a film like *Bundy* (2002), a recent attempt to mine the serial killer theme, is its moral cowardice; treating atrocities with the same self-satisfied 'sick humour' that gave us serial killer playing cards and 'World's Coolest Killers' websites. By contrast, the few moments of humour in *Don't Go in the House* are chiefly at the expense of the killer, which really does make all the difference.

The aforementioned disco scenes may bear the hallmark of a low-budget production whose reach has exceeded its grasp, but in general the small cast is turned to the film's advantage; it helps us to understand how Donny's evil mother, and his consequent hatred of women, have cut him off from social interaction. One shot that always comes to mind when I think of this film is a deep-focus image of Donny simply walking along a jetty, with lowering grey clouds above a deep blue sea whipped into foaming waves. Scenes where Donny visits a lone priest in an otherwise empty church, or wanders disconsolately around town after the shops have closed, are as memorable in their way as the violent set-pieces. As I said, the killer is both pathetic and terrifying, utterly sunk in his psychosis, but lacking the swagger and intellect of the clichéd movie psychopath. His abductions of women are the result of wheedling, forlorn persistence rather than cunning. He certainly knows what he intends to do and is therefore a genuinely chilling figure, but his abductions work despite him, not because he's a born predator. All of which means that neither Grimaldi's performance nor Ellison and Hammill's screenplay pander to a vicarious identification with the killer.

GTO FILMS Presents

YOU HAVE BEEN WARNED!

DON'T GO IN THE HOUSE

...Threshold into terror.

SYNOPSIS

Donny Kohler is sick. Very sick. He was cruelly abused as a child.

He is 27 years old now and his mother is dead. Her death changes him — a long-dormant psychosis is brought to life. He methodically prepares his revenge. His first victim is a beautiful young girl. He burns her alive in a metal room he has built for vengeance. He cannot stop killing once he's committed this first gruesome murder. He keeps the horribly charred corpses in the house with him, dressed in mother's finest gowns. He shares his feelings and thoughts with them in a way he never could with *living* people, but suddenly a form of conscience begins causing him nightmares and hallucinations.

Donny Kohler is lost in the horror of his own life . . . and the final revenge comes from his victims!

CAST

Dan Grimaldi	Donny Kohler
Robert Osth	Bobby Tuttle
Ruth Dardick	Mrs. Kohler
Charlie Bonet	Ben
Bill Ricci	Vito
Dennis M. Hunter	Worker
John Hedberg	Worker
Johanna Brushay	Kathy Jordan
Darcy Shean	Girl in the car
Mary Ann Chin	Woman on street
Jim Donnegan	Clerk in market
Claudia Folts	Body no. 1
Denise Woods	Body no. 2
Pat Williams	Body no. 3

CREDITS

PRODUCER: ELLEN HAMMILL
DIRECTOR: JOSEPH ELLISON
DIRECTOR OF PHOTOGRAPHY: OLIVER WOOD
EDITOR: JANE KURSON
MUSIC: RICHARD EINHORN
STORY: JOSEPH R. MASEFIELD
SCREENPLAY: JOSEPH ELLISON, ELLEN HAMMILL, JOSEPH R. MASEFIELD
ASSOCIATE PRODUCERS: MATTHEW MALLINSON, DENNIS STEPHENSON

Certificate: 'X' Running Time: 81 Minutes

above:
"...Unless you're into the wild look, which is really passé..." David McComb offers fashion advice to Dan Grimaldi's dowdy psycho. Note: the shop is playing the same track (L'Ectrique's **Struck By Boogie Lightning**) that we'll hear in the forthcoming disco scene.

left:
British promo sheet for the film, in which the Kohler house gains a few creepy tombstones in the foreground, giving it a Lucio Fulci, **House by the Cemetery** vibe.

The asbestos suit is a masterstroke – an iconic image, memorable and genuinely frightening. Its bulk transforms nervous Donny into a forbidding, almost alien figure, and the tinted glass of the visor ensures that he's utterly inscrutable. His chosen costume makes sense first, of course, in relation to his desire to burn his victims, but it's also a great metaphor for the detachment of a psychopath: no arguing or pleading is going to get through to him. When he flings open the door to the steel room and stands there, framed in the doorway, dressed head-to-toe in white asbestos, it's a heart-stopping moment to rival Leatherface's sudden appearance in *The Texas Chain Saw Massacre*. And while *Don't Go in the House* can't quite compare to Hooper's flawless debut, it does share with it an aesthetic dimension that amplifies the horror.

One can hardly fail to notice a degree of bitterness and anger in this movie, directed with some ferocity towards the mother figure. The film closes on a coda showing a little boy being shouted at and slapped by a mean-tempered mom. The abused boy stares coldly into space, with the same voices that haunted Donny whispering in his mind. It's an ending not unlike that of David Cronenberg's *The Brood* (also 1979): it too ends with a child showing signs of incipient madness passed on by a violent mother. And in both cases, the films have been attacked by some critics for misogyny. So are they right?

It's a weakness of some otherwise intelligent people that they find it hard to face the phenomenon of bad motherhood. With legitimate feminist concerns about the repression of women to bear in mind, and awareness of the ugly aspects of patriarchal dominance in history and culture, it's understandable that there should be hesitance, but not to the extent that it interferes with the truth. *Don't Go in the House* portrays two horrendous mothers, one

seen throughout the story (Donny's mother, usually in flashback) and another at the end (a nameless mother, beating her small son in a fury because he's disobeyed her). Neither of them are dishonest representations – Mrs. Kohler is perhaps given to more baroque expression than the mundane shouting and slapping of the other mom, but when we read the newspapers, we know that worse still is happening in the real world. It seems that *Don't Go in the House*'s focus on the sins of the mother, coupled with Donny's sadistic killing of women, equates to misogyny in many critics' minds. This is symptomatic of a cultural trend wherein it's impossible to critique the mother figure without being portrayed as a woman-hater or – worse still in many ways, not least because of its lack of compassion – as merely a whingeing male who doesn't like women being 'in charge'. It's surely worth recognising that parents of either gender hold power over their children, and that both can abuse it. Motherhood is the locus of special power, and from it can flow both good and evil. It's uncontroversial to say that 'power corrupts', and yet many who would use the truism glibly for sins of the father lose their nerve when it comes to women. The fact is that children are far more at risk from their parents than from strangers. Ellison's film unflinchingly addresses evil within the family, and as far as I'm concerned, that makes it progressive.

Don't Go in the House has attracted few defenders, yet its commercial success runs counter to the prevailing disdain with which it was met by reviewers. I strongly recommend that you give this film a chance, if you haven't already – it's one of the movies that made me want to write this book, and if (like me) you respond to ambience as much as atrocity in a horror film, you'll find it has more to offer than is commonly claimed. And I guarantee you at least one image that you'll never forget!

below:
Horror house.

"So many people hated that movie! There were a few good reviews, but you could easily count them on one hand. And the bad reviews were *vehement*."
– *Joseph Ellison on Don't Go in the House.*

"As if the grammatically inelegant title, the blatant thefts from Hitchcock […], and the voyeuristic female nudity were not enough, *Don't Go in the House* makes matters even worse by its cynical pretence at an anti-child-abuse message." – *The Aurum Film Encyclopedia: Horror.*

"A real sick one. For fans of *Maniac* only."
– *Michael Weldon, The Psychotronic Encyclopedia of Film.*

"Sickening rubbish."
– *Elliot's Guide to Films on Video.*

"Joseph Ellison's *Don't Go in the House*… may be taken as representing the cycle at its most debased."
– *Robin Wood, "Returning the Look: Eyes of a Stranger".*

Joseph Ellison, lucky for him, has a sense of humour about the way his infamous horror movie has been vilified over the years. However, it's over twenty five years since the film was released, and Ellison is far from preoccupied with bad reviews. After his second feature film, a romantic coming-of-age drama called *Joey* (1986), failed to find an audience (it's been snarled up in rights clearance purgatory ever since), Ellison returned to his first love, music. Today he's a singer-songwriter special-ising in a contemporary brand of country rock / R'n'B. Although his movie-making days are well behind him, he was happy to speak to a true fan of *Don't Go in the House*, and describes here how one of the most shocking horror tales of the 1970s came about…

above and below:
Ellen and Joseph Ellison in Hollywood, during the spring of 1981.

Early Days

Joseph Ellison was born in Manhattan in 1949, and before film – certainly long before the sort of extreme horror for which he became infamous – he was drawn to music. Indeed, he believes music shaped his sensibilities even earlier: "I was boppin' to the muffled melodies of Hank Williams, Thelonious Monk and The Maguire Sisters wafting through the placenta walls," he says. Other than this pre-natal recollection, however, family history is something he feels is largely irrelevant to his filmmaking: "I was partly raised by a Texan, a great man; a redneck raised in the old ways, but he wasn't a bigot. He taught me so much about women, and he was a great role model; he taught me all about that culture from a very early age. I was not just a typical New York kid! I lived in Manhattan, and Tallahassee, I lived in Virginia and DC, I lived in Connecticut for a year – I moved round quite a bit. I had a very broad spectrum of experience. I had sort of a raucous youth, I was in trouble a little bit, and, let's put it this way, I got help when there was a crisis. My mom really stepped up when I was in a jam at fourteen. I've got to tell you, she was nothing like Mrs. Kohler! It worked out okay: 'Life's been good to me, so far.'"

The possibilities of cinema first made an impact on Ellison during high school, as he vividly recalls: "On a rain-soaked November night, a fellow classmate/chemical enthusiast and I happened into the RKO on 23rd Street to view a film from Italy, *Juliet of the Spirits*. The opening titles rolled. Nino Rota's spooky organ music played. I was hypnotised. Brilliant sounds, surreal scenes and psychedelic drugs produced an event more special than the Oscars, even. A life-altering experience! Standing on the platform that night waiting for the Double A train, I knew. I must make art like this. Wild images, dazzling colour, outrageous music, all mushing together like huskies led by Balto[1] himself to speed the sled, bearing life-saving soul medicine, to the ice-bound and blue needy of the world. Just a stoner trying to carry the message!"

Watching the new Fellini, on drugs, in the 1960s? Heady stuff indeed, and, with the Italian maestro at the height of his powers, hundreds of would-be film directors must have emerged from *Juliet of the Spirits*, or *8 1/2*, or *Satyricon*, knocked off their feet just like Ellison, dreaming of creating their own such wonders…

And, as often when the psychedelic shuttle lands and the reveller returns to *terra firma*, the morning after brought a slight recalibration of priorities. Ellison dryly reflects, "Another wannabe film maker would have picked up an 8mm camera and produced his first Academy Award-winning short that very night. I, however, was busy bluffing my way through high school, working in the hardware store on 8th Avenue, playing gigs with my band, chasing girls, and indulging in aforementioned chemical experiments…"

Hedonism aside, the gigs were Ellison's mainline. As one of 'Wayne and the Exceptions', he recorded a single, 'Have Faith', and went on tour: "The band was black, except for me," Ellison recalls. "Just the six of us, trying our best to sound like James Brown and the Famous Flames *and* his thirty piece band. People liked us and we worked all the time. We toured the South not long after Goodman, Chaney and Schwerner were murdered there.[2] There were still separate black and white facilities, even though they had been outlawed. The black audiences loved us. The white café owners didn't, especially when we tried to get served breakfast together. We recorded original music and hit the charts. But the band broke up when first one, then another member had to run from 'the authorities'. I would've joined or started another group but I couldn't understand why I was only able to sound like Sonny Rollins or Charlie Parker for a few notes and then fall apart. It never occurred to me that they practiced eleven or twelve hours a day. I practiced, on average, zero. Depressed and downhearted I took to cloud nine."

Despite his dreamer temperament, Ellison graduated high school and went to George Washington University in Washington DC. It was here that Ellison developed skills that would lead him to the film industry, studying drama and stagecraft with the University drama department, who recruited him to provide music and lighting for their productions. This in turn led to a job with the National Ballet, "touring the South again, only this time as an assistant stage manager. I drove the truck, loaded in, worked the day, then drove to the next town and did it again. When I returned to DC for some sleep, I landed a job as a PA with a production company doing Texaco spots with Jack Benny and Dennis Day, in Virginia."

With a spell in the music industry and the theatre already under his belt, Ellison turned his attention to the cinema: "I went to see classic and current movies several times a week, and by the time I transferred to NYU I was committed to being a filmmaker. I moved to New York and studied acting with Lee Strasberg and his crew in 1970-71. Lee was a short man who would attack with the ferocity of a rabid raccoon if you made an artistic choice he did not approve of." Ellison remembers tuition as, "An embarrassing trip with flying egos, but after more than a year of that I thought I had a handle on directing. In the year and a half I was at NYU I took every film course I could, and graduated."

Enter the Dubber

Leaving NYU in 1971 determined to get involved in the film industry, Ellison gravitated to post-production sound work. "I had learned how to do post synch and dubbing at school. So when I went up for an audition to dub Italian films into English, I got the job. Humble beginnings indeed, but I was working in film. Italian film! 35mm!!!" It was at this time that he made his first short: "A young blonde European woman I knew invited me to Jones' Beach. We drove out there at 110mph in her GTO convertible. On the sand, she offered me a new Alfa Romeo if I would marry her. I was completely confused until she explained that she wanted to be a US citizen. I couldn't go for it. But I did make a short 8mm film that day using her camera. I shot in sequence. It had some surreal elements and the sea. I used her as two different female characters and it worked. It was my first film." With a disdain for modesty that Fellini would have approved, he adds, "I think Federico would have liked it!"

In 1973, Ellison was still dabbling with other career options: "I was trying to be an actor, but it was very short-lived with nothing exciting to tell you, except this. George Romero wanted to cast me in *The Crazies*, and I read for that on video. I did an audition, and then I was on the road with the Harkness Ballet in Alabama, putting up shows. I get word from Romero's assistant, and she says, 'Mr. Romero likes you for the part and would like to see you

again.' And I said, 'I'm in Alabama, I'm working a job and it's going to take me through another month and a half. I could conceivably fly back, but I'd really be putting them in the lurch here. Is there any assurance? How close am I?' She said, 'It's down to you and two other guys, and he really favours you, but I really can't guarantee anything.'" Ellison let the opportunity go and stayed to finish his job in Alabama. "But I really never considered myself an actor anyway, I was doing it for the experience, to know how to handle myself and to learn about film. I'm not an actor type. I'm a musician, I'm very uninhibited when it comes to playing music, not for the self-aggrandisement of getting up in front of people but to share the music, that's where I'm comfortable. With acting, I become very self-conscious."

Ellison was hungry for more filmmaking experience, however it would be several years yet before his first feature materialised. In the meantime, he took whatever work he could to keep the wolf from the door: "Simon Nuchtern ran a great little production and post-production house in the Technicolor building. It was a wonderful place to get your hands on 35mm film and equipment. He approached me to dub, re-mix, score and re-edit movies that he and his clients would bring in from overseas. It was an excellent training ground. He was an editor, DP, tech wiz. It was there I had the opportunity to do all kinds of work on features, industrials, Hanna Barbera cartoons." Ellison worked on scores of titles that passed through Nuchtern's company: "I could never remember all the projects we did there," he laughs. "Sometimes I would come onto a picture where Simon had already done some work on it and pulled the title." Among the films Ellison recalls dubbing are: *The Bodyguard* (dir: Simon Nuchtern, 1976); *Revenge of the Streetfighter* (aka *The Streetfighter's Last Revenge*, dir: Shigehiro Ozawa, 1974); and the Bruce Lee biopic *Bruce Lee: The True Story* (1976) in which he voiced the actor playing Lee, 'Bruce Li' (real name Ho Chung Tao).

above:
Another GTO Films press sheet for the film.

top:
"You hear that, old lady? I'll punish you again!" Donny Kohler talks tough to the ghost of his mother, in **Don't Go in the House**.

above:
Ellen Hammill, in New York, 1978.

below:
The Ellisons in Hollywood, 1981.

Nuchtern's August Films handled a very wide range of film projects. This being New York in the 1970s, some were more 'august' than others, as Ellison explains: "We had every kind of movie coming through that place at the time. I remember at August you'd be showing a client, from say Ingersoll Rand,[3] through the place, and we'd be talking about drill bits and oil pumps, and you'd look in on the editing suites and somebody would have something on the screen that… 'Oh my God! Oh excuse me sorry,' and you'd quickly move onto the next door! It was just stunning what was going on up there! But the reason you didn't just cut and run was it was a place where you could get your hands on 35mm and really work with film, and where the hell were you going to do that in NYC? There was a very small film community there, and you were lucky to be in on it. Your clients would be United Artists, or you'd have really prestigious films like the IMAX film *To Fly!*, and also the sleazy guy down the hall who needed Simon to sync up the tracks for his porno film. I mean, it was amazing. A lot of people who went places went through there, and then there were a few people who were probably doing really bizarre things, too!"

Ellison found the experience of working with Nuchtern immensely enjoyable: "Simon was a very nice person to work with. I was really struggling in those days and he said to me, 'You know how to dub movies, don't you? Well I've always wanted to do that here, so how would you like to run my dubbing service? I'll get all the jobs, and you do all the work, and we'll split it fifty-fifty.' And I said, 'Hey, sounds like a deal to me!' He was great, he gave me an office, we got on well."

It was during this period, in the late Autumn of 1975, that Ellison met his future wife, Ellen Hammill: "Ellen and I met when I was location-scouting for a film Bob Megginson asked me to line-produce called *Pelvis*, which, when I worked on it, was an off-beat, low-budget comedy." *Pelvis* aka *Toga Party* was released two years later, with additional sex scenes said to have been directed by horror maestro Andy Milligan, although Ellison has no recollection of him: "Bob [Megginson]

told me years later that the producer of the film, not knowing what to do with it, shot additional sex footage, in a pathetic attempt to get some fast money out of the picture." When scouting locations for a café scene with the cameraman, Ellison happened into The Prince Street bar in Soho, New York: "It was a cold, grey November day, the 16th of '75 to be exact. We were waiting to order, scoping out the huge bar and century-old architecture, when a breathtakingly beautiful waitress smiled at me and asked what I wanted. After a few brief conversations, I told her what I really wanted was to take her out when she got off work. We have been together ever since. The day I met her was her second day of work at the bar and she quit on her third. She'd had a childhood wish to be a waitress, kind of romantic you know, but when that dream became a reality, it paled. She went on to work on *Saturday Night Live*, and help me with my various film projects."

In 1976, in Hollywood at the Todd-AO Studios dubbing one of the first IMAX films, *To Fly!*, into Japanese and Spanish, Ellison and Ellen Hammill took the opportunity to hawk the script for a "wholesome action film" of their own around town. "We had written it at the request of Alice Hsia, one of the owners of the Chinese production company that shot *Bruce Lee: The True Story*," explains Ellison. "She had requested that we write it, but she didn't pay us anything to do so. When we were done she said it would be too expensive for her company to make so we sent it to Hollywood. While we were out there we set up at the Beverly Hills Hotel, rented a [Mercedes] 450SL, and made the rounds like hot shots. Trying to turn 'no's into 'yes's takes time and money. We ended up staying at the Saharan Motor Hotel on Sunset. The 450SL was history. Everyone 'loved' the script but it was free love and nobody was eager to have a first time director on the project. Ellen asked me, 'What are we gonna do now?' Anyway, I said, 'We're going back to New York and make a horror film.' She said, 'You're crazy.'"

Crazy or not, Ellison was on the right track. A horror boom was just around the corner, and the genre was about to enter a new golden age. In 1977, while still looking for the ideal script for his own debut feature, Ellison saw an Italian film that blew him away: "There was a movie that I screened for Terry Levene of Aquarius one time, he asked me to look at some pictures for him when I was in Rome, to see if they were worth buying. Terry would buy something that had maybe two or three decent scenes in it, but the rest of it was junk, and then he would try to make it work. One of the films I saw was called *Ultimo mondo cannibale*, by Ruggero Deodato. You know that film? I gotta tell you, I think that's a brilliant movie! I saw it at a private screening in Rome, and it was stunning. So I called Terry that day and said, 'I think it's great.' He said, 'Yeah but they want too much money for it!', so that was the end of that. But that was an amazing piece of work, I thought."

The Europeans were gearing up for greater excesses, although the Italian market would only truly hit the motherlode with Lucio Fulci's *Zombie Flesh-Eaters* aka *Zombie*, in 1979, and Deodato's follow-up to *Ultimo mondo cannibale*, the astonishing and infamous *Cannibal Holocaust* (1980). America's horror renaissance was about to get under way: the success of John Carpenter's *Halloween* in 1978 set everyone's pulses racing, thrilling teen audiences and tantalising independent producers with its massive return for a relatively small investment. "When we got back to New York, I started asking around the editing rooms and barrooms, everywhere, looking for a story, script, something that would be a different, shocking film," Ellison says. "I was sure that with the successes of *Carrie* and *Halloween* it was the right way to go to get 'on the boards' – and after being sweet-talked to near-death in L.A. I knew I better do a project that required the least amount of dollars to make it happen."

"How did *Don't Go in the House* get made? Some people ask 'Why?'" - Ellison

Enter Joe Masefield, New York producer, scriptwriter and movie fanatic. Ellison met him in 1978 at an edit suite where he was cutting a picture. Masefield had a script that sounded perfect – nasty, but perfect: "Joe's treatment was about a disturbed man, abused as a child, who burns people to death. I said, 'It sounds creepy.' He said, 'I'll bring it in tomorrow.' The next day, he walked into my office and put on my desk a blue-laminated treatment, *The Burning Man*. I kind of got the chills. Reading it disclosed more promise than substance *but*, it had a twisted mother-son relationship reminiscent of *Psycho*. It had a unique weapon, the flame thrower, reminiscent of *Chain Saw Massacre* (and *The Flying Guillotine*) without the blood. I never thought blood was cinematic, sorry. It had the burnt corpses. Terrifying. And what if they could come to life! And what if we could actually spend time with this madman in the house? View his insanity. It wouldn't be a funhouse roller-coaster perhaps, but it would be dark and disturbing." Ellison found his mind racing with the possibilities: "The film would be blue, like the lamination on the treatment. Blue with fiery moments. And there was 'the metal room,' a most frightening place. And the story had a heart. A desperate child is taught to torture, then grows up and does what he's been taught to do. It was very sad. Perhaps too sad but horror has always been sad to me. I'm not a big horror film fan. I'd rather be scared doing spins in an airplane or driving too fast. Waiting for someone to murder someone else is really not my cup of tea. But, I believed that I had to make one and this seemed like the perfect nightmare. We could make most of the film in the house or sets that doubled for the house. We wouldn't need much money. We could do it! Joe Masefield said he would like to write the script. He would meet with us almost daily and then produce pages along the lines Ellen and I had discussed. But we were writing too. Masefield was moving fast but in the wrong direction, we thought. We had a meeting with him and told him we wanted to take the script another way. He said, 'You're pulling a Thalberg on me,' or something like that, meaning we had been working on an alternative version as we went. Apparently Irving Thalberg would hire multiple writers on the same project unbeknownst to the other writers. But Joe was okay with it all and we parted friendly – he was paid some up front and was paid in full when we'd raised enough to do so."

For Ellison, the iron was in the fire, and beginning to glow. He and Hammill pressed on with the script together. "I wish we had the writing skills we possess today back then, but we did the best we could with the very disturbing subject. We researched child-abuse and various psychoses.[4] We location-scouted while we wrote. After weeks of knocking on the doors of creepy houses all over the New York, New

Jersey area, and discovering scary stories unfolding within, we found it. We turned a corner in Atlantic Highlands, New Jersey and looked up the steep hill to the scariest house we had seen so far. Meeting the strange owners and looking through the cluttered but magnificent old place, we were spurred on to write scenes with specific rooms in mind. I was able to block the script in my mind as we wrote."

Once the screenplay was in place, a budget was assembled by associate producers Masefield, Matthew Mallinson and Dennis Stephenson.[5] "They did what they could to help us in production and we gave them a nice title," Ellison says. "Matt Mallinson was Ellen's assistant for a while. I was trying to get a camera to shoot the film. I did not want to use the blimped 16mm Arriflex that was owned by the post production facility I worked in. There was also an old 35mm Arri that looked like it had literally gone through the war. Then Matt came up to me and said that Ellen had left me a message. She had been to General Camera (Panavision in New York) and Dick DiBona, a great guy who had helped so many filmmakers get started, was enthralled with her. She just wanted to know if I wanted to shoot anamorphic or 185 Panavision. I felt like I had just won the Irish Sweepstakes. We had about enough money to rent that equipment for a day. Dick let us have it for *eight weeks*! There was a Screen Actors Guild strike on, and production was pretty slow. When we ran out of money and couldn't shoot for two weeks, Dick said to Ellen, when she called to ask if we had to return the equipment, 'Just finish your movie.' He was dynamite. In addition to Dick, there were some old gentlemen at Precision Labs without whom we could not have shot the film. Mr. Duryea and Walter Pruscewiecz were awesome. Lou Salvatore and Joe Dirito treated us like we were shooting a picture for Paramount. These guys knew what we were up against and wanted to help."

Matthew Mallinson recalls the arrangements slightly differently: "Neither Ellen nor Joe had done very much production, whereas I had done quite a bit. So I was giving them the nuts and bolts, setting up the labs, the camera deals, the footwork to get the stuff in place. We found a way of setting up a Panavision package for [dp] Oliver Wood if we trimmed out a lot of the accessories – what kills you on a

above:
Joe Masefield visiting the Ellisons, Friday, 21 September, 1984, New York City. (*left to right*): Elly and Joe Masefield, Ellen Hammill holding baby Catherine Lee, and Joe Ellison

below:
Joe Masefield (*left*) and John Tibbetts (*centre*, of the National Film Society) welcome the legendary Frank Capra (*right*) to the Artistry in Cinema Awards Dinner at the Beverly Wilshire Hotel in Hollywood.

Panavision package is the accessories. The reason people like to hire Panavision is that you can use every known conceivable gizmo that you might need, lenses, filters, and you can go a little bit crazy after a while, and the cost mounts up. So we cut a flat deal to use just the basic camera."

As pre-production warmed up on *The Burning Man*, Ellison was forced to leave his post with Simon Nuchtern's post-production facility: "He was a great guy but he didn't want me shooting a feature out of his place," Ellison explains. "I went off on my own in the middle of production and that was basically the end of our relationship."

Because Joe Masefield was withdrawing from the movie at this stage, Ellen Hammill's role was suddenly expanded to include producing the film as well as writing. "When Joe Masefield declined to line produce, Ellen asked me, 'Who is going to produce this movie?' Ellison relates. "I said, 'You are.' She said, 'You're crazy.' She did a super-human job." Matthew Mallinson recalls that Ellen Hammill cut a formidable figure as producer: "We had one kid who came down with pneumonia on the set. I said, 'We've got to get this kid back to the city,' and Ellen said, 'No we will not, if he goes back it'll be demoralising for the crew when they see what happens when someone gets a little sick.' I said, 'Ellen, it's pneumonia!' She gave in eventually because it became such a heated argument."

below:
The charred corpses of his victims advance on Donny Kohler in the climax of **Don't Go in the House**. Note: The stills set was prepared when the film still went by its original title, **The Burning**. Unfortunately, Tony Maylam's summer-camp slasher movie of the same name (incidentally an early production credit for future Miramax mogul Harvey Weinstein) beat it to the punch, necessitating a change of title.

"Donald! Come here!"
Shooting *Don't Go in the House*

Filming commenced in the suburban Atlantic Highlands, New Jersey, and Jersey City, about fifty miles out of New York City, in the winter of 1978. The first scenes to be shot were explosions on the freezing, wintry beach near Atlantic Highlands. "They were tests really," Ellison recalls, "but we used some of them in the dream sequence. We shot in an area where there were concrete bunkers, much like the ones the Germans had in Normandy, built to protect against a potential invasion during WWII. Seeing them while wearing my usual surplus field jacket and having twenty five people running around and blowing up things on my cue made me feel somewhat drunk with military power!"

The prime location, Donny Kohler's house, was used for both interior and exterior shots. There was no heat, few amenities, and little choice than to duke it out against the elements and pray that no one would curl up exhausted in an upstairs room and die of hypothermia. "That scary house was a dangerous place," Ellison stresses. "When we shot the mother's[6] dead scenes, we left a glass of water on the night table, broke for 'lunch' at about 8pm, and when we came back later that night,

THE BURNING

© MCMLXXIX Turbine Films, Inc.
All Rights Reserved

atlas
international

the water was *frozen*. We had a sub-zero set without the expense that William Friedkin went to on *The Exorcist*! When you see breath coming out of Donny's mouth at the end? Yes it was *that* cold. Same in the Jersey City Incinerator where we shot the fire scenes."

Cinematographer Oliver Wood, a Brit who started out as an assistant cameraman for BBC West in Bristol, moved to the USA in the 1960s. He lists Gianni Di Venanzo (who worked with Fellini) and Raoul Coutard (Godard's regular DP) as his primary influences. In 1970 he shot the astonishing black-and-white true-life crime story *The Honeymoon Killers*. "I was brought in by Martin Scorsese who left after a week because of creative differences with the producer," he recalls. "Leonard Kastle, who wrote the script, took over the direction of the movie." As for *Don't Go in the House*, he remembers discussing with Ellison that, "When the killer put on the mask we decided that we did not want to see his face. And we made a sort of doll's house out of the dead bodies. Jo and I had very similar views on how the movie should be shot, and he liked the way I lit it, although every now and then he wanted it to be darker – which was easy because we had no money to make it brighter!"

"The first shot at the main location was in the foyer of Donny's house, when he answers the phone call from Ben," says Ellison. "I remember the light broke through the clouds in the middle of a take and blazed through the bevelled glass windows. Oliver and I got an excited chuckle out of our good fortune. It was a memorable moment, just to be under way."

Ellison was very pleased with the performance of his lead actor Dan Grimaldi. The two first met when they were studying acting together and they remained friends, with Ellison occasionally hiring Grimaldi to do voice work on the movies he was dubbing. "He was not the obvious first choice for Donny Kohler," Ellison reflects. "I first envisioned him blond and frail, with a thoroughbred nervous twitch. But Danny brought a provincial, childish naiveté to the character. He was eager to get into the role even though it was quite a stretch. With the Strasberg technique we both had in common, and with the willingness we both had to play this thing out, we worked very well together. He gave a brave and convincing performance. Perhaps too convincing. Audiences seemed stunned and upset that this horror trip was somehow real." It's certainly true that audiences tend to be rattled and disturbed by the film more than excited in the lighter way. "Joe realised that what is lacking in most horror pictures is a focus on performance," says Matthew Mallinson, and it's true; we spend an awful lot of screen time with Donny Kohler. His childlike quality, and his torment, get under your skin.

If audiences were disturbed by Grimaldi, they were shocked almost out of their skins by the film's most rugged set-piece. Ellison recalls: "Oliver took sick the day we shot the fiery death scene. I was running camera, which was locked down. The effect was set up on two stages positioned ninety degrees from each other and the image came together in the lens. I was terrified that we were actually killing someone because it looked so real. I had to take my eye away from the eyepiece to be sure she was all right. The illusion was totally believable even to me. It upset me and I wondered 'What in the hell am I making here?' What would Fritz Lang have done? I was

trying to make my *Dr. Caligari* complete with off-angles, bizarre angular sets (although Donny's bedroom was not a set but an actual room in the house.)"

Matthew Mallinson remembers the night of the burning: "It started shooting around ten or eleven p.m. and went on until the early hours, maybe four a.m. We were having a lot of trouble getting the prism to line up the real body and the burning body. It was done in a space we had, a mini-sound stage. It was an in-camera effect, basically you saw what the end result was through the camera on set. We had a split prism: we were filming two hanging bodies simultaneously; one was a hanging dummy that we would burn, the other one was the victim. The split prism was then angled so they are superimposed in the camera and it looks like she's burning. The actress would wriggle around, of course, and so we would have to wriggle the burning body in the same fashion to follow her."

The brave actress whose naked writhing is the focus of the scene was Debra Richmond (billed as Johanna Brushay on the credits). "Debra modelled nude and studied art at Hunter College, where Ellen, who was there to paint, met her," Ellison recalls. "She and Debra became fast friends. Debra was a Playboy Bunny when I met her. She used to crack me and Ellen up talking about 'the Bunny Mother.' Ellen asked her if she would do the role and told her what it would demand. An actress we had booked for the part backed out when her boyfriend insisted that she quit." Fortunately, Richmond loved to take her clothes off on camera, and Ellison agrees with me that she gives a sterling performance: "As you say, she was a trouper. She didn't need any 'coaxing' but Ellen stayed with her throughout her scenes, just off camera. During the fire scene, which Peter Kunz had designed so simply and brilliantly, I was actually more upset than Debra was. As I mentioned earlier, she was nowhere near the fire but in the lens it sure looked like she was burning up. No one else on the set could see what I was looking at. The unblimped Arri 35 had the potential to leak light onto the frame if the operator took his eye off the eyepiece. But that's what I did, because I *could* believe my eyes. Then I'd look at her stage and she was fine, except for screaming and pretending to be burning. It was a surreal moment I assure you. I also must say that I was quite uncomfortable after shooting that

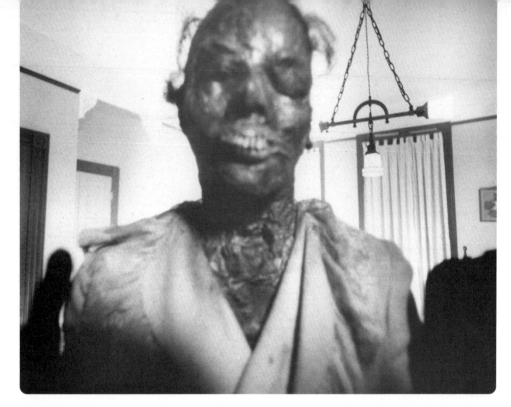

scene. It was just too disturbing. I kept telling myself that the audience wants to see this. And the story would not be complete without it. In those days, everything, *everything*, was being shown in film. If you tried to be 'tasteful' with a cutaway, especially in a low-budget film, you wouldn't get your picture out."

Having devised such a fiendish highlight of cinematic horror, the question then arose of how to realise the aftermath, with its wizened, blackened corpses. "To get the burnt corpse look was a quest in itself," says Ellison. "I had found a black and white photo of a GI hanging out of a tank on Guadalcanal. He was burnt charcoal black. I showed this picture to every make-up artist I interviewed. People would try all kinds of techniques to reproduce that look. One guy came in with tissue paper and some black liquid stuff and crumpled and moulded a burnt corpse cheek on the spot. But it was Tom Brumberger who was able to plan the whole thing: moulding the full suits, doing the detail touch-ups. I used ballet dancers for the corpses because I wanted them to move in a rather stylized way. Plus I knew they wouldn't quit. Dancers are great to work with; talk about troupers. Those girls shot take after take in the freezing cold *on the beach* in February for the dream sequence. I remember them shivering, but never complaining." Oliver Wood confirms the conditions were extreme: "For the beach scenes it was so cold that the batteries kept freezing and we could never get long enough takes."

Tom Brumberger told *Fangoria*'s Bob Martin,[7] "I suggested to them that we not try to attach prosthetics to the actresses, because the prosthetics could only make them look larger – and when you're burned you *shrink*, as you lose fluid. The director wanted the victims absolutely charred black, and skeletal, so I suggested that he use dancers who would be much slimmer than the actresses, but the same height. So that's what we did. I saw it a couple of times with audiences, and it worked. They assumed these were merely lifeless manikins – and at the end, when they came to life, the audiences *freaked*."

Something that may come as a surprise to the film's fans (it certainly surprised me) is that the film was entirely

dubbed, with nothing more than a guide track recorded on set. As a fan of Italian cinema I've grown used to dubbing, which in the case of the Italians was often done in a rather slipshod, hurried fashion. Perhaps due to a combination of Ellison's experience in dubbing other people's pictures, and the fact that he had his own cast re-recording their lines in the correct language (a rare occurrence in Italian productions), the results are pretty well indistinguishable from the 'real thing'. "There was camera noise right through the lens of those old 'Pan-Arris' – Panavision lenses fitted onto unblimped 35mm Arriflex cameras," Ellison explains. "They took a great picture but sounded like a coffee grinder. Much of the film was post-synched later, something which, as you know, I was quite familiar with. I guess that gives the film another Italian touch. I much prefer direct sound but when you're faced with options like 16mm blimped vs. 35mm Pan-Arri there is no contest."

As filming progressed, the mood lightened. "The clothing store scene was a Joe Masefield idea. I remember when I read 'The Matador,' I thought, 'Wow, what the hell is that?' But Ellen and I re-wrote the dialogue. David McComb, the actor in the scene, really got it, but the irony had been laid out far in advance. We were doing a cliché make-over scene – on a psychopath!" The levity increased as the crew moved to a discothèque to shoot Robert Osth as Ben, taking Donny out on the town. Ellison laughs: "I thought Bob was great. Some of the lines were written for a New York Italian *paisan*. But when Bob said those lines in his audition, we laughed like crazy and I realised he brought a whole different thing to the part. It was better his way. I cast him on the spot. The disco scene was shot in a club in New Rochelle, New York. We searched for months before we found a place that would let us set someone's hair (a special wig) on fire. That was another extremely long day. That night, before he succumbed to exhaustion, Oliver said to me, 'It's getting very near the end.' We just barely finished the scheduled work, doing the fight scene in the parking lot with the sun threatening to come up. Ellen and I still quote him, sounding like a burnt out Sgt. Pepper!"

"May I PLEASE use the phone?"
Post-Production and Marketing

And so, with the chills and thrills of the shoot at an end, February 1979 saw *The Burning*, as it was then known, whisked off to the post-production suite. Matthew Mallinson recalls, "Since it was low-budget we worked out of a place called 'Fantasmagoria', owned by this guy Keith Robinson. It was like, 'Give me a few bucks and you can work in my place when I'm not using it.' At the time, Keith was doing a lot of work for *Saturday Night Live*, the film segments, and so that was his bread and butter."

Ellison prepared a rough cut, and screened it for Aquarius Releasing's head honcho, Terry Levene. For Ellison this was the crunch time. He respected Levene's opinion on marketing and knew that he was guaranteed a fair shake: "Terry was a tough guy. When I met him he was in the business of buying very inexpensive pictures from Italy, Japan, wherever he could buy them from. He paid cash for them – people loved that, even if it was very little, they could count on *getting* that very little! He'd buy these Italian pictures that were great in the first half, and then the hero, after helping the kid and saving the girl would, like, shoot the cop or shoot the kid, and all of a sudden blow away his heroic standing: and we'd be just, 'Whoa!' Maybe there'd be some really amazing stunts, but no story. You'd see the first half-hour and think 'Wow, this is great,' and then they'd take this stupid turn and the whole movie would go down the drain. So we'd be charged with re-editing it, remixing it, dubbing it with a reworked script, doing new titles etc. It was great because I learned a lot from working on these things. But the point is, I valued Terry's advice about how to get a low-budget picture out. I invited him to a screening with some other people there. We screened it mid-day, and of course the sound is rough and it's a work cut, scratch music thrown in, and about halfway through the picture… Terry's snoring! I was traumatised! There were others there, young filmmaker types, and I felt like the loneliest man in the world! It was a disaster. And I remember saying to [editor] Jane Kurson at the time, 'Sharpen up your scissors, Jane!' And she said, 'My scissors are sharp! My scissors are sharp!' I thought, well if I don't do this… it may be a work of art but no one's going to see it. So I had to become an enemy of the original concept, try to compromise with what the audience wanted. And that's where I made some mistakes, but I also made the film viewable, and I was able to make a deal. The original running time was probably 98-102 minutes. It's 81 minutes now." And the difference between the two cuts? "I wouldn't say the longer version showed a positive side to Donny Kohler exactly, but it may have shown more of the victim side, a more innocent side."

With Levene's unenthusiastic response to goad him on, Ellison leaned hard into the wind to recut the film. Post production went on and on, and the money ran out twice. Kurson's experience as an editor proved invaluable (she had just come from editing *Pumping Iron*, the documentary that helped to launch Arnold Schwarzenegger in the USA), but in his haste to rescue the film, Ellison allowed Kurson to cut scenes that, on reflection, he wishes he'd kept in: "I had this wrestling match with her, she was being a good editor and saying, 'This isn't working, it's too long', but the problem was that she was really trying to trim it down so she wouldn't bore anybody, or make a bad cut, instead of trying to smash it together so that it would be shocking. There was a scene where Donny kisses one of the corpses and much more interaction between him and the girls in the room. Jimmy Kwei, who worked on the picture beginning to end and who became a successful editor, said, every time I saw him for years, 'I would have left the kiss in.' I loved that scene, and she took it out because it didn't cut. But it could have cut as part of a montage or something, maybe with an optical or two. Jane fought hard to keep it out and eventually I relented. I shouldn't have. And Donny talked back to the voices in his head a lot more, reading stories to the corpses and seeing them seemingly react. It was all much more developed."

So does the footage still exist? Ellison has both good and bad news for devotees of the film: "Actually it does. We did a TV version – which I don't believe was ever shown on TV! – and Viacom bought the rights for six years, I think, from Ed Montoro. When we recut the picture, that corpse-kissing scene was added because we needed more time – we'd had to cut so much of the graphic stuff that we needed to put stuff back in. I have a 35mm print of the picture, but I've lost my 16mm copy of the Viacom version, and that would have been interesting to see. It has other material that we didn't use in the theatrical cut."

Richard Einhorn, whose marvellous score adds muscle to the film's tension and unease, was a busy man at the time, scoring *Shock Waves* and *Eyes of a Stranger* for Ken Wiederhorn, and *The Prowler* for Joseph Zito. "He did some brilliant work for us," Ellison agrees. "He and I worked very well together. The disco tracks and the other source music I produced. When Richard played a cue for me, I would push him for more, and in the end he delivered sounds that I hear copied to this day." Apparently, there are no plans for a soundtrack album, which is a pity: Donny's disco infatuation and Einhorn's eerie electro-xylophone motif, plus his more abstract swampy electronics, would make a highly desirable collection.

At last, with a finished cut of the movie completed, it was time to seek distribution. And for once in this book the story does not take a sudden nosedive into the depths of despair. Ellison describes the marketing process: "My friend and colleague, Dieter Menz of Atlas International, for whom I had dubbed many foreign films – German, Italian, Japanese, Chinese, Filipino, etc. – asked me to let him represent *House* at MIFED in Milano. I had shown the film to Paramount who said, 'Let us know what other people think.' (Really.) We had not made a deal instantly as I had expected. We had no money left. I trusted Dieter more than almost anyone in the film business, so I said okay. My friend Varoujan 'Peter' Aghbolagi accompanied me and Ellen to Milano to market the movie. He loved the idea of coming and he paid for the trip. (He was paid back when we sold the film.) I'm sad to say, Peter died a couple of years ago. Arriving in grey Milano in October of '79, Dieter informs us that he has set up only one screening, for Thursday. We had to wait most of the week to see if we were to make any real progress. Dieter showed us an offer for Argentina by Tuesday, and we had a few other offers for places like Sri Lanka, but we had to wait for our big screening to see what we could expect. Everyone had warned me, 'Don't be surprised when they walk in and walk out of your screening. The buyers there have to see a lot of films and they have to keep moving.' Thursday came. Ellen, Peter and I sat in the screening room. A few people wandered in. Then a few more. By the time the film

above:
James 'Jimmy' Kwei edited **Don't Go in the House**, and went on to become a regular collaborator with Martin Scorsese, acting as assistant editor to Scorsese's regular editor Thelma Schoonmaker on **After Hours**, **The Color of Money**, **Goodfellas**, **Casino**, **Bringing Out the Dead** and **Gangs of New York**. He also assisted Frank Henenlotter, editing his brilliant lysergic monster movie, **Brain Damage** (1988).

below:
Donny models the only outfit he feels truly comfortable in…

started, the screening room was full. Soon after, the three of us had to leave to make room for more. Dieter was outside, shoving people in and forcing the door closed behind them like a Japanese subway conductor! The room was packed. Only two people left the screening, buyers from Sweden. It was explained to me that they did not allow nudity and violence in the same film in Sweden. When the film ended, the doors flew open and Dieter, Ellen and I were attacked – by hopeful buyers! I saw some people I knew from Italy, some from Asia, and I was chatting with an Italian distributor when Dieter grabbed me forcefully by the arm and said, 'Come meet Mr. Montoro,' as he basically pushed me toward Ed Montoro, President of Film Ventures. Dieter was helping me get a US distribution deal while he himself was only asking for rights outside of the US. See what I mean about Dieter? He of course would gain from a good US deal: better publicity, a good US track record, which of course would help him sell worldwide. But he never asked for anything from the US deal he helped to make happen. Meanwhile, Bob Shaye (New Line Cinema, whom I had worked for dubbing Sonny Chiba movies and others) made a bid for the picture. So did AVCO Embassy. But by making a deal with FVI and keeping worldwide rights exclusive of the US for Dieter, we were able to pay our investors."

Don't Go in the House opened wide, reaching Seattle, New York and Los Angeles, and was promoted on TV, with ads running in prime-time during *Saturday Night Live*. It also played drive-ins, with John 'Bud' Cardos's *The Dark*, and did fair theatrical business in the UK (where it was savagely cut for an 'X' certificate). Most importantly in Britain, the film performed excellently on video rental, with the uncut version unleashed by VideoSpace in the days before video certification.

"You scarred my sister for life!"
– Audience Reaction

Don't Go in the House is not a film that warms the heart of your average horror hound. Which is ironic, given the way horror fans virtually beg the genre to assault their sensibilities. Horror films *should* shock, they should leave you wrung out, troubled, shaken. Your mind should be plagued with images that linger for days. It's a lesser brand of horror that merely tickles the belly of your fears. For me, *Don't Go in the House* easily transcends its low-budget limitations, and the occasional flaws count for nothing next to its ferocious violence and seeping morbidity. There are popular films in which men kill tens, hundreds, even thousands of people, with the sort of gung-ho mindlessness that makes Donny Kohler seem like a struggling Saint. *Don't Go in the House* makes sure you *feel* the fear and horror. Donny is stuck inside his sickness, and the film portrays him as a lost soul, a feeble creature driven by forces he can never overcome. His 'wickedness' is truly horrific, but he's pathetic, victimized. No one is going to get their aggressive jollies by 'identifying' with Donny Kohler.

Ellison took the trouble to discuss his script with psychologists before shooting began: "We described the patterns of behaviour in the script, and they said yes, as a matter of fact it's classic. The conversations were not too in-depth because it was so obvious that the material was a classic case. It was perhaps a little obvious that he would use fire, I mean that wasn't necessarily part of the psycho-

logical make-up, but we knew that child abuse could bring out psychosis. We tried to keep a logic to it so it wasn't just gratuitous. I remember one review that said there's an attempt to make this seem like a socially redeeming picture but it's just an exploitation film and it's pretentious that the filmmakers were trying to do this. A lot of people seemed to get really angry."

During the horror boom of the early 1980s, it was common for mainstream reviewers to review the audience as well as the movie, in their efforts to 'prove' that the new wave of explicit horror was a bad influence on society. If someone cheered or laughed during a murder scene, it was reported with the relish of a born killjoy, and used to demonstrate that horror pandered to the worst in human nature (egregiously implying that the film would therefore stimulate real-life violence in its audience). Even a clever writer like Pauline Kael routinely propped up her subjective opinions by conducting a specious survey of audience reaction. But according to Ellison, no one was ever likely to make such a case against *Don't Go in the House*: "We'd play in the same multiplexes where they were showing *Friday the 13th*, for instance, and I'd go into the other theatre playing that film and you'd hear screams and giggles and see kids hugging and getting all excited and having fun being grossed out by all the blood. But then you'd go in to *Don't Go in the House*, you know, and there'd be like dead fucking silence! [laughs] Nobody was hugging *anybody*! They were just agape, you know, like 'Oh my God what *is* this?' I thought, gee I've failed."

"You didn't fail," I interject, "You just made the archetypal bad date film!"

"Exactly! The perfect description!" Ellison laughs. "What I was trying to do was get this 'being at home with the monster' thing, you know? I wanted to be at home with this fellow. What does he do in the afternoon? I was curious. What does a madman do when he's not killing? I didn't mean it to be a misogynist statement, but I can understand why people took that from it. I felt I was making something different to all the other films of its type. To say that sounds egocentric, because I was not a film master, it was my first feature; but that was my attempt to do what I thought the material called for. I knew there were exploitative aspects from the start, mind you. That scene in the metal room was key to getting the film released. And yet there are no other scenes quite like it in the film – no other scenes quite like it, period! I did some work at NYU but I did not actually shoot another film of my own until *Don't Go in the House*. That's my student film! And when people criticise it I look at things like *Who's That Knocking at My Door* by Scorsese or that first Coppola picture *Dementia 13*, and think, well, kicking off with *Don't Go in the House* isn't so bad."

"Can I play my music loud?"
Joey and After…

After *House*, Ellison was, if you like, burned out with the horror genre. Even when Ed Montoro offered him the opportunity to make another horror film straight away, to be shot in Los Angeles and with the money already lined up, he said no. As a devotee of *Don't Go in the House*, I resist the temptation to scream at him and, as calmly as possible, ask why: "Sometimes even Ellen doesn't get this," he laughs. "The idea of making a slasher film purely for marketing was something I couldn't do. I could only imagine Ed calling me on location to say that he had seen the dailies and 'We need more blood, Babe!' But the fact that I was so turned off horror created an opportunity: a horror film send-up. Ellen and I came up with *Scary Movie*. And yes, it was exactly the concept which has recently been so successful. Take the most popular horror films of the past few years, and exaggerate them. Pay the screams off with laughs. We wrote a very funny script which some producers wanted to buy/steal and probably kick us out of the picture. But just as we were sending the script all over Hollywood to agents, producers, anyone who would read it, Frank Lanziano, 'Frankie Lanz', a friend who had invested in *House*, made me an offer. Frankie was a Wall Street guy who produced and hosted the Royal New York Doo-Wop Show. He was a natural talent who had been a DJ in his former life. Loved the music and produced one hell of an oldies show, first at the Beacon Theatre in New York and later at Radio City Music Hall. Frankie wanted to make a film about his show. I had seen far too many documentaries on Golden Oldies. No one cared. In fact, Radio City people told me that the show sold out for two or possibly three days a year but if they ran more than three shows, the place would be empty. 'It's always the same people that come to the show every year,' is what they told me. It seemed essential that a feature film should involve the younger generation in the story. Oldies and new music. A father/son story. I went to work on *Joey*. When Warners screened the picture, they said, 'It's really wholesome, yeah, kiss of death.' But, 21st Century offered double the negative cost of the movie and Frankie, in good faith, took the deal. They were a public company and they went broke by the fourth payment. It was extremely difficult to replace the distribution deal. Everybody wanted to make sure 21st Century no longer had rights to the film. It went on and on. Finally, another company opened the picture in limited theatrical release designed to live up to the bare minimum of their contract. It got good reviews but with no advertising, this 'wholesome' film with *great* music, old and new, was pulled by the distributor who didn't want to invest a dime in getting it properly exposed. They spent almost nothing on advertising. They just made a great deal for themselves selling it to HBO and then other ancillary markets. We used a guy to clear the music and several of the recent rock producers reneged on their deal. They claimed *Joey*'s music rights were limited and were expiring. It was a nightmare. That's why copies of *Joey* are so rare. We had The Silhouettes ('Get a Job'), The Elegants ('Little Star'), Screamin' Jay Hawkins ('I Put a Spell on You'), The Manhattans ('Boy from New York City'), Vito and the Salutations, ('Unchained Melody'), The Teenagers ('Why Do Fools Fall in Love?'). The oldies groups were great and we never had a problem with them. We created an oldies group, The Delsonics, who seemed like an original group but were fictitious. Their oldies song was new but sounded like an old hit, 'Moonlight Love'. With the insurmountable problems releasing *Joey*, I realised that I could no longer go to an investor and say, as I had said with *House*, 'Let me have some money to make my film, and if I'm alive when it's done, you will get your money back.' There were too many dishonest people in the picture business. The deals were at the indie producer's disadvantage. Living with the FVI deal was bad enough. At least I was able to force some payments out of Ed and between that and Atlas get my investors money to them. But this *Joey* thing was impossible. You end up with no control and therefore no

ability to do what you would want to do. You can't make promises because you won't be able to keep them."

Ellison reflects on his latter-day film experiences: "My best scripts, which I wrote on spec, were never produced. I worked in Hollywood doing scripts for TV, I was hired to write a script for Carol Burnett, and I started doing post-production again, as Ellen went to law school and had two daughters with me. (I've asked them not to watch *House* but if they ever did to please find it within their hearts to forgive me!) I also had some work stolen from me. While I acknowledge that similar ideas and 'high concepts' can be generated by different people in different places, I am sure that *The Thirteenth Floor*[8] was stolen from me at least twice. I exposed it to many people, some of them the wrong people, and I've seen pathetic versions of it, not just using the title."

In the 1990s, tired of the film business, Ellison returned to his music, and by reinvesting in his first passion made a new life for himself: "In the end, while taking better and better meetings, writing better scripts, and being

above: Those were the days… Horror fans were spoiled for choice in the early summer of 1980, with the newly released **Friday the 13th** and Ellison's contribution to the genre playing the same theatre. According to writer and documentarian of the era Bill Landis, the Cinerama, located on Broadway and 47th Street, was "an upscale grindhouse" which charged a dollar-fifty more than the others for admission, a pricing policy that kept out the dangerous "Deuce riffraff" who prowled the sleazier theatres. Cinerama 2 was actually the converted balcony of the old one-screen Cinerama, and boasted plush red seating and décor with a Roman Coliseum theme. Ellison must have known it well – during the mid-seventies it played many of the kung-fu action movies he worked on for Simon Nuchtern's August Films.

opposite:
The big scene, sure to have sent a few distressed punters to the exit…

THE BURNING

© MCMLXXIX Turbine Films, Inc.
All Rights Reserved

atlas international

above:
"He wasn't evil but it covered him up... the cover of the flame..." One of Donny's workmates at the New Jersey incinerator plant suffers an accident, while Donny (not pictured) looks on without assisting.

right:
Ellison at work on the film.

below:
Look out for Donny on the dancefloor, with this 12" single released in 1979 featuring the wonderful "Struck by Boogie Lightning" as used in the film's unforgettable 'disco inferno' scene.

encouraged to death, it was all bologna. It was wrenchingly difficult but I turned my back on the film business. By getting away from the whole right-brain thing for a while, I found that my musical abilities came back stronger than ever. I started composing music again and that is what has saved my soul. As for the future, I won't rule out the possibility of making another film, but it seems a remote possibility. I have found that my favoured medium of expression is a two-and-a-half-minute song rather than a one-and-a-half-hour movie."

Even if Ellison does return to the cinema, it's unlikely that he'll do so in the extreme mode of *Don't Go in the House*. The film is a glorious, shocking experience, utterly of its time, and never to be repeated. For star Dan Grimaldi, *House* is the highlight of his career so far... unless you count a recurring role in the smash TV show *The Sopranos*, as 'Patsy' Parisi. It's about time, though, that *Don't Go in the House* was re-assessed; for providing the horror genre with one of its most shocking set-pieces, on a par with the best work of Lucio Fulci, Dario Argento and Tobe Hooper, and for its accomplished mix of humour, horror and melancholia. Let's light a candle for the burning man...

Footnotes

[1] An heroic Alaskan husky dog immortalized as a statue in Central Park, New York City.

[2] Michael Schwerner, Andrew Goodman and James Chaney were civil rights workers murdered by the Ku Klux Klan in Mississippi in 1964 – the case forms the basis of the film *Mississippi Burning*.

[3] A top-line American business specialising in construction and mining machinery.

[4] My own research led me to the case of Joseph Kallinger, apprehended in 1975 for several home invasions involving sexual molestation and culminating in murder. Kallinger's is a truly bizarre case: he murdered one of his sons to claim an insurance policy, and took the other, aged just twelve, out with him as an accomplice to his attacks on women. Whilst it's overly simplistic to lay the blame for any adult's behaviour at the feet of their parents, Kallinger's childhood was horrendous. Adopted by extremely sadistic Catholic parents, he suffered gross mistreatment and humiliation. When he was admitted to hospital for a hernia operation at the age of six, his mother told him the surgery was to stop his penis growing. Like Mrs. Kohler in *Don't Go in the House*, Kallinger's mother exerted her discipline by making the boy hold his hand over an open flame, beating him if he cried. And like Donny Kohler, Kallinger grew up to take pleasure in torturing others. Kallinger was also an arsonist in his youth. He wrote poetry on the subject, an example of which is striking in this context:
> *Oh, what ecstasy setting fires brings to my body!*
> *What power I feel at the thought of fire!*
> *...Oh, what pleasure, what heavenly pleasure!*"

[5] When I asked Matthew Mallinson who Dennis Stephenson was, he laughed: "All I know is, Ellen said he gave her a thousand dollars!"

[6] Ruth Dardick, who played Donny Kohler's mother, also played Bruce Lee's mother in a film by Matthew Mallinson called *Fist of Fear, Touch of Death* (1980).

[7] In *Fangoria* #27.

[8] A script Ellison copyrighted in 1986.

JOSEPH ELLISON: FILMOGRAPHY AS DIRECTOR

1971	*Untitled* (8mm short – 7mins)
1979	*Don't Go in the House* aka *The Burning* (original screen title) aka *The Burning Man* (script title)
1986	*Joey*
1990	*World of Horses* (TV)

chapter 9

If You Go Down in the Caves Today...

Mark Sawicki & Chris Huntley on the making of The Strangeness

The Strangeness (1980)

The Gold Spike mine has a bad reputation. It was abandoned several times until its final closure in the 1890s, and rumours abound of a ravening creature lurking in its depths, said to have killed scores of miners. Now, an exploration party comprising Hemmings, a mining engineer (Rolf Theison); two mining consultants, Calvert (Dan Lunham) and Ruggles (Chris Huntley); Angela Platt, a geologist (Diane Borcyckowski); and writer Dan Flanders and his wife Cindy (Mark Sawicki and Terri Berland), have hired Morgan (Keith Hurt), a British-born miner with knowledge of the tunnels, to help them assess its suitability for re-opening. Flanders is researching a book about the place, and both he and Morgan regale the rest of the party with stories of the Gold Spike's violent past. As the party travel further and further into the maze of tunnels, the stories seem less and less fanciful...

The Strangeness is a real team effort, made on a very low budget by a dedicated band of friends, and its abundant charm is a credit to their ingenuity. Concerning a Lovecraftian menace lurking in an abandoned mine, it rewards the viewer's persistence with an ominous atmosphere, flashes of humour, and a particularly startling monster tucked away in the film's final reel. Among the difficulties encountered on the way are a few too many dialogue scenes, over-ambitious low-level lighting that slips off the scale into eye-strain territory, and some lapses of logic and continuity, meaning that it's easy to lose track of what's going on. It's a film that's never going to win over sceptics, but if you're a monster movie fan or a cine-spelunker accustomed to rooting around in the further-flung caves of the genre it's definitely worth your while.

"For a mine it sure looks like a cave," says Cindy, as the group descend into the dark. Well, for a set it sure looks like a location! Explanations of how the film was created follow in the interview with Sawicki and Huntley, but suffice to say the sets are superbly realised – certainly enough to fool this viewer, who believed the film was shot in real mine workings throughout. Once we're underground the illusion is watertight, compensating well for the shortcomings of the script.

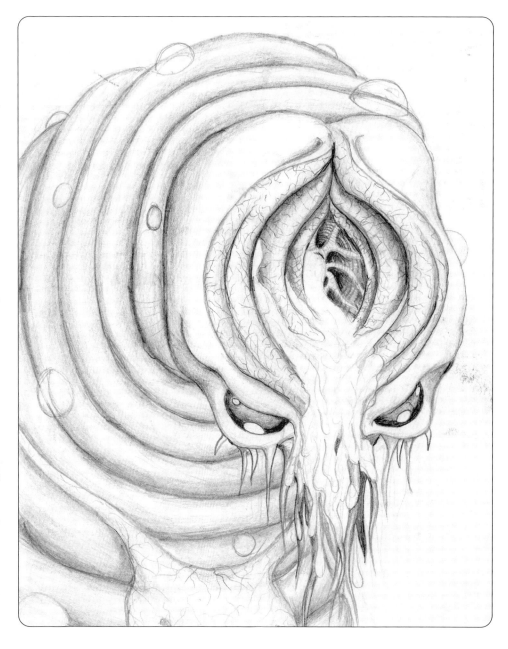

The Strangeness
© 1980. Stellarwind
A Stellarwind production.
director: David Michael Hillman. producers:
David Michael Hillman, Mark Sawicki, Chris
Huntley. writers: David Michael Hillman, Chris
Huntley. cinematography: Kevin O'Brien,
Stephen Greenfield. editor: David Michael
Hillman, Andrew Rodney. special visual
effects: Mark Sawicki, Chris Huntley. additional
scenes director: Chris Huntley. camera
operators: Kevin O'Brien, Stephen Greenfield,
Bob Zalk. camera assistant: Andrew Rodney.
sound recordists: Bob Zalk, Anthony Probst.
matte artist/additional animation: Ernest D.
Farino. music: David Michael Hillman, Chris
Huntley. key grip: Kathy Hanau. sound editor:
Tom Scurry. negative cutter: Anthony Probst.
re-recording engineers: Tom Scurry, Chris
Huntley. processing: HFE. re-recorded at Scott
Sound. main title design: Ernest D. Farino.
Special thanks to: Frank & Gertrude LaBash;
Robert & Trudie Hillman; Dave Bell Associates;
Tech Camera; L.A. County Fair Association;
Mr. & Mrs. Emmett Irwin; Title House; Sean
Phillips; Harry Miller; Tom Meshelski; Larry
Nielson; Jim & Marlene Kazen; Kip Hanan;
Mike Berland; John Phillips; Dr. Marvin
Rodney; Chuck Klasky; Mr. & Mrs. G.N.
Huntley; Richard Huntley; Richard Gill; Susan
Nicola; Robert Anders; Jamie Garrison; Steve
Champagne; Robert Huntley; The City of
Newport Beach; Kevin Gilson. A Very Special
thanks to Mary Hillman. filmed in the city of
Newport Beach.
Cast: Dan Lunham (Geoff Calvert). Terri
Berland (Cindy Flanders). Rolf Theison [Pavo
Bloomquist] (Myron Hemmings). Keith Hurt
(Morgan). Mark Sawicki (Dan Flanders). Chris
Huntley (Tony Ruggles). Diane Borcyckowski
(Angela Platt). Robin Sortman (Brian). Arlene
Buchmann (Amy).

previous page:
One of Chris Huntley's preliminary drawings
for the monster.

First to die is geologist Angela, and we can deduce that she's the least popular member of the party from the rather casual way the others move on after she's trapped, presumed dead, in a rock fall. The film needed a death at this point, for sure, but the lack of an emotional aftermath makes the group seem rather callous. Perhaps realistic shock and hysteria would have been difficult to sustain at such an early stage (after all, it would surely propel everyone to the surface again), but it's something that should probably have been addressed in the script. Structural errors like this show the writers (director Hillman and actor/spfx man Huntley) getting to grips with their craft, and while there are decently-written character scenes throughout, the fact that they take place aside from the storyline suggests that narrative structure was not the team's strong suit.

The screenplay makes up for its callowness in other ways. As if to pre-empt criticisms of hokiness, Sawicki – playing would-be writer Dan Flanders – provides a running commentary, breathlessly exaggerating everything as the party enter and explore the mine. It's as if the film is taking the mickey out of its own clichés: you can imagine Flanders's words, spoken perhaps by John Carradine, gracing a lurid, hyperbolic movie trailer. It's a risky approach that could have lessened the atmospherics and kept the viewer at arm's length, but the filmmakers get away with it by depicting Flanders as a bit of a dweeb (and like Woody Allen at times). In one of the best dialogue scenes, he 'interviews' sardonic old Morgan, supposedly seeking material for his book. The older man spins him tall tales and elaborate jokes – but the humourless Flanders fails to notice his leg is being pulled. When the penny finally drops, he acts as if Morgan has been wasting his time, instead of recognising the man's teasing as exactly the kind of 'colourful' character material a writer could use.

Fans of the film must surely be holding their breath for a DVD transfer from the original negative, because if ever a film needed the strong blacks and heightened clarity of the digital medium, this is it. What is at least clear from the video release (and the marginally better, though extremely rare, budget DVD from 23rd Century) is that the film stands or falls by its lighting – a precarious position considering the unforgiving nature of early 1980s video transfers. O'Brien and Greenfield's cinematography wrings variety from a succession of rock walls and cramped tunnels by employing coloured gels and eerie lighting effects on the actor's faces, but when the image dwindles down to a couple of weak torch-beams the production hits the limits of audience tolerance.

top right:
One of the UK video releases for
The Strangeness, this one from the
excellent VTC label.

right:
A grisly fate awaits explorers of the
abandoned Gold Spike mine…

The Strangeness has no need of excuses for its fabulous stop-motion monster, a demented tentacled phallus with a gaping, undulating urethral opening. Such a provocative combination of phallic and vaginal imagery is spot-on when it is considered that the story is set almost entirely in caves, suggesting fear of the womb, castration and all the Freudian/Kristevan baggage that accompanies such notions. (You'll forgive me if I don't get out my pickaxe and shovel here: I'm *so* over psycho-analytical theory.) In the interview accompanying this review, monster designer Chris Huntley admits that he worked on this Freudian nightmare without considering its symbolic aspects, but it's thanks to his naiveté that the film can boast a genuine creature from the Id. It's a guaranteed 'Wow!' for monster fans and well worth the wait for the moment when it finally appears. Huntley's monster looks like a country cousin of H.R. Giger's creations for *Alien*, and for fans of the BBC's long-running horror/sci-fi show *Doctor Who* it also brings to mind the similarly obscene Fendahleen in the creepy 1977 tale *Image of the Fendahl*. In fact it's such a treat that it's a pity the filmmakers didn't give it more of an airing earlier in the story.

The Strangeness is a light-weight entertainment and there's no point trying to say otherwise, but it's exactly the sort of film that makes rooting around at film fairs such fun; for all its flaws it's been made with guts and spirit and determination. From its wonderful title (which was my initial reason for buying the video) to its eye-opening, gender-busting monster finale, this precursor to such recent hits as *The Descent* and *The Cave* may not win any prizes, but it's well worth a look if you love the shadowy recesses of the genre.

Introducing Mark Sawicki

Mark Sawicki, personable star, co-producer and effects designer of *The Strangeness*, was born in Jackson, Michigan on 10 September, 1956. "My father was a Russian dancer during the Depression, but by the time I came along he and my mother owned a neighbourhood grocery," he explains. "We lived above the store. When the supermarket chains wiped out small groceries they moved into real estate and insurance sales. They were about my age now when they did this and I'm particularly impressed with them, since now I'm facing the demise of traditional camerawork, with the digital era."

Like monster-movie fanatic Doug McKeown (see chapter on *The Deadly Spawn*), Sawicki caught the stop-motion bug early: "I started playing and sculpting with clay at the age of three. My first memories of cinema came from drive-in movies that my older brother Tom would take me to. He would sit in front with his date and I would sit on books in the back, as chaperone, and witness Godzilla or Vincent Price light up the screen. Two of my favourite films were Roger Corman's *The Raven* and Ray Harryhausen's *Mysterious Island*. I became a Harryhausen fan and a stop-motion fanatic. When I was about twelve years old I discovered my parents' seldom-used Super-8 home movie camera and discovered that I could animate my clay characters with it. From then on through high school and early college I would make short little animated clay films. I was also exposed to acting and appeared in numerous school plays and community theatre productions."

On leaving high school, Sawicki found that his passion for the movies was ably supported by his parents, who sent him to USC Film School for two years. It was there that he met all of the friends with whom he would go on to make *The Strangeness*, including director David Hillman, Sawicki's partner in film class. "We made two films together in our second semester," Sawicki recalls. "At USC these films were referred to as 310s, which was the number of the class: the assignment was to make two black and white 16mm films with sync sound and no dialogue. The purpose was to force the student to relate a story visually without reliance on verbiage, an excellent exercise that handed down the traditions of silent film and pictorial language. Two students would partner up and trade places being director and cameraman. I went first, with my film *It Stalked the Night*, which related a true story of me trying to sneak a girlfriend out of the house without my parents noticing. All the action was counterpointed with a made up movie soundtrack that played on the television the father character was watching during the 'escape'. Unfortunately, by the time David got to direct his film he had to leave school to support his wife and family, so he became an absentee film partner. We nonetheless finished his film, starring Pavo Bloomquist [credited as Rolf Theison in *The Strangeness*), about a man who loses himself in a fantasy world that goes awry. The film had many in-camera effects and was an early training ground for me. It was entitled

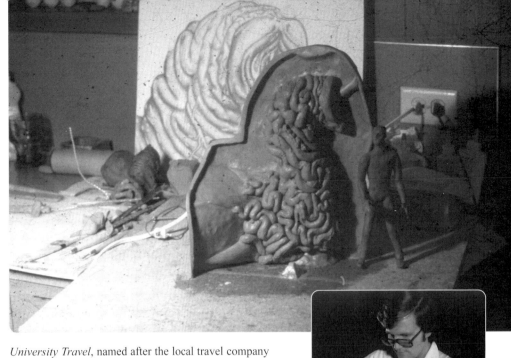

University Travel, named after the local travel company that allowed us to use their storefront as a 'looking glass' that Pavo could pass through into his fantasy world."

Sawicki directed his graduate film *Origins* at USC, winning both a Silver Hugo and a Cine Silver Eagle. The film drew heavily on his youthful interest in special effects: "*Origins* depicted the creation of an alien world from an explosive starburst, the genesis of life in the sea, rising continents and the spawning of alien life on the land, all to be destroyed by yet another starburst that became the alpha and omega of everything. Pretty ambitious. The one big failure in the film was the recognition by the audience that I shot a lava lamp for some of the effects sequences, which gave the trick away. Other than that I think it was pretty successful as a mood piece."

On graduating, Sawicki returned to Jackson, Michigan, but after the excitement of USC, Jackson appeared to offer little advancement. For a while it seemed as though the film school adventure might lead nowhere… "Then I received a call from Peter Donen of Cinema Research Corporation, an optical printing facility. He had seen *Origins* at USC and invited me back to Los Angeles to clean film elements and run a black-and-white processor. I owe my entire career to Peter and I'm sorry to report that he passed away on 1 January, 2004. He was the son of Stanley Donen and he gave many untried people their first break."

above:
Mark Sawicki at work.

top:
The mould for the monster.

below:
Sawicki comments: "A shot of me sculpting a small tentacle. The hairdryer in the foreground was used to create veins. I discovered that by using the hairdryer I could melt the surface of the oil base clay and blow it about to make subtle veins and arteries."

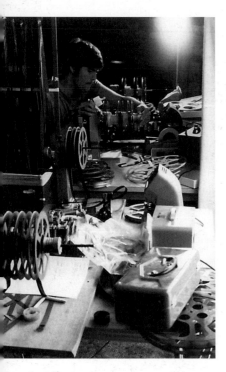

Introducing Chris Huntley

Chris Huntley was born in Long Beach, California in 1958. Like Sawicki, for as long as he can remember he's loved sci-fi, fantasy, and horror movies. "My earliest nightmares were inspired by *20,000 Leagues Under the Sea*, *The Outer Limits*, and later even *Star Trek*," he recalls. "I went on a summer-school field trip to Los Angeles when I was fourteen, and went to several studios including Warner Bros. – they had recently finished filming *Willard* (1971). They still had lots of fake rats around the special effects and prop house. I was in heaven!"

Work on *The Strangeness* provided Huntley with valuable new experience, thanks to his fellow artists. "Most of the effects expertise came from Mark Sawicki, with some help from Ernie Farino. Mark knew how to create paraffin wax explosions, knew a lot about stop motion animation, and more. I knew how to make miniature models and build sets. I'd been making (and blowing up) models since I was a child. The rest we sort of figured out on our own. I'd been making short films since I was in the single digits. There was one occasion when I staged a fire outside my parents house on the cement driveway. I had my brothers run in to tell the babysitter about the fire. She ran outside screaming as I tried to film her. Unfortunately, there was a technical problem and the film jammed. The babysitter wouldn't do a second take... I also made films in high school."

At USC, Huntley met Mark Sawicki and David Hillman: "Mark was a junior and I was a freshman," he explains. "I tagged along with Mark most of the time. He was very patient. At that time Mark and I also shared an apartment on campus with two other fellows. David had big aspirations and was really good at inspiring others to get involved. In the summer after their 310 [graduation] projects, the three of us decided to write a script together, called *The Terminator* – unfortunately, not *that* Terminator!"

The Elusive David Michael Hillman

Sadly, director David Hillman, born in 1955, has remained impossible to trace for this book. Sawicki has nothing but praise for him: "David was a wonderful gentle man, born and raised in Burbank, California. A true native. He was very happy-go-lucky and easy to work with. He always had grandiose ideas and a dollar-ninety-eight to do them! He could talk you into doing anything, and after you did 'the impossible' he was genuinely grateful. He didn't nitpick everything apart as many people do when they get things for nothing. If a shot didn't work as well as he hoped, he would edit around it. David was an editor by trade and prided himself on using editing to make up for filmic shortcomings. After *The Strangeness* I worked with him several times more, mostly on low-budget educational films, but it was always fun. No money, but fun." Sawicki has no idea where he is now, though: "He's pulled an *Eddie and the Cruisers*, if that means anything to you. It's a film about someone who willingly fell off the face of the earth. So David, I guess, will remain a mystery wrapped in an enigma..."

above:
Chris Huntley examining some footage.

top right:
The ever-mysterious David Michael Hillman viewing a scene on the editing table.

above:
Mark Sawicki adjusts focus on one of the fx cameras.

right:
The monster in the cave interior model.

Pre-Production

According to Huntley, the planned film began, not with a script or even a title, but a budget. In order to arrive at the lowest possible 'realistic' budget for a full length feature, the decision was taken to shoot in 16mm, aiming for a 4:1 shooting ratio. They estimated that they could make a film in this way for the tiny sum of just $15,000. Spurred by a single investor's offer of $10,000, Huntley and Hillman began work on a script. The team decided that a horror movie was not only the ideal means to exploit their skills as model-makers and effects designers, but also fell within their modest financial reach. Not only that, but in 1979 horror was enjoying another of its frequent upswings in popularity, with big hitters like *Halloween*, *Phantasm*, *Alien* and *Dawn of the Dead* packin' 'em in and attracting good notices. "Having decided the genre, we needed a story and location," explains Huntley. "We put the cart before the horse – that is, we let the location determine the story. I suggested a terrific location in northern California that my brothers had recently introduced me to: an old, abandoned coal mine. We figured we could shoot the film on a two week schedule at the mine, thereby keeping equipment rental to a minimum, and obtaining incredible production value for minimum cost. Unfortunately, after we had completed our outline and were half way through the treatment, the logistics involved in moving an entire cast and crew that far, for that period of time, with no money budgeted for travel expenses, proved to be insurmountable. By the time that little bomb sunk in, it was too late for us to change the setting, because the backer wanted to see some script immediately and that was the only product we could show him. We began to contact other individuals, both to supply the remainder of the budget, and to join the cast and crew."

Points were offered in lieu of payment, and because money was now being discussed, it was time to establish a legally binding contract with the chief investor. "About this time, our initial investor skipped town with his ten thousand bucks," says Huntley. "Two thirds of the entire budget suddenly disappeared."

Unwilling to cancel the production, for reasons of pride as well as the commitments made to cast, crew and smaller investors, the team continued in the hope that somehow the money would turn up. Hillman, Sawicki and Huntley decided to trade as Stellarwind Inc. to cover themselves against any personal liability should the project suffer further financial setbacks. They got themselves a lawyer, and for $800 he drew up an incorporation contract. A further contract was signed to establish the production as a limited partnership, both to guarantee the investors a return, and to prevent them from interfering with the creative side of the production. This cost a further $400 in legal fees. Huntley explains: "In essence, we, the producers, became a Board of Directors in a corporation, acting as the General Partner designated as the Producer in a Limited Partnership Contract."

The problem of where the location work for the mines would be shot came to a head when the team discovered, to their dismay, that the only other mine they could shoot in was 200 miles away, would cost $4,500 a day in location fees, and had no electricity. The decision was taken to build sets.

Meanwhile, the remaining investors had still not actually signed anything, and the production was

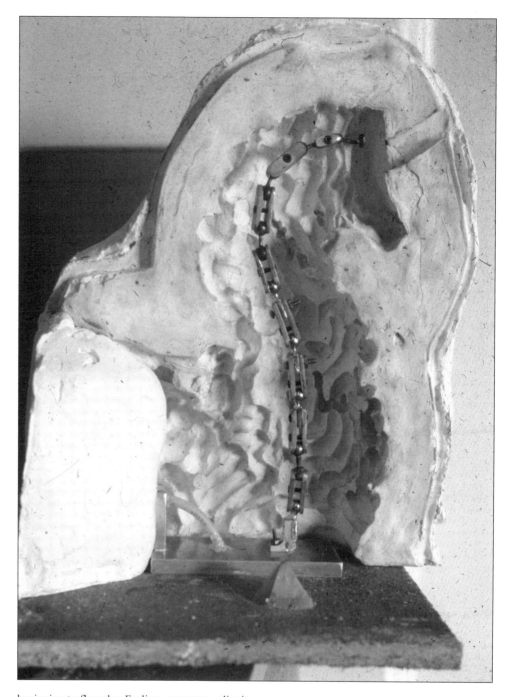

beginning to flounder. Feeling momentum slipping away, Hillman, Sawicki and Huntley decided to arrange a two-day shoot at their own expense. The shoot was completed – and then the other investors dropped out. Disaster loomed. It was at this point that Hillman's luck changed, although in a way none of the team would have preferred – a relative of Hillman's died and left him a small inheritance. As Huntley recalls, "Good fortune – although I hate to look at it that way. Unfortunately, the inheritance was to be tied up in probate for a year, with only small amounts occasionally available earlier. This was to become our production budget." "David had some investors," recalls Sawicki, "but after we'd shot a couple of weekends using borrowed equipment from David's job, they inexplicably pulled out. Then fate stepped in and one of David's relatives passed away, leaving him with just enough inheritance to finish the picture. We literally only had enough for film and lab. Cast and crew alike would be hauling equipment and building sets and everything."

above:
Sawicki comments: "This picture shows the rather skimpy armature inside the mould of the creature. The tube toward the back end was for an air bladder that was intended to make the back of the monster expand and contract. It was never used."

above:
Director of photography Stephen Greenfield prepares a shot.

right:
Ernie Farino shooting an ocean plate for later compositing with his matte painting.

below:
Sawicki comments: "This is the actual matte painting transparency that was used for the mountain explosion at the end of the picture. The painting was by Ernie Farino and an 8x10 inch transparency was made of the art for compositing on the Oxberry aerial image animation camera at Title House. The smoke for the aftermath was interesting in that it was a black and white negative of the explosion that was put out of focus and laid atop the mountain painting. I achieved the movement of this pseudo smoke by slowly dissolving from one frame of the negative fire 'smoke' to the next frame, thereby greatly slowing down the movement to create a massive smoke effect."

Shooting *The Strangeness*

The Strangeness was truly a shoestring venture. Shot on 16mm reversal stock, academy ratio (a hoped-for 1.85:1 blow-up never materialised), its final budget weighed in at a svelte $20,000 (Huntley pegs it at closer to $25,000). It took nearly a year to complete, beginning in 1979 and finishing in 1980, seven months over its original three month schedule, and was shot entirely at weekends, since most of the cast and crew already had regular jobs. Exteriors were photographed at the Red Rover Mine in the Canyon County region of Los Angeles and also along the rocky coast of a private beach belonging to Chris Huntley's grandparents. Specialised locations were not easy to afford on such a low budget, but the nature of the film demanded them nonetheless. "There was one great set we had, which was a mine exhibit at the Pomona Fair Grounds," Sawicki remembers. "David sweet-talked his way into using that for a couple of weekends, for free. It was great!"

For the majority of the film's underground scenes, however, the team had to come up with the goods themselves. "We needed a quiet place to build the set as we could not acquire the use of a soundstage," Sawicki explains. "We tried a ranch in Malibu, but they wanted $100 per weekend. So we ended up in a backyard in Burbank. Another relative's property." The sets ended up costing a mere $700. For fans of the movie, the sheer extent of good material shot on these homemade sets can come as a bit of a shock; on a very low budget, the team created a fantastically convincing illusion of underground mine tunnels and disused workmen's chambers.

"The main set was created in David's grandparents' backyard and garage," Sawicki reveals. "The garage was a cavern, and an L-shaped tunnel led out from that. At first we were puzzled as to how we were going to create the set

with no money. Plaster was discussed, foam rubber was tried but found to be way too time consuming. We eventually wound up using chicken wire covered with industrial strength aluminium foil painted to look like rock. It looked absolutely great, especially when illuminated by a single flare. The only drawback was that you didn't dare touch it or it would flutter like mad!"

As shooting began, Sawicki was working as an animation-stand cameraman for Title House, and David Hillman was working as an assistant editor for Dave Bell Associates, a firm who made industrial films. Chris Huntley and Steve Greenfield were still at USC. "The only seasoned fellow we had was Ernie Farino, who did the titles and helped shoot some plates and did the mould work on the monster," says Sawicki, "I think he may have also animated a large tentacle. Unfortunately Ernie had to leave the production before it was completed to go on to a paying gig. He just recently won an Emmy for visual effects on the TV show *Children of Dune*." Sawicki's job at Title House meant he was able to use their animation camera, an aerial-image Oxberry that doubled as optical printer and animation stand for the optical compositing, while Hillman was initially able to borrow a 16mm camera from Dave Bell Associates.

In keeping with the production's 'all hands to the pump' ethos, Sawicki made use of his early acting experience to essay one of the lead roles; know-it-all journalist Dan Flanders. He has fond memories of working with Keith Hurt, who played grizzled old mining expert Morgan: "I very much enjoyed working with Keith. I don't believe he was even a working actor outside of community theatre. What a creative fellow – a true natural. The scene where I'm interviewing him about his past and turning his 'coal mine' into a 'diamond mine' was completely improvised and written by Keith. We had rented all this camera equipment and were prepared to shoot several scenes with one of the female actors, who suddenly couldn't show. Keith saved the day by inventing that scene on the spot, and it wound up in the picture."

Sawicki found that lack of money sometimes stymied the confidence of the production: "Money is always a pressure, but you can't worry about it to the point of being frozen. We'd have discussions like, 'But we need a permit to shoot there,' and the solution was that we'd do it anyway and worry about it later. Nine times out of ten you can get away with it. You can worry yourself to a standstill." Sawicki also feels that the production was slowed down rather too much by discussions about plot: "We all got along very well on *The Strangeness*, but I seem to recall far too many 'film school' philosophical discussions. The biggest problem we faced was that all the principals went to the same film school and we were all experts on how to make the film. Too many cooks spoil the broth. The director has to be the final word in order for a production to go smoothly. If you sign on to be the director of photography, be that and nothing else. If you get someone on your crew to be the make-up person, let them be the make-up person and don't second guess them. If you feel that the director has made a bonehead decision it's your job to keep it to yourself, not argue, and accomplish his or her request to the best of your ability. Of course there will be times when you have a disagreement. As an actor you might feel that a certain request is totally out of character. It is your job as an actor to *make it* your character and *make it* work. It's not productive to defend your point of view by refusing to perform. After all it's only a movie. I was proud of one contribution I made – our main characters were stuck in the lowest part of the mine with the creature and no one knew how to get them back to the surface. I came up with the idea of the underwater explosion that blows them out to the sea. It was met pretty coldly at first, but no one could come up with a cleaner ending that would get them out of the fix fast. I thought it played pretty well."

The film credits two cinematographers: Kevin O'Brien and Steve Greenfield. Sawicki explains: "Kevin O'Brien was associated with the Dave Bell company from whom we originally borrowed camera gear. I think that deal may have fallen through, and with it so did Kevin. Steve Greenfield was a USC chum as well and he did most of the camera work." In a film rife with shared roles, Chris Huntley is credited with directing additional scenes: Sawicki admits, "I don't recall which scenes Chris directed but I do know that he was the horror film aficionado and was quite excellent with that type of material. So if there was anything creepy or disturbing it was probably his." Huntley elaborates: "I wrote and directed the teaser sequence that appears before the titles. The same is true for the scene in which Geoff breaks down after Tony's death and runs through the mines after Hemmings. There was also a scene where Geoff and Dan are talking about the possibility of running into pockets of gas. I think there were a few more but it's been a long time since I've seen the movie."

Sawicki's character exits the film rather abruptly, with a jump and a glitch on the soundtrack that led me to wonder if something has been removed: Flanders turns to see the creature waving its tentacles, and then there's a cut to a shot of Geoff, asleep in a nearby cavern. Geoff is then woken by Flanders's scream. So is there a shot missing? "No, that's how it was intended," Sawicki says. "The 'less is more' strategy again. By not seeing me 'get

it', the audience could imagine anything, sort of like radio." He pauses: "It might have been better in retrospect to have seen more!"

The aftermath of Flanders's demise also requires some explanation, as the British video release from VTC renders it somewhat mystifying. "That's me stuck to the ceiling!" Sawicki explains. "There was a clever set-up to avoid attaching me to a ceiling for real. I was actually lying on the floor with my arm raised to make it look like it was dangling. We arranged the angle of the shot to match Geoff's point of view, but upside-down as well. We purposely composed the image upside-down to take advantage of the fact that regular 16mm is perforated on both sides of the frame. If you splice the film end over end (bottom to top) then the image rights itself and the action runs in reverse, hence any ooze that was dripped *on* me appeared to fall *from* me. It's a very clever old camera trick that eliminates the need for an optical. I do remember Chris being a bit of a brat and purposely pouring some of that dreadful methyl cellulose stuff in my mouth during the shot!" Huntley treasures the memory… "We had plans to shoot that scene in our own garage (Mark, Stephen Greenfield and I were housemates at that time). I made up

above:
The 'Weegenay Monster' is ready for its close-up, Mr. DeMille…

below:
David Hillman filming Mark Sawicki stuck to the 'ceiling', as Chris Huntley and Steve Greenfield look on.

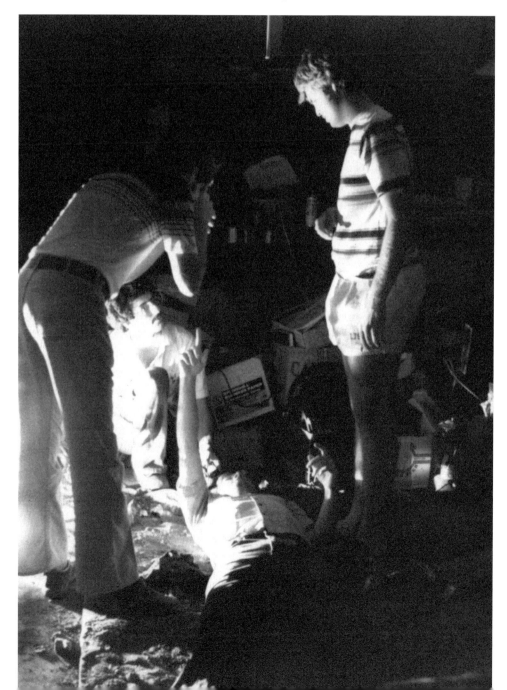

If You Go Down in the Caves Today…

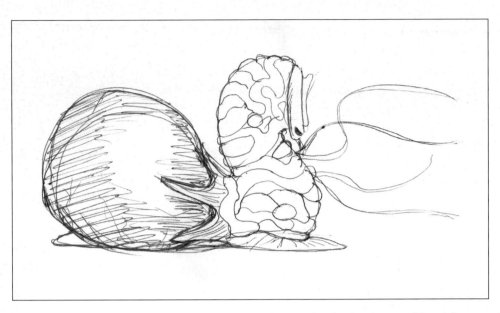

the corn starch goop, but the shooting was delayed for
some reason. We rescheduled and shot the sequence on the
following weekend. By the time we got around to actually
shooting the effect, the goop had soured. I was the one to
drop the stuff on Mark's face. I took a particularly large
handful of the rancid, stinking goop and dropped it right in
his mouth. Ah, the fun of being roommates!"

One of the creepiest images in the film is the discovery
of Chris Huntley's character Ruggles, drenched in monster-
slime and oozing white foam from his mouth. "Oh, this
was a fun shot," Huntley recalls. "The goop was boiled
corn starch. I was laying down on the floor of the mine set
inside David's parents' garage (the set stretched from inside
to outside and then some). It was two in the morning. It
was freezing – you can see steam rising from me if you
look closely enough. Once we got all the lights and camera
set up and took the wide shots and reverse angles, it was
time for the 'money' shot. The effect is simple. Someone
filled my mouth with vinegar. We rolled film. Then David
dropped a chunk of baking soda in my mouth. I closed my
mouth and held it as long as I could before the stuff
erupted from my mouth. Of course, it also went down my
throat, up my nose, everywhere. But in the end, it was
worth it for the shot we got. We only did it once!"

The low-level lighting of *The Strangeness* is its most
distinctive but also its most problematic feature. Sawicki
explains the thinking behind the movie's lighting style:
"Well, we couldn't afford lights! And we didn't want the
fantasy cave lighting 'look' of studio pictures like *Journey
to the Center of the Earth* and *The Time Machine*. It's a
trade-off. If you see the cave, there is absolutely no logic to
the light source. If you hold to strict rules of motivational
lighting you get really dark shots. We shot on 16mm ECO
which had an ASA of 25, at the time, so you pretty much
only saw the flame of the flare in the wide shots. Video
only made this situation worse. We would try to make the
image better on close-ups by holding lanterns very close to
our faces and filling the screen with the lit character. If it
was a wide shot with just flares or lanterns there wasn't
enough ambient bounce to record an extensive area. One
technique that helped was to fog up the interiors with stage
smoke. It created a heavier atmosphere and gave the
limited light sources something to work against, and we
achieved more ambience and haloes. The use of smoke also
helped the miniature sets, providing eerie shadows."

Miniatures played a significant role in the visual
effects. Sawicki, whose childhood fascination with clay
animation stood him in good stead for this, recalls: "We
built the miniature set in our garage then closed the door
and ignited an 'open ocean' emergency smoke flare, which
filled the garage with bright orange smoke. We held our
breath as best we could and grabbed as many shots as
possible before asphyxiating. Our handkerchiefs were
stained orange for a week! I don't recommend this to your
readers! Buy a respirator or something. When you're young
you don't think about safety, but it can come back to bite
you years later. Our group is okay, but I've known many
talented model-makers who are no longer with us due to
cancers probably caused by the materials they worked with
earlier in their careers."

The Monster

The Strangeness boasts a mind-boggling creature design –
part penis, part vagina – and those with a psychoanalytical
turn of mind may wonder, bearing in mind the film's
setting, whether castration anxiety played a part in the
design process. So was there a conscious attempt to work
with such symbolism? "This is kind of embarrassing for
me," laughs Huntley. "Consciously, I didn't think of those
things when I designed the monster. The earlier designs
even had a large, translucent sac attached to it so that it
looked more snail-like. Everybody *else* saw the
resemblance right away, and the monster soon got the
nickname 'The Weegenay Monster' after one crew-
member's nickname for a vagina! The sac disappeared
because it was too difficult to make, so we were left with
the man-eating penis/vagina monster that secretes caustic
goop on its victims. The reason I say it's kind of
embarrassing for me is that I feel it is such a cliché that I
designed it without consciously realising what I was doing.
You see, I was closeted at that time and struggling with my
sexuality. The only one I was fooling, obviously, was me. I
finally came out as a gay man a couple of years later.
Though I'm sure I wouldn't have found it funny then, I
find it very funny now!"

Chris Huntley designed the monster, which Sawicki
then sculpted and animated. "I was the monster fan – and I
could draw – so I went about designing it," Huntley says.
"The film cost about $18,000 originally, with an additional
$7,000 added later. Almost nothing of that budget went
toward the monster effects. At the most, I'd say $1,500-
$2,000, but probably more like $500. It basically went on
materials. Mark was working at a place where we could get
the opticals composited for free (he did the work). We only
had to pay for the film and development. I don't remember

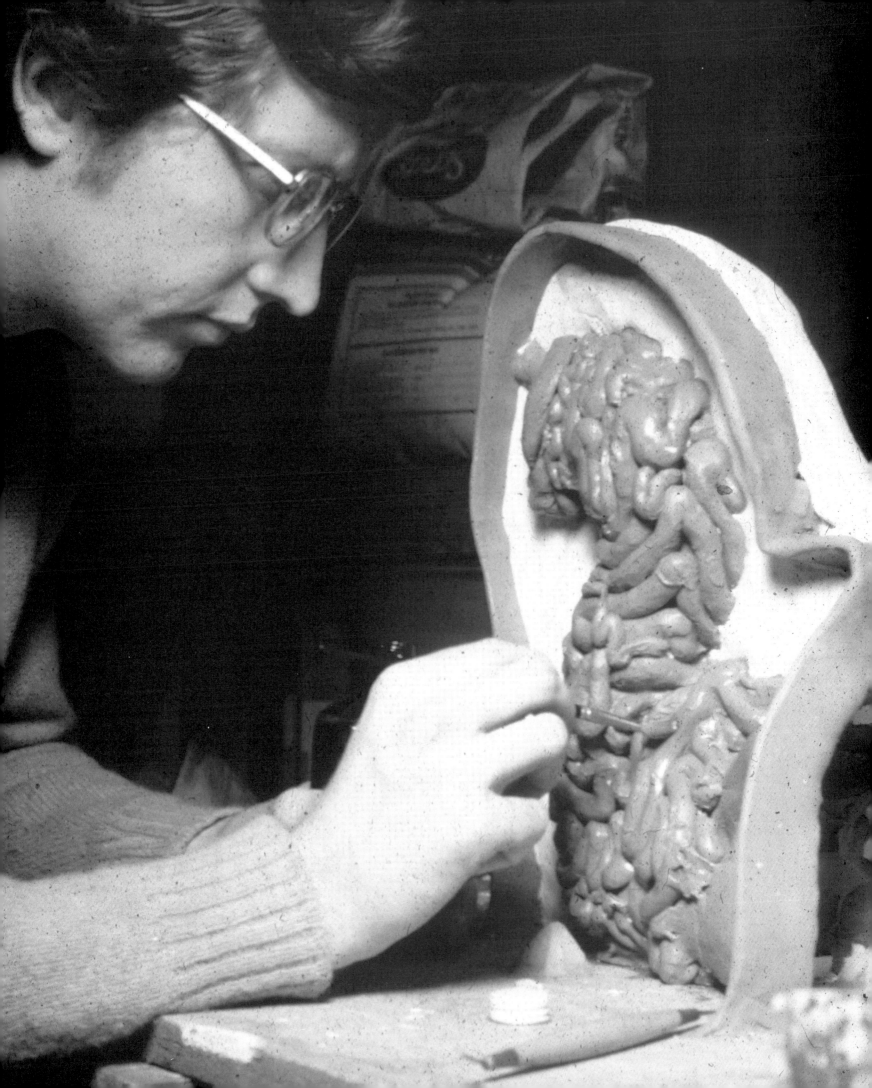

above:
Filming the sea-set climax of the film.

Post-Production, Screenings and Distribution

The film score is quite basic, but uses some effective synthesizer ambience to give the mine more atmosphere. Again, the core team were largely responsible. "David wrote and performed all the music," Sawicki remembers. "I thought it was quite nice. At that time, electronic synthesizers were becoming affordable. Our sound men were Tony Probst, who did a lot of good sound work on my student film *Origins*, and Tom Scurry. If Chris was credited with sound he probably worked closely with Tony to generate the creepy tones. Tony also did our negative cutting in the closet of the house that Chris, Steve, Sean Phillips and I rented. We used the swimming pool for some of the underwater footage, the garage for the miniatures and animation, and my bedroom as a looping stage. We covered my bedroom floor with plastic and dirt and used a double system projector to simultaneously project and record at the same time to 'loop' the sound. The projector was placed outdoors and projected an image through a window into the bedroom. The sound recorded at the beach was unusable due to the crashing waves. We looped all of that material. The projector constantly ate the film and the process was very slow going."

Huntley adds, "I'd spent the previous couple of years taking electronic music classes at USC, because it was easy and fun. It came in handy during our production, because I was able to use the USC recording studio. David also rented a synthesizer which we both played. We also did lots of layering in the soundtrack to help with the mood."

Initially, a film editor acquaintance had promised to 'keep up' with the film as it came in: but when an 8,000-foot backlog had built up and he still had done nothing, it fell to Hillman to begin the task. With the aid of an assistant editor, he took fifteen days to synch up the dailies and a further thirty days to edit together a rough cut. When a distributor was referred to the production by a mutual friend, a ten-minute 'taster' was hurriedly assembled for his benefit. Without a completed 16mm print, the team were reluctant to let anyone see the rough footage, but to their surprise, they were swiftly offered a foreign distribution contract.

While the first distributor was drawing up a contract, a second got in touch. By this time, Hillman had assembled a rather shaky 85-minute rough cut. Huntley was downbeat: "The film was horrible. The first reel should have been, and eventually was, thrown to the four winds. It was so boring. Additionally, the rest of the film lacked any transition scenes, special effects, and the entire ending. It was far from in the can. The distributor was suitably unimpressed, and offered us some rather candid, as well as useful, criticisms. Subsequently, we slipped into an unproductive two week depression. This might well have been the end of the film. Months of work, thousands of dollars, and every last drop of creative energy, appeared to have been spent for the making of a boring, predictable piece of dreck."

Still, the first distributor had yet to see the completed version. There was still time to make changes. Shaken but resolute, the team dragged their asses back to the project. "We cut the first ten minutes of the film out entirely," says Huntley, "and incorporated as many of the second distributor's suggestions as possible. Finally we arranged a screening for the initial distributor." It went better than

a whole lot about working on the script. What I do remember is that it was sporadic. David would write something, then I'd write some more, then we go back and forth some more. It was pretty haphazard. We were more concerned with getting the 'plot' right." "Most of the discussions revolved around protagonist, conflict, structure and all the story things we learned from school based on Lajos Egri's teachings," Sawicki remembers. "We never dealt with anything psychological."

Although *The Strangeness* trades successfully on its claustrophobic setting, the movie takes a while to deliver the dramatic goods; in other words, it's quite a while before we see the monster. Given that Huntley designed the creature, would he agree? "Certainly. I think there are bigger structural problems in the story than that, but from an entertainment point of view it could easily benefit from more monster. Having little money, we wanted to save the bang for the end. Unfortunately, there is little else in the story to hold attention long enough to *get* to the end. We were trying for a *Jaws* or *Alien* type of feeling. We just didn't have the budget to have the payoff of either of those two stories."

right:
Sawicki comments: "A production still of the Hemmings character used as reference to sculpt his puppet, so he could be eaten by the monster."

the first: "The distributors weren't overly impressed, but they offered a welcome optimism and they even seemed to enjoy it. They too made suggestions, which were immediately incorporated into our reshooting plans. They liked it enough to hand us a contract right then and there. Though incredibly tempted to sign immediately, discretion won out, and it's a good thing too. We discussed the contract with our lawyer and managed to include a couple of self-protecting clauses to prevent us from financial responsibility for such things as 35mm blow-up and subtitled versions. We would only have to supply these items after the distributors had sold sufficient territories to cover the cost."

Huntley found the legal advice they received absolutely invaluable. "I can't overstate the importance of showing everything to a lawyer," he stresses. "Although parties in a contract may be on the best of terms, if it isn't in writing it isn't so. For example, unless specified, one party may be construed to have the authority to run up debts in the name of the other. This is a clause of omission. It's easy to spot something wrong that is there, but it takes a lawyer to spot what *isn't* there and *should* be. Although the omission was not intentional on the distributor's part, it could have been used to their advantage should disagreements arise at a later date. The distributors gladly agreed to the change." One expense the team did have to swallow was the provision of advertising materials – pressbooks, promo reels on videotape, artwork, written copy, etc. – which had to produced pronto in time for the film to be ready for sale at Cannes, just a month later.

When a sale to video was clinched, that was the end of the process, and a less than rewarding end it was too. "All I remember was a very dark office where David, Chris and I were gathered to sign a distribution contract," says Sawicki. "It reminded me of the atmosphere of *The Godfather*. All of David's money was tied up in the film and he needed to recoup something. Chris and I were not about to stand in his way so we signed. It probably wasn't a great deal – I remember only receiving a royalty check for $25 and I was one of the producers! But I only had sweat equity in the movie, so it didn't much matter to me. We all received experience and some great footage for a reel."

Huntley elaborates: "What I remember about the video deals is that we got screwed several times by several low-life distributors before we got it to a semi-legit group. We had people selling foreign rights to *The Strangeness* who didn't even have a contract with us. If there was a slimy, dishonest, Hollywood shyster around, he'd find us. That was, by far, the worst part of making this film. After the initial screening of the first answer print, I pretty much dropped out of the loop. David kept the film alive and is responsible for its eventual release on air and on video."

A cast and crew screening was arranged at the Norris Theater on the USC campus. Sadly, it was to be the first and only time *The Strangeness* would play on the big screen. It never did secure cinema distribution, and instead, as was becoming the norm in the 1980s, went straight to video. Sawicki wryly recounts the only time he came into contact with a paying member of the audience: "I do remember seeing it at a local video store in the hands of a patron. I rushed up to the fellow and asked why he decided to rent that particular picture, and his response was... 'I've seen everything else'."

So how would Chris Huntley describe the strengths and weaknesses of the film? "For the most part it was technically competent, especially for the cost. Decent title sequence. Intriguing monster. Some good horror effects and explosions. Weaknesses? It's boring (a cardinal sin for exploitation films). Most of the creative elements are pretty bad. The dialogue is corny. The story structure is non-existent. It's lucky it makes any sense at all. Much of the darker material does not translate to video. In film, the dark scenes are at least visible. Hokey acting. Need I go on?"

Sawicki readily concedes that the film has flaws: "I regret that there was little 'follow through' with the characters. We see the old miner take a swig of booze but nothing comes of that. We see the young miner make a pass at the reporter's wife and nothing comes of that either. We had some good characters who were under-utilised and so the film suffers, as did many of the horror pics of this calibre, from too many scenes of people walking here to there and back again. I would like to have seen some sex or titillation. All we get is one brief underwater wet T-shirt shot. We seemed to pull too many punches and that may have been because David relied on his family a great deal to make the picture. They fed us, they let us keep a cave set in the yard for a year etc. I think, in many ways, David made a nice film for his folks to see. Aside from racy things, I do think that we could have seen much more of the monster. We were trying for the *Jaws* approach, because we didn't think the monster would hold up under close scrutiny. We certainly didn't want it to start looking comical. I think, in retrospect, it might have been nice if there was a spin-off threat spawned by the monster that would lend excitement in an ancillary way: the people who get slurped by the thing becoming zombies, or something. The only other weakness I can think of is that my character was killed off much too soon!"

above:
Sawicki at work.

left:
Sawicki comments: "This is my favourite **Strangeness** picture. Dan Lunham is just walking out of frame, Mark Sawicki is in the centre followed by a very pensive David Hillman. This photo was taken in David's grandparents back yard, where the main mine set was built as an L-shaped tunnel that ended in a cave room, which was built in the garage in the background. You can see the partial chicken wire frame work that made up the walls of the set. This was probably shot at the start of the set construction."

below:
Sawicki comments: "This picture shows the aluminium foil cave chimney that we did our explosions in. The crumbled foil was painted on the inside of the chimney to look like rock. We set off an explosion at the base and filmed the fireball rocketing through the cave miniature from the top. This is how the climactic explosion sequence was done."

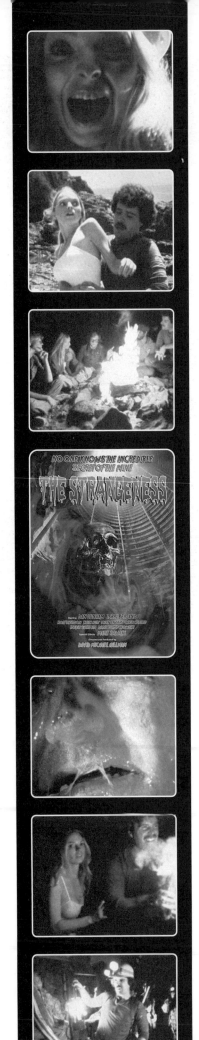

Out of the Mine

After *The Strangeness*, Hillman made one more feature film called *Brothers of the Wilderness* (1983), a 'G'-rated children's adventure about a boy and his dog on a treasure hunt. Sawicki played the lead villain: "My character was a bit of a disgruntled nincompoop type. Needless to say I very much enjoyed that part! I thought it played pretty well, and it was fun to work on. It was financed by a fellow who made or distributed suitcases, I believe. His name was George Bamber. It was all shot in Big Bear, California. After that, David continued making educationals. The last film I worked on with him was *Cincinnati Bones and the Temple of Health* (1988). This was an anti-drug educational that David starred in and produced. I did the visual effects. It was quite well received in schools."

Huntley recalls his own trajectory after *The Strangeness*: "We finished *The Strangeness* the summer after I graduated from USC film school. I promptly got a job waiting tables. Six months later I landed a job at Graphic Films, a special effects house with alumni such as Douglas Trumbull, Ben Burtt, and John Dykstra. I spent two years working on an Omnimax space film called *Tomorrow in Space* (1982). It should have been called 'Tinkertoys in Space'. During my work on that, Stephen Greenfield and I started our own software company called Screenplay Systems. We created *Scriptor*, a screenplay formatter, for which we received the 1994 Technical Achievement Award from the Academy of Motion Picture Arts and Sciences. We created *Movie Magic Budgeting* and *Movie Magic Scheduling*, which have been the industry-standard estimation and production management software since their introduction in the 1980s. We developed the *Dramatica* software, and other writing software as well. We're still business partners, twenty two years and going. We changed our company's name to Write Brothers, Inc. in 2002, to better represent our product line. For me, I'd say that making the film did not directly help me to get other work. *But...* it was an essential step in the long evolution and development of a new theory of story. Some of our conversations during *The Strangeness* became the basis of work David and I later did in 1990. We ended up creating a new theory of story called *Dramatica*.[1] We did a *lot* of philosophical talking about story structure, before, during, and after *The Strangeness*, trying to discover the basic patterns of characters and plot in stories. What were the essentials? What parts were fluff? We obviously didn't figure *any* of that out during the production of *The Strangeness*! In fact, it was the film's bad structure that got David and me thinking about story structure in a big way. From these discussions we determined that there were generally eight archetypal characters found in most action-adventure-type stories. We also determined that they came in pairs. There were the protagonist-antagonist pair; the sidekick-sceptic pair; the reason-emotion pair; and the guardian-'contagonist' pair (we created the name contagonist because we couldn't find any reference to this character; he is the hindering tempter, such as Darth Vader in *Star Wars*). This was a simplistic view of characters, but there seemed to be some fundamental truth associated with it."

Sawicki's film career leapt forward in 1984 when he snared a job with up-and-coming director James Cameron on his sci-fi adventure classic, *The Terminator*. "Ernie

Farino was responsible for getting me on *The Terminator* after Fantasy Two's optical man quit in the middle of the production," Sawicki recalls. "I came up with a variety of processes for the original Terminator vision. I owe my jump to the big leagues to Bill Taylor ASC of Illusion Arts. Bill came into my life a bit later, in 1986. After *Terminator* I worked for Celestial Mechanics with Sean Phillips, doing opticals for television commercials. We also did almost all of the 3D feature title sequences during the 3D Summer. *Jaws 3-D*, *Friday the 13th Part 3*, *Metalstorm*, they were all titles that Sean Phillips devised. Sean, as you recall, was one of the roommates at the house we shot *The Strangeness* in, and provided the spray paint compressor to paint our set. He's a brilliant 3D specialist. Sean now directs and does visual effects in large format venues like IMAX.[2] With *Friday the 13th Part 3*, I seem to recall that we didn't work on the film proper but did many last minute hurried tests to prepare the film for anaglyphic projection for drive-ins. You see, most successful 3D processes use polarized glasses and a silver screen that can reflect the different polarities of the right and left eye. Conventional screens or those found in drive-in theatres need to separate the eyes through colour separation, typically cyan and red filters. This 'anaglyphic' system can create the 3D and some sensation of pseudo colour. It is usually not very successful. I believe the studio passed on the making of special anaglyphic prints once they saw the tests. It was quite an experience though, as Paramount opened up Movielab in Hollywood for us, at the cost of $20,000 for the weekend. My test footage was the only film that was processed and printed on that weekend and I was able to experience walking through all the processing steps at the lab. I sort of felt like royalty!"

Sawicki continued to pick up new knowledge of cameras and optical technology, as film industry techniques went into development overdrive in the 1980s and 1990s. "While I was at CMI (Celestial Mechanics) I began to experiment with blue screen, and went back to the original Vlahos patent to learn how to do it from the source. I always seemed to be the sole cameraman wherever I worked and therefore was self taught to a great extent. I had heard that Bill Taylor was one of the best practitioners of blue screen in the business. He was Albert Whitlock's matte cameraman. I called him one day to ask about blue screen and he invited me over to Universal to look over my notes and blue screen tests. He was very generous with information and a great help to me. I think he must have been impressed with my self study, because when Universal dissolved their matte department and Bill formed Illusion Arts with his partner Syd Dutton, he called me to ask if I would work for him. I was working on rock videos at the time, having a lot of fun but making no money. When he called I couldn't believe it. I accepted, and overnight I was in the feature film matte painting business. My first project was *The Gate*, which was supervised by Bill and Randy Cook. Randy went on to be one of the principal effects artisans on *The Lord of the Rings*. Illusion Arts was a great experience. I became one of the last latent-image matte cameramen. The digital age, unfortunately, wiped out that wonderful tradition. A terrific book that I would highly recommend is *The Invisible Art* by Craig Barron. It covers the history of matte painting from its origins in silent cinema to the digital age. I was happy to see that some of the paintings I composited are featured in the book. Alas my name is not mentioned, but I feel truly blessed to have been part of such a spectacular art-form. I spent ten wonderful years at Illusion Arts, and then was asked by Tim McHugh of Area 51 to come on board as a co-supervisor for *From the Earth to the Moon*, produced by Tom Hanks. Ernie Farino was the principal supervisor. After the Hanks project finished I was out looking for work again and discovered the down side of being with one company for ten years. The digital transition took over the industry and I discovered that my network of people were no more. Most of the small effects shops went out of business and were replaced by large corporate entities like Cinesite and Sony. The schools had flooded the market with inexpensive digital labour and the normal demand for experience was replaced with whoever knew the latest software version. The globalisation of the workforce has also had a devastating effect on Hollywood employment. I was fortunate in that my wife was an early adopter of digital processes – she went on to work for all the major studios around that time. Her last feature was Disney's *Dinosaur*. She all too rapidly saw the decline of the digital effects business into a sort of glorified secretarial pool. She has transitioned into teaching, and I have gone back to optical camerawork. I may very well be the last of the optical cameramen. I have been at Custom Film Effects working on features for about five years now, and spend my spare time creating fine art sculpture and acting on occasion. Custom Film put the optical printers out to pasture in 2005 and I went on to be a digital colourist and on set visual effects cameraman. Before the printers were replaced I made a short film homage to the craft called *Twilight Cameraman*.[3] I am very fortunate to still be working in the field in Hollywood."

Sawicki is upbeat about recent developments in video technology and their possible impact on filmmaking. "It is a fabulous time to be a filmmaker now. The technology is completely accessible. Anyone can afford to make a movie and not go broke. I recently appeared in a mini-DV feature, *Rectuma* (2004, dir: Mark Pirro), that was made for a fraction of what *The Strangeness* cost, with much more production value. The ability for new filmmakers to get exposure is tremendous. I acted in a film directed by visual effects supervisor Keven Kutchaver for the 48 Hour Film Festival, where the challenge is to make a film in that allotted time. Kevin's film, *Mysterious Tales of Unexpected Horror*, is now broadcast over the Internet, and will be seen at the Arc Light Theater across from the Cinerama Dome in Hollywood. The world is at your feet. The *challenge* is that cinema has become the paperback novel of the 21st Century. It will be hard to stand out from the crowd."

The Strangeness, too, has had difficulty standing out from the crowd these past twenty years. Lost in the shuffle during the early eighties video explosion, it's never received much attention in the horror press, and what reviews there have been have scarcely looked beyond the film's murky lighting. But even if the film really *is* like a dusty old paperback novel, something one might pick up with idle curiosity in a bookshop crammed to the ceiling with forgotten titles, Sawicki and Huntley show us that it's often incredibly rewarding to investigate the shady corners, away from the hard-cover 'classics' and the groaning racks of Stephen Kings. Because flaws and failings and all, there's still so much to learn from *The Strangeness*, and from the men who made it happen.

Addendum: *Chris Huntley wrote these tips for filmmakers on a low budget back in 1980, and they're still worth repeating today:*

1) Make sure your script is completely locked down before you begin production. You risk shooting several scenes that are no longer necessary, as well as creating many discrepancies and loose ends in plotline and character development that can never be fully corrected.
2) Unless you are absolutely sure of someone's abilities as an actor, and this includes friends especially, have them read through scenes extensively, preferably with other actors who have already been cast.
3) Never start your production without your entire budget in the bank. It is quite possible to run completely out of money midway through a film and never get it completed.
4) Never underestimate your budget in your enthusiasm to get the project off the ground. Allow 25% of your budget for advertising expenses. If this is your first film you will likely be required to pay for all advertising materials used

above:
Sawicki comments: "A closer view of the monster. There are small human figures in the background that we used to cast shadows on the wall for one of the mysterious introductions to the creature."

initially by the distributor. In addition, the best planned films allow at least a 20% contingency for those unconsidered situations.

5) Get yourself a lawyer. This is not a place to cut corners on your budget. He can and most likely will save your neck. Insurance policies are a must, especially when you, as the producer, might have a personal liability.

6) Not only should everyone have clearly delineated responsibilities, they should know exactly where they begin and end. In our case, we couldn't get things done because no one had been made personally responsible for each area, and a job that should have been a one man responsibility was spread among three or four.

7) Feed everyone well. People will work their hearts out for you if you show enough consideration to provide them with a good meal.

8) Have your shooting schedule planned well in advance, not just for your benefit and for the renting of equipment, but for the benefit of all those who are giving up their free time to conform to your needs. Be prepared with alternate scenes for every shooting day.

9) When striking deals, remember: everything is negotiable. Don't be afraid to suggest getting something for free. Often, companies will accept screen credit, deferred payment, or points in return for goods, services, or discounts.

Footnotes

1   See dramatica.com for details.

2   Phillips was Digital Effects Supervisor on the IMAX version of Robert Zemeckis's *Polar Express* (2004).

3   Distributed by Firstlightvideo.com.

DAVID MICHAEL HILLMAN

FILMOGRAPHY AS DIRECTOR:
1977   *University Travel* (16mm student film)
1980   *The Strangeness* aka *Down to Hell* (also co-prod/co-writer)
1983   *Brothers of the Wilderness*
1988   *Cincinnati Bones and the Temple of Health*

MARK SAWICKI

FILMOGRAPHY AS DIRECTOR:
1977   *It Stalked the Night* (16mm student film) (writer/director)
1978   *Origins* (graduation film, U.S.C.) (writer/director)

OTHER CREDITS:
1977   *University Travel* – dir: David Michael Hillman (16mm student film) (cameraman)
1979   *Gravesite* – dir: Chris Huntley (actor)
1980   *The Strangeness* (actor/co-producer/co-writer/effects)
1984   *The Terminator* – dir: James Cameron (special optical consultant: Fantasy II Film Effects)
1987   *The Gate* – dir: Tibor Takács (production coordinator: Illusion Arts)
1989   *Star Trek V: The Final Frontier* – dir: William Shatner (matte photographer)
1990   *Frankenstein Unbound* – dir: Roger Corman (matte photography)
1991   *Shattered* – dir: Wofgang Petersen (matte photography)
1991   *The Butcher's Wife* – dir: Terry Hughes (matte photography)
1991   *Cape Fear* – dir: Martin Scorsese (matte photography: Illusion Arts)
1991   *Steel and Lace* – dir: Ernest D. Farino (actor)
1992   *A Few Good Men* – dir: Rob Reiner (matte shots) (as Mark A. Sawicki)
1992   *Dogs Bark Blue* – dir: Claudia Hoover (actor)
1993   *The Age of Innocence* – dir: Martin Scorsese (matte photography: Illusion Arts)
1994   *Naked Gun 33 1/3: The Final Insult* – dir: Peter Segal (matte photographer)
1994   *The Shadow* – dir: Russell Mulcahy (matte photography)
1994   *Speechless* – dir: Ron Underwood (matte photography: Illusion Arts)
1996   *From Dusk Till Dawn* – dir: Robert Rodriguez (matte photography: Illusion Arts)
1996   *The Birdcage* – dir: Mike Nichols (digital advisor)
1996   *Courage Under Fire* – dir: Edward Zwick (matte photography: Illusion Arts)
1996   *Daylight* – dir: Rob Cohen (camera operator: miniature production crew: Illusion Arts)
1996   *Skin and Bone* – dir: Everett Lewis (actor)
1997   *The Jackal* – dir: Michael Caton-Jones (optical effects: Illusion Arts)
1998   *Behind Enemy Lines* – dir: John Moore (optical camera)
1998   *From the Earth to the Moon* – dir: various (TV mini-series: 1st episode) (effects co-supervisor)
1999   *Austin Powers: The Spy Who Shagged Me* – dir: Jay Roach (optical camera)
1999   *Boys Don't Cry* – dir: Kimberley Peirce (optical camera) (uncredited)
1999   *Bats* – dir: Louis Morneau (optical camera)
1999   *If I Had a Hammer* – dir: Josh Becker (actor)
2000   *X-Men* – dir: Bryan Singer (optical camera)
2000   *Men of Honor* – George Tillman Jr. (optical camera)
2000   *Meet the Parents* – dir: Jay Roach (optical camera)
2000   *Thirteen Days* – dir: Roger Donaldson (optical camera)
2001   *The Caveman's Valentine* – dir: Kasi Lemmons (optical camera)
2001   *Sugar & Spice* – dir: Francine McDougall (optical camera)
2001   *Get Over It* – dir: Tommy O'Haver (optical camera)
2001   *From Hell* – dir: Albert & Allen Hughes (optical camera) (uncredited)
2001   *Shallow Hal* – dirs: Bobby & Peter Farrelly (optical camera)
2001   *Joe Somebody* – dir: John Pasquin (optical camera)
2002   *Blow* – dir: Ted Demme (optical camera)
2002   *One Hour Photo* – dir: Mark Romanek (optical camera) (uncredited)
2002   *Death to Smoochy* – dir: Danny DeVito (optical camera)
2002   *About Schmidt* – dir: Alexander Payne (optical camera) (uncredited)
2002   *Far From Heaven* – dir: Todd Haynes (optical camera)
2002   *Phone Booth* – dir: Joel Schumaker (optical camera)
2002   *Antwone Fisher* – dir: Denzel Washington (optical camera) (uncredited)
2002   *Gangs of New York* – dir: Martin Scorsese (optical camera)
2003   *Shanghai Knights* – dir: David Dobkin (optical camera)
2003   *Daddy Day Care* – dir: Steve Carr (green screen photographer)
2003   *The League of Extraordinary Gentlemen* – dir: Stephen Norrington (optical camera)
2003   *Scary Movie 3* – dir: David Zucker (optical camera)
2003   *Timeline* – dir: Richard Donner (blue screen consultant)
2003   *Mysterious Tales of Unexpected Horror* – dir: Kevin Kutchaver (actor)
2004   *Eternal Sunshine of the Spotless Mind* – Michel Gondry (effects photography)
2004   *Vanity Fair* – dir: Mira Nair (optical camera)
2004   *A Dirty Shame* –dir: John Waters (model photography)
2004   *Rectuma* – dir: Mark Pirro (actor)
2005   *Rescue Rocket X-5* – dir: Kevin Kutchaver (actor)

BOOK:
2007   *Filming the Fantastic: A Guide to Visual Effects Photography* (Focal Press, ISBN: 978-0-240-80915-1)

CHRIS HUNTLEY

FILMOGRAPHY AS DIRECTOR:
1977   *The End* (Animated short)
1978   *Daddy's Gone a'Hunting* (Animated short. Note: Shown before the world premiere of George Romero's *Dawn of the Dead* at the 1978 FILMEX International Film Festival in Los Angeles)
1979   *Gravesite* (Note: this was Huntley's Graduation Film)

OTHER CREDITS:
1980   *The Strangeness* (co-writer / actor / co-producer / composer / special visual effects / re-recording engineer/dir. additional scenes)
1982   *Tomorrow in Space* – dir: Lester Novros (IMAX effects camera operator; asst. sound editor)

chapter 10

Vigilante of 42nd Street

Robert Endelson on Fight for Your Life

Fight for Your Life (1977)

Is *Fight for Your Life* a firecracker tossed into the lap of political correctness? A tell-it-like-it-is slice of action melodrama? Or a callous exploitation flick having a laugh by grating the liberal viewer's nerves? Any and all of these I would say, but contrary to common misconception it's not racist. The film has been attacked over the years for making an unacceptably indulgent window-display of its villain's racial prejudice, and it's true that the hateful Kane (William Sanderson) enjoys the lion's share of screen time: but viewers of a suspicious nature who wish to ascribe the villain's values to the filmmaker should think again. Taken as the energetic tabloid fiction it is, *Fight for Your Life* is a bruising, nerve-rattling experience as pacy and unpretentious as the blaxploitation films it resembles. The title says it all really, making clear the film's ultimate sympathies: this story of a nice suburban black family attacked by a trio of deranged killers charts the slow, painful accumulation of their rage, and their justified thirst for vengeance.

Endelson sets up a broad, almost cartoonish conflict, between three lowlife hoods and a family teetering on the verge of sainthood. From this basis, the committed cast take Straw Weisman's pungent, demonic script into orbit. Sanderson is the focus of the film, and although the script gives him the ammo, the actor's skill and guts deliver the killer shot. A glimmer of restraint on his part would ruin the film: we really need to see the worst in Kane's character, and Sanderson duly delivers. His energy and passion account for the nervousness with which the film has often been greeted. Here is an actor really sinking his teeth into a role, with an abandon to the imperatives of character that ranks alongside better-known, more fêted 'dark-side' explorers like Harvey Keitel and James Woods.

The bravest performer of the film, next to Sanderson, is Robert Judd, playing the black middle-class pastor and father whose New Testament values are challenged by the attack on his home, his family and his masculinity. Seen from this angle, *Fight for Your Life* is the antithesis of a white power fantasy – it's virtually a Black Panther recruitment film, delaying the righteous violence of the suitably named Turner family until the last possible

moment. The incendiary sado-masochistic tension is so acute it's almost pornographic. One thing's for sure – a white man watching this film in a black area of New York would feel pretty nervous as he left the theatre…

Stylistically, *Fight for Your Life* is no-nonsense get-the-story-told exploitation. Conflict is explored chiefly through the dialogue and acting, with the editing occasionally used for heightened directorial emphasis. There are few camera tricks to abstract what we're seeing: Endelson keeps the lid on his film technique, pushing the viewer's buttons without drawing attention to himself. It's hard-nosed, professional NYC filmmaking, never

below:
Jessie Lee Kane (William Sanderson, *right*) and Chino (Daniel Faraldo, *left*) menace Ted Turner (Robert Judd) and his family.

Fight for Your Life
aka **Staying Alive** (US theatrical re-release title) aka **Getting Even**
aka **Held Hostage**
aka **The Hostage's Bloody Revenge**
aka **Bloodbath at 1313 Fury Road**
© 1977. Fightin' Family Productions Ltd. William Mishkin Motion Pictures presents a Robert A. Endelson film. Released by William Mishkin Motion Pictures, Inc.
director: Robert A. Endelson. producer: William Mishkin & Robert A. Endelson. executive producer: William Mishkin. original screenplay: Straw Weisman. director of photography: Lloyd Freidus. music composed & conducted by Jeff Slevin. words and music by Jeff Slevin. strings and horns arranged by Ron Carran, ©1977 Elsmere Music, Inc. music production services by Candue Music, Inc. recorded at Big Apple Studios, N.Y.C. original motion picture sound track available on Fire Sign Records, Ltd. associate producers: Rick Endelson, Straw Weisman. assistant director: Ralph Coleman. assistant cameraman: Phil Holahan. gaffer: Jim Falconer. grip: Dwayne Arthur. sound recorder: Carl Kriegeskotte. assistant sound: Steve Morris. make up artist: Joan Puma. script supervision: Janet Merwin. art director: Ronald Merk. costumes: Sara Brook. special effects: Doug Hart. production manager: Rick Endelson. editor: Robert A. Endelson. assistant editor: Janet Merwin. sound editor: Steve Brand. associate editor: Larry Taymor. sound mixer: Aaron Nathanson. production assistants: Philip Schaefer, Robert Scannell, Peter Jonas, Michele Berdy, Ed Donohue, Bob Boyoort, John Doyle. The Producers would like to extend their sincere gratitude and appreciation to the following persons and organizations whose cooperation and assistance helped make this film possible: Hudson N.Y. Police Department; Columbia County Sheriffs Department; Chatham Rescue Squad; Chatham Courier; New York City Film Commission; Michael Colton; Seymour Cohen Opticians; Klein Uniform Company; Chatham Travel Lodge; Larry Walker; Steve Goodman; Norman Hollyn.
Cast: The Turner Family: *Robert Judd (Ted Turner). Catherine Peppers (Mrs. Turner). Lela Small (Grandma Turner). Yvonne Ross (Corrie Turner). Reginald Bythewood (Floyd Turner). Ramon Saunders (Val Turner). Queenie Endelson (Queenie, dog).* The Convicts: *William [J.] Sanderson (Kane). Daniel Faraldo (Chino). Peter Yoshida (Ling)* with: *Bonni [sic] Martin (Karen). David Cargill (Lt. Reilly). Richard A. Rubin (Captain Hamilton). David Dewlow (Joey). Nick Mariano (Tony). Robert Whelan (liquor store owner). Lenny Chance (drunk driver). Peter Charbonneau (gas station victim). Stephen Griffith (reporter). Maxine McCrey (prostitute). David Francis (pimp). Billy Longo (police van driver). William Spitz (store robber). Jane Endelson (baby in liquor store). Claudia Angelos (police radio voice). Steve Hasday (Sgt .Hasday) and Cliff Balder. David Balder. Joe Battaglia. John Doyco. Ronald Gauthier. Daniel Herrick. Timothy Jones. Olivia Solomon. Jeffery Seymour. Mary Jane Walsh. James Bertram. Paul Morris. James Blass. Franklyn Schaefer. Rick Endelson. Steven Rosenbloom. Thomas Heald. William Vick. John Laccetti. Larry Walker. Jack Massar. Bob McKinnon. Gary Mazzacano. Mitchell Rothman. Dick Punch.*

top:
Kane cements his image by threatening a baby with a gun in a store holdup. Note the rather perplexing German title, **Ausbruch zur Hölle** ('Break-out to Hell'), which seems to sympathise with the convicts!

William Sanderson + Robert Judd in
Ausbruch zur Hölle
'Fight For Your Life'

dreaming of intruding on the story with lyrical, expressionistic or 'arty' flourishes. But what *Fight for Your Life* may lack in poetry it makes up for in brass-necked nerve. Not only does it take the race issue by the horns; it also bulldozes another taboo area, unusual even for exploitation.

How can I put this delicately… they kill the kid!

So what's the big deal? Well, even the most cynical horror films tend to sidestep the murder of children. Honourably nihilist exceptions include Romero's *Night of the Living Dead*, Lucio Fulci's *The Beyond* and Michael Haneke's art-house horror *Funny Games*, but you can tell how rare this is by the way the hairs stand up on the back of your neck when Ling (Peter Yoshida) offs the little tyke (which one I won't say – there are two in the film…). The shock is even more profound because the boy is set up as the family's potential salvation.

The movie's climax is deferred perhaps a shade too long, but it's a close call. When it comes it's immaculately handled, and when Turner humiliates Kane by taunting him about the *"big black bucks"* who punked him in jail, you could even argue that the script shows a glimmer of sympathy for Kane's wretched character. The sight of the weaselly little monster flustered and deflated, as these words probe the truth, suggests how psychological understanding could have undone the villain's authority. Instead Turner's taunts are simply a nasty and effective *coup de grâce*.

"Vengeance is mine," sayeth the Lord (allegedly), but *Fight for Your Life* is having none of it. The script privatises heavenly judgement, relentlessly berating Christianity as a force which keeps the good guys down: in one of the film's most joltingly aggressive sequences, the Pastor is beaten around the head with his own Bible (in footage that Endelson speeds up slightly, creating a genuinely weird, disturbing effect).

An eleventh hour collusion between sympathetic cop and vengeful father provides a liberal-baiting last squib, something to argue about in the bar afterwards, proving that *Fight for Your Life* is consummate tabloid cinema; rabble-rousing exploitation in which a sense of social responsibility begins and ends in the ticket hall. If it does have a political conscience it's essentially non-racist, right-libertarian, pro-gun, anti-liberal. Like most 'What would you do if *your* family was attacked?' tales, there's a goading quality to the movie, a desire to see social restraints on retribution stripped away. The racial aspect of *Fight for Your Life* is ultimately less crucial – and less problematic – than its appeal to vengeance, with Endelson aligning his sympathies to such urban nightmare cure-alls as *Death Wish*.

Robert Endelson Interviewed

"The racism exploitation movie to end them all. Calculated to drive inner city audiences berserk with rage for an hour and a half before giving whitey his comeuppance, it would also be suitable entertainment for a Ku Klux Klan barbecue." – *Bill Landis, Sleazoid Express (book).*

*F*ight for Your Life, shot in 1976 by Robert Endelson, and released in '77 by New York distributor William Mishkin, is one of the most widely misunderstood movies of the era. Denied a certificate to this day in Great Britain, it's a perfect illustration of the way content can cast a shadow on the character of the filmmaker. It portrays a black family held hostage by vicious racist criminals, and uses dialogue as unflinching as the action. Perhaps it's a testament to the grim intensity of *Fight for Your Life* that reviewers have frequently assumed racism *behind* the camera…

It's certainly something that crosses your mind when watching for the first time: the dialogue crystallizes racist contempt in such a forceful way that one initially has difficulty separating the speaker from the spoken. The situation has been exacerbated because Endelson dropped out of the film industry, and has until now declined to speak about the movie.

So who is Robert Endelson? When Martin Scorsese first went to meet David Cronenberg, having seen the Canadian's early films *Shivers* and *Rabid*, he admits he was expecting someone who looked, "like Renfield… slobbering for juicy flies." If even a genius like Scorsese can assume a direct link between subject matter and artist, imagine how distorted our mere mortal impressions of Endelson have become over the years…

I first made contact with Bob in 2002, just after he was contacted by Blue Underground, who were about to reissue *Fight for Your Life* on DVD. He turned down their request to participate on the commentary track, but he did agree to talk to me for this book, which makes this the first time his views have been set down anywhere. I found him as forthright and vigorous as his movie suggests, with a very firm declaration to make about his personal views on race. It's time to let Robert Endelson speak for himself, and set the record straight…

A Pause for Clarification

Robert Endelson: "The first point I want to make is, I watched the movie this morning with a friend of mine, a woman of colour, who had never seen the movie before. And she said to me, 'This is not a racist film. This doesn't promote racism, it does precisely the opposite, it shows you how terrible racism is. And there's racism on both sides of the family, when the mother says 'Why do you invite that white girl to the house?'" He pauses, then adds, "It's a story about racist confrontation. It doesn't promote racism."

There's no doubt that Endelson is sensitive to the way the film has been perceived. The friend to whom he referred is his 'Family Assistant' (that's 'maid' to English readers), and I had the unexpected pleasure of chatting briefly to her on the phone one day. Endelson insisted, and put aside the receiver calling, "Dorothy! You got a moment?" Moments later Dorothy is on the speaker-phone. I ask her what feelings the film stirred up: "No bad feelings really. I don't think it's racist. I'm gonna watch it again, because I liked it!" Endelson interjects: "I was surprised. She said, 'Leave it in the video, I wanna watch it again this afternoon!'"

Dorothy, a cheerful woman with a no-nonsense attitude, gave the impression she was surprised to even be asked if the film was offensive: if Robert Endelson is running a plantation in deepest New Jersey, he's a *mensch* when it comes to labour relations…

Early Days

Robert Allen Endelson was born in 1947 and raised in New York City. His paternal grandfather emigrated from Russia, via Paris, where he worked for a while as a set painter for the French filmmaker Georges Méliès. "He was a very artistic person before he came over to America, when he went into the textile business," Endelson explains, "I think he may have worked painting the backdrop on things like *Trip to the Moon*."

Robert himself came to the movies via photography: "When I moved from New York to Long Island, one of my best friends was into photography and I thought this was really cool, so I became a still photographer during grade school and high school. I started making short movies, nothing of any significance. The senior car wash, that sort of thing, surreptitiously filming the physics class antics on 16mm. I never shot on Super-8 because I had 16mm

equipment belonging to my father. An old wind-up camera, the sort that took cartridges, actually. Before Bolex. In college there was no cinema club, so I decided to start one. All you had to do to was get twenty five names on a petition, so I walked around and said, 'Would you like to have a cinema club at the University?' And I got the names. The school gave me a thousand dollars, so I became a director! We made a couple of little shorts, two-minute films. I never really studied film but I was an accomplished still photographer. When I was a sophomore in college I was the photography editor of the Yearbook, which was usually a position reserved for a Senior."

Endelson left college for a summer job at a television commercial company, where he was introduced to real filmmaking. "I became the best production assistant that anybody ever had!" he laughs. "I was offered a place in the cinematographer's union by a very famous cameraman at that time called Gayne Rescher[1] and I turned that down because you had to apprentice for five years, and when you're twenty years old, five years is an eternity. So I said no and I got a lot of experience in the television commercial area. This was around 1969-70. There were only so many things I could do as a production assistant in commercials. I was never going to be a commercials director or cinematographer, so I went to work for this documentary producer called Herman Kitchen[2] who has made several quite successful documentaries. He hired me because I had a pilot's licence: he flew his own plane around the country and

above:
The Spanish seem to have caught the spirit of the film rather better than the Germans, with their title, **Defiende tu vida** ('Defend Your Life')!
below:
Uncannily resembling the young David Cronenberg here, Robert Endelson (*centre*, with camera) lines up a scene with Lloyd Freidus (*right*).

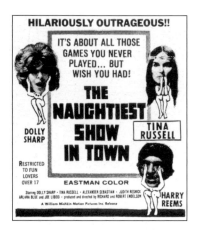

he figured I would be a good co-pilot. I started flying when I was sixteen and had my licence by the time I was nineteen. There was a seaplane base near our home on Long Island and I used to hitchhike down, without my parents' permission, and take flying lessons. Even before I got my full licence, I would land in the nearby backwater swamp areas in a seaplane, pick my friends up from their boat, fly around, then land and drop them off again, because if I came back to the seaplane base with passengers they would have taken my student licence away. We were very near to Kennedy Airport; those were the days before all the restrictions, I lived about twenty miles from Kennedy Airport and as long as you stayed below five hundred feet nobody bothered you. Today they would send a jet and shoot you down! The rule-book then was a quarter of an inch thick, and today it's two inches thick! I haven't flown in the last three years because 9/11 made everybody crazy, but I still hold my pilot's licence."

Endelson feels that the very reason he did poorly in school helped him find a niche in the film industry: "I had what they would call today 'attention deficit disorder' – I was lazy, didn't do well in school, but I had a talent for very specific things, like building ham radios. I liked building and putting things together and taking things apart. I never took my friends' stuff apart though, only my father's stuff! So I was very mechanical-minded, which made picking up the mechanics of cinematography easy, especially with my background in still photography. I became a cinematographer and worked on several low-budget films, some of which were porno films, which most young filmmakers of my generation made when they were in their twenties. If you look in the American Film Institute catalog under 'Francis Ford Coppola', the first movie listed is called *Flesh and Lace*! When you're a hungry young filmmaker all you want is to run film through a camera and have somebody pay for it!"

Today, Endelson's memory of this fascinating period is frustratingly vague, but he remembers enough to make you wish you could hire a hypnotist: "We were given the script on three three-inch by five-inch cards showing the beginning, middle and end, and we would have to make everything else up. One of them was *The Student Nurses* –

my name isn't on it, but it was one of the more successful.[3] Some of them were full hardcore, but a lot of it was faked. We had our own special effects, a lot of milk and sugar-water! And turkey-baister bulbs with little tubes. You could only go so far with some actresses but they didn't mind the sugar water. The actresses would fill out these question-naires: you know, which orifices? Will you do animals? [laughs] There was a guy called Curt Russell who would hire you, and you did anything just to shoot film, and see the result, and experiment. We used to shoot on hundred-foot rolls that he would buy somewhere cheap, so every minute you had to change the roll, you couldn't shoot anything longer than a minute. We used ends, anything that we could run through the camera that would produce an image! I never saw any of them finished. I saw the rushes when they came back from the lab, just to see what the cinematography looked like, but then I had no further interest."

Ladies and Gentlemen: The Filthiest Show in Town!

Working in New York's commercial underground, Endelson came into contact with various phosphorescent figures in the shadows of the industry: "Gerry Damiano I knew. I never worked with him but I met him once at a distributor's office and I had someone who was a mutual friend. I met him at a little gathering after he had made *Deep Throat*. Herb Streicher, who was 'Harry Reems', I knew very well because he worked on my picture *Filthiest Show in Town*.[4] He was one of the brightest, nicest, sweetest people you could imagine."

Filthiest Show in Town, shot in 1972, was Endelson's first feature film.[5] As he recalls, "I said to my father, I wanna make a movie, and he gave me $25,000 to do it, which was a lot of money in those days. I was lucky my

father had the money. He was a very practical man and he would rather invest in his son's movie than some school or university fee. So I went out and made that movie – it was shot in four days, in two locations – and we showed it to twelve distributors, who turned it down, because it's a pretty terrible movie! The thirteenth distributor was William Mishkin, who was a very smart man. It was originally called *The Maiden Game*, a take-off of *The Dating Game*, a nude version.[6] Mishkin was brilliant enough to retitle it *Filthiest Show in Town*, and paid for it to be blown up from 16mm to 35mm. He knew how to promote it, and the movie made quite a bit of money over the next three years, between domestic and international sales."

Pre-dating the similarly themed box-office hit *The Groove Tube* by two years, *Filthiest Show in Town* (the onscreen title omits the definite article) is a sex-oriented skit on dating shows and television commercials, featuring Harry Reems and 'A'-list porn star Tina Russell. When tapes of a sexually explicit game show, 'The Maiden Game', are seized by police, the station bosses, a Jew and an Italian-American, find themselves prosecuted for obscenity. During the court-case, the jury are shown clips from the show, featuring nudity, sex and obscene language. A State prosecutor seeks to prove that the 'moral decay' of society can be laid at the door of shows like 'The Maiden Game', while the defence argues on the basis of freedom of speech. Various witnesses are summoned: the prosecution calls the recent winners of the 'Family of the Year' competition, who assert that their once polite children have turned bratty and unmanageable since exposure to the show; while a representative of a Women's Rights organisation, called to offer her views on the corrosive effect of pornography, announces that she buys piles of the stuff to prevent it falling into the hands of perverts. The defence calls a psychiatrist who tells the court that the real sickos are the moral majority, who damage society by withholding sexual information from children and repressing sexuality in adults. Happily, despite the obvious bias of the Judge (Marshall Anker) in favour of the prosecution, the jury are more interested in watching further clips from the show…

Okay, it's not the most sophisticated sex comedy in the world. It's the sort of film in which a judge inadvertently uses a dildo as a gavel (in fact dildos seem to be an obsession here, as they feature both physically and verbally throughout – look out for a brief scene with Sandra Cassell (Mari Collingwood in *The Last House on the Left*) handling an angry, red-veined example in one of the film's numerous mock commercial spots). But while the constant sexual references become rather exhausting (the characters have names like 'Doris Dryhole', 'Phyllis Phallus' or 'Peter Ramrod'), the underlying argument about the hypocrisy of censors is at times quite sharply conveyed. Given that the film was released in 1972 when the *Deep Throat* trials were under way and XXX cinemas were being raided by the police, it's admirable that the Endelson brothers should have gone for tub-thumping libertarian advocacy on top of their softcore full-frontal orgies (even if they are 'preaching to the perverted'). The puns are awful, the obscenities are corny and juvenile (I'm sure I would have laughed myself sick over this when I was fourteen), but the witticisms about religious attitudes still raise a smirk or two. You can get a flavour of the mix from this example, in which a 'Maiden Game' contestant (a very fresh-faced Reems) is introduced to the studio audience thus: *"He advocates the theory that going to the toilet is unholy; and he holds the world record*

for constipation! From Rottencrotch Missouri, it's my pleasure to welcome – Barney Scrotum!"

The tone of the film is consistently scornful of the Church: something that comes over in *Fight for Your Life* too. At one point, a Catholic priest informs the jury that, *"Watching the show is alright, as long as you hate yourself for it afterwards!"* Well, I didn't hate myself, nor the filmmakers, because despite the film's silliness and repetition, it's still a fairly watchable time-waster if you're interested in the period, and the context in which it was made.

With his first movie completed and sold to one of New York's foremost ballyhoo distributors, Endelson made plans for a follow-up. "I developed another movie, that never got made, called *The Vigilantes of New York*. It was written by the now-famous Jesse Kornbluth. I paid Kornbluth $5,000 to write it; the most money he ever got paid for a project, up 'til then. He was a great, intelligent, well read, sophisticated young guy (whose education and ego got in the way of learning anything from a pipsqueak like me). He was a terrible scriptwriter from the get go. I think twenty years later he taught scriptwriting – if you can't do it, teach it! With me working literally over his shoulder, a script was turned out. We were within a week of starting – this was around 1973, a year before *Death Wish* came out in 1974. It was like there was something in the air. And the investor, a big wheeler-dealer, suddenly lost a lot of money in the commodities market, and he says, 'I'm sorry, I can't complete my commitment to you to make the movie.' This was a big $65,000 movie, and it was very depressing because we had cast it – Sylvester Stallone had come in, this was before he was cast in *The Lords of Flatbush*." Recalling his encounter with the future star of *Rambo*, Endelson adopts a creditable Stallone inflection: "'I'm gonna be one o' duh best actors dere ever is. I know I could be one of dese vidgie-landies!'"

Filthiest Show in Town
aka **The Naughtiest Show in Town**
(US theatrical re-release title)
aka **The Maiden Game** (original title)
© 1972. DVC Productions, Inc.
Joseph Brenner presents. A William Mishkin Motion Pictures Inc presentation.
producers/directors: Rick & Bob Endelson. screenplay: Rick Endelson. director of photography: Bob Endelson. assistant director: Victor Milt. gaffer: Steve Silverman. sound: Phil Pearl. script girl: Sue Town. assistant camera: Jeff Burnham, Stan Fortmeyer. assistant sound: Todd Crandall, Brad Pagano, Mike Spera. editor: Bob Endelson, Rick Endelson. editing consultant: Chic Ciccolini. make-up: Vince DeLeo, Pat Green, Jane Rothchild. still photography: Peter Kaplan, Seth Pinsker, Irving Schild. aerial photography: Tony Sheldon Moir. graphics: Joel Blashka. music editors: Arlon Ober, Larry Kogen. sound mixing: Sound one. set design: John Annus. costume, prop and product design: Rick Endelson. associate producer: Phil Pearl. production assistants: Gretchen Bleicher, Basil Cox, Bryon Gordon. Ross Lumpkin, Eric Markowitz, Linda Maslow, Gary Rich.
Cast: Rudy Hornish. Bernard Erhard. Alexander Sebastian. Richard Tenbroke. Herbert Manguso. Ronald Risman. court cast: Marshall Anker. Marge Davy. Delli Dorfman. Rob Kendall. Richard Manche. Mae Marmy. Carlo Masana (peeping tom). Richard Riker. Gloria Spivak. Stan Watin. the jury: Alan Marlow (jury foreman). Linda Bernard, Shiela Brome, Pierre Chamberlain, Marjorie Endelson, Jack Feintisch, James Zamparel, Janis Klazkin, Edward Kotkin, Lucy Massar, Leslie Shurgin, Franklin Feldhammer. reporters: Rodney Clegehorne, Alex Kreger, Jacob Oken, Joan Stark, Deborah Weiss. commercials: Don Alter (soldier). Bill Buck (dentist). Sandra Cassell (Olga). Hettie Hurtes (dental patient). Michael Mao (1st Viet Cong). Linda Maslow (girl with dog). Dana Ohlmar (Gretchen). Judy Resnick (NGT girl). Jack Russell (love potion jinni). Donna Sands (daughter (REEM)). Charles Seals (man in bed). Blossom Schultz (mother). Stan Watin (man on street). Mel Winkler (man from feces). Frank Young (2nd Viet Cong). seizure at NGT network: David Brooks (Harry). Billy Longo (Sergeant Gardner). Mike Murphy (Lieutenant Corona). Richard Rice (Joe). game show: Ron Alexander (announcer). Chuck Beard (Whitey). Arlana Blue (dancing girl). Patrice DeBauer (Jill). Earl Edgerton (Von Mole). Sam Elias (stagehand). Barbara Grumet (Phyllis). Doug Martin (Peter). Ralph Redpath (Robert). Tina Russell (Doris). Dolly Sharp (Mona). Peter Straight [aka Harry Reems] (Barney).

left:
The man from Mountain is at it again: The reverse side of the UK video cover for **Filthiest Show in Town** features this knowing if bizarre caricature (running shoes?) of the country's then-foremost 'morality campaigner' Mary Whitehouse, head of the National Viewers and Listeners Association. Whitehouse, whose archaic views were thankfully rendered obsolete even before her death in 2001, was instrumental in bringing about legislation against the so-called 'video-nasties' in the mid-1980s.

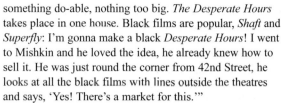

Fortunately, some of the effort was compensated financially: "After it fell through for me, we sold the script to Paul Williams and Ed Pressman for $15,000." Endelson also recalls an amusing irony in having made the sale to Williams: "Sometime between 1963-1967 I saw this ten-minute short in a theatre titled either 'Hooked' or 'The Fisherman'. Fade in: Dusk, a fisherman is surfcasting from the beach – gets hungry – finds a sandwich in a bag on the beach – bites into it and a *hook* goes through his *cheek!* He grabs the line and is dragged down the beach into the surf flopping like a fish. I think it was made by Paul Williams…" A decade later, the script for *Vigilantes of New York* features, "a scene where the vigilantes, with an electric shark rod and reel, *hook* a bad guy who's eating a sandwich at a diner – drag him down the aisle, out the door, down the street to the back of the vigilantes' van where they had a fishing chair mounted. Williams and Pressman read this and had to have the script. It still never got made."

Fight for Your Life

With *Vigilantes of New York* down the tube, Endelson took a sidestep, and came up with the basis of *Fight for Your Life*. However, we almost never got to see a second Endelson film: "After *Vigilantes* fell through I sort of left the business and got involved with some people who were flying planes, like WWII bombers. I don't want to mention what they occasionally carried on these planes, but I had a very close call! You don't know what paranoia is until you've stayed one night at a friend's house that had $2,500 of marijuana in the garage! So I walked away from these people and thought, I need to make a film tomorrow – because this is crazy. Okay, what am I gonna do? I've always liked *The Desperate Hours*, I need a film with one location,

something do-able, nothing too big. *The Desperate Hours* takes place in one house. Black films are popular, *Shaft* and *Superfly*: I'm gonna make a black *Desperate Hours*! I went to Mishkin and he loved the idea, he already knew how to sell it. He was just round the corner from 42nd Street, he looks at all the black films with lines outside the theatres and says, 'Yes! There's a market for this.'"

A great idea doesn't always lead to a great script, but here fortune smiled in the form of a Mishkin employee called Straw Weisman. Endelson explains: "Straw Weisman worked in Mishkin's office as a film booker, sitting at a little desk in the corner, sending prints on buses to Syracuse and Rochester. He was a clerk, but he'd gone to school to study writing and film, and he says, 'Oh, I can write this film'. So great, there's a free scriptwriter! I said, 'Okay, this is how we're gonna do it.' I gave him the plot summary, and he typed it out and he contributed a lot. I would say 85% of the dialogue is his – heavily edited, mind you, because he has a tendency to ramble, whereas for me everything has to lead to the next thing, to propel you on to the next scene. He didn't know very much about film structure or plot or suspense, so for the structure I had to lead him by the hand, but when it comes to putting dialogue in the actors' mouths, he's brilliant." Between them, the two men forged a no-holds-barred script which fairly leapt out of the typewriter. Endelson's strong concept and structure, plus Weisman's pungent, straight-to-the-point dialogue, delivered an exploitation movie-script to die for: almost literally, as it transpired…

But first the movie had to be cast, and with a script so aggressively confrontational it could all have gone horribly wrong: "In those days you put an ad in *Backstage* because all the actors were out of work. There would be lines outside your office, of actors waiting to audition. And that's how it was with Bill Sanderson, who we cast as Kane. He actually wouldn't leave the office! He says 'I know I could do this character and I'm not leaving until you give me the part!' And I said, 'Well, I got other people to talk to,' so he went outside and sat down in the hallway for several hours until I was finished casting and then he came back in, and he says, 'Well, whaddaya think?' And he was just so intense about it I said, 'Well, sure, you're Kane!' He was from the South, he was educated, he had a law degree, he'd discovered acting, and here was a part with teeth, and he gave it hundred-fifty-thousand percent."

Endelson was on a roll. His project had attracted not only Weisman but also Sanderson; an unknown for sure, but a powerful new screen presence without whom the movie could have disappeared into C-list obscurity. No doubt about it, a bad actor playing Kane would have sunk the project. *Fight for Your Life* balances on a knife-edge of taste and morality, and in the wrong hands it would have been a disaster…

One aspect of the script that addresses black American identity head-on is the focus on the family's Christianity. I asked Endelson if he wished to expose Christianity as a negative influence on black culture: "I'm not a religious person, I don't believe in organised religion. I think organised religion is one of the worst things that's ever happened to the world. In pagan times it did have its place, to somewhat civilise the world and give a set of rules, but it's been so distorted and skewed. My philosophy when it comes to symbolism and messages is, if you want to send a message, send a telegram! Not in my movie! Mishkin or Straw Weisman said, 'Wouldn't it be cool if Kane beat the

Deacon with his own bible!' That's not something that would ever come out of my mouth; it must have been Mishkin or Straw's, but I did say, 'Oh, that's not a bad idea!' The question for me is, how the hell do I shoot it? That was a technical challenge, a little room with no moving walls, how do you shoot this and make it effective even though you may have to suspend your disbelief – how do you show someone beaten senseless with a bible? So instead of 24fps I shot it at 8fps, and then you move very slowly, with the head flopping back and forth. When it's run back at 24fps it looks like he's going *whup-whup-whup-whup*."

The script was also influenced by Mishkin himself. Endelson explains, "William Mishkin would edit certain things, add things. For instance he said, 'We need to make the father dance a jig.' William understood emotion and reaction, so he would say, 'We have to do this in order for the revenge to be sweet.' For instance, he wanted me to make little Reggie eat from the dog food bowl, and I put my foot down, I said forget it, it's too degrading, I will not do that – I will not have Kane make the kid eat from the dog food bowl."

Mishkin's fabled parsimony[7] also meant that corners could be cut where others might have shelled out precious cash. "His wife had a hip problem and used a wheelchair, and so in the film, grandma's wheelchair was actually the producer's wife's wheelchair, and she had to stay in bed while we were shooting the scene! He was so cheap he wouldn't let me rent a wheelchair! He would call me every day and ask 'Are you finished with the wheelchair?' On the other hand, as a filmmaker he paid you to the penny. He actually did pay you and send reports, which I believe were honest. His son, on the other hand, was a different story. He was banned from the set."

It was time to begin shooting, and Endelson set off to the locations in New York State with the cast and crew: "The only way to get a film like this made on this budget is to literally kidnap the cast and crew, so we brought everybody in cars and trucks upstate, made a deal with a motel that had a restaurant next door, made a deal with the restaurant. We had everybody at the location for the whole fourteen day shoot. Then it was three days of pickups, like the gas station in New Jersey: we just got in the cars, one with the cameras and one with the actors, and we paid the gas station guy twenty bucks to let us set up the lights, and 'knife him to death', paid him the twenty bucks and then left! So the guy at the gas station plays himself in the movie, but I don't think he's credited because I never asked him his name. We said, 'We're making this low-budget movie, business here looks a little slow, do you mind if we set up some lights and kill you?' [laughs]. We stabbed him with one of these retractable knives and I said, 'As soon as you fall to the ground you gotta twitch.' I think I might even have shot it myself because there were a lot of shots that I did, on pickups and as second camera, certain shots I knew we would only get once, that I shot because I wanted it shot a certain way, like when Ling goes through the window and falls and you see the big piece of glass sticking out his back. Lloyd [Freidus] was an unemployed cinematographer and – I hate to say anything negative – let's say, he didn't have a great eye for composition, but he had a great eye for lighting. That's what I needed, because I had the eye for where to put the camera. Every angle and every shot was designed by me. For instance there's one shot that I know I did, when Kane, after he shoots the baby, comes up into the camera frame and says, 'I knowed it was empty'. I shot it because I knew

Straw Weisman – Kane Creator

Writer, producer and director Straw Weisman possesses excellent recall for the balmy days of New York Exploitation. He also has a natural sense of pride regarding Fight for Your Life, *for which he contributed a truly unforgettable screenplay. This interview, conducted in April 2006, is too detailed to merge with Bob Endelson's story, but as it provides valuable extra detail regarding both the production background of* Fight *and the drives and intentions of the drama, it's reproduced here as both complement and illumination.*

On Meeting and Working for the Mishkins:
"I got out of college 1973, after three years, and worked from April 1973 for an advertising agency, which was the first job I could find. Within six months I saw an ad in the *New York Times* for a film booker. A film booker is a guy who works in a distribution company and he's responsible for tracking the release prints of movies, moving the film round the country, checking the box-office statements, and analysing the advertising money spent. I was all of 22, 23. So I take this job with William and Lewis Mishkin, father and son respectively. I started on Columbus Day, 9 October, 1973. The Mishkins were a unique, oddball couple. William had been in the box business, selling cardboard boxes, at least that's what I was told, and eventually wound up with some powerful friends on 42nd Street, one by the name of Bingo Brandt. Bingo owned the Rialto, which was the premier porn theatre on 42nd Street. Will was a kind, gentle, on the surface, soft-spoken but very, very shrewd guy. And he wound up hiring his son Lewis, who was big, gregarious and prone to being loud and outspoken, who was a graduate of the Wharton School of Business, and a lawyer. The business basically consisted of the two of them, and they sat on opposite sides of a wall, they had matching little offices and a little lobby out front. The day I got hired, I was asked to sit in this little anteroom, the lobby, and it was fifteen minutes before they got to me because they were having an argument! Happened almost every single day, like a morning performance and an afternoon performance, and it lasted the entire three-and-a-half years I was there. And it was always about the same thing. Lew would be saying, 'You don't know how to run this business, this is all wrong,' and Will would be, 'Oh Lewis, this is how I do it, it works Lewis, don't break it if it's not broken!' Lewis would get so frustrated he would throw a chair across the room. Will had his way of doing things, which was old and staid and not modern, but it worked like gangbusters… everything Will touched worked. He would make these sex movies – *Sexual Practices in Sweden* (1970), *All About Sex of All Nations* (1971) – these pictures would be shot in a few days on 35mm, a guy called Kemal Horulu [Karl Hansen] who has since passed on, made both of those pictures as director and cameraman, everything. They'd cost $10,000 or $12,000, and they would play at the Rialto instantly, and each one I think played for a year. For an $11,000 investment and a week's work, he would create something that would play for a year in Times Square, 42nd Street New York! Will's first movie was called *Orgy at Lil's Place* (1963) shot in black and white, with one scene in 'scintillating color!' And the legendary orgy was one scene, and it wasn't even an orgy! It was all about the title. At the time it was the *most* scandalous thing – an orgy? Whoooh! It made quite a bit of money; he rolled that money in. As well as titles, Will was really good at designing front-of-house displays, called 'fronts'. It was like designing a piece of artwork. He had a guy who came in, and Will put his stills together, 'here's how I want 'em and here's the type' and he'd write his little catch-lines, and two or three days later there'd be this thing! A gaudy, glorious scandalous thing! Will tried to involve Lewis as a producer, and Lewis produced about three or four movies, none of which really worked. He made a movie called *That Man Is Pregnant* (Simon Nuchtern, 1972), and *Love-In '72* ('Karl Hansen', 1972). The difference was, we were all crazy and passionate about movies, but for Lewis, it was a widget. He was not a filmmaker *per se*. Will was a feisty penny pincher, and Lewis got that from him. When porn got more lavish, *Deep Throat* changed everything, Will didn't care to do it, he didn't believe in putting that money up on screen. Will's adage was, 'What we make is what we don't spend.' These were brilliant, iconoclastic, make-it-any-way-you-can scrappers, who did whatever they could think of to make a buck."

On How the Distribution Set-up Worked:
"If you were a little distributor, you made ten or fifteen prints, 35mm, and the prints were 'bicycled' all around the country. The country was broken up into 15-20 key cities, territories. New York was a territory, Boston and Newhaven, representing the entire Northeast, was a territory. Florida was a territory. Atlanta-Jacksonville was a territory. Dallas-Fort Worth was a territory. And the 13 Western states were one territory! – including North and South California, Arizona, Nevada, part of New Mexico… And each of these territories had a couple of sub-distributors who knew the theatre owners, and you made your deal with the sub-distributors and they booked the theatres and you would pack up your fifteen or twenty prints and ship 'em down there by bus, they would work the prints all at one time, moving them around and playing all the little key cities in their territory, and then when they were done they'd say, 'Okay we've played the picture out,' and you would move all your prints on the bus to the next territory."

On the Neighbours:
"Jack Bravman [see *Janie* in the review section] worked for Bunny Atlas in the office next door. This was the 13th floor, ironically enough, of 1501 Broadway, it was a mini film distributor's haven and in the office next to the Mishkins' was this woman called Bunny Atlas, a housewife from Queens with an incredible voice, kind of a big blousy girl, who somehow had the ability to attract cash money from Detroit. Bunny's movies all cost $20-25,000, and Jack Bravman cranked that porno out for her, in a few days, shooting with short ends. It was like the Wild West. When I left the Mishkins and went to work for Bunny next door, part of my job was to make her Martinis – mostly vodka, on the rocks. 'Hi, it's eleven thirty, make me a drink.'"

exactly what I wanted. You asked how many setups we got through – well, I went through the old shooting schedule and I counted, in one day, forty seven setups!"

The first day's shooting began with the scene where two boys, Floyd and Joey, black and white, perform a blood-brother ritual in the woods behind Floyd's house. "Joey was such a flat actor I was ready to kill myself," shudders Endelson. "After that day I just said to myself, 'Just get it in the can and don't worry about it.' Basically, we shot outside at first because the prop people were propping the house with all the black family's paraphernalia, the pictures of Bobby Kennedy and Martin Luther King."

If you've ever noticed just how swiftly and confidently *Fight for Your Life* is paced, it's fascinating to hear how precise it all was during the shooting: "Everything was virtually one take. I had been a film editor on documentaries after I'd done television commercials, so I knew exactly how I was going to put everything together. And I was on a Mishkin budget so I had no choice but to shoot virtually everything in one take. What you got was what you got. For one night, we rented a room and did a read-through, only one night, so there was no real rehearsal, apart from one other night where I had everybody come over to my tiny apartment and we had a few drinks and talked about what we were going to do."

One of the film's meatiest roles is that of Ted Turner, father of the household, played with great commitment by Bob Judd. Endelson rates his black leading man very highly: "I was blessed to have Bob Judd, who was a Broadway actor. A bottle of bourbon a day and he was happy! Then he would come in front of the camera, do his line, and retreat to the upstairs of the house, which we never showed because it's where we had the make-up and where everyone hung out. We called him One-Take Judd; every take was virtually perfect. I wish I could have done a second take when he had Chino at the mirror by the front door, because I wanted to see him on both sides of the mirror. That mirror just happened to be there and I used it in order to entrap Chino on both sides. For a while he did hit the mark and we see him on both sides, by the door, but it wasn't perfect. Any other film would have just shot it again so he was in the proper place but I didn't have the luxury. The black daughter [Yvonne Ross] and the white girl [Bonnie Martin] were the flattest. The white girl was picked because Mishkin needed a blonde with tits for advertising! That's why during the chase scene she's running with her tits hanging out, chased by Ling – that was a shot for the trailer! You have to make compromises. I mean, I don't hold myself up as a cinematic artist beyond story and plot and making something that gets under the skin of the audience. Watching it again this morning, it reminded me just how much dialogue I had to go back and dub later. 3/4-inch video had just come out and I put the film on video, and I would have the actors come up to my apartment one at a time, and I would re-record them over the second track on the video – it had two tracks. I would play the original track and they would talk into the microphone in order to dub; this is like the poorest man's dubbing studio you can possibly imagine! And then I would have that track transferred over to film (we shot in 35mm but edited a 16mm workprint to save money). It works because I'm a perfectionist, I synched it all up afterwards by hand. The worst thing in low-budget film is lousy sound."

When I ask Endelson to describe his own directorial style, he laughs: "Basically, I direct like Hitler! They

actually called me that! I'm very *'Achtung! – this* is how it's going to be done!' No discussion. It's very much the Hitchcockian approach, the actors are puppets, the crew are there to help you record it, and it's my way or the highway! There's no time to discuss character or motivation. All that there is time to discuss is how to get the actors into the mood for a scene. There are various psychological, manipulative ways – you have to be a psychiatrist. I held such a tight rein on everything – I was the first to arrive on location in the morning and the last to leave at night. It's the 'X' factor, either you have it or you don't. A good director knows how to help and inspire the actor to hit the mark that you're looking for, either physically or in his expression. When Kane is first in the living room and he steps on a table, I told him to do it. It's so intimidating, to step on someone else's furniture! He crosses over and says, 'Any of you coons wanna tie the feedbag on?' And then puts the gun to the nose of the daughter, and little Reggie is sitting there during this whole thing – you look at Reggie during this scene and he is truly terrified! His father was there, though. He came to the casting call, his father or his mother brought him. He wanted to be an actor, and he walked away from this movie, I assume, profoundly affected, because he went on to become a writer."

Endelson continues, "Only once did anyone have tantrums. It was Chino, when it came to shooting him in the balls. I wanted him rigged so that when the squib exploded in his pants – I had a special guy come in and do this – I had him rigged with foam rubber over the back of his legs and back and neck, and roped to a pulley so that we could pull him and explode his crotch at the same time. I could only do one take. And he says, 'No, you do it and I'll jump.' And I said, 'No. It'll never work, we could never explode it and you jump at the right time. There was a big row but finally he submitted to having this thing rigged up around him, we pulled, and it worked very well. But that was the worst."

Endelson is in no doubt that the cast saw the movie in a positive light. "They thought this was an important movie that needed to be made, because it shows how terrible racism is. That's why they worked for almost no money – Sanderson got $1,000 to do the film, and he was the highest paid. Grandma and some of the others probably got around $500 for all of this time, plus hotel and meals. They certainly didn't do it for the money! They did it because they felt it was an important film to be made, and that's why they got into it so much. They had all read the script, we had no revolts, no arguments on the set."

Throughout the remainder of 1977, Endelson worked on post-production. Thanks to the very tight shooting ratio, the movie was impossible for anyone else to recut. "Mishkin saw it when it was finished. There was so little material there was no question of 'Make this shorter, or this longer, change this, change that,' because what you saw was what there was! The cut was done fairly quickly but then I spent a lot of time on the sound, the breaking of glass, the swigging from bottles, the footsteps, the running of the dog in the woods, in order to give the sound real depth. I spent a tremendous amount of time doing this. It's what brings a film alive. Even the creaking of the floor as someone walks. I collected most of my own sounds – we would punch water-melons and record them! I moved the editing equipment into my apartment. The Steenbeck was under my loft-bed, and I spent twelve hours a day putting together all these snippets of film and sound."

234

Public Screening and Sales

With the movie completed, Endelson was ready for test screenings. "We took it out to Newark, New Jersey. We showed it to an unsuspecting black audience, who went absolutely nuts. Bill Sanderson was there, wearing a hood, slinked down in his seat. He was afraid someone might recognise him, get up from their seat and kill him! We realised at that screening that it was a hot potato. The black audience is yelling and screaming, 'Don't take that! Get up, do it, grab him!' and jumping out of their seats. We made a quick exit! I wasn't going to stick around and introduce myself to the audience and say 'Hi, I'm the director, what did you think of my film?' I was afraid for my life!'

Fight for Your Life has become a must-see item for anyone interested in American exploitation cinema. "It went out all over the country, to drive-ins, and it played in Baltimore for a long time. John Waters wrote about it in one of his books. I went to the next Cannes Film Festival and met him, and he told me how much he liked the movie. Then I met this Chinese guy there called Ed Kong. He bought the movie for all of South-East Asia and paid $60,000. He kept saying, Bob how much did the film cost? And I said, 'I can't tell ya until the deal is closed.' We became very friendly. He resold the rights to Korea and Taiwan, and he released it in Hong Kong where he was based – he was the son of a theatre owner there. Finally we closed the deal and got the $60,000 and I told him the movie cost $77,000 to make!"

Journey East

During 1978 and 1979, while living in Los Angeles, Endelson worked up a project that was as far removed from the incendiary commercialism of *Fight for Your Life* as it's possible to imagine. "Ed Kong wanted to do a film, based on stock footage, all about the Japanese invasion of China and Korea. Most of the people in Hong Kong were refugees from the Japanese. The story had never been told, it was before major TV coverage. We made this movie called *Rising Sun*, which was never shown in this country, it was only shown in Asia. We took silent footage, using several books as historical guides, and created a theatrical soundtrack, putting in footsteps, tank tracks, etc. It was released in Hong Kong in 1980/81. Ed calls me and says 'Bob, you have to fly to Hong Kong – there are lines around the block. Everybody is telling their children to see it, and the grandparents are telling them 'This is why we're all here.' It outgrossed *Close Encounters of the Third Kind*! It made a tremendous amount of money, translated into Cantonese, Mandarin… The Hong Kong reviewer in *Variety* gave it a very good review. It was so successful that Ed and I made another movie called *The Wonders of Life* (1983), also made out of documentary footage. No one in Asia at that time had seen pictures of embryos inside women's bodies, and this was all about nature. It made money but it wasn't as big a hit. And then my life turned towards inventing, and the river started to flow another way…"

Endelson is referring to his life post-cinema: he is now a very successful businessman, whose inventions – including a better flossing tool – have made him far richer than William Mishkin ever could. He doesn't miss his movie-making days: "I think I'm too lazy to make a movie these days. Even now in my business I don't get into day-to-day operations. A good use of my time is looking at the wall for an hour! There are one or two movies I'd like to make but I don't think they

On Writing at the Mishkins':

"At the time, my wife and I lived in a basement apartment in Greenwich Village, I would get up super-early, at 5a.m., and take my motorcycle up to Times Square and get on my IBM Selectric typewriter, which in those days was a very advanced machine, because you could erase! And I would write my own stuff. While I was there I wrote *Pelvis* aka *All Dressed in Rubber with No Place to Go*. And I wrote *Fight for Your Life* and *The Fox Affair* during that period. I co-wrote a thing called *Fear City*, which was eventually made by Chuck Vincent's ex-partner Howard Winters [Cecil Howard] and they changed the title to *Dead Boyz Can't Fly* (1992). For Chuck Vincent's *American Tickler* (1976) I wrote the sketch where there are people at the beach, and then the scary music starts, you know, you can guess, right? Der-der… der-der der-der, and this black shape breaks the water, and people are screaming and running and pointing, and then out of the water comes a Hassidic man, in his hat, and his beard and his Tallis, and the people pointing at the water go, 'Jews! Jews!' And that was my big contribution to *American Tickler*!"

On Spicing Up/Splicing Up Porno:

"Most of these sex films played in three versions. There was the original version; the soft-'X' version, which had touching and nudity; then there was the hardcore version with maybe three or four hardcore scenes. If there was any possibility in the movie that two bodies might get close enough to rub together, that was the basis for a sex scene insert! Two people on a train, and they touch? Cut to 'Ohh! Ohh!' And part of my job at that time, as I knew how to use a splicer, was to go into the editing room and turn the hardcore version to the softcore, or vice-versa, by lifting the inserts out, or putting them in."

On Meeting Bob Endelson and Writing Fight for Your Life:

"After Bob and Rick had made *Filthiest Show in Town*, which the Mishkins distributed, Bob would do some insert work for Will. I met Bob and I was already writing some trailers, generating titles [Straw was the man who retitled *The Slasher Is the Sex Maniac* as *Penetration*!], copy ideas and such, so when I heard Bob's idea for *Fight for Your Life* I said, 'I can write that, I can definitely write that.' I think it was called *Fightin' Family* when I wrote it. I did it in a month. I don't think Will realised how far we were going to go with the element of race baiting in the movie. When I waded into the material and realised where I was, I took the gloves off. The goal was to be as incendiary and inflammatory as possible. The goal was, we're going to torture this family for the first two acts, we're going to bait them and do everything we can to make them boil over, and in the third act the family will get retribution and revenge. What was good for me when I saw it in the editing room was that Bob took the written word very seriously. I would write a scene, and the dialogue I had written almost always came right back as I had written it."

On William Sanderson:

"Sanderson came to audition, he was maybe the last that day, and we looked at him, and his hair was blonde and straggly, he was wearing a sailor's cap, like a yachting cap, and he had on this dirty white shirt and dirty khakis. And he's like, this Tennessee drawl, 'Hi I'm Bill Sanderson, an' I'm here to read for that guy….' And we thought hmm, this is kinda interesting. So we gave him the script and he sat and he looked at it for five or ten minutes, and we said, okay it's time to read, and he opened his mouth and he *was* Jessie Lee Kane. We looked at each other, and the feeling in the room was positively electric – we knew this was the guy. It was brilliant."

On Fight for Your Life:

"I'm a dramatist. I came to the business to tell stories. *Fight for Your Life* came along at a time when playwrights like David Rabe and David Mamet were putting anti-war plays on and off Broadway, they were pushing the boundaries of language. The gloves were off. Race was a strange topic at that time. I'm born Jewish, I was brought up Jewish, I've lived around racial and ethnic epithets. A black can say to another black, 'Hey nigger, wassup?' God forbid that another person should call a black person by the 'n' word. It was forbidden and taboo. Which of course meant that it was fair game for something like this. The goal was, let's see what we have to do to push the buttons of this non-violent, God-fearing black minister, and what would it take to push him over the edge? Okay, he's a minister. So what does that mean? It means he espouses very traditional values of 'turn the other cheek'. Well, in Exploitation, 'turn the other cheek' means 'I can fuck with you'. The bible-beating scene was my idea; the under-cranking of the camera to really make the best of it was Bob's idea. Bob should have stayed in the business. He had great potential. But it's not an easy mistress, the film industry. Will was sure this movie was going to work, but Bob and Lew did not get along at all. They had many fights. On one occasion, Lewis tore the checkbook up! Literally tore it up and threw it in the air, yelling, 'There it is, there's your production!'"

On the Message of the Film:

"What sort of feeling do I want a black audience to carry with them as they leave the theatre? "Those are some damn hateful crackers, an' they oughta die!" And then I give them exactly what they want, and what those characters deserve. I'm a moral, ethical guy, so I ask what should happen to a person who goes that far over the edge? An eye for an eye; retribution. The cop who lets the family get their revenge represents a moral imperative that says – there's a higher law. There's a moment when you know that the right thing to do is to let these people get the revenge that they're entitled to, after everything they've been put through; and that's justice. If you go back to the Holocaust, as a kid hearing about it, I always said, well, why didn't they fight back? That tradition of fighting back, not taking it, that's a core belief for me – if you believe that there's a point beyond which you won't take it any more, you have to fight back. And how far do you have to push someone before they fight back? That's the point on which the movie turns."

will ever realistically happen. In *Rising Sun*, there's this story about a group of five hundred Chinese defenders in Shanghai against the Japs, who retreat to a warehouse. They hold out under constant bombardment for a week. A Chinese Olympic female swimmer swam across the Yangtze river with a Chinese flag, under Japanese gunfire, to give a flag to the defenders. It flew for a week above the warehouse, where ultimately they fought to the last man. And I believe she did that because there was someone in that warehouse she loved, and so she went against the Japanese invasion. I see that as a very compressed, no-way-out, *Das Boot* sort of story. They're under siege, they know they can't win, but valour dictates that they must fight to the last man."

So how does Endelson see the film he's most notorious for, today? When I spoke to him, he had just re-watched the movie for the first time in several years… "I find *Fight for Your Life* a stomach-wrenching film to watch due to the intensity of the racial tension. I felt very queasy watching it. I know I did it, but I'm not sure *how* I did it, because filmmaking is such a complex art, the juxtaposition of the screenwriting, the acting, putting it all together, all the way through to the finest details of sound. A lot of it fell on my shoulders to do and I find it amazing that I had the energy!"

9/11

Endelson addresses any suggestion of racial prejudice with aplomb, and a genuine desire to make himself understood. ("Van Peebles was one of my favourite directors when I was young," he says, adding with a low-budget director's genuine admiration, "On *Sweet Sweetback's Baadasssss Song*, when he needed fire trucks for a scene they just pulled the fire alarm!") However he's far from your standard liberal torch-bearer. Conversations about political matters are fraught with post-9/11 anger and suspicion, bordering at times on paranoia. Says Endelson, "My feeling on gun control is, think how much money we would save if every airline passenger was required to carry a gun, instead of the government spending hundreds of billions of dollars trying to keep them off planes. There would never be a hijacking again if everybody was armed!" He pauses, perhaps sensing my alarm at the image of a Boeing-747 packed with gun-toting Americans, then laughs: "You can say I have an extreme view on the subject!" Echoing Woody Allen's character in his 2003 movie *Anything Else*, he continues: "I'm pro-gun ownership, and I would fight for my right to maintain and have a gun, which I do. It's for home security, and in the back of my mind it's for the day the world goes crazy. After 9/11 I was telling people you have to be very careful coming to my house because the front lawn has land-mines on it! I see an accelerating breakdown in values, promoted by the media. There's really a terrible breakdown of morality, things are being turned topsy-turvy. One of the most popular magazines is called *Self*, you see all the women reading it on the beach. We're turning into a *me-me-me fuck-you* society, and it really distresses me. Children don't come to see their parents or grandparents any more. I don't know what it's like in England, but we used to go to grandma's house. Now the parents have to go see the children and then the children wanna pick the restaurant! When I was growing up they said, 'We're going out to eat' and if I didn't wanna go there my father would say, 'You can stay home and eat a mustard sandwich for all I care!' I think the media is distorting the world. I have two daughters, I don't know what they watch, I'm more worried about what they smoke!" He laughs, adding: "They don't, but then I'm very blessed."

In the right-libertarian tradition, Endelson is thankfully not the sort of guy who thinks the problems of the world would be solved by sweeping censorship; no matter how bad the media scrum can be: "I'm strongly opposed to gagging people, no matter what they have to say, because the more radical they are the more stupid they sound." And he's not swayed by the political influence of his own racial background: "I'm Jewish, but I won't contribute to any Jewish causes." A pro-gun anti-Zionist Jewish right-winger who believes to the utmost in free speech, Endelson is his own man; but then, after watching *Fight for Your Life*, should we expect anything less?

1 Rescher shot Elia Kazan's *A Face in the Crowd* in 1957 and *Star Trek II: The Wrath of Khan* in 1982, but worked mainly in television.

2 Herman Kitchen ran a documentary production company in the early seventies with George S. Ansell, called Unit 1 Productions Inc., specialising in industrial films. He also worked on a Canadian TV documentary series called *Audubon Wildlife Theatre*, directing titles such as *Wildlife By Air*.

3 The credited cinematographer on Stephanie Rothman's 1970 Corman production *The Student Nurses* – probably not the film to which Endelson refers – is Stevan Larner, one of the three who shot Terrence Malick's *Badlands*.

4 Billed as 'Peter Straight'.

5 Adds Endelson, "I made my first TV commercial 'Cliffhanger' about 1970-71. Who would pay an inexperienced kid to make a commercial that would actually be aired? Well, the idea was an anti-smoking spot (which would air for free) pitched to a room of smokers at the American Heart Association. Couple driving in car – man lights cigarette, coughs, drops cigarette into lap, struggles with seatbelt, swerves off road, over cliff. Smoking car on its back with tires still turning – pan down to cigarette in foreground, smoking. Title: 'Cigarettes kill in many different ways.' Title: 'Ask your Heart Association.' Seemed like a good idea, they paid for it, but would not show it when they saw it. I said, 'Fuck it, I'm going to make a feature!'

6 *The Dating Game*, the ABC TV show that provided the blueprint for the UK's *Blind Date*, ran from 1965 to 1986.

7 For more on Mishkin's thriftiness, read *The Ghastly One: The Sex-Gore Netherworld of Andy Milligan*, by Jimmy McDonough.

ROBERT ENDELSON: FILMOGRAPHY AS DIRECTOR

1972	*Filthiest Show in Town* aka *The Maiden Game* (co-directed with Rick Endelson)
1977	*Fight for Your Life* aka *Getting Even* aka *Held Hostage* aka *Staying Alive* aka *The Hostage's Bloody Revenge* aka *Bloodbath at 1313 Fury Road*
1980	*Rising Sun* (documentary)
1983	*The Wonders of Life* (documentary)

OTHER CREDITS:

1969-72	uncredited cinematography on numerous sex films
1970	*The Student Nurses* – dir: unknown (uncredited cinematographer)

chapter 11

The Living Dead at the All-Night Mall

Willard Huyck & Gloria Katz on the making of Messiah of Evil

with contributions from editor Morgan Fisher and designer Joan Mocine

Messiah of Evil (1973)

"*Messiah of Evil* was my view of the San Fernando valley... That bleak high street? If you walk through San Fernando valley at night, that's what you saw."
- *Willard Huyck.*

"A pretentious horror cheapie which wastes its atmospheric camerawork in telling a badly plotted story about cannibalistic zombies. […] Scott Conrad's editing includes too many shots of clouds." – *Variety*

"A strangely surreal movie, shot through with the pretensions one might expect from fresh film school graduates […] but rich in narrative convolutions and peculiar atmospherics." – *Kim Newman, Nightmare Movies.*

True horror fanatics love to ferret out morbid treasures from the undergrowth of low-budget production, but sometimes you wonder if you're beginning to prefer the taste of junk to the occasional truffle. Fortunately, a neglected marvel like *Messiah of Evil* vindicates your persistence. Stephen King writes eloquently about the horror fan's taste for 'prospecting' in his non-fiction book *Danse Macabre*, citing David Schmoeller's *Tourist Trap* as an example of why we should continue to sift the genre for gems. If you're asking *me* to illustrate the point of it all, I would choose George Barry's *Death Bed: The Bed That Eats*, Daniel DiSomma's *Victims*, and Willard Huyck's *Messiah of Evil*. The latter is hardly the most obscure film in this book, but it has never really enjoyed the acclaim it deserves; a shame, as were it not for a tiresome theme song imposed on the material by the producers, and an unnecessary voice-over, I would place it alongside John Hancock's *Let's Scare Jessica To Death* as one of the most unfairly neglected horror films of the 1970s.

Arletty (Marianna Hill), a young woman who has recently lost touch with her artist father Joseph Lang (Royal Dano), sets out to visit him at his studio in a small town called Point Dune, on the California coast. Just outside town she speaks to an all-night garage worker, who seems spooked for no apparent reason. He urges her to turn back. Continuing to Point Dune, Arletty can find no trace of her father, though his studio-cum-home has clearly been lived in recently. She reads his rambling diary entries but learns little of any use, and so drives into town to investigate. The snooty owner of a local art gallery (Morgan Fisher) directs her to a motel, where Thom (Michael Greer), a playboy adventurer interested in her father's paintings, is staying with his two female companions, Laura (Anitra Ford) and Toni (Joy Bang). Arletty finds Thom tape-recording an interview with Charlie (Elijah Cook Jr.), an old vagrant who describes a sinister local legend concerning 'the blood moon'. Leaving the motel, Arletty is accosted by Charlie, who grows agitated and tells her that she must burn – not bury – her father. The following day, back at her father's studio, Arletty awakens to find Thom, Laura and Toni settling in. Thom explains they've been thrown out of the motel and mentions that Charlie has been murdered. Arletty succumbs, through fear and loneliness, to Thom's sexual advances, a development that causes first Laura then Toni to leave and head off into town: a decision they both come to regret. Laura discovers the town's terrible secret in a late-night supermarket, while for Toni a trip to the cinema becomes a nightmare. The next day, Arletty is called to the beach and is told her father has been found dead, crushed beneath a sculpture he was building: Arletty tells Thom the body was not her father's. Meanwhile she is beginning to show symptoms of a strange sickness afflicting the townspeople. At last her father returns home, warning his daughter of danger – then he attacks her. Arletty stabs him and, remembering Charlie's words, sets him on fire. Thom witnesses horrific scenes during a night-time walk through town and returns for Arletty; but there can be no sanctuary for either of them…

Messiah of Evil is a very strange, very innovative spin on the zombie film. Like Robert Voskanian's *The Child* and the aforementioned *Let's Scare Jessica To Death*, it

below:
The US one-sheet for **Messiah of Evil**.

Messiah of Evil
aka **Return of the Living Dead / Revenge of
the Screaming Dead / Dead People**
(US theatrical re-release titles)
aka **The Second Coming** (pre-shooting title)
aka **Deep Swamp** (UK video cover title)
© 1973. A V/M production
A V/M production.
director: Willard Huyck. producer: Gloria Katz.
executive producer: Alan Riche. administrative
executive producer: James P. Graham.
screenplay: Willard Huyck and Gloria Katz.
director of photography: Stephen Katz
(Technicolor). film editor: Scott Conrad. art
directors: Jack Fiske [Fisk] and Joan Mocine.
post-production supervisor: Raymond Nadeau.
electronic music: Phillan Bishop. [song] "Hold
On to Love" music and lyrics by Eliane Tortel,
sung by Raun MacKinnon. associate producer:
Alan R. Howard. assistant to producer: Candace
Lawrence. production manager: R.J. Louis.
associate editors: Morgan Fisher, William [Billy]
Weber. assistant editor: John Simons. script
supervisor: John Dorr. assistant cameramen:
John Swain, Sean Doyle. production sound: Alex
Vanderkar. boom-man: Michael Katz. assistant
director: Alan Howard. wardrobe: Jodie Tillen,
Rosanna Norton. make-up: Budd Miller. gaffer:
Mark Hyer. key grip: Paul Tampourlos. grip:
James F. Huyck. production assistants: Cheryl
Stein, Charlotte Jupiter, Victoria Swain. still
photographers: Judy Fiskin, Ron Batzdorff. titles
and opticals: Opticals West. dubbing: Audio Tran
Sound (Hollywood). sound effects: Gil Marchant.
Cast: Michael Greer *(Thom).* Mariana Hill
(Arletty). Joy Bang *(Toni).* Anitra Ford *(Laura).*
Royal Dano *(Joseph Lang).* Elisha Cook, Jr.
(Charlie). Charles Dierkop. Bennie Robinson
(albino van driver). Morgan Fisher *(antique shop
proprietor).* Emma Truckman. Dyanne Simon
[Asimow]. Herb Margolis. Alex Michaels. Walter
Hill *(pre-credits victim).* Laurie Charlap-Hyman.
B.W.L. Norton. stunts by Stunts Unlimited.
uncredited: Gloria Katz *(cinema ticket-seller).*
Willard Huyck *(scuba diver).* Billy Weber *(staring
ghoul in supermarket).*

illustrations on forthcoming pages...

p.240, strip of images, top to bottom:
The (unexplained) pre-credits assassin – all is
not well at Point Dune's out-of-town garage –
Arletty (Marianna Hill) explores her father's
unsettling home – Charlie (Elisha Cook Jr.) has
some unsettling advice for Arletty – Thom
(Michael Greer) lets himself in – a local of Point
Dune – Laura (Anitra Ford) discovers that 24-
hour shopping is not all it's cracked up to be...

p.242, strip of images, top to bottom:
Thom blends in – a local exhibits signs of
Rouge's Malady? – Toni (Joy Bang) vainly
tries to escape through the screen – Arletty
finds she's riddled with bugs – Arletty's father
(Royal Dano) at one with his art – Patricide
(Robin Wood's favourite bit?) – Arletty attacks
– the living dead swarm the house...

below:
Bennie Robinson – do *not* cold-call this man...

achieves much in an over-subscribed subgenre by setting
out in an altogether different direction, before taking a
metaphorical turn through the cemetery.

Now, for purists out there I have to qualify this
statement: these are not the classic flesh-eating ghoul-
spawn of Romero's *Night of the Living Dead. Messiah of
Evil* was made soon enough after that seminal classic not
to have the weight of formula on its shoulders. Huyck and
Katz take the blank, hollow-eyed silence of the Romero
zombies, and their taste for flesh (in this case both dead
animal and living human), but instead of repeating
Romero's explanations they dispense with them, leaving
the ontological status of these beings largely unspecified.
Are they really 'dead people', as one release title
suggests? Or are they under some sort of mesmeric
influence, mindless acolytes of the mysterious 'dark
stranger' referred to in Lang's rambling diaries? When
Thom witnesses attacks against the police, it seems that
bullets have no effect on the advancing hordes. But their
actions seem less random than the brain-dead shambling
we usually associate with zombies. The story also
mentions disease – the signs of which are a numbness of
the extremities and trickles of blood from eyes and ears,
not unlike the signs of 'Rouge's Malady' in David
Cronenberg's *Crimes of the Future* (1970), or, the slowly
encroaching signs of death in Dan O'Bannon's *The Return
of the Living Dead* (1985). Are the numb yet murderous
townspeople simply infected with a malignant virus?

So these are not your typical zombies. Their behaviour
is governed by Huyck and Katz's desire to populate a
particularly nightmarish vision of sterile Californian
consumerism with symbols of soulless humanity. In this
it's actually a forerunner of Romero's *Dawn of the Dead*:
one scene in particular, in which Laura discovers a pack of
dishevelled-looking 'shoppers' gathered round a
supermarket freezer unit munching cuts of raw meat, is
both a pure nightmare image and a symbol of slavery-to-
consumption as effective as any in *Dawn*.

The other standout scene is Toni's trip to the cinema, a
paranoid nightmare that Alfred Hitchcock would surely
have loved (especially since it quotes a standout scene
from *The Birds*). Like much of the film, it achieves an
oscillation between the mundane and the macabre that
writers of American dark fantasy like Dennis Etchison and
Peter Straub would go on to explore in literature. *Messiah*
accomplishes this under considerable negative pressure:
for instance, Huyck never had the chance to finalize
which film the zombies are 'watching' in the cinema – it
was added by the producers after he and Katz were ousted
from the project. In the film as released, a cinema sign
announces 'Kiss Tomorrow Goodbye', although what we
actually see is a confusing montage of Wild West clips
culled from Bernard (*A Name for Evil*) Girard's *Gone with
the West*, a troubled production starring Sammy Davis Jr.
that languished unfinished for several years. *Gone with
the West* was owned at the time by International Cinefilm,
who were responsible for finishing *Messiah* without
consulting Huyck and Katz (presumably they wanted to
get at least *some* use from the Girard footage). The whole
disorienting mess is cut out of sequence, and scored to
music more typical of a blaxploitation B-movie: the result
is a garbled, senseless entertainment which the slowly
gathering audience of 'dead people' stare at with dull-eyed
disinterest. Yet despite the odds, someone, somewhere,
chose well – while the scene may lack Huyck's

brushstrokes, it conveys a frantic, affectless confusion that
feels entirely right. If you remade *Messiah* today, some
randomly edited Michael Bay footage would no doubt do
the trick...

Overall, this is an accomplished movie in which style
and theme dovetail beautifully. The way in which the
cinematography and art direction align the puzzled,
increasingly spooked Arletty with the looming, alienated
figures in her father's paintings is especially striking. Her
father's home seems actually *built* from art, of a chilly,
forbidding variety: the rooms have become giant
canvasses, with wall-paintings depicting stylised, near-
characterless figures staring blankly from collisions of
geometric planes and disappearing perspectives. The effect
is of the ominous dark-coated men of René Magritte's
paintings invading the post-*Yellow Submarine* psychedelic
poster art of the late sixties. Arletty is almost lost in her
father's graphic domain – which could perhaps be seen as
a reproach to artistic parents who neglect the more
essential creation of their children.

With its heavy emphasis on design, *Messiah of Evil*
reminds me of the extravagant Italian horrors of Dario
Argento. The use of painting to destabilise the film frame
is particularly clever and shows the hand of a director
unafraid to play with the medium, in a way that's rare for
the more pragmatic, commercial American horror film.
And there's a scene where Arletty's father covers his face
with handfuls of blue paint before screaming and attacking
his daughter that wouldn't be out of place in Argento's
(much later) film *The Stendhal Syndrome.*

By the time the 'zombie' secret is out, the viewer has
already been rattled by the film's paranoid perceptions.
Brittle mundanity seems to vibrate with a danger that may
be imaginary, or all-too real. Huyck turns the late-night
car parks and shopping malls of the San Fernando valley
into a hyper-real nightmare, where horror lurks in multiple
window displays, endless store fronts, row upon row of
parked cars. He captures a sense of unease that you
sometimes get in our mechanised society when the fever
of daily traffic is subdued by nightfall. If you've ever
hitch-hiked and found yourself stuck for hours beside
motorway slip roads near industrial estates, with their
giant arc-lit loading bays, you'll have some idea of the
picture I'm trying to draw – inhuman, hostile places,
emerging after dark from behind the façade of banality.
The lighting by Gloria's brother Stephen Katz (a talented
cinematographer later responsible for *Gods and Monsters*)
brings that hard-edged *frigidaire* ambience in from the
periphery and onto the city streets, turning unremarkable
shopping areas into glittering consumerist cemeteries. *"If
the cities of the world were destroyed tomorrow, they
would all be rebuilt to look like Point Dune,"* says (Royal
Dano's) voice-over. *"Entirely normal. Quiet. Silent though
because of the shared horror. I know, it's hiding now
beneath the stuccoed skin."*

Another indication that the filmmakers are aiming
high is the constant attention given to sound. Once you
get past the excruciatingly histrionic title song ("Hold On
to Love" sung by minor folk artist Raun MacKinnon),
Huyck treats sound-mixing as another field of creativity
instead of a simple matter of matching Foley and
dialogue. The pulse of the sea maintains a constant level
of unease, over which an effective, if at times rather
strident electronic score adds an array of ring modulated
efflorations. (Phillan Bishop's weirdy electronics can also

be heard on *Kiss of the Tarantula* and *The Severed Arm* –
see review section). However, it's this skill in orches-
trating sound and vision that makes Arletty's voice-over
so regrettable. It would be a service to cinema if her
intrusive internal monologues were erased one day, like
the unnecessary Marlowisms once given to Harrison
Ford's Deckard in *Blade Runner*. On the other hand, the
diary voice-overs of Arletty's father are more appropriate,
bringing to mind the books of H.P. Lovecraft (whose
protagonists frequently left their disturbed ramblings in
diaries for others to find), fostering the idea that this is
actually a Lovecraftian horror film filtered through
contemporary fears about loss of identity.

Juxtaposed with the conformity of the ghoulish
townspeople is the central character of Thom. He's a
dandy and a dropout, probably a rich kid burning off some
fantasies of alienation and freedom while waiting for his
parents to leave him the estate. In keeping with the times,
he sleeps with two women and seduces a third. However,
there are numerous ironies attached to the depiction of this
'modern' bedroom arrangement: I'd suggest a parallel
with the cynical viewpoint of Lucio Fulci's thrillers of the
time, *A Lizard in a Woman's Skin* and *One on Top of the
Other*. We are clearly dealing with the fallout of the sixties
in the brattish Toni, the sophisticated but possessive Laura
and the dilettantish, emotionally manipulative Thom.
There's the feeling that some kind of socio-cultural bomb
has dropped, but instead of liberation and revolution, a
sort of *laissez-faire* fatalism has descended; perhaps the
true fall-out of the nuclear age. A languid quality soaks
through the drama, echoing the coastal setting and the
endless lapping of the waves. It's a shade short of pretentious in this respect: employing measured performances
and dreamlike pacing, Huyck manages by the skin of his
teeth, I think, to avoid straying into idle portentousness.
I'm reminded very strongly of the mood of Peter Fonda's
Idaho Transfer, also released in 1973, in which hippy
indecisiveness was counterpointed by reckless science.

There are loose ends and confusing issues still
unresolved at the climax. How is the blood affliction
passed on? What is the nature of the seashore ritual? Who
is the dark figure seen amassing his mindless followers?
Doubtless much of the confusion stems from the
unhappily truncated involvement of Huyck and Katz. Still,
Messiah of Evil has some unforgettable, truly disturbing
images. The theme of social alienation is creepily
followed up at the bodily level, as Arletty sticks a needle
into her leg and burns her hand on a gas stove, yet feels
no pain; in another repellent scene she vomits beetles,
maggots and a small lizard into the sink. Bernie Robinson,
a giant, basso-voiced albino who pops up in two
especially alarming sequences, is terrifying enough on his
own to guarantee sleepless nights in the nervous. Unlike
say, Peter Medak's *The Changeling*, another supernatural
tale from a mainstream director, *Messiah of Evil* is clearly
the work of people with an appreciation of the genre. It's
always intriguing when someone not generally known for
their work in the horror field 'has a go' at scaring us.
Kubrick set the benchmark with *The Shining*: Huyck and
Katz, who wrote this as a time-out from the screenplay for
American Graffiti, also have that canny grasp of how to
expand a genre's horizons. *Messiah of Evil* has 'first film'
written all over it, but it's a *great* first film, and you can't
help but fantasize what would have happened if it had
been a hit...

Morgan Fisher on Messiah of Evil

"Since the late '60s, Morgan Fisher has made films which foreground the industrial basis of all filmmaking,
ironically combining narrative and non-narrative forms and underscoring the common ground between the oft-
unreconciled poles of the independently produced 'experimental' film and industrially produced commercial
product." – *Steve Polta, San Francisco Cinematheque.*

MORGAN FISHER FILMOGRAPHY

1968	*The Director and His Actor Look at Footage*	1974	*Cue Rolls*
	Showing Preparations for an Unmade Film	1974	*240x*
1968	*Documentary Footage*	1976	*Projection Instructions*
1968	*Phi Phenomenon*	1977	*Southern Exposure* – 16mm installation
1968	*Screening Room*	1979	*North Light* – 16mm installation
1970	*Production Stills*	1979	*Passing Time* – 16mm installation
1971	*Production Footage*	1980	*Color Balance* – Super-8 installation
1973	*Picture and Sound Rushes*	1984	*Standard Gauge*
1973	*The Wilkinson Household Fire Alarm*	2003	*()*

(Of particular interest here is *Standard Gauge*, which includes anecdotes about *Messiah of Evil* and two outtakes
from the film.)

**Morgan Fisher's detailed and thoughtful responses to my questions would have been difficult to edit into
the main text of this chapter without overbalancing the piece away from Gloria and Willard. However,
they're equally fascinating in their own right, so they are presented in (more or less) unexpurgated form
below, with the rest of this text continued in the sidebars on the following pages.**

How did you first get to know Willard and Gloria?

I met Willard when I was at film school at USC. He was an undergraduate. He dropped out to pursue his career
as a screen writer. He already had a career. He had written some scripts for American International Pictures. I can't
remember the titles. Willard can tell you, I'm sure. I remember that when I met Willard's parents they were worried
that he had made a terrible mistake in dropping out of college, but I assured them things would work out for Willard.

How did you become involved as an editor on *Messiah of Evil*?

Willard and Gloria needed an editor. I had worked as a second editor on *The Student Nurses* so I had some
experience. And I would work for cheap. I think they turned to people they knew because they wanted to work
with their friends, and they could also ask their friends to work for next to nothing. I had met Willard, and Willard
had met and married Gloria, who was in the film program at UCLA. So through Willard I met Gloria. Willard and
Gloria, in asking that we work for next to nothing, assured us that we would all work together on some future
project when we would all be paid more generously. I was on the set a lot, and Willard would ask me for suggestions about how to lay out the shots so they would cut. There was one time when I suggested a specific shot and
Willard rejected the idea. This was in the supermarket scene. Anitra Ford is trying to make the door open so she
can escape, and it won't. I thought the audience would think that she was mistakenly trying to get out through the
entrance door, which naturally would not open, when the point of the scene was that she was trying to get out
through the exit door but that it would not work. My suggestion was to shoot an insert of her feet stamping on the
treadle, so that we see the treadle and see her stamping on it and so we understand that it's the exit door but that
her efforts are unavailing. Willard said it would be an ugly shot and he refused to do it, but then said that if I insisted
on the shot, I would have to direct it myself, and so I did. Of course it is in the nature of inserts that they are often
visually awkward, but they have their part to play in making things clear. I feel vindicated in insisting on the shot,
because it survived in the later cut made by others.

**Willard Huyck said that post-production suffered on *Messiah* due to budget difficulties. Were you aware
of these problems as you worked on the first edit?**

Not until the difficulties began. We worked first in a cutting room at the Technicolor plant in Hollywood as
a part of our deal with them. The film was shot in Techniscope, a patent process developed by Technicolor: the
frame is not four perforations high, but two, so on the film you get a scope ratio, and you get twice the running
time per foot of camera negative than in four-perf 35mm. It's grainier than four perf, of course, but the savings
are significant if you're a director who likes to shoot a lot. *American Graffiti* was shot in Techniscope. Then, for
reasons I don't recall, Willard insisted that we sneak out of Technicolor as if in the middle of the night. I think
Willard was afraid the film would be seized because we were behind on paying the lab bill. We took refuge first
at Willard's parents' house. But Willard at the screening at UCLA earlier this year said something I had never
known, that the neighbours objected to the blood-curdling sounds that were coming from the house, so we had to
move again. Maybe the sounds weren't blood-curdling, maybe they were just loud and repetitive. The same
dialogue over and over again, and so forth. So we moved to the warehouse for the company that Willard's father
owned. Somewhere in here the money ran out. Willard made us work very hard. The days were ten hours, and we
also worked on Saturdays. I remember this particularly from the time when we worked in the warehouse, because
it was in the far reaches of San Fernando Valley, a long drive from Santa Monica, where I lived.

But someone found someone from Texas to step in with more money. It was a young kid with rich parents who
I think wanted their son to be something more respectable than a racing car driver, and they thought being a movie
producer would fill the bill. So the film became a Podno Production. He hung around the cutting room to watch us
work, then when he realised how boring it was, he stopped hanging around. When we all got our first paychecks
from Podno, in freshly printed envelopes, we found that no one had bothered to sign the checks. Not a good sign,
of course, and then the money ran out again. That was when the post-production that I was involved in was broken

Willard Huyck & Gloria Katz Interviewed

Willard Huyck and Gloria Katz are the internationally renowned writers of *American Graffiti* (1973), a bittersweet tale of small-town American life in the early sixties, described by the US critic Roger Ebert as, "not only a great movie but a brilliant piece of historical fiction." It won many more such plaudits, did spectacular box-office business, and launched the commercial career of its director, George Lucas. When Lucas later ran into difficulties writing a sci-fi flick called *Star Wars* (1977), Huyck performed what has to be one of the most wisely accepted 'uncredited rewrites' in cinema history, injecting more humour into the script and earning himself points on the most lucrative and influential film of the century. In the '80s, Huyck and Katz wrote *Indiana Jones and the Temple of Doom* (1984) for Lucas and director Steven Spielberg. The film was criticized at the time for being too bloodthirsty, although it's not a complaint you'll hear from many children. Once again, the writers helped to create a massive commercial smash. However, trouble was waiting in the wings: after a poorly-received comedy called *Best Defense* (1984), which the couple wrote and Huyck directed, their working partnership with Lucas finally hit the rocks with *Howard the Duck* (1986), a resounding flop. Critics ritualistically mutilated Huyck and Katz, plucking out their steaming hearts and lowering them into a pool of molten lava – metaphorically speaking, of course. *Howard the Duck* later received a 'Razzie' for Worst Film of the Decade, putting it in the illustrious company of *Can't Stop the Music* and *Showgirls*, which must be some consolation, but the fuliguline fallout that followed proved hard to overcome, and since 1994's *Radioland Murders*, the names of Willard Huyck and Gloria Katz have been absent from the screen.

But there is one more film of which they can be proud. At the back of the cupboard, so to speak, almost hidden behind the couple's extraordinary A-list adventures, there lies a strange, rarely-screened low-budget horror film, *Messiah of Evil*, made right at the outset of their careers. It was initially written to be sold to another director, but when deals fell through Huyck and Katz decided to direct it themselves. At the time, *Messiah of Evil* did them few favours in the industry, but over the years a few attentive critics and fans, attuned to the film's icy mood, have championed it as one of the most unsettling of the 1970s…

The Team

"We both grew up in Los Angeles," Huyck begins. "I grew up in the San Fernando valley. When I was a kid we used to play out in the ranches out there in the West Valley, the Warner Brothers ranch where they shot movies. So I was interested from then. And then I was interested in journalism and went to USC, ostensibly as a journalism major, and then didn't tell my parents and switched over to film. In those days being a film major was easy. I mean you walked by the film department and they asked you if you wanted to be a major. Now it's incredibly difficult. It was there I met George Lucas. We were in the same class."

"There were very few people in the film department," recalls Katz. "I was a history graduate student and was overloaded with amazing amounts of work. This friend of mine just always seemed to be having such a good time because he went to see movies all the time, and I asked him what was he majoring in – I wanted to do whatever he was doing!"

Huyck and Katz have been together as a couple, and as creative collaborators, for forty years. They first met in 1966, thanks to a shared interest in the work of Roger Corman: "A mutual friend said that Corman, who was of course a god at that time, was going to be showing a first cut of *The Wild Angels* at UCLA," Huyck remembers, "so I drove to UCLA and he introduced me to Gloria. I sat next to her and she had just come back from Europe and was wearing the first miniskirt I had ever seen. It was great! For our first date we went downtown. In L.A. in those days they used to show three films for a dollar at those beautiful Art Deco theatres, like the Mayan Theatre downtown. We went to see this weird double bill – *Rio Bravo* and *Chelsea Girls*!"

Huyck's social life was steeped in film, and it was only a matter of time before he began making as well as watching movies. He first got together with his old roommate at college, Curtis Hanson (who also went on to make movies, including the consummate neo-noir *L.A. Confidential*) and made an hour-long film, in 'Straight-8' format: "Our parents financed it and they had to pay to see it," he laughs. "It was a very odd experimental film: it had war things and a thirties gun chase and car chases. We both had thirties cars so we used our cars prominently and had a whole gangster movie section. I spent my junior year abroad in Paris and went to the cinematheques every day. When I got back to Los Angeles, Curtis was editing *Cinema* magazine, which his uncle ran. Someone called to say they needed a reader at AIP studios. So I became [AIP producer] Larry Gordon's reader. That involved looking over scripts and writing synopses. Gloria was editing at the time and she would help me write the synopses. I told Larry that I could write as well as the people he was hiring. So he said, well, there was a film that needed more work. I had gone to school with John Milius, so I said John and I could rewrite it. So our first screen credit was something called *The Devil's 8* (1969). And then Gloria was writing a script with her friend and the friend bailed out on her, so she and I finished that script and just kept the collaboration going."

Katz meanwhile had made a splash at UCLA with a stop-motion movie called *A Day with Barbie and Ken*. "It was an exploration of the sex lives of the iconic Barbie dolls," she laughs. "That sort of made my career at UCLA film school. It enabled me to go forward in all these various projects; which doesn't seem like a big thing until you realise that Paul Schrader was also parallel to me in class, flunked out and wasn't allowed to continue." Adds Huyck: "Paul was seen in the halls crying and trying to get people to sign a petition so he could get back into film school." Remarks Katz, "UCLA had more taste than the rest of the world." Another of Katz's student films was a split screen 'happening' called *The Bride Stripped Bare By Her Suitors*: "I got into a lot of trouble with that at UCLA 'cos there was nudity and so it was heavily censored."

Katz's friend Joan Mocine, who would later work on the art design of *Messiah of Evil*, remembers, "Gloria and I and another woman shared a house near campus. Gloria hadn't gotten interested in film yet. She was taking lots of different classes and floundering a bit. I was an art major and so was our other roommate. I really started painting a lot in my last year. I moved up to Berkeley with my boyfriend, Arthur, and Gloria stayed in L.A. and went to film school. We stayed in touch. Arthur and I moved back and forth from Berkeley three times from 1965 to 1977. I saw Gloria's *Barbie and Ken* short and another one with an orange moving around, but it's hazy after all these years."

AIP

In 1968, Huyck, now a regular script-reader at AIP, found himself involved in reworking a film that was to become a horror landmark: Michael Reeves's *Witchfinder General* (1968). "AIP had all the Edgar Allan Poe story titles that they would just put on, you know, any film. This one came out as *The Conqueror Worm*. This was in '68 when I was working there. I did some dialogue rewrites on it. I remember I did a great funeral speech!" He laughs: "But there's a very funny story. While I was there I worked my way up from reader to Larry Gordon, who later became a film producer and head of 20th Century Fox, to his assistant. We got a message from an agent at William Morris that John Elder, who had written a lot of the Hammer Horror films, was in Los Angeles and looking for work. So I of course got John Elder's credits together for Larry, and John came in and he was a young guy and, y'know, I spent a lot of time talking to him: 'God it must be wonderful working for Hammer' and so forth, him having done all these films. And he said yes. We had him write a treatment for *The Conqueror Worm* and I was the first one to read it. Larry called and said 'Did you read the treatment over the weekend?' I said 'Yeah. It was awful. It's just terrible.' Larry says, 'The guy can't be that bad - just look at his credits.' So I gave it to him and he said, 'You're right. It's just terrible.' Then we get a call. Larry says, 'You won't believe this. I just got a call from Fred Gwynne, the guy from *The Munsters*. Somehow Fred Gwynne had some kind of weird relationship with John Elder – it's California – and they had a spat or something and he ratted on him. What had happened was that John Elder was the name Hammer put on all their horror films. It's a company name. So what we found out was that this guy had maybe done one little thing at Hammer and had not done any of these films that he gave as his credits. So Larry said, 'He's coming in today and you've got to sit with him while I talk to the lawyer.' So I sat with this guy who was pretending to be John Elder, who was getting nervous. I asked him more questions like 'What was it like on the set of...' Eventually he was called upstairs, and Sam Arkoff, who was the head of AIP, told him that they were going to sue him unless he gave all the money back. But he didn't have anything left."

For 'John Elder' the game was up, but Huyck also helped to bring in real talent, encouraging his bosses to take on Joan Mocine, as she explains: "Willard got me a job at AIP, reading scripts. This was in addition to a full time job teaching elementary school. I was working about fifty hours a day. I'd pick up the scripts on my way home from school, read and synopsize at night, teach and then drop them off. Whew! Later AIP gave me the job of looking for movie ideas, but it was very unrewarding because they always said, 'This is a good script, but it's better suited for an art house.' They used to say that all the time…"

off for good. I don't know how the film came into the hands of the people who finished it. I believe that when it was finally released, in 1975, the releasing company was Crown International. In the meantime, *American Graffiti* had come out and was a huge hit. *Messiah of Evil* was reviewed in the *Los Angeles Times*, and the review did not have kind things to say about it, particularly since Willard and Gloria had co-written *American Graffiti* with George Lucas in the time since. And the reviewer even saw fit to mention how disappointed he was in relation to the promise that Willard showed in his student film *Down These Mean Streets*, which I have never seen.

How did you and Billy Weber collaborate on the film? Were there scenes that you worked on independently of Weber?

Gloria had a friend named Billy Weber, who started out as the assistant editor. I don't know how Gloria met Billy. But as we were editing, we would divide the scenes, so that Willard and I cut some, and Gloria and Billy cut others. In the end, Gloria asked that I share editing credit with Billy. It was only fair for her to have asked, and only fair that I agreed. And Billy went on to have a very distinguished career as an editor. He's worked for Martin Brest and Walter Hill, among others. Martin Brest was the executive producer for a film that Billy directed called, I think, *Josh and S.A.M.* He was a dream to work with. Totally professional and competent, mild-mannered, no temperament. Billy is the ghoul in the supermarket who pauses and looks directly into the camera. The clerk at the ticket window who sells Joy Bang her ticket is Gloria. Willard is the scuba diver who rises up into the shot in a scene late in the film. Alan Riche, who started out as the producer, went on to become a producer in Hollywood. I think his thing is to make film versions of old television shows, like *The Mod Squad*. I play the assistant in the art gallery. I saw the film in a big old theatre in downtown Los Angeles when it came out. I sat behind two women, and when I came on the screen, pale and with a voice that quavered from nervousness, one of the woman said to the other, "He gives me the creeps."

What sort of conversations do you remember about the 'look' of the film?

Billy Weber helped with the location scouting. When we were editing Billy said to me that Willard told him to look for a motel that had the same sort of sleek perfection as Ed Ruscha's paintings and prints of gas stations. At the time, I didn't understand this, and neither did Billy. We agreed with each other that the motel should have been seedy and run down. At the screening of the film at UCLA earlier this year, Willard and Gloria explained that in thinking of Ruscha they were interested in the contrast between the façade of sleek perfection and the ominous and dark things going on behind it. That is certainly a commendable conception with an august history. It's what *Blood of the Beasts* turns our minds toward in its closing moments, and in a less glorious register it's the idea behind *American Beauty*, at least as the makers of that film would have us believe.

So, as I say, it's a commendable idea but I wonder if it is brought out as fully as it might have been in the film, and even if it had, whether people would have understood it, even subliminally. One of the things that makes Ruscha's gas stations what they are is that they are seen from a very specific angle, low and a little oblique, so you have a sense of the building as a mass. It's not just flawless, it's monumental too. And there is no sense of light in Ruscha. There are shadows, but even so you don't sense a source of light, of the scene being bathed by the sun. Of course in photography the sense of a light source is inescapable, unless you shoot under a silk or on a day that's overcast. But then you don't get shadows. It's possible that the motel when viewed from the front may have had a Ruscha-like perfection, but it could have been shot from an angle that would bring out the comparison more clearly. And perhaps this same idea could have been more consistently brought out in treating other architecture in a similarly specific way. It's a question of lighting too, lighting so that the imperfections in the façades are less evident. That takes time, because you have to wait for the light to be right, and we didn't have the time. Or if you can't wait, you light, and lighting on that scale takes money, and we didn't have the money, but this kind of perfect surface is easy to achieve in painting, and above all in a silkscreen or lithograph. It's just a matter of creating a uniform tone. In photography this effect is very hard to achieve, because photography picks up all the details, all the imperfections, in the surfaces that you want to be absolutely plain and perfect. Best that you start with buildings that are already as perfectly flawless as possible, then you have to shoot it in just the right way. What that really means is building sets, and of course that was out of the question.

Willard recalls that at one time the film was being edited 'in hiding' from the producers. Were you involved at this point?

This is what I talk about above. I don't think it was the producers we were hiding from, it was the lab, Technicolor, and we hid simply by decamping with all the footage. It wasn't as if they had sent out the bloodhounds to track us down, at least as far as I was aware. The producer was Alan Riche, at least until well into the production, when under circumstances that I am not clear about, Gloria became the producer. So this established the pattern they have followed since in their own films: they write together, she produces, he directs.

There are two voice-overs in the film – one from Arletty and the other from her father. What do you think of these voice-overs – were they imposed later or were they part of the original approach?

These were in the original script. I think in principle voice-overs are fine. I mean, look at *A Man Escaped*. And Royal Dano's voice has the most fabulous expressivity. His voice creates a world. I think for the film they wanted to make, which was in essence a drive-in film or a programmer… I mean this matter of factly, not as being in any way judgmental… I love drive-in movies and programmers. But I think that for films of this kind, genre films, maybe voice-over is a little arty. And I think it's fine if they wanted to exercise their ambitions in an unlikely context. Their film *Best Defense* is audacious too in what it expects an audience to respond to.

What differences can you point out between the film that you and Willard were trying to make and the one that eventually got released?

At the screening earlier this year the thing that Willard talked about as being the biggest disappointment in the film as others finished it was the music. I don't know what he had in mind, we never got to the point where we had to think about music. But I think what Willard and Gloria wanted to do was to make a quick and dirty low-budget genre film, and at this I think they succeeded, even if the film's treatment at the hands of critics was at first very unkind, as I note above.

There's a scene in the film, set in a movie theatre, where one of the female leads (played by Joy Bang) watches a film, unaware that the theatre is gradually filling up with dozens of the 'undead'. Onscreen there's a montage of shots taken from a cheap western called *Gone with the West*. Willard and Gloria mentioned that they never got the chance to edit this scene as they wished. What do you remember about it?

Messianic Conception

"We wrote *Messiah of Evil* for six weeks in 1971, not long before we shot the movie," Huyck begins. "We had just finished working on the treatment for *American Graffiti*. Our young agent had quit being an agent to become a movie mogul and said he could raise $100,000 for us to make our first movie. A group of private investors in Texas had been convinced to put up money for a 'commercial' genre movie - and they decided they all just loved horror films. It wasn't like we had to satisfy a studio or anything, we just finished the script and showed them and they said, 'Yeah, it seems like a horror film.'"

Two companies are credited for production on *Messiah of Evil*: International Cine Film Corp. and V/M Productions. "I have no idea who those people are," says Huyck. "The Texas investors actually made another film called *Summer Run*, a film by Leon Capetanos, and they raised the money for that too. They ended up making his film, which was about teenagers in Europe, and our film, before they went out of business." The film was supposed to have been budgeted at $100,000 but only $85,000 ever showed up: Huyck explains, "We later learned that the 'finders' of the investors had skimmed $15,000 of the money to re-roof their houses. So, we tried to make the film for $85,000."

Messiah of Evil takes place in a modern-day California setting of strip-lit superstores and modernist architecture, but it achieves something quite unexpected given such a setting, as it radiates the chill influence of Rhode Island horror specialist H.P. Lovecraft. "Curtis Hanson and I used to spend a lot of time in second-hand book stores in L.A.," Huyck recalls. "There was this great place called Acres Books on Long Beach. We came across a lot of horror books and Lovecraft was somebody you read if you were into that area." Gloria Katz also enjoyed Lovecraft's tales: "If you're at all familiar with the genre, it's like reading Edgar Allan Poe," she says. "He gives you that sense of doom and perversity." With Curtis Hanson fresh from scripting AIP's own Lovecraft adaptation *The Dunwich Horror*, there was clearly a whiff of Cthulhu in the breeze. Interestingly though, while *The Dunwich Horror* is based on an actual Lovecraft tale, it deviates wildly from the source material and misses the Lovecraftian essence by a mile. Huyck and Katz, on the other hand, were not adapting Lovecraft directly, but they nonetheless forged a script with sympathetic resonance to 'the Master of Cosmic Dread'.

There still remained the question of what to call the film. Huyck recalls, "We had originally planned for the film to be called *Blood Virgin*, but we couldn't get actors to audition because they considered the title 'cheesy'. So we came up with what we thought was a much classier title – *The Second Coming*. But actors still wouldn't audition, thinking it was a porno film!"

Designing Dead People

Filming took place in the summer of 1971, mostly in Echo Park and other cheap areas of Los Angeles. Among the first aspects of the film to require attention were the murals and paintings which adorned the central interior location of the film, the house-cum-studio belonging to Arletty's father. "The paintings in the film were done by Joan Mocine," says Huyck. "They were painted directly on the walls of our rented location and therefore lost to posterity."

Mocine recalls, "The summer of '71 I was house-sitting in L.A. at Dyanne Asimow's house, who was in the movie and had a chewing-the-scenery part, and Gloria and Willard were filming *Messiah* nearby in an old mansion above Echo Park. They were working frantically, trying to get it together to start filming, and they asked if I'd help out. I said okay. Jack Fisk had been working for some time on the set and we began painting the murals inside the big old house. The ceilings were extremely high as you can see, especially in the escalator mural. I can't remember who thought of what, but Jack – at least at first – was making all the decisions. Gloria and Willard were worried that Jack was going to make the place look too 'horror-filmy', and thought I might have ideas to make it more subtle. I don't remember anything about how I was supposed to do that, but I think they were mostly having first film jitters and wanted me around to bounce ideas off of."

I comment to Gloria Katz on how the film frequently blurs the visual relationship between three-dimensional characters and two-dimensional backdrops. "That was the idea," she agrees, and Huyck adds, "Actually when we were doing *Indiana Jones and the Temple of Doom*, that's how we came up with the idea for a scene where the Thuggee comes out of a wall painting in the palace."

I ask Mocine if she recalled what the script required of the artworks. Were there specific written demands, or was she given a free hand? "I remember that they wanted the murals to reflect his [Arletty's father's] morphing into *One of Them!!!* and to project an empty feeling, one of slight dread without any real violence. Gloria and Willard had a very clear picture of what they wanted. We worked inside the house (which contained one of the sets), using ladders and scaffolding. We also painted a bathroom with murals – which was really difficult because it was a small room, so it was hard to move around. I worked on all the murals and I'm almost sure I painted the whole mural in the bathroom."

Mocine followed her stint on *Messiah of Evil* with a gig as designer for one of the most perversely beautiful films of the seventies: Terrence Malick's *Badlands*. So did *Messiah of Evil* play a part in landing her this iconic assignment? "Yes. I think that Jack Fisk recommended me to Terry Malick. I know I flew down to L.A. to meet with him. I brought a bunch of photos of my work on *Messiah* and he was very polite but said he was looking for somebody who could paint a folk art type billboard and that these works were too realistic. I had also brought along a bunch of photos of my own work – which at that time was (if I may say so) whimsical. He loved it and hired me right then. I painted the large billboard that was supposed to be done by Warren Oates playing Sissy Spacek's father. There was a big scene at the billboard, when Martin Sheen first confronts Oates, and Oates tells him to get lost. After the film was shot, Terry asked if I wanted them to bring the billboard back with them so I could have it. I had no place to store it or display it and I thought it'd be a neat idea to leave it on the Colorado plains outside of La Junta where the film was shot. I wish I'd gone to visit it… must be long gone now…"

Casting Dead People

Taking the lead role of Arletty was TV actress Marianna Hill, whose prior work included spots on shows like *The Tall Man*, *Gunsmoke*, *Bonanza*, *Perry Mason*, and an episode of *Star Trek* ('Dagger of the Mind'). Two years prior to making *Messiah*, she'd appeared in Haskell Wexler's cult movie *Medium Cool*, but was relatively unknown as a screen actress: "Marianna Hill was fun to work with," Huyck recalls. "She had a kind of dreamy *Alice in Wonderland* take on her character – punctuated by crude off-camera jokes."

Michael Greer, an accomplished actor in films like *The Magic Garden of Stanley Sweetheart* (1970) and *Fortune and Men's Eyes* (1971), took the lead male role. Says Huyck: "Michael Greer was more reserved, he was very serious, mostly because he was nervous doing his first straight role. He was primarily known as a female impersonator."

A relatively minor character – Charlie, the bum who informs Arletty that she must burn her father – went to the instantly recognisable character actor Elisha Cook Jr. "Originally we wanted Hank Worden to play the Elisha Cook role because, you know, he was crazy in *The Searchers*," says Huyck. "He was very excited about doing it, and then he called me to say his wife had read the script and was offended because the guy was having a relationship with two women simultaneously, and Hank said he couldn't do it unless we were willing to change it." Fortunately, Cook was a little more laid back: "Elisha Cook was totally professional. You know, 'What do you want me to do?' We were in horrible motels at 150 degrees – I mean, he was a little odd. He was Elisha Cook! He said, 'I want you to know, this is the first time in my career I've ever looked into the camera. I spent my whole career learning and being told, 'Don't look into the camera' and you're telling me to look into the camera.' He found it hard to do."

"Gloria and Willard were really excited about Elisha Cook and Royal Dano being in the movie," Mocine recalls. "I personally was thrilled about Cook because I have always loved *The Maltese Falcon*. But I didn't ever get to talk to him much." Of the other cast members, she adds, "Joy Bang was going through a religious phase – Theosophy. I remember this because I was raised as a Theosophist; until I got old enough to say 'Assez!' Anitra Ford gave me the impression that, while you were talking to her, she was watching her reflection in your eyes. Marianna Hill seemed nice enough. Michael Greer seemed to be the most "*Actor*ish" type, he never lost his arch way of speaking or moving – always 'on'."

One member of the cast sure to lodge in the mind of all who see the film is Bennie Robinson, the very tall, very strange albino actor who appears twice in the film, like a totem of some parallel world.[1] "He was actually black," Huyck recalls, "I guess it happens a lot more with black people. He's a black albino. I don't know who found him. We had a problem because I wanted him to look into the camera but his eyes wouldn't focus. He had this stuttering eye thing and it was really weird. We did a sort of dolly in, and his eyes were sorta jumping all over the place." I mention that he reminds me of the actor Tom Noonan, with whom Huyck and Katz worked in their film 1984 *Best Defense*: "Yeah. That's actually true. Tom also has that strange look. It's interesting because that's why we cast Tom Noonan. And I loved him in the Michael Mann *Manhunter*, which is a film I really liked. He was wonderful in that."

Of course the model for the scene of people gathering in the theatre behind Joy Bang is the scene from *The Birds*, as Willard and Gloria cheerfully acknowledge. They knew films, and they knew successful scenes when they saw them. If we had been able to retain control of the cutting of the film all the way to the end, I don't know what Willard and Gloria would have wanted on the screen in the theatre in that scene. I'm guessing that the people who in the end made the decision used something that they either had the rights to, or else they didn't but they thought they could get away with using it. If the specific choice of the film has any significance, I would say that it signifies the movies in a generic way, that is, movies in general without being any particular movie, because if it were recognised as a particular movie, the audience would want to understand it as commenting on the scene. And the footage also suggests an exaggerated idea of a certain kind of movieness: frantic non-stop action, but of a cheesy kind. I am very impressed with your scholarship, that you recognised the film that it came from. Of course there is the contradiction between what the marquee says is playing, *Kiss Tomorrow Goodbye*, and the movie that is on the screen, which, whatever it is, is certainly not the film of that title.

That scene was cut by Billy and Gloria. Willard may have told you that it wasn't exactly as they would have wanted it, as if there were something wrong with it, but speaking for myself, when I saw the film last year after not having seen it for decades, I found that scene truly terrifying. I forgot I was watching a movie and just responded to the scene.

I understand that your own film, *Standard Gauge*, addresses your experience on *Messiah of Evil* and incorporates clips from the movie. Could you tell me a little about the project and its connections with *Messiah*?

In 1984 I made *Standard Gauge*, in which you see in close-up a series of pieces of 35mm film, as if you are looking at them on a light table. I talk about where I got the pieces, so it's an autobiography, but it's also about Hollywood. There are several pieces that have to do with *The Student Nurses*, and two from *Messiah of Evil*. I talk about how Marianna Hill's performance was such that we couldn't do the scene in a two-shot. Here is what the relevant narration from the film says:

"*In this scene I was opposite the female lead, but because of an idiosyncrasy in her delivery, it wasn't the big moment for me that it might have been. After I gave a line she would pause inordinately before giving hers, so it wasn't practical to do the scene as a two-shot. Instead, the director gave us each a close-up, and the pauses were eliminated in the editing. So, as I recall, I never appeared in the same shot with her.*"

I guess sometimes some of the actors were temperamental, but I didn't have to deal with them, except in my scene with Marianna. In the cutting room afterwards we certainly allowed ourselves some wisecracks about moments in some of the performances. At any rate, I had seen *Red Line 7000* when it came out in the middle sixties, and Marianna Hill had been in it, then an ingénue in the making or a starlet in the making. And there I was, five years or so later, on the screen with her.

And perhaps linked to the previous question: what do you think are the strengths and weaknesses of the film, and what sort of commentary do you think it makes on the time and place in which it was made (if any)?

I think the film at its best moments is truly, truly scary. I don't know if it makes a commentary on the time in which it was made. The reflex would be to want to connect it to Vietnam and civil unrest in this country, but I don't know if the connection can be made. I know the film has its admirers, but I had felt that it was dogged by being without conviction in its material. That's really not so surprising, since Willard and Gloria wrote the script when they were hard-up for money so they wrote it quickly to sell quickly. So the project began as a potboiler, and then their agent, Alan Riche, suggested that he produce it and that Willard direct it. So something they wrote to sell quickly, material to which they were not exactly committed, became a script that Willard directed. But at any rate, for me the film suffers for most of it from what I will call its lack of conviction. But not in the scene in the movie theatre, and not the scene in which Marianna Hill's father tries to kill her and she has to kill him. I get goosebumps recalling that scene as I write this. The pathos and degradation of Royal Dano floundering in the blue paint, and then this soiled, obsessive, deranged man coming after Marianna Hill is truly moving and terrifying. He's piteous and pathetic and pitiable, driven by both love and hate, a man covered with this slimy pasty mess, and you feel it, that there on the screen is an actual human being who to do the scene had to endure this horrific ordeal, which comes off almost as a sort of degradation. It's the actor undergoing this degradation, not the character, but you sense the actor's degradation and it becomes a part of what you respond to in the scene. Of course it's the character's degradation too, but the person who had to undergo it was the actor. You really feel what he's going through, he being both the actor and the character.

Willard and Gloria thought of the moment when Joy Bang is seated in the bathtub and puts a blue wash cloth over her face as an allusion to *Pierrot le fou*, and perhaps the blue paint that Royal Dano is covered with at the end too. If so, it certainly is a far more powerful one than the moment with Joy Bang, and even more powerful than the moment in the Godard, because in the Godard our physical distance from his death, and its being over in an instant, keep us from really seeing it, so we are shielded from its full impact. It has an ironic quality that one could even call a little easy, even cheap. It usually gets a laugh. Not the death of Royal Dano. It's protracted, you see it from very close up, in all of its agonising and gruesome detail. You really see his suffering. You more than see it, you feel it. He's not just being stabbed to death by his daughter, he's wallowing in this grotesque dreadful mess. The sympathy we feel for him is reflexive, we can't help it.

Of course the meaning of this allusion to *Pierrot le fou*, its purpose, is not clear to me, but perhaps Willard and Gloria saw it as recapitulating Godard's allusions to American films. It's the sort of thing that young people who have seen a lot of films and love all kinds of movies might be prone to do, make allusions that let you know the people who made the movie know movies.

What do you make of things like the depiction of Michael Greer and his two female friends?

I don't know what to make of the relation between Michael Greer and Joy Bang and Anitra Ford. Of course it's a triangle, but you don't get the shifting degrees of attachment, being unfaithful, deceiving someone, and so on, the tensions and conflicts that would come with those things. It's a triangle without the development that a triangle by its nature makes possible and is the reason for. Michael and the two women

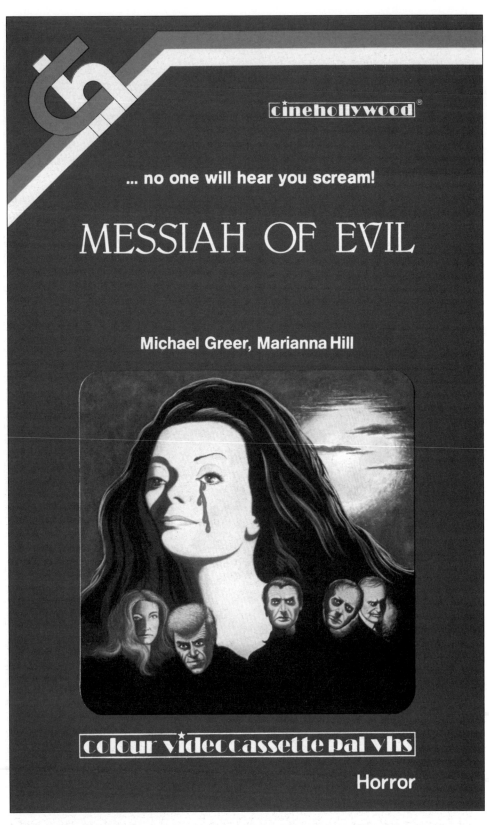

... no one will hear you scream!

MESSIAH OF EVIL

Michael Greer, Marianna Hill

cinehollywood®

colour videocassette pal vhs

Horror

above: Cinehollywood released films by such collectible Eurocult directors as Jess Franco (**Cannibals**, **Devil Hunter**) and Lucio Fulci (**Colt Concert**). When it came to American cult directors, their aim was less true: Huyck's film found itself in the less than stellar company of **Ten Violent Women** (Ted V. Mikels), although the company did at least recognise **Deathdream** (Bob Clark) as a valuable asset.

opposite top right: Don't Look in the Van!

supposed to be very very spectacular. That was never shot. Obviously we had a much different idea for what they were watching, but that never got shot." Huyck adds: "And we never really shot the movie theatre, what they were watching, the way we really wanted to shoot it. When we were cutting the film, only because one of our editors found it in the trash bin, what they were watching in the theatre, for our purposes of trying to sell it, was a trailer for *Stanley*. It looked great. Because it was the original trailer, it had beautiful colour."[2]

Huyck continues, "We actually took the work print at one point and were editing it in hiding. We had to sneak the workprint out of Technicolor, who had been very nice to us because they were happy to have somebody use their unappreciated Techniscope lab equipment, which they sold to China after we finished our film. Another consequence was that we got a frantic phone call from Michael Greer one night: he'd been arrested in Hollywood by two disgruntled cops who had worked doing traffic control on our film. The cops demanded their money before they'd let Michael out of jail. The two cops ended up being the only people ever fully paid. A lot of people were promised that when the film was sold they would get some money. They didn't realise that it was taken away rather than sold."

Body-Snatchers

As Huyck explains, their troubles were far from over once the film was in the can: "We then tried to sell it, but were unsuccessful. Our new agent Jeffrey Berg (who later became the CEO of ICM[3]) told us to quit screening it for people because it was ruining our careers!" "Because the response was so bad," adds Katz.

Huyck continues: "Eventually a group of the original investors sued the executive producers: and one day we sadly watched our workprint and outtakes driven off in a U-Haul. People we never met did some recutting, scored and finally released the movie – several times under different titles. Somebody finally released it under the title *Dead People*, which led to two interesting footnotes: in *Annie Hall* Woody Allen shows a montage of 'tacky Los Angeles' that includes a shot of *Dead People* on a drive-in marquee. The second footnote was that one day my poor dad (Willard Huyck, Sr.) was served a court summons stating that he was being sued by George Romero for title infringement.[4] I don't know who came up with *Messiah of Evil*, but it is catchy. There was a law suit and the investors finally got the rights back from the money-raising young guys we dealt with, and they gave it to some production company in Hollywood to finish it. There's a guy named Scott Conrad on it as editor. He was not our editor." "Actually he's not a bad editor", Katz interjects. "We could have done so much worse than Scott. At least he was a real editor."[5]

"Our editor was a guy named Billy Weber," Huyck continues, "who went on to become very successful."[6] The other editor was somebody we went to film school with, an experimental filmmaker named Morgan Fisher. He was sort of our group intellectual, but he loved the movie, so he was the other editor. Morgan made a film called *Phi Phenomenon*, which was famous because it was one camera on ten minutes of a clock and he was trying to show that you couldn't really see the clock moving yet it did. But it was hard for him to find a clock that didn't actually click." "He plays the art dealer," Katz adds, "the tall sort of strange looking guy. That's Morgan."

With the budget skimmed of $15,000, quite a few people were still unpaid by the end of the shoot. For Huyck, this diminishment of funds led to desperate measures: "It was post-production that suffered. We finished shooting, though there were some pick-ups and things that never got shot, and we edited the film and put in a temp track and so forth, and then we just couldn't sell it."

"Actually, two sequences were never shot," Katz explains. "We never shot the scene on the beach really, the way we wanted to shoot it. You see, the last sequence was

Huyck adds: "I was thinking back on our crew. The art director was Jack Fisk[7], who also did Terry Malick's films, married Sissy Spacek and directed her in *Raggedy Man*. The cameraman, Stephen Katz, is Gloria's brother, and he's shot a lot of movies, including *The Blues Brothers* and *Gods and Monsters*." Gloria adds, "The photography is very, very good and it was in Techniscope so the colour was really really rich." Huyck continues: "I don't know if the version of *Messiah of Evil* you saw starts with a prologue of a young man running, who then gets his throat slashed by a little girl next to a swimming pool? The young man was Walter Hill, who went on to write and direct."[8]

Afterlife

"Executed with a good deal of imaginative stylish panache." – *Messiah of Evil* reviewed in *The Aurum Film Encyclopedia: Horror.*

Messiah of Evil was shot in 1971, edited in 1972, and sanctified with a copyright date in 1973. Its fortunes have been highly variable ever since. Editor Morgan Fisher (see interview) recalls "In a poll in *Sight and Sound*, or maybe *Film Comment*, in the late seventies I think at least two critics placed *Messiah of Evil* on their best films of all times list." Today, *Messiah of Evil* has lapsed into undeserved obscurity. "We have no idea who owns the rights," Huyck sighs, "and we don't have a print of it. I have a bad VHS released by somebody called Woodhaven Film. I've never watched it." One can understand Huyck's reluctance; not only was the film finally edited without his involvement, but so far all video versions have left a great deal to be desired when it comes to picture quality. (The best is probably the Video Gems NTSC release.)

Designer Joan Mocine offers her perspective on the final product: "I do remember thinking it was wonderful in parts, uncomfortably artsy in others. I don't think they could make up their minds whether it was a horror movie or an artistic movie that had some horror in it. An example of this is calling the lead 'Arletty' (the French actress from *Les enfants du paradis*). I do, however, agree that it conveyed a feeling of subtle dread, and it looked great."

"When we couldn't sell it we were despondent," Katz admits. "I don't think we showed it to Francis [Ford Coppola], but George [Lucas] liked the film, so we went back to working on *American Graffiti* and then we stopped being despondent. Many years later, when they were screening my student films from UCLA actually, I ran into

enter the film together, and the relations among them change very little if at all. Michael seems to be equally caring for both, or equally indifferent, since he doesn't seem to have a lot of ardour for either one, but presumably has sexual relations with both. I think that to him they are interchangeable. It's sex with one, then sex with another. Of course this is all off screen, and perhaps before the story begins. I don't think there is any implied sex between Michael and either of the two women within the body of the film. The two women are a little jealous of each other, but I think that's about as far as it goes. The tensions or conflicts between them are hinted at but not developed. One doesn't try to drive the other away, or make Michael hate her rival. They actually seem to be sort of friends, not rivals. Then one leaves, then the other, but I think out of boredom or frustration with Michael, or boredom with the situation at the house. There are no knock-down drag-out showdowns between either of the women and Michael, or between the women. So it's as if the stability of the triangle makes it a character, but one consisting of three people. I know this is a bizarre way to put it, but I do so to make the point. I forget if Michael is devastated by one leaving, then the other, but my sense is he's not.

But something else could be said. It could be that Michael's relations with the women in the film is not sexual. It could be that the script suggests it's sexual, and that Michael's character wants other characters in the film (and us) to think that it's sexual, when in fact it's not. I think Michael's persona, and how we tend to read his physical appearance, and the costuming tend to suggest that it's not a sexual relation, i.e., that he's gay. That could have been made more interesting if it had been developed. If the character is gay, then the relations between him and the two women are altogether different, and this could have been brought out with interesting results. I think it was Alan Howard who suggested that they cast Michael Greer. There is that history in Warhol of relations between heterosexual women and gay men: *My Hustler* and so on. Alan would have known these films, and I imagine Willard and Gloria too. Alan's own identity might have led him to want to have a gay man play a part that is written straight but that, in the absence of the characters being more developed, and in the context of the details of the production (the costuming, the production design), could be understood as being gay. Or perhaps the part was deliberately written so that Michael's sexuality was ambiguous. If Michael's relation with the two women is not sexual, it only suggests that he's gay, it doesn't go farther than that. But I believe it is implied that his interest in Marianna Hill is sexual (isn't it? I'm suddenly wondering). So he could be not sexual with the two women, but sexual with Marianna. But then there's that ironic tone in his voice when he introduces Joy and Anitra as his two "travelling companions," which to me has always implied that he's screwing both of them. But that is not, as I say, implied as occurring off-screen within the body of the film (he never wakes up in bed with one of them, for example, or with both of them). It's all vague, maybe through oversight, or maybe entirely on purpose. It could be that Michael is asexual, not straight despite his implying he is, not gay despite his possibly seeming to be. Maybe his asexuality is deliberate, and comes from the fact that when you're the anti-Christ you are as without sexuality as Christ himself is presumed to be. I really don't know what Willard and Gloria's original conception of the character was, or their conception of his relation with Joy and Anitra. But at the UCLA screening Willard made some remark about how the casting of Michael was due to Alan Howard, as if in some way this explained something about the character as we see him in the film, almost to suggest (this is too far of a reach, really) that Alan had foisted onto him an actor who would have an effect within the film that Alan foresaw but that Willard did not.

But at any rate, the triangle could have been a subplot, but for whatever reason, it wasn't developed into one. Two straight women who are jealous of each other. Or who at first are not, then something happens to set them against each other. Or one of the women is straight and in love with Michael, the other gay and in love with the one who loves Michael, but Michael likes to have sex with the lesbian to dissuade the straight woman who loves him, because he can't return want her love. And the lesbian wants the straight woman to watch because she knows it both torments this other woman and also turns her on to the possibility of a lesbian relationship. I know this sounds like Fassbinder, and maybe it could have been too much for a subplot. Maybe? Almost certainly. But things could have been suggested without giving up a lot of screen time to do so.

So the two women are there to give us scenes between them that aren't really about the main relationship, the one between Michael Greer and Marianna Hill, they're there to provide complications when we need them. They go off by themselves, first one, then the other, but these episodes, in relation to the main thrust of the plot, don't go anywhere, they branch off and stop. But I suppose that it could be said that this elimination of two of the characters who are intimates of Michael raises the suspense. As these characters are killed off, it raises the tension in respect to the remaining character. When I say that the main thrust of the plot is the relation between Michael and Marianna, it could be that people who don't like the film find it not developed enough: the relation that by convention is promised when a man and woman meet does not occur in the film. **How would you describe the experience overall, and what effect did it have on your career?**

What I should stress is how much fun people had on the production. Or at least that is how it now seems to me as I look back on it. Of course production is a lot of work. The hours are long, there is lots of tedium, lots of standing around and waiting, but we liked each other and we got along. But I think that is often the way it is when you are young and full of enthusiasm.

To give you an idea how we scrounged and improvised to get things done, and how close we all were, Willard and Gloria asked if I would lend my car to the production. It had recently been in a wreck and so had just been painted. So my 1967 Volvo 144 was given to Marianna Hill's character to drive in the film. She complained that it was beneath her character, as of course it was, but that was the car she drove because there was nothing better. The white Mercedes that Michael Greer drives was borrowed from Willard's parents. The orange pickup truck that Bennie drives (he was the albino who eats the rat) belonged to Jack Fisk.

I was paid a pittance, that goes without saying. I won't embarrass myself by saying how much it was, but it wasn't much, although it was enough at the time, and in any case it was more than I was paid for my work as associate editor on *The Student Nurses*, which was downright humiliating, except that I misrepresented my qualifications to get the job on *The Student Nurses* so in the end I was grateful for the chance and for the credit. The normal career path would have been to build on the credit on *The Student Nurses* by editing a feature, which is what I started out doing on *Messiah of Evil*, and then go on to other and bigger features, but I didn't. Instead I edited a documentary called *Eadweard Muybridge, Zoopraxographer* that a friend made, then felt that editing features just wasn't the thing for me to do.

above:
Royal Dano attacks his own daughter while
smothered in blue paint.

Robin Wood, the critic. He saw my student film and really
liked it. He said, You're Gloria Katz? Oh, *Messiah of Evil*,
the greatest horror film of the seventies. So I realised the
man was a genius!" She laughs, adding "Actually I said,
'What are you talking about?'"

Huyck and Katz are frank and unpretentious when it
comes to acknowledging the shortcomings of their debut:
thanks to them we now know that the film did not reach the
screen as intended. But while few fans would argue that the
final product is perfect, I feel that *Messiah of Evil* survives
its flaws and emerges (with a bit of leeway granted for that
awful theme song!) as a wonderfully macabre and
unnerving experience, with numerous sequences that stand
up with the best the genre has to offer.

right:
Who really is the mysterious figure controlling
the 'Blood Moon' massacre? Thanks to the
film's foolish producers, who removed Huyck
and Katz before they could finish it, we may
never know...

Footnotes

1 I can vouch for the fact that this man, like Michael Greer, is
always 'on'. But his 'on' is another planet. I called him and had
possibly the creepiest telephone conversation of my life: I have to
assume he was unwilling to be interviewed, so I'll say no more, but
believe me, he is *still* one scary dude…

2 The finished version uses a montage from Bernard Girard's
Gone with the West, cut together in a surrealistic way. Morgan
Fisher, *Messiah*'s editor, also recalls another film being used for the
cinema sequence: "The scene that was playing on the screen in the
movie theatre when we cut it was a trailer for *The Band Wagon*.
Technicolor, where we had a cutting room for a while as a part of
our deal with them, was throwing away a lot of stuff from their
vaults, including A-rolls of the short trailer for *The Band Wagon*, so
we simply cut it in as a stopgap expedient, just as you would lay
some music that you didn't have the rights to over a scene that you
would later replace with music that was composed for the scene or
that you had obtained the rights to. If the scene were ultimately to
have music, especially a scene with no dialogue, you didn't want
dead silence when you screened the cut, you needed music, so you
put in something that everyone understood was temporary. It was
the same thing with our using the trailer from *The Band Wagon*, it
was just a diagram for the fact that ultimately there would be
something on the screen. Of course it was a little sacrilegious to cut
up an IB print of a trailer for *The Band Wagon*, but that is what we
did. We had a whole one thousand foot roll of them."

3 The top-flight talent agency International Creative
Management.

4 The lawsuit was probably because of the retitling *Revenge of
the Screaming Dead*.

5 Scott Conrad went on to edit *Rocky* (1976) and Curtis Hanson's
The Bedroom Window (1987), as well as cult items like *A Boy and
His Dog* (1975) and *Up in Smoke* (1978).

6 Weber is credited on the film as 'associate editor'. He went on
to cut Terrence Malick's *Days of Heaven* (1978), Walter Hill's *48
Hrs.* (1982), Tim Burton's *Pee-wee's Big Adventure* (1985), and
Tony Scott's *Top Gun* (1986).

7 Credited onscreen as Jack Fiske.

8 Hill of course made a splash with his excellent street-gang film
The Warriors (1979) before hitting the Hollywood A-list with *48
Hrs.* (1982).

WILLARD HUYCK FILMOGRAPHY

FILMOGRAPHY AS DIRECTOR:

196? *Down These Mean Streets* (short)
1973 *Messiah of Evil* aka *Dead People* aka *Revenge of the Screaming Dead* aka
      Return of the Living Dead aka *The Second Coming* aka *Bloody Virgin*
      (co-director / co-writer / co-producer)
1979 *French Postcards* aka *Were Geht Denn Noch Zur Uni?* (also co-writer)
1984 *Best Defense* (also co-writer)
1986 *Howard the Duck* aka *Howard: A New Breed of Hero* (also co-writer)

AS WRITER:

1968 *Witchfinder General* – dir: Michael Reeves (uncredited script rewrite, AIP
      version as *The Conqueror Worm*))
1969 *The Devil's 8* – dir: Burt Topper (co-writer)
1973 *American Graffiti* – dir: George Lucas (co-writer)
1975 *Lucky Lady* – dir: Stanley Donen (co-writer)
1977 *Star War*s – dir: George Lucas (uncredited rewrite)
1979 *More American Graffiti* aka *Purple Haze* – dir: Bill L. Norton (co-writer)
1984 *Indiana Jones and the Temple of Doom* – dir: Steven Spielberg (co-writer)
1989 *Mothers, Daughters and Lovers* – dir: Matthew Robbins (co-writer; producer)

1994 *Radioland Murders* – dir: Mel Smith (co-writer)
2007 *Secrets of a Hollywood Nurse* – dir: Sasha Rovin (co-writer)

GLORIA KATZ FILMOGRAPHY

FILMOGRAPHY AS DIRECTOR:

196? *A Day with Barbie and Ken* (short)
196? *The Bride Stripped Bare By Her Suitors* (short)
1973 *Messiah of Evil* (co-director – also co-writer / co-producer)

AS WRITER:

1973 *American Graffiti* (co-writer)
1975 *Lucky Lady* (co-writer)
1979 *More American Graffiti* (co-creator of characters)
1979 *French Postcards* (co-writer; actress)
1984 *Indiana Jones and the Temple of Doom* (co-writer)
1984 *Best Defense* (co-writer)
1986 *Howard the Duck* (co-writer)
1989 *Mothers, Daughters and Lovers* (co-writer)
1994 *Radioland Murders* (co-writer)

chapter 12

Hollywood After Dark

The Films of John Hayes

with interview material from the director's widow, Ellen Hayes, and actress Rue McClanahan

Dream No Evil (1971)

"In a way *Dream No Evil* may have explored some of the darker aspects of John's life, although he'd probably deny it. But there they are; childhood abandonment, insanity (his sister Dolly's) and religious excess (also Dolly)."
- *Ellen Hayes.*

Prologue: Eight-year-old Grace lives in an orphanage run by nuns. Convinced that one day her daddy will come back to retrieve her, she suffers terribly when rescue fails to materialise. There's not a shred of comfort from the nuns, who are stern and indifferent. One day, she and a long line of other orphans are examined by an imperious well-dressed woman. After this dehumanising ritual, Grace is adopted. Twelve years later, Grace (Brooke Mills) has grown up into a troubled young woman working as a performer in an evangelist roadshow; a sort of travelling circus with religious overtones. Her act involves leaping from a precarious thirty-foot pole onto an air-cushion, to demonstrate the Fall of the Damned, and God's mercy. This cheap, hucksterish charade is run by Jesse Bundy (Michael Pataki), a fiery preacher of dubious morality. He desires Grace, but reins in his lust because Grace has entered a chaste relationship with his brother Patrick (Paul Prokop). Patrick has 'fallen from the faith' and now studies medicine. He is conscientious, loving, and patient; but the longer Grace denies him physical intimacy, the harder it is for him to ignore the overtures of a pretty med-student whom he's coaching. Grace, meanwhile, is still obsessed with finding her father. When the Bundy Roadshow visits the town he once lived in, she decides to hunt him down. Wandering into an old hotel, she meets an elderly pimp (Marc Lawrence) with a harem of old-West floozies. The pimp is also the town undertaker, and he tells Grace that he has the body of her recently deceased father 'on ice'. At the mortuary, Grace sees her father (Edmond O'Brien) rise from the slab and kill the undertaker. She subsequently breaks off her relationship with Patrick and moves in with Daddy. The two live on a ranch in regal Deep-South splendour, and Grace is blissfully happy. Others, however, suspect that something is amiss, and when they attempt to intervene, Grace's mind snaps…

Dream No Evil is a modern Gothic in the Flannery O'Connor vein, an emotionally involving tale that's both macabre and terribly sad. Hayes kicks off in the bleakest way: a little girl in an austere, barely furnished convent school, screaming for her daddy as rain fills the night. Unsympathetic nuns assure her she's quite alone in the world. (*"Daddy's coming to get me out of this place!"* *"You have no daddy!"*) Such scenes have been done elsewhere (another great example is the extended prologue of Charles Sellier Jr.'s *Silent Night, Deadly Night*, where it's a little boy in the same situation), but Hayes brings a sort of drab, unadorned realism to Grace's misery, setting up her disturbed reactions for later. So far so good, but it's here that we bump into the first major obstacle to *Dream No Evil*'s reputation…

"From year to year, town to town, Grace stayed on with her adopted church to continue searching for her father. She became engaged to young Patrick Bundy who gave up the ministry to study medicine. Now only his older brother Jesse remained, turning a once respected church into a carnival."

Like Willard Huyck's *Messiah of Evil*, John Hayes's *Dream No Evil* labours under an intrusive and completely unnecessary voice-over, which 'explains' the film at the expense of its magic. It would seem that the overdubs were added to make things easier to understand, probably after the film tanked under its original title *The Faith Healer*, but they're so heavy-handed they simply insult our intelligence, in one instance sabotaging the film's most beautifully timed surprise. Basically (and jump to the next review now if you'd rather not know) the voice-over telegraphs a switch from fantasy to reality. Grace is shown sitting in a beautiful *Gone with the Wind*-style bedroom, which changes in the slash of an editor's razor to reveal her true surroundings: the same room, but run-down and derelict, a mouldering reality of smashed timbers and mildewed carpet. This would have been startling if the voice-over had not already told us there was something unreal about what we were seeing.

The late Marc Lawrence, film noir icon of *Key Largo* fame, and director of the fabulous *Pigs* (see review section), gives the story a boost in a small but pivotal role, while another grandee of classic Hollywood, Edmond O'Brien, who co-starred in *White Heat* (1949) and *D.O.A.* (1950), appears as Grace's father. Both actors play illusory figures, summoned by Grace's imagination. That these important roles are taken by two such iconic actors seems to suggest the way cinema can become a refuge from real-life misery and loneliness. And when it comes to casting, where better

below:
British video cover for **Dream No Evil**, released (with typically atrocious '80s typography) by AVR, one of the first post-Video Recordings Act companies to venture back into horror (they also released films like **The Creeper** and **The Scaremaker**).

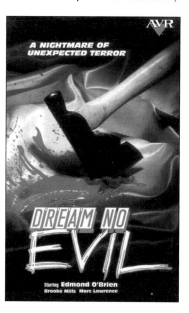

Dream No Evil (US theatrical & UK video title)
aka **The Faith Healer** (original US release
title) aka **Now I Lay Me Down to Die** (MPAA
title)
© none [1971].
Clover Films presents.
writer/director: John Hayes. producers: Daniel
Cady, John Hayes. director of photography:
Paul Hipp. music: Jaime Mendoza-Nava. film
editor: Luke Porano. assistant director:
Jerome Guardino. production manager: Tony
Vorno. camera: Ron Johnson. sound
recordist: Mike Glaser. art director: Lee
Fischer. property master: Rufus Herrick. set
decoration: Michael March. makeup: Ronald
Sallon. costumes: Logan. stills: Paul Turner.
grips: Bret Pearson, Glenn Gondy, George
Engelson. assistant to director: Rebecca
Vorno. sound mixing: Cinesound, Inc. titles:
Willard Tidwell. opticals: Van Der Veer Photo
Effects. colour: Cinechrome.
Cast: Michael Pataki (Jesse Bundy). Paul
Prokop (Patrick Bundy). Marc Lawrence
(undertaker). Brooke Mills (Grace). Arthur
Franz. D.J. Anderson. Nadyne Turney. Vickie
Schreck. William Guhl. Pearl Shear. Elizabeth
Ross. Mary Carver. Jay Scott. Joe Pronto. Teri
McComas, Ray Saniger (stunts).

right:
One of several different UK video covers for
Grave of the Vampire, this one from Guild
Home Video.

below:
Patrick (Paul Prokop) in bed with Shirley, the
student to whom he turns when Grace rejects
his love in **Dream No Evil**.

to find your ghosts than the flickering celluloid of days gone by? O'Brien made nearly a hundred Hollywood pictures, while Lawrence chalked up nearly two hundred. Both have faces that just about anyone who loves the American cinema of the 1940s and 1950s would recognise, even if their names are harder to summon.

In a 'rubber reality' trick that has been played again and again in modern cinema, most notably in *Fight Club*, it turns out that illusion has dominated the film for longer than we've suspected. When Patrick searches for the funeral parlour to investigate what happened there, he can find no such building. It's a simple ghost story ploy, of course, but done with considerable economy and atmosphere, making the unnecessary voice-over all the more annoying.

As a director, Hayes does not strive for surrealistic effects, nor does he exaggerate the technical artifice of cinema. *Dream No Evil* achieves its strange, disconsolate atmosphere without flamboyance. The emphasis is on feeling, with a tragic scenario in which the heroine's struggle to find happiness is doomed because of her childhood. It all gains extra resonance when the circumstances of the director's family life are known (see remainder of this chapter): the name Patrick, given to Grace's boyfriend, a humanist doctor who has turned his back on the family religion, suggests that John *Patrick* Hayes was angry about the role the Church played in the distortion and demolishment of his sister's psyche. Yet he cannot bring himself to critique her childish fantasy; instead he shoots Grace's dream of life on the farm with a loving glow that cradles her yearning. Grace is deeply immersed in her imaginary world, and it's Hayes himself who so tenderly lays it out for her on the screen. It's a genuine wrench when we cut abruptly to reality, and the decaying emptiness in which Grace really lives.

It's possible that Hayes himself identified with Grace. The recurrence of abandonment as a motif throughout his work suggests such a reading. In a way, Grace becomes a surrogate through whom Hayes can more 'legitimately' explore his own feelings of abandonment; feelings he might have found hard to express directly. As a bluff Irish-American brought up in the 1930s, it can't have been easy to find acceptable outlets for his own anguish. The naïve hearts-and-flowers romance of Grace's father-fantasy is not criticised by the film, which will perhaps alienate more cynical or demanding viewers. We are asked to feel sorrow for Grace's ultimate disillusionment, whereas a more rigorous filmmaker would see this as tantamount to encouraging her self-delusion. However, if Grace is in some way Hayes's surrogate, then the very fact that he has written this film about the stripping away of a character's illusions is honesty enough. For a commercial filmmaker with little avowed interest in 'art', Hayes brings an emotional reservoir to *Dream No Evil* that one doesn't always find in the horror genre. Looking at this, along with Hayes's early films, and the astonishing *Baby Rosemary* (see later in this chapter) you can't help but wonder what might have become of this very creative man if he'd been blessed with more money and better feedback for his movies.

Note: The film was first submitted to the MPAA in 1972 as *The Faith Healer*, when it received an 'R' rating. A year later it was re-rated 'PG' as *Dream No Evil*. I can find no record of the differences between the two, nor any indication of when the version called *Now I Lay Me Down to Die* was released.

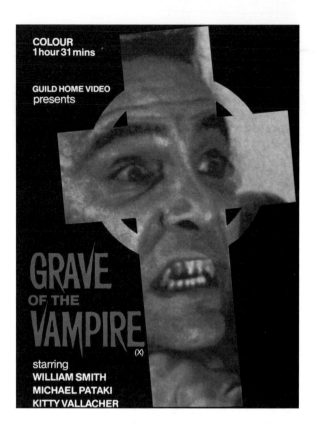

COLOUR
1 hour 31 mins

GUILD HOME VIDEO
presents

Grave of the Vampire (1972)

"This is one of the great blood-sucking pictures coming in the wake of *Count Yorga*. It is perverse, interesting, and exciting in concept and presentation." – *Richard Meyers, For One Week Only*

"A mixture of savagery, compelling strangeness and dumb exploitation." – *'Dr. Cyclops', Fangoria*

"Grim and unusual." – *Kim Newman, Nightmare Movies*

The 1930s. A vampire called Caleb Croft (Michael Pataki) rises from a crypt to attack a young couple making out in a foggy graveyard. The young man (Jay Scott) is killed, his back broken over a tombstone. The vampire then rapes the woman, Leslie (Kitty Vallacher) in an open grave. Dawn breaks and the fiend staggers off, seeking cover as the sun comes up. The victim recovers in hospital, only to find that she's pregnant. She spurns the advice of doctors, who tell her that the child is not alive, but rather a "parasite", drawing blood from her body while lacking life itself. Leslie checks out of hospital and resolves to have her baby at home. When the child is born she's concerned that it looks unusually grey. It refuses milk, but when an accidental cut spills mother's blood on its lips, the eager tot laps it up. Her maternal instinct aroused, Leslie cuts her breast, and at last the baby feeds...

Grave of the Vampire begins with an abrupt deluge of Gothic clichés that really shouldn't work. A combination of swirling fog, gravestones explored by a prowling camera, a vampire emerging from his coffin, and a pumping heartbeat on the soundtrack: surely these archaic horror trappings need time, some sort of context to work their magic? Yet somehow, *Grave of the Vampire* taps us directly into the Gothic horror mother-lode. A subdued twinkle of organ under the heartbeat feels like leakage from Amando de

Ossorio's *Tombs of the Blind Dead* (a Spanish horror masterpiece dripping its sepulchral way across Europe during 1971), and the image of the vampire in his coffin, bedecked with a frosting of cobwebs, looks like cover art from the horror comics of the 1950s. (With their lurid visual style at least twenty years ahead of the movies, these pulp mini-masterpieces had an effect on American horror cinema that cannot be over-estimated.)

Grave's writer David Chase turned his hand to horror again soon after, with eight episodes of the spooky TV hit *Kolchak: The Night Stalker* (1974-75). Nowadays he's busy as the writer of an obscure little TV show called *The Sopranos*, but hey, not everyone can make the big time… He certainly shows promise here: the script, based on Chase's own novel *The Still Life*, keeps hitting us with bold twists on the vampire movie tradition. When we see a mother use a syringe, drawing blood from her own arm to fill up a baby bottle, it's a genuinely haunting image that updates tired vampire clichés and adds a deep irony – mother's milk itself is likened to a drug, and *vice versa*. As the story unfolds it takes a distinctly Oedipal turn, and this image of a mother feeding her blood to a vampire baby resonates with all sorts of inferences. It taps into women's fears about maternity, exploring ambiguous emotions in a way that suggests both Polanski's *Rosemary's Baby* and Larry Cohen's *It's Alive* (the latter made two years later); and it suggests how children can be shackled by the 'drug' of motherhood and the inescapable influence of bloodline.

Grave swerves recklessly through a ninety-degree turn about thirty minutes in, when we're rushed through a thick-and-fast flurry of voice-over revelations. The blood-loving baby has grown up to be a strapping young man; his mother died due to his sanguinary needs, and the vengeful son has set out to hunt for his father, who has sequestered himself in a university teaching history (under the assumed name of Lockwood). All of this is communicated in less than two minutes screen time, a narrative body blow from which the movie takes a while to recover. The present-day setting also temporarily robs the film of its atmosphere. The fog and the gloom are gone, and we're in a banefully familiar world of too-old college students being helpfully lectured on the film's occult themes by the villain. The elision is enough to make your ears pop: something tells me that Chase's original story was too long! Hayes performs a bypass on the narrative, and in his haste creates an expositional blood-clot, necessitating a tedious catch-up lecture from Croft/Lockwood. The rhythm of the film heads dangerously close to pulmonary failure…

All is not lost though, because seventies horror mainstay Michael Pataki (also to be seen in Hayes's *Dream No Evil*) delivers a dish of actorly cold cuts that revives the scary ambience of the first half-hour. He's one of those actors who can command the screen while holding something back to indicate that he's playing with us. Vincent Price was the master of this tactic, both inhabiting and standing aside from his roles. Pataki is less well-known, but his forte is much the same. He turns up in many an enjoyable B-movie romp, and always acquits himself well within the framework of what is being offered. I would cautiously recommend his directorial debut too: *Mansion of the Doomed* (1976), a spin on *Les yeux sans visage*, is doggerel compared to Franju's haunting poetry, but it has a streak of malicious energy that appeals just the same…

Once *Grave*'s slackly-directed college-class scenes are out of the way, we're introduced to eager-beaver student Anita (Diane Holden), whose fervent desire to actually *become* a vampire not only invigorates the screenplay but, one could argue, pre-empts the entire Goth subculture. She tries to seduce 'Professor Lockwood', but despite the mystical décor of her apartment (Tarot card blow-ups on the walls), and her insight that he is truly a vampire, the undead object of her desire remains frustratingly *cold* to the idea of marriage. Just to rub it in, 'Lockwood' murders her with a kitchen knife – cruelly depriving her of the vampire status she craves. And that, you might think, would be that. But Hayes and Chase have another surprise for us, during a séance convened by the killer…

Without a doubt the film's biggest liability is biker-movie stalwart William Smith, who plays the challenging role of the vampire's son with all the expressive zest of a breezeblock. It's not really his fault; he's simply miscast. Smith's screen presence is primarily physical, macho, and imposing; he's like an off-duty pro-wrestler who's stumbled onto a movie set. There are plenty of roles for which his emotional immobility would be ideally suited, but the conflicted rage required of this character eludes him. *Grave of the Vampire* is essentially an Oedipal story, baldly so at times, with the son seeking to kill the father for molesting the mother. The knock-down, drag-out fight scene between Smith and Pataki plays to the younger man's strengths, but when he finally kills his father, only to sprout fangs himself, he simply doesn't have the range to express the necessary horror and despair. (And speaking of Oedipus, this final twist is of course another Freudian reference: the son kills the father but he doesn't erase patriarchy; he simply takes the father's place, thus perpetuating it.)

Comparing this film to George Romero's *Martin* would be wildly overstating things (*Martin* is after all the most beautiful of American horror films), but *Grave of the Vampire*, like Romero's masterpiece, rings some thrilling changes on vampire lore. Scenes we've sat through a hundred times in the genre are succeeded by others which come right out of the blue. Instead of a nothing entry in what was by then a pretty moribund subgenre, *Grave of the Vampire* rises above its generic origins. Rather than playing the vampire for camp amusement (as was more common at the time: see *Dracula (The Dirty Old Man)* (1969) or *Guess What Happened to Count Dracula* (1970)), it finds fresh and interesting nuances, nurturing hybrid possibilities that were perhaps only later embraced through the New Wave horror fiction of Clive Barker.

Grave of the Vampire
aka **Seed of Terror**
© none [1972]
Entertainment Pyramid presents a Millenium [sic] production.
during production: Clover Films.
director: John Hayes. producer: Daniel Cady. screenplay: David Chase. screen treatment by John Hayes. cinematographer: Paul Hipp. music composed by Jaime Mendoza-Nava. film editor: John Hayes. assistant director: Jerome Guardino. art director: Earl Marshall. makeup: Tino Zacchia. wardrobe: Logan Costume. still photographer: Elliot Marks. screen titles: Earl Marshall. filmed in Eastmancolor. laboratory: Cinechrome. assistant cameraman: Ron Johnson. sound recording: Henning Schellerup. production manager: Tony Vorno. sound effects editors: Jack Cheap, Jack May. stunt co-ordinator: Joe Pronto. special effects: Cliff Wingren. gaffer: Ray Atkinson. grips: Mike Petrich, Ron Evans, George Engleson. filmed from 22 January 1972 in Los Angeles (California, USA).
Cast: *William Smith (James Eastman). Michael Pataki (Caleb Croft / Professor Lockwood). Lyn Peters (Anne Arthur). Diane Holden (Anita Jacoby). Lieux Dressler (Olga). Eric Mason (Lieutenant Panzer). Jay Adler (Old Zack). Jay Scott (Paul). William Guhl (Sergeant Duffy). Margaret Fairchild (Miss Fenwick). Carmen Argenziano (Sam). Frank Whiteman. Abbi Henderson (Carol Moskowitz). Inga Neilsen. Lindus Guinness. Kitty Vallacher (Leslie Hollander, the unwilling mother).*

left:
Two different pieces of US promotional art for **Grave of the Vampire**.

Garden of the Dead (US DVD title/shooting title) aka **Grave of the Undead** (US theatrical title) aka **Tomb of the Undead** (UK theatrical/video title)
© 1972 [no company].
Millenium [sic] Productions presents. An Entertainment Pyramid release.
director: John Hayes. producer: H.A. Milton. writer: Jack Matcha. cinematographer: Paul Hipp. assistant [camera]: Ronald Johnson. art director: Earl Marshall. sound recording: Henning Schellerup. production manager: Jay Sodet. gaffer: Bob McVay. grips: Mike Petrich, Mike Evans. special effects: Richard Helmer. make-up artist: Joe Blasco. music [uncredited]: Jaime Mendoza-Nava. assistant director [uncredited]: Jerry Guardino. filmed from 17 May 1972 in Los Angeles (California, USA).
Cast: Phil Kenneally. Duncan McCleod [McLeod] (Dr. Saunders). John Dullaghan (sergeant of the guards). John Dennis (Sergeant Jablonsky). Susan Charney (Carol, Johnson's wife). Marland Proctor (Johnson). Tony Vorno (Mitchell). Jerome Guardino (gravedigger). Lee Frost [Robert Lee Frost] (McGee). Eric [Erik] Stern.
The Dead: Virgil Frye. Phil Hoover (Donovan). Carmen Filpi. Jack Driscole. Rod Manilla. Ted Frost. John Piazza.
Lewis Sterling (guard). Bob Hunter. Barney Tiernay. David Copperman. Bill Condit. Frank Tawlor. Robert Linder. Wally Burns. Greg Cooper. Burk Halter. Ronald Marriot. Eloise Condit. Chuy Castro. Avil Williams. Morton Lewis. Nick Raymond. John Willard. Erwing Berlin and Moe Pronto.

Garden of the Dead (1972)

Inmates of a country prison camp are put to work manufacturing formaldehyde. Unbeknown to the guards and the Governor, many of the prisoners have become hooked on the fumes. Some of the men plan and execute a breakout, but they are swiftly hunted down and shot. That night, as they are buried in hastily-dug graves, the dead come back to life and march on the prison camp, where they force entrance, seeking revenge on the prison staff and craving another hit of their beloved formaldehyde…

Horror cinema in the early seventies was slowly absorbing the influence of *Night of the Living Dead*. In the half decade after its release in 1968, Romero's landmark film enjoyed gradual word-of-mouth exposure throughout America (spurred on in the public consciousness by a pricelessly hostile review in *Reader's Digest*). A ragtag number of variants followed, including John Hancock's *Let's Scare Jessica To Death* (1971), Bob Clark's *Deathdream* (1972), and Willard Huyck's *Messiah of Evil* (1973). What unites these disparate movies is their idiosyncratic refusal simply to mimic the Romero film. In fact it's debatable whether we're actually dealing with zombies at all in Hancock's film – if we are, the definition of the term has to be broadened, rather than consolidated around Romero's template. Nevertheless, the influence is certainly there (as it is in David Cronenberg's 1975 film *Shivers*, whose zombie-like sex addicts want to fuck you, not eat you). It wasn't until Romero's *Dawn of the Dead* (1978) reiterated that zombies are flesh-eating reanimated corpses that other films finally toed the line.

Night of the Living Dead was undoubtedly a factor in the funding of John Hayes's *Garden of the Dead*, but this is not a film that can be ranked alongside the other post-*Night*

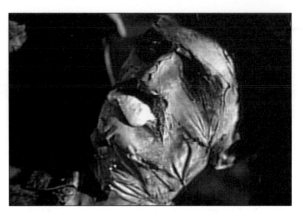

films mentioned. Instead it's a blatant rush job from Hayes that must count as one of the most cack-handed efforts of his career; sex films included. It is, however, thankfully short (around 58 minutes!) and there's fun to be had with it if you're willing to suppress your desire for a decent film and just marvel at the creaky contrivances. If anything, Hayes made a film that harks back to the likes of Monogram's *Revenge of the Zombies* (1943) or Edward L. Cahn's *Zombies of Mora Tau* (1957) – the latter produced by 'Clover Films', coincidentally the name of Dan Cady's and John Hayes's own (unrelated) production company! It makes you wonder if Hayes ever really saw *Night of the Living Dead*; perhaps he merely responded to producer Cady's suggestion of a cash-in on the Romero hit by reaching back to his memories of the Monogram films for inspiration.

That said, it's amusing to note that Hayes has his zombies emerge from the grave with skills it would take Romero's another thirty three years to embrace! Just as in Romero's comeback film *Land of the Dead* (2005), the zombies in *Garden of the Dead* can use tools, understand their surroundings, and plot revenge; they're also sufficiently socialised to follow a leader. Sorry, George, but John Hayes got there first… This bunch can even speak, and issue ultimatums, which takes them way beyond the crowd (although Bob Clark's zombie soldier in *Deathdream* does likewise). Some of Hayes's other innovations, though, are less likely to be adopted in future exploitations of the theme. His zombies are frequently felled by a shotgun blast to the chest, and in the film's most bizarre scenes they pour formaldehyde over themselves, drink it ecstatically, and wash their faces in it. It's certainly an unusual sight in a zombie flick to see the undead grinning with pleasure, but something tells me the actors were reluctant to actually *swallow* the foul-looking red liquid that passes for formaldehyde in the film: certainly no one risks getting it in the mouth, and Hayes instead has to accept his cast merely splashing it over themselves, like super-criminals gleefully playing with stolen money.

On the other hand, a quick browse through *The Home Poisoner's Handbook* (don't get married without it) suggests that Jack Matcha, who wrote this script while contributing to *The Brady Bunch* the same year, undertook at least *some* research to back up his mad idea. Formaldehyde can be inhaled as a gas or vapour (as seen in the early scenes) but it can also be absorbed through the skin as a liquid, so maybe having the zombies bathe in it isn't as silly as it first seems. In every other respect, though, the formaldehyde notion is just crazy. A colourless, strong-smelling gas commonly suspended in fluid and used as a preservative in medical laboratories and mortuaries, formaldehyde is extremely irritating to the eyes, nose, and throat. Using it as

above:
Tool-bearing zombie ahoy!

top right:
Something the film could have used a lot more of – the 'ick' factor…

right:
For all its ropiness, **Garden of the Dead** received a couple of UK video releases in the pre-cert era. KM, who titled it **Grave of the Undead** (complete with gratifyingly ghoulish artwork redolent of the old 'Weird Tales' magazine covers), also put out such video flotsam as Edoardo Mulargia's **Hell Prison**, Al Adamson's **Smash the Crime Syndicate**, Eberhard Schroeder's **Sweet 16**, and Jack Wood's **Equinox** (the latter also available from Mountain).

DEATH WAS THE ONLY LIVING THING..

GRAVE OF THE UNDEAD

filmed in DEAD colour

we see the convicts doing (i.e. breathing it neat from a tube) would cause severe inflammatory reactions of the mouth, throat and lungs, and concentrations over a hundred parts per million are immediately life-threatening. What's more, when the convicts emerge from their graves, having being killed only hours before, they already look discoloured, decayed and mouldy. This would be ridiculous in any film, but since they've been ingesting formaldehyde too, they ought to rot more slowly, not more quickly, than usual; formaldehyde kills most bacteria, destroys fungal growths, and is commonly used as a disinfectant. But while this is one zombie innovation that has to be filed under 'D' for 'Dumb', I can't help liking it anyway. There's something about the flagrant disregard for logic and basic science that's charming even if it *is* bloody stupid.

Garden of the Dead began filming in mid-May of 1972, and it seems likely that it was made purely to fill up the second half of a planned Hayes double bill with the far superior *Grave of the Vampire*, shot earlier that year. Several key crew members were held over: both films were shot by Paul Hipp, with camera assistant Ron Johnson; both had Henning Schellerup as soundman; and the art direction on both films was by Earl Marshall. At least one of the grips, Mike Petrich, also worked on both shoots, so it's reasonable to assume that the second film was hastily convened to make use of the crew from *Grave*. (The double-bill theory also explains why *Garden* is so short.)

Notable faces in the cast include: Eric [Erik] Stern, best known for his role in *The Love Butcher* (here acting without his hairpiece); Marland Proctor, a Hayes regular also familiar from Leonard Kirtman's *Curse of the Headless Horseman*; and Tony Vorno, Hayes's regular collaborator on both sides of the camera. The special make-up was handled by future luminary of the field, Joe Blasco (he invented the bladder effects used to simulate movement under the skin seen in David Cronenberg's *Shivers*, and handled the grisly mutilations in *Ilsa, She Wolf of the SS*). Here, as well as providing your basic discoloured zombie countenance, he creates an especially putrefied example that looks like it was assembled from wet tissue-paper spray-painted onto the actor's face. Somehow it works rather well, and when the actor coughs up a mouthful of thick white goo, the combination provides *Garden of the Dead* with its only bona fide 'Yuk!' moment.

Scored with jazz music more suited to Hayes's earlier work like *Walk the Angry Beach* or *Five Minutes to Love* than a modern zombie film, *Garden of the Dead* is never going to earn a place in horror's Hall of Fame; so it's just as well Hayes eclipsed it with its immediate neighbours, *Dream No Evil* and *Grave of the Vampire*, both of which deserve far more attention.

The Career of John Hayes

This chapter would never have taken flight without the contributions of the director's widow, Ellen Hayes, or his long-time friend and colleague, actress Rue McClanahan; I extend my sincerest gratitude to them both.

The name of John Hayes draws the attention of horror fans thanks to a brace of offbeat seventies movies: the inventive *Grave of the Vampire* and the melancholy *Dream No Evil*. However, curiosity would just as quickly be crushed by a viewing of *Garden of the Dead*, or the slow-moving sci-fi venture *End of the World*, two further Hayes titles awaiting the unwary on video shelves during the 1980s.

But these four movies are only the tip of the iceberg. Starting out in the late fifties as a purveyor of gritty b/w dramas, Hayes journeyed along the highways and alleyways of the independent US exploitation industry, right the way through to the mid-1980s, when the advent of hardcore porn on videotape finally put the mockers on his favoured brand of dark erotic melodrama. Along the way he gave a major TV comedy star her first breaks, contributed to the 'roughie' subgenre of semi-explicit sexploitation films, and made two striking and unusual horror pictures, before crashing and burning in the ghetto of eighties straight-to-video porn.

What's striking about this writer/director's career trajectory is the way that he returns, time and time again, to the experiences of his childhood, revisiting familial traumas in a variety of settings, from melodrama to horror to hardcore. It's this obsessional quality that reveals a true artistic temperament. Hayes often wrote his own films, or at least contributed to the screenplays, which guarantees a degree of personal investment on his part. While the huge variation in quality between, say, *Five Minutes to Love* (1963) and *The Cut-Throats* (1969) would require some formidable, not to say absurd, theoretical gymnastics to make an auteurist point, it's fair to say that the best Hayes films share a definite stylistic persona. Taken at a glance, the mordant theatrical flair of *Five Minutes to Love* and the nihilistic despair of Hayes's darkest film, *Baby Rosemary*, scarcely feel like the work of the same person. But if we can see beyond the sexual explicitness of the latter, both films display a characteristically downbeat worldview, an acute ear for profane dialogue, and a real concern for the lost souls of life. The films Hayes made with Paul Leder in the early sixties are classy, intelligent and well shot; the later erotic films are seedy, cynical and technically ramshackle. Between these two extremes, Hayes journeyed through many of the major genres, following the ups and downs of the exploitation film market for nearly forty years. This in itself would make a study of his films worthwhile; and when we consider the emotional qualities of his best work, it's clear that Hayes deserves credit for genuine creativity too.

Early Days

John Patrick Hayes was born on 1 March, 1930 in New York City. His grandparents were Irish immigrants and his father's family worked on the Manhattan docks. His parents went through a bitter divorce when he was just four: consequently he was taken in by an alcoholic paternal uncle and an elderly grandmother, who shared a home

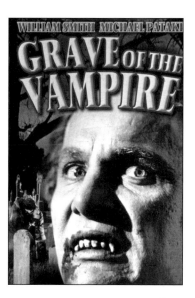

above:
DVD artwork for a budget release of
Grave of the Vampire.

left:
A pastiche of Jean Genet's smoke-sharing prisoners in **Un chant d'amour**? Probably not, but this strange scene from **Garden of the Dead** has an inadvertent erotic quality that might have amused the writer of 'The Thief's Journal'…

Walk the Angry Beach
aka Hollywood After Dark
(1969 US theatrical re-release title)
aka The Unholy Choice
1959
[re-release version] © 1969. a Headliner
release
Headliner Productions present.
director/producer/screenplay: John Hayes.
director of photography: Vilis Lapenieks.
music: Bill Marx. editors: Esther Poche,
Ronald Thorne.
Cast: Jack Vorno [Daniel DiSomma] (Tony).
Rue McClanahan (Sandy). Paul Bruce (Nick).
John Barrick (Tommy). Ernest Macias (Ernest).
Lea Marmer (Mrs McVea). Leslie Moorhouse
(Shakespearean). Doug Rideout (Fitz). Joanne
Stewart (Patti).

together. His sister Dolores fared worse: she was raised in a convent and, after two early marriages and several children, developed schizophrenia marked by religious fanaticism.

At seventeen, Hayes joined the Navy. When he was discharged a couple of years later, his mother pointed him towards the New York Dramatic Workshop across from her apartment, telling him that he needed to get some culture. (It was the same building where, in 1944, Maynard Morris 'discovered' the young Marlon Brando). Watching the students working on a scene from *Death of a Salesman*, Hayes fell in love with the theatre and began attending evening classes. He also studied playwrighting with Lajos Egri (whose milestone book *The Art of Dramatic Writing*, first published in 1946, made him the Robert McKee of his day).

As an actor, Hayes lacked nothing when it came to aesthetic daring, and – as encouraged by the teaching of the day – he drew on his personal experiences to govern his acting choices. In 1953 he appeared in the Actors Studio production of Calder Willingham's play about sadism in the army, *End As a Man* (filmed in 1957 as *The Strange One* with much of its homosexual subtext removed), performing at the Studio and on Broadway.[1] He also appeared in *A Hatful of Rain*, another play critical of the Army. Michael Gazzo's tale of a soldier returning from Korea addicted to heroin (*"Hello Police? I want to report a drug addict: it's my husband!"*) was originally created in 1954 by members of the Actors Studio, including Shelley Winters, Ben Gazzara and Anthony Franciosa. Hayes played the role of Chooch in the original Broadway production, and then ploughed onwards with the Road Company through the summer of 1957. In the Fall of that year he was cast in the original production of *West Side Story* as Lt. Schrank (a part played by Simon Oakland in the movie adaptation). He opened out of town to good reviews but to his disappointment did not continue to Broadway.

Then came the movies…

Awards and Ambitions

Acclaimed actress Rue McClanahan, best known as 'Blanche Devereaux' in the much-loved 1980s sitcom *The Golden Girls*, knew Hayes very well at the time: she appeared in four of his early films and remained a close friend throughout his life. She recalls: "John got a role as one of the policemen in the musical *West Side Story* on Broadway, and it was while he was playing that little part that he sat backstage and wrote a short black-and-white film called *The Kiss* (1958). It was delightful, very funny; it's about a young man who is inept with girls. He goes around various people trying to learn how to kiss – he's very shy with women. He finally takes a girl he likes on a Ferris wheel, and at the top of the Ferris wheel he gets up the nerve to kiss her – and the whole movie turns Technicolor! They float back down to earth for a happy ending. It's a delightful little film, I think it was about twenty nine minutes long. He borrowed $5,000 from his mother to make it. He wrote and produced and directed it, and did the whole thing in New York. He got nominated for an Oscar, which took him to Hollywood. Disney won that year with *Grand Canyon* – that was a blockbuster, and John's was this sweet little personal film. I met him right after that."

With an Academy Award Nomination under his belt, Hayes moved to Hollywood and began hustling for a feature film gig. He was to live in Los Angeles for the rest of his life, though he occasionally returned to New York. He always felt attached to the 'Big Apple', that most iconic of American cities: his widow Ellen Hayes feels that, "The fantasy world of Coney Island and Luna Park played a large role in John's imagination, as did Radio City Music Hall and the old vaudeville skits, undoubtedly for the escape they provided from the harsh realities of his childhood."

Hayes gained his first feature film experience working on the script for Alexander Singer's *A Cold Wind in August* in 1960. Burton (*Rio Lobo*) Wohl took the headline writing credit, with Hayes noted for 'additional dialogue', although it's said his contribution was far more than that. The film is a sleazy heartbreaker about an ageing stripper (played by Lola Albright) who seduces the horny teenage son of a local dignitary. For a precious while the stripper knows sexual bliss, until her toyboy's buddies maliciously tell him what his older lover does for a living: it's like a May-September variant on Sam Fuller's *Naked Kiss*. (In his book *Crackpot*, John Waters lists *A Cold Wind in August* as one of his all-time film favourites, alongside Bergman's *Brink of Life* and Pasolini's *Teorema*, explaining: *"[It] may not have been a cult film anywhere else in the United States, but it played forever in Baltimore. Every time an art-house would book a flop, they'd yank it and bring back* A Cold Wind in August.*"* (If you should chance on it, look out for Hayes himself, who appears briefly as a hot dog vendor.)

Walk the Angry Beach, The Grass Eater, and Five Minutes to Love

Having settled in Los Angeles, Hayes made the necessary contacts and began his feature directing career with a sombre melodrama called *Walk the Angry Beach*. It stars Daniel DiSomma (aka 'Jack Vorno') as Tony, a young man who hits the skids when his wife leaves. Soon after, his junkyard business folds and he's forced to consider joining Nick (Paul Bruce) and Tommy (John Barrick), two crooks who offer to cut him in on a waterfront hold-up. They plan to rob a wage-truck and then toss the money-bag off the pier into the sea, where Tony (a skilled scuba-diver) can lie in wait and retrieve it. While visiting Nick's burlesque joint, Tony meets Sandy (Rue McClanahan), a stripper and aspiring actress. Like him, Sandy is losing a grip on her ideals: Nick wants her to reveal more flesh and dance more provocatively. She attends a 'reading' with a sleazy film producer but ends up drugged and ravished. Disillusioned, she grows ever more resigned to her fate as a mere sex object. Tony too gives in, and joins Nick and Tommy. After participating in the robbery, returning with the bag of money to a motel where Sandy is staying, Tony offers to take Sandy away with him, but she refuses. He goes to the strip joint to deliver the money, intending to decline his cut and regain his self-respect, but Tommy knifes him. Tony makes it back to the motel but dies in Sandy's arms.

It's not easy to establish the original release date for this film: it was re-issued as *Hollywood After Dark* in 1969, and this is the only version to have made it onto video, with all original credits excised. However, Rue McClanahan is sure of when the film was shot: "That one was done in '59, between September and the end of the year. My agent called and said, 'There's this wonderful

opposite page:
Scenes from **Walk the Angry Beach** aka **Hollywood After Dark**.

from top:
Sandy (Rue McClanahan) is angered by the burlesque club-owner's demands;
Tony Vorno (*left*) and Rue McClanahan argue with the boss;
A slightly more risqué burlesque dancer possibly added to the film when it was re-released as **Hollywood After Dark** in 1969;
Rue McClanahan performs onstage…
…to an appreciative audience.
Nick (Paul Bruce) prepares his criminal caper;
Tommy (John Barrick) tries to kill Tony, but gets a lamp smashed in his face;
The police chase Tommy off the road, killing him.

little independent film and you're just right for the lead, can you come out and audition for the producer and director?' I walked into this somewhat rundown little office in Hollywood and first I met Paul Leder. He said, 'the director John Hayes is doing the casting, here he is now': and there's this six-foot-four, thirty-year-old blond from New York. He put me into a little inner office and we started reading the scene: he loved my interpretation and acting style and he hired me. I mean hired, but for no money! Everything was done with a hope that it would get distributed and then you would all get paid accordingly. But it didn't get distributed. It made its premiere in 1960, as I recall. I got a wonderful review in one of the trade papers, *Variety* or *The Hollywood Reporter*. John got good reviews for the writing and directing, but it really did need some money behind it. We were shooting on short ends. It was a very gruelling experience physically, because, not being union, you just worked until they said okay we're stopping. We would work eighteen hours a day very regularly, and one day for twenty four hours. Someone asked John, 'Don't you guys fall asleep on the set?' And he said, 'No, but we faint quite often!' Vilis, our cameraman, really *did* fall asleep one night, with his eye resting on the eyepiece of the camera! I sort of fell for John, and he sort of fell for me. We began an affair. He was shy of getting married – he'd already been married and had two little girls, in fact at the time he wasn't quite divorced because his wife wouldn't give him one. John was jolly and funny, and I thought he had a good career ahead of him; he was such a talented director and writer."

McClanahan's first marriage broke up in 1958, after only a year: by which time she was five months pregnant. When she met Hayes in 1959, her son Mark had been born and she'd already remarried, to actor Norman Hartwig [aka Norman Hartweg]. "I wanted to get a home established for my little boy back in Oklahoma, and Norman and I just weren't working out," she recalls. "In *Walk the Angry Beach* I played a stripper who's stripping because she can't get a job as an actress. She falls in love with an actor, and hates being a stripper. There were a couple of scenes where I had to cry and it was easy to do because all I had to do was think of Mark, who was now living with my mother in Oklahoma, and who I missed sorely."

Hayes's key supporter and ally on his first three movies was Paul Leder, a multi-talented writer, actor and producer. Leder co-produced *Walk the Angry Beach*, produced and starred in Hayes's next two films, *The Grass Eater* and *Five Minutes to Love*, and co-wrote the latter. He would later go on to forge a long and varied directing career, with work including the psycho-thriller *Poor Albert & Little Annie* (better known as *I Dismember Mama*) and the moody psychological horror *My Friends Need Killing*. *Walk the Angry Beach* also marked the first time Hayes worked with actor/director Daniel DiSomma (aka Sebastian Gregory, aka Tony Vorno, aka Jack Vorno). DiSomma became a regular friend and collaborator, working on many of Hayes's films in one capacity or another. (See interview with DiSomma elsewhere in this book). The jazzy score was by Bill Marx, who went on to compose music for Ray Danton's *Deathmaster*, Bud Townsend's *The Folks at Red Wolf Inn*, and the *Count Yorga* films, while the cinematography was by Latvian émigré Vilis Lapenieks, who shot Curtis Harrington's extraordinary directorial debut *Night Tide* and collaborated with Hayes on several more films in the early 1960s.

Walk the Angry Beach only really comes to life when Rue McClanahan and Jack Vorno are onscreen together. The couple's first meeting, when Sandy goes backstage to discuss her stage act with her boss, is a well-written exchange that shows off Hayes's theatrical experience. Sandy has never met the owner of the club, so when she finds Tony in the boss's chair she assumes he's the person demanding that she make her routine more risqué. In fact, Tony is there to discuss the heist. The two of them talk at cross-purposes, before Tony embarks on a cynical speech about the futility of maintaining moral scruples. With Sandy left in tears by his angry words, Tony apologises and so begins their relationship. Apart from their scenes together, the most effective sequence is one in which Sandy goes to audition for a role with Ernest (Ernest Macias), a writer who uses script-reading sessions as an opportunity to ply girls with alcohol (or maybe drugs, though it's not made clear) to get them into bed. McClanahan conveys the optimism and naivety of her character without her seeming simple or foolish, while Vorno, having followed covertly, is excellent as the furious lover who sees his new girl emerge from this sleazy encounter with her clothes in disarray, and resolves to beat the crap out of her abuser.

As would become the norm for Hayes, this is a sombre tale, described as "too risqué and downbeat for its time" in the *New York Times All Movie Guide* – an estimation which may explain why it proved so hard to distribute until much later in the sixties. However, it's also a very moral tale, to a degree that can seem archaic and a little stuffy today. Tony sees his role with Sandy as lifting her "out of hell", a rather extreme estimation of the burlesque scene. (Compare the far more positive testimony of Russ Meyer's star, and one-time burlesque performer, Tura Satana.) In the late 1950s, however, it was difficult to show what else might be required of a good-time gal like Sandy, so the bump-and-grind dance McClanahan seductively performs must stand in for the more licentious possibilities. Certainly, the encounter with Ernest makes it clear what a stripper-cum-actress can look forward to in the scummier echelons of showbusiness. The film does at least hinge upon a considered reflection between Sandy's slide into sleaze and Tony's slide into crime. The moment when Tony decides to hand back his share of the money means that although modern audiences, post-*Bonnie and Clyde*, will find him rather strait-laced, we at least don't think he's a hypocrite.

We can assume that John Hayes did not regard the burlesque scene with the same negative eye as Tony, given the increasingly erotic fixations of his later films. However, it is of course a common trait in exploitation films that the very spectacle being offered for consumption is decried by characters in the story – it's the classic showman's way of satisfying the prurience of the audience while maintaining a pose of moral rectitude. Double standards? Maybe – but America at the time was hardly the most sexually liberated of places. If you wanted to film something racy, you needed your excuses cued up and ready: the House Un-American Activities Committee had only just disbanded, in '59…

When *Walk the Angry Beach* was re-released as *Hollywood After Dark* in 1969, it was shorn of at least ten minutes, possibly more. Sadly, the latter version is all we have today. The original began with scenes showing Tony's marriage crisis, and made it clear that he loses his business too. In the later version, we join the film during Tony's first encounter with Nick at the yard, dropping the marital

Five Minutes to Love (US DVD title)
aka **The Rotten Apple** (US theatrical title)
aka **The Wrecking Yard** (shooting title)
aka **It Only Takes Five Minutes**
© none [1963]
director: John Hayes. producer: Paul Leder.
screenplay: William Norton, Paul Leder.
director of photography: Paul Hipp.
Cast: Rue McClanahan (Sally, 'Poochie'). King
Moody (Blowhard). Will Gregory (Ben). Gaye
Gordon (Edna). Norman Hartwig [Hartweg]
(The Kid). Michael De Carlo (police captain).
William Guhl. Paul Leder (Harry, junkyard
owner). uncredited: Geraldine Leder (Ben and
Edna's daughter).

conflict altogether; and after Tony visits the strip-joint, his junkyard business is never mentioned again. Several other scenes have been shortened, including a long discussion between Tony and Sandy that instead rushes impatiently to their lovers' clinch. Just how much of Hayes's material is missing is hard to verify after forty five years, and to confuse matters new scenes have clearly been added. McClanahan does not recognise the burlesque routines performed by two other girls: for a start, the set is not the one on which McClanahan dances, and considerably more flesh is revealed (the girls 'shake their booty' with nothing but small tufts of fake fur stuck on their nipples). For a film ostensibly shot in '59, these extra scenes are at least eight years too explicit. It seems likely that the film was eventually bought by someone who chose to slash Hayes's script back to basics, to make room for more sexy dancing.

Questions abound regarding this period in Hayes's career. For instance, just after *Walk the Angry Beach* he directed a children's film, title unknown, that has never turned up on any filmography and remains utterly obscure. Rue McClanahan recalls, "It was a children's movie about a dog… a brilliant German Shepherd. We shot that one in Oklahoma, four weeks, a great deal of it shot on a houseboat on a lake North of Tulsa… This amazing dog called 'London' had done a film called *The Littlest Hobo*, and he was the star of this one. I played the mother of a little girl who gets involved with the dog, a small role. I was the script supervisor on that one, for fifty bucks a week, and John was the director. I think that was in 1960."

Daniel DiSomma recalls that Hayes made his third feature, *The Grass Eater* (1961), almost immediately after *Walk the Angry Beach*: clearly he was not inclined to hang around waiting for distribution of his debut. He was joined on the project by playwright turned scriptwriter William W. Norton. Born into a prominent Mormon family in Utah, Norton was a firebrand whose participation in the early progressive political movements of the 1950s resulted in him being called before the House Un-American Activities Committee. Having maintained a more than casual interest in politics, he was arrested in the 1980s for assisting the passage of arms to the IRA, and spent two years in prison. He would go on to pen *I Dismember Mama* for Leder in 1972, as well as mainstream fare like *The Scalphunters*, *Gator* and *Brannigan*.

The Grass Eater, adapted by Hayes from Norton's stage play, depicts a cynical wanderer (Paul Leder) who convinces a romantically-inclined young girl that marriage is a meaningless absurdity. To prove his point, he chooses a married couple at random and proceeds to wreck their union by seducing the other man's wife (a story with similarities to Roman Polanski's under-rated *Bitter Moon*, made nearly thirty years later). Rue McClanahan appears again ("I play a nice, tipsy wife," she says, "which was funny but it's not my favourite role"), and gaining what may be his first feature film credit was Jaime Mendoza-Nava, a prolific composer whose scores have graced many an indie horror, from Charles Pierce's *The Legend of Boggy Creek* and *The Town That Dreaded Sundown* to Jim Feazell's *Psycho from Texas* and John Hayes's own classic, *Grave of the Vampire*.

Hayes's next outing was *Five Minutes to Love* (1963), an overheated but engaging crime melodrama about a crooked junkyard owner, Harry (Paul Leder), who runs a car theft operation on the sly. Holding court to his dope-addled flunkies – Blowhard (King Moody) and The Kid

(Norman Hartweg; misspelled here as Hartwig) – Harry rules the roost, supplying drugs to his associates, keeping a prostitute called Poochie (Rue McClanahan) in a shack behind his office, and generally lording it over anyone who strays into his domain. When out-of-work family man Ben (Will Gregory) comes by, looking for a spare part for his car, Harry introduces him to Poochie, who attempts to seduce him. Meanwhile, Harry sneaks off downtown and frames Ben for auto theft in order to pay off a corrupt police captain (Michael De Carlo) who's been sniffing around for an arrest. While Ben is beaten by Harry and the cops, Blowhard makes a move on Ben's young wife Edna (Gaye Gordon), attempting to rape her on a pile of tyres. Ben evades arrest and Harry implicates Blowhard to take the heat off himself. Harry returns to the yard, but the chickens are coming home to roost…

Unless *The Grass Eater* turns up and steals the crown, *Five Minutes to Love* is probably the best of Hayes's early films, with a taut, well-constructed plot, acerbic dialogue, and excellent performances throughout. Rue McClanahan is outstanding as the mentally disturbed prostitute (billed on the poster as "Poochie, the Girl in the Shack!"), bringing a credible female presence to a film predicated mainly on the failings and aspirations of men. "I thought my role was meaty and challenging," she says, and she's right: this is a cut above your average B-movie fare. McClanahan embodies the character with subtlety and economy, conveying profound derangement through vocal inflection and an emotionally evasive manner instead of grandstanding and rolling her eyes as a lesser actress might have done. 'Poochie' has slipped the rail somewhere, her light and breezy manner is just a bit too flippant. Her incredulous dismissal of questions about her estranged child is genuinely disturbing, and far more effective than a burst of hysteria. The title of the film, drawn from a wonderful monologue delivered by McClanahan, is both a riff on *Five Minutes to Live* (aka *Door to Door Maniac*), a Johnny Cash vehicle made in 1961 (which allegedly features McClanahan in an uncredited bit part, although she can't remember doing it), and also an example of clever misdirection. Judging by the poster and its salacious ad line, 'five minutes to love' sounds like the countdown to some gratuitous sexy frolicking; what it actually means in context, as the cynical Poochie explains, is something quite different: *"Five minutes, that's all. Did you ever look at a clock? That's all it takes, actual time. Five minutes and it's all over […] that's all it is, the real of it. If you make it any more than that it's your own fault. You're crazy."* All in all, a rather less lubricious spin on the words than audiences might have been expecting! The downbeat flavour – typical of Hayes's films in the following years – is redolent of punk-rocker Johnny Rotten's bitter dismissal of sex, nearly twenty years later, as "five minutes of squelching."

William Norton's stagy script is awash with scenes where men rage at each other in the manner of Tennessee Williams, Edward Albee or Arthur Miller. Paul Leder and Norman Hartweg in particular let fly with some sustained screen ranting, sounding off on topics as varied as Nietzsche's Superman, the failure of hope, and the inevitability of corruption. When Poochie freaks out seeing 'The Kid' drinking from a baby's bottle (threatening her repression of memories of her own estranged child), she yells, *"I don't wanna see anybody sucking on a baby's bottle!"* In response, Hartweg summons the authentic bravura and grandiosity of the Beatnik poets: *"I don't*

below:
Blowhard (King Moody) in
Five Minutes to Love.

either; it's a symbol! Like a brass cymbal or a ruptured spleen, and a brass monkey, and a flight of the bumblebee, and a fare-thee-well, and a well-digger's butt in Montana, and a home-is-where-the-heart-is, and a homily, and an early to bed and an early to rise, and a Poor Richard's Almanack! Benjamin Franklin was right! The homilies of life! Like get up in the morning, and go to work, and save your money, and do a good job... it all goes around in a circle, but a desiccated liver is still a penny saved is a penny earned, and any kind of a racket, any kind, is still gonna be crud!" ("John gave him pretty free rein with that scene, as I recall," says McClanahan). Paul Leder is particularly good as Harry in his prolonged diatribe against the cops: "The trouble with you fellas is you're all alike," he snarls, goading a meatheaded sergeant to punch him, "you're either too dumb or too lazy or think you're too smart to work for a living. And then you've got a nasty streak, or else you'd be firemen instead!" Harry walks with a limp, a likely reference to Brick Pollitt in Tennessee Williams's *Cat on a Hot Tin Roof*, and the script seems to make the same insinuations about Harry's potency and sexual orientation. He's a little sleazier than Brick, though: using a home movie camera, he films his cohorts – the muscle-bound, dope-dealing 'Blowhard' and skinny intellectual 'Kid' – making out with Poochie. Not only do we see him getting off on his voyeurism, he also seems far more interested in the men than the girl: *"Do some push-ups, Blowhard,"* he cajoles the big lunk, when they're hanging out at the junkyard together, commenting to Ben, *"There, look at that, a real man!"* If the film ultimately declines to explore the relationship between Harry and his male friends, it compensates with a storyline that foregrounds amorality and exploitation, while retaining compassion for those, like 'Poochie', who've been permanently bent out of shape. 'Blowhard' is drawn with a critical eye for the workings of the inarticulate male psyche, as the menacing bequiffed hunk moves from a clumsy seduction of Ben's girl towards a drug-fuelled attempted rape. *"I know all about how a woman works. She says no, she means yes. She don't know what she wants 'til she gets it,"* he ruminates. Finally, although there's no explicit violence, a scene in which Harry pushes Ben into the darkened maw of a vehicle inspection pit and then heaves chunk after chunk of heavy auto scrap after him is startling in its implication.

With Blowhard shot by the cops and Ben granted a last minute chance to beat the crap out of Harry, the film ends – on a tin roof, naturally – with something close to a moral resolution, albeit one with a bitter-sweet quality, as the emotionally detached Poochie offers a near-comatose Harry her mindless words of comfort. It's a satisfyingly ambiguous and cynical end to a well-told tale. Not that it helped the film make much money. Like *Walk the Angry Beach*, the film went through much retitling to try to find an audience, leading to an eventual outing as *The Rotten Apple*, a re-release featuring an unexpected bonus: a direct to camera address by producer/writer/star Paul Leder himself, which is worth quoting here:

"Why would anyone want to make a story like this? What good purpose would it serve? After viewing tests, the studio called and said they were ready to cast me as Harry. But after going over the story, I told my wife I wouldn't play that role for a million dollars. Next day, we returned the script to the studio. My associates opened a cabinet and spread a dozen large binders in front of me. They were

full of press clippings, magazine stories, police files and medical documents. Now, like many of you, my wife and I are busy parents too. We have three children and we simply didn't realize that we could be raising a rotten apple right here in our own home! I changed my mind and agreed to produce the film. In a minute, you'll see me as Harry, a wrecker of human beings. I'm sure you'll hate me. At least, I hope you'll hate me..."

Shell Shock, and Farewell

While shooting *Five Minutes to Love*, McClanahan's personal affairs grew more and more complex. Her husband Norman Hartweg's beatnik aspirations meant that notions such as monogamy and marriage were far from fixed: "We had a four year off-and-on marriage and I went back and forth between Norman and John Hayes three times during that period," she explains. "I was married to Norman first before I met John but our marriage was on the rocks." Hartweg was growing more and more eccentric at the time: "Norman was a remarkable man, up until then probably the most brilliant man I'd met. He was extremely tightly wired, capable of doing difficult roles. But it really wasn't working out. He hadn't bathed in eight months, or brushed his teeth, or combed his hair. He never washed his hair. And I asked him one time why he was choosing to be so... repulsive! He said, 'Because I want people to like me for my inner self.' And I thought, well we can't *get* to that inner self because you smell so bad! He was really confused. None of us had ever really had therapy. He got into LSD then, and got involved with the Ken Kesey group. He was part of that for a year, and he took fifty trips, and the fiftieth trip was a horror, and he figured he'd had enough. It did change his thinking, and it straightened him out quite a bit. He got some kind of therapeutic advantage from LSD."[2]

Shell Shock
aka **82nd Marines Attack** (export title)
© 1963. Canyon Prod.
A presentation of Westhampton Film
Corporation.
director: John Patrick Hayes [John Hayes].
producer: Charles B. [Beach] Dickerson.
screenplay: Randy Fields and John Patrick
Hayes. original story idea: Don Ford. photography by Vilis Lapenieks. music composed and
conducted by Jaime Mendoza-Nava. editor:
Thomas Conrad. sound: Frank Murphy.
recorded at Ryder Sound Services. titles and
opticals by Ray Mercer. production manager:
Paul Lewis. assistant cameraman: Ron
McManus. key grip: Tom Ramsey. assistant
director: Jack Pierce. special effects: Ross
Hahn, Sam Altonian. set decorator: Chips
Evans. makeup: William Roblin. script
supervisor [uncredited]: Rue McClanahan.
Cast: Carl Crow (Johnny Wade). Frank Leo
(Gil Evans). [Charles] Beach Dickerson
(Rance). Pamela Grey (Maria). Dolores Faith
(Gina, the American girl). Bill Guhl (Prof
Wrigley). Max Huber (the major). Martin Brady.
Rolan Roberts. Bill Roblin. Henry Segfried.
Jack Pierce. Phil Patchen. David Brenner. Jon
Cedar. Robert Sable. Gary Scott. uncredited:
Norman Hartweg (soldier)

opposite page, top right:
Daniel DiSomma (acting under his 'Tony
Vorno' pseudonym) molests the bordello girls
in Hayes's erotic western **Fandango**.

opposite page, bottom right:
Four scenes from **Help Wanted Female**,
Hayes's first film under the pseudonym
Harold Perkins. The male in each is 'Tony
Vorno' aka Daniel DiSomma.

Help Wanted Female
© none [1968]
Clover Films presents.
director: Harold Perkins [John Hayes].
executive producer: William Dancer. photographer: John Lyons. film editor: Patrick Hipp.
art director: Joe Barrett. makeup: Ruth Onion.
sound: Cinesound.
Cast: Sebastian Gregory [Daniel DiSomma]
(himself). Inga Olsen. Dianne Michaels. Lucki
Winn. Joy Kahl. Michael Lincoln (the
salesman). Don Jones (horny neighbour).

Shell Shock (1963) was next for Hayes, a WWII picture echoing some of the themes of Calder Willingham's *End As a Man*, dealing as it does with an abusive relationship between an authority figure and a common soldier. With the Hollywood Hills passing for 1940s Italy, the film has a few credibility problems, but it's the class-conscious psychodrama that matters more than the spectacle: *"I wonder what's going on in that orphanage head of his?"* sneers Beach Dickerson's Captain Rance, as Johnny Wade (Carl Crow), one of his more sensitive men, succumbs to 'combat fatigue' after seeing a fellow soldier (Norman Hartweg) shot in the face during a raid on enemy positions. There's an emotional tenderness in the buddy relationship between good-looking but troubled young Wade and his older 'brother' from the Orphanage, Gil Evans (Frank Leo). *"It's awfully lonesome without you, Johnny,"* says Gil as he watches over his crazed, traumatised friend. Rance, on the other hand, harbours a homicidal grudge against the younger man, whose decorations for bravery he resents: *"First chance I get – American bullet or German bullet; who knows? But you ain't getting' outta here!"* The plotline is rescued from the further implications of its all-male set-up by Wade's escape from the bullying Rance into the arms of a beautiful Italian woman, Maria (Pamela Grey), and Rance's dalliance with an American girl, Gina (Dolores Faith); a sultry apparition in the Italian hills, wrapped in a bath-towel and dancing to jazz records in her back garden, her brassieres hanging on the washing line. The script uses this female character as foreclosure: an afternoon's dancing with a pretty girl is enough to transform psychotic Rance into a reformed character, aghast at his wicked ways. The not unreasonable thesis seems to be that military life creates psychosis due to the absence of women.

Shell Shock owes much to the AIP war films of the late fifties, such as *Jet Attack* and *Tank Commandos*, but it's distinguished from the average by the decent photography of Vilis Lapenieks and its compelling human drama, which emphasises emotional conflict. War films are not among my favourites, generally speaking, but Hayes makes this a lot more involving than I was expecting. Crow is a likeable lad, and his 'shell-shocked' demeanour is adequately believable for the period, while Dickerson, better known for more genial roles, is impressively nasty as the villain of the piece.[3]

McClanahan was script supervisor on *Shell Shock*, and recalls the following incident: "During the shoot the set was visited by representatives of the Screen Actor's Guild, and by this time I was a member. So was one of the cast. We had to pay a hundred dollar fine for being caught doing non-union; but we went right on shooting anyway. That was an exciting afternoon! We had to pick up all our equipment and run, but they caught us. I was really chewed out about it by Ricardo Montalban, who was head of the SAG at the time. But we were at the far outskirts of the movie industry. These movies were shot on the sly, for pennies. The only time I got paid was when I was script supervisor on *Shell Shock* and that little dog movie; and I got paid fifty dollars a week for those. But John was passionate about all of them."

The relationship between Hayes and McClanahan was destined never to end in marriage, due to a combination of wariness and bad timing. She recalls, "When I moved to New York in 1964, I got a call from John, saying that he had got a job with an aircraft company on Long Island, making industrial films, and he was flying his own plane to New York! So he set off and he said he'd like to see me. By then I was involved with 'the Italian', who turned out to be my third husband.[4] But before I married him, John came to New York; it took him a week to fly cross-country. It turned out that he didn't have a job on Long Island, he was coming to see me. When John arrived I saw him mid-week and the Italian at the end of the week. And the Italian said, 'Now look, this has gone on long enough, I'm not putting up with it! You tell that man tonight that you can't see him any more, I want you to promise me you're gonna tell him that.' And I was under his thumb back then and I said yes, okay. Then John took me to a lovely restaurant on Long Island, and proposed! And I said, 'Oh John, I've been waiting four years to hear that and now I've made a promise that I won't see you any more, and I can't break my promise.' (That's really how I felt when I was thirty.) And he said, 'You're making the wrong decision, you're taking second choice and you shouldn't do that.' And I said, 'I made a promise, what can I do?' It was raining, and we left the restaurant and he was crying, tears were just rolling down his face; and that was the last time I saw him before he hooked up with Ellen's sister. John did come to see me after he was involved with her. I was so unhappy with that Italian by then that I sort of made overtures to him during his visit, and he would have none of it. He'd had enough of my dashing back and forth and turning him down."

Hayes worked once more with Leder and Norton, on *The Farmer's Other Daughter* (1965), which later rejoiced in the glorious reissue title *Haystack Hooker*. It stars Norman Hartweg in his last screen role before driving off into psychedelic adventures with Ken Kesey and the Merry Pranksters. The film, a comedy about a poor farmer who plans to sell his lovely daughter to a rich sleazeball, features cornpone humour and music from the Kentucky Colonels, with Ernie Ashworth, of the long-running *Grand Ole Opry* country music radio show. Lusty ole Hicksville was the intended market, quite unlike the urban focus of Hayes's previous films. *The Farmer's Other Daughter*, an otherwise chaste sex comedy, marks the beginning of Hayes's transition from psychological melodrama to explicit erotic drama. The sexual revolution was getting started, and Hayes, though a generation behind, was ready to play the game…

Clover Films, Daniel Cady and the Birth of 'Harold Perkins'…

Walk the Angry Beach, retitled *The Unholy Choice* and then *Hollywood After Dark*, was at last released theatrically in 1969, but it was a 1968 Hayes project that would really point the way towards his future in the industry. Back in 1961,[5] parallel to his feature film career, Hayes had begun producing and directing industrial training films for North American Aviation, who had a contract with NASA for the Apollo project, as well as other government and private agencies.[6] Around 1965 he formed a company, Clover Films, with a friend called Daniel Cady. After a few non-fiction jobs for NASA, the two men produced a spate of independent horror and sexploitation items, beginning with the extraordinary *Help Wanted Female* in 1968.

As would become the norm for his more erotically inclined films, Hayes adopted the pseudonym 'Harold Perkins'. The story kicks off with Jo-Jo, a hooker who robs johns of their dough with a few well-placed karate chops.

After a typical afternoon beating the shit out of some schmuck (Michael Lincoln), she returns home to her lesbian lover Luana, who has just been offered $200 to spend an evening with creepy client Sebastian Gregory (Daniel DiSomma, playing 'Himself' under his 'Sebastian Gregory' pseudonym). Settling in for an evening of mind-games with Luana, Gregory takes an LSD sugar cube and proceeds to tell her how he and his similarly freaky girlfriend Barbara recently butchered a pretty young hitch hiker, whom they persuaded to model for 'intellectual pin-up' shots. Luana thinks he's bullshitting, or having an acid freakout, but when she opens a trunk in the kitchen she discovers there may be more to Gregory's tale…

No doubt liberated by his pseudonym, Hayes packs the film with all the kink and sadism the times would allow. At just over an hour in length, it's a fast-paced hustle through the back-alleys of sleazy cinema, sixties-style. The relationship between Gregory and Barbara is frankly sado-masochistic, echoing Ian Brady and Myra Hindley in its depiction of a swinging couple's predatory *folie à deux* (*"To inflict pain with pleasure only led to the inevitable: to kill for pleasure!"* avows Gregory) and anticipating, however faintly, *Videodrome*'s Max Renn and Nicki Brand (with intimate sex-play involving burning embers and knife-cuts). Gregory, however, is determined to be the master of his pleasures, not the victim. After they've killed Tina, he frets to Barbara that they're putting themselves at risk of the death penalty. Barbara, however, is wantonly unconcerned for their safety, so Gregory takes drastic steps to ensure his liberty. But then twist follows twist, and our interpretation of what we've already seen changes again and again…

On the one hand, *Help Wanted Female* is an eerie, cynical tale of sex and sadism – and on the other it's a black comedy with a hefty dose of sixties camp, in the form of several burlesque dance numbers and some fabulous hair-dos. I guess it all depends on what you've swallowed beforehand. Jo-Jo is very cool indeed with her big hair and shark-fin specs, and she has killer lines to go with her moves: *"I could rip your arm off if I choose, but instead I think I'll just rip your back muscles a little."* Luana, the older woman, has the authentic wear-and-tear of the burlesque scene etched into her features: she's another tough cookie with whom you wouldn't want to argue. But the campy pleasure afforded by these tough girls is absent in scenes such as the one in which Tina is stabbed in the stomach by Barbara, to the accompaniment of a relentless strip-club jazz tune. The music carries on as the nude victim staggers confused and bleeding into the bathroom, where she's finished off by Gregory. The fact that the girl doesn't die immediately, and the way the two killers follow her dispassionately as she stumbles away from them, brings to mind Wes Craven's *The Last House on the Left*, although let's be clear about this, *Help Wanted Female* is nowhere near as graphic or intense. It's simply that the scene, with its blaring, unsympathetic soundtrack, has that element of callousness that was to prove so alarming in Craven's shocking debut. And while I'm comparing this obscure flick to the classics, there's a scene where 'Sebastian Gregory' begins carving up a female corpse that's framed in almost exactly the same way as the first killing in David Cronenberg's *Shivers*, complete with bare-chested middle-aged man wielding a blade, shot from a low angle, and a prostrate female victim in the foreground.

It's a thrill to see this film, not least to enjoy 'Sebastian Gregory' aka Daniel DiSomma, director of the superlative *Victims* (see chapter on DiSomma). Here he gives us just an early glimpse of the black heart he can summon to the screen. DiSomma's forté is playing the weirdo square, who can 'get down' with hookers and druggies yet remains detached and sarcastic in his demeanour, smooching and 'grooving' in a way that's part bourgeois conman on-the-make and part piss-taking psychopath, mocking the delusions of the young and liberated. He resembles a depraved Bob Hope here, exuding Hope's smarmy showbiz vibe, but with that gimlet-eyed insincerity ratcheted up a little too tight for comfort. (Also appearing in a small role, as a horny neighbour who makes out with Barbara behind Gregory's back, is director/cinematographer Don Jones – see chapter on Jones elsewhere in this book).

Gregory appeared again in Hayes's next film, a western sex comedy called *Fandango* (*"Wagons filled with wicked women!"*), made under Hayes's own name in 1969 and starring James Whitworth (Jupiter in *The Hills Have Eyes*). Also in the cast this time were Jay Scott (Paul in *Grave of the Vampire*) and two actors who would go on to become directors themselves: Jim Feazell, who made *Psycho from Texas*; and Roger Gentry, director of the sexploitation biker film *Sleazy Rider*. Back in the cinematographer's chair was *The Farmer's Other Daughter* DP Paul Hipp (like DiSomma a friend of the Hayes family), who went on to shoot *The Hang-Up*, *Grave of the Vampire*, and *Garden of the Dead* (plus numerous horror films for other directors, including *Blood and Lace*, *Devil Times Five*, *Psycho from Texas* and *The Boogens*). Hipp received co-producer credit on *Fandango*, along with Henning Schellerup, himself a cinematographer responsible for shooting indie horrors like *Kiss of the Tarantula*, *Curse of the Headless Horseman* and *Silent Night, Deadly Night*. Schellerup also became a regular DP for Schick-

Fandango (US theatrical & US video title)
aka **Mona's Place**
aka **Cowboy Brothel** (UK video title)
© none [1969]
Tivoli Productions presents.
writer/director: John Hayes. producer: Henning
Schellerup, Paul Hipp. director of photography:
Paul Hipp. camera operator: Rick Eisman.
editor: John Hayes. sound: Sam Nesor.
production manager: Roger Gentry. music:
Mario Toscano. key grip: Ray Atkinson.
Cast: James Whitworth (Dan Murphy). Shawn
Devereaux (Mona DeLys). Sebastian Gregory
[Daniel DiSomma] (Muck Mulligan). Jay Scott
(Billy Busby). Marland Proctor (Sissy Sam).
Paul Harper (Greaser). Donna Stanley
(Pauline). Neola Graef (Joy). Jim Gentry.
Maxine DeVille Franche. Jeannie Anderson.
Frank Teichman. Miller Petit. Beverly
Fredericks. Jeff Latham. Bonnie Cooper.
Wendy Sweeney. Paul Hipp. Paul
Brunton. Ray Saniger. Jerry Seay. John
Dennis. Roger Gentry. Gene Connor. Byron
Wardlow. Earl Newell. Allison Racy Young.

top right:
John Hayes can be seen in this cast photo
taken during the making of **Fandango**.
Hayes is the tall man in the front row, with his
arms round two of the female cast members.

below:
More frivolity from **Fandango**...

Sunn Classic Pictures in the 1970s, shooting their patent brand of earnest docu-dramas for producer/director Charles Sellier. Ellen Hayes recalls: "Paul and Henning were good friends of John's who worked with him on early projects. They were cinematographers he met when working at NASA as a director in the film department for the Apollo project. I believe he got Daniel [DiSomma] a job there, too."

For all the interesting credits, there's not a lot going on in *Fandango*. With his workers fighting and drinking too much, Wild West mining foreman Dan Murphy (Whitworth) takes two employees, Sam (Marland Proctor) and Billy (Jay Scott), to Fandango's, a bar-cum-whorehouse. He asks Madame Mona, an old flame, for a wagon full of girls to take back to his brawling workers in order to soothe industrial relations. Mona allows him to choose the cream of the crop, accompanying the girls herself to Murphy's remote mining encampment. However, Dan has made an enemy of local villain Muck Mulligan (Sebastian Gregory). Mulligan, a mean-spirited varmint who wears a leather patch to conceal his mutilated nose, mobilizes a gang to ambush Mona's pussy posse. Sam's favourite 'working girl' Pauline (Donna Stanley) is gang-raped during the raid, and another girl is shot, but the attack is repelled and the party continue on their way. Once at the camp, the good-time girls are put to work, then – after a few nights' fun and frolics – they're chaperoned back to town. On the return journey Mulligan strikes again, this time killing Billy and injuring Sam and Murphy. Thinking he's won the day, Mulligan begins a slavering sex attack on the assembled whores, but pays for his crimes when the girls descend upon him and skewer him with their hairpins. The story ends with Sam and Pauline married and Murphy hinting that the mine may soon be exhausted, leaving him free to get back together with Mona.

Fandango is a minor effort, a sentimental fantasy where hookers are happy and even the odd rape here and there doesn't spoil the fun. In fact the only females we see are employees of Madame Mona, lending a literal twist to the phrase 'all women are whores'. There's a general lack of characterisation, and the theatrical thirst for psychodrama is far less apparent here than in Hayes's previous films. When Pauline is gang-raped we can just about accept the proposition that she's escaped trauma because her line of work inures her: but it's a bit harder to swallow when soppy Sam seems not only unfazed but blandly accepting of his new girl's molestation. It's a failing of the script that Sam doesn't get to take revenge on the gang, instead being shot in the leg and sidelined during the final gunfight. Sebastian Gregory is a suitably scurvy villain, although his broad, supposedly 'Oirish' accent frequently veers South to the Caribbean. Other cast-members make an effort, but without a decent script to chew on they rarely stand out. Hayes manages a few token flickers of creativity, such as the cut from a hanged man's thrashing legs to a high-kicking floozy hoofing the Charleston, but *Fandango* is thin gruel for film fans, except for those who can forgive a movie anything if the female cast reveal their breasts. Even then, there's not much incentive to pitch your trouser-tent: made in 1969, the film plays safe, with tits and ass permissible but full-frontal male or female nudity *verboten*.[7] At least the film will titillate Charles Manson groupies: it was filmed on the Spahn Ranch, with a dateline that puts it at the crest of the Family's helter-skelter...

Cady and Hayes made three 'Clover' films in 1969. The most 'respectable' of them was *The Cut-Throats*, which Hayes put out under his own name. It concerns a Captain who recruits five American soldiers, dubbed 'The Cut-Throats', to capture battle plans from a German stronghold. However, his real motive is to steal a cache of jewels plundered by the Nazis. The enemy soldiers are gunned down, but then the film tilts into softcore sexploitation: the beautiful women of the compound seduce the Cut-Throats, commencing their fiendish plan with a sexy stage show. Prominent among the girls is softcore queen Uschi Digard, whose more than eighty screen credits include a few of the horror persuasion: Ron Garcia's sex-horror weirdy *The Toy Box* and his pro-monogamy diatribe *Swingers Massacre*; Kentucky Jones's *The Manson Massacre* (in which Uschi plays Charlie's Mum!); Brianne Murphy's *Blood Sabbath*, starring Dyanne Thorne; Don Edmonds's *Ilsa, She Wolf of the SS* and its sequel *Ilsa, Harem Keeper of the Oil Sheiks*,

also with Dyanne Thorne; and Ray Nadeau's dire *The Beauties and the Beast*. *The Cut-Throats* is set during the Second World War, but that's about all it shares with Hayes's previous war movie *Shell Shock*, which at least had a decent script. Here the scenario is indifferently explored, with softcore romping in place of characterisation. For some reason about a third of the film is without music, which makes the proceedings feel even more threadbare. If this was the only John Hayes film I'd seen, I wouldn't bother looking for more. There are a handful of mildly salacious sex scenes, I suppose, including one that takes place between an American soldier and a German girl in a bedroom festooned with Nazi swastikas. On the whole, though, this is little better than *Fandango*, certainly no match for *Help Wanted Female*, and is not recommended.

For the other two Clover films in 1969, Hayes employed his 'Harold Perkins' pseudonym. One of them, *Alimony Lovers*, is possibly the most obscure and hard-to-trace of his entire career. No one seems to have recorded their thoughts on this film, nor any plot information, save for a meagre tally of cast and crew. It does at least feature two names familiar from many of the Clover titles: make-up artist Ruth Onions (who turns up in the credits for *Help Wanted Female*, and the later *Baby Rosemary*), and cinematographer John Lyons, who shot all three.

Fortunately, we know a little more about *Baby Vickie*, Hayes/Perkins's third film in '69. It's a morbid tale about a sexually-repressed young woman, Vickie (Sharon Matt), who plays out sexual fantasies with the dummies in her father's tailor shop. Rejecting Steve (Bill Moore), the man her parents (Will Gary and Dana Raven) approve of, Vickie heads for the waterfront, where she is beaten and raped by Tony (Sebastian Gregory). Her parents cover up their daughter's 'disgrace' by arranging a marriage with Steve. A year later, after Vickie and Steve are married, the deeply disturbed bride returns to the waterfront, seeking another 'tryst' with the rapist… Elusive as yet on video and DVD, this may well emerge one day as another Hayes classic…

The Hang-Up, released in 1970 as a John Hayes film, is distinguished by an *outré* plot involving a cold, moralistic cop, Bob Walsh (Sebastian Gregory), who goes undercover as a cross-dresser to apprehend phoney detectives suspected of shaking down the clientele of a transvestite bar. Far from being sympathetic to the plight of blackmailed trannie-lovers, the homophobic Walsh views the cross-dressing scene with undisguised contempt. When his landlady speculates that his work must be very glamorous, he snaps, *"I catch queers, Miss Howard […] homosexuals, transvestites, child-molesters, pimps, pushers, whores."* Raiding a whorehouse on another assignment, he falls foul of Perano, a wealthy sleazeball *á là* Hugh Hefner. Perano, working for a rich trannie-lover, Killjan, whom Walsh offended during the earlier raid by calling him a pervert, sets up an underage honey-trap with a seventeen-year-old hooker called Angel (Sharon Matt, from *Baby Vickie*): the gullible Walsh falls for her, hook, line and sinker. Perano reveals the sting during a free love orgy in the woods, to which Angel has lured Walsh. As smirking hippies snap photos of the naked cop *in flagrante*, Perano explains that Angel has been in on the scheme all along. Perano's price for the kinky snaps is for Walsh to clear Killjan of involvement in the transvestite scene. Later that night, furious with Angel, Walsh gets drunk and rapes her on an open window-ledge (*"I'm gonna show you what rape's really like!"*), then sets about extricating himself from the blackmail scheme...

Did Paul Schrader see this movie? Some of the similarities to *Taxi Driver* are uncanny. Walsh's lines about hatred of perversion are a virtual ringer for Travis Bickle's musings, and when Walsh decides to rescue Angel from the imminent vice-bust because he believes she's an innocent in need of his protection, we see the relationship between Travis and Iris in nascent form. True, Walsh is a cop, not a psychotic drifter; but then, as Harvey Keitel's pimp observes in *Taxi Driver*, Travis sure as hell *looks* like a cop!

The 'hang-up' of the title is of course Walsh's bad attitude to sexual difference, and his inability to love. However, when he falls for Angel/Lori he seems to be entering a thaw. The film then plays a dangerous game by invoking sympathy for Walsh after he's been betrayed. Perano and Killjan are associated with corruption, using their wealth and social standing for nefarious ends, while Walsh is made to look like a poor unfortunate, trapped in a blackmail scheme just as he was starting to emerge as a 'nice guy'. Even his explosive sexual attack on Lori is forgiven by Lori herself, who accepts the rape as punishment for betrayal. As Lori lies dying in a car wreck caused by Walsh, she denies to police that Walsh had sex with her, thus frustrating Perano's hold over him. (And it's an interesting choice of name for this villain, considering that the Peraino family were notorious Mafia kingpins of the porno film industry.) Walsh is left a broken man, having lost the girl he loved, and realising she loved him too despite her involvement in the blackmail scheme (shades of *North By Northwest*). With no further dialogue to address Walsh's contempt, we're left with a homophobic bigot unlucky in love: not, for me, the most compelling candidate for tragic anti-hero. *The Hang-Up* also suffers from an identical flaw to the earlier *Help Wanted Female*: languid jazz muzak that wafts through the film without rhyme or reason, where a more supportive score

The Cut-Throats (US theatrical title)
aka **She-Devils of the SS**
(US theatrical/Danish video title)
aka **Cut-Throat Kommandos**
aka **SS Cutthroats**
© none [1969].
Clover Films presents.
writer/director: John Hayes. producers: Daniel Cady, John Hayes. director of photography: Paul Hipp. film editor: Luke Porano. art director: Lee Fisher. production manager: David Chase. assistant [art director]: Michael March. makeup: Ron Sallon. costumes: Logan. stills: Michael Cramer. asst. to director: Evelyn Rudy. camera: Henning Schellerup. assistant: Ron Johnson. sound recordist: Jim Stenberg. sound editor: Patrick Price. key grip: Jim Frazel. gaffer: David DiSchweintz. grip: Glenn Gondt. German equipment: Hollywood Military Hobbies. technical advisor: Lee Wentel. stunt coordinator: Ray Saniger. special effects: Harold Volman. title background: Linda Devenport. color lab: Cinechrome. music: Jaime Mendoza-Nava. [songs] "Ballad of Jimmy Johnson", "Just Tell Them We've Paid" lyrics by: Ellen Bender. sung by: Ernie Macy. *Cast*: Uschi Digart [Digard]. Jay Scott. E.J. Walsh. William Guhl. Joanne Douglas. Marland Proctor. Jeff Letham. George Garwin. Pat Michaels. Inge Pinson. Heather Belbin. Barbara Lane. Roger Steel. Michael Plamondon. Eric Norman. Ritva Werner. Oliver Aubrey. Damian Zisk. David Neale.

above:
US promo sheet for **The Hang-Up**.

left:
Australian video cover for the same film (featuring no images from the film), released in that country as **Vice Cop 69**.

The Hang-Up
aka **Vice Cop 69**
©none [1969]
uncredited: Clover Films.
writer/director: John Hayes. producer: Daniel B. Cady, John Hayes. photography: Paul Hipp. music composed and conducted by Mario Toscano. editor: J. Hayes [John Hayes]. [camera] operator: Henning Schellerup. makeup: Ruth Onion. key grip: Richard Ray. production: Michael March. sound: Sam Rose. Cast: Sebastian Gregory [Daniel DiSomma] (Sgt. Bob Walsh). Sharon Matt (Angel). Genene Cooper. Peter Balachoff [Balakoff]. Luke Perry. Bonnie Clark. Michael March. Gene Blackey. uncredited: Eric [Erik] Stern (Sergeant Richards). Karen Swanson (master of ceremonies).

top right:
The cops close in on **Mama's Dirty Girls**, and Candice Rialson riles another hapless male...

Mama's Dirty Girls
© 1974. Lasky/Carlin Productions II
A Lasky/Carlin production.
director: John Hayes. producer: Ed Carlin and Gil Lasky. writer: Gil Lasky. director of photography: Henning Schellerup. film editor: Luke Porand [Porano]. music: Don Bagley and Steve Michaels. production manager: Peter Cornberg. assistant film editor: Milt Citron. sound recordist: Tony Vorno. sound ass't: Dan Ansley. script supervisor: John Dorr. ass't camera: Ray Isley. costumes: Jodie Tillen. art director: Jim Newport. make-up: Jan Hines. re-recording: Glen Glenn Sound. negative cutter: Clay Marsh. key grip: Robert Decker. grip: Paul Dillingham. gaffer: John King. still photography: Peter Cornberg. titles, opticals & processing: Consolidated Film Industries.
Cast: Gloria Grahame (Mama Love). Paul Lambert (Harold). Sondra Currie (Addie). Candice Rialson (Becky). Christopher Wines (sheriff). Dennis Smith (Roy). Mary Stoddard (Cindy). Joseph Anthony (Willy). John Dennis (husband). Anneka de Lorenzo (Charity).

would have given things a lift. 'Sebastian Gregory' though is always compelling as the hard-nut puritan Walsh, giving us a very different performance to his murderous fruitloop in *Help Wanted Female*. He invests the film with enough edge to counteract Hayes's miscalculations (there's a particularly sappy scene in which Walsh runs with horses through lush fields, representing his new-found freedom with 'Angel'). The rest of the cast are unremarkable, although it's worth mentioning an appearance, in drag, by Erik Stern, star of the Mikel Angel/Don Jones horror weirdy *The Love Butcher*.

Sweet Trash (1970) is, like *Alimony Lovers*, a mystery title in the Hayes filmography. According to the American Film Institute Catalog, it was a Clover project with Dan Cady. The Catalog entry describes the sorry tale of an honest New York dockworker, Michael Donovan, unwittingly sucked into the loan shark business through his association with hookers and shady businessmen. He turns, catastrophically, to drink, unable to cope with the double-dealing life in which he's mired. Such a story has similarities to the earlier Hayes triumph *Five Minutes to Love*, with its focus on a decent man sucked into criminality. However, the *New York Times*'s online film review database claims that the AFI entry is erroneous, and asserts that *Sweet Trash* is actually an alternative title for *The Hang-Up*; a claim given extra credibility by the US Copyright Office's entry for *Sweet Trash*, which lists its alternative title as *The Hung Up* – a likely misnomer. I don't know if we'll ever learn more about Michael Donovan's misfortunes in the loan shark business, but as an outline it sounds authentically Hayes-esque...

Vampires, Gold-Diggers, and the Collapse of Clover

It's here, at least fourteen films into his career, that we see John Hayes's first full-blooded contribution to the horror genre: a dark, despairing tale of childhood trauma and madness best known today as *Dream No Evil* (see review). It stars Michael Pataki, who would remain friends with Hayes for several years, and (in a small part) Marc Lawrence, famed for his gangster roles in the classic Hollywood cinema of the thirties and forties.

All the Lovin' Kinfolk was Hayes's fourth movie that year and the third to be produced by Clover Films. Cindy (Mady Maguire), a naive young mountain woman, and her cousin Zeb (Jay Scott) head for the big city, but their dreams lead only to heartache. Cindy becomes a prostitute, seducing her cousin when she discovers that he's having an affair with the daughter of his boss. Another of Hayes's least known films, it remains very hard to elaborate beyond this brief synopsis.

After *Grave of the Vampire* and *Garden of the Dead* in 1972 (see reviews), Hayes made *The Sensuous Manicurist* (1974), a phenomenally obscure title starring Frances Buchanan, Alberta Steinberg and 'Penny Walters' (aka Dyanne Thorne), about which little is else known. In the same year he turned to comedy action melodrama with *Mama's Dirty Girls* (1974), which received much better distribution. The film opens with nineteen-year-old sex kitten Becky (Candice Rialson) squeezing into a skimpy bikini before heading out to the pool where a fat, wealthy, pantingly attentive middle-aged man (Johnny Dennis) serves her drinks. Becky teases the slob to the limit, until finally he tries to rape her – at which point Becky's mother, 'Mama' Love (Gloria Grahame) arrives to reveal that the man molesting her daughter is her newly-wed husband! In exchange for the attack going unreported, hubby writes a full

confession of his crime. This admission is then used as a suicide note, after Mama, Becky and oldest daughter Addie (Sondra Currie) slash the fellow's wrists in the shower. Mama and her two oldest daughters have used their ploy before: preying on wealthy men, marrying and then murdering them for their inheritances. As Mama explains, *"A man is only a man; but property is security."* Youngest of the brood, Cindy (Mary Stoddard), is the only one not in on the scam. The next intended victim is motel owner Harold (Paul Lambert), but unbeknownst to the conniving family, Harold already drowned his first wife to collect *her* inheritance, and intends to do the same to Mama.

With frequent near-nudity from Rialson and Currie, and a script that leans more on the humour than the nastiness of the premise, the film comes across as a black comic variant on the classic *femme fatale* narrative. Headline star Gloria Grahame, who won Best Actress Oscar for *The Bad and the Beautiful* in 1952, was enjoying a late bloom in seventies B-pictures, playing hard-hearted bitches in films like this and Philip Gilbert's *Blood and Lace* for AIP, as well as appearing in Michael Pataki's creepy *Mansion of the Doomed* and Armand Weston's effective haunted whorehouse tale *The Nesting*. Her role here as a matriarch at war with family life is *apropos*, given that Grahame married both Nicholas Ray the movie director and then later his son Tony – her former stepson! According to Ellen Hayes, the actress was a real trouper, very co-operative to the production: but formidable, a woman who lifted weights every morning when filming on location! She's supported well by pretty Candice Rialson, who essays another great bitch-kitten role to set alongside her man-raping 'Bonnie' in Raphael Nussbaum's *Pets*.

Mama's Dirty Girls was not released by Clover, but instead by Premiere Releasing (who distributed *The Manhandlers*, *Swinging Barmaids* and imports like Lucio Fulci's *The Challenge to White Fang*). Sadly, Hayes's relationship with Daniel Cady had foundered after thirteen years, with a dispute over money. Ellen Hayes explains how the rift with Cady came about: "John did everything involved with production. He wrote, directed, edited (story, sound and music), cut negative and could pinch-hit as photographer and sound recordist. The one area in which he had no interest or expertise was finance, and this led directly to his conflict with Dan Cady and the demise of Clover. Also, there were differences between the two on the direction they wanted to take the company."[8]

Baby Rosemary

With Clover now folded, Hayes directed films for other low-budget indie producers, as well as continuing his 'Harold Perkins' career with companies such as Essex Pictures, porno specialists responsible for nuggets like *Sex World* (Anthony Spinelli's 1978 porn take on *Westworld*). In 1976, picking up a thread from his earlier film *Baby Vickie*, he made *Baby Rosemary*, a brutal sex drama that stands as one of his most disturbing films, with strong echoes of the family trauma theme that incessantly coloured his career. Long-standing friend and actor Daniel DiSomma began work on the film as sound-man, but dropped out, finding the unrelenting pornographic focus too depressing. One has to sympathise: the film is certainly a million miles away from the light-hearted sex satire of DiSomma's own foray into sexploitation, *Come One Come All*. Squeamishness aside, though, this was to prove a surprisingly powerful, arresting piece of work. Earlier films can claim to be better made, bedecked with the virtues of Hayes's theatrical background, but if there's an infernal core to his filmmaking, *Baby Rosemary* is it…

Rosemary Price (Sharon Thorpe) is a sexually tormented and confused young woman who is unable to settle down with a man. Her mother died when she was very young and her alcoholic father put her in an orphanage, only visiting her occasionally. (*"It was such a nightmare to be a child. Now I'm the adult, I do what I want."*) When her current lover, John (John Leslie [John Nuzzo]) announces that he's going to join the police force and wants to move in with her, Rosemary turns him down flat. (*"Sex is always so degrading. So unclean."*) She tells him she's going to get a job as a teacher and will be too busy to see him any more. John leaves to seek solace with a hooker called Eunice (Leslie Bovee), whom he addresses as 'Rosemary' while orally worshipping her ass on the stairs of her skanky apartment block. Rosemary visits a flophouse where she believes her father still lives, although she hasn't seen him for several years. Finding he's not there, she waits in his room. A young couple, Tate (Monique Cardin aka Samantha King) and Mick (Ken Cotton), let themselves in, claiming to be her father's friends. After taunting her with pornographic photographs they claim were taken by her father, the couple subject her to a bisexual rape at knifepoint (*"Suck that cunt or you're dead!"*). The story then jumps forward two years: John, now a police officer, approaches Rosemary and informs her that her father has died. However, she's emotionally distant and shows little interest. She introduces John to two of her students, Tracy and Marsha, who are members of *"an occult group that believes that all of life is sexual."* Rosemary and John, accompanied by Tracy and Marsha, attend a funeral home to see Rosemary's father in his coffin. Tracy is unimpressed by the undertaker's soliloquy about death and rebirth (*"All that stuff about a human turning into a flower? It's bullshit"*): the two girls demonstrate their take on death by seducing the undertaker (John Seeman) into a threesome. John tries to reawaken his relationship with Rosemary but she can't relax with him in bed. After a dysfunctional bedroom tussle in which Rosemary makes John come without allowing him to penetrate her, she sneaks off back to her father's old flophouse and voluntarily has sex with Mick, the man who raped her before, achieving her only orgasm of the film during rough, verbally abusive sex. In an 'only in the seventies' twist, the rapist turns sweet on her, cleans up his

act, gets a job, promises to quit drinking and buys her frilly underwear, acting like a bashful schoolboy (*"I ain't never had a girl like you. Clean, and, you know, decent."*). Unfortunately, it doesn't work out – as soon as love is involved, Rosemary turns frigid (*"What's wrong?" "I don't know – it's different!"*). The rejection flips lover-boy back into rapist-scum mode, but his plans for an evening of degradation (*"I'm gonna sit here and drink my beer, 'n' maybe when I've had enough I'm gonna piss it all up your nose, you fuckin' cunt."*) are forestalled by the arrival of John, looking for Rosemary. A fight ensues – Mick knocks John out cold and Rosemary grabs John's police pistol; however she is unable to shoot. Mick leaves, swearing vengeance on Rosemary (*"The next time I catch you alone, I'm gonna fuck you over real bad. An' when I'm through fuckin' with ya – I'm gonna kill ya"*). John agrees to Rosemary's plea not to report the incident, but extricates himself from Rosemary when she tries to rekindle their relationship. Her repeated frustration of his desires has finally dampened his ardour. After a lesbian threesome with Tracy and Marsha, Rosemary hears her father's voice imploring her (*"Rosemary, help me. Don't let them bury me. I'm alive."*). She enters the funeral parlour and sits down in front of the open coffin. As dry ice wafts everywhere, all the characters in the film – John and Eunice, Tracy and Marsha, Mick and Tate, the Undertaker – enter the room and draw Rosemary into a gangbang in front of her father's casket. The film ends on a shot of Rosemary clawing her way out of a morass of naked bodies and reaching out in despair to the corpse, crying, *"Daddy? Take me away from this place!"*

This is one hellishly mixed up film. Sombre, sensitive moments jostle with some of the harshest clichés of seventies porn, in a compelling but relentlessly grim story that seesaws between bad-taste shocks and genuine psychological honesty. The problem is that the film's

Baby Rosemary
aka **Baby Rosemarie**
© none [1976].
Essex Pictures Company presents.
director: Harold Perkins [John Hayes].
producer: Bill Steele. screenplay: Ruth Price and Virgin Rove [approx: illegible]. production manager: John Seeman. music editor: George Correro [approx: illegible]. camera: John Lyons. boom: Ken Roberts. editor: Luke Porano.
Cast: Sharon Thorpe (Rosemary Price). John Leslie Dupree [John Nuzzo] (John). Leslie Bovee (Eunice). Ken Cotton [aka Ken Scudder] (Mick). Monique Cardin [aka Samantha King] (Tate). John Seeman (undertaker). Candida Royalle (Tracy). Melba Bruce. (Marsha). Dale Meador. Tina Castedo [approx: illegible]. Ralph Johnson. Rhonda Fortes.
Note: the American film poster erroneously credits Hayes as 'Howard Perkins'.

below:
Images from **Baby Rosemary**:

clockwise from top left:
Mick (Ken Cotton) fights with John (John Leslie);
Rosemary (Sharon Thorpe) can't shoot her rapist;
Sinister visions at the funeral parlour;
Rape;
John tries to get close to Rosemary;
Eunice gets into lesbian antics during the macabre final orgy;
Rosemary's dead father;
John seeks solace with Eunice (Leslie Bovee).

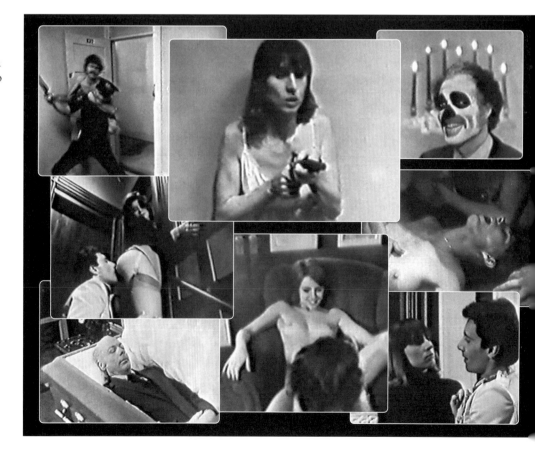

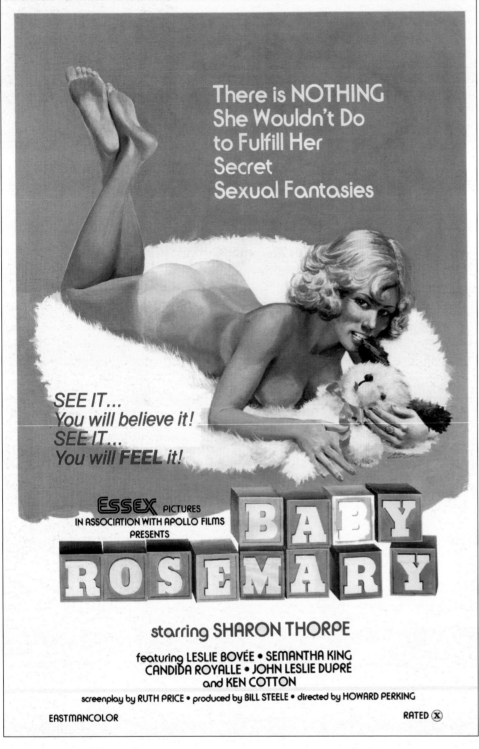

idea from the reverse angle. So, can a porno film also deal seriously with psychological portraiture? On the evidence of a film like this it's harder to dismiss than you might think, despite what the trade paper *Variety* (who mocked its "ludicrous stab at plot narrative") had to say. The porno template for such adventures is often assumed to be Gerard Damiano's downbeat, existential *The Devil in Miss Jones* (1973), but a look at the pre-hardcore nudies and roughies reveals that Hayes, like James Bryan and Don Jones, was already toying with darker character-driven sex stories and looking to make them more and more graphic (If Hayes had made *Help Wanted Female* four years later, it could have been an S&M nightmare to rival the films of Zebedy Colt). *The Devil in Miss Jones*, while undeniably impressive, was simply part of a continuum: Hayes was already seeking a blend of gritty psychological realism and pornography, even before Damiano's hit went mainstream.

What is most haunting about *Baby Rosemary* is the way Hayes once again draws on aspects of his troubled family background for material. The suggestion is that Rosemary was abused in the orphanage where her father left her, and this combination of traumatic sexual experience and parental abandonment has ruined her chances of emotional and sexual happiness; leading, in the end, to madness. Brutal, abusive sex is her only carnal satisfaction, while affection (even from a one-time rapist) turns her frigid. It is certainly not for me to speculate any further as to the links, if any, between Rosemary and Hayes's unfortunate sister, but it's clear that he felt compelled to explore his feelings on the subject even here, in a setting that many would consider hopelessly debased.

By drawing parallels from his own life experience, Hayes makes *Baby Rosemary* resonate with emotional honesty, but he also generates cross-currents, with some misogynistic scenes that confuse the film's moral centre. When the previously sympathetic, apparently sweet-natured John has sex with the hooker Eunice, his surrogate Rosemary, his sexual adoration of her asshole initially casts him as the lovelorn victim. However, the sex then swivels back to a contradictory set-up with the male in the traditional power role: John fucks Eunice, cums over her face and leaves her frustrated, denied her own orgasm. The scene ends up embracing the macho notion that hookers are nymphos who can be left gasping for more, instead of the far more honest depiction that would have shown Eunice able to turn her 'desire' on and off like a faucet. By showing her plaintively calling after the departing 'John' whilst frigging herself off on the stairs, the scene panders to male fantasies of total control over the sexual act. It's as if the earlier sexual submission has to be assuaged, by gestures like John dismissively tossing money at Eunice as he finishes. However, after he's departed, we see Eunice cease masturbating, and mutter incredulously to herself, *"Christ. What a way to make a fucking living!"* – before staggering back up to her room, complaining about her aching back. Considering that John and Eunice later become a couple, with the hooker merging raw sex and emotional commitment in a way Rosemary could not, John's macho trip in the stairwell stands out like a sore, ahem, thumb. Perhaps the actor John Leslie, a big name in porno at the time, took control of the power dynamic as the camera rolled, against the grain of the script, and Hayes felt obliged to keep his star's reaction in the film?

And then there's the rape scene. In psychological terms, poor abused Rosemary might conceivably respond to being raped by 'getting into it'. Not that she does with any great

moral compass (if I dare to presume such a thing) is inevitably steamed up by the graphic, aggressive sex and pungent verbal hostility, swamping the depiction of a traumatized woman in prurient close-ups and raw, pornographic spectacle.

In recent years, art-house movies like Lars von Trier's *The Idiots* (1998), Catherine Breillat's *Romance* (1999), Virginie Despentes's *Baise-moi* (2000) and Michael Winterbottom's *9 Songs* (2004) have once again raised the issue of whether film as a narrative art can sustain pornographic imagery. Earlier art-house hits like *In the Realm of the Senses* (1976) are usually cited as examples of how this can work, but it's rare that anyone gives credit to the porno industry itself for experimenting with the same enthusiasm, it has to be noted; she exudes an attitude of, 'Well, if it's going to happen you may as well ride with it'. The issue is not one of fictive plausibility – the problem lies in the way we're invited to watch. As feminist critics would explain in far more detail, the placement of the camera and use of film style are crucial. They can facilitate amoral complicity; or mindless complicity (two very different attitudes, neither of which require critical engagement with the morality of the camera): or thirdly, a moral engagement with the image (which asks how we may detach our point of view from complicity with the rapists). In this case, I can see no evidence that Hayes intended to distance the viewer from the rapists' sexual pleasure. The rape scene is a pure spectacle of cruelty, and we are invited to the feast either as sadistic voyeurs mindful of our amoral enjoyment, or mindless voyeurs for whom the question is too complicated to care about. In comparison to the rigorous detachment of Meir Zarchi's *I Spit on Your Grave*, Hayes treats the rape as just a rougher-than-average sex scene.

The most shocking aspect of the rape is not visual; it's verbal. In fact, the language throughout is frequently crude and gloatingly abusive. This is one of the strengths of the film. I've quoted a few examples, but you have to watch *Baby Rosemary* in order to appreciate the way that Hayes plays hardball with the audience through obscene, tellingly realistic dialogue. Even if the sexual politics of the era elude the director, he maintains a frank, unflinchingly honest grip on vernacular. Verbal abuse tells us more about the speaker than the spoken-to, and Hayes the theatre-lover still knows how to shorthand his characters' identities through a few well-chosen words, even in this unpromising locale. *Baby Rosemary* is one of Hayes's best films, but it's also one of his most problematic, revealing a terrible cynicism that plays strangely against the compassion to be found elsewhere in his work.

Genre-hopping

After a brief stint editing a sex comedy called *The Boob Tube Strikes Again!* (1977) for roughie specialist Lee Frost, who'd guested as an actor in *Garden of the Dead*, Hayes turned for the first and last time to sci-fi for *End of the World*, a 'star vehicle' generally regarded as a dud. One fashion that never pales is the exploitation trick of hiring old time 'names', even if only for just one day – which is how *End of the World*'s roster of talent was conceived. (Quentin Tarantino's knack of rediscovering out-of-favour actors upgrades the process, which used to be confined to the B- and C-lists). *End of the World* was made in 1977 for producer and soon-to-be low-budget mogul Charles Band, and stars perhaps the most prestigious acting talents Hayes had worked with: Christopher Lee, Dean Jagger and Sue Lyon. Not that life was made easier by the presence of greatness: Ellen Hayes says: "I remember John being amused that Mr. Lee rarely blinked, and one bit of direction would often be, 'All right Christopher, now blink!'"

In 1978, after a bland 'Harold Perkins' sex film for Essex Pictures called *Hot Lunch*, starring Juliet Anderson and Desiree Cousteau, and notable only for its unusual *absence* of strife and misery, Hayes made the erotic melodrama *Jailbait Babysitter* for Group 1, a daring distribution house responsible for thrusting Silvio Amadio's *Amuck!*, Richard Robinson's *Poor Pretty Eddie* and Mario Caiano's *Nazi Love Camp 27* onto the sleaze-thirsty audiences of America. This downbeat sex drama

(Ad-line: *"She's Pure Temptation!"*) revisits the cautionary vibe of Hayes's 1960s work, with its casually amoral, underage female lead causing merry hell in the lives of sex-hungry mankind.

It was followed in 1979 by *Up Yours*, which Hayes co-directed with writer Edward Ryder. This "rockin' comedy" as the subtitle has it, was produced and co-written by Chris Warfield for Warfield's own Lima Productions, and features walk-ons by Belinda Balaski, Ryder and Warfield themselves, and Warfield's buddy, B-movie stalwart George 'Buck' Flower.[9] A compendium of woeful skits, *Up Yours* wants a piece of the *Kentucky Fried Movie* action, but the gags are so limp and artlessly protracted you squirm instead of laughing. I did find the central conceit amusing, simply because it's so tacky: a 'living, speaking' apartment block, as represented by an actress (Cindy Morgan) superimposed

above:
A scene from **Jailbait Babysitter**.

below:
Promo sheet for Hayes's **End of the World**.

Up Yours (UK video title)
aka **Up Your Ladder**
aka **Up Yours: A Rockin' Comedy**
(US theatrical title)
© 1979. The Ladder Film Co., Ltd.
A Lima Productions present.
directors: John Hayes, Eddie Ryder. producer: Chris Warfield. writers: Chris Warfield & Edward Ryder. cinematography: Hanania Baer. assistant cameraman: Mosh Levine. set designer: Marshall Reed. associate producer: George Flower. editor: Bill Christian. assistant editor: Meri H. McDonald. effects & music editor: Frank A. Coe. lighting director: Guy Nicholas. lighting assistant: Stuart Lancaster. best boy: Robert Harris. key grip: Chuck Dawson. grip: Arnold Riehm. set dressing: Richard Gillis. set assistants: Earl French & Scott Gillis. sound mixer: Harold Perkins [John Hayes]. boom man: Eric Myers. wardrobe: Sherrie Goldberg. make up: Kelly McGowan. carpenter: Albert Jones. electrician: Wilson Talmadge. assistant director: Walt Hill. production manager: Olle Farac. script supervisor: Helen Irem. production secretary: Dee Bower. production assistant: Betsy Holt. still photographer: Joel Sussman. production equipment: Cine-Pro. caterer: Village Catering. music: Harry Wylde. lyrics for Up Your Ladder: Frank A. Coe. special effects consultant: G.W. Paulsen. special effects & titles: FX. title setting: Title House. opticals: Hollywood Optical Systems, Inc. colour by Technicolor. sound mixed by Cinesound Co., Inc..
Cast: Eddie Ryder (man on the street). Mike Heit (tenant). Cindy Morgan (Elaine). Rick Dillon (bachelor). Talie Cochran (lady). Thomas Newman (doctor). Mike Heit (dad). Danny Williams (son). Chris Warfield (Doctor Gold). Don Edmonds (patient). Eddie Ryder (obscene caller). Belinda Balaski (Helen). Thomas Newman (plainclothesman 1). Walt Hill (plainclothesman 2). Thomas Newman (soup man). Mike Heit (soup waiter). Lola French (Miss Victor). Caleb Goodman (Virgil). Caleb Goodman (VIrgil's father). Ray Halpern (Francis). Stafford Morgan (Steven). Jill Jacobson (lady patient). Chuck McCann (Doctor Lude). P.J. Williams (barber shop owner (Guido). Fred Nelles (Fungus). John Simmons (Michael). Penny Walters [Dyanne Thorne] (manicurist). John Hayes (cop). George Ranito Jordan (Black). Mike Chan (Yellow). Rick Dillon (White). Chris Warfield (cold man). Debbie Daws (pretty lady). Odette Wyler (Mary Lou Perkins). Buck Flower (beggar). John Hayes (gent). Ray Halpern (maitre d'). Eddie Ryder (chief looney). Thomas Newman (Tommy). Andy Veneto (Andy). George Ranito Jordan (George). John Goff (Johny). Debbie Daws (Betty). Stafford Morgan (Atlanta man). Rick Dillon (elephant man). Chris Warfield (Doctor Gold). Alice Shane (mom). Paul Childs (Donald). Joe Carafello (suicide man). John Goff (devil). George Ranito Jordan (anxious husband). Chuck McCann (doctor). Colleen Meeker (cheating wife). Paul Childs (Roger). Ray Halpern (irate husband). Don Edmonds (friend of bee man) Chris Warfield (bee man). Anna Lopez (flamenco dancer). Chuck McCann (Mr. Hubbard). Alice Shane (Mrs Hubbard). Mike Chan (grocery boy). John Hayes (cop on beat).

opposite:
US one-sheet poster.

over the brickwork, delivers cutesy homilies that segue between stories tenuously linked to the building, to the accompaniment of 'quirky' music that sounds lifted from the seventies TV hit *Soap*. Essentially though, this is the pits. No one sets out to make a bad film, especially a bad comedy, so we must assume that either comedy simply wasn't Hayes's metier, or more likely, that he had little actual control over what went into the script. After all, he didn't write this one: Edward Ryder and Chris Warfield must take the rap there. At least the film offers us several chances to see Hayes himself, including an appearance as a cop in a barbers' shop, and later as a pompous gentleman refusing to give money to a beggar, played by George 'Buck' Flower: *"'Neither a borrower, nor a lender be: for loan oft loses both itself and friend' – William Shakespeare,"* the gentleman says, to which the beggar responds, *"'Fuck you' – Tennessee Williams."* If I tell you this is one of the funniest scenes, you'll know what to do if you ever see this tape in a video sale. The real problem is that simple one-liners are being set up as sketches, stretching the jokes way too thin. For example: a cash-strapped man develops a taste for dog food. He later dies, we're told, but not from the dog food – he falls from the sofa and breaks his neck whilst trying to lick his own balls. Boom-boom! Except it takes five minutes to play out this scenario – and we don't get to see the guy licking his testicles either; surely an oversight in any comedy …

Dyanne Thorne of *Ilsa, She Wolf of the SS* fame appears in the film as a seductive manicurist, using the pseudonym 'Penny Walters' (and leaving one wondering what the connection could be with the earlier obscuro Hayes title *The Sensuous Manicurist* – could Thorne's scene in *Up Yours* be culled from the earlier picture?). Don Edmonds, Thorne's director on the first two *Ilsa* films, appears too, as a psychiatrist's patient looking at ink-blots who delivers the old 'You're the one who drew the dirty pictures' gag, with Chris Warfield as the psychiatrist. In fact the cast is an exploitation-specialist smorgasbord: John Goff, Buck Flower's writing partner on *Drive-In Massacre* and Matt Cimber's collaborator on the screenplays for *Fake-Out* and *Butterfly* (and who played the abusive father in Cimber's *The Witch Who Came from the Sea*) turns up as The Devil, while Stafford Morgan, who also appears in *The Witch Who Came from the Sea* and Don Jones's *The Forest*, essays another couple of roles. You have to wade through an awful lot of rubbish to see them, but anyway, now you know…

The 1980s saw the pornographic movie world change beyond recognition, and although Hayes gave the New Video Order a shot it's clear that his style was never going to make the transition from story-driven sex dramas to video-age smut. In 1982 he directed *Pleasure Zones*, as 'Harold Perkins'. This online description gives you a good idea of how times had changed: *"Beautiful newcomer, Rachel Welles, is our "Pleasure Guide," as she uses her incredible body as a sensuous, living road map while she describes the ecstasy derived from the proper caressing of the Pleasure Zones. As her gentle hands lovingly fondle her magnificent breasts, expertly massaging herself into a state of sensual excitement, she takes us on a visual voyage. Thus begins an overwhelmingly erotic avalanche of visual stimulation that will leave you limp with ecstasy."* Sixty minutes of fondling may take the viewer on a 'visual voyage' of some sort, but it doesn't make for cinema as such, and Hayes, whose roots were in psychological drama and the theatre, must have felt the game was up.

Back to the Theatre

After directing an episode of *Tales from the Darkside* called 'The Madness Room', starring Stuart Whitman, and one more 'Harold Perkins' outing, comprising two segments of the 1985 multi-director porno film *Working Girls* (namely 'Male Hooker' and 'Learning the Biz'), Hayes – and 'Harold Perkins' – retired from the film industry. Instead, he turned back to his first love, the theatre, staying active through the directors unit at the Actors Studio, and through Theater East in Los Angeles. His one-act play *The Front Room* was produced at Theater East as part of the 1987 Fringe Festival.

Hayes married Ellen, the sister of his second wife, in 1986. The two of them had been good friends ever since the mid-sixties, but their romantic relationship took off in 1983, when John helped Ellen through a serious illness. With a stable and loving relationship to rely upon, Hayes varied his endeavours and maintained numerous interests outside of the movies. He ran a catering business for a while and spent a lot of time studying the saxophone, listening to jazz and classical music, and rebuilding old pianos. In the nineties he learned to edit on computer and studied a variety of digital camera systems. He even re-opened Clover Films, with plans to write and direct short dramatic films on tape. His last produced drama was a half-hour piece called *The Neighborhood*, with his friend Paul Carr as actor/producer: the themes were drawn, as so often, from his Irish American, New York youth. He was planning to tighten and re-edit the result before becoming ill. He died of cancer in Burbank California, on 21 August, 2000. He is survived by his wife Ellen, and two daughters from his first marriage; Alisa Shepard and Deborah Copher.

Ellen Hayes recalls: "John was fast and decisive as a director but always relished the rehearsal process most. He trusted actors and listened to their input but believed the director was ultimate dictator. His concentration was fierce and he believed total effort and loyalty were due every project, no matter what its artistic merit. If this sounds humourless, the opposite was true. He was a very funny man who didn't take himself too seriously. In writing he didn't like gags or one liners, preferring situational humour. Jack Colvin, actor, director and acting teacher, was a close friend, having met John, I believe, at Theater East. They would schmooze for hours on the phone about movies, the theatre, vaudeville, burlesque, old songs and New York.[10] Among the films John admired most were *The Entertainer*, *Who's Afraid of Virginia Woolf?*, *Our Town* and *Laura* (for its photography). Good acting moved him emotionally. I once caught him with tears in his eyes watching a comedy. It was Glenn Close's performance in Altman's *Cookie's Fortune*."

Rue McClanahan also stresses Hayes's sense of humour; "During *Shell Shock* I remember him saying to me, 'You know, a lot of people come up to me and say, 'You're so authoritative. You never seem flustered. How do you do it?' I'll tell you how I do it, Rue… I stand there and I look into the distance and I look as if I'm thinking of something, like I'm planning the next shot: all I'm really doing is looking like I'm planning the next shot! And it fools everybody 'cause it looks like I know what I'm doing!'"

McClanahan was well aware that Hayes's humour was set against a background of personal trauma: "He'd had a difficult childhood, raised by his grandmother and his uncle. He wrote short stories that were funny, but touching, sad. He was so disturbed and unsure of himself as a person because of his bad upbringing. His father died, whom he never lived

HER FRIENDS CALL HER JAIL BAIT...

HER CLIENTS CALL HER ANYTIME!

Jail Bait Babysitter

But Not A Baby!

above:
Extremely rare poster for one of Hayes's sex comedies, **All the Lovin' Kinfolk** (1970).

with, and he took it very hard, then his mother Kate died, whom he was very fond of, and he took that very hard too. I visited him and Ellen in Hollywood every time I went out there to do something, and the last time I visited was about a year before he died of cancer. He was obviously very weak and rather frightened, because it was not curable. I'd had breast cancer by then, and I tried to boost him up and explain that he was going to get better. The last time I saw him he was standing in his sitting room with Ellen as I was leaving, and he had a big smile on his face, as he often did: he was a wonderful man."

John Hayes was a tireless lover of cinema whose best work has frequently been either ignored or lost in the commercial shuffle, with only his more avowedly cultish films, the horror titles, tending to attract attention. I hope this chapter has shown that there are many more Hayes films deserving of scrutiny. Personally, I find that with nine of his feature films still to see, I have not yet assuaged my curiosity about the man and his work. Perhaps this chapter will serve as a springboard for other writers, who will eventually add these tantalizing missing titles to their own studies. And for horror fans who, like me, love *Grave of the Vampire* and *Dream No Evil*, the career of John Hayes provides a startling example of the complex life stories that can lie behind those battered old VHS tapes…

and broke his back; he was a paraplegic from then on. "He had been on his way for an interview," McClanahan sighs. "His sister told me: 'I'm pretty confident that Norman was being considered for the position of drama critic at the *New Republic* magazine, and my memory is that he was heading East to explore that possibility.' The others in the crash weren't even injured. He went through a lot of therapy after that and became very independent in his wheelchair. He lived with me for six weeks in L.A., during my fourth marriage, and my husband did not take to that at all! But by then I was thinking of Norman as my best friend."

Footnotes

1   *End As a Man* by Calder Willingham; workshop performances 10 and 17 May and 11 June 1953, Actors Studio. Cast: James Dean in a nonspeaking role as a scribe; also Ben Gazzara, Arthur Storch, Williams Smithers, Albert Salmi, Anthony Franciosa, Peter Mark Richman. Director: Jack Garfein. As listed in Val Holley's book *James Dean: The Biography*.

2   Hartweg was on his way from Las Vegas to New York one night, as a passenger in a friend's car, when the driver fell asleep at the wheel. In the ensuing crash, Hartweg was thrown from the car

3   The film came out on tape in a sepia-tinted version in the USA, from Paragon Video.

4   Rue refers to her third husband Peter DiMeo solely as 'the Italian' and refuses to speak his name!

5   Rue McClanahan thinks it was closer to 1964.

6   "I know John, Paul Hipp and Henning Schellerup did a film on the original group of astronauts, but I don't know the title," says Ellen Hayes.

7   The cover of Something Weird's cassette promises seventy nine minutes but the actual print runs barely seventy, so perhaps the sex scenes were racier in some versions.

8   Cady followed *Mama's Dirty Girls* with two blaxploitation films, *Black Samson* and *Black Starlet*, both 1974, and *Kiss of the Tarantula* by Chris Munger in 1976.

9   The original title was probably *Up Your Ladder*: which is the name of the title song, and is referenced in the production company name set up for the project, The Ladder Film Co. The film appeared on the British video label Apex as *Up Yours*, with a title card slapped over the opening credits to back it up. The title *Up Yours: A Rockin' Comedy* is harder to attribute specifically.

10   Colvin was an actor in TV's *The Incredible Hulk*, in which he played the regular character of nosy reporter and Hulk-hunter Jack McGee.

JOHN HAYES: FILMOGRAPHY AS DIRECTOR

1958	*The Kiss* (short: also writer/producer)
1960	*Walk the Angry Beach* aka *Hollywood After Dark* aka *The Unholy Choice* (also writer/producer)
1961	*The Grass Eater* (also co-writer)
1963	*Five Minutes to Love* aka *It Only Takes Five Minutes* aka *The Rotten Apple* aka *The Wrecking Yard* (also co-writer)
1963	*Shell Shock* aka *82nd Marines Attack* (also co-writer of screenplay)
1965	*The Farmer's Other Daughter* aka *Farm Girl* aka *Haystack Hooker*
1968	*Help Wanted Female* (as 'Harold Perkins')
1969	*Fandango* aka *Mona's Place* (also writer)
1969	*The Cut-Throats* aka *Cut-Throat Kommandos* aka *SS Cutthroats* aka *The Cutthroats* aka *She-Devils of the SS* (also writer/producer)
1969	*Alimony Lovers* (as 'Harold Perkins')
1969	*Baby Vickie* (as 'Harold Perkins')
1969	*The Hang-Up* aka *The Hang Up* aka *Vice Cop 69* (also writer/producer/editor)
1970	*Sweet Trash* aka *The Hung Up* (also writer/editor) ***
1970	*All the Lovin' Kinfolk* aka *Kin Folk* aka *Kinfolk* aka *The Closest of Kin* (also writer/producer)
1971	*Dream No Evil* aka *The Faith Healer* aka *Now I Lay Me Down to Die* (also writer/producer)
1971	*Garden of the Dead* aka *Grave of the Undead* aka *Tomb of the Undead*
1972	*Grave of the Vampire* aka *Seed of Terror* (also co-writer/editor)
1973	*Heterosexualis* (also writer)
1974	*Mama's Dirty Girls*
1974	*The Sensuous Manicurist*
1976	*Baby Rosemary* aka *Baby Rosemarie* (as 'Harold Perkins')
1977	*End of the World* (also editor)
1978	*Hot Lunch* (as 'Harold Perkins')
1978	*Jailbait Babysitter* (also writer/editor)
1979	*Up Yours* aka *Up Your Ladder* aka *Up Yours - A Rockin' Comedy* (co-dir Edward Ryder – also sound mixer)
1982	*Pleasure Zones* (as 'Harold Perkins' – also writer)
1985	*Working Girls* (as 'Harold Perkins' - two segments: "Male Hooker" and "Learning The Biz")

*** for an explanation of this film's dubious accreditation, see the text.

FOR TV:

1984	*Tales from the Darkside: The Madness Room*

AS 2ND UNIT DIRECTOR:

1979	*She Came to the Valley* – dir: Albert Band

UNFINISHED PROJECTS:

The Neighborhood

chapter 13

What Really Happened to Tony Vorno's Victims?

Daniel DiSomma on Victims

Victims (1977)

Paulie (Tony Vorno) is in trouble. He's coming apart. His shrink Dr. Russo (Jerome Guardino) believes hypnotherapy will tap the root of his problems, but for Paulie it's already too late. Every close encounter he has with the opposite sex costs another woman her life, while stirring up memories of his prostitute mother Paula (Lois Adams), who left him at the tender mercies of Sheila (Brandy Carson), a sexually abusive alcoholic hooker, and Charlie (Bud Greene), her far-from-tender pimp...

This deeply downbeat serial-killer tale never received an American release, and sank without trace when released in Britain on the Video Unlimited label in the early '80s. It has been criminally neglected ever since. *Victims* has the studiedly grimy ambience of Joseph Ellison's *Don't Go in the House* (1979) and the no-bullshit verisimilitude of John McNaughton's *Henry: Portrait of a Serial Killer* (1986) – it may be hard to find, but sourcing a copy should be a priority for anyone interested in low-budget, high-quality American horror.

Central to the film is a carefully-observed performance by actor-turned-director Daniel DiSomma. Describing his approach as "a composite psychological profile drawn from my interest in psychology and sensitivity to the subject," DiSomma offers a portrait of a man weakened by childhood trauma, a fragile vessel set to explode at any of life's frustrations. Billed under his pseudonym 'Tony Vorno', DiSomma plays Paul/Paulie as a 'bad actor' – in the American vernacular – someone whose mask of glib sincerity sets our nerves obscurely on edge. When the mask slips, Paul lurches into madness, in a nervy, alarmingly plausible way that captures the enraged disappointment of a loser-turned-killer. When it comes, the violence – although not especially graphic – has a grim intensity born not of lovingly detailed flesh wounds, but of palpable fear and fury.

The backbone of *Victims* is its cast, and their experience in Los Angeles theatre shines through in scene after scene. The film suffers none of the drawbacks one associates with actors in low-budget movies. Each and every part is played well: in particular, the key scenes

between Paul and his female victims are fraught with ferocious tension and believability. *Victims* has none of the kitsch value you get from bad acting; and just as importantly there's no inappropriate grandstanding, of the sort you might expect from stage actors unaccustomed to the screen. Instead, DiSomma draws measured perform-ances from his cast, giving what could have been just another psycho-killer movie much greater credibility.

The brain behind the backbone, so to speak, is DiSomma - as writer, director and star. He treads a fine line in the earlier scenes, with 'Paulie' coming across as both sad and rather comical. We see him driving around the sleazier streets of L.A., fulminating under his breath about the permissive evils to which he's clearly drawn, like a middle-aged, deglamorised Travis Bickle. Spying a cop (James Pascucci) shaking down a passer-by, he sidles up, removes his sunglasses and winks conspiratorially, as if to congratulate the officer – before replacing his shades and striding into a sex store. Once inside, Paulie looks around, seething with the sort of hypocritically aroused moral ire that British readers will recognize as the *modus operandi* of the tabloids, before haranguing the store-owner about the 'shit' he's peddling. Having made his 'point', he struts out with an absurd *"I'll be back"*, underlining his threat with a handful of popcorn thrown, with comic pettiness, at the store owner.

But when Paulie encounters the *opposite* sex, we see what a danger he really is, and the smile is wiped from our faces. *Victims* shares little with other psycho-horror films; there are no virginal 'final girls' here. DiSomma views all the female characters equally and makes no moralistic connection between their career choices and their fates. They're all just trying to make a living, and the whore who has to deal professionally with Paulie's hair-trigger violence is treated with as much sympathy as the unfortunate psychiatrist's secretary (Lenore Stevens) who finds herself stuck alone with him during her dinner break, or the luckless housewife (Patsy Sabline) renting out a room in her pleasant, sunny home. Perhaps the only difference between them is that the whore is harder to fool, since her work often brings her into contact with the dark side of masculinity. Initially unfazed, if watchful, she plays

below:
This rare American admat for **Victims** stresses the realism of the film.

Victims
aka **Paulie** (original title)
aka **Day of the Rapist / Surfside Strangler /
Portrait of a Strangler / The Strangler**
© 1982. Paulie Productions [filmed in 1977]
Paulie Productions presents.
writer/producer/director: Daniel DiSomma.
executive producer: Jeanine DiSomma.
camera: Ray Icely. music: David Kinzie.
editors: Stan Gilman, Robert Freeman, Barry
Schneebeli. post production supervisor: Paul
Jasiukonis. sets and costumes: Ron & Laura
Borenstein. sound: John Patrick Hayes [John
Hayes]. gaffer: Don Brown. camera assistant:
Larry Snodgrass. makeup: Ravon, Tino
Zachio. associate producers: Paul Dvorin,
Jane Dvorin, Sandra Bridge, Norma Chalfin.
script consultant: Frank Dana. production
manager: David Kinzie. negative cutter: Ron
Mathias. title layout: Paul Jasiukonis.
transportation: Mike Weiner. boom: Dallas
Clarke. grip: Mike Deason.
Cast: Tony Vorno [Daniel DiSomma] (Paul).
Jerome Guardino (Doctor J.A. Russo). Lenore
Stevens (Marian). Lois Adams (Paula). Bud
Greene (Charlie). Brandy Carson (Sheila).
Sandy Champion (Louie). Ray Powers
("john"). Janet Dey (hooker). Patsy Sabline
(housewife). Leonard Rogel (bookstore). Peg
Shirley (nice girl). Danielle Ferguson (hitch
hiker). M.B. West (transvestite). Dayna Cooper
(skateboard girl). Laura Borenstein (her
mother). Ron Borenstein (smoker). Dallas
Clarke (gas station). James Pascucci (cop on
beat). Don Brown (gets ticket). Victor Vasquez
(bartender). Hal Gordon (man in bar). Jeffory
Frangos, David Kinzie (patrol). Mike Deason,
Gerald H. Meeks (ambulance). Mike Weiner,
Larry Snodgrass, Ray Contera (others).
Michael Pataki, Leigh Kavanaugh (talk show).
Frank Dana (news). David Kinzie, Jeanine
LaPorte (commercials). Ingvar Grimsgaard
(announcer). John Patrick Hayes (latin mass).

top right:
Dr. Russo (Jerome Guardino) at the site of
one of Paulie's murders.

below:
Paulie attacks another victim.

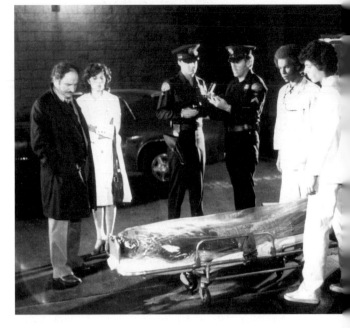

along with Paulie's escalating violence, very little of which
is actually sexual. She tries to manage it, contain it, to let
him blow off steam and hopefully leave. The tension and
sadness of the sequence comes from seeing this woman
feel her way through the encounter, with a mixture of
workaday familiarity and fearfulness. She knows Paulie's
dangerous, but sadly she needs the money. Perhaps he's
only as dangerous as the last fruitloop; perhaps he's a big
spender. It turns out that Paulie can't afford to pay, so he
trashes the apartment, rips the woman's clothes, smacks her
around, and generally runs up a bill – before handing her a
paltry fistful of cash, promising to cough the rest up later.
The victim is just glad that he's gone – but she counts her
blessings too soon…

Paulie's attempted rape of Marianne, the psychiatrist's
secretary, is quite honestly one of the most harrowing and
realistic depictions of sexual assault that I've seen in the
movies. Rather than showing rape from the point of view
of the rapist, *Victims* shows the reverse angle, as Marianne
finds herself trapped with a man she knows to be insane.
Social awkwardness inhibits her ability to control the
situation, and the camera sides with her attempt to get rid
of him without showing fear. The rape, when it comes, is
nowhere near as graphic as *I Spit on Your Grave* (the high
watermark for sexual violence outside of pornography), but
the psychological detail and pinpoint-perfect acting still
take us terrifyingly close to the situation. This is no
exploitation tease, no salacious fantasy. The horror is
conveyed through naturalistic dialogue and skilled
performances. Perhaps the reason this movie failed to find
an audience was that it took too realistic an approach to
something most buyers would prefer to market as
titillation?

Fittingly, *Victims* has a claustrophobic quality. The
outside world only gets a look-in via a radio phone-in show
heard from time to time in the background, debating such
topics as whether women secretly want to be 'ravished'.
DiSomma underlines the hell within which his characters
live by means of the glib talk-radio format, a forum that
offers itself as socially valuable when in fact it's either
aural wallpaper for the terminally bored, or a meaningless

corral from which lonely human cattle bellow into the void.
Far from offering a 'healthier' life beyond Paulie's psychopathic delusion, radio feeds the listener back to himself as
cultural junk food…

Movie flashbacks can be a pain in the ass. Badly
written scripts often use them as a cheat, a lazy back-up.
Not so here. DiSomma uses them to show why Paulie has
become such a danger to women, and they're so extensive
that we could just as easily call the other scenes flash-
forwards. The way they're incorporated ensures that the
past is always there alongside the present; as befits Paulie's
mind-set. There's an agonising *verité* feel to the scenes
where desperate, alcoholic Sheila 'seduces' Paulie, and a
similarly painful reality in the scenes where his mother, a
prostitute at the mercy of her violent pimp, tries unsuccessfully to incorporate child-rearing into her disordered life.
You could show *Victims* on a double bill with Asia
Argento's superlative *The Heart Is Deceitful Above All
Things* (if you wanted to send the audience home in search
of a razorblade).

Victims risks alienating the hang-'em-and-flog-'em
crowd by extending sympathy to the killer, but it's
DiSomma's insistence on showing Paulie as a victim too
that gives the film moral weight. Even the use of the name
'Paulie' instead of Paul stresses the ever-present child in
this psychotic ruin of a man. The abuse of a child is
something no civilised person argues to defend, and yet
we're often unwilling to extend sympathy to those whose
crimes are borne of childhood suffering. "Give us the child
and we'll give you the man," say the Catholics: it may as
well be the child-molester's motto. Those who try to show
such consideration are frequently accused of being more
interested in defending the killer than the victim.
DiSomma dismisses such heartlessness, showing his
humanity as a director by expressing compassion for all
his characters. Even Sheila, the sexually abusive hooker
who molests little Paulie, is depicted as a pitiful wreck,
caught in the toils of drugs and drink and loneliness.
Echoing both *Psycho* and the sorely under-rated *Deranged*,
DiSomma includes a shot of Paulie speaking, with his
mother's voice coming from his mouth. In this final
conflation of victim and aggressor, we're reminded that the
title of the film embraces Paulie too.

Daniel DiSomma Interviewed

Early Days and Hayes Days

Daniel DiSomma (aka Tony Vorno, aka Sebastian Gregory) was born 12 April, 1927 in the city of White Plains, New York, of Italian immigrant parents. He entered the US Navy in 1945, and after his discharge studied acting with Joseph Anthony and Lee Strasberg, subsequently landing Broadway roles in Tennessee Williams's *Camino Real* and Arthur Miller's *A View from the Bridge*. Off Broadway he appeared in Cocteau's *The Eagle Has Two Heads* with Colleen Dewhurst. These early acting experiences were to play a significant part in the genesis of *Victims*, as DiSomma explains: "The Actor's Studio in New York inspired me to work the way I did. In the 1950s, two plays that made it to Broadway – *End As a Man* and *A Hatful of Rain* – were both developed in a workshop atmosphere at the Studio. At the time I envied those at the Studio with the opportunity to work in such a concentrated form for months on end, much like I imagined The Moscow Arts Theatre did. The results could be very rewarding. This is the way I wanted to work and eventually I did, with *Victims*. Michael Gazzo, playwright of *Hatful*, lived on my block in Manhattan, in an area known as Hell's Kitchen. His apartment cost thirty two dollars a month, mine fourteen-ninety-five! These were cold water flats which meant no heat, no hot water, most with toilets down the hallway. One was able to survive on very little in those days..."

This insalubrious setting, however, was to play a major part in DiSomma's career development: "Mike Gazzo made it big and moved out, and John Hayes moved in. John was a dear friend of mine for years and years." Both Hayes and DiSomma moved from New York to California in the late 1950s. Hayes was looking for financial backing to make his first feature, having produced a short film called *The Kiss*, nominated for an Academy Award in 1958. Once settled in Hollywood, Hayes parlayed the success of *The Kiss* into a feature deal: the result was *Walk the Angry Beach* (1959), written, produced and directed by Hayes and starring DiSomma as 'Tony Vorno', alongside future TV star Rue McClanahan, here making her feature debut. The film, which is explored in more detail elsewhere in this book, played a few dates in the Southern States but went unreleased elsewhere until 1968. Other productions with John Hayes would follow, including starring roles in a handful of Hayes's early, less explicit sex dramas: "I was the 'lead stud' in his sex movies," jokes DiSomma, "but we were not hardcore, it was boobies and panties, that was as far as it went. *Help Wanted Female* was the first softcore John Hayes wrote and directed, with me playing the male lead. John was billed as 'Harold Perkins', I was 'Sebastian Gregory'. John and a typewriter salesman, Dan Cady, formed their own company, Clover, to make and distribute softcore films."

DiSomma has used several pseudonyms over the years: "As a young student actor in New York, I was told by an agent that he saw stardom for me with the name Antony Vorno - Hell, he could call me Archibald Leach if it was going to make me a star! So many actors changed their names in those days, notably Tony Curtis, originally Bernie Schwartz. I used Tony Vorno as actor in *Paulie* because I felt a separation between myself as actor and writer-director."[1]

On the Road with Hopper and Fonda

In 1968, DiSomma took a job on one of the defining films of the decade, *Easy Rider*. A crew list for the film shows DiSomma as 2nd Assistant Director, although the screen credits have him listed as Location Manager. This dual credit is typical of the nature of this production, where participants wore many hats and unionized regulations were largely ignored. Although location manager responsibilities usually took DiSomma away from the day of shooting and on to the next location, he remembers: "When I returned to the set on occasion, I would take over as Assistant Director, although the job was no more than a traffic cop."

As Peter Biskind details in his book, *Easy Riders, Raging Bulls*, months before principal photography on *Easy Rider* began, several scenes were shot in 16mm in a New Orleans graveyard, depicting the central characters on acid. This footage, shot February 1968, was then presented to the studio to secure financing. Only then was the film mounted

below:
A call-sheet for **Easy Rider**.
Note Tony Vorno's credit.

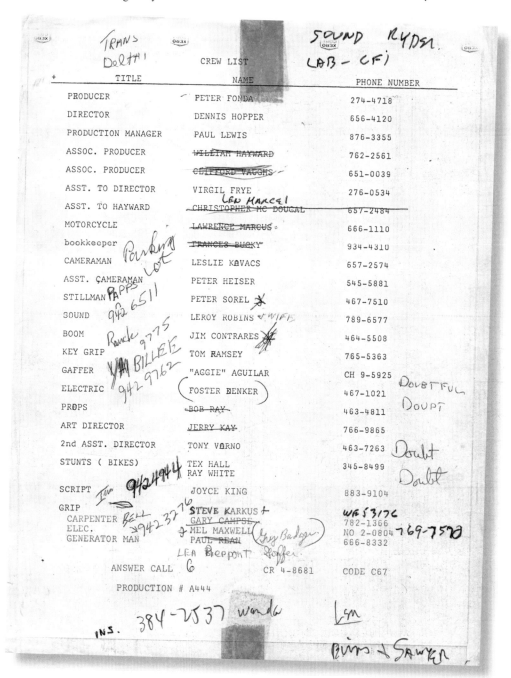

above:
Sebastian Gregory evicts Goldilocks (Christine March) for non-payment of rent in DiSomma's frivolous sex comedy **Come One Come All** (1970).

below:
Rich voluptuous Geraldine (Gina Montaine) digs the lash and Sebastian Gregory obliges.

with a more typical pre-production schedule. As DiSomma recalls, "Dennis [Hopper], Peter [Fonda], and Paul Lewis [production manager] drove across country to New Orleans – most of the trip was along Route 66, an important highway in those days. They would enter a town or some other location and make notes on the places where they wanted to film. I was given these notes, clipped them to my legal size clipboard and, with a New York production car, went on the road." One of the sequences DiSomma worked on was the redneck café scene, where Hopper, Nicholson and Fonda encounter small-town bigots whilst trying to buy breakfast: "I found lots of young people, a Deputy (he was for real), character people – great faces. My job was to set the locations and arrange for people to appear in the scenes. When I entered the café, the owner was behind the counter. I told her we would be shooting a movie in town and would like to film in the café. She knew everyone in town and in the fish camps nearby. Travelling ahead of the company much of the time, the telephone was my ally. While I'd be setting other locations miles away, I'd call her two, three times a day, making sure that everything was taken care of. When the company arrived in town, everything was ready, the townspeople were waiting to participate. I remember when I returned to the set that morning Dennis excitedly asked, 'Where did you get all these people?' 'Hell', I said, 'I just turned out the whole town.' Of course, with my lady behind the counter it was easy."

Another challenge DiSomma managed was the arrangement to shoot the Pueblo of the Taos tribe of New Mexico, as DiSomma evocatively relates: "This scene was but a moment on screen, yet meeting with the Council one night to discuss filming there was only one concession they made to the White Man's civilisation: Coleman lanterns lit the cool adobe walls and the manicured dirt floor. I felt privileged being there. Their spokesman was the only one who spoke to me in English. The others spoke through him in their own language. A dispute arose from the fact that the

tribe was under the impression a photographic unit was going to take some stills. They were not aware it would be a movie company. I was able to solve the financial arrangement differences with a plea to the Council that a compromise had to be reached or we couldn't afford the location. I felt I was in a John Ford movie negotiating a treaty on the frontier!"

Then came the parade sequence: "Santa Fe Springs, New Mexico. Brief shots of Peter and Dennis riding their bikes in Parade, getting arrested, landing in jail. With police and Chamber of Commerce cooperation I was able to have those involved standing by early in the morning waiting for the company to arrive. By that time I was in Texas. Amazing what faith people had in a man with a clipboard!" And if subterfuge was needed, DiSomma rose to the occasion: "I think they thought *Henry* Fonda was coming to town. I did slur over the first name at times..."

Like all low-budget features, corners simply had to be cut on *Easy Rider*, sometimes at risk to the (nonetheless willing) crew: "The script called for the final scenes to be shot in Florida, but we ended outside of New Orleans, Louisiana. The heat and humidity were terrible. The last shots of the movie, taken from a helicopter, would have been banned that day if the authorities had known a helicopter was going to try to lift off in such heavy humid air. That is what the pilot told me. With a great deal of effort he lifted off. Cameraman Laszlo 'Leslie' Kovacs was taking his life in his hands that day. The cooperation I received on every location we needed was magical. People were so willing to be a part of the project and at so little pay. During the time we spent in Texas, Dennis, Peter and Jack wouldn't spend the night there; they would drive to Taos, New Mexico – at least a thousand miles round trip – and return the next day, spaced out. Texas, then and now, has such ridiculous laws about drugs. A little pot would land you in jail."

Come One Come All – this far and no further…

Having seen his friend John Hayes cut a parallel career making softcore sex films, DiSomma decided to try his hand at the directing game. The result was *Come One Come All* (1970). This frivolous erotic comedy, about a put-upon Lothario (DiSomma) so exhausted by the demands of his female admirers that he fakes his own suicide to escape them, is considerably lighter in tone than the Hayes films and *Victims*. A vanity project built around DiSomma's central performance, it could perhaps have used a little more air, plot-wise, as the central conceit is overstretched. The most enjoyable parts of the film come when DiSomma/Vorno, playing an aspiring writer, touts his idea for a screenplay around the Hollywood B-picture studios, giving the viewer a rare glimpse into the subterranean film industry of the late sixties. However, DiSomma's light hearted spoof lost out to the rising trend for more explicit, raunchier sex films, and although it received a few good notices it failed at the time to ignite his directing career. The times they were a-changin', and fast: perched as it was on the lip of the new porno-decade, *Come One Come All* suffered from bad timing on two counts. When it was shot, in 1970, the sexual frankness of *Deep Throat* was still two years away: "In *Come One Come All* I showed pubic hair and the distributor was up the wall!" DiSomma remembers. Then gallingly, two years later, when the film eventually received some distribution, he found he had missed the boat: "It hit right at the time that hardcore came in, and softcore just didn't matter any more.

A Cunning Cocktail In COLOR SEBASTIAN GREGORY PRESENTS **COME ONE, COME ALL!** RELEASED BY ENTERTAINMENT VENTURES, INC.
A FILM FOR THE ERECTOR SET !! - So Adult It Smarts!

6 Angels for Satan

A SABASTIAN GREGORY PRODUCTION

RELEASED BY CLOVER FILMS

Come One Come All
aka **6 Angels for Satan**
(US theatrical re-release title)
© none [1970].
Sebastian Gregory Productions presents...
writer/producer/director: Sebastian Gregory
[Daniel DiSomma]. camera: Henning
Shellerup [Schellerup]. music: David Hinrie.
makeup & costumes by Danielle. sets: Byron
Fallbrook. titles: Gina Gregory. sound: Sam
Rosen. post production supervisor: Robert
Freeman. song "I'm Ready for More" by David
Hinrie & [illegible].
Cast: Sebastian Gregory [Daniel DiSomma]
(Himself). Gina Montaine (Geraldine). Henry
Dillon (Michael). Diane Lamport (Louise).
Roberta Landis (Monica). Loretta Tyler
(Shirley). Peter Ferris. Bruce Porter. Dorothy
Campbell (dancer). Leon Randall. Christine
March (Goldilocks). Burt Powers. Francis
Kauffman. Beatrice Buckingham.

left:
'The Dancer' (Dorothy Campbell) drives
Sebastian Gregory to the brink of exhaustion
after a torrid go-go dancing session in **Come
One Come All**, here pictured under its
alternative title, **6 Angels for Satan**.

Showing pubic hair was nothing compared to what took place." DiSomma was unlucky: making just a modest payday at a time when porn movies were about to go through the roof. "*Come One Come All* cost me on the outside about $15,000 and I made maybe 50% profit, paid everyone off and made a little myself," he shrugs.

Prior to shooting his own picture, DiSomma had appeared in one of John Hayes's sex-themed 'Harold Perkins' movies, *Baby Vickie* (1969), in which he played a rapist with whom Vickie is obsessed: "I also helped with production in San Francisco," he remembers. "In those days Los Angeles was out of bounds for hardcore. Now the San Fernando Valley, part of Los Angeles, is dotted with small

studios making hardcore." But seven years later DiSomma was to reach his tolerance limit, when it came to working on one of Hayes's bleakest, hardest, most pornographic films: "I didn't last long on *Baby Rosemary*. Two days into shooting, as sound man, I couldn't handle it - it all seemed so meaningless and degrading. I left, returned home to Los Angeles. John's distributing company needed product and hardcore was in – but I was out."

below, left to right:
Gregory with the SM-loving Geraldine;
Gregory gets down with 'the Dancer';
Gregory's funeral descends into erotic chaos.

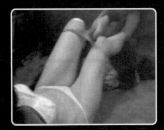

Paulie

Instead, Daniel DiSomma turned to the horror genre – writing, directing and starring in *Victims*. The project began life as a script called *Paulie* prepared by DiSomma at Theater East in Los Angeles. Theater East was a workshop for the presentation of new material written by members, critiqued by a moderator and others in the group. DiSomma remembers that, "At times plays would be presented for paying audiences. Actors Equity, our stage union, has a policy allowing actors to perform with very little pay if the theatre has a seating capacity of ninety nine or fewer seats. If not acting, members would help with costumes, props, and sets. I joined Theater East with a specific project in mind – *Paulie*."

After honing the script through repeated exposure at Theater East, principal photography took place over four weekends during the Spring of 1977 on locations in the Hollywood area – Mulholland Drive, San Fernando Valley and Santa Monica – with a budget raised by DiSomma's wife at the time, Jeanine, who acted as executive producer. The budget was limited to 'in-the-can' costs only – enough to pay for a work print and for all the 16mm photography to be shot, developed and synched. "My low budget dictated the shooting schedule," DiSomma explains, "I rented camera and equipment on weekends. We would pick up late Friday afternoon, having to pay for Saturday only. We would start shooting Friday night, continuing on Saturday and Sunday. Equipment was returned Monday morning. Each sequence in the film was designed to be shot as a contained unit. One weekend for the mother, another for the psychiatrist and another for the hooker's apartment, etc. Film takes were at a minimum ratio: two or three to one. All

major scenes were presented on stage at Theater East prior to the start of film production, and all cast members, with the exception of the psychiatrist, belonged to the group. I had the opportunity to work in close collaboration with the actors to develop my characters: this meant that most of the time our shooting schedule was devoted to camera angles, lighting, sets, etc. The actors knew what their tasks were, so that even when some nudity was expected, they were effortless in expression." As for his own performance, "As a director and an actor, I could do no wrong," he laughs, "so the best and the worst comes out!"

Initially the film was to have been shot by Henning Schellerup, the DP on some of John Hayes's films and DiSomma's *Come One Come All*. At the last minute, Ray Icely, an assistant cameraman on several Dan Cady productions, stepped in: "Ray Icely didn't have the pace I wanted, but I got a quality with Ray which I couldn't duplicate with my other DP, Henning Schellerup. I was shooting in negative stock 16mm, very difficult to light, and Ray was not quick at lighting. So we went for reversal stock, where less lighting was involved. But it turned out that all the scenes I shot in reversal stock were the scenes in flashback with the hooker and the mother. If I'd known I'd be going to TV and video only, I would have shot it and printed it in 16mm and never gone to 35mm, because 35mm blow-ups cost me half the budget."

He continues: "Small as the budget was, everyone involved in the production was paid. I hired a small projection room and showed the film to small groups of friends and business people to raise enough money to finish the project." Scraping by in this way, the film was readied for screening to potential distributors…

Distribution Hell

The last chapter of the *Paulie* story is a familiar one to those who've studied independent filmmaking. DiSomma explains: "Distribution became a nightmare in part because of our naivety. We had several private screenings for average movie-goers and professionals, soliciting their comments with a questionnaire. The distributor, Shel Haims of Films International, said he had an angle. Every low-budget, independent film has to have an 'angle', I guess. At the time the Hillside Strangler dominated the news. Hyping the similarities, adding narration and some additional cuts, would add to the shock value. At first I bought the program. Publicity began to go out – an article in the *The Hollywood Reporter* – publicity to theatre owners for bookings. As I was working on the changes, he presented us with a contract. It called for all monies received from foreign distribution to be his without a share returned to our company and investors. I pulled the plug. I had the sense to realise he would pocket any monies received, foreign or domestic. Professionally, I might have received some media recognition. A clip of the film was shown on ABC Network News tying it to the Hillside Strangler case. According to the distributor, I was unavailable, and he himself appeared, clip in hand, for his moment of fame. Knowing I would no longer cooperate with him, he attempted to seize my negative at the lab, under the ruse that he was now the owner. He took us to court and tried to get a judgement that I turn over all material pertaining to the film. He failed. A dream turned into a nightmare and the film has never been released in the United States, Canada, Mexico and South America. In 1982, Transcontinental Pictures Industries

above:
Paulie attacks Dr. Russo's secretary Marian
(Lenore Stevens) in **Victims**.

became our distributors. They never made it clear that the only market open to them was foreign home video. Their sales pitch was they would guarantee a sale to the UK for $15,000. Other sales were Australia/New Zealand $4000, S. Africa $4000, Taiwan $3000, Holland $3000 and Israel $900. Total received by Somma Films after distributor's percentage and additional lab costs was $1,699. Disappointing to say the least."

For DiSomma, this insulting payday for so much work and creative effort was the last straw: "I just dropped right out. I got the film released in Europe, it was on home video, I said okay that's it, I can't handle it any more. I went back and sold some family property, made a few bucks, took off in a motor home and travelled off, cross-country, went to Mexico and Canada. Even at this point, I'm wanting to do things, at seventy six years old. I'm living now up in the mountains, about sixty five miles from L.A., an hour away, which means I'd have to drive the freeways to get into Hollywood. I've been there, I've done that. I've done just about everything you can do – whether people recognise it or not, *I* do! Sometimes as an actor you might have an

experience on stage that is so unbelievable that it encompasses everything that's religious, or whatever's beautiful in life, and you're completely free as an actor, and I've had that happen to me, so nobody can say to me, 'Gee don't you want to still act?' I'd say, 'Jeez – I've been sublime!' [laughs] And fortunately there were critics at that very moment, an article in the papers about *Hatful of Rain*, that says: "*Hatful* powerful, Vorno great!" Crazy things like that have happened in my life, but you know, I'm just not a recognised person, that's all."

Note: At present all contracts in the home video market have run their course and DiSomma possesses sole rights to any and all distributions of **Victims** *and* **Come One Come All**.

Footnotes

opposite page, strip from top to bottom:
Images from the attempted rape of Marian in
Victims.

opposite, bottom left:
The film's British video cover.

1 The poster using the title *The Strangler* credits DiSomma as lead actor, contrary to his instructions.

DANIEL DISOMMA: FILMOGRAPHY AS DIRECTOR

1970	*Come One Come All* (also writer)
1977	*Victims*

AS ACTOR:

1960	*Walk the Angry Beach* – dir: John Hayes (as 'Jack Vorno')
1968	*Like Mother Like Daughter* – dir: Robert Vincent O'Neill (as 'Sebastian Gregory')
1968	*Help Wanted Female* – dir: Harold Perkins [John Hayes] (as 'Sebastian Gregory')
1969	*Alimony Lovers* – dir: Harold Perkins [John Hayes] (as 'Sebastian Gregory')
1969	*Fandango* – dir: John Hayes (as 'Sebastian Gregory')
1969	*Baby Vickie* – dir: Harold Perkins [John Hayes] (as 'Sebastian Gregory')

1969	*The Hang-Up* – dir: John Hayes (as 'Sebastian Gregory')
1970	*Come One Come All* (as 'Sebastian Gregory')
1972	*The Erotic Adventures of Zorro* (as 'Sebastian Gregory')
1972	*Garden of the Dead* – dir: John Hayes (as 'Tony Vorno')
1977	*Victims* (as 'Tony Vorno')
1978	*Jailbait Babysitter* – dir: John Hayes (as 'Tony Vorno')

OTHER CREDITS:

1969	*Easy Rider* – dir: Dennis Hopper (as 'Tone Vorno') (location manager)
1971	*Dream No Evil* – dir: John Hayes (production manager)
1972	*Grave of the Vampire* – dir: John Hayes (as 'Tony Vorno') (production manager)
1974	*Mama's Dirty Girls* – dir: John Hayes (as 'Tony Vorno') (sound recordist)
1976	*Mansion of the Doomed* – dir: Michael Pataki (as 'Tony Vorno') (boom operator)

chapter 14

If At First You Don't Succeed...

The Films of Tony Malanowski

Night of Horror (1981)

"The movie runs, I believe, about seventy five minutes: the longest seventy five minutes of my life. I think it takes longer to watch than it did to actually make! I confess that I haven't been able to endure it in its entirety for as long as I've owned it." – *Steve Sandkuhler, star of Night of Horror.*

*N*ight of Horror's first shot is of a brick wall – a suitable choice, as you may feel like beating your brains out on one by the end of the movie. The extended opening scene declares what's to come in uncompromising fashion. Two guys, Steve (Steve Sandkuhler) and Chris ('Tony Stark' aka writer/director Tony Malanowski) perch on stools facing a wall. We see them in long shot, backs to the camera. Their forlorn dialogue concerns musical aspirations (they're in a band, which is obviously going nowhere – as represented by the wall). There's a bare minimum of cutting, and we're granted no close-ups; just a couple of opaque mid-shot profiles (and they're especially unrevealing since Sandkuhler's luxurious rock-star mane obscures much of his face). Their dialogue – mumbled, morose and directionless, not to mention peripheral to the actual story – accounts for the first ten minutes of the film! Now that's hardcore: it's like Andy Warhol in a major snit.

But sorry, lovers of emptiness, the story has to begin sometime. Rest assured though that it will all be conveyed with the same flat, ungarnished glare throughout. Things creak into first gear when Steve tells Chris what's really on his mind: he's back from a trip to the country, and what occurred there has been troubling him ever since. In prolonged flashback we see why...

Steve and three friends – Colleen (Gae Schmitt), Jeff (Jeff Canfield) and Susan (Rebecca Bach) – take a weekend's drive to look at a property Jeff's father has left him in a will: but their camper van (which receives so much screen time it should have its own agent) breaks down before they arrive, stranding them in the wilds. Sounds like a typical lead-in for a rural-set horror tale? Not quite: this simple set-up gobbles nearly a third of the running time. Before we can progress to the nub of the story, we're treated to a long, long take of the camper van driving from city to countryside. It's actually quite mesmerising. If you've ever recorded a holiday jaunt with a film or video camera, you can appreciate where this sequence is coming from. The camera gazes raptly through the window and one can almost feel the excited enthusiastic energy behind the lens, the camaraderie of the cast and tiny crew (very tiny as it turns out), little more than a group of friends out for the weekend , hoping to make a movie in the process. This 'outboard' shot is held so long I found myself somehow transported, watching the motorways and bridges and country roads slip by as if I were there on the day, a ghost haunting the filmmakers. (The downhearted music also helps, as long as you're amenable to slightly overwrought vamping on a cheap synthesized piano. I know I am.)

Eventually, the four friends jump out to stretch their legs. Then – to gasps of astonishment from the unwary viewer – they re-embark and hit the road again. Steve takes

Night of Horror
© 1981. Little Warsaw
Little Warsaw Productions presents. producer/director: Tony Malanowski. executive producers: Anthony Malanowski, John Simmons. production manager: Giff Bradford screenplay: Tony Malanowski, Rebecca Bach, Gae Schmitt. original story concept by Tony Stark. creative lighting director: Jeff Canfield. editor: Tony Malanowski, Jackie Jones. art director: Jackie Jones. special effects designed by David Donoho. sound by John Simmons. still photography: Denise Major, Demetrius Francos. unit publicist: Katie Gregg. set designer: Jackie Jones. camera operators: Ben Mario, David Kirkwood. assistant camera operators: Ali Malanowski, John Simmons. sound by John Simmons. boom operator: Stanley Bava. original music written by Jim Ball. all music in this film is copyrighted by Jim Ball. music performed by Off the Wall. script supervisor: Tony Malanowski. special effects designed by David Donoho. special effects crew: Ali Malanowski, Denise Simmons, Denise Major. head gaffer: Denise Simmons. make up by Cynthia Wood. location correspondent: Robbie Zimmerman. costume co-ordination: Gae Schmitt. creative lighting director: Jeff Canfield. titles created and directed by Tom Griffith, Dan Taylor. stunts director: Don Johnson. production assistants: Cliff Malanowski, Jr., R.C. Cussler, Will Anderson. this film was processed and printed at Pete's Quality Film Labs (5800 York Road, Baltimore, Maryland 21212 (1-(301)-435-1212). Special thanks to the following people without whom this film could not have been made: John Kirkwood; John Simmons, Sr.; Dorothy Simmons; Don Dohler; Pete Garey; Dave Ellis; Cliff Malanowski, Sr.; Cliff Malanowski, Jr.; Anne Malanowski; Jim Vykol; Gae Schmitt. Good luck to Don Dohler and Jack Tydings. Editing equipment provided by Brenner Cinesound; Talis and Associates. Special thanks to the 23rd Army of Northern Virginia. 'this film was photographed in Maryland, USA: America in miniature'
Cast: Steve Sandkuhler (Steve). Gae Schmitt (Colleen). Rebecca Bach (Susan). Jeff Canfield (Jeff). Tony Stark [Tony Malanowski] (Chris Marker). Phil Davis, Mark Trunk, Lewis Ellis, Ray Cooper, Jeff Belt, Doug McEvoy, Bruce Nelson (confederate ghosts).

below:
The cover for **Night of Horror**'s scarce US video release.

a shine to Colleen, who's been getting *"the worst vibrations"* since the funeral. She reads Poe aloud, and predicts problems ahead. When the van malfunctions, the previously unflappable Steve, who must never have encountered a Goth before, is freaked: *"That was the first real problem of the trip. Colleen knew something before it even happened. They all went out to see what was going on. I sat frozen in the back. No way was I going out where the rest of them were going."*

By the way, do you like the music yet? Please try, there's lots more to come. If you're to accept Malanowski's slow, uneventful takes and static, stubbornly unaesthetic compositions, you'll need the score as your ally. It has a bright but somehow morbid quality, like sunlight through a hearse window. Somewhere, heartstrings are being tugged, although on whose behalf the script declines to elaborate. I find myself sinking deeper into the music, and I wonder for a moment if I'm being hypnotised when, forty minutes in, it occurs to me that I would like to buy the soundtrack album...

As the camera directs its moribund gaze at the broken-down van, Steve's plaintive voice-over seems to emanate from the vehicle itself: *"It sounded like the muffler, maybe the whole exhaust is shot."* It's like a talking van explaining its own failure, a perception which makes me realise that *Night of Horror*, for all its apparent simplicity, is playing with my head. Perhaps I shouldn't have eaten those funny little mushrooms...

Spook time. A patrol of undead soldiers gather in the shadows... There's been much debate among fans about the relative merits of slow-moving versus running zombies, but no one's ever lit a torch for Malanowski's version; the standing-still zombie. In fact I'm cheating a

bit, calling them zombies: they're really more like ghosts. Only later, in the remake (*The Curse of the Screaming Dead*) do they chew flesh. But even as ghosts they're a reticent bunch: a half-dozen soldiers standing in a blur somewhere, never straying into the same shot as the main cast. Steve, Colleen, Jeff and Susan sit blank-faced around the campfire, listening to the undead's leader as he describes – in a hoarse, virtually incomprehensible voice – the misfortunes of his Confederate army unit. Each syllable is drawn out like a death-rattle; so much so that you can easily forget the one before. The monologue becomes detached from humanity: it's barely a voice any more, it's more like listening to a faulty central heating system when you're running a fever, or playing a gigantic, unfinishable audio version of 'Hangman'. Totally abstract-minimal. Ten minutes of footage shot at a War Games Society (Yankees vs. Confederates) sends the bemused viewer on vacation from the plot, while a vocal/guitar rendition of the main theme plays on and on. At last, Steve summarises the essence of the zombie soldiers' story: *"I couldn't believe what I was hearing! They actually thought that Colleen was the reincarnation of a woman from over one hundred years ago..."*

The four friends decide they've heard enough of this lunacy and, to sobs of gratitude from the audience, get to their feet and head back to the road. Steve trudges behind, fantasising heroics over Colleen: *"It was my last chance, a chance to possibly save her from all this madness. But all I could think of was getting the camper fixed. I was obsessed. If I could do that, maybe everything would be sane again. I followed Colleen into the darkness, the darkness broken only occasionally by the now harsh moonlight..."* The three friends bury a skull at the exact spot requested by the ghosts (for reasons lost somewhere in the wrinkles of that fourteen-minute soliloquy). *"It was here that the hauntings were laid to rest,"* assures Steve. *"Then... then Colleen... now thoroughly... in a deep trance... she prayed over the grave."* The piano theme swells yet again, the zombie-ghosts gasp their appreciation, and the brownish video transfer sucks the actors away into a rectangle of soil bulging from my television like rising bread...

...1,2,3, you're back in the room: and, like a true cyclical nightmare, we return to hear Steve telling Chris his problems, both men still perched on stools against a plain wood-finish wall. No camera movement. His brain aching, Chris goes outside and stares into the swimming pool... *"Try not to expect too much,"* mumbles Steve off-camera, in the last, epigrammatic words of the film...

It's almost impossible to explain why this film should give me pleasure, even as it drives me nuts. Tony Malanowski has concocted an experience beyond the pale for all but the most dedicated students of anti-cinema. It feels like a dream you might have had under the influence of a bad drug, or a nightmarishly depleted and inertial scenario circling round and around in your brain during detox. Maybe I'm enthralled because I feel like it's at the end of the line for horror, for bad films in general. Is that it? Is *Night of Horror* the worst film I've ever seen? I have to say no: despite its extraordinarily slow pace and its total lack of action and thrills, *Night of Horror* pleases me more than a whole cartload of bigger, more prestigious productions. By most 'objective' standards it's the bottom-of-the-barrel and beyond, but I've watched it three times and will probably watch it three more. 'Bad movies', as we all know, are not the *worst* movies. Mediocrity is the only real crime in cinema, and *Night of Horror* is, in some mad way, extraordinary.

I've always been sensitive to mood in the movies, and I'm frequently drawn to films where the mood is dominant over plot and coherence. *Night of Horror* is a case in point. I respond to its moroseness, its ambience of dereliction, its sludgy melancholy, and on a humorous level to its perversity, its lack of all the things you expect from even the cheapest exploitation films. And if you disregard notions of entertainment in the usual genre sense, there's still some tiny flame alive here, captured in the fragile trust of the director that we might keep watching, wrapped up in the lugubrious music, in the inescapable nostalgia of film itself. Cinema is a time machine: in some strange way I feel as if I've lived a day in the life of Tony Malanowski, tagged along with Steve Sandkuhler and friends – an experience that feels almost as real as the ones preserved in my own ancient photographs from the early eighties, places I went, days spent idling and wandering, friends I used to know. *Night of Horror* is a terrible horror film, but against the odds it has an unexpected warmth, a peacefulness, and a glow in its flickering nothings.

Postscript from Steve Sandkuhler: "...Understand, though, that the finished product was not the real final product at all. *Night of Horror* evolved into the bad - but better - *The Curse of the Screaming Dead*. Not many people get the opportunity to be in something that even remotely resembles a feature length film. And *Curse* - without even trying - was soooo camp! All five of my kids love making their friends watch it..."

The Curse of the Screaming Dead (1982)

The Curse of the Screaming Dead follows the adventures of three couples as they head into the woods on a drinking, shooting and arguing holiday. Before long they've added to their woes by stumbling upon an unmarked graveyard occupied by belligerent, if initially dead, Confederate soldiers. When selfish, hot-headed Mel (Christopher Gummer) steals a stray artefact precious to the soldiers (linked to their painful torture during a Union massacre), the scene is set for a mass zombie uprising, Baltimore style.

This is Tony Malanowski's second stab at the same story, and at first glance *The Curse of the Screaming Dead* and its precursor *Night of Horror* are cut from the same cloth. They're each of them rife with padded dialogue and actionless *longueurs*: both are built around the same very specialised theme in an already specialised sub-genre – not just Zombie Movies, but Zombie Confederate-Soldier Movies! – and they feature many of the same cast members. There's good reason for this, as Tony explains in the interview later in this chapter, but initially you tend to recoil from the repetition: the ultra-low energy levels, long takes, and drawn out elaborations of the simplest set-ups. The meandering dialogue is perhaps the biggest stumbling block for most viewers. Talk is, after all, frequently the genre's enemy; unless it's very well written it stymies both mood and action. *Night* goes further, interspersing very long dialogue scenes with actionless mooching around. *Curse* too opens with a good forty minutes of verbal filler, but eventually digresses from its predecessor by handing the viewer a lifeline, in the form of some genuinely actionful horror.

Watching both films gives us the chance to adjust to the director's style. *Night of Horror*, easily the most 'difficult' of the pair, takes on a battered poignancy next to the more polished *The Curse of the Screaming Dead*: whilst *Curse*, seen after *Night of Horror*, assumes heroic dimensions, a triumphant second stab at the same story, showing growth and advancement in just about all areas. The two are twinned so closely it'd be fun to see them projected alongside each other like some avant-garde underground movie – the *Chelsea Girls* of zombie films. Well, I'm funnin' you a little, but don't get me wrong - I cherish these movies. No one is going to claim them as neglected masterpieces, but there's a windswept, *Night on the Bare Mountain* frugality, a determination to make something out of almost nothing, that shames many a more complacently budgeted horror.

For all this talk of limitations, *Curse* really springs to life when the living dead attack. The zombie make-ups and mask designs are almost Fulci-esque at times, and the scene where the ghouls rip yards of intestine from the abdomen of a policeman is wonderfully gruesome and convincing (summoning fond recollections of Jorge Grau's *The Living Dead at Manchester Morgue* and Jess Franco's *Devil Hunter*). There are numerous incidental pleasures along the way: the music, for instance, has an unexpectedly jazzy feel redolent of The Mike Westbrook Orchestra, whilst some cues, built around a chugging bassline and choppy strings, resemble Michael Nyman's work for Peter Greenaway (I kid you not). Try imagining the movie burdened with a regulation synthesizer score, like the one that screws up Charles McCrann's *Forest of Fear*, and you'll appreciate how much the composer has enlivened the film by thinking outside the genre box.

The Curse of the Screaming Dead aka **The Curse of the Cannibal Confederates**
© 1982. A Little Warsaw production. Little Warsaw Productions presents. director/producer: Tony Malanowski. screenplay: Lon Huber. original story concept by Tony Starke [Tony Malanowski]. sound by John Simmons. special sound effects by Lon Huber. special pyrotechnic effects by David Donoho. make-up by Mark Redfield, Linnea Sandkuhler, Larry Schlechter. special make-up effects by Bart Mixon. associate producers: Ali Malanowski, RA Bach, R. Sommerwerck [Bump Roberts], Dick McLung [Richard Ruxton]. film editors: Jackie Jones, Sharla Darke. unit photographers: Richard Geiwitz, Gary Becker. unit publicist: Katie Gregg. set designer: Conway Gainesford. camera operators: Ben Mario, Bobby Ogden. assistant camera operators: Stephanie Safka, Tina Waters Ogden. head gaffer: Dayton Alfred. location correspondent: Randy Robbins. stunts director: Chris Gummer. casting by The Walter Paisley Organization in conjunction with Max O'Hara Enterprises. props by Alice Starr Leggin, David Donoho. creative lighting director: Skip Garrett. focus puller: Paul Pudde. second unit director: Mark Redfield. music: Charlie Barnett. Special thanks to the following people without whom this film could not have been made: David Kirkwood, Pete Garey, Anne Malanowski, David Insley, Jim and Laura Vykol, Cliff Malanowski Sr., Mr. and Mrs. Frank Gummer, Rebecca Bach and the gang at the Woodstock Hotel. Camping equipment provided by Ridgerunner Outfitters. Special thanks to the 21st Army of Northern VA. Police lighting courtesy of Federal Signal Columbia (Maryland). This film was photographed in Maryland (USA) - America in miniature. Lon and Lendon: I'll be there soon! *Cast:* Steve Sandkuhler (Wyatt). Christopher Gummer (Mel). Rebecca Bach (Sarah). Mimi Ishikawa (Blind Kiyomi). Judy Dixon (Lin). Jim Ball (Bill). Richard Ruxton (Police Captain Hal Fritz). Bump Roberts (Deputy Franklin). Mark Redfield (Captain Matthew Mahler). uncredited: Tony Malanowski (voice on radio).

opposite page, top:
David Donoho, **Night of Horror**'s special effects wizard, uses his "smoke paper" to create an atmospheric mist for a Confederate ghost.

below:
Mel (Christopher Gummer) runs to shoot a marauding ghoul in **The Curse of the Screaming Dead**.

above:
The South Rises again, in **The Curse of the Screaming Dead**.

right:
From **The Curse of the Screaming Dead**...
Malanowski says: "Kiyomi meets her death at the hands of revenge-crazed living dead confederate zombies! (OK, mostly guys in rubber masks and old cloths, but you know what I mean...)"

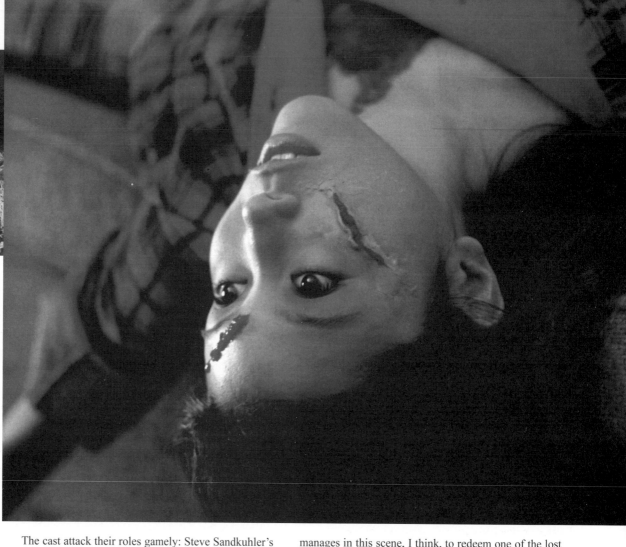

below:
The Australian video cover.

The cast attack their roles gamely: Steve Sandkuhler's Wyatt is a livelier creation than his ineffably morose character in *Night of Horror*, and Rebecca Bach is also more likeable here as the argumentative Sarah (even if the dialogue does give her extra vim only to mock it with snipes at Women's Lib). An emphatic performance from Christopher Gummer makes mean-spirited Mel the most perversely likeable character, as if the actor has personally taken charge of ensuring the film doesn't slide back into the *Night of Horror* doldrums. There are a few misfires though: Mimi Ishikawa, the pretty young actress who plays paranormally sensitive Kiyomi, struggles through an unsuccessful blindness act that makes her un-PC credit as 'Blind Kiyomi' essential in clarifying what she's up to; nevertheless, her air of doe-like nervousness is a credible alternative to the standard screamer role. Tilting the film into Ed Wood territory are two am-dram cops whose magnificent implausibility is clinched when the Sergeant theorises that psychopaths are faking the zombie attacks by arranging stolen cadavers on a pulley-system mounted in the trees! We are wearily accustomed to the police in horror films being unimaginative plodders, so this bonkers flight of fancy is a rare treat and worth quoting in its entirety: *"These kids think they were attacked by corpses. I think whoever dug up those graves is swinging the bodies out of the trees on ropes, like puppets. Spooky business. I'm sure glad I never up-took undertakin'. Anyway, this guy and his pals steal a few bodies every now and then and wait for some campers to come along [...] Now in the middle of the night it's easy to get fooled. They know that. They get some rope, drop the bodies down from some trees and sort of dance them around a little."* Wow. Malanowski

manages in this scene, I think, to redeem one of the lost causes of the horror genre – cop dialogue. They are usually the least interesting characters in a horror film; here I find myself hankering to see them again, maybe talking crazy old Donald Pleasance down off his Boogeyman trip in Carpenter's *Halloween* with some theory about Bill Shatner on the rampage...

There's something about the zombie as a figure in horror's pantheon that invites a tolerance and even a love of the cheaper manifestations. Vampires require some style, and preferably a splash of money to be spent on décor at least, but there's something plebeian and unpretentious about the Living Dead, as if the abjectness of bodily decay sets a base standard which can then be inverted into a sort of glamour. Provided the director avoids the simple-minded fan posturing of 'films' like *Zombie 90: Extreme Pestilence* or *House of 1000 Corpses* (burdened with performances that scream, 'Graaar! look at me, I'm a gut-munching zombie ghoul monster!') he or she can draw on something akin to the energy of the dispossessed, the rotting belly of the underdog. Tony Malanowski's zombie soldiers, defeated in the American Civil War and clinging to the symbolic worth of their flag, emerge from the soil with a similar raddled poignancy to the wasted Etruscan ghouls in Andrea Bianchi's Italian gore marvel *The Nights of Terror*, or the unexpectedly soulful German troops of Jean Rollin's *Zombie Lake*. *The Curse of the Screaming Dead* stands alongside these European titles, shoulder to shoulder, adding a US battalion to the French, Spanish and Italian hordes: they're at the arse-end of the genre spearheaded by George Romero, to be sure: but what price an army without a rearguard?

Baltimore, Maryland. The 1970s. Home of John Waters, Divine and the Dreamland repertory company. Home as well to Don Dohler and his merry band of monster-makers. Two very different groups, similar only in their devotion to the region, and their commitment to creating an alternative movie reality with the absolute minimum of cost. Waters and Dohler have always shot their movies in and around Baltimore; indeed there are times when their woodland locations look uncannily similar, as if a shaky pan to the left in *Desperate Living* might reveal Don Dohler's Inferbyce creature staggering around in the trees, or a hand-held lurch to the right in *The Alien Factor* would spot Dawn Davenport making out with Earl Peterson on an abandoned mattress. Well, there are no skidmarked skivvies in Dohler's films, and no mutant aliens in Waters's (the only shared feature being George Stover, a local actor who worked for both directors). But there was another player in the Baltimore woods, whose work has received almost no exposure even in the cult environs of horror publishing.

It's 1980. Waters is preparing *Polyester*, his first semi-'respectable' movie. Dohler is prepping *NightBeast*, a gory monster flick. And out there in the trees a third camera grinds away, a third minuscule-budget epic is being harvested: except this one will make *Female Trouble* look like *Gone with the Wind*, and *NightBeast* look like *Alien*: the film is *Night of Horror*, and the director / writer / cameraman / producer is Tony Malanowski; a one-time assistant to Dohler, now directing a film of his own.

Waters once commented that his favourite art-house director, Marguerite Duras, "makes the kind of films that get you punched in the face for recommending them to even your closest friends […] Her films are maddeningly boring but really quite beautiful." *Night of Horror* chalks up a noble two out of three on this scorecard, as it's likely to have a similar deleterious effect on your friendships, is as maddeningly boring as any art film, and only loses out in the final furlong by falling short of beauty. But you can't have everything: *Night of Horror* was made for the kind of money that Marguerite Duras sprinkles on her *pommes frites*, so if the cast look a little *déshabillé* and the photography is on the brown side, we can surely make allowances. And besides, as I explain in my review of this movie, there is something *near* to beauty in the film: an elusive charm that perhaps you need to be half-crazy to appreciate, but which nevertheless *counts*…

Malanowski is a genial, good-humoured man who works today in the comfortable offices of Ascent Media in Hollywood, prepping smash-hit TV shows like *Seinfeld* for their DVD and HD upgrades. On the way, he became a skilled film and sound editor with a long list of credits for prolific dynamo directors like David Prior, David DeCoteau and Fred Olen Ray. He is justifiably pleased at how far he's come since the early days of his career, but he's happy to stress just how important those days were in making the later achievements possible. He doesn't simply dismiss *Night of Horror* as an embarrassment, even though he readily concedes its failings. Tony Malanowski's recollections provide one of the most vivid

above:
Tony Malanowski mans the Arriflex BL 16mm camera, during the filming of **The Curse of the Screaming Dead** at the horse ranch location owned by Randy Robbins.

illustrations in this book of the painstaking process of low-budget filmmaking; the thrills and the trials and the grinding frustrations of working with virtually no money, struggling to get a feature-length movie on the screen by hook or by crook. Even if you never see *Night of Horror* (I would recommend it to masochists, students of poverty-stricken filmmaking, lunatics, and insomniacs in need of a celluloid cosh), his follow-up *The Curse of the Screaming Dead* is well worth seeking out for all zombie-movie devotees: if you've opened your heart to Jess Franco's *Oasis of the Living Dead*, or spent money on a DVD of Girolami's *Zombie Holocaust*, I'm sure you'll find pleasure in Malanowski's entertaining contribution to the form!

Early Days

Antony Malanowski was born on 26 January, 1957 in Baltimore City, Maryland, the region where he would go on to work, first as assistant to Don Dohler and then as director of his own brace of curious, extremely low-budget horror movies. "When I was about nine months old, my parents moved to the suburbs," he recalls. "My father got a job at the Bethlehem Steel Mill in Sparrow's Point, Maryland, so the family moved to the Bear Creek area, which was about five miles away from the Steel Mill. My dad had a pretty good job at the Steel Mill as a machinist, so we were doing alright. My dad's parents were both immigrants from Poland, while my mom's mom was from Poland, and her dad was from Russia."

It was cinema as giant spectacle that first attracted his attention: "There were two films that really got me.

above:
Tony Malanowski (*left*) with a Confederate ghost. This shot was taken during the filming of **Night of Horror**.

opposite page:
Images from **Night of Horror**.

camera, I started using it to make my own films. I corralled my friends in the neighbourhood, and did pictures with the kinds of special effects I read about in *Famous Monsters*. I scratched the film to make ray-gun blasts; I super-imposed weird colours over images. I even converted two GI Joe dolls into a white-fur covered gorilla, and a giant, mutated astronaut. They fought on a card table with a Christmas garden town built on it. The effects were actually rather smooth at points, which was very encouraging!"

Malanowski left high school in 1975, by which time he was working on 16mm films with Bill George, a film-poster collector studying at the University of Maryland, Baltimore County. "Bill and I (along with a friend named Charlie Hicks), formed a company selling movie posters at shows in Baltimore and New York City," he recalls. "We'd go up to NYC every six to eight weeks for conventions, make a few bucks, and meet a lot of film people (I met Peter Cushing at the 1974 *Famous Monsters* Convention). It was at one of these shows that I met Scott MacQueen, who would later get me involved in film restoration at the Walt Disney Studios. I eventually went to UMBC myself to study film, at the time the 'noted multi-mediaist' Stan Van Der Beek came to teach."[1]

It was at this time that Malanowski first met Don Dohler, soon-to-be director of rough and ready regional monster flicks like *The Alien Factor*, *Fiend* and *NightBeast*. "I met Don through Bill George and Charlie Ellis (another film-fan-friend)," Malanowski recalls. "Gary Svehla was probably also involved in there somewhere. The filmmaking/film-fan community was pretty tight back then – if you went to one amateur screening, or the annual BaltiCon science-fiction convention, you could meet pretty much everybody who shared your interests. And remember, this was way before VHS and DVDs. If you wanted to see a picture, you either waited for it to run on TV, or you went to a screening at the local school or library. Very restrictive, but it made even the most pedestrian picture a special event! Around this time, Don Dohler was thinking about making a low-budget feature. He got a group of us together, and we kicked around a few ideas. I think what really got us to take the plunge was when George Romero was a guest at BaltiCon one year. I was one of four people who acted as 'Guest Liaisons' for the convention, volunteering to be general goodwill ambassadors and guest 'gofers'. We were made up in pseudo-*Planet of the Apes* make-ups and leisure suits! We picked up Isaac Asimov at the train station, and tended to George Romero as well. By this time, I had acquired a 'portable' 35mm projector, so I brought that along to screen George's then-new feature *The Crazies* (1973). So I got to know him pretty well over those three days. One night over drinks, he really pushed us to make a film, the same way he made *Night of the Living Dead*. Make it in 16mm, get your friends to work for free… you know, the same thing we all had been doing in Super-8mm for the last few years! Over the next few months, what would become *The Alien Factor* began to gel. I went to my teachers at UMBC and told them that I was dropping out of film school and throwing away my scholarship! Stan told me what a mistake I was making. Funny thing is, a year or so later, he read about me in the local paper, and called me in to lecture!"

The first was John Wayne's *The Alamo* at the Carlton Theater in Dundalk. It was such a *huge* film. I remember just sitting there mesmerized! I guess I was about four years old. At one point, I told my mom that I needed to go to the bathroom, and she let me go by myself (which was not dangerous back then, even in Dundalk!). Instead of going to the back of the theatre where the restrooms were, I sneaked up to the front row and just stared up at that big Todd-AO Cinemascope image. It was breath-taking! Even then (around 1964), I loved watching films like *King Kong*, *Gunga Din*, and *The Thing* on TV, so I was already leaning towards fantasy and adventure films. My mom took us to see Jerry Lewis's *The Nutty Professor*, and they showed the trailer for *King Kong vs. Godzilla*. I was totally hooked. I begged my mom to take me the next week, which she did. My life hasn't been the same since! Incidentally, I got to relate this story to Haruo Nakajima, the actor who played Godzilla (and, in most scenes, King Kong). You should have seen his face when the translator told him that I held him responsible for my working in films!"

With his appetite whetted by screen superstar Godzilla, it would only be a matter of time before the youngster noticed a certain hugely influential film magazine on the racks: "I was really falling in love with movies and the entertainment industry, when, like so many others of my generation, I spied my first issue of Forry Ackerman's *Famous Monsters of Filmland* magazine. For me it was issue #26, with *The Outer Limits* on the cover. I learned a lot from *Famous Monsters* – Forry's style of writing (bad puns and all) brought to life the people who made the films. It stopped being a 'royalty only' kind of job, and became more accessible. Reading the life stories of Ray Harryhausen, Boris Karloff, Roger Corman et al, I realized that working in the film business was an attainable goal. Since my dad had an 8mm (and later Super-8mm)

Malanowski gained his first practical feature film experience as co-producer and assistant director of *The Alien Factor*: "I put in $500 cash (as did everyone else) and we formed a company (Cinemagic Visual Effects, based on Don's magazine *Cinemagic*), basically working for percentages. I was supposed to be involved in the editing, but I tore the ligament in my right index finger doing temporary construction work for the money. Remember, when we made *The Alien Factor*, I was the youngest partner in the company. I had just turned eighteen years old and still lived at home, so I had a little advantage in the economics department! And since I wanted to learn everything I could, I was always the first to volunteer. I remember one day, Don had to get his two kids from softball practice, and he left me with some notes and told me to direct the scene. It was after Don Leifert as Ben Zachary had killed the Inferbyce (the bug-creature) and he was arguing with Mary Mertens (Leifert's then-wife), and George Stover. You can tell I directed that scene, because the eye-lines of the actors aren't quite right! The screen direction is wrong - not by much, but it is noticeable! I was kinda bummed by it when I saw it, but everyone else was learning too, so I didn't feel that bad."[2]

Working with Dohler was, for Malanowski, an inspiration and an encouragement to try making movies himself. "Though I had learned a lot doing *The Alien Factor*, there were still many areas of the filmmaking process that I didn't feel I knew well enough. So, I figured that the only way to learn all aspects of making a film, was just to make one from beginning to end. At the time, money was starting to trickle in from *The Alien Factor*, and I had been working as a radiographer testing structural materials for the Maryland State Highway Administration. I had a few bucks put away, and I figured the time was right. Around this time, I was working with Diane Hammond, who was a marvellous make-up artist in the Washington DC area.[3] She was trying to make a sequel to *Battle for the Planet of the Apes* as a glorified demo reel for her make-up effects. Since I loved the original *Apes* films, I got involved. She introduced me to a group of Virginia-based players which included Jeff Canfield, Gae Schmitt, Rebecca Bach and Mimi Ishikawa. We were all supposed to work on the 'Apes' film (now called 'Beyond the Planet of the Apes'). I wrote the first couple of drafts of the screenplay, and was slated to be the DP, with Jeff being director. Eventually, since Jeff was more of a theatre director, it became obvious that he wasn't really right to direct a film, especially one that was being shot in Cinemascope! So, after some measure of conflict, I was made director (along with cinematographer), and Jeff would handle directing the dialog. Unfortunately, 'Beyond the Planet of the Apes' fell apart just after we had cast the picture, built some of the sets, and made most of the costumes. I figured that, since it wasn't going to happen, it was time for me to do my own picture. At the time, it was still considered an expensive proposition to make an independent film. But, with *The Alien Factor*, I had already seen that it could be made relatively cheaply. And since I was planning on paying most of the budget and doing most everything myself, I guessed that the film could be sold rather quickly (the video boom was growing fast), and I could make a profit."

Making *Night of Horror*

Malanowski set to work in the summer of 1980: "I went to Pete Garey at Quality Film Labs (the only film lab in Baltimore), and made a deal to cover the processing and printing costs (Don Dohler had made a similar deal with Pete for his film *Fiend*). I then ordered the raw stock from Kodak through Pete. I paid cash – a couple of thousand dollars. I jumped in feet first, guessing that no matter how scared I was (and, though I was very confident, I was still plenty scared), this put me in a position where I either made the picture, or lost a lot of money! I then wrote the script during lunch breaks at my State job, and during the evenings. It wasn't much of a script – just some disjointed scenes strung together. Again, my main thing was to learn the technical side, so I'm afraid I let the story slide! I looked at the picture as a glorified student film that I could make a few bucks from. Better dropping out of college and making a feature than spending four years and having a handful of shorts, right? I was also naive enough to believe some of the things written about Roger Corman, how his actors would improvise. I guessed my actors could do that too! So the script was pretty threadbare. I took the title from a goofy Bela Lugosi melodrama called *Night of Terror*. During shooting, we called the picture *Night of Malarkey*, and when the first dailies came in (with Jeff doing some improvisations that just didn't work – my fault, not his) I started calling the picture *Night of Bankruptcy*! But *Night of Horror* was always the title."

From the start, it was to be a lower-than-low-budget endeavour: "I had less money than we had on *The Alien Factor* – and no crew. Remember, I wanted to do everything myself, so the picture had to be pared down so that I could work the camera, do the lighting and all grip and prep work. This would also carry over into editorial and post-production duties. Naturally, everything was shot in 16mm on mostly ECO and EF stocks. These stocks were very 'slow', which means they needed to be well-lit. Since I didn't have many lights, that became a problem during night shoots. But, by using the ECO during the days, and the slightly faster EF during the nights, I think we came out pretty good. Contrasty, but good. And, of course, the shots with the 'ghosts' in the mist got reprinted several times. So sometimes the already underexposed shots were duped and cut into the picture, with less than perfect results! Incidentally, that made my actual shooting ratio around 0.85 to 1, which means that by duping up much of the 'ghost' footage, I actually achieved the impossible! I used more film than I shot!"

Ask Malanowski what the budget was for *Night of Horror* and he laughs. "I always get a kick out of questions like this! It presupposes that I really *had* a budget, that this was a 'professional' movie! I remember one reviewer said of *Night of Horror* and *The Curse of the Screaming Dead*, that they were '...the kind of pictures made to play drive-ins in the South.' Like they were shot on 35mm and really played in theatres of *any* kind, *any* place! The money raised for the picture came from my own piggy bank. I arranged a 'semi-open' account at Pete's, and, as I said, I bought the raw stock to make sure I was locked into doing the film. Then, when I was hanging out with my friend 'Big' John Simmons (a huge man with a huge heart!), I was talking about how I was going to make the picture. John worked for the State as well, on the roads, and he asked if he could toss in a few bucks. I agreed, and John came on as a silent partner (he

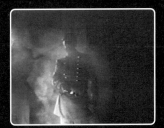

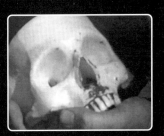

above and below:
Tony Malanowski (*left*) talks with Rebecca Bach (*centre*), and Jeff Canfield (*right*), just after the **Night of Horror** shoot.

also ran the Nagra and recorded the audio for *Night of Horror* and *Curse*). John put up $1,000 and received points like everyone else in the picture. The entire 'budget' came to about $4,000 for everything. But, since I did it to learn filmmaking, you can say that $4,000 bought me a college film degree… and in about one eighth of the time!"

Night of Horror commenced shooting in the summer of 1980 over four weekends, with a couple of extra nights for pickup shots. Malanowski invited Jeff Canfield, Gae Schmitt and Rebecca Bach from the aborted 'Beyond the Planet of the Apes' project to act in it, and added Steve Sandkuhler, a friend at the State Highway Administration who played in a rock group called Off the Wall, as the lead. "Since I was working from script pages, and not a real finished script, the shoots were a little bit chaotic," Malanowski admits, "but everyone pulled together, and worked very hard. I was greatly encouraged by this. Maybe we were all kind of pretending to be working on a film, considering how things were really going. But everyone has to start somewhere!"

With the cost of a Hollywood liquid lunch to play with, every decision had to be made with thrift in mind. "I decided on using a camping trip as the premise, because it was cheap!" Malanowski recalls. "All we needed were some trees! Actually, most of the film was shot at John's parents' house. They had a little plot of land surrounded by trees. We had a dirt road leading in, easy access to electricity, and a place to crash if we shot too late – it was perfect! The house that Jeff and Colleen came out of belonged to John Kirkwood – he was the father of a very close friend named Dave Kirkwood. I met Dave in college, and he owned the Bolex SBM camera that we used for handheld and MOS shots.[4] I eventually shot a bunch of commercials with that camera, and Dave ended up selling it to me, since I always seemed to have it with me! The back of the house was where the door that Chris enters and exits from was located. Also the pool. We had a lot of great parties at that house!"

Night of Horror's opening scene, an extended and barely audible conversation between Steve Sandkuhler as Wyatt and 'Tony Stark' as his friend Chris, is surely one of the most viewer-unfriendly openings ever achieved in the horror genre. Being a big fan of perverse directorial choices, I asked Malanowski to elaborate: "The bar that Steve sits at was in my brother's basement (it was one of those famous 'club basements' that you find in Maryland). I always found it interesting that some people think that the two were in a public bar, instead of just in some guy's house, which is how it was intended. The reason they were talking so low was that my brother was upstairs studying for a medical exam, and we were being considerate, since he was letting us shoot there and all! 'Big' John was stuffed behind the bar with the Nagra, and the mike was hidden behind the roll of paper towels on the bar! And yes, I was 'Tony Stark' (I also provided the voice of the ghosts, doing my best Dr. Phibes impersonation). I played the part of Chris when my original choice, Chris Gummer (another Dohler alumnus) had to go to a casting call and couldn't make it. So I set up the lights, turned the camera on, and jumped into the scene! I didn't have time to learn the lines (even though I had written them) so Steve and I had our 'scripts' on the bar in front of us. Also, I had the tripod for the camera, but didn't have a 'spreader', the thing that acts as a base and holds the tripod's legs in place. So we put a throw rug on the tile floor, and just kinda hoped that the

contraption would 'behave'. That's why the camera itself kept slipping, which gave us those 'Dutch' angles!"

The idea of resurrected Confederate soldiers, the cornerstone of both Malanowski's films, came from his own fascination with the American Civil War. "That's why I joined the 23rd Army of Northern Virginia prior to starting *Night of Horror*," he says. "I loved the re-enacting part, but I couldn't march worth a darn! The group had weekly meetings in a National Guard Armory in Baltimore, and I just couldn't get the hang of simply walking in formation. So, I dropped out shortly after *Night of Horror* was made. It was a great group, and very helpful to me on a personal level. The Civil War battle was shot somewhere in Virginia, I believe. I shot that with Dave's Bolex, and had to stay with the audience – they wouldn't let me on the actual 'Field of Battle', so you only had the one angle. It gave the film a bit of production value, and most of the re-enactors signed model releases, so it was all legit."

For a horror film about ghostly undead soldiers, *Night of Horror* is, to say the least, sparing in its special effects. "They were handled by Dave Donoho," Malanowski recalls. "He was a physical special effects guy, used black powder and such. I remember that he seemed to have singed off all his fingernails from working with it. He designed a kind of chemically treated newspaper that he crumpled up and set a match to. The paper would then emit a *ton* of smoke! Dave was introduced to me by Don Dohler, and we used his 'Smoke Paper' extensively in the 'ghost' scenes." As for the film's conspicuous lack of violence, Malanowski is disarmingly candid: "Well, violence costs money! Action? That needs planning! You can't waste time planning when you've got to drive to DC to pick up the equipment! But seriously, I hoped to get a little 'atmosphere', and get some mileage out of the 'love story'. It may have worked with a real script and more experienced actors, but hey, remember: to avoid puking just keep repeating 'It's only a glorified student film… It's only a glorified student film…'"

Post-production took around six or seven months, allowing for unexpected delays, as Malanowski explains: "When I cut the film together, I found it was too short. That's when I latched onto the extension Corman shot for his film *The Terror*. He brought back a couple of actors, and had one explain what happened in the film to the other! Thus were born the opening and closing scenes with Steve and Chris in the 'bar'." The audio was mixed at a commercial mixing house: "I'll never forget the looks of horror that I kept getting from the owner!" laughs Malanowski. "He'd want to go back and redo something, and I'd say 'No, it's fine, don't worry!' I knew that no amount of 'massaging' would make it sound good, and I just didn't have the money to spend. My feeling was, I learned what I needed to, I was going to at least make my money back (well, almost…), and I didn't see the need to go the extra yard at that point."

Malanowski's 'mentor' at the time, Don Dohler, offered valuable practical assistance, although he was less than encouraging about the actual results: "Don helped me a lot with contacts, especially in distribution. At the time, he was working on a picture (the first *NightBeast*, I think[5]) and had some camera equipment that he sub-rented to me. It was a CP 16mm camera outfit. Now CPs are notoriously tough to thread – they have a lot of gears and sprockets. Not like the Arriflex Cameras, which only need two sprockets. But if the CP camera is 'tight', as this one was,

you won't have a problem. And the camera Don sub-rented to me was a very good one. I think I shot all of the sound scenes with that rig. My pickups were all done with Dave's Bolex. When Don watched the workprint to the film, he was kinda appalled! I don't think he got what I was going for – he really thought I had no idea what I was doing!"

Malanowski, who ended his association with Dohler not long after, pauses and then laughs, "It's funny to look back on it now. Did Don really appreciate that I was doing everything by myself? That there was no crew to speak of? That I was absorbing all of the technical aspects that I could? Well, eventually, bad blood came between Don and myself (this is fairly well documented elsewhere, so I won't go into it now). But, I will say that I now work for several major motion picture studios in Hollywood, pulling in a comfortable six figures, and Don was making digital pictures in Perry Hall, Maryland. So, I guess I knew what I was doing..."

Night of Horror is a film with abundant failings, but for its director the important thing was simply to have *made* something: "Working on *The Alien Factor* was so enjoyable, mostly an ensemble kind of feeling. *Night of Horror* was more of a solo flight... kinda lonely, actually. But I saw it as a step in the right direction. I was reading *Famous Monsters* as well as showbusiness biographies, and I didn't see why I couldn't work in the business too. I mean, I didn't feel that *my* dreams were unrealistic, because I wasn't trying to be a movie star, I was going for the technical end. And *my* story wasn't that much different from the stories of John Landis, Joe Dante, and Roger Corman. I was very pragmatic, and had done my homework. These little films, coupled with the burgeoning 'Video Revolution', gave me a window of opportunity that I was determined to take advantage of. And, even though it was

above:
Tony Malanowski (*left*) with Steve Sandkuhler (looking like a young Roger Daltrey) on John Simmons's property, shooting pick up shots for **Night of Horror**.

only a 'little' film, and we were banging beer cans together because I couldn't always rent a slate, and we only had a maximum of three lights at any time, and we didn't have a 'real' script... well, there was still something magical about standing behind that camera, and saying 'Action'..."

Malanowski is as frank in his assessment of the film as he is about the difficulties making it: "Well, it pretty much stunk as badly as I thought it would! I didn't have any illusions. But it *was* exciting to see my name in the credits as a Director and Producer. It solidly legitimised my dream... if I got hit by a bus the next morning, there was still a picture floating around with my name on it. And the most

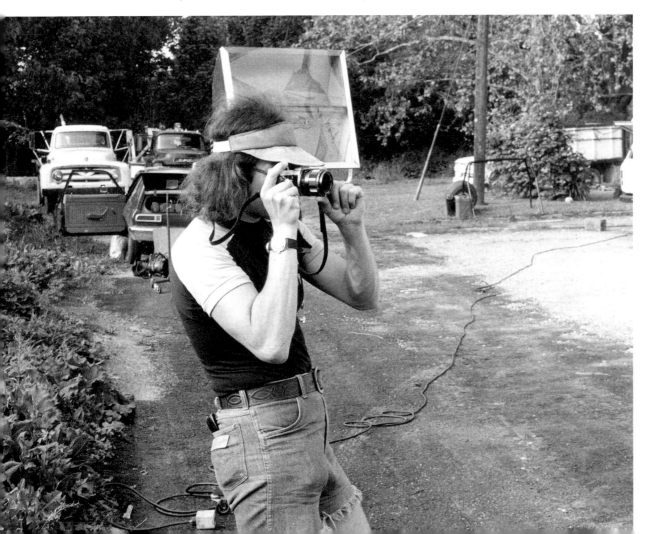

left:
Malanowski takes photos on the 'set' of a phoney shoot designed to generate publicity shots for **Night of Horror**.

above:
Malanowski checking the script with Rebecca
Bach. The legendary camper-van is visible
behind them...

Night of Horror Redux!
Or *The Curse of the Screaming Dead*

With the money given by Alexander Beck to add gore scenes to *Night of Horror*, Malanowski set out instead to remake it. The result, *The Curse of the Screaming Dead*, is still flawed, but it's a big leap on from its forebear. As Samuel Beckett once said, "Fail again, fail better" – a mantra against discouragement and despair that Malanowski's films illustrate perfectly. *Night of Horror* is probably only compelling if you're a student of low-budget cinema or you've got a screw loose: *Curse*, on the other hand, is fun to watch, achieves many of its simple aims, and won't get you beaten up for recommending it to your friends. And if like me you find a certain beauty in images of people chewing guts, then even poetry gets a look-in!

The first lesson Malanowski learned from *Night of Horror* was that it's a good idea to spend some time on your script. "I didn't have a final script for *Night of Horror*, it was mostly just a few pages of dialogue, some disjointed scenes that I kinda made up as I went along. For *Curse*, I decided right away that I needed a real script, a story that was better structured and thought out. Since we were going to basically 'remake' *Night of Horror*, adding what the distributors thought necessary to sell the picture, we already had the basic framework. I had a friend in San Rafael, a city just north of San Francisco, named Lon Huber. Lon was a writer and burgeoning sound designer, so I asked if he would be interested in writing the script based on my outline. He thought it was a good idea, and also asked to help with some of the sound effects. The sound work Lon did mostly entailed going out into the hills with a friend and recording some gunshots at varying speeds. These were used in the film, and, to this day, when I cut and design sound effects, I always prefer recording new effects where feasible. They always have a better, more realistic 'feel' to the ear than library, or 'canned' effects. Or I mix canned effects with similar sounds from the production tracks to sweeten the overall effect. The other main contribution from Lon – and it was a *big* one – was the audio of the actual screams of the 'Screaming Dead'. That was Lon and a few friends tearin' up their vocal chords for the sake of the project."

Whereas *Night of Horror* had been paid for almost entirely by Malanowski, *Curse* benefited from a handful of other investors: "We were still getting cheques from *The Alien Factor* from our TV syndication deal, Big John Simmons dropped another $1,000 into the pot, and Pete Garey made another deal at the lab. But this time, I guess based on my enthusiasm and the fact that I actually made *Night of Horror*, we got a couple of 'outside' investors: my sister; Rebecca Bach; and Richard Ruxton and 'Bump' Roberts, who played the two cops in the film. Dick and Bump wanting to invest was a surprise – I hadn't expected that other people would be at all interested in 'my' dream. I guess it helped that I was giving investors gross points, which means they start getting their money back from dollar one, right along with me. I think that sounded like a good deal to them, that I was being honest. To me, I was keeping so much of the final profit potential myself (by doing all the work), that I could afford to allow some points out. I even gave some upfront money to the players – not a lot certainly, but something."

He continues: "This time, my deal with Pete Garey at Quality Film Labs would cover *all* the lab work through a final answer print. That meant, no matter how much trouble I

important thing was I learned so much! I actually saw where I had made mistakes, had done things wrong. Not so much budgetary problems, because there wasn't much I could do about that, but technical things. I knew that next time I needed to pay more attention to the script and the acting, for example. Plus, I needed more coverage in the editing room. And I was very intrigued by the sound editing. I didn't have a lot of experience, but I knew that I wanted to play around and try things. The *process* was still amazing me. The *feel* of putting the project together was invigorating."

With the film completed, a promo was assembled on three-quarter-inch video, and shown to Bruce Kaufman at distributors Alexander Beck. "They looked at the picture, and said it was slow, and nothing happens," says Malanowski. "I said that I was aware of that. I wasn't looking for *a lot* of money... just enough to get me started on the next film. They told me that I should reshoot some new scenes that would play well in a trailer. They suggested standard horror stuff, you know, ghouls coming out of the ground and some blood and guts. With that, they said, they could make good sales on the picture. Well, I had already decided to cut my 'losses' on *Night of Horror*. I guessed (rightly, it turned out), that it would be better to dump the picture elsewhere for whatever I could get, and use the new money (plus the experience) to make another picture. *That* picture would incorporate these new ideas, would allow me to take the next step in 'quality', and would have as much of a 'guarantee' for success as you could get in the picture business. But I still knew, at that time, that people automatically assumed you needed a lot of money to do even a low-budget film. They couldn't conceive of one person doing all the work. So that gave me an advantage. Nowadays, with digital cameras and the like, well, you aren't fooling anyone. But back then... So, if I upped my budget a little, was wiser in my job as director/producer, took my time, and obeyed the distributors, I figured I could do alright. That was the starting point for *The Curse of the Screaming Dead*."

opposite page:
A selection of images from
The Curse of the Screaming Dead.

got into budget-wise, I would still be able to have the work done for cost, with an open end to how long it would take to pay off that cost. The other consideration, and it was an important one, was that I suddenly found myself working for Pete at the lab. I went in one day to pick up something, and Pete was bemoaning the fact that a new employee had run off. Pete's was a 'Mom and Pop' kind of business – he had only one other full time employee, and his kids would sometimes come in to work. So I said, 'Hey, what about me?' Pete didn't think I was serious at first, but I needed a job and it seemed like a perfect fit."

The Curse of the Screaming Dead went before the camera the first week of October 1981. Malanowski's new job dovetailed neatly, if exhaustingly, with the shoot: "I worked Monday through Friday at Pete's. I would leave the lab (which was in Towson, Maryland just outside of Baltimore) in the late afternoon on Friday, and drive about forty miles to Washington DC to pick up the rental equipment. Then I would drive directly to the location, meet the cast, and start setting up. We'd shoot Friday night, crash at the location then get up and shoot Saturday during the day, and then at night. We repeated the process for Sunday. Then, I'd crash late Sunday night, and have to get up early Monday morning to take the equipment back to DC, then get to the lab by 9a.m. for work. I got to process my own film in the regular developing run, and, since it was a reversal film, I could check out the original as it was spooling through the dryer onto the take-up reel! That way, I could get a decent idea of how the shots turned out! Let me tell you, you don't know pressure until you run the machines that process your own film!"

The shoot brought Malanowski's first brush with sexploitation, although the inclement October weather hindered any potential eroticism: "I was worried because it was getting colder and we had a scene with the girls in bikinis. It was a totally gratuitous scene, just to show some skin, but I was worried that they would be uncomfortable if the weather was too chilly! I even planned on shooting the scene in *my* bathing suit, just to show them that I wouldn't ask them to do something I wouldn't. The day we shot that scene, however, I forgot my bathing suit, and ending up just talking my jacket and shirt off! I guess the effect was the same!"

Malanowski's plan this time was to shoot with the main cast over three weekends, then do pick-ups as needed, with most of the more difficult scenes, like the zombies coming out of the ground and the attack on the house, filmed separately later. However, circumstances dictated otherwise: "That first weekend, when I went to DC to pick up my camera rig, they did not have what I ordered. I had reserved an Arriflex BL 16mm camera, but they had rented it to someone else, leaving only a CP16 camera. Well, as you remember, a CP has many gears, and is a pain to thread. And if you don't thread it just right, (or if the camera gets finicky), you get a blurred image. That happened so often, the film world came up with a derisive name for it: the 'CP Shuffle'! Well, I was stuck, and I had used a CP before on *Night of Horror*, so I figured I'd just go with it. We got to our location, which was a large horse ranch outside of Ellicott City in Maryland. I set up, and we started shooting with the cast walking through the trees, trying to get most of Mimi's scenes done first, because she wasn't 'local'. We shot for three days (and into the evenings). Come Monday morning, I take the CP back and speed up to Pete's where I start loading my film in the magazines in the darkroom.

Since we wouldn't run that machine until later in the day, I left the film closed in the magazine, waiting in the darkroom for a few hours. Finally, the machine was ready, and I started the processing run. Now, I had shot a few thousand feet of 16mm film, and as it was coming out of the dryer, *something* didn't look right! My heart just sank! Without being on a projector (with a shutter separating the frames), I couldn't be positive, but it sure looked like a kind of 'glow' was hanging over my actors! It seemed like forever until I could break down a roll and put it on a projector, where my worst fears were then confirmed. Every damn foot of that shoot had the old 'CP Shuffle' on it. It was all ruined; totally worthless! I just couldn't believe the bad luck!"

Another unexpected problem arose with the prop design: "Dave Donoho had made me graveyard headstones out of Styrofoam. I dirtied them up a little, but kept them their original white colour. Well, on screen, those things flared out like mini-A-Bomb blasts! More unusable footage! Well, it all became a moot point within a week. Seems I never really studied the autumnal cycle in Maryland very closely, 'cause the next weekend we drove to the same horse ranch and discovered that almost every damned leaf had fallen off the trees! Even without the 'CP Shuffle', I would have had to reshoot for the difference in the trees! But actually, it turned out for the best. The trees were now gaunt and dead-looking, making for a better background, (esp. at night). Plus, I had a chance to paint the headstones. Dave Donoho told me not to use oil based paint, as it would 'eat' the Styrofoam. I bought some acrylic spray-paint in a flat grey, but also a small can of oil-based grey paint. By using the oil paint in small amounts, I could cause pitting and texture in the Styrofoam. Then, I painted the whole thing over with the acrylic. It really looked convincing. I still have those headstones, and loan them out for Halloween parties!"

Thanks to the difficulties, shooting extended into spring of 1982, with Malanowski deciding on the need for further pick-up shots during the editing process, grabbing his Bolex camera and adding or reshooting material where needed. "We did the scene where Rebecca Bach, as Sarah, falls off the cross in the graveyard the morning of New Year's Day 1982," he recalls. "Boy, were we hung over! Since the cross was also made of Styrofoam, Rebecca couldn't actually 'sit' on it as the script indicated, I just had her sort of lean on it. Didn't make much sense even when you think about it in context, but we weren't feeling too good that morning! We shot on the horse ranch, which was owned by a friend named Randy Robbins. He had a small cottage that we crashed in, though some of us actually stayed in the tents that we used in the film. After the second weekend, it got too cold at night, so we all ended up inside. We shot the opening camper shots, and some of the night footage there. The house we used was the one that Jim Ball was renting. I think a couple of people stayed there. It was three stories, with that great porch! We shot the scenes with the cops there as well, and some of the soldiers attacking the house, you know, coming out of the woods. The old ruined church we used was right up the street. I don't know who owned it, we just sorta used it! It might have been County property. I think it looked great! The first zombie attack and most of the tent scenes were shot in Chris Gummer's back yard – the 'Gummer Backlot' we called it."

As difficulties arose, anything that could possibly benefit a shot was pressed into service. One night, the lamps started blowing out, and with no spare bulbs lighting was becoming more and more difficult. "It got to the point where I pulled

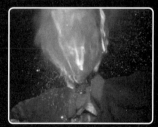

my little Pinto car up to the actors, and put the high beams on!" laughs Malanowski. "Chris even brought out a red heating lamp that we used in close-ups of the ghouls – anything that would help!"

The last scene to be shot was a genuinely effective 'coming-out-of-the-grave' sequence. "We did that one in Mark Redfield's back yard," Malanowski recalls. "Mark played Captain Mahler, and did a lot of make-up effects. So he did his own make-up as the undead Captain. He had a real beard, but, for some reason, he shaved the darn thing just before we shot! So he had to create a false beard, which never really matched. Some reviewers even think he is a different ghoul, so I guess it's okay! Those last scenes were intercut with some shots I had already done at Jim Ball's house. Hey, talk about an *auteur*, I even dug the holes for most of the graves!"

One thing that's noticeable when watching Malanowski's films together is that the actors are far more animated and confident in the second outing. This was in part down to having the first film for reference as a 'how-not-to' guide, and also due to Lon Huber's script: "Lon did a great job of 'fleshing out' the personalities of the people in the story. We took more time with it, since it was the most glaring problem with the first film. Now we had a complete script, written by, of all things, a writer! The players had something to work with, and I think it showed, especially Rebecca Bach and Steve Sandkuhler. Now both of them were in *Night of Horror*, but they were so much more accomplished in *Curse*, which was only shot a year later."

Malanowski is unfailingly generous when discussing his cast: "Jim was a member of Steve's group Off the Wall, and was recommended when I was having a hard time filling that slot in the cast. He was very personable and had done some acting, so it wasn't much of a stretch to bring him aboard. I think he did very well. He was mostly at ease in front of the camera, which is so important in low-budget filmmaking. I'm glad I agreed to including Jim before I found out that he brought along that *big* house as a location! It might have been prejudicial in my judgement at the time! Jim's best scenes were mixin' it up with 'Mel', played by Chris Gummer. Chris was a friend from the old *Alien Factor* days. He could play a very forceful character, and we chose to have him be the 'bad guy' in our film. Mimi Ishikawa as 'Blind Kiyomi' was industrious, hard working, and most of all very photogenic, and incredibly cute! I guess I can be honest and say that I regret putting 'Blind' into the credits, when referring to the character. I originally thought that it added a kind of dignity, like the character 'Susan the Silent' in *Finian's Rainbow*. But, it only seemed to make the character stand out for ridicule, and I'm sorry for that. The other problem was, after we had to reshoot for the 'CP Shuffle' hassles, Mimi came up with an idea. Instead of using the standard 'Blind Look' that a sighted person usually employs when playing a blind person, she thought that her character might seem normally sighted when standing or sitting in one place, but revert to a modified version of the 'Blind Look' when moving or reaching for something. That sounded great to me, and I told her to try it. Well, we shot most of her scenes that second weekend, and when I got the footage back, I realised that it just didn't work. The theory was fine, but the look just seemed incongruous. We changed it for her final scenes, but the damage was done. Especially in close-ups, it really called attention to itself. I hoped that her performance otherwise would cover up these problems. I thought she was especially good in the scene in the tent,

where she talked about losing her puppy when she was younger. Now Mimi was part Japanese, so I needed another Asian actress to play her sister. A friend suggested a woman who was from Korea – she was a war bride, actually. We met, but she was a little older than the part as written. I figured we could probably pull it off with a little script change, but then she suggested her daughter. That's how we found Judy Dixon. I met with Judy, and she was quite excited to get the part. She had a little stage experience, I believe, but she read and I knew she could handle it. Richard Ruxton (Dick McLung) I had met through Don Dohler, and he brought along 'Bump' Roberts (R. Sommerwerk). I thought they did a great job! They wore old Baltimore County Police jackets that I got through a surplus house. And Dick was named 'Captain Fritz' after the Maryland State Police Officer who pulled Big John and myself over on one of our more boisterous outings!"

During the scenes where zombies emerge from the graveyard, tiny flashes of light can be seen in the darkness. Malanowski laughs when I ask what they were: "Oh, yeah... those! Somehow, the idea came up to have glowing lights cover the gravestones as the ghouls came out of the ground. That's why the characters are talking about lights over at the old church. The idea was to make it a little more of a 'mystical' event, while also giving another bit of production value for the distributors. Dan Taylor would've needed money for optical effects like those, and I didn't have it in the budget, so I couldn't impose on him. So what I *did* manage to do was to get some little powder-filled 'cones' from Dave Donoho. These were about an inch tall, and, when lit, would produce a white 'flash' every few seconds. I thought I needed *something* to get the players' attention, you know, that something was happening at the graveyard. So one night I took those 'cones', and my Bolex, out in Dundalk to a local shopping area. They were building an extra parking lot in the area, so I parked my Pinto, set up my Bolex, and lit my cones! Well, those little suckers started spitting out flashes all over the place. I thought I'd shoot a bunch from different angles, and superimpose them over the already-shot footage of the ghouls coming out of their graves! Well, I shot a few takes, and in the distance, I heard fire trucks! I didn't

above:
Malanowski coaches one of his ghouls...

opposite page:
Zombie action from **The Curse of the Screaming Dead**.

below:
They're coming to get you, Baltimore!

think too much about it and kept shooting, but they sounded like they were coming closer! Well, the light bulb went off over my head, and I threw my gear into my Pinto and sped off! In my mirror I could see a couple of fire trucks pulling up and turning into that parking lot! On a similar subject, I needed some shots of fireworks going off when the guys throw the bag of fireworks into the campfire to distract the zombies. I knew that the Baltimore Orioles were having a fireworks display at one of their games at old Memorial Stadium on 33rd Street, so off I went with my ubiquitous Bolex to grab what I could. I parked a coupla blocks away and waited. When the display started I filmed several shots using the zoom lens on the camera. Then the roll of film ran out and I just put the roll back in, and exposed it again. I thought it would 'double-expose' more fireworks, and I would have twice as much on the roll that I could then superimpose over the ghouls! Well, putting the film back in the camera without *rewinding* it first, meant that you had two exposures of fireworks – one going forward normally, and the other going *backwards*! It dawned on me on the ride home, but by then it was too late. When I saw it, it looked kinda silly, but I had a deadline, and nothing else to use."

A highlight of the film is the police captain's theory that the zombies are merely a prank staged by psychopaths who are stealing bodies and rigging them up on wires. "That was all in Lon's original script. Every word. Incidentally, the voice on the radio is mine. I also did the crying sounds that Franklin makes as he is attacked by the zombies, plus the scream that Captain Mahler gives when he stumbles upon his men eating the bodies. Oh, and Rebecca Bach and I perform most of the sounds of the zombies eating the guts!"

Ah, the gut-chewing scenes – where Malanowski's film earns its exploitation stripes and at last joins the grisly legions following George Romero's *Night of the Living Dead* and *Dawn of the Dead*. As actors chomp into glistening entrails, with nary a flinch, the startled viewer wonders how on Earth Malanowski persuaded his cast to be so carnivorous…

"Everyone got into it! I guess you're asking because much has been made about the zombie extras in *Night of the Living Dead* getting grossed out by the real animal parts that were obtained from a slaughterhouse. Well, I read those interviews too! But, even more relevant, I was a vegetarian at the time, and thought phoney entrails made from latex would be better all round – and they were! Larry Schlechter (who created the 'Inferbyce' creature in *The Alien Factor*) made a stomach piece for me, which could fit on an actor's belly. This was big enough to have a few 'organs' and 'entrails' stuffed inside, which were made out of upholstery foam, covered with latex. The ghouls could simply pull these out as needed! Pour some Dave Donoho 'blood' all over everything, and you had yourself an instant gross-out! But I guess we did that part right, because reviewers *always* cite that scene, and say that we used real animal parts! And, as the blooper reel attests, the players had a lot of fun with the gut eating scenes!"

Adding to the much improved goriness of *The Curse of the Screaming Dead* are some capably grotesque zombie make-ups. Malanowski explains how they came about: "I had started talking with Fred Ray, who was down in Florida, prior to his move to Los Angeles. He gave me the name of Bart Mixon, who did make-up effects in Texas. Bart agreed to do a set of pull-over zombie masks for me. He had sent me a résumé and pictures of his work, and it was obvious that he could do it. I thought having these ready to wear masks would help me time-wise, and could also add numbers to any scene where I needed background zombies. The only 'main' mask was the one that would become 'the Flag Bearer'. Bart worked from the description Lon had written in the script, and I think that mask was particularly effective. I remember that Bart wanted $150 for the job to cover expenses. The rest would be points and a credit – and he wanted the masks back at the end of shooting! We also had several other make-up artists on the shoot. As I noted, Larry Schlechter did our guts and that stomach piece, and Mark Redfield did most of our main 'highlight' ghouls. When we did the final coming-out-of-the-grave sequence in Mark's backyard, I had brought some friends over, and Mark made up his brother, Eric. One of the guys had brought along his girlfriend, and I stuck a mask on her and added her to the group. Steve's wife Linnea had done some stage make-up, and he suggested that she would like to come along and help out. You can tell Linnea's ghouls – they have the white, pasty looking faces with a few highlights. Mark's ghouls have a heavier base, with darker highlights. And the blood was made up by the gallon by Dave Donoho. Dave also made some blood 'pools' that he carried around with him. They were done on wax paper sections – he mixed gelatine with food colouring, and painted it out onto the wax paper. When it dried, it looked like pools of blood that you could just lay on the floor and touch up with a bit of fresh liquid. Pretty clever!"

He continues: "The costumes were leftovers from the Civil War re-enactment group. One was an artillery shell jacket with sergeant's stripes, another was a straightforward grey jacket. That became Captain Mahler's costume, along with an old, floppy grey country hat of mine. Since I knew costumes would be a problem, I had told Lon to put something in the script to help us out! So Lon dutifully wrote the section of the diary where Captain Mahler exclaimed, '...most are boys, clad only in rags'."

If *The Curse of the Screaming Dead* has a problem, it's that the comings and goings of the characters are hard to follow, as they split up or disappear from the frame rather

haphazardly. Malanowski acknowledges the problem, but explains, "Well, Lon was very familiar with the kind of film I was making. He kept scenes almost as separate vignettes, to help facilitate the shooting. This did tend to make it a little choppy, but I felt that was an acceptable trade-off. And I probably made it worse by shooting around people's schedules. I'd have people walk into a scene and sit down, and you wouldn't see them for the rest of that scene. This was because, if someone could only give me a half day, then I got them in and out in a half day! Even with storyboards, it's hard to see how something will work until you put it together. A good example of that, is checking out the various 'Kiyomi' body doubles, wearing that long, black Halloween wig! The red and black flannel shirt that Mimi wore in the film was mine. I deliberately had her wear that, because I knew I would be using body doubles to cover for her being away at college! That's another reason why she passes out in the script, and has to be carried all over the place by Mel! Most of the time, it's really my sister Ali, or Jim Ball's then-girlfriend Ridia that Chris is schlepping around! But, again, all of those problems sure seemed to melt away once I got into the cutting room, and starting piecing it all together. It was really magical... just going through the actual process of putting a film together. At that time, I was editing scenes where the players were my friends. But I knew this project would lead to other films where I would be editing scenes with actual, well-known stars. And within a few short years, I would be editing Tony Curtis, Glenn Ford, Angela Lansbury, Roddy McDowall, et al! That's what I was setting my sights on, as I edited away in my parents' basement and garage. I got some flack occasionally; one uncle recently told me, 'You know, behind closed doors, none of us thought you'd ever really amount to much!' But I kept going!"

At the editing stage, Malanowski added the score, written for the film by Charlie Barnett. Unlike many ultra-low-budget films of the period, Barnett's score is surprisingly sophisticated, sounding more like the Mike Westbrook Orchestra than the regulation droning synth so familiar from the genre. "You're the second person to mention a similarity between Charlie's score, and Mike Westbrook," smiles Malanowski. "I've never heard Mike's work, so I can't say. I believe Charlie was recommended by a friend of Gae Schmitt. As I recall, Gae had a friend who did some experimental pieces for another zombie film that I was thinking about doing. I remember his work was very good, but when time came to actually do the film, he was unavailable. But he got me in touch with Charlie, and we arranged to meet. Well, Charlie showed up at my place wearing a tie! He introduced himself, and I promptly told him to remove the tie! I said that we were going to have our meeting up the street in a local lounge. So we got in the car, and I took Charlie (now minus his tie) to the bar. We had a great meeting, and we pretty much agreed to work together at that point. Charlie was a 'classical score' kind of guy. He wanted to get some of his friends from the Kennedy Center and the Washington Opera to come down and record. I told him that I didn't think I could afford that, but he said he'd pull in a few favours. Well, being a producer as well as a composer, Charlie wrangled quite a few friends! I don't remember the exact amount (I'd guess ten or twelve musicians), but they were all real pros. Also, Charlie wrote in a very clever way. He did a couple of main pieces, some transitional pieces, and some 'stingers' for accenting. By mixing and matching, the score could be made to sound more complex and varied than it really was. This also gave the musicians less actual music

to learn, and kept down our time in the studio. On the day of the recording session I bought a couple of cases of beer and sodas for the fellas. I remember carrying them into the studio myself. Charlie later told me that the assembled musicians asked him who I was, and he told them, 'That's the producer!' The guys were so impressed by the fact that 'The Producer' was schlepping drinks for the band that they immediately agreed to stay longer than planned, if we needed extra time. That always stuck with me, that those guys could see how much I was trying to cut corners and all, but also was keeping their comfort in mind as much as I could. The recording session went really well. Charlie sure knew what he was doing. All told, I think we came out with about forty minutes of score! It felt positively uplifting listening to a live performance of what would be the score for your own feature film!"

Malanowski was now far more optimistic about *Curse*'s chances in the marketplace: "Well, since the entire production was designed around the distributor's ideas about what would sell, I didn't expect any problems. In the first couple of shoots, I got enough material (including some of the 'money' shots with the ghouls) to make a decent promo. I rushed that up to Bruce Kaufman, since Alexander Beck was going to a film market, and they needed any kind of a promo as soon as possible. Surprisingly enough, Bruce called right after the market, and told me that they had pre-sold the picture in the United Kingdom for $15,000! How soon could I get it? Man, I was pretty bowled over by *that* news. It sure sounded like everything was going along according to plan. By this time, I had cut a lot of the film together, and needed only pieces of scenes and the large-scale scene of the ghouls coming out of their graves. This did take a little longer than Bruce wanted. I eventually had to rush through the audio mix to deliver the movie. Then the UK agents started quibbling over the picture, but we eventually agreed on the price, and they accepted the film (once I threatened to pull it from them). I went back into the studio and redid the mix, adding some things and taking a little more time with it. That became the official 'final version' of the picture. I don't know if that early mix still exists in the UK or not. Apparently, we were even pirated in a couple of territories, New Zealand was one. Since *Curse* had a final cost of about $12,000 (including the remix of the soundtrack), I was actually seeing some money. I think the distribution fee was fairly high, maybe 40% or so. But I was new to the game, so I couldn't complain. I figured that later in my career I would have more leverage on making deals, and that is pretty much how it turned out. I remember one funny distribution story. Bruce called me and told me that he had interest from an agent who represented Canadian video. They were offering, I think, $4,000 for the rights to *Curse*. Only, they wanted to change the title to *The South Shall Rise Again*, which was the tag line for the picture. When Bruce told me that, I readily agreed. Bruce then said that he had already told the agent that the title change would be acceptable. 'Don't you need to check with the producer?', the Canadian agent asked Bruce. 'Look, I know the producer,' Bruce answered. 'You can change the name of the picture to *My Bar Mitzvah* for all he cares, just as long as you pay him!' Now how's *that* for a distributor who's looking out for you! By this time, I had made a sale for *Night of Horror*, and Bruce got me a domestic video deal with Mogul for *Curse*. They made up a superb ad campaign, with a full colour painting of a ghoul eating some red 'flesh'. Bruce sent me ads from video trade magazines, and I could

see how the picture was being marketed. Later, we were setting up an outright sale deal on *NightBeast* to Troma. I thought that it would be good to get a final deal for cash, since my main sales through Bruce and Alex were slowing down. This worked out fine for me. I was able to get $12,000 from Troma which, when coupled with the money I was making as a Special Commissioned Officer with the Maryland State Police (don't ask...), would finally give me the seed money to move to Los Angeles."

Looking back at the second movie, Malanowksi feels justifiably pleased: "I think it was a lot better than it had any right to be. I was much happier with the acting, the story, the editing, pretty much an improvement in all areas. Still, there was so much more I would have liked to do if I had the time and the money. I envisioned an opening sequence under the credits that showed, via flashback, the Confederate soldiers being tortured. But, I would have needed to shoot it on a sound stage with some wagon props, cannons, Union uniforms, et al. Just no way I could have afforded that."

His next remarks raise the possibility of yet another treatment of the Undead Confederates story – truly the concept that wouldn't die! "I have toyed with the idea of somehow remaking the film, and shooting the script I have for the sequel (*Revenge of the Screaming Dead*) at the same time. But, I'm doing so much better now working on other people's projects, that I just don't feel the need to do the same story for a third time! I will get back into production someday, probably within the next five years, the way that my company is going."

After directing *The Curse of the Screaming Dead*, Malanowski moved into sound and film editing for a string of exploitation notables of the eighties and nineties, beginning with Fred Olen Ray: "I packed my car and drove out to Hollywood in 1987. I started working immediately for Fred Ray where I did the sound editing/design for *Phantom Empire*, *Evil Spawn* (I also re-edited the picture), and *Hollywood Chainsaw Hookers* (I was also the assistant editor). Then, I moved over to work for Dave DeCoteau. I cut picture and sound on *Nightmare Sisters* and *Deadly Embrace*. Then, I cut picture for *Dr. Alien*, *Ghettoblaster* and *Ghost Writer*. I next became the house editor for Action International Pictures (another 'AIP Studios'). They also hired me to first cut sound (*Future Zone*, *Deadly Dancer*, *Final Sanction*), then picture and sound (*Raw Nerve*, *Center of the Web*, *Mardi Gras for the Devil*, *Good Cop/Bad Cop*). All these were for director David Prior. When David left AIP, I went with him, and cut *Felony* and *Mutant Species*. I did several other smaller-budget films, and then joined

Scott MacQueen in the restoration dept at the Walt Disney Studios. There, I did a slew of pictures including the full-scale restorations of *Bedknobs and Broomsticks*, *The Happiest Millionaire*, the *Davy Crockett* TV shows and *Fantasia*. I moonlighted at Crest Labs in Hollywood, doing element evaluation and digital spotting for most of the Anchor Bay titles, and then worked for two years editing and producing DVDs for Disney. I'm especially proud of the work I did on the DVDs of *20,000 Leagues Under the Sea*, *Old Yeller*, *Swiss Family Robinson* and *High Fidelity*. I oversaw the mix on the deleted scenes for *Unbreakable* and the director's cut of *Nixon*. All in all, I worked on dozens of pictures in various capacities. I would even cut promos and trailers on the side. Then, I got into TV restoration with Ascent Media. I recut the first two seasons of *thirtysomething*, and am now heading up the recut of all nine seasons of *Seinfeld* for DVD – a multi-million dollar contract..."

And the moral of the story? I'll leave the final word to Malanowski: "And all of this is through my company Little Warsaw Productions – the exact same production company that brought you *Night of Horror*! I owe it all (I repeat *all*) to the experience I got from making *Night of Horror* and *The Curse of the Screaming Dead*!"

Footnotes

[1] Van Der Beek is an experimental filmmaker and animator whose 1964 film *Death Breath* Terry Gilliam says inspired his animation style.

[2] Amongst those learning their craft on *The Alien Factor* was production assistant John Dods, who went on to design the monster for Dohler's *NightBeast* and, most notably, the amazing monsters in Douglas McKeown's *The Deadly Spawn* – see interview with McKeown.

[3] Hammond went on to do make-up on such films as *The Basketball Diaries* and *Minority Report*.

[4] The origin of this term is uncertain and hotly debated, but it either means "Motor Only Sound", "Minus Optical Sound" or "Mit Out Sound" – the latter supposedly resulting from a German director asking for a shot 'Without sound' in a thick accent! Basically, MOS indicates a shot taken without sound.

[5] Dohler began and then abandoned a version of *NightBeast*, before starting again and completing a second version.

TONY MALANOWSKI: FILMOGRAPHY AS DIRECTOR
1981   *Night of Horror*
1982   *The Curse of the Screaming Dead* aka *Curse of the Cannibal Confederates* aka *The South Shall Rise Again*

OTHER CREDITS:
1977   *The Alien Factor* – dir: Don Dohler (co-producer / assistant director)
1982   *NightBeast* – dir: Don Dohler
1986   *Phantom Empire* – dir: Fred Olen Ray (sound editor)
1987   *Evil Spawn* dirs: Kenneth J. Hall / Ted Newsom / Fred Olen Ray (uncredited) (sound editor + re-edit of film)
1987   *Nightmare Sisters* – dir: David DeCoteau (sound editor/editor)
1988   *Hollywood Chainsaw Hookers* – dir: Fred Olen Ray (sound editor / assistant editor / post-production supervisor)
1988   *Dr. Alien* – dir: David DeCoteau (editor)

1989   *Deadly Embrace* – dir: David DeCoteau (sound editor / editor)
1989   *Ghettoblaster* – dir: Alan Stewart (editor)
1990   *Ghost Writer* – dir: David DeCoteau (TV) (editor)
1990   *Future Zone* – dir: David Prior (sound editor)
1990   *Deadly Dancer* – dir: Kimberley Casey (sound editor)
1990   *Final Sanction* – dir: David A. Prior (sound editor)
1991   *Raw Nerve* – dir: David A. Prior (sound editor / editor)
1992   *Center of the Web* – dir: David A. Prior (sound editor / editor)
1993   *Double Threat* – dir: David A. Prior (editor)
1993   *Mardi Gras for the Devil* – dir: David A. Prior (sound editor / editor)
1994   *Good Cop/Bad Cop* – dir: David A. Prior (sound editor / editor)
1995   *Mutant Species* – dir: David A. Prior (editor / creature voice design / post-production supervisor)
1996   *Felony* – dir: David A. Prior (editor / post-production supervisor)
1996   *Dinosaur Valley Girls* – dir: Donald F. Glut (editor)

chapter 15

Punished By the Sun

Marc B. Ray on Scream Bloody Murder

Scream Bloody Murder (1972)

Marc Ray's *Scream Bloody Murder* is often confused with Robert J. Emery's Florida-shot character-piece of the same name (aka *My Brother Has Bad Dreams*). Purely by coincidence, both films were released in 1972, which has led many a reference work to confuse them. Emery's film has a slow-burn style of its own and is definitely worth seeing, but Ray's film is the bigger crowd-pleaser, featuring a host of gruesome deaths, and a pleasingly lurid visual style.

You know you're in for something special when the pre-credits sequence shows Matthew as a young boy (J.M. Jones) in the family orange groves, deliberately driving a bulldozer over his father (Ron Max). Somehow, though, he falls off and gets his hand mashed beneath the vehicle's treads – surely the epitome of the 'bizarre gardening accident'. This blatantly Oedipal opening riff is dressed up with weird camera angles and wide-angle lenses, giving the film its first blast of lunatic energy. (It's interesting to note that director Marc Ray also wrote Thomas Alderman's horror flick *The Severed Arm* the same year.)

The story proper begins ten years later. Returning home unannounced from the nuthouse, his crushed hand now replaced with a hi-tech claw, Matthew (Fred Holbert) arrives just in time to see his newly remarried momma (Leigh Mitchell) canoodling with husband number two (Robert Knox). This is hardly the homecoming he's been anticipating, and it's not long before he expresses his displeasure by gruesomely axing the interloper (in a scene which appears slightly cut for the UK video release). Understandably, momma takes a dim view of this, and in the ensuing struggle she falls, bashing her brains out on a rock. Taking to the road, the deeply disturbed Matthew accepts a lift from a young couple (Suzette Hamilton and Wiley Reynolds), only to murder them too, hallucinating that they're his mother and her new husband. Such visions will haunt him throughout the movie. He winds up broke at Venice Beach, and falls into conversation with a young woman called Vera (Leigh Mitchell, again), a hooker whom he sees painting abstract canvases on the porch of her wooden shack. Matthew resolves to 'save' her from the men who 'defile' her, but first he needs a home, somewhere impressive to woo his new love. With this in mind, he talks his way into an uptown mansion, murders the occupants, and *voila*! Posing as the wealthy son of a millionaire, he lures Vera back to the house. However,

Vera disappoints Matthew by declining to move in, so he trusses her up in the bedroom: she's going to live with him, like it or not. All seems hopeless for Vera, until she realises there's one weapon she can use to intimidate Matthew – her body...

I know, I know: another flick about a momma-obsessed nut on a killing spree. Stay with it though, because there's enough oddity and imagination in the staging of this tale to make it fly. The premise may be shop-worn, but *Scream Bloody Murder* is top quality exploitation: it's well shot, fairly well acted, and the killings are bloody and alarming, not to mention generously scattered throughout the film. Ten murders in seventy-five minutes is pretty fine for a film made in 1972! Matthew's axing of his stepfather is a grisly montage of chopping and bleeding, while the death of the maid (A. Maana Tanelah), hacked to death with a meat-cleaver in a white-tiled kitchen (all the better to smear with blood) is an OTT mélange of wild camerawork, cheap gore and piercing screams that brings to mind the climax of *Don't Look in the Basement*, made the same year. The murder of one of Vera's clients, a sailor (Ron Bastone), is also impressively nasty – he's slashed across the face with a palette knife then stabbed through the palm of his outstretched hand, in a sequence that wouldn't look out of place in a Dario Argento film.

Given its excessive qualities, I'm surprised that the film is so infrequently reviewed. Most of the bloodier

below:
Admat for **Scream Bloody Murder**, crediting the film to 'John B. Kelly'. Who? No one of that name is remotely connected with the movie. Marc Ray comments: "I have no idea who John B. Kelly is and why he would wish to be attached to this film. Imposter! Throw him into the moat!"

Scream Bloody Murder
aka **Claw of Terror** (alternative US title)
aka **The Captive Female** (Canadian theatrical title)
aka **Matthew** (US video title)
© 1972. Alan Roberts Productions in association with University Film Company First American Films. John B. Kelly presents. Alan Roberts presents.
producer/director: Marc B. Ray. screenplay: Larry Alexander and Marc. B. Ray. executive producer: Alan Roberts. director of photography: Stephen Burum. editor: Alex Furke. music: Rockwell. Matthew's Theme by Bob Bagleey. associate producers: Ron Mitchell, Larry Alexander. make-up & set decoration: Gale Petersen & Ron Mulderich. script supervisor: Lorelei. assistant to the director: John Herzog. gaffer: Roy Harbett. key grip: Chuck Wells. boom operator: Ira B. Slugerman. set grips: Steven Vance, Mark Miller, Bruce Miller. negative cutter: B. Robert Barton. colour by Crest Laboratories. opticals by Consolidated Film Industries. titles by Title House. sound transfer by Producers Sound Service.
Cast: Fred Holbert (Matthew). Leigh Mitchell (Vera / Daisy Parsons). Robert Knox (Mack Parsons). Ron Bastone (Calley, sailor). Suzette Hamilton (Brenda). Wiley [Willey] Reynolds (Tom). A. Maana Tanelah (Bridey-Lee). Florence Lea (Helen Anatole). Rory Guy [aka Angus Scrimm] (Doctor Epstein). Cecil Reddick (Mr. Simpson). Gloria Earl (Mrs. Simpson). J.M. Jones (young Matthew). Norman (candy seller). Ron Max (Matthew's father). Winnifred (the dog).

above right, and below:
Scream Bloody Murder gets off to a great start with a bizarre patricidal scene.

horrors of the seventies have had their champions, but *Scream Bloody Murder* is relatively uncelebrated. True, Matthew – played with grim-faced intensity by Fred Holbert – is not one of the more 'sympathetic' psychos of the cinema; indeed I spent much of the second half of the film willing someone to kill him. He's a prudish, mother-fixated killjoy (how's that for an understatement?), convinced that decent women should hate sex, and he bends every situation into an opportunity to relieve his Oedipal rage. This is one serial killer whose bad attitude is not meretriciously polished up to make him a sleazy audience surrogate. Fixated on the notion of his mother's 'purity', and regarding with thin-lipped hatred anyone he sees as a 'corrupter', he's unlikely to set the stalls cheering *á là* Jason Voorhees, which deflects all sympathy onto his hapless victims.

It's interesting to contrast Holbert's performance with that of John Amplas in George Romero's *Martin*. The prosaic voice and demeanour are very similar, and the characters are roughly the same age and build, but Matthew lacks Martin's self-consciousness. If anything, Matthew's spitefulness towards women, his self-obsessiveness and lack of empathy, are actually closer to the serial-killer mark than Romero's creation who, despite being one of the most intricately drawn characters in the entire horror genre, seems to exist outside of therapeutic realism. *Scream Bloody Murder* is like *Martin* without the sleight of hand that turns a killer into a tragic anti-hero: there's nothing sweetly sorrowful about this guy. Even when Matthew callously slaughters the maid and the old lady, then sobs as he kills her dog, he merely demonstrates a typical attitude among murderers (Myra Hindley for example), who often reserve tender feelings for animals that they withhold from human beings.

Despite the claustrophobia, the goriness, and the fundamentally downbeat premise, Stephen Burum's agile camerawork and the rather campy 'afternoon TV' score ensure the film is impossible to take too seriously. Matthew's insane visions of blood-caked ghoul-women provide both scares and visual amusement: cackling and taunting like the female apparitions in *The Evil Dead*, they are shot using a filter beloved of psychedelically inclined directors, with waves of 'transparent treacle' appearing to wash over the image. Far out, man… That's not to say all the laughs are accidental: when Vera asks Matthew what he can see in her painting, he gazes at the abstract mulch for a while and says he sees a figure: *"He's been punished by the sun, he's been punished for*

chopping up the man who took his mother away from him." *"I didn't know I was such a good artist,"* Vera deadpans.

There's humour too in the way that Ray stages the sequence in which Matthew sets himself up as a phoney 'millionaire's son' – it's shot with a directness of purpose that matches the killer's single-mindedness. The youth simply marches up to the first big house he sees, asks to use the telephone, then murders the friendly black maid with a cleaver before racing upstairs, smothering the old lady who owns the place, and cutting her pet dog's throat on the kitchen slab! Easy. The whole sequence is so neatly, concisely and shockingly done you have to laugh, horrible though it all is. Plus, it fires up the transgressive mood of the film even as it demonstrates the ruthless self-interest of the killer.

The film's major flaw is that people give the clearly unstable killer too much credence as a regular guy. Being a hooker, Vera really ought to spot her loony admirer's symptoms for what they are, as he fulminates against her sexual activities. The same goes for the maid who allows Matthew to use the phone. Other absurdities include scenes where Vera tries to escape while Matthew is out of the house. In one instance, all too common in films involving trussed up victims, a caller knocks at the door but, with help just a few feet away, Vera fails to make more than a squeak; as if all it takes to completely silence a captive is a piece of cloth tied over the mouth. There's another irritating moment when Vera dislodges a ringing phone from its wall-mounted hook, then stupidly uses the phone-cradle lever to dislodge her gag, thus ringing the caller off! She calls the operator, using her nose to dial, but can't form the sentences required to ask for help, until she's interrupted by Matthew who hangs up the phone. This last failure is at least explained by hysteria and panic, but the preceding silliness has made us impatient with Vera, when we should be rooting for her.

Depending on your mood, the film can feel either amusingly trashy, or unpleasant and claustrophobic. Despite its intended status as a schlocky exploitation pic, the second half of the film, concerning Matthew's attack on Vera's freedom and identity, is pretty tense and unsettling, like a slasher-film take on John Fowles's *The Collector*. *Scream Bloody Murder* isn't as smart or disturbing as Fowles's book, but it still has power. The killer's gauche tirades are simultaneously funny and horrible, as he buys his captive 'presents' in order to secure her co-operation: *"Look at this – a steak! Well who else ever bought you a steak before? Nobody, that's who. And paints, and an easel… an easel! How do you like that? There's more damn stuff here than you've ever seen in your life. But do you appreciate it? No, you don't appreciate it. Fine dresses and nice food, the best art stuff they had in the whole store. I'd like to have seen the sailor buy you stuff like this. Well he wouldn't – would he? WOULD HE?"* The stalker's lair scenario culminates in a battle of wills between free-spirited Vera and her repressive captor, and Ray engages our utmost sympathy for the woman. But will our feelings be mauled by one of those bleak endings so typical of the early seventies? Or can the feel-good factor prevail? You'll have to watch and see. In the meantime, let's hope *Scream Bloody Murder* eventually receives a much deserved overhaul on DVD, where I'm sure it will captivate a whole new generation of fans.

Marc B. Ray Interviewed

Early Days

Marc Benton Ray was born in 1940, in Klamath Falls, Oregon, an 'army brat' whose father was a Captain in the medical corps. His family moved to New York when he was just five, and Ray spent the rest of his childhood and adolescence there. After leaving school he studied method acting under Elia Kazan and Lee Strasberg at New York's famed Actors Studio, from 1956 to the early sixties, but he also studied the opposing tradition of classical theatre: "Between studying and teaching, I probably had the chance to play every major and secondary role that Shakespeare wrote," he recalls. Ray decided to move to the West Coast and continue his career in Hollywood. "I came to California to pursue acting, but I woke up one day, I was about twenty seven, and I wasn't an actor any longer. And I don't really know why for sure, except I know that I don't like actors! I like rehearsing, but there's something about being an actor in California, where it's mostly sitting around with other actors, and they're a totally different breed in California. You could be in a play in California and your leading actor will not show up because he just got a commercial somewhere – and I've directed plays where this has happened. You say to him, we've got an audience sitting here, we've been rehearsing three months, and he says, 'I have a commercial tomorrow morning, I have to get up at six o'clock or I'll get bags under my eyes, so I'm not coming!' No one in New York would do that."

In place of acting, Ray found himself writing for television; everything from variety to comedy to drama to children's shows. One of his earliest writing commissions came when a friend, producer/director David Winters,[1] invited him to write a documentary about motor racing. *Once Upon a Wheel* featured contributions from celebrated racing driver Mario Andretti and movie stars like Paul Newman and Kirk Douglas. Ray then collaborated on a lavish TV Special featuring Ann-Margret: "David Winters was my best friend at the time, we were actors together in New York. He was in the original *West Side Story* and he became a choreographer, much in demand. Ann-Margret's career as a young ingénue/sexpot was basically over, so she mounted a Las Vegas show after about a five years absence from film, to renew her career with a different image as a sexy multi-talented singer/actress. David was called in to choreograph it, and it was a big hit. David and his partner Burt Rosen sold it as a TV Special during the golden era of variety shows. David asked me if I wanted to write it, take a look at the nightclub act and convert it to TV. I said I'd never written anything, but he said he didn't trust Hollywood writers and wanted to work with someone he knew. We put the show on, it was a huge hit. I started doing specials for Bobby Gentry and Noel Harrison and Goldie Hawn, through the sixties and the beginning of the seventies. I did a Tom Jones TV show in Great Britain called *The London Bridge Special*, with Jennifer O'Neill, Kirk Douglas and Rudolph Nureyev. Douglas was in Rome at the time doing a movie called *Scalawag* (1973), and he was supposed to come to London to do his routines with Tom Jones, but he couldn't get there so we took everybody to Rome."[2]

above and below:
Scenes from Ray's debut **Wild Gypsies** (1969).

But, as a life-long movie fan, Ray realised that there was still one ambition he hadn't explored: "I wanted to apply my talents and skills to the cinema," he says. "My ex-wife's father was Ed Goldman, who along with her brother Michael Goldman owned Manson International and also some sister companies, including Taurus Films. At the time they specialised in distributing foreign-made independent movies in America and American independent movies overseas. I made a deal where I'd write and direct a film for them for nothing, for the experience. They asked for a softcore sex film about hot-blooded gypsies, and v*oila*!"

Wild Gypsies and *Scream Bloody Murder*

That film was *Wild Gypsies* (1969), which Ray helpfully summarises: "Hot-blooded gypsy guy meets fair-skin girl with big boobs, seduces her, fights with other guys, other hot-blooded gypsies dance around camp fires, get turned on, make out with each other, more fighting, more making out, gypsy music, fighting, breasts, music..."

This more or less covers *Wild Gypsies*, which is exuberant in places, but essentially a filler item that would only really pay off as a double bill with something a bit meatier. And something meatier was precisely what Ray had in mind for his next movie: "I approached Alan Roberts, who was successful producing and distributing porno films and wanted to go 'legit' with exploitation films. I made the same deal that I made with *Wild Gypsies* – I'd write and direct for nothing for the experience." Ray made several suggestions and the film script Roberts liked most was *Scream Bloody Murder*: once Ray had promised Roberts a set number of gory deaths, a budget of nearly $80,000 was raised. "He made an interesting deal with me," Ray explains. "In my contract he stated that the film 'must be gory' and that I would provide 'one gruesome murder in each reel of a ten reel film'. I outdid myself. We had ten gruesome murders, plus a gruesome killing of a dog. I did not get a bonus for the dog!"

For the leading role of Matthew, the mother-loving only child with a penchant for murder and kidnapping, Ray needed a young actor who could convey derangement and obsession. He struck lucky with Fred Holbert: "Fred was a messenger with a post-production company who came to an open audition," Ray recalls. "Earnest, hard-working, and sincere. He'd only done community theatre before. He was years older than he looked and brought an innocence and vulnerability to the role, as well as seeming to be off-kilter. He was gay, but didn't have a gay 'affect'. Because he was older playing younger it kind of leaked through as being vulnerable in a sort of Tony Perkins, Keir Dullea sort of way, and I liked him for that reason. He was never heard of again after our film." His co-star Leigh Mitchell, the victim of Matthew's love-obsession, was married to Ron Mitchell, the co-producer. "I don't know what became of her. I knew of her acting ability for years before hand. You know, of course, that she plays two roles in the film, the hooker and the mother. I did this so that the hooker would remind the killer of his mother." Ray describes this as "a corny device that didn't work", although interestingly it's precisely the approach used by David Cronenberg in his acclaimed adaptation of the Patrick McGrath novel *Spider* (2002). Another key member of the cast may not have seemed so important at the time, but he was to become one of the horror genre's most popular villains. Playing the doctor who sees through Matthew's pretense is 'Rory Guy', aka Angus Scrimm, the 'Tall Man' of the *Phantasm* films, who probably enjoys more dialogue in this one scene than in the four Coscarelli movies combined! Ray recalls "a quiet, reserved, and mysterious man. Kept to himself. Seemed to be quite smart. He was this ominous presence with this resonant voice, and when he spoke it seemed... very important!"

Conventional Hollywood wisdom says you can't build a film around an unsympathetic character. I don't agree, but having found that the coldness and spitefulness of Matthew's attitude prevented me from feeling much sympathy for him, I asked Ray his opinion on the subject: "I don't think there's a hard and fast rule about building a film around a sympathetic or not sympathetic character. If it works, it works. If it doesn't, it doesn't. You can illustrate either point with successful films based on one or the other side of the coin. Personally, I felt sympathy for Matthew because he was a victim of his obsessions and delusions and his warped childhood. It doesn't excuse his pathological behaviour, of course, but it does make him a more interesting and conflicted character, driven by inner demons and real psychosis rather than sheer evil. Matthew is sociopathic. He has no sense of other people's feelings, only his own wants and needs. He needs a car, he gets one. He needs a girl, he kidnaps one. He needs a house, he commandeers one. I just connected the dots. What did Matthew need next? Watch him get it, without a moment's concern for anyone else's wants, needs, feelings, or life."

The combination of bloody violence, added to the very bleak and downbeat mood, was common in seventies horror but is much less popular today. I asked Ray what could have influenced this nihilistic strain in his writing, where even the family dog gets butchered: "I was and am in fine spirits and take each day with humour and a grain of salt. My money-man wanted gore, and Technicolor blood was one of our biggest expenses. It was in the contract! There had to be one murder in every reel, so basically we were pacing them ten minutes apart. 'Gorenographic', as the original one-sheet said. As soon as I saw the film put together, I wished I had used much less blood. It would have been more frightening and more realistic. The excessive blood made the film too over-the-top and kept you from entirely suspending your disbelief. I wanted Matthew to kill the dog so (a) he could, in his mind, create a peaceful and trouble-free world for him and the hooker, (b) so we could shock the audience, and (c) to live up to my contractual obligation to provide lots of gore. By the way, the immobile dog with the cleaver in its neck never blinks its eyes because during the zoom in, I did a freeze frame on his opened eyes which made him look dead."

At which point, we British viewers of the film do a double-take: there is no such cleaver-in-the-dog's-neck shot in the British pre-certificate release on the 21st Century Video label. Despite his qualms about excessive gore, Ray laughs when I tell him this: "Too bad about those edits. A few of those closing shots are as gory as hell. Lots of blood. Hollywood filmmakers are always told to make it sexier for some countries, tone it down for others, more blood and guts for these countries, less violence for those. I guess some distributor didn't think you Brits have the stomach for some of the mayhem that went on so they cut it down for you. Toughen up. Americans like all the sex and blood they can get, and then some!"

The film defies its low budget by hopping energetically through several different locations. Ray recalls that the action was shot "all over L.A., wherever we could steal scenes without a permit, without insurance, and without getting caught. Once Matthew kills his folks, it's basically a road movie, he hits the road and makes murderous stops along the way, with no real destination in mind. The mansion he commandeers is now owned and occupied by Muhammad Ali and was used in the last *Rocky* film as Rocky's residence. It was owned by a minister, a very old man, who had a Christian radio show. His pool was fouled up and one of the guys in the crew was willing to go into the pool and remove the pump or filter and fix it for him. And he said, if you can fix it you can use my house for three days. So we fixed his pool pump and we got to use it."

As always with low-budget production, the film demanded 110% effort from the cast and crew: "We worked for ten days, eighteen hours a day, no days off, in order to maximize use of the rental equipment and keep the budget way, way down. Because I didn't attend film school or have any on-set experience other than as a writer or actor, I was compelled to concentrate on my weakness, the technical side, rather than the acting and character development, which was my strength. I was also solely responsible for getting the film done on-time and on-budget, so every minute detail down to gasoline for the trucks and coffee and doughnuts became my focus. I wish I could have concentrated on the actors and visual look and had someone else worry about the nuts and bolts, but, *c'est la vie*."

The hand-held camerawork, wide lenses, and tilted 'Dutch' angles used for the violent scenes were the work of Stephen Burum, a brilliant cinematographer who was just starting out at the time. He went on to shoot *The Outsiders* and *Rumblefish* for Francis Ford Coppola, before becoming a regular collaborator with Brian De Palma, shooting *Body Double*, *The Untouchables*, *Mission Impossible* and others. Ray knew he'd struck lucky with his DP: "Steve Burum is a born genius as a cinematographer. He starting filming when he was just a little kid, always knew he wanted to be a cinematographer. He taught at UCLA, and is among the very best there is. He was the cinematographer on some TV

specials I wrote, for Ann-Margret, Bob Hope, Raquel Welch, etc. We became friends and admirers of each others' work. He did the film as a favour to our friendship. He's truly gifted. His talent makes me and the film look much better than either of us deserve."

When it came to the editing, low-budget restrictions were very much to the fore: "My choices were limited to cut-and-paste. I was allowed very little time in editing due to cost constraints (rented room, rented Moviola), so most of what we did was splice. When you shoot so fast, you have very little coverage and very few retakes, so you're basically using the few shots you were able to get and don't have much room for editorial experimentation or creativity. I am proud of the editing in the kitchen scene where Matthew kills the black maid. It was filmed in two takes: Matthew pursues the camera, hacking at it. The camera pursues the maid who behaves like she's being hacked at."

Release and Reflection

Distribution was handled by producer Alan Roberts. Ray remembers: "The film played in many small towns and cities and lots of overseas venues. It's impossible to get a small film with no names into a major city or chain theatre. I didn't attend any early screenings but I saw the film much later in a theatre in Washington DC (they had two reels out of sequence) and opening night during a wind storm in a drive-in theatre in either North or South Carolina. A few hours after the theatre closed, the wind blew the screen down and the rest of the run was cancelled. By the way, the film was a big hit in Guam. I have no idea how successful the film was financially. We all worked for percentage points and none of us saw a dime. Distributors, though, always make money. They pass on what's left to the producers who deduct production costs and expenses. Add a little creative book-keeping and there's nothing left. It's common practice in the movie biz. If you want to hire a Certified Public Accountant and auditor and invest a lot of bucks to dig around, you might come up with a few dollars, but probably not. On little films, a distributor sells rights to a package of films, so you never have any idea how much of the package is your film. It happens every day. Even to movie stars and major directors. There are auditing firms working 365 days a year in Hollywood doing nothing but looking for clients' money."

Scream Bloody Murder was also released as *The Captive Female* and *Claw of Terror*, a choice made by the distributors, says Ray, "to maximize income potential and to re-release the same film under different titles at a later date." Of course, such capricious retitling is yet another factor which keeps the filmmaker in the dark about the true extent of his movie's profits: "Because it was produced by the distributors, they played the hell out of it, at home and overseas."

Marc Ray's shocking and enthralling horror film may be overdue for a revival, but he's far from convinced of that himself, admitting: "I'm afraid I didn't and don't attend horror films. I shouldn't have made this one, but it was a chance to get some much-needed filmmaking experience. I'm sure that someone who loves the genre would have done a much, much better job than I did. The same goes for *Wild Gypsies*. I'm 30 years older than I was when I made the film. The world has changed, I've changed. Nobody would give me a movie to direct and I wanted to learn and get one or two on my résumé. First time around, they wanted a nudie. I could have said no. I didn't – I made a nudie.

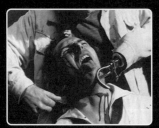

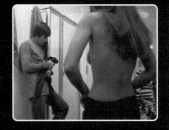

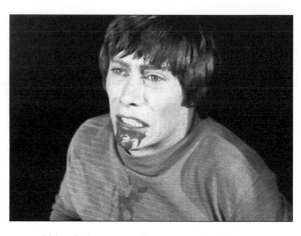

Second time around, they wanted blood and gore. Nobody forced me. I made blood and gore. I was hoping to make *Forrest Gump* one day. It would be best if the director was passionate about the kind of film he was making. I knew and know nothing about horror films. I'm a perfectionist and although the film was shot very, very fast on a tiny budget, all I can see are its huge imperfections. I think of the film as a cheap little exploitation film that doesn't elevate the human condition in any way, there is no moral or ethical lesson to be learned from it, its intent is to entertain by slaughter. It's just not who I am. I appreciate that you see merit in the film, I really do. But the way I'm wired, I can only see how much better it could have, and should have been. Given the money and time constraints, it could have been a five or a six. I missed by a mile."

Referring to the friends and colleagues who made *Scream Bloody Murder* with him, Ray reflects: "We were a fairly relaxed, counter-culturish group. It was, after all, Southern California during the height of the hippy, free-love, smoke pot, peace-and-love era. I was and am a liberal, civil-rights advocate, ex-freedom rider, pacifist. I had the privilege of having my two front teeth broken in a jail in Montgomery Alabama when I was punched in the face with my hands cuffed behind me. And sitting on the floor we were all made to sit side by side with our hands cuffed behind our backs, and this cop or Mountie came along and took out his dick and urinated on all of us, so that was a wonderful experience. Then when I was here in California there were a lot of anti-war demonstrations. When the last riots broke out here my mother called me up, she lived in Brooklyn, and she said I know you're gonna get involved, but please don't. I ended up going to hospital and rolling bandages, and driving people to hospital who had been beaten and dumped on the sidewalk."

Back to the Mainstream

After *Scream Bloody Murder*, Ray continued writing for film and television. For horror fans, the most notable of these credits is *The Severed Arm*, directed in 1972 by Thomas Alderman and produced by Gary Adelman (see review section). Ray explains how the script came about: "My father was an Army physician in World War II. He had told me about some sailors who were stranded for days in a raft and drew lots to consume one another's body parts in order to survive. Soon after severing one guy's arm and eating it, they were rescued. The guy without the arm always resented the other sailors, and they always lived in guilt. I thought it was a great basis for a story. Years later, on location for *Scream Bloody Murder*, a passer-by approached me and introduced himself. He said he was Gary Adelman and wanted to be a movie producer. He was looking for an idea for a horror movie. My mind was on watching them set up the next shot (Matthew meeting the hooker as she was painting in Venice), and I off-handedly told him my idea for the severed arm story. He took my phone number and called me a day or two later. He bought the story from me (I think for one hundred dollars), and the rest, as they say, is history."

After writing another lavish TV special, this time featuring Burt Bacharach and pop singers The Fifth Dimension (*"Up, Up and Away"*) grooving in 'Shangri-La', Ray's next major credit took him to the very heart of American culture. Strange though it may seem, the man behind *Scream Bloody Murder* became the only director interviewed for this book to have had his own parking space at the Disney Studios, when in 1976 he was entrusted with

stewardship of *The New Mickey Mouse Club*, the Disney Corporation's relaunched children's variety show. The original ran from 1955-59 and then in syndicated re-runs through the sixties and seventies. By the mid-seventies, though, the series was looking distinctly old-fashioned, and the Disney top brass decided that a new version was required. Ray explains the thinking: "In the mid-70s, Disney studios decided to recreate the *Mickey Mouse Club* TV series. Times had changed significantly since the original cutesy-poo version. The new version would be shot on multi-camera videotape, which Disney had never done before (only single camera film), and they wanted a contemporary feel to the show. My agent submitted me as head writer because I had a lot of experience in videotaped variety TV, and I was into the pop and rock music scene. They took a long, hard look at me, swallowed hard, and hired me to be the contemporary pulse of the show. In addition to my writing chores, Peter Martin and I wrote the theme songs for the daily shows, and I introduced them to 'Walkin' the Dog', 'Joy to the World', and some other rock classics. It was fun. I had a lot of independence, since they were brand new to this world. The old guard at Disney regarded me with some suspicion, especially in the executive dining room which I was privvy to. They wore white shirts and ties, I had long hair, a beard, and blue jeans. They also approached videotaping in the same manner as film, which I happily educated them in. There was a distinct hierarchy at Disney – which building your office was in, how nice your office was, where you parked, ate, who your visitors were, etc. – but since I had such a pivotal role in the production, I leapfrogged past some of the old-guard, which they weren't that thrilled about. Having said that, I want to emphasize that some of the most creative, intelligent, talented, sane and wholesome people I have ever worked with were employed at Disney studios. It was a pleasure to watch them work and get to know them."

However, as time went on, Ray found the film and TV world gradually less appealing: "I started writing movie pilots for TV, fixing other people's shows. I wrote one hundred episodes – five a week for twenty weeks – of *The New Mickey Mouse Club*, but of all those on the air, I don't think I've seen any. I'm just not interested. I don't think television's that good. I always had a movie under option until about ten years ago [1992] when I decided to get off the merry-go-round. I was doing okay pitching and getting things optioned but then you'd get a star attached and you couldn't get a director, or a director attached and you couldn't get a star. And I'm not the only one; that's the norm, the people who get a movie made are the lottery winners." So were any of these scripts likely to lead Ray back into the territory of *Scream Bloody Murder*? "I wrote a movie that I suppose could be called a horror movie because it concerns this woman who kills lots of people, and the guises she wears, a very intense psychological study called 'Who's Afraid of Junie Frequent'. It was optioned, and at one time it had Mia Farrow attached to it, and then it was called 'Season's Greetings' with the very young Winona Ryder attached to it. I was very strenuously trying to get Adrian Lyne to take a look at it. I really admire his directing."

Scream Bloody Patients!

Today, Ray's main avenue of work is psychotherapy, a field he first entered in the mid-1980s: "I was always fascinated by psychology, people's personal inner demons, and conflicted characters. Acting and writing, for me, are closely aligned with psychology because they're both interested, primarily, in mood and behaviour. 'Why did the character do that? What if he did this instead? What was he thinking? How did it affect other characters? How did he feel afterwards?' I got started in psychotherapy because as a young professional actor it was time to declare a major in college. I was thinking of medical school, paediatric psychiatry and neurosurgery. Since I was already severely bitten by the acting bug, the lure was much too great. Plus, that's where all the tasty babes were... certainly not in med school. Years later when I was a single parent of two small children, my ex-wife, a well-known model, left us for a young and dashing cardiologist. Since I was a freelance writer-producer-director with a feast-or-famine career, I knew that when college time for the kiddies rolled around, I'd better have a Plan B. So I went to grad school and

became a shrink, to supplement my income in case I needed it for their tuition. Parenthetically, I met and married a fabulous woman when I was interning in a Beverly Hills mental health clinic, a successful psychotherapist herself. My kids are terrific young adults and all is well with the world – except for the Middle East." He describes his therapeutic approach as: "Flexible, eclectic, it depends on who walks in the door, and what their issues are. People who get stuck in any one modality and have to cram every square peg into that one round hole find their patients leaving therapy very early. You have someone coming to see you and you present yourself in as real and authentic way as possible. Don't put on any airs, don't be 'the therapist' for them, don't be their 'guru', get into a real human relationship. It's actually very close to being a method actor, doing a real life improvisation."

So finally, as a therapist and a filmmaker, what does he think of the arguments surrounding the issue of screen violence? "It's a valid and ongoing debate with much fodder from both camps. Highly suggestible and unstable folks might (the operative word being 'might') get ideas and impetus from a movie and go out and do a bad thing. The average Joe can separate fact from fiction and knows what's appropriate behaviour and what isn't. There's always the occasional loose nut who'll put on a ski-mask and carve up the neighbourhood with a chain saw because he saw it on cable. He's one in a million and if he didn't learn it at the movies, he would have figured it out some other way. Billy Crystal said it best: 'If we're so influenced by films and TV, how come sit-coms don't make people funnier?'"

Footnotes

1 Winters is the British-born director of *The Last Horror Film* (1982), which reunited *Maniac* stars Joe Spinell and Caroline Munro.

2 Ray is referring to *Tom Jones' London Bridge Special*, in which the Welsh singer boards a double-decker bus in London searching for the famous London Bridge, and is magically transported to Lake Havasu, Arizona. Guest stars included Jennifer O'Neill, The Carpenters, Kirk Douglas, Rudolph Nureyev, Elliott Gould, Jonathan Winters, Chief Dan George, Lorne Greene, Charlton Heston, George Kirby, Michael Landon and Engelbert Humperdinck.

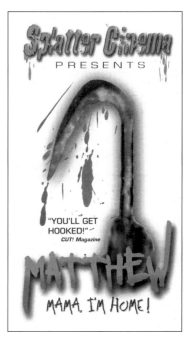

above:
Cover art for a US video release of **Scream Bloody Murder**, re-titled as **Matthew**.

opposite page, strip of images, from top:
Matthew's new stepfather (Robert Knox) finds that his stepson has issues;
A sailor (Ron Bastone) is gored to death for despoiling Matthew's new love;
Vera (Leigh Mitchell) held captive by Matthew (Fred Holbert);
Vera is forced to eat, in a tense dinner sequence;
Vera decides to use her feminine charms to intimidate her captor;
Matthew goes off the deep end;
Will that neck wound prove fatal?;
A figure from Matthew's tormented visions attacks him.

opposite page, top right:
Matthew as victim of his own sickness.

opposite, bottom right:
Plentiful gore and mutilation made **Scream Bloody Murder** a horror trailblazer in 1972.

MARC B. RAY: FILMOGRAPHY AS DIRECTOR

1969	*Wild Gypsies*
1972	*Scream Bloody Murder* aka *Matthew* aka *The Captive Female* aka *Claw of Terror*

AS WRITER FOR FILM & TV:

1968	*Once Upon a Wheel* (TV documentary) – dir: David Winters
1969	*Ann-Margret: From Hollywood with Love* (TV Special) – dir: David Winters
1971	*Lidsville* (TV Series pilot) – dirs: various
1971	*The 5th Dimension Traveling Sunshine Show* (TV Special) – dir: unknown
1972	*The London Bridge Special* (Tom Jones TV Special) – dir: David Winters
1972	*New Zoo Revue* (TV Series pilot) – dir: Tom Belcher
1972	*The Stoolie* – dir: John G. Avildsen
1973	*The Severed Arm* – dir: Thomas S. Alderman
1973	*Burt Bacharach in Shangri-La* (TV Special) – dir: Dwight Hemion

1975	*Ellery Queen* (TV Series) aka *The Adventures of Ellery Queen* (TV movie version) – dirs: various
1977	*The New Mickey Mouse Club* (TV Series) (75 episodes) – dirs: various
1979	*The Seeding of Sarah Burns* (TV movie) – dir: Sandor Stern
1984	*Kids Incorporated* (TV Series) (13 episodes) – dirs: various
1992	*Stepfather III* aka *Stepfather 3: Father's Day* – dir: Guy Magar

OTHER CREDITS:

1982	*Sandahl Bergman's Body* (exercise video)

AUTHOR:

1988	*Going All the Way: men and women talk about their first sexual experiences and the loss of innocence* (co-written with Eve Athey Ray)

SONGWRITER:

1977	*The All-New Mickey Mouse Club Album* (various songs)

They took away everything he
loved and cared for — and now he's

The ORPHAN

"The Orphan" is a gripping
psychological thriller —
don't watch it alone!

Written and Directed by JOHN BALLARD
Starring PEGGY FEURY ● JOANNA MILES ● DONN WHYTE
and introducing MARK OWENS as David with STANLEY CHURCH ●
ELEANOR STEWART ● AFOLABI AJAYI ● JANE HOUSE ●
ED FOREMAN ● JIM BRODER
Art Director, Production Supervisor SIDNEY ANN MACKENZIE
Production Supervisor PETER MULLER Theme song by JANIS IAN

©Sole distributor Hello Video Ltd. Licensed through Video Film Investments Ltd.

chapter 16

Growing Pains

John Ballard on the making of Friday the 13th: The Orphan

with contributions from Sidney Ann Mackenzie

Friday the 13th: The Orphan (1977)

The 1930s. When wealthy explorer Kevin De Ropp (Donn Whyte) and his wife Terri (Joanna Miles) are killed in a domestic shooting accident, their ten-year-old son David (Mark Owens) is left in the care of his Aunt Martha (Peggy Feury), who moves into the De Ropp family home, a large estate set in rambling grounds. David, an imaginative and sensitive boy who idolised his father, finds life without him difficult, and his relationship with stern, repressive Aunt Martha soon deteriorates. Martha, who means well but has no empathy for children, makes the mistake of criticising David's father; her subsequent attempts to guide and discipline David fall on stony ground, and he begins to despise her. For a while, he becomes close to Akin (Afolabi Ajayi), an African friend of his father's who lives on the estate, and enjoys playful banter with Dr. Thompson (Stanley Church), another of his father's old buddies who visits occasionally. He also forms a close connection with Mary (Eleanor Stewart), a servant woman. However, Aunt Martha grows resentful of these bonds, and when she sees Akin sharing a pipe with David in an African smoking ceremony, she orders Akin to leave the estate, demanding also that he should dispose of a live chicken David keeps in an old coop at the bottom of the garden. The coop is the boy's private den, almost hidden in the trees at the edge of the grounds where Aunt Martha rarely strays. Although forbidden to say goodbye to David, Akin sends him a note explaining that Martha demanded the chicken be killed. Consumed with rage at his Aunt, David spends more time down at the coop, collecting objects of talismanic significance and constructing his own belief system, drawing on African mysticism gleaned from his father and Akin, mutated by his own fevered imaginings. Central to his private iconography is 'Charlie', a stuffed chimpanzee, who occupies centre-stage on a raised dais. When Aunt Martha accidentally kills David's pet dog by slamming a door on it, he becomes fixated on prayers and rituals to destroy her. His friendship with Mary ends after he overhears her saying she doesn't care about him. While Mary is hanging sheets in the laundry room an unseen assailant attacks her, stabbing her to death. David runs in his pyjamas across snow-covered countryside to the Ford house, claiming to have heard Mary being murdered by Aunt Martha, but the Fords simply return him back home. Martha tells David she's decided to send him away to boarding school: falling asleep, he has a nightmare in which he's admitted to an orphanage with filthy interiors, broken furniture, and rusting beds upon which disturbed children are tied up: Dr. Thompson and his Aunt, the latter disguised as a man, take him to a filthy operating theatre and cut out his tongue. On waking, David sees his Aunt go down to the coop. Enraged at the thought that she might destroy 'Charlie', he follows her...

Literary in both source and style, *The Orphan* is a secret garden in American horror, barely acknowledged in genre writing so far but worthy of much closer inspection if you appreciate subtle psychological chills. Director John Ballard's resolute emphasis on character, and relative disinterest in physical violence, may have contributed to *The Orphan*'s neglect since its initial release, but I urge you to see this highly individual film. It's loosely based on *Sredni Vashtar*, a marvellously mordant short story by the British writer Saki (aka H.H. Munro) – whose tales, though rarely drawn upon, provide excellent material for film adaptation (Claudio Guerin Hill's *La campana del infierno* (1973) used Saki's story *The Open Window* to great effect for one sequence). It's also worth checking out *The Orphan* if you enjoyed Bergman's *Fanny and Alexander* (1982), and I was reminded of it too when I saw Neil Jordan's brilliant film *The Butcher Boy* (1997), but there are few precursors; perhaps *The Orphan*'s only cinematic parent is Jack Clayton's *The Innocents* (1961).

Vital to the film's success is young Mark Owens, who makes David a credible and sympathetic figure. His expressions of incandescent rage at 'The Woman' (as he twice refers to Aunt Martha) have the primal energy of hatred that many a child, powerless to act in an unjust world, can summon. As is often the case when the powerless have nowhere to turn, religion provides an outlet, and Owens is particularly outstanding in the scenes where he assembles his religious iconography and prays, sometimes in the clasp-handed style of Christian worship and other times in emulation of African tribal trance-states. His sleepy, slightly deer-like features suddenly animate into blazes of emotion. It's a pity he didn't go on to act in other films, because in *The Orphan* he shows the promise of a young Wil Wheaton: he could certainly have held his own in a movie like *Stand By Me*.

opposite page:
This UK video release from Hello Video, who also released George Romero's **The Crazies** and **Martin**, wisely dispensed with the **Friday the 13th** tag (on the cover at least) and marketed the film as **The Orphan**; although the sleeve's promise of a 100-minute version was a trifle misleading – the 'Hello' version actually weighs in at just under 74 minutes.

below:
Mark Owens as David.

Friday the 13th: The Orphan
aka **Betrayal** (shooting / pre-release title)
aka **Killers of the Dream** (pre-shooting title)
aka **Killer Orphan**
© 1977. The Fragment Co.
World-Northal Corporation presents a Cinema
Investments Co. & Gilman-Westergaard
production in association with Trimedia
Southwest Associates.
writer/director: John Ballard. suggested by the
short story "Sredni Vashtar" by Saki (H.H.
Munro). producers: John Ballard, Sidney Ann
Mackenzie, Sondra Gilman, Peter Muller,
Louise Westergaard. director of photography:
Beda F. Batka. art director: Sidney Ann
Mackenzie. editor: John Ballard, Sidney Ann
Mackenzie, Susan E. Morse. musical score
composed and conducted by Teo Macero. "I
Need to Live Alone Again" composed and
performed by Janis Ian, an exclusive Columbia
Records Artist produced by Ian Janis and Ed
Sprigg, arranged by Janis Ian, recorded at the
Hit factory, New York, November of 1977,
©Mine Music Company, 1977. "Don't Make Me
Laugh" and "Did You Ever Dream" vocalist:
Judy Roberts, lyrics: Carl Sigman, music: Teo
Macero. musical score composed and
conducted by Teo Macero. additional orches-
trations: Homer Dennison. associate
producers: Rita Fredricks, Anne Murphy,
Lance Bird. production supervisor: Peter
Muller. additional photography: Robert Kaylor.
editorial consultant: Ralph Rosenblum A.C.E.
music editing: Dan Pinsky. assistant editors:
Nancy Attas, Barbara Kopple, Susan Behr,
Laura Morgan, Susan Bradoon, Stephane
Wallach. production managers: Joseph
Mansfield [Joseph Masefield], Boyce Harman.
assistants to the producers: Chip
Kurtzenhauser, Joshua Silver, Jim Reiser, Bob
Warden. production stills: Patrick Owens, Lee
Owens, Mark Owens. additional art director:
Laura Morgan. sound effects: Ross - Gaffney.
sound editor: Bud Nolan. mixer: Richard
Weigle. negative matching: Irving Rathner,
Scott Rathner. opticals: E.U.E. Opticals. in
appreciation: Ann and Tom Payne; John
Hammond; John Mackenzie, Jr.; John and
Adele Ballard, Sr.; Peter and Charles Schulze;
Michael Shiffrin; Chenko Studios; Phyllis
Craig; Lucy Meyer. filmed in 1968. Town
sequences filmed on location at Waterloo
Village (New Jersey, USA).
Cast: Mark Owens (David). Peggy Feury (Aunt
Martha). Joanna Miles (David's mother). Donn
Whyte (David's father). Stanley Church
(Doctor Thompson). Eleanor Stewart (Mary).
Afolabi Ajayi (Akin). Jane House (Jean Ford).
Ed Foreman (Percy Ford). Jim Broder. Dennis
Watlington. Gregory Juviler. Lynn Kirchoff.
Jeanne Graham. Romero Rochan. Malachy
McCourt. Marion Clark. Cathrine Andrea. John
Grossman. Elizabeth Astrid. Elin Payne.
Cheryl Blodget. Tory Payne. Emil Grundtvig.
Hadley Rowena. Charles Evan. Kermit Stang
and Henry.

opposite page, from top:
Scenes of **The Orphan**:
David's dead father (Donn Whyte);
David;
Aunt Martha (Peggy Feury);
David with Dr. Thompson (Stanley Church);
Martha and a party guest discuss David's
father;
Symbolic – but what can it mean?;
Jolly Dr. Thompson...
...hands David a gun.

Then there's Peggy Feury, a skilled and thoughtful actress who demonstrates here how she came to be one of the guiding lights in her profession. (She taught acting at the Actors Studio, alongside Lee Strasberg.) The role of Aunt Martha is already well-written, but Feury brings her own subtle shadings to the part. It would have been easy for Martha to become simply an ogre or mad-woman, but despite the film giving emotional bias to the boy's point of view, Feury's performance shows us a complex and troubled woman who sometimes tries – and then fails – to do the right thing. Of course there's much to criticise about Martha: like many of the adults in the film, she's appallingly racist, screeching *"Don't you touch me, you black nigger man!"* when Akin tries to protect David, and then informing him in more 'reasonable' tones later that she doesn't want David associating with anything 'dirty'. She's referring to the smoking ritual she saw the two of them practising, but the careless ambiguity of her words speaks volumes for the way racist whites felt towards blacks in the thirties. Feury's watchful, hooded, grey-blue eyes have a potential for cruelty and scorn, but she softens this by adding a sort of defeated weariness; this is a woman whose life has gone sour years ago, and the presence of her sister's child in her life merely underlines her lack of love and intimacy. There's a suggestion that she once had a relationship with Kevin, David's father, until he dropped her and married her sister instead, but since we only see this as a sort of midnight reverie on Martha's part, it's unclear whether it's true or just a fantasy. Later, in a sexually loaded context, Mary says to her, *"You knew Kevin as well as I did,"* but this statement hinges on a double ambiguity – we're also unsure whether Mary might actually be David's true biological mother. And in one of the film's saddest scenes, we see Martha trying to reproduce the rapport she witnessed Mary enjoying with David earlier (during a game of 'statues') by compelling the boy to dance an awkward waltz with her around the sitting room.

At the heart of this story is a boy who feels a powerful need for the love and companionship of a father. When David's father dies, Martha tries to control the boy by denying him the companionship of others. In a trait that leads to her downfall, Martha resents David's love for his father, and tries to corrupt it. The boy has a persistent asthmatic cough, and Martha makes a point of claiming he inherited this 'weakness' from his dad. As with David's friendship with Akin, his love for his pet chicken, and the contents of his shed, Martha is motivated by resentment of anything that might mean independence of mind for the boy, and at the film's emotional core is the repudiation of that oppression.

Perhaps the film's only real mis-step is that David's fantasy image of his father is conveyed in such a sentimentalised way; in fact at first I was tempted to read it as parody. On a snowy mountainside, David runs to his father and the two embrace, while twirling round in slow-motion to the strains of a rather slushy orchestration. David's father is handsome in a Kay's Catalogue sort of way, and his slightly bland Marlboro-Lite features further enhance the feeling of parody. Once you accept that the feelings are genuine, though, it's worth making an allowance for this sentimental miscalculation: the psychological dimension of the story proves to be far more subtle and accomplished than this early scene suggests. What's more, one must be careful not to bring adult

cynicism into play when dealing with a child's percep-tions. The music and the slow-motion may be miscalcu-lated, but the snowy mountainside setting fits a boy's vision of his father as a hero; it's like a fantasy drawn from the novels of Jack London. And declarations of love between parents and children, though sometimes too casually slipped into American speech, do have real emotional currency. In short, if you rescore the scene with ambient wind sounds and the crunching of snow underfoot, the whole thing would work just fine.

Ballard began *The Orphan* in 1968, a very loaded year for inter-generational relations. Out of step with the zeitgeist, he chose to tell a story which actually values the father as a symbolic figure, running counter to the revolu-tionary fervour of the Youth Movement, with its iconoclasm and rejection of patriarchal authority. Jim Morrison was killing his father and fucking his mother in his song 'The End' (1967) but Ballard looked back into childhood with a different eye. Traditionally, in Freud, the son sees the father as a rival for the mother's affection, and begins the process of socialisation only when he repudiates his desire for the mother and accepts the Oedipal father's authority (leading to a mixture of hate/adoration of the father that propels many Oedipal narratives). *The Orphan* is unusual in two ways: it fails to explore the protagonist's feelings for his dead mother (a directorial oversight one could regard as significant in Freudian terms), and it sees David's feelings running contrary to the conventional love/hate dynamic. The father here is far from a traditional authority figure: more anarchist than lawgiver. He's the archetype of the daring explorer, absent for long stretches but affectionate to his son when he returns, and full of inspiring stories about the wonders of the wider world. He thus represents freedom from domestic structures, where women are traditionally in control. The father's oblique relationship to conventional patriarchy puts him in cahoots with his son, not against him. The fact that he is often absent from the family home means that he appears 'irresponsible' to other adults, a point made by one of the Fords: *"If Kevin had stayed at home with his son where he belonged, instead of jackassing around Africa, he would never have died... Being a father means being there at all times."* Dr. Thompson, Kevin's friend, replies: *"Oh hell, Kevin was away from David for years, but I'd be willing to bet that David has a better sense of his father as a man than most boys have."* And it's borne out by other scenes which reinforce Thompson's argument: the father retains the love of his son because his adventurer's life in Africa inspires the boy. *"Oh David, you'd love it there. All the animals run free,"* he says. It's when this powerful ally and compatriot is (accidentally) killed by the mother, who then kills herself, that David enters a darker psychological realm; and when he is forced to live with the puritanical, overbearing Martha, and suffers a variety of emotional losses (his hen, his dog, and his relationships with Akin and Mary), we see what may be the birth of a future psychotic. (The film retains some ambiguity about this – see interview.)[1]

One face of Western patriarchy that Ballard summarily dismisses in *The Orphan* is Christianity. We see David placing 'Charlie' on a makeshift altar and kneeling before it, with his hands pressed together in prayer. Ballard then cuts to a shot of David kneeling in church as a line of Catholic worshippers take the communion wafer in their mouths. When it's his turn, David refuses the sacrament and throws the wafer on the floor. *"He's not my father,"* he explains. David's choice of a chimp as his Godhead is also significant, both because of the suggestion of nature-worship (paganism) and for the particular antipathy Christians have for Darwin (whose theory of Natural Selection is often condensed to the image of a chimpanzee). The relationship between Akin and David also brings in non-Christian associations, especially during the scene in which Martha finds the two smoking together. David has already absorbed African influences from the tales his father told to him, and his worship of his new god involves dancing to achieve a trance state. Christianity did its utmost to stamp out religious practises built around intoxicating drugs or dancing to trance-inducing music (although the latter snuck back in via the Pentecostalists), and it's obvious that, for Martha, intoxication (and by inference hedonism, physical pleasure) is associated with sinfulness and depravity. When she finds David and Akin sitting cross-legged, both dressed in African robes and exchanging the pipe together, we see the ritual through her suspicious eyes, and to her it seems alien. Shot from her paranoid point of view, there's a homoerotic charge to the fingering of the mouthpiece, the wiping of the nozzle with the thumb, the slow, measured exchange of the pipe between two males. The exclusion of women is something that many African tribes practise, and twice Akin tells David to remember that he is his father's child. This advice, and similar remarks from Dr. Thompson, suggest the way in which traditional male identity is predicated on a rejection of the feminine.

This 'cult of masculinity' is complemented by the story's concurrent depiction of women as variously possessive, neurotic, untrustworthy or soul-denying. In the most questionable of the film's choices, David's mother is given almost no screen attention at all. David never even mentions her death, even though it's implied that he saw the accident in which she shot her husband and then herself. Mary, on the other hand, is both sister, mother and wife. She looks out for his interests like a protective older sibling. She says to David that she knows she can never be his mother, but hopes that he will come to think of her as such: David then places a ring on her finger and says *"Til death do us part."* Thus are all the familial feminines incorporated. It's Mary who is the sole repository of feminine value, and for most of the film she's a good balance for the paternal weight of the narrative. (In constructing Mary like this, Ballard softens Saki's tale, which refers to the unnamed servant only as "sour-faced".)

As Ballard reveals later in this chapter, *The Orphan* went through a pruning process at the hands of its female producers before its eventual screen debut in 1978 (ironic, considering the story). Several subtleties were lost, a shorter running time was imposed, and the overall structure was distorted. Watching *The Orphan*, one can sense that there were difficulties in production, but after a rather bumpy first ten minutes even this shorter version (which is, after all, the only one we have) stands up as a genuinely thoughtful exploration of child psychology. If Ballard loses Saki's sly humour, and his maliciousness (the original *Sredni Vashtar* is as funny as it is macabre), he brings to the tale enough compassion and seriousness to repay our close attention.

John Ballard & Sidney Mackenzie Interviewed

"Vincent Canby said, 'It's always refreshing when a director's first film isn't autobiographical,' and I had to laugh, because in a really subtextual way it was."
– *John Ballard*

The Orphan is one of the most literate, intelligent and unusual films covered in this book. Its journey to the screen was long and troubled, and the fact that it did eventually see a release is a testament to the tenacity of its director, John Ballard. I was fortunate enough to meet Ballard when he came to England with his wife, the renowned jazz singer Jackie Ryan, for her concert at Ronnie Scott's Jazz Club in Soho, London, in October of 2003. He's a tall, rangy man, soft-spoken and thoughtful, and he gave very generously not only of his time but also of his personal memories. The story of *The Orphan* is drawn partly from a literary source, but Ballard adapted his screenplay by drawing creatively on aspects of his own childhood experience. Where some genre filmmakers are happiest working, at least at the conscious level, with material outside of their own lives (Bill Rebane's *The Giant Spider Invasion* for instance is not a film you would scrutinise for psychological undercurrents), *The Orphan* is a truly individual piece of work that has to be considered in a different aesthetic framework. It explores aspects of what Freud called 'the family romance', bringing insight and empathy to the story of a young boy's slide into madness.

The film has only ever been available on video as *Friday the 13th: The Orphan*, with a copyright date of 1977. In fact, *The Orphan*, or *Betrayal* as it was first called, actually began shooting in 1968! The film's release came after many years during which the director struggled to complete a final cut, and in order to secure that release Ballard had to accept some last-minute changes inflicted on the film by the latter-day producers. Keen, after ten years of effort, to at least have *some* version of the film released, Ballard agreed to these changes, and the film had its brief time in the sun. Since then, however, it has been neglected by horror fans, something I hope this chapter will change. *The Orphan* might not have the shock value of some of the other great films covered in *Nightmare USA*, but it's stylish and well-acted, and it explores a troubled child's experiences in an honest, unexploitative way.

Beginnings

John Ballard was born in Manhattan in 1947. A child prodigy and accomplished oil-painter by the age of seven, his talent was soon recognised by his parents, who sent him to art school in Vance, Canada. His talents were many and varied: he drew cartoons and painted, as well as writing plays and short stories. His parents initially harboured business hopes for their son, but once they saw how advanced he was as an artist, they wound up supporting his creative ambitions.

Ballard left school and went to Harvard, where he became good friends with Peter Muller, soon-to-be co-producer of *The Orphan*. "In those days there were no film programs in college, so we started a film club," he recalls.

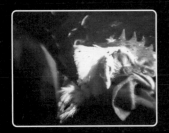

While studying at Harvard, Ballard found himself drawn in another direction: "I was deeply interested in aberrant psychology. At Harvard they called it 'Nuts and Sluts' – that's what I majored in! I was especially interested in autism, and also child abuse. In 1963/64 people really weren't 'into' child psychology at all. My thesis at Harvard was about role models and identity, I studied with Erik Erikson, who was a disciple of Freud's."

After leaving Harvard, Ballard went to NYU (New York University) Graduate School for Film and Television. NYU, along with UCLA in California, was one of the few places in the country at the time to offer such a course. "It purported to offer a year studying film in New York, a year at a Hollywood studio, and then a third year in Europe as apprentice to a European filmmaker," Ballard recalls. "None of that came about! They got the *crème de la crème* to go to that school but they had no funding and no equipment. So we went off and made our own films." In his class were: Jeremy Paul Kagan (future director of *The Chosen*); Ron Maxwell (*Gods and Generals*); Jeff Young (*Been Down So Long It Looks Like Up to Me*); and Paul Caponigro, one of the country's top black and white photographers and a disciple of Ansel Adams. Adams himself occasionally lectured at NYU, and Ballard recalls: "The school was so badly equipped that his lectures on the use of the light-meter were done entirely by drawing on a blackboard, because we didn't have any light meters! Most of us quit school and joined the school of hard knocks and made our own films after a year. I had a little Bolex and I shot a lot of surrealistic, sort of macabre Buñuelish fantasy things."

The first of these was a thirty-minute movie called *The Toy*. Ballard explains, "At the time I was dating one of twins, and so that worked well for the film, they're both in it. And I met twin teenage boys and they're in the film too." So given the time the films were made and the surrealistic nature of the subject-matter, were hallucinogens a research tool for Ballard? "Drugs were certainly something I experimented with, but at the same time I did not admire or respect Timothy Leary one iota. Whereas Bob Dylan…" Ballard's respect for Dylan inspired him to act as cinematographer and assistant director on Jeff Young's 1967 short film, *The Lonesome Death of Hattie Carroll* (the title comes from a Dylan song of the same name based on a real life murder case, in which a rich young white man beat to death a black barwoman but received a mere six-month sentence). He also shot a documentary on the celebrated writer Jorge Luis Borges. "He was lecturing in New York so I filmed the lecture and then interviewed him. I took kind of a straight-ahead, very cerebral approach." He laughs: "And then I just jumped into a making a feature. I didn't know you weren't supposed to do that at twenty one!"

Pre-Production

Ballard's interest in psychology naturally found succour in his cinema-going. It was the mid-1960s, and the European art film was a major force. Ballard loved Ingmar Bergman's movies for their intense psychological explorations ("In *The Orphan*, when the boy is trying to get some emotional strength by building this altar to his father and keep that memory alive, there's a point where there are two mirrors, and the father and son's images merge together – I was drawing on Bergman's *Persona*," he admits). The early films of John Cassavetes (particularly *Shadows* and *Faces*) provided an American

equivalent. Roman Polanski also registered strongly on Ballard's creative radar, with *Repulsion* in particular striking a deep chord.

In 1967 John Ballard met Sidney Ann Mackenzie, who became his partner and collaborator for the next eight years, until the couple broke up, amicably, in 1975. Mackenzie is credited as producer, and fulfilled many other roles. She was Ballard's friend, creative lieutenant, and lover: "Everything I didn't do, she did!" he laughs. "All you need is two people on camera and sound, and lights, and away you go." Together, they began setting up production on *The Orphan*, which began life as a script called 'Killers of the Dream' (a title borrowed from a Lillian Smith novel) built on the foundation of a short story by Saki, aka H.H. Munro, called *Sredni Vashtar* (of which more later). Says Ballard, "I was looking for a story and it just resonated with me. I started to build on it, using the emotional underpinnings."

Ballard received a strong initial boost from his father, who invested in the project: Sidney Mackenzie recalls, "Money came from friends and family. John's dad put some money in at the start. Independent investors came in later: at one point there were two very suspicious characters from New Jersey who said they had a laundry business – I didn't know what it meant at the time! I thought it was very odd that they didn't want to see the script and they didn't want to see any of the footage! We were a little on the naive side!"

Casting was obviously key to such a character-led film, and for the central role Ballard found a talented young unknown called Mark Owens: "I went to a professional children's acting school. Most of the kids I saw were really kind of spoiled, you know, Pepsodent-smile types. Most child actors in those days were doing toothpaste commercials. It came down to two: Clark Collins, the son of Judy Collins, the folk singer – he had red hair and green eyes, and I was attracted to that as I had red hair, so it fitted the role. But then I noticed this one shy kid in the cafeteria, Mark Owens, and just immediately screen-tested him. He was a bit aloof, very inward-looking, and hadn't done a whole lot of commercials, and when I worked with the two doing tests I realised he was the one, with the right sort of interior life."

As the makers of the Harry Potter films realised, there are problems working with young actors; they mature at lightning speed, so that scenes shot a year apart reveal the swift growth of the actor, making it difficult to match shots. "Fortunately, Mark had a nice supply of kid brothers," laughs Ballard. "Two younger kid brothers for the voice – you know, your voice changes at thirteen. Mark was ten when the film began shooting. When we finished he was about seventeen! For the birthday party, in the still shots at beginning, we had to use a different boy who looked exactly like him."

For the role of Akin, Ballard cast Nigerian actor Afolabi Ajayi: "We had the first African in a lead role, Afolabi Ajayi. We filmed a whole lot and then he died, and we had to stop; we wound up using doubles for a lot of scenes." (Ajayi, a footballer, collapsed and died while playing in Central Park.)

Behind the camera, Ballard began with Robert Kaylor[2] and for a while Bill Butler.[3] Eventually, as the fragmented shooting schedule made it difficult to hold a team together, Ballard was joined by the talented Czech émigré Beda Batka, who shot the majority of the film. Batka brought an inventiveness and openness to new ideas that reflected his experience making critically-lauded films in his homeland. Ballard recalls him coming up with unusual solutions to technical limitations: "Beda Batka was quite capable of doing the fluid camera we wanted. He was from

Czechoslovakia, he trained Milos Forman, he trained Ján Kadár, he did twenty six feature films there. Then he came over here and he couldn't get a job as a DP. They wanted him to start as a focus puller! He was a teacher at NYU and he moonlighted to do this job, but unfortunately he had these union problems and it was hard to get work. We had an Arriflex, blimped so we could do the sound scenes, but we were doing a lot of hand-held stuff as well. For the low angles under the bed, we had a little metal pipe on the floor and we rolled the camera back and forth and swivelled it around on the pipe to get that 'five inches from the carpet' feel, which gave us flexibility of movement without jerking. We only had tracks for a few early scenes, in the town at the beginning, the meeting at the teahouse etc."

Sidney Mackenzie recalls, "Most of the horror films, the really raunchy ones, were filmed over a weekend because New York at that point was mostly used for commercials. The commercials people would return all the rental equipment to F & B Ceco, which was the main place where everybody rented from, and then the horror film people and the independent people like us would come in on Friday and rent over the weekend because it was cheaper. There were people shooting just unthinkable things out in warehouses in Queens over the weekends that way! There was one Latino guy who raised Chihuahuas who rented his equipment from F & B Ceco's, then he would go out to this warehouse in Queens and film things about naked women being impaled on gigantic phalluses on the wall – and then he would take them down because it was a meatpacking warehouse during the week! It was a *really* attractive crowd! He was sweet, the dogs were really nice!"

I asked Mackenzie about her responsibilities as a producer: "Well… Peggy Feury was a narcoleptic, so it would usually start with trying to get Peggy to wake up at six in the morning for an early call. Calling it 'producing' is a joke really, we all did everything. John was director so he took most responsibility, but Beda did a lot of it, I did a lot of it, you know, holding the mike boom, getting coffee, digging around for things, doing props, doing continuity, I mean, anything. One of the things that was a big fat joke was that according to the union we had to have a production manager. So even at that point Joe Masefield got paid, I think, $500 a day. Unbelievable. All he had to do was screech and yell 'time is money!' at people every five minutes! At one point they made us have a Teamster boss; there was some ridiculousness where he had to be paid a thousand dollars a day to come and check on us."

Exterior shooting incorporated some footage taken in the Catskill Mountains, and the North shore of Long Island, near Oyster Bay. David's bedroom was actually cinematographer Beda Batka's New York apartment. Sidney Mackenzie recalls, "The estate was actually my uncle's. We went to look at everybody's house who might possibly put up with us. My uncle was away for most of the shoot and we never filmed on the inside." Ballard continues, "We did most of the shooting in 1968, about 75% of it, some in 1969, and over the years until 1978 we'd shoot a little scene here, a cutaway there. The orphanage scenes were shot in 1968 on Roosevelt Island, where bits of *The French Connection* were filmed. We were experimenting with a really wide-angle lens, which you couldn't get for a Panaflex, you couldn't get a real fish-eye. So we had to jury-rig one from a Nikon. For the long orphanage tracking shot, we used a spider dolly, where the wheels on the dolly narrow so you can get it through a doorway."

Inevitably, some scenes were cut together from footage spread over several years shooting, as Ballard explains: "There's the scene where Mary is in the basement hanging up the sheets, and it's obviously some sort of fantasy scene because there are a lot of sheets there! So she senses someone else is in the room, there's a little wind, the sheets flapping, and she sees the shadow behind a sheet. She pulls the sheet back and there are just clothes hanging there and she thinks that's it. Then she's grabbed and rolled in the sheets by these unseen hands, and stabbed. And that was done with hardly any blood back in 1968, with the bloodier shots added in 1970-71."

Post-Production

When it came to making sense of the patchwork of material, Ballard was fortunate to work closely with one of the film industry's most respected editors, Ralph Rosenblum. Mackenzie recalls, "We got stuck on the editing at one point, so I said, 'Okay John, you tell me all the films that you've liked the editing of,' and he went through a list of films and believe it or not every one of them had been edited by Ralph Rosenblum! He had edited *On the Waterfront* and a lot of amazing things." Ballard adds: "Ralph Rosenblum had edited *The Pawnbroker*, he really saved the career of William Friedkin, who had made a movie called *The Night They Raided Minsky's* that was a year-and-a-half in the editing room; and he edited all of Woody Allen's early films. I worked as an editor for ten years off and on, on this film of mine, a lot of it at Ralph's place, where Woody would be in one room and I'd be in another room and Ralph would be going back and forth. So I got to go to all the early mixes of *Annie Hall*, *Sleeper* – just four of us in a room."

Rosenblum's skill at salvaging troubled productions helped when Afolabi Ajayi died during production (just as it had when Bert Lahr died during the shooting of Friedkin's *The Night They Raided Minsky's*). Ballard was also editing the film at home, as he explains: "I bought an old Moviola and taught myself how to edit. My whole apartment was filled, I was living with the film. I was definitely obsessive with some of the cutting. It's so physical; you develop a

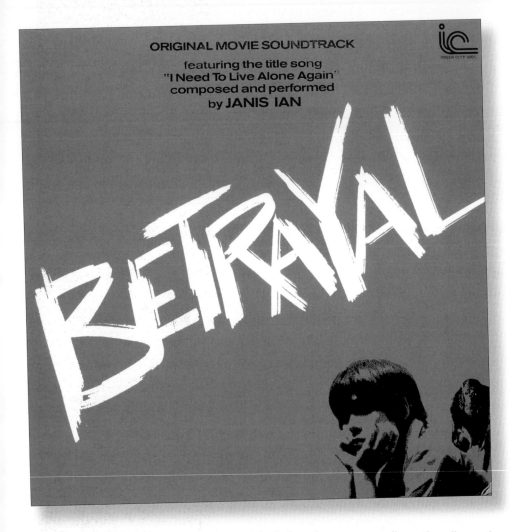

ORIGINAL MOVIE SOUNDTRACK

featuring the title song
"I Need To Live Alone Again"
composed and performed
by JANIS IAN

INNER CITY 4001

BETRAYAL

above:
A soundtrack album was released prior to the film's retitling by the Westergaards, and bore the earlier title **Betrayal**.

opposite page, from top:
Akin kills the hen;
David's rage builds;
A quote from Bergman's **Persona**;
Akin says goodbye to David and gives him his father's ring;
Sometimes Aunt Martha does dreadful things...;
David's father and mother argue;
His mother takes her own life;
Mary the maid is stabbed to death while entangled in cotton sheets.

certain rhythm where you can really see the splices go by as they're screened. You rent a little theatre, bring some reels up, look at it on the big screen, bring it home, edit on that little postcard-size screen on the Moviola, and then there's the sound editing, when you get into multiple tracks... it's just like a giant sewing machine basically! Some scenes, like the ape attack, you keep shortening and shortening things, there's a tendency to do that, and then you wind up with perfectly cut individual scenes, but when you put them with other scenes they're out of balance. So what Ralph was good at was looking at the whole and then coming down from there. Ralph did all the finishing." (Incidentally, *The Orphan*'s assistant editor, Rosenblum's protégé Susan E. Morse, went on to edit all of Woody Allen's films between *Manhattan* in 1979 and *Celebrity* in 1998.)

It was during this long process that Ballard came within an ace of a directing job that could have put his name on the big-time circuit: *The Exorcist*. "My agent brought me in. We were down to like three directors. I was interested in the material but I really wanted to do something very different with it. I thought it was very wooden, in a way. I really didn't think it would go very far! [laughs] I didn't care for it that much."

Last Minute Changes

In 1977, with the film stalled and still unfinished, Ballard began to think about another project, based on his observations of inner-city black youth. The planned project was called 'Hoops'. Unexpectedly, however, this new idea provided the impetus for *The Orphan*'s belated completion: "I started work on 'Hoops' and I had these two people come to

see me, Sandra Gilman and Louise Westergaard, who wound up producing on Broadway but they hadn't done any entertainment before, so I was kind of their guinea pig. 'Hoops' was going to be a totally opposite thing to *The Orphan*, a drama-documentary about inner-city basketball, which was unknown at the time. Sandra and Louise wanted to see something else I had done so I showed them *The Orphan*, and they said, 'Well, why don't we finish this off first?'"

Ballard has mixed feelings about their influence on his fortunes: "They were great in getting the money together, but they also had a kind of puritanical streak. Because they had children, they didn't want their children seeing certain films. As it turned out it was just a tax shelter deal for this Texas investor who came in. So they wound up hacking apart Ralph's work on the film. We filmed some extra scenes which were good. We had to shoot an alternate scene of the dad, so the parents die in the fight. First the boy has an idealistic view of his parents, but then you see them arguing at that same birthday party where she's dressed up in the wings and bird feathers. She lunges at him and he has a toasting fork and it goes into her neck. So we did all that and it was just too bloody for them, so we staged the gun scene. But then they cut out the sexual scenes and the little surrealistic scenes that had all these other meanings."

Gilman and Westergaard also insisted on a title change, quite breathtaking in its meaninglessness. Says Ballard, "It was called *Betrayal* when they first saw it, but they wanted to make it more of a horror thing. The *Friday the 13th* title wasn't my idea at all, although we were actually ahead of the other production. They put in these clunky-looking block lettering titles. I thought *The Orphan* was fine, and then they wanted to do *Friday the 13th: The Orphan*. They wanted a gimmick, a hook, and they just imposed it on the film. They put in these dates, captions, you know, and then the last date was Friday the 13th."

Ballard's final cut, as finished by Ralph Rosenblum, was 110 minutes. However, by the time the Westergaards had finished with it, the film was down to 80 minutes. "We had so much beautiful stuff that's not in there, things that added dimensions and texture," Ballard says, ruefully.

Another area of contention was the score, handled by Teo Macero. Ballard recalls, "I had met him – I was going to get Joe Zawinul and Weather Report, but they were too far out for Sandra and Louise. Then it was between Leonard Cohen and Janis Ian to do the title song; Sidney knew John Hammond the legendary record producer with Columbia, and he had Leonard Cohen and Janis Ian see the movie, and we ended up with Janis."

Janis Ian, who provides the theme song 'I Need to Live Alone Again' (recorded in 1977) was riding high at the time thanks to a million-selling single, 'At Seventeen', in 1975, and a succession of international hit albums: 'Between the Lines' (1975), 'Aftertones' (1976) and 'Miracle Row' (1977). Ian's first hit single, 'Society's Child' (1965), told the story of an inter-racial love affair and was consequently banned on some American radio stations at the time, although it went on to be her first major hit. Unfortunately, 'I Need to Live Alone Again' adds a histrionic mawkishness to *The Orphan*, and is one of the least persuasive elements of the package. It's a pity – you can't help thinking that Leonard Cohen's tender, mournful baritone would have fit the film like a glove. Teo Macero, whose contribution to the rest of the score is much better, is best known for his groundbreaking collaborations with Miles Davis. He was the prime architect of Davis's electric sound on such albums as

Bitches Brew, On the Corner and the stunning *Get Up with It*, for which he developed a number of new electronic treatments. Macero and Davis pioneered a 'cut-and-paste' approach, recording long open-ended jams with the Miles Davis Band and then looping sections, editing, and assembling albums that were dense with multi-tracked and treated sounds (ideas that were heresy to jazz purists but helped bring Miles's music to a new generation of rock and avant-garde music fans).[4]

So, in its drastically compressed and pointlessly retitled version, *Friday the 13th: The Orphan* finally opened, at the 1978 Miami Film Festival. It went on to play in Times Square in November 1979, and drew headlines such as "New York adopts The Orphan!" from *Variety*. The trade magazine *Boxoffice* listed it as their highest rating film for that month. However, the momentum was not exploited by distributors World Northal, and without a second film waiting in the wings, the opportunity to capitalise soon died away.

Missing Scenes

The version of *The Orphan* available today is missing around thirty minutes from the original Ralph Rosenblum cut. (The UK video runs 73m 45s.) Here, John Ballard describes a few of the scenes that were removed:

1) "I was forced to remove a scene where Martha sees Mary showering, and fantasizes first that the girl is making love with a man in the shower; and then that she herself is in the shower with the man."

2) "There was a scene in which Peggy Feury has an erotic fantasy about Afolabi Ajayi. She goes to his cabin and has oral sex, where we see her going down his stomach. I didn't mind that being taken out."

3) "The other key scene was with the doctor, before the boy's tongue is removed. The aunt is worried about his coughing all the time, and the doctor comes and they have him stick out his tongue. It was a precursor of the tongue scene later. It's all done with these wide-angle lenses, nightmarish, with a flashlight in the dark, but it was cut out."

4) "A dream sequence: we start off with a lamp, and a moth circling the bulb. David reaches for it, and gets a shock, looks at his hand, and sees all these ants pouring out of his palm and up his forearm. So he rubs them off, and as he's rubbing his arm, his arm comes off. He doesn't know what to do and he's frantic, so he runs into the bathroom and that's where he starts flushing his clothes down the toilet."

5) "There was a structural design to the film, to do with pastel autumnal scenes at the beginning and cold winter scenes at the end, but because the film was restructured for its final release, this structure is compromised, with scenes from winter added to the early stages."

6) "At the very end – you've seen the cook killed in the basement and then the aunt shot by David – at the end he's making the toast and the maid, Mary, reappears in the door with her suitcase because she's leaving because she just can't stand it any more, and says, 'Where's your aunt?' – and he just looks at her like he's seen a ghost, and says, 'Oh, I think she went down to the chicken coop a while ago,' which is the line from the Saki story. So then you're left thinking, 'Well she's still alive, so maybe he actually did kill the aunt?' So it makes you rethink the whole film, which of course they did in *The Sixth Sense*!"

Sredni Vashtar

Sredni Vashtar, like many of Saki's stories, is so short I could probably reproduce it here in its entirety (especially as it's out of copyright). In order to look at Ballard's treatment of the tale, here instead is a *précis* with quotes:

Conradin, a ten-year-old boy, is bitterly resentful of his cousin-guardian Mrs. De Ropp: *"In his eyes she represented those three-fifths of the world that are necessary and disagreeable and real; the other two-fifths, in perpetual antagonism to the foregoing, were summed up in himself and his imagination."* For her part, *"Mrs. De Ropp would never, in her honestest moments, have confessed to herself that she disliked Conradin, though she might have been dimly aware that thwarting him "for his good" was a duty which she did not find particularly irksome."*

With this conflict comes hatred, and defiance: *"Conradin hated her with a desperate sincerity which he was perfectly able to mask. Such few pleasures as he could contrive for himself gained an added relish from the likelihood that they would be displeasing to his guardian...."*

Conradin's sanctuary is a disused tool-shed at the edge of the grounds: *"...Within its walls Conradin found a haven, something that took on the varying aspects of a playroom and a cathedral. He had peopled it with a legion of familiar phantoms, evoked partly from fragments of history and partly from his own brain, but it also boasted two inmates of flesh and blood. In one corner lived a ragged-plumaged Houdan hen, on which the boy lavished an affection that had scarcely another outlet. Further back in the gloom stood a large hutch [...] This was the abode of a large polecat-ferret [...] Conradin was dreadfully afraid of the lithe, sharp-fanged beast, but it was his most treasured possession. Its very presence in the tool-shed was a secret and fearful joy [...] And one day, out of Heaven knows what material, he spun the beast a wonderful name, and from that moment it grew into a god and a religion."*

Mrs. De Ropp begins to resent the boy's hide-away, and escalates hostilities by getting rid of his beloved hen. However, far from providing an anguished and furious reaction, Conradin remains silent. Mrs. De Ropp is disconcerted: *"Something perhaps in his white set face gave her a momentary qualm."* Down at the shed, Conradin redoubles his devotions, concocting a hymn in worship of his furry idol and making an unspecified request: *"'Do one thing for me, Sredni Vashtar.'"* When Mrs. De Ropp makes another visit to the shed, to throw out the ferret, Conradin observes her from his window, furiously chanting a self-written hymn:

"Sredni Vashtar went forth,
His thoughts were red thoughts and his teeth were white.
His enemies called for peace, but he brought them death.
Sredni Vashtar the Beautiful."

His mind consumed with the threat of losing his *"wonderful god"*, Conradin watches... and watches... in dread that The Woman will emerge victorious. He chants his hymn, over and over, and at last there emerges through the doorway, *"...a long, low, yellow-and-brown beast, with eyes a-blink at the waning daylight, and dark wet stains around the fur of jaws and throat."* A *"sour-faced maid"* asks where the mistress is, and Conradin calmly states, *"She went down to the shed some time ago."* As the household staff go looking, screaming and sobbing at what they find, Conradin calmly makes himself some toast at the fireplace...

Saki's story, barely 1,700 words in length, has an economy of line that guides us back to our own childhood recollections. The details of the tale are spare and archetypal, through which our private memories sweep like visiting ghosts. Even 'well-adjusted' adults can probably remember, if they try, the sensation of being thwarted by a parent or controlling adult: prevented from doing this, ordered to do that. You don't need to have borne a psychotic grudge to empathise with the bright flare of Conradin's childhood rage. Meanwhile, the writer's elegant, sardonic phrasing weaves a cradle for the fury, and the sweet satisfaction of the ending settles the old score: wit eclipses bitterness.

A motherless child, Munro was raised by strict, socially hidebound female relatives who, he believed, exhibited cruelty and spite in the maintenance of their authority. (He is said to have based Mrs. De Ropp on his aunt). While some have accused the writer of misogyny, Munro merely reserves his anger for women whose parenting skills revolve purely around the exercise of power. Of course, for a child even a small thing, like the forbidding of toast in *Sredni Vashtar*, can assume the status of a mountainous injustice and inspire incandescent moments of rage. Such flash-flood hatreds are thankfully 'civilised' out of the majority. But when the injustice takes the form of isolation, or the destruction of one's private world, this leads to deeper pools of anger, and it's here that the Saki story touches, lightly but succinctly, on the way psychological disorder is constructed by childhood experience.

Ballard describes his approach: "It was not meant to be a story of a bad seed, a killer kid. It was around the time of 'The Son of Sam', and it was more about what turns a normal healthy child into a killer? He is systematically betrayed by all the adults in his life. The cook walks out on him, the African guy walks out on him, and this well-meaning aunt has all these good intentions about reforming him from the bad influence of the father, and confines him to his room, and the boy just retreats into this fantasy world. So you blur this distinction between killing and willing someone to die. Even infants can be filled with hate and rage when they're abused or hurt in some way."

Saki is not the only literary influence on *The Orphan*. William Faulkner and Henry James are also touchstones. The aunt's paranoia is very much in the style of the James novella *The Turn of the Screw*, and the child's encounter with truth through eavesdropping is consciously drawn from Faulkner, as Ballard explains: "There's a scene I stole from a Faulkner book, where the boy is under the bed, and the two adults come in and there's complete frontal nudity in the scene, not in an erotic sense, but it's terrifying to the child. In Faulkner, a boy locks himself in a closet and there's this sex scene going on outside and he's ingesting toothpaste, and that always stayed with me." (The scene is from Faulkner's 1932 novel *Light in August*. A five year old orphan boy called Joe Christmas – so-called due to being left at the orphanage on Christmas day – suffers a traumatic encounter that will warp his future relationships with women: while hiding in a closet, eating toothpaste, he becomes an inadvertent eavesdropper on the orphanage's female dietician having sex with another member of staff. He has no understanding of what's really happening, but he's discovered when the toothpaste he's eaten makes him vomit. From thereon, fearing reprisals, he lives with a constant sense of imminent punishment; but also confusion, because the woman gave him a dollar. Joe doesn't realise that the woman fears exposure as much as he fears reprisal: the

dollar, intended to buy his silence, merely cements in his mind the notion of women as capricious and irrational.)

So in what way does *The Orphan* relate to the director's own experience? Ballard explains, "It's autobiographical on a psychological level. The conversations that you hear as a kid really shape you. You can shake them, but sometimes it takes making a movie to do it! There were a lot of arguments behind closed doors; they created an emotional well for the film. My mother was incapable of being around and raising children, she just didn't have a gift for that, and she was very neurotic and self-centred. It somewhat psychologically destroyed my sister, who was older than me. She was kind of a buffer, it all got acted out on her. So I have always had a deep feeling for people who are picked on, for instance for their weight, or some deformity. In terms of horror, what's really horrifying to me is someone mistaking someone's outward appearance for what they are – for instance, when I was sixteen I wrote a screenplay about the Elephant Man."

I mention to Ballard that while the Aunt is portrayed as destructive, Mary the maid (against the grain of the Saki story) is likeable and sympathetic. "The aunt is a harridan, yes," Ballard says. "Which kinda echoes my own childhood! I've done some soul-searching on that. You don't realise until you've worked it all the way through, and then you say 'Ah!' As far as the maid goes, I think when you're fortunate the redeeming factor can be if you have someone else. My older sister was a very loving person who I was very close to, so that can help in your future relationships. In the film, David speaks of her as a mother, we even had some insinuation that she and the father had a relationship and the child could be the offspring."

Sidney Mackenzie says, "John had a penchant for Saki because of the very dark turn in there that isn't quite resolved. I'm surprised more people haven't adapted Saki's work because it's very psychological, it's very complex and true. John had gone to Harvard and majored in psychology and sociology, and one of his teachers was Robert Coles,[5] so he'd had a lot of exposure to stuff on early childhood."

A major component of Saki's story that remains unchanged in the film is the boy's rejection of Christianity, in favour of his own hybrid religion. Mackenzie: "At that time in America, in the late 1960s, there was this odd mix of drug culture and people coming from Tibet and various parts of the East to teach in this country. There was a mélange of hallucinogenic trips that people came back from and reported about, and a terrible longing to find something in Eastern meditational traditions that, you know, nobody had found in the Southern Baptists. This filtered in and out of the discussions we had. The religious impulse in children is something that John has always been interested in, and it certainly interested me an awful lot too, especially when it has to do with compensating for a severe abandonment or trauma that happens very young. The rage and violence that results from that sort of early trauma is a very complicated and confusing combination for a child."

And the idealised father, so important in *The Orphan*? Mackenzie's perspective as a Jungian psychologist is interesting: "It's a big problem in American culture right from the beginning. If you look at us, rushing over here to get away from the King, in one form or another, and then setting up one idealised father figure after another. It's very immature what's going on here, and very scary. And now they're all toppling; corporate heads, idiot presidents, the fathers of the Church, and of course people are suffering unthinkably here: the depression and despair and hopelessness. It's a terribly important point of maturational growth in the culture, but whether or not we're going to make it over the hump or around the corner…"

For Ballard, the idealised father figure in *The Orphan* is partly a response to the fact that his own father was 'removed by age' – "I used to listen outside the door: my father was fifty one years older than me, and I'd listen to see if he was asleep or if he was going to die. I was afraid he was going to die. My father was distant inasmuch as he was so much older than me, but I loved him and worshipped him."

Hoops

After *The Orphan* was released,[6] Ballard went back to work on 'Hoops': "Basketball was not the phenomenon it is now. I had shot some screen-tests with Earl Monroe, captain of the New York Nicks, and Sheila Frazier who was in *Superfly*. I had lined up The Jackson Five, I was running screenings trying to raise money to finish it – I had Dino De Laurentiis there, a lot of people lined up. We had James Earl Jones's father, Robert E. Jones. Eventually I was flown out to Hollywood… and they wanted us to change the coach to a white person! Whereas it was really a father-son story between a black kid and a black coach! So we refused to do it, and a year later *The White Shadow* came out on TV about a white coach and black inner city kids; from the same studio we showed our thing to."

Ballard took one more body-blow before retiring from film: "I did a script about extreme sports. We had all the finance in place, it was going to be done by Cannon Films and I was all set to direct it, and one of the key actors pulled out to make *The Pirates of Penzance*." (TV movie, 1980).

Race and human rights issues were nothing new to Ballard. In the mid-1960s, while still at Harvard, Ballard made contact with activists in the Civil Rights movement. The flashpoint was the infamous occasion in Selma, Alabama on 7 March, 1965, when a peaceful civil rights protest highlighting the region's violation of black voting rights was blockaded and prevented from marching on the State capital, Montgomery. Police attacked the protestors with appalling violence, but their tactics were captured on the TV news, nationwide, providing a clarion call for hundreds of supporters to converge on Selma for two further marches. The third was at last given right of way. Ballard was one of those who headed down to the region to lend his support. He worked alongside Martin Luther King, and spent time in an Alabama jail for his outspoken and practical involvement in the protests. Sidney Mackenzie attests, "When he was at Harvard it was in the middle of a lot of the really difficult racial stuff in this country, so he went with Robert Coles, and on his own a lot, to Alabama on all those marches; Montgomery and so on. He's a very tall red-headed guy and he stands out in a crowd. He has a tremendous empathy for the plight of people who are discriminated against in one way or another, whether racially or in a family circumstance."

Back in New York, Ballard continued to seek ways to assist black youth in the city: "I was working up in Harlem at the time – Mayor Lindsay was trying to run a 'fusion' ticket and I and this young girl called Melba Hill[7] opened a community centre so that disenfranchised black people there could have a voice to help them get what they should from the city. For instance, we helped Claude Brown, who wrote *Manchild in the Promised Land* [published in 1965]; we introduced him to Tom Wolfe."

Ballard's passionate concern for racial equality rose again, undimmed, in the 1980s. After the abortive attempt to film 'Hoops', he turned to publishing. Ballard says, "In the early eighties, when I started to write books on Afro-American themes, I hired an Afro-American writer, Walter Dean Myers, to write the novel *Hoops* and it was turned down by various different publishing houses who said, 'Black kids don't read.' We finally got a publishing house to do it and won a best book of the year award." (*Hoops* was published in 1981 by Delacorte Press. A sequel called *The Outside Shot*, also written by Myers from a screenplay treatment by Ballard, was published in 1984.)

Ballard followed with several books for children and young adults, inspired by his trips to India and the African continent as a voluntary worker during the mid-eighties: "I've always been interested in anything which shows up how people are. So when you collide two cultures, what comes up in that collision is who you are, what your identity is. I didn't have much money but I talked my way onto a relief flight in 1985 to Sudan, which was a war-torn area, and Ethiopia, delivering food during the famine. That provided the basis for my books." The books concern a recurring character called 'MacBurnie King', a white teenage girl who travels through the Third World keeping a diary of her experiences. She first appears in *Monsoon: A Novel to End World Hunger*, published in 1985. The saga continued in 1993 with *Brothers and Sisters: Real Love Knows No Boundaries* (which featured an introduction by Nelson Mandela), doubled-up with another Ballard book, *The Soul Guide to African-American Consciousness: Reclaiming Your History*. The books have met with wildly diverse responses from the trade. Kirkus Reviews called his work *"a sprawling mix of fact and fiction [...] mostly exhortatory, Afrocentric essays on African history and culture"*, going on to say, *"Though obviously a labour of love, and packed with worthy information, these well-meaning but impossibly cluttered and disorganized volumes will be less useful than non-fiction of narrower scope."* The School Library Journal offers a quite different perspective: reviewing *Brothers and Sisters: Real Love Knows No Boundaries*, a contributing teacher described it as, *"A real hodgepodge of both fact and fiction. There are a lot of different typefaces used: bold, small print, large print, and borders. It is an interesting and arresting way of writing and of putting a book together, and should appeal to young adults' creativity."*

Blaxploitation, Separatism, Humanism

I asked Ballard, considering his interest in race issues both in cinema and writing, what he thought of the spate of 'blaxploitation' films made during the 1970s, and their current vogue in the popular cinema of Quentin Tarantino: "*Sweet Sweetback* was creative; most of the others were

above:
Peggy Feury, who gives the role of Martha the benefit of her formidable screen presence.

right:
Finnish video sleeve, with the original title clearly typeset in a hurry…

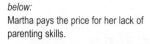

below:
Martha pays the price for her lack of parenting skills.

really stupid. It's the same feeling I have about Tarantino. He has a wonderful talent with actors, but what is he doing? He's like a wannabe black person. It's understandable, now that things have shifted, but having lived through all the violence in the sixties… Tarantino is a genius with actors, but to what end? When he discovers that, if he ever does, he's going to be unstoppable."

In the 1960s, when Ballard and Melba Hill were working together in New York, Ballard had his first encounter with black separatism: as a white man writing on black culture, it would not be the last: "Melba Hill was part of a group called 'Voices of East Harlem' singing black history songs, from slave days through jazz. They had a show doing this in 1968. She took me to a theatre where LeRoi Jones was, and he refused to let me in the theatre; which basically showed me his racist thinking."[8] Sometimes there's a feeling that you have to be black to write about black people, you have to be a woman to write about women. I don't subscribe to that at all. As an artist, if you operate that way you could never write a character. You may never know or understand the full depths of what another person goes through, but it's in the effort to do that that you're going to find art. You know, we inhabit a bag of skin, we're looking out through two eyeholes, and you and I have no choice over the family we were born into, the colour of skin we were born into, the life we were born into. What you do have some choice over is to do something with that life – depending on where you're born! To me the essence is seeing yourself in another person. The extent to which you can do that is the extent to which you can be human."

Epilogue

Ballard and Mackenzie – he honest and engaging, she insightful and humorous – are among the most thoughtful and genuine people I've encountered in the writing of this book. They make the perfect team for a film that explores the trauma, magic, fears and desires of childhood. Like young David in the film, *The Orphan* was nurtured carefully for its first ten years, before the well-meaning but clumsy ministrations of an interloper. Unlike poor Aunt Martha, Sandra Gilman and Louise Westergaard made it away with their lives, and of course we should be glad – they at least showed an interest in the film. More importantly, *The Orphan*'s proud parents, Ballard and Mackenzie, unlike their onscreen counterparts, lived to see their offspring reach a kind of maturity – achieving a brief spell in the New York limelight, with the *Variety* headlines to prove it.

Footnotes

[1]   Ambiguities are central to the finale of this film, and cast a special light on the earlier scenes.

[2]   Future director of *Carny* (1980) and *Nobody's Perfect* (1989).

[3]   Best known for shooting *Jaws* and *The Conversation*.

[4]   Macero was deeply influenced by his friend, the composer Edgard Varése, whose *Poème electronique* (1957) first convinced him of the possibilities of electronic music allied to acoustic instrumentation. Macero's music for *The Orphan* is largely orchestral, although there are significant sections utilising studio effects and electronic treatments. Homer Denison, credited with additional orchestration on *The Orphan*, would work with Howard Shore as his regular orchestrator throughout the 1980s and 1990s, on *The Fly*, *Dead Ringers* and *Naked Lunch*.

[5]   A child psychiatrist and professor at Harvard, author of more than fifty books specialising in the moral, political, and spiritual sensibilities of children.

[6]   A novelisation by Samantha Mellors, from Ballard's screenplay, was published by Jove Publications in 1980.

[7]   Went on to become Melba Moore, the singer.

[8]   Everett Leroy LeRoi Jones: poet, playwright, polemicist. Involved with the Beats in the late 1950s/early 1960s, he eventually left their sphere to concentrate exclusively on racial subjects. In 1961 he helped start the American Theater For Poets, and in 1965 The Black Arts Repertory Theater. After the assassination of Malcolm X in 1965, Jones felt that racial integration was impossible and began espousing black nationalist ideology. In 1968 he became a Muslim, changing his name to Amiri Baraka.

JOHN BALLARD: FILMOGRAPHY AS DIRECTOR
1966   *The Toy* (short)
1967   *Borges* (documentary)
1977   *Friday the 13th: The Orphan* aka *The Orphan* aka *Betrayal* aka *Killers of the Dream*

OTHER CREDITS
1967   *The Lonesome Death of Hattie Carroll* (short) – dir: Jeff Young (as cinematographer / assistant dir.)

chapter 17

Blood Relations

The Films of Irv & Wayne Berwick

with Wayne Berwick, and friend and film producer Ted Newsom

Hitch Hike to Hell (1977)

Geeky, mother-loving Howard (Robert Gribbin) is a delivery driver for loveable old grouch Mr. Baldwin (John Harmon). The job brings Howard into contact with a constant stream of hitch hikers; mostly girls, running away from cruel or oppressive parents. Ignoring their reasons for leaving, Howard begs them to return to their mothers. If they refuse, he develops a bad case of the nervous twitches and drives them off-road for sexual molestation and murder. The reason? Howard's sister Judy hitchhiked out of town and broke momma's heart. When Howard's mutilated victims start turning up dead, Police Captain Shaw (Russell Johnson from TV's *Gilligan's Island*) tries his best to increase awareness that a killer is on the loose, although the self-absorbed parents of a runaway girl brought in for jaywalking provide a glimpse of what he's up against. Howard, meanwhile, barely remembers his atrocities afterwards; and as for his mollycoddling mother (Dorothy Bennett), even when her son suffers flashbacks and goes into psycho meltdown, she does nothing. Eventually, after Howard murders a little girl of eleven, Shaw tracks him down to Baldwin's business and arrests him, with the help of the killer's shocked workmates.

Although the narrative is overstretched and the psychology is rudimentary, this is an effective shocker with a gradually more oppressive awareness of the reality behind the headlines that inspired it. Perhaps unintentionally, Berwick sets up a strong *frisson* between generic subject matter and the earnest social commentary of the script. Like any exploitation picture with a moral point to make, *Hitch Hike to Hell* is a confused and confusing experience. Is it a shameless piece of trashy fun, or a grim warning to teenagers and their parents, delivered at the height of America's serial-killer onslaught? Schizophrenically a bit of both, *Hitch Hike to Hell* shakes the dust off problems that lie undisturbed in other less conflicted exploitation films.

The commercial horror cinema of the 1970s demanded victims, preferably female. Given the excesses of the day, a sexual emphasis was par for the course, and *Hitch Hike to Hell* is no exception. So far so sleazy. Irv Berwick, however, cut his teeth on a series of noirish melodramas in the early 1960s – *The Seventh Commandment*, *The Street Is My Beat* and *Strange*

Compulsion – which gained their narrative energy from putting characters through various moral crises. Something tells me that Berwick automatically sought to include a moral dimension here too, even though the context is so different. It may just have been the natural impulse of a man whose screen model was more likely Edgar Ulmer than Herschell Gordon Lewis, but despite *Hitch Hike*'s shallow storyline by John Buckley, Berwick takes the themes seriously enough to complicate our responses. As the script badgers the audience about the need for parents to take better care of their children, the latter part of the film aims for a feeling of appalled grief. However, as this comes hot on the heels of a couple of gloating rape-murders shot for maximum excitement, an unforgiving audience could easily read the film's moral concern as hypocrisy…

Part of the problem is the lead character. Robert Gribbin's 'Howard' is a meek, wimpish cartoon nerd, all tics and twitches, an out-of-date cinematic cypher mired in a post-*Psycho* rut. He's an amusing creation, but given the then-current reality to which the film alludes, he makes a poor fit with the horror. It's not the actor's fault: it's just that the film is freighted with references to horrors beyond his dramatic range. There's the chill of contemporary anxieties in the script's reference to San Francisco's 'Zodiac Killer' (never caught), L.A.'s 'Skid-Row Slasher' (Vaughn Greenwood) and *"that nut down in Houston,"* (Dean Corll). Berwick's sixties films were dark, certainly, but they were essentially moralist melodramas, stories with convoluted plots and stylized acting, taking place in a parallel world of film. For all their grubby, unglamorous glimpses of the real world, they keep a degree of dramatic distance. Berwick's *The Seventh Commandment* plays almost like a nastier, grimier *Twilight Zone* episode. *Hitch Hike to Hell* uses the rash of brutal serial killer slayings that plagued California in the 1970s as meat for a plot, in the same way that a headline about corrupt priests dealing drugs, or somesuch, would generate noirish material for the thrillers Berwick used to make. The horrendous crimes of men like Ted Bundy, Vaughn Greenwood, Edmund Kemper or Dean Corll, however, probably require a darker, more realistic tone, which is precisely what *Hitch Hike* lacks.

We seem to be getting rather heavy – so I should point out that I do enjoy this film, and besides, this book covers

below:
One of two UK video releases for **Hitch Hike to Hell**, this one from DVS, who also put out Bernard Girard's **A Name for Evil**, George Fenady's **Terror in the Wax Museum**, Robert H. Oliver's **Frankenstein's Castle**, and Antonio Margheriti's **Web of the Spider**.

Hitch Hike to Hell
© 1977. An A.B.A. Film Corporation
production, Encino, California
Boxoffice International Pictures, Inc. - a Harry
Novak presentation.

producer/director: Irv Berwick. executive
producers: Frances Adair, Joseph V. Agnello.
screenplay: John Buckley. photography:
William de Diego. editor: Dan Perry. assistant
cameraman: Miles F. Blum. sound: Wayne
Berwick. production co-ordinator: Michael
Frischer. makeup: Leslie Howard. script
supervisor: Jeanne Marie Rummans. music:
Perry Daniels. sound boom: Loren Schein. still
photography: Michael Dale. key grip: Yosef
Paso. production assistant: Nancy Friedman.
set decorator: Saul Edwards. property master:
Jerry Klein. producer's assistant: Wayne Elliot.
[song] "Hitch Hike to Hell" sung by Nancy
Adams, music by Floyd Huddleston, lyrics by
Tom Kelly, harmonicist: Wayne Berwick.
Cast: Robert Gribbin (Howard Martin). Russell
Johnson (Captain Shaw). John Harmon (Mr.
Baldwin). Randy Echols (Lt. Davis). Dorothy
Bennett (Mrs. Martin). Mary Ellen Christie
(Mrs. Burke). Kippi Bell (Evelyn Davis). Sheryl
Lynn (Lisa). John Grant (Mr. Burke).
Jacquelyn Poseley (Sharon). Beth Reis
(Pam). Jane Ratliff (Gail). Don Lewis (gay
boy). Gail Bowman (Lydia Welles). Vincent
Lucchesi (Mr. Lathrop). Ginny Morrel (Mrs.
Lathrop). Melanie Sutherland (Connie). Petra
Michelle (Phyllis). Gary Frischer (drunk).
Jackie Miller (policewoman). Jayme Feinstein,
Diane Hirshberg (basketball players). Debra
Draper (main title victim).

films far more depraved, explicit and brutal than *Hitch Hike to Hell*, and they don't *all* get hauled over the coals. It's worth taking a second, then, to understand why these thoughts are coalescing around Irv Berwick's movie. The two main murder scenes are not totally explicit (we see breasts but no full nudity, and the violence – both victims are beaten and strangled – is bloodless) but they achieve power through the frenzied performances of the victims and the frantic, fast-paced music, which cranks up the illicit excitement to the max. (Elsewhere the music cues are lifted from the same library record David Cronenberg used for his second feature film *Rabid*.) The first onscreen killing (Jacquelyn Poseley's 'Sharon') has the most impact, and it's one reason why the moral themes create so much friction: there's a leering, in-your-face quality that cues you up for a gloating, amoral exercise in sadism. The second killing we see (Jane Ratliff's 'Gail') also has a charge, despite Gribbin's poor acting (he's meant to be miming rape, but he never even gets his flies undone). Nevertheless, when he strangles the teenager with a coat-hanger, in the back of his grimy old van, recollections of similar real-life crimes (see postscript) send a chill down your spine.

On the plus side, there's little in the way of crass moralising when it comes to the victims. These unfortunate young women hitching their way to Doomsville are shown sympathetically – at no point does the film side with the killer and his pathetic diatribes. In fact blame is often landed squarely on the parents, especially in the case of one couple who refuse to collect their runaway daughter after she's picked up by the police: *"Seems there are delinquent parents as well as delinquent children,"* a cop observes, helpfully underlining the film's moral theme. Significantly, the killer's doting mother is shown to have a distinctly un-maternal streak when the subject of her own runaway daughter is brought up. Seeing a newspaper article about the rape and murder of a hitch hiker (one of her son's victims), she speculates that maybe the same thing happened to Judy: *"If it did she had it comin'."*

The parade of pretty young victims is eventually complicated by the introduction of a young man and a little girl. It's as if halfway through his cautionary tale, writer John Buckley became anxious about the sexploitation elements and sought to remedy things by making the victims less titillating. Unfortunately, Berwick chooses not to show these later murders onscreen, which means the chance is lost to shock audiences with less salacious footage of a young man and a child being attacked. The depiction of the (flamboyantly gay) male

victim (Don Lewis) is another slight miscalculation. He's introduced with a silly piece of music clearly meant to overdetermine the character: none of the female victims are treated humorously, so why this one? Geeky, unworldly Howard fails to pick up on the verbal hints the young man drops about his sexuality, so maybe the comical music was the director's gauche way of making sure the same couldn't be said of his audience?

More successfully, it's with child victim Lisa (Sheryl Lynn) that the mood really darkens. Although the murder itself is not shown, the scene where cops take Lisa's mother to a rubbish skip to identify her daughter's body crashes the film right down off its exploitation high. When the police captain opens the lid of a rubbish skip to reveal the child's dead body, the film at last confronts the darkness inherent in its subject matter. Full marks to Mary Ellen Christie, who plays the distressed mother: her cries shred our nerves as she freaks out, fights with the police, and tries awkwardly to reach her dead daughter.

Viewers can probably have more fun than I seem to be having here by simply ignoring the moral angle, instead watching *Hitch Hike to Hell* as a slightly cheesy, slightly nasty horror/exploitation flick. That's just what I did on first viewing, and a fine time I had too. Thinking about it, I seem to have been affected by just a handful of scenes, and a couple of almost casual details: perhaps all I'm really saying is that the film doesn't go far enough in evoking the chill behind the tabloid headlines that inspired it.

POSTSCRIPT: Certain details of the film are uncannily echoed in the vile sex crimes of Lawrence Bittaker and Roy Norris – committed two years after the film was made, in the summer and autumn of 1979, barely twenty miles south of the film's Malibu and Topanga locations. Bittaker met Norris, a convicted rapist, in jail in 1978 when he was serving time for assault. The two bonded, and hatched a plot to kidnap, rape and murder teenage girls, tape-recording the events for their later amusement. Paroled in November 1978, Bittaker bought a silver van he nicknamed 'Murder Mack' and when buddy Norris was released on 15 June, 1979, the pair were soon driving round the streets of Hermosa and Redondo Beach, Los Angeles. Their first known victim, sixteen-year-old Lucinda Schaeffer, was abducted on 24 June, 1979, to be followed by at least four more girls between the ages of thirteen and eighteen. Several of the victims were hitch hikers. Sixteen-year-old Shirley Ledford, the fifth known victim, was abducted on 31 October and found the next morning in a residential district. After mutilating her breasts with pliers and beating her repeatedly with a hammer, Bittaker had strangled her to death in the back of his van – with a coat hanger. On 20 November, Bittaker and Norris were arrested on charges stemming from the testimony of a woman who had escaped after being abducted in Bittaker's van. While in custody, Norris cracked and admitted to the murders. He stated that he and Bittaker approached girls at random, offered rides, then drove them to a remote mountain road where they were tortured, raped and murdered. Tape recordings of the victims' final moments proved so horrific when played in court that jurors fled the courtroom to be sick. Norris pleaded guilty on five counts of murder, turned State's evidence against Bittaker, and received a sentence of forty five years to life. Bittaker denied everything but was declared guilty and sentenced to death in 1989. At the time of writing he remains alive on Death Row.

right:
Howard at work in **Hitch Hike to Hell**...

opposite page, main image:
Astra Video released **Microwave Massacre** on UK video in the Spring of 1983. Their impressive roster also included such grindhouse classics as H.G. Lewis's **Blood Feast**, Don Jones's **Abducted**, Meir Zarchi's **I Spit on Your Grave**, George A. Romero's **Season of the Witch**, and Michael Findlay's **Snuff**.

opposite page, bottom right:
May's severed head continues to express her disgust at her husband...

Microwave Massacre (1978)

Massacre. It's a word that really gets your attention. Moviemakers certainly thought so, because hot on the hooves of *The Texas Chain Saw Massacre* came *Northville Cemetery Massacre*, *Mardi Gras Massacre*, *Massacre Mansion*, and *Massacre at Central High*. Films without the word in their titles were quickly 'massacred up' for re-release: Frederick Friedel's *Axe* became *California Axe Massacre*, for instance. The word seethes with connotations of indiscriminate violence: post-Manson, in the serial-killing seventies, it promised a nerve-shredding, gut-churning movie experience. But to hell with the serious overtones; it was only a matter of time before some enterprising joker seized upon this over-worked horror buzzword for comedic purposes. Enter, Wayne Berwick. Wayne had a Massacre for us, alright; heated up and ready to go… a *Microwave Massacre*!

Microwave Massacre? Ha-ha, you're thinking – surely a one-trick-pony, a total waste of time? Well, some might say so… ("Overplayed for cheap laughs […] the film ends up being neither horrific nor funny." – *The Aurum Film Encyclopedia: Horror*). For me, though, it has a curious charm. *Microwave Massacre* is no one's *Citizen Kane* – who would be dumb enough to demand such a thing? – but I've watched it more times than *Kane*, which must count for something!

When I first saw *Microwave Massacre* on the video shelves in 1983, I'd only just begun to explore what was out there. Comedy in horror was anathema to me; I wanted my horror films nasty, brutal and sick. I wanted *Last House on the Left*, or *I Spit on Your Grave*. *Microwave Massacre* sounded… well, silly. And it is. Very silly. There's no point hiding the fact; *Microwave Massacre* is just as daft as it sounds.

But if you can roll with that, you're laughing.

Donald (Jackie Vernon), a depressed blue-collar slob, is stuck in a hellish marriage to his shrewish wife May (Claire Ginsberg), whose obsession with 'cordon-blue' cookery is driving him to the edge of madness; a situation made worse by his spouse's mean tongue. *"You're a walking contraceptive,"* she snaps. Bad food, no sex, verbal humiliation – why, it's inevitable: after a drunken domestic argument, Donald beats May to death with a giant continental pepper grinder. Next morning, he discovers that in the previous night's drunken frenzy, things had gone even further beyond the marriage vows: drunk to the moon, and taking advantage of his wife's extravagant taste in kitchen accessories, he'd stuck her in the microwave. Mortified, he hides the body by cutting it up and shoving the parts in the freezer, but after a while he forgets which foil-wrapped parcels are which. Soon, he's sharing the meat with his work buddies, who develop a taste for Donald's lunch-time treats. And when he runs out of May, Donald stocks up on more prime cuts, from a succession of glamorous prostitutes…

Guilty pleasure time: I don't know quite how this one has worked its way into my life but I've watched it at least six times, and I'll probably watch it six more. It's like a seventies sit-com as re-envisaged by a moonlighting *Saturday Night Live* scriptwriter aiming to blitz the video nasty market, with all the rough edges that description suggests. The humour is a mixture of bitter one-liners, blue-collar coarseness and classic hen-pecked husband routines. The latter were old-fashioned even in 1978, based

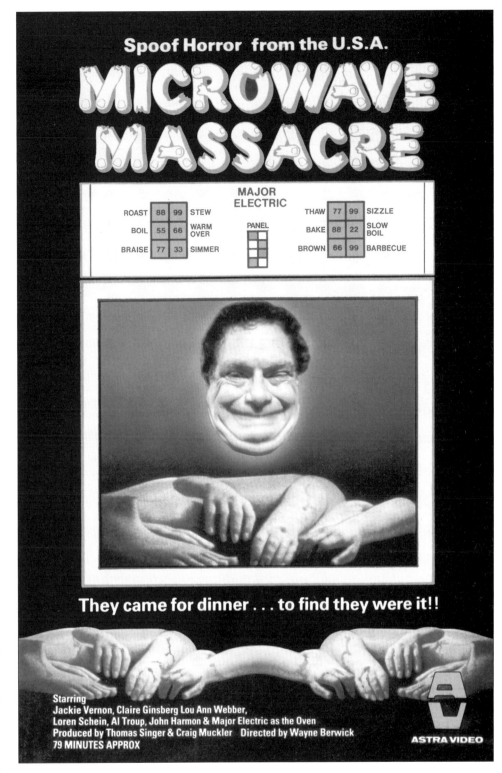

around the sort of 'Take my wife... I mean it, *take her*' gags of fifties stand-ups like Henny Youngman or Bob Hope. Jackie Vernon, famed for providing the voice of *Frosty the Snowman* in the US, mooches like a whipped cur through the story, giving the film a cartoon dimension that is picked up and amplified by the glaringly awful interior decor, which resembles some seventies hellhole ripped from a period catalogue.

Donald's difficulties with his food-obsessed wife are lifted wholesale from Hitchcock's *Frenzy*. At one point we see him at work, wrestling with a whole crab stuck in a large bap. It's not all film buff references though. Gags such as the 'glory-hole' in the building-site hoarding,

Microwave Massacre
© none [1978]
Reel Life Productions presents a chez Reel
Life creation (condemned by Good
Housekeeping).
director: Wayne Berwick. producers: Thomas
Singer and Craig Muckler. screenplay: Thomas
Singer, based on an original story by Craig
Muckler. director of photography: Karen
Grossman. music: Leif Horvath. editor: Steve
Nielson. art director: Robert Burns. 1st
assistant director: Donald P.H. Eaton. Le Staff:
Le Maitre D' production manager: Donald P.H.
Eaton. La Checker continuity: Rebecca
Drenick. L'Hostess makeup: Christy Newquist.
Le Bartender sound mixer: Susumo Takumo.
Les Garcons gaffer: Roberto Quesada. key
grip: Daryn Akoda. boom: Matt Lane. Le
Second Banana assistant cameraman:
Arledge Armenaki. L'Autre Second Banana
2nd assistant director: Gerry James. Les
Jacques of All Trades best boy: J.G.
Featherstone. production assistant: Mitchell
Polevoi. props: Marc Pally. La Muse technical
adviser: Betty Crockpot. The producers wish to
express their thanks to Microwave Ovens,
without which this movie would have taken
much longer. Remember, dismember a friend
for lunch!
Cast: Le Chef: Jackie Vernon (Donald). Les
Cooks: Loren Schein (Roosevelt). Al Troupe
(Philip). L'Aperatif: Marla Simon (knothole girl).
La Specialite De La Maison: Claire Ginsberg
(May). L'Hors D'Oeuvre: Lou Ann Webber
(Dee Dee Dee). La Poultry: Anna Marlowe
(Chick). La Dessert: Cindy Gant (Susie
Grubb). La Pain: (Sarah Alt (Evelyn). La
Cocktail: Karen Marshall (neighbour). Le
Chaser: Phil De Carlo (Sam). Le Wierdo [sic]
Aaron Koslow (salesman). Le House Doctor:
Ed Thomas (Dr. Von Der Fool). Le Shrink:
John Harmon (Dr. Gestalp). Le Buffet: Norman
Friedman (Mr. Goodbite). Les Condiments:
Debra Draper Berwick (la nurse). Malvina
Ackerman (la waitress). Al Mannino (le fruit).
Elaine Barker (la greasy delight). Brad Ford (le
drunk). Joel Hurwit, Greg Walter, Luigi
Bercovici (les movers). Rory Hurwit (le juicer).
John Beyrooty, Bill Ingwersen, Tonedeaf
Jackson, Bob Shebop (les fried pipers). Sticky
Digits, Inc. (le vibrators). Les Leftovers Larry
Allen (le drunk, too). Harry Evans (le worker).
Craig Muckler (le lover). Only He Knows (le
shadow). Dick Nibbler (le reader). Allison
(Allison) (la danceur) and introducing Major
Electric (the oven).

top:
Donald (Jackie Vernon) fantasises about
murdering his wife in **Microwave Massacre**.

right:
Appealingly cartoonish video box art for the
Stateside release of the film.

through which a passing chick inserts her breasts, establish the, shall we say, less cine-literate aspect of the film's humour. It's a live action version of the stuff that turns up in the funnies section of men's magazines, like it or lump it.

There's a self-loathing, self-pitying quality to Donald. He thinks life is good for everyone except him, expressing the disgruntlement of working guys stuck in arduous, badly-paid jobs – men with nagging wives, little money and no sex. He's a classic Joe Schmoe who views life as an endless drudge. *"When I get really bored I like to drive around and see how many squashed dogs I can count on the freeways,"* he says. Even a visit to the pub doesn't help. *"You know what it was today?"* he asks an even more depressed bartender: *"Tuesday,"* comes the reply, to which Donald adds, *"Just keeps gettin' worse and worse."* The barman is no Ted Danson either: his favourite way of cutting short unwanted intimacies from customers is to describe his personal health problems: *"Haemorrhoids... That's why I had to take this job standing up. Didn't I ever tell you about my haemorrhoids? They get really bad when it's humid, you know."*

Of course, there are flaws: yes, even here. Wayne Berwick told me that the target audience for *Microwave Massacre* was the stoner crowd, and it's quite likely this was the best bet, although Vernon is a shade too anachronistic for the plan to work. The veteran comedian seems a touch under-rehearsed too, stumbling through lines here and there in a way that makes you wonder if his mind is on the job, or just the 'refreshment' he's promised himself at the end of it. And if Donald simply bought his own lunch rather than eating whatever his wife puts in his lunchbox, there would be no story. Furthermore, it's never made plausible how Donald develops a taste for human flesh. One day we see him grab something from the fridge at random and start gnawing at it, until the camera pulls back to reveal that it's May's hand. Donald sees what he's eating, pauses a beat, then continues chewing the stump. It's a gag, of course, but are we to accept that he's happy to eat such an unappetizing cut? It seems a bit much to base the central plot development on a sight-gag! Soon he's tempting his workmates into cannibalism with choicer cuts, but his transition from hungry slob to cannibal gourmand is unconvincing. Then there's the microwave itself. Firstly, it's gigantic, like something from the hotel kitchens in *The Shining*, so God knows how they could afford it on Donald's wages. And May's obsession with fancy cuisine seems utterly at odds: who on earth makes lavish connoisseur dishes using a microwave? It's a contraption

noted for convenience not finesse. But the biggest flaw is that the film never really gets to grips with Donald's change of character. When he starts murdering prostitutes, it's a bit of a wrench, credibility-wise. Killing his wife was a *crime passionnel*; killing whores is simply murder. The fact that the script continues to paint Donald as a hapless schmuck doesn't really gel with his new role of cold-blooded killer.

Quite a list of complaints, Sir. So what is it that makes the film so enjoyable? I must admit it's difficult to explain. Perhaps it's the incongruity of a cannibal murder story framed by a comedy routine from a bygone era. Viewers in the UK should imagine a British version of the film, starring Les Dawson as the cannibal, and Mollie Sugden as his wife. The relentlessly lowbrow humour also has its appeal, even though most of the actual jokes have mouldy grey whiskers and a glow-in-the-dark quality. The setting – a suburban purgatory Mike Leigh might have dreamed up if he came from Los Angeles – is another feature, but the charm is somewhere in-between these not entirely plausible explanations. Maybe it's just that Donald's sympathetic loser persona strikes sparks against the increasingly cynical and cold-blooded action. In terms of visual style, there are some arresting shots of naked women lying on a black table in a black room, being sliced with a kitchen knife as blatantly phoney stage blood emerges. And Robert Burns's prosthetics are impressive, including some convincing severed hands (perhaps 'held over' for Alfredo Zacharias's *Demonoid*, on which Burns worked later). It really is hard to sum up, but I don't want to make too much of a meal of the conundrum. Some of you can probably already scent the aroma of simmering movie-trash (not to be confused with badly burnt art, although a mixture of both would be junk movie heaven). If so, my picky-eater caveats will seem like just the simperings of a quiche-loving art-snob.

A final word of warning: if you're finding *my* food jokes a touch indigestible, you'll get the runs from *Microwave Massacre*. If you give it a try, though, you may find the film a diverting, genially bizarre curio – even if it *is* as much of an acquired taste as a crab in a bap.

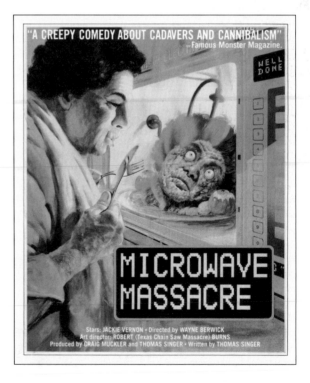

The Careers of
Irv Berwick &
Wayne Berwick

When you think of father-son film directing dynasties in the movie industry, who comes to mind? Melvin and Mario Van Peebles? Carl and Rob Reiner? How about father-daughter combos like David and Jennifer Lynch, or Dario and Asia Argento? Well, horror fans can add another pair to this roll-call: Irv and Wayne Berwick. While there are few similarities between the work of father and son, apart from the low budgets with which they had to work, it's somehow very pleasing to know that while Berwick Jr. was prepping a comedy-gore number called *Microwave Massacre*, Berwick Sr. was shooting a sadistic psycho-movie, *Hitch Hike to Hell*. To quote Jim Siedow's Cook in *The Texas Chain Saw Massacre*: *"This family's always been in meat!"*

Early Days

Irvin 'Irv' Berwick was born in 1915 and raised in The Bronx, New York, one of a family of Romanian Jews originally called Bercovicci. A child prodigy, he was playing concert piano before the age of ten. Although he never abandoned the instrument, he decided to seek a film career instead, hopping on a Greyhound bus to California when he was just seventeen. He first obtained work as an acting extra, and appeared as a billboard model for White Owl cigars. His son Wayne recalls, "He talked about a guy called Max Arnow,[1] he used to say that's the guy who got him started, brought him to Universal. He lived in Hollywood with four or five friends, who stayed friends throughout his life." One of these friends was John Harmon, a character actor who would go on to appear in well over two hundred film credits during a fifty-year career. Harmon became a talismanic presence in many of Berwick's films, including *The Monster of Piedras Blancas*, *The Seventh Commandment*, *The Street Is My Beat*, *Hitch Hike to Hell*, *Lawn Party*, and *Malibu High*.

After military service in World War II, Berwick returned to Hollywood and was hired by Columbia Pictures as a trainee director and dialogue coach. The extent of his work at that time is difficult to verify completely, as much of it went uncredited. Some of the jobs he accepted were for smaller production companies away from the Columbia lot, including the 1947 Groucho Marx 'solo' vehicle *Copacabana*, with Carmen Miranda. In addition to the verified titles listed in his filmography, writer and documentary filmmaker Ted Newsom, a long-time family friend to the Berwicks, recalls that Irv spoke of having worked with William Castle, who was at Columbia Pictures adapting mystery series' such as *The Whistler* and *Crime Doctor* from radio to the big screen. Castle moved to Universal in 1949 and Berwick followed, settling in as dialogue director for a string of westerns and crime melodramas, starting with Alfred E. Green's *Sierra* (1950) and continuing throughout the fifties, for directors like Kurt Neumann, Hugo Fregonese, Budd Boetticher and George Sherman. (Newsom recalls that in 1952 Berwick worked on Sherman's Errol Flynn picture *Against All Flags*: "[Irv] told me he had to spend time as the Flynn-wrangler. He

was pissed off at the end of shooting because Flynn gave him a gift, a bottle of expensive liquor. Irv was angry, because he didn't drink. Jesus, if he still had that bottle he could probably sell it for $1,000 on eBay. 'Booze from Errol Flynn!'") One of his most regular employers was one-man B-movie factory Lew Landers, with whom he first worked on *The Power of the Whistler* in 1945. Landers became a close friend of the Berwick family – he was known to young Wayne and his sister as 'Uncle Lew' and he often put work Berwick's way, including a useful regular job as dialogue director on the CBS 'friendly ghosts' TV series *Topper*, which ran from 1953 to 1956.

The Monster of Piedras Blancas

In the early 1950s Berwick moved to Universal-International, working with the great Jack Arnold as dialogue director on his crime melodrama *The Glass Web* (1953) starring Edward G. Robinson, and the western *Red Sundown* (1956). When Universal-International laid-off many of its employees in the late fifties following a merger with MCA, Berwick formed his own production company called VanWick Productions (later IrvMar) with Jack Kevan, a gifted make-up designer and one of those responsible for the Gill-Man in Jack Arnold's *Creature from the Black Lagoon*. With Kevan eager to develop his own talents, the choice of genre was a no-brainer: their first picture, *The Monster of Piedras Blancas* (1958) was a *Creature from the Black Lagoon* 'variant' shot entirely on location at Point Conception (which provided the lighthouse scenes) and Cayoucos, California. Piedras Blancas ('White Rocks') itself, a real town on the California coast north of San Simeon, was rejected as insufficiently photogenic.

Although the film was an independent production, Universal supplied equipment and crew members from their recently laid-off staff. In an act that neatly (if unintentionally) summarises the incestuous nature of genre pictures, Kevan made the monster suit from bits and pieces of the Universal monsters he'd worked on: the hands were borrowed from *The Mole People* (Kevan had designed their faces), and the feet were from the famous Metaluman monster in *This Island Earth*. Kevan simply built a new head, and bingo! The Piedras Blancas monster was born.

The Monster of Piedras Blancas is a film very much of its time, and for a certain audience it will evoke happy memories of a cinema that is no more: where men in bizarre rubber monster suits stalk the denizens of small

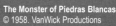

The Monster of Piedras Blancas
© 1958. VanWick Productions
A VanWick production.
director: Irvin Berwick. producer: Jack Kevan. screenplay: H. Haile Chace. director of photography: Philip Lathrop [black and white]. film editor: George Gittens, A.C.E. sound [mixer]: Joe Lapis, [recordist]: James V. Swartz. set operation: Walter Woodworth. lighting by Tom Ouellette. property master: Eddie [Roy] Keys. script supervisor: Luanna Sherman. interiors filmed at Point Conception (California, USA). story [uncredited]: Jack Kevan, Irvin Berwick. production manager [uncredited]: Ben Chapman. assistant director [uncredited]: Joseph Cavalier. monster suit [uncredited]: Jack Kevan.
Cast: Les Tremayne (Jorgenson, the doctor). Forrest Lewis (George Matson, the constable). John Harmon (Sturges, the lighthouse keeper). Frank Arvidson (Kochek, the storekeeper). Jeanne Carmen (Lucy Sturges, lighthouse keeper's daughter). Don Sullivan (Fred, the boy (a biologist)). Pete Dunn (Eddie/the monster). Joseph La Cava (Mike). Wayne Berwick (little Jimmy) and the monster of Piedras Blancas.

left, and above:
The Monster of Piedras Blancas on the prowl, and examining a recent kill...

above:
Video artwork for
The Monster of Piedras Blancas.

town communities, homing inexorably on the prettiest young female and her Brylcreemed, T-shirt clad boyfriend. For those brought up on later strains of horror cinema, such movies can seem slow-moving to the point of boredom, but *Piedras Blancas* has a few brief shots that sufficed to make it an alarming experience for the teenagers of its day. When the monster eventually goes on the rampage, it bursts into a room full of shocked citizens, brandishing the severed head of a recent victim in its scaly claw. There's even a hint of blood around the neck. For 1958, this was strong meat: blood was a rare sight indeed in the horror films of the time. A later shot of the severed head, discarded on the beach, is given an extra *frisson* by the added detail of a live crab crawling over it: it's a grotesque image, not unlike a similar scene in Mario Bava's *Twitch of the Death Nerve* (1971), in which a squid slides over the face of a corpse fished from the water. These details aside, though, it's a film whose appeal is very firmly rooted in its time. For modern audiences, the storyline of *Piedras Blancas* (written by H. Haile Chace) is unremarkable, and more than half an hour passes before we actually see the monster. Perhaps the young Don Dohler was watching, resolving to make films just like it: but with monsters that pounce every ten minutes!

Ted Newsom, who first met Berwick while attending a class Berwick taught at UCLA in the late 1970s, remembers that, "Irv was rather diffident about *Piedras Blancas*, even embarrassed when I asked him about it. Several years later, long after such a thing was necessary, he remained concerned that I shouldn't bring the film up when talking to Jack Arnold – Arnold and Berwick were long time friends – because he thought Arnold would get upset that *Piedras* was a lift from *Creature from the Black Lagoon*. I asked Arnold if there was some sort of ill-feeling and he just laughed and said no, of course not. The common denominator was, of course, Jack Kevan, who was Irv's friend and partner in VanWick Productions. Kevan had grown extremely disillusioned with the studio system and (rightly) felt he never got proper credit for the monster creations at Universal. Taking the bows was the job of Bud Westmore, who apparently would come in when the work was done, pose with 'the tool' (a little pencil-shaped sculpting stick) and *voila!* Another masterpiece from the great House of Westmore! Kevan said to hell with it and became a producer. This lasted with Irv until about '62 or '63, when Kevan, at the suggestion of his wife, got out of the movie business entirely. He started a cosmetics company and apparently did well financially. However, he would never, ever discuss his movie make-up career with anyone. After Kevan went on to other things, Irv formed IrvMar Productions, a contraction of his name and his wife Mary's."

Making *The Monster of Piedras Blancas* as an independent, Berwick developed a thriftiness that would stand him in good stead for his later work. Newsom continues: "Irv was always leery of what he thought was big production expense, like special effects. He often said the Piedras Blancas suit cost $30,000... which would've been true had it been done from scratch at Universal, and was probably the approximate price tag Kevan put on it. However, Kevan was able to pull new moulds from the various other elements at Universal, which saved time. Latex itself didn't cost that much, and since Kevan was co-producer, he didn't charge for his time. It probably cost about $4,000 max, maybe as little as $1,000 in actual

expense. It later shows up in colour in an episode of *Flipper*, by the way: Ricou Browning [who played the original *Black Lagoon* Gill-Man] was the co-producer of the show, and Browning and Kevan were old pals. So Irv avoided projects that needed anything elaborate or special. He had this one crappy script around the office for years, written by Haile (pronounced 'Hallie') Chace, and had a latex burn make-up in the office for at least five years... I guess he thought it would be so expensive to re-do this prosthetic appliance, he should keep it around in case he ever did Chace's burn-victim movie. So that's why he didn't do any more horror movies (except psycho-stuff like *Hitch Hike to Hell*). He occasionally returned to assistant directing and second unit stuff. He worked on Larry Buchanan's *The Loch Ness Horror* for instance. Uncredited, I think. He shot the action stuff.[2] He also worked on *Spartacus*, although he dismissed it and in fact wanted it kept quiet, saying, 'Nobody's supposed to know Kubrick had help on that'".

Berwick's Noir Trio

As the sixties got under way, Berwick's output continued, but in a darker vein. It's a major leap, stylistically, from the lightweight *The Monster of Piedras Blancas* to the lurid, noirish thrillers Berwick made in the 1960s, beginning with *The Seventh Commandment*, a complex guilt-and-cruelty tale which he directed and co-wrote (with Jack Kevan) in 1960. Described by one admirer, director Frank Henenlotter, as "an improbable mix of noirish sex, spirituality, and obsession", it concerns Ted Mathews (Jonathan Kidd), a young man who suffers amnesia after staggering away from a car accident involving him and his girlfriend Terry (Lyn Statten). He's taken in by a travelling preacher (Frank Arvidson), and several years later returns to his hometown as the Rev. Tad Morgan, a genuine healer with supernatural powers, still unaware of his previous life. Meanwhile Terry, who was injured in the accident and is now a bitter ex-convict living in a sleazy apartment with Pete (John Harmon), her crooked boyfriend, decides to take her revenge on the now-respectable preacher by blackmailing him. Ted ends up marrying her while drunk out of his mind, wrongly convinced by this mean-spirited vixen that he caused the crash that started the whole sordid tale. As things spiral downwards for the luckless 'Reverend', the story's cocktail of guilt and revenge leads inexorably to murder...

The Seventh Commandment was shot in Dallas, Texas, and featured soon-to-be horror specialist S.F. Brownrigg as sound mixer. It's a great advertisement for Berwick's newly matured style: it has some great sniping dialogue (When the hero mentions his educational achievements, Terry sneers, *"B.A.? What's that? Bad apple?"*) and an intriguing take on religious hypocrisy. When the Reverend's past catches up with him – or Terry's manufactured version of it, at least – Ted/Tad is tempted to do the decent thing and give himself up to the police. However, with business in the miracle trade booming, and donations skyrocketing, his business partner (and fellow Christian) argues thus: *"No, you will not give yourself up. That would ease your suffering. That would make everything alright in your eyes. But what about His eyes? What right does a sinner have to question His wisdom? If it were not the Lord's will, you would never have started this work. No, you will not give yourself up to any authorities. There's only one authority*

below:
The film shared a bill with **The Dead One**,
Barry Mahon's 1961 voodoo tale.

for you." It's the sort of self-serving argument masquerading as piety you can imagine Jim Bakker (convicted on twenty four counts of fraud and embezzlement) or Jimmy Swaggart (photographed with a Louisiana hooker outside a Travel Inn) having with themselves as they snort cocaine, commit adultery, or steal from the collection box.

Berwick made many friends in the Dallas region, including trash film maestro Larry Buchanan, returning there to shoot several times over the next twenty years. He followed *The Seventh Commandment* with two similarly dark and twisted noirish melodramas. Unfortunately, they cannot be further explored here, as both *Strange Compulsion* and *The Street Is My Beat* are unavailable on either DVD or video. *Strange Compulsion* is particularly hard to research: few critics seem to have caught this Berwick effort, shot in Texas in 1964 and released in December that year. At least the American Film Institute Catalog preserves a brief synopsis, revealing that the story concerns a young medical student afflicted with compulsive voyeurism, who turns to psychoanalysis; whereupon the origin and nature of his obsession is revealed. *The Street Is My Beat* (1966) is a variant on *The Naked Kiss*, and reputedly has some genuine subtleties: according to Ted Newsom, it was Berwick's favourite of his own films. It was written by Jack Kevan and Harold Livingston (the latter a regular scriptwriter for *Mission: Impossible* who later wrote the screenplay for the first *Star Trek* film) and tells the tale of seventeen-year-old Della Martinson (Shary Marshall), who marries an older man, Phil Demarest (Todd Lasswell) to escape from the misery of life with her shiftless father (John Harmon) and domineering mother (Annabelle Weenick aka Anne MacAdams, leading player of the S.F. Brownrigg repertory). But her happiness is short-lived: she discovers

that Phil is a professional procurer for out-of-town businessmen. In order to control her life, he entraps Della in a hotel-room prostitution sting – the court case and subsequent scandal make it impossible for Della to get regular work and she gives in to Phil's suggestions, becoming a high-priced call-girl. When Della catches Phil in bed with another woman she informs on him to the police and goes it alone. Soon she's on the slippery slope to ruin, gaining a drink problem, living in cheap hotel rooms – just another cheap streetwalker. One night she gets involved in a fight with a drunk and falls into the path of an oncoming car. She's admitted to hospital, only to be confronted by her parents…

Ready for Anything!

It was in Texas that Berwick shot the first of his sexploitation films, *Ready for Anything!* (1968), which has never previously been included as part of the Berwick canon. (The film is credited simply to 'Darcia'.) Wayne Berwick informs me that his father began making 'nudies' with *Ready for Anything!* and essayed perhaps as many as ten more in the following ten years, although some may have been unreleased. The Texan provenance is indicated by the presence of one of the Buchanan clan, R.L. Buchanan, as cinematographer (he was the assistant cameraman on two Larry Buchanan pictures from 1967: *Creature of Destruction* and *In the Year 2889*) and Ludwig Moner as assistant cameraman (Moner, another fixture of the Dallas film scene, worked on *Dracula (The Dirty Old Man)* and regularly teamed up with Ron Scott, a director of nudies who appeared in several Larry Buchanan films). Wayne doesn't remember the name 'Darcia', which initially had me worried that there could be two films of the same title kicking around in '68, but nevertheless – judging by the Dallas connections – this is apparently a genuine Irv Berwick film. Wayne Berwick explains, "He was making 'X'-rated pictures around 1970 – including *Ready for Anything!* and *Sexual Hangup* (IrvMar Productions). He felt uncomfortable with me working on *Ready for Anything!*, I think. We talked about it one time and I said, 'If you're not uncomfortable with it then I'm certainly not.' It was just a job. I worked on *Sexual Hangup* and some others that never got released and I don't even remember the titles. He probably made about fifteen altogether. He always used the same DP for every single movie and that was Bill de Diego, a real fast cameraman who I think my dad met when he was looking for people to do his first girlie picture. Dad used a pseudonym on *Sexual Hangup*, but it was my name! It was 'produced' and 'directed' by me. Actually the work I did was the sound, the music and the editing – I edited quite a few of my dad's girlie pictures. When I got back from Europe in '72, my dad and my mom put together this

below, left:
The Seventh Commandment invites you to be the judge: let's hope we can agree on which commandment the seventh one actually is…

below centre, and directly below:
Irv Berwick's nudie **Ready for Anything!** featured numerous cast members from Larry Buchanan's **Mars Needs Women** (1967), including Byron Lord, Larry Tanner, Barnett Shaw and Patrick Cranshaw (the latter of whom also appears in Berwick's **The Seventh Commandment**).

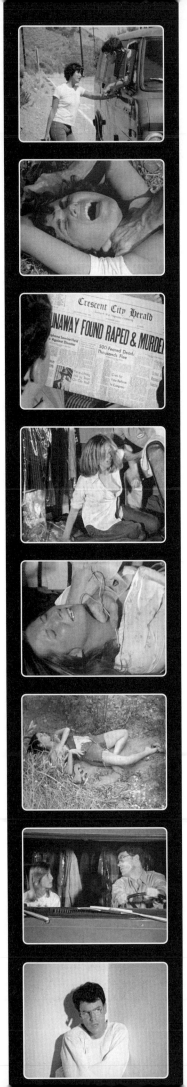

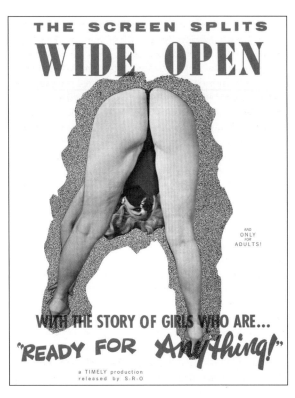

THE SCREEN SPLITS

WIDE OPEN

AND
ONLY
FOR
ADULTS!

WITH THE STORY OF GIRLS WHO ARE...

"READY FOR *Anything!*"

a TIMELY production
released by S-R-O

company called New Directions and they were going to make educational films, about things like drug abuse, stuff like that. I would do the sound and edit all of those. *Sexual Hangup* actually got a release, it played in a huge theatre in Hollywood. It was a big opening, a big deal. It was softcore. There was never any penetration, it was all simulation. Now I don't know if he went further in the couple of films he did without me – I remember there was a time when he said to me look, I gotta go a little more hardcore here 'cos I'm not making any money."

Both *Ready for Anything!* and *Sexual Hangup* are fiendishly obscure titles, and little else is known about them. *Ready for Anything!* apparently stars Larry Tanner, who appeared in Larry Buchanan's *Mars Needs Women* and *The Eye Creatures*, but it remains seemingly impossible to obtain on video or DVD. *Sexual Hangup* is even more obstinate: I've been unable to find another reference to it anywhere. Somewhere, in the garages and film-laboratory vaults and storage vestibules of America, there's an entire shadow industry of lost and forgotten films, and sadly it seems that Irv Berwick's sexploitation films reside there…

Hitch Hike to Infamy

Horror fans on both sides of the Atlantic know the name Irv Berwick chiefly through his psycho-killer movie *Hitch Hike to Hell*, a lurid slice of seventies sleaze that enjoyed wide distribution on video. At the time it was made, Berwick had begun teaching, as Ted Newsom recalls: "Irv taught non-credit adult education classes for the UCLA Extension, which is how I met him. He'd cadge cigarettes from me on break... his wife Mary didn't approve of him smoking, so he had to do it when he was away. The class was called 'Low-Budget Film Production.' Probably 1977 or '78. I'd talk to him about William Castle during a break, and he remembered him fondly (he'd worked with Castle at Columbia prior to the big horror-gimmick breakthrough). During the time he was teaching, the Hillside Strangler case was ongoing in L.A. Irv was either producing or

ghost-directing something like 'The Hillside Strangler Meets the Whateverthehell,' which I think is credited to Ray Dennis Steckler, who's pretty incompetent."[3] At the same time, during the same eight or ten week period, and while he was still teaching, Irv made *Hitch Hike to Hell*."

Hitch Hike to Hell is a classic piece of exploitation cinema, ripping its topically tasteless story screaming from the newspaper headlines. In some ways quite an old-fashioned film, with a twitchy, nerdy killer more suited to the 1960s than the darker 1970s, *Hitch Hike to Hell* nonetheless bears the hallmarks of the more brutal cinema of its day. Although the rape scenes are not sexually explicit, there's a pulse-racing thrill-seeking vibe to the editing, and in particular the music, sending the bad-taste meter way into the red – although in the film's defence, it doesn't commit the cardinal sin of suggesting that the victims either asked for or came to enjoy their violation. This is still not enough to prevent the film from being decried as sexually exploitative: indeed, as Ted Newsom remembers, it was just this charge that was levelled at it by Berwick's female students when, perhaps unwisely, he screened the film for his UCLA class!

But given the moralist thread running through *Hitch Hike to Hell*, to do with the evils of bad parenting and the plight of teenage runaways, can the film can be defended on some levels? Newsom is dismissive of the script's moral equivocation, and cites Berwick: "Irv, in class, used the old phrase 'to take the curse off.' This meant, when doing a sleazeball picture, you toss some redeeming bullshit in there to pacify the blue noses."

Wayne Berwick agrees: "I don't really know how deep his morality went, in terms of his work or anything like that. He projected an attitude of 'Hey, it's exploitable, let's do it.' I don't remember dad's attitude toward the industry being anything but practical. Making films was what he did, and a gig was a gig. He viewed his own work as nothing more than what it was supposed to be. Master shot – over shoulder – close-up – and out. On budget and exploitable. Although he was very pragmatic about the business, he was very much into being 'part of the industry' and the glamour that went with it. I really don't remember much about the period of his life during *Hitch Hike to Hell* other than he was just pluggin' away trying to raise money to make films. The film came about the same way they all did, private investors. John Buckley was a writer buddy of my dad's whom my dad liked to work with because he was fast. That's all he ever said about him, he's fast. I enjoyed working as a soundman on my dad's films more than anyone's. Bing, bang, next set-up. *Hitch Hike* was no exception. A skeleton crew of film students who worked for experience, a professional DP, me on sound and a friend I would hire as a boom operator, and of course always John Harmon, my godfather and my dad's best friend. Since my dad knew he wasn't making Academy Award films, he never treated any shoot like it was life or death."

Hitch Hike to Hell was snapped up for distribution by Box Office International's Harry Novak. Wayne recalls, "Irv had been friends with Harry Novak for a while, through the 'girlie' pictures. He always had a good relationship with him and I always liked him too. It gave my dad the chance to play the gangster role, because Harry was mixed up with some tough guys. My dad came from The Bronx and every now and then he'd like to get back into that tough-guy thing. He was alright with these kinds of people, he grew up with them."

Bad Girls

Berwick turned back to melodrama for *Malibu High* (1978), an entertaining if rough-edged film that saw him hook up with a young tyro producer called Lawrence D. Foldes (best known to horror fans as the director of *Don't Go Near the Park*). Foldes irked rather a lot of people at the time, as Newsom explains: "Larry Foldes hired Irv to make *Malibu High*. Apparently, he was quite brilliant as a child, a genuine prodigy who graduated college by nineteen. But a prodigy is not always the best person to have as a producer. The problem with that sort of thing is, they never have the time to gain social skills. In any case, Irv produced the film *de facto*. I've seldom dealt directly with Larry Foldes, so I can't really say a great deal from personal experience. I know he and Victoria Meyerink were a number for quite some time.[4] They're still married – they just produced a film together a couple of years ago. She apparently was very, very ill for some time and he got her through it. It sounds like he's matured into an extremely nice guy. Of course, he's nearly 50 years old now... But I always got the distinct impression Larry was gay as Christmas. Maybe he was and he didn't realise it. I don't say the latter entirely in jest. I was at the premiere screening of [Foldes's film] *The Great Skycopter Rescue*, an abomination if there ever was one. What a cast! Aldo Ray at his drunkest, William Marshall at his hammiest. Now understand, this was a cast and crew screening with potential investors and distributors there as well. So it should have been a pretty positive, receptive audience. (Larry had fired the experienced second unit DP, deciding he could shoot better stuff himself. He botched it and cost his father, who funded the film, a huge amount of dough to reshoot.) ...So, the itinerate hero wanders into town and buys a burger at a stand. The local thugs show up and molest a nearby girl, tearing her blouse off and posing, huffing and puffing *á là* Brando in *The Wild One* (this is in 1978, a little late for that shit.) The Local Hood (read 'James Dean') weighs in and beats the shit out of the bad guys, who of course vow that they'll have their revenge. Okay, the Hero has met the Local Hood. Hero says, 'You want to come over and have a beer?' 'Sure'. Cut to: Interior, warehouse. Decorated with large airplane models hanging from the high ceiling. Camera starts on the planes and slowly descends down to floor level as we hear the two guys talking: 'So, you're new around here?' 'Yeah, you know, just trying to get to know people…' The camera finally reaches ground level, and here these two mokes are, sitting side by side on a couch – in this *huge* room – side by side in their underwear, drinking beer. The audience absolutely roared. And Larry apparently didn't understand why this was screamingly funny. Maybe he didn't think it was unusual that two total strangers would sit cheek by jowl in their undies in a huge room, immediately after meeting. He made a sequel to *Malibu High*[5] which was plagued with problems, including replacing the director."

Wayne Berwick has similar feelings on the subject of Foldes: "Dad and Bill de Diego worked together on some fifteen films, and they always had the same line with each other: 'Wouldn't it be funny if this was the one!' And after they did *Malibu High*, they said, 'Would you fucking believe it – this is the one – with *that* asshole!' Because they hated Larry Foldes. Everybody hated Larry Foldes! He was just a total egomaniacal spoilt rich kid who thought he was a producer. He'd labelled himself – and the press

caught onto it – as 'the youngest producer in Hollywood', but he'd never done anything. Then *Malibu* got picked up immediately by Crown International, that's why everybody was going around saying, 'I don't believe it, this kid got a picture into immediate distribution.' He hired my dad, who was his teacher at film school at the time, to direct. I remember my dad saw Larry giving direction to an actor one time – I was actually scared that my dad was going to take him apart. He just flipped, and right in front of everybody said, 'You don't EVER, EVER go to my actors!" He reduced him to a kid again. I remember someone telling me that the sound man on *Don't Go Near the Park* punched him out!"

Ted Newsom recalls that *Malibu High* received the odd decent review, although Newsom himself is harder to please: "I remember the *L.A. Times* reviewer Kevin Thomas called *Malibu High* 'a sleazy gem' and compared it to *Pandora's Box*! I caught it at a local multiplex, coming in a few minutes after it started, and hooted and laughed at the obviousness of it all, the goofy/silly transition music. (Hey, this movie is supposed to be serious, and the little music bridges make it sound like a game show!) When the lights came up, I realised Irv and several other people were about six rows from me. They wondered who the horse's ass was who was laughing through the movie. 'Gee', I said, 'I dunno, yeah, I heard it, too!'"

Malibu High does indeed wilt under an absurdly inappropriate score, some of which sounds like shopping-mall-music or something from a twee sixties ad-campaign. It's a shame, because it's actually a fairly tough little drama with some great misanthropic dialogue. Jill Lansing plays Kim Bentley, a teenage tramp with a sociopathic streak a mile wide, who intends to get on in the world no matter what it takes. She's full of contempt for her frumpy mother, harbours a severe grudge against the boyfriend who ditched her, and seduces her teachers in order to blackmail them into giving her top grades. When the headmaster drops by, intending to tell Kim's mother that her daughter's been caught cheating, Kim (home alone) gives the old fool a heart-attack by inviting him in, stripping naked and rubbing her tits in his face. This girl is *dangerous*…

The classroom scenes have a John Waters feel to them; you can imagine Kim hanging out with Divine's 'Dawn Davenport' in *Female Trouble*. She tells her mother she's doing *"relief work"* when the poor dear asks where the new car and fancy clothes are coming from, and as she moves up through the ranks, from hooker to high-class escort to contract killer, she grows to love delivering paybacks on the stupid world around her. Lansing has a slightly gawky coltishness that's almost androgynous at times, and she possesses a great pancake-flat attitude when delivering lines like, *"I really got off on the power of that trigger. Now, when do I get paid?"* – the movie's worth seeing for her performance alone.

The racy, exciting rape-music from *Hitch Hike to Hell* puts in another appearance, this time accompanying a scene in which a punter tries to handcuff Kim and subject her to an S&M violation. The rest of the music is really a puzzle though. Did Berwick and the inexperienced Lawrence Foldes think the film was too dark, and needed cheering up with muzak? Or were they under the impression that cheesy stock-commercial cues would improve the film's chances with the MPAA? This ill-advised use of music dates the film terribly, even as the script tries to upgrade the clichés of wild youth from the fifties to the late seventies. Another handicap

Malibu High
© 1978. Star Cinema Productions
A Star Cinema production.
director: Irv Berwick. producer: Lawrence D. Foldes. screenplay: John Buckley & Tom Singer. original story: John Buckley. cinematographer: William de Diego. editor: Dan Perry. property master: Donald Eaton. sound: Wayne Berwick. assistant cameraman: Nick Vincent. production coordinator: Craig Muckler. associate producer: Tom Singer. script supervisor: Candy Strock. makeup: Joyce Petterson. assistant makeup: Cambra Zweigler. boom operator: A.D. Ackerman. grips: Matt Lane, Richard Buendia. lighting: Kim Haun, Billy Oakes. still photography: Mako Koiwai. title song "Lovely But Deadly" by Steve Myland. filmed on location in Southern California. Interiors at Gabor Lovy Studios & R.F.Studios.
Cast: Jill Lansing (Kim Bentley). Stuart Taylor (Kevin). Katie Johnson (Lucy). Phyllis Benson (Mrs. Bentley). Al Mannino (Tony). Tammy Taylor (Annette Ingersoll). Garth Howard (Lance). John Harmon (Mr. Elmhurst). John Grant (Mr. Donaldson). Jim Devney (Mr. Wyngate). Robert Gordon (Harry Ingersoll). Ken Layton (Mr. Mooney). Cambra Zweigler (Valerie). William Cohen (jeweller). Susan Gorton (Miss Primm). Bill Burke (Mr. H). Scott Walters (paper boy). A.D. Ackerman (henchman).

opposite picture-strip, top to bottom:
More mayhem from **Hitch Hike to Hell**.

below, and opposite top:
Although **Ready for Anything!** has seemingly been lost, we do have these evocative and exuberant admats, one of which thankfully preserves Berwick's pseudonym of 'Darcia' for posterity.

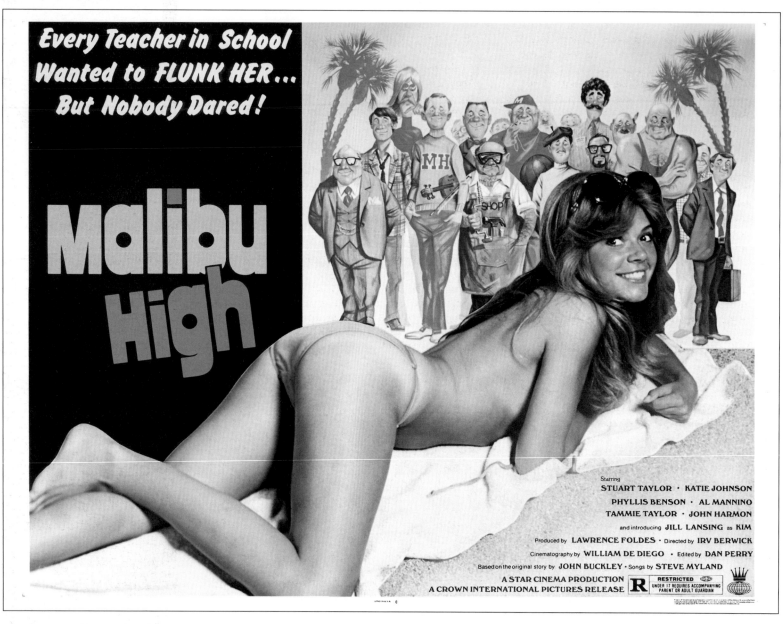

Every Teacher in School Wanted to FLUNK HER... But Nobody Dared!

Malibu High

Starring
STUART TAYLOR · KATIE JOHNSON
PHYLLIS BENSON · AL MANNINO
TAMMIE TAYLOR · JOHN HARMON
and introducing JILL LANSING as KIM
Produced by LAWRENCE FOLDES · Directed by IRV BERWICK
Cinematography by WILLIAM DE DIEGO · Edited by DAN PERRY
Based on the original story by JOHN BUCKLEY · Songs by STEVE MYLAND
A STAR CINEMA PRODUCTION
A CROWN INTERNATIONAL PICTURES RELEASE

above:
In a decision that must have offended Jill Lansing, who stars in **Malibu High** as the amoral Kim, this poster (and all other artwork I've seen for the film, including the UK video cover) replaces the coltish, distinctive actress with a bustier, bimboish model.

opposite page, strip of images:
The chaos continues unabated in **Microwave Massacre**.

is Bill de Diego's camerawork, which is unadventurous and unhelpful. The camera often just stares at the actors, when a livelier approach could have broadened the film's appeal. It's a testament to the lead actress and the pulpish script that such deficiencies don't cut the whole thing off at the knees. If Berwick was the sort of guy to attempt satire, this story could profitably have been played as such: setting off as a light and frothy comedy and then becoming gradually more sleazy and misanthropic, it could have ended up rather like Michael Lehman's wonderful *Heathers* (1989). Still, it's a strong enough tale well served by the cast, and definitely worth checking out. Not that you'd guess from the promotional artwork for *Malibu High*, which gives no hint of the blackness of the content. Wayne Berwick explains: "Crown International hired a model to do the one-sheet, and she wasn't even in it. It was a T&A shot of this sexy girl on the beach looking flirtatiously at the camera; a complete 180-degree turn from the film, which was a real dark, almost sleazy movie. But then *The Street Is My Beat* and *The Seventh Commandment* were kinda sleazy too, what my dad called his 'early-girlie pictures' – only *Monster of Piedras Blancas* was any different!"

At least one version of *Malibu High* spared the audience's blushes, although it's unlikely to appeal to exploitation fans, as Newsom explains: "Another thing that

kills it, in its TV version, is the editing to cover the nudity and *faux* sex scenes. They just cut to the same damned shot of a field of grass at sunset near the beach, panning over it for as long as the scene takes – 15 seconds… 45 seconds… three minutes… That's a *lot* of grass."

As noted, Irv Berwick continued making adult films through the seventies, but he tried his hand at other fare too – no matter how incongruous. Wayne explains: "He made this thing called *Suddenly the Light* – a religious film. In between the porn he was doing religious films! This was 1978, same year as *Malibu High*. I did two films that year with him. We shot it out in Dallas, with Baptist money, spent the summer out there in the Dallas heat, with a film student crew and Bill de Diego. My dad loved to shoot in Dallas, one because there was a studio there called Jamieson Studios and a great film lab that he liked, plus it was a 'right to work' State, so there was never any problem with the unions. He loved Dallas."

Ted Newsom was involved in another of Berwick's religious pictures: "I worked for Irv on the crew once, on a short film that was tentatively titled *Lawn Party*, a 16mm thing done for some Baptist folk down in Texas, I think. I ended up playing a part in a scene with the lead kid when our actor didn't show up. And that was shot out here in California. It was retitled something else. When we were shooting it, I thought *Lawn Party* was the lamest title I'd ever seen. Irv had a 16mm print of it and showed it one night at his house to friends (contemporaries, so they were all in their sixties). I'm afraid Craig Muckler and I, and perhaps Wayne, were not very respectful to it. It was some silly thing about a kid who loses his faith when he realises his dad is working with a crooked real estate guy. The Good Kid falls in with a Bad Kid and robs a grocery store (John Harmon played the owner). The kids leave, have an off-screen auto accident and the Good Kid ends up in the hospital, clinging to life. A cop takes the despondent father aside and says, 'He wasn't making much sense. He was saying something like, 'Please, God, don't let my father go through with this crooked real estate scheme.' What do you suppose he meant by that?' Honest to God, that was the dialogue verbatim. I loved it and memorised it, it was so lame. Irv wasn't a bit religious though. Not unreligious, either. He was Jewish, for goodness sake, and he's directing films for the holy rollers! Irv would do anything if it paid the bills and looked pretty fun."

Farewell to Berwick Sr.

Things got tough for Irv Berwick in the latter stages of his life. Wayne feels that his father grew more cynical about his work, and felt ground down by the process, over the years: "He would have preferred to be an actor. He started out working with actors, and he was an actor at heart. He used it in his life – he could be the tough guy when he was with the tough guys, and he could play the charmer too. He was an incredible charmer, especially with the ladies – not in a philandering way, but he really loved women. We'd sit in a coffee shop and an elderly woman would come in, and he'd say to me, 'Look at her eyes and her make-up; she's spent some time, I'm gonna go over to her and tell her how beautiful she is.' You'd see her face just light up, and he'd come back and finish his lunch. He was a very emotional guy, but not on the set. He was very easy-going but it was all about speed, and keeping in budget. And that's why Bill de Diego was so important, they knew the next thing to do immediately, there was never any need for discussion."

Ted Newsom recalls: "A lot of the life went out of Irv when his wife died in 1982. She was a rock. She was a teacher as I recall, and worked steadily. Irv's productions were sporadic, since that's the nature of the business. Late in his life he moved from their house to a condo. He was burgled and lots of his memorabilia was stolen. Really rotten." Wayne adds, "He just worshipped my mom, and everybody figured he's not gonna last long, but he toughed it out." Irv Berwick did indeed tough it out, for another fifteen years. When he finally died of heart failure on 29 June, 1997, he was 82.

It's a great pity that many of Irv Berwick's films are impossible to see today. That may not matter too much where his sex films are concerned, but on the strength of *The Seventh Commandment*, the obscurity that bedevils *Strange Compulsion* and *The Street Is My Beat* is infuriating. If Wayne Berwick is right, we're lacking at least eight if not ten further film credits for his father, and although these are likely to be ephemera, it would be good one day to have a true picture of the entire scope of his work. In many ways, Berwick's career parallels that of John Hayes (see chapter on Hayes), in that both men directed a handful of accomplished black-and-white melodramas before moving

into the horror genre and sexploitation material in the 1970s. A viewing of Hayes's pseudonymous sex films actually sheds valuable further light on his creativity, and although Berwick would seem perhaps less motivated to create art under such unpromising conditions, you never can tell. At least we have four good examples of his craft: a classic fifties monster movie; a lively pulp melodrama; a lurid horror film; and – perhaps the most unusual – a curious, bitter-edged 'coming-of-age' crime story. Even these few movies guarantee Irv Berwick a place in the history of American independent cinema.

Wayne Berwick – Early Days

Wayne Berwick was born on 10 July, 1949 in North Hollywood, CA. Movies have been an intrinsic part of his life for as long as he can remember: "I literally grew up on the soundstages at Universal Studios. My dad was a dialogue director there for the first eight years of my life and my mom would hang out there and take me with her. Guys like Tony Curtis, Burt Lancaster and Edward G. Robinson would be liftin' me up, rufflin' my hair and chattin' with me all the time. I think the first movie I saw was a Ray Harryhausen Sinbad thing.[6] Whatever it was, it hooked me enough that forty five years later, if I don't get my movie fix I get uneasy."

Like his father, Wayne Berwick is also a musician – but unlike his father he has turned this talent into a career. Initially, the idea of directing a movie didn't occur to him: "It was something my dad did, but after high school when I moved out of the house, I needed a real job. I moved to Venice Beach and lied my way into a gig as a sound recordist for an educational film company. Turned out to be a one man operation. This guy did everything – he was his whole crew and he needed someone to at least run sound, to take some of the load off. So naturally I learned and did everything as well. It was during this time that I became enthralled with the process, and for the next two years he and I made dozens of ten- and twenty-minute mini-movies with some sort of health or safety message – usually whatever was hot at the time. I remember getting a lot of mileage out of VD! [laughs] He wanted to make a career out of it, but I wanted to go to Europe, so I packed a guitar, some harmonicas and some underwear and went. I played in and visited just about everywhere except Eastern Europe." Berwick left midway through 1970 and returned in 1972. Once back home again, he began supplementing his musician's income by working as a soundman on low-budget films, ranging, as he says, "from 'G' to 'X' rating. It was during this time I started making Super-8 films. On one of my soundman gigs in the summer of 1978, I became good friends with a couple of the associate producers. One of them had an outline for a tongue-in-cheek but creepy horror film. The other one claimed he could write the script and raise the $75,000 that I said I could make it for. By October '78 we were shooting. Problem was, the script he turned in, two days before principal photography was to begin, was ninety pages of bad one-liners. What had been creepy, understated humour was completely over the top – in your face. It was quite an adjustment, so my take on it was to make it even more blatant, as if to say, 'You thought *that* was stupid? Well we're havin' so much fun that, here, have some more!' When I saw the script, I knew there was only one way to go with it, and that was to aim for the alcohol and reefer crowd."

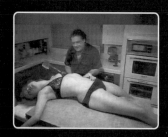

Ingredients

The script, of course, was *Microwave Massacre*, and Berwick's partners in crime were Craig Muckler and Tom Singer. Singer was, and still is, an L.A. sports reporter for newspapers, while Muckler, who had been involved in the production of Berwick Sr.'s *Malibu High*, hosted his own cable TV show at the time, called *Craig Muckler's Hollywood Showcase*. Among his guests were Aldo Ray, William Sanderson, Misty Rowe, Bo Svenson – and the soon-to-be star of *Microwave Massacre*, Jackie Vernon. Muckler came up with the title, helped Berwick whip Singer's script into shootable form, and made the introductions to Vernon, who was quite a significant catch for a low-budget film by a young unknown, as Ted Newsom explains: "Vernon was famous in the early sixties as a stand-up comedian, with a Buster Keaton-style deadpan delivery. Very put-upon character on stage; background in improv comedy *á là* Shelley Berman, Nichols & May, etc."

"Jackie Vernon came on board before the script was finished," recalls Berwick. "He was at a point in his career where he needed the work more than he needed a script to read. He was a very recognisable comedian, his claim to fame is he's the voice of *Frosty the Snowman*, which is shown a few hundred times every December. Was it a stretch for him to play a drunk? He wasn't much of a drinker and was a total pro, but lord have mercy if he ran out of Quaaludes."

Vernon is undoubtedly top banana in the cast, but he's supported by several notable eccentrics: not least the woman who plays his crazy wife. "Claire Ginsberg was a piece of work," laughs Berwick. "She was hired because she *was* the character she played. I remember the day she had to put her head inside the oven so when Jackie opened it we'd see her. She wouldn't do it. Didn't want to get electrocuted. The oven was cardboard! She got hysterical, I got pissed off, and I remember her sitting in the corner on the floor shaking and sobbing uncontrollably about the way I talked to her." As for the role of the bad-tempered barman, Berwick says: "When Phil De Carlo read for the bartender role, we immediately sent everyone else home. We were afraid if we didn't hire him he'd have us whacked! Turned out to be the nicest guy in the world."

Devotees of *The Texas Chain Saw Massacre* will probably have rented *Microwave Massacre* as soon as they noticed that Robert Burns was involved. Burns's design work for the classic Tobe Hooper film is, along with Charles D. Hall's work on James Whale's *Frankenstein*, probably the most creative and influential piece of set dressing in the genre's history. Berwick found him charming: "Robert Burns sent a résumé, I didn't know who he was but I sure as hell knew *The Texas Chain Saw Massacre*, so we met at his funky place at the beach, where he shared the place with all kinds of bodies and heads and limbs. What more could someone who was directing a cannibal comedy want? Plus Robert was a great guy: creepy, but great. By the way, I'm glad you noticed the tacky seventies brochure interior. Robert and I had discussed it, and were going for it. He was very very low key, just a weird guy but very nice. All these severed heads and mummies and stuff all over the place at this little two-room place he had down at the beach. He was just moving from Austin Texas out here to Venice Beach, California, and he sent us his résumé, came out for an interview. Which he

didn't have to do: I mean, we saw *Texas Chain Saw Massacre* and he was hired! He was great. No ego at all."

The film was shot quickly in the fall of 1978, and Berwick enjoyed the process enormously: "Because of the attitude I took when I got the finished script (which was 'this better be a good time'), I really didn't have a lot of pressure. I knew from my low-budget experience, and the corners I'd learned to cut by watching my dad, that I could bring it in for $75,000. I found out after the shoot that there wasn't one day when we had enough money to shoot the following day. The producers withheld this info so I wouldn't have to think about it. We shot fifteen days straight. The locations were all local. The house belonged to Mickey Dolenz and he'd just moved out, so it was empty. The opening scene with the girl bouncing down the street was done last minute. The opening credits were supposed to be shot in a market, and as someone is shopping in the meat department, the credits are on the meat packages. The market pulled out at the last second and we (the whole crew) were sitting around the producer's apartment trying to figure out what to do, when my dad's old T&A influence hit me. The DP[7] had a friend with her. A cute busty friend. So that's her walkin' back and forth on the sidewalk in front the producer's apartment. We were pretty brazen in how we shot exteriors. We'd set up anywhere and act like we belonged. I remember shooting one day on Santa Monica Boulevard. The police just assumed we had a permit and would just drive by. When two biker cops finally stopped, I told the production manager to send over a couple of the girls we were using. They flirted with them for quite awhile, plenty of time to finish what we had to do. When you're stealing shots, staying low-key and keeping it out of the press to avoid any union hassles is the goal."

Garnish and Serve

Berwick got a further blast from editing his picture: "The editing process is what hooked me when I was doing the educational films. It was the illusion you could create in that room with those pieces of film that blew me away and made me want to make movies. It wasn't working with actors, I'll tell ya that. Editing took eight weeks, a lot of all-nighters, usually resulting in too much coffee, not enough food and then dry heaves for breakfast."

The first version Berwick cut together attempted to send up not only the cannibalism concept but also its genre style and pacing: "I wanted to go so over the top, because it was so stupid. I said look, let's break some rules, so I would keep Jackie walking from the sidewalk to the house to the garage and I would deliberately keep the camera on him so it went on and on until people would just think 'Oh my God' like when he was loading the meat into the refrigerator, I made that go on forever! But it was probably a wise decision to cut out all that stuff, and instead we went back and shot more nudity and more gore."

So, a fun-filled experience from start to finish? Nearly... "I had already enjoyed the filmmaking process and I thoroughly enjoyed the idea of being a movie director. It was just a flat-out rush: until distribution. Nobody wanted it. I mean, can you blame them? Very few people 'got it'. They weren't ready for it. Is it supposed to be gory, is it supposed to be funny? I remember we were screening it for a distributor one time, and by this time I couldn't watch the film anymore, so I was sitting in the lobby. Turns out the distributor left through the back exit and when the film was

320

over, out walks Timothy Leary with an entourage of freaks. He loved it! To this day, I have no idea what they were doing there. Anyway, we went back and re-shot some scenes, added some more gratuitous nudity and it was picked up. I don't know which version you've seen. If it's the one distributed by Rhino, that's the softer version. The other one was released by Midnight Video: we went back and reshot some stuff and cut out some of the slower stuff, and that had a picture of Jackie looking in at May in the microwave, drooling." (The British video release from Astra is the stronger version).

It was Berwick's misfortune to have directed an irreverent gore comedy three years before the smash success of a film like *An American Werewolf in London* (1981) popularised the format. For nearly five years the film sat on the shelf, unloved: later, Berwick says, "People were comparing it to *Eating Raoul*." I asked him if there had been much of an influence from comedy skit packages like *The Kentucky Fried Movie*: "I'm sure that's where Tom Singer was coming from, and I had to sort of settle into that and accept it. John Landis was an influence because of that film, and a lot of it came from stuff like the Corman picture, *The Little Shop of Horrors*. A very creepy comedy, that's what we originally had in mind, where you'd be laughing at something but you'd set someone up with actual fear. I was always into the Sam Raimi stuff, *Evil Dead*, the stuff that had a sense of humour. Although the thing that turned me on to horror was when I was a kid and I saw Peter Lorre in *The Beast with Five Fingers* – that movie just freaked me out! The severed hand, the whole atmosphere of that movie. I was always wondering, 'How do you get people scared like that?'

Ted Newsom was not directly involved in *Microwave Massacre*, but he figured in the film's journey to video. He adds these observations about the movie: "I just rewatched that, and it's not as awful as it ought to be. It's a $70-80,000 budget, with ten or twenty grand going into Vernon's pocket. They had nothing but problems with the distributors. It did actually play in theatres; released on tape by Select-a-Tape and I later sold it to Rhino for re-release. I had nothing to do with the making of *Microwave*; nobody asked, although I lived less than a mile away. I've always been miffed they didn't at least ask me to come work on the crew for free! Later on I got my revenge, selling it to Rhino and at least taking a small commission, so I probably made more than I would have at twenty dollars a day on the crew! I did do a photo shoot for a little bit in *Oui* magazine (a girl with an apple in her mouth, carrot slices on her nipples and parsley on her bush, being loaded into the giant prop microwave like a loaf of French bread.) and I got it a nice little three-page blurb published in *Famous Monsters*."

After-Dinner

Newsom and Berwick remained friends, and in 1985 they began working together on Berwick's second and so far last directorial credit: *The Naked Monster*, known for several years in its unfinished state as *Attack of the B-Movie Monster*. "Wayne directed, I wrote and produced," says Newsom. "In the cast are the late John Harmon, Les Tremayne, and Jeanne Carmen. And a lighthouse. My little tip of the hat to *Piedras Blancas*."

Filmed in Super-8, with the idea of reshooting later in 16mm or 35mm, *Attack* was, Berwick readily admits, more Ted Newsom's baby than his own: "He was the fifties

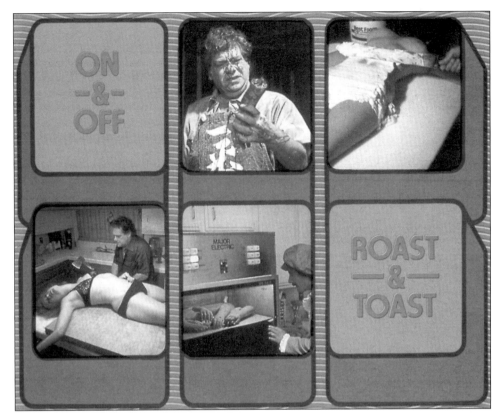

above:
Microwave Massacre stills montage taken from the back cover of the Astra video release.

monster movie freak, I just happened to have the connection to *Monster of Piedras Blancas* and I really enjoyed monster movies, but I didn't know who these people were as much as Ted." To begin with, Berwick and Newsom shot initial footage with John Harmon. It proved to be a fortunate decision, because Harmon died soon afterwards. His appearance in *The Naked Monster*, a film dedicated to the heyday of American monster movies, is a lovely coda to a career spanning half a century. After soliciting the involvement of iconic actors Kenneth Tobey and Robert Cornthwaite (*The Thing*), John Agar (*The Mole People*), Robert Clarke (*The Hideous Sun Demon*), Les Tremayne (*The War of the Worlds*) and Gloria Talbott (*The Daughter of Dr. Jekyll*), Newsom then sourced a selection of soundtrack cues from the Perma Music Library to give the movie an authentic period flavour: "Ronald Stein was the composer," he says, "I was involved in the Perma company with his widow Harlene. It's the same music that was tracked into AIP pictures like the Buchanan stuff, *The Eye Creatures*, *Zontar the Thing from Venus*, from even earlier things like *The Terror* and *Attack of the 50 Foot Woman*." Added to these classic music cues are about ten minutes of footage drawn from old movies, which when combined with the new footage create an affectionate spoof that echoes some of the strategies of the Steve Martin comedy *Dead Men Don't Wear Plaid*. Thanks to a starry cast drawn from the height of the post-war monster movie craze, some of whom reprise their former roles, and a scattershot *Airplane*-style humour tinged with welcome doses of irony, *The Naked Monster* is a genuinely inventive piece of cine-bricolage. It was finally completed in 2005, credited to Newsom and Berwick as co-directors, and is now available on DVD. Let's hope that one day a future Ted Newsom or Wayne Berwick will do the same for the much-loved B-movie stars of seventies horror!

One project that might have brought both Newsom and Berwick to renewed prominence in the horror genre

opposite page, strip of images:
More **Microwave Massacre** madness.

above:
A scene from **The Monster of Piedras Blancas**; Ted Newsom reveals that there was once an option for a sequel to Irv Berwick's B-movie classic.

sadly never saw the light of day. Ted Newsom explains: "Wayne and I, along with FX guy Mark Williams (he died eight years ago at the age of 38) planned to do a sequel to *Piedras Blancas*. Mark had done a script which I didn't think was very good; I wanted to do something else. I started working on an idea that involved two tabloid reporters who are looking for a story to make up *á là* UFOs… they get marooned in Piedras Blancas at just the wrong time. Mark Williams had made up a head for it, based on the original. He was really nuts about the movie. He, and Bob & Denny Skotak (both Oscar winning FX guys), were working together; there was a plan to blow up the lighthouse (in miniature, of course, the Skotak speciality) in the climax. But we hadn't reckoned on one thing – Irv had sold off ALL RIGHTS to the picture to the distributor NTA… for about $250. He didn't think 'those old pictures' were worth anything. Jeeezuss!!!"

Berwick's only other screen directing credit is a short film called *The Shooter*, made right after *Naked Monster*'s first shoot, in 1986. "It got a lot of cable play," Berwick says. "It was a featurette showcase about a crapshooter that played in the early days of Pay TV." Today, though, Wayne Berwick is a musician first and foremost, and he's quite clear that he would only be interested in returning to the film industry if it were, as he puts it, "No bullshit – the

money's there and it's all ready to go." With bullshit-free experiences in film production as rare as hen's tooth pâté, we probably ought not to hold our breath, but we can at least be grateful that Berwick gave us a unique, offbeat and insane film like *Microwave Massacre*. After all these years, there's still nothing quite like it…

Footnotes

[1] Maxwell Arnow was casting director on *Gone with the Wind*.

[2] Berwick receives an associate producer credit only.

[3] Newsom is referring to Steckler's *The Hollywood Strangler Meets the Skidrow Slasher*, and his judgement is, if anything, too lenient…

[4] They married in 1983 and are still together.

[5] *The Graduates of Malibu High* aka *Young Warriors*, made in 1983.

[6] Probably *The 7th Voyage of Sinbad*, 1958.

[7] Karen Grossman, who shot *The Slayer* in 1982.

IRV BERWICK: FILMOGRAPHY AS DIRECTOR

1958	*The Monster of Piedras Blancas*
1960	*The Seventh Commandment* (also producer / writer)
1964	*Strange Compulsion* (also producer / writer)
1966	*The Street Is My Beat* (also producer)
1968	*Ready for Anything!* (as 'Darcia')
1972	*Sexual Hangup* (credited to Wayne Berwick)
1977	*Hitch Hike to Hell* (also producer)
1978	*Suddenly the Light*
1978	*Lawn Party*
1978	*Malibu High*
plus	between 10-15 adult titles between 1968 and 1977 – titles unknown

OTHER CREDITS:

1945	*A Guy, a Gal, and a Pal* – dir: Oscar Boetticher Jr. (dialogue director)
1945	*Blazing the Western Trail* – dir: Vernon Keays (dialogue director)
1945	*Lawless Empire* – dir: Vernon Keays (dialogue director)
1945	*Song of the Prairie* – dir: Ray Nazarro (dialogue director)
1945	*The Power of the Whistler* – dir: Lew Landers (dialogue director)
1945	*Youth on Trial* – dir: Oscar Boetticher Jr. (dialogue director)
1946	*Death Valley* – dir: Lew Landers (dialogue director)
1947	*Copacabana* – dir: Alfred E. Green (dialogue director)
1947	*Danger Street* – dir: Lew Landers (may have contributed to dialogue)
1948	*Adventures of Gallant Bess* – dir: Lew Landers (dialogue director)
1948	*Bungalow 13* – dir: Edward L. Cahn (dialogue director)
1948	*Inner Sanctum* – dir: Lew Landers (dialogue director)
1949	*I Cheated the Law!* – dir: Edward L. Cahn (dialogue director)
1949	*Zamba* – dir: William Berke (dialogue director)
1950	*Sierra* – dir: Alfred E. Green (dialogue director)
1951	*Apache Drums* – dir: Hugo Fregonese (dialogue director)
1951	*Cattle Drive* – dir: Kurt Neumann (dialogue director)
1951	*The Raging Tide* – dir: George Sherman (dialogue director)
1952	*Against All Flags* – dir: George Sherman (dialogue director)
1952	*Aladdin and His Lamp* – dir: Lew Landers (dialogue director)
1952	*Horizons West* – dir: Budd Boetticher (dialogue director)
1953	*Topper* [TV Series] (dialogue director – uncredited)

1953	*City Beneath the Sea* – dir: Budd Boetticher (dialogue director)
1953	*East of Sumatra* – dir: Budd Boetticher (dialogue director)
1953	*Law and Order* – dir: Nathan Juran (dialogue director)
1953	*The Glass Web* – dir: Jack Arnold (dialogue director)
1953	*The Lone Hand* – dir: George Sherman (dialogue director)
1954	*Border River* – dir: George Sherman (dialogue director)
1954	*Playgirl* – dir: Joseph Pevney (dialogue director)
1954	*War Arrow* – dir: George Sherman (dialogue director)
1954	*Yankee Pasha* – dir: Joseph Pevney (dialogue director)
1955	*The Private War of Major Benson* – dir: Jerry Hopper (dialogue director)
1956	*Red Sundown* – dir: Jack Arnold (dialogue coach)
1957	*The Land Unknown* – dir: Virgil Vogel (dialogue coach)
1958	*The Big Beat* – dir: Will Cowan (dialogue coach)
1958	*The Saga of Hemp Brown* – dir: Richard Carlson (dialogue coach)
1958	*The Thing That Couldn't Die* – dir: Will Cowan (dialogue coach)
1958	*Wild Heritage* – dir: Charles Haas (dialogue coach)
1960	*Spartacus* – dir: Stanley Kubrick (unknown)
1967	*Rough Night in Jericho* – dir: Arnold Laven (dialogue coach)
1979	*The Hollywood Strangler Meets the Skidrow Slasher* – dir: Ray Dennis Steckler (uncertain: possibly writer)
1981	*The Loch Ness Horror* – dir: Larry Buchanan (associate producer + uncredited 2nd unit director)

WAYNE BERWICK: FILMOGRAPHY AS DIRECTOR

1978	*Microwave Massacre*
1986	*The Naked Monster* aka *Attack of the B Movie Monster* (also actor) (completed in 2005 – co-dir: Ted Newsom)
1986	*The Shooter* (7min short, for cable TV)

OTHER CREDITS:

1958	*The Monster of Piedras Blancas* (actor)
1961	*The Seventh Commandment* (actor)
1972	*Sexual Hangup* (sound recordist / music / editing)
1981	*The Loch Ness Horror* (sound recordist)
1993/2001	*"Diagnosis Murder"* (writer)

chapter 18

Mind Before Matter

Robert Allen Schnitzer on The Premonition

The Premonition (1975)

"Strange, complex and haunting, in the Val Lewton tradition."
– *The Aurum Film Encyclopedia: Horror.*

"Though some of the film is clumsy and amateurish, Robert Allen Schnitzer […] creates a genuinely eerie spell."
– *Variety*

Little Janie Bennett (Danielle Brisebois) lives happily with her adoptive parents, Sheri (Sharon Farrell), a painter, and Miles (Edward Bell), a college professor. She has no knowledge of her real mother, Andrea Fletcher (Ellen Barber), who has until recently been incarcerated in a mental institution. Now free, Andrea is scouring the area looking for Janie, with the help of Jude (Richard Lynch), a circus employee whom she met while he too was under psychiatric supervision. When Janie visits the circus with her parents, Andrea and Jude spot her, and hatch a plan to snatch the girl from her bedroom and take her with them to live in a broken-down house in the country. Andrea gains entry to the Bennett's house and even Janie's bedroom. However, due to her mental instability, she ends up fleeing with only a doll. At the abandoned house, Andrea sinks into fantasy, until Jude can take no more…

When Andrea's dead body is recovered from a lake, to which Sheri guides the police after seeing it in a vision, the danger would seem to have passed. And yet something is *still* reaching out for Janie, some force that transcends death. Sheri sees terrifying visions, and after a supernatural attack on her car sends it careening off the road, she wakes in hospital to be told that her daughter has disappeared from the crash site. Desperate for help, Sheri turns to Miles's colleague, Jeena Kingsly (Chiitra Neogy), a parapsychology lecturer. As Jeena helps Sheri to piece the truth together, and Miles reluctantly overcomes his scepticism, a most unusual plan is hatched to draw Janie back to her loving parents…

This bold and imaginative movie comes out of left field, with a tone and ambition that sets it apart from the norm. The story of an unbalanced mother trying to take back her daughter from the couple who adopted her is hardly a hackneyed plot for a horror tale, and to make things even stranger, Robert Allen Schnitzer – who wrote as well as directed – gleefully adds telepathy and precognition to a topic one would normally encounter in a rationalist context. The acting is strong and assured, especially from Barber and Lynch, and Schnitzer's directing builds up some powerful suspense, dotted with genuinely startling shock moments.

The tale is told in a non-linear way, with information patched together piece by piece, and not always in a way that makes immediate sense. The viewer has to work to understand what's going on, and certain ambiguities are left to float for a while as other strands of the story dominate. All of which adds up to a highly individual effort from Schnitzer, the quality of which makes you sorry that he never returned to the genre. If his ambition had outstripped his ability, this would have been something of a mess, but he brings skill and sensitivity to the storytelling, a firm hand to the technical aspects, and a clear aptitude for working with actors. Whatever your feelings about the parapsychological concepts Schnitzer raises, there's no doubting his sincerity and his genuine imaginative involvement.

In the hands of a more conservative director, the tale would concern a nice adoptive family being threatened by a psychotic blood relative; you can imagine what kind of a mess Adrian Lyne would make of it. Instead, Schnitzer

below:
Sheri (Sharon Farrell) clutches daughter Janie (Danielle Brisbois) to her bosom in **The Premonition**. Brisebois returned to the horror genre in 1987 to star in a **Tales from the Darkside** adaptation of a Clive Barker short story, 'The Yattering and Jack'.

The Premonition
aka **The Adoption** (script title)
aka **Turtle Heaven** (shooting title)
© 1975. Galaxy Films Productions, Inc.
A Galaxy Films production. A Robert Allen
Schnitzer. An Avco Embassy Pictures release.
producer/director: Robert Allen Schnitzer.
executive producer: M. Wayne Fuller. associate
producers: Laurie Silver, Dale Trevillion.
production manager: J. Boyce Harman. written
by Anthony Mahon, Robert Allen Schnitzer.
director of photography: Victor C. Milt. music
composed and performed by Henry Mollicone.
electronic music: Pril Smiley. editor: Sidney
Katz, a.c.e. associate editor: Virginia Katz. art
direction: John Lawless. 1st assistant director:
Norman C. Derns. sound mixer: William
Meredith. lighting director: William W. Lister. key
grip: Lester Berman. make-up artist: Rita
Ogden. costume supervisor: Jennifer Nichols.
script supervisor: B. Alexander Fedack. 2nd unit
cameraman: Carter Lord. assistant cameraman:
Justus Taylor. 2nd assistant cameraman:
Michael Kantrowitz. boom operator: Albee
Gordon. 2nd grip: Jeff Wolf. colour stills: Janet
Knott. 2nd assistant director: Laurie Silver. 2nd
electrician: Jerry Johnson. production
associate: Mark Weisel. financial counsel:
Robert Feinschreiber. assistant art director:
Stephen Finkin. assistant production manager:
Patricia Kirck. special effects: Ken Newman.
additional dialogue: Louis Pastore. vocals: Ellen
Barber. production coordinators: Pam Pritzker,
Steve Maurer. re-recording: Emil Neroda. sound
editor: Dan Sable. opticals: EFX Unlimited.
casting consultant: Sylvia Fay. consultants:
Harvey Rochman, Stephen F. Kesten, John E.
Quill, Hal Schaffel. Lenses & camera by
Panavision. colour by TVC. toys and
accessories furnished by Gloria Shavel, Inc.
vehicles furnished by International Harvester.
Milky Way photo courtesy of The American
Museum; Hayden Planetarium. Special thanks
to The State of Mississippi Film Commission
and The Mississippi Highway Patrol. filmed in
Mississippi (USA).
Cast: Sharon Farrell (Sheri Bennett). Edward
Bell (Miles Bennett). Jeff Corey (Lt. Mark
Denver). Chitra Neogy (Dr. Jeena Kingsly).
Richard Lynch (Jude). Ellen Barber (Andrea).
Danielle Brisebois (Janie Bennett). Rosemary
McNamara (Lenore). Roy White (Doctor
Larabee). Margaret Graham (landlady). Thomas
Williams (Todd Fletcher). Wilmuth Cooper
(gypsy lady). Mark Schneider (patrolman).
Robert Harper (night watchman). Stanley W.
Winn (Dean Fuller). Tamara Bergdall (nurse).
Bonita Chambers (receptionist). Edward L.
Emling, Jr. (student).

Beyond the power
of an exorcist...

✶ ✵ EMBASSY
Home Entertainment

The Premonition

Starring
SHARON FARRELL,
RICHARD LYNCH,
JEFF COREY

gives Andrea and Jude first bite of the cherry, making them
into protagonists deserving of our interest and concern
before going on to reveal what they're doing. The truth
takes some time to emerge, and in that time we're allowed
to imagine that they are perhaps simply devoted, if
unconventional, parents of a missing daughter. The result
of this strategy is that we cannot simply look upon Andrea
and Jude as monsters. At times, the taut, neurotic Andrea
and compressed, ticking-bomb Jude are more sympathetic
and compelling than the cosy but somewhat complacent
family they're stalking. They are certainly terrifying at
times, but we're always encouraged to view them with
compassion. Schnitzer uses camera style to contrast the
two couples: dialogue sequences between Andrea and Jude
are filmed hand-held, conveying nervousness and urgency,
while similar two-header shots of the Bennetts are more
stable and restrained.

Schnitzer's film is about the bond of motherhood, to
which even some sceptics are willing to attribute a quasi-
mystical quality. Sheri's psychic sensitivity and Andrea's
supernatural bond with her daughter are examples of
'extreme motherhood', and the battle that takes place for
the child is all the more striking for its lack of conventional aggression. There's a creepy scene early on at
Janie's school, when Andrea watches through the school
fence and tries, unsuccessfully, to speak to her estranged
daughter. The camera moves from a shot of Andrea's
fingertips poking through the wire fence, to a diagonal
angle revealing Andrea in her entirety, peering through. It's
an uncanny effect, emphasising her desperation, and her
desire to transgress barriers (including, ultimately, that of
death itself). Sheri sees this strange, agitated woman and,
without knowing why, feels unsettled. Perhaps she has had
some prior knowledge of Andrea – a photo in a case file
glimpsed at the adoption agency, for instance – but the
film wastes little time breeding such doubts, dispensing
with ambivalence about the paranormal fairly early on: it's
clear that Sheri's heightened instinct goes beyond the
realm of conventional psychology.

In a film with many great sequences, perhaps most
powerful is the one in which Andrea, wearing heavy make-
up and a red evening gown, enters the Bennett house and
sneaks into Janie's bedroom. It's more than just creepy; it's
a first class piece of cinema. Schnitzer plays it quietly,
without grandstanding, but tension is powerfully conjured
by the lighting, camera and acting. Because we've begun to
understand just how unhinged Andrea is, the suspense is
initially linked to fears for the child. The fact that
everything seems to go right for Andrea, as she slips into
the house and past the sleeping Sheri, endows her with a
kind of gliding invincibility – interestingly, many killers
have referred to this sensation, of being propelled smoothly
along on the wings of fortune. But Andrea, who is not a
killer, is undone by the perfection of what she sees – the
little girl asleep in her bed. Instead of taking Janie away,
she lingers, cradling the sleepy child in her arms, sitting
there in the dark, soaking up this brief spell of happiness.
It's a terribly sad and eerie moment. Downstairs, Sheri
wakes, and hearing an unaccustomed creaking from Janie's
room, goes upstairs to find Andrea in the child's rocking
chair, clutching the sleeping Janie. After a brief, resonant
silence, the two women fight, and this is where the tinder is
at last allowed to burn. After shrieks and wild reactions
from both women, Andrea runs out of the house, without
Janie, taking only a doll.

It's an electrifying scene that draws on childhood fears
(someone sneaking into your bedroom to abduct you),
parental fears (failing to protect your child in the family
home), and the forlorn fantasies of displaced mothers
(being an outsider in your child's life). Schnitzer ultimately
favours the adoptive parents, but this is a story where
sympathy is open to all characters. Far from being a
conservative fantasy about 'responsible' parents versus
'irrational' or 'crazy' parents, *The Premonition* demands
nothing less than mind-expansion from the 'good' family.
In a sense, the nice, intelligent Bennetts must meet the
wounded, obsessive Andrea half-way. Miles is required to
expand his rationalist understanding of the universe and
embrace a new cosmological paradigm, and Sheri must
engage with artistic creation far in excess of her own
(rather mundane) painterly talents. The only painting by
Sheri that we see, close up, is a portrait of her daughter. It's
blue and open and feminine but it lacks edge, something
Andrea certainly has (judging by the agile, modernist
music she writes, and her difficult relationship with Jude).
If Sheri wants her daughter back, she must match the
passionate, complex Andrea; she must in some way enter
Andrea's world. The fact that she does so means that the
ambiguous ending – is Sheri still 'possessed', has Andrea
'won'? – is even more intriguing: perhaps Andrea and
Sheri have fused psychically, with Sheri providing the
stability and Andrea the creativity? If so, *The Premonition*
becomes an imaginative, unorthodox wish-fulfilment
fantasy in which the writer constructs his ideal mother: a
woman both nurturing and challenging.

Richard Lynch, a sorely underused actor, is fantastic in
the role of Jude. He brings a concentrated, unhistrionic
danger to the role, and he's truly petrifying when he
explodes. Schnitzer gives him a great intro scene: on a wet,
overcast afternoon, among the caravans of a rundown
circus closed to the public, we see him, unsmiling, doing
dance exercises outside his caravan. As he dances he looks
into the camera, while the music summons echoes of
vaudeville long ago. Later we see him plying his trade as a
mime: the accompanying circus tunes have a whimsical but

knowing quality redolent of the Beatles song 'Maxwell's Silver Hammer' or George Harrison's snide, malignant 'Piggies'. Twice during the film, Jude loses control, and Lynch's performance makes the hairs on the back of your neck stand up. He summons a pressurized, resonant tone from deep in his chest, one that sounds virtually electronic (think Tim Buckley circa *Starsailor*): it will haunt you long after the film is over. The cry ascends like a nuclear warning, from inhuman oscillation to frenzied shriek. Normally he'd be the villain, pure and simple. Instead, even he is shown with love; indeed, love is what motivates him. He adores Andrea so much that he donates his every waking moment to her obsession. He only snaps when Andrea settles for less. Clutching a mere doll, she sinks into her delusion, and Jude, having staked all on their joint venture, is left high and dry: a psychotic who's bet his heart and lost. Richard Lynch is the sort of actor that *David* Lynch ought to seek out, and after seeing *The Premonition* I found it hard to watch him in less demanding roles (for instance *Delta Fox* or *Deathsport*): in their mundanity they seem disrespectful.

The Premonition would have played very well in an all-night programme with *Don't Look Now* and *The Brood*, two great films also concerned with parapsychology, metaphysics, and the nature of the bond between parent and child. Like *Don't Look Now*, the focus of attention here is a 'missing' girl (in this a case a living one), whose parents have to come to terms with a new vision of the universe if they want to be reunited. When Andrea is pulled from the lake in her red dress (a striking and melancholic image) the *Don't Look Now* echoes are undeniable. Likewise, although *The Premonition* may have been shot in Mississippi, the locations have the chilly bleakness of early Cronenberg; and as in *The Brood*, the expressive psychosis of a possessive mother is contrasted with a decent but slightly bland (and in this case adoptive) father. Miles, a lecturer on cosmology, is a sceptic when it comes to metaphysics. Ironically, during Sheri's diagnostic session with Jeena, Miles is lecturing to his students on black holes and the structure of spacetime: that is, a branch of theoretical physics which throws up untestable hypotheses just as bizarre as the paranormal ideas Jeena is expressing. Less subtly, Schnitzer uses conversations between Miles and Jeena to shoehorn in some theoretical musings from the fringes of philosophy and Eastern religion: for instance, Miles says: *"So what you're saying is that consciousness is more primordial than matter..."* Meanwhile, Jeena sets up the bizarre developments of the last reel by commenting, *"The clairvoyant reality is totally rejected by science, and finds expression only in art, music and religion."*

In the name of surprise, it's best to draw a veil over the latter stages of the film – suffice to say there's a commitment to the poetic and illogical that would scarcely disgrace Dario Argento in his prime. That's not to suggest there's a motherlode of violence in the final reel, far from it, but there is a similarly heroic disregard for narrative plausibility. *The Premonition* may be just a little too restrained for most fans of modern horror, and perhaps Schnitzer incorporates his metaphysical interests a shade too earnestly in the dialogue at times, but there's a great deal to admire in this impressively unformulaic sleeper. It has ambition, imagination, and the power to linger in your thoughts, and like Thom Eberhardt's *Sole Survivor* or Willard Huyck's *Messiah of Evil*, deserves a far greater genre profile.

Robert Allen Schnitzer Interviewed

above:
Andrea (Ellen Barber) savours the air at the derelict shack to which she and lover Jude have fled.

opposite page, top right:
Ellen Barber as Andrea.

Robert Schnitzer, the Chairman and CEO of California's New Age-oriented Oasis TV, was surprised when I called him up to discuss his 1975 horror movie *The Premonition*: "I thought in the age of *The Matrix* and *X-Men* it would be part of the movie graveyard," he laughs. It's easy to see how he could have formed this impression, since *The Premonition* has not really been accorded much attention or admiration in cult film circles, despite it being, in my opinion, an unusual, intriguing and well-made horror tale, with few obvious similarities to other films of the day. Stylistically it's like a more mystic-friendly neighbour to the films of David Cronenberg: plot specifics differ, of course, but the off-centre conception, with ideas hovering between science-fiction, horror and metaphysics, has a similar maverick sensibility throughout.

Robert Allen Schnitzer was born in New York City in 1950. He started making films at his high school, which was located on the border of Greenwich Village. It was the mid-sixties, and New York was humming with cultural activity. Schnitzer took a lively interest in the underground film scene, attending screenings by Warhol and Kenneth Anger: "I was really interested in what they were doing in film and I just picked up a camera when I was about seventeen; my father bought a Bolex 16mm at a junk shop. I called up a friend of mine who was a still photographer and said, 'Do you know anything about making movies?' He said no, so I said, 'Well, I want to bring this thing over to you, let's learn how to use it and start making movies!' So, after school and at weekends I would start making these, I guess you would call them experimental, 16mm films. We shot them on the streets of New York."

opposite page, bottom left:
The UK video cover from Embassy.

below:
Disturbed circus mime Jude (Richard Lynch) is questioned about Janie's disappearance.

above:
Andrea sinks into fantasy after her failure to abduct Janie.

opposite page, from top:
Andrea examines a photograph of Janie;
Jude takes pictures of children who visit the circus;
Sheri paints her daughter's portrait;
Jude goes off the deep end;
Andrea talks to Janie's doll;
Andrea's body is dragged from the lake;
The portrait bleeds;
Jude throttles a carny worker who knows too much...

Schnitzer's first film was "an impressionistic love story" called *Vernal Equinox*, a forty-minute 16mm piece which he wrote, produced and directed in 1967. It was screened at the famed Bleecker Street Theater in New York City, home of the avant-garde and host to the likes of Andy Warhol, Paul Morrissey, Jonas Mekas and Jack Smith. There was more excitement to come: Schnitzer was surprised and delighted when he received an invitation to enter the film at the Mannheim Film Festival in Germany. A few weeks later an award arrived through the post – Schnitzer's spirits were boosted and his film career was off to a good start. "That really got my attention! I thought wow, my first film won an award in Europe! So I went to college, which had no film program, and I started the first filmmaking club there. We made films on campus, there was no teacher showing us how to do it, but having made films in high school I knew what to do."

Schnitzer directed two more projects at college: "I made a picture called *Terminal Point* in 1969, which was about an hour long, shot in black-and-white, about a student who starts to disintegrate mentally and has a series of psychotic and hallucinogenic experiences. About six years ago I dug up those reels of film and had them cleaned and rejuvenated and put into a temperature and humidity controlled facility. Unfortunately I never transferred them to video. I also did a short documentary called *A Rumbling in the Land*, about the anti-war movement, also in 1969."

Schnitzer's opposition to the war in Vietnam was further expressed by a series of thirty-second anti-war 'commercials' which played at the prestigious Walter Reade cinema chain in Manhattan.[1] The clips were shown before the main film, as Schnitzer explains: "I gave them 35mm prints and they stuck them on like a trailer to their movies, so for about a month these four thirty-second commercials were playing throughout Manhattan in movie theatres."

Like director James Bryan in California, Schnitzer identified with the substance of the hippie revolt of the late 1960s: "I guess I was a hippie, so to speak – I never thought about myself as such, but as time went on and I look back, I think well yes, I wore the beads and the jeans, I went on the marches, I felt that war was already obsolete and that there was a better way. Around that time I also got involved in what would now be called the 'New Age' movement; I felt that this thing we call reality is a mindset and that there are other levels and other realities and other universes existing at the same time, and that everything is a function of consciousness, and so I became increasingly frustrated with going to college. Initially I lived on campus making these films, but I found myself going into Manhattan more and more, until ultimately I dropped out in the early seventies to make what became my first feature film, *Rebel*, which was a reflection of where I was at the time."

Rebel, made in 1972, is the story of an anti-war activist called Jerry Savage (Sylvester Stallone) who falls in love with a flower child, Laurie Fisher (Rebecca Grimes). She feels that the only answer to war is love, whilst he favours direct violent action. After trying and failing to see Laurie's point of view, Jerry joins a cell of the terrorist group The Weathermen, who are planning to blow up a New York skyscraper. However, unbeknownst to him, an undercover FBI agent is about to spoil the bombers' fun. A film exposition of the dilemma expressed in John Lennon's Beatles song 'Revolution 1': *"But when you talk about destruction/Don't you know you can count me out (in),"* it was made just before Stallone starred in *The Lords of Flatbush* (1974).[2] Schnitzer recalls: "It was his first starring role. He was one of about four hundred people we interviewed. I made that film – it was originally called *No Place to Hide* – in 1972, then, because it took a while to finish, we ran out of money and it stayed in my refrigerator for a year while I raised the finishing money. Finally in 1975, when *Rocky* was about to come out, I thought gee, well instead of *No Place to Hide* why don't we call it *Rebel*, you know, to reflect the individual star more. Then *Rebel* was able to get distributed and sold."

Making *The Premonition*

Schnitzer's next film, *The Premonition* (1975), marks a shift from the political to the personal, being concerned primarily with the mystery of human consciousness. A strange and unsettling tale, it seems to spring partly from the arguments of Laurie in *Rebel*, who is more concerned with persuading Jerry to examine his aura than in helping him blow up a corrupt capitalist system. Schnitzer was deeply affected by the work of Timothy Leary, the ex-Harvard professor whose adoration of the LSD experience led him to become both a political radical and a believer in dropping out of the system to pursue spiritual enlightenment. *The Premonition* turns away from politics to explore family identity, the spirit world, and psychic sensitivity.

Just as he had done with *Rebel*, Schnitzer raised the money for *The Premonition* independently. However, this time there was greater security than usual for an independent production, thanks to Avco Embassy Pictures, who entered into a distribution deal with Schnitzer just before the film was shot, after seeing the script and budget proposal. *The Premonition* was to be a non-union film, something that Avco Embassy could not be seen to condone. Therefore the film was not taken onboard as part of their production slate, but rather was bought as a finished negative after the completion of the film: a deal known in the industry as a 'negative pickup'. Avco guaranteed a distribution and promotion budget of $500,000, as long as the film stuck reasonably to the proposal, and so Schnitzer was able to shoot knowing that as long as he kept the film on the right track, a well-supported national release was waiting.

He decided to shoot in the state of Mississippi, where local authorities had a generous attitude toward visiting film crews. Mississippi came out on top because hotel accommodation was cheap, the fire department provided their fire hoses for rain scenes, sales taxes were waived, and location clearance was easy to obtain. "Mississippi was also what was called a 'right to work' state," adds Schnitzer, "and on our budget there was no way we could have shot it with a union crew, so we were able to bring non-union people down there and legally work on the film without having to pay overtime and weekends and so forth."

So what drew Schnitzer to the subject of the movie? "It was a definite outgrowth of my interest in the paranormal. Anthony Mahon came to me with a script named *The Adoption*. I read that and the psychic elements resonated with me, so with Mahon I went through the usual dozen rewrites. Then Louis Pastore did what's called additional dialogue, so the script was about ninety percent done. The contributions were probably forty five percent Mahon, forty five percent me, and ten percent Louis Pastore. He did the polish. The title when we were shooting was *Turtle Heaven*: during the kidnapping attempt there's a fight and the child's pet turtle dies. They bury the turtle and the little girl says 'Is there a heaven for turtles?' and the foster mother says, 'There's a heaven for each of us.' But Avco Embassy thought that *Turtle Heaven* was not the greatest title in the world. I've come to wish we kept that title because it's so much more unique, it creates a definite image, as opposed to *The Premonition* which is very abstract."

The Premonition is constructed obliquely, so that we must constantly strive to piece together clues and implications. "That's how it is in the psychic world," says Schnitzer, "things are hinted at. I remember I wanted the film to feel like a dream, that was the idea. We kept a lot of the violence off-screen. I was a student of Greek theatre at the time and I liked the idea that things were kept off-screen and in your imagination."

Prominent in the cast is Richard Lynch, an idiosyncratic actor who has been somewhat underappreciated, and understretched, although he worked like a dog throughout the seventies, eighties and nineties. Schnitzer agrees that Lynch had something special, although working with him was not without its difficulties. "Well, I've worked in Hollywood where the standard answer is always, 'Oh he was a pleasure to work with, he's a terrific actor and I'd work with him again.' In truth, he was a great actor, but he was going through an emotional period in his life so we had to work around that. There were rumours that he had set himself on fire. I never was able to get a straight answer from him on that. There were rumours he did it as a protest against the war, that he just went nuts and did it to himself, but I learned on *Rebel* that a director sometimes has to be very tough and not take gruff from actors, and so… there were times, being a sensitive actor, which he was, that I would have to lay down the law and give him very strong direction. But that comes with the territory. Actors are artists and artists are temperamental. It took a toll on me though."

Editing and post-production were conducted back in New York. Avco Embassy made good on their guarantee to spend half a million dollars on distribution, prints and advertising. The agreement was for the movie to open in at least ten cities, from a list including the major population centres, like New York, Los Angeles and Chicago. Schnitzer lent his hand to the pump, taking part in promotional activity across the Mid-West: "Avco put me on the road to do publicity for the film around the country," he recalls. "That was fun; it went on for about three weeks, it was very enjoyable. I got the inside look on how a movie gets opened, the relationship between distribution and exhibition. I remember arriving in Des Moines, Iowa, and there was only one limo company in the city and that company was also the funeral parlour. All the limos were taken and all they had was a hearse!"

The Premonition was a moderate success (making the *Variety* top 50 films for a week or two), and so Schnitzer moved to Los Angeles to further his career. However, he soon discovered that having a successful movie in circulation was not in itself a guarantee of further opportunities: "Unless you have an absolute blockbuster, it's like starting again from the beginning. Had I stayed in New York it might have worked out better because my reputation and contacts were there, and New York is itself a media centre, but I wanted to try something different and L.A. was the film capital of the world."

Hollywood, and Beyond…

With the hoped-for follow-up movie deal proving elusive, Schnitzer moved across to television, taking an internship with Steven Bochco, soon-to-be producer of the classic *Hill Street Blues* series. It was 1976, and Bochco was working on a show for Universal called *Delvecchio*, a police drama starring Judd Hirsch and Charles Haid that some have seen as a precursor to *Hill Street Blues*. Schnitzer tracked the production, observing the first season with a view to working as director on the second. But the series was pulled and the job never materialised. "I had mixed feelings about it anyway," Schnitzer says, "because it was so much like a factory, a totally different world. I saw up close the pressures that the producers had with the networks and the studio, having to answer to the management at Universal television etc. When it fell through I decided to stick to things that had something of myself in them. I began a long period of developing properties, some written by me and others based on scripts by others." It was a fallow period in terms of screen credits, but the work was not without financial compensations: "That went on for nine years or so. The old joke was the producers with the fancier cars were the ones who never got films made, and the ones that had the old bangers clunking along are the ones who actually got movies made but didn't make any money on them!"

Schnitzer's experiences on his third feature film, *Kandyland* (1986), were in stark contrast to the relaxed working experience he'd enjoyed on *The Premonition*, and acutely at odds with the frothy, light-hearted slant of the material. The producers, Roger Corman's New World Pictures, were a constant thorn in the director's side, insisting on interfering and second-guessing, criticising and obstructing the embattled director. "I raised the money independently, and had a similar deal to *Premonition*, this time with New World. Even though again this was a negative pickup, they were more involved, they showed up on the set, and we did get more 'guidance' from them." He pauses: "Yes, that's a euphemism! It was brutal, in fact. For about a week I was fighting for my job. They wanted a

above:
Sheri tries to convince her rationalist husband Miles (Edward Bell) that her sinister visions are real.

below:
Sheri's visions of Andrea begin after the latter's death.

harder edge. I saw this as a love story set against a night-club, with music and dance, and they saw it more as a sex film and wanted more nudity. I would get these three- or four-page memos every day, based on their watching the dailies. I was working twenty two hours a day and instead of getting support from them I felt I was getting nothing but criticism. But I came through it, on budget and on schedule. It came out alright, a few more breasts than I was intending, but it was very well reviewed in the trade papers and the cities where it played."

Kandyland may have reached the screen alright, but Schnitzer found the experience so gruelling and unpleasant that he hasn't produced or directed a movie since: "After *Kandyland* I didn't want to direct anymore because the stress was just unbearable. I decided it wasn't worth it. After we finished shooting, for about a week when I woke up in the morning, instead of waking slowly and gradually my eyes would pop open with my heart beating rapidly. I would look at the time, it might be about eight in the morning, and I would jump up out of bed and run to the closet, and it would be two or three minutes before I realised, hang on, we're not shooting any more, we wrapped, I'm not late, I don't have to be on the set at five or six!"

For about six or seven years, Schnitzer acted as producer's representative, helping to package scripts. He made a good living, but felt unfulfilled at a deeper level. It all came to a head towards the end of 1996, leading to a major revision of his life and work: "Even when I made a deal on a project – and some deals did get made – I just wasn't fulfilled as a person, I wasn't enjoying my relation-ships in the Hollywood community. I had a lot of so-called friends in there but they were really just business relation-ships. So I sub-leased my office in Beverly Hills, except for one little room which I kept for myself. I let everybody go. I gave myself ninety days to figure out what to do with the rest of my life. I said I'm gonna be open to everything: I'll go back to school, I'll become a doctor, I'll become a lawyer, a farmer, anything. I wanted to finally give myself the freedom to evaluate anything and everything else that was out there. After thirty days it occurred to me that what I should do is combine my media experience with my personal interests. I started a cable TV network called Body-Mind-Spirit, which is the new phraseology for what used to be called New Age. At college, I had started getting interested in Eastern philosophy, I read the works of Alan Watts, Timothy Leary, I actually met someone I later found out was working for the government on campus at the time, doing research on mind-altering drugs, and I became an aficionado of that whole area. I took acid, I would have to say minimally. Enough to find out what it was all about, then gave it up after that. An educational experience. I found out that reality as we know it is based on subjective consciousness. The thing that sustains life and this thing we call reality is love, and we are evolving creatures. I never joined any group or organisation, and I never practised any one thing. In fact the very thing that people use to put down New Age ideas, dilettantism, so to speak, to me that's the strength of it. Elitism, thinking that one path is better than another, leads to animosity and antagonism, and to what we see going on today with religious fundamentalism. Since I started Oasis TV, one of the most disappointing things I discovered was that once you get a guru of some sort, or join any exclusive-thinking community, you're subject to the same nonsense that afflicts more orthodox mainstream religions.

With Buddhists, one sect is at war with another; and even in India, the very role model for Eastern spirituality, the Buddhists are killing the Hindus and the Hindus are killing the Buddhists! So I think the answer is this so-called dilettantism. Borrow, examine, and make your own mind up. Never sign up for anything. I feel weird signing up for a mailing list!"

Bearing in mind that the New Age movement has frequently been criticised for woolliness and an inability to find a role for 'negatives', except to deny them or sweep them under the carpet, I suggest to Schnitzer that these antagonisms are hard-wired, an inescapable part of the human animal: "I definitely see there's a duality – you can't have light without dark. And I also realise that we're to a large extent members of the animal kingdom, and animals are sometimes aggressive when it comes to their own domain. But I think that's the beauty of spirituality and evolving consciousness, that we can move away from that."

Robert Schnitzer's arguments for the rejection of dogma carry more weight now than ever, even if Oasis TV's rolling menu of Tibetan healing, personal growth therapy, toddler's yoga lessons and David Icke can seem like a mystics' Tower of Babel. Schnitzer struck me as a decent and unpretentious man in our (admittedly brief) conversations; neither soft in the head nor nurturing some new intransigence under cover of a 'global consciousness' MacGuffin. Although the long-term benefits of New Age dilettantism, if any, are yet to be seen, anyone who sets out to provide alternatives to the power of orthodox religion is probably doing the human race a favour right now. And as can be seen in *The Premonition*, with its story of the living reaching an understanding with the angry dead, there's a role for an exploration of humankind's dark corridors along the way.

Footnotes

1   The long established Walter Reade chain of cinemas was bought by Cineplex, allied to MCA/Universal, in 1986. The last remaining Walter Reade Cinema in New York is located in The Lincoln Center, and continues to represent the more experimental and diverse cinemas of the world.

2   Schnitzer: "I'm a tremendous fan of John Lennon, I was in New York the day he died, and as soon as I heard what happened I dropped what I was doing and I went to The Dakota in the rain and joined the mourners there. He was a very unique soul on this planet."

ROBERT ALLEN SCHNITZER:
FILMOGRAPHY AS DIRECTOR

1967	*Vernal Equinox* (short)
1969	*Terminal Point* (b/w short)
1969	*A Rumbling in the Land* (documentary)
1972	*No Place to Hide* aka *Rebel* aka *A Man Called Rainbow* (also co-writer / co-producer)
1975	*The Premonition* aka *The Adoption* (script title) aka *Turtle Heaven* (shooting title) (also co-writer)
1986	*Kandyland* (also co-writer / co-producer)

OTHER CREDITS:

| 1969 | *Series of four 30-second anti-war 'commercials' shown as shorts before movies.* |

chapter 19

Spawn of Venice Beach

Stephen Traxler on Slithis

Spawn of the Slithis (1977)

Wayne Connors (Alan Blanchard), a high school journalism instructor living in Venice Beach, Los Angeles, visits a crime scene where a local couple have been murdered, and finds strange organic matter. He hands it on to a zoologist friend, Dr. John (J.C. Clair) who identifies it as a piece of marine exoskeleton mixed with 'Slithis', a protoplasmic substance discovered in the wake of a nuclear accident several years ago. Connors's girlfriend Jeff (sic) (Judy Motulsky) warns him not to get involved, but he ignores her. On the night of another slaying, a local beach bum (Rocky Fumarelli) sees something come out of the sea. Connors speaks to the man, and approaches the police with his suspicions that some sort of marine creature is involved, but they're convinced the deaths are the work of a 'mutilation cult' and dismiss his findings. Connors strikes up a friendship with a local sailor, Chris Alexander (Mello Alexandria) and persuades him to take his boat out to sea to draw soil samples from the seabed. Connors and Dr. John also close off the canal from the incoming tide, thus blocking the Slithis creature's entry to the Venice Beach area. Instead the monster turns its attentions to the nearby Marina del Rey, savagely killing a sleazy boat-owner and his ingénue pick-up (Steven J. Hoag and Wendy Rastattar). An attempt to trap and kill the creature on land fails, and Connors heads off to sea with Alexander and his crew, where they must battle with the enraged mutation...

This affectionate pastiche of fifties monster movies was the industry calling card of Stephen Traxler, a director-turned-producer determined to make his mark via the horror genre. Complete with scientific gobbledegook about 'living mud' (*"It is organic, there's no doubt about that; but it's also inorganic"*), it transplants the man-in-a-rubber-suit likes of *The Monster of Piedras Blancas* into the seventies, like a prehistoric fish found alive in modern waters. By having his creature stalk L.A.'s Venice Beach (an area best known for its bohemian community and cheap accomodation), Traxler benefits from an interesting, untypical backdrop, and though the movie maybe lacks the pace that would ensure a wider cult following he nevertheless conjures some pleasingly bloody moments. To cap it off, the

'Slithis' itself boasts one of the most charmingly ugly mugs of monsterdom – a vital consideration for such movies, which operate like beauty contests in reverse.

I'm not altogether fond of genre retro-itis, but Traxler spices things up with some gory wrestling between man and beast that would have had fifties kids choking on their popcorn. The 'explanation' for the creature's existence may have its roots in fifties atomic paranoia – a nuclear radiation spill – but when you consider the Three Mile Island incident happened just two years later, Traxler's film is hardly anachronistic. And as well as its numerous fifties references, *Slithis* also borrows from *Jaws*, as the leading man, in a Paul Michael Glaser woolly cardigan, takes to the waves with a salty old Jamaican seadog, Mello Alexandria, to catch a monster the authorities deny exists.

A detail which is either hilarious or irritating, depending on your mood, is the way the monster sees the world through the neck of a bottle; and I don't mean he's a heavy drinker.

below:
'Hell Hath No Fury Like a Slithis...'
Spawned?? The copywriter appears to have run out of nerve for what could have been a great pun...

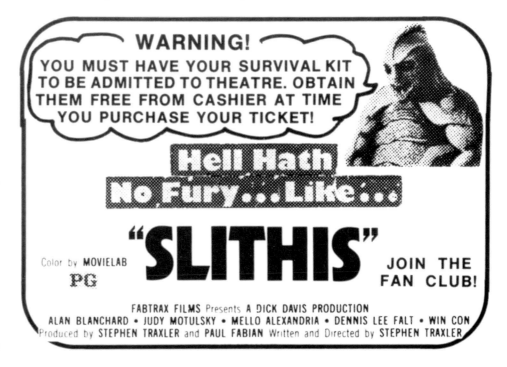

Spawn of the Slithis
aka *Slithis*
© 1977. Fabtrax Films
A Fabtrax Films production.
writer/director: Stephen Traxler. producer:
Paul Fabian and Stephen Traxler. executive
producer: Dick Davis. stunt coordination:
United Stunts of America. director of
cinematography: Robert Caramico. editor:
Robert M. Ross. production manager: Paul
Fabian. assistant to the director: James Speth.
assistant directors: Judy Bring, Dave Peltzer.
music: Steve Zuckerman, recorded by Corey
Bailey, produced by Don Buday original music
copyright ©1977. Fabtrax Music and Steve
Zuckerman Music. gaffer: Jim Bowie. assistant
cameraman: Tony Palmeri. 2nd assistant
cameraman: Richard Lance. best boy: Tar
Webster. key grip: Marshall Reed. electrician:
Robby McClure. sound mixer: Craig Felburg.
boom man: Gord Connon. art director:
Catherine Deeter. set designer and property:
Russ Davis. assistant [set design / property]:
Nipper Larson. wardrobe and make up: Penny
Gotlieb. assistant [wardrobe / make-up]: Kathy
Lober. production co-ordinator: Donna King.
script supervisor: Mimi Leder. production
secretary: Arlene Garelick. transportation:
Travis Hathaway. sound effects editor: Bill
Shippy. sound services: Cinesound. colour by
Movielab. titles and opticals by Pacific Title.
Cast: Alan Blanchard (Wayne Connors). J.C.
Claire (Dr. John). Dennis Lee Falt (Dr. Erin
Burick). Mello Alexandria (Chris Alexander).
Win Condict (the monster). Rocky Fumarelli
(Preston, wino 1). John Hatfield (Bunky, wino
2). Hy Pyke (Jack Dunn). Daphne Cohen
(Helen Dunn). Stephen J. Hoag (Doug).
Wendy Rastattar (Jennifer). Don Cummins
(Rex). David Ridenour (policeman at house).
Dave Carlton. Dale Caldwell. Ken Stimson.
Gregory Clemmons. Ed Fournier. Prudie
Butler. Jack Kelly. Alejandro Vass. Gary Dyer.
Alisa Estes. Abraham Columbus. Michael
Hudson. Drew Deeter. Marcus Harvey. Larry
Dunn, Larry Phillips, De Ette Adams (stunts).

right:
The **Slithis** creature exhibits a pleasingly
Seventies approach to mutilation...

opposite page, main image:
Finnish video cover art for the film – such
being the effectiveness of the original promo
campaign that few countries deviated from
the basic ad design.

opposite page, strip of images:
One of the ugliest mugs in Monsterdom,
and gore into the bargain. Who could resist
Slithis?

Someone decided it would suffice to attach what looks for all the world like a coke bottle to the camera lens for the monster's P.O.V. The film does at least nod to the audience regarding its own absurdity. (After hearing Dr. John's theory of the formation of complex life from irradiated silt, Connors says, *"Oh sure - by combining organic matter, a little bit of bacteria and substituting the pressure of a million years of environmental change with a dose of radioactivity."*) There's also a brief dip into the transient population of a run-down Venice Beach that anticipates Traxler's only other directorial credit, *Sam Churchill: Search for a Homeless Man* (1999).

On the downside, the film is hampered by too many talky scenes, and a leading man you don't give a rat's ass about. Blanchard has a face you'd forget in a line-up, and his way with dialogue has an 'untransmitted TV pilot' quality that eludes your attention. He and his similarly unimpressive girlfriend, played by Judy Motulsky, squash the fun out of their scenes together. *Slithis* spends too much time indoors with these two, and given the 'PG'-level production, there's nothing doing in the bedroom either. Their drawn-out conversations have no other function than to pad the running time between glimpses of the monster. It's left to the supporting cast, especially the likeable Alexandria, to try and lift the energy levels, although Alejandro Voss as the Police Chief perhaps goes a bit too far in the opposite direction, turning in an eye-rolling caricature that even *Police Academy* fans would find a touch broad.

Spawn of the Slithis was made by a Vietnam veteran who fought through some of the most violent days of the conflict, which perhaps explains why he chose to focus on the gentler 'horrors' of a bygone era, drawing on the cinema of his childhood rather than the contemporary horrors of, say, Bob Clark's *Deathdream*. Not every ex-soldier is going to want to revisit their worst memories on film, despite Tom Savini's example. (Savini, who'd been a combat photographer in Vietnam, built a career as arguably the foremost purveyor of realistic grue in the business.) Nevertheless – without wanting to overburden the film – perhaps the alliance between Blanchard's white-bread hero and Alexandria's black sailor (not a typical plot development in fifties monster movies) reflects the way friendships developed between black and white soldiers in the pressure-cooker of Vietnam warfare.

Spawn of the Slithis may not be the most sophisticated film in this book, but it went down a treat with kids at the time, and inspired a much-loved promotional campaign that probably wedged itself in the audience's minds as much as the movie itself, as Traxler now recalls...

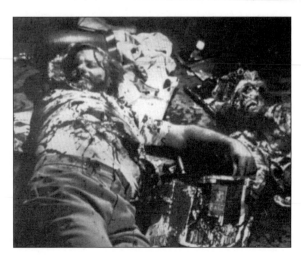

Stephen Traxler was born in San Francisco in December, 1945 and raised, from the age of four, in the San Fernando Valley, Los Angeles. His first brush with the power of cinema came when he saw a re-issue of *The Wizard of Oz* with his grandmother: "Those damn monkeys scared the hell out of me," he laughs. "As a kid I went to the movies whenever possible. The local theatre had Saturday matinees that I attended religiously. Cartoons, comedies and all the sci-fi and horror films, including re-issues of forties serials." The Traxlers couldn't afford a film camera for their young movie fanatic, but they did have a Brownie (a simple, inexpensive still camera). "In our backyard I'd put together a set and place little action figures (army men, cavemen and dinosaurs, cowboys and indians) in various positions, usually conflict of some kind, and find interesting angles to photograph the scene," Traxler remembers. "Ultimately I'd have a storyboard, although I didn't realise it at the time."

His career in the movie industry began while he was still in high school, when he got a role in a TV commercial. "A friend of mine was one of the original 'Mouseketeers' – his mother liked me a great deal and helped me get into the business. When I left school I worked in films as an extra. I also had an extremely short and undistinguished career as a Grip: I think I lasted three days at Paramount." Traxler's ambitions were ultimately to write, produce and direct his own work: "I always enjoyed writing as a kid," he explains. "I wrote my first screenplay when I was in my teens. It was a horror story having to do with native Americans, a shaman curse, an unscrupulous developer despoiling the land in a sacred place and a horrible creature summoned from the spirits. It sounds terribly clichéd but it was way ahead of its time. We saw several of those done some years later."

These nascent ambitions were put on hold, however, when Traxler got drafted to serve in the infantry in Vietnam, during the initial 'big build-up' of February 1966. It was, by most accounts, the nastiest part of the war before the Tet Offensive in 1968. "I was trained as an airborne infantry-man (did jump school at Fort Benning, Georgia) but was placed in a mechanized infantry unit once I arrived in country," Traxler recalls. "I served in 'B' Company of the 1/5 mechanized infantry of the 25th Infantry Division. We were located in Cu Chi and our area of operations included the Viet Cong strongholds of the Bo Loi Woods, the Ho Bo Woods and the Michelin Rubber Plantation, plus the Tay Ninh Province. This area was hot, hot, hot. I was a Forward Observer with a mortar platoon – this was a rather hairy position and volunteer only. I did a night ambush about every third night, when we were in the jungle – which was most of the time. I made the rank of Sgt. E-5, a three striper if you're into old war movies. During my thirteen months in combat I received several Unit Citations, the Bronze Star, the Purple Heart and various medals for various reasons. Our unit saw a great deal of action but there was always a lot of hurry-up-and-wait. 20% terror and 80% boredom, as someone once said."

Traxler made it back home in one piece in November of 1967, and resumed his college studies, majoring in film and broadcasting. "After I graduated from college I moved to a beautiful ski area," he recalls. "Going from high school to

Vietnam to college, I needed a break. I spent several years there and at the close of one season I was racing and broke my leg, very severely. I moved back to L.A. and lived with a girlfriend on one of the canals in Venice, California. I was in a full leg cast for a year, so I had plenty of time to contemplate the area and its funky surroundings. It was then that I thought about doing a modern sci-fi/horror film with roots in the fifties radioactive monster genre. Kind of a 'creature from the green canal' thing."

The Spawning of *Slithis*

Without a real apprenticeship or contacts in the film studios, Traxler knew that if he was to realise his dream of becoming a producer and director he would have to strike out on his own, as an independent. "I took my completed script to a friend, Paul Fabian, who also worked in the business, and suggested that we partner up," he recalls. Fabian agreed, and became co-producer and production manager on the film. "The key was to do the picture for a very low-ball number, an amount that we might be able to secure ourselves from private money. We came up with $100,000, then we worked backward with our budget to make the project fit that number. With a budget in hand along with a slide show of potential atmospheric locations, an illustration of the monster, etc., we started giving a series of presentations, looking for investors. The traditional dog and pony show. Southern California was undergoing a real estate boom at the time and a lot of young people, especially in Orange County, had some money to play with. We concentrated on that area and came up with four $10,000 investors."

That still left sixty thousand dollars. Finally, against all advice, Traxler advertised in the *Daily Variety* and, much to his surprise, got a phone call. "In general, people who solicited investors in trade papers didn't have much luck," he explains. "The advice was to save your time and money 'cause it ain't gonna happen. In my case, it did." The call was from an Iowa theatre exhibitor called Dick Davis, who'd recently invested in a low-budget picture called *The Hazing* (aka *The Curious Case of the Campus Corpse*), directed by Douglas Curtis in 1977. "He'd read my ad and wanted to talk about the project," says Traxler. "We got together, along with a production manager he'd used on his last film. As luck would have it the production manager knew Robert Caramico, the director of photography I planned to use - the fastest cameraman in the business and the only one he felt could allow me to complete the picture in my twelve day shooting schedule."

After some discussion, Davis agreed to chip in the other $60,000. For this investment, however, he also wanted distribution rights. "I was desperate," Traxler admits, "so I immediately agreed and we had a deal. Since our deals with the other investors were about to run out, we didn't have much choice. Also, since my partner and I owned 50% of the film and I personally owned remake and sequel rights, we felt we were adequately covered. We knew embarrassingly little about distribution; it was always a murky area. Quite intentionally kept that way, I imagine, by the distributors."

Also involved, although not as an investor, was another Mid-West exhibitor called Robert Fridley, an occasional partner of Davis's. "Fridley owned a chain of theatres and was the quieter of the two," says Traxler, "whereas Davis was a small man and often loud and obnoxious. He boasted

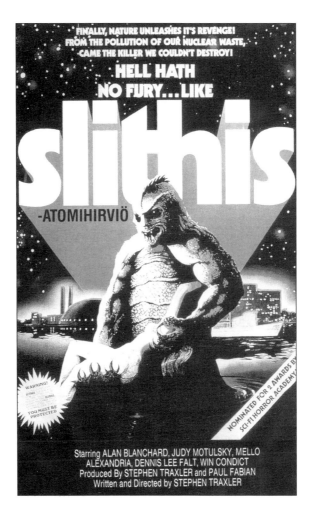

of his friendship with Mickey Rooney and apparently was a financial backer in a dinner show that Rooney starred in. He used to laugh loudly and say 'Let's be friends now 'cause the fuckin' comes later'. Prophetic words for Paul Fabian, myself and our other investors. Davis and his sons made some real money by owning a number of adult theatres in several Midwestern states. He catered to the farm folks in these rural areas and used to say his success could be judged by the number of pick-up trucks in the theatre parking lot. There were no Pussycat Theaters in these areas and this was before porn went directly to video. He also owned several drive-in theatres and later turned the large sites into shopping malls. Unfortunately for Bob Fridley, he had no money in *Slithis*. Davis said he gave him the opportunity but Bob declined to invest - I don't know this for a fact. I was later told by Davis that *The Hazing* was a financial failure and his and Fridley's investment was lost."

Traxler's cinematographer, Robert Caramico, was an experienced professional whose career began, less than promisingly, with Edward D. Wood's go-go-fest *Orgy of the Dead* in 1965. He went on to alternate respectable gigs shooting *The Waltons*, *Lou Grant* and *Dallas* with movies like *Octaman* (1971), *Boss Nigger* (1975) and *The Happy Hooker Goes to Washington* (1977). He also rose to the occasion for more demanding and creative jobs, such as Richard Blackburn's poetic reverie *Lemora: A Child's Tale of the Supernatural*, and Tobe Hooper's hallucinatory *Death Trap* (aka *Eaten Alive*, 1976). "Bob Caramico and I met through a sound mixer that I was working with at 20th Century Fox," Traxler relates. "Bob and I got together, we got along well, he said he'd do *Slithis* if we secured the financing and that was it. Bob Caramico is the only reason

all images this page and opposite:
Slithis director Stephen Traxler drew on the fifties not only for monster movie inspiration but also for the sustained and inventive promotional ballyhoo. Newspaper editors and cinema owners were given a wide range of admat slogans to choose from, many of which also pushed membership of the **Slithis** fanclub. A glance through the entries at the Internet Movie Database proves how effective the Fan Club and the promised (though not always received) 'Slithis Survival Kits' were – indeed, the latter has even generated its own IMDB Message Board thread!

my partner and I completed this picture on time and on budget. He may be the only reason we completed the picture at all. Bob was a genius. He ran his guys hard (small crew of grips and electricians) and treated them tough, but they worshipped him. Soon after my film Bob went legit and basically did union work for the rest of his career. Paul and I visited him on the set of the *Lou Grant* TV show - it was the last time I saw him."[1]

Shooting at the Venice locations began in the spring of 1977, for twelve days: "Seven of those were actually nights and three were on the water, in and around the Marina del Rey," Traxler explains. "The first day of filming was the interior of our hero's apartment. It was the place where I'd stayed while my broken leg was healing and the place where I'd written the screenplay. The locations were as important as the cast, maybe more so. Venice and the Marina were extremely photogenic: before the area was as gentrified as it is today. This was my production value, and my partner Paul and I spent a lot of time finding the most atmospheric location sites possible. There was no studio – everything was filmed at practical locations. You should see some of the cool places that we filmed but didn't end up in the movie. Because of the canals and overall ambience, Venice was absolutely unique and totally conducive to the story."

A classic 'man-in-a-rubber-suit' monster flick, *Slithis* most clearly resembles Irv Berwick's *Creature from the Black Lagoon* knock-off *The Monster of Piedras Blancas* (see chapter on Berwick). "The monster suit was beautiful - but deadly," laughs Traxler. "It was designed and constructed by the artist Catherine Deeter and her staff, who had absolutely no experience in costumes of this type. It looked terrific but was totally impractical. Catherine had a small studio connected to her place in the Hollywood foothills. I believe she was a fine artist (who worked in a variety of mediums) and a designer. I cannot, for the life of me, remember how we got turned onto her. I don't think she continued a career in film. The *Slithis* experience had a way of doing that to people! Once Win Condict – a friend of mine who was a great water man and all-round athlete – was in the suit, it literally had to be sewed up, then glued shut with rubber cement. It took a long time to get him in and even longer to get him out (for fear of damaging the thing). When we filmed, Win would be in the suit for hours. Extraction for a pee was not an option."

Rather like the fifties movies Traxler drew upon, no one really shines in the acting department. Traxler remarks, "Alan Blanchard, the lead, was a nice young guy, a little bland but that's just what I was looking for. I wanted him to be the normal-Norman type who aspires to something more and suddenly finds himself in the middle of events he doesn't understand and can't control. Judy Motulsky was attractive and smart. I wanted her to play the girlfriend who was slightly irritating. The character was happy with where she was at and didn't understand why her boyfriend didn't feel the same way. Some have said she comes across as annoying – shame on me but that's what I wanted. Mello Alexandria was terrific as the Jamaican seaman that became pivotal to the adventure. That's his real accent. I had not originally planned on that character being black but I knew Mello and suddenly I couldn't see it any other way. It was lucky. Mello brought in a huge black audience. The film played to sell-out crowds at the Adams Theater in Detroit for three weeks in a row (at the time I was told that it was the largest black house in America). The film has been accused of having six kinds of bad acting. These were very inexperienced actors (it was a non-Screen Actors Guild shoot) being led by a totally inexperienced director. Under the circumstances I feel they all did a great job."

Traxler vividly recalls the excitement and exhaustion of his first time behind the camera: "Directing the film was a trip. Initially, even though I'd worked on film sets for years, I was terrified. That lasted about half a day because fear was a luxury I couldn't afford. We had a very ambitious schedule, a lot of locations, inexperienced personnel in almost every position and no money. There was virtually no room for error. I was determined, in the look and feel of the film, to make the lack of money work for us instead of against us. Luckily, all the preparation time had paid off. Things moved so fast that we moved by instinct. The post-production went on forever because our editor, Robert Ross, was a buddy, working for me for almost nothing, who had a day job as an assistant editor at Universal. He'd come to our office (the production office had turned into our editorial space) after working all day at the studio. He was usually beat to death and would work on our film for only a couple of hours before he faded. During the day I'd do the clean-up work and continue to carefully cut the film on our Moviola. It was a horrible experience that went on for months and months. We had so little money that we would get bumped at the lab (their TV clients took precedence over our low-budget deal), and almost everywhere else. Our post sound was done by Bill Shippy, who had a studio in his home. Our music was done by Steve Zuckerman who hired ten musicians, rented the music room at the local junior college and recorded the entire score in half a day."

Slithis was conceived as a kid-friendly 'PG' rated film, although the occasional bursts of violence caused a few headaches when it came time to submit the film to the MPAA: "Our original rating was the equivalent of today's 'R', which was unacceptable. We went back twice, cutting more and more shock and violence, until we were given a 'PG' rating. Then we went back to the editing room, put some of the deleted material back in, and had the negative cut!"

On the *Slithis* Trail

In 1978, with the film now completed, Dick Davis showed it around the more established minor distributors, including AIP and Crown International: "Truthfully, the picture was not very good so no one felt compelled to pick it up," Traxler says. "Also, the other companies already had their slates of summer release films. Essentially we were told that there were no bookings available that summer for our picture. So, to his credit, Davis determined to release the film himself. He did this through a number of sub-distributors that then existed throughout the country. A sub would take a film and release it regionally. One sub (Crest Films for example) distributed only in Los Angeles, while another might release in a portion of a state or in several states (depending on the number of theatres). I believe Davis used twelve to sixteen subs to distribute *Slithis* countrywide. He originally ordered less than a hundred prints – that was the deal with going through subs. The film played for a week or two in one region and then the prints were shipped to the next sub-distributor, unlike major releases of today where a film opens in 2,500 screens or more across the country, all on the same day. Davis started the release in the Mid-West, where he had connections with other exhibitors: Des Moines, Iowa, Omaha, Nebraska, Kansas City, Kansas."

Traxler put his shoulder to the wheel, travelling the Mid-West bergs to promote the movie locally: "I was employed at about $300 per week to go to these garden spots, make personal appearances with the creature and occasionally show up on local TV or radio for interviews. I remember sharing a couch with the guy who did the farm report on 'Good Morning Omaha'. It was pretty wacky but a lot of fun, and the picture played to amazing business. Held over for two or three weeks in many theatres, sold-out houses and drive-ins. Our old-fashioned marketing really worked. And as word of mouth of our picture's success spread, and the majority of films on the other independent producers' slates went in the crapper, there was more and more interest in our film. *Slithis* broke onto the weekly *Variety* Top Fifty films in the nation at something like number fourteen. This was absolutely amazing considering the picture cost $100,000 and there were only a hundred or so prints!"

Promotion didn't end with a few local TV spots. Indeed, the distribution and promotion of *Slithis* was uncommonly resourceful for the late seventies, and probably the real reason the film did so well. Traxler explains: "One night, prior to distribution, Davis and I sat around in my apartment in Playa del Rey and thought about what we could do to get an edge for the picture. It was a retro film, harking back to the atomic mutation movies of the fifties, so an old-fashioned gimmick felt right. A throwback to the Joseph E. Levine and William Castle era. I came up with the Slithis Survival Kit, which was tongue-in-cheek instructions on what to do in case of a Slithis attack. Davis loved the idea and had a bunch printed up. It was a cheesy, folded cardboard give-away that turned out to be enormously successful. It also included an address (or was it a phone number?) where you could become a member of the *Slithis* Fan Club and order *Slithis* swag – T-shirts, hats, etc. The only problem was that Davis never had an inventory of goodies. He wanted to see how the audience would react before he spent money on the merchandise. As it turned out, a lot of people sent money in for stuff and never received it. I have no idea how Davis dealt with that."

In addition to the extravagant claims on the presskit, Traxler arranged ever more personal appearances for The Slithis: "We put a local high school kid in the creature costume and made a well publicised personal appearance at the largest drive-in in seven Midwestern states, outside of Omaha, Nebraska. We'd made an earlier stop at a nearby small town walk-in and as we approached the drive-in in our van, the kid (in costume except for his head) and I saw the lights in the distance. It looked like an international airport. We pulled in and the place was sold out - maybe a thousand cars and pick-ups, I'd never seen anything like it. We got the kid's head on and stopped at the snack stand - the size of a supermarket. They sold everything from pizzas to cornbread to cold beer. Suddenly the word was out - he's here, Slithis is here! A huge crowd (it was intermission and *Spawn of the Slithis* was next up) gathered... and as the creature began to wave to his fans, the mob surged forward. It was like a rock concert - Mick Jagger couldn't have set off a bigger riot. People lunged at the monster, grabbing at the rubber fins and appendages. The drive-in employees hurled themselves in front of the rushing mob and the terrified kid inside the costume began to cry. I spotted a large wooden ladder that led to the roof of the concession building. With the help of the theatre manager we muscled the creature over to the ladder and pulled and pushed him up onto the roof. On the

roof there was a series of spot lights shining out onto the cars below. I walked the creature to the front of the building and turned several of the spots onto him. From this location we could give the crowd their look-see while holding them at bay. It was easy to defend the ladder. People screamed and carried on for about ten minutes, until the close of intermission when the lights went out and the film began. Opening credits sent folks scurrying back to their vehicles. Under cover of darkness, we helped the kid down the ladder, into the van and we got the hell out of there. The film wasn't very good, but it hit a nerve with our target audience and turned into the popcorn picture of the year. *Slithis* played to sell-out crowds at that drive-in theatre for three consecutive weeks. I was later told that it was the theatre's most popular movie of the summer of '78."

Into the Mainstream

Traxler's career has since taken him to the very top of the Hollywood tree, with prestigious gigs as production supervisor on massive productions like *Waterworld* (1995) and *Windtalkers* (2002). He remains, however, appreciative and affectionate when it comes to his slightly less than stellar debut: "Other than combat in Vietnam, directing the picture was the most exciting thing I'd ever done. The entire experience was at times the highest high and alternately the lowest low. I learned more from making the movie – my partner and I having to do literally everything ourselves – than I'd ever imagined. I walked away from the project bruised, battered and with the knowledge and experience that has allowed me to do everything I've since accomplished in the film industry. There is no greater teacher than the hands-on experience of making a low-budget film. I wrote it, scrounged up the money to make it, produced and directed it, edited it (under the supervision of my friend Robert Ross). I was integral in distributing it, including creating the marketing gimmick and making personal appearance tours around the country with the creature. All things considered, I was happy with most of what we'd done. The true sign of a low-budget film is the unevenness of it all. Some things are good and some just suck. I saw so many things I'd have done differently. So many places we wasted a day on material that didn't end up in the picture, time and money that could have been spent on coverage, not just masters. Having said that, the picture was a huge success, so it's clear we did more things right than wrong. On TV, Siskel and Ebert called it the 'doggy of the week', *Us Weekly* put it in their 'Don't Bother' category for three weeks (along with *Foul Play*, *The Eyes of Laura Mars*, and *Sgt. Pepper's Lonely Hearts Club Band*) – negative reviews, but major reviews nonetheless. As Leo Penn (Sean's dad) told me at the time, 'Hell, you've made a hundred thousand dollar movie that's playing all over the country, and they're taking you seriously'. The movie played throughout the country to packed theatres and drive-ins, it sold foreign for $450,000 (four and half times what it cost) and I have no idea how much money it actually generated overseas (presumably millions). It played twice on late night network TV (CBS), it was an early success on video for Media Home Entertainment, it played on syndicated TV for years and it's still alive today, mentioned on many, many internet sites. So I guess I'm happy with the way it turned out. My goal with the film was to make sure my investors got their money back. I assumed that if it were at all successful I'd be given the opportunity to direct

above:
Dr. Erin Burick (Dennis Lee Falt) reveals his deformity as he discusses the history of the Slithis substance.

below:
The love-child of **The Monster of Piedras Blancas** and **Godzilla**...

another. I made the picture with a very specific game-plan but never took it at all seriously – there was a whole lot of tongue-and-cheek going on. My first target audience was the crowd that goes to the movies to laugh and hoot, answer back to the dialogue and sail popcorn boxes at the screen. These folks used to exist, big time. Not so much anymore. Second, I was going for the hardcore sci-fi and horror fans who would automatically go to any film, good or bad, in the genre. The *Fangoria* groupies. Finally, and this was presumptuous of me, I was hoping that somehow the film might get noticed by a higher level of moviegoer who would get the intentional humour, the mundane references, the more literate aspects of the film. Ultimately, we got extremely lucky and snagged a good portion of all these audiences. We had one early screening for the Sci-Fi/Horror Academy – a fairly sophisticated association of fans. The house was packed and the reception was amazing. They laughed a lot, which was exactly what I was hoping for; and generally for the right reasons. There was a gasp or two. Even a scream. All in all, we'd appealed to one of the core groups I was after."

The only part of Traxler's plan that didn't come off was his desire to secure a return for his investors. Like so many distribution weasels, Dick Davis disappeared back into the woodwork without paying what was owed to the other investors, even though he did try to persuade Traxler to pen a sequel: "I refused to make a sequel for the distributor because the son of a bitch wouldn't pay me a penny more than I made on the first one – which was nothing – and wouldn't increase the budget. I worked with several attorneys (all acting *pro bono* because they'd read in the *L.A. Times* how I was being cheated) to try and force the distributor to give my partner and I (and the other investors) our fair share: all in vain. The film did well, but my partner and I got screwed by Dick Davis, and our Orange County investors never got their money back. This one hundred thousand dollar movie, shot in twelve days, generated untold millions of dollars in profit: and my poor investors never even got their money back."

Stung by the experience, Traxler took the lessons he'd learned from *Slithis* and parlayed them into a highly successful career in production. And when it comes to production logistics, it doesn't get any bigger and crazier than the Kevin Costner star folly, *Waterworld*. "On that film, I ran the longest and largest Second Unit in film history, or so I've been told," he says. "Both *Slithis* and *Waterworld* were extremely challenging and just as gratifying in their own way. *Waterworld* was the most expensive film ever made, prior to *Titanic*. It was a massive logistical effort and difficult beyond imagination because our unit worked out on the water – beyond the breakwater – virtually every day. That experience is worthy of a book all by itself. *Waterworld*, in my action oriented mind, is a classic. It was the most difficult project I've been involved in; both physically and mentally. I was on the big island of Hawaii for almost ten months. I'm proud of the work we did. The hubbub on this one was the price tag: $180 million. An obscene amount of money. It could cure cancer or pay for 180 smart bombs dropped on America's enemies: the latter being the crime against humanity of our time. What most people don't know is that *Waterworld* made a lot of money, and not for the company that financed it. That was the Japanese conglomerate Matsushita. The winner in this deal was Seagrams. They bought the studio from the Japanese corporation. *Waterworld* cost approximately $180 million, not to mention prints, promotion and advertising. I was told that our Second Unit alone cost $20 million dollars (although we did not have a dedicated accountant). The film did about $91 million, domestic. What wasn't reported by the media is that the film eventually did gangbusters, both foreign and on home video, and ultimately made many millions of dollars profit. By the time the film went solidly into the black Matsushita had sold the studio to the Canadians (Seagrams - the Bronfman family) and that's the company that benefited."

Meanwhile, Traxler's TV movie *Sam Churchill: Search for a Homeless Man* (1999) has played regularly on Sky Movie Max. "It certainly isn't as whacked as *Slithis* but it shares some of the same sensibilities. We shot the picture in Santa Barbara for $1 million in sixteen days, financed by a company in Beverly Hills who made movies for TV for foreign distribution only. It's shown all over the world and made the distributor a great deal of money, many millions. My partner and I got screwed on our back-end but I did make some money up front. See a pattern here?"

And for the future? "I'm currently prepping a very expensive independent ($30 million) on which I will be the primary producer. But I can't wait until my next mini-budget independent – they're really the most fun."

Footnotes

[1]   Caramico died on 18 October, 1997.

STEPHEN TRAXLER: FILMOGRAPHY AS DIRECTOR

1977	*Spawn of the Slithis* aka *Slithis* (also writer/co-producer)
1999	*Sam Churchill: Search for a Homeless Man* (also writer/producer)

OTHER CREDITS:

1982	*Lookin' to Get Out* – dir: Hal Ashby (production supervisor: second unit)
1983	*A Minor Miracle* – dir: Raoul Lomas (production manager / first assistant director / second unit director)
1985	*Invasion U.S.A.* – dir: Joseph Zito (production supervisor: second unit)
1986	*Thunder Run* – dir: Gary Hudson (production manager)
1987	*Mannequin* – dir: Michael Gottlieb (2nd unit director: uncredited/location manager)
1989	*Dracula's Widow* – dir: Christopher Coppola (producer / production manager / first assistant director)
1989	*Gleaming the Cube* – dir: Graeme Clifford (production supervisor: second unit)
1990	*Come See the Paradise* – dir: Alan Parker (location manager)
1991	*Delirious* – dir: Tom Mankiewicz (production supervisor)
1993	*Born Yesterday* – dir: Luis Mandoki (co-producer)
1994	*Tryst* – dir: Peter Foldy (production manager / line producer / first assistant director)
1995	*Waterworld* – dir: Kevin Reynolds (production supervisor: second unit)
1997	*McHale's Navy* – dir: Bryan Spicer (production supervisor: second unit)
1998	*Meet the Deedles* – dir: Steve Boyum (production supervisor: second unit)
2002	*Windtalkers* – dir: John Woo (associate producer / uncredited production supervisor)
2003	*Legally Blonde 2: Red, White & Blonde* – dir: Charles Herman-Wurmfeld (co-producer)
2003	*Out of Time* – dir: Carl Franklin (associate producer / production supervisor)
2005	*Be Cool* – dir: F. Gary Gray (production executive)

chapter 20

Beyond the Black Room

The Films of Norman Thaddeus Vane

The Black Room (1981)

A wealthy, sophisticated brother and sister, Jason (Stephen Knight) and Bridget (Cassandra Gaviola), advertise a special room for hire in their Hollywood Hills mansion: a high-class passion-pit specifically designed for 'swingers'. The walls are swathed in black velvet, the floor is strewn with cushions in plush fabrics, and the candle-lit ambience is given a hi-tech spin by a glowing green-white cube which acts as a table. There's also a luxurious bed, and the room is equipped with speakers from which classical music plays constantly. Meanwhile, on the sly, two-way mirrors facilitate Bridget's voyeurism and Jason's passion for erotic photography. Into this honey-trap strays Larry (Jimmy Stathis), a married man looking for a place where he can explore the sexual fantasies he feels unable to indulge with his loving wife Robin (Clara Perryman). So far so kinky, but there's a further sting in the tail – Jason and Bridget are really vampires, using the enticements of the Black Room to entrap a succession of unsuspecting 'blood donors'…

Modern-day vampires have been done to living-death since the 1980s, but *The Black Room* was made before the deluge that brought us such over-stylised efforts as Tony Scott's *The Hunger* (1983), Richard Wenk's tiresome *Vamp* (1986) and Jerry Ciccoritti's limp *Graveyard Shift* (1987). Perhaps because the film still has one foot in the 1970s, it's more than just a coke-fuelled MTV Gothfest, and balances the seductive fantasia of the Black Room with a more naturalistic look for exteriors and daytime scenes. Five years later and the same story would have been filmed with a suffocating obsession for coloured gels, slow-motion billowing curtains and fatuous camera movement.

The Black Room's sense of style hovers at the edge of camp, although the film is made with a straight enough face to avoid seeming comedic. The décor of the Black Room itself is moneyed kitsch, like a boxer's idea of the high life. What makes it work is the extra element of surrealism, as the 'posh' accoutrements seem to hover in blackness, the swathing folds of velvet smoothed into invisibility by the contrasting glow of the illuminated table centrepiece. The 'sexiness' of all this depends on how much you associate fucking with good wines, tasteful music and the rustle of silk bedspreads. It's not for me, I have to say, but I like it as a pastiche of how the other half loves: there's a fun moment when Jason tells Larry that the room, with its hooked-on-classics sound-system, is ready for his next hot date, purring: *"How about some Chopin for a change?"*

And yet, for all its air of lascivious decadence, at its heart *The Black Room* is a morality tale about infidelity, and a portrait of the way marriage can stifle sensuality. It's also a look at the hypocrisy of men who seek adulterous freedoms for themselves, but find the idea of their wives enjoying extra-marital sex infuriating and unacceptable (see *Swingers Massacre* for a less enlightened treatment of the same theme). Vane summarises all this so neatly it's a pity Stanley Kubrick didn't watch the film before dragging much the same topic out to three hours in his stately but overstuffed *Eyes Wide Shut* (1999). (Funnily enough the party scenes at the chateau in Kubrick's film look like a big-budget *Black Room* rip-off!) Dramatically, the best scenes come when Robin discovers that the 'Black Room' of her husband's 'bedtime fantasies' is actually a real place. Shocked, she retaliates by embarking on a sexual tryst with the archly seductive Jason (although the scene requires a ten-ton weight to suspend our disbelief, since Jason is as camp as Liberace's bedspread…)

As a genre piece, *The Black Room* succeeds admirably, with plenty of tension to go with its good ideas. It's the sort of low-budget 'B' pic that makes you weep at the way the Hollywood mainstream squeezed such small but rewarding treasures out of the running. It's well-acted, well-written, and the careful use of Steadicam brings a dash of elegance that thankfully doesn't degenerate into aimlessness (a chief drawback of Steadicam being a director's inability to unclip the damn thing and go back to the dolly). In particular there's a wonderful scene, powerfully shot through a wide-angle lens by cinematographer and future director of *The Hitcher* Robert Harmon, in which a female victim breaks free from the killers' macabre blood-draining apparatus and makes a run for it. The moral themes and horror movie trappings don't overbalance or contradict each other, and the blood-draining sequences are suitably

below:
A 1983 admat for **The Black Room**, Norman Thaddeus vane's directorial entry into the horror genre.

The Black Room
aka **Vampires of the Black Room** (shooting title)
© 1981. Ram Inc.
Lancer Productions presents a Butler-Cronin production.
writer/co-director: Norman Thaddeus Vane. co-director: Elly Kenner. executive producer: D.P. Cronin. producer: Aaron C. Butler. associate producer: Ami Amir. music: Art Podell and James Ackley. editor: David Kern. director of photography: Robert Harmon. steadicam cinematographer: Andrew (Jeff) Mart. art-set decorator: Yoram Barzilai. associate producers: Dan Sather, Leon Feldman, Gerald Lembas, Kathleen Francis. script supervisor: Karen Golden. production manager / assistant director: Ami Amir. second assistant director: Pierre Wennagel. production sound mixer: Robert Marts. boom operator: Jim Stanley. first camera assistant: Lee Grover. second camera assistant: Michael Saunders. set construction: Eugene Harris. key grip: Mike Moad. assistant grip: Rami Ayali. gaffer: Gary Shore. best boy: Hudi Iceland. wardrobe - costumer: Lidia Priestly, Audrey Kasof. wardrobe assistant: Dona Leavy. make-up artist: Silvia Florez. associate make-up artist: Lars Ferguson. special effects: Mark Shostrom, Yoram Barzilai. still photographers: Rick Davis, Lauren Recht. background photographs courtesy: Ave Pildas. assistant to the producer: John Thomas. assistant to the director: Sheh Pourzand. props: Julian Banks. production assistants: Robert Lee Noble, Suzanne Thomas, John Schmidt, Lisa Gay Cronin, Yehuda Kassiff. post production under the supervision of Aaron C. Butler. post production coordinator: Herman Candler Grigsby. sound editor: David Kern. sound effects editor: Patrick O. Winters. electronic sound effects by Art Podell, James Achley. re-recording mixers: Hiroaki (Zom) Yamamoto, David M. Weishaar. sound by Cinesound. associate camera: Virgil Hammond. second associate camera: Thomas Cooke. Special thanks to David Hewitt, Dick Heronimus. autos & trucks courtesy Vincent Brady's Autos (Riverside, CA). original song "Dancin' to the Music" written and sung by Chris Mancini ©1981. Chris Mancini Music.
Cast: Stephen Knight (Jason). Cassandra Gaviola (Bridget). Jimmy Stathis (Larry). Clara Perryman (Robin). Charlie Young (Lisa). Geanne Frank (Sandy). Linnea Quigley (Milly). Christopher McDonald (Terry). Allisun Kale (Jenny). Bill Anglemyer (Mark). Sheila Reid (female lover). uncredited: Doug Cronin.

Where the rent is blood...

THE BLACK ROOM

Starring
Stephen Knight
Cassandra Gaviola • Jimmy Stathis • Clara Perryman
Produced by Aaron C. Butler • Directed by Elly Kenner

top:
Intervision's artwork for the UK video release in March 1983.

right:
Larry (Jimmy Stathis) and Bridget (Cassandra Gaviola). Stathis's few genre appearances include Burt Brinckerhoff's **Dogs** (1976), Boaz Davidson's **X-Ray** (1982) and Paul Leder's **Vultures** (1983); while Gaviola (aka Cassandra Gava) appeared as 'The Witch' in John Milius's Nietzschean fantasy gone haywire, **Conan the Barbarian** (1982).

horrible (easily a match for *Invasion of the Blood Farmers*, a rural spin on the same imagery). Sceptics among you might wonder how the hell Jason manages to obtain clear photographs of people in the black room through a pane of glass, when the room he's standing in is fully lit, but let's not get too cynical – who *knows* what tricks vampire photographers have up their sleeves?

The film ends with Larry and Robin forgiving each other, as they drive off with their rescued children and their partially exsanguinated babysitter (Linnea Quigley) in the back seat. It's a disappointingly staid conclusion to a story that has suggested far more interesting avenues. Jason and Bridget are left in a narrative limbo, apparently back from the grave, more like zombies than vampires, but presumably needing a new home when Larry calls the police. A better (if obvious) ending would have seen the married couple slay the vampires only to take over where they'd left off, and put the room back on the market. Still, minor quibbles aside, *The Black Room* is an entertaining horror tale that drips intelligence, imagination and style.

The Horror Star (1981)

"A stylish little thriller with a sense of humor and a good command of horror clichés. Compared to most of the movies it will be sharing double bills with, it's a masterpiece." – *Roger Ebert, Chicago Sun-Times.*

"Writer-director Norman Thaddeus Vane, an experienced man of the theater, has hit upon a clever notion and developed it with wit and humor. [The film] may be modest in budget but has style in abundance." – *Kevin Thomas, Los Angeles Times.*

Ailing horror movie icon Conrad Ragzoff (Ferdinand Mayne) is determined that his funeral will be as macabre and magnificent as his films. He even installs a video screen in his mausoleum, from which, in a pre-recorded message, he can bid extravagant farewell to the mourners. Ragzoff dies, and all goes according to plan: his funeral is a hi-tech marvel. However, after the ceremony a group of horror fans – Saint (Luca Bercovici), Oscar (Alan Stock), Donna (Donna McDaniel), Stu (Jeffrey Combs), Meg (Jennifer Starrett), Bobo (Scott Thomson), and Eve (Carlene Olson) – decide to steal the star's corpse and give him a last impromptu party. Big mistake. Ragzoff takes a dim view of irreverence, coming back to life and punishing those who would rewrite his final scene. Soon the revellers are learning the hard way that *no one* upstages Conrad Ragzoff; and if you want him at your fanboy gathering, you'd better be ready to pay...

With three 'death' scenes in the first fifteen minutes, veteran actor Ferdinand Mayne is given a suitably heroic introduction in *The Horror Star*, Norman Vane's paean to the grand old masters of horror. Mayne, who is probably best known to discerning fans for Roman Polanski's *The Fearless Vampire Killers*, can count this role as another feather in his cap. Unlike Peter Bogdanovich's *Targets*, which cast Boris Karloff as a horror icon rendered obsolete by modern life, *The Horror Star* is designed to give the old masters the last word. There are traces of Christopher Lee (not to mention Orson Welles) in Conrad's speech to a blasé TV commercial director – *"You're not only talking to a horror star, but an eminent actor. I played Julius Caesar on Broadway before you were born. I did Oscar Wilde and George Bernard Shaw on the London stage before you were a gleam in your daddy's eye!"* And of course Ragzoff's screen persona owes much to that beloved old *prosciutto* Vincent Price. The film is chock-full of screen references, from the relationship between Conrad and his German director Wolfgang (Leon Askin) to the corpse-stealing idea itself, which takes its cue from the oft-told Hollywood story of Errol Flynn 'borrowing' John Barrymore's corpse for an evening's partying. Last but not least, Ragzoff's elaborate send-off is the funeral dear old Bela Lugosi might have dreamed of – like Lugosi, Ragzoff is buried in his cape, relishing his iconic status to the end.

As we join Ragzoff, his career is on the skids. He's reduced to trotting out his vampire shtick for TV commercials, although judging by the opulent house in which he lives, and the no-expense-spared funeral arrangements, he's making these low-rent appearances because he's addicted to the limelight, not because he needs the money. Perhaps, when an irritated Ragzoff kills the TV director by shoving him off a balcony, Vane blurs the line between Ragzoff-the-man and Ragzoff-the-monster a bit too soon; but at least it

The Horror Star (US theatrical re-release title)
aka **Frightmare** (original title)
aka **The Body Snatchers**
(alternative UK video title)
aka **The Sacrilege**
aka **The Inferno** (title on copyright application)
© 1981. Screenwriters Productions Co., Inc.
director: Norman Thaddeus Vane. executive
producer: Henry Gellis. producer: Patrick Wright,
Tallie Wright. associate producers: Harold
D.Young, Hedayat Javid. screenplay: Norman
Thaddeus Vane. cinematographer: Joel King.
music: Jerry Moseley, arranged by Jack Manning.
editor: Doug Jackson. holographic effects by
Laserworld, John K. Foy. masks & poster
provided by Forrest J. Ackerman and Monster
Magazine. Special thanks to the Old Spaghetti
Factory (Hollywood). 1st assistant director: Sam
Baldoni. second assistant director: Bill Collard.
second unit camera: John Dirlam. extras coordi-
nator: Jack Marston. assistant editors: Philip
Malamuth, Jennifer Houston. creative sound: C
and D Recording. effects editor: Robert
C.Jackson. dialogue editor: Mark J. Garamella.
music editor: Fred Schwartz. special effects:
Knott Ltd. Chuck Stewart. special effects
makeup: Jill Rockow. makeup/hair: Sylvia Flores.
wardrobe mistress: Julie Schaefer. wardrobe
assistant: Verkina Flower. assistant makeup: Lars
Ferguson. wardrobe for Nita Talbot: Profits Du
Monde (Beverly Hills). new wave hair: Atilla of
Hollywood. assistant art director and prop
master: Glenn Neufeld. mausoleum set design:
Stephanie Hughes. mausoleum construction
crew: Tom West, Kevin Galbraith, Bill Manning.
script supervisor: Mori McDonald. sound
engineer: Mary Jo Devenny. boom operator:
Cindy Jones. still photographers: Marcel
Eskenazy, Glenn Neufeld, Hector Mendoza. first
camera assistant: Julio Macat. second unit
director: Sam Baldoni. second camera assistant
and loader: David Chung. key grip/gaffer: Darryn
Okada. gaffer: Doug Yellin. electrical grip: Les
Percy. electrical grip: Robert Duffin. best boy:
Chris Morley. dolly grip: Peter Van Eynde. grips:
Tommy Bias, Mark Thomas, Chris Centrella, Mike
Lee, Walter Hill. assistants to the production:
David Wildman, Erin Wright, Glenn Neufeld,
Sylvia Aimerito. casting: Johanna Ray and Steve
Foster. art director: Anne Welch. sound transfer:
Ron Curfman, Glen Glenn Sound. sound re-
recording: Glen Glenn Sound. titles, opticals,
colour: C.F.I. paramedic: Bill Collard. Thanks to
Adolph Coors Co.; Golden Co.; Tri-Tronics; Koss
Co., Milwaukee (WI). Special Gratitude to Abdul-
Wahed Al-Saihati and Adnan-Ali Sultan.
*Cast: Ferdinand Mayne (Conrad Ragzoff). Luca
Bercovici (Saint). Nita Talbot (Mrs. Rohmer).
Leon Askin (Wolfgang). Jennifer Starrett (Meg).
Barbara Pilavin (Etta). Carlene Olson (Eve).
Scott Thomson (Bobo). Donna McDaniel
(Donna). Jeffrey Combs (Stu). Peter Kastner
(commercial director). Chuck Mitchell
(detective). Jesse Ehrlich (professor). Ancel
Cook (nightwatchman). Michael Linder
(newscaster). Patrick Wright (first policeman).
Jack Marston (second policeman). Tallie
Cochrane (corpse). Alan Stock (Oscar). Twyla
Littleton. Joe Witherell. Janet Lee Orcutt.*

explains his eventual sojourn in hell (without it, we would have had to conclude that overacting is a mortal sin). Straight after this, we see Ragzoff at a film convention, graciously accepting an award from his adoring fans (many of whom are styled in that weird 1980s no-man's-land between New-Wave-Lite and Leather-Jacket-&-Perm). Thoroughly charmed by the adulation, Ragzoff suffers a heart-attack, and he's only saved by the intervention of nice-girl Meg, who revives him mouth-to-mouth.

The fun continues when Ragzoff stages a death-bed ruse, fooling Wolfgang into revealing his true feelings, but the highlight of the film is the star's video eulogy to himself at his own funeral. (Quite why everyone doesn't do this, now that video cameras are so cheap, I don't know.)

The wry, sardonic script gives Ferdinand Mayne plenty around which to roll his tongue, and as he addresses the startled guests, the combination of neon-tube kitsch and imposing marble gives the film a stylistic lift – it's like *Liquid Sky* crossed with *Phantasm*. These video messages are dotted throughout the film, as various characters break into the star's mausoleum: in one of the film's funniest ideas, Ragzoff has wired his crypt to detect intruders, so he can scare the shit out of them from beyond the grave.

Yet it turns out Ragzoff barely needs such techno-logical marvels, as he's soon back on his feet, exacting what many would feel was a fair price for defilement of his tomb and the theft of his corpse. In the film's best scene, the grave-robbing horror fans seal their fate by spinning

above:
A female horror fan demonstrates why she has to die (prêt-à-porter monster masks are *so* gauche), in the barbed genre satire, **The Horror Star**.

Scenes from **The Horror Star**.

above:
Oscar (Alan Stock) wishes he'd shown more repect for the dead.

right:
Exploring the attic in which Ragzoff's body is stashed by his 'fans'.

below:
Oscar makes out with Donna (Donna McDaniel).

Ragzoff's corpse around the room for a dance. Mayne acts the scene beautifully, giving Ragzoff's features a hint of mortification as his cadaver is subjected to an undignified twirl, and Vane knows how to milk the scene for maximum creepiness, scoring it with waltz music that gradually skews out of control, making the most of a whirling camera and wide-angle lenses. Brian De Palma himself would have been proud of the result.

I don't know if Vane intended to make the 'film fans' as hateful as possible, but they certainly raised *my* blood-lust. Perhaps *The Horror Star*'s biggest problem is that we're left in the company of these appalling characters for too long before Ragzoff gets even. Believe me, having their eyes pierced and popped, or their entrails eaten while they watch, is the least these jokers deserve. There's a plausi-bility problem too – nice girl Meg actually revived Conrad with the kiss of life when he collapsed during a fan convention, so it seems a bit unlikely that she would go along with the stealing of his corpse and its treatment as a figure of fun. It's also a bit of a stretch to believe that truly committed horror fans would abuse their idol like this. Perhaps if they were common-or-garden high schoolers instead of your actual film geeks… Still, with a tongue ripping, an immolation, a decapitation, a gassing, a skull-mash via flying coffin, and an enforced cremation, we who sympathize with Ragzoff are pretty well-served by events. (And if unsympathetic teens put you off this film, it's worth taking a look at Vane's *Midnight*, which largely dispenses with the young, following up *The Horror Star*'s 'Horrorwood' theme by scrutinising the life and loves of an ageing 'horror hostess'. The two would make an ideal double bill.)

There are some continuity problems, such as a séance which seems to take place in daylight while a supposedly simultaneous resurrection takes place at night; and it seems a bit unlikely that Bobo should return unhindered to the mausoleum the night after stealing the corpse, as the police are already aware of the theft. Perhaps the over-zealous séance lighting is to blame for giving the wrong impression in the first instance, but there's a rather hurried, ad-hoc approach to the film's time-frame, especially in the second half of the story. The grave-robbing and the party take place at night. We then have a single shot of the police at the mausoleum, in daylight, before the séance begins and Ragzoff is revived, again at night. Just what the seven grave-robbers have been doing during the day is never explained; since the girls are still in nightdresses and the guys are mostly topless, perhaps they've spent the day making out on coke?

More seriously, *The Horror Star* suffers from a second half that fails to be quite as amusing or interesting as the first. Most, though not all, of Ragzoff's best scenes are concentrated into the first forty minutes, and the remainder of the film plays out a supernatural stalk-and-slash scenario that's fun, but not as clever. *Fangoria*'s video reviewer 'Dr. Cyclops' claimed that, "[The] second half abandons the sense of humor of the first half and becomes a mechanical and unimaginative slaughter picture…" I think this is overstating things (I laughed out loud, for instance, at the flying coffin sequence, hardly the most conventional of murder methods), but there's a grain of truth here. Perhaps it's the dampening effect of all those teenagers in a film that began by concentrating on the lives of complex adult characters, but *The Horror Star* could do with a smidgeon more innovation in its last two reels.

Ultimately, what *The Horror Star* really needs is a decent widescreen DVD release to make the most of the lustrous cinematography, especially when it comes to the copious shadows amid which the latter stages unfold. Vane's framing looks unnaturally cramped on 4:3 video and we would doubtless sing his praises far more readily if we could see what he intended us to see. It's clear, even on video, that the film is very well lit and composed, but sadly *The Horror Star* has not appeared on any home video format since the 1980s. Like many of the most interesting films in this book it seems to have been consigned to Video Hell. But never mind – as Ragzoff says, *"Hell is not as bad as you think. It's actually quite pleasant. Maybe the food is a trifle overcooked, and the champagne… Californian; but you do meet the most* interesting *people…"*

Like most British horror fans, I first became aware of Norman Thaddeus Vane thanks to two horror films released on UK video – *The Black Room* and *The Horror Star*. However, Vane's career has stretched much further, from experimental improvised dramas to scriptwriting credits on major studio productions, spanning some forty years and three continents. He has enjoyed success as a playwright, lived and worked in Great Britain during the swinging sixties, moved in the higher echelons of *Penthouse* magazine, and contributed a script for an Australian fantasy/horror TV series...

Norman Thaddeus Vane was born in Patchogue, on Long Island, New York in 1933. He studied at the University of British Columbia for two summers, spent one year at Florida State University when he was in the Air Force, and two years at Columbia University in New York, plus two years at the Actors' Studio in New York. He began his creative career as a playwright, becoming a member of New York's New Dramatists Committee (alongside luminaries like Paddy Chayefsky). His first play, *The Penguin*, starring Martin Landau, was a modest hit off-Broadway in 1956. A year later he landed a writing job on an episode of the popular TV series *Kraft Television Theatre*. For his first screen credit, he contributed an episode called *Collision*, transmitted on 13 March, 1957. The story takes place on a foggy night in the Atlantic Ocean. Two passenger ships collide, and in the rescue one life is lost. An investigation reveals that the captain of one ship had served under the captain of the other for many years. When details of personal conflict between the two men emerge, it casts doubts on the true nature of the accident.

left:
Director Norman Thaddeus Vane.

above:
Vane clowns with a prop from his horror-melodrama, **Midnight**.

Soon after *Collision* aired, Vane moved to Great Britain: "I lived in England during the sixties and up until 1974, when I returned to the USA," he explains. "I had two English wives and thus was able to stay in England and work." He hit the British tarmac running, with two plays, *The Man Who Played God* and *The Deserters*. The latter starred Elizabeth Sellars and was directed by the highly respected Russian émigré, turned luminary of American theatre, Alan Schneider, famous for his groundbreaking Stateside productions of Samuel Beckett's *Waiting for Godot* and *Endgame*. Schneider would later go on to direct Buster Keaton in Beckett's only cinema project, *Film* (1965). It was a testimony to Vane's writing that Schneider was willing to take time off from the American stage (where he was greatly in demand), as he rarely directed plays outside of the United States. *The Deserters* was produced by Wolfe Mankowitz (*The Day the Earth Caught Fire* and *The Millionairess*), and for a while it looked as if the play might be adapted for the screen, until a proposed movie deal to be financed by Sidney Box at Rank fell through. All was not lost, though, as Rank would play a role in the handling of Vane's next project…

The British Films

In 1960, Vane obtained financing for his film debut, a sixty-seven-minute drama called *Conscience Bay*. The story concerns Nelly (Rosemary Anderson) and Fred (Marc Sheldon), childhood sweethearts in a dour Nova Scotian fishing village, who discover that Ben (John Brown), a good-looking youth with a hunchback, has been stealing the lobster catch. Ben lives in a semi-derelict fishing boat called the 'Seabird', which lies isolated in the estuary. Nelly, the adopted daughter of local evangelist Caleb (Mark Dignam) and his sick wife Aunt Boo (Catherine Willmer), discovers that Ben is Aunt Boo's illegitimate son. He has run away from his cruel foster-parents and now lives in Conscience Bay, fending for himself. He steals

bottom left:
Meg (Jennifer Starrett) prepares to defend herself against Ragzoff's supernatural attack, in **The Horror Star**.

below:
Body Snatchers, a retitling of **The Horror Star** for UK video.

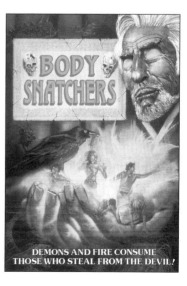

BODY SNATCHERS

DEMONS AND FIRE CONSUME THOSE WHO STEAL FROM THE DEVIL!

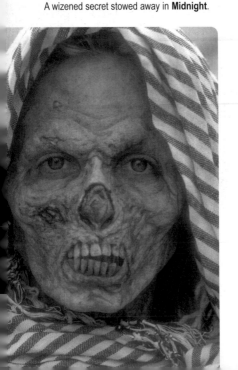

because it's the only way to earn a crust: the local fishermen won't give him a job, so he sells purloined lobsters to a travelling trader. Nelly and Ben become friends and then lovers; soon their relationship supersedes Nelly's feelings for Fred. When Aunt Boo's illness deepens, Nelly brings Ben to the house; mother is reunited with son and asks his forgiveness. Ben returns to the 'Seabird' with Nelly, and the two make love. The next morning, Caleb arrives and finds the young lovers in bed together. Furious, he informs them that Aunt Boo died during the night and curses them for their 'sin'. After a further confrontation with Caleb, Ben runs away, telling Nelly not to come to him again. He returns to his stealing. A jealous Fred tells Caleb that Ben is the lobster thief, and Nelly must sacrifice her inheritance to save Ben from mob violence at the hands of the fishermen. Disillusioned with small town life, and realising she has never really loved Fred, Nelly chooses to leave Conscience Bay with Ben at her side, to seek their fortune together in the wider world…

Vane shot the film on Cornish locations in seven weeks, at a cost of just £20,000. However, *Conscience Bay* was not a commercial success. Rank, who had picked up the film for release as a 'B' feature, pulled it out of circulation, and Vane – who also wrote and produced – quickly re-edited it, but to no avail; little would be seen or heard of the film again.

He had better fortune back in the theatre, where his play *The Expatriate* was a success at The Croydon Pembroke (now The Peggy Ashcroft) Theatre in February of 1961. It starred Gordon Heath (who narrated the famous 1954 adaptation of *Animal Farm*), Frances Cuka, and Noel Harrison (Rex Harrison's actor/musician son, who had a Top Ten hit with 'Windmills of Your Mind' in 1969). Vane recalls that *The Times* called it, *"an important theatrical event: not quite as important as* The Marriage of Figaro *was to the French Revolution."* Sarcasm, of course, is the lowest form of wit, so we must assume that a writer for the lofty *Times* was being sincere: but regardless of such matters, Vane was now making a name for himself on the British theatre scene.

Unfortunately, Vane's next play was one he himself describes with a shudder as "my flop." This 1961 production, called *O'Malley the Duck*, starred fading Hollywood star Linda Darnell, who was at the time largely retired from the screen. (Four years later, Darnell tragically burned to death in a fire at her secretary's home, while watching a TV rerun of her first rags-to-riches movie success, *Star Dust*). *O'Malley the Duck* opened and closed within six days at The Oldham Rep, and even when Columbia Pictures bought an option on the script it did little to salve Vane's disappointment.

As well as writing and directing for stage and screen, Vane dabbled in property and entertainment management, running various nightclubs, casinos and bars in London, including La Discothèque on Wardour Street, The Green Street Club in Mayfair, The Apartment on the King's Road, and, for a while, the notorious gaming club Esmeralda's Barn, in Kensington. "I had three gambling clubs, which turned out to be a lot more profitable than the film business," he recalls.

His partner in some of these endeavours was Mim Scala, one of the movers and shakers of the swinging sixties, a wide-boy turned gaming impresario and rock manager, whose memoir, *Diary of a Teddy-Boy*, is a fascinating glimpse into London post-*Absolute Beginners*. He knew everyone, as they say: or, if not quite 'everyone', then a friend-of-a-friend of everyone. His reach included The Kray twins, who bought Esmeralda's Barn in 1960; and worse, the archetypal evil landlord, Peter Rachman, from whose name the term 'Rachmanism' was derived.[1]

Tiring of the unpleasantness he was encountering in the 'hospitality industry', Vane decided to mount a second feature film, *Fledglings* (1965; shot in 1964). In a recursive vein bordering on the postmodern, he told the story of two struggling filmmakers, Mike (Mike Ross), an artist, and Iain (Iain Quarrier), a male model, who live together in a *ménage à trois* with their girlfriend Julia (Julia White). The two young men are making a film in the *nouvelle vague* style, set in their own Chelsea environs, when they run out of money half-way through production. A prominent American businessman, Reev Passmore (played by Victor Lownes, the *Playboy* magnate) agrees to bankroll the project, and to further ensure the success of the venture, the two *auteurs* persuade Julia to bed him. Subsequent developments lead to the break-up of the trio as their youthful idealism founders on the contradictions between their attitudes and the cold hard reality of international financing.

The story is built around numerous equivalences between fiction and reality: Mike Ross plays a painter interested in the French New Wave cinema, which he was in real life; Julia White was an actual model; and in a further twist, when the film was shown to a Hollywood agent, he became very interested in White, began to date her, and took her off to Hollywood. The chief locations are a Chelsea artists' studio belonging to Mike Ross, and Victor Lownes's lavish house in Montpelier Square. Money did indeed run out half-way through production, at which point one-time theatrical agent Leonard Urry, then joint managing director of film producers Anatole de Grunwald Limited, stepped in as fairy godfather and stumped up the required cash (whether for the same inducements and sweeteners is not on record…).

It's an intriguing proposition and would make a fascinating revival one day, as it's enmeshed in connections to the sixties entertainment industry. Leading man Iain

Quarrier went on to form Cupid Productions, in partnership with upper-class hedonist Michael Pearson (now Viscount Cowdray), to make Godard's *Sympathy for the Devil*, shot in Great Britain during the height of the Paris Riots in May 1968. Quarrier acted in a deluge of sixties cult movies: his friend Roman Polanski's *Cul-de-Sac* and *The Fearless Vampire Killers*; George Harrison's *Wonderwall*; and the multi-director minestrone *Casino Royale*. An unusual casting coup came in the form of Victor Lownes, right-hand man to *Playboy*'s Hugh Hefner. Lownes arrived at *Playboy* in the mid-fifties, and soon made his mark by charming reluctant businessmen into advertising with the magazine. He was so successful that he once boasted he had "a cupboard full of ten foot poles" from businesses he'd persuaded onboard. In 1960 he became closely involved with the newly emerging *Playboy* clubs, before launching the *Playboy* empire's considerable British gambling interests in 1966. A complex individual, he went on to produce Monty Python's *And Now for Something Completely Different* and, having befriended Roman Polanski in the mid-sixties, prevailed upon Hefner to support Polanski's flagrantly uncommercial *Macbeth* with *Playboy* cash.

Made in just eight days, and billed as "The first completely improvised feature film ever made in England," *Fledglings* met with a mixed response in the press, mostly due to its improvisational nature. *"Much as I admire a man who can play the flute standing on his head, I cannot help wondering how much better he could play it on his feet,"* opined the *Daily Mail*, who also described the story as featuring *"two young louts"* who *"receive the rebuff that all such pimps deserve"* for their treatment of Julia: before adding that the *"pretty little model"* herself contributes some *"cleverly ad-libbed"* scenes to the bedroom skirmishes. *The Daily Telegraph*'s reviewer began by stating that the film, *"has considerable academic interest"*, and remarked that, *"some party scenes are caught rather well, and the photography […] has a lyrical quality"*, but concluded that, *"innumerable scenes prompt an uncomfortable comparison with the work of Jean-Luc Godard."* However, while Godard was valorising the existential criminal drop-out in films such as *À bout se souffle* and *Pierrot le fou*, Vane was practicing what Godard could only preach: "The movie was made on stock stolen from the BBC!" he laughs. "The cameraman worked there, and every day he turned up with more stolen film." As a result of this Fassbinder-esque approach to cost management, Vane brought the movie in for a mere £2,500.[2] He describes the film today as, "improvised… arty", and says it's his favourite of the early films. It played for a while at the Classic in Chelsea, but like *Conscience Bay*, it's now diabolically difficult to see.

Swinging Scriptwriter

Turning to screenplays, Vane made a series of career moves that would eventually take him back to the USA. The first was a script based on his own mildly scandalous personal life at the time. He recalls, "My wife then was Sarah Caldwell; we had a very notorious elopement, got married in Scotland. She was only sixteen. Our marriage became the basis for *Lola*, or *Twinky* as it was known in England, a comedy which Richard Donner directed." Exploring the love affair of a fortyish writer of porn novels and a boisterous teenage schoolgirl, *Twinky* starred a nineteen-

year-old Susan George as the sixteen-year-old Sarah ('Twinky' in the film), with Charles Bronson as Vane's surrogate: "Which was disastrous," sighs Vane, "he was as funny as a kippered herring."

"Never had a girl like this for me/Dumb but pretty like a schoolgirl should be," sings Jim Dale, who wrote this Humbert-ish lyric himself, along with, *"Pretty young girl on a two wheel bike/All I see is a Jezebel just like Twinky"*. It's all a bit shocking to anyone who's lived through the change in attitudes to gymslip fantasies over the last thirty years. Nevertheless, *Twinky* did fairly well on its release in 1969: little wonder, with a strap-line that lassoed many a passing male's gaze: *"She had just reached the age of consent: and the first word she said was 'Yes!'"* *Twinky* was released by Rank in England, and AIP in America, and received mixed reviews, but Vane had scored big with the project and things were on the up.

Released before *Twinky* but written after it, *Mrs. Brown You've Got a Lovely Daughter* (1968) – a musical vehicle for the dubious talents of Herman's Hermits – is not a film of which Vane is proud, even though it featured his new wife in her screen debut. "It was a silly kid's movie. I never even tell anyone I wrote it, it's not on my credits, I never mention it. The guy who did the music was called Mickie Most. He was not a friendly guy. A great talent though. I respected him." The film was to have been young Sarah Caldwell's entrée into the movies, but it didn't work out: "Sarah was terrible in the movie," says Vane. "She could have had a film career, she was a top model with Eileen Ford and was on the cover of many magazines, but she turned down a contract at Fox for a lot of stupid reasons and blew it. She lives now in Bath, England, and has three kids – not by me!"

Vane made a tidy sum from the film, although the price of success was having to deal with producer Allen Klein, one of the American entertainment industry's most demonic figures: "I was literally a prisoner in the Hilton hotel for two and a half months during that shoot. I had an

above:
Lynn Redgrave as Midnight, a TV 'horror hostess' coming apart at the seams.

below:
Vane (*middle*) with Midnight stars Tony Curtis (*left*) and 'The Riddler' Frank Gorshin (*right*).

THE BLACK ROOM

INTERNATIONAL FILM SALES DIVISION

THE ROBERT G. HUSSONG AGENCY, INC.
Talent Agency
8271 Melrose Avenue
Los Angeles, California 90046
(213) 655-2534 • TELEX 194629
CABLE ADDRESS: RGHAGENCY
Frank Sacks/Associate

above:
Pressbook artwork for **The Black Room**.

below:
Jason (Stephen Knight) seduces Robin
(Clara Perryman).

Despite ructions with Klein on *Mrs. Brown...*, by the early 1970s Vane found himself spending more and more time working for the infamous mogul's ABKCO Films Inc, in California. This brought him into proximity with a number of Klein's associates, one of whom was Saul Swimmer. Klein had produced his 1962 film *Without Each Other*, which starred Tony Anthony, an actor whose association with Swimmer dated back to *Force of Impulse* (1961). All three – Swimmer, Klein and Anthony – produced the well-regarded spaghetti western *Blindman* (1971), directed by Italian genre specialist Ferdinando Baldi from Anthony's story and screenplay, and starring Anthony in the title role. For added boxoffice, Klein and Swimmer drew on their Beatles connections to snag Ringo Starr, who plays one of the villains (Swimmer was co-producer of the *Let It Be* movie, while Klein's business dealings with the band have been well documented, not least by *The Rutles...*)

Like many who have come into contact with Allen Klein, Vane is scathing about the man often credited with driving a financial wedge between Paul McCartney and John Lennon: and he has claimed to have a theory about Klein's and Swimmer's involvement in George Harrison's 'Concert for Bangladesh' (one of the most fêted charity events of the 1970s, the movie of which Swimmer co-directed and Klein produced) that is impossible for us to verify. The final straw came when Klein allegedly deprived Vane of a decent payday: "Klein was such an asshole, don't get me started. I wrote a script for them called *The Tunnel* which didn't get made, finally got ripped off by [a major Hollywood actor-director] who did his own version of it, which bombed. But at the time I had a publisher who wanted to do a book of *The Tunnel*, and Klein just wouldn't give me the rights. I said, 'Allen it's not costing anything – he's giving *us* money! Let me do the book, he's gonna give me a big advance!' I think he was still mad with me about the incident in the hotel room. I tried to take him to the Writer's Guild and make him pay, he was a signatory, but they said they couldn't do it because he was out of the country."

Indians Are Indians...

Moving on from Klein and ABKCO, Vane, now living full-time back in the States, set about researching material for a spooky drama about Native American mysticism, called *Shadow of the Hawk*. The film was released in 1976, but the transition from typewriter to movie screen was far from smooth. Says Vane, "*Hawk* was a horrible experience for me as I was replaced by no less than nine or ten writers and I worked with four or five different directors. The original title was *Journey Into a Nightmare*, and the script was a really scary and beautifully written story based on a synopsis that a cameraman, Peter Jensen, sold to me. I was working with Peter Guber on *Shadow of the Hawk* and he was not the easiest person in the world to work for, kind of a hate relationship, but I made a lot of money, about $75,000, on that movie. Guber's brother-in-law was Henry Gellis, the producer, and I worked with him on a couple of movies – he was the co-producer of *The Horror Star*. Henry brought a lot of artistry to the project, but completely lost control of the shooting. *Shadow of the Hawk* was a really interesting script. I'd gone to an Indian reservation, researching the Navajos, the Hopis. Then Peter left the movie to do *Jaws*. When he did that, Stanley Jaffe,

enormous fight with Klein: he was showing off with about seven people, and he came to my suite at the Hilton and demanded a rewrite at two in the morning. I was in bed with some girl. I was furious that he woke me up. He was showing off to all these women in mink coats, and I said, 'Okay Allen, you want a rewrite? *Here's* your rewrite!' and I picked up the table which was full of coca-cola bottles, maybe about a hundred of them, and I threw it all over them, and the coke went on the minks, they all ran out of my suite and I went back to bed. They couldn't fire me, I was the writer! If they fired me who was going to do it? Instead, he stuck me with a $4,000 hotel bill!"

"I kept going back and forth between England and the USA from 1969 to 1974," he continues. "In '69 I was the editor of *Penthouse* as well as the theatre, film and book critic." Vane had problems with the head honcho of *Penthouse*, Bob Guccione: "He was trying to fuck my wife, Sarah, under the pretence of him photographing her. I wouldn't let him. I knew better, and quit the magazine."

who's the son of Leo Jaffe, one of the founders of Columbia, took over and said, 'We'll do the movie in Canada, 'cos we got money up there.' I called him up and said, 'Stanley, all the research is real and it all came from me living with the Navajos and the Hopis. Canadian Indians are blood Indians, they have totem poles and it's a totally different thing, they're mountain Indians – we have desert Indians in this story, that's what makes it so spooky.' And he said, 'Oh I don't give a shit about that, Indians are Indians.' So we did it in Vancouver. Many writers came in, there had been some big director attached to it. In the end, the stuff that I'd implied, that made it really scary, they added literally – there's an idiotic mask that keeps following them around – it was ridiculous… it's hard for me to look at the movie."

Despite its troubled history, Vane was glad of the big payday, and he still holds some affection for the film. "It was much scarier in it's original form, but it is still not too bad a movie, all things considered. Somehow or other, a lot of it still came through. I still get royalties on it. It opened big in Los Angeles and played pretty well across the country in theatres."

Shadow of the Hawk was a Columbia Pictures release, and so falls outside the more detailed ambit of this book, but it's hardly an over-exposed title these days, and I have to say I found it a lot more fun than I was expecting. As Vane points out, the constant apparition of the Indian mask gets to be a pain, although its first three appearances – including an excellent underwater manifestation and a floating-at-the-window shock that trumps *Salem's Lot* – are genuinely alarming. The storyline is structured around a haunted road-trip: 'Old Hawk' (Chief Dan George) turns up in the big city and persuades his grandson Mike (Jan-Michael Vincent) to return to the village of his birth and help fight a witch's malediction. The journey back to the village, with a nosy reporter/love interest in tow, forms the backbone of the narrative, and along the way the initially sceptical city-dwellers see enough manifestations of evil to convince them that the old guy is not as crazy as they first believed. (Lovers of Lucio Fulci's *City of the Living Dead* may see a resemblance and wonder what he might have done with the material!) There are several well-conceived set-piece scares that make it all worthwhile: look out for a stunning scene involving a car and a magical barrier, which could hold its own in a far bigger production. *Shadow of the Hawk* is solidly directed, with the occasional imaginative flourish, by George McCowan, whose *Frogs* is one of my guilty pleasures, and although the overall feel is more 'skip work to watch TV in the afternoon' than 'late night scary movie' (hardly surprising, given McCowan's work on *Starsky and Hutch*), it's still worth seeing if you can.

Into the Black…

"Darkly erotic … The ultimate frightmare of the bored married man's search for casual sex gone horribly wrong." – Bill Landis, *Sleazoid Express (book)*.

After *Shadow of the Hawk*, Vane's career went into recession for a while, with one of his few credits of the period being a second unit directing gig on the porno-horror spoof *Dracula Sucks* (1979), starring Jamie Gillis, Annette Haven and genre icon Reggie Nalder (the latter appearing under the pseudonym 'Detlef Van Berg'). By 1981, Vane was looking to direct one of his own scripts again.

The result was *The Black Room*, a slyly amusing chiller about posh vampires hiring out rooms to swingers in their desirable L.A. mansion. The inspiration for this story is surprisingly autobiographical, as Vane reveals: "I'll tell you something I haven't told anyone else. While I was working for *Penthouse* I was married to Sarah, the sixteen-year-old model and actress. We were both very unfaithful to each other, but neither told the other about it. I kept meeting all these beautiful women at *Penthouse* who wanted to fuck my brains out and I had no place to take them. So I rented a small room in the basement of a house of a South African painter. This was the deal: I would call him up when I was coming over, and he would go down to this lovely room in his basement, put on the music, light the candles, and open a bottle of cold wine and leave it on the table. When I arrived there with a girl - usually the latest *Penthouse* centrespread - and she saw the room with the candles lit, the wine cold, and Vivaldi playing, she couldn't believe it. What I *didn't* know was the South African painter had a hole in the wall and was watching everything that we did. One day I saw a little gleam of light coming from a hole in the wall and I followed it around to the next room and caught him in the act, and for the first time understood what was going on. I immediately terminated our arrangement. By then however, four or five ladies had been through the room, and it became the basis for the movie."

Vane showed the script to a producer, Aaron Butler, and an Israeli director called Elly Kenner. "Elly Kenner had read my script – I think the original title may have been *The Vampires of the Black Room* – and they decided they wanted to do it on a budget of approximately $30,000," Vane recalls. "It finally cost $40,000 including post-production. That meant we had enough to shoot the film but we had no idea how we were going to get it finished. Elly was an Israeli who had never directed a movie and I had directed two small ones in England, so I directed the actors, and he directed the camera. We didn't get along very well, obviously, especially as he would stop and say things like 'I want you to cry on this line.' I explained to him that actors didn't cry on cue. I found this particularly offensive, as I came from the Actor's Studio in New York, where we had a very realistic approach to acting and did not impose objectives on the actors but let it come naturally from within."

The shooting lasted for roughly ten fifteen-hour days in 1981; a surprisingly quick turn-over for such a handsome, professional-looking film. Says Vane, "It was shot in a big house in the Hollywood Hills which was owned by the Mafia's literary representative in America. During the shooting there was a big candle scene, if you remember, and when we took a break, one of the tall candles melted into the curtains and set the room on fire. In total panic we put the fire out, but came very close to burning down the house of a mob producer who probably would have had us all killed!"

Vane had mixed feelings about his two producers: "The first twenty or twenty five thousand dollars was contributed by Doug Cronin, a former football player, and he insisted on being in the movie. He has a small scene in the beginning of the movie which makes no sense, in which he is killed and buried. I look at that scene with great pain whenever I see the movie, which isn't very often, and wish we could have gotten Doug the hell out of there, for his sake and ours. Doug was a nice guy, and I was very fond of him, but he did not fit into the movie at all. Aaron Butler,

above:
Bridget suffers a setback during the final moments of **The Black Room**.

below:
A cosy social gathering in **The Black Room**…

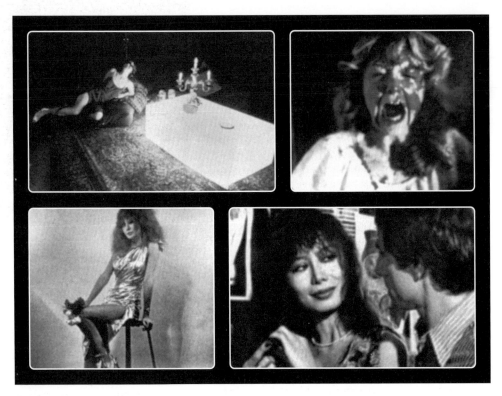

above, clockwise from top left:
Sensuous times in the Black Room;
Bloody horror erupts;
Bridget the seductress;
Bridget homes in on Larry.

the producer, was a big red-headed Irishman of Jewish descent. He wore a Star of David around his neck, drank like a fish, cursed everybody and was totally obnoxious. I found it very difficult to be friends with him after that movie. I do see him now and again, the last time at [film distributor] Billy Fine's funeral."

It's unusual for two directors to collaborate simultaneously on a shoot, and it's a situation ripe for conflict. Vane, not surprisingly, is less than complimentary about his erstwhile colleague: "Elly and I obviously did not get along, especially as just before the shooting began he was fighting with his new South African wife Anne, who I put up in my Hollywood Hills home on Doheny Drive. (I had a live-in girlfriend at the time, Ruth Ann Lorenz [Llorens], who starred in a horror movie called *Graduation Day*). Anne refused to go back to him for a week. During this time she told me that Elly had said, 'As soon as Norman signs the contracts I'm going to fuck him.' After she shared that information with me, I made damn sure I had everything in writing with Elly and the producers before they got the script." (Kenner is currently hard to trace for his comments, having moved to Israel soon after the film was finished.)

Vane has no complaints about the look of the film: "I thought the Israeli art director was very good considering he was working with no money. It was his idea to have the green luminescent table in the Black Room." *The Black Room*'s talented cinematographer, Robert Harmon, would himself go on to direct, scoring a sizeable international hit with *The Hitcher* (1986), starring Rutger Hauer and C. Thomas Howell. Vane recalls, "Robert Harmon did a really good job as DP. After the movie, he did a demo reel for $10,000, got an agent at William Morris, and directed quite a few horror movies himself. One actor that I got a SAG card for was Christopher McDonald, who later starred in quite a few television movies, and was featured in several regular movies as well. But I did start him on the road, as I have done with many, many actors and actresses. Linnea Quigley was in *The Black Room*. I picked her out of a

reading, and she went on to become a 'Scream Queen' in many horror flicks. I thought she was basically terrible. Cassandra Gava was truly marvellous and I see her at parties occasionally, including one a few months ago at Christmastime at a studio. She starred opposite Arnold Schwarzenegger in *Conan the Barbarian* where she played an erotic witch."

With the relish of a born storyteller, he continues: "Now I'll go even further and tell you a couple of things I really shouldn't. The lead actress was Clara Perryman, a girl of Scottish descent about twenty or twenty one at the time, tall and very pretty with red hair. I was mad about her from the first moment I saw her and fought very hard to get her the lead. In the end, in order to get Clara the lead, I had to trade other choices. The truth is, during the readings and the casting, which was about three or four weeks, Clara and I had an affair of sorts. She really blew my head. I was half in love with her – however, as soon as we signed the contracts it ended. But she was a terrific actress and she was great in the movie and a delight to work with and I never had any regrets. After the movie started shooting I heard from everyone that Stephen Knight, the very good looking leading man, was having an affair with Clara and continued to do so during shooting as well as during post. I lost track of Clara and have never seen her again, except as the lead in the play *Nuts*, which played at a nice theatre in Hollywood."

The Black Room was eventually released, two years after it was shot. Says Vane, "The post-production went on forever and I pretty much dropped out of it. We kept getting money in dribs and drabs from Robert Hussong until the movie was finished. Hussong, an agent and a distributor, put up the finishing money and he controlled selling the movie. He died six or seven years ago and he avoided paying almost everyone. I did get a fairly large check a few years ago for the writer's share of the video rights, which surprised me. It was sold basically to video all over the world and I am forever hearing about it from horror fans who seem to think it's a classic. Cassandra Gava tells me whenever she goes to a festival she is swamped by people asking for her autograph."

The Black Room proved to be ahead of the pack in its association of vampires with contemporary style, although one would not wish to blame Norman Vane for what came next. Tony Scott's *The Hunger* (1983) treated vampirism as a chic appurtenance to fashion-magazine aesthetics, and although it failed to set the box office alight the film was embraced by Goth-lite *fashionista* yuppies as a symbol of their *so-decadent-dahling* pretentions. Of course, there was an earlier precedent: Count Dracula himself cut rather a dash, and his castle – all original features, house-hunters! – was hardly a slum tenement. Essentially, though, the Count was 'old-money' and his style was a function of his aristocratic ancestry. When the vampire was updated in the 1980s (passing over such earlier, proletarian anomalies as George Romero's *Martin*), the 'greed-is-good' ethos saw the yuppie bourgeoisie arriving at the castle gates. Vampires became the avatar of choice for coke-sniffing clubbers in touch with their 'dark side'.[3]

Despite the less than congenial circumstances of the production, Vane remains proud of the story's idiosyncrasies: "It was the only vampire film ever made where the people were real and really did have a blood disorder and their need for blood was real and not based on some mythical vampire legend."

Shooting *The Horror Star*

Turning away from the drawn-out post-production hassles of *The Black Room*, Vane took another of his scripts into production, this time without a co-director to cramp his style. "*The Horror Star* was vaguely based on a famous old Hollywood story," he explains, "which was that several Hollywood actors, including Errol Flynn, kidnapped the dead body of John Barrymore for one night and brought it back to his Hollywood mansion for a farewell dinner. In essence that is what inspired me to do *The Horror Star*. The movie was financed by an Iranian real estate tycoon I met at a party, and two Saudi Arabian princes. How I met them I can't even remember. I put in a little money myself, and so did a lawyer in New York. My partner was Henry Gellis, who had produced *Shadow of the Hawk*."

Despite its 1981 copyright date, Vane maintains that *The Horror Star* went into production in the spring of 1982, with a three-week shoot, although it too was not released until '83. "*The Horror Star* was shot partly in a studio, partly in a cemetery in Hollywood, and mostly in an old mansion I found near USC," Vane recalls. "The minute I walked into the mansion and walked up the stairs and went into the library and saw that the bookcases turned completely around into the wall I knew this was the place."

With Ferdinand Mayne, Vane knew he had a strong central performer to rely on, and so spent more time coaching his young supporting cast, which included Jeffrey Combs, soon to find fame as 'Herbert West' in Stuart Gordon's hit *Re-Animator*. Vane also worked very closely with Joel King, who had gone from a gig as camera operator on Brian De Palma's *Carrie*, to cinematographer on Paul Leder's *Sketches of a Strangler* and Jeff Lieberman's *Just Before Dawn*: "Joel was a brilliant cinematographer, but a nutcase beyond all belief. I used him again on *Club Life*. We were at loggerheads quite a bit, but I appreciated the artistry he brought to the shooting. If he hadn't had problems he might have become a major cinematographer, his work was that good. One of the problems is that we were on a limited budget and I would be happy getting to 'take three' or 'take four', but he would insist on going to 'take nine or ten' because he wanted to do it better. We kept running out of money and I had to keep going back to the investors. That's okay on studio films, but not on films like *The Horror Star*, which was being made on a budget of $120,000."

After the movie was finished, MGM showed some initial interest, but eventually decided to pass. The film was instead put out by Saturn International Pictures, which led to an amusing encounter with a future 'king of the world', as Vane reveals: "One of the posters which was not used, but tested very well, was the one with all of the hands coming out of the ground trying to kill the leading lady. This was done by James Cameron! At the time, Saturn was also distributing his film *Piranha II*. Anyway, James did a wonderful poster except he couldn't draw the young girl's face. The face that he drew was that of a twenty-five-year-old woman, not a seventeen-year-old girl. So since we were paying for the poster – I think he got $200 at the time – I got another painter to draw in a young girl's face. When Cameron saw this, he started to tear up the poster just a week or so before the movie was scheduled to go out. I went nuts. I ran across the room and punched him. He punched me back. We rolled all over the floor punching each other before the two distributors pulled us apart. I'm sorry I did that, I obviously didn't know he was to become a famous director, but he did tear up our poster. We shook hands later and sort of made up."

above:
A horror fan dresses as the Bride of Frankenstein to dine with the corpse of Conrad Ragzoff, in **The Horror Star**.

below left:
Ragzoff uses post-mortem telekinesis to chase a victim with a flying coffin.

below:
Promo artwork for the film under its alternative title **Frightmare**, designed by the director of **Titanic** and **Piranha II: Flying Killers**, James Cameron.

bottom:
Ferdinand Mayne oozes evil in a role that would not be out of place in one of the great Hammer or Amicus outings.

A Saturn International Pictures release © 1983.

"FRIGHTMARE"
Released by Saturn International Pictures

The flying coffin in the movie "FRIGHTMARE."

above:
Another piece of artwork for **The Horror Star** aka **Frightmare**.

He continues: "For the opening night in Los Angeles, the movie was in about fifteen drive-ins and thirty five theatres around the city. That Friday night was the worst rain storm in years and it rained all over the weekend, which didn't help the box office. But the movie did go out in various cities and got really good reviews, people seemed to like it. The Manson company gave us $100,000 up front to distribute the movie foreign. They did a good job in selling it, but were very crooked with the books, as all foreign film distributors based in America are. There is no exception to that statement. If you are going to get into the foreign distribution business you are going to get well and truly fucked. The movie grossed, to the best of my knowledge, about $350,000 foreign and they got two-thirds of that, and we got to pay back our advance and a bit more. The investors basically got almost no money and so they didn't come back for another movie as they would have. Eventually we sold the movie to Troma, a distributor in New York, but by then almost everything had been sold already so I'm not sure what they were buying."

Vane found *The Horror Star* a much easier shoot than *The Black Room*: "I was much more in control of everything. Ferdinand Mayne, though, was not easy to work with. If his make-up was not to his satisfaction he would throw a tantrum and would refuse to work until we sent people around Los Angeles trying to find the shade he wanted. But he did win several awards for the film, one particularly from the Horror and Sci-fi Festival here in Los Angeles. I would not let them screen the movie, because they wanted to screen it before it was released, and I didn't want anyone to see it before the reviews came out, which turned out to be really good. People always seem to remember the young girl dancing with the corpse of the film star and they always seem to talk about the flying coffin, which killed people. That was very difficult to do, requiring a very light coffin, and a real one, and scared our leading lady, Jennifer Starrett, who would cry before each shot. Her father was the famous director Jack Starrett [*The Strange Vengeance of Rosalie, Cleopatra Jones*]. It went out big in Europe, especially in France, where it played in fifty-plus theatres. It won second prize at the Avoriaz Film Festival, a silver medal which I still have. Roger Ebert, probably the top American critic, called it a masterpiece compared to any other horror films of that year. The domestic distributor was Saturn International Pictures and they bicycled seventy five prints from one theatre to another. It was bought by Vestron for video and it went out big, so much so that they offered me another horror movie called *The Night Has a Thousand Eyes*, but my line producer screwed up the deal by coming in with a budget for $900,000 – $300,000 *over* the figure I was supposed to bring it in on. The head of Vestron flew in from Connecticut, said, 'We told you it would have to be $600,000, what is this?' They were furious. I could never get the thing back on track."

Club Life and *Midnight*

Vane's next venture was *Club Life*, aka *King of the City* (1985), a crime thriller about Cal (Tom Parsekian), a tough motocross racer who goes to Hollywood looking to become a star. He takes a job as a bouncer at a nightclub run by Hector (Tony Curtis) and gets sucked into underworld violence. But Hector is in trouble with the Mafia, having turned down their offer for his club; Cal's old girlfriend turns up with a drug problem; and his best buddy at the

club is shot by local hoods. Should Cal stay, seek revenge, and sink to the same level as his enemies, or get out of town and leave L.A. to the scumbags who run it?

Club Life's big catch is Tony Curtis, who looks great here as the debonair, silver-haired Hector, trying to resist the blandishments of the Mob and keep drugs *"at arm's length"* instead of letting the dealers have free play in his venue. He's ably assisted by laconic Michael Parks as 'Tank', the resident enforcer at Hector's bar. The starring role of Cal goes to newcomer Tom Parsekian, a handsome guy with a bad perm who had the looks but apparently not the luck to continue in Hollywood – *Club Life* was his third and final screen credit. The film is brisk and fairly diverting, although it was made at the height of the power-ballad craze, meaning that histrionic FM soft rock plays incessantly. A scene that could have been touching, such as Tank's funeral inside the club, is ruined by some irritating rock chick belting out a tacky 'requiem' that sounds like Bonnie Tyler fronting Huey Lewis and the News. The whole thing plays like a cross between *Fear City* and *Footloose*. What hampers it is a flimsy storyline with little in the way of character development, too great a reliance on mediocre dance scenes, and an air of uncertainty revealed by a handful of needless voice-overs. *Club Life* ends fatuously with Cal dragging his junkie girlfriend out of the club, shoving her on the back of his motorbike, and heading back to small town life, leaving Sin City behind: although as anyone knows, if a junkie wants a fix, they'll find it in Missoula if necessary.

right:
US video art for Vane's **Club Life** (1985).

below:
Eve (Carlene Olson), who betrothed herself to Ragzott in a Goth-fantasy ceremony in **The Horror Star**.

Club Life is well outside the ambit of this book, but Vane has a few comments to make about it. He was especially galled when a recent television interviewer implied that Tony Curtis had taken the role as a favour to the director: "Well, I remember it was the exact opposite, he hadn't worked in about three years! We paid him $100,000 for a week's work! I was doing *him* a favour and he kept saying how grateful he was that I had chosen him. Of course I was honoured to work with him, and he was a pleasure to work with; although at that time he was still a bit of a drug addict, and there were times he would come down on the set and his nose would be all red, and he wouldn't let the make-up girl anywhere near him and I'd say, 'Tony, look in the mirror! Look at your nose. She's gotta do something with it, especially since we're in colour – you're gonna look like Rudolph!' He finally did. *Club Life* made a lot of money, very little of which I saw until I stole the negative from the lab (CFI), hid it in the cellar of a friend and wouldn't give it to them until they paid me, which they did. They came over to the US *en masse* – some idiots whose names I won't even mention – and tried to have me arrested. They finally coughed up some serious money and then I gave them back their negative; which I shouldn't have done, since they still owed me six figures. My lady partner stole the negative out of the editing room when we were halfway through editing it, because the distributor said I was taking too long.

In 1988, a female friend of Vane's introduced him to a representative of the Sony Corporation. Vane showed them the script he wanted to shoot next, a horror-comedy he'd started working on in 1984, when it was called *Vampira* (or *Vampirelle*, presumably in anticipation of legal action from the real 'Vampira'). By 1988, Vane had changed the title to *Midnight for Morticia*: he received the green light, and Sony agreed to finance the film for around a million dollars. Further hesitancy over rights issues resulted in the film eventually reaching screens as, simply, *Midnight* (not to be confused with the John Russo horror film of the same name).

'Midnight' (Lynn Redgrave) is a manic, unstable but hugely popular TV horror hostess, struggling to keep control of her brand identity and fighting off her one-time manager and lover, now her arch-nemesis, Mr. B (Tony Curtis), who wants to buy the copyright to the 'Midnight' character and doesn't care how low he stoops to get it. Meanwhile, Midnight (real name Vera Kunk), well into middle-age, falls in love with a leather-jacketed young stud called Mickey Modine (Steve Parrish), an aspiring actor and 'Midnight' fan, who turns up late one night outside the gates of her Beverly Hills mansion and talks his way into her Spandex leggings. Watching over the various indulgences, rows and indiscretions are Midnight's housekeeper Heidi (Rita Gam) and butler Siegfried (Gustav Vintas). As Midnight comes unglued and paranoia bites, her relationship with Mickey is subject to pressure from Mr. B, who arranges for the young stud to score a leading role in a new movie and then pays the female co-star, Angel (Karen Witter), to seduce him. Mickey, not the monogamous sort, screws Angel in Midnight's bed. When Midnight returns unexpectedly, she throws them out. One evening, before a big Hollywood party at Midnight's place, Angel is murdered in the swimming pool by an unseen assailant. Next to die is Mr. B, hanged by the neck. Has the vampish star finally gone over to the dark side?

Midnight
© 1988. Midnight for Morticia Inc.
A film by Norman Thaddeus Vane in association with Gomillion Studios.
writer/director: Norman Thaddeus Vane. producer: Gloria Morrison. producer: Norman Thaddeus Vane. executive producers: John O'Donnell, Jeff Ringler, Ron Gell and Gloria Morrison in association with Gomillion Studios. director of photography: David Golia. editor: David Bartholomew. music: Misha Segal. casting by Barbara Remsen and Associates. line producer: Chaim Sprei. associate producer: John Kelly. stunt co-ordinator: Ric New. production manager: Devorah Hardberger. 1st assistant director: Patrick Wright. 2nd assistant director: Janice Doskey. additional 2nd assistant director: Steve Thomas. script supervisor: Jan Luce. art director and FX: Mark Simon. art department: Lex Crow. prop master: Doug Abrahamson. set dresser: Chris McCann. 1st assistant camera: Rick Osborne. 2nd assistant camera: Jeremy Briggs. underwater photography: Ron Vidor. assistant underwater photography: Lance Fisher. production stills: Donna Jensen. additional still photographer: Barry Seybert. key grip: Randy Ratliff. best boy grip: Dante Cardone. grip: Bill Flick. gaffer: Steve Gero. best boy electric: Alan Frazier. electrician: Steve Price. electric: Donna Lederer. key make-up/hair: Jill Rockow. makeup/hair assistant: Elena M. Breckenridge. special fantasy makeup: Elena M. Breckenridge. wardrobe: Verkina Flower, Lauren Roman, Perri Sorel. sound mixer: Marty Kasparian. boom: Hugh Milstein. location manager: Fred Tate. transportation captain: Fred Tate. production accountant: Maxwell Meltzer. production secretary: Renee Russelle. assistant to producer: Chris Hansen. set utility: Barry Seybert. production assistants: Jonathan Brooks, Frankie Lambert, Wade Alberty, Clark Lewis, Scott Jensen, Matthew Marden, Kelby Bryant, Linda Theroux. craft service: Frederique Lassovani. 1st caterer: Lori's Kitchen. 2nd caterer: Delite Catering. dialogue director: Russell Bekins. assistant casting: Steve Fuji. extra casting: John Kelly. snake wrangler: Natalie Cole. post production supervisor: David Bartholomew. 1st assistant editor: Allen Cappuccilli. 2nd assistant editor: Michael Westmore. post production assistant: Mary Ellen Blair. music production assistant: Randy Tobin. rerecording mixers: T.A. Moore, Jr. CAS, Mark Ettel, Jeff Gomillion. recordist: Tim Gomillion. additional sound recording: Susan Chong Audio. sound F.X. editors: Dennis Diltz, Don Lee Jorgenson, Leland Thomas. ADR editors: Leland Thomas, Stephen Isaacs. music editor: Frank McKelvey. assistant F.X. editor: Charles McClelland. looping by "Walker Talkeez" Raymond Cruz, Lisa Altamirano, Melissa Scott, Annette Hammes, Dale Swann, Mark Murphy. foley artists: Duane Hensel, Ginny Grady. voice artists: Elaine Thomas, Kim Fowler-Esser. post production by Gomillion Studios. additional post production: Candlewick. titles by Mercer Titles and Optical Effects Ltd. title design: Tony Ip, Huck Penzell. opticals by Hollywood Optical Systems. negative cutter: West Coast Editorial. film processing: United Color Lab; Filmservice Laboratory, Inc. sound transfer provided by Film Completion Service. film to tape transfers: Howard A. Anderson Co. video consultant: Steve Austin. stock footage provided by The Stock House. Panaflex lenses provided by Panavision. recorded in Ultra-Stereo. cameras provided by General Camera West. the producers would like to thank the following: Sony Corporation; Status on Sunset; Ciro's Restaurant; New York Seltzer; General Motors - Buick Division; Life Fitness; Sundance Sparklers; Lifecycles; Gustav Vintas (Siegfried). Wolfman Jack (himself). Gloria Morrison (girl reporter). Robert Spectra Systems; Head Tennis Equipment; New Balance; Aaron Biston; Revo Glasses; Adidas; Adajian Fine Oriental Rugs; Hollywood Reporter; Brown Foreman Liquor; Gucci; San Pellegrino Water; Levi's Jeans; Frenry Company; Land Pirate Party Supplies; George Dichels Whiskey; Leaf Candies; Ocean Spray; Graveline Tours; United Product Placement; Creative Film Promotions; Krown Entertainment; Cine Video; Carl Mirano; Arai Helmets - Sammy Tanner Productions. [songs] "Midnight" words and music by Harriet Schock and Misha Segal, performed by Marinna Ricci; "Too in Love" words and music by Harriet Schock and Misha Segal, performed by Pazzi Brooks; "Me and You" words and music by Harriet Schock and Misha Segal, performed by Cyndie Fee and Kop Lennon; "Love Song" (instrumental) music by Misha Segal, performed by Misha Segal; "Savage Streets" written and produced by Jay Lexy and Terry Shaffick; "Heart" written and produced by Maria Cain and Warren Hamaan, performed by Maria Cain; "Young Lover" words and music by Gloira Morrison and Bob Cressberg, performed by Adrianna Miller; "This Is the Night" words and music by Kelly Grosscutt, Terry Pardon and Mik Kamisnki, performed by Orxestra; "Beyond the Dream" words and music by Kelly Grosscutt, Terry Pardon and Mik Kamisnki, performed by Orxestra.
Cast: Lynn Redgrave (Midnight). Tony Curtis (Mr. B). Steve Parrish (Mickey Modine). Karen Witter (Missy Angel). Frank Gorshin (Ron Saphire). Robert Miano (Arnold). Rita Gam (Heidi). Gustav Vintas (Siegfried). Wolfman Jack (himself). Gloria Morrison (girl reporter). Robert Axelrod (Ozzie). Barry Diamond (Wally). Nathan Le Grand (Hank). Virginia Cole (TV reporter). Steven Arnold (doctor). Ron Max (detective). Tom 'Tiny' Lister, Jr. (security guard). Kathleen Kinmont (Party). Suzan Hughes (Suzette). Hank Woessner (Oscar). Renee Russelle (maid). Paul Scallan (restaurant customer). Robin Diamond (clown). Maryanna Phillips (standin for Miss Redgrave). Bud Graves, Lincoln Simons, Ray Saniger, Mary Peters, Eric Megisow, Paul Moddy (stunts).

Midnight is a genuinely oddball production, set in a world of low culture and high artifice. It's pitched at a hysterical level, with something that feels strangely real curled up inside the clichés: or is that itself a cliché? There's a reverberant, disorientating quality to the film that conveys the giddy paranoia of life in la-la land; a story of actors hoist by their own petard, unstable flakes paid fortunes to fake it up, trying to work out what's real in the land of make-believe. Lynn Redgrave's performance is so soaringly OTT that you just *have* to pay attention, if only because the moment she walks onscreen you feel you may be about to see the acting equivalent of a gruesome train-wreck. There's the weird, acid tang of something like real-life lunacy to her performance. She plays Midnight as a bossy Barbra Streisand-ish diva, a Gloria Swanson-style egomaniac, a calculating Bette Davis gargoyle, and an Elvira-esque toilet-mouth, all rolled together. What gives this grotesque a much-needed extra dimension is her underlying sadness and vulnerability. Midnight is getting too old for her own shtick; but it's all she knows. Without it she's 'Vera Kunk', an ageing ham actress too identified with one role to get any more. Vane writes the love affair between Midnight and Mickey with enough subtlety to keep us guessing, along with Midnight, as to whether there's any real emotion behind Mickey's physical charms. Such assignations are of course well known in Hollywood: the older actress and the young, up-and-coming hunk looking for a way into the business. *Midnight* suggests that, in Hollywood, these real life melodramas are mired in their screen echoes. In a strange way, I was reminded of the

below:
Tony Curtis in a scene from **Club Life**.

above:
Lynn Redgrave in full plumage as 'Midnight' in the film of the same name.

Says Vane: "*Midnight* was based on Vampira and Elvira. We parodied both of them. Originally Karen Black was to have played the woman, with George Segal in the Tony Curtis part. Karen Black, who is crazier than a loon, would call me up in the middle of the night and say, 'I want to do this part but I want her to have an accent.' And I said, 'Why? she's an American girl, there's no accent.' She says, 'The original woman, Vampira, she had an accent.' I say, 'Yeah, but she was from Germany or Hungary.[4] Karen, there's no accent. She's from Brooklyn.' So she quit." Vane next approached Lynn Redgrave, who said yes; but there were further complications: "George Segal said, 'If you use Lynn Redgrave I'm quitting. I'm not going to act with her.' It turned out that Lynn's agent, who fired her, also handled Segal, and he seemed very mad at Lynn. He told George, 'You're not going to work with her.' Lynn had a bad reputation at that time because she breast-fed her baby on set and caused a huge scandal, she was dropped by her agency… she was doing it right on the set in front of about thirty or forty people, and it was a big story in the press. She was without an agent when I hired her.[5] After Karen and George quit, I had a problem: Tony Curtis wanted $100,000, George Segal only wanted $50,000. In order to pay Tony I had to pay that out of my salary so the movie could continue!"

Set in the lush, rarefied environs of the Hollywood glamour-set, *Midnight* looks expensive and, if you share the tastes of the Hollywood movers and shakers of the late eighties, it exudes a class beyond its budget. Vane bought plenty of bang for his buck by negotiating to film in an enormous Beverly Hills mansion: "It was owned by a gay German Baron," he explains. "We shot there for about three weeks, for about ten or fifteen thousand dollars a week. We had a terrible time with the neighbours because of the generators at night. The police were called, we were threatened with fines, we had to stop shooting at two in the morning. We were on a small street way up in the hills, the very top, a beautiful mansion. Stevie Nicks rented it after me for quite a while, at twenty five grand a month. She always made big money. I was doing really well at that time, I had a really big home up there, in what they call Birdland. I lived on Warbler Way for about seven or eight years. Stevie Nicks lived right down the street from me."

Midnight's plot bears similarities to the real-life circumstances of its star, in a way that suggests Vane was again blurring art and life as he had in his experimental film *Fledglings*. Midnight is embroiled in a bitter struggle with her ex-husband, Mr. B, who had also been her manager, over the copyright to her screen persona. Says Vane, "Lynn Redgrave was married to this guy John Clark, there was a very nasty divorce. He was unfaithful to her with the maid who was also the secretary – he had a child with her. Lynn was so furious she kicked him out of her life, cut him off from all of her money – he had been her manager – penniless, the last I heard."

Vane feels that he got top dollar from Redgrave: "Lynn is terrific, in fact it is really her best performance ever on film. Many people have said this, but you judge for yourself. Lynn and I are not very friendly, because the shooting was difficult. We had a lot of fights. There was a scene in the cellar where the body was hidden and I wanted to cut it down to about seven or eight lines, there were about twenty-five lines, she said if you cut that I'm not gonna do it, she wouldn't come out of her trailer. So I knocked on the door and said "Look, Lynn, come out, we'll do it your way. But you have to understand that when I get in the editing room I

films of Andrzej Zulawski (*La femme publique* and *La fidélité*), whose work is often concerned with the porousness of life and art, and the difficulty of locating truth. Vane is a lot less cerebral than Zulawski, but even/especially in its trashy moments *Midnight* has art to it: certainly more so than *Club Life*. The reason *Midnight* will probably remain a curate's egg rather than a cult favourite is that Vane leaves it too long before adding a genre dimension to his tears-behind-the-glitter tale. Two-thirds of the way in, murders happen, and we're somewhat brusquely deposited in the horror genre. The model is probably *What Ever Happened to Baby Jane?*, in which Robert Aldrich took his time moving from melodrama to horror. *Midnight* lacks the inexorable grip of that masterpiece, but still Vane achieves something different and commendable. The first time I saw *Midnight* I thought I didn't like it at all… but it kept coming back to me. I couldn't *quite* say I hated it, and by second viewing I liked it. On reflection, it conveys a true psychological shudder, thanks to the hall-of-mirrors story and Redgrave's unsettlingly weird performance, and may actually be Vane's best film.

can cut it all out, so I'm just trying to save a lot of film now. It's just too talky, we don't need all those words. I wrote them, now I wanna take them out! But if you wanna say 'em, you say 'em, and if they're terrific and I'm wrong, they'll be in." And that finally mollified her. She was very funny at times… In the restaurant scene I remember we were very slow in getting started and she yelled, 'If we do this in two takes, I'm gonna fuck Norman Thaddeus Vane!' And I said, 'I'm gonna hold you to it, too!'"

There were conflicts too with Tony Curtis, although the two men got on well. Vane found Curtis's propensity for ad-libbing easy to deal with, perhaps as a result of his own improvisational experiments on *Fledglings*. "Tony Curtis is a great actor who requires very little direction," Vane enthuses, "He likes to improv, he'll go all over the place. I said to him, 'I don't mind if you go off and improvise, but you got to come back to the cue line 'cause if you don't the others don't know when to come in.'" One scene called for the veteran Hollywood legend, then in his late sixties, to be hoisted into the air by a noose round his neck: in reality of course, with a harness, to stage the illusion of a hanging. Says Vane: When we hung him it was on a Saturday night, we were in Raleigh Studios, on Melrose here in Hollywood. We had a big soundstage for the day, but we had parking problems, make-up problems, people were fucking up; by the time we were ready to hang him it was after midnight. So he pulled me aside before the shot and said, 'Listen, I hate to tell you this but we're in Sunday, so it's double time, and I'm getting twenty thousand a day, so if you do this shot now, you owe me forty thousand.' So I took him for a walk and said, 'Tony, don't do this to me. There's no way I can pay you forty thousand. We're over budget now, I've lost pretty much all my director's salary, there's a penalty with the completion bond people so if we go over budget it comes out of my salary. The only money I'm even getting off this movie is as the writer and part of being the producer. If you do this to me they'll take my writer's salary too!' So he said, 'Well I don't know, I'm just sticking to the rules and it's now Sunday.' So I said, 'Tony, don't do this – I'll spread it all over town and you'll have a real problem working again if you do this. It's a small town. Don't do it please, I beg you.' And he didn't."

Vane's difficulties with Redgrave continued into post-production. He recalls, "Lynn did not show up for the dubbing. I had to dub a full day, five or six hours, it's quite expensive, usually about five hundred dollars an hour. We were all set to go and there was a miscommunication and she didn't show, so I got another girl who could do an English accent and she did Lynn's voice quite well, so it kinda worked out okay. The completion bond company made me sue Lynn for two or three thousand dollars, the cost of the dubbing. We won the first time, but she – to my amazement – won the appeal. She kept telling the judge about her long and distinguished theatrical family, her sister, her father Michael, and so on, and he was so impressed that he reversed the original ruling. The fact was she just didn't show up for the dubbing and we had notified her many times and a lot of money went down the drain."

Vane completed his preferred cut of the film, but it did not go down well with the Sony executives. For its eventual video release, the film was cut down by nearly ten minutes. Vane explains, "They decimated Lynn's scenes, cutting out most of the best ones. Gloria Morrison, the executive producer, said the reason she did this was because she wanted to get another deal with Sony and would do anything to get it, including destroying the movie, which she did. To

above:
Missy Angel (Karen Witter), who seduces
Mickey Modine away from **Midnight**.

top left:
US admat for **Midnight**.

this day she doesn't understand the damage she did sending the negative back to New York to the distributors to cut up like a herring. The editor and I were broken-hearted. The distributor was a foreign sales guy in charge of Sony, a total idiot. He insisted, in order to sell the film to foreign markets, on cutting out four or five of Lynn's best scenes, her emotional scenes, the love story."

Midnight did at least receive a limited theatrical engagement. "I showed it at The Royal, a very nice prestigious theatre here," says Vane. "We showed it there at midnight, and that was the best I could get out of it, theatrically." There were even a few positive notices, such as this from the *Los Angeles Times*: "The film is fascinating for going over the top so totally, so deliriously in every way possible."

Taxi Dancers and After…

"Pills are bitter, rope can give, jumping is scary: fuck it, I'll live." – Sparkle, *Taxi Dancers*

Dorothy Parker's words, updated for the early nineties, are as brilliantly cynical as ever, but Dorothy never had to sit through *Taxi Dancers*. By a long way the worst film in Vane's career, this is the sort of movie Joe Eszterhas must have been watching on late-night cable when he wrote *Showgirls*; but if only *Taxi Dancers* had one-hundredth of that film's energy. Waterlogged in softcore muzak, inertial to the point of coma, it hovers around the idea of sexy lapdancers without ever getting close to the action, like a cheapskate punter with nothing but five dollars in his pocket and a will to waste time. Beneath the sexy trappings is a dour warning that this is prostitution and thus 'a bad thing' for a gal to get into – which may or may not be true, but is hardly enough dramatic meat to hang your hat on. A host of averagely pretty chicks strike up relationships with a handful of averagely handsome guys, while being menaced by two of the cinema's least convincing hoods (and boy, is *that* crown contested…) Meanwhile, the more conventional clientele for such dives – the ugly rich – are conspicuous by their absence. Seemingly built around the availability of a genuine L.A. nightclub, *Taxi Dancers* has nothing to offer visually except the tired glitz of an off-duty bar. Only Robert Miano as the bar owner suggests he might be capable of delivering something better; as for the rest, supporting roles in *Red Shoe Diaries* would seem about

below:
Midnight makes a personal appearance to
her adoring fans.

above:
Promo sheet for **Taxi Dancers**, Norman Vane's last film to date.

top:
Three of the 'Taxi Dancers' – Billie (Brittany McCrena), Candy (Michele Hess), and Star (Tina Fite).

the limit. It's all a long way from the experimental drive of Vane's early work, and lacks either the exploitation verve of *The Black Room* or the idiosyncratic genre awareness of *The Horror Star* and *Midnight*.

Unfortunately, so far it has proved to be the last Norman Thaddeus Vane movie to reach our screens. Not that the director, now in his seventies, has given up trying: "At the moment, I'm working on a story called *The Magical Ponies*, which is in the Harry Potter genre. It was a near miss at Dreamworks. They had lunch and meetings on it and passed, probably because I'm with a small agency now and not with William Morris, as I was for twelve to fifteen years. When my agent there, Bill Hart, got fired they dropped me too. My best shot at a production at this point is a political thriller called *Cuba Libre* which is with a lady producer in Florida who has a lot of contacts. I will be the writer on this one and also one of the producers, but will not be directing, although I should. Then there's *The Ram*, with Tapestry Films currently. I wrote it as a book, which is awaiting publication. A real horror film: I'm hoping to interest Lynn Redgrave. It's about a cult in Hollywood. A young girl who was a former member of the cult has an affair with a New York writer who moves out to L.A. She goes back to the cult, is murdered, and comes back as a spirit and kills all the members of the cult."

Stop Press: As of spring 2007, Vane is due to start shooting a horror comedy called *You're So Dead*, starring teen heartthrob Nick Carter of The Backstreet Boys! The story concerns a cemetery where the dead are able to take over the bodies of unwary visitors. Maybe there is yet another chapter to be added to Norman Thaddeus Vane's horror legacy?

Footnotes

1 Rachman, a Polish Jew who fled the Nazis and came to Britain during the war, became notorious for a scam in which he would buy dilapidated properties where sitting tenants paid fixed rents, then use intimidation tactics, such as moving deliberately rowdy neighbours into adjacent rooms, to drive them out: after which, thanks to Conservative housing policy in the late fifties, he was free to increase rents as high as he liked. He would cram West Indian immigrants into the properties and charge them extortionate amounts for the privilege: and since black people at the time faced frequent racism from property-owners, they were stuck with him. Rachman was Vane's landlord at La Discothèque, and it was only when Rachman ran into the Krays in 1960 that he met his match. In an amusing twist, the Krays extorted from the extortionist, setting their heavies on Rachman's thugs. As an emollient, Rachman 'sold' the club Esmeralda's Barn to The Krays, although he didn't actually own it and simply steamrollered Stefan de Faye, the actual owner at the time, into selling up. Rachman died in 1962 of a heart attack, the timing of which led many to suspect that he had faked his own death and absconded.

2 Reported to the *London Evening News* at the time as £5,000.

3 The whole thing gained an extra dimension when 'transgressive' fetishism went mainstream in the 1990s, leading to a hideous brand of all-snarl-and-no-spunk 'eroticism' that had more to do with looking 'freaky' in nightclubs than anything approaching the bedroom.

4 Vampira was born in Finland.

5 How twisted is it that while movie after movie wants the leading leady to go topless or nude, as soon as she pulls out her breast to feed a baby the deal is off!

NORMAN THADDEUS VANE: FILMOGRAPHY AS DIRECTOR

1960 *Conscience Bay* (also writer / producer)
1965 *Fledglings* aka *The Fledglings* (also writer / producer)
1981 *The Black Room* aka *Vampires of the Black Room* (writer / co-dir with Elly Kenner)
1981 *The Horror Star* aka *Frightmare* aka *Body Snatchers* aka *The Sacrilege* (also writer)
1985 *Club Life* aka *King of the City* aka *The Bouncer* (also writer / producer)
1989 *Midnight* aka *Midnight for Morticia* aka *Vampira* aka *Vampirelle* (also writer)
1993 *Taxi Dancers* (also writer / producer)

OTHER FILM CREDITS:
1968 *Mrs. Brown You've Got a Lovely Daughter* (writer)
1969 *Twinky* aka *Lola* (writer)
1972 *Piazza pulita* aka *1931: Once Upon a Time in New York* aka *Pete, Pearl and the Pole* (writer)
1976 *Shadow of the Hawk* aka *Journey Into a Nightmare* (script title) (writer)
1979 *Dracula Sucks* (2nd Unit director) dir: Philip Marshak

FOR TELEVISION:
1957 *Kraft Television Theatre*: 'Collision' (writer)
1968? 'Collision' remake for ATV (British)
1974 *The Evil Touch* (Australian TV series): writer of episode *'They'* aka *'They, Them & the Others' (transmitted 2 June, 1974)*

FOR THE STAGE:
1956 *The Penguin* (Off Broadway)
1957 *The Man Who Played God* (UK)
1959 *The Deserters* (UK)
1965 *The Expatriate* (UK) - US production in 1974/75 w/ Ray Sharkey
196? *Parables of Our Time* (a series of one-act playlets for Penthouse magazine)
1974 *The Alligators Are Coming* (US)
1975 *Kinky* (US) stage version of *Twinky*

NOVELS:
1971 *Lola* (movie tie-in novelisation from his script for *Twinky*)
1974 *The Exorcism of Angela Gray* (horror)
1975 *The Caves* (children's western co-written with Randy Rude)

PHOTOGRAPHY BOOKS:
1966 *Six Nymphets* (editor: photography by David Larcher and Philip O. Stearns)

MISCELLANEOUS:
1975 *'Ginny & Snow'* - feature in July 1975 issue of *Penthouse*

chapter 21

Raising The Child

Robert Voskanian & Robert Dadashian

The Child (1976)

A young teacher, Alicianne Del Mar (Laurel Barnett), is hired as governess for Rosalie Nordon (Rosalie Cole), a little girl who lives with her father Joshua (Frank Janson) and older brother Len (Richard Hanners) in a remote house in the woods. There's something a little odd about the Nordons: Rosalie's mother has died recently in mysterious circumstances; Joshua Nordon is off his rocker; and strange little Rosalie herself is in contact with zombie-like creatures who live in the cemetery. As kind-hearted Alicianne tries to reach out to the child, Rosalie demonstrates psychic powers, summoning 'friends' from the graveyard to do her bidding. First to suffer Rosalie's wrath is nosy neighbour Mrs. Whitfield (Ruth Ballan), followed by a thieving gardener (Slosson Bing Jong). Finally, Rosalie turns her attentions on Alicianne, who must flee for her life as the zombies attack…

If, like me, you're a sucker for off-the-wall horror movies, *The Child* is a thing of beauty. It has a beguilingly deranged amateur feel, unleashing a cache of scary cadavers in the last twenty minutes and packing the rest of the running time with strange music, wild camera angles and warped acting. It has that unpredictable quality you find in the best seventies exploitation, where weird digressions and *non sequiturs* lurk at every turn. For instance, Mrs. Whitfield, the old lady who lives near the Nordons and who by rights should be a peripheral figure, exceeds the mundanity of her role thanks to Ruth Ballan's eccentric performance. Some might call her terrible, but for me her stilted line readings help to loosen the viewer's grip on reality, so that the camera, tilting and weaving like a sick sailor, can send you sliding into oceanic disorientation. As you fall, you'll perhaps hear music that sounds likes Liberace playing for Bela Lugosi's stage show, accompanied by the wounded shrieks of a synthesizer – if so don't worry, it'll pass; just relax and enjoy it…

The score by Rob Wallace and synth rocker Michael Quatro nurtures *The Child*'s strange aura from beginning to end. Wallace's lush, overly-dramatic piano theme (like a cross between *Love Story* and the music for Mario Bava's *The Whip and the Body*) sounds freakish next to Quatro's ancient synthesizer with its primitive swoops and snorts. The effect is beyond bizarre: a bodice-ripping melodrama being invaded by creeping psychosis. When the smoke machine kicks in and the camera goes Dutch, so too the music cuts loose into free-form freak-out, not unlike the more extreme Morricone recordings: the combined effect is a heady brew of experiment and *cliché*, noise and *nous*, amateur and *avant-garde*. The acting further contributes to *The Child*'s unstable energy: the 'bad' actors are not simply wooden or inexpressive, they're if anything *too* expressive, too broad and emphatic. The instability of the performances is heightened by extensive use of post-synch dubbing, adding an extra layer of dislocation.

We're carried along like this for nearly forty minutes without really understanding what *The Child* is about. It's just a fever dream and refuses to become a normal movie. You feel immersed, like poor Alicianne staggering through the foggy woods at the start of the film, but to what end and in what dramatic current is unclear. Plot and characterisation are minimal at best; Alicianne has 'problems' in her past (*"The death of parents when a child is very young… it leaves you feeling so alone."*) but we don't hear much about them. She's troubled enough to sympathise with creepy, unfriendly Rosalie, and that's all we need to know: it explains why she doesn't just bolt for the next train out of town. Much of the back-story remains abstract. Rosalie's mother was robbed and killed, Len explains; possibly by tramps. Rosalie says that her mother was fascinated by the powers of the mind, suggesting a flair for the paranormal passed from mother to daughter. These comments are almost thrown away, and the film is all the better for it. Writers often tell the viewer too much, mistaking this for realism. Alicianne blunders into the Nordons' crazy lives and then departs at the end of the movie really none the wiser, just a great deal more frightened. Disorientation, not storytelling, is the key to the film's pleasures. We're thrown the curveball of telepathic empathy between a child and the denizens of the local graveyard, and we're inclined to *accept* this insane idea: not because it's coherently elaborated, but because we've been lost in the fog for so long we're ready to believe anything! This brand of straight-faced narrative absurdity is something I particularly like, maddening though it may be to students of the dramatic arts. *The Child*'s disconcerting oneiric shiver is intimately bound up in its lack of sense.

Admittedly, there's not a lot going on at a thematic level; at least nothing I can put my finger on. I've earnestly trawled the subtext and still can't find a

below:
Rosalie (Rosalie Cole) glowers at the new arrival, in **The Child**, Robert Voskanian's delirious 'bad seed' horror story.

The Child
aka **Children of the Night** (1973 shooting title)
aka **Child of the Living Dead**
(1976 shooting title)
aka **Zombie Child**
(British and German video title)
aka **Kill and Go Hide**
© 1976. Panorama Films.
Boxoffice International Pictures, Inc. – a Harry Novak presentation. A film by Robert Dadashian/Robert Voskanian. A Panorama Films presentation.
director: Robert Voskanian. producer: Robert Dadashian. executive producer: Harry H. Novak. writer: Ralph Lucas. director of photography: Mori Alavi. music: Rob Wallace. film editors: Robert Voskanian & Robert Dadashian. production manager & assistant director: Smith Johnson. assistant to producer: Julie Connors. art director: Mori Alavi. lighting: Wendell Hudiburg. camera operator: Katsuhiko Ogawa. assistant cameraman: Steve Baiza. sound man: John McDonald. Polymoog synthesizer performed & programmed by Michael Quatro. creatures & special make-up effects: Jay Owens. boom man: Robert Rosen. special audio effects: Andy Sells. assistant make-up: Francine Cornfield. wardrobe: Jane. script supervisor: Rod Medigovich. dialogue coach: Ralph Lucas. assistant editor: Larry Max. sound effects: Bungalow A. musical production supervisor: Bob Platt. music editor: Muckandmire Music Company. still photography: Jeff Widen. grips: Henry Black & Shaw Lance. dubbing: Audio Services. opticals: Modern Film Effects. filming from 1 October 1973 on location in Boyle Heights (Los Angeles) and again from 5 October 1976 in Los Angeles.
Cast: Laurel Barnett (Alicianne). Rosalie Cole (Rosalie Nordon). Frank Janson (Joshua Nordon, Rosalie's father). Richard Hanners (Len Nordon, Rosalie's brother). Ruth Ballan (Mrs Whitfield). Slosson Bing Jong (gardener). Rod Medigovich (priest). Wendell Hudiburg (pall bearer). Chris Tieken (Jefferson). Ralph Lucas & Rod Medigovich (creatures). Jim Dickson, Chick Cavanaugh & Anoosh Avan (additional creatures).

below:
Modestly titled 1975 album by **The Child**'s synth maestro Michael Quatro!

sideways comment on Vietnam, the Kennedy assassination, Nixon's impeachment, or the fuel crisis. So much for horror as social commentary… It's possible that the name Rosalie Nordon was intended by writer Ralph Lucas as an allusion to the occultist and painter Rosaline Norton, but the significance is minimal. The script breeds *Night of the Living Dead* with the possessed child of *The Exorcist* (although it pre-dates *Carrie* and *The Omen*) and operates almost entirely as a horror amalgam; and yet for me there's a fascination beyond the sum of the parts. The movie makes a virtue of its cheapness and its variable acting, while adding truly bizarre and imaginative images to the mix, like the scene in which Alicianne dreams she's dancing in the graveyard with a scarecrow. We're not even sure quite where we are in time. The old cars driven by Alicianne and Mrs. Whitfield suggest the 1940s or '50s, and Alicianne's occupation reminds us of Henry James's celebrated 1897 novella *The Turn of the Screw*. Unlike the neurotic narrator of James's tale, however, Laurel Barnett's Alicianne is a gentle innocent (in fact she's rather more like Rosie Holotik's unfortunate 'Nurse Beale' in S.F. Brownrigg's gore masterpiece *Don't Look in the Basement*). Her lack of worldliness or cynicism makes her more child-like than 'the child' herself. Rosalie, on the other hand, has a slyness and sense of mockery beyond her age; like *The Turn of the Screw*, *The Child* taps into paranoid fears about the secret malice of children. Fortunately, Alicianne finds an ally and a witness to the horrors. Not for her the Jamesian burden of proving that her young charge has been corrupted – Rosalie's brother *sees* the monsters attack, and accompanies the terrorized teacher in her flight from the undead. The plotless miasma lifts at last, and the story suddenly jumps into fourth gear, adopting a chase and escape format. (A gentleman's word of warning: if you prefer proactive females, the sort who are unfazed by blood, horror and violence, I'm afraid that you will have to look elsewhere for your Amazonian jollies – Alicianne proves to be an ankle-twisting hysteric in the grand old tradition – in fact Barnett's frantic screams suggest that Voskanian was looking to Marilyn Burns and *The Texas Chain Saw Massacre* for inspiration.)

The Child climaxes in classic mode with a siege, as Alicianne and Len seek refuge from the zombies in a boarded up building. It's a blatant steal from *Night of the Living Dead*, with an added kick – the couple find their bolt-hole attacked, not just on all sides, but through the floor as well (Romero's film reserved the cellar as sanctuary). It's essential that a zombie film should come to this, with humans barricading themselves ineffectually against a relentless barrage of the living dead. Hands reaching blindly through boarded-up windows while the living huddle inside: it's an image of nightmare clarity, and although it was originated by George Romero it's well worth recycling – if you going to steal, steal from the best. *The Child* may not stand as tall as Romero's formidable *Night* or *Dawn*, but I can think of few better examples of why the independent US horror scene is worth investigating. Yes, *The Child* is illogical, it trails loose ends like spaghetti, it's not 'about' anything important. But by hook or unconscious crook, Robert Voskanian, Bob Dadashian and Ralph Lucas created a film of twilight lunacy, one which – for all its cheap and cheerful production values – is soaked in the borderless confusion of dreams.

Robert Voskanian & Robert Dadashian Interviewed

"I was really surprised to learn that there are still people like yourself, who remember my movie." – *Robert Voskanian.*

The otherworldly weirdness of *The Child* seems to exist outside of time, and it's difficult, at least at first, to imagine what its makers might be doing today. As it turns out, both director Robert Voskanian and producer Robert Dadashian are very comfortably ensconced in the real world.

Voskanian is currently the owner of The Stock Exchange, a nightclub in Los Angeles. The building was originally built by Italian sculptor Salvatore Cartaino Scarpitta in 1929 to house the Los Angeles Stock Exchange (it closed during the Great Depression in 1931). Voskanian bought the building in 1997, and made his mark immediately: for instance, he designed the club to be entered not through the front, but through the back doors, via an alley, a deliberate style choice inspired by several classic New York nightclubs. Inside too, he made his own mark, having designed the interior of every club he's owned. He has been active in the nightclub business since leaving college, when a friend offered him a partnership to purchase a club on the Westside of L.A., called Bootleggers. He learned the business fast, and soon expanded his domain, approaching the management of the prestigious Bonaventure Hotel in Los Angeles with a proposal to establish a nightclub there too. Recently, he has signed a long-term lease for the Million Dollar Theater, built in 1918 on L.A.'s South Broadway. He plans to book concerts and theatre productions, and turn the lobby into a cafe.

Dadashian has remained attached to the film industry, as a post-production supervisor for Family Home Entertainment (allied to Artisan Entertainment), overseeing picture and sound editing, and graphic design. Both men were happy to discuss their one and only entry into the horror film history books.

Parents

Robert Voskanian was born in Tehran in the 1950s. His mother and father were Armenian but moved to Iran shortly before he was born. "We were Christian, so we had our own school, church and our own community," he says, "but in general Persians respected us and let us do our own stuff." Voskanian's father was in the cargo trucking business, and his uncle on his mother's side was the noted Armenian artist Azik Vasken, whose intriguing semi-geometric paintings hover between abstraction and figuration. "Actually he was not a painter 'til later on in his life," Voskanian recalls. "As a kid he was a genius, in fact he was so good that the Iranian government sent him to France to learn mathematics. After he graduated he went back to Iran for a short period of time, then moved to France, where he became a professor at the Sorbonne."

After graduating from high school in Tehran, the seventeen-year-old Voskanian moved with his family to America, arriving first in New York and then heading for California. In Los Angeles county he enrolled first at Whittier College to study business, then joined Columbia

College in Hollywood, as a Film Major. It was there that he hooked up with Robert Dadashian, forging a friendship that would lead to the making of *The Child*: "I met Bob Dadashian while I was going to Columbia. We became good friends, and after we graduated we formed a small company called Panorama Films. We did a few little projects here and there, and of course Panorama Films was not making enough money so I had to get another job in order to pay my bills, as I was married then. The film school was good for its time, it was more of a 'hands-on' place. We always had small projects happening that we used to shoot on 16mm. At Panorama Film we made a couple of small training films, and also edited twenty minutes of documentary for Yamaha International, but there wasn't enough income so I had to get another job working for Bank of America."

Robert Dadashian, producer of *The Child*, was born in Germany in 1946. His family moved to the United States in 1950, settling first in Philadelphia, then moving west to Los Angeles. The young Robert was quickly drawn to the cinema by the early low-budget horror films of William Castle and Roger Corman: "What fascinated me was their ability to make films on a low budget that were surprisingly well done," he says. "I always knew that I would pursue a career in the film industry. I attended Columbia College in Hollywood in 1966. I was fortunate to be taught by experienced teachers who were actively working in the motion picture industry. Years later I returned to Columbia to teach motion picture editing." Meeting Robert Voskanian there, he discovered that the two were of the same ethnic origin (although German by birth, Dadashian is an Armenian name). "This brought us together," he explains, "but most importantly we had common goals and interests. Working with him was very comfortable, and whenever conflicts occurred they were quickly resolved."

After leaving Columbia, Dadashian worked as a film editor at Warren Miller Enterprises, producing documentaries on skiing and surfing. When he and Voskanian set up Panorama Films, they had hoped to become self-sufficient, but the training film and corporate documentary market was already jam-packed. If the two friends were to make a mark they would have to do more than scratch a living in industrials. It was time to consider building a cinematic world of their own…

Conception

Whilst hovering at the fringes of the film industry, Voskanian and Dadashian noticed a small, black-and-white horror flick that was making waves despite its low budget. As Voskanian recalls: "While we were at film school there was a movie out called *Night of the Living Dead*, which made lots of noise: everybody was talking about how some guys from somewhere in the Midwest made this movie, a big success, with very little money. After Bob and I saw the movie we told ourselves we too could make an independent low-budget movie, and we decided that a horror movie was the best choice. We put an ad in *The Hollywood Reporter* for a horror movie script, and we had lots of replies. One that got our attention was a screenplay by Ralph Lucas called 'Children of the Night'. Bob and I liked the script, the next day we called Ralph, and told him that we liked his screenplay and we wanted to make it into a movie. But we could not pay him up front - instead we offered him a percentage of the film. He agreed."

LET'S PLAY HIDE AND GO KILL. . .!

HARRY NOVAK presents
THE CHILD

starring RICHARD HANNERS · LAUREL BARNETT · FRANK JANSON and introducing ROSALIE COLE
produced by ROBERT DADASHIAN · directed by ROBERT VOSKANIAN
written by RALPH LUCAS · director of photography MORI ALAVI · music by ROB WALLACE
music performed by MICHAEL QUATRO executive producer HARRY NOVAK
a BOXOFFICE INTERNATIONAL PICTURES release [R] RESTRICTED

Robert Dadashian expands on what he and Voskanian saw in Lucas's script: "Ralph Lucas was a serious artist, a hard worker and very reliable. He always came through with the rewrites and always met deadlines. What drew me to the theme was the plot from the film *The Exorcist*. As you recall, in *The Exorcist* a little girl was possessed by the Devil. I tried to modify the same theme by having a young girl overcome by telekinesis. The little girl in our film utilised her powers to avenge her mother's death. She controls zombies through telekinesis."

With a script in hand, the next step was to look for a good cinematographer. Voskanian called Mori Alavi, a friend from film school, who agreed to shoot the movie

above: Classic poster artwork for **The Child**.

below: One of Rosalie's friends…

under the same terms as Ralph Lucas. "From there," explains Voskanian, "we put more ads in *The Hollywood Reporter* asking for a cast to act in a low-budget horror movie without pay, against part ownership of the movie. We were able to put our movie together without any upfront payment to the cast or the crew. After all this we put a budget together for raw stock, lab work, equipment rentals and so on, and we asked our family and friends to help us produce the movie. We were fortunate enough to raise money to start the production this way."

Gestation

The Child was apparently shot during 1973 and 1974 for around $30,000, at several locations in Los Angeles: Culver City, Boyle Heights and Montebello. I say 'apparently' because, unfortunately for those seeking to pin down the exact chronology of the production, both Robert Dadashian and Robert Voskanian are extremely vague about dates. The onscreen copyright date for *The Child* is 1976; however, in the book *Gods in Polyester*, lead actress Laurel Barnett speaks confidently about *The Child*, claiming that it started shooting in late 1973 and continued throughout 1974. Even when we consider that Voskanian and Dadashian began showing their finished work to potential distributors in 1976, it would still seem that *The Child* went through rather a long gestation. Voskanian is puzzled by this: "I really don't remember the dates. I am almost positive it didn't take us from '73 to '76 to finish the film but why the discrepancy I can't recall."

Luckily, Voskanian does recall the circumstances of locations and shooting: "Most of the interiors were shot in a house that was built around the early 1920s and was at that time the property of the city of Los Angeles. We talked to the housing department and they told us they were planning to demolish it and build low cost rental housing there. We asked them if they would let us shoot our movie inside the house without a fee as we did not have much of a budget - they agreed if we would provide them with liability insurance, which we did. Some of the other interiors were shot at Bob Dadashian's parents' house. For our exterior shots there was a huge oil field that was the property of Standard Oil Company. We approached them, told them that we were shooting a student film, and asked if they would be kind enough to let us use their property. They agreed and gave us permission to shoot on their oil fields. It was a great opportunity because on their property was this old house which we used as the exterior of the Nordon house. Also, there were lots of trees and bushes that we were able to use for the cemetery and other exterior shots."

Voskanian and Dadashian prepared the shoot rigorously to stay within their means. Voskanian remembers, "When we got the okay from Ralph for his screenplay, we made a production board in order to come up with a shooting schedule, and also rentals and ultimately a shooting budget. When it came to doing the shooting on a day-to-day basis, I transferred all the scenes onto four-by-six inch cards and that's how I knew which scenes I was shooting. I had a card for every scene I had to shoot."

I asked Voskanian what aspects of the filmmaking process he was most involved with during the shoot: "I was very much involved with camera angles and the general mood of the film, with both the technical and also the performing end of it, as a matter of fact all hand-held shots were shot by me with a second camera, with Mori shooting the master shots." Dadashian adds: "Mr. Alavi was from Iran and he had an avant-garde flare for composition. He was a great cinematographer and I believe his style enhanced our film."

The cast's abilities vary wildly, although much of this is to the film's advantage when it comes to establishing an off-centre mood. Voskanian admits: "Our cast was mostly amateur because no professional would work in a movie without getting paid. The one with the most experience was Frank Janson, I had fun working with him, he was easy going and followed direction fairly well. The one person I had a lot of problems with was Ruth Ballan. She was originally a stage actress and when she started acting in the movie, she was acting as if she was on the stage, exaggerating every scene. I had to slow her down, and constantly remind her that there are close-up shots in the film, or when you walk, walk natural, you don't have to project things, the camera will do it for you. Even though Rosalie Cole had never acted before, I had an easy time with her, I think she followed direction well and with some training she probably could have been a good little actress. Laurel Barnett had done some stage acting before, and from time to time I also had to remind her that she was in front of a camera, not on the stage, but overall she was not difficult to work with. Richard Hanners was a quiet person and that was reflected in his acting. Slosson Bing Jong was a classmate of ours, I don't remember where was he from. After the movie was finished I only saw Rosalie once, and Richard twice. The last time I saw Richard he told me that he was giving up acting and moving to Washington state. I also saw Laurel Barnett on television once (she had a small part on a TV show). Mori Alavi moved back to Iran. If you remember, at the end of the movie we had a lot of names listed as crew, but there was no crew - we made up those names! The crew was me, Bob Dadashian, Mori Alavi and maybe a few other people helping us, just because they were on a movie set! Ralph Lucas too, he was a nice person, he helped us a lot during the shooting, mostly keeping track of the dialog continuity. We met [special effects designer] Jay Owens through a friend, he was getting divorced and he didn't have anywhere to stay, so we let him sleep in our office temporarily. He claimed that he could do the make-up for the zombies and also the special effects. Me and Robert, not having anybody for our special effects, agreed to his proposal and it turned out that, for the budget we had, he did a fairly good job. Every zombie took about a couple of hours to do, we usually scheduled the zombie shoots at the end of our day. The movie was supposedly set in the 1950s, but we didn't have an art director or any custom design, so we gave some money to the cast and let them buy their own clothes - some even wore what they had available."

After completing the shoot, the two friends were completely out of money, as Voskanian recalls: "Bob and I started to edit, and we got all the way to a work print and a dialogue track, at which point we started to show the movie as a dual projection system, meaning at one side was the work print and at the other the dialogue track. Perhaps two or three people looked at it, and Harry Novak was the one who liked the movie - he said he would forward the money to finish the film and would distribute it too. At that time we were very happy that our movie was going to be finished and was going to play in the theatres. Not being business-minded at that time we didn't pay great attention to our contract, we were just happy that our film was going to be released. We put another ad in *The Hollywood Reporter* for a composer to do our music track and met [composer] Rob Wallace."

Dadashian remembers that: "[Wallace] had access to Michael Quatro, who did the opening theme to *Rollerball*. He was very proficient in synthesizer music. Quatro and Wallace collaborated to achieve the most fitting score." Voskanian however has mixed feelings about the result: "In the beginning I liked his music but I was not happy with the finished soundtrack. But Harry Novak said he thought the music was fine so I had to agree with him."

School (Hard Knocks)

Harry Novak quickly changed the title of the movie from *Children of the Night* to *The Child*, and in 1977 the movie at last hit theatres. Voskanian recalls: "The movie played in approximately 1,200 to 1,300 theatres all over the United States. I never saw it inside a theatre, I guess I didn't have the nerve to see it with the general public. I went to a few theatres and watched people going inside, but I never went in. The movie did okay, but when the monies started coming in to Boxoffice International we found out that, per our contract, we had a very small cut of that income. We never made any money, and we were only able to pay part

of the money back to our investors. If I knew what I know now, I definitely would try to make a different distribution deal than we made then; but then again, unless you have a solid project, or you have a name, they would take you for a ride, so you should consider the deal as a stepping stone." Dadashian concurs: "My experience with Harry Novak was frustrating. I feel that we never received a fair shake. Distribution was a nightmare. The producer reports that we received were from regions that were small payoffs. We never received reports from the larger regions that obviously earned more. The film played throughout the United States and Europe, to the teen market..."

The film was certainly marketed well. James Bryan, the director of *Don't Go in the Woods* and sound effects editor on *The Child*, remembers the genesis of the iconic, much-reproduced artwork for Harry Novak's release campaign: "*The Child*'s artwork was done by Rocky Schenck, who followed Bill Paxton (*Twister*) from Texas to L.A., where they both worked for Peter Jamison."[1] Bob Voskanian and Bob Dadashian connected with Rocky Schenck at Bungalow A [Bryan's post-production house] by means of my introduction."

opposite page, from top:
Scenes from **The Child**:
Mrs. Whitfield (Ruth Ballan) suffers for her nosiness;
A previous victim?;
Rosalie playing innocently with her teddy? Not likely;
A zombie struggles to cope with Michael Quatro's synth score;
Len (Richard Hanners) realises that his little sister's 'friends' are real;
Alicianne (Laurel Barnett) freaks out;
Alicanne and Len held siege in a shed;
Rosalie keeps on coming...

below:
Lobby card depicting Rosalie Nordon exuding a Manson-girl contemptuousness.

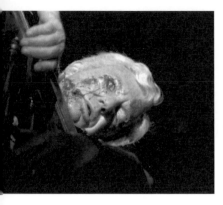

above:
Joshua Nordon (Frank Janson) is added to **The Child**'s death-toll.

right:
Atmospheric artwork for the film's well co-ordinated release by Harry Novak's Boxoffice International.

below:
Alicianne is attacked by the living dead.

So is Voskanian pleased with the movie, in retrospect? "Yes, and I will tell you why. I've read lots of comments that different people wrote about *The Child*, the majority of them knocked the film and made fun of the cast and even the director; but the majority of them, at the end of their comments, said 'I liked it' or 'I recommend you to see it'. Someone even wrote they'd like to see a remake of *The Child*. As the director of the movie, I know what went wrong: we simply did not have enough money to make a good movie." Dadashian says: "I was very pleased with the end result because it reflected all of our work. *The Child* helped form a few alliances. It helped me get a job as a post production supervisor at Family Home Entertainment, who were the first video distributors of the film."

Sadly for fans of *The Child*, the trio of Voskanian, Dadashian and Lucas never worked on another feature together. Lucas clocked a few more screen credits: he wrote a screenplay for *Planet of Dinosaurs* (1978) by James K. Shea, with stop-motion effects by Doug Beswick; adapted *Zipperface* (1992), a comic murder-thriller by Mansour Pourmand; and wrote the screen treatment for *The Boys of Cellblock Q* (1992), a gay-themed prison drama adapted by Lucas from a stage play of the same name.

Robert Dadashian worked as sound editor on several features, including: Richard Sarafian's *Street Justice* (1989); the David Duchovny back-catalogue entry *Julia Has Two Lovers* (1991); erotica specialist Philippe Blot's *Born Wild* (1995); and *The Sweeper* (1996), by the indefatigable Joseph Merhi. James Bryan also recalls that Bob Dadashian edited his sci-fi comedy *Sex Aliens* (1987). Dadashian is now a back-room boy, working post on numerous productions for Family Home Entertainment.

Robert Voskanian still harbours a desire to direct again, so we must hope and pray he gets the chance: "At the present time I'm into the nightclub business, but at the same time I'm writing a horror/suspense thriller called *The Silent Sea* - hopefully I will be able to make it into a movie sometime in the future. The film is a suspense thriller, most of which takes place underwater. It's a survival game between some recreational wreck divers, as they come face to face with a group of killer divers inside a sunken vessel sunk by the US coast guard (of course there is a lot more happening than this one line!)"

Footnotes

1 Jamison's art directing career stretches from Gus Trikonis's *The Evil* (1978) to Victor Salva's *Jeepers Creepers 2* (2003).

ROBERT VOSKANIAN: FILMOGRAPHY AS DIRECTOR

1976   *The Child* aka *Children of the Night* [script title] aka *Zombie Child* aka *Kill and Go Hide*

ROBERT DADASHIAN: FILMOGRAPHY

1976   *The Child* (producer/co-editor)
1987   *Sex Aliens* – dir: Morris Deal [James Bryan] (editor)
1989   *Street Justice* – dir: Richard C. Sarafian (sound editor)
1991   *Julia Has Two Lovers* – dir: Bashar Shbib (sound editor)
1995   *Born Wild* – dir: Philippe Blot (sound editor)
1995   *Lover's Leap* – dir: Paul Thomas (editor)
1996   *The Sweeper* – dir: Joseph Merhi (sound editor)
1999   *Out in Fifty* – dirs: Bojesse Christopher & Scott Leet (sound editor)

chapter 22

Who's the Ghostest with the Mostest?

The Films of Fredric Hobbs

Troika (1969)

"Where Fellini is deified, Kenneth Anger respected, and *Andalusian Dog* considered a classic, Hobbs will be hailed as a genius. Squarer technicians will acknowledge him as a big spender, a wild but talented modern artist, set decorator, costumer and sculptor, a disciplined film craftsman, not a bad comedy director, and possibly mad as a hatter." – *Variety, Nov 1969.*

"An apocalyptic fantasy that creates a sustained crescendo of excrutiating intensity." – *San Francisco Chronicle.*

There's little to prepare you for *Troika*, an extraordinary piece of art that comes straight out of left field. It's variously a wild and weird exercise in symbolism, a glimpse of late sixties political foment, and a visit to another world. Along the way it provides a humorous portrait of Hobbs himself, and a sardonic commentary on the processes that stand in the way of making art cinema in a country more routinely interested in popcorn entertainment.

Okay, so this introduction sounds a little grandiose. But *Troika* – particularly in its extended third movement – comes at you with banners fluttering, a phalanx of mysterious heraldry, and the pomp of alien orchestras blaring: it's no wonder you reel away at the end, straining for superlatives. So to let the mist and madness subside and the mind refine its bearings; what exactly is *Troika*?

To begin with, it's a film about creation. The first thing we see is a brightly lit canvas, blank, maybe ten feet square, occupying the entire field of vision. Into the frame comes Hobbs himself, striding with coiled yet calm purpose to the centre of the screen. Swiftly, steadily, he attacks the canvas with paint, pulling from nothingness a shape and form, a violent tableau. A female figure reclines, extending her arm from which hang faces and forms of flayed humanity. A bird (an owl?) sits triumphantly astride her extended limb, with various grisly horrors dangling below. It's partly a quotation of Goya's *'Great Deeds! Against the Dead!'* (one of his celebrated 'Disasters of War' series), but its very Hobbs. It's also a magnificent *coup de théâtre*, a fantastical painting produced in real time before our eyes. Picasso had a

reputation for similarly rapid work (and Rolf Harris of course), but with the camera rolling and film being so expensive the scene demonstrates Hobbs's absolute confidence in his ability. You can't help but be impressed by such a clear statement of intent – and it's also an inspired way of suggesting that the film should be considered 'as one' with Hobbs's fine art endeavours.

Troika ('a group of three' in Russian) then develops into three individual short films, set within a framework charting the encounters of filmmaker Fredric Hobbs (as himself) with a Hollywood producer – one 'Gordon Goodloins' (Richard Faun). After his telephone calls are ignored, Hobbs leaps from the bushes and literally rugby-tackles the wealthy Goodloins in his own driveway. Goodloins relents and grants Hobbs a conversation. The two men sit in the bath together discussing cinema's relationship to art and life, while a mariachi band, also crammed into the bathroom (and led by Carlos Santana's father, José), plays along. Goodloins suggests that Hobbs's dreams of art cinema are unrealistic when set against the tastes of the general public. *"Do you know how many movie theatres there are in this country?"* he sneers, *"Do you know how many art museums*

below:
Hobbs (*right*) with William Heick, his friend and cinematographer, at Hobbs's studio in California.

Troika
© 1969. Inca Films presents.
art / colour imagery / direction / story / dialogue:
Fredric Hobbs. editor / collaborating director:
Gordon Mueller. camera: William R. Heick,
Gordon Mueller. "Black and White People"
photographed by Richard Faun. unit manager:
E. Prentice Welles. property master: Julianne
Warner. robes: Theodora Skipitares. location
sound & electronics: Michael Riskin. music
consultant: David Johnson. sound consultant:
Richard Birnbaum. acknowledgements:
Mariachi Mexicali de Jalisco. Anchor Steam
Beer Company. Bay Area Electric Railroad
Assn. Treble Clef Society. The Glinden Estate.
John BollesGallery. print by Multichrome
Laboratories.
Cast: Nate Thurmond *(Attenuated Man).* Gloria
Rossi *(Mediterranean Woman).* Parra
O'Siochain *(Warrior).* Morgan Upton *(Rax).*
T.G. Rossi *(Boy).* Richard Faun *(Mr. Gordon
Goodloins).* Basilio O. Holowaty *(Basil).*
Sigmund Harris *(Linesman).* R. Gordon
Henderson *(Professor of Astrology).* Elmer
Moore *(Professor of Folklore).* Ronald Wheeler
(Professor of Classics). Sigmund Harris
(Professor of Economics). Kenn Davis
(Professor of Engineering). Patricia Gaunce
(Professor of Dance). John Feldman
(Professor of Ecology). Fredric Hobbs *(Chef,
Phantom, Hobbs).*

above:
Hobbs as 'The Chef' in **Troika**'s first 'panel'.

opposite page, main picture:
Rax on the move in **Troika**...

opposite, strip:
Images from the mysterious 'ice-cave'
sequence, in which Rax encounters the
Attenuated Man in a scene dense with
religious imagery.

below:
'The Soldier in White' receives unorthodox
medical treatment from The Chef.

*there are? When they stop building movie theatres and start
building art museums, then Hobbs, talk to me about art."*
The conversation turns to the interests of youth audiences:
Goodloins tells Hobbs he should modify his dreams by
engaging with contemporary reality. *"Grab the minds of the
young people, Hobbs, and you grab six figures a year"* (a
cynical point of view that would reappear in *Alabama's
Ghost*). Hobbs approaches Goodloins one last time, but he
drives off in his limousine, dismissing 'art' out of hand,
dubbing it 'garbage' and snapping, *"Stop trying to feed
garbage to popcorn eaters."* What follows is the funniest
image in Hobbs's cinema, as the incensed director chases
down the street, running like crazy and waving his fist,
yelling, *"Up yours, Mr. Goodloins!"*

These linking scenes are amusing and cleverly scripted.
They demonstrate the director's artistic self-consciousness
and give him a soapbox from which to attack Hollywood
small-mindedness, mock the high-life fakery of the
establishment, and position himself as a visionary outsider.
What saves all of this from self-aggrandizement is that
Hobbs plays 'Hobbs' without grandstanding, more like an
anxious private investigator than an artistic giant, which
grants him great likeability. And when it comes to show-not-
tell, his unique visual artistry requires no further hype…

Although the three shorts comprising *Troika* have no
onscreen names, they can loosely be referred to by the
following titles, which Hobbs uses in conversation:

Film One: The Chef
The Chef plays out like an alchemical ritual, with a mad
cook (Hobbs again), chef's hat on head, indulging some
unimaginable culinary experiment. Hobbs, virtually
unrecognisable under Aztec-styled face-paint and a bizarre
false nose like an insect's proboscis, throws various symbolically loaded items into a giant brass tank full of brown
foam (actually a brewer's vat in a brewery). It seems at first
as if the chef is enacting a kind of 'creation/deconstruction
of the self', set to a whimsical, surrealistic soundtrack not
unlike the incidental music for The Beatles' *Yellow
Submarine*, or the later episodes of *The Prisoner*. If so, it's
undertaken in a distinctly satirical vein, mocking the sanctity
of selfhood and the 'deep and meaningful' processes of
symbolic art itself (it makes you wonder what Hobbs would
do with Alfred Jarry's absurdist *Ubu* plays). A stiff, lifeless
homunculus made of clothes, its 'face' entirely swathed in
bandages (referencing, says Hobbs, the enigmatic 'Soldier in
White' in Joseph Heller's *Catch-22*), is plundered for
ingredients (three strips of Air Force decorations) and fed
with bakerlite shrapnel from smashed 78rpm records (on the
prominently displayed 'Vocation' record label). Not content
with symbols alone, the chef then dances a tango with a
heavily painted young woman before tossing her into the
vat. The rose she has held between her teeth is the last thing
to go – the chef gazes at it sentimentally, then tosses it in
anyway. A written text brandished at the camera declares
that after the Emperor Nero, the US Air Force now holds the
record for 'kitchen flambé', giving an unmistakeable whiff
of Vietnam-era critique to the otherwise hermetic
proceedings. Hobbs himself served in the Air Force, so the
scene in which he tosses Air Force decorations into the vat
can be seen as his symbolic disengagement with the military
objectives of the era. The whole thing can thus be said to
double as a metaphor for US militarism: "I don't know what
that one's really about," admits Hobbs when asked about
The Chef, "except that it's an anti-war statement." Hobbs,
who presides throughout the wide-angle weirdness, ducking

and diving like a macabre children's entertainer, ends up
inside the metal cauldron, laughing like a lunatic, making
this dense and rather disturbing piece feel like some
Chinese-box depiction of madness. Hobbs suggests another
reading (optional of course), which is that the actions of the
chef are predicated on destruction – all is consumed and
destroyed until only self-annihilation or madness remain. In
its ironic play with images of creation and negation, its use
of Air Force trimmings, and bearing in mind the self-
consciousness of the wraparound scenes, I found myself
looking for an autobiographical element (although Hobbs
told me there was no intended significance to the fact he
played the chef himself). Whatever the reading, Hobbs hits
the ground running with a genuinely bizarre and arresting
short, photographed with startling clarity and invention by
his regular DP William Heick.

Film Two: Alma Mater
The second short film could be termed an 'Expressionist
documentary', about the student demonstrations of the late
sixties. The sequence contains footage shot at a student sit-
in, taken both inside the college amid tired or downcast
students, and outside where the police amass threateningly
on horseback. Hobbs, doing his best to coax out the implicit
violence cinematically, intercuts between the verité tension
of the documentary footage and images from his own
artworks, drawings with a Goyaesque violence inspired by
the infamous Kent State riots seen on TV, as well as by the
footage Hobbs himself shot (he confirmed to me that he
drew some of the pictures before and others after the film
shoot). This documentary passage (the marvellous drawings
excepted) would fall into the 'dull but worthy' category were
it not for more of Hobbs's inventive Expressionist theatrics.
In a white walled space (defined as a schoolroom by a
handful of props), a dunce-capped teacher bangs a gong,
after which a succession of more and more absurd lessons
take place: one lecturer demonstrates a black inflatable
beach-mattress concealing a bevy of frogs and toads; and an
economics class takes place before the painted legend 'God
Bless the Gnomes of Zurich!' (the 'Gnomes of Zurich' being
British Labour prime minister Harold Wilson's term for
manipulative Swiss bankers). The surrealistic classroom,
dotted with toilet seats and *chaise-longues* instead of chairs,
is populated by students with thickly painted Caligari-esque
faces who eventually boo the dunce-capped teacher out of
class. Most impressively of all, a hillbilly singer (Elmer
Moore) performs the traditional hobo song 'Wabash
Cannonball' against a bare wall, continuing to lip-synch as
the recording grotesquely slows down – a scene that
prefigures the surrealistic performance motifs in David
Lynch's cinema. *Alma Mater* may be the slightest of the
three shorts in *Troika*, but it only looks that way in relation
to the others that flank it; and basically *nothing* could
withstand comparison to what comes next…

Film Three: The Blue People
*"Fred, if you don't like this world that we live in, why don't
you create a new one?"*
It's here, with this challenge to his creativity, that Hobbs
takes *Troika* into the stratosphere. A fantasical biped, its
mask-like face nodding within a carapace resembling some
wondrous beetle, takes a journey by old-West train. The
creature (end credits refer to it as the Bug-Man; its onscreen
name is Rax) disembarks to walk the hills, before being
attacked by a savage seen burning a chicken with a
blowtorch. Beaten with a stone axe and left for dead, the
Bug-Man staggers to a beach and collapses, twitching feebly,

whereupon a deep reddish-orange woman emerges from the sea pushing a sculpture mounted on wheels. She attempts an erotic encounter, caressing the Bug-Man and fingering his wounds, but as he lies there unable to respond she ends up pleasuring herself instead. Perhaps the encounter was not so one-sided after all; as if rejuvenated, we then see Rax enter an ice-cave, where he encounters a black Shaman called the Attenuated Man, a seven foot tall giant who speaks in drastically slowed-down Arabic. As red smoke billows through the cave and the Shaman shares his vision with Rax, another Hobbs sculpture, 'Three Thieves', protrudes from the ice-ceiling, creating an effect halfway between ossuary and church (the three figures, blue faced and dead, are clearly corpses post-crucifixion). Meanwhile, cutaways have shown a mysterious procession making its way who-knows-where through strange, alien countryside. Comprising a phalanx of 'Blue People' carrying banners and accompanied by a strange vehicle (Hobbs's 'Trojan Horse' car sculpture), they are suddenly joined by Rax. Seemingly embraced by the blue people as a saviour, Rax is escorted in regal splendour – yet a sadness envelops proceedings as we cut to scenes of a train passing through a ghost town, from whose empty wooden houses blue and purple people either stare, wave, or shake their fists. The procession arrives at a railway terminus, and amid a collection of ancient carriages and railway ephemera, Rax leaves by train. The blue people wave goodbye and the film comes full circle, with the departure as point of arrival. A final enigmatic shot merges Rax with the Three Thieves in a shadowy tableau…

As can probably be gleaned from this synopsis, the *Blue People* segment of *Troika* is a treasure-chest of visual riches and symbolic enigmas that has to be seen to be believed. The only point of comparison I can make is the work of Alejandro Jodorowsky, but Hobbs is basically out on his own here, creating a mysterious realm populated by astonishing anomalous constructions and conveyed through exceptional dreamlike imagery. Every element is unique: the landscapes are either hauntingly alien or like desolate fragments of a decayed past. Hobbs shot some scenes in an honest-to-goodness California ghost town, Collinsville, by the Sacramento Delta. One breathtaking long-shot was obtained by marching the Blue People down a country path between fields burnt black by a recent summer fire. (Ironically, the Blue People were actually played by a group of Berkeley student activists whom Hobbs had rigorously drilled to march in step!)

As if the visual imagination on offer were not enough, *Troika* boasts astonishingly effective music (composed by the director himself with his editor Gordon Mueller) which sets the tone for this new world. The two men create a ritualized musical environment not unlike LaMonte Young's Theatre of Eternal Music, a drone music that suggests all the journeys of mankind. Hobbs uses slow drumbeats and a backwards musical tone, ebbing and flowing timelessly, joined here and there by gongs and cymbals, or Japanese pipes, or strange arabesques from an early synthesizer. For nearly forty minutes this remarkable score creates an elastic, suspended moment in which the mythic, mysterious action unfolds.

Along with the vivid sound design, Hobbs unleashes his extraordinary colour sense. The final act of *Troika* is an orgy of deep, vibrant hues; cobalt blues, rich purples and glowing reds – colours applied to the faces and bodies of his cast, and of course the sculptures themselves. Hobbs has in effect created a moving painting, or a three-dimensional animated sculpture, incorporating machines, found objects, skies, fields, trains, derelict houses and human beings. The oft-stated desire to merge art and reality finds a credible praxis here. As the imaginary occupies the real, Hobbs's sculptures are set free to encounter each other in a world beyond galleries, exhibition spaces, or museums. The cast too enter a world defined by Hobbs's art, being encased in his sculptures or smothered in his paint. It's incredibly imaginative: at a time when optical solarisation effects were so popular (as a *de rigueur* indicator of psychedelia), it's refreshing to see someone take colour and apply it directly to the actors; in other words, changing the reality *before* the camera not after it. Rather like Antonioni, who had swathes of grass painted red to suit his needs in *Il deserto rosso*, Hobbs enters the real world with his colour (and with less disrespect to the environment!).

Symbolically speaking, it's the sort of odyssey tale that leaves doors wide open to interpretation. A young boy, seen from time to time staring out of a train window, may hold a key to the structure – perhaps all this is his fantasy, or a vision of his internal life? Religious themes are clearly apparent – Rax for instance seems to be accepted as a saviour of the Blue People, albeit a departing one. The Arabic statements of the Attenuated Man, chosen without knowledge of their meaning at the time, are slowed down

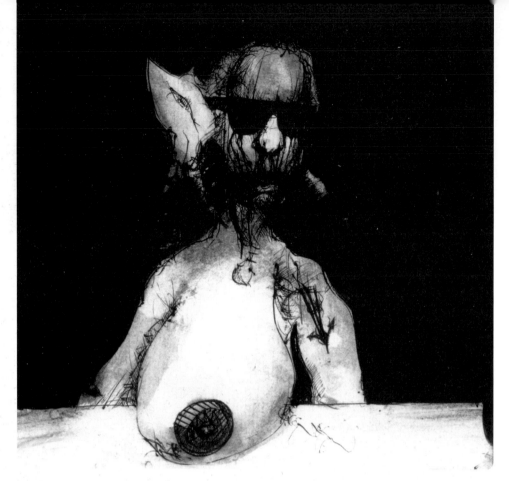

above:
'Anarchy' – one of Hobbs's stunning drawings used in the 'Alma Mater' sequence of **Troika**. Did Ralph Steadman see a Hobbs exhibition before embarking on his famous illustrations for Hunter S. Thompson's **Fear and Loathing in Las Vegas** (published in 1971)?

below:
One of Alabama's magic-show assistants about to feel the prick of something sharp during the old 'Death of a Thousand Swords' act, in **Alabama's Ghost**.

by tape manipulation to the point of obscurity, but according to Hobbs they turn out to be Koranic statements of Universal Brotherhood. The blue faces recall certain rituals of the Navajo Indians, and the Attenuated Man is clearly a Shaman, so like Jodorowsky's films, *Troika* strives towards a multi-faceted religious symbolism in which Christianity (most clearly present in the 'Three Thieves' sculpture) takes its place as a single card in a kind of multi-denominational tarot deck…

With a shot of the painting we saw at the start now completed, Hobbs leaves the studio, and *Troika* ends. The version that Frederic Hobbs has allowed me to see is still not the 'final cut', but it's already apparent to me that this is an important, original work by an artist of genuine vision. While his subsequent movies veer between astounding and frustrating, *Troika* is his masterpiece, and its eventual release on DVD should be awaited with the utmost anticipation.

Alabama's Ghost (1973)

I have to admit, some of this book was written under the influence. I don't mean the hard stuff; no acid, or heroin, or speed; just the occasional bottle of wine or two. There are advantages to this – the odd leap of inspiration, greater connectivity. And there are drawbacks: go too far and you lose clarity. Knowing where to draw the line is not always easy: and of course I edit the results the following day…

Judging by *Alabama's Ghost*, Fredric Hobbs would call my next-day rewrites chickenshit. (In fact, he confirmed to me that he never rewrites his scripts, an artistic choice that coincidentally aligns him with the Beat writer Jack Kerouac.) His stories positively delight in devil-may-care flights of fancy. This presents difficulties when interpreting his work. Should we try piecing the ideas together looking for an overall standpoint? Or 'relax and float downstream', as The Beatles recommended in 'Tomorrow Never Knows',

with Hobbs as our 24fps spirit-guide? Either way the experience is unique: so stand by, dopers, druggies, acid-heads, and trainee magicians; *Alabama's Ghost* is a 23.3-carat mindwarp…

Hobbs hits the ground running with an opening narration about good and bad Zeta Energy that, frankly, renders the upcoming proceedings as clear as mud. You feel as if the acid is coming on too fast. Onscreen, a night-time cityscape roils in superimposed smoke, curling through the air like dope fumes from some imaginary spliffhead in the front row. After a jazz number called 'Who's the Ghostest with the Mostest?' performed by The Turk Murphy Band, the story follows the fortunes of a young black man called Alabama (Christopher Brooks) who, while working as handyman for a San Francisco theatre, accidentally smashes a cellar wall with his fork-lift truck and discovers a secret passage, leading to a treasure trove of stage magic props belonging to the deceased 'Carter the Great' (E. Kerrigan Prescott). Despite warnings from Carter's ghost (yes, we're dealing with the spirit world, not Penn & Teller), Alabama decides to exploit his discovery for personal gain, embarking on a successful tour as a freaky West Coast stage magician and 'King of the Cosmos'. Along the way he makes an enemy of the magician's alleged sister, 'Granny' Carter (Ken Grantham), and meets Otto Max (Steven Kent Browne), a besuited major-domo with a Terence Stamp demeanour and an accent midway between Liverpool and the Caribbean. Max becomes Alabama's manager, declaring, *"Surrealism is where it's at,"* and he's unfazed when Alabama mentions Carter's ghost, sneering, *"If Carter ever shows up I'll book him into Miami for the squares."* Also interested in Alabama is media Svengali Jerry Gault (Ken Grantham again), whose pallid skin is a clue to his real identity...

Alabama's Ghost is unique in its relation to the horror genre, thanks to the director's background in avant-garde art and design. Drawing on his previous work in sculpture and mixed media art, Hobbs populates the movie with anomalous constructions and costumes: Alabama's car, for example, is an enormous sculpted edifice, sprouting bone-like protuberances and embellishments. The vehicle, called 'Trojan Horse', was first used in Hobbs's 1963 work *Parade Sculpture*, a concept whose origins lay in what he refers to as, "ancient religious processions and self-propelled tableaux". These 'parade pieces' (including his *Sun Chariot*, *Three Thieves* and the *Trojan Horse*) were Hobbs's imaginative way of removing art from its museum environment and bringing it to the attention of a mass audience, "in the circumstances of everyday life," as he puts it. His driveable 'art vehicles' were exhibited in a travelling show entitled *The Highway*, which crossed the USA from San Francisco to New York City in 1964, and 'Trojan Horse' can also be seen in his debut feature, *Troika*.

In terms of design, and the director's wildly unpredictable way with a story, *Alabama's Ghost* is a wonderful *sui generis* experience, amalgamating horror motifs, theatrical stylings and counterculture satire in a sort of demented bricolage. No one makes movies like Hobbs: he is probably the most unusual, idiosyncratic director in this book, and it's a shame that this, his strangest and most potent genre assemblage, is not more widely known.

However, this is not a film without difficulties for a modern audience. The racial aspect of the film is, to say the least, ambiguous (which led to difficulties finding an audience on the film's release). The title suggests that race will be central to the story, the Southern state of Alabama being, at the time, virtually emblematic of racism. You wonder at first if the 'ghost' is meant to suggest America's bad conscience. But Hobbs is not concerned with making easily digestible racial statements. His disdain for didacticism is admirable, but it means that the film's racial incongruities take enigma to the point of frustration. Carter the ghostly magician is white, and Alabama has stolen his secrets – it's like a reversal of white trumpeter Roy Castle stealing black Voodoo rhythms for his jazz band in the Amicus horror film *Dr. Terror's House of Horrors* (1965). Carter's ghost warns of dire consequences if Alabama goes ahead with his performance, and when Alabama protests, Carter cries: *"Silence, black man! Heed my warning!"* Alabama replies, in a kind of bizarre pre-echo of *Ghostbusters*, *"I ain't afraid of no white racist ghost!"* So far so strange, but when Carter retorts, *"Your ambition will contaminate the planet!"* one's mouth hangs open in amazement. For a 'white racist ghost' to lecture a black man on the evils of global greed is so skewed a concept that it enters the realms of the surreal. *Alabama's Ghost* arrived just a year after Melvin Van Peebles's *Sweet Sweetback's Baad-Asssss Song*, and in a climate where such angry black movies were finding an audience, the checkerboard detachment and unaligned ambiguity of Hobbs were massively out of step (an occupational hazard, I suppose, when your work marches to the beat of a different drum).

Hobbs is an intelligent, globally-conscious artist and in no way a bigot, but it can be hard, certainly on first viewing, to work out just what *Alabama's Ghost* is saying about race. What emerges after the dust has settled is a sort of allegory in which the black man is herded by white commercialism, and his own opportunism, into trading with the devil. The racial angle is given a further twist when Alabama runs off to the shanty town where his mother lives, chased by a black female vampire whose face is painted purple. One's mind reels, and the films of José Mojica Marins feel just a gravestone away. Terrified, Alabama arrives at Mama's house, and promptly suffers a seizure (here, Christopher Brooks offers perhaps the only realistic performance of the film, going beyond his studied theatricality elsewhere to offer a glimpse of a plausible mental breakdown). If the viewer is expecting the weirdness to let up now, though, they're mistaken. Mama, a resolutely sensible woman in appearance, says: *"There ain't no vampires livin' here in this town. Why, the only vampires I heard about moved into the city after Prohibition."* Just as we're about to ascribe a terminal weirdness to the film, we see Voodoo paraphernalia in Mama's kitchen. She's not crazy – she's just hip to metaphysics. What's strange, though, is the way this excursion into Alabama's racial heritage is then deployed. Voodoo could have offered Hobbs a means of engaging with a black audience: after all, in a story about magic, starring a black man being haunted by a powerful white magician, Voodoo offers racial empowerment. But Voodoo does not raise the character's consciousness: after partaking in Voodoo rites (and some Brazilian-style 'psycho-surgery'), Alabama believes he can repel Carter's magic, and so ploughs on with his intention to offer Carter's disappearing elephant trick to the villainous – and *very* white – Gault. It turns out that Carter's warnings are correct; by ripping off Carter's act and allowing ambition to blind him to Gault's true nature, Alabama very nearly *does* "contaminate the planet", and almost destroys himself to boot. Just to cap it all, it's Carter, not Alabama, who sorts out Gault, in a weirdly heroic finale. I guess it's no wonder black audiences declined to embrace the film…

Blaxploitation, horror, psychedelia, pop satire… 'How about some sci-fi?' you're probably asking. Not to worry, Hobbs has covered this angle too: a scene where Otto Max briefs Gault is futuristically surreal, with bleeps and whirrs on the soundtrack, flashing lights and bizarre technology in the set design, and faceless goons hanging around in freaky sunglasses, like something from the weirder episodes of *The Prisoner*. Coincidental echoes of Patrick McGoohan's TV allegory can also be detected in the extensive use of wide-angle lenses and the obsession with global media control, while the word 'hip' is used repetitively between Otto and Gault in a way that recalls Alexis Kanner in *The Prisoner* episode, *Fall-Out*. Technology is used here to suggest control and surveillance, the dominance of the masses by a handful of media moguls. It's a product of its time in this sense, with its vision of the Global Village as Global Brainwashing Machine.

So what is Hobbs saying about the counter-culture? The vampires hand out free dope at a concert where Alabama is to play to the world via TV satellite link-up. They intend to transmit their malevolent spell worldwide during Alabama's act. Heavy… *"Free admission to all who want to come,"* says Gault, Master Vampire of Media Hall. In a film of relentless mixed messages, this is perhaps the most damning comment of all. Gault is the voice of commercialism. Yet when it's time to mount Alabama's great spectacle, he specifies that entry should be free, declaring, *"I want the world to see an ocean of bodies, like a great human tidal wave."* What is this saying about the treasured late-sixties notion of free festivals, what is it saying about the whole hippie dream? The notion of 'everything for free' was espoused in particular by a faction of hippies called the Diggers, who set up shops in which all the contents, including food, drink, and works of art, were free. Criticism of the hippies has more commonly centred on their willingness to *sacrifice* these high ideals. Gault has this to say: *"This is much greater than gate receipts. I want their bodies – their minds will come later."* Such a pointed reversal of 'free your mind and your ass will follow'[1] suggests a director truly at odds with the counterculture, a fully paid-up member of the awkward squad: rather like Derek Jarman, whose punkily anti-punk film *Jubilee* (1977) gave many safety-pinned members of the Blank Generation a more effective dose of alienation than their Sex Pistols records. One thing's for certain: *Alabama's Ghost* is no simple pleasure-fest for stoned drop-outs!

Whatever the political implications of Hobbs's musings, his approach reveals a deeply nonconformist sensibility, as you can tell from the movie's antagonistic, contradictory tone: acting in *Alabama's Ghost* veers from crazy comedy to malevolent parody; allegory jostles with surrealism; and in sequences like the one in which a pack of vampires suck blood from girls tied screaming to a rickety wooden conveyor belt system, Hobbs visualises truly dreamlike variations on familiar themes. You sense a free-thinking artist in full flow, unencumbered by notions of how things are *supposed* be done. What's more, his antic sense of humour is never far away: an arch, satirical style tilts everything into a carnival whirl of half-glimpsed ideas and leering exagger-ation. Some viewers may find the film's eccentricity a little too close to the studied wackiness of, say, Frank Zappa, but it's nonetheless defiantly out of the ordinary. Heroically oblivious to the trail of wrecked convention he leaves in his wake, Hobbs goes his own sweet way without giving an inch, either to the commercial pressures of genre, or to the constricting seriousness of 'art cinema'.

Alabama's Ghost
© 1973. Fredric Hobbs Films, Inc.
Robert S. Bremson presents a Fredric Hobbs film.
writer/producer/director: Frederic Hobbs. director of photography: William Heick. camera: William Heick, Gordon Mueller, Laurence Grunberg. unit two: Harold Zegart, Susan Heick. best boy: Michael Waldear. key grip: Raymond Theriault. editorial assistant: Evalyn Stanley. production: Harry Maplas, Dorothy Sauer, Judy Clute, Stevie Lipney, Jack Hooper (negative conformer). unit manager: E. Prentice Welles. costumes by Squeak Krauthamer, Ann Wagner Ward, Elaine Joines, Dr. Caligari's cabinet, Yarmo, Lux. production design: Frederic Hobbs. assistant director: Karen Ingenthron. resident magician: Pat Lakey. acknowledgments: Earthquake McGoon's Magic Cellar; Magic Theater; Freeway Barter Theater; The Cockettes; Ted and Pat Derby (elephant trainers). special guest appearances by Turk Murphy Jazz Band with original songs by Turk Murphy and The Loading Zone with original songs by Tom Coster. musical score by Andre Brummer. associate producer: William L. Sullivan. technical director: editing, sound, continuity: Richard S. Brummer. Robert S. Bremson presents a Fredric Hobbs film
Cast: *Christopher Brooks (Alabama). Peggy Browne (Zoerae). E. Kerrigan Prescott (Carter's ghost). Steven Kent Browne (Otto Max). Ken Grantham (Granny, Moxie, Gault). Karen Ingenthron (Dr. Caligula). Ann Weldon (Mama-bama). Ann Wagner Ward (Marilyn Midnight). Joel Noble (Doc). Linda Shelburne, Squeak Krauthamer, Erica Shapiro, Lani Freeman, Hillary Roth, Patricia Shallcorss, Catherine Keir, Rebecca Sand, Richard Marion (groupies). John Carter (Sandor). Evalyn Stanley (Vampira). Ralph Mountain (voodoo drummer). Philip Gerson (sailor). Michelle Marrus (witch). Timmy Cole (monkey). Cedric Clute (doctor). Turk Murphy Jazz Band (themselves). Neena (the elephant).*

above:
Hobbs's Trojan Horse hits the street.

below:
Alabama's Ghost: made in San Francisco…

Godmonster of Indian Flats
aka **The Secret of Silverdale** (screenplay title)
© none [1973]
Bremson International, Inc. presents a Frederic Hobbs film.
writer/director/producer: Fredric Hobbs. executive producer: Robert S. Bremson. director of photography: William Heick. musical score: Henri Price. technical director, editing, continuity, sound: Richard Serly Brummer. associate producer: William L. Sullivan. production manager: George Costello. unit two camera: Susan Heick. best boy: Michael Waldear. key grip: John Carter. costumes: Ann Wagner. monster design: Fredric Hobbs. production technicians: Raymond Theriault, Stephen Williams, Joan Zerrien, E. PrenticeWelles, Evalyn Stanley, Joan Carson, L.G. Beaupre, Harold Zegart, Barbara Pohras. acknowledgements: The Castle; Gold Hill Hotel; Savage Mansion; Union Brewery Saloon; Crystal Bar; Primadonna Club; Fortune Telling Parlour; Reno Jaycee's Ghostriders; Washoe Horsemen's Association. filmed on location in Virginia City (Nevada, USA).
Cast: Christopher Brooks (Barnstable). Richard Marion (Eddie). Marianne Browne (change girl). Terry Wills (Elbow Johnson). Erica Gavin (bar girl). Evalyn Stanley, Joan Zerrien, Ann Wagner (Alta's girls). E. Kerrigan Prescott (Dr. Clemens). Peggy Browne (Madame Alta). Robert Hirschfeld (Sheriff Gordon). Steven Kent Browne (Phillip Maldove). Jack Curran, Chip Cash, Murray Mac, Bruce Ratcliffe (banjo band). P.S. Kreiger, Frank Ford, Walter Daniels, Richard Walton, George Costello (deputies). Karen Ingenthron (Mariposa). Stuart Lancaster (Charles Silverdale). Andre Brummer (Garbage Mike). Gordon Lane (bartender). Ann lane (Lady Barker). Reno Jaycee's Ghostriders (shootout stuntmen). Washoe Horsemen's Association (Silverdale's posse) and the Citizens of Virginia City (themselves).

above:
Barnstable (*centre*) finds a hostile reception from the grandees of the town in **Godmonster of Indian Flats**.

below:
The Godmonster is caged and displayed to the townspeople as 'The Eighth Wonder of the World'.

Godmonster of Indian Flats (1973)

A sheep farmer called Eddie (Richard Marion) is fleeced of his gambling winnings after falling in with the wrong crowd during a boozy celebration in Reno, Nevada. Experimental biologist Dr. Clemens (E. Kerrigan Prescott), recognising the luckless fellow as a neighbour, drives him back home to his flock. Drunk and exhausted, Eddie falls asleep with his livestock. During the night he experiences a strange vision, and discovers a mutant sheep embryo in the pen. Dr. Clemens returns the next morning to check on Eddie, with his assistant Mariposa (Karen Ingenthron) in tow. Eddie shows them the mutant, and Clemens insists on taking it back to his lab for analysis. Meanwhile, a businessman called Barnstable (Christopher Brooks) comes to the nearby town of Virginia City, trying to persuade the townspeople to sell their land rights to a major mining corporation owned by the shadowy Rupert Reich. The Mayor, Charles Silverdale (Stuart Lancaster), and his ally Philip Maldove (Steven Kent Browne), who have their own nefarious plans for the region, meet with Barnstable and tell him that his offers are not welcome. When Barnstable insists on staying in town, Silverdale and Maldove, in cahoots with the local sheriff (Robert Hirschfeld), stage the accidental shooting of a dog, and blame it on the visitor. After a phoney dog-funeral, staged in the local church, Barnstable finds that people in the town are no longer prepared to listen to his propositions. Maldove takes his vendetta against Barnstable a step further, and frames him for attempted murder. A lynch mob descends on the police cell and drag Barnstable off to be killed by a shadowy group called 'The 601 Society', but he escapes and makes for Clemens's laboratory. Meanwhile, at the lab, the mutant sheep is growing rapidly. Clemens theorizes that phosphates from turn-of-the-century mining techniques have combined with mutant sheep DNA to produce this new creature, a theory that also explains various myths about mine-monsters dating back to the 1890s. As the vigilantes converge on the area and Barnstable tries to gain entry, the monster breaks free and rampages across the country, destroying a gas station and scaring children. It's finally hunted down by a posse of cowboys, dragged into town at the behest of the Mayor, and exhibited to the townspeople in a cage at the town rubbish dump. However, Silverdale has betrayed everyone by selling out to Reich's corporation. In fury, the townspeople trash everything, including the monster, until Silverdale is left alone, ranting on a podium overlooking the dump. Far away on the opposite hillside, yellow phosphate gas emerges from the soil and enshrouds a pair of grazing sheep…

Thanks to Something Weird's DVD release, *Godmonster of Indian Flats* is probably the best known and most widely distributed of Fredric Hobbs's films today, which is ironic considering that *Godmonster* went virtually unreleased back in '73, except for a couple of L.A. screenings (see interview). In fact its commercial failure brought Hobbs's film career to an end. Looking back at the four films Hobbs made, however, it's strange to think it was this one that failed to get distribution, because in many ways it's his most conventional movie, with acting of a far more ordered kind than the chaotic, satirical declamations seen in Hobbs's previous movies. It's also tangibly more accessible in its subject matter: small-town corruption juxtaposed with monster-movie mayhem. Where *Alabama's Ghost* has four or five themes jostling for attention, *Godmonster* has a parallel montage structure that charts the petty villainy of

Silverdale and his cronies alongside the birth, development, and eventual destruction of a monster. The film could almost be ranked along with Bill Rebane's *The Giant Spider Invasion*, in which religious revivalists in a small rural town fail to respond to an attack of mutated spiders.

So, a normal, regular B-movie from Fredric Hobbs? I'm teasing, of course. Once you actually watch the thing, you'll realise that it's as far-out and idiosyncratic as his other films, and as stubbornly resistant to formularisation. Hobbs creates a diptych, with the monster theme set alongside a political plot exposing the venality of the town's most influential citizens; although there's no direct causal link between the financial exploitation perpetrated by Silverdale and the appearance of the creature, the two stories vibrate against each other in a resolutely uncliched way. Mining techniques from the heyday of the Comstock Lode are responsible for the mutation, and the film can be seen as an indictment of big business pollution, reaching all the way back to the gold-rush. The theme of greed is mirrored by the actions of Clemens, who thirsts for the scientific glory he hopes will be his when he reveals the mutant sheep to the world. It's a commonplace in monster movies for the monster to represent some current evil, whether it be nuclear radiation (*Fiend Without a Face*), or environmental pollution (*Godzilla vs. the Smog Monster*). Hobbs embraces the format, taking a pop at a symbol of American big business by having his monster destroy a gas station; a concern for the world's dwindling resources that allies the film with Hobbs's ecological track record, as expressed in his 'Art Eco' paintings and sculptures.

Now, to the monster. If you can't love this shambling, ungainly mound of fluff and bone, tottering through the countryside like a giant elderly drunk in a rotting kaftan, then you simply have no soul. Some have apparently chided the construction, claiming it's unprofessional, or unconvincing, but it seems to me that the whole point of designing a monster is to come up with something we haven't seen before. What would be the point of sculpting another Creature from the Black Lagoon? Another King Kong? The best screen monsters positively revel in their own unlikeliness: that's why even the rock-bottom budgeted *Robot Monster* has an ineffable charm that you simply can't ignore. If a monster looks implausible, that's a major plus. Bearing in mind, anyway, that it's a mutation whose growth has been artificially speeded up, it's hardly surprising that it looks as if it's going to fall apart at any second. Surrounded by humans who're seeking to exploit it for their own ends, The Godmonster (never named as such in the film) becomes the only real focus of sympathy in the film. Even a character like Barnstable is simply a lackey working on behalf of big business. He may be the victim of scurrilous allegations by the mayor, but he's also out to secure the sale of private land holdings to a major corporation – so he's far from the Everyman hero one might expect. It's typical of Hobbs that his characters are never drawn with a view to establishing conventional rapport or identification. Barnstable is probably the nearest thing to a lead character in the story, in terms of screen time at least; and given that he's the only black man in a town run by corrupt whites, you might expect him to assume some vaguely heroic function. That such a condescending use of race never materialises is testament to Hobbs's unsentimental approach to character.

Godmonster of Indian Flats is a film of indelible images. The setting evokes the American past, courtesy of the town of Virginia City, maintained as a tourist site where

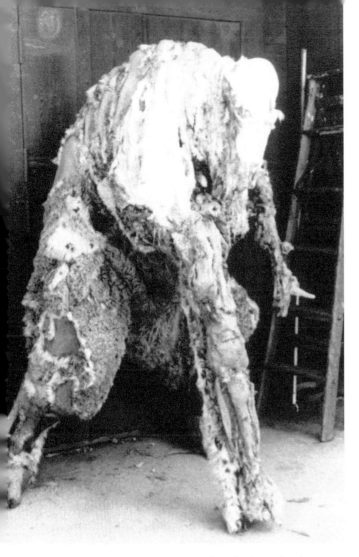

Fredric Hobbs Interviewed

"Hobbs's approach to film courts comparison to Fellini in sweep and style, to Bergman in concentration and intensity, and to Truffaut in the whimsical use of plagiarism and paraphrases of old movie classics and in deft juxtaposition of moods and genres, all adding up to a kind of one-man American New Wave." – *Rolling Stone Magazine.*

Fredric Hobbs is first and foremost an artist, specifically a painter and sculptor, and he has maintained a presence in the art world from the 1950s to the present day. By contrast, his film directing career spanned just four years, from his debut, *Troika*, in 1969, to his swansong, *Godmonster of Indian Flats*, in 1973. It's worth bearing this in mind before considering his movies, which, for all their abundant qualities, are best seen as a wild, feverish digression from his fine art work.

Hobbs was born 30 December, 1931 in Philadelphia. He graduated from Cornell University, where he obtained a Bachelor of Arts degree. After serving as an Air Force Officer he maintained a studio in Madrid, where he attended the Academia de San Fernando de Bellas Artes. Since the late 1950s, when he moved to San Francisco, his work has been committed to issues of spiritual and environmental consciousness. Between 1960-69 he founded the San Francisco Art Center, the city's first integrated 'live-and-work' real estate for the creative professions. He himself conducted master classes there, as well as directing a fine art program, with studio classes in drawing, advanced painting, and mixed media at The Academy of Art College, San Francisco. He was for a while the Chairman of the Department of Fine Art at Lincoln University, San Francisco. He even opened a shop for a while, called 'Fredric Hobbs Fine Arts'.

top left:
Hobbs's wonderful 'Godmonster' sculpture in all its glory, at the artist's studio near San Francisco, in 1972.

bottom:
Hobbs (*left*) with William Heick, at an exhibition of his paintings in San Francisco, 1994. Behind them is Hobbs's 'Murder of the Buffalo Woman'.

below:
'Portrait of Fascism As a Child', a 36-inch-high Hobbs sculpture exhibited in 1980.

the 1800s live on. It's the sort of production value that would add millions to a film budget if you had to start from scratch, and it demonstrates Hobbs's canny knack for choosing 'found objects' (in *Alabama's Ghost* the expensive-looking magic props, in *Godmonster* a whole town) that add lustre to the quality of the finished work. Hobbs also gets maximum visual interest from his monster: in one of the film's most mind-bending sequences, Mariposa, ostensibly the Professor's assistant but actually a sort of loopy flower-child, tries to communicate with the escaped mutation by dancing with it on a hillside, in a slow-motion sequence that's psychedelic in quite the strangest way. Then there's the scene in which the monster staggers onto the manicured lawn of a well-to-do household, terrorizing a group of happily picnicking children. Perhaps the strongest, most pointed (and poignant) imagery of the film is concentrated in the final act, as the Mayor unveils the recaptured monster in a cage at the town rubbish dump, declaring that he is to charge admission for a glimpse of it. As the symbolic end-point of human greed, the rubbish tip is a fitting climax for Hobbs's ecological allegory, and the townspeople's unceremonious destruction of this 'Eighth Wonder of the World' when they learn they've been conned out of their land-rights (another sign of Hobbs's unsentimental way with narrative) suggests how little time people have for wonder and amazement when they're focused purely on self-interest. *Godmonster*, a story about manipulative businessmen and corrupt science, ends up indicting the whole town; it would seem that the ominous curl of yellow smoke emerging from the soil of a neighbouring field signals just desserts for the whole greedy community.

above:
Hobbs photographed in 2006, standing alongside a wood and acrylic 'Art Eco' piece. This painting is part of his Highlands series.

below:
Hobbs creating a picture in the dramatic scene that opens **Troika** (1969).

In the early 1970s, he pioneered an art form he dubbed 'Art Eco', combining environmental technology, fine art, solar architecture and interactive communications, with the aim of pointing the way to an ecologically balanced lifestyle. One-person exhibitions of his pioneering artworks have been held at museums and galleries, including: the Museum of Science and Industry, Los Angeles; The San Francisco Museum of Modern Art; California Palace of the Legion of Honor; the Sierra Nevada Museum of Art; and other venues in New York, San Francisco, and Los Angeles. Numerous works are represented in the permanent collections of: the New York Museum of Modern Art; the Metropolitan Museum of Art, New York; the San Francisco Museum of Modern Art; the Fine Arts Museum of San Francisco; the Oakland Museum of Art; and the Sierra Nevada Museum of Art.

In April 1984 Hobbs suffered injuries from a major automobile accident, requiring lengthy convalescence – an experience which inspired a new 'Pacific Series' of Art Eco Icons and drawings. In 1988-89, he co-produced four PBS Network Programs, under the group heading, *Taiwan: The Other China*. Since the mid 1980s, Hobbs has been at work on *Fastfuture*, a kind of video notebook featuring thoughts on modern culture, commentary on environmental and political crises in modern life, and recontextualized fragments from his movies. He is also the author of several books that combine portfolios of original artworks with text exploring both his ecological concerns and the history of his beloved Monterey coast.

Triptych

Hobbs's first involvement with the moving image came in 1967, when, in collaboration with filmmakers Ron Bostwick and Robert Blaisdell, he assembled a documentary called *Trojan Horse*, recording the public unleashing of Hobbs's 'parade sculpture' of the same name. Hobbs drove his 'Trojan Horse' – actually a Chrysler chassis with newly sculpted bodywork bolted over the top, turning the vehicle into a phantasmagorical bonelike construction – across America in 1964 (it can also be seen in all its glory in Hobbs's later film *Alabama's Ghost*).[2]

Feeling drawn to the cinema after this collaboration, Hobbs decided it would be worth taking over the directorial reins entirely and making his own film, drawing on his design and sculptural skills to fashion a full-length dramatic feature. The result was typically uncategorisable: a three-part avant-garde surrealistic comedy with polemical asides and documentary footage, called *Troika* (1969).

Hobbs describes the film as, "a miracle play – but not underground." He reserves his greatest satisfaction for the film's final segment, saying, "Each section gets stranger and more interesting until the last part really takes off." Sadly, as yet *Troika* remains unavailable both on video and DVD. Hobbs is determined that this should remain the case until he has secured the right deal, and until he has finished re-editing the film. Like his neighbour George Lucas, he is obsessively motivated to correct perceived flaws in the original, and refuses to release *Troika* in its original version. It's very much to be hoped that he will one day soon settle on a satisfactory version, so that audiences can sample the source of his cinematic vision and perhaps better understand how to approach his later, more narrative-oriented work.

Shooting the film, and all of Hobbs's subsequent screen endeavours, was Kentucky-born William Heick. Heick was a film photographer in the US Navy during the Second World War, who moved to San Francisco in 1946 and became embroiled in the burgeoning experimental film scene. Heick worked with another San Franciscan director, Sidney Peterson, the avant-garde short filmmaker, between 1948 and 1953. He met Hobbs in 1962, and warmed to him as a friend and also an artist of vision: "Hobbs films are sorta unique, they don't fit into any category," he says. This laconic observation is a typical understatement from Heick, whose steady technical hand helped guide the wilder visions of Hobbs to the screen. The two men forged a strong creative alliance that persisted all the way to *Godmonster of Indian Flats* and their friendship has lasted to this day. First, though, came Hobbs's scattershot send-up of the sexual revolution: without a doubt the oddest movie ever paid for by veteran exploitation producer Harry Novak…

The Sexual Revolution and Its Discontents

Roseland (1970) is the sort of film that could get you kicked out of the room on your ass if you showed it to your friends during an acid trip. It's a bit like The Rolling Stones' *Their Satanic Majesties Request*: it might *seem* like a trippy idea to begin with, but after ten minutes you're ready to kill someone.

E. Kerrigan Prescott is Adam: a man addicted to pornography to the degree that he actually steals film prints of porno movies, dressing in disguise and adopting the moniker of 'The Black Bandit'. In one of the film's more amusing conceits, we learn that Adam became fascinated with pornographic imagery through his early exposure to the work of Hieronymus Bosch, in particular his *Garden of Earthly Delights*. If you're wondering what the hell made a sleazeball like Harry Novak pick this up for distribution, all is explained by several prolonged sequences of hippie nudity, and some extended burlesque numbers that accommodate the exploitation entrepreneur's taste for pre-hardcore pulchritude. "They wanted a skinflick," Hobbs recalls. "It's not a porno or anything, but my intention was a sort of satire of the sexual revolution."

The highlight of the film is an extended flashback revealing that Adam lost his job in television after mounting a lavish musical spectacular called 'You Cannot Fart Around with Love'. With elements of big-band TV specials, off-kilter carnival jazz, and a zaniness that recalls Frank Zappa's satirical recordings, it manages to be both freakishly weird and teeth-grindingly silly, with Prescott's eye-rolling-to-camera wackiness breaking the fourth wall *á là* The Monkees. *Roseland* is as unique as any of Hobbs's other films, but for me it's his least successful venture. Of course, with such highly personal work, responses will vary wildly all over the spectrum, so you can still take it as read that *Roseland* is worth checking out if you have an interest in sixties Americana and the counterculture. It's certainly strange: whether it's good is very much a matter for you!

Hobbs and the Sixties

Hobbs, the very definition of a square peg in a round hole, benefited from a brief, narrow window of opportunity in the late sixties and early seventies. Film industry businessmen were casting around for clues after the mysterious success of *Easy Rider* (1969). Dennis Hopper and Peter Fonda had delivered the late sixties equivalent of the Sex Pistols' 'Anarchy in the UK' – a trailblazing shock to the system that came roaring out of left field. Its sudden redefinition of the youth market left the cultural establishment confused and out of touch. In the wake of *Easy Rider*, the film industry tried to come to terms with the counter-culture, and for several creatively fertile years, it opened up and diversified, almost in desperation. Rogue elements were able to infiltrate the hallowed ground of the mainstream: this was the time when films such as *Putney Swope* and *Medium Cool* found funding, the latter even gaining distribution through Paramount.

Hobbs entered the fray with his avant-garde epic *Troika* and his 'lunatics have taken over the orgy' sex-satire *Roseland* to show would-be financiers. Five years earlier or later and he would have been shown the door. But as the decade turned, producers looking for 'far-out' filmmakers saw in Hobbs both a genuine craftsman (thus, orthodox points for skill), and a 'bohemian artist' (thus, counter-culture kudos as well). Perhaps Hobbs would turn out to be one of those indefinable weirdoes headed for a breakout financial success, like that crazy-ass Dennis Hopper? Hobbs's financiers must have hoped that they'd found a left-field cash-cow whose work would tap the unpredictable youth market. Since 'the kids' were taking acid, dropping out, painting their faces, rioting, and refusing to sign up for Death-Nam, maybe Hobbs, with his extraordinary 'Art Eco' and fierce individualism, would light their fires?

Hobbs's agent George Litto would be the catalyst for his future forays into cinema, as Hobbs explains: "He heard about my first ultra-low-budget movies and called me up, asked me to come to Hollywood. In my case I made such fantastic movies for so little money they figured it was best to leave me alone and let me do my thing, as long as the script was okay." Hobbs later introduced his producer on *Godmonster*, Robert Bremson, to Litto, which paid dividends for the latter when Bremson supported Litto's subsequent move into film production, with projects for Brian De Palma (*Obsession*) and Robert Altman (*Thieves Like Us*).

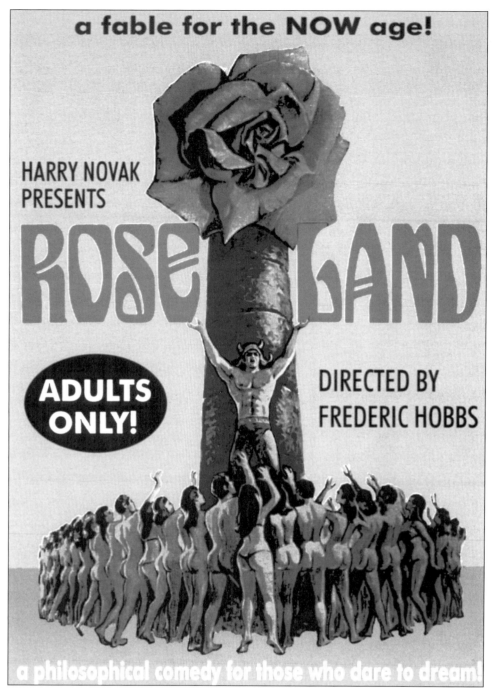

above:
Poster artwork for **Roseland**, Hobbs's satire of the sexual revolution.

Futuristic Jazz-Age Horror-Satire

Hobbs's next film, *Alabama's Ghost*, is a quantum leap on from *Roseland*. It's a gobsmackingly outlandish affair that left even the normally unflappable Elvira, Cassandra Peterson, lost for words when she introduced it, years later, on her cable show and subsequent video label. Imagine Alejandro Jodorowsky remaking Russ Meyer's *Beyond the Valley of the Dolls* – blaxploitation style. With vampires. And Voodoo. It's a film that could *only* have been conceived in the sixties/seventies Interzone, spilling a Satan's brew of allegory and irony across a sprawling canvas unhampered by considerations of genre. It's also yet another 'stoner' film to critique the hippie movement, a common feature of counter-culture cinema through *The Trip* to *Easy Rider* and *The Holy Mountain* (Hopper's *"We blew it"* being the defining perception of the era). The film again leans heavily on satire, this time adding a sardonic enunciation of the horror genre's clichés. Yes, it *is* a horror film of sorts, encompassing the

below:
It's easy to see why **Roseland** attracted the attention of Harry Novak, entrepreneur and horror/sexploitation distributor.

supernatural and replete with monsters, both human and superhuman. We have witchcraft and magic, madness and hallucination, fangs and blood and freakiness. Typically, though, Hobbs straddles the intermediate area between genres: it's a horror film, but it's never really scary; it's a comedy, but you don't exactly laugh. It's debatable whether Hobbs knows *how* to set up a scare, or a joke for that matter, in the traditional sense – but it's a moot point, as he's not making that sort of a film. *Alabama's Ghost* is an act of cine-bricolage – using off-cuts from the horror genre, and locations and props bequeathed for free by theatre acquaintances – all assembled with a sly artistic awareness. Meanwhile, the cast attack their roles with such broadsword swipes that conventional characterisation is chopped into mincemeat, a side effect of the theatre background from which the actors came. It's typical of Hobbs's approach that instead of demanding the cast tone it down for the screen, he incorporates their theatrical performances as 'found objects' to be pressed into the dense impasto of his script. The result is an uncompromisingly individual piece or work with few obvious precursors in genre filmmaking.

The pop satire of *Alabama's Ghost* stands in stark contrast to its traditional jazz score and Houdini-era backstory. Hobbs is an outsider to the sixties youth movement, and some would say that a satirist should have personal investment in whatever he or she satirises. But Hobbs's detachment is an artist's detachment, not an uncomprehending old-timer's, and by welding a critique of the Love Generation's dalliance with the dollar to his own love of the jazz age, he ensures that his work remains personal. By his own admission he could not engage at all with the sensory overload of Hendrix, Led Zeppelin, et al: "I never have been and never will be interested in rock music. Some of it is interesting as pageantry, some of the things they do with lighting, and some of the folk-rock is okay, you know, Pete Seger and those guys. I don't *hate* rock music, but it's over-amplified, and I don't like that. I don't like that it damages people's eardrums. Some of it's okay, The Rolling Stones sometimes, The Beatles, The Beach Boys, the people who do it best. I'm not attacking rock music in the film, I just used that to make the thing work as a story."

Alabama Song

It was Hobbs's connection to the jazz world that led to *Alabama's Ghost*, as he explains: "When Turk Murphy, one of our beloved San Francisco jazz musicians, and Pete Clute, Turk's partner, a great ragtime pianist, were opening up the basement of the William Tell Hotel, they found many trunks containing the life's works, costumes and paraphernalia of 'Carter the Great', a great magician of the 1920s and '30s. He was Houdini's partner, and when he died they made a spirit pact that he would come back. So Turk found all this stuff, and decided they would open a Magic Cellar, not in the cellar where they found the junk, but beneath Earthquake McGoon's Nightclub, and they called it Turk Murphy's Magic Cellar. Turk's band played there. All sorts of people, musicians, underground cartoonists, would show up, along with people interested in magic. Robert Crumb was around. It was popular, they would put on great shows there. Woody Allen was a great fan of Turk Murphy's; he would come from New York and play his clarinet with him once in a while. One day a friend of mine, Arnold Passman, the writer and critic who wrote *The Deejays*,[3] told me about it. I went down there with Passman and I said, 'My God what a

movie! This whole thing is a movie!' Carter the Great was into all kinds of fantastic, strange magical stuff. He made a live elephant disappear! And he's very theatrical, he was considered the most theatrical of the famous magicians of the pre-WWII period."

Hobbs decided to pitch the idea to his friend, the film producer George Litto. Litto had recently been involved in the successful low-budget horror movie *Count Yorga, Vampire* (Bob Kelljan, 1970), and responded immediately to Hobbs's plans for a vampire film set in the world of stage magic: "I told him about the idea for *Alabama's Ghost*, and he said, 'That's great, a horror movie, we can do that.' 'A Hip Head Horror Movie!' is what they called it! I wrote the treatment and it just worked terrifically. I created a Hobbs script, another allegory. I had the idea that an evil guy, Gault, a rock impresario in control of all media, is trying to take over the world by turning young people into vampire slaves, using electrified music and a drug, 'Khartoum Khaki'. In fact he's really a vampire who wants to take over the world by infecting young people through music. I said, 'we'll start with Christopher Brooks, and we'll call him Alabama, a failed jazz musician.' I wrote the treatment pretty fast, in a few days."

Warming to the theme, Hobbs describes his outline thus: "You meet Alabama, and he talks like Lord Buckley,[4] who was a fantastic jazz hipster. What a guy, he could really talk! So I gave Alabama his dialogue in the style of Lord Buckley, like, *'Yeah, that's cool, man. Like a hundred yellow pussycats dancing on jade…'* That's my original stuff, incidentally, Buckley had his own way, but he spoke in this poetic way. So Alabama works for Turk, and one night he goes down to the cellar and his forklift breaks through the wall and he discovers the life's work and belongings of Carter the Great, who disappeared in the thirties and was never heard from again! So Alabama decides that he's going to become a 'rock magician', he's going to go out on the rock circuit and be world famous. Then he calls on these people who have some relation to Carter, like Carter's old sister, Agatha Carter-Crone, who's the world's first transvestite vampire! She's played by that terrific actor Ken Grantham, a very good actor, perfect for this because he had this Josef von Sternberg look. So Carter the Great's sister lives in Sausalito, in a ferryboat. It's a real Sausalito ferryboat; people live in houseboats in a community there. Alabama goes over to see Carter's sister, and he's got 'Khartoum Khaki', and she says, 'What ya got there, boy?' And it turns out the old girl likes to smoke Khartoum Khaki! So they smoke it together. Then he goes along to study magic with the next guy, Moxy the Magnificent. Guess what? The same guy. He tells the audience more about the sort of tricks Carter did. He's a sort of teacher of magic, and has a magic museum. Then there's Doré, played by the lovely Peggy Browne, and she turns out to be a vampire too. And then they meet Otto Max, they're going on the rock circuit, and he dresses like Papa Haydn.[5] That's Steven Kent Browne. He liked to say he was Welsh, but I'm not sure, I think it was because he wanted to be like Richard Burton. He was always after being a romantic hero, but I said, 'No, you're the perfect villain: everybody hates you, you're horrible!' So he played the role even more vindictively, you know! Among the other people, the groupies, one was Richard Marion, who is now the director of *Everybody Loves Raymond*. Christopher Brooks, Steven Kent Browne and Richard Marion were all members of the Magic Theater, which is the big avant-garde theatre at the University of California. It wasn't as big then, but now it's quite famous.

Anyway, Alabama goes to New Orleans where he puts on one of his shows. And the ghost of Carter comes out of the one-sheet for one of his old shows. Alabama accuses the ghost of racism. but it turns out Carter's trying to save Alabama from the vampires. Then the purple vampires show up, and like all good boys he runs home to his mother. She's played by Ann Weldon, who became one of the stars of *Roots*. I gave her her first acting role; she was a singer before that. So she says, 'Come on boy, I'm gonna take you to the doctor.' And she takes him into the Bayou, and the doctor's a witchdoctor! With a lisp, no less! He's kinda fruity, this guy, we don't make a big thing out of it but, who knows. So Alabama's gonna be protected by black magic. The witchdoctor proceeds to sew a frog over his heart! This is all Hobbs, it's all original stuff, I might add. So Alabama's not afraid any more. He's sorta childlike, he's like the Everyman Artist…"

Having elected to continue with the concert, Alabama attempts to stage Carter's disappearing elephant trick. All does not go well, but in the end the bad guys are defeated. Hobbs continues:

"The elephant was borrowed from *The Ed Sullivan Show*, a friend of Turk's brought her up to the location. She was called Nina. We had crowds but we couldn't have them clapping, because elephants riot if you clap, so everybody pretended to clap and we added the sound later. For the crushing of Otto Max, we intercut between the real elephant, which put its foot on his chest, and then we bought one of those elephant foot umbrella stands, you know, and we pushed that down on him, and he screamed and blood came out of his mouth – and that got rid of Otto Max! We had about five hundred extras, including all these little theatre groups. We had The Cockettes, who were famous, gay, crazy-looking people; they were in it. But at the end of the day, about 3p.m., all the fog rolls in from the ocean. It was shot right on the coastline, at Lawson's Landing; Dunecrest, it was called, in Marine County. So that was it for the day, because the sky and everything had to match. It took us several days to shoot the whole thing, the rock concert with the attack of the vampire bikers and all, with five cameras!" Amid the frenzied activity at the climax of the movie, the death of Otto Max's henchwoman Dr. Caligula was originally a more extreme affair: "We had a much better scene, but Bremson insisted it had to be 'PG'-rated. I made a really awful scene where he humiliated her, ate her up, oh, it was so funny! But the censor said you can't do that, so we cut that back. But it was wild. You see, everything Bremson wanted to do had to be 'PG'-rated. He didn't want anything like *Roseland*. And he wanted the young people to see it of course, which was okay with me. So finally, in the last scene, after Alabama and Midnight embrace, they look up in the sky, and there's the ghost smiling benevolently, and we hear the *'Who's the ghostest with the mostest'* music…"

Hobbs, the Interviewer's Nightmare

So there you are: *Alabama's Ghost*, synopsized for you by Fredric Hobbs. Normally, I would consider a detailed account of a movie's plot from the director surplus to print requirements. Thankfully, Hobbs peppers it with a few anecdotal details, and given the film's oddness it's perhaps useful to have confirmation of what is, after all, a fairly bizarre narrative. At the risk of abusing the writer's 'last word' here, though, I would like to share with you the agony and the intrigue of interviewing Fredric Hobbs…

There were many times during the above synopsis when I interjected, or tried at least to do so, without receiving the faintest acknowledgement. If you wonder why I have not asked some pressing question relating to the film, probably Hobbs's most dense and ambiguous work, well, what can I say: it ain't easy. For an artist fond of symbolism and allegory, he's a cagey devil when it comes to interpretation. In fact, he not only resists offering interpretations himself (quite reasonably – many artists dislike doing so); he also blocks questions that would aid your own interpretative process. The classic reticence of the creative soul who feels his work has given all it has to give? Perhaps, but the difficulty goes further: for instance, attempts to place Hobbs in relationship to other artists progress little further than a grudging nod to Expressionism and a willingness to discuss a few of the Old Masters: while discussion of Hobbs's fine art contemporaries – Pollock, or Warhol for instance – is shot down within seconds.

For me the most frustrating of all Hobbs's discursive idiosyncrasies is his unwillingness to digress in your direction. All of your conversational gambits meet the same fate. Light and playful, provocative or serious, surreal and inappropriate, frivolous or tactless: you can utilize any or all of these approaches, and nine times out of ten, Hobbs will walk on by. Never has the term 'train of thought' been more appropriate: trying to change the subject or divert the flow is doomed to failure. You might as well stand before an express train and ask it to swerve! I have even tried rudeness to jolt a conversation in my direction. Not to worry: Hobbs sails merrily by, and if he notices your desperate measures, he barely lets on. Dialogue is very difficult in such circumstances: our telephone 'conversations' frequently became a sort of annotated monologue, in which I spoke not to elicit a reply but to remind myself on the recording of what it was I wanted to ask. A forlorn process? Well, it's not *quite* so bleak. Hobbs will store things that you ask him, and somehow, half an hour later, you recognise features of an earlier question being glancingly addressed. Nothing so easy as a simple thirty minute delay: it's more like adding drops of a different colour to a slowly churning mass of paint. Gradually you see the shade changing as your colour blends in…

I'm sure that Hobbs has always been a very stubborn personality. What's clear from talking to him (and we've talked for many hours) is that he and his films are hewn from the same rock. If you want the films the way they are, then you have to accept his character. Like Hobbs, *Alabama's Ghost* sails blithely through the tempests it stirs, with never a sideways glance, and it's to these storms in a long-forgotten teacup that we now turn…

Alabama's Controversy

Having gambled (rather modestly, with a budget of $55,000) on a counterculture hit from an unusual director, the producers did not get what they expected with *Alabama's Ghost*. It's easy to be wise in retrospect, but Hobbs was not a mass-marketable 'voice of the people': he was never going to catalyse the energy of the youth movement into a saleable product, and he would score no allies in the youth art arena. It's interesting to compare the fate of another 'far-out' amalgam of art and genre filmmaking, Alejandro Jodorowsky's metaphysical western *El Topo* (1970), which gained the attention of John Lennon. On the say-so of Lennon and Yoko Ono, Allen Klein's

above:
This shot, and all others on this page and opposite are from **Alabama's Ghost**. Here the Trojan Horse is driven by Alabama (in turban).

opposite page, from top:
Alabama (Christopher Brooks) crashes his forklift into a false wall;
…and finds a casket belonging to Carter the Great;
…full of the magician's paraphernalia;
He decides to take on Carter's mantle;
…but encounters the sinister Granny Carter (Ken Grantham);
…and Moxy the magician (Grantham again);
…before taking Carter's show on the road, as Alabama, King of the Cosmos;
…supported by a bevy of female assistants.

below:
A magic trick goes wrong, but who was responsible?

above:
This shot, and all others on this page and opposite are from **Alabama's Ghost**. Here Carter's ghost warns Alabama that he is endangering the planet...

opposite page:
A vampiress reveals herself in Alabama's bed;
...but foolishly Alabama accepts an invitation to visit Gault (Ken Grantham again), Master Vampire of Media Hall, seen here with one of his flunkies;
During the night, Carter's ghost appears to Alabama and warns that the vampires are about to take over;
A victim;
On the bloodsucking production line;
Gault in fury;
Alabama decides to perform Carter's greatest trick;
Another vampire manifests.

below:
Alabama, in bed with his latest floozy, recoils in horror from Carter's ghost.

ABKCO financed and distributed the Chilean director's next epic, *The Holy Mountain* (1973), to the tune of $750,000. Hobbs, unfortunately, was not so lucky. We can only speculate as to what he might have delivered with similar financial muscle behind him.

One reason why *Alabama's Ghost* perhaps failed to ignite a 'midnight movie' buzz in the manner of Jodorowsky was that Hobbs was forced to keep actual onscreen violence to a minimum. *El Topo* on the other hand was blood-drenched, as befitted Jodorowsky's conviction that blood equates to life force. As his comments make clear, Hobbs would have liked to go further in this direction: *Alabama's Ghost* has a few moments of graphic horror, but they're brief and unlikely to trouble the squeamish. It's a shame, because Hobbs clearly has a natural well of anger from which to draw. There's a real symbolic violence in some of his paintings and pen-and-ink drawings, with their aggressive arcs and splashes: at times his style brings to mind Francisco Goya, famed of course both for his unflinching portrayals of war and madness, and the bold gestural violence of his pen and brush work. Had Hobbs been able to film images just as unrestrained for the movie screen, he might have caught the attention of a wider audience.

However, there are other reasons why *Alabama's Ghost* failed to become a countercultural hit. Hobbs's detachment from the youth milieu he depicts creates a subtle but appreciable alienation effect, one that perhaps forecloses his chances of scoring with young people. In *Alabama's Ghost*, opposing forces are coldly marshalled: the greed of big business, the power-lust of mystics, the conformity-in-nonconformity of youth; and amidst it all, Alabama, no more inspiring a 'hero' than 'Barton Fink' in the eponymous Coen Brothers movie (another film about a man in need of guidance from a threatening spectre).

But of course, Barton was a Jewish character created by Jewish filmmakers. Hobbs is white, and yet his film satirises the opportunist ambitions of its leading Afro-American character. This need not have been a sticking point however, were it not for the character of Carter the Magician. It apparently never occurred to Hobbs that hip audiences might not 'dig' a film in which an opportunist black protagonist needs guidance from a white racist ghost! Of course the ghost is a pompous creature, from a time when attitudes were such that he would naturally address Alabama with a line like, *"Silence, Black man!"* Hobbs is not indulging racist sentiments, he's simply accommodating the speech habits of a bygone era; yet by following the dictates of his storyline, sublimely unconcerned about the way it might be perceived, he left in his wake a slew of confused and angry viewers. Ironically, for a period when the youth movement was aspiring to sanctify individual nonconformity, it was to be Hobbs's devil-may-care individualism that would sink his film commercially.

Hobbs explains: "*Alabama's Ghost* was cheap, it cost $55,000, but for a lot of reasons it didn't make the money the producers thought it would. It had trouble because of the black issue, and because there wasn't enough violence; it was a 'PG' movie. It played a lot, and a lot of people liked it, so I never considered it a bomb. I thought if they'd only put it in the art-houses it would have been a big success. The distributor was a good guy, too: there were no bad Hollywood people involved, they were all gentlemanly guys. They tried to help me. I was already shooting *Godmonster* by the time they got somebody to take *Alabama*. In a nutshell, it bombed, but all the magicians

showed up and thought it was wonderful. Then they took it up to Atlanta, during the first week of December. So first they had it in a pretty good theatre in Atlanta, and the film bombed. They said, 'Gee, you've got a wonderful interesting film, but it's bombed.' So then they had it playing on a Sunday, and there was a football game going on between the San Francisco 49ers and the Atlanta Falcons, and whoever won that would go through to the Superbowl. You think nobody's gonna come, right? Well guess what? All *kindsa* people showed up, and they were dressed in costumes, and they filled up the place, and they loved it, and everyone was asking, 'What the hell happened? What's going on?' Well, this is before *Rocky Horror*. Nobody knew what this film was. I was on holiday, and I got the word that the film was gonna make so much money, because of the Atlanta screening, you know? But the story I got – the truth, I think – is that they booked it next in Cleveland and Chicago, in black-oriented areas, and they got all these theatrical bookings, and then they changed the advertising so that you had this black guy saying, 'Hey Man, go see the ra-ra-ra-ra', you know, instead of this wonderful refined campaign [laughs]. I didn't hear it, I heard only tiny bits of it, but I can imagine. It was a hard black sell. Based on violence, you know, 'see honky get beat up'. They had it in *Variety* as No.38 in the country, for a week or two! But *Variety* grosses don't mean a thing. The promotional guys make 'em up. Unfortunately, the audience wanted to see whitey get beat up, but they see this strange magician and vampires, and they were very angry. So it was a complete bomb. The black community was furious because they felt the advertising had taken them for a ride, or that's what I heard."

Hobbs is uncomfortable discussing racial interpretations of *Alabama's Ghost*: he's happy to describe the hostile responses, but he's reluctant to be drawn on what exactly might have created the wrong impression: "What I was trying to do was to bring the 1920s back, pre-Barrymore, you know; 'Silence, black man,' that kind of phoney Shakespeare stuff. I tried to give it that feeling. But I didn't consciously try to make a racist of him." Unfortunately, when Carter cries "Silence, black man!", and Brooks, a charismatic black performer, dubs Carter a "white racist ghost", the audience pretty much buys Alabama's point of view...

After its unfortunate first run, *Alabama's Ghost* entered a period of confusion over rights as it flitted between owners, none of whom managed to extract much commercial mileage. Hobbs recalls, "They played it off at the drive-ins with a movie called *Black Girl* (Ossie Davis, 1972). I don't know if it made any money, I never saw any if it did. They eventually sold it but nobody wanted to touch it because the black people were very unhappy with it."

Thankfully, in 1985 *Alabama's Ghost* gained a US video release. Although not the kind of release Hobbs might have wished for – it emerged as part of a series of tapes 'Hosted by Elvira, Mistress of the Dark' – the deal did at least ensure that the film gained a new lease of life. Hobbs explains, "Eventually Bremson repossessed the film, and sold it to this guy in Hollywood, a film buyer, a very nice guy, really intelligent and very friendly, not a Hollywood type. He owned it for a while but he couldn't sell it to anybody, and then he sold it to the Madame Elvira people."

Hobbs remains proud of *Alabama's Ghost*: "I like the fact that my movie is, well not funky exactly, but... I saw a bit of *The Rocky Horror Picture Show* and I thought my stuff was much more elegant." Oddly, though, he feels the film would have been better served in another format entirely: "Danny Selznick, David O. Selznick's son, was a producer at Universal, and oh boy, he liked my work. He loved *Alabama's Ghost*, and he wrote me this wonderful letter. He wanted to make it at Universal as animation! He told George Litto, but Litto was known for making hits outside the establishment and he told Selznick he didn't need to take it to Universal. As animation? What a great idea! And I would have done it, because I would have been chief artist, instead of making Walt Disney cartoonish things, I'd have made these fantastic Hobbs expressionistic drawings, pieces of sculpture, and no artist has ever done anything like that. And then I think it would have been a sensational hit."

High Tide on the Desert

After completing *Alabama's Ghost*, but before the film went out on release, Hobbs signed a three picture contract with Robert Bremson. "For me it was fabulous," he recalls, "Three pictures at $200,000 each and I'd actually get paid, and have a nice piece of it too. That was in 1972, so it was pretty good for a low-budget deal. But then, because of the eventual failure of *Alabama's Ghost*, they didn't want to go through with three pictures. Bremson said he would do one of them, he said 'I'll give you one more shot, but not at $200,000.' So he changed the contract, and he reduced the budget, to $125,000 or $130,000. It finished at $135,000, I think, and I put up the overage myself, out of my salary. So I only had one more shot, I didn't have the full three-picture deal. It was up to me to write the original screenplay. I had six months to do it – the whole thing took more or less a year to do the whole project – so I sat in my studio on the hills out back of Stanford there, the beautiful hills overlooking San Francisco Bay. My mother and stepfather lived further down the same hill. I had a big studio and a Kentucky racing stable there that I had designed, rebuilt and so forth, so I had a really nice place to work. And I wrote a screenplay, originally called *The Secret of Silverdale* (which Bremson liked, and I think it's a good name), and then for various reasons it was turned to *Godmonster of Indian Flats*. Don't ask me how that happened, the idea was to make it more commercial."

Faced with a sudden decline in budget, Hobbs made the inspired decision to shoot in the small town of Virginia City, Nevada; a 'ghost town' turned tourist attraction outside of Reno. It was a place Hobbs knew intimately: "Warren Hinckle[6] and I had written a big hardback book for Houghton, a famous publishers, called *The Richest Place on Earth: The Story of Virginia City and the Heyday of the Comstock Lode*. It got rave reviews; didn't sell lots, but great reviews. I wrote the second half and Warren wrote the first, and I did forty four drawings for it. It was about the fantastic Comstock Lode, Virginia City Nevada, which at one time was the richest place on Earth, during the Civil War and afterwards. It was the last period of Romanticism in the American West: a fantastic story. I knew a lot about that, and later got quite involved with various projects in Virginia City – it influenced a lot of my artwork. So I thought, we'll use this place and it'll look like a really expensive movie! The people all said we'd love to be in the film. We paid them very little, just enough so that everybody participated and the whole town loved the idea of doing it, and they loved that I was doing it, it wasn't just some Hollywood yo-yo. They like artists up there. A lot of artists live in Virginia City, it's

sort of an artists' colony during the summer. I thought, what a great idea, I can take the story and history of Virginia City, and bring a contemporary monster movie into this fantastic historic landmark, where thousands of tourists come every year. During Bonanza Day, in the summer, it's a tourist attraction. They have three hundred people who actually live there and they wear costumes, you know, Western costumes, so you have all these extras and all these crowds. They have camel races up there too, because camels used to bring the water. And ice, because the mines were so hot. So I decided we'll shoot it all during that time, as much of it as we can. I'll work that into the script."

As Hobbs already knew the Virginia City trustees, clearance for filming was easy: "Virginia City is full of characters. They knew me because of my art, my books. I did a lot up there. We did some restoration of old buildings, and we had a company. I was a leader, I'd been going up there and having a great time in all the old saloons; this was in the days when I used to drink, which is many years ago. All those houses you see were all restored. And they had whorehouses that were legal! And they still do! Not right in the town, but they *used* to have them in the town. The whorehouses used to be on D Street but now they've moved down the canyon. You know, Italian fellows run them… but Nevada's known for that. We didn't make a big deal of it, although we had a Madame character."

For Doctor Clemens's scientific base, Hobbs used a striking old concrete edifice at the edge of the town: "Yeah, the place that looks like the Roman Coliseum? It's called American Flats. Not many people know about it. It's the American Cyanide Factory, and cyanide is how they used to separate the silver from the gold in the early twenties. The bonanza days were all over and all they had were these mounds, these enormous mounds, stories high, of 'tailings' they're called, which is what's left over after all the cyanide has been used, it's what's left. And they call it a 'dump' but the dump is still worth money. Because you can distil enough to refine silver from the tailings."

For his *dramatis personae*, Hobbs began with the corrupt Mayor Silverdale: "I made this Machiavellian mayor, who is partly my grandfather, who was a fantastic old capitalist, very close to me, who helped bring me up. He was an outrageous character. So I used him, Robert F. Hobbs Jr., and the famous writer Lucius Beebe, to make this character Silverdale. Beebe had lived up there and started the *Territorial Enterprise*, which is the paper Mark Twain worked on briefly. We used Lucius Beebe's Rolls Royce in the last scene. So the mayor, Silverdale, wants to keep the town as a historic landmark where he can move and walk around in his costume, and all the people have to do the same, and he's actually quite a fascist as it turns out. And he's paranoid – Silverdale is so paranoid he's even spying on the dump! You know, he's got surveillance on the town dump! Then we just used the idea of a billionaire, Rupert Reich, based on Howard Hughes, sending a black air force general in to buy all the mining leases from these townspeople so he could strip-mine the area. It's a terrible ecological thing, illegal, but they do that to the mines up there. All the ghost mines are there, huge piles of tailings all over the Comstock Lode. Hughes, of course, was involved in Nevada during his life. He was into mining and gambling, you know, and Las Vegas. There are fantastic stories about him. Then I got E. Kerrigan Prescott in there, and people from the Magic Theater. Prescott played the part of the professor who finds relics, old pieces of a strange creature in

above:
Action from **Godmonster of Indian Flats**: Barnstable eludes the vigilante lynch-mob as the Godmonster blows up a gas station in the distance.

below:
The Godmonster at large.

Monster Movie

If there's one thing that grabs the attention of the curious when it comes to *Godmonster of Indian Flats*, it's the monster itself. Not just any old monster, of course, not in a Hobbs film: this is a ten foot tall mutant sheep that walks on its hind legs and looks as though it's been created by dipping a flayed animal carcass into a giant candy-floss machine. Sculptural yet chaotic, the 'Godmonster' is one of my favourite movie mutants: simultaneously grotesque, pitiable and hilarious.

The monster movies of the 1970s work mainly to a 1950s template – films like *The Crater Lake Monster*, *Bog*, *Creature from Black Lake*, and *Monstroid* either echo the dinosaur-cum-fishman epics of the past, or take the Bigfoot legends as their template. So what inspired Hobbs to choose a sheep – surely one of Mother Nature's least threatening offspring – as the springboard for his monster? Surprisingly, the decision does have a rational basis, as Hobbs explains: "Okay, there was a local legend about a mine monster, so I used that, but it was my idea to make him look the way he looks. I said, what kind of monster could it be? I don't know how to make monsters, I can draw them, I can paint and I can sculpt them, so I'm going to make a Hobbs sculpture of a giant sheep, because probably if there was such a monster, firstly these miners would be hallucinating anyway, and have hangovers, they would see any kind of fantastic thing – so why not have them see a great big fucking sheep! Which is what it could have been because there are sheep ranches all around there. Those guys up there were drunk all the time, they were the best paid miners in the 1860s and '70s. There are still maybe 30-40 saloons in a street about four blocks long, open all the time 'cause it's Nevada. But it was so hot down there, and then they'd come up and drink and they'd have oysters! Oysters in the desert! They brought in oysters, and the shells are still down there, by the dump, thousands and thousands of oyster shells! Because it was the richest place on earth. Rothschild, the Scottish bankers, everybody came from all over the world and it was a fantastic place, they had the biggest hotel in the West there, the International, which burned down. San Francisco was a shitty little town back then, compared to Virginia City. So I decided that if there was a monster, why not a sheep? We used the Episcopal church, where we filmed the dog funeral, as our production office and studio, down in the basement where I kept everything. It's an early church and it's in perfect condition. I created the flying sheep down there, in the darkness of the Episcopal church basement, which I kinda liked. We hauled these sheep up in the air and they're going, you know, 'Baaaaaa!', and we were all wearing black capes, to hide ourselves in shot. We didn't have any money to make these effects, but that didn't stop me because I know how to create stuff using magician's techniques, just like we did in *Alabama's Ghost*."

Hobbs is justifiably impatient with those who scorn his monster design: "Some monster people think, 'Oh what a cheap monster, I don't like it', but the art people think it's great. Mainly they don't understand the long arm that it has, they think I did that because I don't know any better. You know, stick the Monster in a museum, as part of an Art Eco show, and make an ecological point, then people would think, 'Oh, great artwork, nice sculpture.' The monster was based on a myth, but I made him from an artistic standpoint,

the mines, and he discovers that the fabled Mine Monster really did exist. The mines for silver are hugely deep, 2,500 feet deep and very dangerous. They were some of the most famous engineering feats of the 19th Century, and the wealth they created built San Francisco. We went and shot in one of the small ones, we didn't go in the big ones."

After the drubbing *Alabama's Ghost* received for its perceived racial insensitivity, Hobbs could have been forgiven for overdoing the racial tolerance angle with his next film. That he doesn't do so, but instead incorporates Christopher Brooks into the story without making an issue of his colour, is probably as clear a signal of Hobbs's true feelings on the subject as you could wish; certainly a more sincere approach than concocting some earnest panegyric on the subject of integration. Once again, Brooks plays someone who would not impress the 'positive discrimination' lobby. But as Hobbs points out, "Barnstable is not a bad guy, he's just a tool of Rupert Reich. Someone once said that they liked that I never made an issue out of the fact I was using a black actor. I didn't do it that way to get reviews, but I'm really happy that people think that about it. You know, they come into the bar and ask, 'Where's Barnstable, which one's he?' and he's at the other end of the bar, and someone says, 'He's over there, he's the guy in the purple shirt.'"

Hobbs is unfailingly appreciative of his cast: "The Hobbs troupe, who played in all my films, they liked working with me and I liked working with them. We were all friends, you know, like Altman and his casts. Stuart Lancaster as the mayor did a great acting job, he was in a lot of Russ Meyer films too. He was a well-known actor in Hollywood. He was a legitimate star, he did Shakespeare, he did everything, a very fine actor. And guess who he was? The grandson of John Ringling North, who founded the circus! Russ Meyer loved him, he learned his lines perfectly, and he loved making these real offbeat movies. He was a great guy."

as opposed to a latex copy of King Kong or something like that. I made him a really distorted fucked-up sheep! He's had a bad childhood, right? [laughs]. He's stuck in that lab and they're tweaking him with things. The early version in the lab, he looks like a giant roast beef, somebody said! And then he breaks out, and he's so unhappy about how the humans are treating him that the first thing he does is blow up the oil station. So he goes on the rampage and the people form a posse, and lasso him. I hired these trick riders who worked for Howard Hawks in the famous westerns. They live out there, they loved to do it, and they did it just for screen credit. So they were all real guys. But I based it all on history, or things that could or did happen, not just some bullshit Mickey Mouse monster movie, right? Everybody played it seriously. Now the best scene in the whole movie is the capture of the monster. You really feel sorry for him. I put that stuff inside him and made it yellow, that was a stylistic thing. I didn't want it to just look like guts, I wanted it yellow, as a symbolic link to the sulphur and phosphor gas. But also we had cow's entrails for the scene in the cage. I wanted a lot more of that but they wanted a 'PG' rating. It could have been much more horrific, in my opinion…"

The Cult Revolution and Its Discontents

Hobbs has strong views on the way his films have been commented upon and criticised over the years: "We had a screening of *Godmonster* in San Francisco in one of the big theatres, five or six hundred people, and they filled out cards and nobody said anything bad about the monster. The only thing they said was they thought you'd have to be intelligent to understand the movie. We had a lot of comments like that, that it was a little bit too intellectual for the monster-movie market. And I take credit for that! The idea was very ecological, because the monster blows up the Standard Oil station! The Americans, some of them get that, but I should think the English do, because they listen to dialogue! The monster blows up Standard Oil, do you maybe think that with all the symbolism that's in that fucking movie, don't you think they'd see that? [laughs] It's been said that my stuff is so dense with visuals, images one after another after another, that people get into it and they don't know where the hell they are. But they're in it. But they don't pay attention to all the details. People have said, 'Why does everyone go crazy at the end?' Well it's in the dialogue – they've been had! Even the distributor, who's a smart guy, said, 'Everybody goes nuts at the end! Is that what you always do, Hobbs? In every movie you make everybody always goes nuts at the end!' I said, 'No, for chrissakes listen to the dialogue! It's in there – people in the crowd shouting 'Silverdale's got our money!'' But you know what? The images were so strong that nobody listened. That's why some of my movies fail, in some things. People say, 'Oh the story's weak, Hobbs doesn't know how to do stories.' That's bullshit! My imagery is so powerful that they can't listen. So we added more lines, my ex-wife screamed a few lines in there, so now you can hear a few more lines. The failure of *Godmonster* was heartbreaking to me. They were all friends of mine, I lived up there a lot. But the failure of it meant that I really didn't want to do any more movies. Later, we were going to get Michael Caine, which almost worked, to play Howard Hughes. We were going to try and buy the picture back from the guys who eventually bought

it, and redo it and try to get Caine to just do a couple of days as Howard Hughes, manipulating the whole thing, and we were going to re-release it."

Sadly, these plans came to naught and *Godmonster* fell into obscurity, until it turned up on the Something Weird catalogue, becoming Hobbs's one and only DVD release to date.[7] With the rights having long since passed from his hands, Hobbs has never seen a penny, of course, from the film's digital rebirth, but at least now the film into which he poured so much of his creative energy has travelled the world and taken up residence in the dreams of a small but appreciative international audience. What's perhaps bitter-sweet is that, for Hobbs, his work's integrity can get swept away in a torrent of 'bad movie' website reviews and kitsch-loving condescension…

The dust has settled, the drugs don't work, the dreams of the sixties are over. Culture has moved on. The terrain is unrecognisable. Whatever context audiences might have brought to a Hobbs film in the early 1970s has been overwritten by thirty years of cult, camp, irony, parody, pastiche: postmodernism. So how does he feel about being thought of as a wacky weirdo cult director? How does he feel about the difference between the serious attention accorded to his art, and the rather more irreverent attitude extended to his films? For once, Hobbs is moved to respond directly: "Well I'd like to see them make a movie on $55,000! You can't just be crazy. It takes ingenuity. You ask an interesting question. How do I feel about it? Greatly disappointed, because nobody got it, half the time, and the way it was distributed was so bad, so cruel – but that's always the story with anything avant-garde or different or independent. You're just lucky if anything happens. But I didn't make a film that was saleable enough. I didn't know how to do that, although today maybe I would. But my films were done so cheaply. They said, 'Hobbs does his films for the price of the light-bulbs!' They ridiculed them, because

above:
Erica Gavin (Russ Meyer's **Vixen**) puts in her cameo appearance in **Godmonster of Indian Flats**!

below:
Roused to anger by Charles Silverdale's treachery, the citizens of Virginia City attack the unfortunate Godmonster.

SEE THE LEGENDARY MINE MONSTER

GODMONSTER OF INDIAN FLATS

color by de luxe

bremson international inc presents a fredric hobbs film · starring stuart lancaster · peggy browne · christopher brooks · kerrigan prescott

above:
Original poster for **Godmonster of Indian Flats** showing the monster in its most sheeplike form.

below:
An 'Art Eco Icon': Hobbs's 78-inch sculpture, 'Aerobic Warrior', first exhibited at his one man show at the San Francisco Museum of Modern Art, 1980-81.

they were so cheap. Otherwise they never would have been made, or I might have had to do something I didn't want to do. So in order to have the freedom to do anything, I had to make 'em cheap. My feeling is that, you know, I had my chance. I was young, but it wasn't like Coppola going in there and getting UCLA guys and major studios to let him make movies for $700,000. He didn't have to worry about the actors; he had real actors, right? He didn't have to tailor the material to somebody who's a stage actor, at best. Stage actors, lemme tell you, are not screen actors. My actors were young theatre actors. They weren't film actors. They would overact, but that's okay, I just made it part of the style and did it anyway. It's expressionistic theatre. But imagine what you could do with real actors! I would have written it differently too. So my films were cheap, and the acting's a bit over the top: but my creativity, nobody who knows anything attacks that! If you take the most successful parts of the films, and put them together with the art, it makes perfect sense. But if you put all the films up there as these movies by a far-out filmmaker, it just doesn't seem to make it."

Part of the problem understanding Hobbs's films has always been the lack of background information. When we see a perplexing painting in a gallery we turn to notes and brochures to orientate ourselves with historical context, or the artist's background and intentions, before returning to the image itself. Without such map references, audiences for Hobbs's films today can be forgiven for stepping back bemused, struggling to engage. I always give primacy to the immediate response of the viewer, devoid of background biographical context (surely in these over-stimulated times the most luxurious way of encountering a work of art?). But I also know that if *Alabama's Ghost* had been the work of a black director – a possibility I considered for a time before speaking to Hobbs in person – my perspective on the film would be quite different. Sad, but true.

Maybe it's not so sad: no artwork is an island. The pungent imagined aroma of hashish and incense drifting from the screen in *Roseland* and *Alabama's Ghost* makes it hard for us to get a grip on what we're seeing. And given that the films have a satirical slant (well outside the norm for the horror genre), the need for a compass is all the more acute. Hobbs the artist; Hobbs the filmmaker; Hobbs the intransigent interviewee; Hobbs the reluctant cult figure; hopefully these facets, shown here, help his extraordinary films to resonate more clearly. He's an American original – a cliché, I know, but what the hell – and the horror genre needs men like him, as much as it needs its die-hard fans, and dynamic entrepreneurs. Hobbs's creative 'troika' is anger; horror; humour – all of which can be found in abundance in his work. Attempts to read his films without

recourse to all three are doomed to failure; which of the troika gains ascendancy is entirely up to you. He is currently working on a script called 'A Tale of Two Cats' (revisiting themes from his 1993 book *William, the Zen Cat*), concerning felines who save the director's life and possess esoteric knowledge. It's a project that sounds ideally suited to animation, and given Hobbs's enthusiasm for the idea of an animated *Alabama's Ghost*, it would be fascinating to see how his formidable drawing skills could be marshalled into a feature. One thing's for certain, whether live action or cartoon, 'A Tale of Two Cats' would have little in common with such anthropomorphized animal tales as *Babe* or *The Aristocats*, and everything to do with Hobbs's own unique film universe.

Footnotes

1 The title of a Funkadelic album: *Free Your Mind... And Your Ass Will Follow* (released in 1971). As a piece of hippie lingo it may have been in West Coast currency for a while before that, but I've been unable to verify it.

2 Robert Blaisdell had previously shot a promotional short for Vincente Minnelli's Burton-Taylor film *The Sandpiper* (1965) called *The Big Sur* (1965), which explored the Monterey coastal region where Minnelli's film was made, and depicted the artists and bohemians who worked there.

3 *The Deejays* by Arnold Passman covers the early days of Top 40 radio, up to the beginnings of Progressive Rock on FM. From the Encyclopædia Britannica online: "Arnold Passman['s] *The Deejays* (1971), was the first attempt at a history of radio in the rock era. Although its writing style is dated and often guilty of overreaching and preaching, it covers most of the pioneer disc jockeys and the major issues."

4 Lord Buckley [Richard Myrle Buckley] 5 April, 1906 – 12 November, 1960. Comedian, monologist, hipster and jazz-age icon whose verbal flights of fancy incorporated black slang, beatnik-speak, 'scat' interjections and the rarefied lingo of the English aristocracy.

5 The 18th Century composer Joseph Haydn.

6 The founder of *Ramparts*, a political and literary review magazine published between 1962 and 1975.

7 *Roseland* is available as a DVD-R from Something Weird, but has not been spruced up for an 'overground' release.

FREDRIC HOBBS: FILMOGRAPHY AS DIRECTOR	OTHER FILM CREDITS:
	1967 *Trojan Horse* (documentary about Hobbs: 30mins – co-directed with Ron Bostwick & Robert Blaisdell)
1969 *Troika* (also writer / actor / designer)	1989 *Taiwan: The Other China* (producer only) (PBS TV show)
1970 *Roseland* (also writer)	
1973 *Alabama's Ghost* (also writer / producer / designer)	**BOOKS:**
1973 *Godmonster of Indian Flats* aka *The Secret of Silverdale* (also writer / producer / designer)	1978 *The Richest Place on Earth: The Story of Virginia City and the Heyday of the Comstock Lode* (co-writer; also drawings by Hobbs)
1979 *The Richest Place on Earth* (15 minute 35mm promotional film with John Carradine)	1980 *Eat Your House: Art Eco Guide to Self-Sufficiency*
1996 *Fastfuture 1 – The Inner Space of the Soul* (26m)	1983 *American Paradise: 400 Years on the Monterey Coast*
2001 *Fastfuture 2 – Wind Plus Sun Plus Water Equals Art* (28m)	1990 *The Spirit of the Monterey Coast*
	1993 *William, the Zen Cat*

chapter 23

To Sleep, Perchance to Scream

George Barry on the making and reawakening of Death Bed: The Bed That Eats

Death Bed: The Bed That Eats (1977)

At the edge of a grand estate, near a crumbling old mansion, lies a strange stone building with just a single room. In the room sits a big old-fashioned bed. Created by a demon, the bed is alive, and seeks the blood and life essence of unwary travellers. On the wall nearby hangs a painting. Behind it, the painting's long-dead Artist (Dave Marsh) sits imprisoned; he's been there for sixty years. Unable to intervene, he watches as a young couple enter the room and lie down. Yellow foam emerges from the bedspread, and the couple are sucked into a liquid core. With a burp, the monster is ready for its next meal. For the rest of the film, interspersed with flashbacks explaining the history of the bed, we follow the fortunes of three young women: confident, practical Diane (Demene Hall); nervous, withdrawn Suzan (Julie Ritter); and detached, supercilious Sharon (Rosa Luxemburg). One by one they are attracted to the bed. First to die is Suzan, who falls asleep and suffers nightmares created by the bed. Diane is next, dragged to her doom by a bed sheet tentacle. Sharon's brother arrives and tries to save Diane but, after reaching into the bed's stomach, he's left with skeleton hands, and slumps into depression. The bed's only weakness is Sharon…

George Barry's bizarre and beguiling *Death Bed* is a fairytale horror story, merging surreal humour, private poetry, and a blithe disregard for the essential strangeness of its own ideas. Rough around the edges, off and away in its own world, it's a precious slice of low-budget madness that reminds us what we've lost in the current overpolished and creatively impoverished horror genre.

I first saw *Death Bed* in 1988: Stefan Jaworzyn, the editor of *Shock Xpress*, discovered it in a cheap video sale and recommended that I give it a try. I watched it at his house one Sunday afternoon, and it knocked me out. 'Who on Earth is George Barry?', we wondered, after sitting there, jaws agape, dreary Sunday dispelled by this shaft of seventies ghost-light. 'How did such a movie get made?' Not only was it an uncommonly strange piece of work, but

there was virtually no information about the production on either the film or its sleeve. The video, from the ultra-obscure Portland label, had amusingly cheesy cover artwork but was completely devoid of credits. The film print did at least carry the words '(c) George Barry 1977', but that was all. Where normally you'd expect the names of cast and crew, the screen offered blackness, with only the word 'Credits' hovering, bereft of the promised information. The effect was so opaque, so mysterious, that you felt both laughter and frustration bubbling up. The mystery only intensified as the film gathered momentum, shifting unpredictably from creepy comedy to poetic folktale to surreal horror: the mood ricocheted between registers in a way that defied categorisation, either as mind-warped outsider art, insane student project, or exploitation film gone haywire. When I saw it I thought, 'I must find out who made this!' But no one knew anything about *Death Bed*: the video label had disappeared, the name 'George Barry' was anonymous enough to belong to a thousand Americans. And so the trail went cold…

Death Bed's British video release in the mid 1980s was, to say the least, under-reviewed. The fanzines were still bedazzled by the more extreme end of the horror spectrum, and we were all rather heavily preoccupied with obtaining an uncut *Cannibal Holocaust* or a complete set of the *Ilsa* films. To notice *Death Bed* you needed to tune your mental wireless away from the noisy gore frequencies to a stranger, more elusive position on the dial, in the space between stations, where the shipping forecasts, foreign signals and dream-voices live.

In the days before the internet, most who saw the film knew nothing about it. This in itself wasn't unusual: in the early 1980s, countless films were released on video without fanfare or context. They would enter your life with the enigma of an archaeological relic; albeit, in this case, a relic that flirted with the nonsensical and the silly, and sometimes veered towards sheer baloney. Baloney? Am I talking 'bad' here, a dog's dinner of cheap turkey to be chewed up and spat out on *Mystery Science Theater 3000*? From the title and synopsis, you could be forgiven for

below:
Rusty Russ copes stoically with an insane world, in **Death Bed**.

Death Bed: The Bed That Eats
aka **The Bed That Eats People** (shooting title)
© 1977. George Barry
writer/director/producer: George Barry. co-
producer & art direction: Maureen Petrucci.
editor: Ron Medico. associate producer: Jim
Williams. cinematography: Robert Fresco.
additional music: Cyclobe (Stephen Thrower &
Ossian Brown). assistant camera: Bob Gallant.
additional cinematography: Robert Handley.
assistant camera: Clyde Stringer. assistant
director: Richard Parker. production assistants:
Robert Andrews, Howard Davis, Les Wears.
gaffer & special effects: Jock Brandis. negative
cutter: Dave Wedlake. sound: Jim Viola & Tom
Sherry. sound mix: Patrick Spence-Thomas.
Cast: Demene Hall (Diane). Rusty Russ
(Sharon's brother). Julie Ritter (Suzan). Linda
Bond (the resurrected girl). Patrick Spence-
Thomas (voice of Beardsley, the artist). Rosa
Luxemburg (Sharon). Dave Marsh (artist). Ed
Oldani (victim). Marshall Tate (side order).
uncredited: George Barry (the eyes of
Demon/voice of the gangster). Bob Gallant (The
Demon in long shot). Jock Brandis (the
minister). Ron Medico (voice of the minister).

opposite page:
The first section of **Death Bed**: 'Breakfast'...

below:
Casting a spell to fight the bed.

anticipating a tacky time-waster like *Attack of the Killer Tomatoes*. It has a ludicrous premise, goofy humour, zonked-out performances and even crazier visual effects. The 'bed' burps after consuming a bottle of wine, and glugs a bottle of Pepto Bismol - what sort of relationship are we to have with such a film? *Death Bed* can be silly alright, but its humour is all over the scale, from slapstick to irony: even on first viewing it's not simply something you laugh *at*.

Of all genres, horror allows the greatest flouting of convention, and George Barry exploits this to the max. One of the things that makes *Death Bed* so appealing is the stubbornness of its concept – a bed that eats people is pretty 'out there' as the basis of a story. It's one thing having a weird idea for a movie, though, and quite another to bring it to the screen with the implicit strangeness intact. All would have come to nought if the thing had been poorly directed. Instead, Barry's way with actors, his unusual pacing, and the fragmented storyline all add to *Death Bed*'s charm and mystique. Flashbacks and vignettes enhance a 'literary' feel, and even the largely unconvincing day-for-night photography achieves something worthwhile by accident, placing otherwise ordinary linking scenes in a space neither sunlit nor shadowed, and a time neither day nor night. The acting has a sort of opiated feel to it, a

pharmaceutical blurriness that reminded me of Werner Herzog's experiments with hypnotism in *Heart of Glass*. On first viewing you wonder if the weird, listless line readings are due to the actors' inexperience, but you tend to dismiss this idea as the film progresses. The actors in *Death Bed* are not wooden; they're holding back, deliberately under-emoting, where a more conventional filmmaker would have had them screaming and chewing the scenery. When Diane frets aloud in the throes of a dream, her words are bled dry of emotion (*"No, no. Not again. Not again. Will it ever end? It will never end."*), giving the scene a far more unsettling undercurrent. Then she wakes, only to enter another dream: you could say that the whole film is like stepping through a series of oneiric Chinese boxes. And as always with dreams within dreams, we're left feeling that borders have been eroded, that *everything* could be a dream. For example, Sharon's silent acceptance as Diane is sucked into the bed asks a lot of our credulity if it's happening in the real world, but seems far more acceptable in a dream-state.

Another factor that uproots the film from conventional moorings is the lack of sync sound, for which Barry compensates with a free-for-all of voice-overs: the Artist, Diane, Suzan, all get to add their thoughts to a scene. My favourite is the Artist's comment about a new victim: *"Ah,*

there's another. She's been brought to you." It's pointless in plot terms (the line is dubbed over a simple scene of Suzan and Sharon in the woods) but the casual, offhand way it's said feels as if we're picking up a stray, idle thought: it's effortlessly weird and hilarious.

When it comes to pacing, most horror films have an attack-and-subside rhythm, building towards a grand finale. *Death Bed*, on the other hand, has a gentle rhythm, without the obvious spikes for which even the crudest horror directors aim. There's no suspense, and there's certainly no sense of the story being manipulated towards a climax. For some viewers this may be unsatisfying, but if you're ever so slightly fed up of being marched through film narratives, trotted through them like a pedigree mutt at a dog-show, *Death Bed*'s loose-leash approach is a chance to relax and try something different.

Death Bed deals in transcendental mysteries (the impossible geometry of the bed, bigger on the inside than the outside; the occult means by which it is created and destroyed), but Barry summons his demons from a fantasy world disconnected from religious tradition, telling a story of demonic seduction that has nothing to do with the Church. Barry signals this twice: when Suzan's neck is sawed by the chain of her crucifix pendant, pulled back and forth across her throat by the bed's power; and during a flashback showing a clergyman dying in the bed while reading the Bible. Both scenes leave us in no doubt that the bed is unaffected by the paraphernalia of Christian faith.

"You aim for the grotesque. You're nothing if you're not grotesque: except hungry, of course." – The Artist.
"I have one aim — the grotesque. If I am not grotesque I am nothing." – Aubrey Beardsley.

Throughout the film, poetic images allow the slender narrative thread to take a back seat. In this, Barry is akin to French director Jean Rollin (*Death Bed* would make a lovely double bill with Rollin's *La rose de fer*). We see blood blossom from the eye-socket of a skull in the bed's fluid interior; roses blooming from the same skull, now magically buried in the soil outside; a shattered mirror fragmenting a face into kaleidoscopic collage; and the pages of a book turning to mirrors that capture the flames of a fire. Such imagery suggests the Romantic tradition, as befits the Artist behind the glass, like a fey whisper caught halfway between English Gothic and the Scandinavian Symbolists…

"Surrounded by my paintings, I decided to draw my death-bed."

So says the Artist, looking around him at the walls where Aubrey Beardsley's 'The Dancer's Reward', 'The Woman in the Moon' and 'The Kiss' are displayed. Beardsley was born on 21 August, 1872 and died from tuberculosis in France, on 16 March, 1898. He became notorious for his illustrations in two 'decadent' periodicals of the period, *The Yellow Book* and *The Savoy*. His designs for books such as the banned *Salomé* of Oscar Wilde added to his notoriety, and his major works include the illustrations for *Le morte d'Arthur*, *The Rape of the Lock*, *Lysistrata* and *Volpone*.

"I've been imprisoned behind my painting in this limbo for sixty years now, since my death."

So is this really Beardsley? Well, later he says he hasn't had a cigarette in seventy years, which, given that the shoot began in 1972, is near enough Beardsley's date of death. Certainly the actor *looks* the right age: Beardsley died young at the age of 25. How he got from France to the United States is debatable, but the bed *does* have transcendental powers…

"You gaze at me as a painting on the wall; and I see you as a serving upon some monstrous silver platter."

But if the Decadent and Symbolist movements provide stimulus and imagery, so too does the world of fairytales. The picnic baskets from which people take food, or from which Sharon's brother produces a knife, spin us back to Red Riding Hood, in which a bed is of course a central prop. The entrance into the bed-chamber involves a flight of four or five stairs, descending, *Alice*-like, from halfway up the wall. And as in fairytales, the fixations are basic: food (the bed's constant hunger; the first two victims and their spoiled meal of fried chicken; Suzan's nightmare about eating bug pupae); sleep, of course (from whence dreams and sickness); sex (the bed pants like a dirty old man when Suzan gets undressed; a flashback shows a 'religious revivalist' orgy in the bed); and death. There's also a fascination with reversal, the undersides of things, turning things topsy-turvy. The Artist lives behind the painting instead of in front of it, the fire in the reflection is upside down, Diane is sucked into the bed through the underside, victims are seen upside-down as they fall into the bed's interior.

"A demon residing in a tree, on a whim changed himself into a breeze. While in this state he drifted one morning by a young maiden. He circled around, and back, surrounding her in his form. Gently he blew through her hair, her mind, and her dreams. For her seduction he decided to create a bed, unique for the occasion. […] But something tragic happened. Though he was a man in shape, he was still a demon, unnatural to her, and she died. […] His eyes turned cold, shattered in their grief. Tears of blood fell onto the bed. […] The blood left behind took root into the bed, and from this root a life sprang; and with this life, a hunger."

The best movies leave something elusive behind, a lingering haze that drifts through the mind like Haven Gillespie's "haunting refrain": a special something that seems to dance out of reach when you look directly. There are skilled directors out there whose work, for all its craft, will never possess this quality, which is a dream quality and far from common. *Death Bed* is steeped in this otherness, even though its conventional limitations are blatantly obvious. It's in this way that such a cheaply produced film, made at the very fringes of the industry, can stay with you after a major production has hurried faceless out of your memory. The lines crossed by *Death Bed* are an index of its eeriness. Set in the twilight between categories – between comedy and horror, art and artless, mundane and insane – it draws on energies lost to more sensible films. How great to see it emerge at last, a dream thought lost and forgotten, now revived in miraculous detail on DVD. Here's to the unique and lingering spell of *Death Bed*!

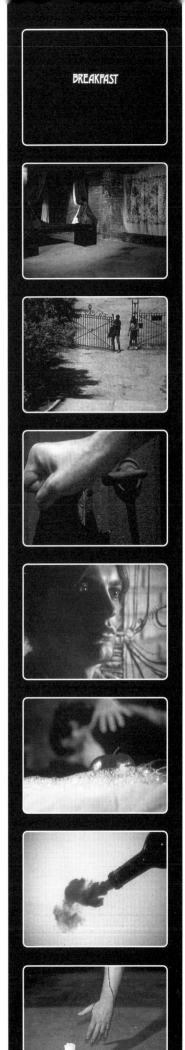

above:
Rosa Luxemburg (looking good for a
100-year-old Marxist theorist) as Sharon,
comforting her unfortunate brother.

opposite page, from the top:
Title card;
Bed;
Four newspaper headlines revealing both the
bed's chequered past and the film's
humorous tone;
A statue;
...and the same statue once the bed's demon
has taken out his rage on it.

Detroit, the centre of America's auto industry, is not the first place you'd think of when trying to place the provenance of *Death Bed*, a film whose blend of cool, faintly ominous countryside locations, crumbling stone houses and decadent daydreams seems to float in some sylvan limbo, far from the smoke of industry. Rock music is more in keeping with Detroit's image: Ted Nugent, Bob Seger, Alice Cooper, Glenn Frey of The Eagles, all came from the city, and cultish heavy rockers The MC5 typify the sort of aesthetic experience one expects from a town with motor oil running through its veins. Detroit's Motown label too, of course, has typically been identified with the city and industrialisation: 'hit factory' or 'production line' being common metaphors for the company's unstoppable momentum. Berry Gordy Jr. established his musical empire in a pokey Detroit house he dubbed 'Hitsville

USA', and many of the artists who made Motown famous, including The Four Tops, Smokey Robinson and Diana Ross, hailed from the city.

Nevertheless, *Death Bed*'s director George Barry was born on 21 August, 1949 in Royal Oak, a suburb of Detroit where he still lives today. In film terms, his most significant 'neighbour' was Sam Raimi, also born in Royal Oak, who began working on his *Evil Dead* dry-run, *Within the Woods*, around the same time that Barry was completing his only film to date, *Death Bed*. You couldn't ask for a greater contrast in fortunes: Raimi scored a cult success with *The Evil Dead*, and went on from there to become a Hollywood giant, director of the *Spider-Man* movies, and one of the biggest wheels in popular cinema; George Barry was, until quite recently, one of the least fêted directors imaginable – in fact, he was a complete unknown in America. *Death Bed* was only released – very briefly, on video – in Great Britain, Australia, New Zealand and Spain. Barry, though, was totally unaware of even this small exposure. In the early 1980s he'd sent the answer print of his movie, which was still without credits at the time, to a small L.A. company who said they were interested in obtaining UK video rights. He was offered $1,000 for a finished video master. Barry, though, was chronically short of cash and unable to shoot the missing credits, for which he needed an estimated $3,000. The answer print was promptly returned, and that seemed to be that. What Barry *didn't* know was that the 'interested party' had pirated a video master-copy of *Death Bed* before sending it back. It was by this route that *Death Bed* snuck out onto tape in Great Britain in the mid-1980s, on the supremely obscure 'Portland' label.[1] No Stateside deal was ever signed, and no bootleg ever ventured onto the shelves there.

But we're jumping too far ahead: let's return to 1950s Detroit, and meet George Barry, a young boy fascinated by the monsters and flickering shadows of the cinema. Our guide, Mr. Barry himself…

"I never thought of myself as being particularly artistic."

"By the mid 1950s I was old enough to go to the movie house on my own," Barry begins, "at least to matinees. I can still remember struggling to stay awake to see *This Island Earth* all the way to the end. The flaming spaceship streaking to its doom over the ocean, and the contrast of the colour of the water and the colour of the night sky surrounding the outdoor drive-in screen. That was yesterday, or the day before, and I was five years old. Now I'm eight, nine, ten years old and that is distant history, because I'm watching TV and the images are small and black and white and grey, but no less important. It's late on a Friday night and I'm watching *Shock Theater*, the Universal horror films of the thirties and forties. Maybe still struggling to stay awake – I'll drink a lot of Pepsi to help me manage. Better than drinking coffee to help you stay awake during your college classes, since the education of the *Shock Theater* classes will stay with you."

For anyone old enough to remember life pre-multiplex, recollections of the cinema are always bittersweet: so much of the magic has been lost. Barry describes the allure of a trip to the movies, pre-video: "Royal Oak had three movie houses, generally showing double bills that often changed twice a week. The heyday of the movie theatres was over, their numbers were dwindling, though I didn't know this as a kid. In a few years I would be taking the bus to downtown Detroit, where the big old movie houses, true picture palaces even in decay, were still surviving. In downtown Detroit there was also the wonderful lure of the smaller, even more run-down triple bill houses, some open twenty four hours a day. You could go in on an evening, catch the last showing of the current triple bill and somewhere around midnight, the new triple bill would start. One ticket, six movies, heaven on earth. In the early morning hours, I saw *Blow-Up* in such a theatre, the Colonial (God have mercy on you if you had to use the rest room). In the row in front of us, an older gentleman, a railway worker by his dress, explained the movie to the empty seat next to him. It seemed to me he had a clearer understanding of the film than the vast majority of critics at the time, at least judging by their reviews."

Barry began making films in the late 1960s while taking Arts and Philosophy courses at Wayne State University: "Like many at that time, I started making films in college," he explains, "though I didn't go to college to make films. Students interested in film were more likely to meet in a Humanities class. It was not a bustling centre of student filmmaking, there was far more activity in Ann Arbor at the University of Michigan. But there was a small film department, offering one or two standard film history courses and a couple of substandard film production courses." Undeterred, Barry began working on short films, his own and others, in 16mm black-and-white: "People seemed to work in either 16mm black-and-white or Super-8 colour. 16mm colour was too expensive and the jump to synced sound was a big one. Film projects often received a class credit, though their subject matter seldom had much to do with the class. This was the sixties of course, and everything was everything: the usual mixture of clumsy melodrama, predictable politics, lame jokes and well worn youthful angst. The work itself could be great fun, however."

Barry's early 16mm efforts are lost, presumed destroyed, but he has been kind enough to dredge up these recollections. A telephone call to an old friend and classmate, Tom Dalton, helped stir the details back into a semblance of order, resulting in the following synopsis for Barry's first short narrative film, shot "no later than 1970": the irresistibly monikered *Night of the Garbage*…

"I haven't a clue where any of the footage for this project is, or even if it still exists. Here's what we can remember of the story. We open with our lead ('OL' from now on) reading his parakeet's suicide note. The bird has hung itself in its cage. His girlfriend tries to console him, to little avail. He crumples up the note, tosses it into a corner filled with debris. The apartment is a one-room, mattress-on-the-floor, unwashed-clothes-strewn-about, posters-on-the-walls, no-furniture affair. OL would, at that time, be described as an underachiever, hiding out in college. He leaves by himself, not aware that his parakeet's note is being read in the corner, picked up off the floor by a hand that appears from a rubbish pile. This is where our memories have hit the wall. The garbage may have come to life through the ingestion (or some other chemical process) of laced roaches. In fact OL may have been smoking as he was reading the note and had thrown the roach into the corner, before he tossed the note. The hand's first appearance may have been to retrieve the still-lit roach, followed by puffs of smoke rising out of the

debris. What follows next, we can't remember. By this time, OL may have realised his garbage had taken on a separate existence. Let's define 'Garbage'. The 'Garbage' was not only waste paper, old food, used prophylactics, and broken guitar strings, but an assortment of all his material possessions; his books, records, clothes, letters, photos. OL may be pursuing his Garbage at this point. The Garbage is drinking, socialising, and OL discovers that his friends like his Garbage better than they like him. We shot a line-up scene. The Garbage has filed a harassment complaint against him. The Garbage lets him off the hook, by purposely failing to identify him." Barry pauses: "You've guessed the end by now. OL dejectedly goes back home, to discover his girl in bed with his Garbage. She's much happier now, so OL takes his dead bird, still hanging in its cage, and departs unnoticed."

Tom Dalton, who helped out on the project, adds, "One memory which sticks with me was rushing into the drugstore on campus, running up to the pharmacist and demanding five condoms – 'And I'm in a hurry!' (For the garbage creature's fingers, to be coated with Karo syrup.) And then there were the trips to a few pet shops, asking if they had any recently deceased parakeets. I think it was after I found myself lingering by a cage with a rather sickly looking bird that I came back to suggest we stick with the fake one."

While the special effects – essentially a chicken-wire-mesh contraption covered in garbage, with an actor inside – were fairly crude, Barry nevertheless remembers that the garbage creature cut a certain dash: "Hard as it may be to believe, it didn't look too bad on film, and we were not seeking realism anyway. It looked better than the *Creeping Terror* carpet monster, which I know is hardly reason to rejoice; but again, that really didn't matter."

The results of his labours assured Barry that film was worth pursuing. "The close-up footage of the parakeet hanging in its cage looked great," he remembers. "In fact, someone watching the rushes got upset with us, thinking we had put to death a real bird. I remember the footage from the opening scene looking as good as anything we shot, and I think the scene may have played well. I can't recall who played OL, but his girlfriend Val was a classmate of mine. Val photographed like a dream. She did the scene topless and was quite fetching. That was a problem with a lot of student films; many had a self-righteous, self-important air with noticeable lack of entertaining, exploitive elements. That's not to say all the stuff I worked on at the time was goofy, parody stuff, though goofy, parody, twist material seemed to suit the shorter film projects better. I later saw a film that used a parakeet or canary suicide/hanging joke. The joke played, and I regretted not finishing my film up."

Sadly, despite a week's filming, *Night of the Garbage* never did make it to the finish line: "We shot about forty minutes of footage," says Barry, "and we processed what we had, but the film was never cut. There might not have been even a rough assemblage, although we thought of *Night* as a fifteen minute film. Some of it looked okay, but I thought we had less than half of what we needed to finish. A few hundred dollars had been spent and I figured it would take another thousand dollars to complete. So that's where the film was left. Not that I gave up on it right away. For a while, I intended to get back to it, but I never did."

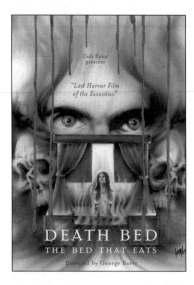

Delving back even further in time, Dalton recalls that *Night of the Garbage* had its roots in a class project to which Barry was assigned, based on what would now be called 'green issues'. Not so easily corralled, Barry had made a five-minute 16mm black-and-white silent short entitled *Mondo Crud*, which extolled the virtues of pollution. "I guess I was sophomoric even then," deadpans Barry, "though I still try to harbour the illusion that once I was a serious person. Young people are supposed to be serious, right? It's only when you get old, you're supposed to get foolish. *Mondo Crud*, I'm told, successfully screened on campus, along with a live musical accompaniment, on the same bill with Warhol's *Bike Boy*. Still, Hollywood failed to call."

In 1971, with his degree on hold (permanently as it turned out), Barry began to contemplate directing a full-length feature. His first impulse was to make a horror film, though he also toyed briefly with the idea of sexploitation. "The hardcore *Mona the Virgin Nymph* [dir: Howard Ziehm, 1970] had just been released," says Barry. "I was told by someone to call 'Uncle Tiny', a friendly fellow who owned a sexploitation house on the West Coast.[2] He confirmed that hardcore had just about taken over the market, and I went off the sexploitation idea. The only project I would have even considered shooting hardcore was *Weekend at Emily's*, a bouncy, literary sex romp graphically detailing the love-life we thought Emily Dickinson should have had. Edgar Allan Poe and Walt Whitman dropped in too, though old Walt might have been problematical relative to market requirements. But I wasn't going to shoot a hardcore sex film, and *Weekend* wasn't really a serious project. There was a script we had that bordered on hardcore due to the nature of the story. A woman has her teeth sharpened to help her to bite off the genitals of a fellow she has issues with. She does this, and is happy in her revenge. He's happy too, since the castration leads to his spiritual renewal. I know this sounds terribly arty, farty, Abélardy; and it may very well have been, though I wrote it as more of a mood piece with the emphasis on a series of obsessive, fetishistic images."[3]

Turning back to the horror genre, though not entirely abandoning the erotic themes he'd being toying with, Barry decided to build a story around a dream he'd had: about an engulfing, possibly carnivorous bed...

Making the Bed

But what kind of horror film to make? Barry describes the process of elimination: "Okay, a horror film. *Willard* opened big, let's do a *Willard* rip-off. If you don't have money, you can't have shame. We were just about to buy the rights (for $1000 – the contracts were drawn and everything) to a Thomas Disch short story about a girl and her roaches [*The Roaches*, written in 1965], when, I think, Leonard Kirtman[4] announced he was going into production on a similar 'girl and her roaches' story. We backed off and the other film was never made. Just as well, rip-offs are a snooze and I don't much care for roaches. I wrote other script treatments, but we must have decided on *Death Bed* by late '71 or early '72."

Barry decided to go for it. A colour 16mm feature film, a horror story of sorts, to be blown up for theatrical release. Part-comic, part-surreal, with the monstrous 'bed that eats' as the focus. Using $10,000 of his own money, he began work on *Death Bed*, a project that would span five years

and cost around $30,000. "I'm not good at approaching people for money," he admits, "though at the end, a few investors came in for a few hundred to a couple of thousand dollars. My memory of the production is spending a few thousand dollars at a time, running out of money, then scraping up a few thousand dollars more to get to the next stage."

Shooting commenced at the Gar Wood Mansion outside Detroit in spring 1972, with two days spent filming exteriors. Hired from a rock band who were encamped there at the time, the location was suggested by actor Dave Marsh ('Beardsley' in the film), then working for the music magazine *Creem*: apparently it had already hosted a number of underground music-biz parties. Says Barry: "We shot only two days at the Mansion, since I was worried we might get thrown off the property at any time. A rock band was renting the place, we rented from them and I suspected they didn't have the right to sub-lease. Sure enough, a representative of the owner showed up the morning of the second day, but to my relief, didn't give us any trouble at all. In hindsight, the fellow may have been disappointed we weren't shooting a naked witches' coven scene on the lawn. I was told later that the owner wanted to buy the adjoining properties, so it was in his interest to be as much of a nuisance to his neighbours as possible, thus encouraging them to sell to him. Later, it was rented out to a motorcycle gang: there was a weekend biker party and the place got trashed. In *Death Bed*, a statue at the Mansion weeps blood: later we dissolve to a still of the broken head of that statue. That was taken from a newspaper photo covering the aftermath of the biker party."

Although not onscreen for very long, the mansion is an excellent location, bringing a decadently aristocratic feel to the film. "It was an odd place," muses Barry, "built by Gar Wood, an inventor who designed and raced speedboats. He could steer one of his speed boats right into the house, an indoor boat dock. The water was close: the old breakwall had failed and the water's edge was getting closer. The marble was quarried and brought over from Italy. A huge impressive ballroom, the full height and nearly the length of the Mansion, almost divided it in two. Gar Wood lived on one side of the ballroom, his wife on the other side. They didn't get along, and that way they wouldn't have to bump into each other unexpectedly in the course of the day. Their son, Gar Wood, Jr., shuttled by a nanny back and forth across the ballroom from one parent to the other, wanted little to do with the Mansion when he grew up. Had I known there would be no trouble from the owner while we shot at the Mansion, I would have adapted the script to the location and extended the shooting time there. But my experience was with productions where there was neither money nor influence to secure locations, so I had developed a catch-as-catch-can mentality." (There was a brief opportunity to film inside the Mansion, which Barry quickly exploited for a flashback sequence exploring the bed's origins. We see the bed at one end of the Gar Wood ballroom, a player organ visible in a corner: the French doors to the rear of the bed lead out onto the stone patio seen at the beginning of the film.)

The interior of the small, windowless stone building, to which the bed is banished for much of the film, was actually a set built a few miles away, in a studio rented from the film's soundmen, Jim Viola and Tom Sherry. The main bedchamber was located upstairs in their old two storey commercial/industrial building in Highland Park,

Detroit. "The entire room was a set," Barry explains, "but most of the brick was real. The fireplace was built into the wall with plastic brick sheeting that we painted. That's why, in at least a shot or two, you can see smoke pouring out into the room, since the fireplace had no venting. In the film, the door to that room was the door to a stone shed in Lapeer, Michigan, some sixty miles away, where we also shot some of the exteriors. The bed met its end in a rock quarry, whose location I can't remember, though it probably wasn't any further away than Lapeer."

The core of the movie was filmed over three-to-four weeks in the spring/summer of 1972 – this being the intended duration of the whole shoot. However, delays soon crept in and further filming resumed in the fall of '72, including key scenes from the fiery climax of the film. Still there was more to do: in 1973 another weekend shoot was arranged, adding further material. "Going over-schedule gave me time to rethink and rewrite elements of the story that weren't working," says Barry. "My script was not a proper shooting script, and we didn't have a production manager: that was probably my biggest mistake, though I made so many mistakes, it's hard to rank them. Most of the time, the actors had their lines beforehand, and at times there was some rehearsal. But I think the longer we went on, the less rehearsal there was. Some of this was due to time restraints and exhaustion, but I was also finding I often preferred the unrehearsed or little-rehearsed takes."

Death Bed's weird, listless acting performances play a key role in generating the film's uniquely dislocated atmosphere. Barry explains how they came about: "I remember at the time of shooting, others on the film being concerned about my seeming lack of regard for the flat tone of some of the performances, and I did think, 'Should I be worried about this?' But I also remember feeling that while the actors are not in a soap-opera and the troubles their characters face are certainly not standard soap-opera difficulties, the delivery of their lines should still range from low-to-middle soap-opera recitation – earnest and banal. This was more of an instinctual notion, that if the story is a bit over-the-top, the acting should run counter. If the bed is outrageous, the people should be 'downed out' a bit. The cast, I'm certain, could have realised more expressive, dramatic characterisations, had they been asked." And was there any 'pharmaceutical assistance' for the spaced-out performers? Barry laughs: "Substance indulgence? No, not really. One performer may have been under the influence of spirits for a brief period of time, but that's about it. I knew none of the principals in the cast before *Death Bed*'s pre-production, except for David Marsh who played Beardsley. It's odd, in a way, to think of Dave as a principal, since, even though he's all through the film, he was on the movie for only two days. We always knew someone else was going to do the voice. We cast from the south-eastern Michigan area. Most of the principals may have been in or just out of college at the time: some were theatre students, though I don't remember if any went to Wayne State. Maybe Rusty did. There were friends, family and crew playing some of the smaller roles. Patrick Spence-Thomas, Beardsley's voice, and Linda Bond, who played the resurrected girl, were from Canada."

Barry's offbeat sense of humour is readily apparent in the film, ranging from broad (e.g. when the bed drinks Pepto Bismol after overdoing it) to surreal (Rusty Russ's reaction to his skeletal hands). "We were shameless with the 'Monty Python' cheap laughs," he admits. "We would go for a laugh at almost any time, no matter how low. My poor grandmother reading a lurid sex paper in the bed. She wasn't worried about it, she thought the camera was so far away, no one would be able to tell what she was reading. Now, a guy who would use his own, truly beloved grandmother for a cheap laugh is capable of any crime against humour."

On a subtler note, the loquacious spirit of Aubrey Beardsley, sharing his poetic reminiscences from behind the painting where he's trapped, adds humour of a different kind: "I was lucky to find Patrick Spence-Thomas," Barry says. "He was the straight man for the bed. I initially did the film's sound transfers at his studio in Toronto. He agreed to do the voice of Beardsley, not to mention mixing the soundtrack on spec. Since I never made any money on the film, he never received payment. At least he's probably forgotten me, since he had no real cause to forgive me. His voice-over was very good, but I wrote too many bridging passages."

In a role that seems perfect for the director of such a personal, idiosyncratic film, Barry appears as the demon, seen briefly in a handful of tight facial close-ups: however, he is quick to dispel any impression that he chose this pivotal cameo for artistic reasons: "Yes, I'm the eyes of the demon. But this was not a preconceived cute cameo – we had something else planned but it didn't work out. I was cheap, available and, as I remember, the only guy around at the time, except for the photographer. We probably should have used someone older. I also did the voice of the gangster. When we were dubbing at the Spence-Thomas sound studio, we ran short on voices. Food was delivered to the studio, so we could work and eat at the same time. If someone said one of the delivery people dubbed one of the characters, I wouldn't deny it." *Death Bed*'s Canadian assistant cameraman Bob Gallant (who worked on David Cronenberg's *The Brood*, as best boy) played the demon in a long shot at the end of the film: "Bob died young, in the early- to mid-eighties," Barry recalls. "I never heard the cause. He was a nice enough looking fellow, but very boyish in appearance, which is why I didn't use his face for the demon." As for the bed and its various rumblings: "I'm almost certain the bed was voiced by more than one person. Patrick Spence-Thomas may have done the laughs/giggles and some of the bed's utterances. I may have done the snoring. Ron Medico did a number of voice bits, he's the minister for sure. Jock Brandis [gaffer and special effects man] played the Minister onscreen, making his acting credits *Death Bed* and *Scanners*!"

Brandis, seen briefly in the 'psychic commune' scene of *Scanners*, worked as a grip on David Cronenberg's *The Brood*, *Scanners*, *Videodrome* and *The Dead Zone*, as well as David Lynch's *Blue Velvet* and John Waters's *Serial Mom* – quite a tally of left-field projects! He also shot a film for Ed Hunt in 1974, called *Diary of a Sinner*. Says Barry: "Jock Brandis left Canada and movie-making a few years back. At the end of the 1960s he met Kurt Vonnegut in Africa. Jock was with a Canadian version of the Peace Corps attached to relief efforts for Biafra, and Vonnegut had flown in to write an article about that nation's impending fall. Vonnegut said something like, 'you know, someone like you, who's been here for a while, should be writing this story'. Thirty years later Jock did just that, in his novel *The Ship's Cat* (2000). He also went back to Africa, and his DIY attitude, so evident in *Death Bed*'s special effects, has lead to an invention which may be a

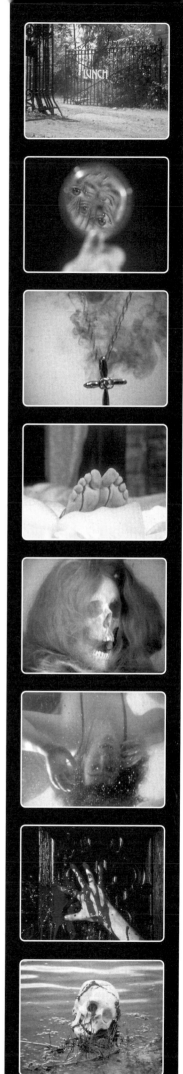

above:
Bob Gallant as the demon and Linda Bond as the girl, who is later resurrected. Gallant was assistant cameraman: he and Bond were in a relationship at the time and lived together in Toronto.

opposite page:
The 'Dinner' sequence:
Diane (Demene Hall) is dragged into the bed (pictures 2, 3 and 4);
Sharon's brother tries to lend a hand but ends up with troubles of his own (pictures 5, 6, 7 and 8).

below:
George Barry with his daughter Darcy in the summer of 1988.

genuine aid in combating Third World hunger."[5] Brandis was responsible for creating the bed's erupting digestive juices (the 'stomach' itself was housed in a tank downstairs from the bed chamber in the Highland Park studio-space). The digestive juices, Barry reveals were, "A water soap mix, heavy on the soap, with yellow food colouring, bubbled out through an air compressor-pump-thingamajig. Jock was really invaluable to the film. He was the gaffer, equipment manager, special effects and everything else guy. For instance, the professional stage blood we bought looked awful. So with water, food colour and a little flour, paste, or something, he came up with phoney blood that not only looked okay, but also, when it spilled out and hit the air, would actually darken like coagulated blood."

The Cronenberg connections keep on coming: *Death Bed* cameraman Robert Fresco shot David Secter's *Winter Kept Us Warm* (1965), a Canadian drama which Cronenberg says converted him from a University of Toronto science major into a filmmaker.[6] Fresco's subsequent work has largely been in Canadian television and documentaries, the latter including studies of jazz musicians such as Cecil Taylor, Archie Shepp and Hugh Masekela. "I had not met Robert Fresco before pre-production on *Death Bed*," Barry says. "I was up in Toronto to talk to a couple of people and check out some motion picture equipment available for budget rental. Someone connected me to Jock Brandis and I think I initially approached *him* to be the cameraman. He was reluctant to be the director of photography, I think he was the one who mentioned Robert Fresco, though they may not have had a close personal or working relationship. I can't remember what I saw of his work, if any, before he agreed to do my movie."

Among the other friends to have played a part in the making of *Death Bed*, Barry found his girlfriend of the time, Maureen Petrucci, invaluable. Her initial role as art director soon grew, Barry admits, to include "endless hours on the film during pre-production and production, taking responsibility for chores far outside an art director's tasks."

Bed-Post Production

Although *Death Bed* was edited piecemeal over the years that it was shot, George Barry and his friend Ron Medico, an experienced TV editor, did the fine cutting in about three months during 1976. As Barry recalls, "The editing room was a spare bedroom in my home and the editing bench was an old door set up on sawhorses with square holes cut out, and pillowcases attached to catch the film." Better equipment was available for short stretches, but *Death Bed* was mainly cut on a Moviola Jr., a little known and technically rather limited machine. Using it was, in Barry's words, "akin to baking a cake over an open campfire!"

It wasn't long before the eponymous bed began to exert its influence on the overall structure of the film. Says Barry: "Whenever we got away from the bed, we seemed to be in trouble. So we cut the footage that seemed too distant from our 'star', based on a principle of, 'Cut out what doesn't work, leave in what does... and do the best with what you've got.'" When pressed on the unconventional style of the film he adds, "Our 'practical' choices came from our tastes and I suppose our tastes weren't very 'practical' at all. Commercial considerations fell by the wayside." Among the scenes to be dropped were a shower scene, and – perhaps most tantalisingly – a sequence featuring actress Demene Hall participating in dream experiments at a mysterious laboratory. Scenes featuring Rusty Russ and Demene Hall visiting a gay bar were also excised. "The cutting of those scenes, like the dream lab scene in the beginning, was no fault of the cast. They were either ill-conceived, or just didn't fit in," says Barry.

Their removal caused a few headaches for editor Ron Medico, when dealing with the scene where Sharon, Suzan and Diane drive out to the mansion. "Ron remembers how he had to push that sequence in the car," Barry explains. "The trouble was: Diane meets Suzan in the dream lab, and Diane meets Sharon in the gay bar, and we cut both those scenes, even though both were shot with synched sound; and we had little enough of that. Neither scene was very good, but the major problem was we felt they kept the film away from the bed too long. So the girls just show up and their interior car footage became more important than originally intended." The solution Barry and Medico came up with was to use the car scene for exposition; but by doing it via Suzan's dazed, child-like voice-over, and the strange sideways glances of Sharon and Diane, a creepy sense of paranoia emerged, justifying the new slant and making what could have been a blatant patch-job into something special.

With a rough-cut established, Barry cast around for someone to provide a music track. He eventually turned to Mike McCoy, "a tall thin fellow in his twenties who had a hearing aid. When he didn't want to deal with things, I remember, he would turn his hearing aid off or pretend to forget to turn it on. We got along well enough and I think he did a good job, apart from the music for the opening and end credits. It was my fault, I had asked him to do something of that nature. What was I thinking about? I thought it would be amusing, but it's not funny 'strange' or funny 'ha-ha'. It's funny 'doesn't work at all'."[7]

"*Death Bed* would have been better served if the music had been planned earlier and we had given greater attention to it," Barry says. "Ron and I talked about this in the last year or so. He wishes *Death Bed* had more music.

I do too. I should have had Beardsley talk less, we should have used music more to bridge certain narrative jumps. Dreams are set down in words, when they're often better represented with image and sound."

Another decision that Barry regrets was adhering to an eighty-minute running time: "Without that standard, the film would have come in at sixty to seventy minutes. It might have had similar pacing, but it definitely would have been shorter." I mention to Barry that *Death Bed*, unlike most other horror films, has an almost gentle rhythm: "I think you're right. If I had thought about that at the time, I would have probably said to myself 'What are we doing? We need slow walks down long dark corridors, things jumping out at you, shocks, more spooky stuff.' While I was never overly fond of those slow walks, dark corridors or things jumping out at you, I do think shocks and spooky stuff can be quite fun. I guess I didn't have them enough in mind, or I wasn't in my right mind, I don't know."

The sound was transferred and mixed at Patrick Spence-Thomas's studio in Toronto, while film processing, editing, the negative cut and the answer print were done in Detroit; by which time the film had cost approximately $30,000. With just a few remaining jobs to be done, including the addition of credits to the beginning and end, the film was virtually finished. All that remained was to find a buyer…

"We like to think we cheat less…"

Unfortunately, Barry's problems were just beginning. "In 1977, just after the 16mm answer print was finally done, we had a screening in Toronto for the Canadian contingent of the crew. A Canadian film distributor was at the screening. He offered me a distribution agreement for Canada, which I signed. Since he had only a small company, he couldn't afford to blow up *Death Bed* to 35mm, but now, he told me, I could go to a Toronto lab and they would blow up the movie on the basis of a deferred payment, secured by this contract. So off I go, contract in hand to the film lab. Now I'm not saying the fellow at the lab wasn't civil, in fact he was very polite. But I remember him handling this Canadian film distribution agreement as if it were used toilet paper."

If the Canadian deal didn't come off, things were no better in the USA. Over the next couple of years, Barry travelled to Los Angeles and New York City several times, making the rounds of the small film distributors. "Most simply didn't like the movie or didn't think they could make any money with it," he recalls. "The late seventies were tough times for some of these operations. The drive-ins and urban action houses were closing, along with the tax shelters that some distributors had been using to finance their releases." Those that did show interest were put off by the blow-up costs. The tenor of these meetings can be gauged by the attitude of one sales manager for L.A. distributors Boxoffice International, who took a fancy to the movie. Barry recalls, "I was in L.A. in 1977/78, screening *Death Bed* on the cheap off a flatbed. Steve Kaplan came over from Boxoffice International, saw the film and expressed interest. His sales pitch was, 'Don't worry about us cheating you because we're going to. But we like to think we cheat less.' A clever line and Steve was a clever lad. Harry Novak was out of the country at the time, his brother would have to approve a deal. I showed the film to him in a proper screening room and he simply

wasn't interested. Steve then said, 'Don't worry about it, you wouldn't have gotten much anyway. We like to think we cheat less, but we cheat just as much as everybody else.' I saw Steve three or four more times over the course of the next year or so. I believe he had burnt his bridges with Roger Corman at New World, and Atlas Films, and he would go on to burn his bridges with Boxoffice International in a big way. Steve maintained healthy relationships with a number of sub-distributors, often (I suspect) at the expense of the companies he worked for. I remember him expressing pride in his TV ad campaign for *Rattlers*. Dark screen with just the title, *Rattlers*, the narration something like, 'This movie is so terrifying, so extreme, we are not ALLOWED to show you any scenes on television.' Actually the movie was so tame, Steve told me, that he couldn't find anything in the film to use in the ad. Steve's way of saying goodbye to Boxoffice International was to give the *actual* grosses of *Rattlers* to its producers. But the mistake they made, at least in Steve's mind, was to sue Boxoffice International, not the Novaks personally. That's when Boxoffice closed and resurfaced, I think, as Valiant International. So the *Rattlers* producers may have ended up with an empty judgment against a defunct company. I called up Boxoffice around that time."[8]

A call from New York raised Barry's hopes for a while: someone had seen *Death Bed* and was ready to pay money up front: "I fly to New York, there's no money. Oops, he didn't know the film would have to be blown up. He'd seen a 16mm print, but assumed the film had been shot in 35mm. He still had a distribution agreement for me. I didn't sign it. I found out he would have signed over the contract to another company. That way he would have had to pay out only a percentage of a percentage. This happened, in one form or another, a few times." The whole affair was becoming extremely dispiriting. As Barry dryly summarizes: "The Nos were Nos, the Maybes were Nos and the Yeses were Nos."

But Barry was determined not to be steamrollered by despair into accepting a crummy deal: "To answer the obvious question, 'After a while, why didn't I just sign anything to get the film into release?' – I was looking for a distributor who would blow up *Death Bed* and who would pay me something if the film made any money. I wasn't being totally naive; I never expected to receive whatever producer's share was in the distribution agreement. But I wanted to get *something*. So I found myself not following up deals or signing agreements where I truly felt there would never be any return. After hawking the movie for two or three years, my only choice seemed to be, 'Sign the film away and expect nothing in return, not even a halfway decent release print.' Even though most of the money in the film was my own, there was still some outside investment in the movie, and people had worked on spec, so I was reluctant to sign a worthless contract. I know that's a contradiction; people receive the same from an unreleased film as they do from a film in release with a worthless distribution agreement: nothing. But still... In the early eighties I talked to a few people about a video release. The last person I remember speaking with was Martin Margulies aka Johnny Legend. We never met, I think we had a couple of phone conversations. He seemed like a nice enough fellow, and at this point all I wanted was for him to put in enough money for *Death Bed* to have a decent video release print. However, he was strapped for

DINNER

above:
Sharon communes with the artist.

cash, since he had just produced *My Breakfast with Blassie* (1983). After that, I pretty much forgot about the movie."

And so there the entire ten-year struggle ended: with an unreleasable film and $30,000 down the drain. A gloomy end for a project steeped in dreams... except, it wasn't the end at all. They say truth is stranger than fiction: in this case, truth took the cliché as a challenge...

The Mouse of Destiny

A lot of things have changed since that day, sometime in the early 1980s, when Barry consigned his print of *Death Bed* to the attic – not least the presence of the internet in our lives. As a research tool the internet is invaluable: a book like this would have taken fifteen years, not five, to complete; and without it, George Barry would never have realised that a pirate release of his movie had attracted devotees abroad. I began researching this book in January 2001, and at the top of my wish-list of directors was George. As luck would have it, in September that year a film fan called Daniel Craddock posted an appreciative review of *Death Bed* on his website *Lightsfade*: which is where the various threads of this story come together at last...

That anyone should even have heard of *Death Bed*, much less seen it and bought it on video, came as a great surprise to Barry himself. With *Death Bed* rejected at every turn, he'd been discouraged from continuing as a filmmaker. "There were a number of projects I tried to get off the ground," he says, "but I was never able to secure enough money to do them on other than a piecemeal basis, the same way *Death Bed* was done. I didn't have the energy, confidence or resolve to continue on that road. If I'm honest, it was really a lack of courage to undergo a similar pounding."

No wonder. One night, though, in September 2001, after working late compiling a database for his book-selling business, Barry decided to unwind by browsing the internet for information on a forties movie actress he'd seen on TV that evening. His enquiries led him to the movie website and fan forum 'Scarlet Street'. While scanning the topics under discussion, he clicked on a post by the French film journalist Jean-Claude Michel, who was asking for information about a very strange, very obscure movie. The title? *Death Bed: The Bed That Eats*...

Barry was astonished: not only was a pirated version of his movie out there in the world, but it was exciting connoisseurs of the *cine-fantastique*: Michel's query included a link to Daniel Craddock's online review. Craddock too was asking readers if they knew anything about the film. Barry wrote to him, and soon an interview was posted to accompany the review.

When I began work on this book a Google search for information about *Death Bed* turned up nothing. Fortunately, my good friend Marc Morris, of the website *Mondo Erotico*, knew of my eagerness to interview Barry, and a year later in January 2002, he too tried a search. The timing was perfect: Marc found the *Lightsfade* link and within days Daniel Craddock put me in touch with Barry.

I was overjoyed, and it wasn't long before the notion of a DVD release for *Death Bed* came to mind. Early in 2002 I'd been approached by Nico B, of Cult Epics DVD, to write liner notes for his release of Agustín Villaronga's *Tras el cristal*: so, when a mooted DVD release of *Death Bed* by Lightsfade fell through, I sent Nico a video copy to

see what he thought. He loved it, and *Death Bed* received, at long last, its debut release in America. There was even a world theatrical premiere, at the San Francisco Independent Film Festival, or Indiefest, on 15 February 2003 – a little late, perhaps, some twenty six years after the film's completion. But unlike Rip Van Winkle, *Death Bed* awoke into a new world that had still not quite caught up with it...

Who's Been Sleeping in My Bed?
– the Fairy Tale Life of a Cult Classic

Now the facts and names and dates have been marshalled for this least documented of silver-screen dreams, there are still questions to be asked regarding its unique provenance. Barry's thoughts on his creative process give some insight into this most idiosyncratic of horror films: "Horror and fantasy films have been my favourite type of movie since I was a child. But I believe a horror film can be more comforting than a fairy tale. Fairy tales possess an unrelenting logic similar to dreams; they can be frightening and inevitable. As a kid and through my early teens, I enjoyed reading science fantasy and horror literature. I read a fair amount of spooky stories, English and American. Poe, of course, H.P. Lovecraft, many others. I was too old to be reading fairy tales when I was a young teenager, but I started college at sixteen and soon I wasn't too old any more to be reading fairy tales again. I liked Oscar Wilde's fairy tales, and that lead me to read *Melmoth the Wanderer*. Years later, this may have lead to my interest in myth and folklore. Why did I use Beardsley in *Death Bed*? Hmmm. I think, early in the writing, I decided the bed was never going to talk, and I needed a device to supply the film's history. Why the picture, I don't know. *The Picture of Dorian Gray*? And if it's a Wilde connection, that could lead to Beardsley. Did I come up with Beardsley because I thought Dave Marsh looked like Beardsley? I went to school with Dave. I know, at least in my company, people were not stopping Dave in the street and asking 'Are you Aubrey Beardsley, famous long-deceased English artist?' Maybe it was because of Maureen Petrucci, the girl I was going with at the time. I felt Maureen would be able to draw a decent Beardsley imitation. Maureen did most of the art and set direction for the film and actually co-produced the movie while we were filming."

Asked about his possible esoteric interests (after all, the period from which *Death Bed* draws was rife with the occult fascinations of Madame Blavatsky and the Temple of the Golden Dawn), Barry offers this response: "I don't *believe in* the supernatural or the occult, but I believe they exist. I don't believe God or the Devil exist outside our bodies, but they may exist inside. A person may have faith there is a God/Devil, they don't need science for proof. A person may have faith there is no God/Devil, they don't need science, either. I've had people tell me true ghost tales. Some I thought were BS-ing me. At least one I took at her word. What about ghost stories and horror movies? Some may be creepy and unnerving, but many are soothing and reassuring. They relate troublesome and fearful things inside us, often using a greater restraint than are granted to us by fairy tales and our dreams." The stakes that Christianity attributes to the occult leave Barry unimpressed, and he explains in terms that make you wish he would direct again, perhaps from the works of

opposite page:
Images from the final scenes charting the end of the bed's malediction.

below:
The bed's fiery demise.

Wyndham Lewis, or even Marlowe: "I'm inclined to find Faust stories a bit silly in their narcissism, the exaggerated value they attach to an individual's soul. The Devil wouldn't really have to make the effort to acquire souls one at a time. What he would need is a very large office with lots of staff. Three shifts of clerks going twenty four hours a day to handle the workload. He wouldn't need to advertise, he could rely on word of mouth. He wouldn't need a prime location, people would come out of their way. The lines of applicants would wrap around blocks and city squares and perhaps the cities themselves. I see shorter versions of these lines every day. The purchase prices could be very modest. If the Devil needed the one-on-one contact of this process, he could spend even less, since so many of us feel so alone. People would give up or offer their souls for nothing, they would be grateful for the attention!"

And dreams? The 'dreamlike' analogy is positively invited for a film about a bed that kills its occupants, not to mention the presence of a shuddersome sequence in which a dreamer is invited to eat bugs from a silver platter, or sees the pages of a book turn into mirrors that capture the flames of the fireplace. If the whole film feels like a dream, these dreams inside dreams are perfect analogies for our own night-time wanderings: cliché or not, 'life is but a dream' is still one of the metaphysical front-runners when it comes to a view of existence. Barry sees the dream angle in an active light; as a warning not to let go of them: "People not only forget their dreams, they often forget *about* their dreams. They forget about the process of dreaming: not only the details, but the event itself. If the journey is more important than the destination, then dreams are constantly changing journeys whose destinations we might not want to reach anyway. Some people use dream books with numbers, and others analyse their dreams according to physiological disciplines, and that's okay, I guess. Better that, than turning your back on yourself and disregarding them altogether. *Death Bed* is not the only instance where I've used a dream I've had for story material. I wish, in *Death Bed*, I'd incorporated the dream elements into the story structure in a less simplistic manner. *Death Bed* came from a dream and, to begin with, I wrote the story as more of a fairy tale than a horror film. We filmed the story as more horror film than fairy tale, then in the editing process, *Death Bed* tried to return to its fairy tale origins. However hazy my thinking might have been, I planned *Death Bed* to be a genre film, an exploitation movie: a fairy tale in the comfort of a horror film with commercial considerations haphazardly thrown in."

As a long-time devotee of European horror cinema, I suggest to Barry that there's a very European feel to some of his imagery, especially the story behind the creation of the bed, and the demon who turns into a breeze. These are not typical drive-in movie notions! Says Barry: "The European look to the film has been mentioned to me before. This was not a preconceived notion. When we viewed the rushes of the first interiors, I can remember feeling they were too bright. Robert Fresco and I talked it over and I remember him feeling the same way. Then I believe, Jock Brandis, the gaffer, told me Robert had a tendency to utilise whatever lights he had at his disposal. So Robert made adjustments and we returned some of the lighting equipment to the rental house. This is a long way of saying, the film became darker, even though we had to keep in mind that the footage was intended to be blown up to 35mm."

If I had to guess which horror fans might appreciate *Death Bed* most, I would hazard a guess at the Europhile contingent, so I asked Barry if he's familiar with European horror cinema, citing a handful of the major players: "Of the directors you mentioned, I've seen Mario Bava's work the most. I certainly appreciate why he's been so influential. Could he be, in the West, the most influential genre director/cinematographer of the sixties? Or is that an overstatement? I quite like Michele Soavi's work. In fact, his *Dellamorte Dellamore*, and del Toro's *Cronos*, are probably my two favourite horror films of the nineties."

Unlike some, Barry is comfortable discussing possible influences: "Films that deeply affect you may not be well remembered. But I remember, when I was seven or eight years old, seeing *Rodan* and *The Hunchback of Notre Dame*, the version photographed by Michel Kelber.[9] I was fascinated, not only by the story of *Rodan*, but by the fact that the people in the film were all Japanese; and I was intrigued, not only by the story, but by the look, the colour of *The Hunchback of Notre Dame*. Now neither of these I would list among my favourite movies, but what might they have started me dreaming about?" As a further guide to the mental world of *Death Bed*, he offers the following list of movies:

The Wizard of Oz
Citizen Kane
La grande bouffe
Persona
Faster, Pussycat! Kill! Kill!
Scrooge aka *A Christmas Carol (1951 version)*
Woman in the Dunes

"I really, really like these movies," he adds, "but I don't know how influential they were on me. I would have seen *La grande bouffe* after the core of *Death Bed* was shot. It may have influenced me during post-production. It certainly is one of my favourite films. Overall, I may like Buñuel as well as any filmmaker." I mention that Cocteau springs to mind when I think of *Death Bed*: "Well, there is that magical bed in *La belle et la bête* isn't there? And I may very well have seen the film before the making of *Death Bed*, though if I had, there wasn't a conscious connection."

Rediscovery

"I drink tea from the cup of my memory,
Strong & bitter, it is my heart's blood & reason,
To say everything has its fixed place, its season,
Denies refuge in the shadows,
Always now just becoming my past."
© George Barry.

George Barry is in his fifties now, with two children, a thriving online bookselling business, and, for which we must be thankful, an attentive cardiologist – 2005 saw him enter hospital for a successful heart procedure. As those who own the DVD of *Death Bed* will already know from his brief but welcome video introduction, he is a warm, humorous, and unfailingly modest man – during the long correspondence he and I have enjoyed these last few years, he has consistently discussed his movie with a dry wit and habitual self-effacement. This modesty, to a degree, characterises his response to its belated 'rediscovery' too,

but there's no doubt he's quietly over the moon, knowing there are people dotted all over the world who adore *Death Bed* and consider it something special. He's aware that for some people it's a film to laugh 'at' as well as laugh 'with': not everyone is uncritical, or forgiving of the low-budget nature of the production. Nevertheless, the majority of those who've commented on the film since its arrival on DVD have done so in a spirit of sometimes bemused, sometimes rapturous admiration: "I've received far more positive response to *Death Bed* than I could ever possibly have imagined years ago when we made the film," he told the editors of the book *Gods in Polyester*.[10] Having watched the film emerge from the shadows, he says, "It seems to me that at least some people like the movie along the lines on which it was designed. Twenty five years ago, at the screenings I had for cast, crew, friends, family and guests, people laughed and told me they liked the movie. But that's what you would expect. The screenings attempting to secure distribution were, for the most part, pretty dismal." Barry is comfortable, even relieved, to know that audiences laugh when confronted by the film's weirdness: "While it's not a comedy, it hard for me to imagine a person liking, or even being interested in *Death Bed*, if they didn't find some parts of it amusing."

It's a far cry from the disappointment of the 1980s: "From the mid-eighties to when I found out about the film's pirated release, I didn't think about *Death Bed* a lot," he says. A painful memory? "No, more a tiring one. During the film's long post-production there were plenty of occasions where I felt like chucking the project, but even though the film was never blown up for theatrical release, when I did think back about it, I found myself feeling glad I finished. Despite a striking lack of financial success, arduous work seen through to the end can offer a certain degree of inner satisfaction. However, discovering that *Death Bed* has found a small, appreciative, if possibly demented, audience, is a great bonus, a gift really, for me. To be honest with you, if I had looked into a crystal ball before shooting the movie and had seen *Death Bed* would take five years to complete and then not receive a theatrical release, I would have rewritten the story and attempted a more conventional, commercially acceptable movie. Whether it would have worked or not, I don't know. If I had looked into the same crystal ball after shooting the movie, I might have adopted a what-the-hell attitude and Ron and I would have edited the film a bit differently. It's funny, had I found out twenty years ago about the *Death Bed* pirate, along with some modest positive feedback, that might have been enough of a boost to see me through to something else. I never stopped writing, though my output, which was never voluminous, diminished and after a while I just wrote for myself."

Epilogue

So with a symmetry as poetic as the film itself, *Death Bed*, a film of fairytale imaginings, enjoys a fairytale happy ending and a wonderful new beginning, emerging on DVD to many a rapturous and admiring review. George Barry's celluloid vision has at last taken its place as one of the strangest treasures of American horror. For sure, its new audience is modest in size, but I know people who adore *Death Bed*, who will probably watch it ten or fifteen times again as the years go by. And I'll be one of them: because even after talking at great length to this most genial and candid of directors, even after viewing the film through the lens of new facts and background stories, *Death Bed* retains a mystery, etched into the grain like a magic spell, ensuring that it will *always* feel like cinema from a parallel universe. It's a movie where dreams and reality are interchangeably bizarre, where humour, horror and surreal imagination are tucked up together so tightly they've merged into a single unique night-beast… There's nothing else like it, and if you love it there is nowhere else to turn: you have to go back to the bed.

Footnotes

1   This pirate copy was then pirated again by someone else for the Spanish version, which is the scarcest of the lot.

2   'Uncle Tiny' can be seen in person in *The Weird World of LSD* (dir: Robert Ground, 1967), playing a man who can score acid, but can't afford to buy any food.

3   Born in Britanny in the late 11th Century, Pierre Abélard was a scholastic philosopher of Aristotelian bent, who brought dialectical thinking to the ecclesiastical teachings of the day, and thus suffered persecution by the Church. As the result of a contested love affair with a female student, Heloise, he was castrated by a gang led by the girl's uncle, after which his teachings took on a more devotional form…

4   Director of *Carnival of Blood* and *Curse of the Headless Horseman* (see review section).

5   The story is at www.peanutsheller.org.

6   *Cronenberg on Cronenberg*, ed. Chris Rodley, Faber.

7   On a personal note, it was my great pleasure in 2003 to accept an invitation from George Barry to rescore the passages he was unhappy with for the DVD release of *Death Bed*, and add music of my own to the beginning and end credits. George suggested a track from *Luminous Darkness*, the first album by my group Cyclobe: we set about adapting it to match the mood of the film, adding piano and phased organ to the album version, lending – I hope – a 'progressive' psychedelic feel.

8   Boxoffice International closed down in 1978, and Valiant International appeared the following year. "'May I talk to Steve?' I naively inquired. 'Kaplan is no longer with us.' SLAM. It's the only time I can remember the phone being slammed down on me – old girlfriends excepted…" see the Frederick Friedel interview for more on Boxoffice International.

9   *Notre Dame de Paris* (1956 dir: Jean Delannoy).

10   Succubus Press, 2004.

GEORGE BARRY: FILMOGRAPHY AS DIRECTOR

1969 (approx)	*Mondo Crud* (short) (also: writer / producer)
1970 (approx)	*Night of the Garbage* (short - unfinished) (also: writer / producer)
1977	*Death Bed: The Bed That Eats* aka *The Bed That Eats People* (shooting title)

above: Video art for **Asylum of Satan**, William Girdler's 1971 directing debut.

left: A Gothic-romantic image from George Barry's **Death Bed: The Bed That Eats** (1977).

below: Stylish UK quad poster for Charles Band's **The Alchemist** (1981).

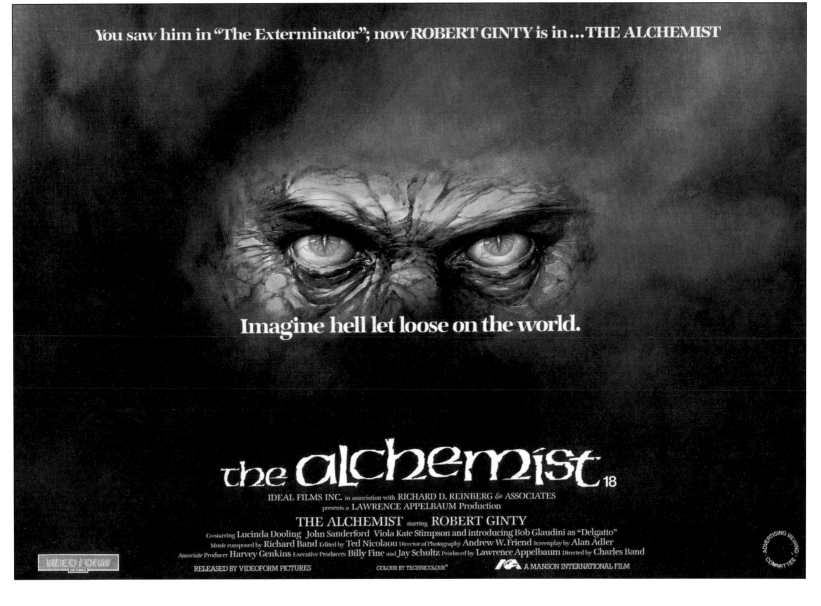

You saw him in "The Exterminator"; now ROBERT GINTY is in ... THE ALCHEMIST

Imagine hell let loose on the world.

the alchemist 18

IDEAL FILMS INC. in association with RICHARD D. REINBERG & ASSOCIATES
presents a LAWRENCE APPELBAUM Production

THE ALCHEMIST starring ROBERT GINTY

Costarring Lucinda Dooling John Sanderford Viola Kate Stimpson and introducing Bob Glaudini as "Delgatto"
Music composed by Richard Band Edited by Ted Nicolaou Director of Photography Andrew W. Friend Screenplay by Alan Adler
Associate Producer Harvey Genkins Executive Producers Billy Fine and Jay Schultz Produced by Lawrence Appelbaum Directed by Charles Band

RELEASED BY VIDEOFORM PICTURES   COLOUR BY TECHNICOLOUR®   A MANSON INTERNATIONAL FILM

IT'S A FIGHT FOR SURVIVAL

ATTACK OF THE BEAST CREATURES

Night of the Cheapskate Monsters!
main picture: Don Dohler's **The Alien Factor** (1977) is a low-budget monster smorgasbord. Here's the Zagatile, a creature too long-legged to fit on this page, ladies and gentlemen!
inset, top: Rare Australian video artwork for Michael Stanley's **Attack of the Beast Creatures** (1983).
inset above: US promo art for the mind-bendingly bad shot-on-video horror epic **Black Devil Doll from Hell** (1984).

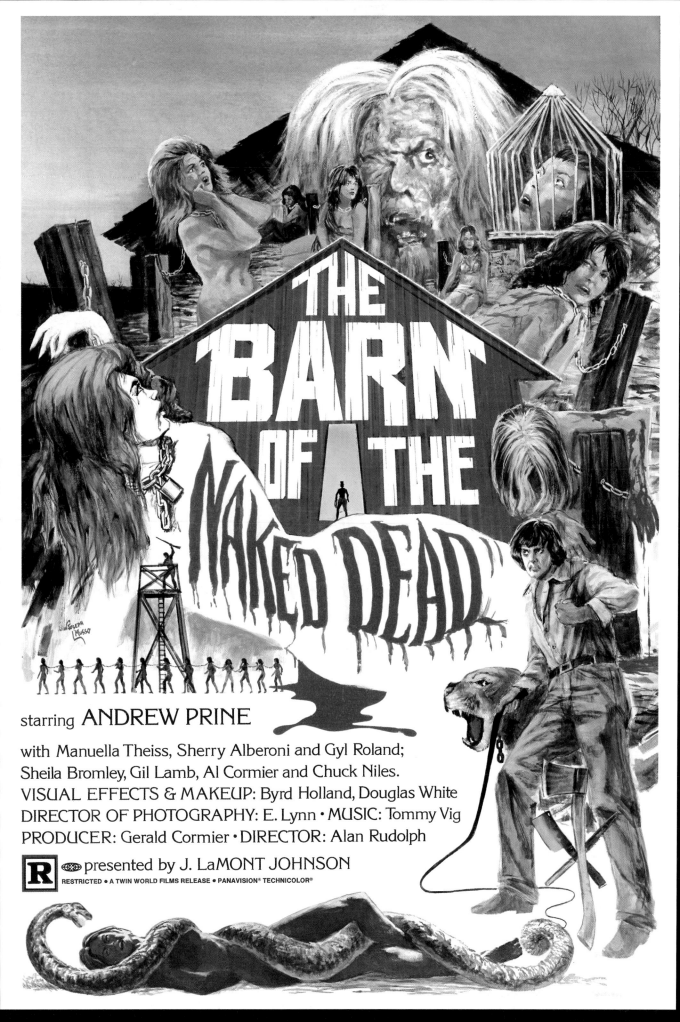

From the respected Hollywood director Alan Rudolph comes **The Barn of the Naked Dead** (1973), complete with ultra-sleazy poster artwork!

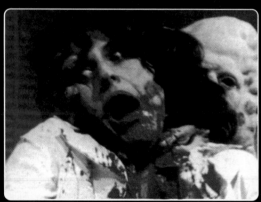

THE TENANT IN ROOM 7 IS VERY SMALL, VERY TWISTED AND VERY MAD!

BASKET CASE

this page: Images from **Basket Case** (1981).
left strip: Dr. Kutter (Diana Browne) pays the price for her callousness – and how; Is Duane (Kevin Van Hentenryck) in danger from his twin brother?; Feeding time; Belial gets even with Dr. Kutter; Belial in a very bad mood.
above: Evocative UK video artwork for the film. Note the 42nd Street marquee advertising John Hancock's **Let's Scare Jessica To Death**.
left: The nailbiting climax of the film as Duane and Belial fight while hanging from a grubby neon sign.

opposite page: More of a Piltdown hoax than a genuine 'Primeval Experience', **The Beast and the Vixens** (1973) at least boasts a great one-sheet poster.

THE UNBELIEVABLE EROTIC ADVENTURE!

THE BEAST

In Exciting Primeval COLOR

AND

THE VIXENS

A Pleasure Weekend Turned Bloodcurdling NIGHTMARE!

BEAUTIFUL MAIDENS PREY OF A CRAZED HUMANOID PRIMATE!

Fantastic Excursion into the PRIMEVAL EXPERIENCE!

ADULTS ONLY

STARRING: JEAN GIBSON, USHI DIGARD, MARIUS MAZMANIAN and BOB MAKAY, with JOE SMITH AS THE INCREDIBLE PRIMATE MONSTER.

Produced by: RAY NADAU & AL FIELDS   Directed by: RAY NADAU

Distributed by SOPHISTICATED FILMS, INC.

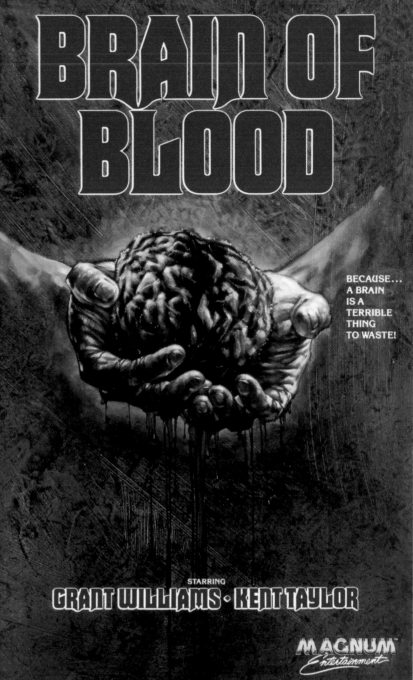

BRAIN OF BLOOD

BECAUSE...
A BRAIN
IS A
TERRIBLE
THING
TO WASTE!

STARRING
GRANT WILLIAMS · KENT TAYLOR

Sometimes
Death is
The Easy
Way Out

THE BRIDES
WORE BLOOD

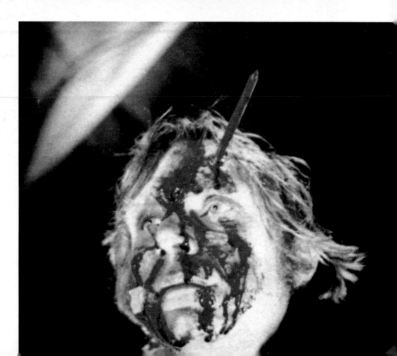

GRITE El terror podría ahogarlo si se queda en su garganta.

Estrella
PETER CARPENTER
Con
MARIA DE ARAGON • VICKI PETERS • REAGAN WILSON • JACQUELINE DALYA
Guion: Producida por   Dirigida por
BOB MAXWELL • CHRIS MARCONI • PETER CARPENTER • ROBERT O'NEIL

COLOR
por Deluxe

CONACINE
presenta

MANIA DE SANGRE

BLOOD MANIA.

un extraño placer

the Demons of Ludlow

The sins of the forefathers come back to haunt the villagers of Ludlow

"CRIMINALLY INSANE"

250 POUNDS OF MANIACAL FURY!

Starring:
Priscilla Alden
Michael Flood

this page:

above: Spanish lobby card for Robert Vincent O'Neill's **Blood Mania** (1971).

far left: British video art for Bill Rebane's Wisconsin-made spook story **The Demons of Ludlow** (1983).

left: US video art for Nick Philips's hilarious 1975 psycho-thriller **"Criminally Insane"**.

opposite page, clockwise from top left:

Ludicrous over-acting in Robert Vincent O'Neill's **Blood Mania** (1971).

Video art for Al Adamson's **Brain of Blood** (1971).

A bloody moment from Richard Cassidy's **Crazed** (1977).

Video art for Bob Favorite's Florida vampire tale, **The Brides Wore Blood** (1972).

DON'T ANSWER THE PHONE!

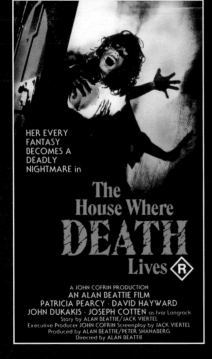

HER EVERY
FANTASY
BECOMES A
DEADLY
NIGHTMARE in

The House Where DEATH Lives ®

A JOHN COFRIN PRODUCTION
AN ALAN BEATTIE FILM
PATRICIA PEARCY · DAVID HAYWARD
JOHN DUKAKIS · JOSEPH COTTEN as Ivar Langrock
Story by ALAN BEATTIE/JACK VIERTEL
Executive Producer JOHN COFRIN Screenplay by JACK VIERTEL
Produced by ALAN BEATTIE/PETER SHANABERG
Directed by ALAN BEATTIE

IT BLOWS THE LID OFF TERROR.

THE JAR

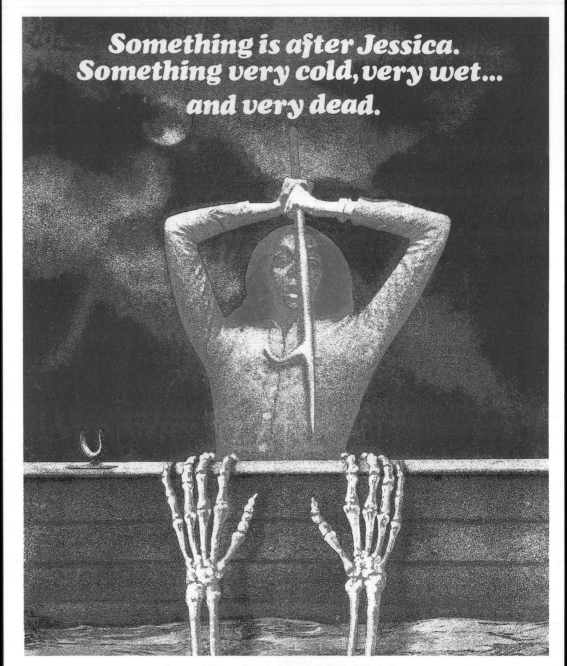

**Something is after Jessica.
Something very cold, very wet...
and very dead.**

Paramount Pictures Presents A Charles B. Moss, Jr. Production

"Let's Scare Jessica To Death"

Starring Zohra Lampert   Barton Heyman   Kevin O'Connor   Gretchen Corbett   Alan Manson and Mariclare Costello
Written by Norman Jonas and Ralph Rose Produced by Charles B. Moss, Jr. Directed by John Hancock   Color   A Paramount Picture

GP

above: Poster for **Let's Scare Jessica To Death** (1971): Paramount acquired the film as a negative pick-up from independent producer Charles B. Moss, Jr.

top left: Video art for Alan Beattie's **The House Where Death Lives** (1980), and Bruce Toscano's intriguing and unusual **The Jar** (1985).

background picture (bottom left): An unscrupulous property developer (Kenneth Tobey) suffers the consequences after trying to evict a group of murderous old folks in Larry Yust's excellent **Homebodies** (1973).

opposite page, left strip: **The Last House on Dead End Street** (1977): Terry's cohort Hardy (Ken Fisher) brandishes a victim's innards; *from top:* Terry Hawkins (Roger Watkins) has a point to make to an unwilling cast-member; The reality film crew from Hell...; Palmer (Edward E. Pixley) finds out who's directing the movie; Steve (Steve Sweet) undergoes a symbolic rape.

opposite top right: Video sleeve for Karen Arthur's disturbing female-psycho tale, **The Mafu Cage** (1977).

opposite bottom right: A young teenager (John Amplas) obsessed with vampirism forces himself on a terrified victim (Fran Middleton) in George Romero's peerless **Martin** (1976).

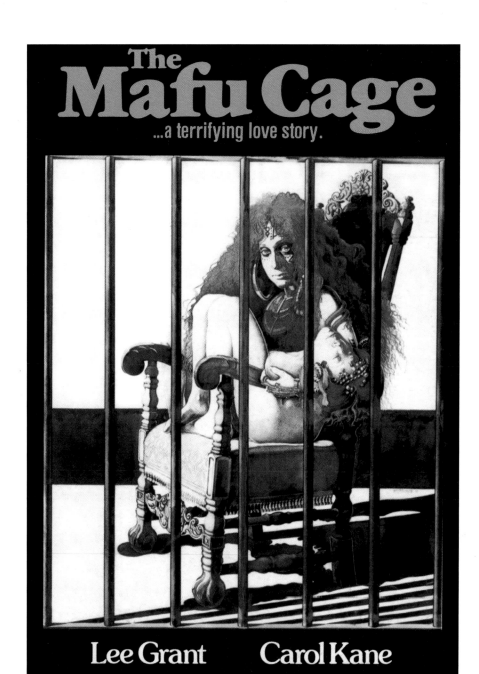

The Mafu Cage
...a terrifying love story.

Lee Grant   Carol Kane

MONSTER

Starring

JOHN CARRADINE   KEENAN WYNN

and

CAROLYN MARTIN

HIS HANDS TEAR THROUGH FLESH AND BONE!

NIGHT BEAST

18

SEE WARNING ON REVERSE   RUNNING TIME 80 MINS. APPROX

ONCE THE PIGS TASTED BLOOD... NO ONE COULD CONTROL THEIR HUNGER!!

A MAD MAN...
A PSYCHO KILLER...
AND MEAN CANNIBAL PIGS...
ALL TOGETHER IN THE SCARIEST FILM
YOU'LL EVER SEE!!!

CLASSIC FILMS PRESENTS
A MARC LAWRENCE FILM

PIGS!

Starring MARC LAWRENCE • JESSE VINT • PAUL HICKEY • JIM ANTONIO
Introducing TONI LAWRENCE as Lynn • KATHERINE ROSS

Produced and Directed by MARC LAWRENCE • Screenplay by F.A. FOSS • Editor IRV GOODNUFF
Animal Consultant MOE DI SESSO • Special Effects BRUCE ADAMS • Set Designer BORIS MICHAEL
R RESTRICTED Under 17 requires accompanying Parent or Adult Guardian • RELEASED BY CLASSIC FILMS

Eastmancolor • Prints by CFI

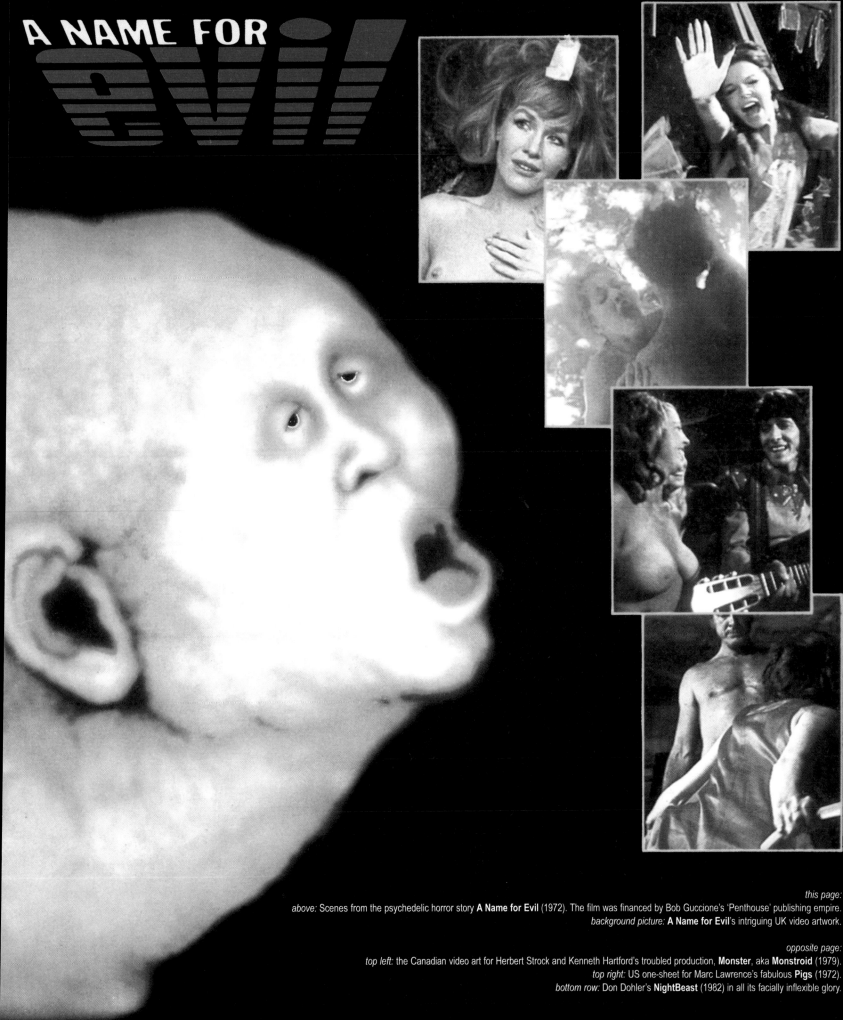

A NAME FOR EVIL

this page:
above: Scenes from the psychedelic horror story **A Name for Evil** (1972). The film was financed by Bob Guccione's 'Penthouse' publishing empire.
background picture: **A Name for Evil**'s intriguing UK video artwork.

opposite page:
top left: the Canadian video art for Herbert Strock and Kenneth Hartford's troubled production, **Monster**, aka **Monstroid** (1979).
top right: US one-sheet for Marc Lawrence's fabulous **Pigs** (1972).
bottom row: Don Dohler's **NightBeast** (1982) in all its facially inflexible glory.

73/48

The dream house that becomes a nightmare.

"A NAME FOR EVIL"

Presented by PENTHOUSE PICTURES · starring ROBERT CULP and SAMANTHA EGGAR
screenplay by BERNARD GIRARD · music by DOMINIC FRONTIERE · produced by REED SHERMAN
directed by BERNARD GIRARD · IN COLOR · C FROM CINERAMA RELEASING   R RESTRICTED
Under 17 requires accompanying Parent or Adult Guardian

Hear Billy Joe Royal sing "Mountain Woman" on MGM Records.

this page:

top: Classic Americana and one of the best horror films of the 1970s – the UK quad for Don Coscarelli's magical **Phantasm** (1978).

above: Lobby card for **Phantasm** under its gormless Australian release title **The Never Dead**.

left: Cleaver madness from Al Adamson's **Nurse Sherri** (1977). The film's UK video title was **Killer's Curse**.

opposite page:
US one-sheet for **A Name for Evil** (1972).

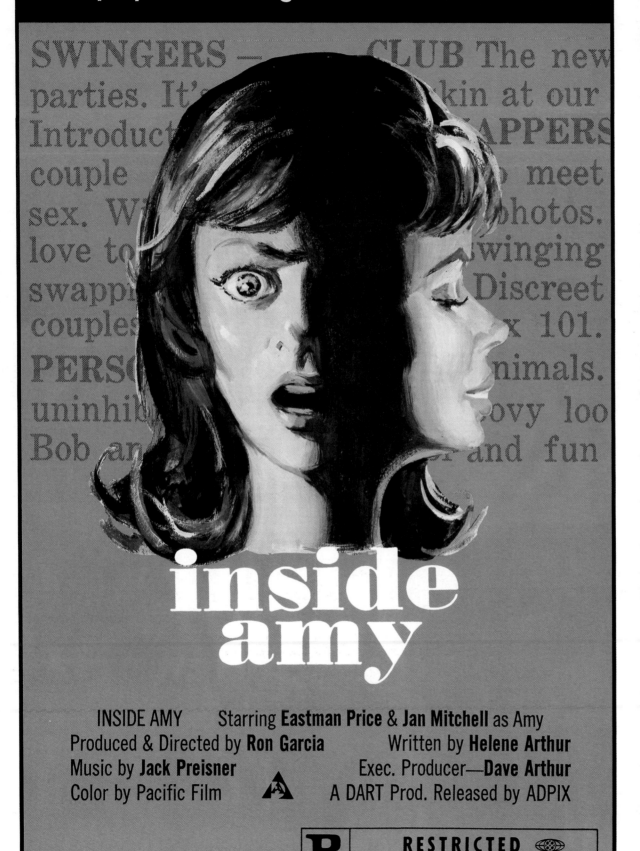

She played the Swingers Games—AND LOST!

inside amy

INSIDE AMY Starring **Eastman Price** & **Jan Mitchell** as Amy
Produced & Directed by **Ron Garcia** Written by **Helene Arthur**
Music by **Jack Preisner** Exec. Producer—**Dave Arthur**
Color by Pacific Film A DART Prod. Released by ADPIX

R **RESTRICTED**
Under 17 requires accompanying Parent or Adult Guardian

COPYRIGHT (C) 1974 ADPIX INC.

74/102

Original one-sheet for Ron Garcia's **Inside Amy** (1973), subsequently re-released as **Swingers Massacre**. Note the text on the poster saying this is a 'Dart Production' – Dave Arthur was the original executive producer and his wife was the writer. Arthur also produced Don Jones's superlative **Abducted**, under its original title **Let's Play Dead**.

opposite page:

clockwise from top left:

UK video art for **The Creature from Shadow Lake** (1981), a retitling of Bill Rebane's late entry in the **Legend of Boggy Creek** mould, **Rana: The Legend of Shadow Lake**.

The US video artwork for Greydon Clark's **Satan's Cheerleaders** (1977) is as exuberantly tacky as the film itself.

group of four stills:
Images from **Satan's Cheerleaders**:
(1) the girls show off their pom-poms.
(2) The sheriff (John Ireland) grapples with the winner of 'tasteless shirt of the year, 1977'.
(3) The sheriff reveals his second job as head of the coven.
(4) Debbie (Alisa Powell) encounters crazy old bum John Carradine.

UK video art for **The Returning** (1983), Joel Bender's story of familial grief and an Indian curse.

INSIDE AMY

THE Creature from Shadow Lake

Under no circumstances watch this film alone

VHS 79 minutes Colour

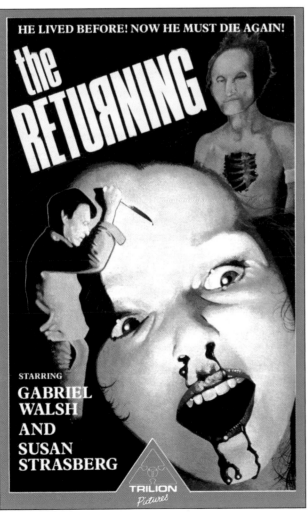

HE LIVED BEFORE! NOW HE MUST DIE AGAIN!

the RETURNING

STARRING
GABRIEL WALSH AND SUSAN STRASBERG

TRILION Pictures

COME SCORE WITH THE CHEERLEADERS

WHEN THESE GIRLS RAISE HELL.... THERE'S THE DEVIL TO PAY!

A GREYDON CLARK PRODUCTION

Satan's Cheerleaders

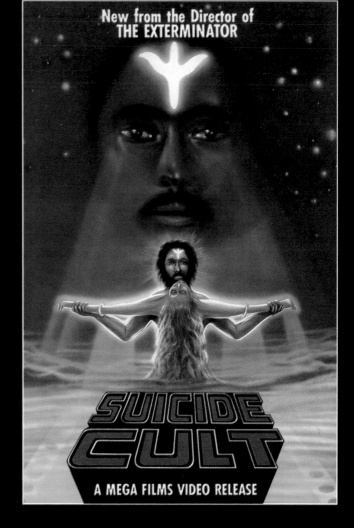

New from the Director of
THE EXTERMINATOR

SUICIDE CULT

A MEGA FILMS VIDEO RELEASE

THE SCAREMAKER

Starring
HAL HOLBROOK

One by one he killed them until
he was trapped in his own game.

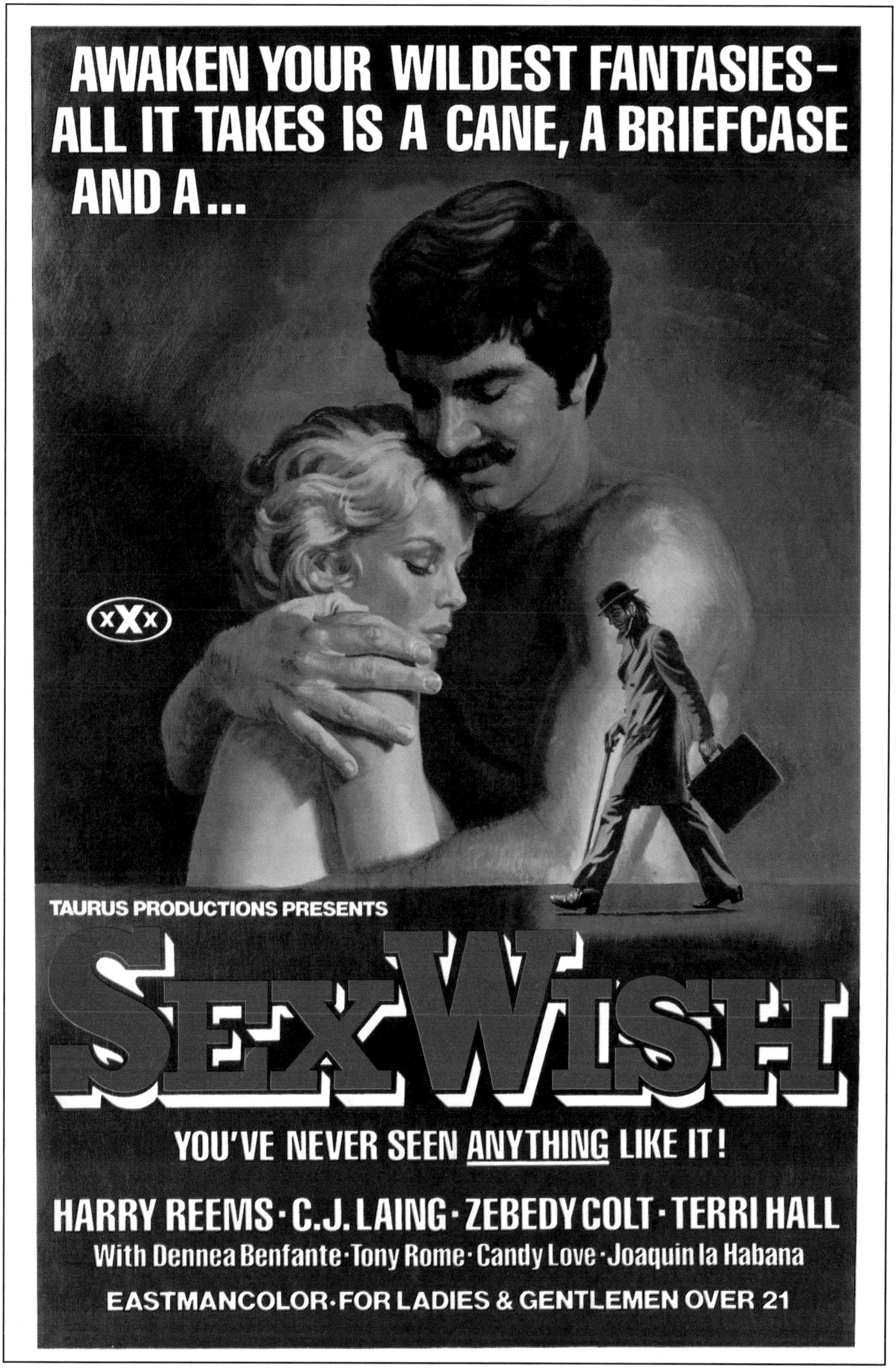
AWAKEN YOUR WILDEST FANTASIES-
ALL IT TAKES IS A CANE, A BRIEFCASE
AND A...
XXX
TAURUS PRODUCTIONS PRESENTS
SEX WISH
YOU'VE NEVER SEEN ANYTHING LIKE IT!
HARRY REEMS · C.J. LAING · ZEBEDY COLT · TERRI HALL
With Dennea Benfante · Tony Rome · Candy Love · Joaquin la Habana
EASTMANCOLOR · FOR LADIES & GENTLEMEN OVER 21

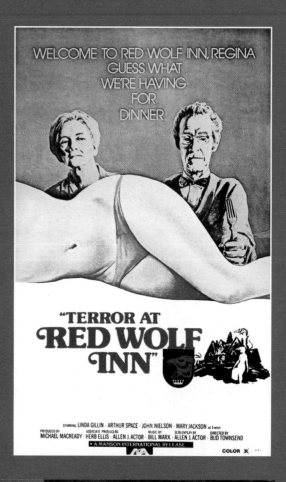

above: An occult ritual about to be disrupted by
Simon, King of the Witches (1971).
right: The film's paperback novelisation.
far right: UK video art for **The Folks at Red Wolf Inn** (1972).
below: Four scenes of mayhem from David Hess's
Xmas-time slasher **To All a Goodnight** (1980).

What he does to your nerves is almost as frightening as what he does to his victims!

THE TOOLBOX MURDERS

starting **CAMERON MITCHELL** PAMELYN FERDIN and WESLEY EURE

Produced by TONY DIDIO
Directed by DENNIS DONNELLY

top: UK quad poster for **The Toolbox Murders** (1977), cut for its 'X'-certificate release but in its uncut version boasting one of the nastiest killings in slasher film history.
above and right: A murder from the late-bloom slasher **Whodunit?** (1982), accompanied by the UK video cover.
far right: Poster for Matt Cimber's moody, disturbing psycho-tale, **The Witch Who Came from the Sea** (1976).

Reviews

ABDUCTED
– Don Jones (1973)
See interview with Don Jones, John Stoglin and Gary Kent.
Made in California.

ALABAMA'S GHOST
– Fredric Hobbs (1973)
See interview with Fredric Hobbs and William Heick.
Made in California.

THE ALCHEMIST
– Charles Band [begun by Craig Mitchell] (1981)

1871: A woman in white, Anna (Lucinda Dooling), is led by dark forces to a moonlight rendezvous with Delgatto (Robert Glaudini), an alchemist who lusts for her body – and her soul. Anna's husband (Robert Ginty) follows her through tangled woodlands: attacking Delgatto with a knife, he accidentally kills Anna. In fury, Delgatto utters a curse, condemning the husband to walk the earth 'as an animal'…

The 1950s. Lenora St. Clair (Dooling again) is heading for Charlotte, North Carolina when she experiences a vision of a woman in white. Shaken, she picks up a hitch hiker, Cam (John Sanderford), infuriating him with her offhand and defensive attitude. Occult powers emanating from an old woman, Esther McCallum (Viola Kate Stimpson), draw Lenora's car off the road and into the woods. The car crashes, and Cam tries in vain to persuade Lenora to walk back to the highway. Instead she heads off deeper into the trees. In a glade, they meet Aaron McCallum (Robert Ginty again), whom Lenora recognises from her vision. Aaron invites them back to his shack and introduces Esther, whom he reveals is in fact his daughter. Aaron has never aged since the spell was placed on him over a hundred years ago, although his daughter is now very old. Disturbed by Aaron's sinister stories, Cam drags Lenora from the house. Aaron calls after them to use his car: Esther has summoned demons to enact the shifting of the curse from her father, but at the cost of Lenora's soul…

The Alchemist would have been fine as the bottom end of a double bill, but alone it's not really strong enough. The plot is garbled and the function of the demons in particular is never elaborated upon. Top-billed Robert Ginty looks uncomfortable, if not unwell. His everyman shtick worked just fine in James Glickenhaus's *The Exterminator*, where he played a normal Joe pushed to violent extremes: as a cursed 140-year-old yearning for his lost love, however, he's out of his depth.

The Alchemist was copyrighted in 1981 but failed to secure a release until '84; Band took over direction from Craig Mitchell, co-director of Don Coscarelli's early credit, *Jim the World's Greatest* (1976). You can tell from the disjointed nature of the film that it was a troubled production, because inconsistencies abound: Esther's death occurs with no explanation or build-up, and when Lenora meets Aaron she says he's the man in her dream, despite having angrily asserted earlier that her visions weren't dreams at all. Also a problem are the tacky and charmless optical effects,

typical of the endless parade of fuzzy blue lights buzzing around low-budget productions in the wake of *Poltergeist* and *Close Encounters*… The demons provide a couple of startling moments, but you can already see in their over-determined sculptural design the beginning of another trend that would sweep the horror genre in the eighties: the overuse of leering monster masks. A cheap prosthetic melt, *Raiders*-style, turns a dummy of the alchemist to latex mush, but it looks more like a demo for the plastics industry than evidence of the supernatural.

Scant use is made of the script's more interesting elements. Alchemy is a potentially fascinating source of imagery for the horror genre; sadly, for all its incidental pleasures, *The Alchemist* is unable to perform a transmutation of its own. The theme is never expanded – Aaron tells Lenora and Cam that the real aim of alchemy is self-transformation, an assertion that should have been the key to the story's climax. However, instead of Delgatto undergoing a dramatic change of form in the latter stages, he is simply stabbed and bisected in the magic gateway. It's a shame the character is wasted, because his feelings for Anna seem genuine: the curse he places on Aaron is born as much from anger for the loss of his love as the thwarting of his will, making him an adulterer and a sorcerer but something less than capital-letter Evil (it's all a bit *Wuthering Heights* really). The effects of the curse are likewise thrown away; after an early scene (borrowed from *An American Werewolf In London*) in which Aaron hunts down a small deer and fondles its entrails for a couple of seconds, we see no more of his lycanthropy. What's left is basically a rather cluttered variant on the old witch's curse routine. At least the woodland location work is atmospheric, and a scene in which Cam and Lenora are attacked in the woods by barely glimpsed

opposite:
Stylish US one-sheet for **The Alchemist**.

below:
Robert Ginty, with slave-girl (not featured in film), confronts demons on this Finnish video cover for **The Alchemist**.

The Alien Dead
aka **It Fell from the Sky** (US theatrical title)
© 1980. Firebird Pictures, Inc.
Firebird Pictures presents.
director: Fred Olen Ray. executive producer:
Henry Kaplan. associate producer: Shelley
Youngren. producers: Chuck Sumner, Fred
Olen Ray. screenplay: Fred Olen Ray, Martin
Alan Nicholas. cinematographers: Fred Olen
Ray, Gary Singer, Fred Gamba. musical score:
Franklin Sledge, Chuck Sumner. additional
music: The American Bluegrass Express, Paul
Jones, Sugar Lee. editor: Mark Barrett. special
makeup design: Allen Duckworth. audio: John
Weyrick, Joe Lang, Malcom Brooks. special
effects: Fred Olen Ray. production assistants:
Mike Gorenfio, John Ray, Cohn Heron-Vanta.
stills: Mac Brooks, Joe Lang, Cohn Heron-
Vanta, Will Harbeson. special animation: Bart
J. Mixon. title graphics: Jon Keck. filmed in
1978 in Orlando (Florida) and Rock Springs
(Florida, USA).
Cast: Buster Crabbe (Sheriff Bernie Kowalski).
Raymond Roberts (Tom Corman). Linda Lewis
(Shawn Michaels). Mike Bonavia (Miller Haze).
Dennis Underwood (Deputy Campbell).
George Kelsey (Emmett Michaels). Martin Alan
Nicholas (Doc Ellerbe). Norman Riggins (Mr.
Griffith). Edi Stroup (Grocery Cashier). John
Leirier (Paisley). Rich Vogan (Krelboin). Ellena
Contello (Mae Hawkins). Nancy Karnz
(Margaret Griffith). Shelley Youngren (angry
wife). Fred Olen Ray (pool player). Chuck
Sumner (Gordon). Bernice Kelsey (farmer's
wife). Ken Triplet (farmer). Jocelyn Davies (girl
swimmer). Domi Adrian (hunter #1). Bob
Wagner (hunter #2). Wesley Place (second
deputy) and Bonnie Irvine. Albert Davies. Lena
Bianton. Steve Kaplan. Carl Bowman. Terry
Stephenson. Ray Duckworth. James Christian.
Barbara Barrs. Mary Jane Kelsey. Nancy Ray.
Terry Droan. Jim Cartwright. Bobby Conwell.
Elton Kemper. Freddy Frei. Mike Dominsky.
Michael Smith. John Ray. Michele De Gurne.
Joe Lang. Denise Thompson. Noli Lagrossa.
Ron Liburn. John Green. Chris Robinson.
Rene McCune. Phil Cardweli.

top:
US admat for **The Alchemist**, making use of
the more familiar 'evil eyes' graphic.

below, clockwise from top right:
Deputy Campbell (Dennis Underwood);
Emmett Michaels (George Kelsey);
...and two Floridian zombies,
all from Fred Olen Ray's **The Alien Dead**.

You saw him in "The Exterminator";
now ROBERT GINTY is in ... THE ALCHEMIST

Imagine hell let loose on the world.
the **alchemist** 18

IDEAL FILMS INC. in association with RICHARD D. REINBERG & ASSOCIATES
presents a LAWRENCE APPELBAUM Production
THE ALCHEMIST starring ROBERT GINTY
Co-starring Lucinda Dooling John Sanderford Viola Kate Stimpson and
introducing Bob Glaudini as "Delgatto"
Music composed by Richard Band Edited by Ted Nicolaou Director of Photography Andrew W. Friend
Screenplay by Alan Adler Associate Producer Harvey Genkins Executive Producers Billy Fine and Jay Schultz
Produced by Lawrence Appelbaum Directed by Charles Band

RELEASED BY VIDEOFORM PICTURES   COLOUR BY TECHNICOLOR®   A MANSON INTERNATIONAL FILM

demonic figures is eerily similar to Richard Blackburn's *Lemora*.
(Bearing in mind the lead character's name, Band may well have
been influenced by the Blackburn film.) Also interesting are a
couple of scenes that pre-empt the imagery of Ridley Scott's
Legend (1985). Lenora's walk through a magic stone gateway in
the trees into a fantastical version of the forest, with a deep red
sky criss-crossed with lightning, resembles a cheap and cheerful
version of the Scott epic, as does a beautiful image of dandelion
seeds blowing through a woodland glade. To round off these
allusions to greater works, the score by Richard Band (the
director's brother) is a classy orchestral affair reminiscent of Pino
Donaggio's work for Brian De Palma.

Charles Band, born 27 December, 1951, is the son of
filmmaker Albert Band. He directed his first movie in 1973, a sex
satire called *Last Foxtrot in Burbank*, starring Michael Pataki. After
several years as an independent producer (he handled Pataki's
Mansion of the Doomed and David Schmoeller's *Tourist Trap*
amongst others), Band started an Italian-based production house,
Empire Pictures. Empire collapsed due to international financing
difficulties in 1989; undeterred, Band started Full Moon Pictures
the following year. The company still thrives today. His drive and
enthusiasm for independent commercial genre cinema parallels
Roger Corman's New World studios (although it must be said that
Band has discovered rather fewer great directors along the way).

Made in California.

THE ALIEN DEAD
– Fred Olen Ray (1980)
aka *Alien Dead*
aka *It Fell from the Sky*

Not as good as Tony Malanowski's *The Curse of the
Screaming Dead* (1982), but better than Joel M. Reed's *Night of
the Zombies* (1981), this early effort from one-man exploitation
factory Fred Olen Ray is more to my taste than his later, campier
films (*Hollywood Chainsaw Hookers*, for example), but even here
you can tell that he's tempted to make a send-up. The script
employs enough (mostly lame) ironies to tip you off that the
writers know how schlocky it all is; although unless such nod-
and-a-wink witticisms are funny, I actually prefer the straight-
faced approach of Don Dohler. Still, *The Alien Dead* is kind of
enjoyable in its cheesy hundred-dollar way; some of the zombies
look pretty good, and once the cheap, unconvincing gore starts to
flow it doesn't let up. If only the performers hadn't taken it upon
themselves to mug for the camera so much: one fellow, clearly
pleased with himself for chewing raw liver on camera, indulges in
a 'Look at me! I'm ker-razee!' moment that belongs in the

blooper reel, not the movie. Venerable *Flash Gordon* star Buster
Crabbe makes a game attempt to take things seriously, and no one
makes fun of him, which helps, but no one's going to watch this
for the acting. The gore scenes have that stagy feeling of everyone
standing just-so in order to conceal wires and tubes: I particularly
enjoyed the scene in which an old lady is stuck through with a
pitch-fork, a laboriously mounted effects sequence giving us
everything *but* the actual piercing. If you're a devotee of zombie
cinema, you might gain a few crumbs of comfort here, but don't
bother trying to make sense of the rationale for the zombie
uprising – something to do with a meteorite killing all the
alligators, I think. Just enjoy discovering this little known tribe of
the cinema's ultimate rejects as they lurch out of the Florida
swamps to join their brethren around the world.

Made in Florida.

THE ALIEN FACTOR
– Don Dohler (1977)

Made for beer and cigarettes in the backyards of Baltimore,
The Alien Factor is, if nothing else, a testament to the persistence
and ingenuity of its director, Don Dohler. As drama it's strictly
flat-pack-furnishing, but as an effects piece it's surprisingly
ambitious, with the balls to put its monsters up there on the screen
in all their twenty-buck glory and to hell with suspension of
disbelief. Dohler, born in 1946, was a film fanatic whose passion
for horror and sci-fi cinema was nurtured by the pages of Forrest
Ackerman's *Famous Monsters of Filmland* magazine. He practiced
special effects make-up and monster designs at home, before
turning up in 1972 as editor of his own magazine, *Cinemagic*,
devoted to the sort of B-movie classics he loved. He made the leap
into film production with this debut horror/sci-fi caper, followed
by a string of similar titles: *Fiend*, *NightBeast*, *The Galaxy
Invader*, *Blood Massacre* and, in 2001, *Alien Factor 2*. Home
video helped his movies reach a bigger audience, but he was to
climb maybe two or three rungs up the industry ladder at best,
always remaining loyal to his home town. Dohler's movies are
usually enjoyable, even if their only *raison d'être* is to mimic the
fifties monster flicks the director clearly fell in love with as a boy.
He operates, albeit shakily, on the level of craft rather than art: the
fun you can have with his films depends on your willingness to
enjoy his no-frills direction, whacked-out monsters and some
unadorned movie clichés.

Filmed between October 1976 and March 1977, *The Alien
Factor* sets the seal on the Dohler style: earnest acting, basic
plotting and rampaging monsters, all shot in woodland or suburban
locations. Sophisticated it ain't, but if you can accept the
cheapness of the production it's a blast. Subsequent Dohlerfests
like *NightBeast* and *Fiend* show some minor technical improvements, but it's fair to say that if you can't get into *The Alien
Factor* you're unlikely to make it through the others. It has the
unselfconsciousness of the fifties monster movies Dohler loved,
and it's all the better for it. The premise is great: a spaceship
shuttling three bizarre alien creatures to an intergalactic zoo
crashes (off-screen, naturally) in Maryland. (The crashed spaceship
itself is really rather special, shown using a clever forced-
perspective shot that bears comparison with movies ten times the
budget.) The monsters run amok, attacking stray hikers and the
usual denizens of Lovers' Lane. Protecting the town are three
(count 'em) cops, led by Tom Griffith as Sheriff Cinder, a
sheepskin-coated stoic who turns up again in *NightBeast* five years
later. Before long, the police are joined by professional monster-
hunter Ben Zachary (Don Leifert), a mysterious, arrogant figure
who seems strangely *au fait* with off-world menace…

For all that he clearly adores his monstrous marauders,
Dohler's stories are usually built around small but resolute groups
of ordinary people struggling to defend their slice of turf. His
scripts are awash with concerned cops, humanitarian doctors,
shopkeepers galvanised into action, and local layabouts turned
monster-hunters. Civic-minded to a fault, he's also at pains to

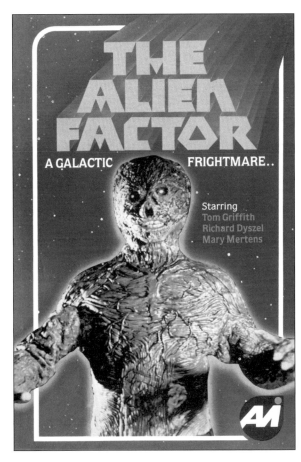

Tony Malanowski (see interview) was assistant director on *The Alien Factor* and plays a small part in the cast. Production assistant John Dods went on to design the monster for Dohler's *NightBeast* and the amazing creatures in *The Deadly Spawn* (see interview with Douglas McKeown). Dohler succumbed to cancer on 2 December, 2006, aged 60.

Made in Maryland.
see also: *Fiend* and *NightBeast*

THE ALPHA INCIDENT
– Bill Rebane (1977)
aka *Gift from a Red Planet*

Scientists discover a space virus on a lump of Martian rock and send samples cross-country by train, in unmarked boxes, to be examined by a specialist. Riding along to protect the shipment is Dr. Ted Sorenson (Stafford Morgan), but nosy old Hank (George 'Buck' Flower), the train-guard, gets suspicious when he notices the stranger is carrying a gun. Once Sorenson is asleep, Hank steals a key and examines the cargo, accidentally cutting himself on a shattered glass vial. When the train stops off at an isolated country station, Sorenson makes a call to a secret government organisation. They inform him that Hank will have been infected with the deadly virus. Sorenson must enforce quarantine, but by now Hank has made physical contact with three more people: station-master Charlie (Ralph Meeker), his secretary Jenny (Carol Irene Newell), and local farmer Jack Tiller (John Goff). Sorenson informs them that they cannot leave the station. As tension, resentment and paranoia mount up, Sorenson must use his gun to enforce order. But what exactly is the virus, and what effects will it have? When an army helicopter airdrops amphetamines, along with instructions not to fall asleep, the fear and claustrophobia worsen…

A shocking look into the future of mankind.

THE ALPHA INCIDENT

Starring
RALPH MEEKER,
STAFFORD MORGAN, JOHN GOFF

point out the evils of drink-driving: a traditional scene where a monster attacks a young couple necking in a car, for instance, follows hot on the heels of said couple swigging from a whiskey bottle. Soon after, a biker comes to grief; also after guzzling while on the road. Such irresponsibility clearly has no place on a real-life Dohler shoot: the ensuing motorcycle crash is filmed with such painstaking sobriety it's a wonder Dohler doesn't throw a few cushions to break the bike's fall. Perhaps the owner was a bona-fide Hells Angel: and besides, replacing a dented exhaust would doubtless have crippled the whole production – when an insectoid creature attacks George Stover in the snowy woods, the actor throws a projectile at the ground *between* them, rather than risk damaging the monster suit.

There are four different monsters in the film and three of them are triumphs of the unlikely, with only the fourth – the stop-motion 'Lemoid' – a conspicuous dud. The insectoid 'Inferbyce' is an escaped *Doctor Who* monster on a par with the creature in Amando de Ossorio's *The Lorelei's Grasp*, and the long-legged 'Zagatile' has a special place in my heart, staggering around like a mutant giraffe or one of Leigh Bowery's more insane creations, propelled by a very brave stilt-walking stuntman. A scene on an icy road, and later in a snow-caked front garden, had me far more anxious for the artiste than the movie characters he was attacking: one slip and the poor sucker could have bashed his brains out on the edge of Dohler's rockery.

Simple and artless as the film may be, there are still moments where the rudimentary style and real-life locations knit convincingly together. Outdoor scenes have a muddy, rainy-day verisimilitude that makes for a pleasurable contrast with the weird creature designs, the photography lending the film a naturalistic sense of place. The wintry weather helps, as well. On the acting front, Don Leifert as Zachary knows a thing or two about scene-stealing, and Kenneth Walker's pulpy music also lifts the spirits, compensating for weaker, quieter scenes with too much of Dohler's drizzling dialogue. The follow-up, *NightBeast*, adds gore to the equation and is better paced – but I'd be a fan on the basis of this first film alone. Every small town should have a Don Dohler!

The Alien Factor
©1977. Cinemagic Visual Effects, Inc. A Cinemagic Visual Effects production. writer/director: Donald M. Dohler. cinematographer: Britt McDonough. music and sound effects: Kenneth Walker. film editors: Don Dohler, Dave Ellis. assistant director: Anthony Malanowski. title logo and trademark design: Tim Hammell. title sequence created by Ernest D. Farino. make-up and special effects: John Cosentino, Larry Schlechter, Britt McDonough. additional photographic effects: Ernest D. Farino. production assistants: Chris Gummer, Dan White, Ed Liztinger, John Dods. technical adviser: Dave Geatty. sound recording and mix: Dave Ellis. "Inferbyce" (insect) designed and worn by Larry Schlechter. "Zagatile" (tall creature) designed and worn by John Cosentino. "Leemoid" designed and animated by Ernie Farino. special effects assistants: Red Richard Rae, Bill Cosentino. we are grateful to the following companies and individuals for their assistance and cooperation in the making of this motion picture: All Media Productions (Baltimore, Maryland); KLM Associates, Inc. (Potomac, Maryland); Quality Film Labs, Inc. (Baltimore, Maryland); Century Studios, Inc. (Dallas, Texas); Gunpowder Falls State Park; Maryland Department of Natural Resources; Baltimore County Office of Central Services; Federal Signal Corporation (Columbia, Maryland); The Anir Lounge (Kingsville, Maryland); WFBR Mad Radio 13 (Baltimore, Maryland); WDCA-TV 20 (Washington, DC); The Baltimore City Police Department; The Baltimore County Police Department; Mr. & Mrs. Frank Gummer; Mr. & Mrs. Ronald Celozzi; Mr. & Mrs. Wilson Smith; John Ashton; Evelyn B. Wagner; Pemla Dohler; Mary Ann Merenda; Donald G. Jackson; Robert Ondira; Lee Jamilik; Tom Phaneuf; Tom Brenner; Mr. & Mrs. Joseph Mistretta. process photography by EUE Opticals. songs "Maybe Someday" and "Jump Back Crackerjack" written by Lon Talbot & performed by Atlantis, ©1976 Mekon Records.
Cast: Don Leifert (Ben Zachary). Tom Griffith (Sheriff Cinder). Richard Dyszel (Mayor Wicker). Mary Mertens (Edie Maretin). Richard Geiwitz (Pete). George Stover (Steven). Eleanor Herman (Mary Jane Carter). Anne Frith (Dr Ruth Sherman). Christopher Gummer (Clay). Don Dohler (Ernie). Dave Ellis (Richie). Dave Geatty (man in bar). Margie Van Tassell (Susan). Tony Malanowski (Ed Miller). Debbie Pietron & Bill Cosentino (couple in woods). Rick Cosentino (biker). Greg Dohler, Kim Dohler & Joey Merenda (three children). Ann Hanks (barmaid). Lon Talbot, Glenn Ruby & Jack Campbell (rock band). Dan White (Vance). Britt McDonough (Ted). William L. Brown (drunk). Cathy Oldaker & Donna Foster (girls in bar). Toni Watcheski & Ed Watcheski (couple in bar). Johnny Walker (Rex).

top left:
British video cover for Don Dohler's debut, **The Alien Factor**. AVI also released Harry Preston's enjoyable **Honeymoon Horror**, Don Schain's **The Abductors**, and Joseph Bigwood [Joe Zito]'s **Bloodrage**, as well as two classic Euro-horrors; Joe D'Amato's **Beyond the Darkness** and Nico Mastorakis's **Island of Death**.

left:
Distinctly misleading US artwork for Bill Rebane's earthbound trudge, **The Alpha Incident**.

One of Rebane's most existentially arid and theatrical films, *The Alpha Incident* really challenges your patience. The refusal of action and excitement, in a story about the spread of an alien super-virus, is so perverse that it would be mistaken for high modernism on the stage. Not only does Rebane restrict events to a couple of small rooms in a rural railway station, he's also extremely parsimonious with visual shocks; there's just one sudden and graphic eruption of horror, and that occurs over an hour into the story! The notion that sleeping makes the virus accelerate its attack on the human body is a good one, but it's tantamount to irony in a film that similarly challenges the viewer to stay awake. Rebane allows weariness to infect the film just as surely as the virus infects the cast, beginning with the musings of two overworked scientists working late at the laboratory, and moving on to Sorenson falling asleep on the train. It's really not a good idea to have your central character doze off around the fifteen minute mark! By the time we arrive at sleepy Moose Point station, the audience need amphetamines more than the characters. Even when the drugs arrive, Rebane is clearly unfamiliar with the side-effects; instead of turning the taciturn quartet into garrulous speed-freaks, all that speed seems to do is loosen Jenny's sexual inhibitions (a throwback to the days when anti-drug films preached that the main effect of illicit substances was to steer 'the kids' into indiscriminate sex). The actors don't do so badly with the material, and there is a sort of claustrophobic intensity to some scenes, but you have to be an obscuro-horror completist to really get a kick out of this one.

William 'Bill' Rebane was born in Latvia in 1937, and moved to Chicago in 1952. In 1966, after making his first film *Terror at Halfday* – an unfinished mess which, with the addition of new scenes shot by Herschell Gordon Lewis, eventually became better known as *Monster A Go-Go* (1965) – he wisely skipped town and moved to Wisconsin. Rebane learned English by going to the movies: he especially loved musicals, westerns and comedies. He recently admitted to the website Bijouflix (www.bijouflix.com) that he never really liked horror movies and became typecast as a horror director against his wishes.

Made in Wisconsin.

see also: **The Demons of Ludlow**, **The Giant Spider Invasion** and **Rana: The Creature from Shadow Lake**

ANOTHER SON OF SAM
– Dave A. Adams (1977)
aka *Hostages* [original title]

A psychopath called Harvey escapes from an asylum and goes on a killing spree at the local college campus. After holing up in a room with two coeds, he's coaxed out into the open by his abusive mother (Ann Owens), and promptly shot dead by the police.

They don't come much worse than this. Boring cops blather on to each other for seventy minutes, while the killer is depicted for the entire film with the exact same close-up of his eyes, regardless of lighting or location. A crudely prowling subjective camera stands in for the rest of him; screaming victims cower as he approaches, but there's no interaction, neither physical nor verbal. As for violence, forget it: we see Harvey's handiwork in brief glimpses, after the killing blow. Only once he's dead do we see his entire body, and since 'Harvey' does not appear on the screen credits, we never even get to find out who played him. One can only assume that former stunt-man turned producer-director Dave Adams did all this deliberately, to express his contempt for murdering scumbags (ten of whom – Jack the Ripper, John Wayne Gacy etc. – are named in a series of captions at the start of the movie). According to production manager Don Cely, the original title, *Hostages*, was changed by Adams to *Another Son of Sam*, to cash in on the case of David Berkowitz, who was in the news at the time; so the director's contempt for serial killers obviously didn't stretch so far as declining their help in selling his picture. What's especially obnoxious about the film is that Harvey, deprived of even a shred of consideration by the filmmaker, is talked into the line of fire by the mother who sexually abused him

as a child! Quite apart from the dubious wisdom of bringing her in to negotiate with her crazed son when he's locked in a room with two teenage girls, there's no recognition of the fact that this woman helped create a monster; she just turns up, does her bit for the police, and that's it. Technically, the whole enterprise is primitive in the extreme, but badly made films I can handle – belligerent, moralistic ones are another matter.

Another Son of Sam was shot in Charlotte and Belmont, North Carolina. The cinematographer was Harry Joyner, the DP on Pat Patterson's *The Body Shop*. The young cast were auditioned at the University of North Carolina, and roles were also given to several local TV and radio personalities, including the self-styled 'Dean of Tampa Bay nightlife,' MOR crooner Johnny Charro, who delivers an Engelbert Humperdinckish number. Behind the cameras, Earl Owensby alumnus and director of *A Day of Judgment*, Charles Reynolds, worked as a grip and acted in a small role. One of the library music cues, used over and over again throughout the film, is a chilling synthesizer motif also used by David Cronenberg for his 1976 film, *Rabid*.

Made in North Carolina.

ASYLUM OF SATAN
– William Girdler (1971)
aka *The Satan Spectrum*

Beautiful concert pianist Lucina Martin (Carla Borelli) needs a rest, but she gets more than she bargained for when a man posing as her father orders her removal to a private asylum run by the sinister Dr. Jason Specter (Charles Kissinger). Unable to secure her own release, Lucina explores the asylum and sees hooded figures converging in the cellar. Her fellow patients are struggling with a variety of phobias, and Specter's methods are crudely confrontational: spiders, snakes… nothing too expensive. Lucina's boyfriend Chris Duncan (Nick Jolley) is denied entrance to visit; undeterred, he spends the rest of the film trying to save his girl before she can be sacrificed to Satan by Specter's coven…

Being incarcerated in a mental hospital and victimised by the therapeutic community is one of the horror genre's favourite riffs. It's a fate that tends to be reserved for pretty girls though, with its outlaw flipside, the escaped lunatic, left mainly for the boys (an honourable exception being Marc Lawrence's wonderful *Pigs*). It's interesting that the most acclaimed study of a person being victimized in a mental hospital is *One Flew Over the Cuckoo's Nest*, with Jack Nicholson's heroic male lobotomised into passivity by a controlling woman; it's a template that was then largely ignored in the exploitation arena, where the female of the species continued to suffer the indignities, invasions and psycho-surgical horrors (see: *Lies*; *The Fifth Floor*; *Human Experiments*). Girdler's frayed and impoverished debut, which of course pre-dates the Forman film, has as much to say about the incarceration of the mentally ill as *Cuckoo's Nest* does about cuckoos, nor does it find much succour in the arms of Satan. The title is really the most enjoyable thing about it: you're probably better off fantasising your own version. If you must see it, look out for Charles Kissinger, who plays two parts, as the wickedly goateed Dr. Specter and (in drag) his Teutonic head nurse Martine. Kissinger was a Kentucky TV horror host, and he's as broad here as a Vincent Price impersonator in a Halloween television commercial. Which would be a liability, except that *Asylum of Satan* is so flat, dramatically speaking, that you welcome his overacting with gratitude. For the rest, it only remains to comment that this is the sort of film that encourages reviewers to bang on about the fashion violations of the cast – but what's the point? Today's sports-leisurewear will look just as ridiculous in thirty years time…

William Girdler, a dedicated purveyor of B-movie trash probably best known for *The Manitou* (1977), was born 22 October, 1947. He learned the rudiments of film while in the Air Force, working on documentaries and educational shorts. Returning to Louisville, Kentucky in 1970, he formed his own production company, Studio One, with his brother-in-law J. Patrick Kelly III. While initially making commercials, Girdler soon gathered a small technical crew and set his sights on a movie-making career. *Asylum of Satan* (from a script titled *The Satan Spectrum*) was the first of his nine theatrical features. It was financed through friends, local theatre owners, and contacts with various Kentucky entrepreneurs. Shooting began in the Autumn of 1971 with a budget of around $50,000. Girdler spotted *Asylum*'s lead actress Carla Borelli through his ad agency contacts: she went on to appear in the well-known US TV soaps, *Days of Our Lives* and *Falcon Crest*. The sinister Dr. Jason Specter was played by Louisville's TV horror host, Charles 'Fearmonger' Kissinger, who would go on to appear in nearly all of Girdler's films. The asylum of the title was an old mansion belonging to an eccentric Louisville heiress. In an interview with Girdler's biographer Patricia Breen, grip Don Wrege recalled: "[She] allowed her poodles run of the place. There was dog shit in every room. She would appear from time to time, leaving in the morning with a good-looking guy... but mainly wasn't around. The […] library with a working pipe organ was covered in dog shit and hadn't been cleaned in what looked like years. Meanwhile the heiress partied every night." The rest of the film was shot at Girdler's Studio One warehouse facility.

For the climax, Girdler secured the use of the Devil costume made for Roman Polanski's *Rosemary's Baby*, a coup perhaps lessened in impact by his decision to top it off with a hokey dime-store mask, allegedly custom-made for the production but more likely won at a carnival. Hearing rumours that Church of Satan leader Anton LaVey had played Polanski's Old Nick, Girdler contacted the California-based Satanist to invite his participation. LaVey was indisposed – virgins to slaughter, babies to roast, etc. – but he despatched one of his demons, who flew out to Kentucky and supervised the final scenes, re-wrote some of the dialogue and littered the background with props from LaVey's collection. What the Horned One thought of the finished product is not on record... Girdler died in a helicopter crash while scouting locations in the Philippines, 21 January, 1978. He was just 30 years old.

Made in Kentucky.
*see also: **Three on a Meathook***

ATTACK OF THE BEAST CREATURES
– Michael Stanley (1983)
aka *Hell Island*

The 1930s. When a ship goes down in the mid-Atlantic, a handful of Gatsbyesque survivors are washed up on a leafy but apparently deserted island, along with a few of the ship's crew. Tensions flare between the sailors and a wealthy passenger called Morgan (John Vichiola), but class friction is the least of their worries. The water on the island is so acidic it dissolves human flesh, and the woods are teeming with little red manikin creatures, with razor teeth and glowing eyes…

If you weren't afraid of lawsuits you could bung this out on DVD as *The Muppet Island Massacre*. Using puppetry techniques that make *Basil Brush* look like the last word in animatronics, Michael Stanley's ultra-cheap monster movie may lack plausibility but at least it gives tedious, glossy efforts like *Ghoulies* and *Troll* a run for their money. A major point of reference is Dan Curtis's wonderful TV movie *Trilogy of Terror* (1975), in which Karen Black fights to the death with a demon doll that could have been the parent of these critters. But *Trilogy of Terror* was professionally directed and tightly edited: *Attack of the Beast Creatures*, sad to say, has no real sense of pacing or dramatic structure. The wacko appeal wears off after a while, due to the static nature of the puppets which, when 'running', are simply being jiggled along from beneath the screen. When first they appear, the red-faced creatures with long black hair

Asylum of Satan
aka **The Satan Spectrum** (working title)
aka **Satan's Spectrum** (MPAA title)
©1971. Studio 1 Associates, Inc.
Studio 1 Associates presents
director: William B. Girdler. producer: J. Patrick Kelly, III. director of photography: William L. Asman. story and screenplay: William B. Girdler & J. Patrick Kelly, III. "The Satan Spectrum Theme", "Lucina's Theme" written by William Girdler, arranged by William Girdler Greg Walker, performed by Eddy Dee and The Blues Express; "Red Light Lady" written and arranged by William Girdler, sung by Nick Jolley. edited by Gene Ruggiero. production managers: Pat Kelly, Lee Jones. production secretary: Clare Bond Pearce. script clerk: Lois Haynie. 2nd unit cameraman: Henry B. Asman, Jr. sound recorders: Warren Maxey, Dave Portugal. assistant editor: Eva Ruggiero. assistant director: Lee Jones. special effects: Richard Albain, Jr. special make-up: James C. Pickett, III. make-up artist: Glen Lawrence. property: Alice Hay. wardrobe mistress: Barbara Girdler. chief electrician: Raymond Jackson. key grip: Tom Todd. head gaffer: Dan Cunningham. still photographer: Mike Kohnhorst. hair styles: Jon Potter of Hairbenders, Inc. Miss Borelli and Mr. Jolley's clothing furnished by Schupp and Snyder, Inc. of Louisville, Ky. publicity manager: Robert E. Lee. technical consultant: Church of Satan. titles and optical: H&H Color Lab. sound mix: Metro-Goldwyn-Mayer Studios. The Producers wish to thank the Jefferson County (Kentucky) Police for their assistance. filmed on location in Jefferson County (Kentucky, USA).
Cast: *Charles Kissinger (Jason Specter / Martine). Carla Borelli (Lucina Martin). Nick Jolley (Chris Duncan). Louis Bandy (Tom Walsh). Claude Wayne Fulkerson (head aide). Jack Peterkin (Doctor Nolan). Sherry Steiner (blind girl). Mimi Honce (cripple). Harry Roehrig (mute). Don Dunkle. Joan Edwards. Gary Morris. Liz Cherry. Don Cox. P. J. Childers. Biggs Tabler. Beth Pearce. Jim Pickett. Nancy Marshall. Ken Jones. Lila Boden. Karen Stone. Lynne Kelly. Pamela Gatz (the creature).*

IT'S A FIGHT FOR SURVIVAL, A RUNNING BATTLE TO ESCAPE THE ISLAND AND THE ATTACK OF THE BEAST CREATURES.

A monstrous storm at sea turns an ocean voyage into a bloody nightmare.
The survivors of the horrifying disaster find themselves stranded on an unchartered island, finding death and disaster at every turn.

opposite page, top right:
This US video cover for **Another Son of Sam** does what the film itself refuses to do and gives the killer a face…

this page, top:
Black magic rites and creepy-crawly weirdness erupt at a private sanatorium, in **Asylum of Satan**.

left:
Strap this video cover for **Attack of the Beast Creatures** to your face and cut out the eyeholes and you too can be one of the Beast Creatures – pretty much, anyway…

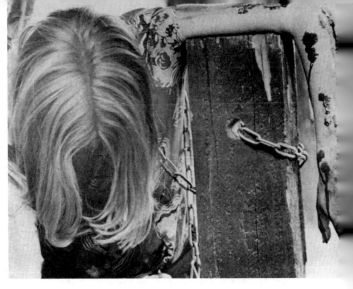

Attack of the Beast Creatures
(Australian video title)
aka **Hell Island** (original title)
© 1983. Obelisk Motion Pictures Ltd.
Obelisk Motion Pictures Ltd. and Joseph Brenner present.
director: Michael Stanley. producers: Michael Stanley, William R. Szlinsky. associate producers: Robert Haborak, Robert W. Sherwood. story and screenplay: Robert A. Hutton. director of cinematography: Robert A. Hutton. music: John P. Mozzi. additional music: Sean H. Lezotte. editing: Robert A. Hutton, Michael Stanley. special mechanical effects: Robert T. Firgelewski. costumes: Sally Sherwood. hair styles: D J's Hair-Inn. property master: Sally Rohac-Hutton. sound: Robert T. Firgelewski, Frans Kal. art director: Robert A. Hutton. assistant director: William R. Szlinsky. 2nd asst. director: Joanne Stanley. special effects: Robert Firgelewski. casting: John Vichiola. camera operator: Robert A. Hutton. 2nd camera operator: Michael Stanley. focus puller: William R. Szlinsky. hair styling: Joseph Garbus, Carol Garbus. percussions: Keith Robinson. guitar effects: Steve C. Pasqua. mattes: Robert A. Hutton. production sound: Robert Firgelewski, Frank Williams. re-recording: Dominick Tavella. property master: Sally Rohac-Hutton. monster design: Robert A. Hutton. gaffers: William R. Szlinsky, Robert Lengyel. editors: Robert A. Hutton, Michael Stanley. assistant editor: Sally Rohac-Hutton. titles: Ian Clark. key grip: Robert Firgelewski. grips: Ronald Haupler Sr., Frans Kal. costume supervisor: Sally Sherwood. catering: Ann Stanley, Arlene Stanley. prop builder: William A. Matzonkai. production secretary: Sally Rohac-Hutton. boats: Robert Bohman. negative matcher: J.G. Films, Inc. timer: Joseph Martocci. dailies: Du Art. equipment: F. & B. Ceco. production assistants: Janis Firgelewski, Ronald A. Haupler Sr., Mildred B. Hauser, Christopher A. Hutton, Joanne Stanley, Gail P. Szlinsky, Mary Szlinsky, Jason M. Szlinsky, Robert S. Szlinsky, Anthony Tranquillo III, Chantel Tranquillo. Special thanks to the town of Fairfield, CT.; the town of Stratford, CT.; Joseph Hauser; Roger Homa. filmed on location in the towns of Fairfield and Stratford (Connecticut, USA).
Cast: Robert Nolfi (John Trieste). Julia Rust (Cathy). Robert Lengyel (Case Quinn). Lisa Pak (Diane). Frank Murgalo (Philip). John Vichiola (Mr. Morgan). Kay Bailey (Mrs. Gordon). Frans Kal (Pat). Robert T. Firgelewski. (Mr. Bruin). Ronald A. Haupler Sr. (first sailor). Robert A. Hutton (second sailor). Joanne Stanley (drowning woman). Christopher Hutton (monster vocals).

and tiny white teeth are funny, even alarming, but I'm afraid the invisible strings suspending my disbelief snapped about halfway through the movie. Essentially, once we've seen the little varmints the film has nothing more to offer, the camera merely following the cast laboriously back to the shore as the monsters pounce and nibble. It reminded me of Italian gore marathons like *Eaten Alive!* and *Emanuelle and the Last Cannibals*: films that force you to pay for your bloodlust by watching actors wandering through endless foliage. There's no explanation of what these creatures are, indeed no one even discusses it. The whole venture would have been vastly improved if we'd learned that the homicidal gonks really *are* puppets; the result would be a sort of alfresco *Puppetmaster*. Instead, what could have been cheerfully bizarre becomes silly and repetitious. Even the last line of the movie is a dud: *"What were those things?"* ought surely to have been, *"What* were *those things?"* Michael Stanley filmed this in Fairfield Connecticut, in 1983. It appears to have been his only contribution to the movie industry.

Made in Connecticut.

AXE
– Frederick Friedel (1974)
See interview with Frederick Friedel.

Made in North Carolina.

THE BARN OF THE NAKED DEAD
– Alan Rudolph (1973)
aka *Nightmare Circus*
aka *Terror Circus*
aka *Caged Women*

Three young dancers on their way to Las Vegas – Simone (Manuella Thiess), Sheri (Sherry Alberoni) and Corrine (Gyl Roland) – spend the night in their car when it breaks down in the Nevada desert. Next morning they are awakened by André (Andrew Prine), a young man who offers to drive them to a telephone. Arriving at his ramshackle farm, the girls explore the outbuildings and discover a caged cougar – and a barn where nearly a dozen women are shackled to posts driven into the ground. André adds the three new arrivals to his collection, but becomes convinced that Simone is the reincarnation of his dead mother…

Shot in the Nevada desert by Alan Rudolph, this is a sleazy 'skeleton in the closet' for the director of *Choose Me* and *Trouble in Mind*. It's also a great vehicle for the wonderful Andrew Prine, star of *The Centerfold Girls* and *Simon, King of the Witches*.

There's not much of a story: things grind to a halt about half-an-hour in, along with the fates of the female cast, who are shackled in the titular barn by Prine's psychopath, and occasionally forced to perform pathetic mock circus acts spurred at the end of his whip. The circus motif, however, feels barely developed, as if the story has been hurriedly convened around a collection of battered cages unexpectedly discovered at the location. (The livestock amounts to the cougar, a snake, two skinny donkeys, and a couple of ducks.) A single dialogue exchange early on, between a theatrical agent and his secretary, refers to the famed Las Vegas venue, Circus Circus (a hotel resort and casino with pulchritudinous live entertainment). Perhaps it's an attempt to link the scuzzy goings on at André's farm to a broader sense of female exploitation, but Rudolph is really pushing his luck: this is definitely not the place to pontificate on such matters!

The Barn of the Naked Dead (or *Terror Circus* as it was originally called) does have some merit as a downbeat exercise in mood. The washed-out earth colours of the desert, the steely glare of the sky, the forlorn disarray of the old farm buildings and the scurvy collection of animals exude a hopeless, depressive feel, which perhaps accounts for the captives' lack of effort to escape. Certainly, the minimal 'brutality' we observe doesn't really explain why the spirit of these women has been so totally broken. We never even see André with a gun, the suggestion being that he has overpowered his captives by force of personality alone. Female viewers in particular will regard the scene where three new girls are captured, apparently without fighting back, unbelievable to the point of offensiveness. (For an interesting contrast, see Don Jones's *Abducted*, where the victims show a great deal more initiative and courage.) Rudolph himself seems embarrassed by the far-fetched scenario, cutting away so as to avoid explaining how three fit young women are shackled by one unarmed man.

Depicting women as physically weak is one thing; to show them as slow-witted is quite another: André unshackles Simone because he thinks she's his dead mother returned to life – but when she's untied she then watches, without a word, as he bullwhips her friend, when it would surely have occurred to her to use her newfound 'maternal authority' to stop him. André drags one victim out to the cougar cage, and as the creature snarls, he daubs the girl's dress with cow's blood – while telling her she can go. That the victim naively imagines she's being freed, when it's blindingly obvious she's about to be hunted down by the hungry carnivore, indicts the scriptwriter not the character.

Frankly, much of this would be quite annoying if it wasn't for Prine, who is by far the most interesting circus act in town. He chews the scenery for sure, but he can swivel on a dime and be genuinely unsettling. Whether he's menacing a bound victim with a python (*"You're going to learn his ways. His movements. You're going to get inside of him. And he's going to get inside of you."*), or explaining to Simone why the victims are never missed (*"No one misses these little animals out in the jungle. The jungle has a very short memory…"*), he plays the part with the gusto it needs, rescuing the film from the doldrums.

The female exploitation theme barely registers, but a recurrent jibe about the Army's use of the Nevada desert for nuclear testing was obviously intended to be noticed. However, for a director whose first film, *Premonition* (1970), took the hippy culture to heart, this lame excursion into fifties atom-bomb paranoia smacks of desperation: if you're going to bash the Establishment in order to beef up your sleazier fantasies, fine, but take a cudgel not a peashooter. Prine's father, deformed and mutated by atomic radiation, stalks the farmstead and occasionally picks off a fleeing victim, although why he attacks his son later on remains a mystery. At least this otherwise arbitrary plot device – sorry, character – ensures that all does not end well for the shed full of victims, leaving the viewer with a fantastically cold, empty sensation.

Alan Rudolph is respected as a left-of-centre explorer of the American psyche, the sort of figure who might one day direct something educated people could agree was the cinematic equivalent of The Great American Novel. How surprising then to discover, lurking at the quieter end of his CV, this considerably less salutary title. Rudolph never talks about *The Barn of the Naked Dead* or *Premonition*, and they are rarely listed in books or serious studies of his career. Of course, they were both made when he was still quite young, but since they're out there on videotape with his name on them, I'm surprised he's unwilling to at least put them into context. There's certainly an interesting tale to be told about the gulf between this movie (shot in January 1973) and his well-regarded drama *Welcome to L.A.*, made just three years later and generally treated as his first film. During this time, Rudolph struck up a close working relationship with Robert Altman, who

gave him the second assistant director's role on *The Long Goodbye* (1973) and *California Split* (1974), and the assistant director's job on *Nashville* (1975): perhaps it was Altman who urged him to suppress his 'juvenilia' and start over?

Technical work on the movie is all fairly competent, and from the frequent tracking shots and confident handling of the actors you can tell that Rudolph has talent. All of the film's real flaws are attributable to the script by 'Gerald Cormier' and someone named 'Roman Valenti'. The print under review is the Australian video with the screen title *The Barn of the Naked Dead*, and Rudolph receives clear directorial credit under his own name. Other sources have reported the film as *directed* by Gerald Cormier, leading to the likely supposition that this is in fact a Rudolph pseudonym; in which case he wrote and produced as well as directed the film (it wouldn't be the first time: Rudolph is credited with all three roles on *Premonition*). The original version, *Terror Circus*, or a subsequent retitling of the movie as *Nightmare Circus*, may have used the Cormier name as director, but I've been unable to check these prints.

Alan Rudolph was born 18 December, 1943. His father, Oscar Rudolph, worked on many classic sixties TV shows like *The Brady Bunch*, *I Dream of Jeannie* and *Batman*. Fans of the animated series *Josey and the Pussycats* may be interested to know that Pussycat voice-artist Sherry Alberoni plays one of the new girls in *Barn*. The plot bears similarities to the later case of Robert Hansen, of Anchorage, Alaska, who between 1977-1981 tortured and sexually abused seventeen women: he then turned the naked victims loose in the country, gave them a head start, and tracked them down with a high-powered hunting rifle. The victims included prostitutes, topless dancers, and barmaids. He was eventually caught thanks to one escapee's testimony: ballistics evidence ensured he received life imprisonment.

Made in Nevada and California.

The Barn of the Naked Dead
(US theatrical re-release title)
aka **Terror Circus** (original US theatrical title)
aka **Nightmare Circus** (US video title)
aka **Caged Women** (title on German DVD)
© 1973/1975. C.M.C. Pictures Corp.
C.M.C. Pictures Corporation presents.
director: Alan Rudolph. executive producer: Shirlee F. Jamail. producer: Gerald [Jerald] Cormier. associate producer: Marvin Almeas. story by Gerald Cormier. screenplay: Roman Valenti. director of photography: E. Lynn. music composed and conducted by Tommy Vig. song "Evil Eyes" by Tommy Vig, Harvey Siders, Chuck Niles, sung by Pamela Miller. editor: M K Productions, Inc. filmed with Panavision equipment. colour by Technicolor. titles by Westheimer Company. special make-up and visual effects created by Byrd Holland and Douglas White. assistant to the producer: Joan Cormier. art director: Bill Conway. production manager: John Patrick Graham. assistant director: Eddie Markley. script supervisor: Tony Lanza. still photographer: Dan Dayton. gaffer: Bobby Jones. best boy: Brink Brydon. key grip: Ken Johnson. sound mixer: John Vincent. boom man: David Keith. property master: Al Cormier. wardrobe: Allen Apone. assistant film editor: Tom Penick. sound effects and music editor: Frank A. Coe. filmed in February and March 1973 on location in Nevada and Southern California locations (USA).
Cast: Andrew Prine (Andre). Manuella Thiess (Simone). Sherry Alberoni (Sheri). Gyl Roland (Corrine). Shiela Bromley (Mrs. Baynes). Gil Lamb (Mr. Alvarez). Al Cormier (Sheriff Stanford). Chuck Niles (Derek Moore). Jennifer Ashley (flower child). Laura Campbell (Laura). Sonja Dunson (Sonja). Karene Fredrik (Karene). Lin Henson (Lin). Julene Lontere (crazy girl). Jean Manson (Jean). Leslie Oliver (Leslie). Marlene Tracy (Marlene). Byrd Holland (club manager). Nick Archondo (1st deputy). Billy Holms (2nd deputy). Bernie Schwartz (1st hunter). Bill Conway (2nd hunter). David Miller (highway patrolman).

Images from **The Barn of the Naked Dead**:

opposite page, top right:
The blood-caked Corinne (Gyl Roland) is tied to a post, in a scene missing from some prints of the film.

opposite page, bottom left:
André (Andrew Prine) with Simone (Manuella Thiess), the victim he comes to believe is his mother.

top left:
André turns against Simone when she tries to help the others.

top right:
André with another cowering victim.

left:
Daddy's home!

bottom right:
Australian press-art for **Basket Case** plays
on the 'ET in a cycle-basket' image to
amusing effect.

opposite page, top left:
Belial attacks and rapes Sharon (Terri Susan
Smith): it's worth noting that in Christian
myth, Belial is said to be a demon of lust.
The word is also frequently translated from
the Hebrew as 'without worth'; significant to
Basket Case, since this is the attitude of the
parents and doctors who separate Belial from
his able-bodied twin.

opposite page, top right:
US video cover artwork.

BASKET CASE
– Frank Henenlotter (1981)

Does this evergreen splatter favourite really need a synopsis? Young Duane Bradley (Kevin Van Hentenryck) moves into a terminally scuzzy New York hotel, with only a mysterious wicker basket for company. A succession of people enquiring *"What's in the basket?"* soon regret their curiosity, for inside is Duane's horribly deformed Siamese twin brother, Belial – an angry distended bollock of flesh, with sharp teeth, powerful claws, and one hell of a temper. Duane and Belial were separated, against their will, by a trio of quack doctors (Diana Browne, Lloyd Pace, and Bill Freeman), who added insult to injury by leaving Belial to die in the trash. Now the brothers are reunited, scouring the Big Apple for the surgeons responsible, so that Belial can reach closure by slashing them all to ribbons…

Shot cheaply on weekends during 1980, this story of "a malignant jack-in-the-box", to quote director Frank Henenlotter, is that rare thing: an exploitation film made by a diehard fan which holds its own alongside the movies that inspired it. It's a splatter-comedy that nevertheless plays the genre game to the hilt. Henenlotter has his cake, eats it, and hurls it at the viewer at the same time, with a film that is simultaneously a slice of authentic Big Apple scuzz, a parody of the same, and a here's-mud-in-your-eye attack on the expectations of cult film viewers who thought they'd seen it all. It's also a gentle piece of character comedy, and intriguingly shows the beginnings of a homoeroticism that would flourish in *Brain Damage* (whose young male lead provided some topless beefcake in a genre where visual 'gay interest' is fleeting to say the least).

Basket Case is touching without being cloying (which for me is where the sequels went wrong). It's sweet and sour, mean and moving, grotty and generous, hovering between extremes in a far more dexterous, playful way than most of the 42nd Street sleaze from which Henenlotter drew his inspiration. The gore is OTT to the point of ridicule, and we know we're being encouraged in our laughter by the filmmaker, who sets up his blood-spewing sequences with the loving eye of a true H.G. Lewis fan. When a particularly deserving victim receives a face quilled with surgical scalpels we're seeing the true progeny of Lewis's *Gore Gore Girls* joyously delivered for the 1980s. Henenlotter was a first generation gorehound, a fan of *Ilsa* and *Olga* before there really *was* a trash-movie cult scene to speak of. Crucially, he was also creative enough to add his own brand of manic humour to excesses borne of Lewis's *Blood Feast* and Andy Milligan's *The Ghastly Ones*. A true midnight movie mutant, *Basket Case* plays like a hybrid of Lewis's jocular sadism and John Waters's affectionate sickness.

And, not unlike the Waters films, *Basket Case* savages to deceive. Despite the gore, the true heart of the film is fraternal love and the sanctity of life. There's a terrific, touching scene where the young Duane (Sean McCabe), having undergone surgical separation from his conjoined twin, sneaks out of the house and finds his twisted little brother in a black refuse sack next to the rubbish bins, abandoned but still alive. Duane lovingly rescues tiny Belial, and it's this almost Dickensian moment that provides the cynical comedy and blood-frenzy of the film with its emotional counter-balance. Echoes of Tod Browning's *Freaks* are perhaps only really explored in the sequels, but the implication is that life – at least post-natal life – is sacred: not exactly a common theme in 42nd Street theatres of the time!

Not that the film is some earnest moral tract. There's intelligence alright, but it's twinned with a grimy quality that unites perfectly with the mangier celluloid denizens of The Deuce. *Basket Case* would happily sit on a double bill with *The Headless Eyes*, and my recommendations don't come much higher than that! Putting a sleazy sexual spin on an old horror movie cliché, *Basket Case* includes a scene where the monster eats-*out* the girl (a sick joke that finds its echo in the blow-job scene of *Brain Damage*). Some reviewers claim that Belial's

rape, murder and necrophiliac molestation of the heroine add a sour note to an otherwise effective black comedy, and it's true that the film lurches into a place less warmly amusing at this point. By opting for such a gloomy climax, though, Henenlotter is simply following the current of the times, before unhappy endings were ushered out of the genre in favour of survivalist heroics or trite 'evil-lives-on' codas.

Judging by Henenlotter's interviews, and his brisk, friendly commentary tracks, deeper discussion of his movies' themes is a non-starter. He embodies a passionately self-effacing, practical, down-to-earth tendency in American filmmaking, where the greatest sin is pretension. He's a terrific raconteur and provides a most energetic commentary on the 'Something Weird' DVD release of *Basket Case*, which I recommend you hear. He's also unstintingly generous to the cast: "It's the people in front of the camera who made this work, because there was nobody *behind* the camera!" You can tell he's a proud parent though, by the way he asserts, "Fifty years from now this is *still* going to be ugly and offensive!"

But for all his bluff, hearty demeanour, Henenlotter is a literate guy whose intelligence cannot help but give itself away. Perhaps the most telling example is the way that Belial's rape of Sharon (Terri Susan Smith) ties in with an earlier scene in which an aunt (Ruth Neuman) reads to Duane and Belial from Shakespeare's *The Tempest*. The lines are Caliban's, beginning: "*Be not afraid; the isle is full of noises, sounds and sweet airs, that give delight, and hurt not.*" The reference is far from gratuitous: in *The Tempest*, Caliban is referred to as a beast or monster by Prospero. He rapes Miranda, Prospero's daughter, and yet Shakespeare gives him a poetic sensitivity. He is depicted with sympathy, not disgust: an outsider who, un-nurtured by society, could hardly be expected to know any better. Prospero calls him, "*A devil, a born devil, on whose nature nurture can never stick…*" It's this assessment that Henenlotter is extending to his 'monster'. Seen in this light, the rape-murder is an inevitable reflection of Belial's savage instincts, and, having already enjoyed his vengeance, we cannot so easily withdraw our sympathy.

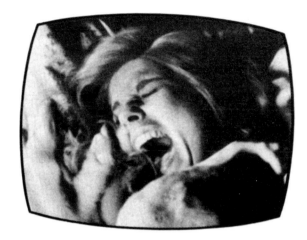

Henenlotter's retirement from directing to shepherd other people's sleazy movies onto the shelves (via his work for Something Weird) may have been a boon to the collector, but it's a loss to the horror genre. Hopefully, by the time you read this, Henenlotter's comeback film, *Bad Biology*, will have joined his best work and revived interest in a true genre talent.

Made in New York City.

THE BEAUTIES AND THE BEAST
– Ray Naneau [Nadeau] (1973)
aka *The Beast and the Vixens*

The Beauties and the Beast is barely an hour long, but tedious direction and the generally wretched tech credits sink this horny Bigfoot tale to the bottom of the creek in half that time. Burdening the film with stock music of the *Lassie Come Home* variety, and a time-wasting straight-to-camera intro about the Bigfoot legend, Naneau plays it for limp comedy and limper sex, with softcore regular Uschi Digard and friends lounging around nude before engaging in tiresome fake humping. As for horror, forget about it – there's not a single scare or *frisson* to be had. This sort of T&A/monster combo might have tickled 'em in the 1950 and 60s (see *Monsters Crash the Pajama Party*) but by the 1970s it took more than the addition of a few shaky beaver shots to make it work.

The film bears a copyright date of 1973, but the softcore frolics feel more suited to the late sixties. Some sources credit the director's surname as Nadeau. The print of *The Beauties and the Beast* however, reads Naneau. To add to the confusion, the credits begin with the phrase "RAYNAD PRODUCTIONS presents". Some sources list actor Marius Mazmanian as co-director, although he's not credited as such on the print I've seen. At least someone connected with this movie had a sense of humour – the production company is Sophisticated Films.

Naneau/Nadeau was the producer of *The Midnight Graduate* (1970) and associate producer of *Snakes* (1974). *The Beauties and the Beast* is his only credit as director. If the Internet Movie Database is correct, he worked as editor (*A Sweet Sickness* in 1968, *The Love Garden* in 1972) and cinematographer (*The Satin Mushroom* in 1969) and acted a few tiny roles in a smattering of studio films. There is apparently another film with the same title, directed the same year by porn maestro Ron Jeremy.

Made in: unknown

BLACK DEVIL DOLL FROM HELL
– Chester N. Turner (1984)
aka *The Puppet* (original title)

Unbelievable. Probably unwatchable, but certainly one of a kind... This shot-on-video story of a possessed, dreadlocked ventriloquist's doll turning a devout church-going black woman (Shirley L. Jones) onto the joys of glove-puppet sex is truly

something to behold, providing you keep your finger no more than an inch away from the fast-forward button at all times. Technically this is as rough and ready as it gets: the dialogue sounds like arguments coming through the wall from the apartment next door, the 'go-motion' animation is beyond primitive, and the ugly videotape 'look' is made even more unbearable by the almost total absence of editing, which leaves uneventful scenes to play in real time. The sexual frisson depends on the glove puppet's brutish machismo turning a Christian woman on to rape-sex, which barely registers as tasteless given how lo-o-ong everything takes. If that wasn't enough, the score is basically one riff played on home organ and drum machine, chugging psychotically away over just about every scene. The stubbornness of this alone is enough to make your mind collapse – I mean, how hard could it have been to write a second piece?

The Beauties and the Beast
aka **The Beast and the Vixens**
© 1973. Sophisticated Films, Inc.
Raynad Productions presents a Second Unit production.
director: Ray Naneau [Nadeau]. producer: Art Jacobs. screen play: Gaynor Maclaren. 2nd unit supervised by E.M. Brown. production manager: Eric Nevil. camera technician: William Foster. sound recording: Art Names. grip - gaffer: Hal Strong. original song: David Ankrum. editorial: Editorial Services. continuity: Paula Ross. colour by Alexander Film Services.
Cast: Jean Gibson. Uschi Digard [Uschi Digart]. Marius Mazmanian. Bob Makay [sic]. Patrick Scott. David Wheeler. Susan Wescott. John Shell. Carol Evins [sic]. Sandra Carey. Sharon Kelly. Tami Lynn. Beverly Wallace. Paul Kalin. Charles David. Brian Jacobs.

top:
US video cover for Chester N. Turner's
uniquely bizarre entry in the possessed doll
subgenre...

opposite page:
This US poster for **Bloodrage** shows a killer
more suited to overpowering women than the
skinny youth who actually stars in the film...

below:
Andy Milligan's marvellous **Blood** made its
so-far-only appearance on video in the early
1980s, via the UK's Iver Film Services.

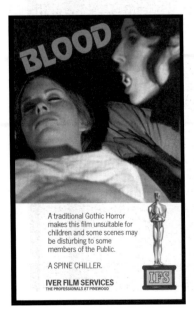

A traditional Gothic Horror
makes this film unsuitable for
children and some scenes may
be disturbing to some
members of the Public.

A SPINE CHILLER.

IVER FILM SERVICES
THE PROFESSIONALS AT PINEWOOD

I've got to be careful not to oversell this: it really is the pits of
Pluto – awesomely awful. At best, *Black Devil Doll from Hell*
stampedes to a distant second in the queue (behind the psychedelic
brainstorm that is *BoardingHouse*) whenever shot-on-video horror
madness is uppermost in your mind. How's that for qualified praise?
The same director essayed a second shot-on-video horror called
Tales from the Quadead Zone in 1987. It falls outside the scope of
this book by a year or two, but if anything could tempt me to write
a follow-up covering the years 1986 to the present day it would be
a conversation with a bona-fide eccentric like Chester Turner. If
nothing else we might find out what on Earth 'Quadead' means...

Turner remains an elusive figure, and the film gives no clues
as to his location. The Rev. Obie Dunson, who appears as himself
in the film delivering a sermon in Church, is currently pastor at the
New Pasadena Baptist Church in Chicago, which suggests that
Black Devil Doll from Hell could well have been made in Illinois.
Therefore we can thankfully assume that our man is not the same
Chester Turner who raped and murdered nine women in the Los
Angeles area between 1987 and 1998.

Made in: unknown (Illinois?)

THE BLACK ROOM
– Norman Thaddeus Vane and Elly Kenner (1981)
See interview with Norman Thaddeus Vane.

Made in California.

BLOOD
– Andy Milligan (1974)

I've been fascinated by Andy Milligan ever since reading a
feature about him in *Fangoria* back in the early 1980s. His films
sounded brutal and bizarre, and the titles – *The Ghastly Ones*, *The
Bloodthirsty Butchers*, *Torture Dungeon* – promised all manner of
depravity. But that's not all: I was also intrigued to learn that many
horror aficionados held his work in contempt, deploring it as
unbearably cheap and sloppy. Here, it seemed, was a director even

H.G. Lewis fans could look down upon. *Blood* was the first
Milligan movie that I saw, and I began by feeling the usual 'bad
film' vibe of detached amusement. Twenty minutes in, though,
and I was totally engaged. I vowed then and there that I would
watch as much Milligan as humanly possible...

Well, the 'humanly possible' clause turned out to be a useful
caveat, excusing me from Milligan's work beyond 1980, but I'm
still very much a fan. Milligan, who died on 3 June, 1991, operated
on a different plane to the rest of horror cinema, but to me he fulfils
one of the major aesthetic criteria: the world he created is
consistent, and distinct from any other. Who cares if that world is –
to put it mildly – a place not everyone wants to visit? Andy
Milligan made movies that deserve to be considered as art. Every
cramped shot and overstuffed line of dialogue communicates an
ethos and a vision of the world. You simply don't *make* films like
this if you're in it for the money, or the prestige of being a director,
or because your investors agreed it was a sound business move.
Andy Milligan, bless his wicked soul, was an artist.

And yet, even some who can appreciate the man's work turn
up their noses at *Blood*, claiming that its comparatively grime-free
35mm photography lessens the Milligan magic. Talk about
specialisation! For you, dear reader, it's probably like insisting
that a broken leg is preferable to a fractured skull. But don't think
you can slither away to A&E yet. In Milligan's universe everyone
is smashed, broken or damaged in some way, or if not then soon
to be. Besides, there's an uncommon lightness in the air this time.
Hang around and ask yourself if this is perhaps Milligan's version
of *The Addams Family*! *Blood* is a Monster-Medley that flaunts
all the classic Milligan hallmarks, but in a way that feels
curiously ironic. Yes, I know; given the dizzying lack of realism
in Milligan's films, it seems a quixotic aim to establish self-
parody. And yet *Blood*, for me, is a horror-comedy; arch and
deliberately absurd. I'd say it's the most sheerly enjoyable
Milligan film.

We open with an image of roses blooming in a well-tended
garden. All seems well with the world: a benign impression that is
allowed to accumulate for just a few precious seconds before
Milligan's unique delirium sweeps it away, along with all
thoughts of 'normal' cinematic values. We are dealing here, in
case you want to know, with a scenario that demands the son of
The Wolfman, Dr. Orlofski (Allan Berendt), should unwittingly
have married Regina, Count Dracula's daughter (Hope
Stansbury). We have to trust that Orlofski believes his wife really
is Dracula's daughter, despite the fact that he sees her plastic
fangs falling out. But these are mere details. Why, downstairs,
Carrie the maid (Patti Gaul) is going about her chores, tending to
Orlofski's collection of carnivorous plants, with a boil on her leg
the size of a watermelon. As the camera struggles, with her, to
negotiate the cramped interior of what was then Milligan's own
home, we're made poignantly aware of the sheer awkwardness of
running this household. Carrie is a devout Catholic, something of
a problem when the lady of the house is, shall we say, indisposed
to The Cross. Walking in to find Carrie blessing a pot roast, a
furious Regina shrieks that the offending symbol be hidden away.
"I have a right to my own beliefs!" snaps Carrie. Imagine – a
Christian and a vampire forced to live in the same house: it's like
a mean-spirited reality TV show, with participants chosen for
maximum friction. Orlando (Michael Fischetti), a legless
manservant on a wheeled trolley, and a senile, slavering woman
called Carlotta (Pichulina Hampi) make up the household. If only
I had time to tell you *their* stories...

Milligan's primary trademark is talk: lots of it. Characters of
at best tertiary importance – like Prudence Towers (Pamela
Adams), Mr. Root's secretary – can suddenly erupt with
passionate intensity (*"I never realised until now how much I
really loathe you"*), often holding forth on their own troubles,
distending the subjective time frame of the movie. These ellipses
continue until the clamour of minor characters obscures the basic
storyline. I don't think it's entirely pretentious to suggest that
there's significance in Milligan's profligate, verbose scripting, his

habit of giving even the lowliest of cast members something meaty and personal to say. I'm not calling him a Communist, an Altman, or a Godard-in-the-rough: but Milligan's generosity with dialogue draws no distinction between the lead actors and the 'hired help', a quality that links him to such alternative universe megastars as John Waters and Paul Morrissey. Perhaps it's part of a sensitivity gay directors can have to the marginalised and excluded (Milligan staged Genet's *The Maids* at The Cino theatre in New York in 1961). Whatever the reason, the hierarchies of Milligan's screenwriting are in chaos: incidental characters usurp the main cast, scenes of doubtful significance swarm the viewer's attention, fleeting asides assume the status of the most favoured aphorism. It's this mélange of the loaded and the casual that gives Milligan's dialogue its deranged excess. It can be over-ripe and theatrical (*"Go to hell."* … *"We're there already."*) or comically adrift between registers (the primly delivered protestation, *"Mr. Root, you are an extremely rude and stingy man."*). The incessant chatter of Orlofski, Regina, Orlando, and Petra (Eve Crosby, as an elderly crone-cum-blackmailer), inspires an auditory dizziness that's matched by the vertiginous camera technique favoured by this most hands-on of directors (Milligan wrote, shot, directed, and edited his films, as well as designing the costumes).

Theatre is of prime importance to Milligan: the films are rarely cinematic. This is a man who devoted a vast amount of his career to greasepaint and boards; who, when he received the occasional pittance to make a movie, drew on theatrical, not cinematic inspiration. As Jimmy McDonough revealed in his marvellous book on Milligan, *The Ghastly One*, Andy's prime contribution to the technical language of cinema is the instruction 'swirl camera' – a phrase written on his scripts to denote a scene of particular intensity. Time and again, climactic sequences in Milligan's work end with the camera shuddering away from briefly glimpsed gore effects to wildly scan the sky, the floor, the walls: as if Milligan, who always operated his camera, had suffered a fit. Bad camerawork? I don't think so. Milligan seems to go for this device when he wants to penetrate the essential detachment of the form. In theatre you don't have to 'swirl' anything; the audience are there to be addressed directly. Milligan's 'swirl camera' instruction is borne of sheer frustration, the act of someone who prefers direct communication. When he says, "swirl camera" he means swirl you!

Milligan is easy to mock and dismiss, as has been proved by many over the years. He's also very difficult to write about, especially if you want to add him to some pantheon or other. His plotlines are so florid you feel like a collaborator with Dullsville if you offer so much as a simple précis. Frankly, I could write another five thousand words about this film alone (so be grateful I'm not in a selfish mood). But I urge you to see *Blood* – it's a Midnight Movie waiting to happen, and in some mad parallel universe it's already playing to packed houses; the audience are dressed as their favourite characters, stars of stage and screen are queuing to appear in the Broadway musical version, and Milligan is the Talk of the Town. God, I wish I lived there…

Made in New York City.

BLOODRAGE

– Joseph Bigwood [Joseph Zito] (1979)
aka *Never Pick Up a Stranger*

Richie (Ian Scott), a withdrawn young man with an implacable hatred of women, kills Beverly (Judith-Marie Bergan), a small-town hooker, during an altercation about money. Carefully concealing his crime, he goes on the run to New York, trailed by Ryan (James Johnston), a cop who's holding a torch for the victim. Living in a seedy apartment block, Richie works his way through several more female victims, before Ryan learns of his whereabouts….

A depressing serial killer story with a cop-vengeance chaser, *Bloodrage* does penance for its many flaws with an effectively grimy mood, playing scene after scene in peeling-wallpaper interiors and piss-soaked New York alleys. Ian Scott, whose hair looks like it dropped onto his head from a tree, is certainly creepy-looking (kind of like Christopher Walken's plain kid brother), but he lacks genuine screen presence and often fails to make the grade dramatically. A scene involving a victim he meets in a bar, Lucy (Blair Trigg), is hampered by the implausibility of this skinny teenager overpowering a healthy older woman. Scott doesn't sell the character, and we can't help but feel that the only reason he succeeds in throttling her is because the director cuts to the attack already in progress and has probably instructed the actress not to struggle too hard.

Joseph Bigwood – actually a pseudonym for the soon-to-be successful slasher director Joseph Zito – amuses himself by using the story to hang out a washing line of influences, perhaps hoping to catch the eye of the studios. (He succeeded, but not with this picture: his efficient 1981 slasher tale *The Prowler* got him a gig directing *Friday the 13th: The Final Chapter* – the fourth film in the series – for Paramount.) Judging by *Bloodrage*, Zito was a big fan of Scorsese and Hitchcock: the urban street squalor and

Blood
© none [1974].
Walter Kent presents.
writer/director: Andy Milligan. lighting: James Vale. sound: Joe Downing. sets: Jim Fox. costumes: Raffiné. titles: B & O Film Opticals. costume supervisor: Agatha Miller. editor: Gerald Jackson. make-up created by Ted Donovan. continuity: Maureen McGrady. technical director: Craig Malcomson. production assistant: Jerry De Coe. unit director: Joseph Miller. production assistant: Walter Springer. production co-ordinator: Irwin Barash. grip: Nicky Guy.
Cast: Allan Berendt (Lawrence Orlofski). Hope Stansbury (Regina Orlofski). Patti Gaul (Carrie). Michael Fischetti (Orlando). Pamela Adams (Prudence Towers). John Wallowitch (Carl Root). Eve Crosby (Petra). Martin Reymert (Mr. Markham). Pichulina Hampi (Carlotta). David Bevans (Jimmy). Hazel Wolffs (nosy neighbour). Joe Downing (Mr. Sharp). Lawrence Sellars (Mr. F). Sophia Andoniadis (Mrs. F). Walter Kent (man in office).

NEVER PICK UP A STRANGER

Starring IAN SCOTT, JUDITH-MARIE BERGAN, JAMES JOHNSTON and LAWRENCE TIERNEY
Music by MICHAEL KARP Screenplay by ROBERT JAHN
Executive Producer TEDDY KARIOFILIS
Produced by JOSEPH ZITO and ALAN M. BRAVEMAN Director JOSEPH BIGWOOD

Bloodrage (UK video title)
aka **Never Pick Up a Stranger**
(US theatrical title)
© 1979. Picture Company of America
director: Joseph Bigwood [Joseph Zito].
executive producer: Teddy Kariofilis. producer:
Joseph Zito, Alan Braveman. associate
producers: William Tasgal, Claire Liberman,
Tom Gioulos, Milton Wolosky. writer: Robert
Jahn. story consultant: Bernhardt J. Hurwood.
directors of photography: Joao Fernandes,
Joseph E. Scherer. music composed,
arranged & conducted by Michael Karp. film
editor: James MacReading. assistant editor:
James H. Nau. art direction: John Lawless,
George Heyward Jr. gaffer: Frost Wilkinson.
assistant electricians: Richard Newhouse,
Michael Sharin, Craig Nelson, Henry
Bronchtein. sound: Gary Rich, Vladimir
Simonenko, Fred Kamiel. boom: Dierk Piffko.
re-recording mixer: Jack Higgins. assistant
cameramen: Fred Pflantzer, Peter Adelaar,
Joel Markowitz, Richard DeStefano. still
photographer: Bobbi Leigh Zito. key grip:
Michael Fedack. grips: John Bolger, Dallas
Garred, Rick Losey, James Gilroy, Ralph
Loggia. location scout: Leo Ryers. special
effects: Deed Rossiter. special effects make-
up: Dennis Eger. make up: Pam Jenrette.
continuity: Jenny Lax. wardrobe: Paulette Aller.
assistant director: Graham Place. assistant to
the producer: Michael Pack. production
assistants: Steven Greenstein, Gary Hill,
Sandra Kaufman, Fred Isola, William Scheck,
Lee Edelman. additional music by David
Mullaney. disco lyrics by Rick Cummins, Neil
Sheppard. sound effects: Roy Valle. titles and
opticals: EFX Unlimited. mixed at: Magno
Sound. colour by Deluxe.
Cast: James Johnston (Ryan). Judith-Marie
Bergan (Beverly). Jerry McGee (Charlie). Ian
Scott (Richard). Patrick Hines (Gus). Buddy
Basch (Motor Inn desk clerk). Harry Linton
(Times Square desk clerk). Pelati Pons (street
murder victim). Jimi Keys (killer). Jerome
Green (1st cop at street murder). Barry
Bernstein (2nd cop at street murder). Shanton
Granger (hometown police captain). Dan
Seymore (pimp in elevator). Copper
Cunningham (prostitute in elevator). Wally
Stern (news dealer). Jery Hewitt (junkie in
police station). Lawrence Tierney (Malone).
Richard Triggs, Tony DeCarlo, Carl Pistilli,
Raymond Martucci (cops in police station).
Eve Packer, Larry Ridell, Erle Bjornstad, Lee
Ford, Ruth Terner, Carol Kosma, Jon E.
Oppenheim (Eastside bar patrons). Blair Trigg
(Lucy). William Richardone (Freddy). Rita
Ebenhart (Candice). Susan Doukas (Myrna).
Bernie Friedman (Abe). Barbara Grace
(Madeline). Kristen Steen (Stevie). Tom Pierce
(Byron). Christine Perdicaro, Susan Lawrence
(Go-Go dancers). Betsy Ramlow (Nancy).
Ralph Monaco (1st bartender). Molly King
(hostess). Leo Tepp (Joe Monroe). Mario
Jensen (2nd bartender). Ramon Rafuir
(Bones). Jessie Hill (prostitute in police
station). Ed Deleo (Karl). Billy Longo (super in
West Side bar). Daniel Revusky (tenant). Wally
Hughes (cowboy). Henry Ferrentino (cab
driver). Rachel Dunn (Richard's dance
partner). Raynor Scheine (Fred). Irwin Keyes,
Clee Burtonya (pimps in hallway).

killer's voice-over mimic *Taxi Driver*; the prologue's post-murder clean-up scene is a direct lift from *Psycho*; and Richie's spying on the occupants of an apartment block from his window explicitly quotes *Rear Window*. Meanwhile, the score by Michael Karp is Hermannesque to the point of plagiarism. Where the film falls down is in its failure to connect these references into an overall style, not least because it seems to have been edited together from separate shoots (Scott's hair changes noticeably between the opening scenes and the rest). The laughably arbitrary resolution (in which Ryan tracks Richie down after seeing him by chance at a hotdog stand, an encounter we hear about but never see) may actually have been forced on the production by lack of money. The running time is a brusque 69 minutes; so either the film had to be finished minus a few days shooting, or some of the material was so weak it had to be excised. Perhaps the biggest problem with *Bloodrage*, though, is that even at such a short length it outstays its welcome, thanks to some repetitious 'peeping tom' scenes that drag on unnecessarily. Rita Ebenhart as Candice, Richie's foulmouthed Jewish neighbour, gives the film a much-needed shot in the arm, and cultish tough-guy Lawrence Tierney turns up to sympathise with Ryan and mutter a few curses about how hard it is being a cop when criminals have rights. The overall tone is not dissimilar to Robert Hammer's *Don't Answer The Phone!*, another serial-killer saga with a right-wing attitude to law enforcement. *Don't Answer the Phone!*, though, is a skilfully obnoxious film that fucks with your head, and it features a blistering lead performance: the bad attitude in *Bloodrage* is not so well decorated.

Zito's first film was *Abduction* (1975), a tabloid headline exploiter which at first glance appears to be about the Patty Hearst case, except that it's based on a novel called *Black Abductor* by Harrison James, which actually preceded Hearst's abduction. By optioning the James novel, Zito was able to make a film seemingly about the Patty Hearst case (the lead character is even called Patricia!) without the threat of a libel action. Patricia was played by Judith-Marie Bergan, i.e. Beverly in *Bloodrage*.

Made in New York City.

right:
Bloodrage somehow avoided being roped into the 'video nasty' controversy, despite its gruesome UK video cover from AVI.

BLOODY BIRTHDAY
– Ed Hunt (1980)
aka *Creeps*
aka *Hide and Go Kill*

Three babies born during a solar eclipse develop into pint-sized psychopaths, who celebrate their tenth birthday by going on a murder spree and killing anyone who gets on their nerves: fathers, sisters, best friends and – probably – people who use the term 'pint-sized'…

The logic behind all this is, to say the least, rather shaky, with the astrological 'explanation' (something to do with Saturn, the planet of emotion, being blocked by the sun and moon) failing to clarify why it takes ten years for the kids to start killing. (A brief Google search indicates that various astrologers consider the 'planet of emotion' to be either Mars, Venus, or that other well-known planet (sic), The Moon. *What*ever…) Nevertheless, I found this a surprisingly taut and enjoyable horror thriller. Basically, it's a slasher movie trifle with a scoop of *The Bad Seed* and some delicious *Children of the Damned* topping, making it another ideal choice for a killer-kid all-nighter, along with Sean MacGregor's *Devil Times Five*, Max Kalmanowicz's *The Children*, John Ballard's *The Orphan* and Robert Voskanian's *The Child* (with maybe Alfred Sole's *Communion* for variation).

I used to see this movie around on video all the time in the early 1980s, but for some reason I never rented it (a mild review from Alan Jones in *Starburst* perhaps stayed my hand). In a way I'm glad I left it so long, as it offered me a time capsule of vintage pleasure from a period I thought I'd more or less exhausted. The last bruised apple at the bottom of the barrel? No, there are some genuinely well-crafted suspense scenes here, along with decent acting and even a slight emotional kick, as the film concentrates not only on the killings, but also on the grief of those, like Melinda Cordell's Mrs. Brody or Lori Lethin's Joyce, who've lost relatives or friends to the mystery killers. It doesn't hurt, either, that the suburban tree-lined locations are so similar to those in John Carpenter's *Halloween*; you keep expecting the kids to bump into Laurie Strode or crazy Doc Loomis. (*Halloween* is sure to have played a big part in the inception of this story.)

Of the three young stars, two are outstanding: Elizabeth Hoy as cunning, manipulative 'angelface' Debbie, and Billy Jacoby (later known as Billy Jayne) as the nerdy but threatening Curtis make even the silliest scenes work. Andy Freeman as Steven is given less to do and consequently loses out, fading into the background somewhat, although he did appear more frequently on the promotional stills. Even the 'good' kid, Timmy (K.C. Martel) makes a go of it, being likeable enough to occasionally deflect our black-hearted, insidious identification with the bad seeds.

Some viewers may find the film tasteless and offensive for casting children as killers, but the kids themselves quite clearly relished their roles. Each of the three were either fresh from another horror project or destined to act in more of the same: Hoy turned up in *Hospital Massacre* three years later, as did Jacoby, funnily enough – he also took roles in *Superstition* (1982), *Cujo* (1983), *Nightmares* (1983), *Demonwarp* (1988), and *Dr. Alien* (1988). Freeman has had the leaner time of it since, appearing in *The Corpse Grinders 2* (2000), poor devil. Martel was already an old hand at the horror game, having played the Lutz family's kid in mainstream smash *The Amityville Horror* the year before. Anyway, given the macabre imagination children bring to their own games, I'd say that adult misgivings are the result of forgetting what it's like to be a child. Ask a group of ten-year-olds which they'd most like to act in, a horror film or a recreation of the Nativity, and I warrant you'll get an answer that would make Jesus himself despair.

The movie has weaknesses though, it has to be said. For instance, why do Curtis and Steven not attack their families, when Debbie attacks hers? The extra killings would mean speeding up the narrative to fit them all in, but fine – that sounds

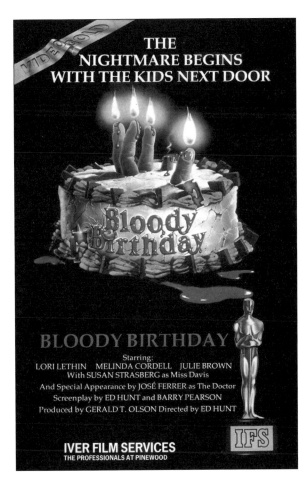

THE NIGHTMARE BEGINS WITH THE KIDS NEXT DOOR

BLOODY BIRTHDAY

Starring:
LORI LETHIN   MELINDA CORDELL   JULIE BROWN
With SUSAN STRASBERG as Miss Davis
And Special Appearance by JOSÉ FERRER as The Doctor
Screenplay by ED HUNT and BARRY PEARSON
Produced by GERALD T. OLSON Directed by ED HUNT

IVER FILM SERVICES
THE PROFESSIONALS AT PINEWOOD

IFS

like an answer to the film's fluctuating tension. Arlon Ober's score is sometimes locked in that TV-movie style of workaday horn and string arrangements, redolent of shows like *Kojak* or *Ironside*. The more exciting moments sound like Harry Manfredini, who of course would have made a better stab at it. And I know it shouldn't really matter, but the story is often extremely far-fetched: a little girl is able to throttle a young woman with a skipping-rope, and a small boy knocks two men unconscious, one with a baseball bat (possible) and one with the flat side of a spade (unlikely). Young Curtis seems to handle a police issue revolver with ease, recoil and all, and a cop is beaten to death, his injuries blamed on a fall down approximately five garden steps. But let's not be too strict about all this; you have to take a forgiving attitude. Regard the flaws with tolerance and look what you get in return: not only is the cop killed early on, but he's set up for it by his own sweet little daughter, who watches impassively as her buddies bash his brains in. One malicious tyke locks his playmate in an old junkyard refrigerator and leaves him to suffocate. And the entire 'rat poison birthday cake' scene had me snickering into my jelly and trifle as if *my* star-chart showed Saturn blocked by the sun and moon. Be honest – movies where kids murder adults are the perfect antidote to that nasty old sadist Steven Spielberg, who routinely victimizes child characters. Sure, *Bloody Birthday*'s gore levels are quite restrained, but when Debbie kills her older sister by firing an arrow into her eye, we can surely cheer the scene without demanding that Lucio Fulci step in to direct?

Bloody Birthday was made in the USA by Ed Hunt, a Canadian who often crossed the border to direct films both in his native country and the States. Hunt began his career with two softcore sex films (*Pleasure Palace* in 1973 and *Diary of a Sinner* in 1974), before turning to sci-fi with a trio of films shot by David Cronenberg's first regular DP, Mark Irwin – *Point of No Return* (1976), *Starship Invasions* (1977) and *Plague* (1978). Producer Gerald Olson went on, during the eighties, to become Director of Production at HBO and a Vice President of

Production at New Line, and later executive produced the comedy hit *Dumb and Dumber* (1994). Writer Barry Pearson wrote two more films for Ed Hunt; the Canada-lensed *Alien Warrior* (1985) and *The Brain* (1988).

Finally, a word about credits. Perhaps you've noticed already that movies starring children frequently credit the adults first, often giving 'above the title' priority to actors who only deserve third or fourth billing, and relegating the young leads who've acted their socks off to also-ran status. It's a convention that strikes me as outrageously unfair, and it gives me an idea for a sequel. How about *Bloody Birthday 2*, with disgruntled child actors bumping off adults who've stolen top billing?

Made in: unknown

BLOOD FREAK
– Brad F. Grinter [Frank Merriman Grinter] and Steve Hawkes (1972)
aka *Blood Freaks*

Who said Franz Kafka's *The Metamorphosis* was unfilmable? This relocates the story from early 20th Century Prague to Miami Florida in the early 1970s, the affliction is poultry-related not bug-related, and I guess some artistic license has been taken with the hero's need for the blood of dope-fiends; but hey, it's a lot more fun than Welles's *The Trial*.

Herschell (Steve Hawkes), a muscle-bound lunk with a greasy quiff and a truckers' rest-room air about him, is dating Angel, a nice Christian girl, who introduces him to her sex-pot sister, Ann. Ann promptly takes a shine to the big fella, and rather than let all that beef go to waste on Miss Goody-Two-Shoes (*"By the time she's through preachin' to him, he'll be so screwed up I won't have a chance!"*), she seduces him into bed by turning him on to marijuana. At first Herschell is resistant to the siren call of drugs, but he caves in when Ann calls him a coward. This tactic of manipulating the hero by casting doubt on his manliness works again soon after, when two agricultural boffins persuade him to be their experimental guinea-pig, using the same strategy. The experiment involves Herschell eating specially modified turkey meat: cue catastrophe, as his body (and mind) go into a drug-cocktail meltdown, leaving him with, well, after-effects… How to put this? His head… *mutates*… into a turkey's head…

A DRACULA ON DRUGS!

BLOOD FREAK

Bloody Birthday
aka **Creeps**
aka **Hide and Go Kill**
© 1980. The Happy Birthday Company, L.P. A Judica production.
director: Ed Hunt. producer: Gerald T. Olson. screenplay: Ed Hunt and Barry Pearson. director of photography: Stephen Posey. music composed and conducted by Arlon Ober. film editor: Ann E. Mills. casting: Judith Holstra. associate producer: Steve McGlothen. first assistant cameraman: Latsi Bielitz. art direction and set dressing: Lynda Burbank and J. Rae Fox. make-up and hairdressing: Julie Purcell. first assistant director: Bill Dodge. second assistant director: Frank Martinez. third assistant director: Wade Mayer. location manager: Gary W. Fuchs. production co-ordinator: Angela Gruenthal. assistant to the producer: Julie Moldo. script supervisor: Joan Diamond. second assistant cameraman: Todd Pike. sound mixer: Anthony Santa Croce. boom operator: Anna DeLanzo. key grip: Robert Feldman. best boy grip: Jeffrey Sudzin. gaffer: Chrtis Tufty. best boy electric: Scott Buttfield. grip/electrician/driver: Stephen Crawford. set construction: Alex Hajou. art department assistant: Nancy Friedman. property master: Angus McLoone. wardrobe: Michele Logan. wardrobe assistant: Patty Koehnen. second wardrobe assistant: Christopher Gibson. stills photographer: Nancy McGovern. assistant editor: Bert Glatstein. special effects: Roger George. stunt co-ordinator: Reed Allen. second unit director: Ted G. Vujovich. second unit director of photography: Fred Aronow. second unit assistant camera: Ron Raschke. second unit grip/gaffer: Ray Bilger. craft service: Lisa C. Cook. production assistants: Monty Montgomery, Mark L. Witzer, Allen Alsobrook. film processing: M.G.M. Laboratories. opticals: Jack Rabin and Associates. sound processing: Producers' Sound Service. sound effects editing: The Provision Company. music editor: Curt Sobel, La Da Productions. re-recording mixers: Wayne Artman, c.a.s., Michael Jirow, c.a.s., Tom Beckert, c.s.a. music supervision: Ira Hearshen. music recording: Sage and Sound. source music: "Woman" music and lyrics by John G. Jones, BMI published by Wallaroo Music ©1975; "Music" music and lyrics by John G. Jones, BMI published by Wallaroo Music ©1978; "My Darlin' Don't You Cry" music and lyrics by John G. Jones, BMI published by Wallaroo Music ©1978. Lenses and Panaflex camera by Panavision. Thanks to Cool Light Company; Rick Enterprises; Fashion Hair Furniture; Calso; Orange Bang; Party World. Special thank you to Ben Marley. *Cast:* K. C. Martel (Timmy Russel). Elizabeth Hoy (Debbie Brody). Billy Jacoby (Curtis). Andy Freeman (Steven Seaton). Lori Lethin (Joyce Russel). Melinda Cordell (Mrs. Brody). Julie Brown (Beverly Brody). Joe Penny (Mr. Harding). Bert Kramer (Sheriff Brody). Susan Strasberg (Miss Davis). José Ferrer (the doctor). Erica Hope (Duke and Annie). Ellen Geer (Mrs. Seaton). Daniel Currie (Deputy Duncan). William Boyett (Mr. Russel). Shane Butterworth (Jimmy Phillips). Ward Costello (Curtis's grandfather). Michael Dudikoff (Willard). Cyril O'Reilly (Paul). Georgie Paul (Miss Lawrence). Norman Rice (Mr. Seaton). Ruth Silveira (nurse). Sylvia Wright. John Avery. Nathan Roberts. Kim Epper (stunt woman).

top:
Iver Film Services released **Bloody Birthday** on video in the UK.

left:
This US promo art for Brad Grinter's **Blood Freak** seems to promise a film with some style…

Blood Freak
aka **Blood Freaks**
(title on application to US Copyright Office)
© 1972. Sampson Motion Picture Production Company.
co-producers/co-directors: Steve Hawkes, Brad F. Grinter. camera and photography: Ron Sill. sound: Randy Grinter Jr. camera assistant: Rafael Hernandez. editor: Gil Ward. music: Gil Ward. filmed on location in Florida. *Cast:* Steve Hawkes *(Herschell).* Dana Cullivan *(Ann).* Randy Grinter Jr. Heather Hughes *(Angel).* Larry Wright. Tera Anderson. Dolores Currier. Bob Currier. Jane Tarber. Anne Shearin. Lee Morris. Linda Past. Sam Taker. Debbie Smith. Francis Sipek. Sandy Kneelen. Linda Preuwet. Dominik Grutta. Steve Vaughan. uncredited: Brad F. Grinter *(narrator).*

top right:
US DVD cover for **Blood Mania**.

bottom right:
This rather appealing US one-sheet promises that **Blood Mania** will 'jolt you right out of your seat' for the last fifteen minutes; although you're likely to get up and leave well before then...

below:
More mania...

Blood Mania
© none [1971].
Crown International Pictures presents a Jude production.
director: Robert [Vincent] O'Neil. producers: Chris Marconi, Peter Carpenter. screenplay: Toby Sacher, Tony Crechales; from a story by Peter Carpenter. cinematography: Bob Maxwell, Gary Graver. music: Don Vincent. supervision: John Caper, Jr. film editor: Patrick Kennedy. hairstyling by Jimie. painting by Mendij. still photography: John Caper, Sr. script clerk: Debbie Maxwell. key grip: Rocky Pebbles. backgrounds: Pierre Decorative Designs. makeup: Nora Maxwell, Sherry Tilley. electronic sound: Wurlitzer. assistant producer: Tony Crechales. production manager: Gary Kent. sound: Clark Will. re-recording: Producers Sound Service. titles and opticals: Imagic Inc. negative cutter: Ruth Shea. colour by Deluxe. *Cast:* Peter Carpenter *(Craig).* Maria de Aragon *(Victoria).* Vicki Peters *(Gail).* Reagan Wilson *(Cheryl).* Jacqueline Dalya *(Kate).* Leslie Simms *(Miss Turner).* Eric Allison *(father).* Arell Blanton *(blackmailer).* Alex Rocco *(lawyer).* Reid "Chippy" Smith *(poolboy).*

"*Gosh Herschell, you sure are ugly,*" says Ann, when she sees his new look for the first time – but turkey-head or not she's still thinking about that body, pledging to stick by her sister's man come what may: "*What will our children look like?*" she sighs. I like Ann; she knows what she wants and she won't be thrown off the scent by a few feathers and a beak.

"*It's so weird. It's like out of Star Trek or The Twilight Zone,*" Ann tells her drug dealer. Well, it's weird alright, and I'm sure Mr. Spock would find the turkey-headed hunk's thirst for the blood of drug-addicts 'fascinating', but what really warps this into lunacy is the coarse thread of Christian propaganda running throughout. I wonder – can *Blood Freak* ever have played in Revivalist venues? If so I'd love to have seen the faces of the congregation on the way out, especially since the film climaxes with an awesome dose of power tool mayhem, a true "*Legs Cut Off!*" moment that could hold its own in *Blood Feast* or *Two Thousand Maniacs!* In fact, with a hero called Herschell, it's possible that all this is some sort of twisted tribute (or dire warning?) to the Godfather of Gore himself: after all, Grinter knew Lewis socially, and acted for him in his obscure nudie, *How to Make a Doll* (1968).

Leading man and co-director Steve Hawkes had suffered serious burns the year before, during the filming of a Spanish Tarzan movie called *Tarzan y el arco iris* (released in the USA as *Gungala and the Treasure of the Emerald Cave*). He must have drawn on his excruciating first-hand experience here, as he simulates toxic shock and drug withdrawal; a scene where he lunges around his sitting room, diving head-first into the sofa and writhing in agony, has some plausibility (now there's a word you don't hear used about *Blood Freak* very often). In general though, this is a very poorly made film, probably cut together from two separate shoots, with no covering material to link scenes together. Grinter himself patches things up with several straight-to-camera homilies about sin, salvation and the corrosive effects of drugs; blithely chain-smoking the whole time, and erupting in a fusillade of coughs at the end that must surely have been intended as a joke.

According to Charles Kilgore in the short-lived but excellent *Highball* magazine, "Grinter entered acting initially through the Florida dinner theatre circuit. [He] occasionally wrote or co-wrote the productions he acted in, which were usually risqué comedies

with literary or sociological pretensions." I wonder how *Blood Freak* would have gone down with a dinner-theatre audience? It's certainly an ideal booking for Thanksgiving parties... As it was, *Blood Freak* failed to secure national distribution, and Grinter retreated from genre filmmaking to knock out a couple of reportedly lame nudies, *Barely Proper* and *Never the Twain* (both 1975). Business remained poor: the films were stubbornly softcore in an age where *Deep Throat* had swept the coyness of the sixties aside. The two were apparently little more than filmed stage productions, a trial of patience for even the most tolerant of Z-film lovers: according to Kilgore, "Filmmaker and ex-Floridian Fred Olen Ray once walked out of a screening of *Never the Twain*, at Grinter's house." How's that for bad publicity?

Made in Florida.

BLOOD MANIA
– Robert Vincent O'Neil (1971)

Like Sergei Goncharoff's *House of Terror*, this starts with a deceptively delirious credits sequence, only to settle down as a thoroughly dull and talky murder-thriller. There's barely a moment to relieve the tedium, other than a few examples of fancy lighting and a blood-soaked death by candelabra. With a title like *Blood Mania*, though, you expect more than a few squirts of ketchup in an actress's hair. The story concerns Victoria (Maria de Aragon), who decides to bump off her rich, ailing father (Eric Allison) and help her boyfriend, daddy's doctor (Peter Carpenter), out of a financial jam. Whoops, the inheritance goes to Victoria's sister Gail (Vicki Peters) instead. Mmm, I wonder what's going to happen next? Well, you'll have to wait an awful long time to find out. Everyone talks too much, the whacked-out psychedelic soundtrack has nothing remotely hallucinatory to grab onto onscreen, and the cameraman tries too hard to make the dialogue scenes interesting by shooting from low angles and generally misframing the action. As noted, the lighting is occasionally ambitious, but with a story this anodyne and predictable it's going to take more than a few coloured gels to turn *Blood Mania* into a Mario Bava film. Arrel Blanton, here playing a blackmailer who helps out with the dumb ending, went on to appear in the aforementioned *House of Terror* a few years later: he really ought to try reading the scripts beforehand...

Made in California.

BLOOD OF GHASTLY HORROR

– Al Adamson (1971)

aka *Psycho A Go Go* (original title given to US Copyright Office)

aka *Echo of Terror* (alternative title given upon submission of *Psycho A Go Go* title to US Copyright Office)

aka *Fiend with the Electronic Brain*

aka *Man with the Synthetic Brain*

When is a horror film not a horror film? When it's a murky crime caper directed by Al Adamson, retitled for the squillionth time to wring hard-earned cash out of unsuspecting punters, some of whom may even have fallen for the same rubbish before, masquerading as sci-fi under the title *Man with the Synthetic Brain*. This began its half-life in 1964 as *Two Tickets to Terror*, and with the participation of Sam Sherman went through a number of retitlings that made it the shingles of the genre; irritating and hard to get rid of. Perhaps I should just laugh and sign up to the 'so-bad-it's-good' lobby, but really, no. Tedious, dishonest, anachronistic, it's the sort of feeble run-around that counts as a waste of your life. The DVD from Troma (who else?) features Sherman in Showman mode, defying critics and playing the fool. He's a charmer, probably a great guy, and by all accounts he was the power behind the throne on Adamson's movies: but I'll leave it to others to tell that story. For me, Adamson's and Sherman's efforts fail to make the grade in all sorts of ways. They lack the demented, chaotic quality that makes films like *BoardingHouse* so compulsive; there are no unintentional howlers like the ones that perk up Ed Wood's scripts; they're neither squalid enough to shock your inner prude, nor arty enough to masturbate your inner aesthete; and the wedge of conventional action melodrama that frequently intrudes has a flattening effect on the trash-horror elements. Having watched four Adamson movies for this book, I find that I haven't smiled once; neither with them nor at them. I consider myself a sucker for the siren call of trash, but as Kim Newman put it in his book *Nightmare Movies*, "Any fool who thinks bad films are uproarious fun would be cured if locked in a cinema during an all-night Al Adamson retrospective."

Made in California.

see also: **Brain of Blood, Dracula vs. Frankenstein** *and* **Nurse Sherri**

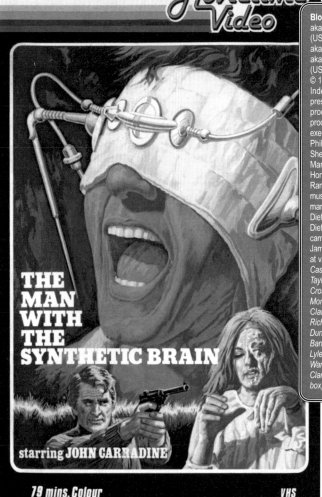

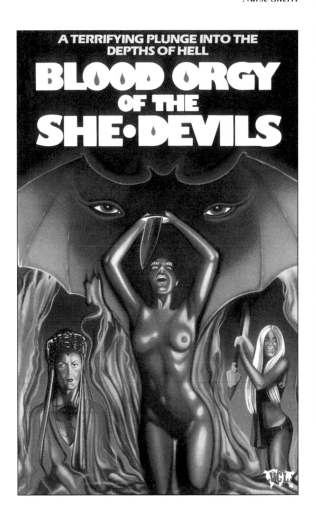

BLOOD ORGY OF THE SHE DEVILS

– Ted V. Mikels (1972)

aka *Female Plasma Suckers* (US video title)

If you'd like a thorough trip through the wacky world of auteur polygamist Ted V. Mikels, I recommend you track down a copy of the Re/Search book *Incredibly Strange Films*, which provides an extensive interview, and talks about his movies in detail. For me though, Mikels is another director in the Al Adamson mould: his films suffer the same plodding adherence to an earlier period of movie-making that we see in Adamson's *Dracula vs. Frankenstein*, or stray anachronisms like Charles Nizet's *The Possessed!*, J.G. Patterson's *Doctor Gore* and Jerry Warren's *Frankenstein Island*. *Blood Orgy of the She Devils* is a case in point: static, talky scenes are interspersed with painfully drawn-out 'occult rituals', performed by scantily clad women whose writhing is supposed to connote mystical sensuality but instead looks simply ludicrous. Mara, a witch queen living in a castle on the outskirts of Los Angeles (actually Mikels's home at the time), offers a service designed to connect women with their experiences in a previous life: in each case, it turns out they were once persecuted for witchcraft. The reincarnated witches gratefully lend a hand in Mara's ceremonies, which climax in the sacrifice of a bound man. Mikels's taste for strong women does at least add some colour to his narratives, but unlike Russ Meyer he's less thorough in pursuing the implications. The witch-queen's plot is thwarted by three men, one an occult expert and one a Christian priest. So much for the awesome power of Woman; but then what do you expect from a man who lives with his own harem?

Made in California.

see also: **The Corpse Grinders**

left:
Video cover for Al Adamson's **Blood of Ghastly Horror** under one of its many retitlings: this version came out twice in the UK, once from Mountain (pictured) and once from Videon.

bottom left:
VCL released this Ted V. Mikels film three times in three years in the UK!

above:
Sacrificial suffering in **Blood Sabbath**.

top right:
Video cover art for the UK release of **Blood
Sabbath**, put out by Avatar through CBS Fox.
Note the (then voluntary) '18' certificate. Two
earlier releases from the sinister sounding
Videoring are fiendishly rare.

right:
A Satanic picnic? No, it's just a bit of
woodland child sacrifice from
Blood Sabbath...

BLOOD SABBATH
– Brianne Murphy (1972)
aka *Yyalah*

Drippy David (Anthony Geary) – allegedly a Vietnam veteran, but temperamentally more suited to sitting cross-legged in a field listening to Donovan – goes hiking through Mexico with his guitar. After a 'scary' encounter with a troupe of naked hippy girls, he knocks himself out in a fall. He comes round to find a beautiful young woman called Yyalah (Susan Damante-Shaw) tending his wounds. Slipping back into unconsciousness, he wakes some time later to find Lonzo (Sam Gilman), an itinerant preacherman, standing over him. Lonzo warns David not to go looking for this ethereal new girlfriend. It transpires that Yyalah is a water-nymph who belongs body and soul to the Priestess Alotta (Dyanne Thorne), who runs a witch-cult practising child sacrifice; an arrangement that the locals accept, to the horror of their local padre (Steve Gravers). If David wants to stay with Yyalah, he must first sacrifice his soul – and Alotta is the only one who can perform the necessary ritual. But Alotta has her own reasons for helping David shuck off his spirit…

I enjoyed this a lot more than I was expecting to, but whatever possessed Brianne Murphy to cast Anthony Geary as the soldier? He looks as though he'd have trouble fighting off a persistent moth, never mind the Vietcong. *Blood Sabbath* draws much of its amusement value from such miscalculations – I love the scene where a thoughtless David, keen to be united with Yyalah, asks a startled Catholic priest how to get rid of his soul. Even better is the later scene where David, now successfully rid of his soul, goes running through the woods, leaping and cheering and shouting, *"I'm free, Yyalah!"* It works because Geary is comically inept at showing joy: picking up fallen tree branches and shaking them emphatically, chucking handfuls of leaves in the air, and, in one priceless moment, swinging on a low-hanging branch and falling gracelessly on his arse. You don't get many pratfalls in witchcraft movies, and let's face it, if ever a subgenre needed a bit of slapstick… The one casting choice that makes perfect sense, however, is Dyanne Thorne, who brings her special brand of charismatic wickedness to the part of Witch-Queen Alotta. There's something about Thorne that lifts even the silliest of material, and although *Blood Sabbath* is refried leftovers as far as witchcraft tales are concerned, she herself is reason enough to watch it. She has a way of purring through dialogue that ensures you listen to every word. Thorne pushes useless Yyalah and dozy David out from centre-stage, with evil Alotta perversely likeable in their stead (as befits a story whose cartoon-like notions of good and evil are divorced from reality).

The red stuff in *Blood Sabbath* takes a while to flow, but it's worth waiting for a great surprise involving a severed head. Full-frontal nudity is frequent enough to raise a few eyebrows, but the sexual content is strictly of the writhing, ritualized variety seen in films like *Blood Orgy of the She Devils* and *Crypt of Dark Secrets*. *Blood Sabbath*, though, is head and shoulders above these examples, and if you simply *have* to watch an early seventies sexy witchcraft tale, this one's probably the most fun.

Director Brianne Murphy (aka Geraldine Brianne Murphy) was born in London in 1933, but moved to America after the war and embarked on a strikingly unconventional career: attending the Neighborhood Playhouse in New York City, working at a rodeo, and performing as a clown for the Barnum & Bailey Circus. She eventually took a slightly more sedate job as a still photographer,

Once a year, a virgin must DIE..!

BLOOD SABBATH

18

The nightmare
half-world
between
heaven and hell…

AVATAR

which led her to Hollywood, where she met and married low-budget movie-maker Jerry Warren (see *Frankenstein Island*). In 1980 she became the first ever female director of photography on a major studio picture (*Fatso*, starring Dom DeLuise) and has had several Emmy nominations (and one win) for cinematography. Presumably Murphy was disenchanted with witchery and *Blood Sabbath*: her second and last film, *To Die, To Sleep* (1994), is a Christian-themed drama of sin and repentance. She died of cancer in Puerto Vallarta, Mexico, on 20 August, 2003.
Made in California.

BLOOD SONG
– Alan J. Levi (1982)
aka *Premonitions* [original title]
aka *Dream Slayer*

Teenager Marion Hauser (Donna Wilkes) is unhappy at home, thanks to her ceaselessly bullying father, Frank (Richard Jaeckel). Not content with having partially crippled her in a drunk-driving incident, he jealously polices her every move, and threatens her with violence if she continues to see her boyfriend Joey (William Kirby Cullen). Worse still, she's suffering bad dreams and visions about an escaped lunatic (Frankie Avalon) committing gruesome murders. Could the visions be linked to a blood transfusion she received, from a patient at the State Mental Hospital?

If you're familiar with Avalon from his *Beach Party* films with Annette Funicello, or as a teen pop star contemporary of Fabian and Bobby Rydell, you'll probably do a double-take at the sight of the former Sultan of Surf slamming an axe into a man's face. If not, you'll simply consider his performance moderately acceptable, but wonder where he got a Bermuda tan when he's supposed to have been incarcerated in a top security loony-bin for twenty years. The best acting here comes from Richard Jaeckel as the über-strict father, and Antoinette Bower as his despairing wife. Damsel in distress Donna Wilkes, however, could do with a bit of tuition when it comes to the *de rigueur* sobbing and screaming.

KAIKKI ALKOI
MURHASTA V. 1955...
v. 1982 VERILÖYLY
VOI ALKAA...

BLOOD SONG

FRANKIE AVALON · DANE CLARK · NOELLE NORTH
WILLIAM KIRBY CULLEN · RICHARD JAECKEL

grab the necessary extra footage. The last few scenes with Marion being restrained and sedated by doctors, and later in bed, seen only in darkened profile, may have been filmed without Wilkes's involvement, and the aforementioned scene with the cops at Marion's house, which not only fails to show the father's dead body but also relegates the mother to a brief dialogue aside, also has the stamp of a scene shot later without the principals.

Robert Burns, the art director on the picture, told me: "The director was Alan J. Levi who was (and still is) one of the most successful directors of television, but somehow he thought this little item was his ticket to the big time. Knowing nothing about what makes horror scary he went for more blood. In a fight to the death between Avalon and Jaeckel he just kept wanting me to pour more and more of it on poor long-suffering Jaeckel. He ended up looking like a squashed jelly donut." Presumably, some of the excess that Burns describes was trimmed later, because what's left is actually the most powerful scene in the film; both for the plausibly nasty knife-wounds Jaeckel receives, and for the emotional dynamic, which has the bad father redeem himself by giving his life to protect his daughter. In fact, without Jaeckel's input this film simply wouldn't work at all; the psychic theme is fumbled, the lead actress is no good, and the soundtrack close to intolerable. Avalon's performance is okay, but it's not enough to hang a film on. I suppose, in the pantheon of horror films starring pop singers, it's better than Bill Rebane's *Blood Harvest* starring Tiny Tim, but it falls some way behind Pete Walker's *The Comeback* with Jack Jones…

Television director Alan J. Levi began directing in high school, making over forty non-fiction films before he even got to college, for groups like the National Conference of Christians and Jews and the National Safety Council. He moved to California in 1960, working for MGM as an assistant to the producer on the TV show *National Velvet*. He later went on to direct more than fifteen television 'Movie of the Week's, and helmed numerous episodes of *Columbo*, *The Bionic Woman*, *Airwolf*, *Lois & Clark*, *ER*, *Buffy the Vampire Slayer* and *Battlestar Galactica*, among many others.

Made in Oregon.

above:
Frankie Avalon plays heavily against type in **Blood Song**.

top left:
Finnish video art for **Blood Song**, with figures bearing little resemblance to anyone in the film.

Filmed in the Oregon coastal towns of Coos Bay, North Bend and Charleston, *Blood Song* at least has these attractive locations to its credit. Sadly, the most interesting story angle – Marion's psychic link with the killer – is left undeveloped. The movie was originally called *Premonitions*, but the psychic idea never really leads anywhere, which is perhaps why the first title was dropped. Ironically, given that Frankie Avalon never sings a note, the film's biggest problem is the music; suspense is constantly undermined by a synth-heavy score that bounces between irritating arpeggio bass-lines and schmaltzy romantic interludes. Thanks to this musical hotchpotch, and some puzzling ellipses in the narrative, the film's momentum is as stumbling as the lead character's gait. You have to be in a forgiving mood too, when Marion, having walked in on the killer hacking her father to death in the sitting room, runs outside and makes no attempt to rouse the neighbours, instead limping furiously off to the deserted saw-mill at the end of the street. It's not even the middle of the night: Marion's mum is still at a PTA meeting, so the neighbours should still be awake. The ensuing saw-mill sequence is one of the highlights of the movie, but for a heroine with one leg in callipers to doggedly ignore the nearest source of help is the sort of weak plotting that hobbles credibility.

The fact that Marion's mother never reappears, even after police arrive to mop up her husband's butchered remains, is a clue to the film's behind-the-scenes problems. Although the sole directing credit at the start of the film goes to Alan J. Levi, the end credits mention additional scenes directed by Robert Angus, and with a different cinematographer, Irwin Goodonov, suggesting that the new scenes were filmed after the initial production wrapped (the first credited DP is Steve Posey [aka Stephen L. Posey], a horror specialist at the time who notched up credits on *Bloody Birthday*, *The Slumber Party Massacre* and *Friday the 13th Part V: A New Beginning*). A *Variety* article called 'Director Shifts During Filming' (3 September, 1986, p.82), listing productions where directors had been replaced for various reasons, mentions Levi and *Blood Song*. It would seem that after Levi finished his shoot, the producers asked editor Robert Angus – who had had some directing experience – to go out and

left:
Marion (Donna Wilkes) prepares to fend off the killer, in **Blood Song**.

above: Typical backwoods attitude (horror movie style) from an old garage attendant (Herb Goldstein) in **Blood Stalkers**.

below: Kim (Toni Crabtree), Jeri (Celea-Anne Cole) and Daniel (Kenny Miller) realise there's something nasty in the wood shed, in **Blood Stalkers**.

There is terror in the backwoods…
In a place where violence is a way of life,
there are many ways to die!

WARNING: Due to graphic displays of violence, viewer discretion is advised.

Starring **KENNY MILLER, CELEA ANN COLE**
JERRY ALBERT and **TONI CRABTREE**
Written and Directed by **ROBERT W. MORGAN**
Executive Producer **BEN MORSE**

VIDMARK
ENTERTAINMENT

BLOOD STALKERS

– Robert W. Morgan (1975)
aka *Bloodstalkers*
aka *The Night Daniel Died*

Terror awaits two couples heading for a restful vacation in a cabin set deep in the Florida Everglades. Despite the rural beauty, their holiday becomes a nightmare that only one of them will survive. Will it be Mike (Jerry Albert) the Vietnam veteran; Mike's missus, the averagely lovely Kim (Toni Crabtree); valiant theatrical Daniel (Kenny Miller); or his nervous wreck of a wife, Jeri (Celea-Anne Cole)? A surly garage attendant warns them to turn back, for they're about to enter *"Blood Stalker country… nobody can survive out there overnight!"* Paying no heed, and ignoring a trio of grimy psychos who drop by the garage to check out the newcomers, the townies stubbornly head for the old wooden cabin once owned by Mike's parents. As they arrive, unearthly, animal-like screams echo across the swamplands, a hulking creature darts through the undergrowth, and huge muddy footprints appear on the car… Just who – or what – are the Blood Stalkers?

Sounds pretty good, huh? Well, I'm afraid me and the guy who wrote the video cover have misled you some. *Blood Stalkers* lifts its set-up from *The Texas Chain Saw Massacre*, but wastes a decent first act and the creepy, run-down backwoods setting by withholding any actual mayhem until the last few minutes. The leads have little to recommend them, certainly nothing to justify spending so much time in their company. If you're like me, you tend to add up the available red meat in a tale such as this, and although a lead cast of four is a touch lean, it could still have worked if the killings had been made to count. After all, four murders were sufficient for Tobe Hooper. Unfortunately, by crowding all the violence into the last five minutes, Morgan makes a truly insane genre miscalculation. As for the soundtrack: there were times when the use of music in *Blood Stalkers* had me clutching my head in dismay. It's unremarkable for the first half of the story, but as things 'hot up' a deeply unhelpful Gospel number takes over, ruining the atmosphere as surely as a Wayne Bell score played at a Revivalist baptism. The offending

tune plays over two key scenes in quick succession: the latter running for nearly five minutes of supposedly nail-biting parallel montage, involving an attack by a hairy humanoid creature and the hero's attempts to dash cross-country to the rescue. As bad decisions go, it's a humdinger, completely destroying the already flimsy tension. Finally, in a twist borrowed from *Scooby-Doo*, the 'Blood Stalker' turns out to be a local smuggler dressed in an ape skin to scare visitors from his stash of ill-gotten gains. Probably the *least* exciting of all possible explanations, and a perplexing one when you consider the following…

Robert W. Morgan was born in Ohio, in 1935. He was a partner in Creative Film & Sounds of Miami, Florida (which provided post-production facilities for *Blood Stalkers*) and worked with Florida based director William Grefé as production assistant. Back in March of 1957, Morgan was out hunting in Mason County, Washington when he encountered a creature he later came to identify as a Sasquatch, or Bigfoot. The experience led to a lifelong obsession – Morgan has appeared regularly on US talk shows to debate the existence of Bigfoot, and between 1968 and 1974, after dropping out of highly paid work in the electronics industry, he mounted a number of expeditions to search for the elusive Forest Giants, as he prefers to call them. He drew on his experiences for Lawrence Crowley's 1971 documentary film *Bigfoot: Man Or Beast?* (originally entitled *The Search for Bigfoot*). Morgan can be seen on-camera in the film, testifying to his Bigfoot sighting and describing his numerous search expeditions. He also appeared on David Wolper's TV documentary, *Monsters: Mysteries Or Myths?* for the prestigious Smithsonian Series. In 1974, Morgan co-founded the non-profit American Anthropological Research Foundation with his friend and attorney, W. Ted Ernst (who appears as one of the townspeople in *Blood Stalkers*). He has continued searching the world for evidence of Forest Giants. Morgan was described by one source as, "The most successful and the most controversial tracker of Bigfoot." One has to query his success, given the stubborn lack of fully authenticated sightings, but Morgan's 'controversial' status is based on his noble attempt to protect 'whatever-it-is' from gun-toting morons who simply wish to shoot the creature for personal glory. Morgan has successfully urged various territorial officials to create County Ordinances protecting Bigfoot from 'wanton slaying'. In response, Rene Dahinden, a Canadian researcher, angrily threatened to, "shoot Morgan if he ever comes between me and a Bigfoot" – so whatever your feelings about the credibility of the phenomenon, Morgan is at least on the side of the angels. (On their side, but not yet living with them. The Internet Movie Database confuses Robert W. Morgan the filmmaker and Bigfoot expert with Robert W. Morgan the deceased Ohio DJ, who died of lung cancer in 1998. In fact the former is still alive and was interviewed by Canadian broadcaster Rob McConnell for his paranormal-themed 'X-Zone Radio' as recently as March 2007.)

Made in Florida.

BOARDINGHOUSE

– John Wintergate (1982)
aka *Housegeist*
aka *Bad Force*

A house where mysterious deaths have occurred is bought by Jim Royce (Hawk Adley aka Hank Adly aka John Wintergate), a Lothario with psychic powers who proceeds to rent out rooms to pretty college girls. His plans for a harem are undone, however, by a malevolent force residing within…

You'd never guess from the synopsis above, but this is one of the weirdest films in this book; truly a one-of-a-kind experience. Some would say that's a good thing; we don't *want* any more films like this in the world. However, I disagree – *BoardingHouse* is unhinged in some wonderful, elusive way that defies criticism. The accumulation of events is so haphazard, and the dialogue so off-the-wall, that you can watch this three times before sense begins to emerge. I know that, for me, the first viewing was a riot of incomprehensible situations. I admit to being in an altered state at the time, but the film is tailor-made for such indulgences: a hallucinatory vibe positively radiates from the screen. I found my notes from that viewing worth drawing on here, because although I've now got a grip on the film (sort of), it's the first-time experience that matters most, so:

[FLASHBACK] After a slow start with some strange goings on at a hospital, a guy in an office, sitting in the lotus position, kick-starts the story by willpower alone. He's called Jim, he's played by the director, and he uses the power of his mind to make the potted plants shake, which is the first demonstration of cause and effect in the movie (or as Einstein would say, 'spooky action at a distance'). Just as you're getting the hang of it, a roaring drunk (Joel Riordan) staggers into the scene and disrupts everything. Back at the boarding house, carloads of *girls* are arriving. They look and sound like 'horror film victims' and for a while *BoardingHouse* feels as if it's going to settle down and act 'normal'. This turns out not to be the case, and we're soon back in Mr. Wintergate's druggy dislocated mind-swamp. It's all strangely compulsive. The girls arrive in such numbers that it's subsequently hard to keep track of who's who, and what they mean to each other. They're a touch mechanical but they add a dash of vigour, and at least they *think* they're in a regular movie, despite the editing, camera and soundtrack conspiring to derail them. A supernatural force pushes a metal spike through one girl's hand. She screams, and her friends gather round to stare. *"All her fingers work; I checked them,"* says Jim. He must be in robotics. A good thing he showed up, as the robogirls are starting to break down: how else could one of them take a shower without seeing a huge blossoming bloodstain on the wall? When finally she freaks, she sees herself as a gargoyle in the mirror; the first of several surprisingly creepy images. Everything is very strange, and now the horror is piling up: a fellow called Richard (Brian Bruderlin) is electrocuted when a hairdryer jumps into the bathwater; gloved hands drag the body away. So far we have telekinesis, supernatural entities, and a gloved killer, each vying for attention. *BoardingHouse* has flaws alright, but it certainly isn't dull. A brunette called Victoria (Kalassu) goes upstairs to steal a meditation tape from Jim. He's in the bath, and says: *"I'm into harnessing cosmic energy so that I can learn the secrets of the Universe."* He demonstrates his power to Victoria by levitating the soap out of the bathwater and skimming it across the suds. *"You mean you just made it move with your brain?"* she says. Downstairs, she makes a startling claim when the girls ask if Jim came on to her: *"He's not physical at all: he's too into metaphysics."* In the garden, the leather-clad gardener brandishes a chainsaw at someone we can't see. A skeleton hand reaches out and touches Victoria as she climbs into bed. It's one of the other girls, banging a saucepan with a spoon. I think madness is entering my brain… From this maelstrom we enter a dream-sequence – a daring move for a film already so close to the edge. Who knows where the dream begins? Perhaps at the start of the tape? Rotting hands reach from the mattress, and Victoria takes to the garden, where a terrifying 'thing' with a pig's head attacks her. Victoria goes to bed in a graveyard, but there's a corpse under the covers. She wakes up and screams – three loud, lingering tones at the same perfect pitch. Jim has some calming words for us, as we approach meltdown: *"Everything's alright. Trust me. Everything is beautiful. And love is beautiful too…"* [FLASHBACK ENDS]

There's more, much more, but you need to see the film yourself without too many quotes to spoil it. Be assured, it just gets freakier. You could quote every line of dialogue, describe every scene and every cut, and still you wouldn't capture the freaked out ambience of *BoardingHouse*. In a film where people say things like, *"I cut myself with the apple… er, the knife,"* what chance is there to make sense of things? Psychics battle each other in a demon-infested house; a woman develops paranormal abilities after being told, *"Anyone can do it."*; people are dying but no one seems to notice; and whole sections of the film ignore each other. There's something thrilling about its immaculate impenetrability.

...Where The Rent Won't KILL YOU, but something else WILL!

Starring
HANK ADLY · KALASSU · ALEXANDRA DAY
TRACY O'BRIAN · BRIAN BRUDERLIN

A HORRORVISION VIDEO FILM RELEASE

COLOUR
MG 006

BoardingHouse
aka **Housegeist** (US video title)
aka **Bad Force** (German video title)
© none [1982].
director: Johnn [sic] Wintergate. producer: Peter Baahlu. music: Kalassu, 33 and a third, Jonema. second unit director: K. Kay [Kalassu Kay]. assistant director: Lanny Williamson. written by: Jonema [John Wintergate]. assistant producer: Elliot Van Koghbe. theme "Boarding House": Christopher Conlan, Chris Cristin. original music: Teeth. directors of photography: Jan Lucas, Obee Ray. editors: Jim Balcom, Johnny Kay. makeup artist: J. Wintergate. boom operator: Chris Cristin. best boys: J. Buxor, T. Campbell, S. Lindley. assistant camera: A'ryen Winter. script girl: Ronesa Roswood. presenter: Howard Willette this film is dedicated in loving memory to: Joel McGinnis Riordan.
Cast: Hawk Adley [John Wintergate] (Jim Royce & gardener). Kalassu Kay (Victoria). Alexandra Day (Debbie Hoffman). Joel McGinnis Riordan (Joel Weintraub). Brian Bruderlin (Richard). Belma Kora (Sandy). Tracy O'Brian (Suzie). Mary McKinley (Cindy). Rosane Woods (Gloria). Cindy Williamson (Pam). Christopher Conlan (Christopher). Elizabeth Hall (Terri). Tom Mones (the agent). Dean Disico (Harris). Elliot Van Koghbe (Officer Weston). John Chase (orderly). A'ryen Winter (Nurse Sherry). Victoria Herron (Su Ling). Michael Burke (lawyer). Jim Vincioni (Officer Paul). Carla Nansel (girl in car). Michele Krieger (photographer). Allen R. Warren (uncle). Tim Campbell (bass player). Jon Buxer (keyboard player). Chris Cristin (guitar player). Mark Prines (magician). 33 and a third (the band).

BoardingHouse is Frank Roach and Renee Harmon's *Frozen Scream* taken even further. After a very slow and obstinate first fifteen minutes, the film begins to accelerate, with something weird happening, or ineffably bizarre being said, in every scene. For instance, Victoria sees some sort of demon, and has a fit. Two friends barge in and find her screaming her guts out, and one of them says, *"Here, have some pizza."* How do you deal with that? *How?* Horrible things keep happening, as the genre demands, but they're churning around in so much technical perversity that there's no sense of development or accumulation. You could reorder the shots back to front and not seriously damage the overall experience.

Just as mathematicians had to invent 'imaginary numbers', like the square root of a minus figure, to make certain calculations work, we need to invent an 'imaginary aesthetic' if a film like this is to yield its pleasures. And the keynote is pleasure, not 'making sense'. The confusion and car-crash plotting are essential to the fun. I don't know what to make of this film; I don't know what I'm supposed to think. I don't know where I am in relation to it, or within it. These feelings are exhilarating, and they happen in only two places: extreme art cinema and the weirdest shores of horror. *BoardingHouse*, like Doris Wishman's *A Night To Dismember* and the films of Renee Harmon, feels like cinema from another dimension: so much is skewed, so many technical and structural flaws proliferate, that you're forced to take it as a new kind of viewing experience. It's cinema anti-matter, and as such, potentially dangerous: if you projected it onto Hitchcock's *Vertigo*, the two would annihilate each other in a flash of pure energy. Go ahead, try it! But don't say I didn't warn you.

It's probably a good thing after all that there are so few films like *BoardingHouse*: we might get used to them, and never enjoy a coherent movie again. There's a great short story by Clark Ashton Smith, *A Star Change* (1933), in which a man's mind is altered by aliens so that he can experience their higher dimensional reality; which is fine until they dump him back on Earth without reversing the process. He goes insane, unable to cope with a now monstrous and terrifying human reality. If only John Wintergate could adapt it for the screen!

left:
Magnum's UK video release of **BoardingHouse** features the only available artwork generated for this extraordinary film.

opposite page, top right:
Blood Stalkers never received a UK video release – here it is in its US version from Vidmark.

below:
'Hank Adly' (or is it 'Hawk Adley'?) aka John Wintergate, and his partner and muse Kalassu, star of **BoardingHouse**, seen here in a recent photograph.

this page:
Artwork and stills from Al Adamson's **Brain of Blood**. The admat at the top right shows the film on a double bill with the similarly creaky Filipino horror movie, **The Vampire People** (1966), by Gerardo de Leon.

Director John Wintergate and star Kalassu, on the making of *BoardingHouse*

"*We read your* BoardingHouse *piece and we could not stop laughing. You seem to have caught the gist of what we meant to portray. We meant it to be a sort of cult oriented, far out, over the top, tongue & cheek, outrageous and insane comic spoof on the horror film genre. Your understanding of it is great, marvellous and very, very funny. Hey, you might have inspired us to do a sequel, 'BoardingHouse 2: The Next Generation'. Who knows, it might be great fun, we'll just have to find the money to do it. You asked about other projects, the last one we did was a family type movie based on a true story, called* Sally & Jess. *We stopped the release when our friend, who was a relatively honest distributor, died before it was finished and the three new distributors we contacted seemed to get ready to shaft us and black market the movie in the Orient, Middle East & South America. We were contacted by someone who informed us, so we pulled the picture each time. We are still looking to distribute it, it's a nice family TV movie. Kalassu and I have been married for more than thirty three years. We have been in the entertainment field, acting, writing, directing as well as music most of our life. We wanted to make a funny comic spoof about horror films, so Kalassu and I thought about the most unlikely scenario to present it and make it over the top cultish and weird. Since we had limited funds, we decided to be innovative and do it in video format, due to the very nature of the film. As you know, with film you don't want to waste too much footage in retakes because it gets very expensive. So since we knew it might take many takes to get the right weird (off the wall) flavour to the scenes, we decided to be daring and be the first to do an entire film project in video format. The video editing in some ways was easier in a physical aspect, but the sheer volume of takes made it quite challenging to pick out the most suitable ones. Kalassu and I had quite a few different opinions from our distributor. We also did all the 'special' (ha ha ha) effects and had a great time playing with them in different ways. We asked a few of our fellow acting friends to work with us to make it all happen, and it was quite a challenge to have some of them come off the way they did, but we all had fun working on the project. (We did use a few of the ad-libs that happened throughout the filming when they were really strange or came off even naive or stupid-feeling.) The metaphysical aspect in the film was meant to give it a deeper scope somehow and also make it more emotionally intricate as well as a bit more crazy. Kalassu's and my love for the metaphysical and spiritual aspect of life seemed like a strange but good and extra ingredient for the film, so we wove it into the fabric of the script along with the computer typing which at the time was pretty strange. A lot of laughter, fun, partying and lots of playful pranks and mischief. When we opted to transfer the movie to film later on, it was quite an interesting decision and a relatively new process, and did not turn out quite as well as we had hoped, but we thought it was good enough for an innovative cult type film and the distributor agreed and released it alongside* Jaws 2, *if we remember correctly.*"

Made in California.

BRAIN OF BLOOD
– Al Adamson (1971)
aka *Brain Damage* (US video title)
aka *The Brain*
aka *The Creature's Revenge*
aka *The Undying Brain*

On the principle that if you've nothing nice to say you shouldn't say anything at all, I really ought not to review Al Adamson's movies, as there's not a single one that I like. It was with a weary heart that I decided I ought to at least briefly touch on his horror output, so forgive me, I'll keep it brief… For the record, *Brain of Blood* has a gory brain transplant, sinister Arabs, hokey mind control, inept car chases, a mad scientist and his dwarf companion, a laboratory full of bubbling vials, a cellar

where screaming girls have the blood drained from their bodies, and the chance to see more of Zandor Vorkov (the screen's worst Count Dracula). If this sounds like heaven to you, well there you go, knock yourself out. For me, this plodding retro-horror is charmless, muddled and oh-so-boring. Adamson made a career pilfering horror motifs from the thirties, forties and fifties, bolting them all together without a spark of ingenuity, and stranding the viewer somewhere between failed pastiche and hoary nostalgia. Wading through his work is like crossing a slurry-pit full of the dead or dying offcuts of bygone genre cinema; you just wish he'd let the cadavers rot in peace.

Made in California.
see also: **Blood of Ghastly Horror, Dracula vs. Frankenstein** *and*
Nurse Sherri

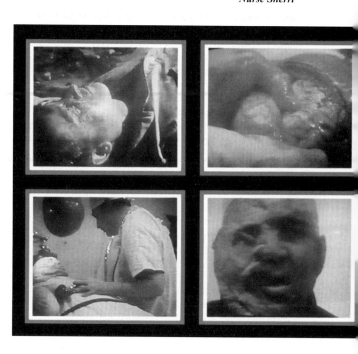

'internal' flashbacks along the way. Technically, Favorite is totally uninspired: shots are held for too long, the camera merely observes and never explores, and nothing in his arsenal aids the performers. The effects are rudimentary too: despite warning that to interrupt a black magic ceremony disturbs the delicate balance between good and evil, the most terrifying manifestation we see is a pot bubbling with dry ice, some camera lens flare, and a ginger-haired mutant in a cape. There's a very explicit and drawn-out injection scene that could perhaps give the squeamish hard time, but *The Brides Wore Blood* is really 'For Completists Only'. Filmed in Jacksonville, Florida. Note: some sources refer to 'the late Bob Favorite' but I've been unable to confirm his death.

Made in Florida.

CARNIVAL OF BLOOD
– Leonard Kirtman (1970)

There's a maniac on the loose at the Coney Island funfair, and when you meet his victims you'll be rooting for him all the way. Trainee district attorney Dan (Martin Barolsky) drags his girlfriend Laura (Judith Resnick) to the carnival to investigate the decapitation of Claire (Linda Kurtz), shrewish wife of Harry (William Grinell). Laura hears noises under the boardwalk, and when she and Dan check it out they find the eviscerated body of a hooker. Later, some broad has her eyes pulled out: no, I'm not being callous, she's *that* important to the plot. The suspects include Tom (Earle Edgerton), balding mild-mannered major-domo of the shooting range, and 'Gimpy' (John Harris [Burt Young]), his scarred and hunchbacked servant… Wanna play 'Guess the Psycho'?

Boy, this is hard work. Right from the opening scenes, following Harry and his harpy of a wife round the carnival, you feel as though you're being punished for heinous sins in a previous life. It's seventeen minutes before Harry and Claire are banished from the screen – she decapitated in the ghost-train, he eternally

The Brides Wore Blood
© 1972. Robert R. Favorite Productions
producer/director: Robert R. Favorite. story: Liz Blanda, Tom Rahner, Bob Smith, Bob and Dottie Favorite. art direction and graphics: Stinson Associates. script consultant: Bill Williamson. sound recordist: Neil Mengle. sound assistant: Liz Blanda. gaffer: Lynn Tidwell. key grip: Lee Hansen. grip: Peter Jannott. script girl: Linda Stinson. make up: Dorothy Favorite, Tom Rahner. film editor: Steve Heape. unit manager: Pat Stinson. production supervisor: Will Smott. music: Lee Peters. chief technician: Steve Heape. camera operator: Rick Voight. associate producers: Tom Rahner, Rick Voight. produced through the facilities of Robert R. Favorite Productions (Jacksonville, Florida). filmed on location in Florida (USA).
Cast: Dolores Heiser (Yvonne). Paul Everett (Carlos). Bob Letizia (Perro). Chuck Faulkner (Juan). Jan Sherman (Laura). Dolores Starling (Dana). Rita Ballard (Vickie). Ben Robinson (guy). Norman Howard (waiter). Art Schill (Perro's father). Robert Carberry (coroner). Jim Billington (lieutenant). Jean Rahner (victim). Dot Favorite (waitress). Leana Lucas (dancer). Mike Sherman, Ken Pacetti (guitarists).

above:
The vampire (Chuck Falkner) is exposed to the sunlight in the Florida-shot vampire tale **The Brides Wore Blood**.

top left:
More images from **The Brides Wore Blood**.
clockwise from top left:
Yvonne (Dolores Heiser) in a negative mood;
One of the rejected brides;
The vampire;
Sinister revelry with retarded servant Perro (Bob Letizia).

THE BRIDES WORE BLOOD
– Robert R. Favorite (1972)

Long ago, the De Lorca family brought a curse upon themselves by dabbling in black magic. Subsequently, the men of the family have turned into vampires and slain their brides. It's up to Juan De Lorca (Chuck Faulkner), his Uncle Carlos (Paul Everett), and their retarded servant Perro (Bob Letizia) to lift the curse, but this by necessity involves taking a bride and impregnating her, after which family friend Madame Von Kirst will exorcise the child. Perro is sent out to invite four young women – Laura (Jan Sherman), Yvonne (Dolores Heiser), Vickie (Rita Ballard) and Dana (Dolores Starling) – to visit the grand De Lorca house, where they are unwittingly 'auditioned' for the role of unwilling mother. Juan opts for Laura, but her boyfriend Guy (Ben Robinson) gets wind of what's happening and interrupts the occult ceremony before it can be completed. Perro is possessed by a demon spirit and turns into a monster, slamming a machete into Guy's head and strangling Laura. Dana becomes a vampire, and Vickie has her throat slashed. Juan decides to make the best of it, and rapes Yvonne. The family keep her locked up in the house to await the birth of her child…

In order to make sense of this story, I've basically ignored the first five minutes. A young man in bed with his girlfriend discovers a hidden cubby-hole in the bedside wall. Inside is a diary written by Carlos De Lorca. *"Who's Carlos De Lorca?"* asks the girl. *"He was my great uncle,"* the young man replies. *"He raised my father and helped raise me, until his death about two years ago. For some reason my great grandfather threw him out of the house. He came back when his brother died and helped raise his nephew, Juan De Lorca, who was my father."* You got all that? Well, since the speaker is supposedly the son of a man who turns out to have been killed, and whose only child was killed too, it's a mystery who the hell he really is. He's never even named – he finds the diary in the opening minutes, the contents of which cue a giant movie-length flashback, but we never return to him! The fact that neither he nor his girlfriend are credited merely proves what a catchpenny effort this is. The seemingly arbitrary Spanish element, complete with flamenco guitar on the soundtrack, merely makes you pine for the far more enthralling Iberian nonsense of *Count Dracula's Great Love* (Javier Aguirre, 1972) and *Werewolf's Shadow* (Leon Klimovsky, 1970). Somehow, although the story could easily provide the basis for a decent Gothic vampire tale, *The Brides Wore Blood* fails to live up to its title. The actors lack confidence, ensemble dialogue scenes hiccup with hesitations and nervous glances off-camera, and the story is structured disastrously: if your tale is told in flashback, it's really not a good idea to include

WIZARD

A HORRIFYING CREEP SHOW!

CARNIVAL of BLOOD

HOW MUCH TERROR CAN YOU TAKE!

BURT YOUNG in CARNIVAL OF BLOOD
Also starring EARLE EDGERTON · JUDITH RESNICK
MARTIN BARLOSKY and JOHN HARRIS
Produced, Written and Directed by LEONARD KIRTMAN

18

left:
UK video cover for **Carnival of Blood**.

below:
This decidedly camp grizzly bear adorns the
UK video cover of **Claws** (one of two different
versions, this one from Shaftesbury Films);
am I imagining things, or is it trying to
replicate David Bowie's pose on the cover
of his 1977 album 'Heroes'? The back cover
blurb is also worth a double-take:
"Having killed several humans in horrific
fashion, a professional animal catching team
try their luck with our grizzly friend…"

grateful – but by then the damage has been done. It would take a
miracle to turn this baby round, and Kirtman is no Paul McKenna.
Instead, tedious Dan and bland Laura patiently walk us through the
same funfair stalls we visited with Claire and Harry: the shooting
range; the palmist; the ghost-train. By the time Laura has daringly
added the Ferris wheel to the list, in the company of the killer no
less, even the Dalai Llama would be baying for her blood. At the
risk of repeating myself (if only that thought had occurred to
Kirtman), I honestly don't think you can say you've known
boredom until you've sat through this movie without a remote
control. Sold on DVD by Something Weird as *"a strange little
sickie"* and *"in the splatter style of Herschell Gordon Lewis,"*
Carnival of Blood gives even the lamest of Lewis (*Color Me
Blood Red*) the lustre of a Dario Argento film. Admittedly, *both*
gore scenes are in the same funny/clumsy vein as Lewis – but
they're over too quickly, and the photography (at least as presented
on DVD) is so abysmal there's barely a chance to see what's going
on. It makes you realise how clever Lewis was to light his dime-
store grue with the flashbulb glare of a paparazzi doorstepper.

Leonard Kirtman made one more horror flick, *Curse of the
Headless Horseman*, before doing the decent thing and moving
over to porno as 'Leo De Leon' and 'Leon Gucci'. As 'John
Kirkland', he was lighting director and Second Unit director on
Eric Jeffrey Haims's *The Jekyll and Hyde Portfolio*, and redeemed
himself by producing films for porno's über-shock merchant
Zebedy Colt (*Sex Wish*, *The Affairs of Janice*, *Unwilling Lovers*
and *The Devil Inside Her*). Most of the rest of the cast and crew
seem to have packed up and left the movie-business without trying
again; although Earle Edgerton went up in the world a few years
later, in Andy Milligan's *Fleshpot on 42nd Street*. Perhaps the
most shamefaced participant here is Burt Young (credited as 'John
Harris'), who went on to appear in the *Rocky* films and made a
memorably evil patriarch in Damiano Damiani's superior horror
sequel, *Amityville II: The Possession*.

Made in New York City.
see also: **Curse of the Headless Horseman**

A SHAFTESBURY FILMS VIDEO PRESENTATION

CLAWS

Starring
JASON EVERS
and
LEON AMES

The story of a
giant devil bear.
A nightmare
thriller of flesh-
tearing savagery.

VHS • Running time 1 hour 30 mins • Colour

THE CENTERFOLD GIRLS
– John Peyser (1974)
See interview with John Peyser.
Made in California.

THE CHILD
– Robert Voskanian (1976)
See interview with Robert Voskanian and Robert Dadashian.
Made in California.

CLAWS
– Richard Bansbach and Robert E. Pierson (1977)
aka *Devil Bear*
aka *Bear Tooth*

Jason Monroe (Jason Evers) leads a bunch of macho types up
into the Alaskan Rockies, in pursuit of the giant grizzly bear that
mauled his son during a boy scout expedition. Monroe's Indian
tracker believes the bear is possessed by a supernatural power,
and Monroe is convinced it can think. As the harsh elements and
the cunning grizzly pick off the quartet of hunters, it seems
Monroe will have to face the beast alone…

This is a serviceable afternoon adventure film with one furry
foot in the horror genre, thanks to some goring of victims and the
emphasis on the Indian's supernatural visions of 'Wailing Women'
foretelling his doom; visions which the film backs up as genuine.
The grizzly's attack on a boy-scout camp is amusing for sure, and
slightly bloodier than you might expect, but this remains an
adventure movie with horror elements, rather than the other way
round. I confess I'm including it here mainly because it happens to
have been shot in Alaska; Juneau to be precise. Evers travelled to
the other end of the country (Miami, Florida) later the same year,
to star in *Barracuda* for Wayne Crawford and Harry Kerwin.

Made in Alaska.

THE CORPSE GRINDERS
– Ted V. Mikels (1971)

Caleb (Warren Ball) and his wife Cleo (Ann Noble) supply
corpses from the local cemetery to Landau (Sanford Mitchell), a
cat-food manufacturer, who puts the bodies, shrouds and all, into
his meat-grinding machine. Landau hit on the idea after using the
grinder to get rid of a troublesome business associate (Ray
Dannis), and when sales of the adulterated cat food increased, he
turned to grave-robbing to keep up with demand. However, the
product has unfortunate side-effects: domestic cats are now
developing a taste for human flesh. When a cat belonging to Nurse
Angie Robinson (Monika Kelly) attacks her boyfriend Doctor
Howard Glass (Sean Kenney), and a dead woman whose throat has
been ripped out by an enraged feline is dropped off at the hospital,
Howard puts two and two together, and with Nurse Angie in tow
sets off in search of the culprits…

I've been pretty unforgiving in this book about horror films
that mimic the styles of earlier decades, but *The Corpse Grinders*
has an essential morbidity and cynicism that rescues it. Although
the stock-cue soundtrack could just as easily have graced a
Monogram cheapie from the forties, there's a grubby, ghoulish
kick to the proceedings, with its bundled up cadavers, low-rent
interiors and bad-tempered, exploitative characters. Although the
story is silly beyond the reach of sarcasm, there's a pulp grossness
to the film that's weirdly charming. The decidedly shaky 'corpse-
grinding machine' (which sadly is only referred to as such in the
film's bonkers trailer) has an ultra-cheap, school-project vibe,
admitting fully-clothed humans at one end and discharging sloppy
mincemeat at the other, a process that contrives to be both
hilarious and revolting. There's also something compelling about
the film's cramped *mise en scène*, with everything shot in such
tight, cluttered compositions, and with so little actual movement
from scene to scene, that you could imagine it all fitting inside a

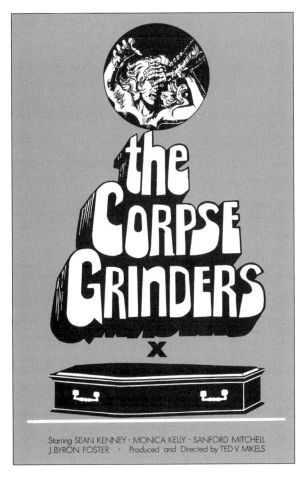

snow-shaker (now there's a marketing idea). The characters too – including a mentally subnormal woman who clings to a doll, and a deaf woman (Drucilla Hoy) who acts like Igor's anorexic sister – add to the general air of dysfunction. Freakiest of all, the man playing Caleb, Warren Ball, is a thyroidal giant who looks like he'd have been happy abducting hitch hikers and torturing them in a soundproof bunker if the acting career went downhill. All of this within a story about flesh-eating cats on the rampage makes the result irresistible: Mikels is not one of my favourite directors, but this shabby, creaky piece of grime is a masterpiece of kino-bizarre.

The Corpse Grinders was written by Joseph Cranston (*The Crawling Hand*, 1963), and Arch Hall Sr. (director of *Eegah!*, 1962). Mikels later directed a shot-on-video sequel, *The Corpse Grinders 2* (2000), following it with *Mark of the Astro-Zombies* (2002). *You* check 'em out, I don't think I dare…

Made in California.
see also: **Blood Orgy of the She Devils**

THE CRATER LAKE MONSTER
– William R. Stromberg (1977)

A cop and a doctor discover cave paintings down a mine near Crater Lake, depicting primitive man battling a plesiosaur – proof that dinosaurs survived much later than believed. A meteor lands in the prophetically named Crater Lake, heating up the water and thus hatching a dinosaur egg that's lain in the silt for centuries… A water-dwelling plesiosaur then takes to the land (?) and kills a hitch hiker, a bull and a fisherman in short order, before the action slows to a crawl and the viewer's mind clouds over…

"I've been stuffin' my shoes with newspaper so long my feet know more about what's goin' on than my head!" This quip aside, *The Crater Lake Monster*, another minor addition to the roll-call of seventies monster-movies, is tough to sit through. Its combination of lowbrow humour, shambolic plotting and occasional bursts of enthusiastic stop-motion animation may charm fans of *The Beast from 20,000 Fathoms* (1953), but even hardcore plasticine addicts will be struggling more than usual between bouts of monster mayhem. The creature's scale varies wildly depending on which prop version we see, but at least Stromberg shows plenty of the beast – and right from the off, too. There's so little actual story though that he opts to waste five long minutes on a comedy brawl between two good ole boys, who slug it out in the shallows of Crater Lake until finally, thank God, they stumble upon a floating corpse. In case you were unsure of how to take their drunken antics, they're helpfully signposted as 'comedic' by the bumptiously chuckling score. An out-of-nowhere sequence involving a man who holds up a liquor store, shooting dead the assistant and a customer, feels cut in from a different movie: the actor gives the only compelling performance in the film. Nevertheless, Stromberg soon has the character drive his car off a cliff and into the monster's maw (or rather, into jump-cut proximity with a shot of its thrashing jaws – a must-see for connoisseurs of 'Will that do?' filmmaking). To give you some idea of the film's pacing problems, the generic scene where cops, local doctor and heroic young couple gather to discuss what to do takes place around the seventy minute mark. At which late point, all that remains is for the locals to duke it out with the plesiosaur using a bulldozer *à là* Sigourney Weaver battling the Mother in *Aliens*. Watch out for that lawsuit, James Cameron…

Shot at Huntington Lake and Palomar Mountain, California, *The Crater Lake Monster* boasts several future luminaries of special effects cinema. Actor Michael Hoover worked as digital artist on *Spider-Man 2*; fellow star Mark Siegel was creature maker on *Dune* and *Naked Lunch*; cinematographer Paul Gentry was visual effects supervisor on the hit TV series *24*; Jon Berg worked as a stop-motion effects man on *Star Wars* the same year he built the miniatures for *Crater Lake*; Randall Crook designed the monster in Larry Cohen's *Q: The Winged Serpent*, and worked on the stop-motion climax of Carpenter's *The Thing*, before joining the effects crew of the first two *Lord of the Rings* films; and Jim Danforth and Dave Allen's combined credits are too numerous to mention here. Perhaps most impressive of all, Phil Tippett went from building *The Crater Lake Monster*'s miniatures to the post of 'dinosaur supervisor' on *Jurassic Park*!

Made in California.

top left:
Pressbook cover for
The Corpse Grinders.

far left:
Grubby leftovers from the
grinding machine…

left:
The Crater Lake Monster;
and a mammal…

Crazed (UK video title)
aka **Slipping Into Darkness** (US theatrical title)
aka **Bloodshed** (US video title)
aka **The Paranoiac** (working title)
© none [1977].
director/writer: Richard Cassidy. producer: Jean Cassidy. director of photography: Doug Hodge. music: Ron Ramin. film editors: Richard Cassidy, Jean Cassidy. associate producer: Randy L. Turtle. production manager: Steven C. Bobek. assistant director: Steve Sherry. 2nd assistant director: David Byron Lloyd. 2nd unit cinematographer: Neil Lundell. 2nd assistant camera: Suzanne Palmer, Robert Payne. art directors: Janice Carr, Jane Mancbach. assistant art director: Susan M. Marcinkus. key make-up artist: Helen Little. production sound: Avi Kipper. boom man: Jeffrey Lawrence Ellis. script supervisor: R.L. Turtle. gaffer: Doug Hodge. best boy: Robert Payne. grips: Eric Butler, Brad Smith, Kevin Burke. key grip: Dan Zarlengo. grips: Philip R. Miller, Jim Arone. production assistants: Benny Landau, Jim Piper, Brian Brosnan, Douglas Horowitz. music conducted by David Spear. song "Rodeo Cowboy" by John McFarland. legal adviser: Evan J. Morris. production services: Sawyer Camera Company. sound: Post-Transfer Services. effects/music editors: Richard Cassidy, Jean Cassidy, Steve Sherry. negative cutter: Fred H. Teetzel. title artwork: Michael Marcus. title photography: Animagraphics. re-recording: TV/Recorders. home style catering: John & Vickie Carey. colour, prints & opticals: United Color Lab.
Cast: Laszlo Papas (Grahame). Belle Mitchell (Mrs. Brewer). Beverly Ross (Karen). TJ McFadden (Rodney). Rigg Kennedy (Chuck). Helen Rogler (Mrs. Dobson). Marguerite Price (room renter #1). Stefanie Auerbach (room renter #2). Jeffrey Lawrence Ellis (room renter #3). Jim Arone (wacko conductor). Robert Payne (market customer). David Kaufman, Martin Rubin (cashiers). Emma N. Benavides (prostitute). Michael Anthony DeLorenzo, James K. Cortez, Roger E. Herbel, Kenneth Hass (students). Leo Salkin (professor). Susan M. Marcinkus, Jim Piper, Evelyn King Kennedy, D.D.S., Robert P. Kaplan, Brad Smith, Gracie Speranza (students). Dorothy Buhrman (lead whore). Sheila Rachel, Carol Holden, Jeannie Morris, Janice Carr (whores). Philip R. Miller (Grahame's father). Janet Marie (Grahame's mother). Chris Smith (Grahame as boy). Barney McFadden (minister). Dorothy Francavilla, Frank Bolger (hotel clerks). Walter R. Feltz, Steve Sherry (farmers). Suzan Campbell (Chuck's wife). R.L. Turtle (telephone operator). Marion Wayne (Brewer's neighbour). Jeannie Morris (nurse).

top left: US video sleeve for **Crazed**.

top right, clockwise from bottom left:
Karen (Beverly Ross) greets her boyfriend Rodney (TJ McFadden) while Grahame (Laszlo Papas) looks on in **Crazed**;
Mrs. Brewer (Belle Mitchell) learns the truth about her sweet young lodger;
Someone is not going to make it to the end of the movie;
Grahame confronts his demons.

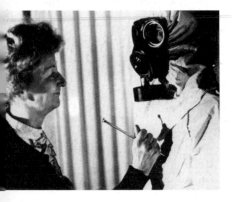

CRAZED

– Richard Cassidy (made 1977, released 1979)
aka *Slipping Into Darkness*
aka *The Paranoiac*
aka *Bloodshed*

Laszlo Papas is Grahame, the Norman Bates figure in this average knock-off of *Psycho*. Sexually abused by his father, dubbed 'retarded' by his mother, and then abandoned in a children's home by both of them, Grahame grows up a quiet but emotionally disturbed young man. Having spent unhappy years in the Army, he's now settling down at a boarding house run by Mrs. Brewer (Belle Mitchell), an eccentric old dear who assumes a motherly role in his life. Into this situation comes Karen (Beverly Ross), a young woman seeking a new life away from her abusive husband. Grahame falls for the new arrival, but all is bound to go wrong...

Crazed is basically too slow, but it's fairly well acted by Papas and Ross. Belle Mitchell as the old lady is a touch off-key, but her eccentricity survives a few clumsy line readings. On the violence front there's one nasty stabbing scene and a strangling, but little else to trouble the squeamish. The emphasis is on mood, and while the story is predictable (save for a decent twist about half-way) I found myself gripped as the old lady finally tumbles to the sickness of her favourite lodger. Cassidy's direction is rather staid, lacking for instance the ambition to visualise the madness of the unhappy lead. Perhaps the main problem is that there are just too few unusual touches to distinguish it from the many other stories of this kind (Curtis Harrington's *The Killing Kind*, Denny Harris's *The Silent Scream*, or David Schmoeller's *Crawlspace* for instance). Enjoyable as you watch it, *Crazed* nonetheless slips all too easily out of your mind afterwards and merges into the crowd of post-*Psycho* horror thrillers. Husband-and-wife team Richard and Jean Cassidy conceived the film together, and in order to drum up interest in the project they initially filmed it as a 35mm short. The film's grip, Dan Zarlengo, recalls that their "beautiful b/w project was an obvious tribute to the suspense and magic of Alfred Hitchcock. Directed by Richard, it featured his wife, Jean as the murder victim." Zarlengo also confirms that the original working title of the film was *The Paranoiac*, and that it was completed and released as *Slipping Into Darkness* by Jupiter Pictures in late 1979. The house featured in the film apparently still stands on Edgemont, south of Wilshire Blvd., a few blocks east of Highland Avenue in Hollywood. Cassidy is sometimes confused with an Australian director of the same name.

Made in California.

THE CRAZIES

– George Romero (1973)
aka *Code Name Trixie*
aka *The Mad People* (original script title)

After the little-seen misfire *There's Always Vanilla* and the flagrantly uncommercial *Season of the Witch*, *The Crazies* sees George Romero rediscover the commercial savvy that propelled his debut, *Night of the Living Dead*, while taking on the breadth of ambition that would characterise his later films. It offers a nightmare vision of chaos surrounding America's first biological weapons spill, and it's so utterly convincing that only blind patriots, or optimists of the fuzziest variety, would find it implausible. Everything goes wrong: technology interferes with the process of communication (a recurring Romero motif); bureaucracy and human error combine into gridlock; and the rub between authoritarianism and individualism puts a spark to the tinder to a point where, dramatically speaking, you hardly need to show the effects of the weapon spill. The fact that the infected go crazy is more a bitter irony than a pivotal plot point.

Romero develops the confusion without the film being confusing itself, packing an emotional punch that transcends the sometimes overstretched acting skills of the cast. And that's the downside: of all Romero's major films, this is probably the least well served in the acting department. The central group of David (Will MacMillan), Judy (Lane Carroll), Clank (Harold Wayne Jones), Artie (Richard Liberty) and Kathy (Lynn Lowry) lack the fine characterisation that distinguishes Romero's subsequent film *Martin*, and more pertinently, his action-horror masterpiece *Dawn of the Dead*. MacMillan and Carroll are serviceable, nothing more; Jones (a David Hess look-alike) is a bit better, providing a dry run for Scott Reiniger's character in *Dawn*; while Richard Liberty (Dr. 'Frankenstein' Logan in *Day of the Dead*) is given little to do until the last reel, when his madness tilts into perversion. The exception is Lynn Lowry, who essays another of her spaced-out child-woman roles with great sensitivity (see also *I Drink Your Blood* and *Shivers*). The best performance, though, comes from Richard France as Dr. Watts, the scientist sent – in a chillingly believable bureaucratic blunder – into the middle of the danger zone, despite being a vital player in the search for an antidote. Romero must have liked Richard France's style: he used the actor's blustering, bear-like persona again in *Dawn of the Dead*, as the pundit whose brutal pragmatism alienates his fellow experts during a rapidly collapsing TV debate. Here, France

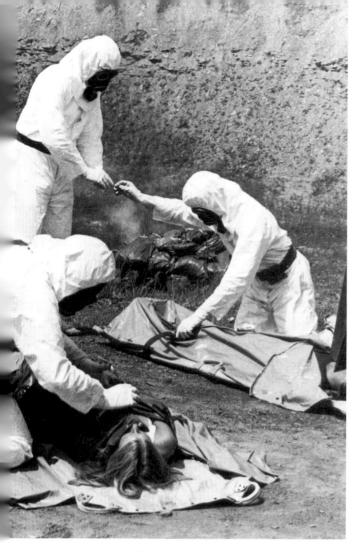

The Crazies
aka **Code Name Trixie** (US theatrical re-release title)
© 1973. Pittsburgh Films.
Lee Hessel presents. Produced by Pittsburgh Films through the facilities of The Latent Image, Inc., Pittsburgh. A Cambist film.
director: George A. Romero. producer: A. C. Croft. director of photography: S. William Hinzman. editor: George A. Romero. based on an original script by Paul McCollough. screenplay: George A. Romero. production managers: Bob Rutkowski, H. Cramer Riblett, Vince Survinski. post production co-ordinator: Bob Rutowski. sound recordists: Rex Gleeson, John Stoll. sound technicians: Eric Baca, Michael Gornick. production co-ordinator: Edith Bell. script girl: Bonnie Hinzman. Miss Carroll's make up: Doris Dodds. make up consultants: Gloria Natalie / Justine Ltd. make up: Bonnie Priore. special effects: Regis Survinski, Tony Pantanello. assistant cameraman: John Fitzpatrick. assistant to the editor: Joe Colazzi. grips: David Meek, Robert Karlowsky, John Atkinson. medical adviser: Barry J. Rosenbaum, M.D. military adviser: Col. Bernard Garred, Ret. song "Heaven Help Us" composed by Carole Bayer Sager and Melissa Manchester, sung by Beverly Bremers, courtesy of Scepter Records, Inc. musical director: Stephen Metz. musical score by Bruce Roberts. associate producer: Margaret Walsh. colour by Movielab. Special thanks to Victrix Productions, Inc. Our thanks to the citizens and officials of Evans City, Pa. and Zelienople, Pa. for their help and cooperation. filmed on location in Evans City and Zelienople (Pennsylvania, USA)
Cast: Lane Carroll (Judy). W. G. McMillan (David). Harold Wayne Jones (Clank). Lloyd Hollar (Colonel Peckem). Lynn Lowry (Kathy). Richard Liberty (Artie). Richard France (Dr. Watts). Harry Spillman (Maj. Ryder). Will Disney (D. Brookmyre). Edith Bell (lab. technician). W. L. Thunhurst, Jr. (Brubaker). Leland Starnes (Shelby). A. C. MacDonald (Gen. Bowen). Robert J. McCully (Hawks). Robert Karlowsky (Sheriff Cooper). Ned Schmidtke (Sgt. Tragesser). Tony Scott (Deputy Shade). Roy Cheverie (army doctor). Jack Zaharia (priest). Stephen Liska. David Meek. Roger Brown. Kim Smith. Billy Hinzman. Richard Lewicki. William C. Kennedy. MaLynda Parker. Walton Cook. Peg Tilbrook. Vince Survinski. Norman Chase. Ross Harris.

CREATURE FROM BLACK LAKE
– Joy N. Houck Jr. (1976)
aka *Demon of the Lake* (US video title)
aka *Attack at Black Lake*

Two Yankee students visit the Louisiana swamps to research stories of a giant bipedal anthropoid – that's Bigfoot, to you and me. First they get themselves into trouble with the locals, and then with a hulking creature that stalks them in the woods after dark…

A likeable though insubstantial affair, this, not to mince words, could have done with a bit more monster mayhem. Despite some fairly effective scenes of tension there are no onscreen deaths, and even for a family-oriented drive-in feature it's just too gentle. Obviously Houck, a cinema entrepreneur well-acquainted with his potential audience, was aiming for a lighter 'PG'-level scare-movie: the young male leads avoid swearing entirely and their attempted courtship of two 'hospitable' Southern girls is discreetly curtailed by the arrival of the creature. However, considering that *Blood and Lace*, released around the same time and featuring several fairly graphic hammer murders, received a 'PG' too, Houck appears to have erred a little too far on the side of caution.

Despite a respectable looking ape-suit for the creature, and the presence of Dean (*Halloween*) Cundey at the camera, the film still wastes its visual possibilities. Bigfoot may be an oral tradition, with sightings passed around as folk stories and local gossip, but it seems a perverse use of the medium to spend more time looking at people talking about Bigfoot than actually showing the thing. There are several scenes where people recount tales of the creature, but only a few of these cross-fade into visual depictions. Perhaps Houck's intention was to approach things in the style of a campfire story, a round-the-log-fire country tale, but it's a shame there's not more emphasis on visual storytelling, except for some rather

opposite page, bottom left:
Grandma gets political in **The Crazies**.

left:
Helping or hindering? Good guys or bad guys? Few horror directors can mix it all up as well as Romero in his prime.

below:
This UK video cover from Replay is crude but likeable – as befits the film.

Creature from Black Lake
aka **Attack at Black Lake** (MPAA title)
© 1976. Jim McCullough Productions, Inc.
A Jim McCullough production.
director: Joy Houck, Jr. producer: Jim McCullough. screenplay: Jim McCullough, Jr. executive producer: William Lewis Ryder. director of photography: Dean Cundey. music: Jaime Mendoza-Nava. title song "Exits and Truck Stops" written, composed and sung by Jim McCullough, Jr. film editor: Robert Gordon. production manager: Al Salzer. assistant director: Bill Baker. location manager: H.B. McCullough. wardrobe: W.L. 'CC' Ryder, Jr. sound: Tommy Causey. art director: Roger Pancake. make up: Carlene Cundey. gaffer: Mark Walthour. key grip: Grant Tucker. script supervisor: Patricia Motyka. second unit cameraman: Jim deBuys. assistant production manager: Edie Houck. assistant cameraman: James A. Borgardt. 1st assistant cameraman: Ray Stella. 2nd assistant cameraman: Bucky Brinson. property master: Douglas Laramore. assistant make up: Karen Brooks. special effects: Sterling Franck. boom man: Joe Brennan. assistant art director: Charlie Hughes. best boy: Tony Kupersmith. best boy: Ron King. grips: Bob Kyle, John Fertitta. set operations: Hugh McCullough. craft service: George Rigg. location auditor: C.C. Colley. assistant auditor: Molly Westbrook. sound effects editors: Dimitri Gortinsky, John Paul Jones, Shelley Tackett. assistant wardrobe: Meleta McKellar. negative editor: Jack LaMantain. locations by Movivan. titles, opticals and colour by CFI. The Producers gratefully acknowledge the assistance in the making of this motion picture to the following: Mator Calhoun Allen and the Shreveport, Louisiana Department of Public Safety; Mayor James Cathy and the Bossier City, Louisiana Police Department; State of Louisiana Dept of Commerce and The Louisiana Film Commission; State of Louisiana Wild Life Department; Shreveport, Louisiana Chamber of Commerce; Dub Allen and mayor, police and citizens of Oil City, Louisiana; Willis Knighton Hospital - Dr Walter T. Snow and James Elrod, administrators. filmed on location in Shreveport, Bossier City and Oil City (Louisiana, USA).
Cast: Jack Elam (Joe Canton). Dub Taylor (Grandpaw Bridges). Dennis Fimple (Pahoo). John David Carson (Rives). Bill Thurman (sheriff). Jim McCullough, Jr. (Orville Bridges). Roy Tatum (Fred and creature). Catherine McClenny (waitress). Becky Smiser (sheriff's daughter). Michelle Willingham (Michelle). Evelyn Hindricks (Mr. Bridges). Roger Pancake (H.B.). Karen Brooks (Orville's mother). Chase Tatum (little Orville). Bob Kyle (Rufus). J.N. Houck, Jr. (Doctor Burch).

brings a touch of ham to the role of Dr. Watts that nonetheless strikes me as appropriate, his manner that of a high-handed private surgeon. Despite his arrogance, Watts emerges as a potential hero, but this being the 1970s, when heroism was extremely unlikely to flourish in the horror genre, all does not go according to plan. The scene where Watts is mistaken for a 'crazy' by gas-masked soldiers, who herd him into an enclosure with the infected, neatly encapsulates the film's message: failure of communication screws us all.

In contrast to Romero's signature zombie movies, bloodshed in *The Crazies* is mostly restricted to bullet-hit squibs. There are no gaping flesh wounds or creative disembowelments this time. In fact the most violent assault is on the ears, thanks to the aggressive sound-mix. The predominant musical element throughout is a rattling military snare drum; to which Romero adds sirens, blaring loudspeaker announcements, crackling radio-sets, near-constant gunfire, muffled yelling from gas-mask clad soldiers, the roar of motor vehicle engines; in short, cacophony. It gives the film a jagged, metallic, painful quality, something that's not in the least bit assuaged by some very tinny sound-recording. As masked soldiers argue or discuss their orders with each other, Romero chooses to dub their voices in an echoey, highly artificial way, always blatantly studio-recorded despite the many naturalistic scenes set outdoors. This adds to the sense of dislocation between the soldiers and the rest of the cast, but further amplifies the headachy tension of the film; *The Crazies* is like walking outdoors in the morning with a hangover, and having sunlight bounce off a car bonnet into your eyes. If it weren't for the quality of the storytelling, it would all be a bit too much. Flaws aside, however, this is a ferociously intelligent and compelling film made by a very talented director about to hit his peak.

Made in Pennsylvania.
see also: **Martin**

The Creeper (UK video title)
aka The Dark Side of Midnight
(original/US video title)
© 1984. Wes Olsen
writer/director: Wes Olsen. director of
cinematography: Wes Page. associate
producer: Mary Ann Olsen. producer: Wes
Olsen. original music composed by Doug
Holroyd, arranged by Tom 'Fingers' Farnsworth.
casting: James Hull. camera: Wes Page.
assistant camera: Bob Napton. sound: Misty
Walls, Tony Medeiros, Bill Prudhomme. film
editor: Wes Olsen. production assistant: June
Asher. make-up: MaryAnn Phillips. special
make-up effects: Susan Frawley. script
supervisor: Gitte Norby. gaffers: Gary Zwald,
Tom Duncan. grips: Vaughn May, John Zoslocki,
Bruce Brown. property master: D.W. Wells.
wardrobe: Suni Walls. art director: Bob Olsen.
set construction: Alvin Olsen. paintings
furnished by Robert Olsen & Merle Maxwell. The
Producer would like to thank the following
people for making this picture possible, Mr. &
Mrs. Bruce Brown; Mr. Amos Hobby; Mr. & Mrs.
John MacArthur; Mr. Louis Niles; Mr. Alvin
Olsen; Mr. & Mrs. Robert Olsen; Mr. & Mrs.
Vernon Olsen; Mr. & Mrs. Pete Peterson; Mr. &
Mrs. Don Phillips; Miss Joie Phillips; Mr. Joe
Phillips; Mr. & Mrs. Bill Shipman; Mr. & Mrs.
Howard Shipman; Mr. William Vieira; Mr. John
Zoslocki; Miss Peggy Zwald; Mr. Bob Rocha; Mr.
John Turner; Mr. Michael DeRuosi; Mrs. JoAnn
Lyons. music recorded & mixed at Musical
Image Productions - sound engineer: Gary
Shriver. This film is dedicated to Harley Lee.
Cast: James Moore (Chief Cooper). Wes Olsen
(Brock Johnson). Sandy Schemmel (Jan
Cooper). Dave Bowling (Mayor Reilly). Dan
Myers (the creeper). Dennis Brennan (Ben
Fischer). Susan Frawley (Cheryl Tompkins).
Eliot Fisher (Timmy Simmons). Rocky Jackson
(Lt. Nelson). Ron Posey (David Griffin). June
Asher (Kathy Freeman). Anthony Medeiros
(Chuck McCalister). Nancy Frykman (Mrs.
Reilly). James Hull (Mr. Freeman). Charline
Freedman (Mrs. Freeman). Christine Asher
(Terri Cooper). Misty Walls (April). Kat
Huddleston (April's friend). Kandis Boven
(mayor's secretary). Lisa Moeglein (Nelson's
girlfriend). Gary Thomas (police sergeant).
Steve Saunders (Mr. Simmons). Rita Thomas
(Mrs. Simmons). Amos Hobby (Mr. Tompkins).
Marian Napton (Mrs. Tompkins). Aubrey Asher
(Dr. Benjamin). Tom Farnsworth (Dr. Jacobs).
Steve Wiegman (neighbour man). Diane Dilday
(neighbour's wife). Bill Prudhomme (Sergeant
O'Hara). Casey Stowers (Linda Parker). Robert
Olsen (arresting officer). Bill Shipman (police
detective). Brad King (vagrant). Sandy Asher
(nurse). Cary Thomas (Mr. Turner). Eren Fisher
(boy#1). Evan Fisher (boy #2). Wes Page (radio
interviewer). Suni Lee Walls (girl in toy store).
Bob Napton (prowler). Mike Hewitt, Denise
Hewitt, Dennis Zambruno, Barbara Page, Dixie
Zambruno (news people).

top right:
The Creeper gets the video-sleeve it deserves.

below:
A victim buys time by playing 'Heads,
Shoulders, Knees and Toes'...

routine stalking in the woods in the last twenty minutes. Despite that, it's a pleasant enough experience, perhaps best watched on a weekend afternoon rather than during a late-night horror session.

The strained relations between North and South provide a little extra detail, as the film shows Southern hospitality and its flipside of distrust, while the visiting Yankees are given to crude assumptions and a lack of country manners. Locals are sensitive to being misrepresented: *"Don't want folks comin' round makin' us look like a bunch o' dumb rednecks,"* says one old-timer. The sheriff is an unfriendly type, but even he has the safety of the visitors at heart. So while the North-South differences are acknowledged, there's little sense of friction. As a film made by a Southern director, *Creature from Black Lake* is ironically less incendiary in tone than *Two Thousand Maniacs!*, directed by Chicago-born but Southern-sympathizin' Herschell Gordon Lewis.

Joy (short for Joinda) Newton Houck Jr. was born on 26 January, 1942. He was the son of a Southern theatre chain owner who produced low-budget films to be distributed to his own cinemas. Houck Sr.'s company Howco International began in the 1950s. Some sources confuse father and son in their credits; for example, the IMDB lists Houck Jr. as executive producer on three films made before he was fifteen! Houck Jr. started his filmmaking career with two horror films which he wrote, directed and produced: *Night of Bloody Horror* (1969) and *Women and Bloody Terror* (1970). He can be seen in *Creature from Black Lake* playing a college lecturer and expert on Bigfoot. He died of heart failure at home, on 1 October, 2003.

Made in Louisiana.

THE CREEPER
– Wes Olsen (1984)
aka *The Dark Side of Midnight*

I rarely turn my back on a slasher (good advice in real life too, kids) but this dismal effort, at an arse-numbing 113 minutes, is so ceaselessly, bloodlessly dull it defeated even my optimism. Cops sit at their desks, arguing on the phone and chewing over the case in question, *viz.* 'The Creeper' – a murderer so badly conceived he can't even stick to his *m.o.* Though he's apparently known for attacking beautiful young blondes with hourglass figures, three of the film's six barely-glimpsed killings are anomalous, including two brunettes (one of them fat) and a six-year-old boy (blond but hardly curvaceous). There is *one* workable and rather unnerving idea, but it's thrown away in a line of dialogue and a single fluffed scene: The Creeper is said to have struck before, often sneaking into victims' houses and hiding in their attics for weeks or even months before emerging, after midnight, to kill without warning. The idea of a psychopath covertly living in his victims' homes is pregnant with possibilities (see Thomas Harris's *Red Dragon*), but it's stillborn here. All that's left by way of amusement is to observe the colossal ineptitude of the two cops in charge of the case. At one point, arriving in an attic where The Creeper has been living, and finding his makeshift bed still warm, they settle down to wait for him, only to nod off and alert the returning psycho to their presence by snoring! The standard of acting is appalling throughout, with the cops unengaging and the various victims and relatives incapable of a convincing reaction: two parents, informed that their daughter has been hacked to death, exhibit a mild grief more befitting the discovery of a smashed ornament than news of bereavement. As this grossly overlong snoozer draws to a close, Officer Brock Johnson (Olsen himself) despatches the killer by luring him into a shack and setting fire to it; at least we *assume* he's despatched, since there's no sign of him burning in the hurried, deeply unimpressive fire scene. Surely this coy approach to the killer's death is simply a shop-worn prelude to a 'twist' where he pops up again *à la* Michael Myers? Oh no – in what may be *The Creeper*'s only slasher-film innovation, this utterly limp finale really is it: the end, *finito*, forget it. *"Well, we won't have to worry about him any more,"* says Olsen: words that could stand as his directorial epitaph…

Made in California.

"CRIMINALLY INSANE"
– Nick Philips [aka Nick Millard aka Steve Millard] (1975)

Ethel Janowski (Priscilla Alden), a big fat 250lb lump of resentment, is released from psychiatric incarceration into the care of her grandmother (Jane Lambert). A doctor suggests to Grannie that she should try to help Ethel lose weight. On her first night of freedom, Ethel wakes up and blunders downstairs looking for food, but Grannie has locked the kitchen cupboard and emptied the icebox. Thwarted, she attacks the cupboard with a knife. When Grannie tries to stop her, Ethel stabs the old dear to death, finishes her midnight snack, then drags the corpse upstairs and locks it in her room. Next morning, Ethel telephones the store and places a humungous $80 food order. When the delivery boy arrives, Ethel realises there's no money in the house (*"I've only got $4.50!"*). Not to be denied, she kills the kid, stashes the body, and tucks in to those groceries. Ethel's prostitute sister Rosalie invites herself over to stay, moves her pimp in with her, and uses the spare room to service her clients. Then a police detective (C.L. LeFleur [George Buck Flower]) arrives, looking for the missing delivery boy. And so Ethel's murder-spree continues, as various interlopers and busy-bodies threaten to expose her as a murderess and – worse still – interfere with her mealtimes.

"Criminally Insane" is a short but perfectly formed little masterpiece. Trimmed to the bone, with a lean running time of just under an hour, it's a model of restraint and concision. What's immediately so impressive is the simplicity and starkness of the concept, and the comic banality of the killer's motive. Abel Ferrara has rightfully been praised for his film *The Driller Killer*, in which a man is driven crazy not by sexual dysfunction but incipient poverty. Ethel is another of the psycho-genre's mis-shapes: she kills because she can't stop eating. Oh sure, you can theorise that this fat woman probably has an unhappy little girl inside screaming to get out, but part of the fascination with this movie is its implacable disinterest in psychological motivation. Everyone's got a sob story, it seems to say, so who cares what made Ethel such a greedy, sour-faced bitch? Of course obese people have problems regulating their appetites, and being slowly smothered by 250lbs of lard is likely to

turn anyone bitter, but the director is having none of this bleeding heart stuff – Ethel's blankly disinterested attitude to anything other than food is echoed by the film's scorn for the niceties of plot and characterisation. I wouldn't want *every* psycho film to be made this way, but I love how flat and bleak this is – it's like a deeply unsympathetic fly-on-the-wall documentary. The lack of a real storyline makes it all feel vaguely Warholian, something the matter-of-fact performances help to foster: you can imagine Brigid Polk in *Andy Warhol's Bad* getting on with Ethel. Most importantly, Priscilla Alden plays the lead with a sullen distance that ensures the subject matter doesn't flare into camp. And Ethel has a bad attitude to go with her hunger-pangs. Like that other hefty horror star, Martha in *The Honeymoon Killers*, Ethel is prone to anti-Semitic outbursts: *"That Goddam Jew doctor gave them orders not to give me enough to eat,"* she explains to her grandma: *"They were trying to save money, and starve me while they were at it."* And when the old lady tries to stop her breaking into the kitchen cupboard, she exclaims, *"You and that Heeb are trying to starve me to death!"* It's a detail that ensures we keep our distance even though we're amused by how awful she is, and it means we don't feel so bad withholding our sympathy. After all, Ethel's problem is nothing a stay in Buchenwald wouldn't cure…

Made in California.

see also: **Satan's Black Wedding**

CRYPT OF DARK SECRETS

– Jack Weis (1976)

Another exercise in tedium from the New Orleans-based Jack Weis, he of the mindlessly redundant *Blood Feast* rip-off, *Mardi Gras Massacre* (1978). *Crypt of Dark Secrets* is fractionally better, but still feels like congealed genre leftovers. For the first ten minutes, all you get is a shot of immortal Voodoo Queen Damballa (Maureen Ridley) dancing in some obscure ritual, and two cops (Herb Jahncke and Wayne Mack) boating through the Louisiana Bayou, explaining the back-story (mysterious woman sighted on haunted Bayou island) with a lack of enthusiasm you soon come to share. The tale eventually grinds into second gear when three jewel thieves, Earl, Max and Louise (Butch Benit, Harry Uher and Barbara Hagerty), move in on Bayou bachelor Ted Watkins (Ronald Tanet), beating him to death and chucking his denim-swathed body in the creek. Damballa takes pity and revives him by performing a sexy nude dance. (Ridley is noticeably better at nude dancing than dialogue, which perhaps gives a clue as to where Weis discovered her.) Back in town, another 'voodoo woman' (Susie Sirmen) is shown sticking huge pins in a man's back while he sits silent and docile by her suburban fireplace. We never do find out why, but it looks like a fun hobby. As smoke curls from between the trees, we see flashbacks to Damballa's tribal origins (perhaps footage from an abandoned production, to judge by the difference in picture grain). Damballa tells Ted that he is one of the living dead: an ontological paradox that bothers him not a jot. She helps him to take his revenge against the thieves, and then marries him, in a ceremony that takes place beyond the vale of death (thus presumably shortening the marriage vows a little). The natural place to bring this story to an end, you'd think; except that Weis, obviously struggling to get this up to feature-length, adds another pointlessly protracted boat ride through the swamps in the underwhelming company of the

police. At least the locations are beautiful, and if you dig Maureen Ridley's oiled breasts you'll be more than happy, but really this is forgettable tripe that belongs in the swamp, beyond even the most powerful Voodoo Queen's ability to retrieve. By the way, despite the pleasingly Gothic title, there's no crypt in the film.

This was Weis's third movie, following *Quadroon* (1972 – co-directed with Herbert Janneke Jr.), about a white boy teaching English to mulatto prostitutes in the 1830s, and *Storyville* (1974), a period drama about New Orleans life at the birth of the jazz age. What's notable is that Weis clearly had a great love and fascination for New Orleans, always shooting there and, as the subjects of his first two movies show, taking a genuine interest in the city's history. Note: some sources erroneously list *Crypt of Dark Secrets* as an alternative title for Weis's later film *Mardi Gras Massacre*.

Made in Louisiana.

CURSE OF THE HEADLESS HORSEMAN

– John Kirkland [Leonard Kirtman] (1972)

Mark Callahan (Marland Proctor) inherits a Wild West tourist trap from his uncle, but a codicil stipulates that he must turn a profit within six months or he'll forfeit the lot. Heading for the ranch with fiancée Brenda (Claudia Ream), and a gaggle of hippie loafers as guests, Mark plans to turn it into a music and theatre venue, but it's not to be. When someone dies after seeing a Headless Horseman prowling the area, it seems that the dire warnings of sinister site foreman Solomon (B.G. Fisher) are coming true…

Ouch. I watched this the day after Kirtman's *Carnival of Blood*, and please, heed *my* dire warning – it's not recommended. The uneventful, meandering story is made harder to take by poorly recorded dialogue and a clueless directorial 'style'. Warhol's Ultra Violet appears as a visiting Contessa (who's given Ultra Violet's real name, Isabelle Collin Dufresne) incongruously toting a

"Criminally Insane"
© [none]
writer/director: Nick Philips [Nick Millard]. producer: Frances Millard. cinematographer: Karil Ostman. editor: John Lincoln. unit manager: Ray Sikes. camera operator: Francois Truchon. continuity: Dave Cox. sound: Ronald Gertz. art director: Charles R. Fenwick. makeup: Gigo. casting: Harold Morris. still photography: Larry Bange.
Cast: Priscilla Alden (Ethel Janowski). Michael Flood. Jane Lambert (Mrs. Janowski). Robert Copple. C.L. LeFleur [George 'Buck' Flower] (Detective). Gina Martine. Cliff McDonald. Charles Egan. Sonny Larocca. Sandra Shotwell. Lisa Farros.

above:
(Relatively) thin people must die…
and:
Here comes Ethel! 250lbs of Anti-Semitic flab.

above left:
I would rent **Curse of the Headless Horseman** on the strength of this US videocassette cover…

bottom left:
Surely somewhere in New Orleans there's an Immortal Voodoo Queen for all of us? Here's Damballa (the exquisitely named Maureen Ridley) astride her beau (Ronald Tanet) in **Crypt of Dark Secrets**.

Crypt of Dark Secrets
© none. [1976].
Associated Productions, New Orleans, presents. Filmed by Associated Productions Inc. AFL - C10
producer/director: Jack Weis. original story: Irwin Blache. screenplay: Jack Weis. director of photography: Irwin Blache. assistant director: Glenn Stewart. camera operator: Don Piel. filmed in New Orleans.
Cast: Ronald Tanet (Ted Watkins). Maureen Ridley (Damballa). Herb Jahncke (Sgt. Buck). Wayne Mack (Lt. Harrigan). Butch Benit (Earl). Susie Sirmen (high priestess). Harry Uher (Max). Barbara Hagerty (Louise). Lois Tillman, Cindy Almario, Nattie Dear (voodoo dancers). Vernel Bagneris (high priest). Jack Flynn (banker). John Simmons (other banker).

Superman lunchbox. Presumably the addled 'superstar' was unable to distinguish between Warhol's experimental 'undirecting' and Kirtman's inability. The final revelations are pure 'I'd have got away with it too, if it wasn't for you meddling kids', and the only highlight is a demonstration of how to fake a headless horseman with some bits of bent wire and a cape. Marland Proctor, a regular for John Hayes (he's in *Fandango*, *The Cut-Throats*, *All the Lovin' Kinfolk* and *Garden of the Dead*), is okay as the lead, but this is a viewing chore you really ought to spare yourselves: when Kirtman crossed over to hardcore porn, he did us all a favour. Writer Kenn Riche, who provides a tiresome, verbose script replete with washed-out purple prose, was even more considerate: he disappeared completely.

Made in New York State.

see also: **Carnival of Blood**

THE CURSE OF THE SCREAMING DEAD
– Tony Malanowski (1982)
See interview with Tony Malanowksi.

Made in Maryland.

THE DARK
– John 'Bud' Cardos (1977 [production] 1978 [copyright] 1979 [release])

This project, presumably called *The Dark* to give its useless alien invader an excuse to hide in the shadows, is a twenty-four-carat time-waster. For a start, the emphasis is relentlessly cop-centric: police, police, police all the way. Someone really ought to explain to horror film writers that telling your tale via a police investigation is the scripting equivalent of moving your lips when you read. Mind you, the alternatives presented here aren't much better: namely a female reporter (Cathy Lee Crosby) who wants to do something 'real' instead of covering the latest Hollywood hairdos; and a supposed writer of horror fiction (William Devane) who never takes his dark glasses off long enough to type a milk-note. The only person to come out smelling of roses is Jacquelyn Hyde, who plays an eccentric psychic with a dash of venom that lifts her from the mire. Meanwhile, the monster, which looks like a steal from William Girdler's *The Manitou*, tears the heads off people you don't give a rat's ass about – and since you can barely see them half the time it's even harder to care. Jesus, even porno director Michael Findlay's *Shriek of the Mutilated* had a better monster. Eventually the production limps to the finish-line, the monster is cornered by the cops,

and the damn thing explodes when someone sets fire to it: a dumb ending for a dumb movie.

I never saw this back in the early days of video, when it was released in the UK by Guild. I was already pissed off that Carpenter's *The Fog* was *not* an adaptation of James Herbert's fantastically brutal novel: Herbert's follow-up novel *The Dark* was even nastier, so when a movie of the same title appeared without Herbert's name on it, I was damned if I was going to subject myself to more disappointment. Well, John Carpenter's *The Fog* turned out to be an atmospheric treasure in its own right; *The Dark* however is dreck, whatever your expectations.

The original director, Tobe Hooper, was sacked very early into the shoot, and replaced by John 'Bud' Cardos. It would be a mistake to place the blame entirely with Cardos, though: stepping in at the last minute, his role was probably just to meet the deadlines, keep the production rolling, and make the best of a bad job. Stanford Whitmore, a scriptwriter of mainly TV movies, is as culpable as anyone. Tobe Hooper has remained close-lipped on why he was sacked (not surprisingly), so we may never know what he thought he could do with such apparently unpromising material.

Made in California.

DARK AUGUST

– Martin Goldman (1975)

aka *The Hant*

After Sal Devito (J.J. Barry) kills a little girl in a road accident, he falls under the vengeful curse of the child's bitter, menacing grandfather, Ned McDermott (William Robertson). Becoming more and more jumpy, Sal sees a cowled figure lurking in the woods around his home. He glimpses the figure again while working with his brother Paul (Richard Alan Fay) on a construction site, his distraction causing a nasty accident. A family friend, Lesley (Kate McKeown), performs a Tarot reading and detects the presence of a 'magician' creating trouble in Sal's life. Lesley, and Sal's wife Jackie (Carole Shelyne), drag him off to meet Adrianna (Kim Hunter), a witch whom Lesley believes is capable of lifting the malediction. After Sal burns down his home in an unsuccessful attempt to lift the curse, Jackie steals a fetish representing her husband from McDermott's basement, which forms the basis of Adrianna's magickal counter-attack...

Unspectacular perhaps, and lacking a satisfying ending, *Dark August* is nevertheless a decent, well-acted tale of guilt, vengeance and witchcraft. Add to this an attractively photographed, unfamiliar small-town milieu (Stowe, in Vermont) and a gentle critique of prejudice against the occult, and you have a quietly unsettling genre piece with a few jolting surprises and enough brooding menace to infiltrate the sleepy pacing. William S. Fischer's music is frequently excellent, with chromatic progressive rock and melancholy piano breathing life into the drama. A recurrently blaring synthesizer is more irritating than unsettling, but it does at least add panic to scenes such as the one where Jackie breaks into McDermott's basement. Generally rather foursquare in style, the film relies for its impact on the acting, which is always solid and at times fairly nuanced. The male lead J.J. Barry, however, is not the most appealing of screen presences. His stocky, slightly dwarfish build and Saturnine, gone-to-seed appearance suggest a miniaturised Eric Bogosian and, as played, his character is riskily unsympathetic.

Although McDermott is clearly shown casting a spell and constructing a magick fetish in the pre-credits sequence, ambiguity regarding the efficacy of the occult is maintained for quite a while. Goldman's script hovers between the rational and the supernatural in a way that recalls Roman Polanski's *Rosemary's Baby* (although one has to say he could profitably have raided Polanski for tension as well as ambivalence). *Dark August* has a literary feel that

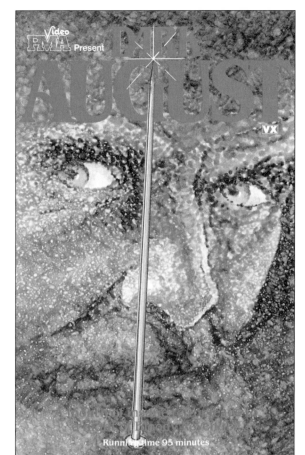

Running Time 95 minutes

Dark August (US theatrical & UK video title) aka **The Hant** (shooting title)
© 1975. Raffia First Co.
Raffia Productions & Marianne Kanter present a Martin Goldman film.
director: Martin Goldman. producers: Marianne Kanter, Martin Goldman. writers: J.J. Barry, Martin Goldman, Carole Shelyne. director of photography: Richard E. Brooks. music: William S. Fischer. editorial consultant: Ralph Rosenblum, A.C.E. assistant producer: Steven Schwartz. production manager/1st assistant director: John E. Quill. 2nd assistant director: Walter Rearick. location sound: J. Lencina. boom man: Bobby Rogow. 1st assistant cameraman: David Anderson. 2nd assistant cameraman: David Elliot. gaffer: Thomas Cestare. grip: Joseph Carrol. property man: Jack Wright Jr. script supervisor: Kay Chapin. make-up: Lynn Donohue. special effects: Ed Drohan. assistant editor: Hanna Wajshonig. colour consultant: Dan Sandberg. negative cutter: Irving Rathner. recording mixer: Al Gramaglia. production co-ordinators: Robert Colesbury, Dale White, William Pankow. psychic adviser: Charles House. illustrations by Sandy Hoffman. art transportation: Allegheny Airlines. wardrobe supplied by Grecophelia; Say Yes; Jaxs. titles and opticals: Eue Screen Gems. Chem-Tone process: T.V.C. Lab. production vehicles courtesy of Ford Motor Company and International Harvester. associate producer: John E. Quill. editor: Dennis Hayes. sound editors: Dan Sable, Harriet Glickstein. production co-ordinators: Dennis Hayes, Susan Kirson. Thanks to the town of Stowe Vermont and Harriet Lewis. filmed from 22 June 1974 entirely on location in Stowe (Vermont, USA). Cast: J.J. Barry (Sal). Carole Shelyne (Jackie). Kim Hunter (Adrianna). Kate McKeown (Lesley). Frank Bongiorno (Theo). William Robertson (the grandfather). Richard Alan Fay (Paul). Martin Harvey Friedberg (town drunk). Kenneth W. Libby (sheriff). Stan Shefler (1st deputy sheriff). Kenneth Kaplan (2nd deputy sheriff). Gerry Lou (accountant). Randie Wilder (sales girl). Captain Haggerty's School for Dogs (Mona). Karen Lewis (the child) and The Stowe Volunteer Fire Department.

makes one think of writers like M.R. James and Fritz Leiber: Sal is another of those 'Doubting Thomas' protagonists so popular in the occult horror sub-genre. There's a focus on 'accidents' and their interpretation that reminded me of Ramsey Campbell's novels, especially *The Count of Eleven* and *Obsession*. As with Campbell's writing, the script for *Dark August* finds unease in the small details of life, in the larval paranoias and anxieties we try to control, but which can hatch and overwhelm us at any moment.

Tarot-reading Adrianna is introduced sympathetically, without stereotyping; she's a practical, sociable woman whose first flicker of witchery is to admit *"an absolute passion for pumpkin seeds"*. Her first idea for lifting the curse is for Sal to burn down his artist's studio – site of the first spectral visit – while reciting an incantation and throwing a vial of potion into the flames. In a painfully comical sequence that again bears comparison to Campbell's *The Count of Eleven*, the fire brigade and police arrive *before* Sal can complete the incantation. As his future plans go up in smoke, burly cops throw him to the ground and arrest him for arson, the spell still unbroken. The second spell involves Adrianna using a clay head stolen from McDermott's basement as the focus of a banishing ritual. That this tense scene climaxes with merely a shotgun blast and a deeply unsatisfying 'shadow of the demon' is a pity, given Kim Hunter's taut and committed performance. Even those who sneer at the monster in Jacques Tourneur's *Night of the Demon* might agree that here, at least, is a film in need of a crowd-pleasing Beelzebub. Without it, *Dark August* appears simply to lack the necessary energy. And the coda, in which Sal blunders into a sacrifice that seems at last to assuage the old man's loss, feels trite; an appeal to tender emotions unsupported by the earlier drama. Weak ending aside, however, *Dark August* merits a higher genre profile, and approaches a topic so often reduced to meretricious titillation with a sober eye and a will to explore ideas.

Goldman had previously directed a blaxploitation western, *The Legend of Nigger Charley* (1972), featuring the formidable Fred Williamson in an early starring role, but after *Dark August* he disappeared off the radar until *Legend of the Spirit Dog* in 1997 (a title that suggests a link to the ending of *Dark August*)...

Made in Vermont.

top right:
Dark August was released twice on UK video. The cover here is by PMA, whose only other US horror title was Ron Honthaner's **The House on Skull Mountain** (1974).

below, left:
Dark August was also issued by HVM, from whose cover art this image originates.

opposite page:
The Dark squanders its urban locales, and refuses to scare us, but at least the graphic designers were trying...
top right: An alien giant zaps humanity;
far left (from the novelisation): A mocking mask enjoys our fear;
bottom left: A passing space-traveller grabs a girl's throat.

THE DARK POWER
– Phil Smoot (1985)

If this film had played its zombie Toltec Indians straight, instead of camping them up with silly growls and slapstick, *The Dark Power* would have been a much more pleasing twist on the old Indian curse subgenre: a twist because, after thirty minutes of build-up on the subject, it turns into a sorority slaughter film! Despite lots of earnest talk about the history of the Toltecs of Mexico and their possible links with the Red Indian tribes of North America, we're eventually steered into slasher territory when a cursed house on a sacred site is converted into dorm space for a quartet of co-eds. All seems to be shaping up well, with lots of unsympathetic teen characters: one girl, a nasty racist bitch, turns against her friends because they've invited a black friend to move in; lots of horrible chauvinistic boys arrive to drink beer and listen to loud music; and a rotting hand emerges from the soil outside... we're on course for a blend of *Sorority House Massacre* and *Children Shouldn't Play with Dead Things* (a combination I never realised I wanted, but which sure looks good on paper). Unfortunately, the spell is broken when the Toltec zombies turn out to be lumbered with atrocious Halloween masks and broad gestures more suited to a campy TV horror-host. Instead of showing us a bunch of college assholes being picturesquely slaughtered by the undead, *The Dark Power* begins to resemble a movie made by the victims. Comedy horror requires a ferocious intelligence and a tight grip on the material; it's not something that can easily survive bad scripting and a low budget. Sadly, the simple pleasures promised at the start of the film are thrown aside in favour of something beyond the sophistication of the filmmakers.

It's worth pointing out that this is actually a star vehicle for Mr. Lash LaRue, a grizzled Southern gentleman who likes nothing more than to show the world his dexterity with a whip. It seems the lash of Mr. LaRue is, among other things, a major bitch-magnet – *The Dark Power*'s spunky reporter-heroine starts off a

liberated gal, but within seconds of meeting Lash she's drooling over his earthy whip-wielding charms. And it's ol' whuppin' dawg Lash who saves the day, defeating the Toltec warriors and rescuing the girls. (Perhaps the title refers to Mr. LaRue, not the monsters?) LaRue, a veteran of numerous Wild West oaters in the forties and fifties, was coaxed out of retirement by North Carolina producer Earl Owensby for Worth Keeter's *Chain Gang* (1984). He stayed around to appear in *The Dark Power* (shot primarily at Belews Creek, North Carolina) and Smoot's *Alien Outlaw*, made the same year. Smoot was also production manager on LaRue's last film, *Escape* (dir: Richard Styles, 1990).

Made in North Carolina.

THE DARK RIDE
– Jeremy Hoenack (1977)
aka *Killer's Delight*
aka *The Sport Killer*

Danny (John Karlen), a serial killer with a hatred of women and a penchant for disguise, is abducting and murdering pretty girls who hitchhike around the San Fernando region. Sgt. Vince De Carlo (James Luisi) and Dr. Carol Thompson (Susan Sullivan) set a trap for him, with Carol as bait: but intelligent paranoid psychopaths are notoriously difficult to fool…

This is a sombre film lacking the visceral kick to compete with more exploitational treatments of the same theme. Of interest, though, is the way *The Dark Ride* anticipates the *modus operandi* of serial killer Ted Bundy, depicting an outwardly respectable man, with a penchant for disguise, picking off young female hitch hikers. (Many sources list *The Dark Ride* as made in 1979; it was in fact shot in 1976. Bundy began his killing spree in 1974 but he wasn't caught until February of 1977.) Of less interest is the time spent in the company of the police: De Carlo suffers the usual problems, a fractious boss and a worried wife, and the script leans heavily on the movie cliché that cops have to break the law in order to save us from psychopaths. The murders are largely of the off-screen variety, although the victim pick-up sequences and crime scene aftermaths have a certain grimness that at least prevents the film from adding triteness to its list of drawbacks. Unlike more sensationalised treatments of the topic, Irv Berwick's *Hitch Hike to Hell* for instance, *The Dark Ride* goes for shock value just once, in a scene where a victim is stripped and molested while her companion is forced to watch; otherwise it's a fairly routine stroll through the nasty newspaper headlines of the mid-seventies. Hoenack makes good use of the scenic but forbidding hills of the San Fernando Valley, Byron Olson's sparse score enhances the subdued atmosphere, and a few gruesome black-and-white photographs of mutilated female corpses are flashed before the camera to compensate for the lack of gore elsewhere, but really the film is efficient without being exciting. It's clear the director has the necessary talents to make a 'normal' movie, but you find yourself wishing for a little more insanity.

The Dark Ride would perhaps benefit from a DVD release one day, if only so we could see what was happening during the film's frequent night scenes. A jump and an audio glitch in the British video release from VRO give the impression of a missing scene: we see the killer menace a victim he's keeping trussed up in his garage, and when we see her again later there's an unexplained flesh wound on her thigh. I doubt though that another fleeting glimpse of blood and violence would do much to change the emphasis of what is basically a police procedural sheep in slasher wolf's clothing.

Hoenack was born in Washington DC, and raised in Bethesda, Maryland before moving to L.A. Although his primary area of specialisation was physics, he finished up at UCLA film school. Soon after leaving college he began working as an editor on films like Ferd Sebastian's *The Hitchhikers* (1971) and Charles Pierce's *Bootleggers* (1974). He was also assistant editor on the groundbreaking *Sweet Sweetback's Baadasssss Song*

(1971), and has since notched up over two hundred credits as a sound editor/sound designer/re-recording mixer, including *Airplane* (1980), *The Beastmaster* (1982), *Yellowbeard* (1983), *Poolhall Junkies* (2002) and Damon Wayans's *Behind the Smile* (2004). In 1981 Hoenack invented a new, feature-film quality, electronic editing system which revolutionised the sound design field. He went on to set up Sound Trax Studios, and is known in the industry as an innovator for film sound. The newest invention to emerge from Hoenack's company is the ADR BRAIN™ which speeds up and hones the accuracy of dialogue looping (dubbing), by utilising digital time-compression/expansion to bring perfect sync to each syllable.

Jeremy Hoenack on *The Dark Ride*: *"Your review is quite fair. If the subject of this film ever comes up in conversation, and not if I can help it, I explain that when I made it, I actually made two films at the same time... my first and my last! The original title was* The Sport Killer, *but only for foreign theatrical and video. It was released theatrically in the US as* Killer's Delight – *not my choice – then for US and world video as* The Dark Ride – *my choice. To our credit, the film was made in 1976, and based on research, before Bundy was caught. Our depiction of his M.O. and psyche turned out to be pretty accurate. On the other hand, the execution left a lot to be desired. I appreciate the kind comments you did make. Things I learned: don't use actors that are friends. I didn't know how to remedy some pretty terrible acting. The story overly relied on inferences and too much cop blah-blah. The film would have benefited greatly from some visceral day-for-night scenes of our villain chasing his prey through the woods and playing with them before the dirty deed. I was and am much too timid to do pain and gore. The finger breaking was actually added after the fact to 'R' it up a bit, but obviously not nearly enough. The interior of the police station, the psychiatrist's office and the nightclub were actually inside my house. The shrink is me. The woods and tow shots are all San Fernando Valley as well as the close-ups carrying the body and beginning to launch it. The real woman flying through the air is Maralyn Thoma in back of my house en-route to my pool. All aerial shots are San Francisco as well as the wide shots of the van parking and Johnny Karlen throwing a weighted blow-up doll off the cliff. So the title scene is shot in four different locations. I used my own money, and Maralyn's, supplemented by some friends and family. The entire cash budget was under 100k – basically the cost of film stock, equipment rental and SAG minimums. Then a little more for lab, titles and mixing. The rest of the costs were deferments. My biggest mistake was turning down a great offer with a big cash advance from Crown International, who intended to do a wide release. They had a great record of saturation releases of films like this. Crown President Mark Tenser was very taken with Susan Sullivan and felt she had the star power to generate very favourable market conditions. Instead, I foolishly listened to a weasely little crook who assured me I would make much more money from him on foreign alone, but I received almost nothing from the crook over the next few years. Then, when I finally got a decent video release from a legit company; they later discovered the crook had sold a lot of territories he never disclosed. They were rightfully upset, causing the video deal to be renegotiated much less favourably. By this time the creep had passed away. I soon went back to my physics roots and developed technology that eventually led to my company, www.soundtraxstudios.com."*

Made in California.

DATE WITH A KIDNAPPER
– Frederick Friedel (1975)
See interview with Frederick Friedel.

Made in North Carolina.

THE DEADLY SPAWN
– Douglas McKeown (1982)
See interview with Douglas McKeown.

Made in New Jersey.

DEATH BED: THE BED THAT EATS
– George Barry (1977)
See interview with George Barry.

Made in Michigan.

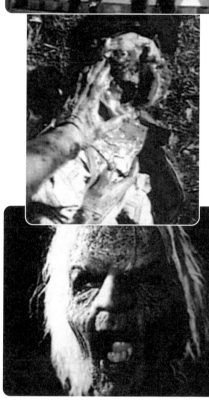

opposite and above:
The Dark Power.

left:
UK video cover for Jeremy Hoenack's downbeat serial killer tale **The Dark Ride**.

The Dark Ride (UK video title)
aka **Killer's Delight** (original US theatrical title)
aka **The Sport Killer** (export theatrical title)
© 1977. Hoenack Productions
A Jeremy Hoenack / Maralyn Thoma presentation.
director: Jeremy Hoenack. producer: Jeremy Hoenack & Maralyn Thoma. original screenplay: Maralyn Thoma. director of photography: Arthur R. Botham. music: Byron Olson. production manager: John Welsh. assistant director: Steve Dunn. 2nd assistants: Gene Bryson, Gale Ricketts. production assistants: Victoria Rocha, Nancy Frazen, Patrick Mickler. dialog coach: Georgia Phillips. art direction: Martin Speer. script supervisor: Hilly Dunlap. wardrobe: Melanie Wirsching. property: Billy Royal. make-up: Sherry Speer. assistant art: Joe Ivy. assistant script: Annie Wareham. assistant wardrobe: Keli Sills. camera operator: Arthur R. Botham. 1st assistant: Jim Bagdonnis. 2nd assistant: John Sliwa. 2nd unit assistants: Jerry Botham, Richard Fichter. camera systems: Cinepro. helicopter systems: Astrocopter. gaffer: Jonathan Silviera. grips: John Murphy, Steve St. John, Richard Dean, Richard Bekins. best boy: Harry Hope. assistant grips: Creighton Holden, Michael Bonnabel, Dennis Sullivan. production sound mixer: Dick Van Dyke. sound editors: Jeremy Hoenack, Jack Woods, Al Kajita. music editor: Maralyn Thoma. re-recording: Cinesound. re-recording mixers: Zom Yamamoto, Wayne Nakatsu, Paul Martin. transfers: Romness Recording. music arranger: Byron Olson. music supervisor: Jules Chakin. recording engineers: Jimmy Hite, Dick Bogert. recorded at Wally Heider and A & M Recording Studios. editor: Jeremy Hoenack. negative cutter: Dennis Brookins. colour and prints: DeLuxe General Laboratories. titles and opticals: Van Der Veer - Pacific Title. RCA Sound Recording. With Special thanks to: American Academy of Dramatic Arts; Tony and Phyllis Riggle; Merrick and Mary Riggle; Al Rattner; Ken and Barbara Isley; Casa Vega; Motorola Corp.; Don Wallen, Security Pacific Bank; Los Anmgeles Police Department.
Cast: James Luisi (Sgt. Vince De Carlo). Susan Sullivan (Dr. Carol Thompson). John Karlen (Danny). Martin Speer (Detective Mike Mitelman). The Victims: Hilarie Thompson (Annie). Eddie Benton (girl with dog). Sandy Serrano (Wanda). Cynthia Nigh (Sheila). Keli Sills (Kay). — Sharon Du Bord (De Carlo's wife). Carol Bilger (De Carlo's daughter). Al Dunlap (Captain Jeter). Buck Flower (Pete the witness). Gene Bryson (Sanders). Victoria Rocha (Miss Ice Cube). Richard Bekins (1st deputy). Creighton Holden (2nd deputy). Richard Dean (Nancy's boyfriend). Joe Ivy (Podunk). John Sliwa (man with the gun). Nancy Frazen (woman with the man). William Royaal & Michael Bonnabel (the boyfriends). James Henriksen (lifeguard). Patrick Mickler (pool manager). Melanie Wirsching (young mother at pool). Arthur St. John (helpful citizen). James Hahn (Wonderful Wally). Jack Kearney (pianist). Gale Ricketts (waitress Sherry). Cynthia Graham (2nd witness). San Francisco P.D.: Mimi Lieber (hooker). John Petrillo (detective). Bill Bufkin (uniform cop). Larry Hannifee (uniform cop). Cari Warfield (clerk). — Sheriff's Department: Jeff Moser (photographer). John Welsh (coroner). Reno Sweeney (3rd deputy). — Janet Cattano, Elie Childs, Phran Schwartz, Margaret Rose (bar patrons). Greg Thoma (little boy). The Blair Bunch (the dog, Nelson). uncredited: Maralyn Thoma (first victim thrown from cliff). Jeremy Hoenack (psychiatrist).

**Keli made a mistake.
Linda should have known.**

Annie knew...

THE DARK RIDE

JAMES LUISI • SUSAN SULLIVAN • JOHN KARLEN • MARTIN SPEER • HILARIE THOMPSON...

THE DARK RIDE based on the novel by MARALYN THOMA
R RESTRICTED
Produced by JEREMY HOENACK & MARALYN THOMA Directed by JEREMY HOENACK
Written by MARALYN THOMA Music BYRON OLSON Photography ARTHUR BOTHAM Color by DELUXE

Death Trap (UK theatrical title)
aka **Eaten Alive** (US theatrical title)
aka **Legend of the Bayou / Starlight Slaughter / Horror Hotel** (MPAA titles)
aka **Horror Hotel Massacre**
© 1976. Mars Production Corporation
A Virgo International Pictures release. A Mars production. Mardi Rustam presents.
director: Tobe Hooper. executive producer: Mohammed Rustam. producer: Mardi Rustam. co-produced by Alvin L. Fast. associate producers: Samir Rustam, Larry Huly, Robert Kantor. written by Alvin L. Fast and Mardi Rustam; adapted for the screen by Kim Henkel. director of photography: Robert Caramico. music composed, conducted and arranged by Tobe Hooper and Wayne Bell. editor: Michael Brown. director of photography: Robert Caramico. editor: Michael Brown. casting: Eddie Morse. sound effects: Echo Film Service, Bill Manger. music editor: Lee Osborne. assistant editor: Andy Ruben. first assistant director: Ron Smith. second assistant directors: Jeff Kibbee, Louie Lawless. script supervisor: John D'Amato. 2nd unit cameraman: Jack Beckett. 2nd assistant cameraman: Jon West. first assistant cameraman: Tony Palmieri. second assistant cameraman: Victor Alexander. still photographer: Heddy [Hedy] Dietz. assistant photographer: Ann McDonald. production sound mixer: Bob Dietz. boom operators: Lowell Brown, Jean Clark. production manager: Sheldon Lee. key grip: Michael Donovan O'Donnell. grip: Ken Kerr, Robbie McClure, Bobby Westwater, Romy Rao, Dennis Glass. gaffer: Lee Heckler, Rich Foster. best boy: Jim Bowie, Gary Zietlow. art director / set designer: Marshall Reed. set decorator: Mike Wiegand. assistant prop man: Richard Gillis. wardrobe: Greg Tittinger, Jane Mancbach. make up / hair: Craig Reardon, Beth Rogers. special effects: A & A. stunt co-ordinator: Von Deming. radio songs by Rick Casual, Eddie Bailes, Cam King, Linda Casady, Jay White, Rick Smith, Oscar Deleon & Napoleon Colombo, Al Bolt. Special thanks to: Hal Freeman of Cin-Kay Records, the Hookers (Bros. Sound, Austin, Texas); recorded by Glen Glenn Sound. rerecording mixer: Jay Harding. titles and opticals: Total Optical Productions. processing by CFI. colour by International Film Laboratory, Inc. production facilities by Producer's Studio. mechanical alligator and crocodile furnished by Bob Mattey. dog trainer / owner: Lou Schumacher.
Cast: Neville Brand (Judd). Mel Ferrer (Harvey Wood). Carolyn Jones (Miss Hattie). Marilyn Burns (Faye). William Finley (Roy). Stuart Whitman (Sheriff Martin). Roberta Collins (Clara). Kyle Richards (Angie). Robert Englund (Buck). Crystin Sinclaire (Libby Wood). Janus Blyth [Blythe] (Lynette). Betty Cole (Ruby). Sig Sakowicz (Deputy Girth). Ronald W. Davis (country boy). Christine Schneider (waitress). David Hayward (the cowboy). David 'Goat' Carson (Marlo). Lincoln Kibbee (first guy in bar). James Galanis (second guy in bar). Tarja Leena Halinen, Caren White, Valerie Lukeart, Jeanne Reichert (Miss Hattie's girls). Scuffy (dog). Minor Mustain, Paula Crist, Donna Garrett, Andy Epper, Jeanie Epper, Gary Epper (stunt doubles).

opposite page:
All images from **Death Trap**:

top: "Snoopy!" Hooper's pitiless **Chain Saw** vibe goes one step further to embrace childhood suffering, as a little girl witnesses her obnoxious pet dog being eaten by an alligator.

middle: Once again, proof that the early 1980s was the peak period for video cover designs...

bottom: Chaos rules as the alligator attacks not only the cast but the rickety set as well.

DEATH TRAP
– Tobe Hooper (1976)
aka *Eaten Alive*
aka *Starlight Slaughter*
aka *Horror Hotel*
aka *Legend of the Bayou*
aka *Murder on the Bayou*
aka *Horror Hotel Massacre*

Crazy old Judd (Neville Brand) runs the Starlight Hotel, little more than a tumbledown shack on the outskirts of Bayou country. The hotel is directly next to a swamp where Judd's 'pet' alligator swims – he insists it's really a crocodile from Africa. When Clara (Roberta Collins), a young prostitute, decides to leave the local whorehouse and look for other work, she fetches up at the Starlight. Judd attacks her and feeds her to the alligator. No sooner has he cleared up the mess than a family – Faye (Marilyn Burns), Roy (William Finley) and little daughter Angie (Kyle Richards) – drop in, looking for a room. Things get off to a bad start when the family dog is eaten by the alligator. Roy tries to shoot the creature but Judd attacks him, pushing him into the swamp where the reptile finishes him off. Judd then trusses Faye to an upstairs bed and chases Angie underneath the hotel, locking her in the crawlspace. Harvey (Mel Ferrer) and Libby Wood (Crystin Sinclaire), Clara's father and sister, stop by, looking for their missing relative. They show Judd a photograph of Clara, but he claims never to have seen her. At Judd's suggestion, Harvey and Libby visit the whorehouse, with Sheriff Martin (Stuart Whitman) in tow. The Madame, Miss Hattie (Carolyn Jones), also denies seeing the girl. Harvey returns to the hotel while Libby heads to the local bar to share her woes with the sheriff. At the hotel, Harvey hears Angie trapped in the crawlspace and goes to investigate. Before he can free her, Judd slams a scythe through his neck and – you guessed it – feeds him to the alligator. He then crawls under the hotel after Angie, who finds herself trapped between Judd and his pet, which has gained entrance to the crawlspace. As the film builds to a frenzied finale, yet more visitors drop in. Libby returns to find Faye bound and gagged in the next room, and everything dissolves in a whirlpool of screaming, scraping, squeaking and roaring …

Death Trap has always lived in the shadow of *The Texas Chain Saw Massacre*, but it nevertheless shares blood with that flawless masterpiece. Perhaps the film's biggest handicap is that it's filmed entirely on indoor sets. *Chain Saw* showed that Hooper was brilliant at milking locations for maximum unease, and you'd expect *Death Trap* to take a similar approach. The film is set in Louisiana, swamp country: and if directors like Jack Weis (*Crypt of Dark Secrets*) or Ferd & Beverly Sebastian (*Gator Bait*) could get good footage out of the Bayou, surely Hooper would excel? Instead, *Death Trap*'s studio-bound sets challenge the planet-scapes of early *Star Trek* for fakery. People staggered out of screenings of *The Texas Chain Saw Massacre* looking almost as freaked as the unfortunate Sally, who escaped the saw with her innards if not her marbles intact. So how did Hooper come to follow a film hailed as almost *too* realistic with something so alienating and anti-naturalistic?

It's part of the charm and enigma of cinema that even the most tawdry of films can achieve fleeting magic through a felicity of location. Incidental details of sunlit stonework, looming skies, or the uncomprehending faces of onlookers, can breathe magic into the image even if the story itself is clichéd. Sometimes directors can harness this quality and make it work as part of an overall vision – George Romero with *Martin*, for instance – but it can also happen by accident. There's a beauty in the indifference of the world, its impassive, enigmatic neutrality, that the cinema can encapsulate effortlessly. On *Death Trap*, Hooper loses this resource, but gains the polar opposite: every shot is unreal, a *trompe l'oeil* construction. As composer Wayne Bell explains, Hooper was living in Los Angeles at the time: it seems likely that the script was written with the intention of filming on location, until lack of money forced a studio-bound compromise.

The film begins with an image of the moon. Wayne Bell's soundtrack takes the dark sky as a cue and fills the air with frantic electronic information. This delirium recurs throughout the film; the audio field buzzes and clamours with atonal sounds and clashing musical styles. Crazy Judd has a mind like a detuned radio, skipping back and forth between mellow and psychotic, and the film employs free electronics, eerie sound-effects and rampaging Country & Western to echo the wreckage of his psyche.

Hooper then fractures the story by superimposing narrative threads, using the hotel itself as a fixed co-ordinate. The Starlight Hotel has three levels, and various strands of the narrative are enacted on each. At ground level there's the foyer, leading to guest rooms and Judd's quarters. On the first floor (or second floor in American usage) are a few more rudimentary guestrooms, and a dirty, shadowy bathroom. Beneath the house there's a crawlspace, full of cobwebby junk. As the film piles horror upon horror in the last twenty minutes, all three levels are occupied simultaneously, creating a layered, chaotic, overcrowded sensation. There are times when *Death Trap* turns to insane cacophony: screams and twanging bedsprings from upstairs, as Faye struggles to free herself; Judd's cracked *basso-profondo* maundering and incessant C&W radio on the ground floor; and creaks and rat-squeaks from the crawlspace as the alligator hunts little Angie, whose pipistrelle screams do battle with Wayne Bell's chittering electronics. There are passages in the film that border on hysteria, and they demonstrate the director's continued ability, not lost after *Chain Saw* as detractors claim, to summon an authentic reek of derangement and mental collapse. The film positively groans with pressure, created by the cramped *mise en scène* and relentless soundscaping. And it's all wrapped up in a flagrantly phoney-looking backlot movie-set masquerading as the great outdoors: could this movie actually *get* any weirder?

Death Trap may summon the craziness of its forebear, but its play with melodrama and artifice is almost diametrically opposed. The supporting actors give stylized performances (the black maid at the whorehouse is like something from *Tom & Jerry*) and the lighting is blatantly cartoonish, with dramatically unmotivated reds and blues as bold and irrational as *Suspiria*. Years later, George Romero and Stephen King would attempt to recreate the design of 1950s horror comics such as *Eerie* and *Weird Tales* in their homage to the era, *Creepshow*. But Hooper was there before them.

This would be nothing but window-dressing, however, if not for an alarmingly plausible performance by Neville Brand, who provides *Death Trap*'s strongest link to *The Texas Chain Saw Massacre*. In his characterization you can see traces of all the *Chain Saw* family: the pseudo-civilized smarm of the Cook, the bloodlust of Leatherface, and the leering sadism of the 'Hitchhiker'. Also, in a pre-echo of 'Chop-Top' in *Chainsaw 2*, Judd is an ex-soldier (as we discover in a great scene where Brand free-associates a sarcastic parody of parade-ground drill). Without Brand, *Death Trap* could have seemed just a gaudy, faintly experimental piece of flim-flam. Fortunately, Hooper knows when he's onto a good thing, letting Brand have his way with the role. In fact, some of the most effective passages of the film occur when only Brand is onscreen. For instance, after killing Roy, Judd wanders off into reverie, and the camera slowly explores his room – a scrappy, barely decorated affair dotted with a few ragged bits of junk. Time slows down, the image drifts, and the electronic soundtrack provides a scree of alien birdsong, over which Judd sings:

> *"Down round, tumble down,*
> *Standin' round in the rain,*
> *Ain't got no ticket, ain't got no bag,*
> *Still waitin' on the train."*

Hooper allows the forlorn, reflective tone of Judd's singing and the eerie electronic shrieks of the Wayne Bell score to blend for two or three minutes, shunting the film down a siding into Judd's strange and solitary world. He's trying on different pairs of second-hand spectacles as he sings, a white-trash detail that's sad and funny and real. Brand's cracked hobo drawl, in a film rife with strange percussive and electronic sounds, recalls such American originals as Howlin' Wolf and Captain Beefheart, while his more manic outbursts invoke the spluttering howls and guttural laughter of Screamin' Jay Hawkins on his classic single 'I Put a Spell on You' (banned from some record stores and radio stations on its release for being 'cannibalistic'!).

There's an air of sexual dysfunction and absurdity in *Death Trap*, from the reluctant whore refusing anal sex, whose screams are accompanied by twanging bedsprings as her frustrated client tries to force the issue, to Marilyn Burns and William Finley and their grotesquely exaggerated portrait of marital discord. (Finley in particular is priceless: his *"You gouged my eye out"* routine gives Brand a run for his money in the Nutjob Olympics). All is relentlessly bizarre, even Judd's coke dealer Buck (Robert Englund) and his cheery girlfriend Lynette (Janus Blythe – 'Ruby' in *The Hills Have Eyes*): the former a cartoon redneck trouble-maker and the latter a mindless coquette babbling about how "cute" Judd is. The poisonous atmosphere and constant sense of absurdity infiltrate even the innocents: there are scenes where little Angie resembles a tiny picture-book hobgoblin trying to outrun a fairytale boogeyman. And of course, there's something both comical and perverse about Judd crooning, *"Little girl... little girl, come on an' see what Uncle Judd done brought you"*, as he hunts the child through the crawlspace. The malignant fairytale ambience is also amplified by the chiming celeste that plays intermittently throughout the film: and when Judd chases Angie through the cobweb-strewn, rat-infested crawlspace, Hooper brilliantly visualises a classic childhood nightmare the Brothers Grimm themselves would have admired.

Death Trap was by all accounts a troubled production. Hooper has kept silent on exactly what went wrong, but it seems likely, looking at the scenes with Stuart Whitman for instance, that pressure was put on him to add some conventional material away from the hotel. These workaday inserts – the sheriff's office, the bar, and a return visit to the whorehouse – are visually uninteresting and feel spliced in from a different movie; Carolyn Jones as the wizened Miss Hattie helps the whorehouse scene earn its place, but the majority of them are simply mundane. It's been suggested that Hooper found it difficult to make the transition from independent 'backyard' filmmaking, where he could take as long as he liked to get something right, to the studio regime where everything has to run to schedule. If so, *Death Trap* perhaps marks the start of his problems, but it nevertheless feels like the work of the man who made *The Texas Chain Saw Massacre*, and *not* the guy who made *Poltergeist*. It was deemed a failure by Hooper and some of his colleagues, but to me it makes good on at least 70% of the promise of *Chain Saw*. It's true that compared to its perfect sibling it suffers from a limp and a stoop and a crooked gait, but in all its malformed glory it still commands respect for its unrelenting weirdness, its vicious hysteria, and Neville Brand's wonderful performance.

Note: The story was inspired by the case of Joe Ball, a killer who lived in Texas in the 1930s. Ball is reported to have fed patrons of his bar to the alligators he kept in a home-made pool out back. He killed himself when the police started asking questions...

Composer Wayne Bell on recording the soundtrack for *Death Trap*:

"I'd had some musical training, and received more in the years between Texas Chain Saw *and* Death Trap. *I was familiar with Stockhausen, Cage, Harry Partch, and Captain Beefheart, although I'd give more credit to Hendrix, early Pink Floyd, and an Austin acid rock band called Shiva's Head Band, but really, it came from our own experimenting, without much thought about anybody else's work. Ron Perryman deserves credit here. He was a pal and collaborator of Tobe's, and I met them both at the same time, a few days after I graduated from high school. Neither he nor Tobe were musicians, but they would have these parlour jam*

sessions that were just pure play, no rules. At some point they began inviting me in, and we had a grand time. Tobe's earlier movie Eggshells *has some abstract cues from those sessions.*

I was living in Austin at the time, where I was working for a one-of-a-kind radio station, Progressive Country KOKE-FM, which I helped originate, and making radio commercials for the now-famous Armadillo World Headquarters and other Austin music spots. My film music career was on hiatus, but I was

above:
Death Trap gets into gear with a grindingly grotesque slaying.

opposite page, top left:
Media's UK video cover for **Demented**.

opposite page, top right:
Two masked morons soon to regret their sense of humour…

opposite bottom, clockwise from top left:
Witchcraft and weirdness descend upon Wisconsin, in **The Demons of Ludlow**.

below:
The wonderful William Finley, as over-the-top being eaten by an alligator as he was while arguing with his wife, in **Death Trap**.

involved in other musical projects. Tobe gave me a call in the spring of 1976 as a heads-up that he would soon want me to come out to Los Angeles, where he was now living and working, to help him knock out a score for the film he was currently editing. (Unlike Chain Saw, I had no part in the shooting phase of this film). It wasn't a high-paying deal, but he would put me up, cover expenses, and promised to introduce me to various moviemaking folks; I believe his idea was that I might find more work and want to stay.

In L.A., I lived in Marilyn Burns's apartment and set up our makeshift music and recording studio in an empty room of Tobe's apartment nearby. I believe we recorded the Death Trap score in the summer of 1976. I can't remember our instrumentation, but I think it was similar to what we used on Chain Saw, with a few notable differences. The bird sounds are actual bird-calling devices of mine, used by hunters and naturalists. One instrument we didn't have that I missed was my upright bass, which we did all sorts of torturous things to in the Chain Saw sessions. The thing was way too big for my little car, and knowing the way we would abuse one if we had it, there was no possibility of renting one. I did bring along my cymbals and percussion instruments and mallets, along with a number of children's toys and toy instruments that we'd used before. I also brought a tape I'd recorded in my studio of processed cymbals that we used. I believe I also brought my Hofner electric bass (the McCartney bass) and lap steel guitar. I know Tobe had some more toys and probably a dulcimer. One new thing he had, which would bite us later, was one of the earliest commercially available small synthesizers. It was the latest wonder toy, and of course we couldn't resist playing with it, and it probably was overused. I remember enjoying its sound as we would play, then find that same sound lacking when I put it up against picture in the editing room. One particular piece I recall played great in the recording room but sounded simply like noise out of a Moviola speaker. I don't recall how much of the cymbal sounds ended up in the final mix. It's a sound I would return to later when Kim Henkel did his turn at a Chain Saw sequel (The Return of the Texas Chainsaw Massacre).

Our method for both Death Trap and Chain Saw was not to score to picture, but to create a library of music and sound, then cut to fit in the editing room; in a way, our version of what was called a 'track job' in Hollywood at the time. A 'track job' was a music editing practice (usually on B-movie schlock stuff and industrials) wherein the editor would simply cull from an existing music library that the producer already had rights to, or that could be bought cheaply. The idea was to very quickly slug something in the music track that at least came close to working, and crank it out by Friday. Our method was to create a library of extended jam sessions done on a basic idea related to the movie (e.g. 'Tension', 'Chill', 'Chase', 'Seethe', 'Madness', etc.), then in the editing tailor them (and in some cases overlap them) to fit the dramatics of the scene. If you've created enough swells, changes, static sections, etc. it is quite possible to cut and splice and make it sound like it was scored to picture. I think this is still a viable method for a film that doesn't require an orchestral or song-based score, and I would encourage filmmakers on a budget to try it. One of the positives of this method is it allows plenty of room for serendipity, trying things you wouldn't have thought of lf trying to compose synchronously to picture. Being overly synchronous was one of the problems I had with Saw 2's score, although I can't fault the guy too much because I made the same mistake on Chainsaw 4.

A regret I have about the music on the original Chain Saw is we had to rush through the music edit. Tobe cut it in very fast because we were under serious deadline pressure. By rights, given our method, the editing phase is an important part of the creative process and deserves plenty of time. But with our situation, Tobe adopted a style of putting in something that worked, and letting it continue 'til it fell apart, then cutting the music there, letting only the music play from that point, spooling right into a bin (probably the trash) until it sounded right again,

splicing it right there, and then continuing on in sync with picture until it fell apart again. Obviously I can't argue too much with success, but I knew what great stuff we had created and that there were better versions of the same ideas that Tobe just didn't have time to find and cut in. If we were to ever do a Chain Saw original soundtrack album I'd love to cut together a suite of some of that great stuff and let the listener use his imagination to fill in the scene.

For Death Trap the music edit fell to me, although I had to work with an old-time Hollywood music editor, Lee Osborne. He was pretty crusty, and had quite a low opinion of the film and the music I was bringing in, although he respected my sense of dramatics, i.e. where to begin a cue, where to cut, where to swell and where to lay back, some of which I did in an unorthodox manner. I knew that what we were doing was from another planet relative to what he was used to, but I also knew his experience was not something to sneeze at. By the time we were finished we had both learned a lot from each other. He kind of took me under his wing and showed me around the lot (we were cutting at Goldwyn Studios on Santa Monica Blvd.) and introduced me to studio life. Lunchtime was especially interesting. We'd go to the haunts of the Hollywood old guys, the kind of place where they wouldn't ask you if you wanted a martini before lunch, but how you wanted your martini. I met a lot of interesting characters.

Once again, the music edit wasn't allowed the time it needed, so we were under quite a deadline crunch. We would be editing reel four while they were mixing reel one on the dubbing stage; consequently I had to make some compromises in places where I would have preferred to take my time. Another consequence was I couldn't be at the mix until about reel seven. Although we recorded some good cues, I found it wasn't as good as what we'd done for Chain Saw, and we hadn't created nearly as much music, given our time pressures. Furthermore, the picture I was cutting to just wasn't as interesting as Chain Saw, so when I'd finished editing I came away feeling only so-so about the work. Good effort; passable, but I wanted better.

There's a signature part of the Death Trap score I cannot take credit (or blame) for. At some point in the middle of the mix, while I was still editing, it was decided, not surprisingly, that there was something lacking in the score. We were mixing at Glen Glenn Sound, a very conventional place, and I'm sure what we were trying to do was a bit of an assault to their ears. In the dubbing theatre were a few musical instruments, most notably a celeste. One of the guys there was playing a lullaby on the celeste and the idea struck to include that in the score, which they did in a few places.

That is about all I can remember. I took the money I made from Death Trap, rented a room at the Montecito, and met people and explored the Hollywood movie scene. I found I could definitely make a living there, but the place gave me the blues. I was especially homesick for Texas music and Texas women. The girls I met in L.A. were all flaky; you'd meet one day and they'd be one way, and the next day they'd put on a different face, different character. I never knew who was going to show up even though it was the same girl. I soon longed to be where you could look a gal in the eyes, see who's really there, carry on a real conversation, and the next time you see her, she's still the same person, and very comfortable in her own skin. I wanted real women, not the L.A. version. I decided to go with my heart, return to Texas, and figure out a way to do music and sound for film and make a living there, and that's what I've done.

I don't share your affinity for the film. I knew Tobe could do much better, and I think he felt the same, as his comments about the film were more about disappointment than satisfaction; he saved his unkindest comments for the producers, about whom I heard nothing positive; I never made it a point to meet them. Tobe's personal title for the film, and the name by which we spoke of it, was 'Crock', as in 'a crock of shit', if you'll pardon my expletive."

Made in California

SANDY COBE Presents   An IWDC film "DEMENTED"

Starring SALLEE ELYSE · BRUCE GILCHRIST
Produced by MICHAEL SMITH · Directed by ARTHUR JEFFREYS · Screenplay by ALEX REBAR
Executive Producer ALEX REBAR · Music by RICHARD TUFO/M.S.R. RECORDS, INC.
Edited by WILLIAM J. WATERS

DEMENTED

– Arthur Jeffreys [and Alex Rebar – unconfirmed] (1980)
aka *Slay the Joker*

Linda Rogers (Sallee Elyse aka Sallee Young) recuperates at her country home after a nervous breakdown brought on by a gang-rape. Her husband Matt (Bruce Gilchrist [Harry Reems]) is seeing a mistress (Kathryn Clayton) who demands his attention just when Linda is at her most fragile. Left alone, she suffers visions of four masked youths invading her house and threatening further sexual assaults. They can't be the same attackers, because all four were caught and imprisoned. So are these new attacks real, or are they all in her mind?

Demented kicks off like one of those 'History of Rape' loops from Alpha Blue Archives: a woman feeding horses in a stable is set upon by four stocking-masked rapists, who subject her to a gang-fuck in the straw. The presence of Harry Reems, all flares and smiles as the husband (and fresh from such treasures as *Sex Wish* and *Forced Entry*) further signifies porno-extremity, although the remainder of *Demented* stays firmly within the constraints of 'R'-rated horror. (Reems appeared in some of the porno industry's sleaziest and scariest movies, but he's also a decent movie actor whose line readings are easily up to scratch for the horror genre.)

Demented, sad to say, sags badly in the middle, turning into a lacklustre marital drama with a rape-and-madness chaser. What's worse, I found myself disliking the put-upon heroine: Linda's shrill, squeaky hysterics make it difficult to sympathise with her. Matt disappears for the second half of the film, leaving Linda and the four grossly unpleasant (but under-characterised) teenagers to hold our attention. At least slutty gold-digger Carol raises a few smiles during cutaway scenes in her boudoir: she can scarcely wait for Matt to have his orgasm before asking, *"How much money did you make last year?"*

People who think that *I Spit on Your Grave* is misogynistic ought to look at *Demented*, and ask themselves if *I Spit on Your Grave*'s unflinching realism isn't by far preferable to such a coy confection. *Demented* is basically a sillier, less skilled and confrontational version of Meir Zarchi's classic; there's even a castration scene with a male character begging for his life and trying to justify his actions. In this case, the recipients of the heroine's vengeance aren't the original rapists, but since they've donned masks and cavorted around Linda's house terrorizing her, knowing that she was raped before, frankly they deserve all they get. But with sympathy at least theoretically stacked up for the character, it all goes to pieces in the final reel. Sallee Young's overacted looniness is too mannered for the revenge scenes to work. *I Spit on Your Grave* does it so much better by making the heroine mostly mute in the latter stages, whereas here, by the time Young has floundered through her faux-crazy shtick for ten minutes, you begin to wonder if the intruders haven't suffered enough…

Scriptwriter Alex Rebar also wrote David (*The Last House on the Left*) Hess's ill-advised foray into directing, *To All a Goodnight*. Little is known about Arthur Jeffreys, which makes you wonder if maybe he was a porno director trying to work overground. *Demented* is his only known credit, so perhaps he later returned to a pseudonymous life in the adult industry.

Made in: unknown

THE DEMONS OF LUDLOW

– Bill Rebane (1983)

Debra Hall (Stephanie Cushna) is back in her home village of Ludlow (population 47) to research its history, when the Mayor (C. Dave Davis) unveils a gift for the 200th birthday of the settlement: a piano that used to belong to the village's founding father, Ephram Ludlow. As soon as the piano is installed at the Community Hall, strange things start to happen: two teenagers (Michael Accardo and Mary Walden) are attacked by a demonic force while making out in a barn; the church pianist's daughter Emily (Patricia J. Statz) turns up strangled; and her mother is hung by the neck by her daughter's ghost. The village priest (Paul Von Hausen) warns the remaining people of Ludlow that evil forces are set to wreak havoc upon them, in Ephram Ludlow's name…

Made in the same remote North Wisconsin location as Ulli Lommel's *The Devonsville Terror*, and with a few of the same actors, Rebane's variation on Lommel's supernatural revenger fails to emulate its style. Lommel used autumn leaves and witchery to lend his film an almost pagan feel, but Rebane, a native of the area,

Demented
aka **Slay the Joker** (title on © application)
© 1980. Four Features Partners Ltd.
IRC. Intercontinental Releasing Corporation presents a Sandy Cobe presentation. An I.W.D.C. film.
director: Arthur Jeffreys. executive producers: Alex Rebar, Rick Whitfield. producer: Arthur Jeffreys, Mike Smith. associate producer: Sharyon Cobe. writer: Alex Rebar. director of photography: Jim Tynes. editor: William J. Waters. production coordinator: Jolie Kramer. sound mixer: Bob Fisher. boomman: Kevin Myers. set decorator: Bryan Ryman. gaffers: Rick Heebner, Bryan England. best boy: John prudy. key grip: Robert Krebsbach. grip: Thoma West. 1st assistant cameraman: Jim Strong. 2nd assistant cameraman: Greg Ferguson. script supervisor: Marvis teague. make-up: Tonga Knight, Steve La Prote. special effects make-up: Robert Burman, Dale Brady. wardrobe: Bryan Ryman. property master: Lisa Lazarus. assistant wardrobe: Judy Meltz. production assistants: Robert Mendel, Jon Frank, Bari Suber. assistants to the producers: pamela Whitfield, Jennifer Landis, Vivienne Raymond. sound editor: James Waters. music editor: Pax Whitfield. assistant editor: Gregory J. Ferguson. rerecording: Ryder Sound Services. title design: William J. Waters. titles and opticals: Pacific Title. sound transfers: Audio Research. catering: Dawn Catering. cameras and lenses provided by Clairmont - Engle. music scored and arranged by Richard Tufo / M.S.R. Records, Inc..
Cast: Sallee Elyse [Young] (Linda Rodgers). Bruce Gilchrist [Harry Reems] (Matt Rodgers). Deborah Alter (Annie). Kathryn Clayton (Carol). Bryan Charles (Doctor Dillman). Chip Mathews (Mark). Mark Justin, Robert Mendel, Douglas Price (jokers). Stephen Blood (detective). Bosco Palazzolo (Manuel). J. Kelly, John Green (police officers). Bill Martin, Jay Belinkoff, Robert Mendel, Mark Del Castille (rapists).

The Demons of Ludlow
© 1983. Ram Productions Inc.
Titan International Ltd. presents a Ram
Production, Inc. film.
producer/director: Bill Rebane. executive
producer: Barbara J. Rebane. associate
producers: Alan Ross, Cheri Caffaro. writer:
William Arthur. additional dialogue: Alan Ross.
director of photography: Ito [Ito Rebane].
original music created and arranged by Steven
Kuether. editor: Brita Paretzkin. 1st assistant
director / production manager: Barbara J.
Rebane. 2nd assistant director: Alan M.
Rebane. sound: Dan Kennedy. boom: Richard
Lange. gaffer: Alan Rebane. assistant
cameraman: Bruce Malm. script & continuity:
B.J. Kress. production design: Bill Rebane. art
director: Denise Bednar. wardrobe: Mary
Walden. special effects prosthetics: Denise
Bednar, Alan Rebane. special effects: Vern
Hyde, Spectacular Effects of Atlanta, Georgia
and The Shooting Ranch Ltd. of Gleason, Wis.
grips: Richard Lange, Randy Scott, Tom Ritz.
production assistant: Jeff Jacobsen. production
secretary: Kathy Leigh. editor: Brita Paretzkin.
assistant editors: Barbara Kress, Bruce Malm.
sound effects & music editor: Bruce Malm.
music mixer: Dan Kennedy. original music:
Steven Kuether, Ric Coken. rerecording
assistants: James C. Moore, Luis Quiroz. re-
recording mixer: Rick Sweetser. negative cutter:
Ron Vitello, Match Cut. rerecorded at Zenith d/b
Studios (Chicago, Illinois). laboratory: Precision
DeLuxe (New York). optical effects: Exceptional
Optics (New York). filmed entirely on location
at the studios of The Shooting Ranch Ltd.
(Gleason, Wisconsin).
Cast: Paul Von Hausen [Paul Bentzen]
(preacher). Stephanie Cushna (Debra). James R.
Robinson (Winfred). Carol Perry (Ann Schultz).
C. Dave Davis (mayor). Debra Dulman (Sybil).
Patricia J. Statz (Emily). Angailica [Angelica
Rebane] (Ludlow's daughter). Mary Walden
(Eleanore). Michael Accardo (Andy). William
Dexter (Doc). Don Arthur (Ludlow). Deanne
Hass, Genevieve Brown, Mary Walden, James E.
Chamberlain III, Paul Bernard, Richard Ausman,
Richard W. Lange (demons). Robert Dawson,
Jose Granados, J.R. Robinson (fencers).

top right:
That's one great big angry Papa Bear!
Devil Times Five.

below:
The Intervision video sleeve.

is unable to pull theme and location together. It begins well, with
wonderful snowbound exteriors that serve to emphasise Ludlow's
isolation; it's just a shame they weren't used more consistently.
Maybe Rebane's crew were unwilling to shoot outdoors in the
freezing Wisconsin winter? Instead, we're served a succession of
dull scenes lacking in dynamism, filmed in the sort of interiors even
motel designers would reject as 'cruel and unusual punishment'.
The priest's wife is stranded alone in her bedroom for half of the
film, like an aspiring starlet being humoured by the director but
hidden away from the rest of the cast. Rebane squanders his story
with much wandering back and forth, and the many minor
incursions of the supernatural – levitating chairs, doorknobs
turning, flaming tree-stumps – are so boring it's a wonder anyone
notices. The haunted piano is an idea with potential, but it's ruined
when someone plays the damn thing, because it sounds like a
synthesized harpsichord. A group of elderly Christians listening to
an old woman play what sounds like a bad Rick Wakeman
composition is as close to genuinely weird as the film ever gets,
especially since the piano – white with gold trim – looks like it
belongs in a Louisiana whorehouse. For the truly persistent, there
are a few spooky splinters of genre amusement to be had: mentally
handicapped Emily's vision of a rich 18th Century family who tear
her gorily limb from limb is certainly creepy, as is the scene in
which Ephram Ludlow's ghostly daughter pelts Emily's mother
with stones, or dead Emily slips a noose round her mother's neck
so that a demon can drag her off to hell through the ceiling. If only
the rest of the film was as action-packed as this!

Studio work was recorded at Rebane's 'Shooting Ranch'
facility in Gleason, Wisconsin. Judging by the snowy exteriors,
Rebane must have mounted this near-copycat project soon after
Devonsville Terror was completed. Among the local actors who
appear in both movies are: William Dexter, who played Aaron
Pendleton in *The Devonsville Terror*; Paul Von Hausen, who
played the Executioner (aka Paul Bentzen); Mary Walden; and
Deanna Haas. Rebane himself was associate producer on *The
Devonsville Terror*.

Made in Wisconsin.
see also: **The Alpha Incident, The Giant Spider Invasion** and
Rana: Creature from Shadow Lake

DEVIL TIMES FIVE
– Sean MacGregor (1973)
aka *People Toys*
aka *The Horrible House on the Hill*
aka *Tantrums*

Rick (Taylor Lacher) and his girlfriend Julie (Joan McCall)
join Rick's colleague, Dr. Harvey Beckman (Sorrell Booke) and
his alcoholic wife, Ruth (Shelley Morrison) at a winter hideaway
owned by Julie's father, Papa Doc (Gene Evans) and his wife,
Lovely (Carolyn Stellar). Meanwhile, five children – David (Leif
Garrett), Moe (Dawn Lyn), Sister Hannah (Gail Smale), Brian
(Tierre Turner) and Susan (Tia Thompson) – survive a road
accident on the slippery roads near Papa Doc's place, and head for
the house. It seems they were being transported from a mental
institution, and the injured driver of the crashed vehicle is
extremely anxious to stop them…

This initially staid horror-thriller takes quite a nasty turn,
paying off as a nihilistic fable depicting children as amoral
psychopaths and adults as their blundering, too-trusting dupes. The
story begins with a gathering of the clan, lorded over by a bad-
tempered patriarch somewhere way down the line from 'Big
Daddy' in *Cat on a Hot Tin Roof*. The visiting adults tolerate
bullying blowhard 'Papa Doc' only because they're thirsting for a
slice of his wealth, and the film initially looks as if it's going to
focus on the usual tiresome power struggles within a conventional
moneyed family. It's like a pilot for a *Dallas* spin-off (Sirk it
ain't), and the omens are far from promising…

It's hard to say if the initial blandness of the film is a result
of unimaginative direction or a sly teasing of the viewer's

expectations. Seen twice, the menace of the early scenes is more
obvious, as we witness a gang of children emerge from a minibus
crash in the snowy wilds, somehow undisturbed by their brush
with death. On first viewing, as the kids trek through the snow in
search of habitation, it's easy to miss the subtle unease. I first took
the film to be a characterless affair, the acting and *mise en scène*
flattened out and lacking in colour. It takes time for the more
unusual features of the movie to kick in. If this was a deliberate
strategy by MacGregor it was high-risk: it would be all too easy to
assume the film was going nowhere. It's only when the murderous
children start to 'play' with their 'people toys' (cf. the film's
original title) that the film's nasty streak emerges…

The only fun to be had in the first act involves a sluttish
woman attempting to seduce a Lennyesque simpleton, followed
swiftly by a cat-fight between female rivals, complete with hair-
pulling and lurid trumpet-meows on the soundtrack. This Russ
Meyer-esque scene tilts the movie from 'dull' to 'cheesy but
amusing', until the plot takes another turn and we enter an entirely
different realm, in the form of an extended sequence shot in
extreme slow motion, depicting the children bludgeoning the bus
driver to death as he tries to prevent them making contact with the
household. The soundtrack slows right down to a montage of
basso growls and blurred human cries, an atonal string
arrangement combines with the childish theme tune, and the image
is reduced to a succession of still shots. This weirdness persists for
something like three minutes; the director is at last thinking well
outside the box!

*"Don't you think there's something strange about those
kids?"* asks Julie. Well, for a start there are some very disconcerting vibes emanating from 11-year-old child star Leif Garrett in
the role of David. He fixates on Harvey, a hen-pecked hubby
unable to tempt his contemptuous wife into sex. David's intense
concentration steers just shy of a seduction, a very weird and
near-the-knuckle twist in a film like this. *"Grey's a lovely
colour,"* he says, stroking a woman's jersey on the bed in
Harvey's room, *"Don't you think it goes with my eyes?"* Things
turn even kinkier, as the boy stares into a bedroom mirror, puts on
a wig, ear-rings and lipstick belonging to Harvey's wife, and
murmurs: *"You're all mine, Harvey Beckman!"* In questionable
taste, perhaps, but I think this scene shows what the film as a
whole ultimately lacks. If each of the children had chosen an adult
on whom to concentrate, it would have given the film a backbone,
a more resonant way to explore tensions between children and
grown-ups. Each of the five killer kids could have embodied a
different slant on inter-generational dynamics, with Garrett taking
revenge for the sexually abusive side of adult/child relations: after
all, what is the Garrett bedroom scene alluding to if not the idea
that children seduce adults into sex crime (a frequent self-justifi-
cation among sex offenders)? There are a few opaque utterances
from prematurely nunnish 'Sister' Hannah to suggest prior
grudges, and the military discipline of Brian, the black child,

NOT SINCE "VILLAGE OF THE DAMNED"
HAS DEATH BECOME SO SAVAGE... OR SURVIVAL SO HOPELESS!

DEVIL TIMES FIVE

Starring GENE EVANS • SORREL BOOKE
SHELLY MORRISON

Executive Producer JORDAN WANK
A BARRISTER PRODUCTION
A SEYMOUR BORDE • Color By DELUXE
and ASSOCIATES
RELEASE

R RESTRICTED
Under 17 requires accompanying Parent or Adult Guardian

Devil Times Five
aka **Tantrums** (alternative UK video title)
aka **The Horrible House on the Hill** (MPAA title)
aka **People Toys** (shooting title)
© none [1973].
Barrister Productions, Incorporated presents. director: Sean MacGregor. screenplay: John Durren. story by Dylan Jones. producer: Dylan Jones, Michael Blowitz. executive in charge of production: Sandra Lee Blowitz. executive producer: Jordan M. Wank. associate producer: Albert Cole. director of photography: Paul Hipp, Mike Shea. film editor: Byron 'Buzz' Brandt. music composed and conducted by William Loose. editor: Byron Brandt. production supervisor: Beryl Gelfond. assistant director: Leo Weyman. 2nd assistant director: Walter Dominguez. art director: Jac McAnelly. production associate: Toby Wank. production assistant: Robert C. Fowler. assistant editor: George Villasenor. music editing: Post Production Associates. wardrobe: Judy Durren. assistant camera: Mike Petrich. gaffer: Bob McVay. best boy: Mike Evans. 2nd grip: Paul Brown. sound: Clark Will. boom: Jeff Jarvis. technical adviser: Leeland F. Cook. stunt co-ordinator: Paul Knuckles, Stunts Unlimited. special effects: Carol Lynn Enterprises. property master: Dennis Nodine. script supervisor: Hannah Hempstead. sound effects: Larry Merrill. still photographer: Mike Paladin - Michael Cohan. unit publicist: Patricia L. Brotz. titles, opticals & processing: Consolidated Film Industries. The producers wish to thank: Inspector Stork (Department of Fish and Game, Sacramento); Captain Sheflin (Department of Fish and Game, Long Beach); AMF - Head Skis; Miles Gupton (Blue Jay Mail, California); Young Set (Baby Town). filmed from 5 March 1973 on location at Lake Arrowhead (Big Bear, USA).
Cast: Sorrell Booke (Harvey). Gene Evans (Papa Doc). Taylor Lacher (Rick). Joan McCall (Julie). Shelley Morrison (Ruth). Carolyn Steller [Stellar] (Lovely). John Durren (Ralph). Leif Garrett (David). Gail Smale (Sister Hannah). Dawn Lyn (Moe). Tierre Turner (Brian). Tia Thompson (Susan). Henry Beckman (Dr. Brown).

left:
An unrevealing, unhelpful ad-design prevents the onlooker understanding what **Devil Times Five** is all about...

below:
Die, adult, die! **Devil Times Five**.

dovetails neatly with his murder of the (white) family patriarch (*"I've got me one big papa bear,"* he announces, impaling the old bully with a sword rigged to the front of a child's swing), but it's not enough to prevent the ensemble becoming a bit of a blur. Garrett's fixation on Harvey seems simply gratuitous, because the script chickens out (if you'll excuse the term) and neglects to make the man a paedophile. Of course, if you think about the use of child actors in such a black-hearted context the film is already shocking enough.

"I was just wondering when the beer commercial is going to come on," says cynical, drunken Ruth when the adults gather to discuss the murderous kids. I know what she means – people are dying left right and centre but the acting never quite shakes off the cosiness of a TV drama. At times the out-there theme of the movie, and the undeniable creepiness of the young actors, takes the film by the throat, but it keeps slipping back to something with the atmosphere of a slightly grubbier *Hart to Hart*. The kids and the

concept are excellent – a tighter script and more urgent acting from the adults would have made this film a classic.

According to *The Hollywood Reporter*, the screenplay was written by actor John Durren from a book by Sean MacGregor. Shooting began in March 1973. MacGregor had previously directed a feature length documentary called *Wounded Knee to Washington DC: The Trail of Broken Treaties*. He also came up with the original story idea for *The Brotherhood of Satan* (1970). *Devil Times Five* was his last film. Tierre Turner worked as an actor in films and TV before turning to stunt work, notching up over sixty credits including regular stints as stand-in for Cuba Gooding Jr. in films such as *What Dreams May Come* (1998) and *Pearl Harbor* (2001). Chief among the kids of course is Leif Garrett, a seventies teenybop idol whose music career began in 1977 and continues, minus the international adulation, to this day. He appears here alongside his sister Dawn Lyn, who plays Moe.
Made in California.

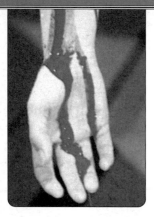

above and top:
Doctor Gore is the title that was used for the re-released version of **The Body Shop**.

opposite page, top:
A scene from **Don't Answer the Phone!** that's missing from the censored UK video print.

opposite page, middle right:
The Strangler claims another victim.

opposite page, bottom right:
Insert your local grindhouse's telephone number here...

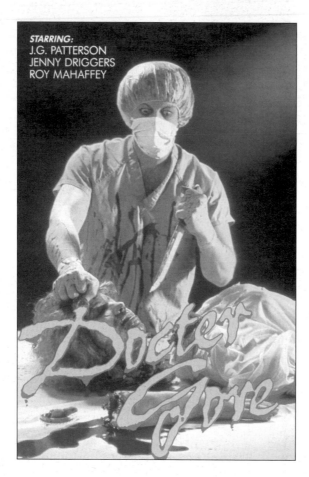

STARRING:
J.G. PATTERSON
JENNY DRIGGERS
ROY MAHAFFEY

Doctor Gore

DOCTOR GORE
– J.G. 'Pat' Patterson (1972)
aka *The Body Shop*

Plastic surgeon Doctor Don Brandon (J.G. Patterson) loses his beloved wife Anitra (Jenny Driggers) in a tragic accident. With his faithful hunchbacked assistant Gregory (Roy Mehaffey), the grief-crazed doctor lures young beauties back to his lab using his hypnotic powers, so that he can create a new woman. But Brandon is a raving chauvinist, and 'love' does not go smoothly…

If ever you wanted proof that the horror genre didn't immediately change its spots after George Romero's *Night of the Living Dead*, you need only watch Pat Patterson's *Doctor Gore* to see the death-throes of the old order, played out in a kitsch-meets-parody format. Patterson's requirements for making a *Frankenstein* rip-off seem to have come down to a list of props: the focus on lab accoutrements at the expense of story and character interaction reminds me of John Cleese's mad doctor in *Monty Python's The Meaning of Life*, presiding over a birth but disinterested in anything except *"the machine that goes 'Ping!'"*

Doctor Gore is silly, shoddy and very very slow. Terrible leaps of plotting suggest numerous missing scenes – but believe me, you're grateful they're not included; anything to speed things up. If you amplified the technical shortcomings of Patterson's film, ratcheted the weirdness past the point of no return, and rattled through the incomprehensible storyline at top speed, you might just get some fun out of it. I say this to stress what's really wrong here – *Doctor Gore* plods, and its basic idea is so hackneyed there's nothing to look forward to. The concept harks back to an older idiom, while attempting to 'update' it with blood and nudity. It's what *Flesh for Frankenstein* would have been without Paul Morrissey's mordant intelligence (and Carlo Ponti's money). Patterson, a stage-magician and spook-show dabbler who wandered into film production, plays the lead role himself, revealing a whole new set of limitations to add to his directorial ones. Swathing the soon-to-arise 'monster' with bacofoil is an odd touch ('inspired' perhaps by Al Adamson's *Brain of Blood*), and

you have to acknowledge the attempt to mimic Arthur Edeson's tilted angles and shadowy photography from the James Whale original, but it simply doesn't work. At least the bloodshed is copious, and clearly provoked by the Southern drive-in successes of Patterson's friend and associate Herschell Gordon Lewis. Patterson's skills as a stage magician ensure some fairly convincing severed limb illusions: it's just a shame he doesn't know how to put them in a context where we give a damn about what's going on. If you're in good company, and drunk as a skunk, the gruesome bits might be enough to get you through, but as for the rest, forget it. Considered unreleasable at the time under its original title *The Body Shop*, and thought lost for many years, *Doctor Gore* is perhaps not the best epitaph for a man whom colleagues regarded as charming and supportive (see interview with Frederick Friedel). A better way to remember him is as director, writer and producer of *The Electric Chair* (1975), a far more creditable Southern-fried drama about the murder of two adulterous lovers (a priest and a trucker's wife!) and the subsequent trial of the murder suspect. It wastes too much time on court-room chit-chat but it's streets ahead of *The Body Shop*, and it's worth seeing for an intense execution scene, shot in a County Prison facility with a genuine 'Old Sparky'.

Made in North Carolina.

DON'T ANSWER THE PHONE!
– Robert Hammer (1979)
aka *The Hollywood Strangler*

Father-loving fitness fanatic Kirk Smith (Nicholas Worth) has issues. To relax, he strangles young women, or phones a radio chat-show hosted by psychologist Dr. Lindsay Gale (Flo Gerrish), posing as a Mexican with psychotic tendencies. Gradually, Kirk moves in on Dr. Gale herself, killing one of her patients before turning up for a personal consultation…

This aggressive, tasteless slasher movie would love to piss you off, especially if you harbour liberal sensitivies regarding the exploitation of women. Watching it is like bumping into a troublesome drunk in a bar; you just know it's looking for a fight. Even the music is parodically, gloatingly sleazy; instead of underlining tension it synchs up perfectly with the killer's sneering attitude. Made in 1979, *Don't Answer the Phone!* was shot as *The Hollywood Strangler*, and so concentrates on that particular murder method rather than axes, knives, boat-hooks etc. Plot-wise, we're in the sub-genre of murder tales that reveal the identity of the killer right from the start, alongside John Peyser's *The Centerfold Girls* (1974), Irv Berwick's *Hitch Hike to Hell* (1977) and, most notably, William Lustig's *Maniac* (1980) starring Joe Spinell, with which it has some telling similarities. Chief among these is the depiction of the killer as a sweaty, parentally abused paranoid sleazebag, frequently seen alone in his apartment, either boasting and preening, or collapsing into tears of self-pity. Both men are, let's say, on the heavy side too – Spinell's maniac is an overweight slob and Worth's is a flabby but bullishly muscled keep-fit nut. They even share the same day-job: when they're not out raping and strangling, they're touting for business as downmarket fashion photographers.

The first thing you notice about *Don't Answer the Phone!* is attitude. Initially it's just the dialogue between cops assigned to the case, which apes the hard-boiled cynicism of dime-store crime novels, as in the following banter: *"Did you get a shot of that breast?" "Which one – she's got two you know." "The one that was nearly bitten off, goddammit."* It all feels quite self-aware, as if our laughter has been anticipated. *"The last thing I need right now is a comedian,"* snarls Lt. McCabe (James Westmoreland), and we might agree, given the severity of the film's subject matter. But a comedian we get, as the director slips us a queasy mixture of sleaze, black humour and outright nastiness. Where it differs from *Maniac* is the prevailing sense of a wind-up perpetrated by the filmmakers – a superior sense of liberal-baiting wit, amplified by the malevolent glee with which Nicholas Worth embraces the role of killer.

Don't Answer the Phone!
aka **The Hollywood Strangler**
© 1979. A Scorpion Production
A Hammer/Castle presentation.
director: Robert Hammer. executive producer: Michael Towers. producer: Robert Hammer, Michael D. Castle. screenplay: Robert Hammer, Michael D. Castle. based on "Nightline" by Michael Curtis. director of photography: James Carter. music: Byron Allred. editor: Joseph Fineman. associate editor: Robert Gordon. assistant director: David Osterhout. production managers: Scott Rosenfelt, Tikki Goldberg. production co-ordinator: Sharron Reynolds. assistant to the producer: Robin Oliver. art director: Kathy Cahill. assistant art director: Elliot Nachbar. script supervisor: Kathy Zatarga. sound mixer: Jan Brodin. boom operator: Douglas Arnold. 1st assistant cameraman: Timothy Suhrstedt. 2nd assistant cameraman: Arthur Krauss. additional photography: Tony DeFabees, Andy LaMarcaq. assistant editor: Robert Cummings. make-up: Teresa Austin. hair stylist: Mira Hammer. wardrobe: Deborah Scott. key grip: Tracy Neftzger. grip: Mike Taylor. gaffer: Christopher Tufty. best boy gaffer: Gary Featherstone. electrician: Van Spaulding. sound effects editor: Ken Collins. production assistants: Thomas Rolapp, Susan Cooley. additional casting: Guderjohn and Sillman. stunt co-ordinator: John Sistrunk. special effects: Dick Albain. re-recording mixers: Wayne Artman, Michael Jiron, Tom Beckert. Lenses and Panaflex camera by Panavision. Metrocolor. titles and opticals: MGM.
Cast: James Westmoreland (*Lt. McCabe*). Ben Frank (*Sgt. Hatcher*). Flo Gerrish (*Dr. Lindsay Gale*). Nicholas Worth (*the strangler*). Denise Galik (*Lisa*). Stan Haze (*Adkins*). Gary Allen (*John Feldon*). Michael Castle (*lab man*). Pamela Bryant (*Sue Ellen*). Ted Chapman (*man in bar*). Chris Wallace (*psychic*). Dale Kalberg (*nurse*). Deborah Leah Land (*police woman*). Tom Lasswell (*police psychiatrist*). Mike Levine (*Gary Markow*). Chuck Mitchell (*Sam Gluckman*). Victor Mohica (*Ventura*). Susanne Severeid (*hooker*). Paula Warner (*Carol*). Hugh Corcoran (*wino*). Gail Jensen (*Joyce*). Joyce Ann Jodan (*roommate*). Corine Cook (*Rikki*). Ellen Kay Karsten (*hooker*). Havoc Oliver (*hooker*). David Osterhout (*policeman*). Peter Fain (*policeman*). Jon Greene (*policeman*). Robin Oliver (*dope dealer*). Shirley Handelsman (*nurse's mother*). Don Lake (*man in plastic*). Eileen Castle (*neighbour*). Danny Disner (*boyfriend*). Marilyn Olsson (*stunt double*).

Yet despite the intelligence, this is a cruel film. The overall attitude is sour, irate with what is portrayed as weakness or woolly-liberalism. Principally, the writers (Hammer, with Michael D. Castle) seem to share the killer's contempt for psychiatry. We first see Dr. Gale with a female patient who suffers from poor self-esteem and a history of victimisation by men. The tender good advice Dr. Gale offers seems to indicate that the scriptwriter values her profession. But then the victim is trapped in her own home by the killer, who mockingly assumes the role of 'daddy' when he intuits the nature of the girl's fears. The scene isn't exactly played for laughs, but it's not tragic irony either: Worth's arch performance and the malicious timing of the scene play a mean game, suggesting that victims attract their own suffering. Later, when Kirk attacks Dr. Gale in her office, he plays up the unstable victim/killer role, repeatedly tricking her and proving himself to be sardonically hip to the clichés of psychoanalysis: the point presumably being that killers are often smart enough to play-act forms of psychosis or contrition for the benefit of psychiatrists, whose gullible testimony can save them from prison, or facilitate their early release. It *is* funny, in a nasty sort of way, but the way the killer pours scorn on the educated standards of his female victim leaves an unpleasant aftertaste. Elsewhere, in a caricature scene expressing a prejudice soon to be stamped out by the novels of Thomas Harris, a psychological profiler is bluntly satirised as a connoisseur of the obvious, windily telling the cops nothing of value. Even psychics get dragged in for a kicking: a clairvoyant approaches the truth when touching a picture of one of the victims, but – ha-ha! – the cops ignore his advice and arrest him as a suspect. I wish I could believe the joke was meant to be on the authorities…

The two main cops in the film are either callous blockheads or hard-headed realists, depending on your point of view. Dr. Gale tells McCabe he's the reason men like the killer exist, before relenting and going to bed with him, so I guess that's the end of *her* credibility. What clinches the seduction? Well, as if to prove that no-nonsense males with an air of authority can tackle mental health issues better than your wishy-washy *innerlekshuls*, McCabe talks a suicidal female down from a fourth storey ledge more efficiently than Dr. Gale, and in a fraction of the time! For the last twenty minutes of the film, police procedure takes precedence over the killings – as if we're to accept this licking of police butt as a Hail Mary for the unmitigated sleaze and sarcasm of the rest. The scumbag killer is traced through his involvement with the porno industry (so much less savoury than the slasher-horror business, right?). McCabe eventually shoots the killer, following the bullet with a dismissive *"Adios, creep!"* – but the similarity between the killer's contemptuous attitude to Dr. Gale and the film's scorn for her profession is just as creepy. All this would matter far less, were it not for the fact that Nicholas Worth makes 'The Strangler' a truly chilling creation, frightening even as he sends up the character's arrogance and self-pity. He would have made a terrifying John Wayne Gacy (a scene where he persuades a young woman to let him handcuff her for what starts as a mildly kinky photographic session carries echoes of Gacy's murder technique).

Despite its California origins, there's something of the New York horror scene to this rough and rancorous film. You find yourself wondering just where the director's head was at. My impression is that it's the brainchild of someone a lot smarter than the material – but with one hell of a bitter outlook. Despite the overwhelming sarcasm, the film has a sliver of truth to it: there's been some thought applied to how one depicts the amoral, sneering satisfaction of a killer. Or perhaps it was simply Nicholas Worth who overbalanced an otherwise superficial crime and retribution tale with his excellent performance. Whatever the answer, the result is a film that gloats at the sleaze and violence it shows, while ingratiating itself with the forces of law and order. Despite all this there's something perversely enjoyable about *Don't Answer the Phone!* I admire Worth's bravura performance, and the prevailing air of provocation: I'm just not a fan of the 'hanging's too good for 'em' attitude that comes with it.

Made in California.

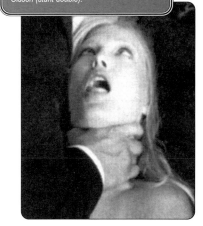

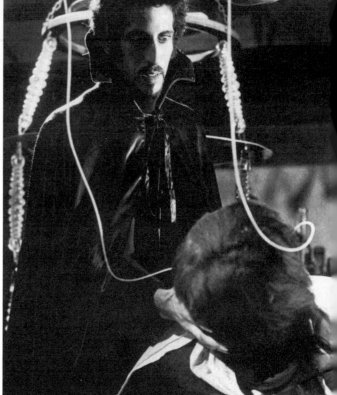

DON'T GO IN THE HOUSE
– Joseph Ellison (1979)
See interview with Joseph Ellison.

Made in New York City and New Jersey.

DON'T GO IN THE WOODS
– James Bryan (1981)
See interview with James Bryan.

Made in Utah.

DRACULA VS. FRANKENSTEIN
– Al Adamson (1970)
aka *The Blood Seekers*
aka *Blood Freaks*
aka *Blood of Frankenstein*
aka *Satan's Blood Freaks*
aka *Teenage Dracula*
aka *Revenge of Dracula*

Wacky send-up, or flimsy attempt to relive the glory days of Universal's monster marathons? Although shot in 1969, completed in 1970 and released in '71, this might as well have been made twenty years earlier. With a retro feel that would shame Paul Naschy, all bubbling test-tubes and screaming girls, this is fun nonsense for a very precise demographic of horror fandom (you know who you are…), but tedious gubbins for everyone else. Unusually for Adamson, it does at least deliver on its title, although Dracula – played by 'Zandor Vorkov' aka Roger Engel, the director's stockbroker – looks like a sibling to Hall & Oates, and the Frankenstein Monster (John Bloom) has a face like a collapsed suet pudding. *"All illusions look real, or they wouldn't be illusions, would they?"* asks Dr. Frankenstein (J. Carrol Naish), in phenomenological mode; a line of dialogue that is as close to the talents of Edward D. Wood as Adamson ever came. Look out for actor-director Gary Kent in a blink-and-you'll-miss-it cameo as a beach-bum making out with his girl before being interrupted by killer Lon Chaney Jr. (so washed up it's not even funny), whose poorly-edited scenes commit the sort of crime against continuity for which Adamson is the benchmark.

In an interview for BijouFlix, Kent (also assistant director on *Dracula vs. Frankenstein*) drew this thumbnail sketch of the director: "Al Adamson was a 'white socker'. The last guy to get a date for the prom. His pants were too short, and his shirts were from Sears. He never smoked a joint in his life. He never drank more than a beer now and then, and was as square as a checkerboard. He really wanted to make movies 'like they did in the forties'. It was his partner, Sam Sherman, who talked him into filming the outrageous, the daring, and the ridiculous. Sherman told Al they had to if they wanted to stay in business in the sixties and seventies. Al's charm was 'employment'. He knew so little about actual acting that you pretty much got to do whatever came into your head."

After Adamson was murdered in 1995, Gary Kent was called as a material witness at the trial of his killer, building contractor Fred Fulford, because of a telephone call Kent made to Adamson two days before the murder. "He was full of plans for a comeback, in a great mood. He told me the only bummer in his life was the contractor he had hired to work on his house. The guy was living with him, and Al had caught him stealing money and running up his credit cards. He told me he was going to confront him, and the guy had better pay up, or Al would 'throw his ass in jail!' That was our last conversation. Two days later, he was dead."

Made in California.
*see also: **Blood of Ghastly Horror, Brain of Blood** and*
Nurse Sherri

DREAM NO EVIL
– John Hayes (1971)
See feature on John Hayes.

Made in California.

ENCOUNTER WITH THE UNKNOWN
– Harry Thomason (1972)
"There are few things as strange as reality, for reality comes to us wearing many faces, disguised as all manner of things. What is reality and what is illusion? Some things we think are real may be merely wisps of smoke from our minds. And some things we think illusion are merely cloaked in that guise, so that they may play their parts without knowing what they really are."

It's downhill all the way after this Creswellian announcement from a presumably cash-strapped Rod Serling, cueing up three supposedly uncanny stories, none of which generate much of a shudder. In the first tale, three young men, Dave (Tom Haywood), Frank (Gary Brockette) and Randy (John Leslie) pretend to set up

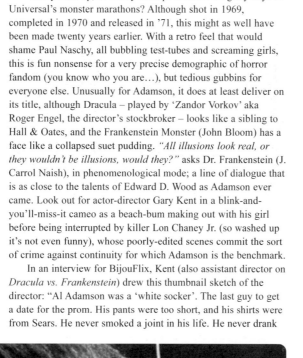
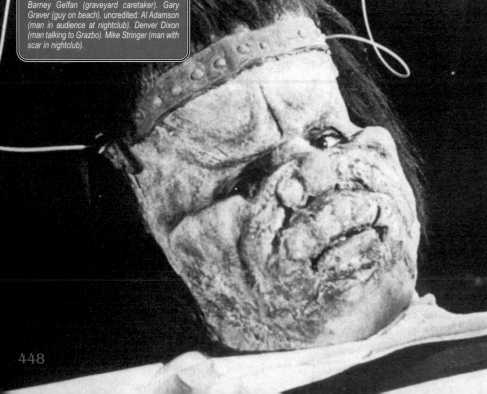

their slightly 'uncomplicated' acquaintance Johnny (John Cissne) with a girlfriend, sending him off on a wild goose chase to a random address. Their jolly jape goes awry though, when the old lady who actually lives there (Mary Jane Wilson) accidentally shoots him: *"I've got my husband's pistol out and I certainly don't want to hurt anybody... Oh!"* At the funeral (presided over by actor Jim Harrell, the conniving doctor from S.F. Brownrigg's *Don't Open the Door*), Johnny's mother puts a 'cryptic' curse on the three. Seven days later, Dave is hit by a car. Another seven days go by, and Frank is fretting over the curse's meaning while on a plane journey. He falls into conversation with Father Duane (Bob Ginnaven) in the next seat. *"Do you believe in the supernatural?"* asks Frank. *"I'm one of many people with a supernatural boss: he's a good boss, one who knows all the answers,"* Father Duane replies. Frank spills his woes, and one is irresistibly reminded of the scene in *Airplane!* where an old lady commits suicide during a fellow passenger's interminable life story. *"Strange things happen to all of us,"* offers the priest, feebly. Departing the plane at its next stop, Father Duane looks back to see a fire-flash in the sky. Two down, one to go: I wonder if Randy's skydiving hobby will play a part in *his* demise?

For the second story, it's sick-bucket time: *"A boy and his dog chase dreams and butterflies back and forth across Saturday. Observe one man-child and one man-child's dog, on their way to a uniquely soul-shattering rendezvous with darkness."* (To be fair, this is just the sort of sentimental guff that would appeal to the likes of Steven Spielberg, who, with the whole of the Twilight Zone to explore, served us a plate of 'heart-warming' gloop about revivified oldsters in *Twilight Zone: The Movie*). A boy (Kevin Bieberly) searching the woods for his missing dog finds a hole in the ground from which smoke and strange moans emerge. (A hippy commune? Charlie Manson? Guess again, fun seekers...) Running back home, he informs his stolid, working-class father (Robert Holton) and kitchen-bound, picture-book mother (played by leading light of the S.F. Brownrigg rep company, Annabelle Weenick). A posse is summoned (including Charlie Dell, of Brownrigg's *Poor White Trash Part 2*), but the men hesitate to explore the hole. Eventually the boy's father decides to climb down. At which point we should get some monster action, right? You must be joking. Dad emerges from the hole and goes running off into the trees, raving mad. End of story – not even a claw seen poking from the earth... Annabelle Weenick is far too good for this material, and here she has little to do, at times responding to the dearth of interesting dialogue by adopting the manner of a silent movie actress. There's little else to add, except to mention the use of a library music cue familiar from the tenement scene in *Dawn of the Dead*.

The third segment begins with Serling in high metaphorical-metaphysical mode: *"There is a bridge in our mind that leads through time and memory from what we know to shores beyond knowing. It sways high above the canyons of our disbelief like some spectral span spun by devils for us to tread. To walk this bridge is to accept all kinds of possibilities, especially the most exciting possibility of all – the possibility of impossibility."* Good Lord, surely he was kidding?

At least this last story is marginally better than the others, based, Serling tells us, on a common American folk tale known in Arkansas as 'The Girl on the Bridge', in North Carolina as 'The Lydia Story', in Illinois as 'Spectre of the Mists', and in Texas as 'The White Rock Lady'. (In deference to the director's roots, Serling favours the Arkansas moniker). Susan is played by Rosie Holotik, leading lady in S.F. Brownrigg's classic shocker *Don't Look in the Basement*. She's joined by Brownrigg's greatest acting asset, Gene Ross (star of all four Brownrigg horror films), who plays her strict, jealous father. Holotik's pixie-ish charm matches the thirties period setting: she'd have made a great Gatsbyesque flapper. The story though is a mild concoction, about Susan's forbidden tryst with a lover her daddy dislikes. Fleeing the old man's anger, the couple fatally crash their car into a river. Every anniversary, the ghostly Susan hitches a lift

Encounter with the Unknown
© none [1972]
Centronics International presents.
director: Harry Thomason. producer: Joe Glass. writers: Harry Thomason, Joe Glass, Jack Anderson, Hellman Taylor. directors of photography: Michael C. Varner, Jeff Kimball. cinematography: Jim Roberson, Charles Thuston. editorial: Erwin Cadden, Jerry Carraway, Brian Hooper. music editor: Eddie Norton. assistant director: Mike Taylor. unit production manager: Jimmie Mundell. post production supervision: Hank Gotzenberg. production assistant: Michelle Rumph. assistant camera operators: Paul Fisk, Tom Lamb. lighting: Robert Dracup. script continuity: Annabelle Weenick. make-up: Jackie Barnes. sound: Ron Roberson, Gary Abbott. sets: Vernon Williams, Ed Hogan, Carol Bean. grips: Gus Blass III, Bill Eubanks Jr., Dave White. [song] "Rememberin' (How It Used To Be)" by Steve Beeson, recorded by Becky Fain. filmed on location in Texas (USA).
Cast: Rod Serling (narrator). Bob Ginnaven (Father Duane). Gary Brockette (Frank Cameron). John Leslie (Randy Powell). Tom Haywood (Dave Terrell). Fran Franklin (Mrs. Davis). Jim Harrell (Brother Taylor). John Cissne (Johnny Davis). Marey Jane Wilson (Mrs. Wilson). Lyle Armstrong (second priest). Charles Rumph (student). Kevin Bieberly (Jess). Annabelle Weenick (mother). Robert Holton (Joe). Frank Schaefer (barber). Ken Carson (doctor). Bob Glenn (constable). David Haney (first man). Billy Thurman (second man)(. Syl Schumann (third man). Charles Dell (Jonas). Rosie Holotik (Susan). Michael Harvey (senator). Judith Fields (senator's wife). August Sehven (Paul). Gene Ross (Susan's father). Beverly Dixon (Susan's mother). Mitchell Wood. Gary White. Phyllis Moore. Becky Fain. Joe Reynolds. Mike Thompson. Rose Hughes. Becky Gaines.

above:
The US video sleeve for **Encounter with the Unknown** promises an experience 'past **The Twilight Zone**'.

back home. But as each new Samaritan rings the doorbell to summon the sorrowful father, she disappears, leaving only a bouquet of flowers... I enjoyed the clichéd but still dreamlike scenes of Susan and her young beau wandering through a misty woodland limbo, near a fairytale house surrounded by gnarled tree-trunks and mossy riverbanks, especially as they're scored to a haunting MOR instrumental called 'Sleepy Shores' (a British chart hit for the Johnny Pearson Orchestra in 1971, thanks to its use as the theme for the BBC's *Owen M.D.*).

"We remain baffled by the power of rational thought," admits the script, *"by the hidden sources of creativity."* Such honesty is refreshing, but it's counteracted by the film's refusal to bow out gracefully. Once the third story has limped to a close, Thomason needlessly drags things out by repeating lots of earlier footage, while the final voice-over (not Serling's) theorizes, *"The dear departed who do not quite depart. Why can't they let go?"* – as if reading our impatient minds. *"Is it because we can't let go of them? Is our love the anchor that holds some part of them near?"* Frankly, in this instance, no.

Harry Thomason was an Arkansas high school football coach who got the movie bug. His other works include *Visions of Evil* aka *So Sad About Gloria* (1973), *The Day It Came to Earth* (1979), and *Revenge of Bigfoot* aka *Rufus J. Pickle and the Indian* (shot in 1978, released in 1979). He and his wife Linda later developed and produced the successful American sitcoms *Designing Women* (1986-93) and *Evening Shade* (1990), the latter drawn from Thomason's own experiences as a footballer, and starring Burt Reynolds. Cinematographer turned director James Roberson (*Superstition*) worked with Thomason several times. Lighting man Robert Dracup was yet another regular from the Brownrigg stable: if ever there was a doubt as to Brownrigg's prowess, it's extinguished by the failure of Thomason to ignite the cast and crew talent here.

Made in Arkansas.

opposite page:
Robert Powell as The Count and Dawn French as The Monster, in Al Adamson's **Dracula vs. Frankenstein**.

The Evil
aka **House of Evil** (UK video title)
aka **Cry Demon** (shooting title)
© 1977. Rangoon Productions [released 1978]
A Rangoon production.
director: Gus Trikonis. executive producers:
Paul A. Joseph, Malcolm Levinthal. producer:
Ed Carlin. screenplay: Donald G. Thompson.
director of photography: Mario Di Leo. music:
Johnny Harris. film editor: Jack Kirshner.
production manager: Harry Caplan. 1st
assistant director: Scott Adam. 2nd assistant
director: Dan Steinbrocker. art director: Peter
Jamison. construction coordinator: Alton
Walpole. scenic artist: Arthur Thomas. set
decoration: Robert W. Sheets. 1st assistant
cameraman: John Bollinger. 2nd assistant
cameraman: Larry Snodgrass. sound mixer:
Bill Kaplan, Jr. boom operator: Earl Sampson.
key grip: Ken Wheeland. gaffer: John Murray.
best boys: Gil Valle, Lawrence Purcell. grip:
David Skenes, Jr. script supervisor: Elizebeth
Gallagher. property master: Michael Bennett.
wardrobe coordinator: Barbara Andrews.
wardrobe assistant: James Alvarez. make-up:
Lynne Brooks. special effects: Hollywood
Mobile Systems. animal trainer: Lou
Schumacher. prosthetic make-up: Jack Young.
assistant film editor: Jan Gershkoff. effects
editors: Robert R. Rutledge, Gordon Davidson.
music supervision: John Fresco. music editor:
Jerry Cohen. production assistant: Judy
Williams. production secretaries: Carol
Shelton, Becky Ditterliner. assistant to
producer: Barbara Strickland. stills: Jackie Di
Leo. landscape coordination: Interior Living
Design. titles and opticals: Jack Rabin and
Associates. re-recording by Ryder Sound
Services, Inc. colour: Movie Lab. (Hollywood).
*Cast: Richard Crenna (Doctor C.J. Arnold).
Joanna Pettet (Caroline). Andrew Prine
(Raymond). Cassie Yates (Mary). George
O'Hanlon Jr. (Pete). Lynne Moody (Felecia).
Mary Louise Weller (Laurie). George Viharo
(Dwight). Victor Buono (Devil). Milton Selzer
(realtor). Ed Bakey (Sam). Galen Thompson
(Vargas). Emory Souza (demon). Buddy Joe
Hooker (stunts).*

above and below:
Key artwork for **The Evil** promises a
'from the grave' riff that the film declines
to elaborate upon.

THE EVIL
– Gus Trikonis (1978)
aka *Cry Demon*
aka *House of Evil*

The Vargas mansion, built by Old Vargas himself over an ancient sulphur pit in what the Indians called the Valley of the Devils, has stood empty since the early 1900s. *"Geothermal activity ended about the time the house was finished – dried out, like he put a seal on it..."* Cue the present day, and husband-and-wife science team C.J. and Caroline Arnold (Richard Crenna and Joanna Pettet) are moving in, sprucing up the place as a rehabilitation home for recovering drug addicts. Will these new arrivals debunk the house's spookshow rep? And what could possibly scare a bunch of tough inner-city drug-fiends?

"Haven't you noticed that since the house closed in on us, the whole place smells of sulphur?" The Evil is a Stephen King wannabe, boiled from the stewed bones of the Maine-man's horror blockbusters. *"Just suppose that over the years this house could soak up some of the natural power around it,"* muses one character, whose job it is to cue a blatant steal from *The Shining*. Of course King himself was hardly a bolt from the blue (as he would happily agree, being wise to the genre's history). In *The Evil*, just as in *Salem's Lot* or *The Shining*, horror's many clichés are in evidence: spirits that only a sensitive female can see; cobwebs and dusty diaries; scared dogs picking up on an underlying evil; thunder and lightning; Indian legends... But unlike King's novels, *The Evil* fails to reupholster these mould-bewhiskered furnishings. The problem is not so much the lack of originality; it's the editing, which goofs the rhythm and fumbles tension. For example: after a young man is electrocuted by a falling cable, the shutters, doors and windows close of their own accord, sealing the exits. We then cut to a character saying, *"Let's get the hell out of here."* Excusing the *Scooby-Doo* dialogue, it would surely have been a more dramatic ploy to insert the line *before* the shutters close? That way the house closes the avenue of

escape in defiance of the victims' words. As it is, the character just seems slow-witted. A 'simplistic' slasher film like *Friday the 13th* makes even its false alarms frightening, and its murders convulsively exciting. *The Evil* fails this basic requirement.

Tension is also squandered between those who believe in the supernatural and those who disbelieve, by giving the group irrefutable proof of the spooks too easily. A scene between Doctor Arnold and his student Raymond (Andrew Prine) at least aims for a little drama, as the younger man challenges his sceptical mentor to approach the topic of haunting with the open-mindedness for which he's renowned. As if to punish himself, soon after this confrontation Raymond 'accidentally' slices his own hand off at the wrist with a circular saw. Talk about Freudian slips... Worst of all, the script fails to capitalise on what could have been its most interesting angle – the tension between druggies and doctors. Having the addicts adjust to the supernatural, unlike their square and uninsightful counsellors, would have given the film some satirical bite. Unfortunately, these poor lambs are the least convincing smack-heads and speed-freaks you'll ever see. They even fail the genre's elementary reefer requirements: that 'Arnold cure' must really be something...

For the climax of the movie, Christian imagery is trotted out to validate the irrational. At least it incorporates a genuinely weird scene with Victor Buono as The Devil forcing an atheist to believe in God, a scene that puts the film in the Jesus Army wing of the genre, along with *The Exorcist* and, er, *Cataclysm* (I'll only genuflect to the latter, personally). It's too little too late, though, and *The Evil*, though watchable, is damned to genre purgatory – destined forever to be an also-ran, and surely no one's secret indulgence.

Scriptwriter Donald [Galen] Thompson also wrote *Superstition* for James Roberson: the story is similar, but Roberson is a more stylish director than Trikonis and turns in the better film. Gus Trikonis started out as a dancer, playing 'Action' in the original production of *West Side Story*. He was married to Goldie Hawn but divorced in 1974. Trikonis's second film was *Swinging Barmaids* starring Dyanne Thorne, a story about a religious nut killing waitresses at a sexy bar. The Vargas house is perhaps a loose reference to *Touch of Evil* – Trikonis shot *The Evil* in New Mexico, and Vargas is the name of the Mexican character Charlton Heston plays in the Welles film (although Welles actually shot his Mexican border scenes in Venice, Los Angeles.). Production of *The Evil* was first mooted in *The Hollywood Reporter* in July 1976, when it went under the name of *Cry Demon*, although it was not released until 1978.

Made in New Mexico.

FATAL GAMES
– Michael Elliot (1983)
aka *The Killing Touch*
aka *Olympic Nightmare*

Here's a light but engaging rarity for lovers of early 1980s slasher movies. It's definitely an also-ran, but fans will relish that warm glow of familiarity as the clichés are put under starter's orders. Athletes at a sports college are being stalked and speared by a cagoule-clad nut. Future Olympic hopefuls disappear from their courses, one by one, but no one seems to suspect foul play. Perhaps one of the faculty is harbouring a grudge? Or is one of the students just not a team player?

Predictable? I guess so. Politically incorrect? Guilty as charged. Formularised? ...oh, sod it, I can't wear this sackcloth any longer: if connoisseurs of black-and-white horror films can wax rhapsodic at some daffy old Lugosi film, I can surely indulge a sentimental moment for this tacky eighties slasher! *Fatal Games* is never going to be hoisted on fans' adoring shoulders and taken for a lap of honour, but personally I have a sneaking affection for its clumsy hop, skip and JUMP! It's even better than its nearest sibling, *Graduation Day*. A warning though: the reason this flick has no chance of winning a medal is that the violence is neither

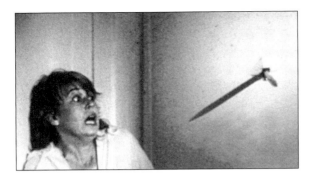

varied nor explicit enough. The killer spears each victim with a javelin, meaning there are no amusing variations to look forward to (discus between the teeth anyone?). The real fun comes with the stalking scenes, as the killer, hampered by that unwieldy choice of weapon, chases victims around the faculty, no doubt wishing to have selected something more practical on corners. And you have to laugh when a star swimmer is javelined from *beneath* the water, a feat requiring extraordinary muscle-power and an even greater perversity on the part of the killer, who could easily have done the deed from above. There's a surprising amount of nudity, female of course, including a few full frontals: and some 'lesbian interest' too, although it's hardly what you'd call progressive... Of the cast, the only one I recognised was Nicholas Love, the retarded brother in Ulli Lommel's excellent fright flick *The Bogey Man*. The director, Michael Elliot, seems to have disappeared subsequently, but never mind – this sort of thing is not your auteurist playground: the slasher movie is more sport than art, and Elliot gets good points from me for completing the course without sending me to sleep.

Made in California.

FIEND
– Don Dohler (1980)
aka *Deadly Neighbor*

A demon possesses a corpse, which rises and sucks the life-essence from an amorous couple making out in the graveyard. Thus refreshed, the dead but *so-o* arrogant 'Mr. Longfellow' (Don Leifert) sets up shop in a quiet suburb of Baltimore, offering violin tuition from his home. Meanwhile, local resident Gary (Richard Nelson) suspects that the outsider could be responsible for a string of horrible murders that have recently plagued the neighbourhood…

Despite a bumpy start and some terribly over-extended dialogue scenes, I find I like Don Dohler's *Fiend*. It may even be his best film, which is ironic, since it was designed as an emergency stop-gap when production was temporarily halted on Dohler's sophomore monster flick, *NightBeast*. The big advantage this time, in the absence of *The Alien Factor*'s fabulous monsters, is the central role given to Don Leifert, who plays the eponymous Fiend with the sort of airy grandiosity Vincent Price would have loved. It's fair to say that, acting-wise, Leifert is the saviour of Dohlerville: his roles as Zachary in *The Alien Factor*, the villainous biker in *NightBeast*, and Mr. Longfellow in *Fiend*, put him head and shoulders above the rest of Don's repertory. In fact he slightly overbalances *Fiend*, by making Longfellow far more compelling than Gary, the nosy neighbour hero; an irony that makes perfect sense in the rest of the genre, but which in Dohler's strait-laced universe is akin to Pazuzu winning Regan's soul. *"Kinda cold and damp down here isn't it?"* asks Gary, who insists on a guided tour of Longfellow's cellar after a girl is found dead behind his house. *"I prefer it that way,"* sneers Leifert, in the tones of a nobleman forced to explain his taste in furnishings to a visiting bumpkin. In a classic Dohler exchange, Gary seems to find this lack of interest in home improvement – *"A little insulation and panelling would make it a lot more comfortable, don't you think?"* – suspicious in itself. The tension is further ramped up by the feeling that we're witnessing not so much a war of nerves as a battle of the moustaches: the hero's looks like a truculent caterpillar, while Longfellow's facial fungus could signify villainy from half-a-mile away (it's all you can do not to hiss the screen when he appears).

Fiend
aka **Deadly Neighbor**
© 1980. Cinema Enterprises
A Cinema Enterprises film. Produced by Cinema Enterprises. A Cinema Enterprises production.
writer/director: Don Dohler. producer: Cinema Enterprises. associate producers: Anne Frith, Ted Bohus, George Stover. photography: Richard Geiwtz. editor: Don Dohler. music composed and performed by Paul Woznicki. special visual effects: David W. Renwick. make-up and set design: Mark Supensky. technical consultants: Chan Sieg, Harris Dinerman. sound processing & mix: Lion and Fox Recordings, Inc. engineer: Jim Fox. print: Quality Film Labs, Inc. colour consultant: Pete Garey. production assistant: Greg Dohler. titles & logo design by David W. Renwick. additional concepts by Don Leifert. graphic artist: Tom Griffith. additional photography by Don Dohler, Mark Supensky. Special thanks to Evelyn B. Wagner; Mr. & Mrs. Joseph Mistretta; Mr. & Mrs. Robert Greenlee; John & Amy Van Popple; Marlene Phillips; Kingsville Volunteer Fire Dept.; San Taylor; Tony Malanowski; Larry Reichman and the fine folks of Moray Court.
Cast: Don Leifert (Eric Longfellow). Richard Nelson (Gary). Elaine White (Marsha). George Stover (Damian Frye). Greg Dohler (Scotty). Del Winans (Jimmy Barnes). Kim Dohler (Kristy Michaels). Debbie Vogel (Miss Waters). Richard Gelwitz (Fred). Denise Gryzbowski (Kristy's friend). Lydia Vuynovich, Steve Frith (couple in cemetery). Pam Merenda (Jane Clayton). Barbara Shuman (girl with dog). Tom Griffith (man with beard). Anna Dorbett (woman). Anne Frith (woman in car). Rosemary Chapman, George Balster, Ron McNeil (ambulance attendants). Phil DeFlavis, Danielle DeFlavis (father/daughter at academy). Steve Vertlieb (radio announcer). Alan Burton (voice of Glaswell) and Pepper the Cat (Dorian).

top left: From **Fatal Games**: Insert your own jokes about 'getting the point' here…

bottom left: The UK video cover.

Fatal Games
aka **The Killing Touch** (US theatrical & UK video title)
aka **Olympic Nightmare** (Dutch video title)
© 1983. Impact Films
Impact Films presents a Michael Elliot film.
director: Michael Elliot. producer: Christopher Mankiewicz. screenplay: Rafael Bunuel, Michael Elliot, Christopher Mankiewicz. co-produced by Rafael Bunuel. executive producer: William Kroes. associate producer: Jonathon Braun. production advisor: Larry Kritt. music composed by Shuki Levy, conducted by Steve Rucker. art director: Jay Burkhart. director of photography: Alfred Taylor. film editor: Jonathon Braun. executive in charge of production: Alan Waite. production manager: Patricia Stallone. assistant director: Wendy Bernier. assistant to the producer: Richard Valentine. assistant to the director: David Scott Kroes. production consultant: Richard Hinds. script supervisor: Sandy Hadar. camera operator: Dick Stuart. assistant camera: Ken Barrows. gaffer: Steve Loew. best boy: Charles "Corky" Baines. electricians: Smitty, Basho Elliot. key grip: Steve McLaughlin. best boy grip: D. Steers. dolly grip: Paul Miranne. production mixer: Rod Sutton. boom operator: Tom Moore. supervising sound editor: Gordon Ecker, Jr. dialogue editor: Stan Gilbert M.P.S.E. sound effects editor: Sandy Berman M.P.S.E. sound editors: Randy Kelley, Anthony Milch, Glenn T. Morgan, Richard Yawn. assistant sound editor: Donald Ortiz. underwater photography: Robert Hayes. still photographer: Victoria Miller. 1st assistant editor: Lida Saskova. 2nd assistant editor: K. Lee. apprentice editor: Flandina Tasca. negative cutters: Suzanne Gervay, Toni Christiansen. propmaster: Woodward Romine, Jr. set decorator: Anne Kuljian. set coordinator: Ric Urbauer. set dresser: Sheri Nuckolls. assistant prop person: Jim Flinn. costume design: Shoko Saito. wardrobe: Christine Leder. assistant wardrobe: Starla Gresham. special effects: Paul Staples, Don J.D. Fox. stunt coordinator: B.J. Davis. make-up artist: Patty Beigel. hair stylist: Celia Brooks. post production sound: Todd-A.O. re-recording mixers: Buzz Knudson, Robert Glass, Don DiGirolamo. additional still photography: Bill Miller. transportation: Julie Hoffman. location manager: Thomas DeSoto. production accountant: Richard Scott. location auditor: Leba Shana. unit publicist: Michael B. Druxman. post production recording: Taj Soundworks. recording engineer: T.E. Sadler. assistant engineer: Greg Orloff. foley by John Roesch, Joan Rowe. music recorded at Sound Connection. engineer: Sheridan Wolf Eldridge. assistant engineers: Nicholas Carr, Andrew Dimitroff. production assistants: Anna Rita Raineri, Richard R. Knight, Patricia Vita, Abbas Moaddab. technical advisors: Tony C. Baker, Shari Smith. casting: Jacov Bressler. titles and opticals by Creative Film Arts. colour by United Color Lab. Arriflex cameras by Cine-Pro. title song "Take It All the Way" by Shuki Levy, Deborah Shelton. original soundtrack available on Saban Records and Tapes. Special thanks to: Aviation High School, Mr. Fish; Gatorade; Speedo Swimwear; Continental Yogurt; Tiger Asics; Converse; Santa Monica Gymnastics Center; Olympia Brewing Co.; Laura Scudders; Farmer Brothers Coffee; Executada for Vector 4 Computer; Maria Caso, Bendix Dixon; Top Video; Intersound, Inc.; Sunwest Productions, Inc.; Alta Marea Productions, Inc.; Haim Saban and Seymour Ziff.
Cast: Sally Kirkland (Diane Paine). Lynn Banashek (Annie Rivers). Sean Masterson (Phil Dandridge). Michael O'Leary (Frank Agee). Teal Roberts (Lynn Fox). Melissa Prophet (Nancy Wilson). Marcelyn Ann Williams (Coach Drew). Angela Bennett (Sue Allen Baines). Nicholas Love (Joe Ward). Lauretta Murphy (Shelley). Michael Elliot (Dr. Jordine). Christopher Mankiewicz (Coach Webber). Edward Call (Mr. Burger). Mel Klein (Annie's father). Alan Waite (waiter). Miguel Elac (singer). Jim Peppers (policeman #1). William G. Sipos (policeman #2). Beverly Schaeffer (waitress). Shari Smith, Steve Malis, James W. Broderick, Nancye Ferguson, K. Stephanie Grimes, Jody Alexander, Thomas Ballatore, Greg Barbacovi, Kiff Kimber, Jennifer McPherson, Claudie Noakes, Cyndi Gallagher, Ron Ortman, Bill Valaika, Noam Ilan, Linnea Quigley, Tori Caplan, Deanna Claire, Larry Lawrence, Joy Hoffman, Ingrid Mesch, Mark Meyers, Steve Leslie, Julie Hoffman (athletes). Kurt Bryant, Eddie Braun, Ray Lykins (stuntmen).

Final Exam
© 1981. Peninsula Management
MPM presents.
writer/director: Jimmy Huston. producer: John L. Chambliss, Myron Meisel. executive producers: John L. Chambliss, Lon J. Kerr, Michael Mahern. film editor: John A. O'Connor. director of photography: Darrell Cathcart. associate producers: Todd Durham, Carol Bahoric. production manager: Mike Allen. music supervision: David Franco. music composed by Gary Scott. dialogue coach: Sam Kilman. assistant director: Charles Reynolds. 2nd assistant director: Dawn Easterling. assistant camera: Irl Dixon. 2nd assistant camera: Roger Painter. sound man: Fred H. Dresch. assistant sound: Al Yelton. sound editor: Bruce Stubblefield. assistant editors: Paul la Mori, Steve Kramer. foley editor: Laraine Mestman. script supervisor: Dawn Freer. gaffer: Dennis Woods. key grip: Fritz Jon Goforth. dolly grip: Gene Poole. grips: Jeff Reep, Dennis Owensby, Herb Greenberg, Chris Carthcart. wardrobe: Alice Taylor. makeup: Barbara Galloway. props: Sarah Robbins. production assistants: Tom Rooker, Mary Ellen Withers. stunts coordinated by Spectacular Effects Int'l. Inc. (Atlanta, Georgia). fight coordinator: Timothy L. Raynor. 2nd unit photography: Dennis Woods, Irl Dixon. titles and opticals by Modern Film Effects. negative cutting: Magic Film Works. sound: Ryder Sound Services. music recorded at The Music Grinder. colour by DeLuxe. special thanks to: Isothermal Community College. filmed at E.O. Motion Picture Studios (Shelby, North Carolina, USA).
Cast: Cecile Bagdadi (Courtney). Joel S. Rice (Radish). Ralph Brown (Wildman). Deanna Robbins (Lisa). Sherry Willis-Burch (Janet). John Fallon (Mark). Terry W. Farren (pledge). Timothy L. Raynor (killer). Sam Kilman (sheriff). Don Hepner (Dr. Reynolds). Mary Ellen Withers (Elizabeth). Jerry Rushing (coach). Shannon Norfleet, Carol Capka (students in car). R.C. Nanney (Mitch). Gene Poole, Fritz Jon Goforth (cafeteria workers). Jeff Beery (stuntman).

right:
Finnish video sleeve for Don Dohler's cheap but loveable **Fiend**.

below:
Will this slasher movie victim really kill the killer, or will he walk again... whoever he is? See **Final Exam** for the answer...

Leifert is not the only asset, though: Dohler's direction is a shade more accomplished here. There's a greater sense of scope in the location shooting (it's amazing what a trip to the supermarket can do), and a number of smoothly executed tracking shots add lustre to the production. However, the editing is pretty choppy to begin with, as if Dohler was straining for atmospheric images which he then had difficulty assembling – for instance, shots of tree branches against the sky feel very awkwardly inserted. If the plot seems to hinge on rather too many murders of women walking through woodland, then at least there's a pleasingly seasonal chill to the scenery (*Fiend* was shot in the early spring of 1980). Pacing, though, is still a problem; waiting for the plot to reach a conclusion involves the viewer's attention in a battle between curiosity and cynicism. The music is generally successful in its pulpish way, but why, when Gary complains about the villain's noisy violin tutorials, doesn't Dohler use a real violin on the soundtrack? A bit of library music or a public domain classical clip would surely have been far more effective than the awful synthesizer which takes its place! Least valuable are the primitive and largely unnecessary optical effects: intended to show an ancient supernatural evil possessing the villain, they serve only to shroud some otherwise effective rotting-face appliances. Nevertheless, *Fiend* is another film to cement Dohler's status as the home-movie horror director it's okay to like.

Don Leifert on *Fiend*:

"Don, a person for who I have much respect, was a gifted editor. I think he saved his films in the editing room. His personal favourite was Fiend*.* Fiend *was tough on me: I was undergoing a painful divorce, drinking heavily (I'm actually intoxicated in a few minutes of footage), and the makeup was downright painful. Latex was used to pull the skin under my eyes as low as possible, thus exposing the sensitive areas under the eyes to the climate when we shot outside. As I'm fair-skinned (red hair as a kid), the make-up caused my skin to break out and I had to go to a dermatologist. There were a few days when everyone was ready to shoot and I refused to get into makeup. The mere thought of applying it sickened me."*

Made in Maryland.
see also: **The Alien Factor** *and* **NightBeast**

*Jännäri...
Ei huonohermoisille!*

FIGHT FOR YOUR LIFE
– Robert Endelson (1977)
See interview with Robert Endelson.

Made in New York State.

FINAL EXAM
– Jimmy Huston (1981)

In the introduction to this book, I made the rather extreme assertion that I would happily watch a twenty-four-hour slasher film. I also admitted that, for some unspeakably perverse reason, I often find myself wishing the early stages would go on longer before the murders begin. It's sick I know, and I apologise for using this book as a confessional booth, but there it is: at least it's a warning to the rest of you. Slasher films can really fuck you up...

Final Exam, however, proved something to me that the rest of you probably knew already: even if the pre-slaughter stages are fun, you can't just dispense with the nasty stuff altogether. At some point, no matter how late, gardening tools or serrated cutlery must make graphic contact with teenage flesh. *Final Exam* is so much fun to begin with that it's painful to see how far short it ultimately falls. After two sketchy killings in the opening sequence (as per usual, we expect no more than a brief splash of blood early on), director Jimmy Huston takes fifty leisurely minutes to get to the next murder, filling up the time with a blissful array of eminently diceable characters. Numbnuts fraternity jocks and dweebish nerds have ritualised confrontations; an airhead chick (Sherry Willis-Burch) agonises about whether her new boyfriend (Terry W. Farren) takes her seriously; a sweet-natured student clearly marked out as 'the final girl' (Cecile Bagdadi) tries to advance her education while dispensing advice to her room-mates... it's all coming together perfectly. El Nerdo numero uno (Joel S. Rice) even has one-sheets for *The Corpse Grinders* and *The Toolbox Murders* on his wall, kindly pointing out who our surrogate is. Thanks, guys. The campus troublemaker (and repressed homosexual) is called 'Wildman' (Ralph Brown), and he and his crazy-ass Gamma Fraternity buddies cut loose with stunts such as trussing a freshman to a tree, stripping him to his underpants, smothering his torso in shaving cream and pouring ice-cubes in his crotch. Mind you, they also fake a school slaughter by driving their black van onto campus, shooting stooge students 'dead' with machine-guns, and then driving off with the 'corpses', which was impressive, I have to admit. The asshole local cop (Sam Kilman) gets bent out of shape about it, but the school's cheery coach (Jerry Rushing, a regular for Worth Keeter) and creepy caretaker (R.C. Nanney) take a more lenient view. (Something tells me that this gag would meet with more disapproval post-Columbine – and for the same reason I doubt you'll ever see this film on American TV...)

So *Final Exam* is heading for straight 'A's. Then the killings begin, and the movie flunks. Huston skimps on the blood, hides the attacks in shadows and medium shots, and neglects to deliver even the simplest of prosthetic wound appliances. It's deeply unsatisfying and very disappointing. The killer (Timothy L. Raynor) doesn't even have a signature weapon, and the absence of close-up stabbing, slicing or crushing really breaks the contract with the audience. (There's a moderately successful death by weight-training apparatus, I suppose, but it was all done so much better in *Happy Birthday to Me*). It was shot at Earl Owensby's North Carolina-based E.O. studios in 1980, which is before the MPAA clamped down hard on gory horror, so the only reasons I can see for circumspection are either lack of money for special make-up, or the director's basic dislike of the grisly stuff. If it's the former, well even cheap gore effects are better than nothing; if the latter, perhaps Mr. Huston, whose real forté would seem to be action drama (e.g. *Death Driver* and *Buckstone County Prison*), should have passed the production to fellow Owensby alumnus Worth Keeter, who would probably have been more willing to spill the red stuff?

He came
out of nowhere
with only
the need to kill....

FINAL EXAM

by Geoffrey Meyer

NOW A MAJOR MOTION PICTURE FROM MPM

So the film is gore-lite, but also quite appallingly concluded. I'm not really a stickler for plotting and characterisation in the slasher subgenre, but frankly you do need *some* sort of explanation for the killer's bad mood. Amazingly, *Final Exam* tells us nothing at all about the murderer. We don't know who he is, or why he's killing people. It's not that he's a mysterious force of nature, a symbolic faceless 'everyman', or a supernatural boogeyman either. He's just, you know, some guy. He's not a teacher who hates exam cheats; nor a student who's so obsessed with getting the best grades that he kills his class rivals; he's not even a common-or-garden escaped lunatic. (Nice girl Courtney mentions that a student once threw herself off the clock tower after being turned down by a sorority, but amazingly this snippet isn't followed up.) There are candidates aplenty: the jolly, laid-back coach could easily harbour secrets; the chemistry teacher (Don Hepner) chasing his female students for a little *alfresco* experimentation could have been more than just a dirty old man; hell, even the caretaker would suffice, and now I'm *really* not being choosy. But no – it's just some guy, with no reason, no dialogue, no back-story, *nada*. You almost have to admire the effrontery, the complete lack of effort. The net result of all this is that *Final Exam* will only ever appeal to slasher-movie completists, and even then it'll never make its way to the top of anyone's chart. If even a hopeless case like myself can't overlook its flaws, I suspect its chances of finding a cult are close to zero.

Final Exam was filmed at the E.O. [Earl Owensby] Studios, in Shelby North Carolina, with location work at the Isothermal Community College, North Carolina (there are two campuses of this name, one in Spindale NC, the other in Columbus NC). The assistant director was Charles Reynolds, aka C.D.H. Reynolds, director of *A Day of Judgment*.

Made in North Carolina.

THE FOLKS AT RED WOLF INN
– Bud Townsend (1972)
aka *Terror House*
aka *Terror on the Menu!*
aka *Terror at Red Wolf Inn*
aka *Terror at the Red Wolf Inn*

An elderly couple, Henry and Evelyn Smith (Arthur Space and Mary Jackson, the latter a regular from *The Waltons*) invite young women to stay at their beautiful seaside inn; then, after fattening them up with lots of home-baked food, they slaughter, cook and eat them, sharing the prime cuts with the remaining guests. Into this situation comes Regina (Linda Gillen), who believes she has won a prize holiday at the Smiths' guesthouse. Once there, she forms a romantic involvement with their nervous grandson, Baby John (John Neilson). But will true love save her from the fate of her fellow guests?

In a country renowned for its jumbo portions, it was inevitable that food would make an appearance in the collective nightmares of American cinema. Kicking off from a very unlikely premise (basically, 'Drop everything, you've just won a holiday in a competition you don't even remember entering, and the plane leaves now!'), this is actually a lot better than it's satire/send-up reputation suggests. A hokey trailer emphasising the humorous possibilities sells the film short, as it's actually an eccentric but reasonably gripping thriller. Such satire as there is extends about as far as dubbing 'Pomp and Circumstance' over an elaborate dining scene, though the scene is also marinated with creepier ideas. For instance, a succession of gluttonous non-verbal sounds are placed unsettlingly high in the sound-mix, while the sly look on old Evelyn's face when one diner cheerfully announces, *"I'm going to get as fat as a pig!"* is more chilling than funny.

In horror movie terms, cannibalism was the food-fad of the seventies, with *The Texas Chain Saw Massacre* as the best possible commercial. Bud Townsend may not deserve as many Michelin stars as Tobe Hooper, but he *did* get there first, serving a weird, unsettling 'acquired taste' akin to Laurence Harvey's *Welcome to Arrow Beach* (1974). Dramatic plausibility, it must be said, is not the film's strong suit: the heroine is far too easily subdued when she finally learns the truth, and the intermittent whimsicality makes an uneasy bedfellow with horror. I must admit I'm completely puzzled by a rendition of 'The White Cliffs of Dover' at the end of the film: it matches up with the use of Elgar's 'Pomp and Circumstance,' I suppose… but to what end? The latter is played during US college graduation ceremonies, but I can think of no American relevance for the former. The tone of the film is thus rather uncertain, which nevertheless accounts for its charm. It's a head-scratcher, a one-off, with an unusual lop-sided feel, and like many of the more curious horrors of the seventies it refuses to settle neatly into the usual genre pigeonholes.

Producer Michael Macready previously hit paydirt with *Count Yorga, Vampire*, while Townsend previously contributed *Nightmare in Wax* (1969) to the genre, before moving on to softcore erotics. Townsend died on 19 September, 1997, at the age of 76.

Made in California.

The Folks at Red Wolf Inn
aka **Terror House** (US theatrical re-issue title)
aka **Terror at Red Wolf Inn**
(UK video sleeve title)
aka **Terror on the Menu!**
(UK and Canadian video title)
aka **Club Dead** (North American video title)
© 1972. The Red Wolf Company
director: Bud Townsend. producer: Michael Macready. screenplay: Allen J. Actor. director of photography: John McNichol. original music: Bill Marx. film editor: Al Maguire. associate producers: Herb Ellis, Allen J. Actor. production manager: Erik Nelson. art director: Mike Townsend. set decorator & props: Elizabeth Nelson. chief electrician: Al York. key grip: Leo Behar. script supervisor: Patty Sue Townsend. sound mixer: Bruce Bisense. casting: Sheila Manning. sound: Ryder Sound Service. sound effects: Rich Harrison. titles & opticals: Modern Film Effects, Steve Orfanos. post production: The Film Place. assistant to the producer: Ted Petit. girl on the set: Nola. [song] "My Dream" lyrics written & sung by Marilynn Lovell.
Cast: menu - hors d'oeuvres: *Janet Wood (Pamela). Margret Avery (Edwina).* a la carte: *Linda Gillin [Gillen] (Regina). John Nielson (Baby John). Arthur Space (Henry). Mary Jackson (Evelyn).* side dishes: *Michael Macready (Jonathan the deputy). Earl Parker (Paul the pilot).* kitchen helpers: *Carl, Jenny, Ray, Pam, Bubi, Ann, Bob, Epeter, David, Johnny, Jeff, Tom, Paul, Joe & Lenny.*

top left:
Often, in the days before home video, the only way to revisit a film was to read the paperback novelisation. Some were truly creative: **Videodrome** by 'Jack Martin' [Dennis Etchison], for instance, which drew on an earlier, even weirder Cronenberg script. So does the novelisation of **Final Exam** throw light on the identity of the killer? You'll have to read it to find out!

top right:
If you're a skinny 'wimp' who hate 'jocks' you'll love this scene from **Final Exam**.

below:
What's the chance that someone's mum kindly agreed to draw a picture for the UK video cover of **Terror at Red Wolf Inn**?

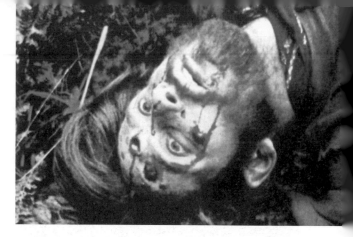

top right: Too much aftermath, not enough violence! But apart from that, **Forest of Fear** is a hoot.

bottom right: **Forest of Fear** also played in Australia as **Toxic Zombies**...

below: ...and it played under its original title on this double bill; presumably with James Wasson's exuberant penis-ripping Bigfoot feature **Night of the Demon** rather than Jacques Tourneur's black-and-white masterpiece?

THE FOREST
– Don Jones (1981)
See interview with Don Jones and Gary Kent.

Made in California.

FOREST OF FEAR
– Charles McCrann (1979)
aka *Bloodeaters*
aka *Toxic Zombies*

As dumb as you please, *Forest of Fear* is an okay woodland zombie romp, no more, no less. Like the films of the 1960s that addressed the multi-coloured counterculture while wearing enough establishment sackcloth to avoid being censored, *Forest of Fear*, seen at a glance, tries to have it both ways, here equating stoned hippies with zomboid murder and running an anti-authoritarian back-story just in case. It turns out the government are to blame, having paid some old-timer to spray the marijuana fields with dangerous untested pesticide (the film trades on the contemporary Paraquat scare). Not that this information shifts the focus of the film that much: the rationale may rail against The Man, but the bulk of the action has naive holiday-making bourgeois types attacked by pestilential hippies, whose drooling madness is far scarier than the underlying anti-government theme. It's a classic case of heart in one place, head in the other.

Of course the truth of the matter is that when you're stoned, tripping, or otherwise off your face, it's a lot more satisfying to watch your representatives foaming at the mouth and tearing chunks out of innocent squares than it is to wade through a worthy defence of the value and beauty of the drug experience. I don't know about you, but if there's one thing guaranteed to give *me* a bad trip, it's a dose of pro-love, hippy-dippy peace-not-war earnestness. That's why *Forest of Fear* can claim to have its finger on the fibrillating pulse of its likely audience.

So there's the tolerant side of the review: now the rest. *Forest of Fear* basically lacks the visceral charge of its inspiration, *Dawn of the Dead*, and there's no stylistic detail or imagination to compensate. To put it bluntly, this is a movie where a bunch of nobodies run around woods and fields, with the cameraman occasionally grinding to a halt to look at the *aftermath* of a zombie attack. Except for a severed hand stunt so phoney Herschell Gordon Lewis might have asked for a retake, and a couple of very fleeting bullet-to-the-head appliances, there are no advances on what you might call the action-gore front. We do see blood-spattered corpses (yawn), a severed leg (zzzzz) and a body with a pool of intestines slopped out beside it (okay, that was nice…), but these are static shots with little impact. The rotting face make-ups are adequate but unmemorable: Tony Malanowski's *The Curse of the Screaming Dead*, filmed in the next field, so to speak, can boast a more grotesque vision of the dead. And David Sperling's photography is merely adequate, which is a shame given that he turned in some beautiful work the same year for Ulli Lommel's *The Bogey Man* and later shot the inventive, hyperactive *Street Trash* (1987).

Forest of Fear was shot on 16mm as *Bloodeaters*, in the Pittsburgh region, with production allies on loan from George Romero, so you can be forgiven for expecting more. It's particularly galling that John Amplas, the gifted, unforgettable star of Romero's *Martin* is tossed an utterly mundane part as sidekick to a hard-ass cop; it's tragic to see this teenage prodigy trudging through such a thankless role. Amplas, I guess, must have shunned the spotlight after *Martin*, or else he'd never have sunk this far, but *Forest of Fear* is tainted by the feeling of such sorely wasted potential.

What can I say about Ted Shapiro's score? It apes both *Halloween* and, more ambitiously, the Goblin of *Dawn of the Dead*, but even if you have a tolerance for cheap synthesizer, it's heavy going. The same uninspired arpeggios plunk away over the action; perhaps intended to grind us down, they simply erode our goodwill. Music aside, there's also a lot of unreconstructed female screaming to be heard, the poor actresses screeching away like tortured

seabirds. All in all, the *Forest of Fear* audio experience is definitely *not* recommended if you're feeling tetchy.

You have to be a little bit soft in the head to stick up for this film: to even vaguely *like* it suggests you've spent too long pining for the early days of video, when these cheap and nasty turkeys were all the rage. What the hell, that's me on both counts. Even though the music can drive you crazier than a toxic hippy, *Forest of Fear* is a laugh. It's like a cheap frozen pizza: you turn up your foccacia-loving nose at it, until late one night you're pissed and starving and there's no gravadlax or goat's cheese flan left in the cupboard. If at times it all feels like a forerunner of those fucking awful made-on-video gut-fests like *Violent Shit* (1987), try not to blame this little movie for the sins of its fans. Relax, watch some Bergman, and stay out of the low-budget woods for a while. Try to enjoy reading Adorno. You'll be back...

Charles 'Chuck' McCrann's career in film stalled after *Forest of Fear*. A Princeton graduate in Law, he moved on to become a prominent figure in the business community, as senior vice-president of the financial services conglomerate, Marsh & McLennan: with an office in the World Trade Center. He died in the Twin Towers terrorist atrocity, on 11 September, 2001. His body was never recovered.

Made in Pennsylvania.

FRANKENSTEIN ISLAND
– Jerry Warren (1981)

Take fifteen minutes of *The Wild Women of Wongo*, ten minutes of *The Island of Dr. Moreau*, half-an-hour of desiccated *Frankenstein*, add a caged Cameron Mitchell (unwashed) and sprinkle with optically composited head of John Carradine; simmer for twenty three years and serve cold in 1981. Don't be surprised if no one wants a bite, what you've made is a flick that challenges Al Adamson for stubborn retro-itis. The difference is that director Jerry Warren actually made this sort of cheesy sci-fi horror flick back in the day, when such monster-mash shenanigans were all the rage, whereas Adamson merely aped them fifteen years too late. Coming from the director of *Manbeast* (1956), *The Incredible Petrified World* (1957), *Teenage Zombies* (1959) and *Attack of the Mayan Mummy* (1964), a goofy flick like *Frankenstein Island* is just more of the patent Warren hullabaloo: if you're feeling grandiose, you could suggest that by making such a defiantly old-fashioned film in 1981 (year of horror hits *An American Werewolf in London* and *Scanners*), Warren was staking his final claim to a territory he helped to shape, just as Billy Wilder bid farewell to his brand of Hollywood with that grand old showboat *Fedora* (1978). I'll leave further debate to those with fonder feelings for Warren's movies. For me, *Frankenstein Island* offers just the mild satisfaction of having finally seen what lies behind that spectacularly awful 'Ambassador Video' cover…

Made in California and Arizona.

FRIDAY THE 13TH: THE ORPHAN
– John Ballard (1977)
See interview with John Ballard and Sidney Mackenzie.
Made in New York State.

FROZEN SCREAM
– Frank Roach and Renee Harmon (1981)
See interview with Renee Harmon.
Made in California.

GARDEN OF THE DEAD
– John Hayes (1972)
See feature on John Hayes.
Made in California.

THE GIANT SPIDER INVASION
– Bill Rebane (1975)

Rebane's best film opens at quite a pace, for him at least, certainly a lot faster than his next, *The Alpha Incident* (1977). Nervy crosscutting gives *The Giant Spider Invasion* an almost modern feel: it could probably play on TV with little embarrassment. The narrative flickers between a loveless husband and wife (Robert Easton and Leslie Parrish) whose farmland is the focus of the horror, and the rather less vivid affairs of an investigating scientific team. There's also a wise-old-bird local sheriff (Alan Hale) breathing laconic humour into the story – the sort of character you'd later find in Stephen King's novels. What with this and an alien invasion that reveals a town rotting from within, no wonder King referenced Rebane's flick warmly in his study of the horror genre, *Danse Macabre*.

The arrival of mysterious meteorites is achieved with enthusiastic if implausible pyrotechnics, courtesy of some brazen matte work. Early stages, as the meteorites trigger increased activity in the indigenous spider population, are as creepy as you could wish: people are constantly sweeping irritably at the air with their hands, dislodging webs in doorways, flicking spiders from the table. One highlight involves a spider making its way across unwashed dishes until it crawls into a blender – just in time for the farmer's wife to switch it on and mix a Bloody Mary. Eventually, rising to the challenge of the movie's title, Rebane gallantly offers us a giant spider the size of a camper van. And it's not bad at all: though it's less obscurely disturbing than the creature which earlier leaped out from the dusty eaves of a barn, like a rag-doll with too many legs…

While the sheriff's cynical comments indicate a less than pious attitude towards the town's Christian revivalist meeting, the eventual arachnapocalypse is overdubbed by a preacher's ranting about sin and deliverance. So are the spiders a judgement on the godless, or are the faithful, locked away in their drawn-out church meetings, being satirized for their irresponsibility? Perhaps Rebane was aiming for the double whammy of Don Siegel's *Invasion of the Body Snatchers*, where opposing interpretations work equally well? Well, perhaps not...

The scientific aspects are shameless gobbledegook, incorporating quantum physics that would flummox Niels Bohr. *"Looks like our black hole has turned into an open doorway from hell,"* says one Einstein. Faced with how to rid the town of a spider the size of a Buick, another boffin suggests, *"We could shower it with neutrons!"* A bit silly then, but this is basically good fun, a light, unpretentious monster movie of the sort that disappeared once the big studios crowded the pitch. There's a poignant moment when the sheriff describes the giant spider, saying, *"Did you ever see that movie,* Jaws? *It makes that look like a*

Frankenstein Island
aka **The Captives** (shooting title)
© none [1981]
Jerry Warren presents a Chriswar production.
producer/director: Jerry Warren. screenplay: Jaques Lacouter. director of photography: Murray De Ately. music director: Erich Bromberg. production assistant: James Daigh. 2nd unit camera: Michael Lambert. sound mixer: Bob Ernst. production liaison: Gloria Warren. grips: Jim Webb, Norman Yoffe. gaffer: Don Bettes. sound assistant: Michael Kellogg. filmed in January 1981 in Baja (lower California), Colossol Cave (Tucson, Arizona), Escondido and Hollywood (California, USA)
Cast: Robert Clarke (Dr. Paul Hadley). Steve Brodie (Jocko, old drunk). Cameron Mitchell (Clay Jayson). Robert Christopher (Mark Eden). Tain Bodkin (Curtis Ryan). Patrick O'Neil (Dino). Andrew Duggan (the colonel) and John Carradine (Dr. Frankenstein). Kathrin [Kathryn] Victor (Sheila Frankenstein Van Helsing). George Mitchell (Dr. Van Helsing). Dana Norbeck. Laurel Johnson. Richard Banks (Jocko's 1st mate). James Webb. Marla Conner. Donna Green. Vic Schneider and Melvin (the dog).

top left:
Ambassador Video's distinctive UK video cover for **Frankenstein Island** was clearly drawn by the same artist who came up with their sleeve for Richard Cassidy's **Crazed**.

below:
Italian locandina poster for Bill Rebane's **The Giant Spider Invasion.**

The Giant Spider Invasion
© 1975. Transcentury Pictures
A Cinema Group 75 film. World wide distribution: The Group 1 Int'l. Dist. Org. Ltd. (Los Angeles, USA).
director: Bill Rebane. executive producer: William W. Gillett, Jr. producer: Bill Rebane & Richard L. Huff. screenplay: Richard L. Huff & Robert Easton. original story: Richard L. Huff. director of cinematography: Jack Willoughby. film editor: Barbara Pokras. associate producers: Jack Willoughby, Dick Plautz. music editors: Ito Rebane, John Arrufat. assistant editors: Ticci Goldberg, Barbara Kress, Andrea Scharf. effects editor: Jim Ryan. special effects: Richard Albain, Robert Millay. first assistant director: Kevin Brodie. second assistant director / unit manager: Barbara J. Rebane. assistant cameraman: Karl Kitt. gaffer: Alan Rebane. key grip: Richard Plautz. sound mixer: Steve Hunter. boom man: Ron Everett. set designer: Ito [Ito Rebane]. continuity & script: Barbara Kress. set decorator: Jutta Rebane. make up: Tom Schwartz. hairdresser: Sue Brodie. wardrobe: Robin Brodie. grips: Rick Plautz, Buck Gillett, Carl Pfantz. production secretaries: Joann McCracken, Pat Phillips. titles & optical effects: CFI. post production sound services: Ryder Sound (Hollywood, California). filmed in Eastman Color. The Producers Wish to Acknowledge the Co-operation of: The University of Wisconsin (Stevens Point, Wisconsin); Nicolet College Sheriff's Department (Rhinelander, Wisconsin); Marathon County Sheriff's Department (Wausau, Wisconsin); Owens of Illinois; Towns of Merrill and Gleason and Lincoln County (Wisconsin); Enstrom Helicopter furnished through the courtesy of the Enstrom Helicopter Corporation (Menomonee, Michigan); vehicles courtesy American Motors Corporation. filmed on location in the towns of Merrill and Gleason (Lincoln County, Wisconsin, USA).
Cast: Steve Brodie (Dr. Vance). Barbara Hale (Dr. Jenny Langer). Robert Easton (Kester). Leslie Parrish (Ev). Alan Hale (sheriff). Bill Williams (Dutch). Kevin Brodie (Perkins). Dianne Lee Hart (Terry). Tain Bodkin (preacher). Paul Bentzen). J. Stewart Taylor (deputy). Christiana Schmidtner (Helga). William W. Gillett, Jr. (Rider). Dennis Wilder, Robert F. Nelson (stunt men).

goldfish!" Of course it was precisely the arrival of Spielberg's mega-film that sealed the fate of cheap, small-town monster movies. Egos got bigger, budgets got bigger, until the B-movie pool was colonised by bloated behemoths of the Hollywood variety, excluding the little fish altogether. Rebane's valiant effort, with its scenes of local townspeople gathering to fight monsters under occasionally visible film lights, was already one of a dying breed…

Made in Wisconsin.
see also: **The Alpha Incident, The Demons of Ludlow** *and*
Rana: The Legend of Shadow Lake

GODMONSTER OF INDIAN FLATS
– Fredric Hobbs (1973)
See interview with Fredric Hobbs and William Heick.
Made in California.

THE GORE GORE GIRLS
– Herschell Gordon Lewis (1972)
aka *Blood Orgy*

Someone is killing the strippers who work at Marz's Heaven, a downtown club owned by Marzdone Mobile (Henny Youngman). Nancy Weston (Amy Farrell), a pretty young reporter, invites sophisticated private investigator Abraham Gentry (Frank Kress) to track down the killer and pass the exclusive story to her newspaper for a cool $25,000. Gentry accepts the deal and sets about uncovering the maniac's identity; meanwhile, go-go girl after go-go girl is being gore-gore-gored to death…

Until *Blood Feast 2* (2002) came along, *The Gore Gore Girls* was Herschell Gordon Lewis's last film, and it's a wonderful send-off for the exploitation classics that made his name. Personally, I think it's his best; *The Wizard of Gore* is the weirdest, and *Two Thousand Maniacs!* has the best premise, but *The Gore Gore Girls* refines the goofy humour of *The Gruesome Twosome* and then confounds expectation by backing it all up with a couple of genuinely likeable performances. Frank Kress plays 'Abraham Gentry' as an American Jason King, with the sort of lordly arrogance typical of all Brits who aren't cleaning chimneys and dancing on the rooftops *á là* Dick Van Dyke. His bickering relationship with reporter Nancy Weston (She: *"If you're done being clever…"* He: *"Never!"*) provides the backbone of the film, ensuring that the entrails don't slide into the narrative gutter in the way that made *The Gruesome Twosome* such a chore between scalpings. And although Gentry's

snobbish attitude towards Nancy initially marks him as a sort of supercilious homosexual with no time for women, there's a gradual thaw between the two that may be the only believable trace of affection Lewis ever attempted.

From its jittery opening jazz theme to its chaotic conclusion, *The Gore Gore Girls* is a blast: it has an amusing script, loveable lead actors, insanely catchy rock'n'roll instrumentals, burlesque atmosphere, bizarre guest-spots (Henny Youngman??) and more sadism and mutilation than you can shake a severed leg at. The violence is pure *Grand Guignol* slapstick, but beware; its nastiness can still get you ostracized if you slip the film on at the wrong party. During the killing of stripper 'Candy Kane', the murderer gets so carried away mutilating the victim's face that the result looks like a spilled Tomato and Beef Pot Noodle; in fact the assailant actually has to reinsert a popped eyeball into the victim's pulverized visage to remind us what we're looking at! The infamous nipple-slicing (white milk from one nipple, chocolate from the other) suggests the gross imaginings of a ghoulish child, as does the pulverising of a girl's buttocks with a meat tenderizing mallet (with salt and pepper added to the resulting mess). Two face-frying scenes compound the impression: one girl has her head shoved into a pan of deep-frying chips, and another has her features frazzled with a hot iron. It's as if two ten-year-old boys are vying with each other to think up scenes for a horror film, which makes even the nastiest moments feel somehow strangely innocent.

The Gore Gore Girls (there's no hyphen in the onscreen title) has another sort of charm, thanks to its status as a kind of super-cheap *giallo* (I'm referring to the Italian style of thriller pioneered by Mario Bava and Dario Argento). Consider the evidence: a mysterious black-coated, black-gloved maniac attacking young women; an inept police investigation upstaged by the efforts of an amateur sleuth; and a handful of blatant red-herrings… One wonders whether young first-time scriptwriter Alan J. Dachman (who appears briefly as a dope-head) had recently enjoyed Argento's *The Bird with the Crystal Plumage* (1970) on its US release? Even the identity of the killer, as revealed in the final scenes, bears comparison with the *giallo* format.

Of course, there's a chauvinism to the film (despite the extreme violence, I'd say chauvinism, not misogyny, is the issue). The relationship between Gentry and Nancy is always skewed towards male superiority, with Nancy either slavering after Gentry's affections, or falling for his manipulation of her sexual jealousy. A viewer of the feminist faith, with no warmth towards the horror genre, would doubtless be appalled by the movie, both for its sadism and its sexual politics. Lewis appears to have anticipated this, lampooning feminists in a scene where a group of them invade a strip-joint and attack the working girls,

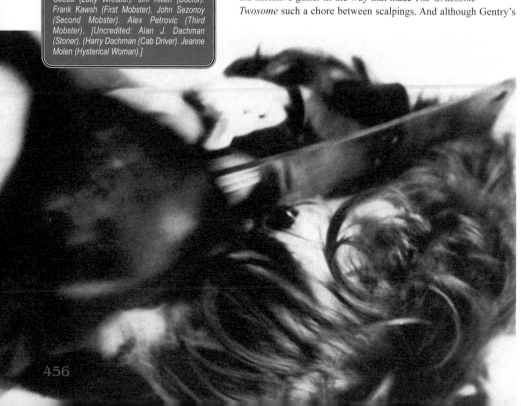

brandishing ludicrous sloganeering banners. The killer's reason for attacking beautiful women (entangled in the final plot twist) also plays to the chauvinist gallery, and if it wasn't for the fact that the film is so obviously pulling the audience's chain, it could all seem quite unpleasant. 'You mean cutting off women's nipples and frying their faces in boiling oil *isn't*?', you ask. Oddly enough, I'd say no. The violence in Lewis's films is so clearly intended to rile and provoke that it's best considered aside from issues of political correctness. By foaming about misogyny one is simply falling for Lewis's *shtick*: if you're the sort of person who's offended by screen violence against women, he has created these extraordinarily graphic provocations just for you, serving them to the screen with a sardonic smirk. He's like a chef who puts extra chillies in your meal just to see the look on your face. Lewis has gone on record as saying that the film was intended for 'sophisticated' audiences, and for sure it helps if you've been round the chopping block a few times. But it's obviously part of the fun for him to offend the 'unsophisticated' (read: everyone who hates the movie).

It's worth noting that when Nancy gets up to dance in the stripper's contest – jealous that Gentry is ogling another woman – actress Amy Farrell doesn't really disrobe; even though the rest of the girls have gone cheerfully topless throughout. Many an exploitation director would have said, 'Do it topless or we get another broad'. Lewis says nothing about Farrell in *The Gore Gore Girls* DVD commentary (a rather unhelpful track with too much digression by the moderators), so it's unclear whether, for instance, Farrell refused to bare her breasts at the last minute, after much of the film was in the can. Whatever the truth, her modesty remains intact. Such would not be the case in the mid-seventies as the horror genre began to seep into the porno arena. In 1972, year of *Deep Throat*, and with porno-chic hot on his heels, Herschell finally bailed out, leaving the new frontier of sexually explicit horror to such driven and dangerous figures as Walt Davis, Shaun Costello and Zebedy Colt.

Made in Illinois.

GRADUATION DAY
– Herb Freed (1981)

When a promising high school athlete named Laura (Ruth Ann Llorens) dies from a heart attack after winning a hundred metre sprint, a killer in a sweatsuit and fencing mask begins murdering her fellow track-and-field stars one by one. Could it be bullying Coach Michaels (Christopher George), obsessed with sporting excellence? Or Laura's tough-cookie sister Anne (Patch Mackenzie), a commissioned army officer who returns all the way from Guam for the funeral, despite the hostility of her alcoholic stepfather Ronald (Hal Bokar)? How about asshole school principal Mr. Guglione (Michael Pataki), or Laura's intense bereaved boyfriend Kevin (E. Danny Murphy)?

"Everybody wants to be the winner," the title song declares, as Laura achieves just that, and drops dead. *"These diplomas are tickets to the adult world. If you want to get in, you've got to pay the admission price,"* says Principal Guglione, who also has a line in sobering cynicism: *"You're only as good as your last mistake."* (actor Pataki was in *Raise the Titanic* the previous year, so perhaps he ad-libbed this remark…) Ideas seem to be gathering focus under starter's orders, and as you hyperventilate for the track-and-field slaughterthon to come, you find yourself wondering if you're about to see the world's first anti-capitalist slasher film! Perhaps a communist critique of competition as wasteful expenditure? Guglione uses the fact that his insecure secretary (E.J. Peaker) has a crush on him to make her work harder. Exploitation in the workplace, too? It's positively Marxian.

Well, an impossible dream perhaps, but *Graduation Day* has a witty script to recommend it anyway. The undercurrent of humour can't entirely redeem what is basically a second-string slasher, but it makes the whole thing a lot more fun to watch. I loved the climactic chase during which a police officer, less fit than the

top:
UK video sleeve for **Graduation Day**

killer, stops because he's suffering a stitch. (When you consider all the running that goes on in the slasher genre, it's a miracle half the victims don't die of a coronary.)

There's more running at the climax of the picture, as Anne sprints all the way across town and then crosses the sports field to sit at the opposite end, on the bleachers. The camera, perched on a much higher seat behind her, looks back over the entire stadium in the direction she came from. No one's there. She sits down and catches her breath, for no more than five seconds. The next shot is the killer's POV, approaching her from just yards away. I know the slasher genre cheats with its POV menace-shots, but this really takes the biscuit. It's the sort of thing that annoys outsiders to the genre, and even I felt cheated. If you're a stickler for tidy plotting too, *Graduation Day* is going to get on your nerves. We never find out, for instance, why Anne's stepfather is so utterly hostile to her, or for that matter, what's so special about Anne that the film should end on a farewell to her as she heads off back to Guam. But that's typical of *Graduation Day*: its final thesis is hopelessly muddled and full of loose ends. Screw the thesis, though, does it 'rock'? Well, the murders are okay, the highlight being a spiked cushion that the killer prepares for a pole-vaulter, and a brief but vivid fencing stab, through the throat and out the other side, but Freed seems more concerned with hyping new-wavey looking but AOR-sounding student band Felony, whose song 'Gangster Rock' gets a full workout in the film as the audience roller-skate around and around the stage… (Note: Felony actually went on to release two albums in the 1980s, *The Fanatic* and *Vigilante*: a track from the latter featured in *Friday the 13th Part VI: Jason Lives*. Formed by Joe and Jeff Spry, the band continued into the 1990s when things hit the skids and Jeff committed suicide.) A time-capsule of the early eighties, *Graduation Day* is the sort of film I really ought to blush for recommending, but which has snuck into my slasher comfort-zone and taken up residence, despite the groans of my better judgement…

Made in California.
*see also: **Haunts***

opposite page, top left:
Bill Rebane's spider movie on a double bill with Patrick J. Murphy's **Riding Tall** (1972), starring Andrew Prine.

opposite page, top right:
Admat for Herschell Gordon Lewis's best movie.

opposite page, bottom:
Can you make sense of this face? **The Gore Gore Girls** takes screen violence to the limit.

GRAVE OF THE VAMPIRE
– John Hayes (1972)
See feature on John Hayes.

Made in California.

HAUNTED
– Michael De Gaetano (1976)
aka *The Haunted*

In Arizona during the Civil War, Abanaki (Ann Michelle), a Native American woman accused of witchcraft, is tied to a horse and left to die in the desert. One hundred years later, Jennifer Baines (Ann Michelle again) arrives in a desert settlement. Once a Wild West movie-set, it is now occupied by a handful of lonely oddballs. Soon after she settles in, people start dying in mysterious circumstances: is Jennifer really the reincarnation of Abanaki?

Haunted is a jumble of themes and non-sequiturs largely unhampered by narrative design. So what is it? A horror western? The combination of a supernatural revenge theme and the abandoned Western film sets almost qualify it as such. An Indian curse movie? Well, it's an element, certainly, but it's barely elaborated upon after the prologue. How about a Hollywood melodrama, in the style of *What Ever Happened to Baby Jane?* A prominent strand of the story deals with bitter old Aldo Ray, hanging out with a senile screen actress (Virginia Mayo, Cody Jarrett's lover in *White Heat*), hoping she'll eventually fall in love with him. Or maybe it's an art film about the impossibility of communication? A subplot involving a public payphone being erected in the dust-blown wilds of nowhere is as oblique and puzzlingly abstract as Antonioni. De Gaetano allows the whole thing to hover between all of these ideas without committing to any of them. Who knows what he was trying to say?

Aldo Ray is on top form as the lovelorn brother, who never recovered from the fact that his sibling stole the woman of his

Starring: Aldo Ray · Virginia Mayo · Anne Michelle · Jim Nager

HAUNTED

NOT FOR MINORS OR THOSE OF A NERVOUS DISPOSITION

M VIDEO UNLIMITED MOTION PICTURES

REINCARNATION or MADNESS?

dreams. Since his brother's accidental death, he's hung around, hoping for a place in her beloved's heart, but willing to settle for a place in her bed in the meantime; even if it's clear that she's seeing his brother in her crazy mind's eye. The depiction of 'old Hollywood' in a modern context, and the relationship between fans and old movie stars, brings to mind the films of Curtis Harrington, although *Haunted* lacks the coherence Harrington would have brought to the story.

Cutting across this mournful tale, and ignoring for the moment the supernatural theme, there's another subplot involving two young men, at least one of whom is decidedly ambiguous in his sexuality. He embarks on a gentle relationship with visiting actress Jennifer Baines. During a romantic night in the desert, *apropos* of nothing, she enquires *"Are you gay?" "No, I don't think so,"* he replies. Not the sort of response that closes the matter for good! Again, though, it's a story idea that appears to be heading somewhere interesting, only to evaporate without reaching a destination.

All of these story strands wave loosely around in the breeze for eighty minutes, sharing nothing more substantial than the designated location. And that's a good thing: *Haunted* is a perfect example of the way story values can be mutated by allowing location to determine action. There's no doubt that the opportunity to shoot the film on a derelict Wild West film-set guided the narrative in directions it otherwise would not have gone. By reacting to the mood and detail of a place, scriptwriters can escape the page-bound clichés of the B-movie. It's an approach that unites unsung heroes like Frederick Friedel, and one-hit-wonders like Robert Voskanian and Michael De Gaetano, with the art-house. *Haunted* may not cohere, but it has a unique vibe which feels like blessed relief after the mundane likes of, say, *Blood Mania* or *House of Terror*. Perhaps only an interview with the elusive Mr. De Gaetano would throw light on the puzzling nature of the film, but until such time I'm happy to let sand drift over the questions and just enjoy the uncertainty…

Made in Arizona.

HAUNTS
– Herb Freed (1975)
aka *The Veil*

When a local girl is found raped and murdered, Ingrid Svenson (May Britt), a reserved young woman living on a farm in an isolated rural community, begins to fear for her own safety. One night as she's walking home from choir practice, she's attacked by a masked figure, but struggles free and alerts her Uncle Carl (Cameron Mitchell) and the local sheriff (Aldo Ray). Ingrid suspects Frankie, the butcher's boy (William Gray Espy), and views a new arrival with suspicion too; but when a second corpse is found – this time in Ingrid's chicken-run – her shock, coupled with memories of an unhappy childhood, make it increasingly difficult for her to distinguish real dangers from the phantoms of her own mind…

Haunts has some of the sombre rural destitution of S.F. Brownrigg's *Keep My Grave Open* or Bill Rebane's *The Demons of Ludlow*, although thanks to Freed's steady hand as director it's closer to the former than the latter. The aptly named May Britt makes a brittle, earnest creature of Ingrid, capturing the prim nervousness of a woman who uses religion to keep desire at bay. Reliable turns from Cameron Mitchell and Aldo Ray bolster her in the later stages of the story, involving plot twists best left unexplained. They're not exactly surprises of the first order, but enough said: the film needs them to maintain interest. There's definitely a touch of the Italian *giallo* here, something that Pino Donaggio's stylish score helps to underline. The use of initially opaque flashbacks to childhood trauma; blatant attempts to throw the audience off the scent; doubt about the female lead's sanity; arresting but *non-sequitur* images (such as Ingrid milking blood from a goat's udders); all of these devices echo the Italian murder-mysteries of, say, Sergio

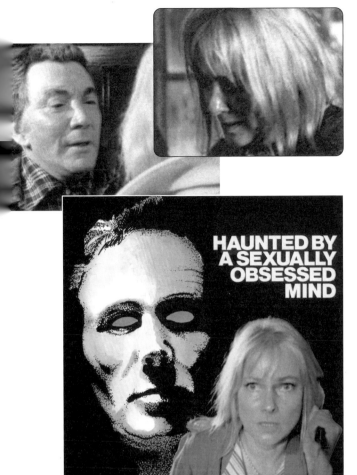

HAUNTED BY A SEXUALLY OBSESSED MIND

HAUNTS

PG

starring MAY BRITT
CAMERON MITCHELL
ALDO RAY

DERANN
VIDEO

Martino or Umberto Lenzi. Then we have a masked killer, several false endings, and the use of scissors to menace the heroine. If the film lacks the erotic fascination with cruelty so essential to the true *giallo*, *Haunts* still has that touch of sadness coalescing around the fate of an unstable heroine that one feels in films like *The Sweet Body of Deborah* or *Paranoia*. A touch of sleaze would have helped clinch the deal, but *Haunts* is nonetheless worth a look for the moody setting and Britt's lead performance.

Made in California.
see also: **Graduation Day**

THE HEADLESS EYES
– Kent Bateman (1971)

A burglar (Bo Brundin) trying to rob an apartment is caught in the act when the tenant awakens. A struggle ensues and the enraged victim turns aggressor, wielding a spoon – yes, a spoon – and gouging the burglar's eye from his socket, like a mollusc from its shell. The unfortunate thief, his eye drooling down his face, crawls from an upstairs window and flees down the fire escape. So begins *The Headless Eyes*: the first and so far premier example of the oft-neglected 'stalk-and-scoop' subgenre. The credit sequence described is so perfect you almost hope the film ends right there. You fear a thoroughly ordinary movie might follow on and spoil it. The cries of the injured thief are priceless in themselves – just a loop of Bo Brundin shrieking *"My eye! My EYE! [undecipherable shrieks] ...My eye!"* as he climbs down the side of a New York slum and skulks off into the night. It's one of the great cheap horror flick beginnings, and yes, it leads into a film just as crazed. The thief – named Mal, although it's easy to miss – has moved on from that humiliating encounter, and now works out his resentment using a sort of mixed-media, sculpture/murder approach, plundering the ocular organs of various, need it be said, unwilling donors to make avant-garde *objets*. His speciality? Eyes suspended in cubes of Perspex. Eat your heart out, Damien Hirst.

Once you're over the initial hilarity, *The Headless Eyes* becomes a bleak and sorry tale with perhaps a smattering of arty ambition (the name of the director's production company, Laviniaque Films, is drawn from Virgil's *The Aeneid*, after all). Although it seems positively zany today, *The Headless Eyes* must have sent a few unwary souls out into the New York dark with an indefinable case of the jitters. It's not a straightforward slasher film (the killer is onscreen from the start) and it's not exactly a gore film (the graphic violence is limited to some red smears and a few fake eyes). As for a thrill-ride, forget it: though not quite plotless, it's certainly getting there, as if narrative too has been scooped out along with the protagonist's orb. No, the essence of the film is a sort of shabby, destitute, gutter-level weirdness: it's the cinematic equivalent of a scary old bag lady.

The emphasis on a grimy street-level reality merges the film with its first intended audience, as Mal stalks his prey past cinemas all too likely to show *The Headless Eyes*. Like William Lustig's *Maniac* and Tim McCoy's supremely nasty *Sex Wish*, inspiration has clearly been drawn from the very stalls and venues in which the film will play – a feedback loop of sleaze. As if mocking the Soho-Boho fantasy of street-level artiness, director Kent Bateman depicts his dropout avant-gardist as merely another damaged sleazo staggering through the 42nd Street slum-pile, no different to piss-soaked tramps and dishevelled druggies limping into cinemas to sleep off their nightmares.

With its focus on a struggling artist in a poverty-stricken urban setting, *The Headless Eyes* resembles Abel Ferrara's *The Driller Killer*, and while the Ferrara film is by far the more ferociously intelligent, they'd still make a great double bill. There are a few quiet scenes that echo the emotional dimension of *The Driller Killer*: a hooker tries to offer Mal sympathy but ends up paying for it with her life; Mal's ex-lover drops in, trying to reach out to him, but is rebuffed by his bitterness; and in another scene we linger on the funeral preparations for a victim whose death we then see in flashback. Sadly, though, Bo Brundin can't match *The Driller Killer* director's ultra-naturalistic lead performance. The Swedish-born Brundin at times reaches silent movie levels of over-emphasis, although if you're in a forgiving mood even this can give the film a whiff of delinquent reality: imagine a real killer agreeing to play himself in a movie, self-servingly trying to convey his 'inner pain' and then overdoing it. Brundin deserves credit for the best moments – heard once, instead of ten times in a tape-loop, his shriek of *"My eye! My EYE! Oh... my eye!"* is as chilling as Tom Towles's agonised, disbelieving screeches for the eye-popping scene in *Henry: Portrait of a Serial Killer*, or Daryl Hannah's in *Kill Bill: Volume 2*.

Haunts
aka **The Veil** (shooting title)
© 1975. Nachson Films.
A production of American General Production Company in association with Entertainment Services International.
director: Herb Freed. executive producer: Norman G. Rudman. producer: Burt Weissbourd. co-producer: Herb Freed. producing associate: Elmer Adams. writers: Anne Marisse & Herb Freed. director of photography: Larry Secrist. music: Pino Donaggio. music arranged & conducted by Nando DeLuca. musical score © Edizionicurci, s.r.l. 1975. song "Father, I Long" by Art Podell & Herb Freed. editor: Richard E.Westover. casting: Anne Marisse. make-up artist & hair design: Jeffrey Angell. locations design: Sheral Hippard & Rosemarie Belden. costume design: Charles Berliner. production manager: Brian Frankish. assistant director: David McGiffert. lighting director: Stephen Slocomb. sound effects editor: John P.Howard Jr. re-recording: Ted Gomillion. gaffer: Jeffrey Briggs. key grip: Gary Cyr. property master: Michael Bossick. location manager & unit manager: Robert Hippard. best boy: Tom Adams. assistant camera: Robert Thomas Mellinger Jr. additional musical effects: Brent L. Lewis. carpenter: C.Allen Tegmeier. painter: Douglas D.Chaney. assistant editors: Franklin D. Cofod, Gregory McClatchy & Brenda Franks. negative cutter: Magic Film Works. recording engineer: Robb Keystone. boom operator: Janusz Cieszkowski. location consultant: Toni Lemos. production co-ordinator: Kathleen Lawrence Gale. production secretary: Carla Jupiter. assistants to the producers: Mark Whalen, Kalika, Linda Girasole & Leslie Tribe. post production: West Ho Films. sound transfer: Magnatronics. sound: Audio Services, Inc. title design: Beau Tekra. with thanks for their cooperation: Tucker Studio Trucking; Leonetti Cine Rentals; Marrero Productions, Inc. titles & opticals: The Optical House. colour: DeLuxe.
Cast: May Britt (Ingrid). Cameron Mitchell (Carl). Aldo Ray (sheriff). William Gray Espy (Frankie). Ben Hammer (vicar). E.J. Andre (Doc). Kendall Jackson (Loretta). Susan Nohr (Nel). Robert Hippard (Bill Spry). Don Dolan (Hellman). Lette Rehnolds (Margaret). Jim McKenny (bartender). Warren Peters (Howard Porter). Judy Franks (Mrs. Peterson). Bob Avery (TV interviewer). Brian Frankish (newscaster). Larry Finnegan (Mr. Lewis). Elmer Adams (Frank Olsen). Norm Rubinfeld, Sandy Rubinfeld, Eddie Rubinfeld & Michele Rubinfeld (Olsen family). Margot Lowell (Brigette). Toni Lemos (Margaret's mother).

opposite page:
From **Haunted**:
Aldo Ray takes out his frustrations; Ann Michelle as the Native American witch Abanaki; The UK video sleeve.

this page, left, from the top:
From **Haunts**:
May Britt; Cameron Mitchell; The UK video cover; A victim of the killer.

below:
"My eye!" – the start of **The Headless Eyes**.

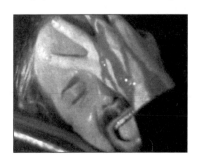

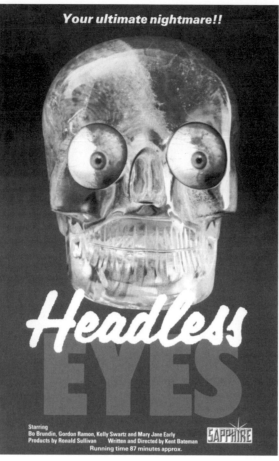

"*We're too hot for his window,*" says a drunken rich-girl to her sugar-daddy, as they slug booze from a bottle and spot Mal lurking in a shop-front display. It's easy to miss the fact that Mal *owns* the store, which makes the scene even stranger. Firstly, the placement of the camera obscures exactly where Mal is. He seems to be outside on the pavement, looking at the couple through a double-sided window display. The illusion is broken when Mal deposits one of his artworks onto a display mount. We see that he's actually *inside*, looking out. Because the director has neglected to introduce Mal as the store-owner, there's a weird shift between inner and outer, suggesting an unstable boundary between the two and thus (if you like) symbolically echoing the piercing of the eye. Mal then follows the couple back to their apartment and gains entrance, killing them both with a hammer, before settling back in a chair to enjoy his latest *tableau-mort*. If nothing else, we see that the petty thief is now an incorrigible aesthete!

Uptight to a fault, though, Mal has problems handling praise. "*I like your work, whoever you are,*" says a pretty girl who enters his shop. Her words send him running out in terror, hallucinating helplessly, through streets of stern, monolithic architecture. A brutalist wedge of corporate art looms over him, mocking the simple compliment he's been paid. Mal is obviously moved by his admirer's words, because the next thing we know he's grave-robbing eyeballs from cadavers, presumably so that he doesn't have to murder anyone else. He's interrupted by a sleazy cop who's pleased as punch, thinking of the acclaim he'll receive for capturing the killer; we therefore feel a twinge of sympathy for Mal as he snivels "*I'm not finished,*" and stabs the greedy pig to death. Abandoning the grave-robbing idea, he chases another victim through a scuzzy market warehouse region at some ungodly hour of the morning. The streets are stained with vile eruptions and discolourations: you can almost smell the stench of putrefying vegetables. The quarry makes a dash for it through a meat refrigeration locker and, lucky for her, Mal manages to screw up, getting himself locked in a freezer. A slew of hectic superimpositions and some out-of-focus camerawork suggest a panicky last-day's shooting, by a director forced to acknowledge that the money has finally run out, and that's your lot…

I'm willing to bet that *The Headless Eyes* was made without a finished script, ending as it does so raggedly without a real conclusion. Nevertheless, it's still a fascinating trip through the slums of exploitation, far away from the gentrified avenues of mainstream horror. It's an absolute must-see if you're interested in the grimier reaches of American horror.

It is sometimes suggested that *The Headless Eyes* was in truth directed by porno producer Henri Pachard, aka Ron Sullivan. This is an interesting hypothesis, but remains unconfirmed. Sullivan is the credited *producer* of *The Headless Eyes*. Kent Bateman certainly exists – he moved to California in 1977, where he notched up his only other confirmed movie directing credit, *Land of No Return* (1977), an entirely ordinary adventure story with Mel Tormé and William Shatner that looks like a trip through the Hollywood Hills, not the scuzzy netherworld of *The Headless Eyes*. He consolidated his journey into the mainstream by creating and directing *Family Ties*, the TV show that launched Michael J. Fox's career, as well as episodes of *Valerie's Family* for Lorimar and *The Hogan Family* for Warner. An early credit has him as production manager on *It's Not My Body* (1970), directed and written by porno filmmaker and writer Ron Wertheim. A project called *The Rogue and Grizzly* (1982/3) was directed by Kent Bateman and Dick Robinson, released on tape by Ranger Rob's Home Video Theater. The cast includes Dick Robinson, Carol Elasz, Don Shanks, and the screenplay is credited to Kent Bateman and James Bryan, although Bryan has no recollection of Bateman's involvement. The presence of Robinson and the mention of James Bryan suggest this was a Utah-based production.

Leading man Bo Brundin was born 25 April, 1937, in Uppsala, Sweden. He later appeared alongside Sean Connery and Henry Fonda in *Meteor* for AIP. Brundin's screams in *The Headless Eyes* prologue can also be heard on the trailer for Doris Wishman's *Another Day, Another Man*. Bateman's daughter is actress Justine, who got her start in her father's sitcom *Family Ties*.

Made in New York City.

THE HEARSE
– George Bowers (1980)

Divorcée Jane Hardy (Trish Van Devere) moves into her deceased aunt's country house after inheriting it in her mother's will. The locals are rude and unhelpful, mainly because the aunt and her lover were said to have worshipped the Devil. Naturally, local children believe the house to be haunted. Estate attorney Walter Pritchard (Joseph Cotten) resents Jane moving in because he feels the house should have been left to him, and the only local handy-man willing to work for Jane is Paul (Perry Lang), a love-struck teenager who forms a potentially troublesome erotic attachment to her. Worst of all, a giant hearse repeatedly tries to ram Jane's car off the road, and glides menacingly up her driveway in the middle of the night. Fortunately, a handsome young man called Tom (David Gautreaux) comes along and sweeps Jane off her feet, although it's strange that he only ever wants to meet her at night…

I enjoyed *The Hearse* immensely, but it's hard to explain why so generic a ghost story should excite me. All of the elements are in place for a by-the-numbers spook-show. We have a divorcée recently recovered from a nervous breakdown, a town full of hostile bumpkins eager to give a city gal a hard time, a suave stranger with something of the night about him, and a spooky old hearse aggressively stalking the heroine down moonlit country roads. Did I mention the diary Jane finds in the attic, explaining her aunt's doomed romance and the devilish death pact into which she had entered? *The Hearse* is stacked to the rear axles with these genre leftovers, right down to windows that fly open of their own volition and a graveside revelation before the finale. So why do I find this Crown International pot-boiler so appealing?

Firstly, Trish Van Devere is touching and sympathetic as the fragile but determined heroine, unwilling to let Joseph Cotten's supercilious estate agent, Med Flory's lascivious sheriff, or sundry surly shopkeepers get her down. Perhaps the script gives her a bit more sex appeal than the average horny teenager would acknowledge (local boys act as if Britney Spears has come to town), but she's brave and witty and deserving of her chance of happiness, and I found myself wishing her well as she embarked upon her blousily Gothic romance with spooky but dishy Tom. I love the main piano theme too, which crops up from time to time throughout; by employing an angular descending motif against a sensuous counter-melody, it dreamily underlines both the romance and the menace of the story. The rest of the soundtrack leans too heavily on a repetitive *Twilight Zone* refrain, but it's serviceable nonetheless.

Perhaps the film's biggest handicap is the lack of a satisfying ending: Jane finds the dead bodies of two supporting characters for no other reason, you suspect, than because the writers needed to erase her doubts and wrap up the narrative. *The Hearse*, like so many ghost stories, never tries to explain how spooks and shades can affect the physical world, ramming cars off the road with

The barrier between Life and Death is no greater than the thickness of a door.

And now... the door is open!

A PINNACLE BOOK ★ $2.25
41-056-5

the HEARSE
by Henry Clement

dented fenders and all. And while some things that befall Jane may be 'all in her mind', the murder of two key characters cannot.

However, the traditional virtues of the ghost story are at least three-quarters present; the hulking 1950s hearse has a satisfying leer to its chrome bumpers, and its scary old driver would not be out of place in one of the BBC's M.R. James adaptations. As in the films of S.F. Brownrigg, the emotional centre of the film concerns the efforts of a single woman to survive various attacks and indignities, while a villainous array of men try to destabilise her. If Brownrigg's films have more integrity, thanks to their powerful rep' performances, unusual plots, and their powerful sense of place, there's still something to be said for a trifle like *The Hearse*.

Trish Van Devere appeared in two ghost stories in 1980, the other being Peter Medak's *The Changeling*. Director George Bowers was best known for directing hit TV series *The Dukes of Hazzard*. After *The Hearse* he made three more films, including *My Tutor* (1983), before settling down as an editor whose career highlights include the brilliantly tense slasher tale *The Stepfather* (1987) and the 'Johnny Depp meets Jack the Ripper' horror-comic *From Hell* (2001).

Made in California.

HITCH HIKE TO HELL
– Irv Berwick (1977)
See interview with Wayne Berwick.

Made in California.

HOMEBODIES
– Larry Yust (1973)

Six elderly tenants – Mr. Crawford (Douglas Fowley), Mr. and Mrs. Loomis (Ian Wolfe and Ruth McDevitt), Mr. Sandy (William Hansen), Miss Emily (Frances Fuller), and Mattie (Paula Trueman) – are threatened with eviction from their old apartment block in Cincinnati. Incensed, they embark on a campaign of sabotage against the nearby building redevelopment which threatens to reduce their district to rubble. Ringleader Mattie persuades the group to go even further, conniving in the death of a relocation worker and murdering a fat-cat property tycoon. As doubts assail the rest of the group, Mattie becomes ever more ruthless, until her fellow tenants must act to save themselves…

I'm not sure if I should be reviewing this. *Homebodies* was picked up for distribution by Avco, and director Larry Yust had previously shot a film for Universal called *Trick Baby*. But it's independently financed, it's a film I adore, and it's rarely mentioned in studies of the genre – perhaps because it lacks the more familiar genre trappings. It is, after all, concerned exclusively with the fortunes of old people; there's not a teenage bimbo or collegiate stud to be seen. If you can get your head around this, however, *Homebodies* is a film of genuine depth and class. There's a bracingly hard edge to the story, and the finale is as complex and morally ambivalent as you could wish. In fact, if you were to recast the film with young radicals and set it during the student riots of 1968, the essential dynamics would cross over quite easily.

The older you are, though, the more the film raises a smirk, as the beloved qualities of older life – peace and quiet, stability of home – are defended with the same zeal that the young bring to their passion for noise and freedom of movement. The first great moment occurs when Mattie witnesses a young man fall to his death from the skyscraper under construction at the end of her street. As his body splats to the ground, the roar and bustle of the building site ceases for the first time in the film, and you see Mattie realise just how useful death can be.

There are flaws here and there, chiefly the depiction of the relocation official, a hard-hearted bitch called Miss Pollack (Linda Marsh), who is scripted with less finesse than the protagonists. Rather like Nurse Ratched in *One Flew Over the Cuckoo's*

Homebodies
© 1973. Cinema Entertainment Corporation
Cinema Entertainment Corporation.
director: Larry Yust. producer: Marshal Backlar. screenplay: Larry Yust, Howard Kaminsky and Bennett Sims. executive producer: James R. Levitt. director of photography: Isidore Mankofsky. music composer & conductor: Bernardo Seg'all. editor: Peter Parasheles. art director: John Retsek. costumer: Lynn Bernay. song, "Sassafras Sundays": music: Bernardo Seg'all, lyrics: Jeremy Kronsberg, sung by Billy Van. key grip: Jack Palinkas. gaffer: Ross Maehl. script continuity: Bonnie Prendergast. camera operator: Frank Raymond. make-up: Louis Lane. sound mixer: Leroy Robbins. special effects: Donald Courtney. set decorator: Raymond Molyneaux. best boy: Jack Flesher. electrician: Calvin Maehl. boom man: Norman Webster. production manager: Carl Olsen. production assistant: Eric Nelson. first assistant cameraman: Roger Smith. sound effects editing: Edit International, Inc. re-recording: Doc Wilkinson. production secretary: Patricia Dalzell. We wish to thank the city of Cincinnati for its cooperation in the making of this film. filmed on location in Cincinnati (Ohio, USA).
Cast: Peter Brocco (Mr. Blakely). Frances Fuller (Miss Emily). William Hansen (Mr. Sandy). Ruth McDevitt (Mrs. Loomis). Paula Trueman (Mattie). Ian Wolfe (Mr. Loomis). Linda Marsh (Miss Pollack). Douglas Fowley (Mr. Crawford). Kenneth Tobey (construction boss). Wesley Lau (construction foreman). Norman Gottschalk (apartment superintendent). Irene Webster (woman in floppy hat). Alma Du Bus (superintendent's wife). Nicholas Lewis (construction worker). SIFT adds John Craig (construction worker). Joe deMeo (construction worker). Michael Johnson (policeman). Eldon Quick (insurance inspector). William Benedict (night watchman).

opposite page, top:
Scenes from **The Headless Eyes**, and the film's peerlessly goofy UK video cover.

opposite page, bottom, clockwise from bottom left:
Trish Van Devere;
Joseph Cotten;
Trish with the hearse;
Dreamboat Tom (David Gautreaux).

this page, left:
The Hearse was novelized by Henry Clement, who also performed the deed on Spielberg's **Sugarland Express** and Cy Endfield's **De Sade**.

below:
Ever wondered about the old woman carrying shopping in **Annie Hall**, who tells Woody Allen, "It's never something you do, that's how people are. Love fades"? She's played by Paula Trueman, and in **Homebodies** we discover she's a septuagenarian murderess…

above:
The elderly decide to 'relocate' their Relocation Officer, in the barbed black comedy **Homebodies**.

right:
Mattie loses sight of the rights and wrongs in **Homebodies**.

below:
The UK video cover.

Cinema Entertainment Corporation presents

Prints by Movielab PG
An Avco Embassy Release

Copyright © 1974 Cinema Entertainment Corporation   LITHO. IN U.S.A. 3 ◎   74/283

Nest, she serves as a sitting target for anger and resentment. Stamping from apartment to apartment issuing eviction decrees, she's rather too easily hateful, when a glimmer of sympathy would have lent the film greater complexity. As it is, we can just about see that she adopts a heartless façade because she's afraid of the burden of caring for people. However, when she fails to persuade the old folks to leave, she falls back on hectoring authoritarian bluster, and we withdraw any shred of sympathy. Her continued heartlessness as she shows four 'old dears' into their drably modern new homes not only fails as characterisation, it also blunts the film's social observation – it would surely have been more cutting if we'd seen a bland public-relations persona come to the fore. Fortunately, the plangent electronic music, ominous bare corridors, and starkly modern rooms take up the slack, giving the old people's home the same necropolitan chill as the apartment block in Cronenberg's *Shivers*.

By making the old folk multiple murderers the film sacrifices credibility as a morality tale, but it gains instead a wit and irony that would perhaps have amused Hitchcock, and should certainly appeal to those who appreciate black comedies such as *Arsenic and Old Lace* and *The Ladykillers*. For instance, when Mattie blithely dumps the corpse of the council worker into the boot of a car parked outside, we think she's crazy – until we realise that stealth is redundant: the entire region is abandoned, awaiting the wrecking ball. Then there's the scene in which Mattie and Mr. Loomis smuggle the corpse of Miss Pollack across town in plain sight, propped up in a wheelchair. It's a beautifully observed piece of slapstick. The elderly criminals have to wheel the dead weight down a steep incline – shots of their frantically racing feet show how close they are to losing control. In fact they *would* have lost control, were it not for the assistance of another group of old-timers who see what's happening and bring the wheelchair to a halt (showing a helpfulness, the film winks, that's more likely from the elderly than the self-obsessed young). Then, as if to counter any suggestion of sanctimony, an interfering old

trout blusters into the situation, wittering *"Perhaps I can help? I like to help people."* Repulsed, Mattie grabs the brim of the woman's hat and yanks it down over her eyes, leaving her squawking in outrage. (There follows an understated moment that really makes use of the premise – after a long walk out of town, Mattie and Loomis finally ditch Miss Pollack's corpse, and Loomis wheels the exhausted Mattie back home in the same wheelchair.)

Yust delays challenging the amorality of his characters, perhaps to give Mrs. Loomis moral authority when she finally confronts her husband about the murders. *"Don't you see, it'll never be the same here after what we've done,"* she says. The characters are motivated by a desire to protect what they have, resisting change as many people do – and yet, by resisting it so passionately and violently, they've irrevocably changed themselves. It's at this point that the elderly's habit of referring to spouses as 'Mother' and 'Father' gains extra irony – when Loomis begs his wife not to go to the police, she assumes maternal authority, and those of the group who remain willing to kill are characterised as children, a perspective lurking behind many exchanges in the script.

If the movie is sometimes a little plain to look at – there's an occasional hint that it might have been conceived as a stage play – there's nevertheless plenty to engage with in this slow-paced but quick-witted drama. For sure, I love the crudity of *The Gore Gore Girls* and the blatant sleaze of *Sex Wish*, but if only more horror films were blessed with the idiosyncrasy of character that Larry Yust brings to *Homebodies*…

Made in Ohio.

THE HORROR STAR
– Norman Thaddeus Vane (1982)
See interview with Norman Thaddeus Vane.

Made in California.

THE HOUSE OF SEVEN CORPSES
– Paul Harrison (1973)
aka *Seven Times Dead* (UK video cover title)

John Ireland plays mean-spirited director Eric Hartman, and Faith Domergue his fading actress-lover Gayle, in this tale of a film crew struggling to shoot a Gothic horror picture in a house where actual murders took place. Glooming around the place like a bad smell is John Carradine, who ought to be enough to give anyone the willies, but despite such bad omens Hartman persists in being a bastard, even after his leading lady's pet cat is found bisected on the lawn. Meanwhile, a minor cast member adds a grimoire's genuine occult incantations into Hartman's script, in the name of authenticity…

What really scuppers *The House of Seven Corpses* is the music. Everything else – the clichéd love/hate romance between director and ageing screen star, the pretentious Hollywoodisms of the supporting cast – could have worked, or at least have been explained away as satire. Sadly, the workaday score flat-lines tension and blurs the potential for irony. This is supposed to be about a 1970s film crew shooting an old-fashioned horror Gothic, but Harrison fails to respond to the challenge, larding the same awful muzak over everything. It's exasperating: how hard can it be to draw a distinction between a modern-day film-shoot and a Gothic period-piece? The whole point is that characters who *think* they're just acting have to deal with a genuine supernatural menace. If the director can't sell the change of emphasis, you may as well pack up and go home. (A similar failure to render two distinct layers of reality afflicts Wes Craven's wannabe-clever *New Nightmare* (1994), for which there really is no excuse!) Crewmembers are murdered while packing away klieg lights and electrical cables, but there's no attempt to give their reality a modern-day inflection. And since the irony of the tale is surely that mediocre actors are being asked to fake terror, it seems a shame if they act just as badly when they're meant to be 'real people'. There is a good idea here, one which could have yielded a *Mask of Satan* redux: imagine a Mario Bava or Terence Fisher surrogate besieged by the very ghouls they've unleashed in the cinema. Instead, Paul Harrison, a TV director who strayed briefly into theatrical releases, stares a gift-horse in the mouth.

Don Jones photographed *The House of Seven Corpses* just after directing *Abducted* (see chapter on Jones). Ron Garcia (*Swingers Massacre*, *The Toy Box*), who also art-directed, appears onscreen in a blink-and-you'll-miss-it cameo as a swiftly-killed period character, in the film's far-too-promising prologue. Actor-director-stuntman Gary Kent was associate producer (see the interview with Kent).

Made in Utah.

HOUSE OF TERROR
– Sergei Goncharoff (1972)
aka *The Five at the Funeral*
aka *Scream Bloody Murder*

A nurse (Jennifer Bishop) hired to look after the disturbed wife of a wealthy businessman (Mitchell Gregg) plots with her boyfriend (Arrell Blanton) to inherit the man's money. When the millionaire's wife commits suicide, the dead woman's identical sister (Jacquelyn Hyde) turns up and latches onto the plan – but who is fooling whom, and who will be the next to die?

A bland title like *House of Terror* virtually begs you to forget it, yet the prologue promises much, an impressionistic charade filmed in a style that recalls the films of Mario Bava (*Hatchet for the Honeymoon* in particular). As soon as the credits are over, though, this misleading signpost leads nowhere but a quagmire of fatuous Dutch angles and TV-movie styling. Actually, I love Dutch angles, fatuous or otherwise. What I hate is mundanity: that dreary brand of drama we get when the director is either unimaginative, or simply bored to tears by a script without a single vivid scene. *House of Terror*'s endless dialogue is shot with a workaday flatfootedness that completely ignores the pre-credits flourish. A nurse and a criminal discuss their tangled lives but it's utterly uninvolving, as they emote in TV movie hell to the tune of the usually reliable Jaime Mendoza-Nava, faking it on their behalf on the soundtrack. *House of Terror* is the sort of movie that can throw you off the scent when it comes to researching a book like this. It's deeply, utterly tedious, like a C-list tele-soap, the derivative of a derivative of *Knott's Landing*. But don't just take my word for it:

The House of Seven Corpses
aka **Seven Times Dead** (UK video cover title)
© 1973. Television Corporation of America Television Corporation of America presents. director: Paul Harrison. producer: Paul Lewis and Paul Harrison. written by Paul Harrison and Thomas J. Kelly. director of photography: Don Jones. editor: Peter Parasheles. music supervision: Synchrofilm, Inc. choral music: Bob Emenegger. executive producer: Dayton A. Smith. associate producers: Gary Kent, Thomas J. Kelly. laboratory: Alexander Film Lab. titles & opticals: Modern Film Effects. equipment: Production Systems, Inc. art director: Ron Garcia. assistant director: Marty Hornstein. sound mixer: Lee Alexander. sound effects editor: Dick Baxter. re-recording: Cine Sound. assistant editor: Mary McGlone. assistant camera: Tom Kantrude. gaffer: Ray Dorn Jr. key grip: Steve Moon. best boy: Joe Dorn. props: John Klotz. script supervisor: Hannah Scheel. make-up: Ron Foreman. wardrobe: Anna Sugand. We gratefully acknowledge the cooperation of The Utah State Historical Society (Salt Lake City) for the use of its facilities in the production of this film. filmed circa November 1972 - three weeks at the Utah State Historical Building in Utah (USA).
Cast: John Ireland (Eric Hartman). Faith Domergue (Gayle). John Carradine (Mr. Price). Carol [Carole] Wells (Anne). Charles Macaulay (Christopher). Jerry Strickler (David). Ron Foreman (Ron). Larry Record (Tommy). Marty Hornstein (Danny). Charles Bail (Jonathan Anthony Beal/ Theodore Beal). Lucy Doheny (Suzanne Beal). Jo Anne Mower (Allison Beal). Ron Garcia (Charles Beal). Jeff Alexander (Russell Beal). Wells Bond (the ghoul).

left:
The House of Seven Corpses was retitled **Seven Times Dead** (on the cover at least) for its second release on UK video.

bottom left:
This artwork for the crude but compelling UK video cover for Video King's release of **House of Terror** is much more fun than the movie.

House of Terror (UK theatrical/video title)
aka **Five at the Funeral** (US theatrical title)
aka **Love Thy Murderer / Scream Bloody Murder** (MPAA titles)
© 1972. Rancho La Paz, Inc.
A Gamalex Associates production. producer/director: Sergei Goncharoff. executive producer: George A. Gade. screenplay: Tony Crechales, E.A. Charles. director of photography: Robert Maxwell. musical director: Jaime Mendoza-Nava. additional source music themes: George A. Gade. film editor: Sergei Goncharoff. art director: Phedon Papamichael. second unit director: John "Bud" Cardos. production manager: Betsy Paullada. assistant director: Frank Bolger. assistant to the executive producer: Mary-Moss Taylor. assistant editor: Hanya Roman. sound editor: Irwin Cadden. production assistants: Tony Crechales, E.A. Charles. make-up: Nora Maxwell. 1st assistant cameraman: Ken Gibbs. 2nd assistant cameraman: Dennis Tyck. gaffer: Skip Karnas. best boy: Vossa Leach grip: Ron Batzdorff. script supervisor: Elizabeth leach. sound mixer: Clark Will. boom man: Chick Bourland. wardrobe: Frances Dennis. "Tell Me More" sung by Kelly Garrett, music and lyrics by George A. Gade.
Cast: Jenifer Bishop (Jenifer Andrews). Arell Blanton (Mark Alden). Mitchell Gregg (Emmett Kramer). Irenee Byatt (Norma). Ernie Charles (lawyer) special guest star Jacquelyn Hyde (Marsha Kramer/Dolores Beaudine).

The House Where Death Lives
aka **Delusion** (US video title)
© 1980. Trauma Associates Ltd.
A John Cofrin production. An Alan Beattie film.
director: Alan Beattie. producers: Alan Beattie,
Peter Shanaberg. story: Alan Beattie, Jack
Viertel. screenplay: Jack Viertel. director of
photography: Stephen Posey. editor: Robert
Leighton. music: Don Peake. associate
producers: David Charles Thomas, Thomas
Viertel. production John Cofrin. casting: Sam
Christensen & Joyce Robinson. art director:
Steven G. Legler. gaffer: Chris Tufty. best boy:
Scott Buttfield. electrician: Michael Garvin. key
grip: Ken Wayne. grip: Robert Fischer. sound
mixer: Mark Harris. boom man: Ken
Beauchene. first assistant camera: Tim
Suhrstedt. second assistant camera: Ayne
Coffey. props: Ivo Cristante. assistant props:
James Gierman. construction: Douglas Dick,
Michael Beltran. first assistant director: David
Blocker. second assistant director: Steve
Jerrom. script supervisor: Anne Warner. stills:
Jennifer Maxon. make up: Pamela Peitzman.
costumes: Ellen Shanahan. production co-
ordinator: Susin Keeler. stuntman: George
Wilbur. prop maker: Tom Shouse. production
assistants: Elizabeth Turnock, Shawn Shea,
Patricia Hall. first assistant editor: Michael
Bloecher. assistant editor: Bill Williams. sound
effects editor: Louis Edelman. re-recording:
Richard Portman, David Horton. electronic
orchestration: Dan Wyman. music recorded at
Sound Arts. music engineering: Jim Cypherd.
[illegible] services: Warren Sound West. title
design: Carol Banever. production equipment:
Selluloid, Inc. caterer: Ellerine Harding.
animals: Frank Inn, Inc. automobiles furnished
by BMW of North America, Mercedes of North
America. furs by Edwards Lowell Fur Originals.
[illegible]: H&R Medical Supplies. Lenses and
Panavision camera by Panavision. location
equipment supplied by Production Systems,
Inc. colour by Metrocolor. titles and optical
effects by Modern Film Effects. re-recorded at
Todd-AO. J.N. Bach Suite [illegible] in C Major,
[illegible] Concerto [illegible] in B Flat Major
courtesy of Musical Heritage Society.
Cast: Patricia Pearcy (Meredith Stone). David
Hayward (Jeffrey Fraser). John Dukakis
(Gabriel). Leon Charles (Phillips). Alice Nunn
(Duffy). Patrick Pankhurst (Wilfred). Joseph
Cotten (Ivar Langrock). Louis Basile. Abraham
Alvarez. Simone Griffeth (Pamela). James
Purcell. Shelby Leverington.

if you search the internet for a synopsis, you'll find that no one
seems to agree about exactly who is employing whom to look after
who; and that's established in the first fifteen minutes! It's no
wonder; I had to trudge through this twice to make the details
stick. To be fair, cinematographer Bob Maxwell tries a few
arresting compositions, and he went on to shoot *The Centerfold
Girls* for John Peyser, an altogether better movie with some
genuine style. On the other hand, he also shot *Blood Mania* and
The Psycho Lover, two excruciatingly dull Robert Vincent O'Neil
movies, both of which lack the same essential spark as this one. If
we're celebrating the weird, unpredictable fringes of American
horror cinema, then *House of Terror* represents the flat, featureless
centre. Technically 'competent' but drainingly uninspired films
like this really are the worst of genre graveyards. I would cling in
eager gratitude to the worst film by Jess Franco in preference.
Polite, made with one eye on a TV sales niche, *House of Terror*
lacks vim, vitality, integrity, or failing all that, sleaziness. Why
Sergei Goncharoff ever thought to make a horror film I have no
idea; he'd have been better off marketing tranquilisers.

Made in: unknown

THE HOUSE WHERE DEATH LIVES
– Alan Beattie (1980)
aka *Delusion*

A young woman, Meredith Stone (Patricia Pearcy), lands a job
as nurse to a wealthy, ailing old man, Ivar Langrock (Joseph
Cotten). Once established, she discovers that Langrock's retarded
son is sequestered in an upstairs room. The old man's ever-present
alcoholic attorney (Leon Charles) and a bustling no-nonsense maid
(Alice Nunn) round out the household. Meredith falls in love with
Langrock's sixteen-year-old grandson, Gabriel (John Dukakis), but
as secrets from both Meredith's and Gabriel's lives are revealed,
murders occur at the house. With so many skeletons dangling in
the Langrocks' closet, who is responsible for the killings?

La-di-da, another day, another 'house of horror'… *The House
Where Death Lives* is well-shot, competently acted, professionally
mounted: so why do I feel like an estate agent trying to sell a
dodgy property? In truth, after twenty minutes of this tedium I was
longing for an Andy Milligan film, or another look at
BoardingHouse. Like a pair of sensible shoes worn to a drag ball,
this under-performs terribly, wandering into the horror genre
without the wit or derring-do to play the game. I'm glad I never
shelled out for this in a theatre; what we have here is another
square pretender, a duller-than-dull housewife's choice that
belongs in the purgatory of afternoon cable-TV, sandwiched

SHE SEDUCES MEN
AND ENJOYS A GOOD KILL!

IF SEX DOESN'T GET YOU,
THE BLOODSHED WILL!!!

The House Where Death Lives

HUMAN EXPERIMENTS

The victims: young female inmates

Linda Haynes
Best Actress

Film Festival of
Science Fiction
and Horror

R

between home makeovers and celebrity gossip features. The cast
features a young John Dukakis, step-son of failed Presidential
candidate Michael Dukakis; a presumably hard-up Joseph Cotten;
and, more notably, Alice Nunn – yes indeed, none other than
'Large Marge' from *Pee-wee's Big Adventure*. She's the highlight.
As for the horror content, well there are a couple of blows to the
head administered by the killer, some glooming around in the
shadows, and that's about your lot.

Beattie's first film was a seventeen-minute short based on an
Ambrose Bierce story, called *The Boarded Window* (1973),
followed by a ten-minute short called *Doubletalk* (1975) for which
he received an Academy Award Nomination in 1976, for Best Live
Action Short Film. He has several credits as an executive producer
for TV through the nineties and beyond.

Made in: unknown

HUMAN EXPERIMENTS
– Gregory Goodell (1979)
aka *Beyond the Gate*

Although the title leads one to expect a sleazefest with
copious torture and nastiness in the style of *Bloodsucking Freaks*
and *The Toolbox Murders*, this is actually a well-acted fair-to-
middling thriller. What do you mean, 'How disappointing'? Rachel
Foster (Linda Haynes) is a toughened pro of the Country-and-
Western circuit, resilient but wary, as befits a woman making her
way in a world populated by the likes of exploitation monster-for-
hire Aldo Ray, here playing a sleazy nightclub owner who puts the
make on her during the film's opening scenes. The tense first act
inflicts a horribly plausible run of bad fortune on the embattled
lead, as she stumbles off the high road into the aftermath of a
family slaying, only to be blamed for the killings herself. Tension
and mood are admirably maintained; Goodell knows how to hold

Human Experiments
© 1979. Pyramid Entertainment
Summer and Edwin Brown present.
director: Gregory Goodell. executive producer: Edwin Scott Brown. associate producer: D.K. Miller. producers: Summer Brown and Gregory Goodell. screenplay: Richard Rothstein. story: Gregory Goodell. director of photography: João Fernandes. music: Marc Bucci. edited: Barbara Pokras and John Gregory. [song] "Hill Country Rain" written by Jerry Jeff Walker, courtesy of Groper Music, Inc. and Free Flow Productions, Ltd. vocals by Linda Handleman, keyboards/synthesizers: Ian Underwood and Michael Lang, woodwinds: David Edwards, flugelhorn: Malcom McNab, trombone: Bruce Fowler. violin: Bobby Bruce. cello: Ray Kelley. bass: Kenneth Wild. guitar: Dennis Budimir, percussion: Jules Greenberg; "Fear No Fear", "Fear No Evil", "I'm Hot" written by Arthur King Williams. production manager: Nicole Scott. assistant directors: Nicole Scott, Jim McCabe. 2nd assistant director: Corky Quakenbush. assistant film editors: Rachel Igel, Bette Cohen. apprentice editors: David Ewing, Mia Goldman. sound effects: J'S Fine Art & Provision Co. sound mixer: Arthur Rochester. boom operator: Don Coufal. re-recording: Samuel Goldwyn Studios. re-recording mixers: Robert Litt, Howard Wollman, Alan Holly. music recording: Gold Star Studios. make-up artist: Alan Friedman. wardrobe supervisor: Julie Dresner. wardrobe assistant: Ivette Silberman. prison uniforms: hamille. production designer: Linda Spheeris. art directors: Todd Hallowell, Kathy Curtis Cahill. script supervisors: Ellen Hibler, P.Tooke. titles & opticals: Pacific Title. special effects: James Dannaldson, Knott Limited, Frank DeMarco. camera operator: Robert Hillman. assistant cameraman: Paul Maibaum. 2nd assistant camera: Phil Sparks. assistant to the producers: Geoffrey Rich. production assistants: Liz Shaner, Rachel Lopez, Mark Goldberg. gaffers: Leroy Heckler, Earl Williman. key grip: Frank Palmer. dolly grip: Patrick Vitolla. best boy: Jerry Posner. electrician: Larry Flynn. grip: Wayne Johnson. set construction: Bill Humphrey & Ken Wolfe. carpenters: Ken Pajor, Rick Bailey. extras casting: Carmen Sarro. dogs: Rick Carlton. video equipment: Metrovonics, Inc. special appreciation: William Alexander, M.D.; Jackie Frame; Douglas Kirkland; David Peoples; Jack and Moira Sher; James Sloyan; Roger Spottiswoode. colour by DeLuxe. filmed in April/May 1978 on location in Newhall.
Cast: Linda Haynes (Rachel Foster). Geoffrey Lewis (Dr. Kline). Ellen Travolta (mover). Aldo Ray (Mat Tibbs). Lurene Tuttle (granny). Mercedes Shirley (Warden Weber). Darlene Craviotto (Rita). Marie O'Henry (Tanya). Wesley Marie Tackitt (Jimmy). Caroline Davies (Pam). Cherie Franklin (cell guard). Jackie Coogan (Sheriff Tibbs). Bobby Porter (Derril Willis). James O'Connell (father). Rebecca Bohanon (mother). Theodora Tate (daughter). Timothy Coyle (son). Roberta Jean Williams (nurse #1). Ruth Stanley (nurse #2). Maryanne Furman-Barrett (Martha). Millicent Crisp (Laura). Ginny Siegel ('pong game' inmate). Jinaki (nursery guard). Joyce Davis Smith (warden's secretary). Arthur King Williams (Lucifer). Mick Walker, Lou Ozonko, Larry Spatz, Steve Halter, Kenny Allen (Arch Angels). Stan Bohrman (judge's voice). Philip Proctor (prosecutor's voice). Sarah Cunningham (loud speaker announcements). Teda Bracci, Gayle Gannes, Laurie Hendricks, Debbie Pierce (inmates).

our attention by feeding us information bit by bit, letting the accumulation draw us in. When Haynes is sent down for the murders, the usual clichés of prison life beckon, but the film plays skilfully inside the formula, with the heroine's gradual collapse under pressure given time to escalate believably. Some films would stampede to the melodramatic end of the scale too soon: Goodell takes his time, letting the drip-drip pressure of prison life and the odious attentions of resident psychiatrist/creep Dr. Kline (Geoffrey Lewis) do their work. By the time Rachel is steered by the mad doctor into crawling through a ventilation shaft seething with creepy-crawlies we accept that she's primed to flip her lid...

Gregory Goodell is the author of *Independent Feature Film Production: A Complete Guide from Concept Through Distribution*, a book first published in 1982. *Human Experiments* was his debut film, after which he moved into television scriptwriting and production, eventually reappearing as a (TV) director in the mid-nineties. The executive producer of *Human Experiments* was Edwin Scott Brown, director of *The Prey*.

Made in: unknown

I DISMEMBER MAMA
– Paul Leder (1972)
aka *Poor Albert & Little Annie*
aka *Crazed*

"What good is breeding if all it results in is a multiplication of worms?" So asks wealthy young fruitloop Albert Robertson (Zooey Hall), before escaping from the low-security mental institution to which his mother (Joanne Moore Jordan) had sent him. Heading for the family home with vengeance in mind, he arrives to find it empty except for the maid, Alice (Marlene Tracy). Demanding to know if she's a virgin, he then rapes and murders her because she says she has a daughter. The daughter, eleven-year-old Annie (Geri Reischl), duly arrives at the door. Albert tells her that Mommy has gone away for a while, and he is to take care of her. The two then embark upon a day of fun and games at the amusement park, with Albert extolling the wonder of Annie's purity and innocence, before the two of them retire to a hotel for the evening. Later that night, with Annie asleep in the bedroom, Albert brings a prostitute (Rosella Olson) back to the hotel and strangles her. Annie wakes up, and discovers the truth about her new friend...

I Dismember Mama was originally called *Poor Albert & Little Annie*, which gives a better *précis* of the film than the more famous and provocative moniker. Matricidal dismemberment is conspicuously off the menu: what we have instead is a character study about Albert, a spoiled rich brat psychopath, and his chaste 'dream date' with Annie, the pre-pubescent daughter of his mother's maid. It's a frequently irritating film though, with music that strips the film of mood, or blaringly overstates the case

(Herschel Burke Gilbert worked primarily on TV shows such as *Gilligan's Island*; and boy does it show). Zooey Hall, a ringer for Richard "The Night Stalker" Ramirez, is perfectly convincing: his intimidation and assault of Alice is genuinely unpleasant and unnerving. But this is another of those psycho horror/thrillers about a nut obsessed with female purity, a psycho character trait I find rather wearing. I usually try to find a point of empathy with the killer in a movie, as long as there's at least some sort of psychological dimension to be considered, but I confess this particular brand of lunatic obsession leaves me feeling distinctly unsympathetic. Marc B. Ray's *Scream Bloody Murder* dresses up the same central character study with enough bizarre excess to get me by, but here the killer's purity fixation is too bald and unadorned for me to get into the picture. Instead I spend the whole film loathing the central character and wishing 'Little Annie' would cut his throat...

Of course the subtext, not so carefully hidden, is paedophilia. Albert never lays a finger on the child, but his obsession with purity and childhood innocence is paedophilia dressed up in denial. His dream date begins with the romantic stand-bys of amusement parks and boating lakes, but a child's day out with an older man doesn't normally end with a night at a hotel. When the unsuspecting Annie falls asleep, Albert grows more and more agitated, staring at her unconscious form and pacing round the hotel suite, trying to deny the contradiction that lies at the heart of his worship of purity: the desire to defile it. Leder's films are all pretty slow, but here, because the central relationship could never be 'consummated' onscreen, the film drags its heels and struggles to maintain tension, ending on a rushed and unsatisfying about-face: Albert realises that Annie has seen him strangling the prostitute, and in a couple of terse lines decides that she's now 'just the same' as other women. Presumably he reaches this

I Dismember Mama (US theatrical title)
aka **Poor Albert & Little Annie**
(US theatrical re-release title)
aka **Crazed** (UK video title)
© 1972. Romal Films
Romal Films presents.
director: Paul Leder. produced by Leon Roth. associate producer: Jack Marshall. screenplay: William Norton. director of photography: William Swenning (Eastman Color / colour by Pacific Film Industries). music composed & conducted by Herschel Burke Gilbert. editor [uncredited]: Paul Leder. camera operator: Mark Rasmussen. lighting: Parker Bartlett. script supervisor: Joseph Bean. assistant editor: Justin DuPont. grips: Terry Meacham, Reuben Leder. sound: Kirk Francis. boom operator: John Westmoreland. theme song "Poor Albert" lyrics by Rocket Roden, music by Herschel Burke Gilbert, sung by Rocket Roden and Wonderclam.
Cast: Zooey Hall (Albert Robertson). Geri Reischl (Annie). Joanne Moore Jordan (Mrs. Robertson). Greg Mullavey (detective). Marlene Tracy (Alice, Annie's mother). Frank Whiteman (Doctor Burton). Elaine Partnow (nurse). Rosella Olson (blonde girl in pool parlor). James Tartan (attendant). Robert Christopher (man in pool parlour).

DON'T OPEN THAT DOOR!

Albert may be there.

Albert hated women...
It started with his mother...
Albert got a knife...
Poor women...
Poor Albert!

ROMAL PRODUCTIONS
presents

Poor Albert
& Little Annie

THESE
WOMEN
TRUSTED
ALBERT...
they
shouldn't
have!

THE NURSE
She deprived him of his
only pleasure.

THE NIGHT LADY
She wanted money —
he wanted love.

THE HOUSEKEEPER
She was dead the min-
ute she opened the door.

ANNIE
The child woman he
wanted to marry, not kill.

starring
ZOOEY HALL as Albert · GERI REISCHL · JOANNE MOORE JORDAN · GREG MULLAVEY
MARLENE TRACY · FRANK WHITEMAN · ELAINE PARTNOW · ROSELLA OLSON
Screenplay by WILLIAM NORTON · Produced by LEON ROTH · Directed by PAUL LEDER
Music Composed & Conducted by HERSCHEL BURKE GILBERT · Produced in Hollywood for EUROPIX Release · COLOR

above:
The US pressbook for **Poor Albert & Little
Annie** (aka **I Dismember Mama**) lays the
character's misogyny on the line.

right: Alice (Marlene Tracy) is raped for being
a mother, by Zooey Hall's nutjob Albert.

opposite page, from top:
The cover of a 'grey-market' release of **Janie**
that may or may not be key artwork;
Ominous hooded figures and Christlike poses
suggest a guilt theme to **The Jar**.

conclusion because, being a self-obsessed egotist, he finds it
impossible to feel guilty for betraying her trust, but the script
refuses to provide the insight so it's really anyone's guess.

The writer is William Norton, who worked with Leder on a
few early John Hayes movies (*The Grass Eater*, *Five Minutes to
Love* and *The Farmer's Other Daughter*) at the start of his career.
Here, unlike the excellent *Five Minutes to Love* for instance,
Norton seems to have given little thought to the overall structure,
with three completely ineffectual and superfluous characters taking
up far too much screen time. Dr. Burton (Frank Whiteman) and the
detective (Greg Mullavey, star of the superior Leder outing *My
Friends Need Killing*) could be removed from the story and no one
would miss them, while Albert's mother is just a criminal waste of
dramatic potential. The actress is more than capable of elevating
the material (she appeared in Cassavetes's *A Woman Under the
Influence* a couple of years later), and any good dramatist would
surely want to bring mother and son together for the *denouement*;
but for some reason Norton misses the trick. I suspect his heart
simply wasn't in the movie.

Thanks to its great 42nd Street hype of a title, *I Dismember
Mama* became perhaps Leder's most talked-about film, which is
a shame because it showcases little of value about him. The only
person to come out with any distinction here is Zooey Hall (fresh
from a star turn in *Fortune and Men's Eyes*), who makes the most
of his role and gives the deeply unpleasant Albert detail and
plausibility.

Made in California.
see also: **My Friends Need Killing** and **Sketches of a Strangler**

I DRINK YOUR BLOOD
– David Durston (1971)
See interview with David Durston and Bhaskar.
Made in New York State.

JANIE
– Jack Bravman (1970)

Janie (Mary Jane Carpenter) skips school and decides to liven
up her daily routine with a few murders. First she talks a school
friend, Carol, into having sex with a man who gives them a lift. She
watches for a while as they make out on the grass, then drives the
car over them. After masturbating in the back seat, she drives
through a posh part of town and decides to go for a swim, choosing
a private pool at random. The owner ('Richard Jennings' aka *Snuff*
director Michael Findlay) comes out to investigate. Janie lures him
onto his private jetty, before stabbing him to death and chucking his
corpse in the water. Driving off again, she runs out of gas, and so
hitches a ride with a middle-aged woman who invites her back to
her apartment, and loses no time coming on to her. Janie flirts
awhile, takes a bath, then straddles her host naked on the bed and
slashes her to death with a razor. She returns home just in time to
see her stepfather killing her mother. Amused, she skips off without
interrupting. In the mood for love, she phones her father and
arranges to visit for a nice relaxing bout of incest. When she arrives
Daddy's still not back, and his lover Roberta (Roberta Findlay) is
also waiting. Janie strangles her, dumping the body in the bathtub.
Daddy returns, and father and daughter take to bed. Janie tells him
all about her escapades (a conversation that has been dotted in
flash-forward throughout the film so far). Daddy thinks Janie's
making it up, until he goes to the bathroom… Cue anger! Shouting!
Slaps! Janie-in-a-psychiatric-cell! The End!

It sounds so fabulous, right? A day in the life of an amoral
homicidal teenage girl: bored, vicious, contemptuous of her peers,
scornfully aware that her body turns men and women into slaves.
This cynical 'heroine' is matched all the way by an equally cynical
'plot' which strings together a succession of sex scenes, each
culminating in murder. With murky 16mm photography shot in
woodland and suburban locations, shakily handheld by Anna Riva
(aka Roberta Findlay), *Janie* looks for all the world like a home

movie made by Sadie from *The Last House on the Left.* So, a classic of seventies sleaze? Almost... except that director Jack Bravman pads the film mercilessly with multiple recaps of what's gone before, extending the aftermath of each murder with umpteen repetitive flashbacks. *Janie* is already short, around sixty five minutes, but if you remove the flashback montages I doubt it would scrape to forty. That's room for another two motiveless murders! It's the soundtrack though that really messes things up. Basically a sixty minute jam by a noodlesome acid-rock group called 'The Fear', it plays continuously throughout the film, seemingly unedited, veering from pedestrian riffing to increasingly tiresome 'freak-outs'. 'The Fear' drizzle their racket all over the film from start to finish; it's possibly the most obtuse and unsophisticated use of film music I've ever heard. Ten minutes would have been a trial, sixty is just a bummer. Imagine the Jimi Hendrix Experience reconfigured as a thumbsy instrumental outfit by three talentless hippies, given vast amounts of dope and then told they're fantastic. Relatively minor problems, like lead actress Mary Jane Carpenter looking closer to thirty than the required sixteen, pale into insignificance. Janie's omnipresent voice-over expressing her schizoid dissociation and contempt for others goes on a bit too, although we're used to such money-saving contrivances in ultra-low-budget filmmaking (see Wishman, Doris). But it's come to something when you can watch a film like this and say you wish it had been directed by Roberta Findlay...

Made in New York State.

THE JAR
– Bruce Toscano (1985)
aka *Charon* (US copyright database title)

Paul (Gary Wallace), a lonely businessman-bachelor driving late at night, is involved in a collision with another vehicle. When he pulls over and rescues the driver, an old man (Les Miller), all the stranger cares about is retrieving a large jar from the back seat. Paul drives home, taking the old man with him, but once there the old man disappears, leaving only the jar – which contains a pickled mutant foetus. Almost immediately, strange things happen. Paul experiences hallucinations and bad dreams, and comes to believe that his lonely existence has been invaded by a malevolent supernatural force...

The Jar is a real oddity, leaning so heavily on looming symbolism that the paper-thin plot plays second fiddle to whatever else was troubling writer George Bradley and director Bruce Toscano. While it's usually inadvisable to attempt amateur psycho-analysis without reference to at least an interview with the filmmaker, *The Jar* seems positively to demand exegesis on the psychological level. So, with the necessary interpretative caveats in place (i.e. I'm guessing), here's what I saw in *The Jar*...

Paul's slightly effete manner and the constant positioning of him as victim, frequently nude or semi-nude, suggests the possibility of a gay reading. (Plus there's something about the way Wallace wears a pair of jeans that just screams 'metropolitan homo'!) The actor's hesitant, resolutely un-macho screen presence, and the character's status as a single man prone to visions of quasi-sexual victimisation, suggest a story about someone struggling with a closeted sexuality. However, given that the film's only other key character, Crystal (Karen Sjoberg), is set up as a possible love interest, it's hard to tell where Paul's sexual confusion ends and the writer's begins.

The recurrent symbolism of the jar and its silent, malevolent occupant points towards a species of guilt gnawing away at the character. Could Paul be guilty that he's not contributing to the continuance of the species? Or else 'The Jar' could represent the closet itself, with a deformed creature trapped within, silently reproaching the dreamer/protagonist. *"I'm not going to let you keep haunting me. I'm not going to let you tear me apart. Get out! Get out!"* Paul screams. The twisted denial implicit here suggests that the very symbol of the character's self-repression is blamed for the repression itself, with truth/self-knowledge blamed for threatening the success of repression. *"You have taken everything away from*

me, and left me alone," Paul accuses, which sounds like the plaint of an unhappy gay man attacking his own orientation. Of course, if this reading is correct it's Paul's guilt, not his sexuality, that condemns him to loneliness, because he fears to share what he feels he should not be.

Paul's dreams and hallucinations are populated by a number of characters. But who are they? The first we see is a boy rising up from a bath full of blood. Then there's the street-kid (Dean Schlaepfer), sometimes broodingly aggressive, sometimes tear-stained, who turns up in a scene where Paul dreams the two of them are standing together on a ledge of a high rooftop. The solipsistic/narcissistic quality of the film suggests that both of these figures are younger versions of Paul, although the latter, with his hustlerish appearance, could also be an illicit object of desire. Paul also dreams of a little girl who lets go of the string of her balloon (like a spermatozoa?) and then reaches out to hold his hand. Perhaps she represents the daughter he'll never have? Who knows? *"Maybe you want to know too much,"* Paul chides, when Crystal persists in asking questions. He drifts off when she blathers about the merits of psychology – the soundtrack fills up with a metallic roaring sound, blocking out what she's saying. Whatever else is going on, this is *definitely* a film about repression!

As for the old man, his status, real or imaginary, remains uncertain. It's tempting to read the car-crash between Paul and the old man in simple Freudian terms as a homosexual encounter, but since no one else ever sees the man, and Paul never shows anyone the jar and its occupant, he could be yet another symbolic reproach; an accusing father, perhaps. In the film's final scenes, Paul seeks comfort from Crystal, daydreaming about the two of them making passionate love together. However, when she answers the door and they embrace, she turns into the old man, an inevitable development that makes it all the more likely that the nature of Paul's problem is suppression of sexual orientation.

An ill-matched lurch into action-adventure in the last fifteen minutes suggests two different production periods spliced, unsuccessfully, together. Perhaps finishing money was only available on condition that the narrative be opened out, at whatever cost to plausibility. Bruce Toscano's strange little film deserves credit for its unusual approach and concept, and if I were you I'd give it a look if you see it around. I hesitate to make comparisons between *The Jar* and *Eraserhead*, as they would set up unrealistically high expectations, but I wouldn't be surprised if Lynch's film was uppermost in Toscano's mind – he certainly prioritises the unstable reality of his central character to a similarly solipsistic degree. It would be interesting to know what Toscano did next: *The Jar*, shot in Denver, appears to have been his only film, but there's enough going on here to suggest that a second Toscano film would have been of real interest.

Made in Colorado.

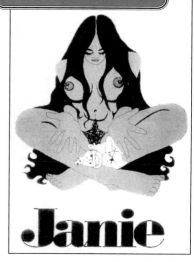

Janie
© none [1970]
Janie Film Company presents.
producer / director: Jack Bravman. screenplay: James Foley. music: The Fear. effects: Phil Savath. sound by John Amero, George Howard. director of photography and camera: Anna Riva [Roberta Findlay]. art director: Jean Paiva.
Cast: Mary Jane Carpenter (Janie). Peer St. Jean. Tina Kraskow [Tina Grasco]. Richard Jennings [Michael Findlay]. William Savage. Berta Molke. Ella Greenberg. William Dunnett. Paul Green. uncredited: Roberta Findlay.

The Jar
© 1985. Nocturna International Limited
A Nocturna International Limited production.
director: Bruce Toscano. assistant director: Marta Simons. writer: George Bradley. music composed and performed by Obscure Nights. production manager: Charles Macleod. production designer: CBM Design Associates. gaffer: Cameron Macleod, Craig Cline, Janet H. Clark. assistant camera: Gary Reed, Craig Baker. editor: Bruce Toscano. key grip: James D. Brown. best boy: Robert Allan. sound recordist: Ron Cramer. assistant sound recordist: John Eidsmore [approx: illegible]. makeup Carol A. VanNatta, Michael Ford. special physical effects: Jeffery Poole, Alan Peacock. production assistant: Daniel Madsen. re-recording: American Recording Studios. music recording: FTM. music engineer/mixer: Steve Avedis. special visual effects and Techniscope conversion [approx: illegible]: Cinema Research Corporation. optical consultant: Sam Bush. film laboratory/colour: Western Cine. negative cutting: Carl N. Hunsaker, Ltd. post production sound engineering: David Emrich. camera equipment: Hill Production Services. support equipment: Film/Video Equipment Service Company. helicopter services: Hoffman Pilot Center. The Producers wish to acknowledge the assistance and cooperation of the following organisations and individuals for their support on the production of this motion picture: Colorado State Film Commission; Colorado State Parks and Recreation; City and County of Denver; Downtown Denver, Inc.; City of Littleton; Bratskellar Bar and Restaurant; Christ The Savior Lutheran Church; Port of Denver Seafood; Jack C. Oakes; Freund Investments; Denver Executive Suites; Sandy Murray; Dwight Ryder; Barbara Macleod; Anthony Toscano; Yukon King. filmed in Todd-AO35.
Cast: Gary Wallace (Paul). Karen Sjoberg (Crystal). Les Miller (old man). Dean Schlaepfer (young man). Robert Gerald Witt (Jack). Don Donovan (jester). Torin Jackson (boy). Robert Cameron Arnold (spectre). Michael Ford (street preacher). Patrick John [illegible] (soldier #1). Vernon Moody, Jr. (waiter). Jose Moreno (butcher). Lowell Noel (bartender). Brent Varner (river man). Paul Jeremy Weissman (road child). Carolyn Murch (bag lady). Lisa [illegible] (playground child #1). Donald Turner (playground child #2). Jeff Greenstein (playground child #3). Christopher Papish (playground child #4). Casey Rountree (playground child #5). Danny [illegible] (playground child #6). Scott Anderson (soldier). Mark Lyon Finley (soldier). Bruce Godsman (soldier). Mike Goodman (soldier). Miles Hames (soldier). Philip Haynes (soldier). Patrick King (soldier). John Knox (soldier). John Marquez (soldier). Kevin Monk (soldier). Duncan Osborne (soldier). Paul Powell (soldier). John [illegible] (soldier). Joe Utsher (soldier). Robert Willocks (soldier).

right:
The Intervision release of **The Jekyll and Hyde Portfolio**, one of the world's rarest videos, and the closest thing to an Andy Milligan film made by a heterosexual…

HORROR–COLOUR
A-AE 0434

THE JEKYLL AND HYDE PORTFOLIO
– Eric Jeffrey Haims (1971)
aka *Jekyll and Hyde Unleashed*

Haims already had form in the medical-horror category, thanks to a porno mind-control effort called *The Sex Machine* (1971). However, it's a wonder he wasn't struck off the directors' register after *The Jekyll and Hyde Portfolio*, a clumsy but often hilarious confection perhaps best appreciated by Andy Milligan fans, thanks to a superficial resemblance to Milligan's work. A period setting, creaky stock music cues, a deformed retarded servant and grainy, blown-up 16mm photography may have you thinking this is an undiscovered epic by the Staten Island maestro, although the absence of Milligan's wall-to-wall dialogue or his thematic obsession with family corruption eventually compromise the illusion. The opening scene, in which a girl on a swing is impaled by a pitchfork, is a haphazardly edited mishmash straight out of *The Ghastly Ones*, but the giveaway is Haims's use of slow-motion, a celluloid-hungry technique the cash-strapped Milligan would never have countenanced!

And so follows a lethargic combo of sex, violence and costume drama, as police investigate the turn-of-the-century Florence Nightingale Institute, where the staff and students – who seem to divide their free time between making-out and staging theatrical adaptations – are being knocked off faster than the lab specimens they ceaselessly carve. Haims delights in showing his actors poke around in the innards of freshly dissected frogs, his camera gawping enthusiastically – rather as René Cardona revelled in gory heart operations in *Night of the Bloody Apes*. This is horror as might be conceived by a twelve-year-old boy, and while the moderately explicit sex scenes would prevent that age group from seeing the film, the overall tone is defiantly immature.

Perhaps to counteract the childishness with a hint of sophistication, there's a self-conscious campiness to some of the dialogue, and the lesbian drooling of the head nurse has a certain broad-brush comedy, but, as failed camp is one of the cinema's least appetising dishes, they'd have been better off playing it straight. Elsewhere Haims tries to mimic the dated conventions of the period-horror setting, a brave move on what looks like a $10,000 budget. Sadly the Gothic approach fails because of the less than stellar actors, who were presumably cast more for their willingness to bare their snatches than for their 'stylized' line-readings. No wonder they're adrift though: Haims has a detective talk directly to camera (a flagrantly modern device), while random electronic squeals on the soundtrack demonstrate a cavalier disregard for period ambience that Jess Franco would admire. As for literacy, a voice-over at the beginning tells you all you need to know: *"Strange tales of evil men and women, monsters some call them, have invaded the minds and imaginations of the superstitious and the curious for centuries and centuries. Such a human monster was the one to whom many have labelled the most sadistic and evil of them all: Dr. Jekyll and Mr. Hyde, a name that conjures up an immediate spectre of corruption, lust and evil. Infamous names that come immediately to mind are those of Jack the Ripper, the Borgias, Bluebeard, Rasputin, the mad monk, the Marquis de Sade, Lizzie Borden, and many others."*

Made in: unknown

KISS OF THE TARANTULA
– Chris Munger (1975)
aka *Shudder*

Young Susan Bradley (Rebecca Eddins and Susan Eddins), loves spiders. She lives with her kindly mortician father John (Herman Wallner) and mean mother Martha (Beverly Eddins) at a big old funeral home. Martha hates John (*"Don't touch me, you smell of chemicals and death!"*); she also hates Susan, and she loathes Susan's little spider friends. The only thing Martha cares about is John's money, and she's prepared to seduce her husband's brother Walter (Eric Mason) to get it. Together, the two of them plot to murder John, but Susan overhears and releases a tarantula into Martha's bed. Martha dies of a heart attack…

Years later, Susan (Suzanne Ling) is still not happy. Shunned by her high school peers, and plagued by amorous innuendos from Uncle Walter, she has retreated into a fantasy world where her pet spiders are her only friends. One Halloween night, a gang of boys break in, intending to steal a coffin. They force their way into Susan's basement and crush one of her tarantulas. Later that night she follows them to a drive-in movie show, intending to scare them by releasing spiders into their car. Instead, she accidentally causes their deaths: in the panic, a window is broken and one victim bleeds to death. Another has his neck broken as his friend crushes his windpipe against the steering wheel. The only survivor is Joan (Rita French), and she's driven insane.

Nancy (Patricia Landon) suspects that Susan is responsible after overhearing her apologise to the comatose Joan. She tells her boyfriend Bo (Jay Scott Neal), the only member of the gang who wasn't at the drive-in that night. Bo seduces Susan then turns nasty, demanding to know the truth about the deaths. Betrayed and angry, Susan sets her spiders on Bo, who dies in terror. Can Susan keep getting away with murder?

Kiss of the Tarantula is great fun, but there are quite a few problems: Suzanna Ling, who resembles a cross between Marilyn Burns and Diane Keaton, is too beautiful to convince as a wallflower and high school reject, and if she loves spiders, why is she willing to put them in confined spaces (a car, a heating duct), with people who are obviously going to thrash around and squash them? (Not that the spiders get squashed for real, you'll be glad to know). Susan is contrite about the fate of the girls in the car, but what did she expect – that they would *dig* having tarantulas crawling over them? Susan is presumably shunned at school because of her father's occupation, but this is never even mentioned by her peers. Walter clearly hates his brother John, but why? What is it that makes Susan feel so close to spiders? The only indication is a scene where her mother sees her playing with one and squashes it, saying it's disgusting. Surely there's more to her love than childish rebellion?

So, if the story is so poorly developed, and the motivations implausible, what is there to enjoy? For me at least, quite a lot: *Kiss*

SO SILENT SO DEADLY SO FINAL

KISS OF THE TARANTULA

of the Tarantula has a morbid setting (much of the action takes pace in and around a marvellously Gothic funeral home, set alone in wintry woods redolent of Lucio Fulci's *The House by the Cemetery*); the girl-and-her-spiders concept is so weirdly charming it can survive the glaring inconsistencies; and the death scenes, though slightly silly, are actually quite bizarre and memorable. I enjoyed this movie in the cinema back in 1982, and the DVD, which restores the clarity of the photography, has sealed the deal. The naive electronic score by Phillan Bishop, who also provided music for Willard Huyck's *Messiah of Evil* and Thomas Alderman's *The Severed Arm*, is disarmingly cheesy and Moogalicious, and there is one great sequence that deserves to be singled out, in which Susan pushes her amorous uncle down the stairs and paralyses him, before dragging him off to the funeral parlour and sealing him in a coffin. The process is shown in fascinating detail, as Susan utilises a mechanical corpse-hoist to finish the job – so if, like me, you enjoyed *Phantasm* and *Phantasm 2*, you'll probably get a kick from all this monkeying about in the morgue.

Kiss of the Tarantula (or *Shudder* as it was called on its UK release) has been dismissed or ignored in most retrospectives of the genre, perhaps because its forlorn quality is not quite pulpish enough. In this it shares a gene with the films of John Hayes, whose erstwhile partner Daniel Cady produced it, and long-time friend Henning Schellerup (*Mama's Dirty Girls*) shot it. There's a sort of Hayesian grimness to the *mise en scène*, while the theme of a disturbed young woman seeking peace and happiness with her father should also ring a few bells for fans of Hayes's *Dream No Evil*. Munger's first film was *California – The Year of the Commune* aka *The Good Life* (1969), followed by *Black Gauntlet* (1974), in-between which he worked as camera operator and associate producer on James Bryan's *Escape to Passion* (1970 – see chapter on Bryan), but sadly it seems he never directed again after *Kiss of the Tarantula*. Features aside, however, Munger continued to work in film. The noted human rights campaigner Dr. Gregory Stanton, wrote: *"Chris Munger, a professional filmmaker, accompanied me on one of my trips in the summer of 1986, and his steady hand on the video camera produced tapes that I hope will someday be made into a documentary film about the Cambodian genocide. The Cambodian Genocide Project won a grant from the United States Institute of Peace to produce a rough cut of a film, but we have never secured adequate funding to complete the film. I have turned over all the videotape to the Cambodian Genocide Program at Yale, and also have originals, so I still hope a documentary filmmaker will be able to use the witness testimony we collected."* [see http://www.genocidewatch.org/the%20Call.htm]

Made in California.

THE LAST HOUSE ON DEAD END STREET
– Victor Janos [Roger Watkins] (1973 [released 1977])
aka *The Fun House*
aka *The Cuckoo Clocks of Hell*

The Last House on Dead End Street is as far removed from the majority of the films reviewed here as Saturn is from the Earth. It's a ferocious, cynical, misanthropic exercise in brutality that nevertheless has a rapier intelligence, making it a far more dangerous psychic experience than your standard blood-and-gore epic. For years known only through a few appalling, virtually unwatchable bootleg videocassettes circulating among the more jaded and obsessive horror fans, it finally emerged on DVD in 2002, in a deluxe edition that brings it as close to visual and auditory clarity as humanly possible, given the rarity of materials and the technical limitations of the original.

Terry Hawkins (Roger Watkins), a filmmaker sick of producing standard porno for his asshole producer, decides to make a snuff film. Assembling a crew of sociopathic associates, and choosing as his location a mouldering, empty house with an overwrought Gothic façade and room after room of bare-walled decay, Terry invites his 'cast' to join the party. Once assembled, these individuals – all of whom have pissed Terry off in some way – are informed of his malevolent intentions. Understandably disinclined to play along, the victims are chased, confined, beaten, mentally assaulted and physically tortured, all the while being subjected to a verbal barrage of contempt from the director. It's no spoiler if I tell you that they don't live happily ever after; I'm merely directing your attention to the film's title, which for once has a clear and direct relevance to events. (Ironically, the title was concocted by a subsequent distributor, replacing the blackly comic original, *The Cuckoo Clocks of Hell*, which Watkins apparently chose from a story by Kurt Vonnegut called *Mother Night*.)

For lovers of cinema extremes, *The Last House on Dead End Street* is the real deal. Everything about it gives off a forbidding, hostile vibe, a malignant radiation that sends your toxicity meter

The Last House on Dead End Street
aka **The Cuckoo Clocks of Hell** (original title)
aka **The Fun House**
© 1977 [filmed in 1973]. Today Productions, Inc. [DVD release ©2001. Roger Watkins]. Today Productions Inc. presents.
director: Victor Janos [Roger Watkins]. producer: Norman F. Kaiser. writer: Brian Laurence [Roger Watkins]. musical supervision: Claude Armand [James Flamberg & Roger Watkins]. director of photography: Alexander Tarsk [Roger Watkins]. art director: Olivia Carnegie [Roger Watkins]. set designer: Gabor Lazlos. make up & special effects: Kevin Heatley. unit manager: Eric Loude. film editor: Brian Newett [Roger Watkins]. sound engineer: Allan Courtney. technical director: Kevin Whitcomb. *Cast:* Steven Morrison [Roger Watkins] (Terry Hawkins). Dennis Crawford [Ken Fisher] (Ken Hardy). Lawrence Bornman [Bill Schlageter] (Bill Drexel). Janet Sorley [Kathy Curtin] (Kathy Hughes). Elaine Norcross [Pat Canestro] (Patricia Kuhn). Alex Kregar [Steve Sweet] (Steve Randall). Franklin Statz [Edward E. Pixley] (Jim Palmer). Barbara Amunsen [Nancy Vrooman] (Nancy Palmer). Geraldine Saunders [Suzie Neumeyer] (Suzie Knowles). Paul Phillips [Paul M. Jensen] (blind man). Ronald Cooper [Ken Rouse] (the whipper). Alan Cooper (young boy). Howard Neilsen (man on couch). Doreen Ellis (woman on couch). Helene Roberts (laughing girl #1). Nora Tucker (laughing girl #2).

top left:
Can spiders kiss? Find out in
Kiss of the Taranatula...

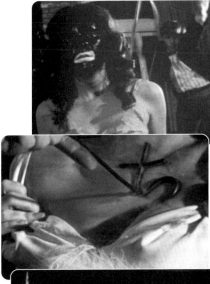

BLOOD-CURDLING TERROR YOU'LL NEVER, EVER FORGET!

A Gothic tale of a house that turned fun and games into an orgy of agony and death!

THE FUN HOUSE
...it will scare you to death!!!

L B S PRODUCTIONS, INC. presents 'THE FUN HOUSE' starring STEVEN MORRISON, DENNIS CRAWFORD, LAWRENCE BORNMAN, JANET SORLEY, PAUL PHILLIPS, ELAINE NORCROSS, ALEX KREGAR, FRANKLIN STATZ, BARBARA AMUNSEN, GERALDINE SANDERS Musical Supervision CLAUDE ARMAND
Written by BRIAN LAWRENCE Produced by NORMAN F. KAISER
Directed by VICTOR JANOS
R RESTRICTED   COLOR

above:
Humiliation, mutilation and obfuscation: three skills essential for torture, in **The Last House on Dead End Street**.

left:
The Last House on Dead End Street really did play as **The Fun House** for a while...

IT'S BACK! THE EVIL THAT HAD YOU SCREAMING...
IT'S ONLY A MOVIE!

LAST HOUSE ON DEAD END STREET

A Production Concepts Ltd. Presentation • A CINEMATIC RELEASE Starring
STEVEN MORRISON • DENNIS CRAWFORD • LAWRENCE BORNMAN • JANET SORLEY • PAUL PHILLIPS
ELAINE NORCROSS • ALEX KREGAR • FRANKLIN STATZ • BARBARA AMUNSEN • GERALDINE SANDERS
Musical Supervision CLAUDE ARMAND • Written by BRIAN LAWRENCE • Produced by NORMAN F. KAISER
Directed by VICTOR JANOS • COLOR   R RESTRICTED ::

above:
This poster art makes the film look scary enough, but it fails to even hint at the nightmare depths of **The Last House on Dead End Street**...

haywire. Of course, the synopsis I've given could yield a far more conventional film. What gives it unique status is the aura of pure hate that oozes from every pore of the project. I can think of no other feature film that so relentlessly portrays such aggressive loathing. You have to look to music for a parallel: there's a proto-punk sensibility there, well ahead of the curve in 1973. Although the Sex Pistols were musically banal, Johnny Rotten was the first 'rock star' to achieve mainstream notoriety entirely on the basis of an attitude of negation, hostility and scorn. Before that, such feelings would only occasionally find expression, in, say, the early albums of Frank Zappa and The Mothers of Invention, or the occasional garage-punk single from the sixties ('No Escape' by The Seeds, '96 Tears' by ? and the Mysterians, 'Shut Up' by The Monks). But Zappa used humour too, and his attitude encompassed a scatological bad-boy pose that may have been hysterically funny to stoned students but never did anything for

me. *The Last House on Dead End Street* has humour alright, moments where you laugh out loud; but it's the laughter of cruelty, and you need to be in that frame of mind to indulge in it.

When Watkins was eventually interviewed by British writer David Kerekes, it came as no surprise to me to read that the director had been high on amphetamine when the film was made. I first encountered *The Last House on Dead End Street* in just such a state, with two fellow speed-freaks, Chris Barber and Grant Pettit (see *The Eyeball Compendium*). It was the late 1980s, a time when we would seek out the most OTT movies to feed our own amphetamine psychosis. We'd been up three nights and days and were entering the fourth, eighty-four-hours of wakefulness sustained by regular intravenous refuelling: a perfect audience for the film's icy, arty antagonism. Speed shuts down your tender feelings, wires you to the harder, colder side of your personality, and when taken for long periods of time fosters a powerful sense of social disconnection. Factor in the hallucinatory state that occurs when you deprive yourself of sleep for such a long time, and it's easy to see how a film like *The Last House on Dead End Street* can speak to your condition like some bubbling vileness from within. The atrocious video copy actively encouraged hallucination, but beneath the fuzzy colour and distorted sound, the movie itself was seething with a deeply weird and nasty energy. The film played with masks at all levels, with shifting identities and ritualistic menace, its cold, echoey voice-over telling the entire story from the point of view of the psychopaths, and the going-for-broke brutality bringing the worst of all possible worlds down on the victims. Here, at last, was a film that succeeded in fingering your every cruel and callous wish for the genre; it didn't falter dramatically, it didn't screw up with trite dialogue, it didn't let itself down with corny music. The overall vibe ricocheted between arty and primitive, and when it came down to the wire, the wire was barbed; red in tooth and claw. It had a *really bad attitude*, not the sort that can be mass-marketed. It felt like outsider art: deranged, unschooled, but full of imaginative detail, and totally idiosyncratic.

Roger Watkins (we can dispense with the 'Victor Janos' pseudonym) not only directs but also plays the lead role, and his portrayal of vicious, contemptuous Terry Hawkins is electrifying. Although at the time I didn't know for a fact that the star was also the director, I never had any real doubt. For a maniacal performer in such an intensely idiosyncratic film to attack another actor in a frenzy, while shouting, *"I'M the director of this fucking movie!"* was just too provocative an image: you believed it came from the heart! Watkins missed his calling as an actor subsequent to this, which is a shame but perhaps understandable. He's a powerhouse performer who would likely have been too hot to handle for anyone else. It would have taken a very strong character, a Herzog to his Kinski, to utilize that energy.

The score is evil psychedelia, assembled from what one suspects were snatches of choral and classical music shoved through a variety of grungy, primitive effects-pedals. It invokes a truly malevolent surrealism, which – far from creating whimsical or wonderful effects – feels like the authentic product of a disturbed mind. What gives the film that extra chill is not that you somehow believe you're seeing 'a real snuff film'; it's just that you believe that the bad attitude required to do such a thing has been authentically summoned in the film. John Waters, whose early films expressed similar feelings at times, once lectured to a class at the Baltimore State Penitentiary, and implored the assembled rapists and murderers, "Next time you want to kill someone, don't *do* it; write it, draw it, paint it; because these films I make are my crimes, only I get paid for them." I guess we should hope that Watkins feels the same.

The Last House on Dead End Street is a horror film alright, but there's a streak of the sixties New York underground there too, thanks to a few distracted, uneventful takes over which characters reel off monologues, placing the film partially in the arty alienation bracket. Shot on 16mm, handheld much of the time, it resembles one of the later 'decadent' Warhols, before the more humanist Paul

Morrissey took over. The use of masks and other symbolic devices, like horns and hooves, gives the killers an otherworldly appearance, sending the viewer's mind spiralling through literary and mythical associations (especially Greek drama: one of the female associates appears possessed by Diana, the Goddess of the Hunt). This is art cinema as made by a penniless psychopath. On the other hand, the 'artiness' of talentless hacks trying to dress up their dogs-dinner porno flicks with pathetic pretension is skewered in the dialogue, and one such perpetrator gets 'skewered' in a 'horny' scene later in the action, so 'art' is not a word to toss around lightly as far as Watkins is concerned. What emboldens me to use the term in relation to *Dead End Street* is the hermetic, self-assured world that he's created, with every part of the filmmaker's arsenal brought into play to achieve the film's sadistic goals. Even though what can be seen today was reputedly cut down from a three-hour version that the director considers definitive, it still comes across as a perfectly honed artwork. One can admire the savage monomania of, say, the early *Guinea Pig* films from Japan, without ever feeling that the 'A' word is appropriate. I doubt those guys would care, but Watkins clearly does; an aesthetic dimension is maintained in *The Last House on Dead End Street*, with varying levels of artifice, clever framing, theatrical tricks and a wonderful visual gag involving a victim attacked through an empty window frame that clearly expresses the desire to lunge out at you across the threshold of the screen (rather as the lank-haired ghost does in Hideo Nakata's *Ringu*). Watkins inflicts a thrilling vertigo by funnelling you towards sights and sounds you've never anticipated, so in a way, the less you know about the fates of the victims the better. It's one hell of a trip: just don't come running to me for the bicarbonate of soda…

Roger Watkins responded to this review with the word:

"Beautiful."

Which was a relief. You don't want an e-mail saying "Die" from the director of *The Last House on Dead End Street* …

"EVERYTHING was pissing me off in the real world at the time and still is. Crystal methadrine only fuelled the matter (the real stuff, not that cow manure/battery acid shit that's going around now. This stuff was straight from Switzerland; the Sandoz company I believe). I only gave it up when, after two years of imbibing I awoke one morning and didn't know what the button on my shirt was for. My friends (especially Ken Fisher) stuck with me through thick and thin during the production of the film. They did not stay in character between scenes, in fact most of them were busy doing homework for their college classes. The entire crew (what little there was of it) was actually quite relaxed between takes save for one scene… the 'operation scene'. The actress (Nancy Vrooman) was visibly shaken during the entire experience… very nervous indeed. She even demanded that the ropes which seem to bind her be tied to absolutely nothing. Nancy Vrooman is my favourite cast member. Why? Because she had never acted in anything before, didn't know the least thing about filmmaking and was called upon to commit a plethora of cinematic crimes all of which she did very well and without complaint."

It's usually very adolescent or film-schoolish – or at least a bit 'cute' – when someone makes a film about making a film. But you get away with it, 100%. Did you worry about this, did you hesitate before making something recursive?

"I agree. Films about the making of films are generally a crashing bore. But I knew this one would work."

Like everyone who admires the film, I'm curious about the original cut. If you could reinstate three passages missing from the existing version, what would they be and where would they fit? And where does the existing version fall down, for you?

"If I could reinstate three scenes: definitely the one where Sweet finds himself in his own house after sucking the deer's leg and just prior to getting his eye drilled out; a long (six minute) tracking shot of Bill wandering through the vast recourses of the building; and a sequence of the two prostitutes in the park surrounded by little children. The film falls apart at the very beginning for me. I wrote and directed the fucking thing and I

hardly know what's going on. The ridiculous flash forward was inserted by the ridiculous distributors. Bernie Travis was a no-talent, show business wannabe who happened to be best friends with Leo Fenton, the distributor of the film. A mere messenger boy who talked Leo into the fact that Terry and his minions should not go unpunished for their exploits, thus ruining the entire film."*

Can you tell me a bit more about how you put the music together?

"The music was stock music culled from the music library of Ross-Gaffney, an editing house on 46th Street in Manhattan. Jim Flamberg and I added the phasing effects."

In *Last House*, Terry seems to have grown sick of working with asshole porno producers. Did things get better for you in that world afterwards, or did you get used to it?

"Funny, the real porno producers I worked with were pretty funny guys whom I liked very much. And as opposed to the 'legitimate' distributors they always paid me the money they owed me. This is a major deal in the film industry."

Roger Watkins passed away on Tuesday, 6 March, 2007. He was just 59.

Made in New York City.
see also: **Shadows of the Mind**

LAST RITES
– Domonic Paris (1979)
aka *Dracula's Last Rites*

When the local funeral parlour attempts to deny Marie Bradley (Patricia Lee Hammond) the right to an open-casket wake for her recently deceased mother (Mimi Weddell), she and her boyfriend Ted (Michael Lally) protest, only to discover that their small town has been taken over by an exclusive cabal of vampires who control the local emergency services. These highly organised bloodsuckers prey on accident victims and then quickly stake them, in case they rise up and give the game away by overpopu-lating the town with monsters. Sheriff Ordell (Alfred Steinel), Doctor Cummins (Victor Jorge) and undertaker Mr. A. Lucard (Gerald Fielding) are all in cahoots, using their positions to hide their exsanguinary extravagances. Thanks to Marie and Ted's intervention, however, Mrs. Bradley avoids being staked, and sure enough goes missing from her coffin…

There's a great premise here, akin to one of my favourite studio horror films of the 1980s, Gary Sherman's *Dead and Buried* (a small town full of the undead), or that wonderfully offbeat French vampire film *Traitement de Choc* by Alain Jessua (vampirism as an exercise in corporate man management). There's even a glancing similarity to Peter Weir's debut flick, *The Cars That Ate Paris*. *Dracula's Last Rites* has an ambitious score, and a seductive, meandering title theme that reminded me of Italy's progressive maestros Goblin. So what's the problem? Well, I've tried three or four times to get into this movie, and each time I've been defeated by director Domonic Paris's *slow-w-w* pacing and

Last Rites
aka **Dracula's Last Rites** (video cover title)
© 1979. New Empire Features, Inc.
A New Empire Features production.
director: Domonic Paris. producer: Kelly Van Horn. screenplay: Ben Donnelly, Domonic Paris. director of photography: Domonic Paris. music: Paul Jost, George Small. editor: Elizabeth Lombardo. assistant director: Ben Donnelly. art director: Robert Johnson. continuity: Jo Anne Small. assistant cameraman: Michael Hirsch. 2nd assistant cameraman: Steve Kaman. gaffer: Joe Bolesta. 2nd electrics: Ralph Petri, Paul Meder. key grip: Phil Devonshire. 2nd grips: Mike Edwards, Jeff Justin. sound: Rolf Pardula. boom: Stu Deutsch. special effects: Cord Keller, Ron Kurash. makeup: Carla White. hair stylist: Thomas Serra. wardrobe: Jane Paul. still photographer: Fred Knepperges. production co-ordinators: Bob DiMiliaa, Jill Marti. transportation captain: Gene Perone. location co-ordinator: Ed Heller. production assistants: Bonnie Stern, Rikki O'Neal. special props: Bob Serra. special thanks: Mr., Mrs. Gordon Bennett; John Patella, D.D.S.; Brody Furniture; Presidential Motor Lodge; City of Vineland; Rone Funeral Service; Holiday Inn; Tri-City Alignment; Linkinchuck Auto; Vineland Volunteer Rescue; Novick Chevrolet; Williams Auto Parts. opticals: B&O Opticals. graphic design: Bob Siciliano. mixed at Du-Art. music recorded at J.D.S. and hometown Studios. music produced by Paul Jost. all music performed by Paul Jost, George Small. colour by DeLuxe.
Cast: Patricia Lee Hammond (Marie). Gerald Fielding (Lucard). Mimi Weddell (Mrs. Bradley). Victor Jorge (Dr. Cummins). Michael Lally (Ted). Alfred Steinel (Sheriff Ordell). Eric Trules (Potter). Gordito (Gasher). John Juback (hearse driver). Joe Perce (Bobby). Rain Worthington (Suzy). Dan Freedman (aide). Suzy Brabeau (young girl). Michael Valentine (young man). Mark Bennett (drowning victim). Rosine Signoriello (stunt woman). Leah Vitale (girl). Steven Vitale, Brian Nonnenmacher (boys). Mark Bennett, Peter Severino, David Yeagle, Harry Limperopulos (stunt drivers).

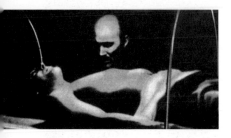

above:
Bloodsucking shenanigans from **Last Rites**...

pedantic visual style. I try not to fast-forward films if I'm reviewing them, but sometimes human frailty intercedes. Paris, who shot the movie himself, has a habit of using slow zooms to show us things we'd noticed within a couple of seconds, and he frequently lets shots dally too long before cutting, which drags down the pace of what could have been an acceptable B-pic. Plot-wise, the film shows its hand in the first ten minutes (hence the apparent spoilers in the above synopsis) and then has nowhere to go, as the hero and heroine plod dutifully towards a truth we already know. It *is* possible to generate suspense under such conditions (Hitchcock thrived on showing the audience things his characters didn't know) but I'm afraid Mr. Paris is not the Master of Suspense's natural heir…

But hold on a second: there is something worth watching, even if you need the patience of Job to get to it. I'm referring to Mrs. Bradley, the old lady who turns bloodsucker and eludes the vampire authorities. She looks fantastic, acting with the bizarre over-emphasis of an Andy Milligan character circa *The Body Beneath*, and her sad, half-assed attempts at vampirism bring something new to the undead repertoire: an air of uncertainty and hopelessness. The more I think about it, the more Mrs. Bradley seems like one of the cinema's most poignant vampires. She's a confused old lady catapulted into the realm of the living dead, and she simply can't hack it. The scene where she menaces a docile fat girl who's taking out the trash, but fails to even scare her, never mind snack on her life essence, left me strangely moved. While vampire movie fans prefer intellectual aristocrats (e.g. the original *Dracula*, or *The Addiction*), slinky lesbians (*Daughters of Darkness*, *Requiem pour un vampire*), or the leather-jacketed likes of Kiefer *Lost Boys* Sutherland, let's spare a thought for the nonplussed undead, wandering through the night displaced and confused, hungry for *something* but with only a vague, Alzheimerish sense of what, exactly. You have to sift through an awful lot of dross in this film to enjoy the fun stuff: in his book *Danse Macabre*, Stephen King likened the horror aficionado to "a prospector with his panning equipment or his wash-wheel," seeking treasure amid the sand and mud of the genre. I think he meant that's how we find good little films among the truly wretched, rather than good scenes in wretched movies – but the principle, if not the degree of desperation, is the same…

Paris has carved a minor niche for himself since the 1980s by compiling trash-movie compilation tapes, including *Afros, Macks and Zodiacs* (1995), which gathers together clips from famous blaxploitation films like *Foxy Brown* and *Superfly* with less well known material like *That Man Bolt* and *The Soul of Nigger Charley*. Various online commentators have castigated *Last Rites* for its occasional technical deficiencies, such as glimpses of film lighting equipment in frame, and shots that reveal the scaffolding and wooden struts supporting the sets. There's no denying these flaws (although cinema matting would doubtless cover up most of these slips), but to call the film 'home-made' as some have done is to ignore the true domestic artisans of cinema, like John Wintergate or Chester Turner. *Dracula's Last Rites* has technical flaws (so does *The Shining*, actually), but its only real problem is pacing. Speed everything up and this could have been as much fun as Alfredo Zacharias's *Demonoid*.

Made in New York State.

opposite:
It's all linked to water in these images from **Let's Scare Jessica To Death**, one of the best horror films of the seventies.

below:
Is Jessica being saved or drowned?

LET'S SCARE JESSICA TO DEATH
– John Hancock (1971)
aka *Jessica*
aka *The Secret Beneath the Lake* (Canadian promotional title)
aka *What Killed Sam Dorker?* (working title)

Let's Scare Jessica To Death is a rural paranoia tale shot in hallucinatory style, which coasts along on a chill wind of spooky ambiguity before drafting The Undead into service for the last reel. It's loose, and sometimes rather careless with its narrative ingredients, but it's still one of the best low-budget American horrors of the seventies, and shares, with other underappreciated films like Willard Huyck's *Messiah of Evil*, a zoned out post-hippy artiness that owes as much to Fonda and Hopper as Romero and Hooper.

Jessica (Zohra Lampert) has recently been released from a psychiatric institute into the care of her musician husband Duncan (Barton Heyman) and quasi-hippy friend Woody (Kevin O'Connor). They take her to a remote spot in rural Connecticut to recuperate at a big old house Duncan has bought. On arriving, the trio discover a beguiling young woman called Emily (Mariclare Costello) squatting the premises: at first startled by her sudden appearance, Jessica is charmed and invites the girl to stay; a decision she comes to regret, as it seems both Woody and Duncan are attracted to her. Strange events accumulate: Jessica finds an old photograph in the attic featuring a young woman who resembles Emily, and a local antique dealer, Sam Dorker (Alan Manson), mentions that young Abigail Bishop, who used to live at the house in the 1890s, drowned in the nearby cove; this tallies with a white-gowned figure Jessica occasionally sees there. One day, the girl appears again, beckoning her to a waterfall, beneath which lies the corpse of the antique dealer. When Jessica returns with her husband, the body has gone, and the girl in white runs away. Troubled by whispering voices in her head, and alienated from her unsupportive husband, Jessica's sanity is giving way. She goes swimming with the increasingly sinister Emily, who tries to drown her. Jessica runs to the village, but the old men there are just as menacing. Duncan finds her collapsed in the woods and takes her back to the house, but by now her entire reality is under siege…

This haunting character study stands or falls with its central character, and while Zohra Lampert's performance may at first seem a little strained and artificial, it soon develops into a *tour-de-force*, at times comparable to Catherine Deneuve's role in Polanski's *Repulsion* (1965) or Harriet Andersson's tormented Karin in Bergman's *Through a Glass Darkly* (1961). Jessica walks with the gauche fragility of a doll hoping to pass for human; her movements are cautious re-enactments of grace, an approach well suited to the role of an intelligent, sensitive woman recovering from a nervous breakdown. Lampert, whom Hancock first saw in a production of Bertolt Brecht's *Mother Courage and Her Children*, looks uncannily like the anorexic, depression-prone pop star Karen Carpenter – superficially wholesome and earnest, yet bony and painfully sensitive, as if she's losing a war with her skeleton.

With its emphasis on sexual and emotional tension, and dialogue scenes that vibrate with brittle discomfort, *Let's Scare Jessica To Death* has a brooding, storm-cloudy feel, even though much of the film is shot in bright sunlight. There's a pressurised, inertial Summer-of-Love hangover lingering in the air, a feeling augmented by Woody's habit of saying things like *"We're all kind of wandering spirits, you know?"* and Emily's fondness for picking out fragments of sad melody on an acoustic guitar. It's never explained what caused Jessica's breakdown, but she has the aura of someone who may have suffered a psychotic reaction after one too many tabs of LSD. The most obvious sign of the sixties is the hearse Duncan and Jessica drive, with a peace symbol and the word 'LOVE' stencilled on the side, the sort of amusing eccentricity one might suppose from ex-students who dig the alternative humour of the counterculture. Certainly, despite Duncan's encroaching baldness and Jessica's sensible attire, the hostile locals see only the car and its irreverence, cursing the newcomers as *"damned hippies"*.

IN COLOUR

PARAMOUNT PICTURES PRESENTS **LET'S SCARE JESSICA TO DEATH** *Starring* ZOHRA LAMPERT • BARTON HEYMAN
A CHARLES B. MOSS, Jr. PRODUCTION KEVIN O'CONNOR • GRETCHEN CORBETT
Written by NORMAN JONAS and RALPH ROSE • Produced by CHARLES B. MOSS, Jr. • Directed by JOHN HANCOCK ALAN MANSON *and* MARICLARE COSTELLO
X CERT. COLOR. A PARAMOUNT PICTURE

Let's Scare Jessica To Death
(Paramount re-issue title)
aka **Jessica** (original title)
© 1971. The Jessica Company.
Paramount - a Gulf+Western company.
director: John Hancock. producer: Charles B. Moss, Jr. film editor: Murray Solomon. photography by Bob [Robert M.] Baldwin. music: Orville Stoeber. co-producer: William Badalato. written by Ralph Rose [John Hancock], Norman Jonas [Lee Kalcheim]. assistant editor: Ginny Katz. assistant cameraman: Sal Guida. set decorator: Norman Kenneson. costume design: Mariette Pinchart. gaffer: Myron Odeguard. continuity: Randa Haines. makeup: Irvin Carlton. grip: Melvin D. Noped. producer's assistant: Judith Spangler. production assistants: Joanne Michels, Barbara Reynolds. sound: Joe Ryaan. electronic music by Walter Sear. colour by DeLuxe. filmed from 16 October 1970 in Essex (Connecticut, USA).
Cast: Zohra Lampert (Jessica). Barton Heyman (Duncan). Kevin O'Connor (Woody). Gretchen Corbett (girl). Alan Manson (Dorker). Mariclare Costello (Emily).

Underlying the drama is a sense of people who are groping towards something they're ashamed to admit: a desire to 'settle down'. Hence the house, with its apple orchards offering the dream of a return to the land, and the hearse, which offers a symbolic reproach later picked up and amplified by the eruption of the undead. Jessica's love of grave-rubbings is another harbinger; when she reads aloud from them, while in bed with her inattentive husband, it's hard to avoid the implication that marriage itself is a sort of burial. You sense that much of the tension here has to do with the reinstatement of conventional moral codes after the flirtation with 'free love' espoused by the hippies. And, as in Willard Huyck's *Messiah of Evil* and James Bryan's *The Dirtiest Game in the World*, it's sexual jealousy that heralds the return of convention and the erosion of alternatives. For instance, as Duncan talks after dinner, an indeterminate female voice-over whispers, *"I desire him."* Is Jessica picking up Emily's thoughts, or simply projecting a paranoid suspicion that Emily wants to steal her man? Jessica fights her suspicions by asking Emily to stay, yet something really *is* going on between Duncan and Emily. Woody detects it: when Jessica leaves the table after noticing Emily's mild flirtation, he tells Duncan, *"Take care of your wife."* But is Woody *really* concerned for Jessica, or merely jealous that the new girl is interested in Duncan? Is Duncan suggesting that his jittery, neurotic wife see a doctor again because he loves her, or is he simply tired of living with a fruitcake, and hoping to get rid of her so he can have a clear run at Emily? The film's emotional dynamic is fraught with such questions. By giving everyone ambiguous motivations it takes on a literary quality, in particular echoing Henry James's *The Turn of the Screw*.

If all that the film had to offer was a drama of marital paranoia, it would scarcely count as a horror film. What makes it work magnificently as horror, even before the story tilts overtly

into the macabre, is the handling of location and the exemplary use of sound. The exterior filming by cinematographer Robert Baldwin is often both achingly ominous and startlingly beautiful: a misty river-crossing for instance, or the dew-soaked morning arrival at the house, not to mention numerous scenes in, on and around an obscurely unsettling lake. Water provides a link to the drowning of Abigail Bishop, but also suggests another world alongside ours, where different physical laws apply. Sound-wise, Hancock turns the time-saving practice of post-synching to his advantage by having Jessica's voice-overs delivered close-miked and *sotto voce*, giving her interiority an intimate and claustrophobic quality. It feels somehow *too* intimate, like eavesdropping, adding to the sense of Jessica as a painfully vulnerable creature. It's as if we can hear her thoughts through her skull. Meanwhile, the music alternates between the strumming of an acoustic guitar, a faux-Satie piece for piano, and lashings of primitive Moog synthesizer from Walter Sear (a combination of elements that anticipates I Libra's music for Mario Bava's late masterpiece, *Shock*). The synthesizer also provides a haunting electronic wind-scape, blurring reality and fantasy as it curls and whistles over shots of the countryside (composer Giuliano Sorgini did something quite similar on the superlative zombie film, *The Living Dead at Manchester Morgue*).

The horror films that followed in the immediate wake of George Romero's *Night of the Living Dead* (1968) were more diverse than the hordes that followed its sequel, *Dawn of the Dead*, post-'78 (although Lucio Fulci's ghostly ghouls in *The Beyond* and Jean Rollin's soppy Nazis in *Zombie Lake* are honourable exceptions). The early seventies saw such diverse oddities as: *Messiah of Evil* (touting a 'hippy dream gone sour' meets 'consumer society gone crazy' theme well before *Dawn of the Dead*); *Deathdream* (in which a Vietnam soldier returns home as a zombie, and fakes it as a living being); *Children Shouldn't Play with Dead Things* (a frivolous send-up that turns surpris-

below:
Artwork from the Mountain video release of
Madame Zenobia.

ingly nasty); *Garden of the Dead* (with its talking, formaldehyde-addicted chain-gang zombies); and from Europe, *Tombs of the Blind Dead* (starring zombie Knights Templar on horseback). Hancock adds his own posse: they're a gang of menacing old men who scare Jessica with their small-town hostility before finally invading her bedroom. They act as though they're the walking dead, but they're not the flesh-ripping sort: they're much harder to define. The post-Romero elements are further spiced by a mixture of paranoia, parapsychology and the supernatural, effective not least because the film withholds explanation about the relationship between them. *"Stay Jessica, stay – you're home now,"* insists a voice in the heroine's head, summoning a blatant shiver of *The Haunting* (1963), a film that provides as least as much fuel to the story as the undead themes discussed so far. Meanwhile, the character of Emily, a sort of emotional vampire, further clouds the obvious genre boundaries. It's interesting too that Hancock incorporates a 'failure of communication' motif, to which Romero himself would return again and again (see *The Crazies*, *Martin* and *Day of the Dead*).

There are flaws in Hancock's film, but they're sins of omission. A certain amount of haziness and a preponderance of loose ends is acceptable in the name of the irrational, but it's a pity the back-story of the house is not more tightly woven into the film; the fate of the Bishops, even the drowning of Abigail Bishop, is strangely peripheral. According to an interview Hancock gave to the editors of *Gods in Polyester*, the 'girl in white' was included in the script purely on the insistence of the producers; sadly it shows, as her existence in the real world (Duncan sees her too) is never explained. Still, there's no doubting the overall effect, which is to wrong-foot the audience and leave us genuinely unnerved.

Let's Scare Jessica To Death was shot in twenty five days for $200,000, on location in Essex, Connecticut. Hancock's original title for this, his directorial debut, was simply *Jessica*, but when the movie became a 'negative pickup' for Paramount, the name was changed to echo such titularly verbose movies as the contemporary MGM acquisition *What's the Matter with Helen?*, and AIP's *Whoever Slew Auntie Roo?* – both directed the same year, 1971, by the same director, Curtis Harrington. (I have to admit a fondness for Celso Ad. Castillo's gloriously silly Filipino variation on the theme, *Kill Barbara with Panic...*) The retitling suggests that Paramount were looking to resolve *Jessica*'s ambiguities by pointing towards a rational explanation; sadly the rational explanation doesn't fit the story! It *is* just about possible to read the film as simply a descent into madness, with everything corralled under the heading of paranoid hallucination, but there's certainly *no* sustainable case for the film as a 'drive the heroine crazy' drama. Fortunately, the film was never recut to force the issue, and remains one of the most mesmerising and haunting American horror films of the seventies.

Hancock, who also wrote the film under the name Ralph Rose, went on to make *Bang the Drum Slowly* (1973), a sports drama with Robert De Niro and the great Michael Moriarty. He's since directed nine films and some TV shows, including episodes of Steve Bochco's cult hit, *Hill Street Blues* and a clutch of eighties *Twilight Zone* entries. *Let's Scare Jessica To Death* was the first movie to be produced by Charles B. Moss Jr., grandson of theatre president B.S. Moss (see chapter on David Durston and his film *Stigma*). It opened at the Criterion on Times Square, a prestige venue run by the Moss family.

Made in Connecticut.

THE LOVE BUTCHER
– Mikel Angel and Don Jones (1975)
See interview with Don Jones.

Made in California.

MADAME ZENOBIA
– Eduardo Cemano (1973)
aka *Zenobia*

Madame Zenobia is an exuberant, drug-tinged tale of necrophilia and witchcraft. It tells of Marcia (Tina Russell), a young woman unable to achieve orgasm since the death of her lover John. We first see her with a new squeeze, her chauffeur Eric, who drives her to the graveyard to pay her respects to the deceased. Marcia's expression of grief is intense, as she frigs her pussy energetically on the flowers and wreaths festooning the grave. We soon discover that Eric cannot bring Marcia to climax, and after a gaggle of sex-crazed friends also fail to get her off during a four-way sex tussle, one of them suggests a visit to the mysterious Madame Zenobia (Elizabeth O'Donovan). Madame Zenobia sends a message beyond the grave to Marcia's lover (currently in heaven banging some celestial floozy), reuniting the lovers via the body of Eric the chauffeur, who 'channels' John in a rather intimate way and at last brings Marcia to her sorely needed orgasm.

The fun of this film is chiefly in the way-out photography, design and music. Madame Zenobia's place looks like *A Clockwork Orange*'s Korova Milk Bar, merged with Jagger's pad in *Performance*. The photography, by Cemano himself, is a delirious free-for-all of hand-held wide-angle lensing, while coloured smoke, bizarre costumes and lots of superimposition add to the incense-heavy aura. A handful of John Waters-ish performances contribute further to the whacked-out psychedelic appeal. There's some irritating classical music during the slower-paced first half, but the soundtrack then turns to bongos and Farfisa organ for a Tangerine Dream-like workout that tallies perfectly with the dope-and-sex imagery. Softcore sex is usually a bore, but *Madame Zenobia*'s sixty five minutes whiz by, giving you some idea of what sexploitation would look like if shot by Nic Roeg or Ken Russell!

Eduardo Cemano was a New York-based sexploitation director who kicked off with the intriguingly titled *The Weirdos and the Oddballs* (1968), before lensing two porno titles, *Lady Zazu's Daughter* (1971) and *Millie's Homecoming* (1972). Another Cemano credit, *Sweet Love*, is possibly an alternative title for one of the others. *Madame Zenobia* was shot in 16mm and blown up to 35mm. Madame Zenobia herself was played by black actress Elizabeth O'Donovan, who was the Empress in Richard Burton's *Doctor Faustus* (1967). Tina Russell (Christina Russel) who plays frigid Marcia, was a porno regular who appeared in all Cemano's films bar the first. Levi Richards, her obliging chauffeur here, went on to work with Doris Wishman on *The Immoral Three* (1975), *Come with Me My Love* (1976) and *A Night To Dismember* (1983). *Madame Zenobia* was produced by Jason Russell (aka Lee Hassel), whose later production credits include Armand Weston's brutal sex epics *The Defiance of Good* (1974) and *The Taking of Christina* (1976), and Shaun Costello's *Dominatrix Without Mercy* (1976).

Made in New York State.

THE MAFU CAGE

– Karen Arthur (1977)
aka *My Sister My Love*
aka *Deviation*
aka *Don't Ring the Doorbell*

Cissy (Carol Kane), spoilt, screw-loose daughter of a wealthy wild-animal trapper, is obsessed with apes and monkeys, persuading her live-in sister Ellen (Lee Grant) to obtain them so that she may keep one caged at all times in their plant-festooned house. On his death-bed, their father made Ellen swear that she would never have Cissy committed, believing that her madness was merely the 'eccentricity' of a creative child. However, Cissy is dangerously unstable and prone to murderous fits of rage, especially if someone touches her. The only person who can do that is Ellen, with whom she has an incestuous relationship. As the apes become the victims of Cissy's destructive rage, indulgent Ellen turns a blind eye, and simply obtains new specimens; and so the sorry process continues. Into this literal and metaphorical hothouse comes Ellen's new boyfriend David (James Olson). Cissy dislikes him intensely, and when he turns up one day while Ellen is away, she proceeds to make him very uncomfortable indeed...

This is a claustrophobic, distressing film with a highly unusual story (based on the play *Toi et tes nuages* ['You and Your Clouds'] by Éric Westphal) and a *tour-de-force* central performance by Carol Kane. Although it's not graphically violent, it's tough to sit through, focusing on a deeply selfish individual with a penchant for cruelty to animals, whose sadism eventually escalates to include human beings. It reminds me of Marc B. Ray's *Scream Bloody Murder*, depicting a disturbed, deeply unsympathetic, but well-drawn central character determined to mould anyone and anything according to their self-centred mania. The theme of lesbian incest is perhaps too subtly incorporated, but the portrait of emotional manipulation between siblings is spot-on, and the African imagery adds unpredictability in a genre not always noted for breadth of cultural reference. (See John Ballard's *The Orphan* for another example.)

This is one of those movies that creeps up on you: Carol Kane builds her tics and mannerisms slowly, from 'kooky' to full throttle mentalist, and though the violence Cissy commits against an orangutan is allusively shot, there are still a few incredibly disturbing shots of Kane snarling and yelling at the caged creature that made my hair stand on end. (I should mention, however, that the American Humane Society gave the film the all-clear.) Kane's appearance is at times quite astonishing, as she adopts a series of African tribal outfits, beginning with a look that's more proto-punkette, then heading dramatically into full-fledged tribal marks, neck rings, Congolese costumes and deep red face-paint. The soundtrack features some extraordinary African music recordings, bringing to the film an alarmingly intense ritualistic ambience. As for Cissy's treatment of David; while the sadistic opportunities are not as luridly explored as those in Peter S. Traynor's similarly themed *Death Game* (1976), *The Mafu Cage* is still likely to chill the ardour of all but the most masochistic of males, so if you ever had the hots for Kane as the girlishly ditzy Simka in the TV comedy series *Taxi*, you may want to avoid seeing this one...

Karen Arthur has since worked almost exclusively in TV (apart from the stalker-thriller *Lady Beware*, in 1987). *The Mafu Cage*'s cinematographer John Bailey had earlier lensed *Premonition* (1970) for Alan Rudolph, and went on to shoot *American Gigolo* (1980), *Cat People* (1982) and *Mishima* (1985) for Paul Schrader.

Made in California.

The Mafu Cage
aka **Deviation**
© 1977. Clouds Productions , Inc.
director: Karen Arthur. producer: Diana Young. executive producers: Karen Arthur, Gary L. Triano. screenplay: Don Chastain, based upon the play "Toi et Tes Nuages" ("You and Your Clouds") written by Eric Westphal; translated into the English language by Richard Cottrell. editor: Carol Littleton. music: Roger Kellaway. production manager: Stuart A. Gross. costume design by Nani Yee Grenell. production design by Conrad E. Angone. visual consultant: John Bailey. drawings and mural by Roger Landry. assistant director: Stuart A. Gross. production mixer: Michael Moore. gaffer: Thomas Stern. key grip: Peter Wagner. propertymaster: Jim Dultz. makeup: Barry Gelber. script supervisors: Kisuna Jacobsen, Betty Goldberg. sound editor: Gib Jaffe. first assistant camera: Raphael Sloan. second assistant camera: Doug Scott. still photographer: Daniele Legeron. boom operator: DG Fisher. best boy electric: Richard Bowen. costumer: Karen Davis. hairdresser for Ms. Grant: Audrey Levy. hairdresser for Ms. Kane: Ann's Attic. assistant to the director: Linda Joan Grant. assistant to the producer: Marcy Gross. assistant editor: Victoria Martin. assistant props: Rick Squire, Barry Gelber, Steven Hirsh. greensman/assistant props: Jim Damalas. food co-ordinator: Truudi Reynolds. production office co-ordinator: Pamela Jaye Smith. production auditor: Melinda Clark Bell. second assistant director: Bart Patton. executive production assistants: James Sherwood, Will Sherwood, Marilyn McAvoy, Kathleen Hughes, Terry Strawn, Guy Paonessa, Ginny Caimari, Tony Vidal. music supervisor: Jules Chaikin. musicians: Roger Kellaway, Edgar Lustgarten, Gene Cipriano, George Calusdian, Ron Krasinski, Jules Chaikin. animal trainers: Kent Douglas, John Dawley. solar co-ordinators: Paul Roques, Bob King. opticals by f-Stop. filmed in Metrocolor. re-recording at Todd-AO. We wish to thank the following: Jean Pierre Hailt; Natural History Museum of Los Angeles County; The UCLA Museum of Cultural History; Jan Baum-Iris Silverman Gallery; Mike Hammer Gallery; David Stuart Galleries; Silverman Collection; Marcy and Edgar Gross Collection; Elaine and Conrad E. Angone Collection; Glenn Swanson Collection; Yves St. Laurent Menswear; David Brown of California; The Brass Tree (Beverly Hills); Patti African Arts & Beads; The African Shop; Clairmont-Engel; Gentle Jungle-Enchanted Village; Sara Mirzah; Leona Wood; Bob Estrin. Bluther piano supplied by Kasmioff (Hollywood). prepared piano courtesy of Russell Reiner. animal photography monitored and approved by American Humane.
Cast: Lee Grant (Ellen Carpenter). Carol Kane (Cissy Carpenter). Will Geer (Zom). James Olson (David Eastman). Budar (Mafu). Will Sherwood (Will).

MAKO: JAWS OF DEATH

– William Grefé (1975)
aka *Shark Killers*

This story of a man (Richard Jaeckel) who loves sharks so much that he murders shark-hunters to protect his fishy friends is more action-adventure than horror. So what's it doing here? Well, he can communicate with sharks, and he's protected by an amulet given to him by an old shaman, adding just enough mystic hogwash to place it in the shallows of the genre.

Apart from that, it's a curious, sentimental drama, which plays like an amoral kids' film, appearing to condone murder as retribution for unlicensed fishing. Much as I personally detest the arrogance of 'gladiatorial' man vs. animal types, murder seems hardly the healthiest solution. Still, for young teens with an angry eco-conscience this will provide fantasy wish-fulfilment, and Richard Jaeckel (the only ray of light in John 'Bud' Cardos's *The Dark*) at least gets to go over the top a bit, with hand-wringing and tears as he talks to his pointy-nosed friends. (The scene in a maritime laboratory where he kneels sobbing, arms outstretched, holding out a dead baby shark to its equally dead mother, rates a Purple Heart on the melodrama scoreboard.). The director, Florida exploitation dynamo William Grefé, had come on a great deal since *Death Curse of Tartu* (1966), handling the action and dialogue scenes with confidence. That said, a little more of the madness of his early work would not have gone amiss.

Made in Florida.

Mako: Jaws of Death
aka **The Jaws of Death** (UK theatrical title)
aka **Shark Killers**
© 1975 [no company]
uncredited: Universal Majestic Inc.
producer/director: William Grefé. executive producers: Doro V. Hreljanovic, Paul A. Joseph. associate producers: Robert Plumb, Bob Bagley. story: William Grefé. screenplay: Robert Madaris. director of photography: Julio C. Chavez (colour by Movielab). underwater photography: Jordon Klein. film editors: Ronald Sinclair, Julio C. Chavez. 1st assistant directors: Adrienne Bourbeau, Gayle De Camp. 2nd assistant director: George Marvin. art director: Roger Carlton Sherman. camera operator: William Walsh. assistant cameraman: Robert Gersicoff. soundman: Bernard Blynder. boom-man: Michael S. Blynder. gaffers: Lane Chiles, Sandy Perales. grips: Jerry Rhodes, Jon R. Grinter, Michael H. Goad. makeup: Susan Kuennen. script: Betty Kerwin. hair stylist: Gary Walker. assistant editor: Michael R. Hoyt. props: Kurt Nagle. wardrobe: Heather Hughes. stills: Emil Deaton. assistants to the producer: Ernest Colonna, Jr., Marlene Ginsberg. transportation: Rocky Parker, Eddie Bykiewicz. generator operator: Reginald Callahan. boat operator: Pat Starbeck. production secretary: Sheila Owens. location accountant: Grace Grefé. equipment by Cine Tech, Inc. underwater crew — director: William Grefé. cameraman: Jordon Klein, chief diver / shark handler: Big John McLaughlin. shark handlers: Courtney Brown, Jerry Klay, Artie Maleschi. location manager: B.J. Johnson. special thanks to Miami Seaquarium; Shark-Quarium; Wellington Hall Ltd.; Fine Prints Unlimited. production services by Mako Associates. The Producers wish to express their sincere gratitude to the members of the underwater crew who risked their lives to film the shark sequences in this motion picture without benefit of cages or other protective devices.
Cast: Richard Jaeckel (Sonny Stein). Jenifer Bishop (Karen). Harold 'Odd Job' Sakata (Pete). John Chandler (Charlie). Buffy Dee (Barney). Ben Kronen (Whitney). Milton "Butterball" Smith (Butter). Paul Preston (2nd patrolman). Bob/Robert Gordon (bartender). Jerry Albert (mate). George Johnson (captain). Luke Halpin (3rd patrolman). Ric O'Feldman (1st patrolman). Dan Fitzgerald (deputy). Bob Leslie (client). Raff Prieto (attendant). Marcie Knight (secretary). Dete Parsons (helper). Richard Sterling (tourist). Mal Jones (1st man). Jack Nagle (2nd man). Don Sebastian (customer). Arthur C. Gulliver, Jr. (1st vigilante). Courtney Brown (2nd vigilante). Herb Goldstein (fisherman). Lucille Blackton (Annie). James Reed Parham (stuntman). Gay Ingram (stuntgirl).

top left:
Images from **The Mafu Cage**.

below:
US video cover for **Mako: Jaws of Death**.

Malatesta's Carnival of Blood
© 1973. Windmill #1 Co. [DVD release ©2002.
Christopher Speeth.]
director: Christopher Speeth. producer:
Richard C. Grosser, Walker Stuart. story:
Werner Liepolt. assistant director: Margret
Turner. director of photography: Norman
Gaines. sound: Hugh Little. sound effects:
Daniel Miles Kron. costumes: Joan Kleinbard.
script coordinator: Leslie Rado. assistant
cameraman: Jeffrey Apple. make-up: James
Lambert. wardrobe: Elaine Bass. engineers:
Michael Kleeman, Barry Gorodetzer. psychoa-
coustics: Dr. Sheridan Speeth. production
assistants: Barbara Warren, Warren Schloss,
Michael Montamura, Fernando Urbino, Lois
Kimmelman, George Hache. sound mix: Tom
Peterson, Motion Picture Sound, Inc.
processing: Movielab, Inc. production design:
"Alley Friends": Wud Stange, Ace Johnson,
Lance Sims and Ruth Horwitz, Arreta Keefer,
Sharon Keefer, Tony Whitfield, Steve Levine,
Lucy Christopher, Patti Stem and others.
Cast: Janine Carazo (Vena). Jerome Dempsey
(Blood). Daniel Dietrich (Malatesta). Lenny
Baker (Sonja). Herve Villechaize (Bobo).
William Preston (Sticker). Paul Hostetler (Mr.
Norris). Betsy Henn (Mrs. Norris). Chris
Thomas (Kit). Paul Townsend (Johnny). Tom
Markus (Bean). Sebastian Stuart (Lucky).
James Lambert (Winston). Rebecca Stuart
(leading ghoul). Jim McCrane (Mr. Davis).
Gloria Salmansohn (Mrs. Davis). Karen
Salmansohn (Toby Davis). Tom Dorff (state
trooper). Ghouls Gary Shaber, M.D. (blood-
letting ghoul). Andy Bass, Kenneth Beerger,
Kenny Berlin, Rissa Berlin, Larry Brookman,
Frank Brown, Madeline Burke, Tom Burke, Ron
Burns, Jim Cader, Barry Carlin, Michael Carver,
Mike Carlin, Priscilla Cashman, Peter
Churchman, Avis Cohen, Murrey Cohen, Steve
Cohen, Kathy Cornfield, Jeff Couzens, Jim
Cunningham, Nick Desipio, Kathleen Distel,
Helene Feinstine, Jean Galliano, Donna Gilbert,
Andye Greenborg, Ronald Glickman, Mike
Goldberg, Richie Grayboys, Rick Gilbert,
Herman Greenstein, Marc Greenstone, Linda
Halverson, Barbara Harvey, David Haupschein,
Donna Hausman, Michael hausman, Jeffrey
Heller, John Henderson, Conrad Herman,
Arlene Kagel, Davida Kagen, Bob Kandall, Gary
Koff, Robin Kulman, Gary Lubell, Margo
Lukeno, Chris Martin, Paul Martin, Keith Mason,
Nina Nocella, Patrice Nocella, Pasquale
Nocella, Barbara Palma, Bunsey Penrose,
Sandy Perlie, Kathy Potts, Tom Randolph,
Steve Rhian, Andrea Rosenbaum, Jayne
Rosenberg, Mark Rubin, Mark Rosenberg, Reni
Schober, Bob Schwartz, Larry Shaw, Linda
Singer, Ferdinand Smacchi, Rona Tractenberg,
Richard Weiss, Lee Wessof, Van Williams,
Dennis Wolk, Perry Yeldham and others.

MALATESTA'S CARNIVAL OF BLOOD
– Christopher Speeth (1973)

Mr. and Mrs. Norris (Paul Hostetler and Betsy Henn) and their daughter Vena (Janine Carazo) pose as new employees at a dilapidated fairground in order to search for their missing son, last seen in the vicinity. An ingratiating fellow called Mr. Blood (Jerome Dempsey) shows them around, but by the time they've met some weird denizens of the fairground community they're convinced their boy has met an untimely end. Vena befriends Kit (Chris Thomas), a young carny worker who runs the Tunnel of Love, and he tells her of his own suspicions: recently a family disappeared into the Tunnel and failed to come out the other end. Everything is very strange, and getting stranger by the minute. Cannibals live under the carnival, vampires take care of the business side, and murderous freaks and lunatics lurk at every turn, all of them working under the shadowy guidance of Mr. Malatesta (Daniel Dietrich). The Norrises try to escape, but they're drawn down into the caverns beneath the rollercoaster. Can Vena's boyfriend Johnny (Paul Townsend) save the day, or is everything just too damn weird?

Believed lost for thirty years, this amateur but genuinely bizarre item allegedly played the Southern drive-in circuit in the early seventies, and then disappeared, leaving only its alluring title in a handful of reference sources. Much to the surprise of collectors, a print of the film emerged on DVD in 2003, having been discovered in the proverbial attic and taken to the American Zoetrope Studios for remastering. Extra footage was also found, including some very gory material snipped from the original version by the censors, now included as a DVD extra.

All of which rather begs the question: after thirty years of obscurity, was *Malatesta* worth uncovering? Well, with a few reservations I'd say it more than deserves a spell in the cult spotlight. It may share three-quarters of a title with Leonard Kirtman's stunningly bad *Carnival of Blood*, but that is *definitely* where the similarities end. Beautifully photographed, imagina-tively designed, far-out in conception and successfully bonkers at least half the time, *Malatesta's Carnival of Blood* is unlike anything you've seen before. Its closest neighbours in outer-space are maybe Jack Hill's *Spider Baby* (1964), Jack Cardiff's *The Mutations* (1973), and Ray Dennis Steckler's *The Incredibly Strange Creatures Who Stopped Living and Became Mixed Up Zombies!!?* (1963) – the latter purely on the basis of the carny setting and the photography.

I'm all in favour of plotless horror films, which is just as well really because there's not much meat on the bone here (just lots of

guts and gravy, and a few oddly textured lumps I can't quite identify…) 'Ordinary folk look for a missing boy in a fairground run by monsters' just about covers it. Like the Euro oddity *Freak Orlando* (1981), it's really a showcase for the director and his art designers to go berserk with acid-tinged visuals. The design team, a Philadelphia-based triumvirate called Alley Friends, pull off tableau after tableau of stylish disorientation: a car suspended upside down from a ceiling with the interior dressed to resemble a huge red mouth; a room half-filled with what seems to be an enormous, partially deflated racing balloon; and many more marvels best left for your first viewing. Interestingly, the Alley Friends troupe have proved to be more than drug-frazzled art-school weirdos by establishing themselves in the world of architecture, where today they design sustainable-energy-based eco-friendly buildings. Partners Bruce Millard, Alan ('Ace') Johnson and Richard ('Wud') Stange have also worked on off-Broadway plays, temporary festival structures, passive solar buildings, and award-winning, multi-purpose, high-rise condominiums. (see www.bemarchitect.com) So if you're living in a strange-looking condo in Pennsylvania and you suspect there are cannibals in the basement, perhaps you've bought one of their creations!

Christopher Speeth should be proud to have made such an unconventional, defiantly stylish and dreamlike film, in a country where the horror genre often falls into predictable pigeonholes. (Not content with having a bunch of cannibal ghouls living beneath a rollercoaster, Speeth makes them silent movie addicts, gathering transfixed before battered prints of *The Phantom of the Opera*, *The Cabinet of Dr. Caligari* and *The Hunchback of Notre Dame*). Several sequences are like nothing else in the genre (a night-time ride on the roller-coaster is particularly breathtaking), and it would be a minor masterpiece were it not for a handful of drawbacks. One is the acting, which veers from eerily unique (Jerome Dempsey's 'Mr. Blood', a creepy cross between Victor Buono and Edward G. Robinson; the extraordinary William Preston with his wildly wandering eye and craggy face) to woefully forced and contrived (i.e. most of the non-speaking actors playing ghouls and vampires). All credit for trying, but the amateur cast provide just the sort of eye-rolling, pseudo-spaced-out silliness that you'd expect if you asked a local college drama class to simulate phantoms from a drug nightmare. The other, more subtle failing of the film is the editing, which can't quite pull the best out of the weirder scenes. A faster cutting style would have given the film more delirium: the photography and design are begging for it, but although the *mise en scène* looks like a madman's dreams, the cutting tends to give us an observer's viewpoint, not the lunatic's. Traditional virtues like pacing and continuity are all at sea too, but that's less of a problem; a really good, creative editor could have made this film a vertiginous experience, whereas Speeth, who I imagine cut the film himself (no editor is credited), leaves us with our metaphorical feet firmly on the ground. Of course, much of this is likely due to lack of money: a tight schedule leaves little time for retakes, and not a lot to play with in the edit suite. Nevertheless, from its sparse electronic soundtrack to its gloriously hi-contrast night-time photography, much of the film is a technical triumph, and in his sheer devotion to the far-side of cinema, Speeth can claim a knock-out against the low-budget odds.

Christopher Speeth studied film under Solomon Wishnepolsky (aka Sol Worth, best known for producing *Through Navajo Eyes*, a series of short films about Native Americans) at the University of Pennsylvania's Annenberg Center. He subsequently produced several experimental shorts and documentaries. He worked for both CBS and ABC, and his documentary footage has appeared on shows such as *America's Most Wanted*, *Final Justice*, and *Nightline*. *Malatesta's Carnival of Blood* was his only feature film. Diminutive star Hervé Villechaize, whose body stopped growing early in his childhood, went on to score fame the following year as Scaramanga's henchman in *The Man with the Golden Gun*, followed by the role that took him to the heart of afternoon TV worldwide – the enigmatic 'Tattoo' in *Fantasy Island*. His career

after this was unsuccessful and dogged by alcoholism and depression. Further health problems contributed to his weakened state of mind, and tragically he shot himself in 1993. Daniel Dietrich, who plays the title role of Malatesta, appeared in Andy Milligan's *Fleshpot on 42nd Street* (1973). The extraordinary William Preston was a book-keeper in a Philadelphia trucking firm, until he began acting at the age of 47. He played 'John the Bum' in Terry Gilliam's hit *The Fisher King* (1991), and also appeared in *The Exorcist III* (1990), *Far and Away* (1992), and *Waterworld* (1995), and was a regular player on the popular comedy talk-show *Late Night with Conan O'Brien*. When Preston passed away on 10 July, 1998, the O'Brien show marked his passing with a specially-filmed eulogy.

Christopher Speeth writes:

"Twice in the past year I have been surprised by developments in the screening of Malatesta's Carnival. In the Fall of 2005, Malatesta won the Grandma Gladys Award at the Eerie Film Festival. Your thoughtful review is the other. When I look back (and it is way back) on this film, I remember playing a minimax game with almost no money. After seeing an Off-Broadway show where the main actor gave a soliloquy to his own tapeworm, I sought and drafted the playwright, Werner Liepolt, to do the script. We had certain constraints, e.g. the free use of a carnival after hours and an old machine shop (Wicaco) for interiors, which was between bankruptcy sales. Malatesta took six weeks to shoot. There was about two months pre-planning and eight months post-production. Neither I nor the two producers were paid salaries. I was to receive 14% of the gross after the theatre nut. One of the producers, Walker Stuart, acted as an in-line producer. He was experienced in managing all the details (equipment rent, contract negotiations, etc.) and went on to do the same for many other productions. The other producer, Richard Grosser, a graduate of the Wharton Business School, helped with special effects and was the principal money man. He sold shares to what he called the local crap shooters: an insurance man, a clothing man, someone who owned a piece of a sports team, and a paper merchant. The eight months of post-production were done in my editing rooms with Daniel Miles Kron as the sound editor, Meg Turner as assistant editor and myself as editor. I insisted on paying the principal actors scale so they could make it through another summer in New York and/or Philadelphia while also extending their unemployment compensation afterward. I am extremely proud of this principal cast and the proof of my selection is borne out by their subsequent successes, some of which you have mentioned in your well-researched review. The ghouls were paid $5.00/day plus doughnuts. Our shooting ratio varied between 3:1 to 1:1, which, as you notice, does not give you much to work with in the editing room. The continuity was further eroded by the Motion Picture Association of America. We needed an 'R' rating in order to have it seen in the drive-in circuit. The MPAA censored all the cannibalism, and we were too small a company to fight their decision. To finish it off, the 'director's cut' was chopped to pieces to make the trailers because we did not have the money to have an extra print made. I would like to mention Walker Stuart and Richard Grosser, two of the original producers who contributed so much to the production, as well as Margret Turner, my very talented assistant. Elfenworks, and Howie Stein at Coppola's American Zoetrope, made the release of the DVD possible."

Made in Pennsylvania.

Film website: www.malatestascarnival.com

this page and opposite: Scenes from **Malatesta's Carnival of Blood**. Director Christopher Speeth first met Alley Friends Architects at Philadelphia's Institute of Contemporary Art in 1970. Alley Friends had set up an inflatable bubble for the ICA's art auction, the same bubble that became the set for Vena's dream in the carnival of blood.

Alley Friends member Richard Stange describes the method used for the film: "The world beneath the carnival was built with materials scrounged from the carnival above: bent wheels, rubber tires, trashed ride cars, wooden pallets, race car track, 3-D cartoon figures with missing appendages, cotton candy, broken mirrors & windows, french fry containers, trash and scraps of wood, discarded neon signs and plywood sign cut-outs."

MANIAC
– William Lustig (1980)

Frank Zito (Joe Spinell) lives alone in a dingy basement flat, in the apartment block where he's caretaker. Abused by his mother as a child, he deals with his resentment by stalking, murdering and scalping women. The victims are prostitutes, nurses, couples making out; any woman who catches his eye, as long as there's a chance to kill. At home, Frank agonizes over his own misery, and wallows in guilt about what he's doing, but the compulsion to kill continues. He meets Anna (Caroline Munro), a beautiful photographer who genuinely likes him, but even with her he's unable to conceal his sickness…

Blowing through the genre like a freezing wind in the wake of 'fun' slaughter pics like *Halloween* and *Friday the 13th*, this totemic slice of Big Apple sleaze from William Lustig sucks the rollercoaster joy out of the slasher format and replaces it with the self-pitying murmurs of a miserable paranoid psychopath. Instead of *Halloween*'s immaculate autumnal suburbia, or *Friday the 13th*'s lakeside idyll, *Maniac* offers skanky red-light districts, graffiti-smothered toilets, grim roadside lay-bys and unmanned subway stations. From the first blue-tinged images of a couple making out on an inhospitable beach, to the final grubby apocalypse in the killer's basement flat, there's about as much light-hearted vim and fizz to all this as a night spent slumped in a piss-soaked doorway.

Naturally, what I'm trying to say is that *Maniac* is head and shoulders above the crowd. Isn't *horror* the name of the game, after all? And if you think not, well maybe you need to do a few 'Hail *Maniac*s' every now and again for getting a cheap kick out of murder and mutilation elsewhere. You wouldn't call this a work of art exactly, but in its strongest moments it reminds you of the gulf between the happy-go-lucky vicariousness of the horror genre and the heartlessness of real murder.

Jay Chattaway's theme tune exudes a defeated, hopeless quality that cues up both the killer's squalid existence and the miserable fates of the victims, with the surface prettiness of the instrumentation adding a tinge of bitter irony. It reminds me very much of Goblin's music for another great downer of the genre, Joe D'Amato's torture and taxidermy classic *Buio omega* (released theatrically in the USA as *Buried Alive*), which was made just the year before. Lustig has admitted to showing his lighting cameraman *The Exorcist* because he wanted to recreate an interior lighting technique for *Maniac*; perhaps he also packed Chattaway off to a 42nd Street grindhouse to bone up on morbid music? Probably not,

but like Goblin did for D'Amato, Chattaway takes the film into a realm of bleakness it might not have reached without him.

Unlike the cheerier slaughterthons of the early 1980s, *Maniac* is going to haunt you; not just later when you're going to sleep, but straight away, as you leave the theatre, or cross town at night. Imagine seeing this in a New York sleazepit, and then walking to the subway afterwards… The film feels hewn from the fear and paranoia of city life, and there's no safety net of fantasy to help dismiss the anxiety, especially for women, whom I imagine find it hard to 'dig' this movie at all. The most alarming sequence in the film is the stalking of a nurse (Kelly Piper), who's hunted down in a long drawn-out chase scene through an empty subway station, and murdered in a public toilet. The scene is brilliantly edited and paced to perfection, toying with the audience as the killer toys with the victim, and the actress makes the character's predicament horribly convincing. Also quite brilliant are Tom Savini's grisly effects, and I'm glad to see he's returned to the fold on this one, after reportedly regretting his involvement in the aftermath of the film's bad-boy profile. Personally, I much prefer Savini coming up with heavy-duty horrors like the scalpings and dismemberments seen here, instead of the cute spiny-toothed monsters he made for *Creepshow* and *Tales from the Darkside*.

There *are* things wrong with *Maniac*: the heavy breathing over Frank's point-of-view shots can make you giggle if you're in that sort of mood, and the device of having him mutter to himself leads to some momentarily toe-curling 'crazy-talk' – there's even a bit where he freaks at the word 'crazy', just like they always do in the movies. But the violence essentially crowds out these problems, and it's harder to giggle after the relentless throttling and scalping of a hooker (Rita Montone), or the subway stalking scene mentioned earlier. The most persistent of the film's drawbacks is the oft-remarked absurdity of Spinell earning a living as a fashion photographer whom glamorous Caroline Munro finds unaccountably loveable. Frank Zito (named after Lustig's friend Joseph Zito, director of *Bloodrage* and *The Prowler*) is not an urbane chameleon like Ted Bundy; he's a drop-out and a slob. Lustig admits on the film's most recent DVD commentary that this development of Frank's character was a mistake, made because he wanted to give Caroline Munro more to do. But he gets away with it, ultimately: you don't really remember these scenes so clearly afterwards – it's the grime and the squalor that stick in your mind's eye, the sorrow of the victims' fates that hangs heavy in your heart, and the chilly paranoia of *Maniac*'s urban hellscape that quickens your step on the way home.

Made in New York City.

478

MARTIN

– George Romero (1976)

Martin (John Amplas), a withdrawn teenager obsessed with drinking blood, goes to live in Pennsylvania with his elderly cousin Tata Cuda (Lincoln Maazel), who believes him to be a real vampire. Cuda, a cold disciplinarian, refers to the boy only as *"Nosferatu!"* and dresses the house with garlic and crucifixes, warning him that he will be destroyed *"without salvation"* if he takes a victim from the town. Martin, however, insists: *"There's no real magic. There's no real magic ever."* Instead, utilizing syringes filled with sleeping draughts, and razor blades instead of fangs, he secretly continues his sick nocturnal activities. As Martin tries to normalise his life via friendship with Cuda's granddaughter Christina (Christine Forrest) and a lonely housewife, Mrs. Santini (Elyane Nadeau), with whom he begins his first sexual liaison (*"without the blood part"*), he also strikes up an odd relationship with late-night listeners to a radio phone-in show, to whom he confesses his crimes. No one believes him, and instead he becomes a figure of fun, dubbed 'The Count' by the radio host (Michael Gornick). Martin attempts to rid himself of his compulsion, but waiting in the wings is Cuda, determined to deal with 'Nosferatu' the old way…

Martin is the most beautiful of American horror films. Although its director George Romero will forever be associated with his indelible zombie films, it is his true masterpiece, the peak by which his talents as a director and stylist should be measured. *Martin* has emotional maturity, technical virtuosity, and a brilliant storyline that blends wit, horror and sadness into something quite unique. It's also Romero's most compassionate work, extending emotional reach to a character others might have cast beyond the pale. In *Martin*, we spend the entire running time in the company of a killer, but Romero contemplates him with such honest sympathy that we're compelled to feel for him, lost in delusion as he is. The humanity extended to this 'monster' is neither trendily callous (as was the case with recent turkeys like *Bundy*) nor unpersuasive (as in *Maniac*, where the character's self-pity eclipses our efforts to sympathise with him). You end up viewing Martin sorrowfully, as you would a much-loved brother or close friend somehow sucked into madness. In fact, such is the persuasiveness of Martin's voice (rather like Alex in *A Clockwork Orange*) that you have to stop and remind yourself he really *is* a murderer: the first victim has her veins slit from wrist to elbow (to mimic an efficient suicide cut), and is left drugged, presumably bleeding to death. Later, Martin pierces a male victim through the throat with a sharpened stick, in an act not of thirst but of petulance. (*"You weren't supposed to* be *there."*)

The reason we're seduced is that *Martin* reaches beyond violence and horror into detailed character-study, while also focusing on environment; with the latter, in my opinion, the most fertile yet least explored of horror's possible concerns. The film is both a portrait of a psychologically disturbed youth, and an affectionate but unsentimental look at a broken-backed town. By finding beauty in the decay of both physical and psychical geography, Romero engages deeply with the Gothic sensibility – and then undercuts it with a series of acute, ironic scenes which challenge head-on the nostalgic complacency of the tradition.

Right from the start there's a powerful investment in location. A train leaves a railway station late at night, the departing carriages haunted by a mournful railroad bell. Donald Rubinstein's peerless music is both ironically *mittel*-European and achingly sad. It's as if we've boarded the latest of late-night sleepers on our way to a dark, romantic adventure. However, instead of Hitchcock's *North By Northwest*, with Cary Grant seduced by Eva Marie Saint, nervous young Martin enters a lady's railroad boudoir only to drug her and drink her blood. In his mind, though, he *is* a Cary Grant of sorts, albeit with overtones of Lorre and Lugosi (with whom, after all, Grant shared a sinister debonair quality).

It's here, during the attack in the railway carriage, that Romero definitively steers away from the norm. In an elegant manoeuvre that's both an homage and critique of the horror genre, we're shown the stark reality of Martin's actions alongside the romantic black-and-white fantasy (or is it memory?) playing in his head. Romero and his prodigiously talented DP, Michael Gornick, deftly mingle desaturated colour and sepia-tinted black-and-white, backing up what could have seemed like abstruse formal experimentation with a strong narrative *raison d'être*. The lush, blowsy fantasy version and the awkward, fumbling reality are both equally well-realised, but it's the clutter and jumble of the sleeping carriage, and its occupant with her face smeared in moisturizing cream, that stick in your mind.

When the train pulls into Pittsburgh, Martin disembarks, leaving his victim locked in her sleeper compartment. A proud, unwelcoming elderly man who introduces himself as Cuda (Lincon Maazel) tells him they must take another train. Looking from the window on this second, suburban journey, we stare along with Martin as desolate downtown Pittsburgh rushes by. When the train arrives at Braddock, Martin's new home, the images and the matchlessly exquisite score unite to present a vision of pure melancholy, a small town both beautiful and bereft of hope for the

Martin
© 1976. Braddock Associates
A Laurel presentation.
director/writer: George A. Romero. producer: Richard Rubinstein. director of photography: Michael Gornick. music composed & arranged by Donald Rubinstein, recorded at Triton Studio (Boston), engineer: Jay Mandell. post production supervisor: Michael Gornick. post production assistants: Michael Di Lauro, Tony Buba. assistant cameramen: Tom Dubinsky, Nick Mastandrea. grips: Steve Lalick, Phillip Desiderio. special effects & make-up: Tom Savini. technical assistance: Regis J. Survinsky, Tony Pantanella. associate producers: Patricia Bernesser, Ray Schmaus. production coordinator: Joyce Weber. assistant to the producer: Donna Siegal. colour by WRS Laboratory (Pittsburgh). titles by The Animators, Inc. (Pittsburgh). financial services: Barney C. Guttman. legal services: Goldberg & Snodgrass. Special thanks to Lakeshore Railway Historical Society; Baltimore & Ohio Railroad; the people of Braddoock (Pennsylvania).
Cast: John Amplas (Martin). Lincoln Maazel (Cuda). Christine Forrest (Christina). Elyane Nadeau (Mrs. Santini). Tom Savini (Arthur). Sara Venable (housewife victim). Fran Middleton (train victim). Al Levitsky (Lewis). George A. Romero (Father Howard). James Roy (Deacon). J. Clifford Forrest, Jr. (Father Zulemas). Robert Ogden (businessman). Donaldo Soviero (flashback: priest). Donna Siegal (woman). Albert J. Schmaus, Lillian Schmaus, Frnces Mazzoni (family). Vincent D. Survinski (train porter). Tony Buba, Pasquale Buba, Clayton McKinnon (drug dealers). Regis J. Survinsky, Tony Pantanella (hobos). Harvey Eger, Tom Weber (men in bathroom). Robert Barner, Stephen Fergelic (police). Douglas Serene, Jeanne Serene (cyclists). Nick Mastandrea, John Sozansky (Marines). Ingeborg Forrest (Mrs. Anderson). Carol McCloskey (Mrs. Bellini). uncredited: Michael Gornick (radio show host).

opposite page:
Attacked by his own trophies – a killer pays the price for his evil in **Maniac**.

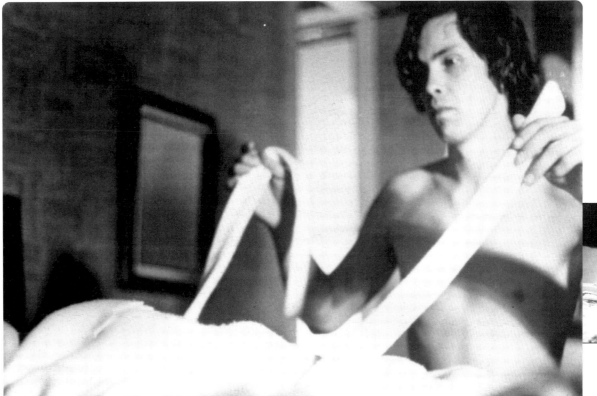

left and below:
Martin enjoys the only kind of sex he can in George A. Romero's sophisticated horror masterpiece **Martin**.

479

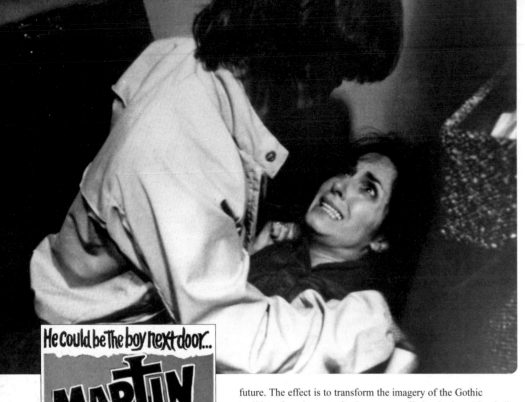

future. The effect is to transform the imagery of the Gothic tradition: from images of pale women suffering in the rotting halls of the aristocracy, to misunderstood modern youth in the collapsing infrastructure of post-industrial cities.

The film can be read either as a naturalistic story with fantasy sequences, or a supernatural tale with flashbacks. To the credit of many critics and fans, there has generally been a reluctance to drive a definitive wedge between the two possibilities, no doubt fostered by the very thoughtful and persuasive interviews Romero has given on the subject. One could tease out the various implications of each possibility for page after page; *Martin* is one of Romero's densest works. For me, the chief interest lies in the realist interpretation; which is not to say the supernatural possibilities lack resonance. After all, if Martin really is a vampire, he's one who's forced to live in a universe without God. None of the traditional protections have the slightest effect: Martin chews a bulb of garlic, kisses a crucifix, and lounges bored during an attempted exorcism. But although he affects contempt for Cuda's religious orthodoxy, he remains afflicted with melancholia. Instead of being assured a meaningful existence throughout eternity, as a powerful outcast from the Kingdom of God, he's adrift without meaning, without special powers, an absurdity in a Godless world. This failure of religious meaning is referred to concretely in the film, through Cuda's arguments with the trendy new vicar of Braddock, played by Romero himself, and implicitly by the secular media confessional offered by the radio phone-in.

Martin's ability to talk frankly about his crimes to a radio interviewer (who ironically regards his 'confessions' as a clever joke) is one of Romero's best ploys, showcasing his habitual theme of miscommunication and his ironic approach to technology. The radio host, of course, is another sort of vampire, smoothly sucking at the troubles of his listeners to provide amusement for his show. He reveals his 'fangs', appropriately enough, during an advertising break, saying off-air to Martin: *"Count? Hey man, where can I get a hold of you? This is really going over big […] I'd like to talk to you, I'd like to have you come down to the station…"* Like many who call to air their views on such shows, Martin has no stomach for a meeting in the flesh; mortified, he hangs up. Of course it's also the case that the last thing *"a real life honest to goodness vampire"* needs is face-to-face publicity, but the situation is, as always in *Martin*, multi-layered. The radio phone-in sequences juxtapose brilliantly observed black humour with a terrible sadness, exploring themes of media manipulation, loneliness, and the need for confession.

Martin has more complex interactions with others than any screen vampire I can think of. He's an aggressor to his victims; a stranger to the citizens of Braddock; a wayward child to Cuda; a surrogate brother and confidante to Christina; a toyboy (and cat surrogate) for Mrs. Santini; a hit property to the radio host; and a fantasy identification figure to the phone-in listeners. But all of these positions are complicated or distorted: Martin the aggressor is a victim of his own violent drives; Martin the stranger is the delivery boy from the store down the street; Martin the child terrifies the superstitious patriarch in a fog-shrouded children's playground; Martin the 'older brother' is left behind as his enterprising 'sister' leaves town; Martin the hot young lover cannot save Mrs. Santini from depression and suicide; and of course neither the radio host nor the clamouring public understand that 'The Count' is for real, not a joke. Finally, as the film reaches its sad, ironic, inevitable end, the final distinctions are blurred; life and death, truth and make-believe – perhaps even death and resurrection.

NB: Romero has said that his original preferred cut of the film was nearly three hours in length, but the only existing print of this version was stolen from his garage soon after the film was completed. The extra material added more scenes of Braddock and its people: as this focus on the town helps make *Martin* so unique and valuable, it's really a crying shame that the long version is lost. Search your neighbours' garages!

Cinematographer Michael Gornick on his experience shooting with Romero:

"The opportunity to shoot Martin *came quite by chance. During the set-up of our first shot (Martin ambles along the tracks of a railroad line as he walks to his first day of work at Tata Cuda's market), George suddenly turned to me (I was to do audio for the film, and was preparing to place my boom mike for some reference audio and 'wild sound' of the approaching locomotive) and offered, 'Say man, I'm tired of shooting. I'd like to direct. Here, take a look and set up this shot.' Dumbfounded, but honoured, I moved to camera. George Romero – the maestro – had asked me to shoot. I couldn't believe it. At the time of our work together on* Martin *I had already known and worked with George for some three years. He was an amazing talent. Always friendly and engaging, probably the most democratic artist I have ever met. In that I mean to suggest that he often solicited the opinions and perceptions of those about him as he crafted his films. Never indecisive or without conviction, George used the criticisms and input of others as a challenge to his creativity and a kind of forum to express his creative logic. Often he found room for the thoughts of others, and at other times he confronted suggestions with the staunch command of a director of German silent cinema. Always receptive to ideas in improving the process or product, one could gauge George's acceptance of a proffered idea as he exuberantly said, 'That's Cool!' Rejection from George came gently: 'Really, man... I don't know...' Nonetheless, either in acceptance or rejection one felt some sense of grand collaboration with the artist."*

George had gone through kind of a dry period after The Crazies*, and just to make a dollar we were making sports documentaries on ABC, but we would constantly save raw footage so that we would one day be able to shoot a motion picture, and we used that footage, which we had saved over two to four years, to make* Martin*! We shot it on colour reversal film 16mm, ECO, at ASA-25, which is very slow. George from day one wanted to release it black and white as opposed to colour, and we maintained that as long as possible until we were trying to get it into distribution. We met with Ben Barenholtz, a distributor from New York, and he said, 'Dammit guys, if only you'd shot this thing in colour!' George, out of desperation, said, 'Alright, I did shoot it in colour!' – and the rest is history.*

At the time we did a test market screening of the three hour version, in black and white, in a theatre in New Jersey, and that was the only screening of the three hour version: that print unfortunately has gone, we don't know what happened to it. It had that one audience screening, and it was our own kind of test screening to see how the film would perform."

Made in Pennsylvania.
see also: **The Crazies**

MESSIAH OF EVIL
– Willard Huyck (1973)

See interview with Willard Huyck and Gloria Katz.

Made in California.

MICROWAVE MASSACRE
– Wayne Berwick (1978 [released 1983])

See interview with Wayne Berwick and Ted Newsom.

Made in California.

MONSTROID
– Kenneth Hartford and Herbert L. Strock (1979)

aka *Monster*
aka *Monster: The Legend That Became a Terror*
aka *It Came from the Lake*
aka *The Toxic Horror*

Colombia, South America. A giant creature living in a lake emerges to attack the locals, and pollution from a nearby cement works is responsible. The company's American owners send a big game hunter to kill it…

Monstroid initially seems set on being an anti-capitalist monster movie, underpinning its drama with earnest speeches about the pollution of the Third World by greedy American multinationals. John Carradine plays a Colombian priest, who together with an investigative female reporter brings down bad publicity on a cement-making corporation responsible for polluting the local water supply. You find yourself wondering what Oliver Stone might have done with the material! Sadly, as events roll on, the eco-angle gets lost in the dust, and the film turns into a tame 'trap it and kill it' adventure. You just know the script's political conscience is going off the rails when the monster kills a pretty young secretary working at the corporation; after all, 'who could possibly blame her for the

STARRING JIM MITCHUM. JOHN CARRADINE. PHIL CAREY. ANDREA HARTFORD. TONY EISLEY. WRITTEN, PRODUCED & DIRECTED BY KEN HARTFORD. DIRECTOR OF PHOTOGRAPHY. JOHN WILDER MINCEY. MUSIC BY GENE KAUER. EDITOR: MIKE JOHNSON

MONSTROID

A HORRIFYING LEGEND COME TO LIFE

"TERROR FILM OF THE YEAR"
—FILM WORLD

R RESTRICTED
UNDER 17 REQUIRES ACCOMPANYING PARENT OR ADULT GUARDIAN
AN ACADEMY INTERNATIONAL RELEASE.

800040

evils of capitalism?' I guess the monster's just bad after all… With the weightier theme silted over by standard generic riffing, it's left to the hired hunter to fillet any remaining social commentary from the story by performing heroically and wasting time with some airborne helicopter hoopla. There's a final shot of monster eggs on the lakeshore that simply plays the obvious 'evil lives on' finale, but it's hardly the sustained attack on big business greed the first reel was promising. The monster itself is kind of cute, for what it's worth, but given the Japanese Godzilla movies, it's hardly groundbreaking. (Someone at least went to a lot of trouble to sculpt a realistic giant claw for the first monster attack; a pity that the full monty, so to speak, doesn't live up to it.)

Monstroid was shot in Colombia and New Mexico, but was not a Colombian co-production. Placing exactly when it was made is quite difficult: the first mention of the film being 'in production' came with a promo set report in *Variety*, October 1975. Two years later, in October 1977, it was still listed as 'in production' by *The Hollywood Reporter*. Another year later, in October 1978, *Variety* ran an advertisement announcing that 'production' was completed. The film finally received a copyright catalogue entry in 1979. Kenneth Hartford grabs the onscreen directing credit, although Herbert L. Strock, veteran director of *I Was a Teenage Frankenstein* and *The Crawling Hand*, actually shot the majority of the finished film. Credits from some sources are erroneous, suggesting that Cesar Romero, Diane McBain and Keenan Wynn feature in the cast, although they were only ever announced prior to shooting and were never actually signed.

Made in Colombia and New Mexico.

MOVIE HOUSE MASSACRE
– Alice Raley [Rick Sloane] (1984)

aka *Blood Theater*

The manager of a beleaguered cinema sees his lover dallying with an usher, so he deliberately sets fire to the place, killing everyone. Some time later, the Spotlite Theater chain decides to revive the cinema, employing staff from a more successful theatre to take over and relaunch it. Before long, they fall victim to the old manager's ghost and some extremely dull murders…

Movie House Massacre is located in a strange, unloved region of town, a crossroads where kitsch meets failed send-up, and where bad jokes and broad-brush performances try to pass themselves off as irony. As bad as only bad camp can be, *Movie House Massacre* cheats horror fans with its near bloodless murders, while wasting a premise that had some real potential. Quite how Mary Woronov, a frequently talented comedy actor, got herself entangled in it is a mystery. Every attempt at humour ends forlornly, with the distant plop of a stone missing its target by hundreds of yards. The shooting, framing, acting, editing and writing are all flawed, leaving little to enjoy. It's so bad that you feel for the filmmakers, forced to get up in the morning to complete something that was probably hopeless on day three. There's a vague New Wave feel (that's post-punk, not Godard), but the attitude-free vibe suggests that the filmmakers have grooved on a punk sense of irreverence without knowing what it is they're supposed to be irreverent about. Unctuous cinema Tannoy announcements aim for a sort of *Saturday Night Live* meets Paul Bartel humour, but they're far too limply written, and the T&A is chaste enough to satisfy the actresses' mothers. For a sense of how badly the movie is written, try this news-reporter's speech to camera: *"We're coming to you live on our opening night, or should we say our grand re-opening. Since its construction in the 1930s this building has been continually opened and closed. Will success smile on the theatre or will it stand empty and crumbling in a short matter of time?"* Ed Wood, eat your heart out…

Where *Movie House Massacre* really falls down is in its contrast between corporate and private movie-houses. In fact it's

Monstroid
aka **The Toxic Horror** (US video title)
aka **Monster** (US video title)
aka **It Came from the Lake** (US video title)
aka **The Legend That Became a Terror** (pre-release title)
© none [1979]
Academy International Distributors presents an Academy International presentation in association with Major Financial Investments. actual director [uncredited]: Herbert L. Strock. credited director [additional scenes only]: Kenneth Hartford [Kenneth Herts]. producer: Kenneth Hartford. story by Kenneth Hartford. screenplay: Kenneth Hartford, Walter Roeber Schmidt, Herbert L. Strock & Garland Scott. directors of photography: John Wilder Mincey & Arthur Fitzsimmons. supervising editor: Rodger Parker. editor: Michael W. Johnson. Colombia cameraman: Jan-Henk Kleijn. associate producer: Kenneth J. Fisher. gaffer: Tim Lightner. camera operator: Robin Willis. assistant cameraman: Mike Sábo. script supervisor: Candice Strock. sound mixer: Pat Vallierra. key grip: Michael Shore. grips: Michael Lamb, Diane Miller & David McCormick. makeup artist: Juliet Wilson. wardrobe supervisor: Elizabeth Scott. set decorator: Gary Hoffman. property master: Mathews / Mathew Sanchez. location manager: Karen Koch. production coordinator: Barbara Waters. special effects: Ken Hartford, Steve Czerkas & Marc Wolf. music: Marshall Lieb. executive in charge of publicity: Bud Testa. additional editing: Will Dent. teamster captain: John Boulton. boom: Gregg Valtierra, Jr. security: Joseph Herrera & John Collins. assistant to the producer: Darlene Gonzales. extra casting: Gerald Sandaval. drivers: Fred Mignardot & Paul Knee. assistant editor: Bill Stewart. post production: Post Transfer Services. processing: CFI (Hollywood); Microstampa (Rome). key art design: Roger Lamanna. filmed in mid-1978 on location in Ambalema (Colombia) & Espanola (New Mexico) and Griffith Park (California).
[additional 'Monstroid' credits]: music by Gene Kauer. publicity: Bud Testa. processing by Getty Film Laboratory. titles by Title House. now in paperback from Carousel books.
Cast: Jim Mitchum (Bill Travis). John Carradine (the priest). Phil Carey (Pete). Tony Eisley (Al Barnes). Andrea Hartford (Andrea Anderson) and Glen Hartford (Glen Anderson). Coral Kassel. Connie Moore. Maria Rubio. Aldo Sambrell. Luis Suarez. Emanuel Smith. Leslie Meigs. Roberto Martinez. John Lamarr. Polo C'd Baca. Carolyn Martin. Henry Gabaldon. Pam Day. Jannine May. The St. Ann Choir and the citizens of Ambalema (Columbia) and Espanola (New Mexico). Fritzie Ross, Darlene Dickquist & Joe Flores (stunt people).
additionally credited on 'Monster: The Legend That became a Terror' prints: Monte Cook. Felicia Robbins. Steven Fisher.

bottom left:
A vague, lumpy shape emerges from the lake… that'll be **Monstroid**…

opposite page, top:
Martin attacks a woman on a late night train.

opposite page, below:
Two well-designed admats for **Martin**.

hard to see exactly what the filmmaker wanted to say on the
subject. The head of the Spotlite cinema chain is clearly meant to
be an asshole, but the tragedy that befell the old cinema was
caused by a selfish manager who murdered his own staff in
furtherance of a personal vendetta. There was scope here for an
attack on soulless multiplexes, from the point of view of those
who admire the old picture palaces, but the film ends up
implying that the older cinemas were as bad as the new. *Not* a
message to warm the hearts of cult-moviegoers! Written with a
half-hearted frosting of satire that fails to cover the underlying
silliness, it's hard to imagine *Movie House Massacre* surviving
an opening weekend out there in the real world. Despite the self-
consciously cultish approach, one thing's for certain: it'll never
be revived as a midnight movie.

The onscreen credit goes to 'Alice Raley', but the film was
apparently made by sexploitation-comedy director Rick Sloane,
who carved a successful niche for himself in the late 1980s with
the tits-and-truncheons *Vice Academy* series…)

Made in California.

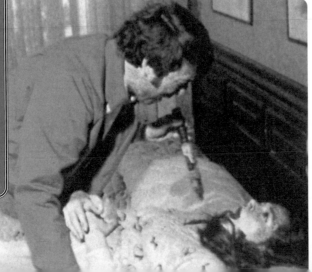

MY FRIENDS NEED KILLING
– Paul Leder (1976)

Gene Kline (Greg Mullavey), a Vietnam veteran who suffers
nightmares about the crimes he and his unit committed against
Vietnamese civilians, writes to four of his old army buddies
proposing to meet up with them again. He sets about murdering
them, one by one, acting as angel of vengeance in retribution for
their shared crimes. First down is Vincent Gray (actor uncredited),
whom Gene drains of blood as punishment for letting an old
woman bleed to death. A stay-over with boorish ex Corporal Gil
Perkins (Clayton Wilcox) leaves him and his wife Susan (Carolyn
Ames) dead (*"They didn't count, they were just gooks,"* Gil
protests). A visit to San Francisco to see Les Drago (Roger Cruz)
results in a drink-and-drugs 'suicide', and a trip back to L.A. to
meet ringleader and unrepentant pig Sergeant Walter Miller (Bill
Michael) ends with Miller gorily stabbed to death. But when
Walter's pregnant wife Georgia (Laurie Burton) goes into labour at
the news of her husband's murder, how will Gene react?

My Friends Need Killing would be essential viewing on the
basis of that wonderful title alone, and there's a good little movie
behind it too. Gene's crusade against his old army buddies has a
satisfying 'And then there were none' structure, with all but the first
(oddly truncated) encounter revealing the character of each victim
before they die. The film was clearly made cheaply (a lot of footage
was shot silent and dubbed later) but the lead character's despair
comes across strongly, not just through the creepy performance by
Leder regular Mullavey (*Marigold Man*, *I Dismember Mama*,
Vultures, *Body Count*) but via the succession of locations – airports,
freeways, Los Angeles and San Francisco streets – all imbued with
a downbeat, one-way-trip-to-oblivion vibe.

It's an odd film, though. Gene is more than a mere psychopath
but less than a true moral force. It's difficult to justify his actions
because he rapes and murders Gil's wife, who of course had nothing
to do with the atrocities he's so steamed up about, and he persists in
his psychological assault on Les even though it's clear the young
man has turned against the war, suffering enormous guilt that he is
seeking to confront through acting in the theatre. Les recites from
Macbeth: *"Out, damn spot. Will these hands never be clean?"* but
Gene merely uses the young man's guilt to make the task of killing
him easier. By persuading him to take an overdose, Gene ignores
the man's contrition and shows the same lack of mercy for which
he's punishing everyone else. And since the dialogue withholds the
exact nature of Les's involvement (was he a killer or a bystander?),
it's particularly hard to tell whether Gene's eye-for-an-eye crusade
makes internal sense. The rape of Susan and the 'assisted suicide' of
Les removes Gene's actions from the realm of poetic justice, and
the film suffers slightly from this: without these unprincipled
actions, the rest of the killings could be discussed as rough justice.
It's as if Leder wanted to detach himself from the actions of his
protagonist, and so makes him commit a blatantly unjustifiable act.

Shot with Leder's characteristically understated camera style,
the pacing occasionally threatens to slip into tedium. Fortunately,
the simplicity of the four-victim structure keeps us orientated so that
we don't feel too adrift. The whole thing has a sort of minimalist
theatrical quality, especially when Walter, Gene's mean old
sergeant, momentarily buys into Gene's fantasy recreation of a raid
on a Vietnamese village and joins him on the ground, as if under
fire from unseen enemies. It's easy to imagine this played against
black drapes with a couple of props in some off-Broadway theatre.
Of course Leder's style comes out of the Actors Studio melodramas
of the 1950s (see chapter on John Hayes), so it's interesting to see
this later chamber piece staying true to the roots of his early writing
assignments; it's just a shame he didn't choose to act in the movie
too. Nevertheless, I'd recommend *My Friends Need Killing* (if you
know what I mean): it makes an essential addition to a Vietnam-
horror-themed video all-nighter, along with Sean Costello's *Forced
Entry*, Bob Clark's *Deathdream*, Buddy Giovinazzo's *Combat
Shock*, and Antonio Margheriti's *Cannibal Apocalypse*…

Made in California.
see also: **I Dismember Mama** *and* **Sketches of a Strangler**

Sheila Sullivan   Robert Culp   Samantha Eggar

A NAME FOR

EViL

directed by BERNARD GIRARD
produced by REED SHERMAN
with MIKE LANE, CLARENCE MILLER,
SUE HATHAWAY
and TED GREENHALGH

DVS

A NAME FOR EVIL
– Bernard Girard (1972)
aka *The Face of Evil*
aka *The Grove*

A Name for Evil trendily takes its cues from the disaffection motifs of late sixties and early seventies cinema, employing a mishmash of psychedelic superimpositions, coloured filters and artsy manipulations. The editing shuffles information in disordered fashion, while free love and nudity cynically ensure the sexual revolution gets a look-in. Visually it resembles Jess Franco's *Venus in Furs* (1969) but without that film's icy commitment to perversity.

The story centres on John Blake (TV stalwart Robert Culp), a disaffected architect who drops out of the family business to pursue his dreams in the countryside retreat built by 'The Major', his great grandfather. John's wife Joanna (played with great skill and naturalism by Samantha Eggar) is quick to pour scorn on his stand, telling him he's irresponsible, immature and all the other things the hippies were accused of by straights. Joanna attacks her husband's airy notions by suggesting his act of rebellion is more copout than dropout, a childish refusal of complex realities. She's adept at slashing holes in her husband's stance but there's no suggestion that she has anything but comfortable self-interest at heart. Joanna is a materialist in love with her husband's wealth and the social status that comes with it. John's onscreen reveries show what he would prefer Joanna to be: a submissive, adoring caricature of femininity. It seems this rebel against conformity has a thing for Stepford Wives.

Despite Joanna's ballbreaking attitude, her criticisms have some validity. John's posturing is indeed half-baked. He turns his back on his family's wealth, but it's not a choice that brings any hardship or sacrifice. He remains comfortable, withdrawing not to join an anarcho-syndicalist commune or tour the Far East but to renovate his great grandfather's country house. How noble! Change will be hard, though: The Major warns in a pre-credits voice-over that he will never allow a single alteration to be made to his property – whether he's alive or dead. Indeed, such is his autocratic mien that he even declares the insects in the grass to be subject to his will…

For all its counterculture trappings, *A Name for Evil* is a spook story, albeit one that links the generational conflicts of the classical Gothic to contemporary tensions in politics and culture. It doesn't take much of a stretch to read The Major and his domineering ego as representing 'the old order'. John sees The Major's indistinct ghost walking around, silhouetted in broken windows, flitting out of sight through doorways and round corners. The dynamic initially points to the dead weight of the past weighing down on John's attempt to start again. *A Name for Evil* is a long way short of a film like *Let's Scare Jessica To Death* or *Messiah of Evil*, but it shares with them a desire to rethink supernatural clichés by firing them through the prism of the counterculture. Or is it rethinking the counterculture by firing it through the prism of supernatural cliché? That's the trouble with *A Name for Evil* – nothing really coheres into the statement it seems desperate to make. When Girard introduces a ghostly white horse, it's the sort of heavily symbolic image that leaps up and licks your face. The supernatural steed appears several times, seemingly belonging to the baneful ghost. One night, leaving his wife asleep, John leaps astride the creature, which bears him out of the woods, eventually depositing him at a raucous country tavern. He joins in the revelry and ends up making love to a beautiful young woman called Luanna (Sheila Sullivan, Culp's wife at the time). The film takes this infidelity as a cue to divest the cast of their clothes, and, in scenes that must have been part of the reason *Penthouse*'s Bob Guccione put up the money, we enter that familiar whirlpool of quasi-occult sexual cavorting so familiar in early seventies horror.

It's around this point that we lose our compass as regards the film's intended theme. If the steed, belonging to the autocratic Major, is symbolic of the patriarchal past, it seems strange that it should have led John to joyful orgiastic celebration. You're left wondering if the film views such sexual freedom as evil. Confusion therefore reigns as the latter stages unfold. The night's dalliance may just have been an illusion. When John returns home in the morning, he believes he has spent the night in rapturous union with a child of nature. His wife, on the other hand, claims he subjected her to hours of sexual brutality and degradation. But the following day John meets Luanna again and confirms her existence in the real world. The confusion is carried through to the 'Debussy Does *Dallas*' score; one minute beguiling, the next banal.

If *A Name for Evil* has a problem it's precisely that it lacks the ability to decide where evil lies. Not because of any tricksiness, but because it hedges its bets so thickly, trying to appeal to both reactionary and revolutionary. Although Girard toys with the visual codes of the counterculture, he also seems to attack it. Through the fog of style, one suspects that in fact a rather conservative tale has been mangled beyond sense. In a terrible, muddled ending, John commits a murder we've been expecting for the last half-hour: cut to a long shot of a funeral taking place in the forecourt, attended by figures too small and distant to recognise. A car stands nearby and someone gets into it, but where is John? Perhaps all is clear on the big screen, but in terms of dramatic structure and pacing this ending is too rushed, and very unsatisfying. Whatever significance the film has been reaching for is lost, and in a pessimistic/reactionary cyclical gesture, we end on The Major's mantra, repeated from the prologue: *"I wouldn't permit it to be changed during my life – why should I permit it just because I happen to be dead?"*

Bernard Girard was born on 22 February, 1918. He began his film career as a screenwriter in the fifties: his feature directorial debut followed in 1957 with the western *Ride Out for Revenge* (an earlier film called *As You Were* runs under an hour in length). Afterwards, he concentrated on television, including assignments for *The Twilight Zone*, *Alfred Hitchcock Presents*, *Rawhide* and *The Virginian*. He made *The Mad Room* for Columbia in 1969, and an unusual sci-fi drama called *The Happiness Cage* (1972), starring Christopher Walken in one of his earliest film roles. After *A Name for Evil*, Girard made one final movie, a western called *Gone with the West* (1975), reputed to have been stitched together with material from an older, unfinished project. (See the feature on *Messiah of Evil*). He died on 30 December, 1997.

Made in: unknown (Partly shot in Canada.)

A Name for Evil
aka **The Grove** (shooting title)
aka **The Face of Evil** (pre-release title)
© 1972. Penthouse Pictures, Inc. Distributed by Penthouse Distribution Inc. A Penthouse Production presentation during production: Interfilm (Canada)/Centennial Productions (Hollywood). director: Bernard Girard. producer: Reed Sherman. screenplay: Bernard Girard; from the Andrew Lytle novel "A Name for Evil". cinematographer: Reginald Morris. music: Dominic Frontiere. cinema editor: Maurice Wright. art director: Cameron Porteous. song "Mountain Woman" lyrics: Ed Cobb, music: Emory Gordy, Jr., performed by Billy Joe Royal. 'production manager: David Robertson. unit manager: Harvey McCracken. assistant director: Bill Lukather. 2nd assistant director: Fred Hatt. choreographer: Grover Dale. music editors: Emma E.Levin & Robert H.Raff. make-up: Al Fleming, Pyllis Newman. hairdresser: Salli Bailey. wardrobe: Ilse Richter & Bobby Watts. still photography: Robert Willoughby. assistant editor: Michael Palakow. assistant camera: Rod Parkhurst. sound: John Guselle, Art Steadman & Rupert Bennett. lighting: Bobby Milligan, Bruce Campbell. grips: Fred Ransom, David Humphries & Don Kosloski. props: John Stooshnov & Peter Young. production secretary: Gail Turner. post production supervisor: Synchrofilm, Inc. re-recording: Samuel Goldwyn Studio, Richard Portman. title design: Hannah Hamilburg. titles/opticals/ processing: Consolidated Film Industries. filming from 15 July 1970 in Vancouver (British Columbia, Canada).
Cast: Robert Culp (John Blake). Samantha Eggar (Joanna Blake). Sheila Sullivan (Luanna Baxter). Mike Lane (Fats). Sue Hathaway (Mary). Ted Greenhalgh (Hugh). Clarence 'Big' Miller (Jimmy). Barbara Tremain (Mrs. Olson). Reg McReynolds (M. Olson). Walter Marsh (minister). D. Goldrick (secretary).

top left:
The UK video cover of **A Name for Evil** uses the same sinister old house that features on the poster art for **The Last House on Dead End Street** on page 470.

opposite page, top:
The US video carton for **Movie House Massacre**.

opposite middle and bottom:
Greg Mullavey as the disturbed Vietnam veteran in Paul Leder's **My Friends Need Killing**.

NATAS: THE REFLECTION
– Jack Dunlap (1983)

Investigative reporter Steve Granger (Randy Mulkey) is fired from a big newspaper job because of his obsession with a local Indian legend. Girlfriend Terry (Pat Bolt), also a reporter, is likewise fed up with hearing about the enigmatic Smohalla, a two-hundred-year-old Indian mystic whom Steve believes is living in a nearby mountain range. Determined to silence his critics, Steve heads off into the hills. He soon finds Smohalla (Nino Cochise), and asks for guidance regarding an Indian riddle about the Natas Tower, where souls are said to be entrapped by the Prince of Darkness. Legend has it that if the Devil can hold the spirits prisoner for a hundred years they belong to him, and down to hell they go. Only human intervention can thwart his plan. Steve takes a talisman and a map from Smohalla and sets out to save some souls. With the help of Terry and a trio of friends, he encounters a ghost town full of zombies, before ascending the mountain in search of Natas…

I used to see this video kicking around in second-hand shops and car-boot sales, although for years I never bothered to investigate because the title was so silly. But it's an odd little film in places, beginning as a tired, poorly acted trudge, and then stumbling across a few genuinely unsettling ideas along the way. A scene in a derelict saloon populated by creepy, mouldering old cowboys carries a real chill: the customers, the barkeep, even a pair of hookers, are caked in grime and dried blood, like ghouls who've been caught in a dust storm. The zombie-lite attack scenes are similarly startling (at least in contrast with the slower sections beforehand). Sadly, some very loose scripting allows tension to dissipate after Steve's buddy Spec (Fred Perry) is murdered in the old ghost town. The four remaining friends, initially scared and angry, split up and search the empty buildings; then for no good reason start fooling around and acting like they've forgotten about Spec's death. *"It was most likely a tramp or a bum or somebody like that, and they've probably already high-tailed it out of here,"* shrugs Jay (Craig Hensley). At least he and Angie (Kelli Kuhn) pay dearly for their cavalier attitude: first Angie, in an effective scare involving sleeping bags and surprise occupants; then Jay, in an entertaining encounter with a falling scythe (which unfortunately seems to be missing a few frames in the British video).

To his credit, director Jack Dunlap obviously took a personal interest in his subject matter. What initially seems like an odd conflation of Native American mysticism and Catholicism turns out to be based on proper research: Smohalla was a genuine historical figure who set up a sect blending the two belief systems in the mid-19th Century (although recent sightings have been rare…) Research aside, Dunlap also deserves credit for the mountain-side climax. It's pleasingly fantastical up there, with

smoke hissing from crevices and an impressive winged demon waiting at the top. It's just a pity that the confrontation is resolved in such a simple and predictable fashion. Still, I found that I warmed to the lead, Randy Mulkey (who dresses like the front-man of a seventies rock act), even if he does seem more concerned with how to look cool in a suede jacket than displaying the extremes of emotion suggested by the script. Things end on a comical note as Terry flings her journalist's notes out the car window at the end: perhaps her flagrant littering of the sacred lands was intended to leave the way open for a sequel. Oh, and in case you're still trying to decipher the enigma of *Natas*: come back Johnny Alucard, all is forgiven…

Made in Arizona.

THE NESTING
– Armand Weston (1980)
aka *Phobia* (shooting title)

Lauren Cochran (Robin Groves) is a successful writer of Gothic mystery novels. She's also agoraphobic, sexually repressed, and suffering writer's block. She decides to rent a house in the country to try and overcome her personal problems – but, as she settles in, her dreams become steadily more disturbing and sexually charged. In fact they're so vivid she believes she may be experiencing visions of the house's past. The beautiful old country dwelling was once a whorehouse, and Lauren comes to believe that the spirits of prostitutes who were killed there one night in the 1930s are reaching out to her. Either that, or she's losing her mind…

Five minutes into *The Nesting* and you already have to re-evaluate your expectations of a horror film made by one of America's most notorious sado-porn directors. There's elegant music (including Bach's 'Air on a G String' cut off brusquely in mid-swoon); the reflexive quality of the story; wide-angle lenses used, for once, to convey something quite suited to the effect – an attack of agoraphobia: all these things and more show how Weston could easily have essayed a career in mainstream genre cinema. Not that he should have, necessarily – his dark-hued brand of porn (see *The Defiance of Good*) possesses a malevolent vitality that already seems to come from an engagement with his muse – but *The Nesting* is a well-paced, well-made supernatural tale that trumps similar films like *The Evil* while borrowing from quality fare like Stephen King's *The Shining*.

We first meet the heroine, Lauren (Robin Groves), as she uses a relaxation tape to alleviate her agoraphobia. The voice on the tape asks her to visualise a walk outside, and the image is then double-exposed to show her leaving her body and walking downstairs (the same method Woody Allen used in *Annie Hall* to show Annie's detachment in bed). On the way to her country retreat, she jokes sardonically about the clichéd writerly escape she's seeking: *"Troubled uptight writer goes to small sleepy town in search of peace and inspiration, instead she finds an erupting volcano of lust and passion."* Lauren's friend Mark (Christopher Loomis) is sceptical when she claims that the house is the same as the one she described to the artist who illustrated the cover of her new book. *"How gullible do you think I am?"* he asks, *"There she is: the frightened girl in the foreground, the brooding mysterious mansion in the background."* So far the entire fiction has lightly but succinctly poked fun at its own clichés. However, the film really doesn't need to be so careful. The beautiful octagonal house that provides the main setting is creepy and impressive enough to work without these ironic caveats.

Sinister eroticism enters the picture when Lauren has a dream in which she fondles herself while gazing into a mirror – another pair of hands join hers and she flinches away. Startled, she's transported back in time to when the house was still a brothel; bound in a beaded curtain, she's made to recline on the Madame's sofa, while curious punters (leaning into the subjective camera) peer at her. Jazz music accompanies the creepier moments, reminding us that what is now considered a 'classy' musical form

Natas: The Reflection
© 1983. Arizona/West Film Productions, Inc.
Arizona/West Film Productions presents.
director: Jack Dunlap. executive producers: Jack Dunlap, Peggy Dunlap. screenplay: Jack Dunlap. director of photography: Donavon D. Bell. casting by: J. Dunlap and Associates. music: Mitchell Markham. producer associate: Ron Dutton. associate producers: Charles Bauman, Charles Branin, Ray Lambert, Bud Mason. production co-ordinator: Peggy Dunlap. first assistant director: Todd Mitzman. second assistant director: Jackie Fuller. camera operator: Don Bell. assistant cameraman: Terry Hall. sound mixer: Bill Frasier. boom man: Rod Stewart. script supervisor: Sibylle Aldridge. makeup and hair: Joyce Clements. special makeup and effects: Chris Bergschneider. assistant special makeup: Regina Gagliano. wardrobe: Jean Brock. special effects: Ray Robinson, Jim Haughlum. production assistants: Jerry Crutsinger, Terry Graybeal, Bobby Graybeal, Rea Orcutt, Will Strickland, Pat Bradford, props set dressing: Ken Cerny. gaffer: Herb Morris. key grip: Cliff Dalton. first grip: Armando Quiroz. construction: Conrad Slonaker. wrangler: Jim Evans. transportation captain: Ted Buford. drivers: Don Getzwiller, Fargo Graham, Pat Knapp, Harold Sargent, John Warner. generator operator: Jim Haughlum. still photographer: Leo Hohler. camera equipment: Ray Baxter (Phoenix, Arizona). honeywagon transportation: Jack Vaughn (Tucson, Arizona). limousine hostess: Carolyn Gervais. editing: D.B.B. Editorial Services. post services: Filmkraft / Wally Soul. post sound services: Quality Sound. visual electronic effects and titles: Ruxton Ltd., Image Transform. lab services: Foto-Kem Industries. catering by: The Hilton Inn of Tucson; Ruiz's Cafe of Benson (Arizona); The Peak Trading Post (Picacho, Arizona). A Special thanks to: Bosa Donuts; Coca Cola Bottling (Tucson); Shamrock Dairy; Finley Distributing Company; Bob's Bargain Barn; Coronado Apartments; Arizona Historical Society; City of Tucson Parks and Recreation; The Hilton Inn of Tucson; Allstate Limousine Services; K-CUB Radio of Tucson. filmed on location in the City of Tucson, Picacho Peak and Mescal (Arizona, USA).
Cast: Randy Mulkey (Steve). Pat Bolt (Terry). Craig Hensley (Jay). Kelli Kuhn (Angie). Fred Perry (Spec). Tom Martinelli (Natas). Nino Cochise (Smohalla). Bob Cota (the killer). Ghost Town Zombies Richard Aufmuth (gambler). Jerry Crutsinger (doctor). Leslie Donnelly (prospector). Gloria Goodman (saloon girl). Ted Karadenes (marshall). Tom Martinelli (barkeep). Rea Orcutt (saloon girl 2). Will Strickland (gunfighter) also Roy Gunzburg (storekeeper). Leo Hohler (rancher). Frieda Smith (old woman) and Billie Cameron (mama). Adam Dutton (boy). April Dutton (girl). Mary Kested (saloon girl 3). David Jankowski (undertaker). Stoney Quinto, Sr. (banker). Stoney Quinto, Jr. (worker). Charlie Smith (papa). Alex Duncan (Lynoff). Jim Sanders (Dr. Cord). Bob Cota (stunts).

was once the music of the whorehouse. Lauren's trip to the attic, and the discovery of clothes and shoes seen in her dream, is a classic Stephen King device. In this context, the old jazz records provide a further echo, of Kubrick's *The Shining* (1980). Instead of a grand hotel, *The Nesting* has a haunted whorehouse, but the similarities are undeniable: the scene where Lauren lurches from room to room, discovering various sexual assignations and being chased through the halls by the clientele is almost certainly inspired by the Kubrick film (or if not, it's inspired by the knowledge that a film of King's novel was on its way!) The back-story aspects also suggest King; for example, the scene where secondary character Daniel (Michael David Lally) traumatically discovers the truth of his parentage. (Coincidentally, lead actress Robin Groves went on to appear in the King-penned *Silver Bullet* in 1985.)

The violence is sparing – which accounts for the film's lower than average profile, given the splatter of the early eighties. The highlight comes when Lauren's psychiatrist Dr. Webb (Patrick Farrelly) is impaled through the eye (see also *The Deadly Spawn* for this classic psychiatrist's fate!), falling face-down on a railing spike after trying to rescue her from a precarious upper window-ledge. This moment of eye violence provides a welcome link to the films of Lucio Fulci, in particular his classic supernatural horror *The Beyond*, which went before the cameras in October of 1980. The decaying old house that used to be a hotel, the spooked female owner, a victim falling from the roof, a time-shift between two eras, creepy manservants, dramatic thunderstorms; the Fulciesque similarities are striking, though in this case accidental. What *The Nesting* lacks of course is *The Beyond*'s fluid visual style, and its gore-drenched irrationality. Like most American horror filmmakers, Weston frames his nightmare scenario in a sensible narrative format. That said, the sequence in which deranged white trash Abner (David Tabor) doggedly chases Lauren, first by car and then on foot through deserted farm buildings, is sustained enough to be genuinely nightmarish, especially since his attack seems so arbitrary. The final explanation from Colonel LeBrun (John Carradine), though, ties up the loose ends in workmanlike fashion. What's salutary, for a film made by an ex-porno director, is that the story is entirely in sympathy with the ghostly prostitutes (destroyed by a stubborn old man and three stupid, vicious youths), and certainly does not blame them for *"the ruin of many a poor boy,"* as the famous song 'The House of the Rising Sun' so egregiously puts it.

It's a shame that Weston (born in 1932) never went on to develop his aptitude for horror. He was fired from the production of *Dawn of the Mummy* (1981), which wound up being made by Egyptian-American director Frank Agrama. While attempting to release *The Nesting* under its original title of *Phobia* in the Spring of 1981, Weston was threatened with legal action by the producers

of the recent John Huston picture, *Phobia* (1980), starring Paul Michael Glaser, and had to rename the film. Some sources have claimed that Armand Weston was a pseudonym for porno producer Anthony Spinelli: this is not the case, as fellow porn director Cecil Howard has asserted. Weston shot Joe Sarno's *Misty* (1975), but he is most notorious for his hyper-sleazy porno-horror flick *The Defiance of Good* (1974), starring *The Last House on the Left*'s 'Weasel', Fred Lincoln, as a sadistic doctor running a psychiatric hospital to which Jean Jennings is sent after being caught taking drugs by her strict mother. She's gang-raped on her first night by three dangerous inmates, but that's nothing compared to what the Doctor has in mind. Subjected to bondage and sadistic torture, collared and chained like a dog, her mind is broken down until she believes that her sole purpose in life is to submit to the deviant desires of others. *The Defiance of Good* is a hardcore pornographic nightmare that actually works as drama, possessing a genuine Sadean quality comparable to Jess Franco. Weston's 1976 film *The Taking of Christina* is reportedly another gruelling but compelling exercise in the same territory. He died on 26 May, 1988.

Cinematographer João Fernandez was a busy man on horror projects at the time: he shot *Human Experiments* for Gregory Goodell, and *Bloodrage*, *The Prowler* and *Friday the 13th: The Final Chapter* for Joseph Zito. *The Nesting* was the last movie credit of Hollywood actress Gloria Grahame, winner of a Best Actress Oscar for *The Bad and the Beautiful* in 1952, and star of hits like *Crossfire* (1947 – Oscar nominated), *The Greatest Show on Earth* (1952), and *Oklahoma!* (1955)

Made in New York State.

NIGHT OF HORROR
– Tony Malanowski (1981)
See interview with Tony Malanowski.

Made in Maryland.

A NIGHT TO DISMEMBER
– Doris Wishman (1983)

Don't be distracted by better-known Wishman titles like *Bad Girls Go to Hell* and *Let Me Die a Woman*: *this* is Doris's finest hour. Unlike the torpid, attenuated dramas for which she's best known, *A Night To Dismember* is a joy from start to finish: that is, as long as you love cinema that confounds your sanity at every turn.

If, by some calamity, the Region 1 DVD has been deleted by the time you read this, you can simulate the experience thus: drink heavily and take a hit of MDA; invite the psychotic S&M freak in your life to bash you round the head until you see stars; then pull back, dribbling, from the brink of unconsciousness... Still with me? What you're feeling is a fair analogue of *A Night To Dismember*, possibly the most whacked-out movie in this book. It's a celluloid embolism, deserving in spades the attention normally wasted on earnest old slowcoaches like Ed Wood and Al Adamson.

Most Wishman films merely exemplify the Bad Movie norm. They sound great when written up in condensed form, but that's as far as you need to go. At best, a well-chosen highlights tape would be fun to slot into a witch-titted study course on women's cinema. But *A Night To Dismember* is something else: it trumps all previous Wishman opuses by consistently creaming your brains from start to finish. The demented soundtrack cuts between stock cues and mutilated sound effects, like some *musique-concret* nightmare by Pierre Schaeffer, John Cage, or Kenny Everett. Garbled information from the voice-over vies with abstract cacophony; nine parts post-synch dubbing to one part synchronised dialogue. Someone's changing channels in your head and you may as well get used to it. Just when you think the film has done its worst, an utterly twee, banal piece of muzak cuts in, ripped from some late-night shopping mall, the sort of thing you get over the Tannoy for special offers on tights and pickled goods...

The Nesting
aka **Phobia** (shooting title)
© 1980. The Nesting Company
producer/director: Armand Weston. screenplay: Daria Price, Armand Weston. executive producers: Sam Lake, Robert Sumner. associate producer: Don Walters. director of photography: J. [Joao] Fernandes. editor: Jack Foster. original music by Jack Malken, George Kim Scholes. production manager: Don Walters. assistant director: Fred Berner. art director: John Lawless. scenic designer: Pat Mann. soundman: Bill Meredith. special effects: Matt Vogel. costume designer: Alexis Balsini. makeup: Lyzanne Goodson. script supervisor: Clea Pricetti. asst. camera: Michael Duff. gaffer: Frost Wilkinson. key grip: Doug Armstrong. 2nd electric: Craig Nelson. grip: Miles Strassner. loader: David Frederick. best boy: Robert Steivers. boom operator: Nicki Tzanis. asst. art director: Fred Isola. props: Will Scheck. production secretary: Pat Finnegan. 2nd unit camera: Michael Duff. 2nd asst. director: Philippe Rivier. asst. scenic designer: Paul Evcritt. asst. special effects: Jeff Schecter, Bruce Martin. special makeup: Richard Alonzo, Jay Perlman. seamstress: Edith Frederick. still photographer: Marco Nero. graphics: Chery Amatuzzo. production assistants: Michele Solatar, Gary Hill, Bob Rudis, Allison Hickey, Bruce Shell, Jill Lashley. bookkeeping: Bondi Walters. assistant editor: Dave Frederick. location co-ordinator: Paul Giacobbe. publicist: R. Allen Leider. legal: Walter Gidali. music mix: Secret Sound. optical effects: Videart Opticals. camera equipment: Panavision.
Cast: *Robin Groves (Lauren Cochran). Christopher Loomis (Mark Felton). Gloria Grahame (Florinda Costello). Michael David Lally (Daniel Griffith). John Carradine (Colonel LeBrun). Bill Rowley (Frank Beasley). David Taybor (Abner Welles). Patrick Farrelly (Doctor Webb). Bobo Lewis (Catherine Beasley). June Berry (Saphire). Ann Varley (Gwen). Cecile Liebman (Helga). Ron Levine (Leland LeBrun). Bruce Kronenberg (young Abner). Jim Nixon (young Frank). James Saxon (Earl). Jeffrey McLaughlin (butler). James Hayden (GI #1). Jerry Hewitt (GI #2). Cliff Cudney (sheriff). Lee Steele (doctor). Cliff Cudney, Jerry Hewitt, Jake Plumstead, Tiffany Lynne (stunts).*

top left:
Robin Groves as the writer seeing ghosts while staying in a converted whorehouse, in **The Nesting**.

below:
One of two UK video covers for the film: this one from Warner Bros., who picked it up for distribution after Vipco let the rights lapse.

A Night To Dismember
© 1983. Juri Productions, Inc.
A Juri Productions, Inc. presentation. producer/director: Doris Wishman. associate producer: Lorenzo Marinelli. story and screenplay: Judith J. Kushner. director of photography: C. Davis Smith. editor: Lawrence Anthony. music composed and arranged by Danny Girlando. recorded at Ian London Productions. post production: East End Co. assistants: Clint Elliot, Paulette Licitra, Noreen Evans, Denise Marino, Tina Botond, Lawrence Marinelli, Jr. promotional consultants: John Rochford, Terry Taylor. special effects: Les Lorrain. colour by Movielab. production manager: Jim Proser. casting: Dawn Whitman. coordinator: Lynn Manwaring. re-recording mixer: Aaron Nathanson. synchronization: Eli Haviv. sound: Steve Rogers. boom operator: Steve Deutsch. additional photography: Robert Lindsay, Anthony J. Spala, Bob Zimmerman. make-up by Miriam Meth. visual effects by John A. Bezich. opticals by B&O Film Effects, Corp. technical adviser: Richard L. Kushner.
Cast: Samantha Fox (Vicki Kent). — The Kent Family: Diane Cummins (Mary). Saul Meth (Adam). Miriam Meth (Blanche). Bill Szarka (Billy). Chris Smith. (Sam). — The Todd Family: Dee Cummins (Vicki). Norman Main [Larry Hunter] (Larry). Mary Lomay (Ann). Rita Rogers (Aunt Bea). — Nina Stengel (Nina). Frankie Sabat (Frankie). Alexandria (Nancy). William Longo, Jr. (Timmy). Robert De Rosa (Marty). Heather Sabat (Sandy). John Szarka (John).

below:
A campy promotional shot for Don Dohler's **NightBeast**, featuring Dohler's regular cast-member George Stover.

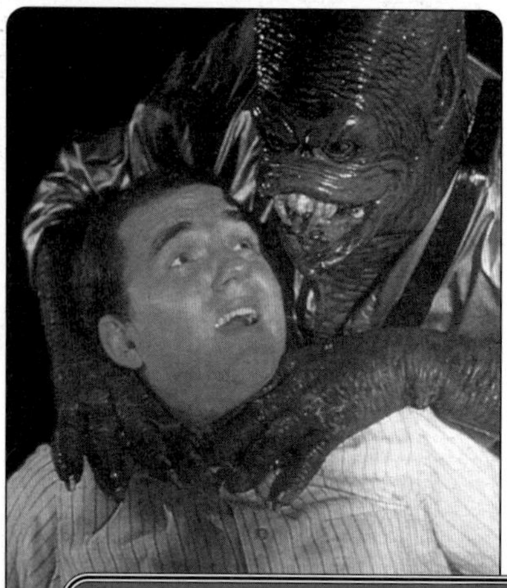

Violence within the family seems to be the theme, but despite a haphazard narration vainly trying to summarise the internecine squabbles, most viewers will find the question of who's doing what to whom impenetrable throughout. Perhaps the best one can say is that roiling away in this miasmic stew there's a murderous intrigue involving two sisters, Mary (Diane Cummins) and Vicki (Samantha Fox).

On second thoughts, maybe 'intrigue' is the wrong word. Armchair detectives be warned: even the unflappable Miss Marple would have a conniption trying to unravel this tale. Characters arrive in the frame, their faces filled with fear, rage or passionate intent, only to exit the scene in the next shot having achieved precisely nothing. The interior of the main house, initially a pokey little condo, turns labyrinthine as characters stagger from room to dimly lit room, racing up multiple flights of stairs until our sense of the interior dimensions is totally chaotic. The fact that this is actually Ms. Wishman's own home (as revealed in the utterly priceless DVD commentary) only amplifies the majesty of *A Night To Dismember*'s assault. When Wishman informs us that Vicki's bedroom was actually the guest-room of her own apartment, the mind reels: imagine actually *staying* there! You can keep your guided tours round Beverly Hills, *this* is the holiday destination cineastes' dreams are made of…

There's plenty of blood and violence, but splatter fans will likely feel as disconcerted as everyone else. Ms. Wishman cares not a monkey's chuff for physical reality: heads are lopped off, for sure, but her personal approach to gory axe attacks involves a leisurely blade gently touching the victim's neck in fake slow motion. By contrast, some later close-ups of flesh being pierced are uncannily convincing (rather like the disturbing gore effects in José Mojica Marins's *Trilogia de Terror*). If nothing else, this woozy swing between the flagrantly phoney and the unexpectedly realistic ramps up the film's powerful hallucinogenic quality.

A Night To Dismember is, on the whole, a 68-minute celluloid car-wreck. It's impressive because we simply can't keep pace with the aesthetic transgressions hurled at the screen. Framing is haphazard; the film stock changes texture; characters come and go senselessly; events contradict themselves; the dialogue cuts in and out like a faulty telephone; eyelines are totally ignored – Wishman and her cameraman cross the line at least a hundred times, until pedantic notions of left and right, to and fro, back and forth, are garbled beyond recognition… for lovers of the terminally weird it's hog heaven.

However, a few scenes break through the ineptitude. Mary dreams that her entire family attacks her with various sharp implements. Wishman shows the deluge of blows in simulated slow-motion, and for once she actually finds a rhythm for the scene; meanwhile, the soundtrack offers quiet groans, pitched somewhere between a dreamer's murmuring, a nymphomaniac's sexual whimpers, and the delirious sobs of the insane. As incoherent, incomprehensible and idiotic as this film may be, Mary's dream is fantastically vivid and authentic. If Ms. Wishman needed to churn out her entire *oeuvre* in order to reach this three-minute apotheosis, well, I'm glad she did it. If you've ever sat bolt upright in bed at five in the morning, shaking from the aftermath of a horrendous but elusive nightmare, you'll applaud Doris's dogged persistence in finding, at last, the true register of her own demented dreams.

Doris Wishman died of cancer on 10 August, 2002, leaving behind a body of work that is nothing if not distinctive. By far the majority of her time was spent making skinflicks of one sort or another, and *A Night To Dismember* is her only dip into the horror genre, *per se*. The story *behind* the film goes at least some way towards explaining why it's so bizarre. Wishman always shot her movie trailers first, and then raised the cash for the film itself using the trailer as bait. (It's included as an extra on the DVD.) In a calamity that would have floored most directors, more than half of the feature material Wishman then shot was destroyed in a fire, after a disgruntled processing lab employee struck back at his bosses by torching the building. Wishman had no insurance so there was no money to start again, but instead of giving up she spent eight months assembling a new version of the film, using 'outs' (outtakes and technically flawed shots), clips from her trailer, and new footage shot as cheaply as possible, added to what was salvaged from the fire. The result is a breathtaking amalgam, of wrongness, madness, and so-wrong-it's-right-ness: she even found room for a few shots from her very first film, *Hideout in the Sun* (1960) – typically, a Warholian screen portrait of a hideous sofa. Wishman edited multiple unused takes together to extend short scenes, straining for the minimum feature running time: the effect is of time hiccupping, or perhaps the projector trying to spit out the film. Certain Wishman trademarks, such as her penchant for repetitive close-ups of feet, preferably in whatever insane shoes were considered stylish at the time, survive into this movie, along with her cost-conscious preference for extensive post-sync dialogue, the latter of which gives her work an autistic separation from reality. Characters rarely feel something directly without a voice-over telling us what it is, or an atrociously dubbed voice filling in for the character as their lips find something else to do. Much of Wishman's eccentric style is governed by lack of money, but it *is* still a style. She could, after all, have stopped making movies altogether. To continue under the burden of such financial depletion is a style statement in itself. By the time this movie made it to DVD, Wishman was struggling to mount a new skinflick production, but without an accumulation of back pay for movies already in production, life was getting hard. In fact, one of the most forlorn and moving aspects of the commentary is her frequent sigh of *"I wish I lived there now,"* as she looks at her old apartment. We also learn that Ms. Wishman wanted to make *another* horror film, possibly culled from a similar slush-pile of out-takes – with the awe-inspiring title, *Axe of Violence*. Never mind a director's cut of *The Magnificent Ambersons*, *here* is a restoration project worthy of AFI funding!

Made in Purgatory.

NightBeast
© 1982. Amazing Film Prods.
Amazing Film Productions presents a Don Dohler film. Produced by Amazing Film Productions. director/writer: Don Dohler. director of photography: Richard Geiwitz. assistant director: Larry Reichman. production manager: Dave Ellis. edited by Don Dohler. music: Rob Walsh, Jeffrey Abrams. additional music: Arlon Ober, Leonard Rogowski, courtesy of Screenmusic West. sound effects: Dave Ellis, Jeffrey Abrams, Don Dohler. sound recording: Greg Dohler. graphic animation effects: Kinetic Image Productions, Ernest D. Farino. spacecraft sequence created by Kent Burton, Phil Cook, John Ellis. spacecraft design by John Poreda. pyrotechnic effects: David Donoho, P.C.E. 2nd assistant director: Anthony Malanowski. talent coordinator: Pam Dohler. production personnel: Anne Frith, Chris Gummer, Kim Dohler. prints by Quality Film Labs, Inc. colour consultant: Pete Garey. sound mix: Lion & Fox Recording, Inc., engineer: Jim Fox. music & sound editors: Don Dohler, Dave Ellis. location coordinator: Anne Frith. locations courtesy of Mr. & Mrs. Frank Gummer; Mr. & Mrs. Bruce Brown; Sharon martin; Jim & Barbara Mintfort; John Minfort; Dr. R. Adolph; Mr. & Mrs. Louis Frith. police car & uniforms designed by Tom Griffith, Richard Geiwitz. additional photography by Don Dohler, Dave Ellis, Larry Reichman, Tony Malanowski. negative cutter: Joan Insley. additional make-up effects: David Donoho, Amodio Giordano. production assistants: Joe Merenda, Missy Taylor, Dan Taylor, Dennis McGeehan, Don Leifert. Special thanks to Peter Anastopolus; KLM Associates, Inc.; Voxcam Associates, Ltd.; Federal Signal Corporation; Baltimore County Office of Central Services; Oregon Ridge Park; Haven McKinney; Rick Neff; Carl Paolino; Steve Fiorillo; Evelyn B. Wagner. beast designed by John Dods. title sequences by Kinetic Image Productions. associate producers: Don Dohler, Dave Ellis, Peter Garey, Richard Geiwitz, Tom Griffith, Tony Malanowski, Larry Reichman, George Stover. story & characters ©1982. Don Dohler.
Cast: Tom Griffith (Sheriff Cinder). Jamie Zemarel (Jamie Lambert). Karin Kardian (Lisa Kent). George Stover (Steve Price). Don Leifert (Drago). Anne Frith (Ruth Sherman). Eleanor Herman (Mary Jane). Richard Dyszel (Mayor Bert Wicker). Greg Dohler (Greg). Kim Dohler (Kim). Monica Neff (Suzie). Glenn Barnes (Glenn). Rose Wolfe (Glenn's girl). Jerry Schuerholz, Hank Stuhmer, Fred Gibmeyer (hunters). Richard Ruxton (Governor Embry). Bump Roberts (Bill Perkins). Don Michaels (Jimmy Perkins). David Donoho (Uncle Dave). Rick Ernest (governor's aide). Richard Geiwitz (Pete). Larry Reichman (Berkeley). Chris Gummer (Clay). Dave Parson (Wilton). Chris Burke, Bill Wieman (Wilton's friends). Richard Nelson (Krebs). Gary Svehla, Dick Svehla (men who find Suzie). Chris White, Dave Ellis, Steve Sandkuhler (laser victims). Christine Herman, Toni Patti, Phyllis Hammond, John Merenda, Mary Hopkins, Charlotte Merenda, Maria Morris, Pam Dohler, Dennis McGeehan, Rick Hammontree, Martha Brown, Chris Gummer, Richard Christensen, Brenda Blanks, C.A. Murray, Norman Belbot (pool party guests). beast portrayed by Christopher Gummer, Dennis McGeehan. Dennis McGeehan (stunts).

NIGHTBEAST
– Don Dohler (1982)

A spaceship crashes near a small Maryland town. With the town's corrupt mayor reluctant to act, it's up to Sheriff Cinder (Tom Griffith) to save the locals from the monster that emerges from the wreckage… Well, the sheriff's perm has got shaggier, but other than that we're back on the same stylistic turf as Dohler's first film, *The Alien Factor*. No mention is made of the events of that movie, though, so I guess Griffiths is not meant to be playing the same character, even if he does have the same name. Besides, it would be tough to explain why *two* alien spacecraft have crash-landed in the same small area of Maryland. Nevertheless, much is the same – essentially, an alien stranded on earth after its spaceship crash-lands goes roaming the woods attacking people. This time, though, the

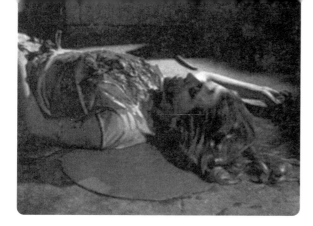

creature wears a shiny jumpsuit, like some interplanetary disco artiste en route for a rollerboogie duet with Olivia Newton-John. The only other difference is that Dohler adds a brief, nervous sex scene and a few bared breasts (presumably at the prompting of distributors – *The Alien Factor* and *Fiend* were totally sexless, probably because it's harder to ask your family and friends to strip off than an actress from a casting agency). The pacing is tighter, but essentially it's *Alien Factor* redux with extra gore: in itself reason to celebrate, of course, especially the cheerfully gruesome decapitation scene.

NightBeast is really a lot of fun, with a monster whose face is so impressively ugly you forgive it for having no moveable features. If the effects aren't up to the standard of, say, *The Deadly Spawn* (although designed by the same make-up artist, John Dods), they are still very satisfying, and the characters aren't given too much unnecessary chit-chat between slaughters. What dialogue there is mostly advances the drama. Fans of John Waters will enjoy seeing Baltimore actor George Stover once again embedded in a cast of local Thesps and the sort of enthusiastic also-rans who populate Dohler's films. Thankfully though, their efforts, no matter how rough-hewn, never descend into snide or facetious camp; a testament perhaps to Dohler's directing skills, and his devotion to the sci-fi horror subject matter. The 1980s saw the emergence of a cinema underclass of gore-fans turned directors, many of whom, without wishing to be too harsh, should have had their efforts shoved down the nearest trash compactor. Dohler, although just as much a fan-turned-director, had enough filmmaking skill to escape that category, coming over as the sort of super-low-budget player who would probably have ended up working for Corman had he entered the field a few years earlier.

Sadly, Don Dohler died of cancer on 2 December 2, 2006. He was 60.

Don Leifert on Don Dohler and *NightBeast*:

"I met Don Dohler over George Stover's house. Stover, a 16mm film collector, hosts frequent viewings in his basement. During the seventies, we met every Tuesday evening. Don Dohler attended a screening and we talked about a variety of film-related subjects. Shortly thereafter, he called me and asked me to play the lead in The Alien Factor. *He said he liked my voice. We became very good friends and socialised frequently. In the nineties, we co-edited a 'zine called* Cinemagic *for seven years before packing it in. Of the five Dohler films in which I appeared,* NightBeast *was my favourite. Incidentally, I needed a double for the motorcycle scenes, as I have never driven one. During the final scene in which I attack the deputy sheriff, she scratched me so many times I thought I needed a tetanus shot. She had no experience with stage fighting and actually fought me. I was not pleased and had nothing to do with her after that.*

I remember Don as an excellent collaborator and as a valued friend. He was easy going, intellectually curious, and hard working, but most of all he was driven to create. He was, in many ways, a contradiction: he was an excellent writer, editor, and organizer, yet he was a high school dropout; he seldom ventured outside his community in Perry Hall, yet he is a relatively well-known movie director; and finally, he was that rarest of all breeds – a filmmaker who never sought praise or accolades. It was the process of moviemaking that he loved. Don was a good friend. I will miss him."

Made in Maryland.
see also: **The Alien Factor** and **Fiend**

NURSE SHERRI
– Al Adamson (1977)
aka *The Possession of Nurse Sherri*
aka *Hands of Death*
aka *Black Voodoo*
aka *Killer's Curse*
aka *Beyond the Living*
aka *Hospital of Terror*

A black magician called Thomas Reinhauer (Bill Roy) suffers a heart attack while trying to resurrect a corpse in front of his followers. He dies in hospital but his spirit possesses Nurse Sherri (Jill Jacobson), sending her on a killing spree: the targets include Reinhauer's black associate (J.C. Wells) and the doctors who failed to revive him…

Adamson's cardboard creativity remains as flimsy and unconvincing as ever, but this is probably the most enjoyable of his horror films. In case you think that's a recommendation, please don't get me wrong: it's still Adamson, it's still at least 75% abysmal. Sherri's murders are the highlights, thanks to Jill Jacobson's bizarre performance. Also of note is some extremely, er, funky animation used to signify the invading spirit, consisting of psychedelic pencil scribbles superimposed with green light (at least I think it's green; it probably depends on the video release). Unfortunately for the hyperactive effects designer, Jill Jacobson undergoes this barrage of overlays with the stoical indifference of a cow pestered by flies. The soundtrack combines forties-style orchestration and buzzing Theremin, of a kind so out of date in the late seventies that to anyone except Adamson it signified nothing but the clapped-out scares of a bygone era.

What's annoying about Adamson's films is that they're prone to wandering from their chosen genre to include brain-achingly generic car chases, comedy sex scenes, or tedious action ephemera. I'm all for mixing it up, genre-wise: but with unerring accuracy Adamson works to the wrong recipe. Producer Sam Sherman, credited as Mark Sherwood, claims the film was inspired by Brian De Palma's *Carrie*; a statement that makes sense for just one shot, when a blood-soaked Sherri advances on her lover brandishing bloody knives, shot from a low angle that makes her resemble Carrie's crazy mother. (Overall, it's more like *Patrick*, really.) NB: In a botch that seems to sum up Adamson's *oeuvre*, the DVD commentary for *The Possession of Nurse Sherri* has Sherman's reminiscences completely out of synch with the actions they describe.

Made in California.
see also: **Blood of Ghastly Horror, Brain of Blood,** and
Dracula vs. Frankenstein

PHANTASM
– Don Coscarelli (1978)
aka *The Never Dead*

Phantasm appeared out of nowhere in the late 1970s and cleaned up at the box-office, introducing us to a new directing talent in Don Coscarelli, and a new denizen of the *fantastique* hall of fame in Angus Scrimm's unforgettable Tall Man. While budget limitations mean that the special effects occasionally challenge our credulity, Coscarelli always has another great idea up his sleeve, so that scene by scene we're given far more than the standard issue for horror films of the period; a perfect fusion of mood, setting, character and music, not to mention a host of wild visual concepts. *Phantasm* mixes genres with such smart but unselfconscious verve that it's only later you realise you've been watching a sci-fi horror film about grave robbers from another world. That's right, the same plot as *Plan 9 from Outer Space*. Could this be the film Edward D. Wood was seeing in his mind's eye? Certainly nothing could be further from Wood's ineptitude in this assured and constantly inventive movie.

Phantasm may be wild and off-the-wall, but underpinning the weirdness is a strong emotional current – it's a film about friendship and fraternal love as much as monsters and alternative dimensions. It's this marriage of feeling and fantasy that accounts

Nurse Sherri (US theatrical title)
aka **Killer's Curse**
(US theatrical re-release title & UK video title)
aka **Hospital of Terror / Beyond the Living**
(US video titles)
aka **The Possession of Nurse Sherri**
(US DVD title)
[Nurse Sherri] ©1977. Independent-International Pictures Corp.
[The Possession of Nurse Sherri] ©1978. Independent-International Pictures Corp.
Independent-International Pictures Corp. presents an Independent-International release.
director: Al Adamson. producer: Mark Sherwood [Sam Sherman]. written by Michael Bockman & Greg Tittinger; based on an idea by Al Adamson. director of photography: Roger Michaels (in Eastman Color). editor: Michael Bockman & Greg Tittinger. assistant director: Adam Roberts. script [supervisor]: Michael Bockman. sound: Robert Dietz. stills: Hedy Dietz. sets: Joe Arrowsmith. makeup: Tom Schwartz. hair: Beth Rogers. post production supervisor: Steven Jacobson. special visual effects & title design by Bob Le Bar. art design: Ann McDonald. gaffer: Romy Roa. key grip: Robbie McLure [McClure]. production assistant: Andrew Lamy. assistant editor: Jan Holling.
Cast: Geoffrey Land (Dr. Peter Desmond). Jill Jacobson (Sherri Martin). Marilyn Joi (Tara Williams). Mary Kay Pass (Beth Dillon). Prentiss Moulden (Marcus Washington). Bill Roy (Thomas Reanhauer). Erwin Fuller (Charlie Stephens). J.C. Wells (Stevens). Clayton Foster (Dr. Nelson). Caryl Briscoe (Nurse Gordon). Jack Barnes (Dr. Andrews).

above:
Mind-control takes its toll in **Nurse Sherri**;
…and the US one-sheet for the film.

top left:
A victim of the **NightBeast**.

for the enduring fascination the film has inspired in fans all over the world. Instead of the currently fashionable notion that the lead cast of a teen horror flick should snipe and bicker at each other, thus giving the scriptwriters the chance to demonstrate their supposedly waspish wit, Coscarelli's script foregrounds loyalty, courage, friendship and perseverance. Instead of simply setting up 'empowerment' clichés, he gives each of his three leads the capacity not only to face the horrors but also to appreciate each other's worth in the process.

Phantasm achieves an almost effortless dreamlike quality, which becomes more and more pervasive as the story develops. Coscarelli was way ahead, slyly undermining our sense of what's real and unreal five whole years before Wes Craven's *Nightmare on Elm Street* came along and seized the mass market with the same idea writ idiot-large. At one point Coscarelli even goes for an 'it was all a dream' twist, and not only makes it work but gives it pathos, a sorrowful bloom of surprise that touches your heart.

What can I say about *Phantasm*'s villain, The Tall Man? Given, I think, just two dozen words, Angus Scrimm propelled this elegant, looming fiend into the Pantheon of horror icons. The scene where Mike sees him walking in ominous slow motion down main street, 'warming' his hands over the chilly condensation rising from an ice-cream van's open refrigerator, is as poetic, funny and strange as anything in the genre. Scrimm's performance is a dream in itself – it straddles the divide between horror and fairytale, being both arch and ominous, knowing and nightmarish. Far more than just a killer in the Michael Myers or Jason Voorhees mould, The Tall Man embodies a primal archetype: the figure at the end of the bed. He represents all childhood fears: an abductor, a killer of parents, a lurker in the dark; and his obsession with Mike has an almost feverish intensity. Invading dreams and intruding into night-lit rooms, he's a negative Peter Pan, trying to draw Mike (like Wendy) into a never-never land beyond adulthood, out of time.

As befits a tale of adolescent anxieties, the subject of sexual awakening is inescapable. Mike, whose older brother Jody is already scoring dates, enjoys the slightly perverse pleasure of spying on his sibling's 'conquests'. But while observing Jody making out at the cemetery with a haughty, ethereal girl (who's more involved in the story's dark side than either of the brothers realise), Mike is attacked by the sinister cowled emissaries of another realm...

...On a story level, this 'other realm' is another planet. But on a symbolic level, it's adulthood. Thanks to The Tall Man's activities, death leads to slavery. In a film where the protagonists are teenagers and the dead are their elders, it's not such a big leap to see this threat of post-mortem slavery as a metaphor for the fears of smart kids, fast reaching the age at which they're meant to choose a responsible adult role in life. Many a dissolute teenager has felt a chill of dismay when faced with the prospect of getting a 'real' job (I should know – I still feel it now...) Perhaps the young Coscarelli (whose parents supported his movie-making dreams and who directed his first film at the age of 21) was disconcerted to see school-friends being lured into dull and meaningless occupations?

When you're very young, the promise of adulthood is a done deal: power, autonomy, staying up late – what's not to like? Come the mid-teens and things change: adult life is apprehended with a curious mixture of fear, exhilaration and contempt. Newly important sexual freedoms beckon, and there are social freedoms too, inasmuch as you can at last decide when, where, and with whom you hang out... Yet the tempting sales pitch masks a dull weight of responsibility. To live after death on The Tall Man's planet is to become a zombie dwarf, a crushed remnant of humanity toiling meaninglessly in a void. A bit like working in an office? No one heroic or interesting has a 'serious job' in *Phantasm*: Jody is an itinerant rock musician; Mike is too young for work; while family friend and offbeat hero Reggie is, of all things, an Ice-Cream Man – a six-year-old's choice of profession. (The extras on the *Phantasm* DVD include a discarded scene featuring Jody as an executive, flirting with a girl in his office.)

Cute though he looks in his flared seventies business garb, the scene would have eroded Jody's symbolic value as the brother who has not 'sold out' and acquiesced to normality, and was rightfully discarded by Coscarelli).

Phantasm also deals with a teenager's conflicting feelings about family. We start with the funeral of Mike and Jody's parents, yet, as the spellbinding music and unpredictable plot weave on, the brothers show little sign of trauma or sorrow. *"In time I guess you can get used to just about anything,"* Jody says. It's like the daydreams you have as a kid, of your parents dying and leaving you to live on at home, without them. You imagine with all due sadness the funeral and the tears, but you also relish the idea of having the family home to yourself. Mike seems to get all the family support he needs from his brother, although this is threatened by Jody's plan to move away and send him off to an aunt. Both are horrified and furious when they realise their parents' bodies are missing from Morningside: but there's no real sense of a hole in their lives beforehand. They basically support each other. In this context, the final scenes are all the more poignant.

There is at least one adult in *Phantasm* (outside of the family) who has rejected the dreary adult grind. The old woman who lives at 'the house on the corner' (in beautifully understated fairytale manner) may be too old for work, but she's obviously too mystically endowed to need it. Her role as a powerful witch counterweights the threat of The Tall Man. The old woman never speaks (refusing the masculine realm of language and definition). Instead, her granddaughter (her familiar?) communicates the old woman's thoughts to Mike: *"Fear is the killer, that's what grandma wants you to see."* (There follows a brief but beautifully achieved demonstration of 'magic' redolent of the similarly entrancing effects in Cocteau's *Orphée*). This short, resonant scene in the old lady's house embodies a positive perception of women, as against the Lady in Lavender, seductress and veil for The Tall Man. The fact that the granddaughter speaks for the grandmother, as if in telepathic accord, is elegant shorthand for the idea that women are a separate species, with different aims and purposes on this planet. When Mike departs, Coscarelli cuts back to the two women indulging a private joke, chuckling in slightly macabre fashion. It's as if they're laughing to themselves at the crises of male development. (I was reminded of the equally sinister laughter of the two elderly women in Nicolas Roeg's *Don't Look Now*.)

But adults, whether dead, benevolently mysterious, or wicked, are not the main focus of *Phantasm*. Instead, young Mike's curiosity provides the dynamo. Cannily playing to the teen audience, Coscarelli has the boy constantly pushing the narrative forwards, always going his own way: declining to attend a family funeral and then spying on it through binoculars, returning to the funeral home to investigate, contriving an explosive device in order to escape from the bedroom Jody has locked him in, and, most importantly, alerting his older brother to the danger of The Tall Man. In a pivotal scene, Mike shows Jody the evidence that proves, once and for all, that the world is going crazy (a box containing a severed, still-twitching finger, oozing yellow blood!) We feel a grateful satisfaction as Jody looks inside and says – after a comic pause – *"Okay, I believe you!"* We're wearily accustomed to the film cliché of the young hero being mocked and disbelieved, always unable to present evidence when it's needed. Such scenes can drag a fantasy film down with too much time-wasting scepticism, halting the flow of the story. Not so in *Phantasm*. The doubting older brother is brought into the fold in a short, sweet, and funny way.

These themes, to do with family and adolescence, fraternity and loyalty, are only part of the film's appeal. *Phantasm* is a wonderful, emotionally engaging whole: it's very hard to tease it apart because the movie has the gentle but startling consonance of a dream. There are marvels in the film I haven't even touched upon here, as I think it's good not to dissect a film best experienced as a carnival of surprises. Leaving almost as many loose ends dangling as there are in the film, I'll end by praising the score (at the time of writing still criminally unavailable on CD). A bad or even indifferent soundtrack would have cramped *Phantasm* so badly that we would today have been mourning a near miss, rather than celebrating a classic. Fred Myrow and Malcolm Seagrave deserve our gratitude for taking the repetitive ostinato of *Halloween* and adding tonal colour. Don't get me wrong, John Carpenter's score for *Halloween* is a wonder; a classic piece of audience manipulation. However, *Phantasm* not only exploits it but also transcends it. Subtle shifts in counterpoint, timbre, and emphasis are far ahead of *Halloween*'s pulsing minimalism. Musical themes are explored not only as clusters of notes but also as textures, with a sensual, fluid quality that reaches the intuitive side of the brain. The title theme, filtered, transposed, and occasionally mangled, matches the director's drift between fantasy and horror. The result is a perfect blend of image and sound second only to the collaboration between Italian director Lucio Fulci and the composer Fabio Frizzi.

Made in California.

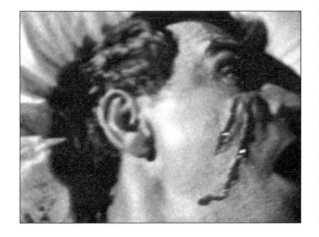

PIGS
– Marc Lawrence (1972)
aka *Daddy's Deadly Darling*
aka *Horror Farm*
aka *Blood Pen*
aka *The Killer*
aka *The Strange Love Exorcist*
aka *The Strange Exorcism of Lynn Hart*

Pigs, a love story in case you're wondering, is a marvellously strange and absorbing film directed by actor and consummate screen villain Marc Lawrence. It's a personal favourite of mine, one of the initial handful of titles that inspired me to embark on this book. Alright, so there's little in the way of action, but the absence of a forward-driving narrative is an essential part of the fun: *Pigs* doesn't fly; it floats. There's a muted psychedelic feel to the film – you feel kind of stoned watching it, a sensation that's cued up by Charles Bernstein's wonderful sixties-style theme song (*"Somebody's waiting for you/somewhere down the road/Keep on driving"*), and his often startling score, which employs lots of Jew's harp (a neglected psychedelic instrument in my opinion).

Pretty but disturbed Lynn Webster (played by Toni Lawrence, Marc Lawrence's real-life daughter) escapes from an asylum where she's been incarcerated after murdering her sexually abusive father. Making off into the countryside, exhausted and out of money, she spies a ramshackle old café. She asks the owner, Zambrini (Marc Lawrence), for a job and a place to stay. We already know Zambrini's odd because we've seen him feeding a human corpse to the pigs he keeps out back. He apologised to the dead man, explaining that the pigs have developed a taste for human flesh ever since snacking on a drunk who fell asleep in their field. But is he actually killing people, or simply stealing their corpses?

Zambrini may be a strange old coot, but birds of a feather flock together, and he takes troubled Lynn under his wing. Quickly intuiting that she's on the run, he refrains from pushing her to explain, even covering for her when the local pig – sorry, sheriff – Dan Cole (Jesse Vint), starts snuffling round asking questions. However, suspicions are accumulating around Zambrini himself, thanks to the claims of two dotty old cows – sorry, ladies – Miss Macy and Annette (Katherine Ross and Iris Korn), who tell anyone who'll listen that Zambrini is killing people to feed to his porkers. Sheriff Cole finds the story a hard turnip to swallow, mainly because Miss Macy insists that Zambrini is stealing the *souls* of his victims (Miss Macy: *"They're not pigs you know... they're dead people. He feeds those pigs dead people, and then he eats the pigs!"* Sheriff Cole: *"I don't think there's a law against turning dead people into pigs."*) Cole tells her that a body has been stolen from the local morgue – a comment that helps to sustain the ambiguity of Zambrini's actions.

Less ambiguous by a long way is Lynn's continuing status as a dangerous psychotic. After she's mauled by an amorous truck driver (Bone Adams), Lynn invites him into bed, then slashes him to death with a straight razor (implicitly castrating him beneath the sheets). Hearing screams, Zambrini discovers Lynn delirious and child-like, crouched in the corner of her room, with the trucker's blood-soaked corpse on the bed. Tenderly, he implores her to forget all about it, then drags the mutilated body out to the pigpen...

Like I said, a love story. Okay, it's a love story between a psychotic teenage girl and a grave-robbing pig-farmer, but love is love, right? Both Lynn and Zambrini are lonely, and as they recognise each others' haunted souls, a bond develops. The incestuous aspect is clearly signalled, but displaced through games and dreams – we never see the two of them kiss, or even embrace. However, the scenario is given an extra level of perversity by the fact that Marc and Toni Lawrence were father and daughter in real life: a metatextual frisson that one-ups even Dario Argento's *The Stendhal Syndrome* (in which the director's daughter Asia is raped in brutal fashion before turning feminist avenger).

Pigs (US/UK video title)
aka **Daddy's Deadly Darling** (US theatrical title)
aka **The Strange Exorcism of Lynn Hart / The Strange Love Exorcist** (US theatrical release titles for new version with additional footage.)
aka **Daddy's Girl** (MPAA title)
aka **The Killer** (UK TV title)
aka **Blood Pen** (unofficial theatrical re-issue title)
aka **Horror Farm**
© [none] 1972
A Safia S.A. production.
produced and directed by Marc Lawrence. executive producer: Donald L. Reynolds. screenplay by F.A. Foss [Marc Lawrence]. photography: Glenn R. Roland, Jr. music: Charles Bernstein. editor: Irvin Goodnoff. production manager: Bill [William H.] Bushnell. production co-ordinator: Lawrence Jason. associate editor: Stephen Michael. assistant to the director: Eric Morris. animal consultant: Moe Di Sesso. property master: Dick Shuyler. special effects: Bruce Adams. script supervisor: Jerri Scott. set designer: Boris Michael. assistant cameraman: Paul Silberman. sound mixer: Lee Alexander. key grip: Sam Dodge. key gaffer: Mike Strong. make-up: Chuck House. sound editor: Nick Elipoulas. boom man: Remus Timasonis. dubbing: Glen Glenn Sound. titles, opticals & processing: Consolidated Film Industries. circus poster: Michael.
Cast: Toni Lawrence (Lynn Webster). Marc Lawrence (Zambrini). Jesse Vint (Sheriff Dan Cole). Katherine Ross (Miss Macy). Iris Korn (Annette). Walter Barnes (doctor). Erik Holland (Hoagy). William Michael (deputy). Jim Antonio (man from hospital). Bone Adams (truck farmer). Larry Hussmann (gas attendant). Don Skylar (oil worker). Paul Hickey (Johnny).

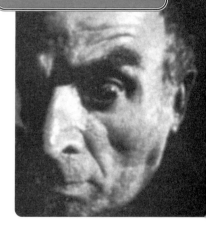

above:
Actor turned director Marc Lawrence, as seen in a disturbing dream sequence from **Pigs**.

bottom left:
This fellow should have let Lynn alone... a scene from **Pigs**.

opposite page:
Promo art and lobby cards for **Phantasm**.

above:
US video sleeve for **Pigs** – great artwork, shame about the cornball tagline!

Toni Lawrence raises goosebumps with her performance as the terminally damaged Lynn. Lynn craves both forgiveness and punishment from her dead father; a common dichotomy with abused children who lash out at their abusers. The first night that Lynn sleeps under Zambrini's roof she dreams of him as a punishing figure, attacking her with a razor. Lawrence directs by initially withholding a distinction between real and imaginary. The scene begins at night with Lynn asleep in bed. We see Zambrini advance across the darkened room. As he prepares to kill her, Lynn stirs. Zambrini hesitates. Then, satisfied that she's asleep, he slashes her face, over and over, accompanied by a cacophony of screaming and the amplified squeal of pigs: at which point Lynn wakes up in panic, to reveal it was 'just' a nightmare.

The local cop is there to stem incestuousness with the voice of Law: *"Are you related to Zambrini the Great?"* he asks, pointedly. Of course, the cop is also a love rival – it seems that Lynn attracts men who want to 'help' her in one way or another. Eventually another 'helper' – Jess Winter (Jim Antonio), an investigator sent by the asylum – tracks her down and tries to persuade her to return (an unusual way of dealing with escaped homicidal maniacs, but this *is* California). Unfortunately, the allure of the nuthouse just can't compete with the new man in Lynn's life. Zambrini wants her to stay, so she stabs the interfering Winter to death, only just managing to conceal her latest crime from the sheriff. Zambrini, her surrogate daddy, helps her to dispose of the body.

The film is set in some kind of limbo, an unreal place between life and death (actually Camarillo, near Los Angeles). I don't mean that Lawrence employs any overt visual flourishes to make the setting fantastical; there are no swathes of mist or quasi-supernatural manifestations to suggest parallel dimensions. Nonetheless, much of *Pigs* feels dreamily displaced from the real world. Zambrini's café-bar sits in the dust of the California desert hills, a last outpost on an abandoned frontier, and the central relationship between old man and young girl feels dreamlike too, as if two fantasy figures have escaped from an imaginary asylum and run off together. A lascivious oil worker at the bar tells Lynn: *"Zambrini always gets the pretty girls, They come here and work for a while and then they disappear. They say he feeds them to the pigs."* Again, there's something dreamlike about this exchange: so many people seem to have guessed Zambrini's pig-feeding habits, yet nothing is done about it. The unpleasant customer continues: *"Let me tell you about him, about Zambrini. He worked in a circus. Fell off a platform five hundred feet up. They say he was dead. They took him to the morgue. And he came to. He's dead, then he was alive. That's what they say. Something wrong with that man."* (It's interesting to compare this back-story with the plot of John Hayes's *Dream No Evil*, in which Lawrence appears as an undertaker killed by a woman who works in a travelling circus.) When Lynn asks Zambrini about the missing barmaids, his answer isn't exactly reassuring: *"Let them come here, let 'em run away, what's the difference? Let 'em run. No one finds out."* Zambrini is similarly terse when Lynn explains her recent nightmare: *"Everybody has bad dreams. Everybody."*

The pigs are a constant presence, a force of nature, harbingers of madness and violence. Shots of snouts pushing at rickety pigpen gates communicate a barely contained savagery. Interestingly, though, the pigs are edited to represent, at different times, both victim and predator. They suggest the bestial in man and woman: at various times, both Lynn and Zambrini are identified with the animals. As already described, Lynn's screams are merged with pig-squeals during her nightmare; and when Zambrini tries to throw a gang of suspicious workmen off his land, one of them snarls: *"Don't touch me, I don't like pigs touching me."*

Conventionally, of course, pigs symbolise greed. In the Jewish faith they represent impurity; in Islam they're symbols of evil, lust and ignorance; and it is after all an evil lust, in the form of a father's rape of his daughter, that sets the story in motion. In general though, *Pigs* doesn't linger at the symbolic level; there's an almost arbitrary quality to the inclusion of flesh-eating porkers. They lack the significance given them in, say, Thomas Harris's novel *Hannibal*, but they brand themselves into your memory with a lucidity that is its own justification.

Composer Charles Bernstein remembers that the production was a long drawn out affair, shot over many months and subsequently re-cut and agonised over for quite some time by Lawrence. Certainly there is a fair amount of confusion in the story, such as the question of whether Zambrini is actually a murderer or just a grave-robber; perhaps Lawrence was unable to decide and ended up fluffing the point? Lynn's name is given as Webster throughout the film, but at the end her death certificate is headed up Lynn Hart, as confirmed in one of the film's many retitlings, *The Strange Exorcism of Lynn Hart*. In Marc Lawrence's autobiography, *Long Time, No See*, this anomaly at least is explained: *"It fell short. Maybe it was the ad. Another distributor took it on and then another. They came to me with an idea they wanted to incorporate — to do an* Exorcist *beginning. I did it gratis. The film was now on its way. The last title it played under, that I know of, was* The Strange Exorcism of Lynn Hart. *I don't know where Hart came from; the girl's name in the film was Webster. I heard they're making money with it."*

According to star Jesse Vint, actor Ross Hagen owned the rights to *Pigs* at one time and was selling the film all over the world under various titles. *Pigs* wasn't reviewed by *Variety* until 1982, when Aquarius played it in New York City as *Daddy's Deadly Darling*. Vint told *Psychotronic Video* magazine, *"We were told it was going to be a little movie that the daughter [Toni Lawrence] was going to use as 'film on herself'. In the pre-video days, actors often submitted 'film' on themselves when audition-ing for a movie role. It took eighty days to film and I was involved for ten of them."*

A contributor to the Mobius Home Video Forum spotted yet another retitling: *"I was inspecting the first reel of an unknown movie labeled* Blood Pen *(complete with what looked like a Filmack-manufactured title card, including stock music!) It opened with a really amateurish-looking scene involving a priest going into a hospital room as a nervous doctor (looking a little like Larry Hagman) advises against it. Inside is what is apparently a possessed young woman (who snarls in a dubbed pig's growl) cavorting with a huge rat. Anyway, the exorcism goes poorly, and she bolts out the window. Then, an audible splice, and I am greeted with the sight of Marc Lawrence about to feed an elderly victim to his pigs, and realized this movie was* Pigs! *Apparently, somebody hijacked this particular print, didn't care for the incestuous opening, and created this new one to explain Toni Lawrence's escape and dementia. (Of course, the "possessed" actress looks nothing like her!)"*

Lawrence of course would, quite reasonably, regard this movie as a mere footnote to a long and illustrious career in the classic Hollywood films of the forties and fifties. Born 17 February, 1910, in the Bronx, he attended the City College of New York. In 1930, he joined Eva Le Gallienne's acting company, and befriended a young man who would eventually change his name to John Garfield. They appeared together in a play for Le Gallienne, and for a while joined the politically radical Group Theater. Lawrence was given a film contract with Columbia Pictures, where he excelled in a series of roles as brooding heavies, gangsters and mobsters. Following the Second World War, Lawrence was charged with Communist leanings. Before the House Un-American Activities Committee, he admitted he had once been a member of the Communist Party, and under pressure, named the names of other Party members. He was blacklisted and departed for Europe. When the blacklist was overwritten, he returned to America. He died on 27 November, 2005, of natural causes.

Made in California.

opposite page:
Caged women in **The Possessed!**, and the US video sleeve for the film.

THE POSSESSED!
– Charles Nizet (1974)
aka *Help Me... I'm Possessed!*

No, not a sleaze/horror Dostoevsky adaptation, you'll be sorry to hear. Instead it's a creaky mad scientist story, similar in style to the contemporary efforts of Al Adamson or Ted V. Mikels, but without the slumming yesteryear cast of the former or the femme-fatale bias of the latter. The setting is an asylum in the desert – or rather what looks like a chunk of leftover skid-row Hollywood scenery, in the form of a patently false castle façade, erected in the ubiquitous Bronson Canyon, California. The doctor is trying to extract the 'Essence of Evil' from various abductees caged in his laboratory, only for the stuff to escape and go rampaging around the desert, attacking various passers-by and a couple of cops. The Essence of Evil, it transpires, looks like a blurry close-up of red worms dangled at the camera. So now you know.

This is a tedious film that feels left over from another era. The actors are tiresomely campy, particularly the limping, retarded manservant and the doctor's wife, whose wig and costume give her the appearance of a soon-to-be revealed cross-dresser. The wordlessly shrieking caged girls and a handful of corny mental patients soon outstay their welcome too. By far the most screen time is taken up with interminable interviews between the doctor and the sheriff, conducted in an ugly, windowless office set. *The Possessed!* is unimaginative camp that fails to add up to genuine style: it's like *Bloodsucking Freaks* without the sex, blood, sadism and nihilism. Imagine that. What's left makes Eric Jeffrey Haims's *The Jekyll and Hyde Portfolio* look like a cult-classic in waiting.

Charles Nizet was born in Belgium on 1 March, 1932. His career has yet to be properly researched, but he turned his hand to war movies (*Mission: Africa*, 1968); nudies (*Slaves of Love*, 1969); and crime dramas (*Three-Way Split*, 1970), before settling on horror for a while with *The Ravager* (1970), *Voodoo Heartbeat* (1972), and *The Possessed!* When Impact Films tried to release a 79-minute print of the latter in Australia in 1982 it was reportedly banned for reasons of sexual violence. The following year it was cut to 70 minutes and awarded an 'R' rating. Nizet died on 4 February, 2003: according to the IMDB, he was murdered during a trip to Brazil. Nizet also made the Vietnam P.O.W. rescue movie *Rescue Force*, starring real life Green Beret and activist Bo Gritz.

Made in California.

THE PREMONITION
– Robert Allen Schnitzer (1975)
See interview with Robert Allen Schnitzer.

Made in Mississippi.

PSYCHOPATH
– Larry Brown (1972)
aka *An Eye for an Eye* (original title)
aka *Mr. Rabbey* (script title)

A mean, lardass mom (Barbara Grover) and her weak-willed stooge of a husband (Lance Larson) kill their young son during a punishment beating that goes too far. This and other parental evils are noted by Mr. Rabbey (Tom Basham), an obsessive children's TV entertainer with an affinity for his pre-teen audience that goes beyond professionalism and into psychopathology. Carolyn (Gretchen Kanne), the producer of the Mr. Rabbey TV series, knows that her star is both a natural children's performer and a few liquorice sticks short of a bundle, and so shields him from the adult world to a degree, but it's the adult world that needs to watch out: Mr. Rabbey is about to assume the mantle of children's protector, embarking on a moral-crusading murder spree, with abusive parents as victims…

This frequently overlooked psycho-thriller, shot in 1972 as *An Eye for an Eye*, is distinguished from the crowd by a fantastic premise and a startling central performance. Director Larry Brown and writer Walter Dallenbach replace the usual victim-parade of

nubile screamers with a string of nasty, abusive parents; and with a prototype Pee-wee Herman as your murdering anti-hero there's nothing trite or formulaic about the set-up. Unfortunately, Brown loses a grip of the material after forty five minutes or so, and while there are still some good scenes later on, the potential this film had to be an out-and-out classic slips away. Nevertheless, *Psychopath* is the sort of wild, unsettling film that makes exploring the waysides of the genre so compelling.

The greater part of the blame for child abuse here is directed at bad mothers, with fathers either absent or weakly condoning their spouses' cruelty. (It would make a good double-bill with *Don't Go in the House*). The film is unrelentingly obsessed with nasty moms: the only parent we see with redeeming qualities is a father who berates his wife and urges her not to beat the child while he's away at work (*"You keep your damn hands off, I don't want her hurt any more. I'm damn sick and tired of every time I come home from work wondering if I'm going to find that kid in one piece!"*). Statistically, men are the more likely abusers, at least when it comes to physical violence – although you could argue that if psychological abuse were easier to quantify, the figures would not look so one-sided. A writer shouldn't have to take a sociological average, of course: they can draw on their own observations rather than aiming for some specious notion of 'balance'. But *Psychopath* does run into problems by posing the story in such a lopsided way. Although it will chime with some viewers' experiences, the film's overwhelming concern with bad moms runs the risk of sentimentalising or excusing the parade of weak-willed or absent fathers.

Having said that, there is a tendency to turn away from the idea of abusive motherhood. Most people will flock to the cause of the child abused by their father, but you can expect a lonelier protest if your concern is maternal abuse. The abusive mother is, some would even argue, a victim herself, forced into cruelty by the distorting pressures of patriarchy. Special pleading of this sort obscures the fact that the abusive mother is an agent of serious emotional damage. It's still a taboo subject today, thanks to a combination of emotional denial on the part of men and defensiveness on the part of women. The mothers in *Psychopath* are all completely believable; from the fat harpy in the first scene, who demands that her husband savagely assault their nine-year-old son simply for playing in the street and getting dirty, to the wealthy career mom who submits her daughter to a litany of scorn in private, but turns on the sweetness and light in front of her friends.

As for Mr. Rabbey; he must be the horror genre's strangest mass killer. Soft-spoken, gentle, he's virtually the embodiment of the whimsical, effeminate homosexual. The character's sexuality is never alluded to, but he is undoubtedly going to be perceived as screamingly gay by most audiences. It's not long before the ignorant suspicion that a man like this must be interested in children for unsavoury reasons is expressed by one hostile mother, after her daughter joins a crowd of children gathered round Mr. Rabbey in a public playground: *"Well, I don't know about you, with all these children, it isn't normal! I'm gonna talk to some people who have some authority about this. Do the mothers of these children know they're out here with you? I bet they don't – and I'm gonna see to it that somebody* does *know about it!"* Her outburst, however, is not as public-spirited as it seems. Rather than expressing legitimate parental concern, she's merely resentful because Mr. Rabbey stared at her when she was yelling abuse at her little girl: Dallenbach's astute observation being that parents often use the spectre of 'stranger abuse' as a way of distracting from their own abusive behaviour.

The moral and emotional core of the film is a scene in the children's ward of a hospital, where a nurse (Margaret Avery) explains to a cop investigating a suspected child-abuse case how she can spot an abused child from their behaviour. *"Once you've seen a child who's been beaten, you know. You know. Not by the marks on the outside, by the ones inside. […] People think that a child who's been beaten will rebel, become incorrigible, but it's*

The Possessed! (video title)
aka **Help Me... I'm Possessed!**
(US theatrical title)
© 1974. Peerless Film Productions Inc.
Will Zens presents.
producer/director: Charles Nizet. executive producer: Si De Bardas. story and screenplay: William Greer. associate producer: Harold J. Stocker. director of photography: Charles Nizet. production manager: J.P. Agostin. electrician: Stuart Spohn. key grip: John Ledon. recordist: John Draulis. makeup: Jeanine. editor: James Spohn. titles: Cinefx. filmed from 20 January, 1974 on location in Los Angeles (California, USA). *Cast:* Bill Greer. Deedy Peters. Lynn Marta. Blackie Hunt. Jim Dean. Pepper Davis. Tony Reese. Pierre Agostini. Dorothy Green. Barbara Thorsen. Alvin Bart.

Psychopath (US theatrical re-release title)
aka **An Eye for an Eye**
(original US theatrical title)
© 1972. Larry Brown Productions, Inc.
[re-release version] ©1975 International Releasing Corp.
Larry Brown Productions, Inc. presents.
producer/director: Larry Brown. screenplay: Walter G. Dallenbach. story: Larry Brown. executive producers: Thomas P. Richardson, Jackson Bostwick. associate producer: Barbara Kieserman. director of photography: Jack Beckett. music: Country Al Ross. assistant cameraman: Dan Foley. production manager: Ron Mitchell. film editors: John Williams & Dennis Jakob. set director: Norma Rosenberg. assistant director: Bruce Kimball. property master: Barry Lieberman. sound mixer: Kirk Francis. sound editing: Jim Bryan. makeup: Ken Osborne. script supervisor: Barbara Kieserman. gaffer: Kerry Magness. key grips: Chuck Wells & Hank Miller. rerecording: Leslie Shatz. puppets by Roger Barnes. budoju-jutsu: Al Thomas System. titles, opticals & processing: Consolidated Film Industries. *Cast:* Tom Basham (Mr. Rabbey). Gene Carlson (Burt Mitchell). Gretchen Kanne (Carolyn). Dave Carlile (Perry Forbes). Barbara Grover (Judy Cirlin). Lance Larson (Harold Cirlin). Jeff Rice (Richard). Pete Renoudet (Lt. Hayes). Jackson Bostwick (Sgt. Graham). John D. Ashton (Sgt. Matthews). Mary Rings (mother in park). Margaret Avery (nurse). Sam Javis (coroner). Brenda Venus (Joanie). Carol Ann Daniels (Mrs. D'Sicca). Bruce Kimball (Mr. D'Sicca).

above:
Video sleeve for **Psychopath**, released by
UK video powerhouse Derann. A second
release through Trytel was apparently mooted
but never emerged.

opposite bottom right, from the top:
Rana, an aquatic reptile frog apparently...
Dr. Hatley (Karen McDiarmid) – where did
she get that Ph.D?;
American gun policy vindicated? A child fights
off a nasty green monster;
Extra production value from Mr. Rebane...

below:
Mr. Rabbey has plans for these shears in
Psychopath...

just the opposite. […] A child who's been beaten is completely docile. He'll do anything you tell him to, just as long as you don't hurt him again." She makes her point by staging a demonstration. Speaking firmly to a young boy of five, lying in his hospital bed with a broken arm and fractured hip, she demands the boy lift his other arm in the air: *"Jefferson, raise your arm. Higher! Now you keep it there."* She turns to another child: *"Beatrice. Raise your arm above your head. Higher! Now you leave it right there."* Turning to the cop, she says quietly, *"The minute I turn my head she'll drop it. And why shouldn't she, she isn't afraid of me. It's only normal."* As she turns away, the child does indeed immediately lower her arm. *"Look at Jefferson,"* the nurse says. The boy is still obediently straining his arm high in the air.

It's a heartbreaking scene, well acted by the children, and by Margaret Avery, who later went on to receive an Academy Award Nomination for Best Supporting Actress for *The Color Purple* (1985). It shows what healthcare and childcare professionals have to deal with: pilloried in the press and the courts if they over-react, yet seeing, on a regular basis, children with the unmistakable signs of abuse, and knowing just how heavy is the burden of proof in family situations, where a child is likely to lie to protect their abuser. If it feels a little like a lecture, the clarity and the emotional clout save the scene from sanctimoniousness. On top of the realistic depiction of hateful parents, it ensures that the theme of child abuse strikes us seriously, and not simply as window-dressing for entertainment.

So how do we treat the film: is it 'more' than entertainment? Should it even *be* entertainment if the subject is approached from the heart? By touching on something real, the question arises as to the morality of bringing an issue like this into the genre film arena. *Psychopath* is a horror film, and to some people this precludes any possibility of seriousness. To make child abuse the subject of a horror film requires some nerve, and to make it genuinely troubling is to step from the comfortable verities of genre action and into a darker and more complex area.

It can work. David Cronenberg's *The Brood* manages to play the genre game while raising the same issue, so it's not impossible. It all comes down to tone. *Psychopath* veers wildly from realistic drama to weird, even campy horror. It's not graphically violent, and it doesn't revel in the spectacle of abuse. (The film received the old 'AA' Certificate when released in the cinema here in Britain in the 1970s, clearing it for audiences over fourteen years of age.) When child characters are physically harmed, Brown avoids the prurient voyeurism that could have made it all tasteless. What does slightly compromise his efforts is the laboured cultivation of suspense involved in the run-up to Mr. Rabbey's killings. When Mr. Rabbey stalks and kills the parents who killed their young son, the film uses clichéd suspense music, and tacky tricks like having the husband discover his wife's corpse and run to the car, only for Mr. Rabbey to pop up in the back seat in proto-slasher movie fashion. If the man had decided to phone the police from inside the house instead of bolting for his car, Mr. Rabbey would presumably have been left waiting in the back seat like a fool. We can overlook such things when a film is essentially frivolous – take any basic slasher pic as example – but it jars a bit when the story relates more closely to the real world.

All of which makes it seem as if I've lost my sense of humour, so I should stress that despite a few misgivings here and there, I found *Psychopath* both creepily disturbing and fantastically weird: the lunatic facial expressions of Tom Basham are laugh-out-loud funny (frequent close-ups of his eyes darting from side to side are as cartoonishly weird as *Blood Feast*'s close-ups of Fuad Ramses), and the strangulation scene, watched uncritically, is a hoot. What's more, right up there in the Pantheon of 'Cinema's Most Bizarre' is the scene in which Mr. Rabbey causes a child-tormenting mom to faint by *flicking her with a piece of cloth*, before steering a lawnmower over her head. By the numbers this ain't. Tom Basham's memorably fey performance would make Paul Reubens look butch, and it's certainly not his fault if the film can't quite find its centre of gravity: he creates a totally compelling lead character.

If it seems like I'm criticising this film too much, considering I'm supposed to like it, it's because it succeeds maybe too well in certain scenes: there's a more heartfelt story going on that might have survived better in a less exploitational framework. As it is, *Psychopath* is located on one of cinema's fault lines. You can't deny that Brown and Dallenbach approach the issue of abuse seriously, but you find yourself querying the method. I certainly would never advocate excluding serious topics from genre pictures, but Larry Brown hasn't quite pulled it off. It's all a bit confusing, likely to give you a case of aesthetic indigestion if you think about it too much. Still, *Psychopath*'s combination of passionate moralism, wacko acting and bizarre murders makes it an unforgettable one-off movie experience. And the ending gives us a good, solid act of audience provocation to argue about afterwards: the film climaxes with an act of matricide, making it a sort of *I Spit on Your Grave* for battered kids – which is no bad thing in my book!

On the technical side, the biggest asset to the production is 'Country Al Ross' – he provides a wonderful score whose central theme for clarinet and wah-wah guitar haunted me for days after. Cinematographer Jack Beckett shot *A Scream in the Streets* and *Legacy of Blood* for Carl Monson; and James Bryan, the director of *Don't Go in the Woods*, turns up as sound editor. (Note: there is another Larry G. Brown out there, director of an eighties movie called *Final Cut*.)

Walter Dallenbach, the writer of *Psychopath*, began as a TV journalist before going on to write for television, including *The Rockford Files*, *Hart to Hart* and *Law & Order*. He teaches a screenwriting workshop for Adult Education in Santa Barbara.

"I'd been working in radio and TV in Pennsylvania, and then I went to USC around 1963-64 for graduate work, and that's where I met Larry. He was a student in the theatre department. A few years later, I was just starting to break into television, around 1971, he came to me and asked if I would be interested in making a film with him, extremely low budget? I said sure, depends what the film's about, so we started talking. Tom Basham also went to USC and he was a good friend of Larry's. Tom was kind of a strange dude [laughs] and Larry thought that was something that would come over in the picture. After spending time with him, and watching him with his 'Rabbey' – he actually had a Rabbey! – I realised this was a truly bizarre character. [Note: Dallenbach is referring to the piece of cloth, or 'Rabbey', that Mr. Rabbey carries everywhere with him in the movie!] I don't know if you ever saw a show called Mister Rogers' Neighborhood? The host was a soft-spoken bizarro guy, kids loved him, but there was something a bit 'off' for me, as an adult, something weird. It suddenly came to me, talking to Tom, that there was something to be done within that framework."

How did Basham feel about having his personal 'quirks' drawn upon to create a movie psychopath?

"Good question! [laughs]. I tend to think he was actually pleased, that he could do this kind of character. I never got a sense that he resented that it was being channelled into a psychotic personality. He played it to the hilt. He trusted Larry implicitly. Larry wanted to do something with Tom Basham, and something to do with the horror genre. I came up with what I thought would be an interesting idea, about this television personality, with a revenge thing to it. I went out and researched at children's hospitals, and then built the story. I must say though that a lot of the macabre effects were really Larry's idea. He was very good at that, the head in the garage for instance. Some of his suggestions about how he wanted to kill these people, I was saying, 'Holy Christ!', you know. But he was right."

And the naiveté of 'Mr. Rabbey'? Was it part of Tom Basham's character, or was it part of his act?

"Actually, he had a bit of that about him. After all, he was an actor, and actors have a certain childishness about them! I don't know the background to his family but obviously he was somewhat wounded, but he was not a nasty person, just bizarre."

How much did the film cost, and how long did it take to shoot?

"It was shot in 35mm for about $90,000, in three weeks with lots of pickups afterwards. Then Larry started cutting it at home. He was living with a lady who was one of the producers, I think, and then he'd occasionally get people together to go out and shoot some scene that he realised he needed. That went on for, I'm guessing, six months."

There's a pretty disturbing realism to some scenes…

"When I wrote the script, I spent a lot of time doing something I tell students not to do, which was to write a lot of verbiage telling what the scene's about – but of course you can do that when you're working with the director. I like realism, and characters that come from reality, but the reality of the thing was one of the reasons it never got major distribution. We showed it to people, they liked the film, but they said, 'Oh, I can't show this. It's appalling. You just can't put this out on the screen, this is terrible stuff'. Now maybe ten years later that would not have been the case, but back then…"

The film seems to concentrate most of its fire on bad mothers…

"I know I didn't deliberately angle it that way, it just seemed to happen, and when you mentioned it I realised that it's probably true, but it wasn't something that I set out as a pattern. I knew some of the actors from USC that Larry was going to use, and I kind of geared it that way because maybe the better actors were women, I don't know. I didn't want to do a film about sexual child abuse, that was not of interest to me, and in just hanging out, I saw many more mothers with children, and I began to notice things. I noticed how incredibly harsh mothers could be with their kids, in seemingly innocent moments in a grocery store or a park, and I guess that probably influenced me. With fathers, I think you find it's usually alcoholism and violence, or they're sexual predators, that sort of thing, but a mother's violence, I think, can be equally injurious, seeing the way they would just squelch a kid emotionally, or slap them around in public, and I think that's the reason I went that way. It was sort of a composite. Like, I noticed that when these mothers would do that, they would look to other adults for approval – you know, 'Look how bad my kid is being' – and they actually want the other parents to go along with it. That was pretty appalling to see. When you're on the lookout you start to notice these things. I think most people normally turn away from it because they don't want to be involved with it. I would be staring at it, thinking 'Jesus Christ, this kid is going to be warped for life.'"

What do you remember about Larry Brown? And did you ever see his 'gay biker' movie The Pink Angels?

"I had a great experience with Larry. I didn't get paid much, maybe 3 or 4,000 dollars for the script, I was not a member of the Guild at that time. But it was fun, it was my first experience of a film production. When Larry did Pink Angels *I was writing trailers for AIP, and one of the films they'd picked up was* Pink Angels *– I think it was them or Crown International. I thought it was a really clever unique idea, he just never got it on screen, in my opinion. He let the actors do a lot of extemporaneous stuff, and the scenes just dragged on and on, there was no rhythm or impact. Larry was straight – I mean, he didn't smoke dope, I don't even think he drank. He was very into wrestling and physicality, but* Pink Angels *wasn't what you'd call a reflection of his private life. He wasn't gay, but Larry had a number of friends who were gay, from the theatre departments, so he was certainly open to that world, but I don't think he really explored that world or understood the emotions or the motivations. Which is evident in the film! He would just say something that came out of nowhere: he was not an articulate guy that you would sit and rap with for a long time, but he would just suddenly come up with these bizarre concepts: 'Wouldn't it be funny if…' Afterwards I would see him occasionally, and then he went off to the Philippines to do another film, with some rock person in the lead, Gary Puckett or someone like that, but I don't think he got distribution for it. He was over there shooting for quite a while. He finally went back to Philadelphia, that's where his money sources were, his dad had a machinery business back there, and I think he ended up taking over the family business."*

Made in California.

RANA: THE LEGEND OF SHADOW LAKE
– Bill Rebane (1981)
aka *The Creature from Shadow Lake*
aka *Croaked: Frog Monster from Hell* (US DVD title)

Yet another monster-in-the-lake movie, sharing with most of its kin a lack of bite, lazy pacing and in this case a needlessly coy approach to the monster. 'PG'-level scares and an old-fashioned music score compound the tedium. An all-nighter of this, *Creature from Black Lake*, *Bog* and *The Crater Lake Monster* would be very hard to take. The fifties-style adventure music dates the film before it even gets started, only stumbling as far as the seventies via an uneasy mixture of old-school orchestral and blaxploitation horns. After an attractively photographed intro of mist hovering over the waters and canoes silhouetted against the shoreline, we meet Dr. Eleanor Hatley (Karen McDiarmid), a 'palaeontologist', allegedly. Examining a scale from the monster, she declares, *"It's from some kind of aquatic reptile, like a frog but much larger."* The needlessly fractured timeline shuttles backwards and forwards, with Kelly reminiscing to his new lover about his experiences on the island as a boy. Add to the stew an Indian Lake God called Rana, and an irritating character called Charlie (Jerry Gregoris), who gives the sort of performance that's intended to amuse children but is likely instead to piss them off, and you'll perhaps understand why I'm out of patience. The influence of *Jaws* can be discerned in underwater shots of a nubile swimmer tugged beneath the water by an unseen aggressor: however, even at the forty-minute mark this turns out to be just a horny scuba-diver, which goes to show how little actual monster fun the film has to offer. Later shots of a torso in a scuba suit, with offal poking out of one end, and a glimpse of the monster's fingers cut off by an axe-blow, give some idea of what the film otherwise lacks. Other sequences, such as the aftermath of the attack on the dinghy, rely on voice-overs from the adult Kelly (Glenn Scherer) to patch over missing footage. But what's the point of being too churlish when the proactive depiction of young Kelly Jr. (Brad Ellingson), seen firing rounds of ammunition at the monster in the last reel, suggests the film was mainly intended to appeal to kids whose tastes had yet to be turbo-charged by the sugar-rush of Hollywood? The monster – yet another variant on the Black Lagoon's favourite son – is at least impressively weird and slimy when it does finally appear, spewing a frog from its jaws in a way that perhaps explains Dr. Eleanor's earlier confusion.

Made in Wisconsin.
see also: **The Alpha Incident, The Demons of Ludlow** *and*
The Giant Spider Invasion

THE RETURNING
– Joel Bender (1983)
aka *The Spirit*
aka *Witch Doctor*

Though lacking tension much of the time, *The Returning* eventually hits its stride with a plausible treatment of a father's grief. John Ophir (Gabriel Walsh) goes to pieces when his beloved son Jason (Brian Poelman) is killed in a road accident, first trying to imitate the boy and then developing a bitter desire for revenge on the hapless driver. (In this respect it's the reverse angle of Martin Goldman's *Dark August*). Alongside this narrative there's a second strand about a cursed stone, taken by the boy from an Indian Reservation, with two warring Indian braves striving to reincarnate their vendetta in the souls of the father and his son's killer.

The Returning would really have benefited from dropping the Indian curse angle and concentrating on the corrosive effects of bereavement. Thanks to a frighteningly believable performance from Walsh as the anguished father, this story takes some surprising turns, transcending the otherwise trite supernatural theme. As it is, lifting the curse involves the dead boy's mother Sybil (Susan Strasberg) watching a Shaman spout

Rana: The Legend of Shadow Lake
aka The Creature from Shadow Lake
(UK video title)
© 1981. Galaxy One Productions
director: Bill Rebane. producer: Bill Rebane and Jerry Gregoris. executive producers: Joost van Oosterum and Larry Dreyfus. screenplay: Lyoma Denetz, Jerry Gregoris, Mike Landers. director of photography: Ito. cinematographer: Bela St. Jon. production design by Will McCrow. art director: Donna McCrow. Rana design by Tom Schwartz. special effects by Spectacular Effects of Atlanta, Georgia, Vern Hyde. associate producers: Jochen Breitenstein and Cheri Caffaro. 1st assistant director and production manager: Barbara J. Rebane. 2nd assistant director: Alan Rebane. sound: Bruce Malin. boom: Richard Lange. gaffer: Alan Rebane. aerial & underwater photography: Jochen Breitenstein. assistant cameraman: Rick Plautz. script and continuity: B. Kress. wardrobe & costume: Jutta Boettcher. makeup & special effects makeup: Tom Schwartz. special effects: Spectacular Effects, Vern Hyde, Robert Babb. grip: Mark Burns. production secretary: Sandra Lange. editor: Bill Rebane. assistant editors: Bruce Malm and Barbara J. Rebane. special sound effects editor: Bruce Malm. music: Valentino Inc. sound services: Zenith D.B. Inc. (Chicago, Illinois). animal handler: Dale Kremsriter. horse wrangler: Art Peters. We wish to thank the following for their co-operation in the making of this motion picture: The Wisconsin Dept. of Development; Lincoln County (Wisconsin); Crystal Caves (Spring Valley, Wisconsin); Owens of Illinois (Tomahawk, Wisconsin); Coca Cola Bottling Co. (Rhinelander, Wisconsin); animals supplied by Warbonnet Zoo (Hazelhurst, Wisconsin). filmed entirely at the facilities of Titan Studios (Gleason, Wisconsin, USA).
Cast: Karen McDiarmid (Elli). Alan Ross (John). Brad Ellingson (Kelly Jr). Glenn Scherer (Kelly Sr). Julie Wheaton (Susan). Jerry Gregoris (Charlie). Jim Iaquinta (Burley). Bruno Aclin (Cal). Michael J. Skewes (Mike). Doreen Moze (Chris). Lorry Getz (Sorenson). Paul Callaway and Richard Lange (Rana). Angel Rebane (baby Rana).

The Returning
aka **The Witchdoctor** (US/UK video title)
aka **The Spirit**
© 1983. The Returning Company
Willow Productions Company Ltd. presents.
director: Joel Bender. producer: Sally Faile.
executive in charge of production: Mark
Silverman. associate producers: Mike Edwards,
Patrick David Dillon. screenplay: Patrick Nash.
director of photography: Oliver Wood. music:
Henry Manfredini. editor: Daniel Loewenthal. art
director: Stephen Flynn. casting: Deborah
Rosen. assistant director: Deborah Reinisch.
assistant to the producer: Jane Harris. crew first
assistant cameraman: David H. Dunlap. second
assistant cameraman: Paul Cheesman. first
assistant cameraman (NYC): Bruce
Mermelstein. gaffer: Robert Chappell. best boy:
Chris Sorensen. third electric: Michael Strype.
key grip: Gregory Grover. second grip: Rhett
Fernsten. third grip: James Miller. location stills:
Hall Hutchison. property master: Randele
Beecher. property assistant: Marc Campbell.
director of special effects: Sam Nicholson,
Xenon Corp. (Hollywood). location sound mixer:
Ron Harris. boom operator: Joe Judd. make-up:
Lorraine Altamura. special effects make-up:
Larry Pennington. Ruth Warrick's make-up: Loa
Filiaga. wardrobe designer: Catherine
McClellan. wardrobe assistant: Yvonne
Peterson. extra casting: Rosen-Knutsen
Casting. stunt co-ordinator: Rick Barker. script
supervisor: Martha Mitchell. special effects
props: Sandy Hamilton, Tom Allen. second
assistant director: Mary A. Kelly. production
manager: Mark Silverman. production office co-
ordinator: Peggy McLain. production assistants:
J. Greg Evans, Kevin Dowd, Julie Fife, Bruce
Anderson, David Timothy, Barbara Atkins, John
Michael Miller, J. Matt Merritt, Janene Weddle,
Lynne Van Dam. production accountant: Lyndal
Cole. first assistant editor: Emily Dillon.
assistant editor: Nancy C. Saunders. dailies
supervisor: Robert Riedener. sound editor:
Emily Dillon. assistant sound editor: Angela
Tiseo. sound effects consultant: John 'Skip'
Lievsay. synthesized effects: Fred Szymanski.
production co-ordinator: Jane Harris. re-
recording: Michel Carton, Magno Sound Inc.
negative matcher: Ron Vitello, Match Cut Film
Service, Inc. opticals & titles: Exceptional
Opticals, Inc. main title design: Jose V. Gallardo,
Exceptional Opticals, Inc. colour grader: Angelo
Russo. colour by TVC. locations (Moab, Utah):
George White. special thanks to: Jill Hixson;
Utah Film Commission; Moab Film
Development Committee; Phantasmagoria
Productions; Doug Miller (News Director, K.S.L.
Radio, Salt Lake City); Oakridge Elementary
School; Salt Lake City Police Department; the
people of Salt Lake City.
Cast: Gabriel Walsh (John Ophir). Babetta Dick
(co-worker). Susan Strasberg (Sybil Ophir).
Brian Poelman (Jason Ophir). Terrell Dougan
(neighbour #1). Beverly Booth Rowland
(neighbour #2). Victor Arnold (Al Lyons). Richard
W. Barker (Spikee). Logan Field (Jimmy the
bartender). Victoria Lopez (Al's girlfriend).
Mostea Oshley (medicine man). Ben Jones
(indian in trading post). David Gardiner (stunt
double as Jason). Fred Schwab (cop with
corpse). Jay Bernard (Mr. Lyons). Yvonne
Robertson (Mrs. Lyons). Lucivs M. Ward (Doctor
Morton). H.E.D. Redford (Mr. Rizer). Ruth
Warrick (Grace). Coleman Creel (police
sargent). Max Golightley (Mr. James). Jere
Clames (Billy). Paul Nicholls (Mr. Lewis).
Heather Hunt (child #1). David W. Jacobs (child
#2). Vikki Gunn (woman teacher). Beth Trauth
(nurse on rounds). Douglas Coleman (stunt
double #1 as Al Lyons). Rick Seaman (stunt
double #2 as Al Lyons). Katherine Shelton (Al
Lyons nurse). David Kirk Chambers (hospital
attendant #1). Kevin Addison (hospital attendant
#2). William C. Moore (patient). Mary Jane Bird
(Nurse Pisu). Oscar Rowland (Doctor Berg).
John Hansen (Kevin). David Breitbarth, Susan
Shopmaker, Allen McCullough, Nancy
Hendrickson, Mike Brennan (voices). Duane
Southwick (traffic report).

incantations over an open fire where rocks housing the battling
Indian spirits are cooking. Blood springs from the stones and
there you have it, problem solved; no thanks to the leading
players. The direction is sometimes wooden, and the elliptical
treatment of the boy's fatal accident is oddly unsuccessful:
perhaps it was intended to divert attention from a less than
committed performance by Susan Strasberg? Harry Manfredini's
score veers between echoes of his famous *Friday the 13th*
themes and some less effective music redolent of TV movie
limbo (rather like his work for Max Kalmanowicz's *The
Children*). What *is* noteworthy is the commitment to telling a
story less familiar in horror movies, where pain and trauma are
generally reserved for the moment of death, not the aftermath.
When it comes to explorations of grief in the genre, only Bob
Clark's wonderful *Deathdream* and the Stephen King adaptation
Pet Sematary come quickly to mind. *The Returning* isn't as good
as either of these, but it's a welcome venture into emotional
territory too often lost in a welter of gore.

The film was lensed in Salt Lake City and on location in the
Mojave desert by cinematographer Oliver Wood (who shot
Joseph Ellison's *Don't Go in the House*). Director Joel Bender
was production manager on Joseph Zito's *Abduction*.

Made in Utah.

SATAN'S BLACK WEDDING
– Philip Miller [Nick Millard] (1975)

When his sister Nina dies in mysterious circumstances,
Hollywood actor Mark Gray (Greg Braddock) returns to the
family home in Monterey to investigate. Someone has
apparently drained Nina's body of blood and severed one of her
fingers, then attempted to fake her suicide: the police lieutenant
on the case confides that several similar murders have occurred
in the area recently. *"That book she was writing had become an
obsession,"* Aunt Lilian informs Mark, *"Renegade priests and

nuns, children sacrificed to the Devil…"* Mark discovers that
Nina, while pursuing her research, had fallen under the spell of a
Satanic priest called Father Daken. Now, at his bidding, she has
become a vampire who attacks members of her own family to
slake her thirst for blood. Aunt Lilian's nurse wants to quit,
having heard something trying to get in during the night, but too
late: she's savaged to death, along with Aunt Lilian, by Nina and
Father Daken. Mark joins forces with Jean, his old girlfriend and
friend of Nina's; together they confront the vampires in Father
Daken's crypt of horrors…

People with ill-fitting joke-shop fangs and blood-smeared
mouths have badly edited fits of the munchies in this curious
gore item from the director of the 'Crazy Fat Ethel' movies.
Satan's Black Wedding is right on the line between mindless
weirdy fun and irredeemable garbage – not a distinction that
many people fret over, but I thought I'd point it out anyway. It's
blatantly absurd, but despite a few dull passages it livens up here
and there, with the last twenty five minutes providing a sort of
hyper-zonked amusement, although be warned: this trashy treat is
sub-Andy Milligan (yes, such a realm does exist). There's also a
sort of *low*-low-budget Amando de Ossorio vibe, for lovers of
Iberian grue – it's as if Miller saw *Malenka, the Niece of the
Vampire* and *The Night of the Sorcerers* on a double bill while on
holiday in Spain, and returned home vowing to make his own
cheesy vampire tale (albeit without the benefit of the Spaniard's
technical facilities). Roger Stein's piano score is, well, *occasionally*
appropriate, whether tinkling away in ominous classical mode or
scraping diligently on the innards of the instrument, and his title
theme is actually rather wonderful, reminding me of Goblin's
sparser moments, or the morbid romance theme in *The Evil Dead*.
On the whole, the music either adds a creepy silent movie feel to
things or drives you round the bend, depending on what sort of
day you've had…

If 'horror' is measured by litres of blood, then *Satan's Black
Wedding* is up there with the greats. As drama though, one has to

Satan's Black Wedding
© none [1975]
I.R.M.I. Films Corporation
director: Philip Miller [Nick Millard]. producer:
Tamara Brown [Frances Millard]. original story:
Philip Miller [Nick Millard]. director of photography: Paul Rogers. film editor: Jack Fletcher.
music: Roger Stein. art director: Carl Lemaster.
production manager: Mitchell Adams. assistant
director: Tom Blake. lighting: Greer Amis.
makeup: Yvonne Cory. sound recording: Frances
Sarra. camera operator: Paul Dixon. sound
mixing: David B. James. costumes: Betty Grapes.
Cast: Greg Braddock (Mark). Ray Myles. Lisa
Milano. Barrett Cooper. Zarrah Whiting. Lisa Pons.
Osa Danam. Georgia Lemaster. Don Lipsey.

above: American video sleeves for **Satan's
Black Wedding** and **Satan's Cheerleaders**;
and a poster for a double bill of Philip Miller
madness...

opposite: Slick but unrevealing US poster and
amusing Finnish video art for **The Returning**.

Satan's Cheerleaders
© 1977. World Amusement Company Inc.
World Amusement Company presents a
Greydon Clark production.
director: Greydon Clark. executive producer:
Michael MacFarland. producer: Alvin L. Fast.
writers: Greydon Clark, Alvin L. Fast. director of
photography: Dean Cundey. music: Gerald Lee.
production manager: Michael O'Donnell. songs
"One for All and All for One", "Who You Gonna
Love Tonight" sung by Sonoma. musical score
orchestration: Roy Phillipe. assistant director:
Donn Greer. 2nd unit photography: Ray Stella.
assistant camera: Chris Davis. wardrobe & props:
Julie O'Donnell. sound mixer: Robert Dietz. still
photography: Hedy Dietz. script supervisor: Debra
Hill. make-up / hair: Dolores Warren. gaffer:
Roman Roa. 2nd unit director: Michael Bockman.
boom: Beau Franklin. production assistants: Stuart
Krieger, Michael Bourne. choreography: Bobbi
Grumley. sound editor: Richard Brummer.
assistant film editor: Jane Kass. film editor: G.D.
Clymer. sound: Gomillion Sound, Inc. colour:
Movielab. titles / opticals effects: Modern Film
Effects. filming from 1st December 1976 on
location in Los Angeles (California).
Cast: John Ireland (Sheriff Bub). Yvonne De Carlo
(Emmy Bub). Jack Kruschen (Billy Brooks). John
Carradine (bum). Sydney Chaplin (monk).
Jacqulin Cole (Ms. Johnson). Kerry Sherman
(Patti). Hillary Horan (Chris). Alisa Powell
(Debbie). Sherry Marks (Sharon). Lane Caudell
(Stevie). Joseph Carlo (coach). Michael Donavan
O'Donnell (farmer). Robin Greer (baker girl). The
Huskies (themselves).

say it stumbles. Bereaved brother 'Mark Gray' is meant to be an
actor, but it's a wonder his real life surrogate ever worked at all:
his reaction to the gory death of his aunt and her nurse is limited
to a brief disturbance of the lips, as if he's attempting to burp
without making a rude noise. The police lieutenant is no better –
when attacked by vampire ghouls in the church crypt, he utterly
refuses to emote, as if the fake teeth and ketchup somehow
offend his Thespian vanity. More than all these shortcomings,
though, it's the editing that gives *Satan's Black Wedding* that
certifiable stamp of seventies lunacy. For instance, Mark's old
flame Jean is attacked by the vampire Nina, but her creditable
performance of screaming horror is senselessly intercut with
shots of a rushing stream, while the sound glitches and jumps
chaotically. To be fair, I suspect at least some of the film's
editing flaws are due to a heavy-handed cut made for American
video; there's enough blood and gore to suggest that the killings
are intact, but the running time may have been truncated by a
video distributor aiming to pick up the pace of his acquisition.

The plot finally hinges on incest: *"Satan himself will rise
from hell to marry you and Nina,"* Father Daken informs Mark.
*"By human standards your offspring will be horribly deformed,
but he will be beautiful in the eyes of Satan."* Apparently Old
Nick saw the brother and sister playing together in the
churchyard as children, and thought they'd make a lovely
couple. Mark's not so sure he wants an incestuous necrophiliac
Satanic wedding and makes a run for it: but Satan, in league
with the film's editor, conspires to thwart his escape, in a
frankly befuddling climax.

Satan's Black Wedding was the first in a series of Nick
Millard films produced by the director's mother, Frances
Millard, aka Tamara Brown, for her own production company
I.R.M.I. Films. Millard is sometimes credited as: Phillip Miller,
Nick Philips, and Nick Phillips.

Made in California.
see also: "Criminally Insane"

SATAN'S CHEERLEADERS
– Greydon Clark (1977)

The sort of film that ten years later would be exaggerated into
tedium by Empire Pictures and Troma, this, for all its bubblehead
effervescence, is a surprisingly enjoyable romp. It might seem the
height of pickiness to stick up for *Satan's Cheerleaders* against the
likes of *Chopper Chicks in Zombietown* (1989), and I should make it
clear there's only a Rizla-paper's difference between them, but fine
distinctions are what being a connoisseur is all about, right?

Partially at least, it's a matter of the decade in which the film
was made. Shot in 1977 by B-movie stalwart Greydon Clark, *Satan's
Cheerleaders* happily pre-dates the extravagant self-aggrandising of
its eighties variants. There's no pretension either, mind you, no 'art'
lurking in the undergrowth (but I guess you figured that from the
title...) The film wants purely to provide a few laughs and titillate
viewers with glimpses of girl's asses bursting from leotard seams: all
grafted onto a few simple horror riffs. Clark revs the genre engine
pretty hard later on, but takes ten minutes out at the beginning to
show us the four principal girls – Chris (Hillary Horan), Sharon
(Sherry Marks), Debbie (Alisa Powell) and Patti (Kerry Sherman) –
cavorting around on the beach with a couple of guys from the
football team, while the coach (Joseph Carlo) tries to prevent his
boys from expending their *"precious bodily fluids"* with the
rambunctious temptresses (and yes, the script really does quote *Dr.
Strangelove*). The girls are smart-mouthed, with a tireless capacity
for sexual innuendo, but they're less cruel than their peers in Brian
De Palma's *Carrie* and a shade less hip than Laurie Strode's ill-fated
friends in *Halloween*, two female-dominated horror films of roughly
the same period. Their strength lies in their friendship, as seen in a
sequence where they cheerfully initiate what almost turns into a
'gang-rape' of a bemused jock – on the soccer field yet. It's girl
power twenty years early, emblazoned on the story with the subtlety
of a T-shirt emblem. The film is mainly for boys of course, but Clark
is canny enough to ensure that girlfriends can get a kick out of it too.

above: John Carradine and Alisa Powell in **Satan's Cheerleaders**.

below: Mild gore and screaming, from **The Scaremaker**.

bottom right: **The Scaremaker** also played theatres as **Girl's Nite Out**, as this ultra-sleazy admat proves!

With the introduction of a middle-aged, sexually frustrated school caretaker (Jack Kruschen), the film sets up its real line of opposition. The tension is between teenagers and adults: the Satanists are mainly bitter and twisted old men, lusting after unattainable jailbait. There's also a town-and-country thing going down, with hip, urbanised schoolgirls versus *déclassé* backwoods yokels, presided over by corrupt sheriff John Ireland and blowsy Satanic matriarch Yvonne De Carlo. The girls flirt with every man they meet, even John Carradine, here playing a tramp whose purported knowledge of devilish secrets is never elaborated by the script. As per usual, Carradine is just a background totem, a 'ready-made' in the Duchampian sense – he was probably only on set for a day…

Once the film gets rolling, it's actually quite surprising how tense and exciting things become. The girls' flight from the Satanist sheriff into a countryside crawling with coven-members offers twenty minutes of good, efficient scares. One girl tries to use a public phone at the edge of a Hicksville town, only to be surrounded by menacing bumpkins. Another is corralled by a fork-wielding relative of the *Chain Saw* family, while a third throws herself at the feet of a man of the cloth, only to screech *"Jesus!"* when she sees his Satanic brooch. *"Not quite,"* he smirks. Replete with fun dialogue (when told that the coven is seeking a virgin, one girl protests: *"I'm no maiden – I've been a cheerleader for three years!"*), this is pure trash but strangely satisfying nonetheless.

Made in California.

THE SCAREMAKER
– Robert Deubel (1982)
aka *Girls Nite Out*

A campus treasure hunt co-ordinated via college radio is the setting for another formula slasher flick. Your first clue: it's 'The One Where The Killer Wears A Cartoon-Bear Costume'…

I'm a pushover for a good stalk-and-slash run-around, but sadly, this ain't one of 'em. I did *try* to like *The Scaremaker*, despite its utterly meaningless title, not least because the cast are the most killable bunch of bozos since the International Mime Society held a Freestyle Poignancy Contest. The first twenty five minutes are oversubscribed with the sort of applicants other slashers restrict to one or maybe two per cast-list: giggling dopers, zany class comics, gurning devotees of alcohol, mincing drama students… why, the possibilities for mayhem are endless. It pains me to report, however, that once the murders are underway, disappointment, frustration and thwarted bloodlust are all you can look forward to. The killer dons a cartoon bear suit – not in itself a hindrance to the film's potential – but he customises the suit with 'claws' made of taped-together kitchen knives, which limits his *modus operandi* to a few maulings of victims' throats, mostly in medium shot. Despite the knives anticipating Freddy Krueger by a couple of years, this radically dampens the amusement factor, not least because all you see is, at best, a gush of blood from the vicinity of a throat, with a giant furry paw obstructing your view. There is at least something curiously homoerotic (and thus faintly idiosyncratic) about the film, with its preference for stripping the male not the female cast; and two of the most obnoxious 'class clowns' are so screamingly gay it's an act of pie-in-the-sky wishful thinking to depict them as popular not just with dopers and dropouts, but the jocks and jockettes too in this Ivy League college, where Senators' daughters rub shoulders with America's richest Remingtons. I too harbour fantasies of a gay-themed college slasher tale to out-butcher them all, but Robert Deubel fumbles the opportunity and delivers a blur of a movie instead. The score gives the film some extra class by treating us to classic sixties songs like The Lovin' Spoonful's 'Summer in the City,' but class ain't what this end of the market needs: less money spent on pop music clearance and more on graphic flesh-wounds would have lifted *Scaremaker* higher up the horror charts. Note: the film is set, at least nominally, in Westville, Ohio.

Made in New Jersey.

The Scaremaker (UK video title)
aka Girl's Nite Out (US theatrical title)
© 1982. Anthony N. Gurvis.
An Aries International Releasing Corp. and Independent-International Pictures Corp. release. Anthony N. Gurvis in association with Concepts Unlimited presents.
director: Robert Duebel. director of photography: Joe Rivers. editor: Arthur Ginsberg. executive producers: Kevin Kurgis, Richard Barclay. producer: Anthony N. Gurvis. production designer: Howard Cummings. associate producer: Arthur Ginsberg. screenplay: Gil Spencer, Jr., Kevin Kurgis, Joe Bolster, Anthony N. Gurvis. based on a story by Gil Spencer, Jr., Kevin Kurgis. production manager: Patrick McCormick. first assistant director: Dwight Williams. second assistant director: Tom Fritz. camera operator: John Soenko. first assistant camera: Lisa Rinzler. second unit cameraman: Roger Dean. script supervisor: Hariotte Aaron. still photographer: Ken Howard. make up / hair stylist: Kathryn Bihr. special effects make up: Tom Brumberger. special effects: Deed Rossiter. costumes by Masija. wardrobe supervisor: Dianne Finn Chapman. wardrobe assistant: Carla Froeberg. property master: L. Scott Moore. set decorator: Neil Prince. set decorator: Jane Musky. music library: FV Sound, Ltd. sound: Magno Sound. rerecording mixer: Jack Cooley. assistant editor: Celeste Hines. assistant to the producer: Kip Miller. title design: William Parks. music supervision: Richard Barclay. casting by Marcia Shulman for Shuman/Pasciuto, Inc. production auditor: Barbara-Ann Stein. production office co-ordinator: Ooty morehead. D.G.A. trainee: Michea Caye. location manager: Edwin (Itsi) Atkins. assistant location manager: Lenny Vullo. production assistants: Ruth Aamon, Loretta Beasley, Geb Byers, Vebe Borge, Louis Di Cesare, Thomas Kudlek, Jim Rosenthal, Viola Rotundo. recordings courtesy of: Buddah Records, Inc. "Summer in the City" written by John Sebastian, performed by The Lovin' Spoonful; "Do You Believe in Magic" written by John Sebastian, performed by The Lovin' Spoonful; "You Didn't Have To Be So Nice" written by John Sebastian and Steve Boone, performed by The Lovin' Spoonful; "Didn't Wanna Have To Do It" written by John Sebastian, performed by The Lovin' Spoonful; "Yummy, Yummy, Yummy" written by Arthur Resnick and Joe Levine, performed by Ohio Express; "Quick, Joey Small" written by Arthur Resnick and Joe Levine, performed by Kasennetz Katz Singing Orchestral Circus; Kaskat Music, Inc. "Indian Giver" written by Bobby Bloom, Bo Gentry and Ritchie Cordel, performed by 1910 Fruit Gum Co.; "1,2,3 Red Light" written by Sal Trimachi and Bobbi Trimachi, performed by 1910 Fruit Gum Co.; "Down at Lulu's" written by Joe Levine and Kris Resnick, performed by Ohio Express; Roulette records, Inc. "Hanky Panky" written by Jeff Barry and Ellie Greenwich, performed by Tommy James & the Shondells; "Do Something to Me" written by J. Calvert, P. Naumann and N. Marzano, performed by Tommy James & the Shondells; "I'm Alive" written by P. Lucia and T. James, performed by Tommy James & the Shondells; "Darling, How Long" written by J. Sheppard and W.H. Miller, performed by The Heartbeats; Su-Ma Publishing Co., Inc. "Judy in Disguise" written by John Fred and A. Bemar, performed by John Fred and the Playboy Band. lenses and Panaflex camera by Panavision. opticals by The Optical House. location equipment by Filmtrucks. colour by TVC. titles by On Film Ltd.
Cast: Julie Montgomery (Lynn Connors). James Carroll (Teddy Ratliff). Suzanne Barnes (Dawn Sorenson). Hal Holbrook (Jim MacVey). Rutanya Alda (Barney). Al McGuire (Coach Kimble). Lauren-Marie Taylor (Sheila Robinson). David Holbrook (Mike Pryor). Laura Summer (Jane). Mart McChesney (Pete 'Maniac' Krizaniac). Carrick Glenn (Kathy). John Didrichsen (Ralph Bostwick). Lois Robbins (Leslie Peterson). Mathew Dunn (Benson). Susan Pitts (Trish). Paul Christie (dancer). Gregory Salata (Hagen). Tony Shultz (Bud Remington). Larry Mintz (Charlie Kaiser). Richard Bright (Detective Greenspan). Kevin Mulvey (Sergeant Parker). Richard Voights (Dean kemper). Page Mosely (pledge one). Rafael Ferrer (pledge two). Steven McGraw (pledge three). Cynthia S. Lee (Carol Rice). Lee Ann Brentlinger (sorority sister). Peter Steltzer (security man).

SCREAM BLOODY MURDER
– Marc B. Ray (1972)
See interview with Marc B. Ray.

Made in California.

SCREAMS OF A WINTER NIGHT
– James Wilson (1979)
See interview with James Wilson and Richard Wadsack.

Made in Louisiana.

A SCREAM IN THE STREETS
– Carl Monson (1972)
aka *Girls in the Streets*
aka *Scream Street*

One of the most stupid, lazy-ass films in this book, *A Scream in the Streets* is a ragbag of scenes thrown together around two charmless cops driving through Los Angeles fulminating against criminality, while searching for a rape-killer (Con Covert) who is also a deeply unconvincing transvestite. *"I hate you! I hate women!"* he yells, as he murders his victims. That'll be psychology covered, then. The two cops – you guessed it, a by-the-book type (John Kirkpatric), and a loose-cannon psycho (Frank Bannon) – wrangle about whether criminals deserve any rights, while the script tosses in a couple of crime-scene shootouts and four or five tedious softcore interludes. In a can't-be-arsed shrug of a 'climax', the cops don't even find the killer themselves; instead, they're given a tip-off on a street corner by a previously unseen old-timer. A showdown between By-the-Book and Killer-Trannie ends with By-the-Book stabbed to death, so Psycho-Partner blows Killer-Trannie's brains out while sarcastically reading him his rights. The only real highlight is a sleazy spanking session in a sauna that turns into G.B.H., as the john smashes a bottle in the owner's face and thrashes the cringing masseuse with a leather belt. *A Scream in the Streets* has occasionally been cited as some sort of trash classic, but if you ask me it's too dumb and indolent to deserve a cult following. It was produced by Harry Novak in cahoots with his buddy Carl Monson (born 2 September, 1932), who directed the tedious *Legacy of Blood* (1971) and the 'comedy' sex film *Please Don't Eat My Mother!* (1973). Monson died on 4

August, 1988. Note: The IMDB alleges that Dwayne Avery was an uncredited co-director: apparently there are three people in the world willing to put their name to this movie.

The film's most bizarre feature, its weird, unconvincing killer transvestite, has echoes of the Jerry Brudos case of 1969. When a young woman went missing in Portland Oregon, shoppers described seeing a tall, strange-looking female hanging around the area where the victim disappeared. A witness who got closer realised that it was actually a man in drag. Brudos was apprehended later that year and found to be both a shoe fetishist and occasional transvestite (he did not, however, abduct women while in female garb). Horror films like *Psycho*, *Dressed to Kill* and *A Scream in the Streets* have depicted cross-dressers as psychotic slashers who hate women. In fact, transvestites are generally non-violent. If they do commit violent acts, their fetish is generally incidental, not causal. For another dose of unconvincing transvestite action, see *Sometimes Aunt Martha Does Dreadful Things*.

Made in California.

THE SEVERED ARM
– Thomas S. Alderman (1972)

In a darkened morgue, an unidentified man cuts an arm from a corpse. The next morning, TV scriptwriter Jeff Ashton (David G. Cannon) receives the arm in a brown paper package addressed to him. Could it perhaps have something to do with the time, five years ago, when Jeff and his friends – Ray Sanders (John Crawford), a doctor; Bill Haile (Vince Martorano), a building contractor; Mark Richards (Paul Carr), a cop; Ted Rogers (Ray Dannis), an architect; and 'Mad Man Herman' (Marvin Kaplan), a radio DJ – were trapped behind a rock fall during a caving expedition? Desperately hungry after more than two weeks without food, they resorted to cannibalism, severing Ted's arm to feed themselves. Unluckily for Ted, just as they crossed this moral Rubicon, a rescue team arrived. Jeff persuaded the group to lie to the authorities, claiming that Ted's arm was crushed in the rock fall. Now someone is stalking and mutilating the remaining five…

The Severed Arm is a missed opportunity, as there's enough in the story to have made a great little horror flick. The cast give the tense, despairing cave scenes a fair shot (I especially liked Herman's quip when cannibalism is first suggested: *"We'll have to hold on until tomorrow. I can't eat meat on Fridays"*), and although the budget doesn't stretch to any make-up miracles, at least the production tries, with crusty face appliances for the starving men that resemble the early stages of zombiehood (not to mention some bizarre bushy beards). The fact that the victims-in-waiting are older men rather than teens or nubile women is a welcome change, and the story is commendably single-minded, never taking time out for superfluous romance or sub-plots. Gradually, though, the film turns from horror into more of a straightforward murder-thriller. Alderman allows the pace to slacken and there are just too many talky scenes; although some of them work dramatically, the film lacks urgency. Perhaps with a more daring shooting style *The Severed Arm* might have been a shoo-in for cult reappraisal, but it's hampered by plodding

bottom left:
He hates women, apparently…
the transvestite killer in action, from
A Scream in the Streets.

below:
UK video sleeve for **The Severed Arm**,
one of two covers that Iver Film Services
gave the film in the UK.

camerawork and functional TV-style editing – unlike *Scream Bloody Murder*, a much more lurid bits-cut-off tale from the same writer (see the interview with Marc Ray elsewhere in this book). At least Phillan Bishop's electronic score is fun, an analogue synth freak's delight that sounds like early Tangerine Dream gate-crashing a Pertwee-era *Doctor Who* story, thus keeping the mood, if not the pace, afloat. (Bishop provided similar pleasures for Willard Huyck's excellent *Messiah of Evil* and Chris Munger's *Kiss of the Tarantula*). And the final twist is cruel and effective, bringing the story full circle with a claustrophobic shudder.

I've been unable to see an uncut print of this movie, which is a shame because it's clear that scenes have been trimmed, in particular the severing of Ted's arm in the cave, where both music and picture jump abruptly. To be fair, demands for extreme gore are probably misplaced anyway; this is the sort of borderline horror/drama we were more used to seeing in the seventies, before *Friday the 13th* and *Dawn of the Dead* upped the stakes, and it's unlikely that an uncut version would add more than a few blood-spurts. Still, for a film about men having their arms chopped off to lose that very image is a bit of a handicap.

Director Thomas Alderman made one earlier film, *Co-Ed Dorm* (1971), which I've been unable to screen but which, according to producer Gary Adelman, was originally blessed with the title *Feruk U* (as in University). It stars *The Severed Arm*'s unfortunate 'Ted Rogers' aka Ray Dannis, as 'Dr. Maurice de Sade', and features softcore actress Uschi Digard in the role of 'Miss Melons', so I think we can guess where that's heading… *The Severed Arm* was shot by Robert Maxwell, whose numerous credits in the horror genre include *The Astro-Zombies*, *The Centerfold Girls*, *Blood Mania*, *The Psycho Lover* and *House of Terror*, as well as the cult blaxploitation film *Sweet Sweetback's Baadasssss Song*. Fans of TV's *Top Cat* may recognise 'Mad Man Herman', aka Marvin Kaplan, as the voice of Top Cat's sidekick, Choo-Choo!

Made in: unknown

SEX WISH
– Tim McCoy (1976)
aka *Love Wish*
aka *Night-Walker*

"Sex Wish was more of a psychological study than a sex film. It raised a notch the level between sex and violence to an absurd point. If you separate sex from love, there is nothing but violence. Nothing but a power trip." – Zebedy Colt (lukeford.com)

This New York sex-and-horror hybrid is so sleazy you can't decide whether to laugh or reach for the carbolic. *Sex Wish* upstages even Italian shockers like Joe D'Amato's *Emanuelle in America*, making you feel like a scumbag as you enjoy the gleeful obscenity. It charts the invasion of heterosexual bliss by a snivelling sicko, whose infantile games of humiliation are motivated by raging homosexual jealousy. That this formula should produce anything other than a hateful homophobic exercise is testimony to the extraordinary commitment and energy of its bisexual star player, Mr. Zebedy Colt.

Colt (real name Edward Earle Marsh) died in July 2004, but he left a body of work in the field of American porn that stands as some of the most ferociously extreme of the seventies. As a performer, he was a law unto himself, and his phenomenal self-assertion is nowhere better vindicated than here. *Sex Wish* is for Colt what *Taxi Driver* was to De Niro, what *Blue Velvet* was to Dennis Hopper, or *The Last House on the Left* to David Hess. The fact that this is a full-on porno film with penetration and cum-shots adds a verisimilitude that Scorsese and Lynch can allude to but never show.

Sex Wish begins with an outstandingly sleazy title theme, played on fuzzed-up beatbox and organ. A gnarly evocation of human trash crawling through the gutters of the mind, it sounds so twisted you feel laughter bubbling up, a discomfiting sensation that recurs throughout. Beneath the credits we see a shadowy figure, 'The Night Walker' (Zebedy Colt), flitting through the New York streets; the *Taxi*

Driver milieu of whores, junkies, buggers. The credits sequence alone is unsettling enough: what follows is Grade-A New York nastiness.

Marital bliss provides the initial anchor. Cue Harry Reems as Ken, sporting a luxurious moustache and playing a nice guy this time (as opposed to his possessed turn in Shaun Costello's *Forced Entry*). As so often, he's a screen natural, easy-going and likeable. His line deliveries could easily pass muster in 'regular' films. After a bath-time frolic with his lovely wife Faye (C.J. Laing) he heads off to work, leaving her home alone – until 'The Night Walker' knocks at the door, forces his way in, and sends *Sex Wish* into overdrive…

Acting with the energy of the truly uninhibited and displaying a conviction that suggests powerful reservoirs of inner-direction, Colt turns the first sex attack into a queasy-hilarious polymorphous playground, a grimy plunge into depravity only rarely seen in the acting profession (Colt could hold his head up high in the company of 'Bad Lieutenant' Harvey Keitel). He taunts, bullies and cajoles his victim into grotesque sexual role-play, murmuring and squealing like a baby: you wonder what on Earth actress C.J. Laing thought she'd stumbled into. Maybe Colt was adept at putting the talent at their ease before a take, but once the camera's rolling there's no turning back. The scene is a horrendous rape-murder played for the blackest comedy. How else are we to react, during sequences such as the one where Colt takes on the persona of a little boy raping a woman with a vibrator, before switching personalities and adopting the tones of a haughty English madam, flouncing his shoulder-length hair, and whipping the victim for *"teaching my boy dirty tricks"*? Teetering between sick and ridiculous, Colt's detailed verbalisation is a wonderful display of acting *cojones*, giving *Sex Wish* the acrid odour of undiluted rape-fantasy.

Things simmer down for a while after this prolonged scene and, when Reems reacts to the rape and murder of his girlfriend by going to a bar and accepting the offer of troilism from two chicks – Bermuda (Deanna Benfante) and Lisa (Tony Rome) – you could be forgiven for thinking the film has resolutely turned its back on plausibility. Not so – those in the throes of grief often hurl themselves into sex as an escape from unbearable loss. Mind you, once *Sex Wish* has introduced us to Zebedy Colt's vicious comedy, it's difficult to see the subsequent 'vanilla' sex scenes in quite the same way. (It's like his twisted revenge on heterosexual porn).

What appears vanilla though is soon subverted again, in an unexpected way. At the climax of his three-way with the two girls, Reems announces he's going to cum. Deanna Benfante drops to her knees to receive the customary facial sacrament: but then, as Reems is shooting over her, she gazes intently up at him and says: *"You know what I'd do if I were you? I'd kill that motherfucker – I'd go out there and I'd search and I'd find him and I'd get me a gun and I'd kill that motherfucker so he could never do anything like that again!"* At the very moment of orgasm, this impassioned statement sends the fury of the film into overdrive, as the woman uses Reems's sexual energy to fuel his revenge (exactly the principle that underlies the occult practice of sex-magick).

Colt prepares for his next atrocity by transferring amyl nitrate to a nasal dropper, threading his genitals through a cock-ring and slipping into a nice white jockstrap before invading the home of Betty and Bobby (Candy and Ronnie Love), a young black couple, and forcing them at gunpoint to have sex in front of him. The dynamics of this scene are fascinating, because they seem to send up the relationship between a porno director and his cast. Colt's sniggering demands are like the funhouse leering of the sickest, weaseliest, woodsiest porno auteur imaginable. By showing a young black couple manipulated by the white psychopath, the film adds a further illicit charge to the exploitation game. It's fascinating to see the couple almost slipping out of character as Colt taunts and laughs and giggles his demands – not only are they facing the challenge of acting in a porn film, they're also dealing with a fantasy so energeti-cally perverse that it's about to break the fourth wall. When the young man leaves off from a clinch with his lover to snap, *"You're sick, you know that?"* there's a real depth to his remark. His girlfriend visibly tries to suppress her laughter when Colt lets loose a torrent of grotesque giggles. Colt insists she take off her panties, and she protests: *"I don't want to do that."* Like a psychotic film director (shades of *The Last House on Dead End Street*), he yells from off-camera *"Take them off!"* The couple start to fuck, and we cut back to Colt watching in rapt enjoyment. *"Is that what you want to see, you dirty motherfucker?"* the actress demands, as we're given a close-up of the man's cock pounding her pussy. Not only is Colt the director's satiric surrogate, he's ours too...

The fourth wall slips again when Colt is heard encouraging the fuck-scene with the words, *"That's nice Gabe, you..."* Suddenly Colt, onscreen, breaks off and jabs his rubber-gloved thumb in his mouth – has he given away the actor's real name? This feeling of the artifice slipping away gives the film an edge that makes the violence even more alarming: *"You clamp down on that goddamned tit and you bite it off!!!"* he yells, sending a chill up the viewer's spine. For a second you believe him, although it's the extremity of his delivery that makes you flinch, more than the image onscreen.

As must have suited the bisexual Colt, humiliation is shared equally between the male and female victims. The man is slashed by The Night Walker's sword, and during the ensuing struggle the actress loses her wig (another shudderingly *verité* moment). He cuts her throat but, as with Jess Franco's sex-horror pictures, we see little actual gore. In fact this is the closest the American cinema gets to a Franco film, and the similarities are very pronounced: right down to the creepy organ music. The scene draws to a close with The Night Walker castrating the dead Bobby, snarling, *"It's all your fault,"* before breaking down and crying.

The pacing is way off in the last fifteen minutes. Police procedural material intervenes where another killing would have fitted neatly. Ken almost catches the killer in the street but Colt escapes to harass a passing shopper, dragging her into a side alley, as bold as you please, for a bit of prêt-a-porter rape-fun. The initially unconvincing actress (Terri Hall, star of Colt's *Terri's Revenge* and McCoy's *The Erotic Dr. Jekyll*) is frogmarched into a good performance by Colt's intensity. She begins in a tacky, self-consciously 'tarty' mode, but by the time Colt has her tied to a ladder, her performance is a lot less 'cute'. But it's a hurried scene, compared to the others. The verbal aggression is muted, and although in any other film it would qualify as disturbing, it's all a bit truncated by *Sex Wish* standards. Maybe the coke ran out... (For the record, Colt denied using drugs.)

In a plot twist that signals merely the desire to wrap things up, Reems attends a gay nightclub 'on a hunch' and recognises Colt performing onstage as a sort of foppish cross-gender entertainer. Leaping to his feet, he points at the outrageously attired killer, and utters the immortal line: *"That's him! That's her! The murderer! The rapist!"* Colt shoots dead a policeman played by Robert Kerman (thus doing what hordes of Italian movie cannibals could not) and flees, before being cornered by Reems in a part of the club that resembles the Korova Milk Bar: *"I did it because I love you!"* he cries. Reems shoots him, but the end credits speculate as to whether we've *really* seen the end of The Night Walker. Sequel, anyone?

So who made *Sex Wish*? Well, the film was originally called *Night-Walker* (the version I've seen has a title card inserted during the credits, bearing the words *Sex Wish* in a different font), with the director listed onscreen as Tim McCoy. However, Zebedy Colt told at least one interviewer that he directed as well as starred. ("Colt regards his best films as those that he directed – *The Affairs of Janice, Playgirls in Munich, Sex Wish*" – see www.lukeford.com.) A third character, Milton Vickers, has been associated with the director's chair on this movie too (his name is on the American Copyright Catalogue entry) – amazing, since it's the sort of super-scuzzy film where you'd expect people to be denying involvement rather than claiming it! Given that Colt essentially governs the course of each scene he plays (especially the one with the black couple, in which he literally sits beside them and directs their sex scene), it's possible that he was responsible for directing his own scenes while McCoy or Vickers (could they be one and the same?) directed the rest of the movie.

Gay viewers of political sensitivity may find the film homophobic, despite its bisexual provenance. It is, after all, about a jealous homosexual who murders any woman who gets close to the heterosexual male he desires: at the end of the film the heavily made-up Night Walker declares that he murdered out of love for Ken, and Ken shoots him dead. For a gay viewer not to be offended by the film, they must be able to enjoy the extraordinary performance Colt contributes; without this enjoyment, *Sex Wish* will probably appear as gay-friendly an experience as William Friedkin's *Cruising*.

It's as well to reflect on your opinions before dissing Zebedy Colt, as music critic Bob Amsel discovered in 1969 when he reviewed Colt's man-to-man love song album, 'I'll Sing for You.' Amsel wrote: "Don't be suckered into buying these old standards just because they're sung by a guy. The orchestrations and male chorus were enough to turn me onto Lawrence Welk, who does that sort of bubble muzak so much better. Zebedy (where did he ever get that name) may be a nice guy, but his taste stems from Early Tacky to Late Forest Hills, and his music (mucous?) album typifies everything that was wrong with the Eisenhower years."

A bad review can set anyone's temples throbbing, but the temptation to respond is usually a mistake. That said, few of us have Zebedy Colt's seething resentment, nor his way with words, as his letter to the publication in question shows: "Who in the fuck is Bob Amsel? Out of what pile of shit did he emerge to decide what is good or bad? His review of my album is so stupidly biased and ignorant of the kind of war I'm waging that his opinions made me want to vomit all over him… If Asshole Amsel wishes to debate publicly, privately or in print, I'm ready to cut his balls off with a rusty razor blade any time." (Thanks to the late Jack Nichols for these quotes, which can be found online at the Gay Today Entertainment Archives.)

So to reiterate: *Sex Wish* is a stunning *tour-de-force* that pushes the envelope while everyone else is still looking for a flat surface to write the letter. I'm not a superstitious man, but I don't want the ghost of Zebedy Colt jumping out at me with a rusty razorblade. Now, perhaps I should go back and rewrite those Al Adamson pieces…

Made in New York City.

SHADOWS OF THE MIND

– Roger Watkins [erroneously credited to Bernard Travis] (1980)
aka *A Heritage of Blood*

After her release from a mental institution, Elise Sayers (Marion Joyce) returns to the house where she was brought up, and where, as a child, she saw her father (Richard McNichol) and stepmother (Marcia Watkins) drown. Soon, her unsympathetic stepbrother Leland (G.E. Barrymore) arrives, and the gardener is murdered by an unseen assailant. The following night, Elise's attentive psychiatrist Doctor Lang (Erik Rolfe) and his fiancée Diana Russell (Bianca Sloane) drop by for a social evening, but jealousy and unresolved tensions between the four lead to further murders.

Talk about contrasts. This film from the director of *The Last House on Dead End Street* could not be further removed from the dementia of that first, extraordinary movie. In an interview with David Kerekes (see the booklet for the DVD release of *The Last House on Dead End Street*), Watkins states that he directed *Shadows of the Mind*, having written it with his friend Paul Jensen, under the title *A Heritage of Blood* (inspired by David Pirie's pioneering film book *A Heritage of Horror*). According to Watkins, one 'Bernard Travis' then improperly claimed the director's credit (Travis had already roused Watkins's ire by imposing a cop-out voice-over on the ending of *The Last House on Dead End Street*). Watkins further alleges that producer Leo Fenton's wife Marion Joyce (star of *Shadows of the Mind*) stole the writer's credit.

It's hard to see what Watkins would gain by lying about this. *The Last House on Dead End Street* is a masterpiece, *Shadows of the Mind* is just awful. It's tedious and poorly conceived on just about every level. Watkins agrees, claiming that he once demanded of his producer, "Leo, why are we making this fucking film? It stinks!" Fenton, referring to the fact that he was making the movie as a sop to his wife Marion, who thirsted for a career as an actress, replied,

Sex Wish (US/UK video title)
aka **Night-Walker** (original US theatrical title)
© 1976. Santini Prod.
Taurus Productions presents.
writer/photographer/director: Tim McCoy.
executive producer: Leo De Leon. producer: Ralph Ell. editor: Charles Lamont.
Cast: Harry Reems (Ken). Zebedy Colt (Nightwalker). C.J. Laing (Faye). Terri Hall (raped woman). Deanna Benfante (Bermuda). Tony Rome (Lisa). Alexis Blassini (M.C.). Joaquin La Habana (dancer). Ronnie Love, Candy Love (young couple). Sue Franklin (Alice). uncredited: *Robert Kerman (policeman).*

opposite page, from top:
Scenes from **Sex Wish**:
Zebedy Colt as the Night Walker, breaking into a house;
...tying up the female occupant (C.J. Laing);
...subjecting her to physical indignities while ranting his bizarre fantasies;
...before kneeling over her;
...and cutting her throat.
Later he attacks a black couple (Candy Love shown with Colt);
...and insists that they make love to his orders as he sits watching avidly;
He is finally brought to book by the husband of his first victim, played by porn legend Harry Reems.

Shadows of the Mind
aka **A Heritage of Blood** (original script title)
© 1980. LBS Properties, Inc.
A Production Concepts Ltd presentation.
director: Bernard Travis. producer: Leo Fenton. executive producers: Leo Fenton and Steven A. Florin. cinematographer: Domonic Paris, A.S.C. music supervision: Claude Armand. sound supervision: Ben Donnelly. editors: Arnold Larschan, Bernard Travis. make-up supervisor: Joan Puma. makeup by Dorothy Klein. main title design: W.H. Lackie Co., Inc. special sound effects: Aquarius Sound. special visual effects: Film Opticals. negative matching: Lou Somerstein. set decoration: Lillian Demroth. property master: Mike Gagliano. stunt co-ordinator: Ed Reilly. post production super: Marshall Blumenthal. art director: Peter Jennings. editors: Arnold Larschan & Bernard Travis. gaffer: Daniel Canton. assistant cameraman: Kelly Van Horn. 2nd electrician: Robert Johnson. assistant sound: Hector T. Austin. key grip: Phil Devonshire. grip: Fred Knepperges. 2nd unit assistant: Fred Knepperges. continuity: Arlene Kaufman. prod supervisor: Jay Marshall. 2nd unit cameraman: Kelly Van Horn. written by Marion Joyce. colour by Movielab.
Cast: Marion Joyce (Elise). Erik Rolfe (Dr. Robert Lang). G.E. Barrymore (Leland Sayers). Bianca Sloane (Diana Russell). Anthony Frank (Andrew). Don Renshaw (Sydell). Marcia Watkins (the mother). Rick McNichols/Richard McNichol (father). Pamala/Pamela Dawn (Elise as little girl). Lisa Suzanne/Lisa Susanne (girl on swing). Len Fine (man in park). Margret Smith (nurse). Dorothy Klein (woman in car).

above:
The video cover for **Shadows of the Mind** makes use of the only gory moment in the film.

bottom right:
This Cannes film market poster for **The Silent Scream** omits the definite article.

opposite page, top:
Silent Night, Bloody Night looks pretty good judging from this montage of stills, the centre-piece of which depicts a horde of lunatics…

"It's cheaper than a divorce!" Well, perhaps a divorce would have been better: Marion Joyce is far too frumpy and unprepossessing to carry the movie. Leland, her mean, money-grabbing stepbrother, is at least convincing in a low-rent *Dallas* or *Falcon Crest* sort of way, but the pacing is woeful, with information drip-fed so slowly that cinemagoers would have time to plan, commit and conceal a murder of their own between each new development.

The only discernible link to Watkins's first film is the relentless unlikeability of the characters. Elise is a mousy bore still obsessed with jealousy over her father's love for her stepmother, Leland is a selfish pig looking to capitalise on the sale of the house, and Diana is a bitch who enjoys stirring up trouble simply because of a lazy twinge of jealousy at her fiancée's concern for his patient. Even Andrew the gardener (Anthony Frank) is an idiot. I usually warm to the kind of movies where people get garden tools through their necks, but *Shadows of the Mind* fails to enliven its dopey story with enough gruesomeness, and it certainly never feels remotely as dangerous or as fascinating as *The Last House on Dead End Street*.

Made in New York State.
see also: **The Last House on Dead End Street**

SILENT NIGHT, BLOODY NIGHT
– Theodore Gershuny (1972)
aka *Death House*
aka *Deathouse*
aka *Asylum*
aka *Night of the Dark Full Moon*
aka *Zora*

1935: Wilfred Butler, the owner of a grand old house used as an asylum, dies in mysterious circumstances. The building stands empty for thirty five years until the heir puts it back on the market. This creates consternation among the town's prominent figures, including Mayor Adams (Walter Abel), Charles Towman the proprietor of the local newspaper (John Carradine), Sheriff Mason (Walter Klavun), and – in a quirk that's maybe the only laugh in the film – the switchboard operator, Tess Howard (Fran Stevens). Butler's lawyer John Carter (Patrick O'Neal) arrives in town and discovers that the four dignitaries are keen to snap up the property themselves. That night, the lawyer and his floozy, Ingrid (Astrid Heeren), are murdered at the house by an unseen figure. The four dignitaries receive a phone call from a woman called Marianne, drawing them one by one to the house, and their doom. Jeffrey Butler arrives and strikes up a relationship with the mayor's daughter Diane Adams (Mary Woronov). Together they try to solve the mystery of what really happened back in 1935.

"You know, one of the great pleasures in life is the pleasure of anticipating pleasure," says Patrick O'Neal, neatly summing up what's wrong with the film, as we slip from anticipation into scepticism, and finally to dismissiveness. I expected to like this, having seen stills of ominous robed figures roaming the grounds of a spooky old house, reproduced in many a film magazine over the years. The fact that it's set at Christmas also whetted my appetite: would it be as much fun as *Silent Night, Deadly Night*? Or *Christmas Evil*? High hopes indeed, and very soon dashed. *Silent Night, Bloody Night* is a painfully slow affair, plotted for maximum irritation, with a deferred mystery structure that will have you screaming with impatience after the first hour. Gershuny shows some visual style, as seen in isolated arty shots here and there, but he directs in ponderous mood, patching over events he can't properly elaborate with snippets

of tiresome voice-over (and the post-synch recording is poor for an American film; it's like a stodgily dubbed Italian drama of the 1950s). Snow-dappled exteriors and leafless trees during the first half of the film exude a forlorn wintry atmosphere similar to David Cronenberg's *The Brood*, and the glowering string arrangements sometimes recall Howard Shore's work on that film, but the similarities really do end there. The latter half of the film is shot almost entirely at night, with scene after scene played in near-blackness. The action limps from darkened roadside to darkened interior, with barely a flicker of imagination about how to animate such a simplistic palette. Of course, a film of relentless shadow is ill-suited to videotape, so it's possible that a decent DVD release may one day reveal more detail and style. But the film has trouble even getting started, wasting everyone's time with half an hour in the company of Butler's lawyer (an awful, leaden performance by Patrick O'Neal). When he and his girlfriend are despatched by an axe-wielding mystery attacker, one's spirit is briefly perked: sadly, Gershuny lets the film slip back into lethargy. At least Mary Woronov suggests an intelligence beyond the reach of the story, but she's wasted in a role that hardly taxes her abilities.

The asylum flashbacks mark an at first exciting shift into grainy, overexposed sepia, yet even this becomes irritating. The appearance here by members of New York's underground film scene is another baited hook the film waves before us, but by the time you get to see Candy Darling, Ondine, Jack Smith and Hetty MacLise cavorting and grimacing as asylum inmates, you're almost ready to swap the experience for a screening of Warhol's *Sleep*.

The film was shot at Oyster Bay, Long Island. Gershuny wrote about filmmaking in an essay called *The Grand Voyage,* for the book *Soon to Be a Major Motion Picture*. *Silent Night, Bloody Night* was eventually picked up in 1981 for a very brief spell in British theatres, playing under the inelegant retitling *Deathouse*.

Made in New York State.

THE SILENT SCREAM
aka *The Boarding House*
– Denny Harris (1979)

Another nice young college girl forced to take off-campus accommodation, another old house with mysterious goings on in the attic, another strange old lady, another nervy young man whose mental stability is in question. Can *The Silent Scream* distinguish itself from the crowd? The answer is yes, but only just. The actors take a fair slice of the credit: Rebecca Balding especially is sweet and plausible as Scotty, the femme lead, and Juli Andelman gives chatty, cheerful Jewish girl Doris a light touch to contrast with her heavy build. The great-looking house is a bonus too, and when Barbara Steele pops up in the latter stages horror fans *d'un certain age* will levitate in their seats. There's also a tense, well-edited stalking, a nasty murder on a lonely stretch of beach, and a pleasantly Gothic climax. So what's the problem?

From its slow-mo prologue and lavish, flagrantly Herrmannesque score to its attractive setting and elegant old-fashioned camerawork, *The Silent Scream* adds a *soupçon* of class to its serving of genre cliché. And 'class' isn't always a good thing in horror. Depending on your tolerance, this movie is either a cut above the nasty old slashers, or a touch too stuffy and tweedy for its own good. Personally, I find I warm to it, despite its unwillingness to go for the jugular. The characterisations are uncomplicated but they're well sketched and likeably played. For instance, although Creepy Mason (Brad Rearden) comes from a long line of voyeuristic post-*Psycho* nerds, we greet him with pleasurable recognition: after all, who would dream of renting out student digs *without* metal grills in all the rooms, linked by hidden corridors just perfect for peeking?

So it's the same old story we've seen so many times before, but it's fun anyway. Peter (John Widelock), a rich, sexist drunk, makes an ideal first victim, and it only remains for me to say we should perhaps have had a little more of the red stuff when he dies (I'm sure I've said that a hundred times in this book already, but

Silent Night, Bloody Night
aka **Deathhouse** (US/UK 1981 re-release title)
aka **Zora** (shooting title)
aka **Night of the Dark Full Moon**
© 1972. Zora Investment Associates
Ami Artzi and Cannon Releasing Corp. in conjunction with Armor films Inc. present a Cannon production in association with Jeffrey Konvitz Productions. A Cannon release.
director: Theodore Gershuny. producer: Jeffrey Konvitz and Ami Artzi. associate producers: Frank Vitale and Lloyd Kaufman. screenplay: Theodore Gershuny, Jeffrey Konvitz and Ira Teller; based on an original story by Jeffrey Konvitz and Ira Teller. director of photography: Adam Giffard (colour by DeLuxe). music composed and conducted by Gershon Kingsley. editor: Tom Kennedy. equipment: Cameramart, N.Y. sound: Magnosound, N.Y. art director: Henry Schrady. assistant art director: Sam Bender. props: Jim Walker. wardrobe: Bill Christians. make-up: Pat Pizza. hairstylist: Neil Barbella. sound recorder: Bruce Perlman. sound assistant: Paul Bang. assistant director: Andrew Geygerson. assistant cameraman: Sal Guida. gaffer: Aristides Pappidas. script continuity: Helga Petrashevics. grip: Joe Bruck. transportation: Rudy Churny. first electrician: Jim Crispi. still photographer: Roy Patterson. production assistants: Jeff Kahan, Brad Pagota, Melanie Mintz, Thomas Sturges, Everett Sherman, Gary Rich. assistant to the producer: Carole Sobel. production secretary: Cheryl Konvitz. sound editor: Nobuko Oganesoff. music editor: James Korris. assistant editors: Jonathan Kroll, Charles Baum. rerecording engineer: Raun Kirves. mixer: Jack Cooley. special effects: Louis Antzes. title design: Sal Vitale, Hugh Valentine. Special thanks to GT.Norris, Inc. filmed from 20 January 1971 in Old Westbury (Long Island, USA).
Cast: Mary Woronov (Diane Adams). Alex Stevens (burning man). Patrick O'Neal (John Carter). Astrid Heeren (Ingrid). James Patterson (Jeffrey Butler). Walter Abel (Mayor Adams). John Carradine (Towman). Fran Stevens (Tess). Walter Klavun (Sheriff Mason). Lisa Richards (Maggie Daly). Phillip Bruns (Wilfred Butler, 1929). Donelda Dunne (Marianne Butler, age 15). Jay Garner (Doctor Robinson). Candy Darling, Charlotte Fairchild, Michael Pendrey, George Strus, Barbara Sand (doctors & guests). Debbie Parness (Marianne Butler, age 8). Tally Brown, Lewis Love, Harvey Cohen, Hetty MacLise, George Trakas, Susan Rothenberg, Cleo Young, Kristin Steen, Jack Smith, Leroy Lessane, Bob Darchi (inmates). Ondine (chief inmate). Grant Code (Wilfred Butler, age 80). Staats Cotsworth (the voice of Wilfred Butler).

The Silent Scream
© 1979. Denny Harris Inc. of California.
director: Denny Harris. producers: Jim and Ken Wheat. executive producers: Joan Harris, Denny Harris. associate producer: Leslie Zurla. writers: Ken & Jim Wheat, Wallace C. Bennett. cinematography: Michael D. Murphy, David Shore. music: Roger Kellaway. editor: Edward Salier. production designer: Christopher Henry. casting: Leslie Zurla. costume designer: Fredda Weiss. special construction consultant: McCoy Wood. production manager: Carol Lee Emrich. location manager: Leslie Zurla. assistant director: Leslie Zurla. production assistant: Mary Jo Thatcher. location auditor: Joan Newstrom. 2nd.unit photography: Denny Harris, George Posedel. propmasters: Skip Troutman, Peter Nigel Williams. assistant propmaster: Michael Feffer. wardrobe: Brian Higby, Betty Nowell. makeup: Dante, Mary M. Hunter. hairdresser: John E. Malone. publicity: The Patricia Fitzgerald Co. production sound mixer: Larry Goga. still photography: Barbara Seiler. assistant cameraman: George Posedel. gaffers: Stuart Spohn, Felix Alcala, George MacDonald, Kerry Magness. electrician: Rachel Jenkins. best boys: Mike Barrett, William Mamches. key grips: Bill Pecchi Jr., David J. Gordon, Jonathan J. Woolf, Robert Stern. grips: Bruce Ward, Bob Fisher. utility: Steven McGrew. special effects: Steve Karkus. stunt coordinator: Joe Pronto. script supervisors: Marion Tumen, Patricia Motyka, Catherine Stoddard. welfare teacher: Jean Gonzales. generators: Bruce Johnston. Chapman crane operator: Alfred DelBoccio. catering: Trudi Reynolds, Scandia Village, Moveable Feast, Lori Hannigan. post production supervisor: Edward Salier. special effects editor: Bonnie Kozek. music editor: Edward Salier. assistant editors: Richard Ross, Ann Hagerman. additional editing: David Tour, Jack Hofstra. assistant post production supervisor: Mori Biener. dubbing: Robert Knudson, Don MacDougall, Robert Glass. re-recording: Todd A-O. titles and opticals: Modern Film Effects. laboratory: MGM. title design: Ernie Potvin. production & post production services and facilities provided by Denny Harris Inc. of California. [songs] "I Love You Baby, Oh Baby I Do" words and music by Roger Kellaway, vocal solo by Ken Barrie, saxophone solos by Tony Coe. filmed from 15 November 1978 in Los Angeles (California, USA).
Cast: Rebecca Balding (Scotty Parker). Cameron Mitchell (Lieutenant Sandy McGiver). Avery Schreiber (Sergeant Maury Rusin). Barbara Steele (Victoria Engels [sic]). Steve Doubet (Jack Towne). Brad Rearden (Mason Engels [sic]). John Widelock (Peter Ranson). Jack Stryker (Police Chief). Thelma Pelish (housing lady). Tina Taylor (Victoria at 16). Yvonne DeCarlo (Mrs. Engels [sic]). Juli Andelman (Doris Pritchard). Annabella Price (T.V. rape victim). Joe Pronto (T.V. rapist). Jason Zahler (Mason Rand at 3). Joan Lemmo (rooming house lady). Ernie Potvin (boarding house husband). Virginia Rose (boarding house wife). Ina Gould (landlady). Rachel Bard (nurse in psycho ward). Jeannie Epper (stunts).

there you are – I'm becoming as predictable as a slasher movie myself). Cameron Mitchell, the man whose face defies Botox, and whose posture makes William Shatner look limber, delivers yet another identikit performance, but then he *is* playing a cop, so maybe it's intentional? No matter – with Yvonne De Carlo glooming around the place and Barbara Steele tucked away in the attic, the film has enough melodramatic weight in the acting department; so much, in fact, that it feels like a latter-day reverie from Curtis Harrington. It's regrettable, though, that the film makes little use of its starry cast in the early stages.

The script's biggest flaw is in using police procedural scenes to disclose a Gothic back-story: far better, surely, for Scotty herself to discover the true history of the family? It would bring the two halves of the cast together, as well as cueing new takes on Gothic staples such as 'leafing through journal entries in the attic' or 'researching family secrets at the spooky old library'. Our interest is hardly engaged by listening to dimwit cops trading shop-worn banter. There are other faults too: the soundtrack sends things up a tad too much when lovers Jack and Scotty (note the *Vertigo* reference) kiss after a day at the beach, swelling to absurd proportions and drenching the scene in horrendous 'sexy' saxophone. Am I being too sensitive? The immediacy of music means it can ruin mood in a split second. Thank goodness for the 1950s record emanating scratchily from the attic, suggesting a house stuck in a time warp, forever replaying the past.

The Silent Scream is a B-stream slasher with a *cinéaste* streak, unassuming in many ways but decorating the standard format with glancing parallels to classic cinema. A victim meets her death in the cellar, cut to ribbons in a scene that replays *Psycho*'s shower murder amidst hanging sheets, culminating in a direct reference to the shot where Janet Leigh grasps the shower curtain as she falls. There's even a swinging light shade. And this after Mel Brooks's *High Anxiety* (1977) placed Hitchcock pastiche beyond the pale for all but the most shameless (which is the category Brian De Palma falls into). On a more obscure note, a great visual trick – involving a portrait in place of a mirror – serves perfectly to cue the obsessional image of guest star Barbara Steele: it's like a scene from the classic Italian horror films in which Steele made her name, such as *The Mask of Satan* (1960) or *The Long Hair of Death* (1964).

The Silent Scream was the Wheat Brothers' first produced script. Having made their own short film called *Stuck on the Screen*, they decided to put together a low-budget feature, to be called *Birthright*. They wrote a story, raised development money, and used it to hire a professional screenwriter. Unfortunately, with an investor, director, cast and crew in place, a change in the tax laws killed the financing. To make matters worse, the screenwriter turned in a lousy script. Back at square one, the brothers wrote another screenplay which was noticed by Denny Harris, then chiefly a commercials director. He declined the script but hired the Wheats to rewrite and produce *The Silent Scream*. (The script Harris declined became *The Return* by Greydon Clark, starring Cybill Shepherd, Jan-Michael Vincent, Neville Brand and Raymond Burr.) Three quarters of *The Silent Scream* had already been shot, and the Wheat Brothers were hired to write and produce twenty minutes worth of material to glue it together. Ken Wheat asserted in *Fangoria* that, "In the end, we eliminated all but twelve minutes of the original footage, and for the same money that was going to be spent on a few bits and pieces, we put together an essentially new film. All but four parts were cut or recast, and we hired Yvonne De Carlo, Cameron Mitchell and Barbara Steele to do a couple of days each. It was guerrilla film making, with twelve days of principal photography, then several months of no-budget inserts and doubles shots." If anyone takes a chance reissuing *The Silent Scream* on DVD one day, it would be fascinating to see the abandoned material along with the finished version. Sadly, for all its charms I doubt whether it will receive such deluxe treatment. Denny Harris has disappeared, and seems not to have directed anything else. The Wheats went on to write *A Nightmare on Elm Street 4: The Dream Master* and *The Fly II*, before scoring a hit with the story and screenplay for David Twohy's *Pitch Black* (2000).

Made in California.

SIMON, KING OF THE WITCHES
– Bruce Kessler (1971)

Simon, King of the Witches is an intelligent, warm and witty addition to the early seventies witchcraft subgenre, starring the ever-wonderful Andrew Prine. It's distinctly left-field in its sympathetic evocation of the life and beliefs of a magickian: refreshingly for the subgenre, Simon's actions are geared not towards material gain or the furtherance of petty squabbles with other magickians. His aim is simple and much higher: he wishes to achieve equality with the gods (note the plural: the theme is not Satanism, and there's no dilly-dallying with the trappings of inverted Christianity). He seeks to move among the higher beings as an equal, and he uses his powers in furtherance of this aim. But because he has not yet ascended, he can be thwarted or thrown off-course, and he's capable of error, making choices which rebound in ways he hasn't been able to anticipate. Even a skilled practitioner can be blind-sided by the immense forces at play in the wider realm of magick. Simon's entire project is destabilized by a single mistake: when a rich sceptic (Angus Duncan) deliberately pays for a Tarot reading with a rubber cheque (*"And I want you to know it was worth every penny of that."*), Simon curses him, and two days later the man is dead. This disproportionate response may be the seed of Simon's eventual failure to achieve his goal. Likewise, he fails to regard the complexities of his actions closely enough, remarking at one point that he is not simply cursing the District Attorney but the entire Establishment! The fact that this spell works *too* well, not only toppling corrupt officials but also screwing the city's drug dealers, whose names are found in the Police Chief's safe, shows just how out of control things can get.

The film's recurrent symbol for elemental power is rain; when we first meet Simon, he is living in a Los Angeles storm drain (*"When it rains, most people go in: I go out,"* he declares to camera in the film's opening seconds.) Rain falls in torrents during several key scenes, including the extended climax in which Simon's curse on the District Attorney (Norman Burton) leads to a chain reaction of arrests of corrupt public figures. The rain is also a dominant force during Simon's final confrontation with the gods, who resist his Promethean efforts to join them by steering an unwitting vessel (a drug dealer) to attack him. This has been foreshadowed: earlier, Simon asked Linda (Brenda Scott) not to take drugs while his most ambitious magickal working took place, because the forces ranged against him can influence the mind of a drug user, guiding them to a bidding beyond their control. (This provides an explanation, if you're so inclined, as to why so many inexplicable, impossible, sometimes terrifying things seem to happen when you're high). The film's liberated view of drug-taking and drug-dealing (neither of which is 'demonized') therefore runs alongside an awareness that for true mastery of the elemental realm, intoxicants must be set aside. Of course in the late sixties and early seventies, drug-taking and black magick were frequently intertwined in the clichés of the era, so it's refreshing to see a film in which the distinction between druggy hedonism and the asceticism of the Magus is made without rancour.

In the area of sexuality, Simon, King of the Witches is again surprising and sophisticated. Thrown in a jail cell one rainy night for vagrancy, Simon befriends a teenage boy called Turk (George Paulsin), who says, with a smile, that he was arrested for *"Loitering: I was just sitting on a kerb."* It's clear that Turk is a hustler, and although the film hedges its bets, making him a heterosexual by choice and a homosexual by profession, it's still a plausible and sensitively handled characterisation. The link between Simon and Turk is the predominant human relationship of the film, and although both characters engage in sex with women, the underlying dynamic is a Platonic bond between teacher and acolyte: that is, homosexual in the Greek manner. For Simon however, Turk is more a friend and confidante than a serious student of magick. Simon is already preparing to go beyond the mortal realm; he doesn't have time to begin nurturing

Simon, King of the Witches
© 1971. Fanfare Film Productions, Inc. Joe Solomon presents. Produced and released by Fanfare Film Productions, Inc. director: Bruce Kessler. writer: Robert Phippeny. executive producer: Joe Solomon. producer: David Hammond. associate producer: Thomas J. Schmidt. music composed and conducted by Stu Phillips. photographer: Vision Photography. editor: Renn Reynolds. art director: Dale Hennesy. set decorator: Robert deVestel. assistant director: Arthur Levinson. casting: Pearl Kempton. sound mixer: Gene Cantamessa. make-up: Maurice Stein. wardrobe: Arnold Lipin. property master: Barry Bedrig. special effects: Roger George. gaffer: Don Knight. key grip: Eugene Barragy. script supervisor: Elaine Newman. production assistant: Larry Bischof. Eastman Color. recording by Producers' Sound Service. music editing by Synchrofilm, Inc. sound effects by Edit-Rite, Inc. optical effects and titles by Cinefx. locations by Cinemobile Systems. filmed from 9 November 1970 at Metro Studios. Cast: Andrew Prine (Simon). Brenda Scott (Linda). George Paulsin (Turk). Norman Burton (Rackum). Gerald York (Hercules). Ultra Violet (Sarah). Michael C. Ford (Shay). Lee J. Lambert (Troy). William Martel (Commissioner Davies). Angus Duncan (Colin). Richmond Shepard (Stanley). Richard Ford Grayling (John Peter). Allyson Ames (Olivia Gebhart). Harry Rose (landlord). Mike Kopcha (lab technician). John Yates, Jerry Brooks (policemen). Ray Galvin (Chief Boyle). Buck Holland (detective). David Vaile (TV newscaster). Earl Spainard, Frank Corsentino, Bob Carlson, John Copage, Bill McConnell (reporters). Art Hern (mayor). Helen Jay (Mrs. Carter). John Hart (doctor). Sharon Berryhill (secretary). Luanne Roberts, Jay Della, Stevi Freeman, Elizabeth Saxon, Avanell Irwin, Harri Sidonie, Jason Max and Eris Tillare (guests).

opposite page: Rebecca Balding, as the intrepid Scotty, gets more than she bargained for after exploring the big old house she's staying at, in **The Silent Scream**.

inset: The UK video cover from Intervision.

this page, bottom left: Horror icon Barbara Steele in **The Silent Scream**.

below: Ultra Violet as a black magician whose methods are derided by **Simon, King of the Witches**.

this page, above and below: Admats from the US pressbook for **Simon, King of the Witches**. Oddly, the lower icon spells out the word 'Tetragrammaton': in Judaism, the Tetragram-maton (Greek for 'word with four letters') is YHWH (or Yahweh) the ineffable Name of God, and is forbidden to be read aloud.
right: Simon (Andrew Prine) is apprehended by the police while carrying his magickal implements.
opposite page: A very rare early Intervision slipcase for **Sisters of Death**.

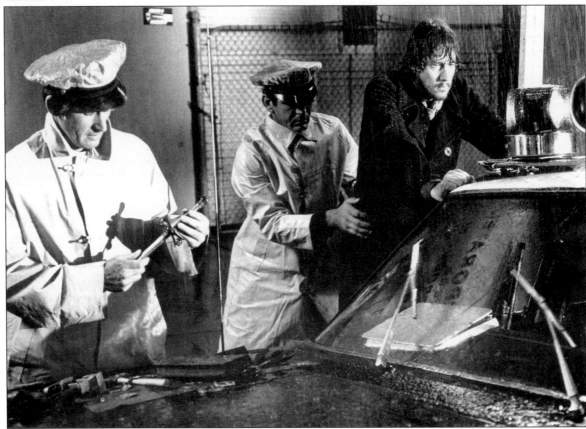

an apprentice. Besides which, Turk isn't really suitable material; he's sweet and trusting, good company for Simon, but he's too naive to make it as a magickian.

Some gay viewers may regard the film with suspicion due to a scene in which Turk asks Simon to curse Stanley (Richard Shepard), an old queen at a party who's been coming on to him too heavily. Simon declines to curse the man, but decides to use him in a magickal ceremony instead. Simon's previous attempt at sex magick, with Linda, failed due to what he calls the *"double bind"* – that is, although the union of partners during sex brings the magickian closer to the eternal realm, the sexual energy summoned also clouds the mind with lust and swallows the will. *"Someone who turns me on will also be someone to make me lose control, right?... And unless I am turned on, there is no charge to control."* In other words, sex magick only works if you can get aroused without getting horny! The scene with Linda collapses into failure, in magickal terms, and the two simply fuck instead. Simon decides to use Stanley, who is willing to go along with any scene with Simon as long as Turk is also present, to achieve arousal without lust, presumably because Simon is bisexual enough to get an erection, but not homosexually orientated enough to get excited. No doubt the unattractiveness of the old queen helps too, and it may explain why Simon doesn't use Turk in the ceremony! But while Stanley is certainly depicted as excessive and ridiculous, he still gets some funny lines (*"Listen sweetie, I've been cursed so many times, one more wouldn't make any difference"*) and there are plenty of fruity old things like him floating around in real life. Just as with the 'Uncle Monty' character in Bruce Robinson's classic *Withnail & I*, gay viewers have to accept that such florid, lustfully incorrigible characters are part of the real world, and not merely invented by homophobic directors. What's more, the homosexual encounter actually works as magick, and Simon's assault on the citadel of the gods (via a mirror at a specially appointed time) can begin.

Some commentators on the film have suggested that Andrew Prine's portrayal sends up the character against the grain of the script. This is, I think, a mistaken view, based on the supposition

that because Simon believes he is a true magickian he must therefore be incapable of self-ridicule or deprecation. To me, Simon's sardonic attitude is simply good, three-dimensional characterisation: belief in magick and reincarnation doesn't require a sense of humour bypass. One of the funniest scenes in the film is Simon's visit to a Wiccan witchcraft ceremony, convened by Warhol starlet Ultra Violet. The scene has much incidental humour: as the chanting and swaying goes on and on, Turk peeks behind a curtain and sees a naked woman lying on an altar, clutching two skulls and lying as if in a trance, until the boy reaches out to fondle her vagina, at which she chides, *"Don't touch me, I'm a religious object!"* Simon meanwhile, has been observing the occult shenanigans with increasing amusement, until he can take no more and breaks the mood with an impromptu song and dance with a domestic broomstick. This irreverence signifies Simon's lack of belief in the value of pomp and pageantry (a similar attitude led to a split between the self-styled Great Beast, Aleister Crowley, and the British artist and occultist Austin Osman Spare: Spare was closely involved with Crowley for a while, but fell out with him because, among other reasons, he regarded Crowley's passionate attachment to ceremonial group workings as egotistical, preferring a solitary approach himself).

There are many other humorous moments to enjoy: when Simon moves into a dismal basement flat, accompanied by a landlord (Harry Rose), who lectures him about the rent, his first action is to draw a pentagram on the wall: the landlord, now flustered, says, *"Please don't think I'm prejudiced, Rabbi: I hope you'll be happy down here!"* And there's no doubt that Prine conveys his character with a humorous glint throughout. In fact, after seeing him play scary, perverted sickos in such films as *The Centerfold Girls* and *The Barn of the Naked Dead*, it's a treat to see him here in such a charming and likeable role. As Simon's tilt at the windmills of the gods falls to wind and rain and death at the climax of the story, you find yourself wishing for a sequel – with reincarnation so prominently discussed (*"Death is only temporary"*), it would be great to see Simon get another spin of the cosmic wheel...

After *Simon, King of the Witches*, Bruce Kessler never worked in the cinema again, instead going on to a busy career in television, directing episodes of everything from *CHiPs* to *Knight Rider*, *T.J. Hooker* to *The A-Team*. *Simon* was not the first time he'd handled gay subject matter: his comedy *The Gay Deceivers* (1969) concerns two straight men who pretend to be gay in order to escape the draft to Vietnam. The film polarises opinion: some enjoy it as a witty time-capsule of the era, and praise it for its daring, while others complain that it resorts to limp-wristed stereotypes. *Simon* writer Robert Phippeny previously co-wrote the screenplay of a Marlon Brando movie, *The Night of the Following Day* (1968). According to Prine, in an interview with the website Kitley's Krypt, "[Phippeny was] a practising warlock. He was dead serious about being a warlock. He had a coven of witches. The movie that he wrote was based upon a part of his life. He was making money at Hollywood parties, doing what he called 'fakery'. And that supported [his] real motives […] to conjure up 'witching' powers. This guy was not kidding. He was a fascinating character. So we attempted to do his life as it really was."

Made in California.

SISTERS OF DEATH

– Joseph Mazzuca (1972 – released 1977)

aka *Death Trap*

Five young women receive an invitation to a reunion party for the Sisterhood they formed at college. But who's pulling the strings behind the scenes? Seven years ago, one member of the group was killed during a sorority game of Russian Roulette, so when the dead girl's father pops up the answer seems obvious, but a quick resolution is deferred by the revelation that one of the girls deliberately placed a live round in the gun. An electrified fence prevents anyone from leaving and cues up some dreadfully acted despair and terror. For the next sixty minutes the girls are menaced by a variety of 'threats', from a ho-hum hairy spider to the inevitable rattlesnake and a less than impressive Alsatian attack. After that, if you care to keep track of the subsequent twists you're more diligent than I…

A ninety-minute no-man's land between TV-movie trash and stalk with no slash, *Sisters of Death* is typical of what happens when boring *mise en scène* and a lack of gratuitous violence get it on. The basic plot suggests a slasher movie along the lines of *Sorority House Massacre*; what you actually get is the sort of thing you might once have flicked past on afternoon television. The trouble with this film is not that it mistakes plot convolution for good writing; it's the drab, workaday *Charlie's Angels* vibe that pervades at all levels. *Sisters of Death* offers no real horror, and not a crumb of style or imagination. The girls' reactions to their predicament are pitiful, and occasionally laughable: one 'babe', who's become a Buddhist since leaving college, copes with the discovery that they're all trapped by squatting down and chanting her mantra. Some films pull through despite their TV ambience – *All the Kind Strangers* for instance, or *The Touch of Satan* – *Sisters of Death*, though, is just the pits.

Oddly, the soundtrack features several moody compositions featured prominently in Jess Franco's *Venus in Furs*, a film that could teach Mr. Mazzuca a thing or two about turning clichés into movie gold. The score for Franco's film is credited to Mike Hugg with American pop-rocker Manfred Mann, although biographies on Mann fail to mention it. If the pieces used in *Sisters of Death* are actually library tracks, they account for a large part of *Venus in Furs*, leaving only one (admittedly central and mesmeric) composition for electric piano and organ unaccounted for. Perhaps it was this theme alone that Mann and Hugg provided? But I digress, because talking about Jess Franco is a holiday from the square-ass mundanity of this film. In the great expanse of American horror cinema, a film like this is the drive-by don't-stop Mid-West burg of the genre. It's not bad enough to amuse, not nasty enough to appal; there's no compelling story to tell, and it's not morbid enough to burn you out. It's just dull – the cardinal sin – and that's all there is to it.

Made in California.

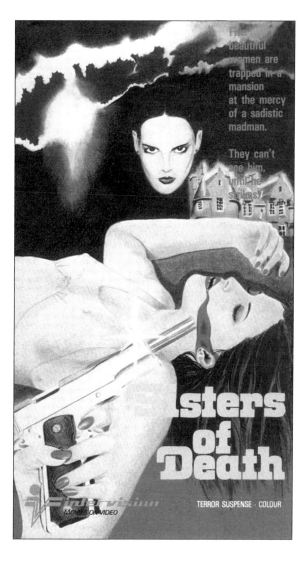

They can't see him, until it's too late!

SKETCHES OF A STRANGLER

– Paul Leder (1978)

Middle-aged art student Jack Garvey (Allen Goorwitz aka Allen Garfield) lives with his religious freak sister Eileen (Jennifer Rhodes), who still treats him like the teenager he was when their parents died. He lets off steam by strangling prostitutes, deviating from his *m.o.* occasionally to take in actresses and strippers. One of the prostitutes he strangles is Margaret Foster, whose twin sister Lynn (Meredith MacRae in both roles) arrives in town to identify her body. Shocked to learn that her twin was not a model as she'd claimed, but a whore working Hollywood Boulevard, Lynn vows to catch the killer and assumes the identity of a hooker to entrap him. She's aided in this dangerous scheme by Artie (Clayton Wilcox), an ex-cop now running a late night bar after being drummed out of the force on a suspected, but never proven, murder rap. Meanwhile, Eileen has begun to suspect that her brother is up to no good, and by tracking him through the streets one night, she inadvertently pushes him into the arms of Lynn. Stunned, and mesmerised, he sees her as Margaret reincarnated…

Sketches of a Strangler is interesting and worth checking out, but it's a bit half-baked by Paul Leder's standards. Gone are the days when his method-school training gave a pugilist aggression to films such as John Hayes's *Five Minutes to Love* (which he wrote and starred in). More to the point, the morose, depressive depths of his previous horror film, *My Friends Need Killing* (1976), run rather shallower here. Although Arlon Ober's music has a predatory sweep to its orchestration, the film on the whole feels like a missed opportunity, and suffers from a lack of credibility. For a start, the stranglings are deeply unconvincing, both in the way Garfield fails to simulate real pressure, and the often ridiculous positions from which he applies it. Two years

STRANGLER

Sketches of a

above:
UK video sleeve for Paul Leder's
Sketches of a Strangler.

right:
Director of **The Slayer**, Joseph S. Cardone,
seen here directing his vampire film
The Foresaken (2001).

friend, a phoney Christian Evangelist, smearing the image of her face with blood, suggests an indictment of the role religion plays in stoking psychosis, but apart from a brief scene showing the 'evangelist' laughing at how much money she makes, it's just another story strand that should have been 'sketched' in a bit more detail.

Star Allen Garfield was a regular for Brian De Palma in his early films *Greetings*, *Hi Mom!* and *Get to Know Your Rabbit*; clearly he was known to the key movie-brats in general, having also appeared in Francis Coppola's *The Conversation*, *One from the Heart* and *The Cotton Club*, as well as Coppola's production of *The Black Stallion Returns*.

Made in California.
*see also: **I Dismember Mama** and **My Friends Need Killing***

THE SLAYER
– J.S. Cardone (1981)

Two couples – sensitive artist Kay (Sarah Kendall) and her husband David (Alan McRae), with Kay's ad executive brother Eric (Frederick Flynn) and his wife Brooke (Carol Kottenbrook) – head for a vacation on a deserted island, staying at a friend's luxurious summer house. Kay, however, recognises the holiday idyll from a recurring bad dream she's been having, and tries to convince the others to turn back: irritated with Kay's moodiness, they ignore her. However, when David is found murdered the following night, Eric and Brooke realise the truth: someone, or some *thing*, is stalking them. But do Kay's dreams really hold the answers?

This atmospheric and absorbing supernatural tale is so nearly excellent, but doesn't have quite enough plot to sustain it and so falls short of its potential. Still, it's well-made, attractive to look at, and it actually prefigures ideas in the *Nightmare on Elm Street* movies by some three years, including a heroine whose dream monster lays waste to her friends in real life, and a final act that revolves around her trying to stay awake to stop the creature gathering strength when she's asleep.

It's always a welcome break when a horror tale casts adults instead of regulation teens, but *The Slayer* could perhaps have done with a more likeable bunch of characters. Kay's brother is the sort of borderline bully who approaches a vacation in the same selfish spirit as his work, obsessed with all the fishing he can do and to hell with his wife. More crucially, Kay herself is a little too morose to really engage our sympathy, and her stubborn warnings about the island are so flatly uncompromising you feel sorry for the others having to deal with her. She makes no effort to communicate her fears in a reasonable way, and her epically self-absorbed response to her husband's death is to mutter *"I told you so"*.

I know I say this a lot, but bear with me, I can back it up: *The Slayer* would have gained enormously by adding to the death-toll. After David disappears (*we* know he's been murdered, head trapped in a coal elevator, but the others don't), there's much wandering around on the island looking for him. Now at least half of this exploration is good, atmospheric stuff, thanks to the great

later, William Lustig would get it right in his benchmark horror film *Maniac*, but here it's a problem, from the otherwise excellently acted first scene onwards. It's a pity: Garfield has the pathetic loser-turned-killer shtick off to a tee, and MacRae is right on the money as a hooker who knows she's dealing with a dangerous john but risks playing along with him anyway. Apart from these two well-acted key roles, however, there's not a lot else to admire. Jack's sketches of young women, referenced in the title, play no significant part in the story, and we rarely get to see them except in medium shot. The act of drawing a beautiful woman whom one intends to kill could have lent a disturbing sensuality to the stalking scenes; the caress of pencil on paper contrasted with the brutality of the murders. Even when Eileen sees Jack's drawing at the site of a recent kill, it adds nothing but a superfluous confirmation that he's the killer. The finale, with Jack shot by police and falling against a giant picture of Eileen's

The Slayer
aka **Nightmare Island** (MPAA title)
© 1981. The International Picture Show Company
director: J.S. Cardone. producer: William R. Ewing. executive producer: Lloyd N. Adams. executive in charge of production: Eric Weston. original screenplay: J.S. Cardone & William R. Ewing. music composed and conducted by Robert Folk. director of photography: Karen Grossman. film editor: Edward Salier. production designer: Lynda Burbank. art director: Charles R. Moore. associate producers: Anne Kimmel & Gerald Olson. unit production manager / 1st assistant director: Peter Manoogian. 2nd assistant director: Brenda Haverstock. script supervisor: Patrience Thoreson. production co-ordinator: Lisa C. Cook. assistant to the director: Cheryl Waters. camera operator / 2nd unit D.P.: Arledge Armenaki. 2nd assistant cameraman: Guy Olds. key grip: Tracy A. Neftzger. grip best boy: John Sorich. grip: Kevin Brennan. sound mixer: Anthony Santa Croce. boom operator: William Flicker. property master: Allen Alsobrook. set dresser: Jerie Kelter. art department assistant: Dix Elliott. carpenter: Vance Thompson. costume designer: Patricia Koehnen. special effects make-up created by Robert Short. make-up and hair: Julie Purcell. gaffers: Roberto Quezada, James J. Gilson. best boy: Greg Gardiner. lamp operators: Jim Grce, Robert Kempf, Mark Crapse, Raymond Perosi. special effects: Spectacular Effects, Robert Babb. generator driver: Floyd Pittman. generator operators: Ralph Hester, Edna Rivers. music editor: Douglas Lackey. assistant editors: Patrica Ann Salier, Jill Bowers. negative cutter: Kay Suffrin. still photographers: Dennis Williams, William Flicker, 'Ace' Armenaki. production accountant: Melinda McRae. executive producer's representative: Larry Adams. helicopter pilot: Les Howell. catering by Annette Anderson, Jack Anderson. production assistants - Georgia: Sherri Scott, Mac Gordon, Lloyd Adams, Sr., William Nichols, Cone S. Bostwick. production assistants - Los Angeles: Tom Rombouts, Kim Maxwell, Paulette Thibault, Vahe Mansourian, Nazareth Darian. stunt co-ordinator / double for Marsh: Hill Farnsworth. double for Kay: Megan McFarland. double for David: Lonnie Smith. double for Eric: Ron Bledsoe. music recorded with The National Philharmonic Orchestra. engineer on the recording session: Eric Tomlinson. music recorded at EMI Abbey Road Studios (London). opticals and titles by Cinema Research. post production sound by Gomillion Sound, Inc. colour by DeLuxe. Lenses and Panaflex camera by Panavision. Special thanks to: State of Georgia; Georgia Film Commission; Gary Womack; The Residents of Tybee Island (Georgia); Ladha Beach Hotel; Carthay Studios.
Cast: Sarah Kendall (Kay). Frederick Flynn (Eric). Carol Kottenbrook (Brooke). Alan McRae (David). Michael Holmes (Marsh). Sandy Simpson (Norman). Paul Gandolfo (fisherman). Newell Alexander (Kay's father). Ivy Jones (Kay's mother). Jennifer Gaffin (young Kay). Richard Van Brakel (young Eric). Carl Kraines (the slayer). stunt pilot: Dick Moore.

location work, but eventually it drags. What's worse, when David's body is finally discovered it's hard for the characters to make the transition from happy-go-lucky to shocked and terrorized, because there's still too much time left to go and they'd be hitting the hysteria button too early. This means that Kay seems to take the death of her husband in her stride, which further reduces her likeability. If two lesser characters had gone missing, a more gradual increase in panic and tension could have been achieved. Still, for a film that involves so much wandering around in gloomy semi-darkness *The Slayer* is a class act, from its surprisingly adept symphonic score to its final out-of-left-field twist, which manages to get away with one of the most hackneyed devices in the genre. The 'Slayer', seen only once, is a marvellous creation, like something dredged from the swampier recesses of *Weird Tales*, and although this is not a splattery gore-athon by any stretch of imagination, a scene in which someone gets a pitch-fork rammed through their chest is as pleasingly nasty as contemporary efforts like *The Bogey Man* or *Friday the 13th Part 2*.

The Slayer was shot on Tybee Island, Georgia. Cardone went on to helm genre items like *Shadowzone* (1990) and *The Forsaken* (2001), perhaps his best work post-*Slayer*. He recently turned up with a straight-to-video 'sequel' to the Nicolas Cage vehicle *8mm* called *8mm 2* (2005), although the retitling was imposed by Sony Pictures after the shoot, against Cardone's wishes. Cardone frequently worked again with cast and crew members from this, his first film; particularly Frederick Flynn and Carol Kottenbrook, the latter moving behind the camera to become his regular producer.

Made in Georgia.

SOLE SURVIVOR
– Thom Eberhardt (1982)

Denise Watson (Anita Skinner), a TV producer, is the sole survivor of a plane crash. As she tries to resume her life, she notices bedraggled strangers – in the streets, in the park, in the hospital garage – staring at her with hollow, malevolent eyes. Plagued by night fears, and a series of terrifying near-miss accidents, she turns to her sweet, attentive doctor, Brian Richardson (Kurt Johnson), and her teenage neighbour Kristy (Robin Davidson). Neither is able to help. Hostile emissaries of death haunt her every move, intent on repossessing her extra lease of life...

Since its low-key release onto video in 1984, *Sole Survivor*'s leisurely pace and lack of gore have cast it into the shadows, which is a shame because it's very well made, sensitively acted, and boasts one of the creepiest 'walking dead' scenarios you could ask for. It's the sort of under-your-skin experience that'll keep you awake at night if you see it just before bedtime. Zombie movies were enjoying a maggoty heyday in the early 1980s, and, with *The Return of the Living Dead* and *Re-Animator* just round the corner, this is one of the last to join the ranks before comedy-splatter became the new default mode for horror. The twist in *Sole Survivor* is to have perambulating cadavers converging on just one person. This leads to some mightily effective shudders, as strange, pasty-faced individuals stalk the jittery heroine, gradually intensifying their efforts to finish off what the pre-credits plane crash started.

You seriously have to wonder if Glen Morgan and Jeffrey Reddick, the writers of *Final Destination* (2000) were aware of this movie: the similarities are marked enough for Eberhardt, who wrote as well as directed, to at least check with his lawyer. Like the *Final Destination* films (which I love, by the way), suspense is brilliantly orchestrated throughout (the multi-talented Eberhardt edits the picture too), with perhaps only a few romantic interludes relaxing us too far. Structurally, there are a few lapses: for instance, a subplot involving a psychic actress (Caren Larkey) is weakly developed, and peripheral to much of the story – but it does at least cue a great final payoff. References to the psychological condition known as 'Survivor Syndrome' are more successfully deployed: rather like the heroine of *Rosemary's Baby*, Denise finds that her supernatural predicament is dismissed by others as mere mental illness, brought on in this case by 'sole survivor' guilt. The chilling statistic that many such individuals 'commit suicide' within two years of their accidents, either deliberately or by 'carelessly' stepping out into traffic, gives the film an extra *frisson*: one can easily imagine the American dark fantasist Dennis Etchison (whose work has been sorely neglected by filmmakers) making hay with the notion of 'careless suicides' whose fates are the handiwork of supernatural agency…

When the heroine of *Sole Survivor* goes on the run at the climax of the movie, Eberhardt takes the slightly shop-worn threat of the living dead and crafts a nightmarishly intimate variant. There's a great scene in which Denise, scared out of her wits, drives at night through the city, eventually running out of gas in a deserted shopping thoroughfare. The poor woman sits in her car, not daring to get out, knowing that *somewhere*, in a nearby morgue

top left:
Images from **The Slayer**.

below:
Anita Skinner survives a plane crash only to be hounded by the living dead, in Thom Eberhardt's spooky and compelling **Sole Survivor**.

Sole Survivor
© 1982. R. & C. Larkey
A Robert D. Larkey/Caren L. Larkey production.
writer/director: Thom Eberhardt. producer: Don Barkemeyer. executive producer: Sal Romeo. associate producer: Dru White. director of photography: Russ Carpenter. music: David F. Anthony. editor: Thom Eberhardt. production manager: Jim Mathers [James Mathers]. associate editor: Steven Wolfe. sound editors: Kurt Bennet, Mike McKay. camera operator: Don Devine. sound recordist: Phil Spinelli. boom operator: Tom Rolapp. gaffer: Rik Faigh. best boy: Joey Alvarado. script supervisor: Jill Gurr. make-up artist: Alice Campbell. hair stylist: Christine Lamano. wardrobe supervisor: Laurie Silver. key grip: Brady Hicks. production secretaries: Rita Ornelas, Jean Kyler. electrician: Don Giroux. sound utility: John Livavi. additional make-up: Robin Beauchesne. assistant editor: Michael Dempsey. production assistants: Michelle Stevens, Willie Vande Kerkhoff. student apprentices: Barbara Scott, William Judkins. special graphics: Tom Scott. still photography: Bosco Kline. technical adviser: Marta Sarmiento, M.D. aviation technical adviser: Gary L. Beck. [songs] "Doing Time" sung by Kimaya Koepke, courtesy of Vince Gray; "Saving My Love" sung by Kimaya Koepke & Tink Williams, courtesy of Vince Gray; "Germs" performed by American Strange, courtesy of James Caine; "Hello, Goodbye" sung by Evan Williams, courtesy of Gregg Thomas; "Come To Me" courtesy of Evan Williams. music recorded at Evan Williams Studios. sound mixed at Scott Sound. sound mixer: Mike Sabo. production services provided by Jim Mathers Video/Films. post-production services provided by Cinemax. colour, titles & opticals by CFI. special effects by AA Special Effects, Inc.
Cast: Anita Skinner (Denise Watson). Caren Larkey (Karla Davis). Peggy McLure, Roberta Kay, Kathleen Blyth, Steve Krause, Dominic Manano, Randolph Stripling, Richard Bosworth (crash victims). Laurie Wendorf (Blake's wife). Andrew Boyer (Blake). Rudy Challenger (air traffic controller). Kurt Johnson (Brian Richardson). Robin Davidson (Kristy Cutler). Brian Zoccola (hospital receptionist). Linda Rose (nurse 1). Cynthia Weislogel (nurse 2). Jennifer Sullivan (girl on loading dock). Wendy Dake (Roxie). Toni Lawrence (T.V. actress). Susan Malter (Rita). Gino Gaudio (Frank). Al Valletta (Dave). Lloyd Stevens (old man in park). Eldon Randall (highway inspector). Thomas Peterson (T.V. director). Leslie Corin (baby Barker). Barbara Reneé (Mrs. Barker). John Zigler (man in parking structure). Richard Kleber (Santa Claus). Clay Wilcox (Randy). Brinke Stevens (Jennifer). Gerald Griffin, Sid Marsh, Joseph Gaudio, Don Worden (police officers). Daniel Carmell (Lieutenant Patterson). Sandra Goldgraben (police woman). Marc Handler (undercover cop). Jaxson Fish (dead boy). William Snare (Artie). Alan Levy (civil service dork). Darian Hays (Salvation Army lady). Stephen Isbell (cabbie). Leon Robinson (gang leader). Anthony Alvarez, Jim Landes, Kip Waldo (gang members). Paula-Marie Moody (stuntwoman). Brian Quisenberry (stuntman).

above: Intervision's UK video release.

right: US video sleeve for **Sometimes Aunt Martha Does Dreadful Things**.

below: From the same film: Stanley (Scott Lawrence) panics when a girl gets too close; and girls who get too close to Stanley usually pay with their lives...

Sometimes Aunt Martha Does Dreadful Things
aka **Damn You, Aunt Martha**
(US theatrical re-release title)
© 1971. Paragon Films Inc.
A Paragon Films production.
writer/producer/director: Thomas Casey. director of photography: H. Edmund Gibson. production manager: Harry Kerwin. art director: Paul Moore. film editor: Jerry Siegel. sound: Jay Ginsberg. assistant director: Chris Martell. executive producer: Eva Barnett. associate producers: Paul Moore, Ronald Sinclair. camera operator: Bill Walsh. 1st. asst. cameraman: Tom Kolowrat. 2nd. asst. cameraman: Ron Sill. gaffer: Charlie Guanci. key grip: Randy Grinter. make-up: Pat Erle, Dante Palmieri. property master: Margaret Moore. wardrobe: Heather Hughes. 2nd unit directors: Harry Kerwin, Robert Woodburn. script clerk: Bonnie Brown. set construction: Luke Moberly. additional editing: Thomas Woodburn, Julio Chavez. procurer's agent: Sandra George. grips: William Kerwin, Harold Glaze, Lane Chiles, Wayne Hagan, Frank J. Ardillo.
Cast: Abe Zwick (Paul). Scott Lawrence [Wayne Crawford] (Stanley). Don Craig (Hubert). Robin Hughes (Vicki). Yanka Mann (Mrs. Adams). Marty Cordova (Alma). Maggie Wood (Dolores). Mike Mingola (Joe). Robert De Meo (Jerry). Sandra Lurie (Mary Lou). Brad Grinter (Lt. Farrell). Charlie Guanci (Sgt. Baker). Francella Waterbury (Mrs. Johnson). Victor Anchipolovsky. Robert Mann. Joseph Bracci. Larry May. Terry Craig. Nanette Mongillo. Rita Dagovitz. Robert L. Rivero. Pat Erle. Harry Rose. Robert Halstead. John Wilson.

or hospital or bed or back-alley, a corpse is coming back to life with the sole purpose of killing her. It's a marvellously paranoid notion that ought to have lifted Eberhardt alongside hotshots of the era like John Carpenter and Wes Craven.

But after the hugely enjoyable sci-fi/horror flick *Night of the Comet* (1984), Eberhardt abandoned the scary stuff and dedicated himself to comedy and teen romance. It's a shame, because he could have been a genuine new voice in the horror genre. Unfortunately for us, he appeared on the scene just as horror was collapsing as a commercial force, buried by the oncoming eighties avalanche of sneering big-budget horror-comedy and fascistic action-violence. I for one would love to see him return, now that the genre is once again attractive to producers.

Sole Survivor features Toni Lawrence, the psychotic anti-heroine of her father Marc Lawrence's *Pigs*, in a small role as an actress suffering multiple takes of a coffee commercial. And while *nothing* can compete with a cross reference to *Pigs* (one of the finest American horror films of the seventies), it's just about worth noting that *Sole Survivor*'s cinematographer Russell Carpenter went on to shoot a tacky love story set on a sinking ship, called *Titanic* (1997)…

Made in California.

SOMETIMES AUNT MARTHA DOES DREADFUL THINGS
– Thomas Casey (1971)
aka *Don't Spank Baby* (shooting title)

This Floridian fumble through the genre's cross-dressing cami-knickers starts off about as much fun as a Stanley Baxter sketch, but it's worth hanging in there, if you can, for a *volte-face* about three-quarters of the way through. A gay criminal duo – dominant, possessive Paul (Abe Zwick) and his childlike bad-boy lover, Stanley (Scott Lawrence [Wayne Crawford]) – lie low in the Miami suburbs after bungling a jewel robbery in Baltimore. Paul dresses in drag as Stanley's 'Aunt Martha', while Stanley – who drives a van apparently borrowed from the Scooby-Doo gang – keeps putting their cover-story at risk by getting stoned and bringing girls back to the house. There's so little charm to these early scenes that you spend the first half of the movie eagerly awaiting the arrival of the authorities. Casey is so determined to make 'comedy' capital out of transvestism that he expects us to believe no one notices that 'Aunt Martha' is a man in a ludicrous wig, not even the various hair-hoppers and hippie-chicks who converge on the area, who really ought to know a thing or two about drag since half of them look like female impersonators. Despite having chosen to depict a gay relationship of sorts (not exactly common ground for an exploitation horror film), *Sometimes Aunt Martha* spends its first hour standing aloof from its subject, essentially playing the scenario for cheap laughs. Stanley explores his confused sexuality by wriggling around half-dressed with hippie girls, while Paul seethes at the situation and occasionally murders the interlopers to calm his nerves. The arch acting style of Abe Zwick probably curries favour with some, but it got on my nerves almost as much as the succession of bland Miami-motel interiors. However, writer-director Thomas Casey turns the film around in the last reel by delving, rather more believably, into sado masochism. It's also a relief that he takes the story out on the road, away from the horrendous interiors. You wonder whether somewhere in Casey's imagination he was reaching for a horror-comedy spin on *The Killing of Sister George*, with an imploding relationship between old queen and young rough trade, but it's so poorly executed you'd have to be as crazy as Paul to fall for it. At least the climax has some melodramatic fizz, as Stanley delivers a baby by Caesarean section (don't ask), and he and Paul hide out at a film studio (another *Sister George* reference?). Paul finally flips his wig completely, ties up Stanley, writes 'Slut' in lipstick on his forehead, and swathes him with the jewelled necklaces they've stolen, before leering into his face and threatening to kill him. Only now, as we reach the

She just isn't herself these days!

Sometimes Aunt Martha Does Dreadful Things

showdown, is Paul frightening. It's too little too late for the film as a whole, but the finale shows what was missing from the rest of the movie: a touch of spite and some aggressive (albeit theatrical) psychological confrontation.

Various notables from the Florida film community helped out on the picture: Brad Grinter, director of *Blood Freak*, played a cop; Harry Kerwin, director of *God's Bloody Acre* and *Getting Even*, directed 2nd Unit; while his brother William, star of numerous local productions including Herschell Gordon Lewis's *Blood Feast*, was a grip. Chief among the Miami alumni of course is Wayne Crawford aka 'Scott Lawrence', who became Harry Kerwin's right-hand man, writing the scripts of *God's Bloody Acre*, *Getting Even* and *Barracuda*, co-directing the latter, and acting in all three. When I interviewed Crawford in 2002, he had this to say about *Sometimes Aunt Martha*: "Tom Casey was a really interesting fellow, a very smart eccentric guy. He started with a schedule of three weeks and shot twelve. I met Harry Kerwin during this movie: he was a friend of Tom's and tried to get him out of his schedule troubles. *Aunt Martha* was his first and only film I think. The script was not very good and in my honest opinion kind of stupid, but it was a lead in a movie and I had never done one. I don't believe a dozen people ever saw it."

Made in Florida.

SPAWN OF THE SLITHIS
– Stephen Traxler (1977)
See interview with Stephen Traxler.

Made in California.

THE SPECTRE OF EDGAR ALLAN POE

– Mohy Quandour (1972)

aka *Leanor*

A story for those who think writers must live what they write in order to create, this could still have been fun if it didn't suffer from an excess of wandering around in dimly-lit interiors. Poe's famous poem *The Raven*, and his stories *The Pit and the Pendulum*, *The Premature Burial* and *The System of Doctor Tarr and Professor Fether* are revealed here not as the phantasmagorias of a creative mind, but simply as events that actually befell the beleaguered writer over a mere couple of months!

When his sweetheart Lenore (Mary Grover) is stricken dead with a malady just as she's swooning into his arms, Edgar Allan Poe (Robert Walker Jr.) is inconsolable. In anguish at the funeral, he throws himself into the grave, thus hearing faint cries from within the coffin. Rescued from her premature burial, Lenore – now white haired and haggard – sinks into a deep catatonic fugue. Dr. Forrest (Tom Drake), a friend of Poe's, recommends a 'rest home' for her, but Dr. Grimaldi (Cesar Romero), the head of the establishment, is up to no good, using patients for despicable experiments. When Poe explores the hospital deep in the night, he finds a cell; and within, a murdered prisoner. He tries to raise the alarm, but he's overpowered and drugged. He comes to in a dank pit, strapped to a wooden board, floating in filthy water writhing with snakes. An overhead pipe gushes more water into the chamber, floating the board higher and higher (although to what end is left uncertain, Quandour choosing to swap Poe's ambiguity about what wriggles in the water for uncertainty about what waits at the top). Drugged again, Poe is set loose (God knows why) and tells his friend what happened. Despite Dr. Grimaldi's attempt to pass it all off as drunken hallucination, further investigations by Poe and Dr. Forrest reveal the awful truth...

While this is a terrible film, it's amusing to think that, had it made money and found an audience, there could have ensued a series of equally ridiculous sequels; all of them staging elements from Poe's stories as chaotic pseudo-biographical simulacrae. Perhaps 'The Fury of Edgar Allan Poe' (comprising *The Black Cat*, *Berenice* and *The Murders in the Rue Morgue*), would have made a good follow-up? Sadly, Quandour's hopeless directing sinks the would-be franchise, and the script fails to assign anything like a truly compelling character to Poe himself, who's played by Robert Walker as a slightly peeved-looking nobleman.

Made in: unknown

STIGMA

– David Durston (1972)

See interview with David Durston.

Made in Massachusetts.

THE STRANGENESS

– David Michael Hillman (1980)

See interview with Mark Sawicki.

Made in California.

SUICIDE CULT

– James Glickenhaus (1977)

aka *The Astrologer*

Suicide Cult is a bizarro story with an expensive appearance that belies its low-budget origins. Made by James Glickenhaus, who would score a solid B-movie hit in 1980 with his vigilante flick *The Exterminator*, it's a very odd piece of work about a secret government research organisation studying the astrological charts of prominent figures, looking for those with the 'Zodiacal Potential' for either great good, or great evil. A crackpot premise at first glance, for sure, but if you sideline your scepticism you've got to admit it's different.

The plot concerns the efforts of Astrological Super-Spy Alexei Abarnel (Bob Byrd) to guide a young woman, Kate (Monica Tidwell), a New Jersey dance instructor, to her cosmic destiny. His 'technique' is to marry her, and thus 'protect' her, since she is believed to have the purest 'Zodiacal Potential' since The Virgin Mary... which is nice, because it seems that she is about to give birth to the Second Coming of Jesus! But while the forces of good are gathering around Kate, across the globe Evil is preparing its attack. An Indian cult leader called Kajerste (Mark Buntzman), a dangerous magician with an almost limitless capacity for evil, is seeking the purest women on Earth in order to destroy them and corrupt the universal balance...

Oddly enough, this had the potential, Zodiacal or otherwise, to be a really good movie. But there's something not quite *right* about *Suicide Cult*; it's as if it's been hurriedly assembled from an incomplete shooting schedule, with huge cracks papered over. The editor receives first mention on the end credits, which suggests a troubled production snatched from the brink of collapse, perhaps at the urging of a desperate producer determined to get at least *something* onto the market. The ending especially is a jolt, no doubt betraying where the bulk of the unfilmed material belongs. The story, based on a 1972 mass-market pot-boiler called *The Astrologer* by John Cameron, progresses through ellipse after ellipse, changing location between America, India and England, with each shift augured by solarised effects (another hint that the film was hard to edit). Within the weirdness, though, are a couple of surprisingly convincing performances. Mark Buntzman as Kajerste lives up to the hype by fairly blazing from the screen, playing a sort of Indian Charlie Manson. The scene where he wills to death a female spy assigned to plant suicidal impulses in his dreams (the film is nothing if not ambitious) could have floundered if the villain had been campy or exaggerated. Instead he gives the sequence a truly malevolent energy.

There's a philosophical angle to the film's astrological mysticism, which, although it might stick in the throat of those raised on the notion that all men are created equal, at least offers

The Spectre of Edgar Allan Poe
aka **Lenor** (UK video print title)
aka **Leanor** (UK video cover title)
© 1972. Cintel Productions, Inc. (Utah)
Cintel Productions presents a Cintel - First Leisure production.
producer/director: Mohy Quandour. production manager: Edward Markley. production controller: Tanya Mamalis. screenplay: Mohy Quandour; based on an original story & treatment by Kenneth Hartford, Denton Foxx. director of photography: Robert Birchall. music composed by Allen D. Allen. "Lenore" words and music by Allen D. Allen, sung by Tom Bahlor. editor: Abbas Amin. editor post production: Abbas Amin. art director: Michael Milgrom. make-up/special effects: Byrd Holland. casting: Marvin Page [sic]. 2nd unit cameraman: Karlo Lohay. production assistants: Ray Jacobs, Carolyn Alban. gaffer: Mel Maxwell. electrician: Brink Brydon. best boy [electrician]: Skip Karness. 2nd assistant cameraman: Danny Dayton. still cameraman: Peter Riches. key grip: Bill Coker. dolly grip: John Graham. grip: John Garfield. sound mixer: Dick Damon. script supervisor: Michelle Logan. assistant make-up: Christian Lyon. property master: Mick Bankins. wardrobe supervisor: Laurel Shaulis. propman: Lee Runnels. music sound engineer: Stan Ross. dubbing: Scottsound. casting: Marvin Paige [sic]. filmed from 17 April 1972.
Cast: Robert Walker, Jr. (Edgar Allan Poe). Cesar Romero (Doctor Grimaldi). Tom Drake (Doctor Adam Forrest). Carol Ohmart (Lisa). Mary Grover (Lenore). Mario Milano (Joseph). Karen Hartford (the night nurse). Dennis Fimple (Farron). Paul Bryer/Paul Bryar [front-credits/end-credits] (Mr. White). Frank Packard (Jonah). Marsha Mae Jones (Sarah). Robert Pearson (mourner #1). Jean Estes (mourner #2). Dawn Krespi (mourner #3). Tanya Mamalis (mourner #4). Ethel Corn (waitress). Carolyn Alban (Virginia). Peter Riches (the priest). Lee Runnels (patient). Dana Grazide (orderly). Inal Quandour (little boy #1). Glen Hartford (little boy #2). Katherine Lewis (day nurse).

bottom left:
The UK video cover for the SVC release of **The Spectre of Edgar Allan Poe**. The film was also released by Vox, with spectacularly poor sleeve artwork, as **Leanor**.

below:
The Astrologer, the occult thriller upon which **Suicide Cult** was based.

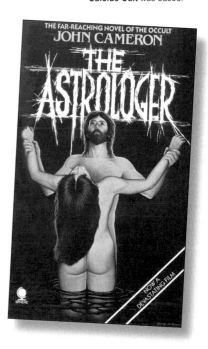

Suicide Cult (US theatrical re-release title)
aka **The Astrologer** (original US theatrical title)
© 1977. Napolis Hoose Films, Inc.
director: Jim Glickenhaus. producer: Mark Buntzman. editor: Victor Zimet. music: Brad Fiedel. director of photography: Francis A. Romero. sound: Rolf Pardula. art director: Meg Cameron. set design: Robert Theis. unit production manager: Joanna Mallas. assistant director: Beriau Picard. assistant to the producer: Susan T. Klein. music recorded at Generation Sound. engineer: Haydn Harris. sound editors: Dan Sable, Ron Kalish; Magnofex. re-recording mixer: Jack Cooley; Magno Sound. optical effects consultant: Mo [Moses] Weitzman. optical effects by EFX Unlimited. equipment rental: General Camera. colour by Movielab. post production services: August Films. Lenses and Panaflex camera by Panavision. head gaffer: James Wilberger. key grip: George Elanjian. extra casting: Robin [illegible]. make up: Simon Deitch. hairstyles: Neill Stern. production accountant: Robert Sesti / Seso. dubbing director: Peter Fernandez. electrician: Craig Nelson. gaffer: Harold Warren. dolly grip: Mark Daniels. production assistants: William Tasgal, Sonja Kobler. UK video sleeve states based on the novel by John Cameron.
Cast: Bob Byrd (Alexei Abarnel). Monica Tidwell (Kate Abarnel). Mark Buntzman (Kajerste). Al Narcisse (Congressman Harkell). Alison McCarthy (Ahau). Julie Raggo (the child). Anaho [illegible] (Mother Bogarde). Nancy Brody (classroom question). Gabriel Buntzman (Senator Wiley). Robert Drug (indian in gas station). Virginia Fedder (Sister Mary Elizabeth). Alf Geisler (agent in airport). Jim Glickenhaus (agent in race car). Kenneth Greene (guard in car). Michael Kreper (male gypsy). Dr. Lloyd Motz (Interzod lecturer). Chandra [illegible] (Indian soldier). John Rasello [approx: illegible] (Whembley). Paul Abhcberg [approx: illegible] (guard with dog). Steven Spicehandler (fighter). Neill Stern (Neil). Chuck Sukharj [approx: illegible] (Indian cab driver). Subbhally Vassant (Indian father). Arjun [illegible] (maiden's father). Lee Wells (steward in plane). Ivy White (Indian maiden). George [illegible] (violinist).

an accurate summary of *one* view in the occult 'fraternity'; that the human race is radically divided between drones and visionaries. As you would expect, those who adhere to this view tend to speak from an assumed position in the latter camp, but there are similarities between this point of view and the aristocratic mercilessness of philosopher Friedrich Nietzsche. Dig deeper into books like Nietzsche's *Thus Spake Zarathustra* though, and one finds telling room for manoeuvre. Instead of the fixed cosmological constants of high and low espoused in *Suicide Cult*, the philosopher proposed 'the Superman' as the next stage in humanity's development. The overcoming of Man was to be undertaken in the will of the individual, and was certainly not the province of some pre-existing oligarchy. *Suicide Cult* has a fascist notion at its core (some people are just destined to rule), but at least it proposes the idea in a way that alerts us to the sad fantasies inherent in such dreams of an over-race.

Philosophy aside, in the post-*X-Files* media environment this is a film whose theme could easily be revisited and developed. The government astrologers in *Suicide Cult* are liars and cheats, so there's plenty here to grip conspiracy theorists, or at least to amuse devotees of *Fortean Times*; for instance, a well-constructed sequence shows how an unsuspecting congressman is hoodwinked into supporting the agency by the creation of ominous 'accidents'. Imagine *Night of the Demon* remade by Oliver Stone…

Despite it's manifest flaws, *Suicide Cult* belongs in the same oddball company as Larry Cohen's *God Told Me To* and Jeff Lieberman's *Blue Sunshine*. What it lacks in coherence it gains in ambition and the nerve to be different, and I'm surprised it has not been cheered or defended before. For all its garbled, unfinished quality, and its half-digested ideas, it feels like the work of someone to watch.

Glickenhaus was born 24 July, 1950, in New York. He co-owned the production company Shapiro-Glickenhaus. Since this debut he has made *The Exterminator* (1980), *Codename: The Soldier* (1982), *The Protector* (1985), *Shakedown* (1989), *McBain* (1991), *Slaughter of the Innocents* (1994), and *Timemaster* (1995).

Made in: unknown

SWINGERS MASSACRE
– Ron Garcia (1973)
aka *Inside Amy*

I was looking forward to this luridly titled obscurity, made back-to-back with Don Jones's *Abducted*. Garcia's sex film *The Toy Box* was weird, if a little tedious, but this rather more conventional murder tale seemed to propose a fusion of *The Toy Box*'s sleaziness with the narrative demands of the horror genre. Sad to say, despite two salacious titles promising all sorts of sleazy mayhem, *Swingers Massacre*/*Inside Amy* fumbles the chance, stooping to a crawl without ever getting its face in the gutter.

Lawyer Charlie Tishman (Eastman Price) petitions his reluctant wife Amy (Jan Mitchell) to join him on the swingers scene, in a bid to liven up their love life. He finally succeeds, browbeating her to attend a swingers party, only to freak out when she actually digs it.

What's more, Charlie is a wash-out with the other women, failing to get it up despite numerous opportunities. One of the husbands waves a vibrator at him, suggesting he buy one: *"Amy'll love it!"* Charlie tries to take his humiliation out on his wife (*"You need an army. No wonder I can't keep you satisfied. I guess I should consider myself lucky you're even coming home with me!"*), but having unleashed her pent-up desires, Amy is not about to let Charlie spoil her fun – especially since he's being so mean and hypocritical. Unable to face the situation he's created, Charlie murders all the men his wife has slept with: Jim (Gary Kent), Bill (Ron Darby) and Rod (Paul Oberon). Allowing himself to be talked into *another* swinging party, this time with Jerry (Philip Luther) and Donna (Ann Perry), Charlie spends the evening yammering about his work, until Amy goes off without him for a bisexual tryst with their hosts. Incensed, Charlie drugs them all, strangles Jerry, hangs Donna, and carts his wife off home unconscious. As a police investigation belatedly closes in on the Tishmans, Amy must confront her crazed husband alone…

It sounds like a decent little thriller from the synopsis. But just as you think the story is settling down to a depiction of chauvinistic jealousy, Garcia – working from a script penned by the producer's wife – has the gall to tell the tale as if Charlie's attitude should be respected. A song played over the scene in which Amy has sex with Jim warns her to return to the marital fold or face the consequences. It's worth quoting the lyrics at length for their breathtaking hypocrisy: *"Who knows what goes on inside Amy?/How did she get to be this way?/Breaking the heart of one who loves her/And giving not a damn about the price she'll have to pay/Amy, you'd better straighten out or be prepared to meet your fate/Go back to what you were before it's too late."*

Swingers Massacre (US re-release title)
aka **Inside Amy** (original title)
aka **Super Swinging Playmates** (US theatrical re-release title)
© none [1973]
Dave Arthur presents a Cinema Seventies production.
producer/director: Ronald V. Garcia. original story and screenplay: Helene Arthur. executive producer: Dave Arthur. director of photography: Don Jones. music composed and conducted by Jack Prisner. associate producer: Jon Klotz. art director: Ron Foreman. assistant director: Dianne Young. editor: Ron Garcia. gaffer: Steve Moon. production sound: Jon M. Hall. asst. cameraman: Tom Kantrud. boom: A.J. Solari. hair stylist: Josh Giannelli. production assistant: Sherri Moon. night club sequence filmed at 'Filthy McNasty's' (Sunset Strip, Hollywood). post production sound: Scott Sound. colour by Pacific Film Lab. opticals by Van Der Veer. sound re-recording: Audio Services. equipment: Production Systems Inc. titles by Title House.
Cast: Eastman Price (Charlie Tishman). Jan Mitchell (Amy Tishman). Gary Kent (Jim Simon). Harrison Phillips. Marsha Jordan (Irene Simon). Richard Stobie. Carmine Marino. Ann Perry (Donna Morton). Paul Oberon (Rod Lewis). Mickie [Mickey] Nader (Marge Lewis). Rene Bond (Diane Stacey). Ron Darby (Bill Stacey). Dawna Kaufmann. [and from the Inside Amy credits: Ushi Digart (Lois). Josh Gianelli. Kenneth Hoyle. Tito Meminger. Lorie Kowan.]

The poster text reads:
SWINGERS MASSACRE
RATED R
BEWARE OF THOSE WHO'LL LOVE YOU TO DEATH
EVEN STEVEN PRODUCTIONS
starring
JAN MITCHELL
EASTMAN PRICE • USHI DIGART
PRODUCED & DIRECTED BY RON GARCIA
STORY & SCREENPLAY BY HELENE ARTHUR

Men who propose open relationships often seem to have thought it through only as far as visualising themselves in bed with another woman; the possibility that their wives may get a taste for other men is far less palatable. One could argue that the song's lyrics are meant to represent Charlie's viewpoint, as he sits there, glass of whiskey in hand, watching his wife make out on the rug with hunky Gary Kent; but the vocalist is a woman, the song is a syrupy lament, and there's no sense of jealous intensity to the music. The scene plays like a directorial 'flourish' expressing an omniscient judgement. Quite how anyone can film a story in which the male is so blatantly the agent of his own misfortune, then turn around and blame the woman for bringing disaster, is beyond me.

There are a few similarities here to James Bryan's *The Dirtiest Game in the World*, but Bryan made his failed swinger Felicia a genuinely tragic figure, and when she erupts into violence it's turned against herself. Charlie never shows a glimmer of self-recrimination and no one gets to tell him what a selfish hypocrite he is. If Charlie had ended his murder spree by killing himself, his anguish might at least have tempted us to extend some sympathy. We're obviously meant to see him as disturbed and deranged, but instead of focusing on how Charlie's lack of self-understanding has led him to murder, the film climaxes with Amy terrorized by her husband and facing the wages of her 'sin'.

I hate this sort of moralistic bullshit in exploitation movies, especially when the film lacks the prurient spectacle to offset its bad attitude. To compound matters, this is way overlength at around a hundred minutes, and could easily have been cut by twenty. For a start, there's way too much dancing, wrangling and schmoozing at a dimly-lit nightclub (the famous 'Filthy McNasty's' on Sunset Strip, Hollywood), which slows the pace to a crawl; by the time we arrive at the tame clinches that constitute Amy's awakening, nothing short of a donkey-show could liven things up.

The original title of the film was *Inside Amy*, and you may suspect that a more pornographic cut was released under that name, and then shorn of its shagging for the 1987 video release (which is where the title *Swingers Massacre* originates). This seems unlikely though – if you added hardcore sex scenes to *Swingers Massacre*, the running time would soar over the two-hour mark with ease. The suggestion that swingers are destined for a life of misery ending in humiliation or painful death is particularly sanctimonious given that the original title was such a porno-rag tease. With murders that aren't explicit, sex scenes that aren't graphic, and a preachy ending showing another young couple about to 'swing' into the marital quicksand, this is one exploitation flick I can find no reason to recommend.

Made in California.

TILL DEATH
– Walter Stocker (1974)

On the eve of his wedding to Anne (Belinda Balaski), Paul (Keith Atkinson) has a nightmare in which he's attacked by a dead woman in a graveyard. Next day, the wedding progresses without incident, but en-route to their honeymoon Paul sees the woman of his nightmare again; terrified, he drives his car off a cliff, killing his wife in the process. Months later, checking out of the hospital where he's been sequestered for depression, Paul visits his wife's tomb and is accidentally locked in overnight. As midnight looms, he hears his wife's voice begging him to get her out of her coffin. Attacking the tomb with a pickaxe left behind by workmen, he discovers Anne is still alive, having woken from a catatonic sleep. Happily, he tells her of all the places they can visit once help arrives in the morning. But as night ebbs away, Anne reveals there's only one way they can truly be together...

Till Death is a clumsy but faintly eerie tale of love beyond the grave, the sort of thing that in the hands of Mario Bava or Jean Rollin would have made the grade as a necrophiliac poem, but in Stocker's mitts ends up as doom-laden doggerel. Rollin's *La rose de fer* for instance, spins a similar tale of lovers locked in a tomb overnight, but imbues the theme with such melancholy

Till Death
© 1974. Pamstock Productions
A Pamstock production.
producer/director: Walter Stocker. co-producer: Marshall Reed. associate producer: Pamela Stocker. original screenplay: Gregory Dana. cinematographers: George Smart, Jack Steeley. production manager & 1st asst. director: Paul Pav. supervising editor: Marshall Reed. editors: Richard Allen, Doug Grindstaff. 2nd unit cameraman: Richard Allen. camera assistants: Bruce Watson, Paul Silberman. set construction supervisor: Roy Combs. head grip: Bill Haas. best boy: Bill Haas Jr. grip drivers: Bob Thornton, Ron Archibald. gaffer: Jim Stemme. best boy: Herman Solomon. script supervisors: Judy Burkett, Chris Minsky. still photographers: Russ Stocker, Don Mazer, Gene Marlowe. wardrobe & props: Pamela Stocker, Bernie Wright. sound recorder: Lowell H. Brown. special effects: Roger George. makeup supervisor: Jerry Soucie. Our Special thanks to Perry C. Zanger M.D. for his invaluable technical advice in the medical and psychiatric clements and to John Arnold & Associates - promotion and marketing consultants. titles, opticals & colour by CFI. sound by Glen Glenn Sound. music: Jim Ed Norman & Chick Rains. title song "Till Death" written & sung by Chick Rains.
Cast: Keith Atkinson (Paul Ryan). Belinda Balaski (Anne Ryan). Marshall Reed (Rev Dustin). Bert Freed (Dr. Sawyer). Keith Walker (Dr. Perkins). Jonathan Hole (Mr. Hilton). Paul Micale (workman #1). Joey Aresco (woman #2). Bruce Kemp (highway patrol sgt.). Ron Roy (highway patrolman). Nancy Mecum (woman in white).

left:
Artwork used for the UK video sleeve for **Till Death**, as released by Videoform.

opposite page, bottom right:
US video cover artwork for **Swingers Massacre**. Was the designer working out his hatred of Farrah Fawcett with this?

opposite page, far left:
Can the fates of a New Jersey dance instructor and a Mansonesque Indian guru be linked? Two images from **Suicide Cult**.

dreaminess that dialogue is hardly necessary. Still, recovering from a bland first reel depicting the saccharine relationship between Paul and his bride, things begin to improve with the appearance of Mr. Hilton (Jonathan Hole), the rather camp *maître d'* of the cemetery where Anne is buried. *"Life is death, death is life,"* he trills. Thank goodness for his arch performance, it livens the film up a bit and signals the start of better things. Proudly giving Paul the guided tour of his beloved cemetery, Hilton waxes philosophical as he points out a new grave: *"Such a beautiful sight, never fails to move me... The mound of freshly turned earth, symbolising the return to the bosom of Mother Earth from whence we all sprang."*

A potentially effective scene in the mausoleum, as Paul digs his wife from her tomb, demands aesthetic imagination and a touch of class, but Stocker's approach is resolutely sensible. Sure, the tomb interiors are lit with coloured gels, but the effect is more Quinn-Martin than Antonio Margheriti, whose *Castle of Blood* (a young man trapped in a haunted mansion who falls in love with a ghost) provides another Euro-parallel. Unfortunately, the stubbornly static camera and Belinda Balaski's emotionally Botoxed performance fail to milk the Gothic potential. Emerging from the tomb, Anne is violent and freaky for a while, but she soon calms down and we're back to the tedious Mrs. Wifeisms of earlier. Perhaps Balaski was unhappy with the production.

below:
Paul sees a vision of putrefaction just before his wife dies in a car crash, in **Till Death**.

"If you can just open your heart to the body of life, you can behold the spirit of death: timeless, beautiful," says Anne to Paul. *"You've never talked this way before, what's the matter with you?"*, is his staggeringly dopey response. *Till Death* suffers from the same lack of sensitivity. Paul's journey from rational day to supernatural night lacks any sort of back-up from the director, the camera or the editing. The sole exception is the score, which although crude does occasionally spark a feeling of otherworldly tension. At the core of the problem is the scene where the reanimated Anne begs Paul to make love to her before dawn. Paul refuses: he points to the sepulchral surroundings and asks her if she's crazy. And yet the whole film is about the yearning desire the bereaved feel for departed lovers! In European horror films about love beyond the grave (and there are many), Paul's lack of passion would cramp the style of the whole enterprise. *Till Death* could have focused on the simultaneous desire and horror of the lead character, with the two feelings shading into each other. Mario Bava's *Lisa and the Devil* (1972) is a perfect example: a film where sex with the dead is not merely a twist but a swooningly erotic centrepiece. The best that Stocker and his cameramen George Smart and Jack Steeley can offer is to tell the bare bones of writer Gregory Dana's story, ensuring that the camera observes the necessary speech and actions without ever *amplifying* the theme. There's an emotional and sensual potential here staring the filmmaker in the face; but like Paul, mystified by his dead wife's delirium, the director just doesn't get it.

Stocker was born 1 September, 1925, in Philadelphia PA, and died 5 December, 2003, in Port Hueneme CA. He earned a bachelor's degree from the University of Miami, a master's degree from Columbia University, taught college in North Carolina and Virginia, and served in World War II in the Army Air Corps. His only other genre credit was as an actor in *They Saved Hitler's Brain* (dir: David Bradley, 1963).

Made in: unknown

TO ALL A GOODNIGHT
– David Hess (1980)

It's the Christmas holidays at Calvin College Finishing School for girls. A group of students arrange a private farewell party, adding a sleeping draught to the night-time milk of their house-mother Mrs. Jensen (Katherine Herrington), and inviting some boys to stay the night. But there's a killer stalking the college, dressed as Santa Claus. So who's been naughty and who's been nice? Only sweet, virginal Nancy (Jennifer Runyon) is in with a chance of surviving; that is, unless she succumbs to the ardour of super-nerd Alex (Forrest Swanson). With darkness closing in, one question remains... how many deaths will we get to see in the murky day-for-night photography?

Yes, it's cookie-cutter time again. A 'two years earlier' prologue, clumsy synth score, tacky performances, a creepy old gardener... no doubt about it, *To All a Goodnight* sets up its stall at the cheap end of Slasherville. The end-of-term Christmas Sorority-House setting is pilfered wholesale from Bob Clark's superior *Black Christmas*, and much of what passes for a *denouement* is nicked from *Friday the 13th*. To be fair, the killer Santa arrives well in advance of the better-known *Silent Night, Deadly Night* (1984), and may even have pre-dated Lewis Jackson's *Christmas Evil* (made the same year). But originality is not the major consideration; visceral kicks are what matter. Sad to say, actor-turned-director David Hess – who gave us one of the screen's most electrifying killers as Krug in *The Last House on the Left* – fails to bring his personal intensity as a performer to his role behind the camera.

High expectations aside, you can still get your jollies laughing at howlers in the script: from *"Bless whoever built that airstrip!"* when help arrives, to *"I think I'll go get a Kleenex"* as a prelude to getting killed. A kitchen floor smeared with blood is dismissed with a curt *"Ralph probably cut himself with the shears"* – and best of all, after Ralph is found dead and two more of the party disappear, someone says, *"Just because weird Ralph got himself murdered doesn't mean anything's happened to the others."* Top class rubbish that dear old Ed Wood might have dreamed up, if he'd ever turned his hand to the slasher genre...

As for the violence, it certainly isn't what you'd expect from the man who carved his name into a screaming girl's throat in *The Last House on the Left*. The killings are okay, but they don't make the A-list: there's a crossbow bolt through the back of the head, a decapitation by axe, a severed head screwed onto a shower-fitting, and sundry stabbings and skull-bashings. There's even a double death by aeroplane propeller, but we don't see it directly, just a splash of grue onto the fuselage.

Bearing in mind its provenance, *To All a Goodnight* ought to have trounced the opposition, but it turns out to require a completist's devotion. If like me you're a lover of formulaic hack-and-slash movies, you'll probably get a mild kick out of this, just the once, but return visits are unlikely.

Made in California.

THE TOOLBOX MURDERS
– Dennis Donnelly (1977)

So, how does an L.A. producer in disco-land 1977 come to make a killing with a sordid little film like *The Toolbox Murders*, three long years before Paramount Studios 'smelled the glove' and snapped up *Friday the 13th*? Well, jobbing producer Tony DiDio noticed that *The Texas Chain Saw Massacre* was back in theatres, enjoying a second bite of the cherry in 1977. As he knew *Chain Saw*'s distributors, he asked them how come the film was being re-released so soon. 'Low-budget horror, even second-time-round, is money in the bank,' they explained, so DiDio put out feelers for a writer and director who could deliver another graphically violent cash-cow. He arranged a screening of *Chain Saw* for writers Robert Easter and Ann Kindberg, and young TV director Dennis Donnelly, telling them to come up with something that would compete in the graphic horror market. The result is certainly violent, although *Toolbox* couldn't be more different to *Chain Saw*.

Shot over eighteen days in the summer of 1977 for $165,000, on Sherman Way and Van Owen Street, Los Angeles, *The Toolbox Murders* is quintessential exploitation, with a first act that delivers jolt after explicit jolt. The image of a balaclava-clad killer hefting a toolbox for torture has an archetypal quality, ripped dripping-red from America's collective psyche. If we've never actually read about a killer lugging a toolbox from kill to kill, we *feel* as if we have. The early scenes echo Ted Bundy, as the killer roams an apartment block with a variety of murder weapons (hammer, screwdriver, nailgun), prefiguring the creative-killing mayhem of the *Friday the 13th* series. *The Toolbox Murders*, with its trashy and vicious ad-campaign, could have been the ultimate urban horror flick – except for a third act that slows the pace to a crawl. The real toolbox nastiness takes place in the first reel, leaving, shall we say, the more *psychological* aspects of the film to drag on and on. Cameron Mitchell is given his head to play his scenes interminably; singing, sucking a lollipop, ranting, hamming it up and no doubt having a whale of a time. If you're a fan of this grizzled exploitation veteran, you'll be in hog heaven. For everyone else, it's like having a drunken old relative gatecrash the party.

Feminists (and censors) have always found the movie's signature nail-gun scene deeply problematic, and it's not really surprising. More so than any other slasher scene I can think of, it combines softcore female nudity and hardcore violence in a very queasy way. Future porn star Marianne Walter (aka Kelly Nichols) is shown masturbating in the bath as the camera leers at her suds-covered boobs. Thanks partially to the actress's performance and partially to the style of filming, the scene feels drafted in from a softcore porno movie. Then, on cue with her orgasm, as if to chastise her pleasure, the killer enters and stalks the naked woman through her apartment, firing a nail-gun. He corners the girl in her bedroom where she kneels nude on the bed, pleading for her life, quivering in acquiescence. The camera simply ogles at this, and the scene's jazz-mag cheesiness, when dropped into such a brutal context, can give even seasoned sexploitation/horror viewers pause, although on closer inspection the victim has chosen to assume the seductive position on the bed as a desperate ploy to persuade the assailant not to kill her. As the soundtrack coldly contrasts the horror with a country ballad on the radio (*"Pretty lady, I'm in love with you"*) it will come as no surprise to anyone that the nails eventually hit their target, leaving the viewer to mull over one of the nastiest and sleaziest slayings in the genre.

Associate producer Jack Kindberg, father of the film's co-writer, went on to become President of Studio Operations and Administration at Sony Pictures Entertainment, thanks to the intervention of Tony DiDio, who first interested him in acquiring a studio property back in the 1980s. Actress Pamelyn Ferdin voiced the brattish 'Lucy Van Pelt' in *Charlie Brown*.

Made in California.

VICTIMS
– Daniel DiSomma (1977)
See interview with Daniel DiSomma.

Made in California.

WHODUNIT?
– Bill [William T.] Naud (1982)
aka *Island of Blood*
aka *Scared Alive* (Australian video title)

This intermittently eccentric slasher tale has largely been ignored by fans. I wouldn't say I was waving a flag for it, but it's good enough to rank alongside the likes of *Graduation Day* at least. A group of actors and filmmakers go to a private island retreat with a director and producer, intending to rehearse a rock musical. But there's no chemistry between the cast, the lead actress is hopeless, the caterer is a grumpy psychotic, and the rock musicians who've been drafted in to help are a bunch of callous assholes. Perhaps it's just as well that a killer is stalking the island…

The first thing to say here is please, if you're making a slasher film, *don't* film some guy strumming tunelessly on an acoustic guitar when you're setting up the plot. *Whodunit?* does so, and you can feel the energy draining out of the film and puddling on the carpet. It also helps if you can decide what you're trying to achieve, and then stick to it. Steve Faith, the film-within-the-film's producer, explains to his cast that they're doing something socially redeeming: a rock musical about kids putting on a show for charity. The contrast between his cheesy project and the nasty horror film we're actually watching ought to have generated a bit more irony, but *Whodunit?* misses the trick. *"These are up, up people,"* says the director about his characters, but apart from calling him Franklin Phlem (I'm not sure, but I *think* that's satire…), Naud fails to have much fun with the premise. It's a shame, because the notion of a tacky showbiz troupe being slaughtered by a maniac has lots of potential – something Italian director Michele Soavi proved in his enjoyable debut, *Stagefright* (1987).

As a result of its fluffed comedy, *Whodunit?* is extremely unsteady on its feet in the first twenty minutes – the attempt to satirize bad filmmaking is maybe a tad ambitious for a movie that can barely get out of the starting gate. As if realising he's barking up the wrong tree, Naud abandons satire after the first reel, as the film concentrates on the simpler task of murdering its teenage cannon-fodder.

We arrive in slasher-land with a flourish that ought to be excruciating but actually helps to fix the movie in your mind: each killing is accompanied by a tape-recorded punk song (well, punk as in The Knack or The Dickies, at least), the choruses of which vary to match each demise: *"Boil me! Boil me!"* for a victim's plunge into a superheated swimming pool; *"Spear Me! Spear*

The Toolbox Murders
© 1977. Cal-Am Productions
Cal-Am Productions presents a Tony DiDio production.
director: Dennis Donnelly. producer: Tony DiDio. associate producers: Kenneth A. Yates, Jack Kindberg. screenplay: Neva Friedenn, Robert Easter and Ann Kindberg. director of photography: Gary Graver. music composed & conducted by George Deaton. film editor: Nunzio Darpino. unit production manager and assistant director: Ann Kindberg. production designer: D.J. Bruno. sound mixer: Robert Dietz. gaffer: Michael Stringer. key grip: Gary Strange. script supervisor: Nancy Hansen. assistant cameraman: Michael Ferris. make-up artist: Ed Ternes. set decorator: Leamon Adams. wardrobe supervisor: Michelle Logan. still photographer: Hedy Dietz. 2nd assistant director: Gary M. Lapoten. sound editor: Ron Moler. assistant editor: Mario S. Anthony. boom man: Beau Franklin. electrician: Jean Clark. 2nd assistant camerawoman: Catherine Coulson. production secretary: Maria C. Dillon. drivers: Tom Gordon, Charles Franchimone. lead man: Frank Armas. production assistants: Anne McDonald, Tony DiDio, Jr., Patty Koehnen. bookkeeper: Jim Magglos. [song] "Pretty Lady" sung by George Deaton & Terry Stubbs; "I've Goy Everything It Takes To Be a Fool", "Carolina in the Morning" sung by George Deaton. music & lyrics by George Deaton. string arranger: Zeke Dawson. keyboard arranger: Walt Cunningham. music engineer & mixer: Frank Evans. music recorded at A.B.E. Sound; Innovation Studio (Nashville, Tennessee). colour by Consolidated Film Industries. sound transfers by T.V. Recorders. Cast: Cameron Mitchell (Uncle Reg Kingsley). Pamelyn Ferdin (Laurie Ballard). Wesley Eure (Kent). Nicolas Beauvy (Joey Ballard). Tim Donnelly (Detective Jamison). Aneta Corsaut (Joanne Ballard). Faith McSwain (Mrs. Andrews). Marciee Drake (Debbie). Evelyn Guerrero (Maria). Victoria Perry (woman in apartment). Robert Bartlett (man in apartment). Betty Cole (middle-aged woman). John Hawker (middle-aged man). Don Diamond (Sergeant Cameron). Alisa Powell (girlfriend). Marianne Walter (Dee Ann). Robert Forward (screamer man). Kathleen O'Malley (screamer woman). Gil Galvano (man). James Nolan (bartender). George Deaton (preacher).

top right and bottom left:
One of the screen's nastiest murderers plying his trade in **The Toolbox Murders**.

Whodunit?
aka **Island of Blood**
© 1982. Creative Film Makers
SRN presents an SRN production in association with C.F.M.
writer/director: Bill Naud. producers: Tom Spalding, Sally Roddy, Bill Naud. line producer: Sally Roddy. director of photography: Tom Spalding. editor: Hari Ryatt. creative consultant: Joel Swanson. original score composed and performed by Joel Goldsmith. title song "Face to Face" written by Richard Dandrea, performed by Factor Four: "Black Hole" music written and sung by Gary Phillips, lyrics by Bill Naud. associate producer: Pamela Scrape. assistant director: Alex Daniels. camera operator: Richard Walden. first assistant camera: Kent Roddy. second unit camera assistants: David Boyd, James Barbour. sound mixers: Dan Oldman, George Hose. boom man: Don McNeil. gaffer: Mike Kovacevich. electrician: Joy Allen Cohen. script supervisor: Sharron Reynolds, Merry Lowry. production assistant: Karen Roddy. assistant editor: Simon Gittins. casting: Lorene Cummins. props: Cyndi Gylov. special effects: Make-up Effects Lab; Image Engineering, Inc. opticals: Imagination Engineering. negative cutter: Peggy Seder. location vehicles & equipment: Cinervan / Telecine Films. audio mix: Soundco. print by United Color Laboratory. camera equipment furnished by Filmtrucks, Inc., Hollywood. locations courtesy of Paradise Cove, Dana Point Marina Co.
Cast: Terry Goodman (Steve Faith). Rick Dean (Jim). Ron Gardner (Franklin Phlem). Steven Tash (Phil). Gary Phillips (Taylor). Bari Suber (Betty Jean, 'BJ'). Richard Helm (Rick). Marie Alise (Donna). Jeanine Marie (Lyn). Red McVay (Bert). Jim Piper (John). Michael Stroka (mayor). Jim Williams (policeman).

above, top left: This victim in **Whodunit?** can't stand the music any longer...

opposite: Molly (Millie Perkins) subverts all those footballers' hotel-room spit-roasting stories with the aid of a simpe razor-blade, in **The Witch Who Came from the Sea**.

The Witch Who Came from the Sea
© 1976
MCI presents a Matt Cimber production.
producer/director: Matt Cimber. writer: Robert Thom. director of photography: Ken Gibb. associate director of photography: Dean Cundey. music composed and directed by Herschel Burke Gilbert. film editor: Bud Warner. post-production supervisor: William Swenning. production supervisor: Jef Richard. assistant director: John Tull. production co-ordinator: Norma Rosenberg. technical supervisor: Dean Cundy. gaffer: Bill Coker. casting: George 'Buck' Flower. assistant camera: Ray Stella. second assistant camera: Mark Buckalew. sound mixer: John Vincent. assistant sound: Jay Kaufman. makeup: Gale Peterson. wardrobe: Caroline Davis. props: Cloudberry - Thunderstone. script supervisor: Lynn Ward. key grip: Jim Salazar. best boy: Jim Andrien. grip: Bill Drake. grip: Gil Valle. grip: Don Coufal. grip: Tom La Monaco. gopher: Robert Lubin. assistant editor: Jan Wesley. sound editor: Colin Waddy. assistant sound editor: Robert Florio. title design: James Yousling. re-recording: Glen Glenn Sound Co. opticals: Praxis. post-production services: Aquarius Films Co. colour: Movielab Hollywood. filmed in Todd-AO 35.
Cast: Millie Perkins (Molly). Lonny Chapman (Long John). Vanessa Brown (Cathy). Peggy Feury (Doris). Jean Pierre Camps (Tadd). Mark Livingston (Tripoli). Rick Jason (Billy Batt). Stafford Morgan (McPeak). Richard Kennedy (Detective Beardsley). George 'Buck' Flower (Detective Stone). Roberta Collins (Clarissa). Stan Ross (Jack Dracula). Lynne Guthrie (Carol). Barry Cooper (newcomer). Gene Rutherford (Sam Walters). Jim Sims (Austin Slade). Sam Chu Lin (newscaster). Anita Franklin (TV commercial girl). John Goff (Molly's father). Verkina (young Molly).

Me!" for an impalement; *"Saw Me! Saw Me!"* for... well, you get the idea. The rest of the score is by Joel Goldsmith, and it bears a distinct similarity to his music for the classic Steve Martin movie *The Man with Two Brains*, made a couple of years later.

The murders are sometimes impressive, my favourite being the one where the killer pipes battery acid into a shower-cubicle, giving a luckless bather a serious skin problem. However, the film's biggest flaw is that it fails to show *all* the killings directly. Once you've showered a naked girl with battery acid, what else can you possibly be afraid of showing? If every murder in *Whodunit?* was as grotesque and unpleasant as the acid scene, it would gladden the heart of slasher-fans everywhere. As it is, a nail-gun attack is promised (*"Nail Me! Nail Me!"*) but we only *hear* the nails going in. Sure, we see the bloody aftermath, but it's not quite the same, is it?

Whodunit?'s characters range from idle cynics to out-and-out morons, interspersed with a few mild and mediocre girls, a forgettable hunk, and a Central Casting nerd (who at least made me laugh when he brandished a lit candle at the suspected killer, saying *"Stay away, or I'll burn you!"*) This lack of sympathetic characters needn't be a problem, but a bit more detail would have helped. One of the script's best ideas is to make everyone so selfish and cynical that they all suspect each other. This could easily have been the saving grace of the film, but in the end the honour goes to that song, that damn song, which I guarantee will be stuck in your mind's ear for days. And the runner-up, the not-quite-saving grace? Well, there's a final twist, one it would be mean to reveal, which at least explains why the actors were so bad in those early scenes...

Whodunit? was filmed at Dana Point, Orange County CA, and Paradise Cove, Los Angeles County. Richard D'Andrea, who wrote 'Face to Face', the song that echoes the murders, was an ex-member of The Motels and The Know, the latter of which he formed with Blondie member Gary Valentine in 1978. By 1980, after gigging extensively without scoring a deal, D'Andrea disbanded the group. His song on the film is credited to a group called Factor Four, but I've been unable to discover any more about them...

Made in California.

THE WITCH WHO CAME FROM THE SEA
– Matt Cimber (1976)

Molly (Millie Perkins) lives near Santa Monica beach with her older sister Cathy (Vanessa Brown). She looks after Todd (Jean Pierre Camps) and Tripoli (Mark Livingston), Cathy's children. Cathy's husband has left her, and Molly has become the boys' friend and chaperone. Although well-liked at 'The Boathouse', the waterfront bar where she works for Long John (Lonny Chapman) and Doris (Peggy Feury), Molly exhibits some unsettling character traits. A fantasist obsessed with her own absent father, whom she claims was lost at sea, she bitterly resents Cathy's dismissal of him as a no-good drunk. Molly's views on other men veer between adoration and rage, a conflict that soon turns to violence...

The only Matt Cimber film I'd seen before this was *Butterfly*, so imagine my surprise when *The Witch Who Came from the Sea* turned out to be one of the strangest and most perversely beautiful horror films of the seventies. It's a beguiling fantasy with a unique texture well beyond the more workaday levels of the genre, the sort of movie you can watch several times and still remain unsure of the exact contents. Not because it's bad, or boring, but because the hazy, downbeat style twists your mind out of focus. Cimber saturates his tale with an off-season seaside ambience, which, blended with the lead character's dreamy psychopathy, produces something extraordinary...

There's no point skirting the central theme of this film merely to avoid spoilers, as the viewer will suspect the truth very quickly. The flashbacks revealing that Molly was abused by her father are nothing like a twist – we can tell from her fervent declarations of love that some paternal wickedness has scarred her deeply. *Witch* is devoid of suspense and fails to ignite as a mystery; instead, it's the acting, the way in which the tale is told, that makes it special.

Millie Perkins's performance as Molly achieves a clarity that reaches into your mind and seriously creeps you out. She's amazing – I would put her performance on a par with Susannah York in *Images* and Carol Kane in *The Mafu Cage*. Her strained, gaunt face conveys Molly's dual life perfectly. We can see that the tide of her fantasies will never wash away her trauma.

Of course this is a horror film, not simply a psychological portrait; what's more, it's a horror film that found its way onto the banned list in the UK back in 1984. So what makes *The Witch Who Came from the Sea* so shocking and objectionable? I suppose it comes down to the 'c'-word. No, not that one (although it does spring from the lips of a couple of unpleasant male characters). I mean 'c' as in *castration*. *"Don't say that word!"* begs Woody Allen in *Bananas*, and he's right – for most men, the syllables themselves are enough to set the nerves on edge. Molly seduces two hulking American Football players, one white, one black, into a threesome; but this is to be no Premier-league 'spit-roasting' session. After the men have smoked some powerful grass, Molly languidly ties their wrists and ankles to the bed. The black player is so stoned he falls asleep at this point, leaving his team-mate to fend off Molly with just one leg untied. To no avail: Molly gags him then emerges from the bathroom with a razorblade, before moving between his legs for a long, leisurely hack-and-slash session...

Gulp. Cimber has sprung this horrorshow on his audience quite suddenly: *so* suddenly, in fact, that for a while we think it may all have been Molly's fantasy; just as earlier, while watching two musclemen working out on the beach, she daydreamed they were strung up mutilated from their exercise apparatus. The castration sequence, heavily reverbed in a way that suggests either druggy dislocation or fantasy, is wedged into the middle of a scene in which Molly argues with her sister. After the footballers have been, shall we say, 'relegated', we return to the same argument, as if the castration scene in its entirety happened somewhere out of time. It's only later, when Molly is with Long John at the bar, that a TV news report confirms the reality.

Motifs relating to Molly's fantasy life are subtle and well-integrated; for instance, her obsessional belief that her father sailed out to sea and never returned makes sense when, in flashback, we're shown the painting of a sailing ship hung above the child's bed. Her fantasies of daddy disappearing into the ocean are rooted in the child's attempt to shut out rape by staring into the picture. Her obsession with mermaids, women of the sea, takes on extra significance after a discussion at a party. Staring raptly at a reproduction of Botticelli's Venus, she enquires as to the meaning of the artwork. The host, McPeak (Stafford Morgan), tells her that Venus was born when her father (Ouranos) was castrated (by his son, Saturn) and his testicles thrown in the ocean, from whence they inseminated the sea. (Amusingly, the predatory but shallow McPeak tells Molly that he learned this nugget of mythology from his chauffeur.) Molly later muses on the nature of mermaids, recounting the notion that mermaids' tails were split in two to make legs. This image, the rending of the

A young woman's nightmare of incest and castration.

THE WITCH WHO CAME FROM THE SEA

mermaid's wholeness to create a woman, mirrors Molly's fate at the hands of her father, a child torn open and forced into sexual knowledge. When Molly has a tattoo of a mermaid inscribed on her stomach, she insists to the tattooist that he be careful to get the placement just right, the fins not too close to her crotch, underlining the symbolism of unsullied maidenhood. (The mermaid is, "An Eve figure overlaid with the cult of the Virgin, a sealed vessel enclosing either sexual temptation or sexual virtue, or some paradoxical and potent mixture of the two," as Canadian writer Carol Shields puts it in her book *The Republic of Love*.) In Molly's mind these myths entangle, until they seem to demand that the birth of a mermaid requires the castration of the father. Later, when Molly kills and castrates McPeak, she massages her breasts with his blood; her mermaid tattoo is visible underneath. (With wonderful economy, she later explains the bloodstains to Long John as blood from the tattoo itself.)

To keep castration in our thoughts throughout the film, the script employs an ever-recurring theme of razors and shaving. Molly sees a TV commercial featuring a male model shaving while espousing the wonders of the blade. The razor killings occur after Molly sees the first of these commercials. (*"Turn on your television set – find out what's happening in the real world,"* she says at one point.) The link between TV and murder isn't simply causal – it's just that everything seems to fit together in Molly's head: images from the beach, images from TV, her own vengeful fantasies, all approaching a sinister confluence that leads inexorably to the castration-killings. *"Headache can strike at any time, but it always seems to come at the wrong moment,"* says a TV commercial, after Molly has hallucinated the man in the razor advert inviting her to slice him from his throat to *"the parts that you want…"*

With the exception of Long John and the two boys, men are depicted unflatteringly. The footballers are initially just laid-back jocks indulging the unthinking arrogance of their breed. It's when Molly strays from the script of their threesome that one of them uses the other 'c' word, exposing a brittle misogyny behind the casual chauvinism. Billy Batt (Rick Jason), a self-obsessed actor, uses the 'c' word too, in a way that underlines his nasty streak. One of the film's most powerful scenes is Molly's attack on Batt,

in his bedroom, during an attempted party seduction that goes awry. Provoked by a stray remark, she hurls herself at him, attempting to bite off his penis and then breaking bones in his hand. After a brief exchange, during which Batt realises that Molly is quite insane, there's another clumsy, agonised scuffle at the door of the bedroom, which propels Molly into a living room packed with media and showbiz hangers-on. Batt stands in the doorway, nursing his injured hand, while Molly slumps silently to the carpet. To the guests, it looks as if Batt has assaulted her. However, instead of explaining the truth, he withdraws back to his bedroom, fully aware of the misunderstanding but preferring to be seen as a bully rather than a victim of a woman's rage.

Molly tries to avoid saying anything that will damage Todd and Tripoli's perception of their 'role models' – the footballers she has castrated. Something of her 'innocence' is artificially preserved by this contradiction, which is obviously intended to maintain our sympathy for the character – one of the few heavy-handed touches in the film. But sympathy or otherwise, Molly's self-delusions are not without price in the lives of those she cherishes. In a chilling scene, Todd and Tripoli react with venom when their mother says Molly is a killer. Molly's self-deception has caused a ripple: just as she was unable to face the truth about her wicked father, now the boys are unable to countenance the truth about her. As they stare coldly at their sobbing mother, we see in their hatred the negative impact of Molly's influence.

The ending has an anti-authoritarian slant: Doris and Long John (*"A pirate,"* says Molly, *"he knows where the treasure is"*) give the murderess a final, loving send-off without alerting the police, even though they know what she has done. Together with the boys, they form a surrogate family around her, enveloping the final scenes with a romantic 'band of outsiders' fantasy. Cimber aligns himself with them: the last shot, taking Long John's point of view, looks out at the approaching police through a faux-porthole in the bar-room door.

The Witch Who Came from the Sea feels hewn from late night conversations, private reminiscences; it drifts and sways like seaweed, like thoughts in a cannabis fugue. The structural timber of the horror genre is cast adrift. Horror, overt horror at least, is concentrated in the early part of the film, and what follows is a sad, sleepy tidal shift into psychological portraiture. Imagery and allusion are uppermost in the latter half, and a first late-night viewing of the film may yield nothing the morning after except a few images and a morbid afterglow. The movie changes the metabolism of its genre; the scares are oblique, the overall tone languid. Matt Cimber would be derided, four or five years later, when his Pia Zadora vehicle *Butterfly* hit the screen. I rather enjoyed that one too, but *The Witch Who Came from the Sea* is in another league, a genre masterpiece deserving of a much higher profile.

Matt Cimber's first film *Single Room Furnished*, starred his then wife Jayne Mansfield in a rare serious role (she plays three stages of the same character). Mansfield died before the film could be completed, on 29 June, 1967 – Cimber completed it with footage featuring the supporting cast. *Witch* was shot by Dean Cundey and written by the writer/director of *Angel, Angel, Down We Go*, Robert Thom, who died in 1979. On the production side, line producer Jefferson Richard, who worked on several Cimber films including *The Black 6* and *The Candy Tangerine Man*, was production supervisor on *Ilsa, Harem Keeper of the Oil Sheiks*, co-producer of *Maniac Cop* and the writer/director of *Berserker* (1987). Millie Perkins, the lead actress, went on to a varied career, returning to the horror genre in 1994 to appear in the Brian Yuzna segment of the Lovecraft anthology film *Necronomicon*. The cop is played by George 'Buck' Flower, who's appeared in several John Carpenter films including *The Fog* and *They Live*. He was also, like fellow cast-member here Stafford Morgan, in Bill Rebane's *The Alpha Incident* (1977) – Flower played the railway guard and Morgan was Dr. Sorensen, the government man. Flower also played Binz, the sleazy, ingratiating doctor in charge of medical experiments in *Ilsa, She Wolf of the SS*.

Made in California.

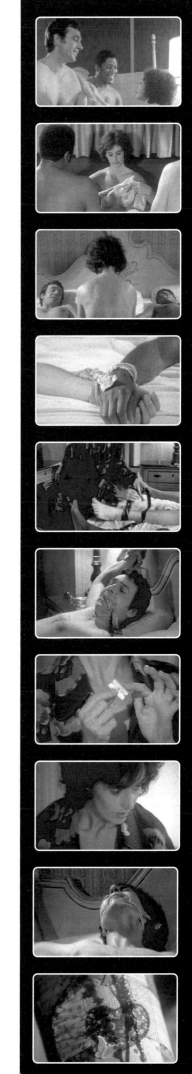

An Exploitation Independent Checklist

Horror, 1970-1985

Deciding what is and is not a horror film can be a fraught affair: thrillers, sci-fi movies and comedies all regularly overlap with horror, and that's before you get started on the adult movie industry. I suspect we would all draw the line slightly differently, so I make no claims here to a definitive categorisation. Likewise, defining an independent production is not always easy. Where there is doubt as to the validity of the 'independent' tag, I have noted the production company. Year of production is drawn, where possible, from the film itself.

The list would grow at least half as long again if I included international co-productions. There are a few tucked away here, in cases where the definitions were particularly ambiguous, but in general they are not included. Films from the 'adult' film industry that combine pornographic imagery and horror (as opposed to horror films with some sexual imagery) are listed here. Finally, space simply does not permit the addition of alternative titles: if you think your favourite is not included, it's probably here under another name. Where possible, I've used the most familiar variant, although American readers may find a British bias to some choices!

Roughly a quarter of the films cited below are covered in this book, with around the same number lined up for *Nightmare USA: Volume 2*. As for the rest, who knows? In some cases, the year of production is approximate or unverified, since I have yet to view the films to confirm their copyright dates.

ABDUCTED – Don Jones (1973)
ALABAMA'S GHOST – Fredric Hobbs (1973)
THE ALCHEMIST – Charles Band (1981)
THE ALIEN DEAD – Fred Olen Ray (1980)
THE ALIEN FACTOR – Don Dohler (1977)
ALIEN ZONE – Sharron Miller (1978)
ALL THE DEVIL'S ANGELS – Peter Balakoff (1978)
ALLIGATOR – Lewis Teague (1980)
THE ALPHA INCIDENT – Bill Rebane (1977)
ANOTHER SON OF SAM – Dave A. Adams (1977)
ARNOLD – Georg Fenady (1973) Bing Crosby Productions
ASYLUM OF SATAN – William Girdler (1971)
ASYLUM OF THE INSANE – Byron Mabe (1971)
ATTACK OF THE BEAST CREATURES – Michael Stanley (1983)
THE ATTIC – George Edwards (1980)
AXE – Frederick Friedel (1974)
THE BABY – Ted Post (1972)
BABY ROSEMARY – Harold Perkins [John Hayes] (1976)
THE BARN OF THE NAKED DEAD – Alan Rudolph (1973)
BARRACUDA – Harry Kerwin (1977)
BASKET CASE – Frank Henenlotter (1981)
THE BEAUTIES AND THE BEAST – Ray Nadeau (1973)
THE BEING – Jackie Kong (1983)
BEN – Phil Karlson (1972) Bing Crosby Productions
BEYOND EVIL – Herb Freed (1980)
BLACK DEVIL DOLL FROM HELL – Chester N. Turner (1984)
THE BLACK ROOM – Norman Thaddeus Vane / Elly Kenner (1981)
BLACKENSTEIN – William A. Levey (1972)
BLOOD – Andy Milligan (1974)
BLOOD BATH – Joel M. Reed (1975)
BLOOD BRIDE – Robert J. Avrech (1979)
BLOOD CULT – Christopher Lewis (1985) *shot on video*
BLOOD FREAK – Brad F. Grinter (1972)
BLOOD MANIA – Robert Vincent O'Neil (1971)
BLOOD OF GHASTLY HORROR – Al Adamson (1971)
BLOOD ORGY OF THE SHE-DEVILS – Ted V. Mikels (1972)
BLOOD RAGE – John Grissmer (1983)
BLOOD SABBATH – Brianne Murphy (1972)
BLOOD SHACK – Ray Dennis Steckler (1971)
BLOOD SONG – Alan J. Levi (1982)

BLOOD STALKERS – Robert W. Morgan (1975)
BLOODRAGE – Joseph Bigwood [Joseph Zito] (1979)
BLOODSUCKERS FROM OUTER SPACE – Glen Coburn (1984)
BLOODSUCKING FREAKS – Joel M. Reed (1976)
THE BLOODTHIRSTY BUTCHERS – Andy Milligan (1970)
BLOODY BIRTHDAY – Ed Hunt (1980)
BLOODY WEDNESDAY – Mark G Gilhuis (1985)
BLUE SUNSHINE – Jeff Lieberman (1977)
BLUE VOODOO – Armand Weston (1977)
BOARDINGHOUSE – John Wintergate (1982)
BOG – Don Keeslar (1978)
THE BOGEY MAN – Ulli Lommel (1980)
THE BOOGENS – James L. Conway (1981)
BOOGEYMAN II – Ulli Lommel (1983)
THE BRAIN LEECHES – Fred Olen Ray (1977)
BRAIN OF BLOOD – Al Adamson (1971)
THE BRIDES WORE BLOOD – Bob Favorite (1972)
BUMMER! – William Allen Castleman (1973)
THE CAPTURE OF BIGFOOT – Bill Rebane (1979)
CARNAGE – Andy Milligan (1983)
CARNIVAL OF BLOOD – Leonard Kirtman (1970)
CATACLYSM – Tom McGowan (1980)
THE CENTERFOLD GIRLS – John Peyser (1974)
THE CHILD – Robert Voskanian (1976)
THE CHILDREN – Max Kalmanowicz (1980)
CHILDREN OF THE CORN – Fritz Kiersch (1984)
CHILDREN SHOULDN'T PLAY WITH DEAD THINGS – Bob Clark (1972)
CHRISTMAS EVIL – Lewis Jackson (1980)
CLAWS – Richard Bansbach / R.E. Pierson (1977)
THE COMING – Bert I. Gordon (1980)
COMMUNION – Alfred Sole (1976)
CONFESSIONS OF A SERIAL KILLER – Mark Blair (1985)
THE CORPSE GRINDERS – Ted V. Mikels (1971)
COUNT EROTICO - VAMPIRE – Tony Teresi (1975)
THE CRATER LAKE MONSTER – William R. Stromberg (1977)
CRAZED – Richard Cassidy (1977)
THE CRAZIES – George Romero (1973)
CREATURE FROM BLACK LAKE – Joy N. Houck Jr (1976)
THE CREEPER – Wes Olsen (1984)
"CRIMINALLY INSANE" – Nick Millard (1975)
CRYPT OF DARK SECRETS – Jack Weis (1976)
CRYPT OF THE LIVING DEAD – Ray Danton / Julio Salvador (1972)
CURSE OF BIGFOOT – Don Fields (1976)

CURSE OF THE ALPHA STONE – Stewart Malleson (1972)
CURSE OF THE HEADLESS HORSEMAN – Leonard Kirtman (1972)
CURSE OF THE MOON CHILD – director unknown (1972)
THE CURSE OF THE SCREAMING DEAD – Tony Malanowski (1982)
THE DARK – John 'Bud' Cardos (1978)
THE DARK ANGEL – director unknown (1983)
DARK AUGUST – Martin Goldman (1975)
DARK DREAMS – Roger Guermontes (1971)
DARK EYES – James Polakof (1980)
THE DARK POWER – Phil Smoot (1985)
THE DARK RIDE – Jeremy Hoenack (1977)
DARK SANITY – Martin Green (1982)
DAUGHTER OF SATAN – Hardi Burton (1970)
DAWN OF THE DEAD – George Romero (1978)
THE DAY IT CAME TO EARTH – Harry Thomason (1979)
A DAY OF JUDGMENT – C.D.H. Reynolds (1979)
DAY OF THE DEAD – George Romero (1985)
DAY OF THE REAPER – Tim Ritter (1984)
THE DAY SANTA CLAUS CRIED – Philip Otto (1980)
DEAD AND BURIED – Gary Sherman (1981)
DEAD END – Emerson Bixby (1985) – *shot on video*
DEADLY GAMES – Scott Mansfield (1980)
DEADLY LOVE – Alexander Newman (1976)
THE DEADLY SPAWN – Douglas McKeown (1982)
DEAFULA – Peter Wolf (1974)
DEATH BED: THE BED THAT EATS – George Barry (1977)
DEATH BY INVITATION – Ken Friedman (1971)
DEATH GAME – Peter Traynor (1976)
DEATH SCREAMS – David Nelson (1983)
DEATH TRAP – Tobe Hooper (1976)
DEATH WISH CLUB – John Carr (1983)
DEATHDREAM – Bob Clark (1972)
THE DEATHHEAD VIRGIN – Norman Foster (1974)
THE DEFIANCE OF GOOD – Armand Weston (1974)
DEMENTED – Arthur Jeffreys [and Alex Rebar] (1980)
DEMENTED DEATH FARM MASSACRE: THE MOVIE – Donn Davison / Fred Olen Ray (1972/1986)
THE DEMON LOVER – Donald J. Jackson (1976)
DEMONOID – Alfredo Zacharias (1979)
THE DEMONS OF LUDLOW – Bill Rebane (1983)
THE DEVIL INSIDE HER – Zebedy Colt (1976)?
DEVIL TIMES FIVE – Sean MacGregor (1973)
DEVIL'S DUE – Ernest Danna (1973)
DEVIL'S ECSTASY – Brandon G. Carter (1974)

DEVIL'S EXPRESS – Barry Rosen (1975)
THE DEVIL'S GIFT – Kenneth J. Berton (1984)
THE DEVIL'S PLAYGROUND – Rik Taziner (1977)
THE DEVONSVILLE TERROR – Ulli Lommel (1983)
DIMENSION – Leon Armand (1984)
DISCONNECTED – Gorman Bechard (1983)
DOCTOR GORE – J.G. 'Pat' Patterson (1972)
DOGS – Burt Brinckerhoff (1976)
DOGS OF HELL – Worth Keeter III (1982)
DON'T ANSWER THE PHONE! – Robert Hammer (1979)
DON'T GO IN THE HOUSE – Joseph Ellison (1979)
DON'T GO IN THE WOODS – James Bryan (1981)
DON'T GO NEAR THE PARK – Lawrence Foldes (1979)
DON'T LOOK IN THE BASEMENT – S.F. Brownrigg (1973)
DON'T OPEN THE DOOR – S.F. Brownrigg (1975)
THE DOUBLE GARDEN – Kenneth G. Crane (1970)
DR. BLACK, MR. HYDE – William Crain (1975)
DR. DEATH, SEEKER OF SOULS – Eddie Saeta (1973)
DRACULA SUCKS – Philip Marshak (1979)
DRACULA VS. FRANKENSTEIN – Al Adamson (1970)
DRACULA'S DOG – Albert Band (1978)
DRAGULA – Jim Moss [with Andy Milligan] (1971)
DREAM NO EVIL – John Hayes (1971)
THE DRILLER KILLER – Abel Ferrara (1979)
DRIVE-IN MASSACRE – Stu Segall (1976)
ECSTASY IN BLUE – Bill Milling (1976)
EFFECTS – Dusty Nelson (1978)
ENCOUNTER WITH THE UNKNOWN – Harry Thomason (1972)
ENTER THE DEVIL – Frank Q. Dobbs (1972)
EQUINOX – Jack Woods (1968/71)
ERASERHEAD – David Lynch (1976)
THE EVIL – Gus Trikonis (1977)
EVIL COME, EVIL GO – Walt Davis (1972)
THE EVIL DEAD – Sam Raimi (1982)
EVIL FORCE – Evan Lee (1975)
EVILS OF THE NIGHT – Mardi Rustam (1985)
EVILSPEAK – Eric Weston (1981)
EYES OF FIRE – Avery Crounse (1983)
FADE TO BLACK – Vernon Zimmerman (1980)
FALL BREAK – Buddy Cooper (1985)
FATAL GAMES – Michael Elliot (1983)
FEAR NO EVIL – Frank La Loggia (1980)
FIEND – Don Dohler (1980)
THE FIFTH FLOOR – Howard Avedis (1978)

FIGHT FOR YOUR LIFE – Robert Endelson (1977)
FINAL EXAM – Jimmy Huston (1981)
FINGER LICKIN' GOOD – Rik Taziner (1974)
FLESH FEAST – Brad Grinter (1970)
THE FOLKS AT RED WOLF INN – Bud Townsend (1972)
FORCE OF DARKNESS – Alan Hauge (1985)
FORCED ENTRY – Helmuth Richler [Shaun Costello] (1972)
THE FOREST – Don Jones (1981)
FOREST OF FEAR – Charles McCrann (1979)
FRANKENSTEIN ISLAND – Jerry Warren (1981)
FRIDAY THE 13TH – Sean Cunningham (1980)
FRIDAY THE 13TH: THE ORPHAN – John Ballard (1977)
FROZEN SCREAM – Frank Roach & Renee Harmon [uncredited] (1981)
GALAXY INVADER – Don Dohler (1985)
THE GAME – Bill Rebane (1984)
GANJA AND HESS – Bill Gunn / Fima Noveck (1974)
GARDEN OF THE DEAD – John Hayes (1972)
GATOR BAIT – Ferd & Beverly Sebastian (1973)
GETTING EVEN – Harry Kerwin (1976)
THE GHOST DANCE – Peter F. Buffa (1980)
GHOSTS THAT STILL WALK – James T. Flocker (1978)
THE GIANT SPIDER INVASION – Bill Rebane (1975)
GODMONSTER OF INDIAN FLATS – Fredric Hobbs (1973)
GOD'S BLOODY ACRE – Harry Kerwin (1974)
THE GORE GORE GIRLS – Herschell Gordon Lewis (1972)
GRADUATION DAY – Herb Freed (1981)
GRAVE OF THE VAMPIRE – John Hayes (1972)
THE GREAT HOLLYWOOD RAPE SLAUGHTER – Charles Edward (1971)
GRIM REAPER – Ron Ormond (1976)
GRIZZLY – William Girdler (1976)
GURU THE MAD MONK – Andy Milligan (1970)
HALLOWEEN – John Carpenter (1978)
HANGING HEART – Jimmy Lee (1983)
HAPPY MOTHER'S DAY, LOVE GEORGE – Darren McGavin (1972)
HARDGORE – Michael Hugo (1974)
HAUNTED – Michael De Gaetano (1976)
THE HAUNTED PUSSY – Doris Wishman (1976)
HAUNTS – Herb Freed (1975)
HAVE A NICE WEEKEND – Michael Walters (1974)
THE HEADLESS EYES – Kent Bateman (1971)
THE HEARSE – George Bowers (1980)
HELL NIGHT – Tom De Simone (1981)
THE HILLS HAVE EYES – Wes Craven (1977)
HITCH HIKE TO HELL – Irv Berwick (1977)
THE HOLLYWOOD STRANGLER MEETS THE SKID ROW SLASHER – Ray Dennis Steckler (1979)
HOME SWEET HOME – Nettie Peña (1981)
HOMEBODIES – Larry Yust (1973)
HONEYMOON HORROR – Harry Preston (1982)
THE HORNY DEVILS – director unknown (1973)
HORROR IN THE WAX MUSEUM – Titus Moody (1983)
THE HORROR STAR – Norman Thaddeus Vane (1981)
HOT SUMMER IN THE CITY – Gail Palmer (1976)
HOUSE OF DE SADE – Joe Davian (1975)
THE HOUSE OF SEVEN CORPSES – Paul Harrison (1973)
HOUSE OF SIN – Carter Stevens (1982)
HOUSE OF TERROR – Segei Goncharoff (1972)
THE HOUSE ON SKULL MOUNTAIN – Ron Honthaner (1974)
THE HOUSE THAT CRIED MURDER – Jean-Marie Pélissié (1974)
THE HOUSE WHERE DEATH LIVES – Alan Beattie (1980)
HUMAN EXPERIMENTS – Gregory Goodell (1979)
I DISMEMBER MAMA – Paul Leder (1972)
I DRINK YOUR BLOOD – David Durston (1971)
I SPIT ON YOUR GRAVE – Meir Zarchi (1978)
IGOR AND THE LUNATICS – Billy Parolini (1985)
IMPULSE – William Grefé (1973)
INSANITY – Christine Hornisher (1973)
INVASION OF THE BLOOD FARMERS – Ed Adlum (1972)
ISLAND CLAWS – Hernan Cardenas (1981)
JANIE – Jack Bravman (1970)
THE JAR – Bruce Toscano (1985)
THE JEKYLL AND HYDE PORTFOLIO – Eric Jeffrey Haims (1971)
JUST BEFORE DAWN – Jeff Lieberman (1980)
KEEP MY GRAVE OPEN – S.F. Brownrigg (1976)
KIDNAPPED COED – Frederick Friedel (1975)
THE KILLING KIND – Curtis Harrington (1973)
KISS OF THE TARANTULA – Chris Munger (1975)
KNEEL BEFORE ME – Phil Prince (1983)
THE LAST HORROR FILM – David Winters (1982)

THE LAST HOUSE ON DEAD END STREET – Roger Watkins (1977)
THE LAST HOUSE ON THE LEFT – Wes Craven (1972)
LAST RITES – Domonic Paris (1979)
THE LAST VICTIM – Jim Sotos (1975)
LEGACY OF BLOOD – Carl Monson (1971)
LEGACY OF HORROR – Andy Milligan (1978)
LEGACY OF SATAN – Gerard Damiano (1973)
THE LEGEND OF BOGGY CREEK – Charles B. Pierce (1972)
THE LEGEND OF HORROR – Bill Davies / Enrique Carreras (1972)
LEGEND OF MCCULLOUGH MOUNTAIN – Massey Cramer / Donn Davison (1965/1976)
LEMORA: A CHILD'S TALE OF THE SUPERNATURAL – Richard Blackburn (1973)
LET'S SCARE JESSICA TO DEATH – John Hancock (1971)
THE LOCH NESS HORROR – Larry Buchanan (1981)
LONG ISLAND CANNIBAL MASSACRE – Nathan Schiff (1980)
LORD SHANGO – Ray Marsh (1975)
THE LOVE BUTCHER – Mikel Angel/Don Jones (1975)
LOVE ME DEADLY – Jacques Lacerte (1972)
THE LUCIFERS – director unknown (1971)
MADAME ZENOBIA – Eduardo Cemano (1973)
MADMAN – Joe Giannone (1981)
THE MAFU CAGE – Karen Arthur (1977)
MAKO: JAWS OF DEATH – William Grefé (1975)
MALATESTA'S CARNIVAL OF BLOOD – Christopher Speeth (1973)
MANIAC – William Lustig (1980)
THE MANITOU – William Girdler (1977)
MANSION OF THE DOOMED – Michael Pataki (1975)
MARDI GRAS MASSACRE – Jack Weis (1978)
MARK OF THE WITCH – Tom Moore (1970)
MARTIN – George Romero (1976)
MASSACRE AT CENTRAL HIGH – Rene Daalder (1976)
MAUSOLEUM – Michael Dugan (1982)
MESSIAH OF EVIL – Willard Huyck (1973)
MICROWAVE MASSACRE – Wayne Berwick (1978 [released 1983])
MIDNIGHT – John Russo (1982)
THE MILPITAS MONSTER – Robert L. Burrill (1975)
MIRRORS – Noel Black (1974/78)?
MONGREL – Robert Burns (1982)
MONSTROID – Kenneth Hartford / Herbert L. Strock (1979)
MOONCHILD – Alan Gadney (1972)
MOTHER'S DAY – Charles Kaufman (1980)
MOVIE HOUSE MASSACRE – Alice Raley [Rick Sloane] (1984)
MURDERLUST – Donald M. Jones (1985)
MUTANT – John 'Bud' Cardos (1984)
MY BROTHER HAS BAD DREAMS – Robert J. Emery (1972)
MY FRIENDS NEED KILLING – Paul Leder (1976)
THE NAIL GUN MASSACRE – Bill Leslie / Terry Lofton (1985)
A NAME FOR EVIL – Bernard Girard (1972)
NATAS: THE REFLECTION – Jack Dunlap (1983)
NECROMANCY – Bert I. Gordon (1972)
THE NESTING – Armand Weston (1980)
NEW YEAR'S EVIL – Emmett Alston (1980) Cannon Films
NIGHT OF HORROR – Tony Malanowski (1981)
NIGHT OF THE COMET – Thom Eberhardt (1984)
NIGHT OF THE DEMON – James C. Wasson (1980)
NIGHT OF THE WITCHES – Keith Larsen [Keith Erik Burt] (1970)
NIGHT OF THE ZOMBIES – Joel M. Reed (1981)
A NIGHT TO DISMEMBER – Doris Wishman (1983)
NIGHT TRAIN TO TERROR – Various (1985)
NIGHTBEAST – Don Dohler (1982)
NIGHTMARE IN BLOOD – John Stanley (1979)
NOCTURNA – Harry Tampa (1978)
NURSE SHERRI – Al Adamson (1977)
NUTRIAMAN: THE COPASAW CREATURE – Joe Catalanotto / Martin Folse (1985)
OCTAMAN – Harry Essex (1971)
DOUBLE JEOPARDY – Ulli Lommel (1981)
ONE DARK NIGHT – Tom McLoughlin (1983)
THE ORACLE – Roberta Findlay (1985)
THE OUTING – Byron W. Quisenberry (1981)
PETS – Raphael Nussbaum (1973)
PHANTASM – Don Coscarelli (1978)
PICK-UP – Bennie Hirschenson (1975)
PIGS – Marc Lawrence (1972)
PLEASE DON'T EAT MY MOTHER – Carl Monson (1972)
PLEASE DON'T EAT THE BABIES – Henri Chan (1983)

POINT OF TERROR – Alex Nichol (1971)
POOR PRETTY EDDIE – Richard Robinson / David Worth (1973)
POOR WHITE TRASH PART 2 – S.F. Brownrigg (1974)
POSSESSED – director unknown (1976)
THE POSSESSED! – Charles Nizet (1974)
THE POWER – Jeffrey Obrow / Stephen Carpenter (1982)?
PRANKS – Jeffrey Obrow / Stephen Carpenter (1981)
PREMONITION – Alan Rudolph (1970)
THE PREMONITION – Robert Allan Schnitzer (1975)
THE PREY – Edwin Brown (1980)
PSYCHED BY THE 4D WITCH – Victor Luminera (1972)
PSYCHIC KILLER – Ray Danton (1975)
PSYCHO FROM TEXAS – Jim Feazell (1971)
THE PSYCHO LOVER – Robert Vincent O'Neil (1970)
PSYCHO SISTERS – Reginald Le Borg (1974)
PSYCHOPATH – Larry Brown (1972)
THE PSYCHOTRONIC MAN – Jack M. Sell (1979)
RANA: THE LEGEND OF SHADOW LAKE – Bill Rebane (1981)
RATS ARE COMING, THE WEREWOLVES ARE HERE – Andy Milligan (1971)
THE RAVAGER – Charles Nizet (1970)
RAW FORCE – Edward D. Murphy (1981)
RED HEAT – Ray Dennis Steckler (1975)
THE REDEEMER – Constantine Gochis (1976)
RETURN – Andrew Silver (1985)
THE RETURN – Greydon Clark (1980)
RETURN TO BOGGY CREEK – Tom Moore (1977)
THE RETURNING – Joel Bender (1983)
REVENGE OF BIGFOOT – Harry Thomason (1979)
THE RIPPER – Christopher Lewis (1985) – *shot on video*
RUBY – Curtis Harrington / Stephanie Rothman (1977)
SACRILEGE – Ray Dennis Steckler (1971)
SAN FRANCISCO BALL – Jack Genaro (1971)
SATAN WAR – Bart La Rue (1979)
SATAN'S BLACK WEDDING – Nick Millard (1975)
SATAN'S BLADE – L. Scott Castillo Jr (1984)
SATAN'S CHEERLEADERS – Greydon Clark (1977)
SATAN'S CHILDREN – Joe Wiezycki (1974)
SATAN'S LUST – director unknown (1971)
SATAN'S TOUCH – John D. Goodell (1984)
SAVAGE ABDUCTION – John Lawrence (1972)
SAVAGE WATER – Paul Kener (1978)
SAVAGE WEEKEND – David Paulsen (1976)
SCALPEL – John Grissmer (1974)
SCALPS – Fred Olen Ray (1982)
SCARED TO DEATH – William Malone (1980)
THE SCAREMAKER – Robert Deubel (1982)
SCHIZOID – David Paulsen (1980) Cannon Films
SCHOOL FOR DEAD GIRLS – director unknown (1972)
SCREAM BLOODY MURDER – Marc B. Ray (1972)
SCREAM FOR VENGEANCE – Bob Bliss (1979)
A SCREAM IN THE STREETS – Carl Monson (1972)
SCREAMS OF A WINTER NIGHT – James Wilson (1979)
SEASON OF THE WITCH – George Romero (1972)
SEEDS OF EVIL – Jim Kay (1973)
THE SESSION – Pasquale Arico (1971)
THE SEVERED ARM – Thomas Alderman (1972)
SEX DEMON – J.C. Crickett (1975)
SEX PSYCHO – Walt Davis (1970)
SEX RITUALS OF THE OCCULT – Robert Caramico (1970)
SEX WISH – Tim McCoy (1976)
SEXORCIST DEVIL – Ray Dennis Steckler (1974)
SEXUAL SATANIC AWARENESS – Ray Dennis Steckler (1972)
THE SHADOW OF CHIKARA – Earl E. Smith (1978)
SHADOWS OF THE MIND – Roger Watkins (1980)
SHOCK WAVES – Ken Wiederhorn (1976)
SHRIEK OF THE MUTILATED – Michael Findlay (1974)
SILENT MADNESS – Simon Nuchtern (1984)
SILENT NIGHT, BLOODY NIGHT – Theodore Gershuny (1972)
SILENT NIGHT, DEADLY NIGHT – Charles E. Sellier Jr. (1984)
THE SILENT SCREAM – Denny Harris (1979)
SIMON, KING OF THE WITCHES – Bruce Kessler (1971)
THE SINGLE GIRLS – Ferd & Beverly Sebastian (1973)
SISTERS OF DEATH – Joseph Mazzuca (1972 [released 1977])
SKETCHES OF A STRANGLER – Paul Leder (1978)
THE SLAYER – J.S. Cardone (1981)
SLEAZY RIDER – Roger Gentry (1972)
SLEDGEHAMMER – David A. Prior (1983)
SNUFF – Michael Findlay (1976)

SOLE SURVIVOR – Thom Eberhardt (1982)
SOMETIMES AUNT MARTHA DOES DREADFUL THINGS – Thomas Casey (1971)
SONS OF SATAN – Tom DeSimone (1973)
SOUL VENGEANCE – Jamaa Fanaka (1975)
SOUTH OF HELL MOUNTAIN – Louis Lehman / William Sachs (1971)
SPAWN OF THE SLITHIS – Stephen Traxler (1977)
THE SPECTRE OF EDGAR ALLAN POE – Mohy Quandour (1972)
STANLEY – William Grefé (1972)
STIGMA – David Durston (1972)
THE STRANGE VENGEANCE OF ROSALIE – Jack Starrett (1972)
THE STRANGENESS – David Michael Hillman (1980)
SUGAR COOKIES – Theodore Gershuny (1973)
SUICIDE CULT – James Glickenhaus (1977)
SUPERSTITION – James Roberson (1982)
SWEET KILL – Curtis Hanson (1971)
SWEET SAVIOR – Bob Roberts (1971)
SWEET SIXTEEN – Jim Sotos (1983)
SWINGERS MASSACRE – Ron Garcia (1973)
TALES OF THE THIRD DIMENSION – Tom Durham / Worth Keeter / Thom McIntyre (1984)
TENEMENT – Roberta Findlay (1985)
TERRI'S REVENGE – Zebedy Colt (1976)
TERROR AT ORGY CASTLE – Zoltan G. Spenser (1971)
TERROR IN THE WAX MUSEUM – Georg Fenady (1973) Bing Crosby Productions
TERROR ON TOUR – Don Edmonds (1980)
THE TEXAS CHAIN SAW MASSACRE – Tobe Hooper (1974)
THE THIRSTY DEAD – Terry Becker (1973)
THREE ON A MEATHOOK – William Girdler (1972)
THROUGH THE LOOKING GLASS – Jonas Middleton (1976)
TILL DEATH – Walter Stocker (1974)
TIME WALKER – Tom Kennedy (1982)
TO ALL A GOODNIGHT – David Hess (1980)
THE TOOLBOX MURDERS – Dennis Donnelly (1977)
TORTURE DUNGEON – Andy Milligan (1970)
THE TOUCH OF SATAN – Don Henderson [Tom Laughlin] (1971)
TOURIST TRAP – David Schmoeller (1978)
THE TOWN THAT DREADED SUNDOWN – Charles B. Pierce (1976)
THE TOY BOX – Ron Garcia (1970)
TOYS ARE NOT FOR CHILDREN – Stanley H. Brasloff (1972)
TRACK OF THE MOONBEAST – Richard Ashe (1972)
TRICK OR TREATS – Gary Graver (1982)
TRIP WITH THE TEACHER – Earl Barton (1974)
TWISTED BRAIN – Larry N. Stouffer (1974)
UNHINGED – Don Gronquist (1982)
THE UNSEEN – Peter Foleg (1981)
UNWILLING LOVERS – Zebedy Colt (1977)
THE VARROW MISSION – Peter Semelka (1978)
VICTIMS – Daniel DiSomma (1977 [copyrighted/released 1982)
VICTIMS – Jeff Hathcock (1985)
VISIONS OF EVIL – Harry Thomason (1973)
VOICES OF DESIRE – Chuck Vincent (1970)
VOODOO HEARTBEAT – Charles Nizet (1972)
VULTURES – Paul Leder (1983)
WAPPER – William Gilfry / Todd Hughes / Tim Kirk (1975)
WARLOCK MOON – Bill Herbert (1973 [released 1975])
THE WARNING – Greydon Clark (1980)
WATERPOWER – Shaun Costello (1976)
WEASELS RIP MY FLESH – Nathan Schiff (1979)
WELCOME TO ARROW BEACH – Laurence Harvey (1973)
WEREWOLVES ON WHEELS – Michel Levesque (1971)
WET WILDERNESS – Lee Cooper (1975)
WHISKEY MOUNTAIN – William Grefé (1977)
WHODUNIT? – Bill [William T.] Naud (1982)
WILLARD – Daniel Mann (1971) Bing Crosby Productions
THE WITCH WHO CAME FROM THE SEA – Matt Cimber (1976)
THE WIZARD OF GORE – Herschell Gordon Lewis (1970)
WOLFMAN – Worth Keeter III (1979)
A WOMAN'S TORMENT – Roberta Findlay (1976)
THE WORM EATERS – Herb Robbins (1977)
WRONG WAY – Ray Williams (1972)
ZAAT – Don Barton (1975)
THE ZODIAC KILLER – Tom Hanson (1971)
ZOMBIE ISLAND MASSACRE – John N. Carter (1983)

Books

The Amazing Herschell Gordon Lewis and His World of Exploitation Films – Daniel Krogh & John McCarty (Fantaco Enterprises, 1983)
American Horrors: Essays on the Modern American Horror Film – ed. Gregory A. Waller (University of Illinois Press, 1987)
The American Nightmare: Essays on the Horror Film – Andrew Britton, Richard Lippe, Tony Williams & Robin Wood (Festival of Festivals, Toronto, 1979)
The Aurum Film Encyclopedia: Horror – ed. Phil Hardy (2nd Edition, Aurum Press, 1993)
Crackpot: The Obsessions of John Waters – John Waters (Fourth Estate Ltd., 1988)
Danse Macabre – Stephen King (Macdonald, 1981)
Easy Riders, Raging Bulls – Peter Biskind (Bloomsbury, 1998)
Elliot's Guide to Films on Video - John Elliot (2nd Edition, Boxtree Books, 1991)
For One Week Only – Richard Meyers (New Century, 1983)
The Ghastly One: The Sex-Gore Netherworld of Filmmaker Andy Milligan – Jimmy McDonough (A Capella Books, 2001)
Gods in Polyester: Or, A Survivor's Account of 70's Cinema Obscura – ed. Suzanne Donahue & Mikael Sovijärvi (Succubus Press, 2004)
Nightmare Movies: a Critical History of the Horror Film, 1968-88 – Kim Newman (revised edition, Bloomsbury, 1988)
The Psychotronic Encyclopedia – Michael Weldon (Ballantine, 1983)
See No Evil: Banned Films and Video Controversy – David Kerekes & David Slater (Headpress/Critical Vision, 2000)
Shock! Horror!: Astounding Artwork from the Video Nasty Era – Francis Brewster, Harvey Fenton & Marc Morris (FAB Press, 2005)
The Sleaze Merchants: Adventures in Exploitation Filmmaking – John McCarty (St. Martin's Griffin, 1995)
Sleazoid Express – Bill Landis & Michelle Clifford (Fireside, 2002)
Splatter Movies – John McCarty (Columbus, 1984)
Wes Craven's Last House on the Left: The Making of a Cult Classic – David A. Szulkin (revised edition, FAB Press, 2000)
The Zombies That Ate Pittsburgh: The Films of George Romero – Paul R. Gagne (Dodd, Mead, 1987)

Magazines

Cinefantastique
Cinema Sewer
Fangoria
Gore Gazette
Hollywood Reporter
Is It... Uncut?
Psychotronic
Rue Morgue
Shivers
Shock Cinema
Shock Xpress
Sleazoid Express
Starburst
Variety

Websites

Critical Condition (www.critcononline.com)
DVD Maniacs (www.dvdmaniacs.net)
Hysteria Lives! (www.hysteria-lives.co.uk)
The Internet Movie Database (www.imdb.com)
The Latarnia Forums (www.latarnia.com)
The Mobius Forums (www.mhvf.net)
Mondo Digital (www.mondo-digital.com)
Mondo Erotico (www.vidmarc.demon.co.uk/mondo-erotico)
The New York Times All Movie Guide (www.nytimes.com)
Pimpadelic Wonderland (www.pimpadelicwonderland.com)
Pre-Certification Video (www.pre-cert.co.uk)
Sex Gore Mutants (www.sexgoremutants.com)

Page references in **bold** refer exclusively to illustrations, though pages referenced as text entries may also feature relevant illustrations.

Nightmare USA: Volume 2

In Preparation:

God's Bloody Florida – The Films of Harry Kerwin.
New York Scandals – Simon Nuchtern on *Snuff, Silent Madness,* and others.
Til Death Do Us Part – Harry Preston on *Honeymoon Horror.*
The Blood-Spattered Feminist – Jean-Marie Pélissié & John Grissmer on *The House That Cried Murder, Blood Rage* and *Scalpel.*
'Hey Little Girl, Where Are You Going?' – Richard Blackburn on *Lemora: A Child's Tale of the Supernatural.*
Geek Tragedy – *My Brother Has Bad Dreams,* and the films of Robert Emery.
Bigfoot Ate My Penis! – An Interview with Jim Ball, producer of *Night of the Demon.*
Oregon Horrors – Don Gronquist on *Unhinged.*
Duke of Earl – Worth Keeter III on *Wolfman, Rottweiler,* and the Earl Owensby studio.
Return of the Killer Kids – Max Kalmanowicz on *The Children of Ravensback.*
A Texas Gent – Robert Burns on *Mongrel, Demonoid, Time Walker, Tourist Trap,* and others.
Every Town Should Have Its Own Monster – Peter Semelka on *The Varrow Mission.*
Sorrow – The Films of S.F. Brownrigg.
Mannequin Split – The Films of David Schmoeller.
Cataclysmo! – The Films of John Carr.
Rapemaster – Meir Zarchi on the Making of *I Spit on Your Grave.*
plus eight further chapters to be confirmed.

120 Titles Planned for Review Section, including:

BLOOD BATH – Joel M. Reed / BLOODSUCKING FREAKS – Joel M. Reed / BLUE SUNSHINE – Jeff Lieberman / BOG – Don Keeslar / THE BOGEY MAN – Ulli Lommel
THE BOOGENS – James Conway / THE CAPTURE OF BIGFOOT – Bill Rebane / CARNAGE – Andy Milligan / CHRISTMAS EVIL – Lewis Jackson
CURSE OF THE ALPHA STONE – Stewart Malleson / DARK DREAMS – Roger Guermontes / DARK EYES – James Polakof / DARK SANITY – Martin Green
DEATH BY INVITATION – Ken Friedman / DEATH GAME – Peter Traynor / DEATHDREAM – Bob Clark / THE DEFIANCE OF GOOD – Armand Weston
THE DEMON LOVER – Donald G. Jackson / THE DEVIL INSIDE HER – Zebedy Colt / THE DEVONSVILLE TERROR – Ulli Lommel / DON'T GO NEAR THE PARK – Lawrence D. Foldes
DOUBLE JEOPARDY – Ulli Lommel / DR. DEATH, SEEKER OF SOULS – Eddie Saeta / DRIVE-IN MASSACRE – Stu Segall / EFFECTS – Dusty Nelson
ENTER THE DEVIL – Frank Q. Dobbs / EQUINOX – Jack Woods / EVIL COME, EVIL GO – Walt Davis / EVIL FORCE – Evan Lee / EVILSPEAK – Eric Weston
FORCED ENTRY – Shaun Costello / THE GAME – Bill Rebane / GHOSTS THAT STILL WALK – James T. Flocker / THE GREAT HOLLYWOOD RAPE SLAUGHTER – Charles Edward
GRIM REAPER – Ron Ormond / GURU THE MAD MONK – Andy Milligan / HARDCORE – Michael Hugo / HOME SWEET HOME – Nettie Peña / HOT SUMMER IN THE CITY – Gail Palmer
HOUSE ON SKULL MOUNTAIN – Ron Honthaner / HOUSE OF THE DEAD – Sharron Miller / IMPULSE – William Grefé / INVASION OF THE BLOOD FARMERS – Ed Adlum
ISLAND CLAWS – Hernan Cardenas / THE KILLING KIND – Curtis Harrington / THE LAST VICTIM – Jim Sotos / LEGACY OF HORROR – Andy Milligan
LEGACY OF BLOOD – Carl Monson / LORD SHANGO – Ray Marsh / MADMAN – Joe Giannone / MANSION OF THE DOOMED – Michael Pataki / MARDI GRAS MASSACRE – Jack Weis
MASSACRE AT CENTRAL HIGH – Rene Daalder / THE MILPITAS MONSTER – Robert L. Burrill / MOONCHILD – Alan Gadney / MOTHER'S DAY – Charles Kaufman
THE DAY IT CAME TO EARTH – Harry Thomason / NIGHT OF THE ZOMBIES – Joel M. Reed / ONE DARK NIGHT – Tom McLoughlin / THE ORACLE – Roberta Findlay
THE OUTING – Byron Quisenberry / PETS – Raphael Nussbaum / PLEASE DON'T EAT MY MOTHER – Carl Monson / PRANKS – Jeffrey Obrow & Stephen Carpenter
PREMONITION – Alan Rudolph / PSYCHIC KILLER – Ray Danton / THE PSYCHOTRONIC MAN – Jack M. Sell / THE RAVAGER – Charles Nizet / RAW FORCE – Edward D. Murphy
THE REDEEMER: SON OF SATAN – Constantine Gochis / THE RETURN – Greydon Clark / REVENGE OF BIGFOOT – Harry Thomason / SAVAGE WEEKEND – David Paulsen
SCALPS – Fred Olen Ray / SCARED TO DEATH – William Malone / SEASON OF THE WITCH – George Romero / SEX PSYCHO – Walt Davis
SHRIEK OF THE MUTILATED – Michael Findlay / SILENT NIGHT, DEADLY NIGHT – Charles E. Sellier Jr. / SLEAZY RIDER – Roger Gentry / SOUL VENGEANCE – Jamaa Fanaka
SUPERSTITION – James Roberson / SWEET SAVIOR – Bob Roberts / SWEET SIXTEEN – Jim Sotos / TERRI'S REVENGE – Zebedy Colt / TERROR IN THE WAX MUSEUM – Georg Fenady
TORTURE DUNGEON – Andy Milligan / TOYS ARE NOT FOR CHILDREN – Stanley H. Brasloff / THE TOY BOX – Ron Garcia / TRACK OF THE MOONBEAST – Richard Ashe
TRIP WITH THE TEACHER – Earl Barton / TWISTED BRAIN – Larry N. Stouffer / THE UNSEEN – Peter Foleg / UNWILLING LOVERS – Zebedy Colt / VOODOO HEARTBEAT – Charles Nizet
WARLOCK MOON – Bill Herbert / WELCOME TO ARROW BEACH – Laurence Harvey / WITHOUT WARNING – Greydon Clark / THE WIZARD OF GORE – H.G. Lewis
WRONG WAY – Ray Williams / THE ZODIAC KILLER – Tom Hanson

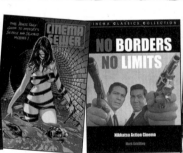